Microsoft®

Office

365

2019 Edition

Nita Rutkosky | **Audrey Roggenkamp**
Pierce College Puyallup
Puyallup, Washington

| **Ian Rutkosky**
Pierce College Puyallup
Puyallup, Washington

PARADIGM
EDUCATION SOLUTIONS

St. Paul

Vice President, Content and Digital Solutions: Christine Hurney
Director of Content Development, Computer Technology: Cheryl Drivdahl
Developmental Editor: Jennifer Joline Anderson
Director of Production: Timothy W. Larson
Production Editor/Project Manager: Jen Weaverling
Senior Design and Production Specialist: Jack Ross
Cover and Interior Design: Valerie King
Copy Editor: Communicáto, Ltd.
Testers: Janet Blum, Angela Niño, Lisa Hart
Indexer: Terry Casey
Vice President, Director of Digital Products: Chuck Bratton
Digital Projects Manager: Tom Modl
Digital Solutions Manager: Gerry Yumul
Senior Director of Digital Products and Onboarding: Christopher Johnson
Supervisor of Digital Products and Onboarding: Ryan Isdahl
Vice President, Marketing: Lara Weber McLellan
Marketing and Communications Manager: Selena Hicks

Care has been taken to verify the accuracy of information presented in this book. However, the authors, editors, and publisher cannot accept responsibility for web, email, newsgroup, or chat room subject matter or content, or for consequences from the application of the information in this book, and make no warranty, expressed or implied, with respect to its content.

Trademarks: Microsoft is a trademark or registered trademark of Microsoft Corporation in the United States and/or other countries. Some of the product names and company names included in this book have been used for identification purposes only and may be trademarks or registered trade names of their respective manufacturers and sellers. The authors, editors, and publisher disclaim any affiliation, association, or connection with, or sponsorship or endorsement by, such owners.

Paradigm Education Solutions is independent from Microsoft Corporation and not affiliated with Microsoft in any manner.

Cover Photo Credits: © lowball-jack/GettyImages.
Interior Photo Credits: Follow the index.

ISBN 978-0-76388-712-4 (print)
ISBN 978-0-76388-707-0 (digital)

© 2020 by Paradigm Publishing, LLC
875 Montreal Way
St. Paul, MN 55102
Email: CustomerService@ParadigmEducation.com
Website: ParadigmEducation.com

Printed in the United States of America

28 27 26 25 24 23 22 21 20 19   1 2 3 4 5 6 7 8 9 10 11 12

Contents

Achieving Proficiency in Microsoft Office

The Benchmark Series, *Microsoft® Office 365*, 2019 Edition, is designed for students who want to learn how to use Microsoft's popular suite to enhance their productivity at school, work, and home. Throughout this text, students are expected to develop and execute strategies for solving information processing and management problems using Microsoft Office. After successfully completing a course using this courseware, students will be able to:

- Analyze, synthesize, and evaluate school, work, or home information-processing needs and use application software to meet those needs efficiently and effectively.
- Create, design, and produce professional documents using Microsoft Word.
- Process, manipulate, and represent numeric data using Excel spreadsheet software.
- Plan, structure, and create databases for efficient data access and retrieval using Access database software.
- Design and create informational and motivational slide shows that contain hyperlinks, tables, images, and animation using PowerPoint presentation software.
- Learn strategies for merging and integrating source data from different applications.

Well-designed pedagogy is important, but students learn technology skills through practice and problem solving. Technology provides opportunities for interactive learning as well as excellent ways to quickly and accurately assess student performance. To this end, this course is supported with Cirrus, Paradigm's cloud-based training and assessment learning management system. Details about Cirrus as well as its integrated student courseware and instructor resources can be found on page xii.

Unit Openers display the unit's four chapter titles. Each program module has two units with four chapters each.

Proven Instructional Design

The Benchmark Series has long served as a standard of excellence in software instruction. Elements of the series function individually and collectively to create an inviting, comprehensive learning environment that leads to full proficiency in computer applications. The following visual tour highlights the structure and features that comprise the highly popular Benchmark model.

Chapter Openers Present Learning Objectives

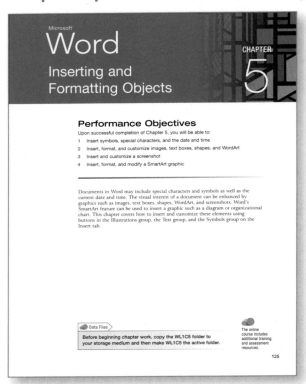

Chapter Openers present the performance objectives and an overview of the skills taught.

Data Files are provided for each chapter. A prominent note reminds students to copy the appropriate chapter data folder and make it active.

Activities Build Skill Mastery within Realistic Context

Multipart Activities provide a framework for instruction and practice on software features. An activity overview identifies tasks to accomplish and key features to use in completing the work.

Typically, a file remains open throughout all parts of the activity. Students save their work incrementally. At the end of the activity, students save, print, and then close the file.

Tutorials provide interactive, guided training and measured practice.

Hints offer useful tips on how to use application features efficiently and effectively.

Check Your Work model answer images are available in the online course, and students can use those images to confirm they have completed the activity correctly.

Quick Steps in the margins allow fast reference and review.

Between activity parts, the text presents instruction on the features and skills necessary to accomplish the next portion of the activity.

Step-by-Step Instructions guide students to the desired outcome for each activity part. Screen captures illustrate what the screen should look like at key points.

Magenta Text identifies material to type.

Chapter Review Tools Reinforce Learning

A **Chapter Summary** reviews the purpose and execution of key software features.

A **Commands Review** summarizes visually the major software features and alternative methods of access.

The Cirrus Solution
Elevating student success and instructor efficiency

Powered by Paradigm, Cirrus is the next-generation learning solution for developing skills in Microsoft Office. Cirrus seamlessly delivers complete course content in a cloud-based learning environment that puts students on the fast-track to success. Students can access their content from any device anywhere, through a live internet connection; plus Cirrus is platform independent, ensuring that students get the same learning experience whether they are using PCs, Macs, or Chromebook computers.

Cirrus provides Benchmark Series content in a series of scheduled assignments that report to a grade book to track student progress and achievement. Assignments are grouped in modules, providing many options for customizing instruction.

Dynamic Training

The online Benchmark Series courses include interactive resources to support learning.

Watch and Learn Lessons include a video demonstrating how to perform the chapter activity, a reading to provide background and context, and a short quiz to check understanding of concepts and skills.

Guide and Practice Tutorials provide interactive, guided training and measured practice.

Hands On Activities enable students to complete chapter activities, compare their solutions against a Check Your Work model answer image, and submit their work for instructor review.

Chapter Review and Assessment

Review and assessment activities for each chapter are available for completion in Cirrus.

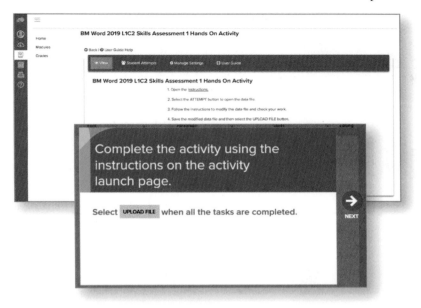

Concepts Check completion exercises assess their comprehension and recall of application features and functions as well as key terminology.

Skills Assessment Hands On Activity exercises evaluate the ability to apply chapter skills and concepts in solving realistic problems. Each is completed live in the Office application and is uploaded through Cirrus for instructor evaluation.

Visual Benchmark assessments test problem-solving skills and mastery of application features.

A **Case Study** requires analyzing a workplace scenario and then planning and executing a multipart project. Students search the web and/or use the program's Help feature to locate additional information required to complete the Case Study.

Exercises and **Projects** provide opportunities to develop and demonstrate skills learned in each chapter. Each is completed live in the Office application and is automatically scored by Cirrus. Detailed feedback and how-to videos help students evaluate and improve their performance.

Skills Check Exams evaluate students' ability to complete specific tasks. Skills Check Exams are completed live in the Office application and are scored automatically. Detailed feedback and instructor-controlled how-to videos help student evaluate and improve their performance.

Multiple-choice **Concepts Exams** assess understanding of key commands and concepts presented in each chapter.

Unit Review and Assessment

Review and assessment activities for each unit of each Benchmark course are also available for completion in Cirrus.

Assessing Proficiency exercises check mastery of software application functions and features.

Writing Activities challenge students to use written communication skills while demonstrating their understanding of important software features and functions.

Internet Research assignments reinforce the importance of research and information processing skills along with proficiency in the Office environment.

A **Job Study** activity at the end of Unit 2 presents a capstone assessment requiring critical thinking and problem solving.

Unit-Level Projects allow students to practice skills learned in the unit. Each is completed live in the Office application and automatically scored by Cirrus. Detailed feedback and how-to videos help students evaluate and improve their performance.

Student eBook

The Student eBook, accessed through the Cirrus online course, can be downloaded to any device (desktop, laptop, tablet, or smartphone) to make Benchmark Series content available anywhere students wish to study.

Instructor eResources

Cirrus tracks students' step-by-step interactions as they move through each activity, giving instructors visibility into their progress and missteps. With Exam Watch, instructors can observe students in a virtual, live, skills-based exam and join remotely as needed—a helpful option for struggling students who need one-to-one coaching, or for distance learners. In addition to these Cirrus-specific tools, the Instructor eResources for the Benchmark Series include the following support:

- Planning resources, such as lesson plans, teaching hints, and sample course syllabi

- Delivery resources, such as discussion questions and online images and templates

- Assessment resources, including live and annotated PDF model answers for chapter work and review and assessment activities, rubrics for evaluating student work, and chapter-based exam banks in RTF format

About the Authors

Nita Rutkosky began her career teaching business education at Pierce College in Puyallup, Washington, in 1978 and holds a master's degree in occupational education. In her years as an instructor, she taught many courses in software applications to students in postsecondary information technology certificate and degree programs. Since 1987, Nita has been a leading author of courseware for computer applications training and instruction. Her current titles include Paradigm's popular Benchmark Series, Marquee Series, and Signature Series. She is a contributor to the Cirrus online content for Office application courses and has also written textbooks for keyboarding, desktop publishing, computing in the medical office, and essential skills for digital literacy.

Audrey Roggenkamp holds a master's degree in adult education and curriculum and has been an adjunct instructor in the Business Information Technology department at Pierce College in Puyallup, Washington, since 2005. Audrey has also been a content provider for Paradigm Education Solutions since 2005. In addition to contributing to the Cirrus online content for Office application courses, Audrey co-authors Paradigm's Benchmark Series, Marquee Series, and Signature Series. Her other available titles include *Keyboarding & Applications I* and *II* and *Using Computers in the Medical Office: Word, PowerPoint, and Excel.*

Ian Rutkosky has a master's degree in business administration and has been an adjunct instructor in the Business Information Technology department at Pierce College in Puyallup, Washington, since 2010. In addition to joining the author team for the Benchmark Series and Marquee Series, he has co-authored titles on medical office computing and digital literacy and has served as a co-author and consultant for Paradigm's Cirrus training and assessment software.

Microsoft® Office

Getting Started in Office 365

Microsoft Office is a suite of applications for personal computers and other devices. These programs, known as *software*, include Word, a word processor; Excel, a spreadsheet editor; Access, a database management system; and PowerPoint, a presentation program used to design and present slideshows. Microsoft Office 365 is a subscription service that delivers continually updated versions of those applications. Specific features and functionality of Microsoft Office vary depending on the user's account, computer setup, and other factors. The Benchmark courseware was developed using features available in Office 365. You may find that with your computer and version of Office, the appearance of the software and the steps needed to complete an activity vary slightly from what is presented in the courseware.

Identifying Computer Hardware

The Microsoft Office suite can run on several types of computer equipment, referred to as *hardware*. You will need access to a laptop or a desktop computer system that includes a PC/tower, monitor, keyboard, printer, drives, and mouse. If you are not sure what equipment you will be operating, check with your instructor. The computer system shown in Figure G.1 consists of six components. Each component is discussed separately in the material that follows.

Figure G.1 Computer System

PC/tower

USB drive

monitor

printer

keyboard

mouse

Figure G.2 System Unit Ports

| Ethernet port | USB ports | microphone connection | speaker connection | video port |

System Unit (PC/Tower)

Traditional desktop computing systems include a system unit known as the *PC (personal computer)* or *tower*. This is the brain of the computer, where all processing occurs. It contains a Central Processing Unit (CPU), hard drives, and video cards plugged into a motherboard. Input and output ports are used for attaching peripheral equipment such as a keyboard, monitor, printer, and so on, as shown in Figure G.2. When a user provides input, the PC computes it and outputs the results.

Monitor

Hint Monitor size is measured diagonally and is generally the distance from the bottom left corner to the top right corner of the monitor.

A computer monitor looks like a television screen. It displays the visual information output by the computer. Monitor size can vary, and the quality of display for monitors varies depending on the type of monitor and the level of resolution.

Keyboard

The keyboard is used to input information into the computer. The number and location of the keys on a keyboard can vary. In addition to letters, numbers, and symbols, most computer keyboards contain function keys, arrow keys, and a numeric keypad. Figure G.3 shows a typical keyboard.

The 12 keys at the top of the keyboard, labeled with the letter *F* followed by a number, are called *function keys*. Use these keys to perform functions within each of the Office applications. To the right of the regular keys is a group of special or dedicated keys. These keys are labeled with specific functions that will be performed when you press the key. Below the special keys are arrow keys. Use these keys to move the insertion point in the document screen.

Some keyboards include mode indicator lights to indicate that a particular mode, such as Caps Lock or Num Lock, has been turned on. Pressing the Caps Lock key disables the lowercase alphabet so that text is typed in all caps, while pressing the Num Lock key disables the special functions on the numeric keypad so that numbers can be typed using the keypad. When you select these modes, a light appears on the keyboard.

Figure G.3 Keyboard

function keys

mode indicator lights

alphanumeric keys

arrow keys or insertion point control keys

numeric, insertion point control, and special keys

Drives and Ports

An internal hard drive is a disk drive that is located inside the PC and that stores data. External hard drives may be connected via USB ports for additional storage. Ports are the "plugs" on the PC, and are used to connect devices to the computer, such as the keyboard and mouse, the monitor, speakers, USB flash drives and so on. Most PCs will have a few USB ports, at least one display port, audio ports, and possibly an ethernet port (used to physically connect to the internet or a network).

Printer

An electronic version of a file is known as a *soft copy*. If you want to create a hard copy of a file, you need to print it. To print documents, you will need to access a printer, which will probably be either a laser printer or an ink-jet printer. A laser printer uses a laser beam combined with heat and pressure to print documents, while an ink-jet printer prints a document by spraying a fine mist of ink on the page.

Mouse

Most functions and commands in the Microsoft Office suite are designed to be performed using a mouse or a similar pointing device. A mouse is an input device that sits on a flat surface next to the computer. You can operate a mouse with your left or right hand. Moving the mouse on the flat surface causes a corresponding pointer to move on the screen, and clicking the left or right mouse buttons allows you to select various objects and commands.

Using the Mouse The applications in the Microsoft Office suite can be operated with the keyboard and a mouse. The mouse generally has two buttons on top, which you press to execute specific functions and commands. A mouse may also contain a wheel, which can be used to scroll in a window or as a third button. To use the mouse, rest it on a flat surface or a mouse pad. Put your hand over it with your palm resting on top of the mouse and your index finger resting on the left mouse button. As you move your hand, and thus the mouse, a corresponding pointer moves on the screen.

When using the mouse, you should understand four terms — *point*, *click*, *double-click*, and *drag*. To *point* means to position the mouse pointer on a desired item, such as an option, button, or icon. With the mouse pointer positioned on the item, *click* the left mouse button once to select the item. (In some cases you may *right-click*, which means to click the right mouse button, but generally, *click* refers to the left button.) To complete two steps at one time, such as choosing and then executing a function, *double-click* the left mouse button by tapping it twice in quick succession. The term *drag* means to click and hold down the left mouse button, move the mouse pointer to a specific location, and then release the button. Clicking and dragging is used, for instance, when moving a file from one location to another.

Hint Instructions in this course use the verb *click* to refer to tapping the left mouse button and the verb *press* to refer to pressing a key on the keyboard.

Using the Mouse Pointer The mouse pointer will look different depending on where you have positioned it and what function you are performing. The following are some of the ways the mouse pointer can appear when you are working in the Office suite:

- The mouse pointer appears as an I-beam (called the *I-beam pointer*) when you are inserting text in a file. The I-beam pointer can be used to move the insertion point or to select text.

- The mouse pointer appears as an arrow pointing up and to the left (called the *arrow pointer*) when it is moved to the Title bar, Quick Access Toolbar, ribbon, or an option in a dialog box, among other locations.

- The mouse pointer becomes a double-headed arrow (either pointing left and right, pointing up and down, or pointing diagonally) when you perform certain functions such as changing the size of an object.
- In certain situations, such as when you move an object or image, the mouse pointer displays with a four-headed arrow attached. The four-headed arrow means that you can move the object left, right, up, or down.

- When a request is being processed or when an application is being loaded, the mouse pointer may appear as a moving circle. The moving circle means "please wait." When the process is completed, the circle is replaced with a normal mouse pointer.
- When the mouse pointer displays as a hand with a pointing index finger, it indicates that more information is available about an item. The mouse pointer also displays as a hand with a pointing index finger when you hover over a hyperlink.

Touchpad

If you are working on a laptop computer, you may be using a touchpad instead of a mouse. A *touchpad* allows you to move the mouse pointer by moving your finger across a surface at the base of the keyboard (as shown in Figure G.4). You click and right-click by using your thumb to press the buttons located at the bottom of the touchpad. Some touchpads have special features such as scrolling or clicking something by tapping the surface of the touchpad instead of pressing a button with a thumb.

Figure G.4 Touchpad

Touchscreen

Smartphones, tablets, and touch monitors all use touchscreen technology (as shown in Figure G.5), which allows users to directly interact with the objects on the screen by touching them with fingers, thumbs, or a stylus. Multiple fingers or both thumbs can be used on most touchscreens, giving users the ability to zoom, rotate, and manipulate items on the screen. While many activities in this textbook can be completed using a device with a touchscreen, a mouse or touchpad might be required to complete a few activities.

Figure G.5 Touchscreen

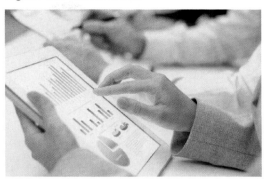

Choosing Commands

A *command* is an instruction that tells an application to complete a certain task. When an application such as Word or PowerPoint is open, the *ribbon* at the top of the window displays buttons and options for commands. To select a command with the mouse, point to it and then click the left mouse button.

Notice that the ribbon is organized into tabs, including File, Home, Insert, and so on. When the File tab is clicked, a *backstage area* opens with options such as opening or saving a file. Clicking any of the other tabs will display a variety of commands and options on the ribbon. Above the ribbon, buttons on the Quick Access Toolbar provide fast access to frequently used commands such as saving a file and undoing or redoing an action.

Using Keyboard Shortcuts and Accelerator Keys

As an alternative to using the mouse, keyboard shortcuts can be used for many commands. Shortcuts generally require two or more keys. For instance, in Word, press and hold down the Ctrl key while pressing P to display the Print backstage area, or press Ctrl + O to display the Open backstage area. A complete list of keyboard shortcuts can be found by searching the Help files in any Office application.

Office also provides shortcuts known as *accelerator keys* for every command or action on the ribbon. These accelerator keys are especially helpful for users with motor or visual disabilities or for power users who find it faster to use the keyboard than click with the mouse. To identify accelerator keys, press the Alt key on the keyboard. KeyTips display on the ribbon, as shown in Figure G.6. Press the keys indicated to execute the desired command. For example, to begin checking

Figure G.6 Word Home Tab KeyTips

the spelling and grammar in a document, press the Alt key, press the R key on the keyboard to display the Review tab, and then press the letter C and the number 1 on the keyboard to open the Editor task pane.

Choosing Commands from a Drop-Down List

Some buttons include arrows that can be clicked to display a drop-down list of options. Point and click with the mouse to choose an option from the list. Some options in a drop-down list may have a letter that is underlined. This indicates that typing the letter will select the option. For instance, to select the option *Insert Table*, type the letter I on the keyboard.

If an option in a drop-down list is not available to be selected, it will appear gray or dimmed. If an option is preceded by a check mark, it is currently active. If it is followed by an ellipsis (...), clicking the option will open a dialog box.

Choosing Options from a Dialog Box or Task Pane

Some buttons and options open a *dialog box* or a task pane containing options for applying formatting or otherwise modifying the data in a file. For example, the Font dialog box shown in Figure G.7 contains options for modifying the font and adding effects. The dialog box contains two tabs—the Font tab and the Advanced tab. The tab that displays in the front is the active tab. Click a tab to make it active or press Ctrl + Tab on the keyboard. Alternately, press the Alt key and then type the letter that is underlined in the tab name.

Figure G.7 Word Font Dialog Box

To choose an option from a dialog box using the mouse, position the arrow pointer on the option and then click the left mouse button. To move forward from option to option using the keyboard, you can press the Tab key. Press Shift + Tab to move back to a previous option. If the option displays with an underlined letter, you can choose it by pressing the Alt key and the underlined letter. When an option is selected, it is highlighted in blue or surrounded by a dotted or dashed box called a *marquee*. A dialog box contains one or more of the following elements: list boxes, option boxes, check boxes, text boxes, command buttons, radio buttons, and measurement boxes.

List Boxes and Option Boxes The fonts available in the Font dialog box, shown in Figure G.7 (on the previous page), are contained in a *list box*. Click an option in the list to select it. If the list is long, click the up or down arrows in the *scroll bar* at the right side of the box to scroll through all the options. Alternately, press the up or down arrow keys on the keyboard to move through the list, and press the Enter key when the desired option is selected.

Option boxes contain a drop-down list or gallery of options that opens when the arrow in the box is clicked. An example is the *Font color* option box in Figure G.8. To display the different color options, click the arrow at the right side of the box. If you are using the keyboard, press Alt + C.

Check Boxes Some options can be selected using a check box, such as the effect options in the dialog box in Figure G.7. If a check mark appears in the box, the option is active (turned on). If the check box does not contain a check mark, the option is inactive (turned off). Click a check box to make the option active or inactive. If you are using the keyboard, press Alt + the underlined letter of the option.

Text Boxes Some options in a dialog box require you to enter text. For example, see the Find and Replace dialog box shown in Figure G.8. In a text box, type or edit text with the keyboard, using the left and right arrow keys to move the insertion point without deleting text and use the Delete key or Backspace key to delete text.

Command Buttons The buttons at the bottom of the dialog box shown in Figure G.8 are called *command buttons*. Use a command button to execute or cancel a command. Some command buttons display with an ellipsis (...), which means another dialog box will open if you click that button. To choose a command button, click with the mouse or press the Tab key until the command button is surrounded by a marquee and then press the Enter key.

Figure G.8 Excel Find and Replace Dialog Box

Figure G.9 Word Insert Table Dialog Box

measurement boxes

radio buttons

Radio Buttons The Insert Table dialog box shown in Figure G.9 contains an example of *radio buttons*. Only one radio button can be selected at any time. When the button is selected, it is filled with a dark circle. Click a button to select it, or press and hold down the Alt key, press the underlined letter of the option, and then release the Alt key.

Measurement Boxes A *measurement box* contains an amount that can be increased or decreased. An example is shown in Figure G.9. To increase or decrease the number in a measurement box, click the up or down arrow at the right side of the box. Using the keyboard, press and hold down the Alt key and then press the underlined letter for the option, press the Up Arrow key to increase the number or the Down Arrow key to decrease the number, and then release the Alt key.

Choosing Commands with Shortcut Menus

The Office applications include shortcut menus that contain commands related to different items. To display a shortcut menu, point to the item for which you want to view more options with the mouse pointer and then click the right mouse button, or press Shift + F10. The shortcut menu will appear wherever the insertion point is positioned. In some cases, the Mini toolbar will also appear with the shortcut menu. For example, if the insertion point is positioned in a paragraph of text in a Word document, clicking the right mouse button or pressing Shift + F10 will display the shortcut menu and Mini toolbar, as shown in Figure G.10.

To select an option from a shortcut menu with the mouse, click the option. If you are using the keyboard, press the Up or Down Arrow key until the option is selected and then press the Enter key. To close a shortcut menu without choosing an option, click outside the menu or press the Esc key.

Figure G.10 Shortcut Menu and Mini Toolbar

Working with Multiple Applications

As you learn the various applications in the Microsoft Office suite, you will notice many similarities between them. For example, the steps to save, close, and print are virtually the same whether you are working in Word, Excel, or PowerPoint. This consistency greatly enhances your ability to transfer knowledge learned in one application to another within the suite. Another benefit to using Microsoft Office is the ability to have more than one application open at the same time and to integrate content from one program with another. For example, you can open Word and create a document, open Excel and create a worksheet, and then copy a worksheet from the workbook into Word.

The Windows taskbar at the bottom of the screen displays buttons representing all the programs that are currently open. For example, Figure G.11 shows the taskbar with Word, Excel, Access, and PowerPoint open. To move from one program to another, click the taskbar button representing the desired application.

Maintaining Files and Folders

Windows includes a program named File Explorer that can be used to maintain files and folders. To open File Explorer, click the folder icon on the Windows taskbar. Use File Explorer to complete tasks such as copying, moving, renaming, and deleting files and folders and creating new folders. Some file management tasks can also be completed within Word, Excel, PowerPoint, or Access by clicking File and then *Open* or *Save As* and then clicking the *Browse* option to browse folders and files in a dialog box.

Directions and activities in this course assume that you are managing files and folders stored on a USB flash drive or on your computer's hard drive. If you are using your OneDrive account or another cloud-based storage service, some of the file and folder management tasks may vary.

Figure G.11 Windows Taskbar with Word, Excel, Access, and PowerPoint Open

Creating and Naming a Folder

Files (such as Word documents, Excel workbooks, PowerPoint presentations, and Access databases) are easier to find again when they are grouped logically in folders. In File Explorer and in the Open or Save As dialog box, the names of files and folders are displayed in the Content pane. Each file has an icon showing what type of file it is, while folders are identified with the icon of a folder. See Figure G.12 for an example of the File Explorer window.

Create a new folder by clicking the New folder button at the top of the File Explorer window or in the dialog box. A new folder displays with the name *New folder* highlighted. Type a name for the folder to replace the highlighted text, and then press the Enter key. Folder names can include numbers, spaces, and some symbols.

Selecting and Opening Files and Folders

Select files or folders in the window to be managed. To select one file or folder, simply click on it. To select several adjacent files or folders, click the first file or folder, hold down the Shift key, and then click the last file or folder. To select files or folders that are not adjacent, click the first file or folder, hold down the Ctrl key, click any other files or folders, and then release the Ctrl key. To deselect, click anywhere in the window or dialog box.

When a file or folder is selected, the path to the folder displays in the Address bar. If the folder is located on an external storage device, the drive letter and name may display in the path. A right-pointing arrow displays to the right of each folder name in the Address bar. Click the arrow to view a list of subfolders within a folder.

Double-click a file or folder in the Content pane to open it. You can also select one or more files or folders, right-click, and then click the *Open* option in the shortcut menu.

Figure G.12 File Explorer Window

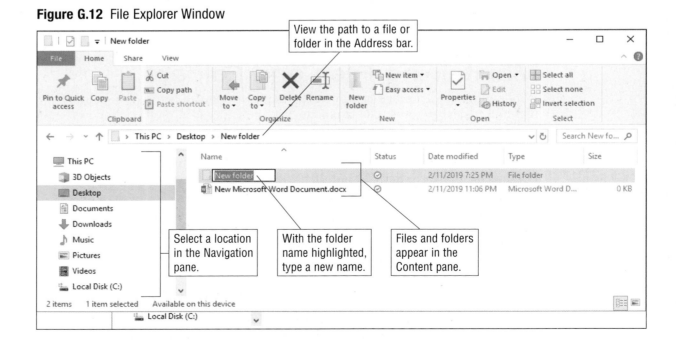

Deleting Files and Folders

Deleting files and folders is part of file maintenance. To delete a file or folder, select it and then press the Delete key. Alternatively, use the Delete button on the Home tab of the File Explorer window, or click the Organize button and then *Delete* in the dialog box. You can also right-click a file or folder and then choose the *Delete* option in the shortcut menu.

Files and folders deleted from the hard drive of the computer are automatically sent to the Recycle Bin, where they can easily be restored if necessary. If a file or folder is stored in another location, such as an external drive or online location, it may be permanently deleted. In this case, a message may appear asking for confirmation. To confirm that the file or folder should be deleted, click Yes.

To view the contents of the Recycle Bin, display the Windows desktop and then double-click the *Recycle Bin* icon. Deleted items in the Recycle Bin can be restored to their original locations, or the Recycle Bin can be emptied to free up space on the hard drive.

Moving and Copying Files and Folders

A file or folder may need to be moved or copied to another location. In File Explorer, select the file or folder and then click the Copy button at the top of the window, use the keyboard shortcut Ctrl + C, or right-click the file and select *Copy* in the shortcut menu. Navigate to the destination folder and then click the Paste button, use the keyboard shortcut Ctrl + P, or right-click and select *Paste*. If a copy is pasted to the same folder as the original, it will appear with the word *Copy* added to its name. To copy files in the Open or Save As dialog box, use the Organize button drop-down list or right-click to access the shortcut menu.

To move a file or folder, follow the same steps, but select *Cut* instead of *Copy* or press Ctrl + X instead of Ctrl + C. Files can also be dragged from one location to another. To do this, open two File Explorer windows. Click a file or folder and drag it to the other window while holding down the left mouse button.

Renaming Files and Folders

To rename a file or folder in File Explorer, click its name to highlight it and then type a new name, or right-click the file or folder and then select *Rename* at the shortcut menu. You can also select the file or folder and then click the Rename button on the Home tab of the File Explorer window or click *Rename* from the Organize button drop-down list at the Open or Save As dialog box. Type in a new name and then press the Enter key.

Viewing Files and Folders

Change how files and folders display in the Content pane in File Explorer by clicking the View tab and then clicking one of the view options in the Layout group. View files and folders as large, medium, or small icons; as tiles; in a list; or with details or information about the file or folder content. At the Open or Save As dialog box, click the Change your view button arrow and a list displays with similar options for viewing folders and files. Click to select an option in the list or click the Change your view button to see different views.

Displaying File Extensions Each file has a file extension that identifies the program and what type of file it is. Excel files have the extension *.xlsx;* Word files end with *.docx,* and so on. By default, file extensions are turned off. To view file extensions, open File Explorer, click the View tab, and then click the *File name extensions* check box to insert a check mark. Click the check box again to remove the check mark and stop viewing file extensions.

Displaying All Files The Open or Save As dialog box in an Office application may display only files specific to that application. For example, the Open or Save As dialog box in Word may only display Word documents. Viewing all files at the Open dialog box can be helpful in determining what files are available. Turn on the display of all files at the Open dialog box by clicking the file type button arrow at the right side of the *File Name* text box and then clicking *All Files* at the drop-down list.

Managing Files at the Info Backstage Area

The Info backstage area in Word, Excel, and PowerPoint provide buttons for managing files such as uploading and sharing a file, copying a path, and opening File Explorer with the current folder active. To use the buttons at the Info backstage area, open Word, Excel, or PowerPoint and then open a file. Click the File tab and then click the *Info* option. If a file is opened from the computer's hard drive or an external drive, four buttons display near the top of the Info backstage area as shown in Figure G.13.

Click the Upload button to upload the open file to a shared location such as a OneDrive account. Click the Share button and a window displays indicating that the file must be saved to OneDrive before it can be shared and provides an option that, when clicked, will save the file to OneDrive. Click the Copy Path button and a copy of the path for the current file is saved in a temporary location. This path can be pasted into another file, an email, or any other location where you want to keep track of the file's path. Click the Open file location button and File Explorer opens with the current folder active.

Figure G.13 Info Backstage Buttons

If you open Word, Excel, or PowerPoint and then open a file from OneDrive, only two buttons display—Share and Open file location. Click the Share button to display a window with options for sharing the file with others and specifying whether the file can be viewed and edited, or only viewed. Click the Open file location button to open File Explorer with the current folder active.

Customizing Settings

Before beginning computer activities in this textbook, you may need to customize your monitor's settings and change the DPI display setting. Activities in the course assume that the monitor display is set at 1920 × 1080 pixels and the DPI set at 125%. If you are unable to make changes to the monitor's resolution or the DPI settings, the activities can still be completed successfully. Some references in the text might not perfectly match what you see on your screen, so you may not be able to perform certain steps exactly as written. For example, an item in a drop-down gallery might appear in a different column or row than what is indicated in the step instructions.

Before you begin learning the applications in the Microsoft Office suite, take a moment to check the display settings on the computer you are using. Your monitor's display settings are important because the ribbon in the Microsoft Office suite adjusts to the screen resolution setting of your computer monitor. A computer monitor set at a high resolution will have the ability to show more buttons in the ribbon than will a monitor set to a low resolution. The illustrations in this textbook were created with a screen resolution display set at 1920 × 1080 pixels, as shown in Figure G.14.

Figure G.14 Word Ribbon Set at 1920 x 1080 Screen Resolution

Activity 1 Adjusting Monitor Display

Note: The resolution settings may be locked on lab computers. Also, some laptop screens and small monitors may not be able to display in a 1920 × 1080 resolution or change the DPI setting.

1. At the Windows desktop, right-click in a blank area of the screen.
2. In the shortcut menu, click the *Display settings* option.

3. At the Settings window with the *Display* option selected, scroll down and look at the current setting displayed in the *Resolution* option box. If your screen is already set to 1920 × 1080, skip ahead to Step 6.

4. Click the Resolution option box and then click the *1920 × 1080* option. **Note: Depending on the privileges you are given on a school machine, you may not be able to complete Steps 4–5. If necessary, check with your instructor for alternative instructions.**

5. Click the Keep Changes button.
6. At the Settings window, take note of the current DPI percentage next to the text *Change the size of text, apps, and other items*. If the percentage is already set to 125%, skip to Step 8.
7. Click the option box below the text *Change the size of text, apps, and other items,* and then click the *125%* option in the drop-down list

8. Click the Close button to close the Settings window.

Retrieving and Copying Data Files

While working through the activities in this course, you will often be using data files as starting points. These files are provided through your Cirrus online course, and your instructor may post them in another location such as your school's network drive. You can download all the files at once (described in the activity below), or download only the files needed for a specific chapter.

Activity 2 **Downloading Files to a USB Flash Drive**

Note: In this activity, you will download data files from your Cirrus online course. Make sure you have an active internet connection before starting this activity. Check with your instructor if you do not have access to your Cirrus online course.

1. Insert your USB flash drive into an available USB port.
2. Navigate to the Course Resources section of your Cirrus online course. *Note: The steps in this activity assume you are using the Chrome browser. If you are using a different browser, the following steps may vary*.
3. Click the Student Data Files link in the Course Resources section. A zip file containing the student data files will automatically begin downloading from the Cirrus website.
4. Click the button in the lower left corner of the screen once the files have finished downloading.

5. Right-click the *StudentDataFiles* folder in the Content pane.
6. Click the *Copy* option in the shortcut menu.
7. Click the USB flash drive that displays in the Navigation pane at the left side of the File Explorer window.
8. Click the Home tab in the File Explorer window.
9. Click the Paste button in the Clipboard group.

10. Close the File Explorer window by clicking the Close button in the upper right corner of the window.

Microsoft® Word Level 1

Unit 1

Editing and Formatting Documents

Microsoft® Word

Preparing a Word Document

CHAPTER 1

Performance Objectives

Upon successful completion of Chapter 1, you will be able to:

1 Open Microsoft Word

2 Create, save, name, print, open, and close a Word document

3 Close Word

4 Open a document from and pin/unpin a document at the *Recent* Option list

5 Edit a document

6 Move the insertion point within a document

7 Scroll within a document

8 Select text

9 Use the Undo and Redo buttons

10 Check spelling and grammar

11 Use the Tell Me and Help features

In this chapter, you will learn to create, save, name, print, open, close, and edit a Word document as well as complete a spelling and grammar check. You will also learn about the Tell Me feature, which provides information and guidance on how to complete a function, and the Help feature, an on-screen reference manual that provides information on features and commands for each program in the Microsoft Office suite. Before continuing, make sure you read the *Getting Started* section presented at the beginning of this book. It contains information about computer hardware and software, using the mouse, executing commands, and managing files.

 Data Files

Before beginning chapter work, copy the WL1C1 folder to your storage medium and then make WL1C1 the active folder.

The online course includes additional training and assessment resources.

You will create a short document containing information on resumes and then save, print, and close the document.

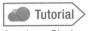

Opening a Blank Document

Opening Microsoft Word

Microsoft Office contains a word processing program named Word that can be used to create, save, edit, and print documents. The steps to open Word may vary but generally include clicking the Start button on the Windows desktop and then clicking the Word tile at the Start menu. At the Word opening screen, click the *Blank document* template.

Exploring the Word Screen

Creating, Saving, Printing, and Closing a Document

When the *Blank document* template is clicked, a blank document displays on the screen, as shown in Figure 1.1. The features of the document screen are described in Table 1.1.

At a blank document, type information to create a document. A document is a record containing information, such as a letter, report, term paper, or table. To create a new document, begin typing in the blank page. Here are some things to consider when typing text:

Quick Steps

Open Word and Open Blank Document
1. Click Word tile at Windows Start menu.
2. Click *Blank document* template.

- **Word wrap:** As text is typed in the document, Word wraps text to the next line, so the Enter key does not need to be pressed at the end of each line. A word is wrapped to the next line if it continues past the right margin. The only times the Enter key needs to be pressed are to end a paragraph, create a blank line, or to end a short line.

- **AutoCorrect:** Word contains a feature that automatically corrects certain words as they are typed. For example, if *adn* is typed instead of *and*, Word automatically corrects it when the spacebar is pressed after typing the word. AutoCorrect will also format as superscript the letters that follow an ordinal number (a number indicating a position in a series). For example, type *2nd* and then press the spacebar or Enter key, and Word will convert this ordinal number to 2nd.

- **Automatic spelling checker:** Word contains an Editor that checks the spelling and grammar in a document. By default, words that are not found in the Spelling dictionary are underlined with a wavy red line. These may include misspelled words, proper names, some terminology, and some foreign words. If a typed word is not recognized by the Spelling dictionary, leave it as written if the word is spelled correctly. However, if the spelling is incorrect, retype the word or position the I-beam pointer on the word, click the right mouse button, and then click the correct spelling at the shortcut menu.

Hint The Status bar includes a book icon. A check mark on the book indicates no spelling errors have been detected by the spelling checker, while an X on the book indicates errors. Click the book icon to display the Editor task pane. If the book icon is not visible, right-click the Status bar and then click the *Spelling and Grammar Check* option at the shortcut menu.

- **Automatic grammar checker:** Word's Editor includes an automatic grammar checker. If the grammar checker detects a sentence containing a possible grammatical error, the error will be underlined with a double blue line. The sentence can be left as written or corrected. To correct the sentence, position the I-beam pointer on the error, click the right mouse button, and choose from the shortcut menu of possible corrections.

Figure 1.1 Blank Document

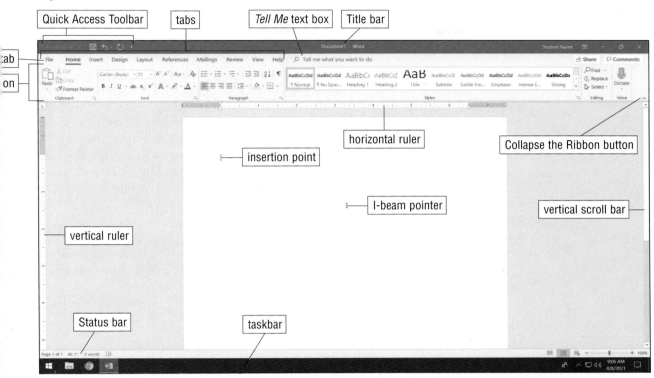

Table 1.1 Microsoft Word Screen Features

Feature	Description
Collapse the Ribbon button	when clicked, removes the ribbon from the screen
File tab	when clicked, displays the backstage area, which contains options for working with and managing documents
horizontal ruler	used to set margins, indents, and tabs
I-beam pointer	used to move the insertion point or to select text
insertion point	indicates the location of the next character entered at the keyboard
Quick Access Toolbar	contains buttons for commonly used commands
ribbon	area containing tabs with options and buttons divided into groups
Status bar	on the left, indicates the number of pages and words in the document; on the right, includes view buttons and Zoom slider bar
tabs	contain commands and features organized into groups
taskbar	contains icons for launching programs, buttons for active tasks, and a notification area
Tell Me text box	provides information and guidance on how to complete functions
Title bar	shows the document name followed by the program name
vertical ruler	used to set the top and bottom margins
vertical scroll bar	used to move the viewing area up or down through the document

- **Spacing punctuation:** The default typeface in Word is Calibri, which is a proportional typeface. (You will learn more about typefaces in Chapter 2.) When typing text in a proportional typeface, use only one space (rather than two) after end-of-sentence punctuation such as a period, question mark, or exclamation point and after a colon. The characters in a proportional typeface are set closer together, and extra white space at the end of a sentence or after a colon is not needed.

- **Option buttons:** As text is inserted or edited in a document, an option button may display near the text. The name and appearance of this option button varies depending on the action. If a typed word is corrected by AutoCorrect, if an automatic list is created, or if autoformatting is applied to text, the AutoCorrect Options button appears. Click this button to undo the specific automatic action. If text is pasted in a document, the Paste Options button appears near the text. Click this button to display the Paste Options gallery, which has buttons for controlling how the pasted text is formatted.

- **AutoComplete:** Microsoft Word and other Office applications include an AutoComplete feature that inserts an entire item when a few identifying characters are typed. For example, type the letters *Mond* and *Monday* displays in a ScreenTip above the letters. Press the Enter key or press the F3 function key and Word inserts *Monday* in the document.

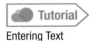

Entering Text

Using the New Line Command

A Word document is based on a template that applies default formatting. Some basic formatting includes 1.08 line spacing and 8 points of spacing after a paragraph. Each time the Enter key is pressed, a new paragraph begins and 8 points of spacing is inserted after the paragraph. To move the insertion point down to the next line without including the additional 8 points of spacing, use the New Line command, Shift + Enter.

Activity 1a Creating a Document   Part 1 of 2

1. Open Word by clicking the Word tile at the Windows Start menu.
2. At the Word opening screen, click the *Blank document* template. (These steps may vary. Check with your instructor for specific instructions.)
3. At a blank document, type the information shown in Figure 1.2 with the following specifications:
   a. Correct any spelling or grammatical errors identified by the Editor as they occur.
   b. Press the spacebar once after end-of-sentence punctuation.
   c. After typing *Created:* press Shift + Enter to move the insertion point to the next line without adding 8 points of additional spacing.
   d. To insert the word *Thursday* at the end of the document, type Thur and then press the F3 function key. (This is an example of the AutoComplete feature.)
   e. To insert the word *December*, type Dece and then press the Enter key. (This is another example of the AutoComplete feature.)
   f. Press Shift + Enter after typing *December 9, 2021.*
   g. When typing the last line (the line containing the ordinal numbers), type the ordinal number text and AutoCorrect will automatically convert the letters in the ordinal number to a superscript.
4. When you are finished typing the text, press the Enter key. (Keep the document open for the next activity.)

Figure 1.2 Activity 1a

Figure 1.2 Activity 1a

The traditional chronological resume lists your work experience in reverse-chronological order (starting with your current or most recent position). The functional style deemphasizes the "where" and "when" of your career and instead groups similar experiences, talents, and qualifications regardless of when they occurred.

Like the chronological resume, the hybrid resume includes specifics about where you worked, when you worked there, and what your job titles were. Like a functional resume, a hybrid resume emphasizes your most relevant qualifications in an expanded summary section, in several "career highlights" bullet points at the top of your resume, or in activity summaries.

Created:
Thursday, December 9, 2021
Note: The two paragraphs will become the 2nd and 3rd paragraphs in the 5th section.

Tutorial

Saving with a New Name

 Save

Saving a Document

If a document will be used in the future, it must be saved. To save a new document, click the File tab and then click the *Save* or the *Save As* option. The Save As backstage area displays, as shown in Figure 1.3. Click the *Browse* option to open the Save As dialog box, shown in Figure 1.4. (Pressing the F12 function key will also open this dialog box.) At the dialog box, navigate to the location where the file is to be saved, type a file name, and then press the Enter key or click the Save button. Continue saving periodically whenever edits are made by clicking the Save button on the Quick Access Toolbar or with the keyboard shortcut Ctrl + S.

Quick Steps

Save Document
1. Click File tab.
2. Click *Save As* option.
3. Click *Browse* option.
4. Type document name in *File name* text box.
5. Press Enter key.

To save a new version of a document while keeping the original, click the File tab and then click the *Save As* option to display the Save As backstage area. (Do not click *Save*, or changes will be saved to the existing file.) At the Save As backstage area, click the *Browse* option to display the Save As dialog box. Type a new name for the document, select a location where the document is to be saved, and then press the Enter key or click the Save button.

💡 **Hint** Save a document approximately every 15 minutes or when interrupted.

Figure 1.3 Save As Backstage Area

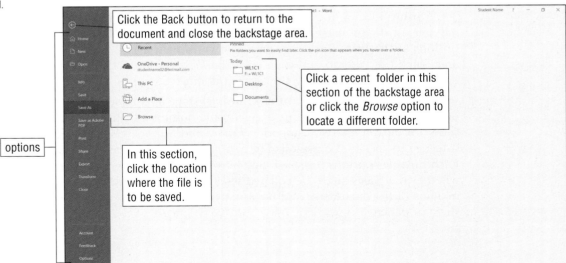

Figure 1.4 Save As Dialog Box

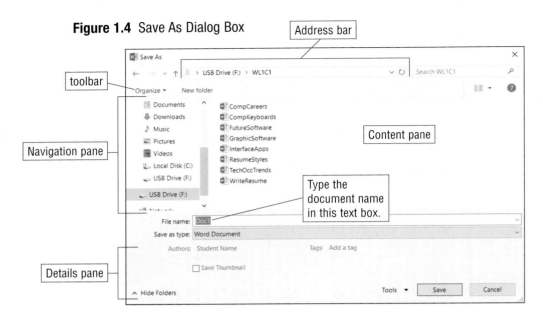

Naming a Document

Hint Word will not allow you to save two documents with the same name in the same folder. This is true even if you make one name uppercase and one lowercase.

Document names created in Word and other applications in the Microsoft Office suite can be up to 255 characters in length, including the drive letter and any folder names, and they may include spaces. File names cannot include any of the following characters:

forward slash (/)   less-than symbol (<)   quotation marks (" ")
backslash (\)   asterisk (*)   colon (:)
greater-than symbol (>)   question mark (?)   pipe symbol (|)

Printing a Document

Tutorial

Printing a Document

Quick Steps

Print Document
1. Click File tab.
2. Click *Print* option.
3. Click Print button.

Click the File tab and the backstage area displays. The buttons and options at the backstage area change depending on the option selected at the left side of the backstage area. To leave the backstage area without completing an action, click the Back button in the upper left corner of the backstage area, or press the Esc key on the keyboard.

A printout of a document on paper is known as a *hard copy*, as opposed to the *soft copy*, or digital version, which displays on the screen. Print a document with options at the Print backstage area, shown in Figure 1.5. To display this backstage area, click the File tab and then click the *Print* option. The Print backstage area can also be displayed using the keyboard shortcut Ctrl + P.

Click the Print button at the Print backstage area to send the document to the printer. Use the *Copies* option to specify the number of copies to be printed. Below the Print button are two categories: *Printer* and *Settings*. Use the gallery in the *Printer* category to specify the printer. The *Settings* category contains a number of galleries. Each provides options for specifying how the document will print, including whether the pages are to be collated when printed; the orientation, page size, and margins of the document; and how many pages of the document are to print on a sheet of paper.

Figure 1.5 Print Backstage Area

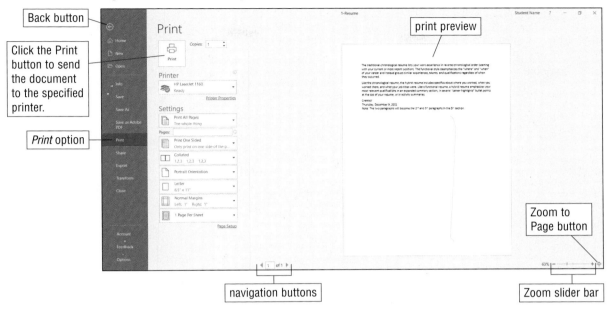

Back button

Click the Print button to send the document to the specified printer.

Print option

print preview

Zoom to Page button

navigation buttons

Zoom slider bar

 Quick Print

Quick Steps

Quick Steps

Close Document
1. Click File tab.
2. Click *Close* option.

Close Word
Click Close button.

 Tutorial

Closing a Document and Closing Word

 Close

Another method for printing a document is to insert the Quick Print button on the Quick Access Toolbar and then click the button. This sends the document directly to the printer without displaying the Print backstage area. To insert the button on the Quick Access Toolbar, click the Customize Quick Access Toolbar button at the right side of the toolbar and then click *Quick Print* at the drop-down list. To remove the Quick Print button from the Quick Access Toolbar, right-click the button and then click the *Remove from Quick Access Toolbar* option at the shortcut menu.

Closing a Document and Closing Word

When a document is saved, it is saved to the specified location and also remains on the screen. To remove the document from the screen, click the File tab and then click the *Close* option or use the keyboard shortcut Ctrl + F4. When a document is closed, it is removed and a blank screen displays. At this screen, open a previously saved document, create a new document, or close Word. To close Word, click the Close button in the upper right corner of the screen. The keyboard shortcut Alt + F4 also closes Word.

Activity 1b Saving, Printing, and Closing a Document and Closing Word   Part 2 of 2

1. Save the document you created for Activity 1a and name it **1-Resume** (*1-* for Chapter 1 and *Resume* because the document is about resumes) by completing the following steps:
    a. Click the File tab.
    b. Click the *Save As* option.
    c. At the Save As backstage area, click the *Browse* option.
    d. At the Save As dialog box, if necessary, navigate to the WL1C1 folder on your storage medium.

1a

e. Click in the *File name* text box (this selects any text in the box), type 1-Resume, and then press the Enter key.
2. Print the document by clicking the File tab, clicking the *Print* option, and then clicking the Print button at the Print backstage area.

3. Close the document by clicking the File tab and then clicking the *Close* option.
4. Close Word by clicking the Close button in the upper right corner of the screen.

> Check Your Work

Activity 2 Save a Document with a New Name and the Same Name 2 Parts

You will open a document in the WL1C1 folder on your storage medium, save the document with a new name, add text, and then save the document with the same name. You will also print and then close the document.

Creating a New Document

Quick Steps
Create New Document
1. Click File tab.
2. Click *Blank document* template.

When a document is closed, a blank screen displays. To create a new document, click the File tab, click the *New* option, and then click the *Blank document* template. A new document can also be opened with the keyboard shortcut Ctrl + N or with the New button on the Quick Access Toolbar. To insert the button on the Quick Access Toolbar, click the Customize Quick Access Toolbar button at the right of the toolbar and then click *New* at the drop-down list.

Additional templates can be found by clicking the File tab and then clicking the *Home* or the *New* option. Double-click the *Single spaced (blank)* template to open a new document with single spacing and no added space after paragraphs.

Opening a Document

> Tutorial

Opening a Document from a Removable Disk

After a document is saved and closed, it can be opened at the Open dialog box, shown in Figure 1.6. Display the dialog box by clicking the File tab, clicking the *Open* option, and then clicking the *Browse* option at the backstage area. Other methods for displaying the Open backstage area include using the keyboard shortcut Ctrl + O, inserting an Open button on the Quick Access Toolbar, and clicking the <u>More documents</u> hyperlink in the lower right corner of the Word opening screen and the Home backstage area.

Figure 1.6 Open Dialog Box

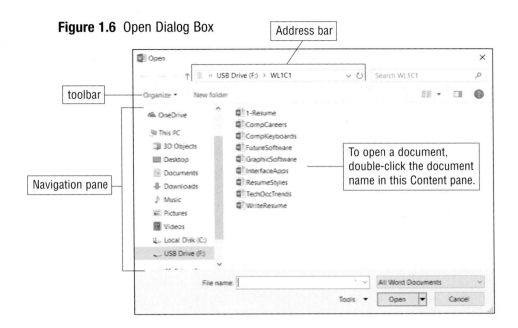

Address bar

toolbar

Navigation pane

To open a document, double-click the document name in this Content pane.

Quick Steps

Open Document
1. Click File tab.
2. Click *Open* option.
3. Click *Browse* option.
4. Double-click document name.

At the Open backstage area, click the *Browse* option and the Open dialog box displays. Go directly to the Open dialog box without displaying the Open backstage area by pressing Ctrl + F12. At the Open dialog box, navigate to the desired location (such as the drive containing your storage medium), open the folder containing the document, and then double-click the document name in the Content pane.

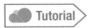

Tutorial

Opening a Document from the *Recent* Option List

Opening a Document from the *Recent* Option List

At the Open backstage area with the *Recent* option selected, the names of the most recently opened documents are listed. By default, Word lists the names of the 50 most recently opened documents and groups them into categories such as *Today*, *Yesterday*, and perhaps another category such as *This Week*. To open a document from the *Recent* option list, scroll down the list and then click the document name. The Word opening screen and the Home backstage area also provide a list of the names of the most recently opened documents. Click a document name in the Recent list to open the document.

Tutorial

Pinning and Unpinning a Document at the *Recent* Option List

Pinning and Unpinning Documents and Folders

If a document is opened on a regular basis, consider pinning it so it can be found more easily. At the Open backstage area, hover the mouse pointer over the document name in the *Recent* option list and then click the push pin icon that appears. The document will now appear at the top of the list in the *Pinned* category, with the push pin icon pointing down. A document can also be pinned at the Home backstage area. Click the push pin icon next to a document name, and the document will display in the *Pinned* tab.

To "unpin" a document from the *Recent* option list at the Open backstage area or the Pinned list at the Home backstage area, click the push pin icon to the right of the document name. More than one document can be pinned to a list.

Another method for pinning and unpinning documents is to use the shortcut menu. Right-click a document name and then click the *Pin to list* or *Unpin from list* option. The shortcut menu also includes the *Remove from list* option, which removes a document from the *Recent* option list and the Recent list. Right-click a pinned document in the *Recent* option list at the Open backstage area and the shortcut menu includes the option *Clear unpinned Documents*, which removes all unpinned documents from the *Recent* option list.

In addition to documents, folders can be pinned for easier access. To pin a frequently-used folder, display the Open backstage area and then click the *Folders* option. Recently opened folders are listed and grouped into categories such as *Today*, *Yesterday*, and *Last Week* to reflect the time they were last accessed. Click the push pin icon to the right of a folder and it will be pinned to the top of the list.

Activity 2a Opening, Pinning, Unpinning, and Saving a Document   Part 1 of 2

1. Open Word and then open **CompCareers** by completing the following steps:
   a. At the Word opening screen, click the <u>More documents</u> hyperlink in the lower right corner of the screen. (You may need to scroll down the screen to display this hyperlink.)
   b. At the Open backstage area, click the *Browse* option.
   c. At the Open dialog box, navigate to the external drive containing your storage medium.
   d. Double-click the **WL1C1** folder in the Content pane.
   e. Double-click *CompCareers* in the Content pane.

2. Close **CompCareers**.
3. Press Ctrl + F12 to display the Open dialog box and then double-click *FutureSoftware* in the Content pane to open the document.
4. Close **FutureSoftware**.
5. Pin **CompCareers** to the *Recent* option list by completing the following steps:
   a. Click the File tab and then click the *Open* option.
   b. At the Open backstage area, hover the mouse pointer over **CompCareers** in the *Recent* option list and then click the left-pointing push pin icon to the right of the document. (The **CompCareers** file will now appear in the *Pinned* category at the top of the list, and the push pin icon will be pointing downward.)
6. Click *CompCareers* in the *Pinned* category at the top of the *Recent* option list to open the document.
7. Unpin **CompCareers** from the *Recent* option list by completing the following steps:
   a. Click the File tab and then click the *Open* option.
   b. At the Open backstage area, click the down-pointing push pin icon to the right of **CompCareers** in the *Pinned* category in the *Recent* option list. (This removes the file from the *Pinned* category and changes the pin to a left-pointing push pin.)
   c. Click the Back button to return to the document.

8. With **CompCareers** open, save the document with a new name by completing the following steps:
   a. Click the File tab and then click the *Save As* option.
   b. At the Save As backstage area, click the *Browse* option.
   c. At the Save As dialog box, if necessary, navigate to the WL1C1 folder on your storage medium.
   d. Press the Home key on your keyboard to move the insertion point to the beginning of the file name and then type 1-.
   e. Press the Enter key.

Saving Changes to a Document

After making changes to a document, save the changes before closing the file. Consider saving on a periodic basis to ensure that no changes are lost if the application crashes or freezes or if power is interrupted. Unless keeping an older version of the document is important, changes can be saved using the same file name. Save a document with the same name using the Save button on the Quick Access Toolbar, the *Save* option at the backstage area, or with the keyboard shortcut Ctrl + S.

Quick Steps

Save Document with Same Name
Click Save button on Quick Access Toolbar.
OR
1. Click File tab.
2. Click *Save* option.

   Note: If a document is stored in a cloud location such as Microsoft OneDrive or SharePoint Online, any changes to it will be saved automatically with the AutoSave feature. AutoSave can be turned on or off by clicking the toggle switch in the upper left corner of the Word screen.

Activity 2b Saving a Document with the Same Name

Part 2 of 2

1. With **1-CompCareers** open and the insertion point positioned at the beginning of the document, type the text shown in Figure 1.7.
2. Save the changes you just made by clicking the Save button on the Quick Access Toolbar.
3. Print the document by clicking the File tab, clicking the *Print* option, and then clicking the Print button at the Print backstage area. (If your Quick Access Toolbar contains the Quick Print button, you can click the button to send the document directly to the printer.)
4. Close the document by pressing Ctrl + F4.

Check Your Work

Figure 1.7 Activity 2b

The majority of new jobs being created in the United States today involve daily work with computers. Computer-related careers include technical support jobs, sales and training, programming and applications development, network and database administration, and computer engineering.

You will open a previously created document, save it with a new name, and then use scrolling and browsing techniques to move the insertion point to specific locations in the document.

Scrolling

Editing a Document

When a document is being edited, text may need to be inserted or deleted. To edit a document, use the mouse, the keyboard, or a combination of the two to move the insertion point to specific locations in the document. To move the insertion point using the mouse, position the I-beam pointer where the insertion point is to be positioned and then click the left mouse button.

Scrolling in a document changes the text display but does not move the insertion point. Use the mouse with the vertical scroll bar, at the right side of the screen, to scroll through text in a document. Click the up scroll arrow at the top of the vertical scroll bar to scroll up through the document, and click the down scroll arrow to scroll down through the document.

The scroll bar contains a scroll box that indicates the location of the text in the document screen in relation to the remainder of the document. To scroll up one screen at a time, position the mouse pointer above the scroll box (but below the up scroll arrow) and then click the left mouse button. Position the mouse pointer below the scroll box and click the left button to scroll down a screen. Click and hold down the left mouse button and the action becomes continuous.

Another method for scrolling is to position the mouse pointer on the scroll box, click and hold down the left mouse button, and then drag the scroll box along the scroll bar to reposition text in the document screen. As the scroll box is dragged along the vertical scroll bar in a longer document, page numbers are shown in a box at the right side of the document screen.

Activity 3a Scrolling in a Document   Part 1 of 2

1. Open **InterfaceApps** (from the WL1C1 folder you copied to your storage medium).
2. Save the document with the new name **1-InterfaceApps** to your WL1C1 folder.
3. Position the I-beam pointer at the beginning of the first paragraph and then click the left mouse button.
4. Click the down scroll arrow on the vertical scroll bar several times. (This scrolls down lines of text in the document.) With the mouse pointer on the down scroll arrow, click and hold down the left mouse button and keep it down until you reach the end of the document.
5. Position the mouse pointer on the up scroll arrow and then click and hold down the left mouse button until you reach the beginning of the document.
6. Position the mouse pointer below the scroll box and then click the left mouse button. Continue clicking the mouse button (with the mouse pointer positioned below the scroll box) until you reach the end of the document.
7. Position the mouse pointer on the scroll box in the vertical scroll bar. Click and hold down the left mouse button, drag the scroll box to the top of the vertical scroll bar, and then release the mouse button. (Notice that the document page numbers are shown in a box at the right side of the document screen.)
8. Click in the title at the beginning of the document. (This moves the insertion point to the location of the mouse pointer.)

Moving the Insertion Point to a Specific Line or Page

Find

Word includes a Go To feature that moves the insertion point to a specific location in a document, such as a line or page. To use the feature, click the Find button arrow in the Editing group on the Home tab and then click *Go To* at the drop-down list. At the Find and Replace dialog box with the Go To tab selected, move the insertion point to a specific page by typing the page number in the *Enter page number* text box and then pressing the Enter key. Move to a specific line by clicking the *Line* option in the *Go to what* list box, typing the line number in the *Enter line number* text box, and then pressing the Enter key. Click the Close button to close the dialog box.

Moving the Insertion Point with the Keyboard

Tutorial

Moving the Insertion Point and Inserting and Deleting Text

To move the insertion point with the keyboard, use the arrow keys to the right of the regular keyboard or use the arrow keys on the numeric keypad. When using the arrow keys on the numeric keypad, make sure Num Lock is off. Use the arrow keys together with other keys to move the insertion point to various locations in the document, as shown in Table 1.2.

When moving the insertion point, Word considers a word to be any series of characters between spaces. A paragraph is any text that is followed by a single press of the Enter key. A page is text that is separated by a soft or hard page break.

Table 1.2 Insertion Point Movement Commands

To move insertion point	Press
one character left	Left Arrow
one character right	Right Arrow
one line up	Up Arrow
one line down	Down Arrow
one word left	Ctrl + Left Arrow
one word right	Ctrl + Right Arrow
to beginning of line	Home
to end of line	End
to beginning of current paragraph	Ctrl + Up Arrow
to beginning of next paragraph	Ctrl + Down Arrow
up one screen	Page Up
down one screen	Page Down
to top of previous page	Ctrl + Page Up
to top of next page	Ctrl + Page Down
to beginning of document	Ctrl + Home
to end of document	Ctrl + End

Resuming Reading or Editing in a Document

If a previously saved document is opened, pressing Shift + F5 will move the insertion point to the position it was last located when the document was closed.

When a multiple-page document is reopened, Word remembers the page where the insertion point was last positioned. A "Welcome back!" message appears at the right side of the screen near the vertical scroll bar, identifying the page where the insertion point was last located. Click the message and the insertion point is positioned at the top of that page.

Activity 3b **Moving the Insertion Point in a Document** Part 2 of 2

1. With **1-InterfaceApps** open, move the insertion point to line 15 and then to page 3 by completing the following steps:
   a. Click the Find button arrow in the Editing group on the Home tab and then click *Go To* at the drop-down list.
   b. At the Find and Replace dialog box with the Go To tab selected, click *Line* in the *Go to what* list box.
   c. Click in the *Enter line number* text box, type 15, and then press the Enter key.
   d. Click *Page* in the *Go to what* list box.
   e. Click in the *Enter page number* text box, type 3, and then press the Enter key.
   f. Click the Close button to close the Find and Replace dialog box.

2. Close the document.
3. Open the document by clicking the File tab and then clicking the document name *1-InterfaceApps* in the Recent list.
4. Move the mouse pointer to the right side of the screen to display the "Welcome back!" message. Hover the mouse pointer over the message and then click the left mouse button. (This positions the insertion point at the top of the third page—the page the insertion point was positioned when you closed the document.)

5. Press Ctrl + Home to move the insertion point to the beginning of the document.
6. Practice using the keyboard commands shown in Table 1.2 to move the insertion point within the document.
7. Close **1-InterfaceApps**.

You will open a previously created document, save it with a new name, and then make editing changes to the document. The editing changes will include selecting, inserting, and deleting text and undoing and redoing edits.

Inserting and Deleting Text

Editing a document may include inserting and/or deleting text. To insert text in a document, position the insertion point at the location text is to be typed and then type the text. Existing characters move to the right as text is typed. A number of options are available for deleting text. Some deletion commands are shown in Table 1.3.

Tutorial

Selecting,
Replacing, and
Deleting Text

Selecting Text

Use the mouse and/or keyboard to select a specific amount of text. Selected text can be deleted or other Word functions can be performed on it. When text is selected, it displays with a gray background, as shown in Figure 1.8, and the Mini toolbar displays. The Mini toolbar contains buttons for common tasks. (You will learn more about the Mini toolbar in Chapter 2.)

Table 1.3 Deletion Commands

To delete	Press
character right of insertion point	Delete key
character left of insertion point	Backspace key
text from insertion point to beginning of word	Ctrl + Backspace
text from insertion point to end of word	Ctrl + Delete

Figure 1.8 Selected Text and Mini Toolbar

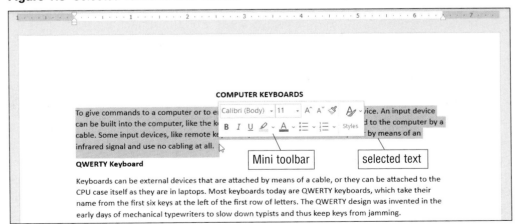

Selecting Text with the Mouse Use the mouse to select a word, line, sentence, paragraph, or entire document. Table 1.4 indicates the steps to follow to select various amounts of text.

One way to select text is by clicking in the selection bar. The selection bar is the space at the left side of the document screen between the left edge of the page and the text. When the mouse pointer is positioned in the selection bar, the pointer turns into an arrow pointing up and to the right (instead of to the left). Click once to select a line of text, twice to select a paragraph, and three times to select all the text in the document.

Another way to select text is by using the I-beam pointer. Position the pointer on the first character of the text to be selected, click and hold down the left mouse button, drag the I-beam pointer to the last character of the text to be selected, and then release the mouse button. Alternately, position the insertion point where the selection is to begin, press and hold down the Shift key, click the I-beam pointer at the end of the selection, and then release the Shift key. To cancel a selection, simply click in the document screen.

Select text vertically in a document by pressing and holding down the Alt key while dragging with the mouse. This is especially useful when selecting a group of text, such as text set in columns.

Selecting Text with the Keyboard To select text using the keyboard, turn on the Selection mode by pressing the F8 function key. With the Selection mode activated, use the arrow keys to select text. To cancel the selection, press the Esc key and then press any arrow key. The Status bar can be customized to indicate that the Selection mode is activated. To do this, right-click on the Status bar and then click *Selection Mode* at the pop-up list. When the F8 function key is pressed to turn on the Selection mode, the words *Extend Selection* display on the Status bar. Text can also be selected with the commands shown in Table 1.5.

Table 1.4 Selecting Text with the Mouse

To select	Complete these steps using the mouse
a word	Double-click the word.
a line of text	Click in the selection bar to the left of the line.
multiple lines of text	Drag in the selection bar to the left of the lines.
a sentence	Press and hold down the Ctrl key and then click in the sentence.
a paragraph	Double-click in the selection bar next to the paragraph, or triple-click in the paragraph.
multiple paragraphs	Drag in the selection bar.
an entire document	Triple-click in the selection bar, or click the Select button in Editing group and then click *Select All*.

Table 1.5 Selecting Text with the Keyboard

To select	Press
one character to right	Shift + Right Arrow
one character to left	Shift + Left Arrow
to end of word	Ctrl + Shift + Right Arrow
to beginning of word	Ctrl + Shift + Left Arrow
to end of line	Shift + End
to beginning of line	Shift + Home
one line up	Shift + Up Arrow
one line down	Shift + Down Arrow
to beginning of paragraph	Ctrl + Shift + Up Arrow
to end of paragraph	Ctrl + Shift + Down Arrow
one screen up	Shift + Page Up
one screen down	Shift + Page Down
to end of document	Ctrl + Shift + End
to beginning of document	Ctrl + Shift + Home
entire document	Ctrl + A

Activity 4a Editing a Document   Part 1 of 2

1. Open **CompKeyboards**. (This document is in the WL1C1 folder you copied to your storage medium.)
2. Save the document with the new name **1-CompKeyboards**.
3. Change the word *give* in the first sentence of the first paragraph to *enter* by double-clicking *give* and then typing enter.
4. Change the second *to* in the first sentence to *into* by double-clicking *to* and then typing into.
5. Select the words *means of* in the first sentence in the *QWERTY Keyboard* section and then press the Delete key to delete the selected text.

6. At the end of the last sentence of the first paragraph, select the words *and use no cabling at all* and the period that follows, being careful not to select the space following the period. Press the Delete key to delete the selected text.
7. Insert a period immediately following the word *signal*.

8. Delete the heading *QWERTY Keyboard* using the Selection mode by completing the following steps:
   a. Position the insertion point immediately left of the *Q* in *QWERTY*.
   b. Press the F8 function key to turn on the Selection mode.
   c. Press the Down Arrow key.
   d. Press the Delete key.
9. Complete steps similar to those in Step 8 to delete the heading *DVORAK Keyboard*.
10. Begin a new paragraph with the sentence that reads *Keyboards have different physical appearances* by completing the following steps:
    a. Position the insertion point immediately left of the *K* in *Keyboards* (the first word of the fifth sentence in the last paragraph).
    b. Press the Enter key.
11. Save **1-CompKeyboards**.

To enter commands into a c
device can be built into the
computer by a cable. Some i
means of an infrared signal.

QWERTY Keyboard

Keyboards can be external d
itself as they are in laptops.
the first six keys at the left o
of mechanical typewriters to

8a–8c

To enter commands into a computer
device can be built into the compute
computer by a cable. Some input dev
means of an infrared signal.

Keyboards can be external devices th
itself as they are in laptops. Most key
the first six keys at the left of the firs
of mechanical typewriters to slow do

The DVORAK keyboard is an alternati
commonly used keys are placed clos
install software on a QWERTY keyboa
keyboards is convenient especially w

Keyboards have different physical ap
that of a calculator, containing numb
"broken" into two pieces to reduce s
change the symbol or character ente

10a–10b

> Check Your Work

Using the Undo and Redo Buttons

Undo typing, formatting, or another action by clicking the Undo button on the Quick Access Toolbar. For example, type text and then click the Undo button and the text is removed. Or apply formatting to text and then click the Undo button and the formatting is removed.

Click the Redo button on the Quick Access Toolbar to reverse the original action. For example, apply formatting such as underlining to text and then click the Undo button and the underlining is removed. Click the Redo button and the underlining formatting is reapplied to the text. Many Word actions can be undone or redone. Some actions, however, such as printing and saving, cannot be undone or redone.

Word maintains actions in temporary memory. To undo an action performed earlier, click the Undo button arrow. This causes a drop-down list to display. To make a selection from this drop-down list, click the desired action; the action, along with any actions listed above it in the drop-down list, is undone.

1. With **1-CompKeyboards** open, delete the last sentence in the last paragraph using the mouse by completing the following steps:
   a. Hover the I-beam pointer anywhere over the sentence that begins *All keyboards have modifier keys*.
   b. Press and hold down the Ctrl key, click the left mouse button, and then release the Ctrl key.

install software on a QWERTY keyboard that emulates a DVORAK keyboard. The ability to emulate other keyboards is convenient especially when working with foreign languages.

Keyboards have different physical appearances. Many keyboards have a separate numeric keypad, like that of a calculator, containing numbers and mathematical operators. Some keyboards are sloped and "broken" into two pieces to reduce strain. All keyboards have modifier keys that enable the user to change the symbol or character entered when a given key is pressed.

1a-1b

   c. Press the Delete key.
2. Delete the last paragraph by completing the following steps:
   a. Position the I-beam pointer anywhere in the last paragraph (the paragraph that begins *Keyboards have different physical appearances*).
   b. Triple-click the left mouse button.
   c. Press the Delete key.
3. Undo the deletion by clicking the Undo button on the Quick Access Toolbar.
4. Redo the deletion by clicking the Redo button on the Quick Access Toolbar.
5. Select the first sentence in the second paragraph and then delete it.
6. Select the first paragraph in the document and then delete it.
7. Undo the two deletions by completing the following steps:
   a. Click the Undo button arrow.
   b. Click the second *Clear* listed in the drop-down list. (This will redisplay the first paragraph and the first sentence in the second paragraph. The sentence will be selected.)

7a   7b

8. Click outside the sentence to deselect it.
9. Save, print, and then close **1-CompKeyboards**.

 Check Your Work

Activity 5 **Complete a Spelling and Grammar Check**   **1 Part**

You will open a previously created document, save it with a new name, and then check the spelling and grammar in the document.

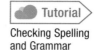

Tutorial

Checking Spelling
and Grammar

Quick Steps

Check Spelling and Grammar

1. Click Review tab.
2. Click Check Document button.
3. Click the Results button.
4. Change or ignore errors.
5. Click OK.

Check
Document

Checking the Spelling and Grammar in a Document

Thoughtful and well-written documents are free of errors in spelling and grammar. Word contains an Editor that checks for spelling and grammar errors in documents and offers suggested corrections. It may also suggest refinements for clarity and conciseness. The Editor's spell checking feature can find and correct misspelled words, duplicate words, and irregular capitalizations. To check spelling, it compares the words in the document with the words in its dictionary. If it finds a match, it passes over the word. If the word is not found in its dictionary, it offers possible corrections. The grammar checker searches a document for errors in grammar, punctuation, and word usage. There are some types of errors that the Editor cannot find, however. Using the Editor does not eliminate the need for proofreading.

To complete a spelling and grammar check, click the Review tab and then click the Check Document button in the Proofing group or press the F7 function key. The Editor task pane opens at the right side of the screen and contains a Results button indicating the number of possible spelling and grammar errors. The task pane also contains options in the *Corrections* section identifying the number of possible spelling errors and grammar errors and a *Refinements* section identifying the number of areas that may need editing. Click the Results button to search and display spelling and grammar errors as they are encountered. Click the *Spelling* option in the *Corrections* section to review all possible spelling errors and click the *Grammar* option to review all possible grammar errors.

Click the Results button at the Editor task pane and the first spelling or grammar error is selected. The *Suggestions* list box contains one or more possible corrections. Click a suggestion to make the correction in the document. Or, click the arrow to the right of a suggestion for more options, as described in Table 1.6. If none of the suggestions seems right and the word is correct as typed, use the other options in the task pane to ignore the error or add the word to the spell checker's dictionary. Refer to Table 1.7 for descriptions of the options in the Editor task pane.

If Word detects a grammar error, the text containing the error is selected and possible corrections are provided in the Editor task pane *Suggestions* list box. Depending on the error, some of the options described in Table 1.7 may be available and a grammar rule will be provided near the top of the task pane. Click the down arrow at the right of the grammar rule and information about the grammar rule displays along with suggestions on how to correct the error.

When checking the spelling and grammar in a document, temporarily leave the Editor task pane by clicking in the document. To resume the spelling and grammar check, click the Resume button in the task pane.

Table 1.6 Suggestion Drop-Down List Options

Option	Function
Read Aloud	reads the suggested correction aloud (speaker necessary)
Spell Out	spells the suggested correction aloud (speaker necessary)
Change All	changes all instances of the error to the suggested correction
Add to AutoCorrect	makes a suggested correction automatic by adding it as an option in AutoCorrect

Table 1.7 Editor Task Pane Options

Option	Function
Ignore Once	ignores the selected error
Ignore All	ignores the error and all other occurrences of it in the document
Add to Dictionary	adds the word to the spelling checker dictionary
Delete Repeated Word	deletes one of two repeated words
Don't check for this issue	ignores a suspected grammar error and no longer checks for this type of error in the document

Activity 5 Checking the Spelling and Grammar in a Document
Part 1 of 1

1. Open **TechOccTrends** and save it with the name **1-TechOccTrends**.
2. Click the Review tab and then click the Check Document button in the Proofing group.

3. The Editor task pane opens and identifies the total number of possible spelling and grammar errors along with information in the *Corrections* section. Click the Results button (displays as *6 Results*) to display the first possible error.

4. The spelling checker selects the word *tecnology* in the document and provides the correct spelling in the *Suggestions* list box in the Editor task pane. Click *technology* in the *Suggestions* list box to change the word to the correct spelling.

5. The grammar checker selects the word *too* in the document and provides the word *to* in the *Suggestions* list box of the Editor task pane. Click the down arrow to the right of the text *Possible Word Choice Error* near the top of the task pane, read the information provided about a possible word choice error, and then click the up arrow to remove the information.

6. Click *to* in the *Suggestions* list box to correct the grammar error.

7. The grammar checker selects the words *downloaded* and *versus*, noting that two spaces appear between the words. The *Suggestions* list box in the Editor task pane provides an option with the words *downloaded versus* with only one space between the words. Click the option in the *Suggestions* list box to correct the error.

8. The spelling checker selects the word *sucessful* in the document and provides *successful* in the Editor task pane *Suggestions* list box. Since this word is misspelled in another location in the document, click the arrow at the right of the *successful* option in the *Suggestions* list box and then click *Change All* at the drop-down list.

9. The spelling checker selects the word *are*, which is used two times in a row. Click the *Delete Repeated Word* option in the Editor task pane to delete the second *are*.

 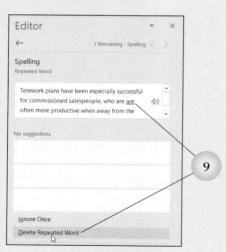

10. When the message indicating the spelling and grammar check is complete, click OK.

11. Close the Editor task pane by clicking the Close button in the upper right corner of the task pane.

12. Save, print, and then close **1-TechOccTrends**.

Check Your Work

Tutorial

Using the Tell Me Feature

Using the Tell Me Feature

Word includes a Tell Me feature that provides information and guidance on how to use various functions in the program. To get help finding or using a function in Word, click in the *Tell Me* text box on the ribbon (or press Alt + Q) and then type the function. A drop-down list displays with options for completing the function. The drop-down list will also include links to find more information online or through the Help feature.

Click the last option in the Tell Me drop-down list to search for more results. A Smart Lookup task pane will open at the right of the screen, providing information from various sources on the internet. The Smart Lookup task pane can also be displayed by clicking the Smart Lookup button in the Research group on the References tab or by selecting text, right-clicking the selected text, and then clicking *Smart Lookup* at the shortcut menu.

Activity 6a **Using the Tell Me Feature**   Part 1 of 2

1. Open **GraphicSoftware** and then save it with the name **1-GraphicSoftware**.
2. Press Ctrl + A to select all text in the document.
3. Use the Tell Me feature to learn how to double-space the text in the document by completing the following steps:
   a. Click in the *Tell Me* text box on the ribbon.
   b. Type double space.
   c. Hover the mouse pointer over the *Line and Paragraph Spacing* option.
   d. At the side menu, click the *2.0* option. (This double-spaces the selected text in the document.)

   e. Click in the document to deselect the text.

4. Use the Tell Me feature to display help information on AutoCorrect by completing the following steps:
   a. Click in the *Tell Me* text box.
   b. Type autocorrect.
   c. Hover the mouse pointer over the *Get Help on "autocorrect"* option.
   d. At the side menu, click the first option (an article on AutoCorrect). This displays the Help task pane with the article information.

   e. Read the information in the Help task pane and then close the task pane by clicking the the Close button in the upper right corner of the task pane.
5. Display information on scrolling in the Smart Lookup task pane by completing the following steps:
   a. Click in the *Tell Me* text box.
   b. Type scrolling.
   c. Click the *See more search results for "scrolling"* option. (The option may display as *Smart Lookup on "scrolling."*)
   d. Look at the information on scrolling in the Smart Lookup task pane.
   e. Close the Smart Lookup task pane by clicking the task pane Close button.
6. Save, print, and then close **1-GraphicSoftware**.

 Check Your Work

 Tutorial

Using the Help Feature

 Help

Using the Help Feature

The Help feature is an on-screen reference manual containing information about Word features and commands. The Help feature in Word is similar to the Help features in Excel, PowerPoint, and Access. Get help by using the Tell Me feature, at the Help task pane, or at the Microsoft Office support website. Display the Help task pane by pressing the F1 function key or clicking the Help tab and then clicking the Help button.

At the Help task pane, type a topic, feature, or question in the search text box and then press the Enter key. Articles related to the search text are shown in the task pane. Click an article to display the article information in the task pane.

Getting Help from a ScreenTip

Hover the mouse pointer over a certain button, such as the Format Painter button or Font Color button, and the ScreenTip displays with a Help icon and the <u>Tell me more</u> hyperlinked text. Click <u>Tell me more</u> or press the F1 function key and the Help task pane displays with information about the button feature.

Getting Help at the Backstage Area

Click the File tab in Word to display the backstage area. A Microsoft Word Help button, labeled with a question mark (?), appears in the upper right corner of the backstage area. The Help button is also available at many of the other backstage areas. Click the Help button and the Microsoft Office support website opens in a browser window with information about the backstage area. After reading the information, close the browser window and return to Word.

Getting Help in a Dialog Box

Some dialog boxes contain a Help button. Open a dialog box and then click the Help button and the Microsoft Office support website opens in a browser window with information about the dialog box. After reading the information, close the browser window.

Activity 6b **Using the Help Feature** Part 2 of 2

1. Open a new blank document by completing the following steps:
   a. Click the File tab.
   b. At the Home backstage area, double-click the *Single spaced (blank)* template. (For Word 2019, click the File tab, click the *New* option, and then double-click the *Single spaced (blank)* template.)

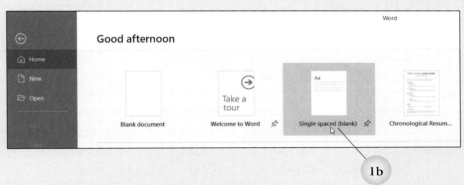

2. Press the F1 function key to display the Help task pane.
3. Type print in the task pane search text box and then press the Enter key.
4. When the list of articles displays, click the Print a document in Word hyperlinked article. (You may need to scroll down the task pane to find this article.)
5. Read the information in the task pane about printing a document.
6. Click the Close button to close the Help task pane.
7. Hover the mouse pointer over the Format Painter button in the Clipboard group on the Home tab.

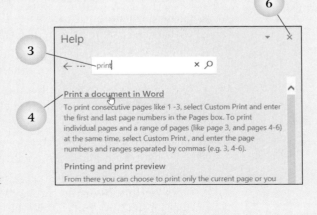

8. Click the <u>Tell me more</u> hyperlinked text at the bottom of the ScreenTip.
9. Read the information in the Help task pane about the Format Painter feature.
10. Click the Help task pane Close button.
11. Click the File tab.
12. Click the Microsoft Word Help button in the upper right corner of the backstage area.

13. Look at the information on the Microsoft Office support website and then close the browser window.
14. Click the Back button to return to the document.
15. Close the blank document.

Chapter Summary

- Refer to Figure 1.1 and Table 1.1 (on page 5) for an example and a list, respectively, of key Word screen features.
- Click the File tab and the backstage area displays, containing options for working with and managing documents.
- Document names can contain a maximum of 255 characters, including the drive letter and folder names, and they may include spaces.
- The Quick Access Toolbar contains buttons for commonly used commands.
- The ribbon contains tabs with options and buttons divided into groups.
- The insertion point displays as a blinking vertical line and indicates the position of the next character to be entered in the document.
- Print a hard copy of a document by clicking the File tab, clicking the *Print* option, and then clicking the Print button.
- Close a document by clicking the File tab and then clicking the *Close* option or with the keyboard shortcut Ctrl + F4.
- Close Word by clicking the Close button in the upper right corner of the screen or with the keyboard shortcut Alt + F4.
- Create a new document by clicking the File tab, clicking the *Home* or *New* option as needed, and then clicking the *Blank document* template or by using the keyboard shortcut Ctrl + N.
- Create a new single-spaced document by clicking the File tab, clicking the *Home* or *New* option, and then clicking the *Single spaced (blank)* template.
- Display the Open backstage area by clicking the File tab and then clicking the *Open* option; by using the keyboard shortcut Ctrl + O; or by clicking the <u>More documents</u> hyperlink at the Home backstage area or the Word opening screen.
- Display the Open dialog box by clicking the *Browse* option at the Open backstage area or with the keyboard shortcut Ctrl + F12.

- At the Open backstage area with the *Recent* option selected, 50 of the most recently opened documents display.

- Pin a frequently-used document or folder to the *Recent* option list at the Open backstage area or pin a document at the Home backstage area by clicking the push pin icon to the right of the document or folder name. Pinned documents and folders appear in the *Pinned* category. Click the push pin icon again to unpin a document or folder from the list.

- Save a document with the same name by clicking the Save button on the Quick Access Toolbar, with the *Save* option at the backstage area, or with the keyboard shortcut Ctrl + S.

- The scroll box on the vertical scroll bar indicates the location of the text in the document screen in relation to the remainder of the document.

- The insertion point can be moved throughout the document using the mouse, the keyboard, or a combination of the two.

- The insertion point can be moved by character, word, screen, or page and from the first to the last character in a document. Refer to Table 1.2 (on page 7) for keyboard insertion point movement commands.

- Delete text by character, word, line, several lines, or partial page using specific keys or by selecting text using the mouse or the keyboard. Refer to Table 1.3 (on page 17) for deletion commands.

- A specific amount of text can be selected using the mouse and/or the keyboard. Refer to Table 1.4 (on page 18) for information on selecting with the mouse, and refer to Table 1.5 (on page 19) for information on selecting with the keyboard.

- Use the Undo button on the Quick Access Toolbar to undo an action such as typing, deleting, or formatting text. Use the Redo button to redo something that has been undone with the Undo button.

- Word contains an Editor that checks for spelling and grammar errors in the document. Corrections are suggested in the Editor task pane. Refer to Table 1.6 and Table 1.7 (on page 23) for a description of options at the Editor task pane.

- The Tell Me feature provides information and guidance on how to complete a function. The *Tell Me* text box is on the ribbon.

- Word's Help feature is an on-screen reference manual containing information about Word features and commands. Press the F1 function key to display the Help task pane or click the Help tab and then click the Help button.

- Hover the mouse pointer over a certain button and the ScreenTip displays with a Help icon and the Tell me more hyperlinked text. Click this hyperlinked text to display the Help task pane, which contains information about the button feature.

- Some dialog boxes and the backstage area contain a Help button that links to the Microsoft Office support website to provide more information about available functions and features.

Commands Review

FEATURE	RIBBON TAB, GROUP/OPTION	BUTTON, OPTION	KEYBOARD SHORTCUT
AutoComplete entry			F3
close document	File, *Close*		Ctrl + F4
close Word		✕	Alt + F4
Go To feature	Home, Editing	🔍, *Go To*	Ctrl + G
Help task pane	Help, Help	⃝?	F1
leave backstage area		←	Esc
move insertion point to previous location when document was closed			Shift + F5
new blank document	File, *New* OR File, *Home*	*Blank document*	Ctrl + N
New Line command			Shift + Enter
Open backstage area	File, *Open*		Ctrl + O
Open dialog box	File, *Open*	*Browse*	Ctrl + F12
Print backstage area	File, *Print*		Ctrl + P
redo action		↻	Ctrl + Y
save	File, *Save*	💾	Ctrl + S
Save As backstage area	File, *Save As*		
Save As dialog box	File, *Save As*	*Browse*	F12
Selection mode			F8
spelling and grammar check	Review, Proofing	abc✓	F7
Tell Me feature			Alt + Q
undo action		�581 ⌄	Ctrl + Z

Microsoft®

Word

Formatting Characters and Paragraphs

Performance Objectives

Upon successful completion of Chapter 2, you will be able to:

1 Change the font and font size and choose font effects

2 Format selected text with buttons on the Mini toolbar

3 Apply styles from style sets

4 Apply themes

5 Customize styles and themes

6 Change the alignment of text in paragraphs

7 Indent text in paragraphs

8 Increase and decrease spacing before and after paragraphs

9 Repeat the last action

10 Automate formatting with Format Painter

11 Change line spacing

12 Reveal and compare formatting

The appearance of a document on the screen and when printed is called the *format*. A Word document is based on a template that applies default formatting. Some of the default formats include 11-point Calibri font, line spacing of 1.08, 8 points of spacing after each paragraph, and left-aligned text. In this chapter, you will learn about changing the typeface, type size, and typestyle as well as applying font effects such as bold and italic. You will also learn to format paragraphs by changing text alignment and line spacing, indenting text, and applying formatting with Format Painter.

 Data Files

Before beginning chapter work, copy the WL1C2 folder to your storage medium and then make WL1C2 the active folder.

The online course includes additional training and assessment resources.

You will open a document containing a glossary of terms and then format the document by changing the font and the font size; adding bold, italics, and underlining; and applying font effects.

 Tutorial

Applying Font
Formatting Using
the Font Group

Applying Font Formatting

One of the most visible aspects of a document's format is the font. Font formatting can be applied to the individual characters of text, including letters, numbers, and symbols. A font consists of three elements: typeface, type size, and typestyle. By default, a Word document is formatted with the Calibri typeface in 11-point size. The typestyle is roman type; that is, regular and not bold or italic. This default may need to be changed to another font for such reasons as altering the mood of the document, enhancing its visual appeal, and increasing its readability.

Hint Change the default font by selecting the font at the Font dialog box and then clicking the Set As Default button.

The Font group on the Home tab, shown in Figure 2.1, contains a number of options and buttons for applying font formatting to characters in a document. The top row contains options for changing the font and font size as well as buttons for increasing and decreasing the size of the font and changing the text case. The bottom row contains buttons for applying typestyles such as bold, italic, and underline and for applying text effects, highlighting, and color. Also notice the Clear All Formatting button in the top row of the Font group. Use this button to remove all formatting applied to characters and paragraphs in the text. To remove only character formatting, select text and then use the keyboard shortcut Ctrl + spacebar.

Hint Use a serif typeface for text-intensive documents.

A typeface is a set of characters with a common design and shape and can be decorative or plain and either monospaced or proportional. Word refers to a typeface as a *font*. A monospaced typeface allots the same amount of horizontal space for each character, while a proportional typeface allots varying amounts of space for different characters. Typefaces are divided into two main categories: serif and sans serif. A serif is a small line at the end of a character stroke. Consider using a serif typeface for text-intensive documents because the serifs help move the reader's eyes across the page. Use a sans serif typeface for headings, headlines, and advertisements. Some popular typefaces are shown in Table 2.1.

Figure 2.1 Font Group Option Boxes and Buttons

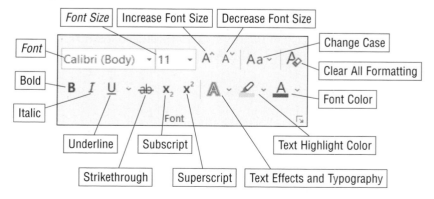

Table 2.1 Categories of Typefaces

Serif Typefaces	Sans Serif Typefaces	Monospaced Typefaces
Cambria	Calibri	Consolas
Constantia	Candara	Courier New
Times New Roman	Corbel	Lucida Console
Bookman Old Style	Arial	MS Gothic

Hint Press Ctrl +]
to increase font size by
1 point and press
Ctrl + [to decrease
font size by 1 point.

Type is generally set in proportional size. The size of proportional type is measured vertically in units called *points*. A point is approximately ¹/₇₂ of an inch—the higher the point size, the larger the characters. Within a typeface, characters may have varying styles, including regular, bold, italic, bold italic, and underlined.

Use the *Font* option box in the Font group to change the font. Select the text in the document, click the *Font* option box arrow, and then click a font option at the drop-down gallery. Another method for changing the font is to click the current font name in the *Font* option box to select it and then type the new font name. Change the font size by clicking the *Font Size* option box arrow and then clicking the font size at the drop-down gallery. Or, click the current font size in the *Font Size* option box to select it and then type the new font size number.

To see a live preview of the text in different fonts and sizes before changing the formatting in the document, select the text and open the *Font* or *Font Size* drop-down gallery. Hover the mouse pointer over different font options to see how the selected text displays in each font or size.

Activity 1a Changing the Font and Font Size

Part 1 of 4

1. Open **CompTerms** and then save it with the name **2-CompTerms**.
2. Change the typeface to Cambria by completing the following steps:
   a. Select all text in the document by pressing Ctrl + A. (You can also do this by clicking the Select button in the Editing group and then clicking *Select All* at the drop-down list.)
   b. Click the *Font* option box arrow, scroll down the drop-down gallery until *Cambria* displays, and then hover the mouse pointer over *Cambria*. This displays a live preview of the text set in Cambria.
   c. Click the *Cambria* option.

Chapter 2 | Formatting Characters and Paragraphs

3. Change the type size to 14 points by completing the following steps:
   a. With the text in the document still selected, click the *Font Size* option box arrow.
   b. At the drop-down gallery, hover the mouse pointer over *14* and look at the live preview of the text with 14 points applied.
   c. Click the *14* option.

4. Change the type size and typeface by completing the following steps:
   a. Click the Decrease Font Size button in the Font group three times. (This decreases the size to 10 points.)
   b. Click the Increase Font Size button two times. (This increases the size to 12 points.)
   c. Click the *Font* option box arrow, scroll down the drop-down gallery, and then click *Constantia*. (The most recently used fonts are listed at the beginning of the gallery, followed by a listing of all fonts.)
5. Deselect the text by clicking anywhere in the document.
6. Save **2-CompTerms**.

Check Your Work

Choosing a Typestyle

B Bold

I Italic

<u>U</u> ▾ Underline

Apply a typestyle to emphasize text using the Bold, Italic, and Underline buttons in the bottom row in the Font group on the Home tab. More than one typestyle can be applied to text. For example, a word may be set as bold italic and also underlined. Click the Underline button arrow and a drop-down gallery displays with underlining options such as a double line, dashed line, and thicker underline. Click the *Underline Color* option at the Underline button drop-down gallery and a side menu displays with color options.

1. With **2-CompTerms** open, press Ctrl + Home to move the insertion point to the beginning of the document.
2. Type a heading for the document by completing the following steps:

   a. Click the Bold button in the Font group. (This turns on bold formatting.)
   b. Click the Underline button in the Font group. (This turns on underline formatting.)
   c. Type Glossary of Terms.
3. Press Ctrl + End to move the insertion point to the end of the document.
4. Type the text shown in Figure 2.2 with the following specifications:
   a. While typing, make the appropriate text bold, as shown in the figure, by completing the following steps:
      1) Click the Bold button. (This turns on bold formatting.)
      2) Type the text.
      3) Click the Bold button. (This turns off bold formatting.)
   b. Press the Enter key two times after typing the C heading.
   c. While typing, italicize the appropriate text, as shown in the figure, by completing the following steps:
      1) Click the Italic button in the Font group.
      2) Type the text.
      3) Click the Italic button.
5. After typing the text, press the Enter key two times and then press Ctrl + Home to move the insertion point to the beginning of the document.
6. Change the underlining below the title by completing the following steps:
   a. Select the title *Glossary of Terms*.
   b. Click the Underline button arrow and then click the third underline option from the top of the drop-down gallery (*Thick underline*).

   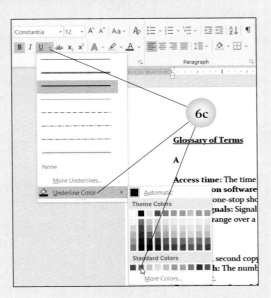

   c. Click the Underline button arrow, point to the *Underline Color* option, and then click the *Red* option (second color option in the *Standard Colors* section).
7. With the title still selected, change the font size to 14 points.
8. Save **2-CompTerms**.

Figure 2.2 Activity 1b

C

Chip: A thin wafer of *silicon* containing electronic circuitry that performs various functions, such as mathematical calculations, storage, and controlling computer devices.

Cluster: A group of two or more *sectors* on a disk; a cluster is the smallest unit of storage space used to store data.

Coding: A term used by programmers to refer to the act of writing source code.

Crackers: A term coined by computer hackers for those who intentionally enter (or hack) computer systems to damage them.

 Tutorial

Highlighting Text

 Clear All Formatting

 Change Case

 Strikethrough

 Subscript

 Superscript

 Text Effects and Typography

 Text Highlight Color

 Font Color

Choosing a Font Effect

Apply font effects with buttons in the top and bottom rows in the Font group on the Home tab, or clear all formatting from selected text with the Clear All Formatting button. Change the case of text with the Change Case button drop-down list. Click the Change Case button in the top row in the Font group and then click one of the options in the drop-down list: *Sentence case, lowercase., UPPERCASE, Capitalize Each Word,* and *tOGGLE cASE.* The case of selected text can also be changed with the keyboard shortcut Shift + F3. Each time Shift + F3 is pressed, the selected text displays in the next case option in the list.

The bottom row in the Font group contains buttons for applying font effects. Use the Strikethrough button to draw a line through selected text. This has a practical application in some legal documents in which deleted text must be retained in the document. Use the Subscript button to create text that is lowered slightly below the line, as in the chemical formula H_2O. Use the Superscript button to create text that is raised slightly above the text line, as in the mathematical equation four to the third power (written as 4^3).

Click the Text Effects and Typography button in the bottom row and a drop-down gallery displays with effect options. The Text Highlight Color and Font Color buttons are used to highlight text or change the color of the font. To apply highlighting, select text and then click the Text Highlight Color button. The default color is yellow; other colors can be selected from the drop-down list. Or, click the button to make the I-beam pointer display with a highlighter pen attached, and then select text with the mouse pointer to highlight it. Click the button again to turn off highlighting. To change font color, select text, click the Font Color button arrow, and then click a color at the drop-down gallery.

Applying Formatting Using Keyboard Shortcuts

Several of the options and buttons in the Font group have keyboard shortcuts. For example, press Ctrl + B to turn bold formatting on or off and press Ctrl + I to turn italic formatting on or off. Position the mouse pointer on an option or button and an enhanced ScreenTip displays with the name and description of the option or button and the keyboard shortcut, if it has one. Table 2.2 identifies the keyboard shortcuts available for options and buttons in the Font group.

Table 2.2 Font Group Option and Button Keyboard Shortcuts

Font Group Option/Button	Keyboard Shortcut
Font	Ctrl + Shift + F
Font Size	Ctrl + Shift + P
Increase Font Size	Ctrl + Shift + > OR Ctrl +]
Decrease Font Size	Ctrl + Shift + < OR Ctrl + [
Bold	Ctrl + B
Italic	Ctrl + I
Underline	Ctrl + U
Subscript	Ctrl + =
Superscript	Ctrl + Shift + +
Change Case	Shift + F3

Tutorial

Applying Font
Formatting Using
the Mini Toolbar

Formatting with the Mini Toolbar

When text is selected, the Mini toolbar displays above the selected text, as shown in Figure 2.3. Click a button on the Mini toolbar to apply formatting to the selected text. When the mouse pointer is moved away from the Mini toolbar, the toolbar disappears.

Figure 2.3 Mini Toolbar

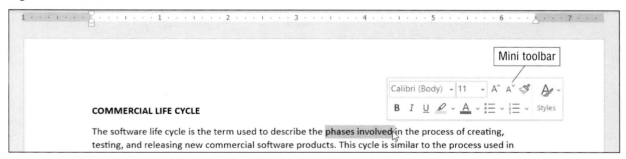

Activity 1c Applying Font Effects

Part 3 of 4

1. With **2-CompTerms** open, move the insertion point to the beginning of the term *Chip*, press the Enter key, and then press the Up Arrow key.
2. Type the text shown in Figure 2.4. Create each superscript number by clicking the Superscript button, typing the number, and then clicking the Superscript button.

3. Remove underlining and change the case of the text in the title by completing the following steps:
   a. Select the title *Glossary of Terms*.
   b. Remove all formatting from the title by clicking the Clear All Formatting button in the Font group.
   c. Click the Change Case button in the Font group and then click *UPPERCASE* at the drop-down list.

   d. Click the Text Effects and Typography button in the Font group and then click the option in the second column, second row (the option with blue gradient fill and reflection).

   e. Change the font size to 14 points.
4. Strike through text by completing the following steps:
   a. In the *Crackers* definition, select the phrase *or hack* and the parentheses around it.
   b. Click the Strikethrough button in the Font group.

5. Change the font color by completing the following steps:
   a. Press Ctrl + A to select the entire document.
   b. Click the Font Color button arrow.
   c. Click the *Dark Red* option (first color option in the *Standard Colors* section) at the drop-down gallery.
   d. Click in the document to deselect text.
6. Highlight text in the document by completing the following steps:
   a. Select the term *Beta-testing* and the definition that follows.
   b. Click the Text Highlight Color button in the Font group. (This applies yellow text highlighting color to the selected text.)
   c. Click the Text Highlight Color button arrow and then click the *Turquoise* color (third column, first row) at the drop-down palette. (This turns on highlighting and the mouse pointer displays as an I-beam pointer with a highlighter pen attached.)
   d. Select the term *Cluster* and the definition that follows.
   e. Click the Text Highlight Color button arrow and then click the *Yellow* color (first column, first row) at the drop-down gallery.
   f. Click the Text Highlight Color button to turn off highlighting.
7. Apply italic formatting using the Mini toolbar by completing the following steps:
   a. In the definition for *Aggregation software*, select the phrase *one-stop shopping* (When you select the text, the Mini toolbar displays.)
   b. Click the Italic button on the Mini toolbar.
   c. In the definition for *Bandwidth*, select the word *bits* and then click the Italic button on the Mini toolbar.
8. Save **2-CompTerms**.

Figure 2.4 Activity 1c

Chinese abacus: Pebbles strung on a rod inside a frame. Pebbles in the upper part of an abacus correspond to 5×10^0, or 5, for the first column; 5×10^1, or 50, for the second column; 5×10^2, or 500, for the third column; and so on.

Tutorial

Applying Font
Formatting Using
the Font Dialog Box

Quick Steps

**Change Font at
Font Dialog Box**
1. Select text.
2. Click Font group
   dialog box launcher.
3. Choose options at
   dialog box.
4. Click OK.

Applying Font Formatting Using the Font Dialog Box

In addition to options and buttons in the Font group, options at the Font dialog box, shown in Figure 2.5, can be used to change the typeface, type size, and typestyle of text as well as apply font effects. Display the Font dialog box by clicking the Font group dialog box launcher. The dialog box launcher is a small icon with a diagonal-pointing arrow in the lower right corner of the Font group.

Figure 2.5 Font Dialog Box

Choose a typeface in this list box. Use the scroll bar at the right of the box to view available typefaces.

Choose a typestyle in this list box. The options in the box may vary depending on the selected typeface.

Choose a type size in this list box, or select the current size in the option box and then type the desired size.

Apply a font effect to text by clicking the check box next to the desired effect.

See a preview of the text with the selected formatting applied.

Click this button to change the default font.

Click this button to display the Format Text Effects dialog box, which contains options with special text effects.

Activity 1d Changing the Font at the Font Dialog Box

Part 4 of 4

1. With **2-CompTerms** open, press Ctrl + End to move the insertion point to the end of the document. (Make sure the insertion point is positioned a double space below the last line of text.)
2. Type Created by Susan Ashby and then press the Enter key.
3. Type Wednesday, February 24, 2021.
4. Change the font to 13-point Candara and the color to standard dark blue for the entire document by completing the following steps:
   a. Press Ctrl + A to select the entire document.
   b. Click the Font group dialog box launcher.

c. At the Font dialog box, type can in the *Font* option box (this displays fonts that begin with *can*) and then click *Candara* in the *Font* list box.

d. Click in the *Size* option box and then type 13.

e. Click the *Font color* option box arrow and then click the *Dark Blue* option (ninth option in the *Standard Colors* section).

f. Click OK to close the dialog box.

5. Double-underline text by completing the following steps:

a. Select *Wednesday, February 24, 2021*.

b. Click the Font group dialog box launcher.

c. At the Font dialog box, click the *Underline style* option box arrow and then click the double-line option at the drop-down list.

d. Click OK to close the dialog box.

6. Change text to small caps by completing the following steps:

a. Select the text *Created by Susan Ashby* and *Wednesday, February 24, 2021*.

b. Display the Font dialog box.

c. Click the *Small caps* check box in the *Effects* section. (This inserts a check mark in the check box.)

d. Click OK to close the dialog box.

7. Save, print, and then close **2-CompTerms**.

Activity 2 Apply Styles and Themes   3 Parts

You will open a document containing information on the life cycle of software, apply styles to text, and then change the style set. You will also apply a theme and then change the theme colors, fonts, and paragraph spacing.

Tutorial

Applying Styles and
Style Sets

Applying Styles from a Style Set

Tutorial

Applying Styles and
Style Sets

Make a document look more polished and professional by applying different styles to the title, headings, and body paragraphs. Word provides a set of predesigned styles in the Styles group on the Home tab. Each style is a different combination of font style, color, and size. Click the More Styles button (the arrow button at the right side of the gallery) to display all the style options. Position the insertion point in the text and then hover the mouse pointer over the options in the gallery to see how the text will look in various styles. Click a style to apply it.

Quick Steps

Apply Style
1. Position insertion point in text.
2. Click More Styles button in Styles group.
3. Click style.

If a heading style (such as Heading 1, Heading 2, and so on) is applied to text, the text below the heading can be collapsed and expanded. Hover the mouse pointer over text with a heading style applied and a collapse triangle (solid, right- and down-pointing triangle) displays to the left of the heading. Click this collapse triangle and any text below the heading collapses (is hidden). Redisplay the text below a heading by hovering the mouse pointer over the heading text until an expand triangle displays (hollow, right-pointing triangle) and then click the expand triangle. This expands (redisplays) the text below the heading.

Removing Default Formatting

The default formatting for a Word document includes 8 points of spacing after paragraphs and line spacing of 1.08. (You will learn more about these formatting options later in this chapter.) This default formatting, as well as any character formatting applied to text in the document, can be removed by applying the No Spacing style to the text. This style is in the styles gallery in the Styles group.

Changing the Style Set

Quick Steps

Change Style Set
1. Click Design tab.
2. Click style set.

To quickly change the look of an entire document, choose a new style set. Style sets can be found in a gallery on the Design tab in the Document Formatting group. Each set contains a different combination of title, heading, and paragraph styles. To apply a new style set, click the Design tab and then click the style set in the style sets gallery in the Document Formatting group.

Activity 2a **Applying Styles and Changing the Style Set**   Part 1 of 3

1. Open **SoftwareCycle** and then save it with the name **2-SoftwareCycle**.
2. Position the insertion point anywhere in the title *COMMERCIAL LIFE CYCLE* and then click the *Heading 1* style in the Styles group.

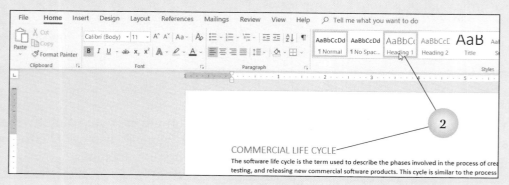

3. Position the insertion point anywhere in the heading *Proposal and Planning* and then click the *Heading 2* style in the styles gallery.

4. Position the insertion point anywhere in the heading *Design* and then click the *Heading 2* style in the styles gallery.

5. Apply the Heading 2 style to the remaining headings (*Implementation*, *Testing*, and *Public Release and Support*).

6. Collapse and expand text below the heading with the Heading 1 style applied by completing the following steps:

a. Hover the mouse pointer over the heading *COMMERCIAL LIFE CYCLE* until a collapse triangle displays at the left of the heading and then click the triangle. (This collapses all the text below the heading.)

b. Click the expand triangle at the left of the heading *COMMERCIAL LIFE CYCLE*. (This redisplays the text in the document.)

7. Click the Design tab.

8. Click the *Casual* style set in the style sets gallery in the Document Formatting group (the ninth option in the style set). (Notice how the Heading 1 and Heading 2 formatting changes.)

9. Save and then print **2-SoftwareCycle**.

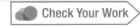

Check Your Work >

Tutorial >

Applying and Modifying a Theme

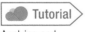 Themes

Quick Steps

Apply Theme
1. Click Design tab.
2. Click Themes button.
3. Click theme.

Applying a Theme

Word provides a number of themes for formatting text in a document. A theme is a set of formatting choices that includes a color theme (a set of colors), a font theme (a set of heading and body text fonts), and an effects theme (a set of line and fill effects). To apply a theme, click the Design tab, click the Themes button in the Document Formatting group, and then click the theme at the drop-down gallery. Hover the mouse pointer over a theme and the live preview feature displays the document with the theme formatting applied. Applying a theme is an easy way to give a document a professional look.

1. With **2-SoftwareCycle** open, click the Themes button in the Document Formatting group on the Design tab.
2. At the drop-down gallery, hover your mouse pointer over several different themes and notice how the text formatting changes in your document.
3. Click the *Organic* theme.

4. Save and then print **2-SoftwareCycle**.

Check Your Work

Modifying a Theme

Quick Steps

Change Theme Color
1. Click Design tab.
2. Click Colors button.
3. Click theme color option.

Change Theme Fonts
1. Click Design tab.
2. Click Fonts button.
3. Click theme font option.

Change Paragraph Spacing
1. Click Design tab.
2. Click Paragraph Spacing button.
3. Click paragraph spacing option.

 Theme Colors

 Theme Fonts

 Theme Effects

 Paragraph Spacing

The color and font of a style or theme can be modified using buttons in the Document Formatting group on the Design tab. Click the Colors button and a drop-down gallery displays with various color schemes. Click the Fonts button in this group and a drop-down gallery displays with font choices. Each font group in the drop-down gallery contains two choices. The first choice is the font that is applied to headings, and the second choice is applied to body text in the document. If a document contains graphics with lines and fills, a specific theme effect can be applied with options at the Effects button drop-down gallery.

The buttons in the Document Formatting group provide a visual representation of the current theme. If the theme colors are changed, the small color squares in the Themes button and the larger squares in the Colors button reflect the change. Change the theme fonts and the *As* on the Themes button and the uppercase *A* on the Fonts button reflect the change. If the theme effects are changed, the circle in the Effects button reflects the change.

The Paragraph Spacing button in the Document Formatting group on the Design tab contains predesigned paragraph spacing options. To change paragraph spacing, click the Paragraph Spacing button and then click an option at the drop-down gallery. Hover the mouse pointer over an option at the drop-down gallery and after a moment a ScreenTip displays with information about the formatting applied by the option. For example, hover the mouse pointer over the *Compact* option at the side menu and a ScreenTip displays indicating that selecting the *Compact* option will change the spacing before paragraphs to 0 points, the spacing after paragraphs to 4 points, and the line spacing to single line spacing.

1. With **2-SoftwareCycle** open, click the Colors button in the Document Formatting group on the Design tab and then click *Red Orange* at the drop-down gallery. (Notice how the colors in the title and headings change.)

2. Click the Fonts button and then click the *Corbel* option. (Notice how the document text font changes.)

3. Click the Paragraph Spacing button and then, one at a time, hover the mouse pointer over each paragraph spacing option, beginning with *Compact*. For each option, read the ScreenTip that explains the paragraph spacing applied by the option.

4. Click the *Double* option.

5. Scroll through the document and notice the paragraph spacing.

6. Change the paragraph spacing by clicking the Paragraph Spacing button and then clicking *Compact*.

7. Save, print, and then close **2-SoftwareCycle**.

☁ **Check Your Work**

Activity 3 **Apply Paragraph Formatting and Use Format Painter**   **6 Parts**

You will open a report on intellectual property and fair use issues and then format the report by changing the alignment and indent of text in paragraphs, changing spacing before and after paragraphs of text, and repeating the last formatting command. You will also format headings using Format Painter and change the line spacing of text.

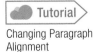

Changing Paragraph Alignment

Changing Paragraph Alignment

By default, paragraphs in a Word document are aligned at the left margin and are ragged at the right margin. Change this default alignment with buttons in the Paragraph group on the Home tab or with keyboard shortcuts, as shown in Table 2.3. The alignment of text in paragraphs can be changed before text is typed, or the alignment of existing text can be changed.

Table 2.3 Paragraph Alignment Buttons and Keyboard Shortcuts

To align text	Paragraph Group Button	Keyboard Shortcut
At the left margin		Ctrl + L
Between margins		Ctrl + E
At the right margin		Ctrl + R
At the left and right margins		Ctrl + J

Changing Paragraph Alignment as Text Is Typed

Center

Show/Hide ¶

Align Right

Align Left

If the alignment is changed before text is typed, the alignment formatting is inserted in the paragraph mark. Type text and press the Enter key and the paragraph formatting is continued. For example, click the Center button in the Paragraph group on the Home tab, type text for the first paragraph, and then press the Enter key; the center alignment formatting is still active and the insertion point is centered between the left and right margins. To display the paragraph symbols in a document, click the Show/Hide ¶ button in the Paragraph group. With the Show/Hide ¶ button active (displays with a gray background), nonprinting formatting symbols display, such as the paragraph symbol ¶, indicating a press of the Enter key, or a dot, indicating a press of the spacebar.

In addition to paragraph symbols, other formatting or formatting symbols display when the Show/Hide ¶ button is active. For example, hide text in a document using the *Hidden* option at the Font dialog box and the hidden text displays when the Show/Hide ¶ button is active.

Changing Paragraph Alignment of Existing Text

Hint Align text to help the reader follow the message of a document and to make the layout look appealing.

To change the alignment of existing text in a paragraph, position the insertion point anywhere within the paragraph. The entire paragraph does not need to be selected. To change the alignment of several adjacent paragraphs in a document, select a portion of the first paragraph through a portion of the last paragraph. All the text in the paragraphs does not need to be selected.

To return paragraph alignment to the default (left-aligned), click the Align Left button in the Paragraph group. All paragraph formatting can also be returned to the default with the keyboard shortcut Ctrl + Q. This keyboard shortcut removes paragraph formatting from selected text. To remove all formatting from selected text, including character and paragraph formatting, click the Clear All Formatting button in the Font group.

1. Open **IntelProp**. (Some of the default formatting in this document has been changed.)
2. Save the document with the name **2-IntelProp**.
3. Click the Show/Hide ¶ button in the Paragraph group on the Home tab to turn on the display of nonprinting characters.

4. Press Ctrl + A to select the entire document and then change the paragraph alignment to justified alignment by clicking the Justify button in the Paragraph group.
5. Press Ctrl + End to move the insertion point to the end of the document.
6. Press the Enter key.
7. Press Ctrl + E to move the insertion point to the middle of the page.
8. Type Prepared by Clarissa Markham.
9. Press Shift + Enter and then type Edited by Joshua Streeter.

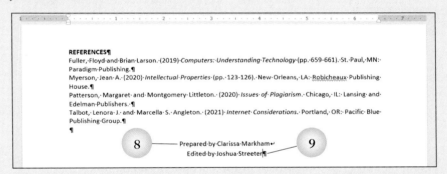

10. Select the two lines of text you just typed and then hide the text by completing the following steps:
    a. Click the Font group dialog box launcher.
    b. Click the *Hidden* check box to insert a check mark.
    c. Click OK to close the dialog box. (Since the Show/Hide ¶ button is active, the two lines of text display with a dotted underline.)
11. Click the Show/Hide ¶ button in the Paragraph group to turn off the display of nonprinting characters. (Notice that the two lines of text you identified as hidden are no longer visible.)
12. Specify that the two lines of text should not be hidden by completing the following steps:
    a. Click the Show/Hide ¶ button.
    b. Select the two lines of text.
    c. Click the Font group dialog box launcher.
    d. Click the *Hidden* check box to remove the check mark.
    e. Click OK.
    f. Click the Show/Hide ¶ button to turn off the display of nonprinting characters.
13. Save **2-IntelProp**.

Changing Alignment at the Paragraph Dialog Box

Along with buttons in the Paragraph group on the Home tab and keyboard shortcuts, options in the *Alignment* option box at the Paragraph dialog box, shown in Figure 2.6, can be used to change paragraph alignment. Display this dialog box by clicking the Paragraph group dialog box launcher. At the Paragraph dialog box, click the *Alignment* option box arrow. At the drop-down list, click the alignment option and then click OK to close the dialog box.

Figure 2.6 Paragraph Dialog Box with the Indents and Spacing Tab Selected

Change paragraph alignment by clicking the *Alignment* option box arrow and then clicking the alignment option at the drop-down list.

Use these options to adjust spacing before and after paragraphs.

Activity 3b **Changing Paragraph Alignment at the Paragraph Dialog Box**   Part 2 of 6

1. With **2-IntelProp** open, change the paragraph alignment by completing the following steps:
   a. Select the entire document.
   b. Click the Paragraph group dialog box launcher.
   c. At the Paragraph dialog box with the Indents and Spacing tab selected, click the *Alignment* option box arrow and then click the *Left* option at the drop-down list.
   d. Click OK to close the dialog box.
   e. Deselect the text.
2. Change the paragraph alignment by completing the following steps:
   a. Press Ctrl + End to move the insertion point to the end of the document if necessary.
   b. Position the insertion point anywhere in the text *Prepared by Clarissa Markham*.

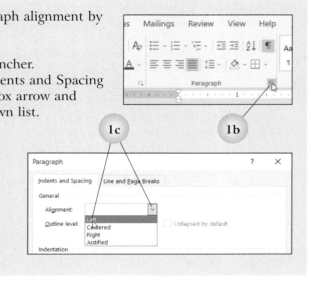

c. Click the Paragraph group dialog box launcher.

d. At the Paragraph dialog box with the Indents and Spacing tab selected, click the *Alignment* option box arrow and then click the *Right* option at the drop-down list.

e. Click OK to close the dialog box. (The line of text containing the name *Clarissa Markham* and the line of text containing the name *Joshua Streeter* are both aligned at the right since you used the New Line command, Shift + Enter, to separate the lines of text without creating a new paragraph.)

3. Save and then print **2-IntelProp**.

 Check Your Work

Tutorial

Indenting Text

 Quick Steps

Indent Text
Drag indent marker(s) on horizontal ruler.
OR
Press keyboard shortcut keys.
OR
1. Click Paragraph group dialog box launcher.
2. Insert measurement in *Left, Right,* and/ or *By* measurement box.
3. Click OK.

Indenting Text in Paragraphs

The first line of a paragraph is commonly indented to show paragraph breaks in a document. Paragraphs may also be indented from the left and right margins to set them off from the rest of the text. For instance, a long quotation or a bulleted or numbered list may be indented in this manner.

To indent text from the left margin, the right margin, or both margins, use the indent buttons in the Paragraph group on the Layout tab, keyboard shortcuts, options from the Paragraph dialog box, markers on the horizontal ruler, or the Alignment button above the vertical ruler. Figure 2.7 identifies indent markers on the horizontal ruler as well as the Alignment button. Refer to Table 2.4 for methods for indenting text in a document. If the horizontal ruler is not visible, display the ruler by clicking the View tab and then clicking the *Ruler* check box in the Show group to insert a check mark.

Figure 2.7 Horizontal Ruler and Indent Markers

Table 2.4 Methods for Indenting Text

Indent	Methods for Indenting
First line of paragraph	• Press the Tab key.
	• Display the Paragraph dialog box, click the *Special* option box arrow, click *First line*, and then click OK.
	• Drag the First Line Indent marker on the horizontal ruler.
	• Click the Alignment button above the vertical ruler until the First Line Indent symbol displays and then click the horizontal ruler at the desired location.

continues

Table 2.4 Methods for Indenting Text—*continued*

Indent	Methods for Indenting
Text from left margin	• Click the Increase Indent button in the Paragraph group on the Home tab to increase the indent or click the Decrease Indent button to decrease the indent. • Insert a measurement in the *Indent Left* measurement box in the Paragraph group on the Layout tab. • Press Ctrl + M to increase the indent or press Ctrl + Shift + M to decrease the indent. • Display the Paragraph dialog box, type the indent measurement in the *Left* measurement box, and then click OK. • Drag the Left Indent marker on the horizontal ruler.
Text from right margin	• Insert a measurement in the *Indent Right* measurement box in the Paragraph group on the Layout tab. • Display the Paragraph dialog box, type the indent measurement in the *Right* measurement box, and then click OK. • Drag the Right Indent marker on the horizontal ruler.
All lines of text except first (called a *hanging indent*)	• Press Ctrl + T. (Press Ctrl + Shift + T to remove a hanging indent.) • Display the Paragraph dialog box, click the *Special* option box arrow, click *Hanging*, and then click OK. • Click the Alignment button, left of the horizontal ruler and above the vertical ruler, until the Hanging Indent symbol displays and then click the horizontal ruler at the desired location. • Drag the Hanging Indent marker on the horizontal ruler.
Text from both left and right margins	• Display the Paragraph dialog box, type the indent measurement in the *Left* measurement box, type the indent measurement in the *Right* measurement box, and then click OK. • Insert measurements in the *Indent Right* and *Indent Left* measurement boxes in the Paragraph group on the Layout tab. • Drag the Left Indent marker on the horizontal ruler and then drag the Right Indent marker on the horizontal ruler.

Activity 3c Indenting Text

Part 3 of 6

1. With **2-IntelProp** open, indent the first line of text in each paragraph by completing the following steps:
   a. Select the first two paragraphs of text in the document (the text after the title *PROPERTY PROTECTION ISSUES* and before the heading *Intellectual Property*).
   b. Make sure the horizontal ruler is visible. (If it is not, click the View tab and then click the *Ruler* check box in the Show group to insert a check mark.)
   c. Position the mouse pointer on the First Line Indent marker on the horizontal ruler, click and hold down the left mouse button, drag the marker to the 0.5-inch mark, and then release the mouse button.

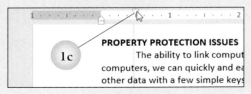

d. Select the paragraphs of text in the *Intellectual Property* section and then drag the First Line Indent marker on the horizontal ruler to the 0.5-inch mark.

e. Select the paragraphs of text in the *Fair Use* section, click the Alignment button above the vertical ruler until the First Line Indent symbol displays, and then click the horizontal ruler at the 0.5-inch mark.

f. Position the insertion point anywhere in the paragraph of text below the heading *Intellectual Property Protection*, make sure the First Line Indent symbol displays on the Alignment button, and then click the 0.5-inch mark on the horizontal ruler.

2. Since the text in the second paragraph in the *Fair Use* section is a quote, indent the text from the left and right margins by completing the following steps:

a. Position the insertion point anywhere in the second paragraph in the *Fair Use* section (the paragraph that begins *[A] copyrighted work, including such*).

b. Click the Paragraph group dialog box launcher.

c. At the Paragraph dialog box with the Indents and Spacing tab selected, select the current measurement in the *Left* measurement box and then type 0.5.

d. Select the current measurement in the *Right* measurement box and then type 0.5.

e. Click the *Special* option box arrow and then click *(none)* at the drop-down list.

f. Click OK.

3. Create a hanging indent for the first paragraph in the *REFERENCES* section by positioning the insertion point anywhere in the first paragraph below the heading *REFERENCES* (on the third page) and then pressing Ctrl + T.

4. Create a hanging indent for the second paragraph in the *REFERENCES* section by completing the following steps:

a. Position the insertion point anywhere in the second paragraph in the *REFERENCES* section.

b. Click the Alignment button until the Hanging Indent symbol displays.

c. Click the 0.5-inch mark on the horizontal ruler.

5. Create a hanging indent for the third and fourth paragraphs by completing the following steps:
   a. Select a portion of the third and fourth paragraphs.
   b. Click the Paragraph group dialog box launcher.
   c. At the Paragraph dialog box with the Indents and Spacing tab selected, click the *Special* option box arrow and then click *Hanging* at the drop-down list.
   d. Click OK or press the Enter key.
6. Save **2-IntelProp**.

Check Your Work

 Tutorial

Changing Spacing Before and After Paragraphs

Hint Line spacing determines the amount of vertical space between lines, while paragraph spacing determines the amount of space above or below paragraphs of text.

Spacing Before and After Paragraphs

By default, Word applies 8 points of additional spacing after a paragraph. This spacing can be removed or it can be increased or decreased, and spacing can be inserted above the paragraph. To change spacing before or after a paragraph, use the *Before* and *After* measurement boxes in the Paragraph group on the Layout tab, or use the *Before* and *After* measurement boxes at the Paragraph dialog box with the Indents and Spacing tab selected. Spacing can also be added before and after paragraphs with options at the Line and Paragraph Spacing button drop-down list in the Paragraph group on the Home tab.

Spacing before or after a paragraph is part of the paragraph and will be moved, copied, or deleted with the paragraph. If a paragraph, such as a heading, contains spacing before it and the paragraph falls at the top of a page, Word ignores the spacing.

Spacing before and after paragraphs is added in points. One vertical inch is equivalent to approximately 72 points. To add spacing before or after a paragraph, click the Layout tab, select the current measurement in the *Before* or *After* measurement box, and then type the number of points. The up or down arrows at the *Before* and *After* measurement boxes can also be clicked to increase or decrease the amount of spacing.

Automating Formatting

Applying consistent formatting in a document, especially a multiple-page document, can be time consuming. Word provides options for applying formatting automatically. Use the Repeat command to repeat the last action, such as applying formatting, or the Format Painter to apply formatting to multiple locations in a document.

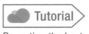 Tutorial

Repeating the Last Command

Quick Steps

Repeat Last Action
Press F4.
OR
Press Ctrl + Y.

Repeating the Last Command

Formatting applied to text can be applied to other text in the document using the Repeat command. To use this command, apply the formatting, move the insertion point to the next location the formatting is to be applied, and then press the F4 function key or the keyboard shortcut Ctrl + Y. The Repeat command will repeat only the last command executed.

1. With **2-IntelProp** open, add 6 points of spacing before and after each paragraph in the document by completing the following steps:
   a. Select the entire document.
   b. Click the Layout tab.
   c. Click the *Before* measurement box up arrow in the Paragraph group. (This inserts *6 pt* in the box.)
   d. Click the *After* measurement box up arrow two times. (This inserts *6 pt* in the box.)

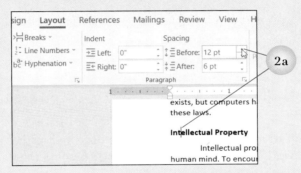

2. Add an additional 6 points of spacing above the headings by completing the following steps:
   a. Position the insertion point anywhere in the heading *Intellectual Property* and then click the *Before* measurement box up arrow. (This changes the measurement to *12 pt*.)

   b. Position the insertion point anywhere in the heading *Fair Use* and then press the F4 function key. (F4 is the Repeat command.)
   c. Position the insertion point anywhere in the heading *Intellectual Property Protection* and then press the F4 function key.
   d. Position the insertion point anywhere in the heading *REFERENCES* and then press Ctrl + Y. (Ctrl + Y is also the Repeat command.) (When a heading displays at the beginning of a page, the spacing above is ignored.)
3. Save **2-IntelProp**.

> Check Your Work

Formatting with Format Painter

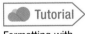 Tutorial

Formatting with Format Painter

 Format Painter

Quick Steps
Format with Format Painter
1. Click in formatted text.
2. Click Format Painter button.
3. Select text.

The Home tab contains a button for copying formatting, which displays in the Clipboard group with a paintbrush. To use this button, called Format Painter, position the insertion point anywhere in text containing the desired formatting, click the Format Painter button, and then select the text to which the formatting is to be applied. When the Format Painter button is clicked, the I-beam pointer displays with a paintbrush attached. To apply the formatting a single time, click the Format Painter button. To apply the formatting in more than one location in the document, double-click the Format Painter button and then select the text to which the formatting is to be applied. When finished, click the Format Painter button to turn it off. The Format Painter button can also be turned off by pressing the Esc key.

1. With **2-IntelProp** open, click the Home tab.
2. Select the entire document and then change the font to 12-point Cambria.
3. Select the title *PROPERTY PROTECTION ISSUES*, click the Center button in the Paragraph group, and then change the font to 16-point Candara.
4. Apply 16-point Candara and center-alignment formatting to the heading *REFERENCES* by completing the following steps:
   a. Click in the title *PROPERTY PROTECTION ISSUES*.
   b. Click the Format Painter button in the Clipboard group.

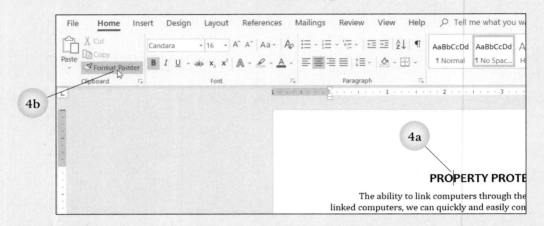

   c. Press Ctrl + End to move the insertion point to the end of the document and then click in the heading *REFERENCES*. (This applies the 16-point Candara formatting and centers the text.)
5. Select the heading *Intellectual Property* and then change the font to 14-point Candara.
6. Use the Format Painter button to apply 14-point Candara formatting to the other headings by completing the following steps:
   a. Position the insertion point anywhere in the heading *Intellectual Property*.
   b. Double-click the Format Painter button in the Clipboard group.
   c. Using the mouse, select the heading *Fair Use*.
   d. Using the mouse, select the heading *Intellectual Property Protection*.
   e. Click the Format Painter button in the Clipboard group. (This turns off the feature and deactivates the button.)
   f. Deselect the heading.
7. Save **2-IntelProp**.

Check Your Work

 Tutorial

Changing Line Spacing

 Line and Paragraph Spacing

Changing Line Spacing

The default line spacing for a document is 1.08. (The line spacing for the IntelProp file, which you opened at the beginning of Activity 3, had been changed to single line spacing.) In certain situations, Word automatically adjusts the line spacing. For example, if a large character or object, such as a graphic, is inserted into a line, Word increases the line spacing of that line. The line spacing for a section or an entire document can also be changed.

Quick Steps

Change Line Spacing
1. Click Line and Paragraph Spacing button.
2. Click option.
OR
Press keyboard shortcut command.
OR
1. Click Paragraph group dialog box launcher.
2. Click *Line spacing* option box arrow.
3. Click line spacing option.
4. Click OK.
OR
1. Click Paragraph group dialog box launcher.
2. Type line measurement in *At* measurement box.
3. Click OK.

Change line spacing using the Line and Paragraph Spacing button in the Paragraph group on the Home tab, keyboard shortcuts, or options in the Paragraph dialog box. Table 2.5 shows the keyboard shortcuts to change line spacing.

Line spacing can also be changed at the Paragraph dialog box with the *Line spacing* option or the *At* measurement box. Click the *Line spacing* option box arrow and a drop-down list displays with a variety of spacing options, such as *Single*, *1.5 lines*, and *Double*. A specific line spacing measurement can be entered in the *At* measurement box. For example, to change the line spacing to 1.75 lines, type *1.75* in the *At* measurement box.

Table 2.5 Line Spacing Keyboard Shortcuts

Press	To change line spacing to
Ctrl + 1	single line spacing (1.0)
Ctrl + 2	double line spacing (2.0)
Ctrl + 5	1.5 line spacing

Activity 3f Changing Line Spacing

Part 6 of 6

1. With **2-IntelProp** open, change the line spacing for all paragraphs to double spacing by completing the following steps:
   a. Select the entire document.
   b. Click the Line and Paragraph Spacing button in the Paragraph group on the Home tab.
   c. Click *2.0* at the drop-down list.
2. With the entire document still selected, press Ctrl + 5. (This changes the line spacing to 1.5 lines.)
3. Change the line spacing to 1.2 lines at the Paragraph dialog box by completing the following steps:
   a. With the entire document still selected, click the Paragraph group dialog box launcher.
   b. At the Paragraph dialog box, make sure the Indents and Spacing tab is selected, click in the *At* measurement box, and then type 1.2. (This measurement box is to the right of the *Line spacing* option box.)
   c. Click OK or press the Enter key.
   d. Deselect the text.
4. Save, print, and then close **2-IntelProp**.

Check Your Work

You will open a document containing two computer-related problems to solve, reveal the formatting, compare the formatting, and make formatting changes.

Revealing and Comparing Formatting

Display formatting applied to specific text in a document at the Reveal Formatting task pane, shown in Figure 2.8. The Reveal Formatting task pane displays font, paragraph, and section formatting applied to text where the insertion point is positioned or to selected text. Display the Reveal Formatting task pane with the keyboard shortcut Shift + F1. Generally, a collapse triangle (a solid right-and-down-pointing triangle) precedes *Font* and *Paragraph* and an expand triangle (a hollow right-pointing triangle) precedes *Section* in the *Formatting of selected text* list box in the Reveal Formatting task pane. Click the collapse triangle to hide any items below a heading and click the expand triangle to reveal items. Some of the items below headings in the *Formatting of selected text* list box are hyperlinks. Click a hyperlink and a dialog box displays with the specific option.

Figure 2.8 Reveal Formatting Task Pane

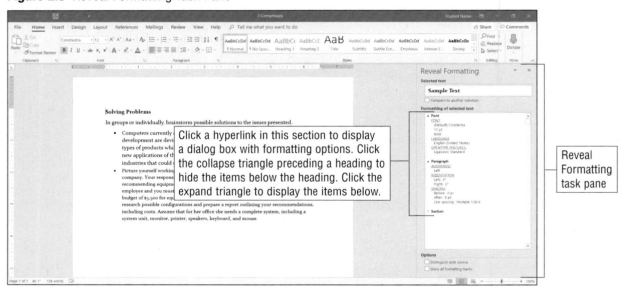

Click a hyperlink in this section to display a dialog box with formatting options. Click the collapse triangle preceding a heading to hide the items below the heading. Click the expand triangle to display the items below.

Reveal Formatting task pane

Activity 4a **Revealing Formatting** Part 1 of 2

1. Open **CompIssues** and then save it with the name **2-CompIssues**.
2. Press Shift + F1 to display the Reveal Formatting task pane.
3. Click in the heading *Solving Problems* and then notice the formatting information in the Reveal Formatting task pane.
4. Click in the bulleted paragraph and then notice the formatting information in the Reveal Formatting task pane.
5. Leave **2-CompIssues** open for the next activity.

Quick Steps

Compare Formatting
1. Press Shift + F1 to display Reveal Formatting task pane.
2. Click or select text.
3. Click *Compare to another selection* check box.
4. Click or select text.

Along with displaying formatting applied to text, the Reveal Formatting task pane can be used to compare formatting in two text selections to determine what is different. To compare formatting, select the first instance of formatting to be compared, click the *Compare to another selection* check box, and then select the second instance of formatting to be compared. Any differences between the two selections display in the *Formatting differences* list box.

Activity 4b Comparing Formatting   Part 2 of 2

1. With **2-CompIssues** open, make sure the Reveal Formatting task pane is visible. If it is not, turn it on by pressing Shift + F1.
2. Select the first bulleted paragraph (the paragraph that begins *Computers currently offer both*).
3. Click the *Compare to another selection* check box to insert a check mark.
4. Select the second bulleted paragraph (the paragraph that begins *Picture yourself working in the*).
5. Determine the formatting differences by reading the information in the *Formatting differences* list box. (The list box shows *12 pt -> 11 pt* below the <u>FONT</u> hyperlink, indicating that the difference is point size.)

6. Format the second bulleted paragraph so it is set in 12-point size.
7. Click the *Compare to another selection* check box to remove the check mark.
8. Select the word *visual*, which is used in the first sentence in the first bulleted paragraph.
9. Click the *Compare to another selection* check box to insert a check mark.
10. Select the word *audio*, which is used in the first sentence of the first bulleted paragraph.
11. Determine the formatting differences by reading the information in the *Formatting differences* list box.

12. Format the word *audio* so it matches the formatting of the word *visual*.
13. Click the *Compare to another selection* check box to remove the check mark.
14. Close the Reveal Formatting task pane by clicking the Close button in the upper right corner of the task pane.
15. Save, print, and then close **2-CompIssues**.

Check Your Work

Chapter Summary

- A font consists of three elements: typeface, type size, and typestyle.

- A typeface (font) is a set of characters with a common design and shape. Typefaces are monospaced, allotting the same amount of horizontal space for each character, or proportional, allotting varying amounts of space for different characters. Typefaces are divided into two main categories: serif and sans serif.

- Type size is measured in points; the higher the point size, the larger the characters.

- A typestyle is a variation of style within a certain typeface, such as bold, italic, or underline. Apply typestyles with buttons in the Font group on the Home tab.

- Apply font effects such as superscript, subscript, and strikethrough formatting with buttons in the second row in the Font group on the Home tab.

- The Mini toolbar automatically displays above selected text. Use options and buttons on this toolbar to apply formatting to the selected text.

- Use options at the Font dialog box to change the typeface, type size, and typestyle and to apply specific font effects. Display this dialog box by clicking the Font group dialog box launcher in the Font group on the Home tab.

- A Word document contains a number of predesigned formats grouped into style sets. Change to a different style set by clicking the Design tab and then clicking the style set in the styles set gallery in the Document Formatting group.

- Apply a theme and change theme colors, fonts, and effects with buttons in the Document Formatting group on the Design tab.

- Click the Paragraph Spacing button in the Document Formatting group on the Design tab to apply a predesigned paragraph spacing option to text.

- By default, paragraphs in a Word document are aligned at the left margin and ragged at the right margin. Change this default alignment with buttons in the Paragraph group on the Home tab, at the Paragraph dialog box, or with keyboard shortcuts.

- To turn on or off the display of nonprinting characters, such as paragraph symbols, click the Show/Hide ¶ button in the Paragraph group on the Home tab.

- Indent text in paragraphs with indent buttons in the Paragraph group on the Home tab, buttons in the Paragraph group on the Layout tab, keyboard shortcuts, options from the Paragraph dialog box, markers on the horizontal ruler, or the Alignment button above the vertical ruler.

- Increase and/or decrease spacing before and after paragraphs using the *Before* and *After* measurement boxes in the Paragraph group on the Layout tab or using the *Before* and/or *After* options at the Paragraph dialog box.

- Repeat the last command by pressing the F4 function key or the keyboard shortcut Ctrl + Y.

- Use the Format Painter button in the Clipboard group on the Home tab to copy formatting already applied to text to different locations in the document.

- Change line spacing with the Line and Paragraph Spacing button in the Paragraph group on the Home tab, keyboard shortcuts, or options at the Paragraph dialog box.

- Display the Reveal Formatting task pane with the keyboard shortcut Shift + F1. Use the *Compare to another selection* option in the task pane to compare formatting of two text selections to determine what is different.

Commands Review

FEATURE	RIBBON TAB, GROUP	BUTTON	KEYBOARD SHORTCUT
bold text	Home, Font	**B**	Ctrl + B
center-align text	Home, Paragraph	☰	Ctrl + E
change case of text	Home, Font	Aa ˅	Shift + F3
clear all formatting	Home, Font	A◇	
clear character formatting			Ctrl + spacebar
clear paragraph formatting			Ctrl + Q
decrease font size	Home, Font	A˅	Ctrl + Shift + < OR Ctrl + [
decrease indent	Home, Paragraph	⇤≣	
display or hide nonprinting characters	Home, Paragraph	¶	Ctrl + Shift + *
font	Home, Font		Ctrl + Shift + F
font color	Home, Font	A˅	
Font dialog box	Home, Font	⌐	Ctrl + Shift + F
font size	Home, Font		Ctrl + Shift + P
Format Painter	Home, Clipboard	✏	Ctrl + Shift + C
highlight text	Home, Font	✐ ˅	
increase font size	Home, Font	A^	Ctrl + Shift + > OR Ctrl +]
increase indent	Home, Paragraph	≣⇥	
italicize text	Home, Font	*I*	Ctrl + I
justify text	Home, Paragraph	☰	Ctrl + J
left-align text	Home, Paragraph	☰	Ctrl + L
line spacing	Home, Paragraph	↕≣ ˅	Ctrl + 1 (single) Ctrl + 2 (double) Ctrl + 5 (1.5)

FEATURE	RIBBON TAB, GROUP	BUTTON	KEYBOARD SHORTCUT
Paragraph dialog box	Home, Paragraph		
paragraph spacing	Design, Document Formatting		
repeat last action			F4 or Ctrl + Y
Reveal Formatting task pane			Shift + F1
right-align text	Home, Paragraph		Ctrl + R
spacing after paragraph	Layout, Paragraph		
spacing before paragraph	Layout, Paragraph		
strikethrough text	Home, Font		
subscript text	Home, Font		Ctrl + =
superscript text	Home, Font		Ctrl + Shift + +
text effects and typography	Home, Font		
theme colors	Design, Document Formatting		
theme effects	Design, Document Formatting		
theme fonts	Design, Document Formatting		
themes	Design, Document Formatting		
underline text	Home, Font		Ctrl + U

Microsoft® Word

CHAPTER 3

Customizing Paragraphs

Performance Objectives

Upon successful completion of Chapter 3, you will be able to:

1 Apply numbered and bulleted formatting to text

2 Apply paragraph borders and shading

3 Sort paragraphs of text

4 Set, clear, and move tabs on the horizontal ruler and at the Tabs dialog box

5 Cut, copy, and paste text in a document

6 Use the Paste Options button to specify how text is pasted in a document

7 Use the Clipboard task pane to copy and paste text within and between documents

As you learned in Chapter 2, Word contains a variety of options for formatting text in paragraphs. In this chapter, you will learn how to apply numbered and bulleted formatting as well as borders and shading. You will also learn how to sort paragraphs of text in alphabetical, numerical, and date order and to set and modify tabs on the horizontal ruler and at the Tabs dialog box. Editing some documents might include selecting and then deleting, moving, or copying text. You can perform these types of editing tasks with buttons in the Clipboard group on the Home tab or with keyboard shortcuts.

 Data Files

Before beginning chapter work, copy the WL1C3 folder to your storage medium and then make WL1C3 the active folder.

The online course includes additional training and assessment resources.

You will open a document containing information on computer technology, type numbered and bulleted text in the document, and apply numbered and bulleted formatting to paragraphs in the document.

Applying Numbering and Bullets

 Numbering

Bullets

Automatically number paragraphs or insert bullets before paragraphs using buttons in the Paragraph group on the Home tab. Use the Numbering button to insert numbers before specific paragraphs and use the Bullets button to insert bullets.

Tutorial

Creating Numbered Lists

Creating Numbered Lists

Quick Steps

Type Numbered Paragraphs
1. Type 1.
2. Press spacebar.
3. Type text.
4. Press Enter key.

Hint Define a new numbering format by clicking the Numbering button arrow and then clicking *Define New Number Format*.

To type a numbered list, type *1.* and then press the spacebar, and Word indents the number 0.25 inch from the left margin. Text typed after the number will be indented 0.5 inch. When the Enter key is pressed to end the first item, the next number, *2.*, is automatically inserted at the beginning of the next paragraph. Continue typing items and Word inserts the next number in the list. To insert a line break without inserting a number, press Shift + Enter.

To turn off numbering, press the Enter key two times or click the Numbering button in the Paragraph group on the Home tab. To turn numbering back on, simply type the next number in the list (and the period) followed by a space. Word will automatically indent the number and the text. (Numbered and bulleted formatting can be removed from a paragraph with the keyboard shortcut Ctrl + Q. Remove all formatting from selected text by clicking the Clear All Formatting button in the Font group on the Home tab.)

When the AutoFormat feature inserts numbering and indents text, the AutoCorrect Options button displays. Click this button and a drop-down list displays with options for undoing and/or stopping the automatic numbering.

Activity 1a **Creating a Numbered List** Part 1 of 3

1. Open **TechInfo** and then save it with the name **3-TechInfo**.
2. Press Ctrl + End to move the insertion point to the end of the document and then type the text shown in Figure 3.1. Apply bold formatting and center the title *Technology Career Questions*. When typing the numbered paragraphs, complete the following steps:
   a. Type *1.* and then press the spacebar. (The *1.* is indented 0.25 inch from the left margin and typed text is indented 0.5 inch from the left margin. Also, the AutoCorrect Options button displays. Use this button if you want to undo or stop automatic numbering.)
   b. Type the paragraph of text and then press the Enter key. (This moves the insertion point down to the next paragraph and inserts an indented number *2* followed by a period.)
   c. Continue typing the remaining text. (Remember, you do not need to type the paragraph number and period—they are automatically inserted. The last numbered item will wrap differently on your screen than shown in Figure 3.1.)
   d. After typing the last question, press the Enter key two times. (This turns off paragraph numbering.)
3. Save **3-TechInfo**.

 Check Your Work

Figure 3.1 Activity 1a

Technology Career Questions

1. What is your ideal technical job?
2. Which job suits your personality?
3. Which is your first-choice certificate?
4. How does the technical job market look in your state right now? Is the job market wide open or are the information technology career positions limited?

Automatic numbering is turned on by default. Turn off automatic numbering at the AutoCorrect dialog box with the AutoFormat As You Type tab selected, as shown in Figure 3.2. To display this dialog box, click the File tab and then click *Options*. At the Word Options dialog box, click the *Proofing* option in the left panel and then click the AutoCorrect Options button in the *AutoCorrect options* section of the dialog box. At the AutoCorrect dialog box, click the AutoFormat As You Type tab and then click the *Automatic numbered lists* check box to remove the check mark. Click OK to close the AutoCorrect dialog box and then click OK to close the Word Options dialog box.

To create a numbered list, click the Numbering button in the Paragraph group on the Home tab. Type text and it will be formatted as a numbered list. Click the button again to turn off numbering, or select existing text and then click the Numbering button to apply numbered formatting.

Quick Steps

Create Numbered List
1. Select text.
2. Click Numbering button.

Figure 3.2 AutoCorrect Dialog Box with the AutoFormat As You Type Tab Selected

1. With **3-TechInfo** open, apply numbers to paragraphs by completing the following steps:
   a. Select the five paragraphs of text in the *Technology Information Questions* section.
   b. Click the Numbering button in the Paragraph group on the Home tab.

2. Add text between paragraphs 4 and 5 in the *Technology Information Questions* section by completing the following steps:
   a. Position the insertion point immediately right of the question mark at the end of the fourth paragraph.
   b. Press the Enter key.
   c. Type What kinds of networks are used in your local area?

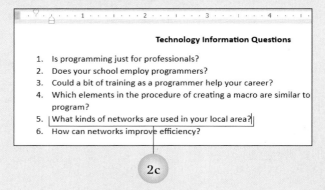

3. Delete the second question (paragraph) in the *Technology Information Questions* section by completing the following steps:
   a. Select the text of the second paragraph. (You will not be able to select the number.)
   b. Press the Delete key.
4. Save **3-TechInfo**.

 Check Your Work

Creating Bulleted Lists

In addition to automatically numbering paragraphs, Word's AutoFormat feature creates bulleted lists. A bulleted list with a hanging indent is automatically created when a paragraph begins with the symbol *, >, or -. Type one of the symbols and then press the spacebar and the AutoFormat feature inserts a bullet 0.25 inch from the left margin and indents the text following the bullet another 0.25 inch. Change the indent of bulleted text by pressing the Tab key to demote text or pressing Shift + Tab to promote text. Word uses different bullets for demoted text.

Bulleted formatting can be turned on or applied to existing text with the Bullets button in the Paragraph group on the Home tab. Click the Bullets button to turn on bulleting, type text, and then click the button again to turn off bulleting. Or select existing text and then click the Bullets button to apply bulleted formatting. When the AutoFormat feature inserts bullets and indents text, the AutoCorrect Options button displays. This button contains options for undoing and/or stopping the automatic bulleting. The automatic bulleting feature can be turned off at the AutoCorrect dialog box with the AutoFormat As You Type tab selected.

Quick Steps

Type Bulleted List
1. Type *, >, or - symbol.
2. Press spacebar.
3. Type text.
4. Press Enter key.

Create Bulleted List
1. Select text.
2. Click Bullets button.

Activity 1c Creating a Bulleted List and Applying Bulleted Formatting   Part 3 of 3

1. With **3-TechInfo** open, press Ctrl + End to move the insertion point to the end of the document.
2. Type Technology Timeline: Computer Design and apply bold formatting and center alignment, as shown in Figure 3.3, and then press the Enter key.
3. Turn off bold formatting and change to left alignment.
4. Type a greater-than symbol (>), press the spacebar, type the text of the first bulleted paragraph in Figure 3.3, and then press the Enter key.
5. Press the Tab key (which demotes the bullet to a hollow circle) and then type the bulleted text.
6. Press the Enter key (which displays another hollow circle bullet), type the bulleted text, and then press the Enter key.
7. Press Shift + Tab (which promotes the bullet to an arrow), type the bulleted text, and then press the Enter key two times (which turns off bulleting).
8. Promote bulleted text by positioning the insertion point at the beginning of the text *1958: Jack Kilby, an engineer* and then pressing Shift + Tab. Promote the other hollow circle bullet to an arrow. (The four paragraphs of text should be preceded by arrow bullets.)
9. Format the paragraphs of text in the *Technology Timeline: Computers in the Workplace* section as a bulleted list by completing the following steps:
    a. Select the paragraphs of text in the *Technology Timeline: Computers in the Workplace* section.
    b. Click the Bullets button in the Paragraph group. (Word will insert the same arrow bullets that you inserted in Step 4. Word keeps the same bullet formatting until you choose a different bullet style.)
10. Save, print, and then close **3-TechInfo**.

9b

> **Check Your Work**

Figure 3.3 Activity 1c

Technology Timeline: Computer Design

➢ 1937: Dr. John Atanasoff and Clifford Berry design and build the first electronic digital computer.
  o 1958: Jack Kilby, an engineer at Texas Instruments, invents the integrated circuit, thereby laying the foundation for fast computers and large-capacity memory.
  o 1981: IBM enters the personal computer field by introducing the IBM-PC.
➢ 2004: Wireless computer devices, including keyboards, mice, and wireless home networks, become widely accepted among users.

Activity 2 Customize a Document on Chapter Questions   **3 Parts**

You will open a document containing chapter questions and then apply border and shading formatting to text.

Adding Emphasis to Paragraphs

To call attention to or to highlight specific text in a document, consider adding emphasis to the text by applying paragraph borders and/or shading. Apply borders with the Borders button in the Paragraph group on the Home tab and shading with the Shading button. Additional border and shading options are available at the Borders and Shading dialog box.

Tutorial

Applying Borders

Applying Paragraph Borders

Every paragraph in a Word document contains an invisible frame, and a border can be applied to the frame around the paragraph. Apply a border to specific sides of the paragraph frame or to all sides. Add borders to paragraphs using the Borders button in the Paragraph group on the Home tab or using options at the Borders and Shading dialog box.

⊞ ⌄ Borders

When a border is added to a paragraph of text, the border expands and contracts as text is inserted or deleted from the paragraph. Insert a border around the active paragraph or around selected paragraphs.

Quick Steps

Apply Borders with Borders Button
1. Select text.
2. Click Borders button arrow.
3. Click border option at drop-down gallery.

One method for inserting a border is to use options from the Borders button in the Paragraph group. Click the Borders button arrow and a drop-down gallery displays. At the drop-down gallery, click the option that will insert the desired border. For example, to insert a border at the bottom of the paragraph, click the *Bottom Border* option. Clicking an option will add the border to the paragraph where the insertion point is located. To add a border to more than one paragraph, select the paragraphs first and then click the option.

1. Open **Questions** and then save it with the name **3-Questions**.
2. Insert an outside border to specific text by completing the following steps:
   a. Select text from the heading *Chapter 1 Questions* through the four bulleted paragraphs.
   b. In the Paragraph group on the Home tab, click the Borders button arrow.
   c. Click the *Outside Borders* option at the drop-down gallery.
3. Select text from the heading *Chapter 2 Questions* through the five bulleted paragraphs and then click the Borders button (The button will apply the border option that was previously selected.)
4. Save **3-Questions**.

> **Check Your Work**

Quick Steps

Apply Borders at Borders and Shading Dialog Box
1. Select text.
2. Click Borders button arrow.
3. Click *Borders and Shading* option.
4. Choose options in dialog box.
5. Click OK.

To further customize paragraph borders, use options at the Borders and Shading dialog box, as shown in Figure 3.4. Display this dialog box by clicking the Borders button arrow and then clicking *Borders and Shading* at the drop-down list. At the Borders and Shading dialog box, specify the border setting, style, color, and width.

Figure 3.4 Borders and Shading Dialog Box with the Borders Tab Selected

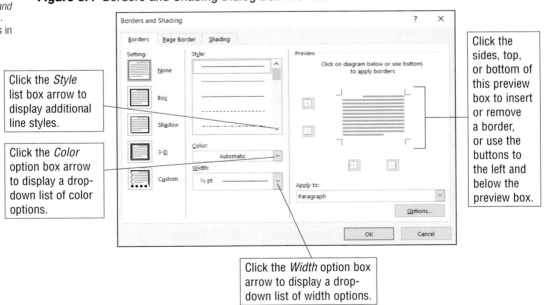

Click the *Style* list box arrow to display additional line styles.

Click the *Color* option box arrow to display a drop-down list of color options.

Click the sides, top, or bottom of this preview box to insert or remove a border, or use the buttons to the left and below the preview box.

Click the *Width* option box arrow to display a drop-down list of width options.

1. With **3-Questions** open, remove the paragraph borders around the heading *Chapter 1 Questions* by completing the following steps:
   a. Position the insertion point anywhere in the heading *Chapter 1 Questions*.
   b. Click the Borders button arrow and then click *No Border* at the drop-down gallery.
2. Apply a bottom border to the heading *Chapter 1 Questions* by completing the following steps:
   a. Click the Borders button arrow.
   b. Click the *Borders and Shading* option.
   c. At the Borders and Shading dialog box, click the *Style* list box down arrow two times. (This displays a double-line option.)
   d. Click the double-line option.
   e. Click the *Color* option box arrow.
   f. Click the *Blue* option (eighth color option in the *Standard Colors* section).
   g. Click the *Width* option box arrow.
   h. Click the *3/4 pt* option at the drop-down list.
   i. Click the *None* option in the *Setting* section.
   j. Click the bottom border of the box in the *Preview* section.
   k. Click OK to close the dialog box and apply the border.
3. Apply the same border to the other heading by completing the following steps:
   a. With the insertion point positioned in the heading *Chapter 1 Questions*, click the Format Painter button.
   b. Click in the heading *Chapter 2 Questions*.
4. Save **3-Questions**.

> **Check Your Work**

> **Tutorial**
Applying Shading

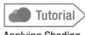 Shading

Quick Steps

Apply Shading
1. Select text.
2. Click Shading button.
OR
1. Click Borders button arrow.
2. Click *Borders and Shading* option.
3. Click Shading tab.
4. Choose options in dialog box.
5. Click OK.

Applying Shading

Apply shading to selected text or paragraphs in a document with the Shading button in the Paragraph group on the Home tab. If no text is selected, shading is applied to the paragraph where the insertion point is positioned. Select text or paragraphs and then click the Shading button arrow, and a drop-down gallery displays. Shading colors are presented in themes in the drop-down gallery. Use one of the theme colors or click one of the standard colors at the bottom of the gallery. Click the *More Colors* option and the Colors dialog box displays. At the Colors dialog box with the Standard tab selected, click a color or click the Custom tab and then specify a custom color.

Shading can also be applied using options at the Borders and Shading dialog box. Display this dialog box by clicking the Borders button arrow and then clicking the *Borders and Shading* option. At the Borders and Shading dialog box, click the Shading tab. Use options in the dialog box to specify a fill color, choose a pattern style, and specify a color for the dots that make up the pattern.

1. With **3-Questions** open, apply shading to the paragraph containing the heading *Chapter 1 Questions* by completing the following steps:
   a. Click in the heading *Chapter 1 Questions*.
   b. Click the Shading button arrow.
   c. Click the *Blue, Accent 5, Lighter 80%* option (ninth column, second row in the *Theme Colors* section).
2. Apply the same blue shading to the other heading by completing the following steps:
   a. With the insertion point positioned in the heading *Chapter 1 Questions*, click the Format Painter button.
   b. Click in the heading *Chapter 2 Questions*.

3. Apply shading to selected paragraphs with options at the Borders and Shading dialog box by completing the following steps:
   a. Select the four bulleted paragraphs below the heading *Chapter 1 Questions*.
   b. Click the Borders button arrow.
   c. Click the *Borders and Shading* option.
   d. At the Borders and Shading dialog box, click the Shading tab.
   e. Click the *Fill* option box arrow.
   f. Click the *Gold, Accent 4, Lighter 80%* option (eighth column, second row in the *Theme Colors* section).
   g. Click the *Style* option box arrow.
   h. Click the *5%* option.
   i. Click the *Color* option box arrow.
   j. Click the *Blue, Accent 5, Lighter 60%* color option (ninth column, third row in the *Theme Colors* section).
   k. Click OK to close the dialog box.

4. Apply the same shading to the bulleted paragraphs below the heading *Chapter 2 Questions* by completing the following steps:
   a. Click in the bulleted paragraphs below the heading *Chapter 1 Questions*.
   b. Click the Format Painter button.
   c. Select the five bulleted paragraphs below the heading *Chapter 2 Questions*.
5. Save, print, and then close **3-Questions**.

Check Your Work

You will open a document on online shopping and then sort several different paragraphs of text.

Tutorial

Sorting Text in Paragraphs

Sorting Text in Paragraphs

Paragraphs can be sorted alphabetically, numerically, or by date, based on the first character or characters in each paragraph. If the first character is a letter, Word will sort alphabetically from A to Z or from Z to A. This can be useful for such things as a list of names or a glossary of terms. Paragraphs that begin with a number, such as a dollar amount or measurement, can be arranged numerically in ascending or descending order.

Sort

To sort text, select the specific paragraphs to be sorted. (If text is not selected, Word sorts the entire document.) Click the Sort button in the Paragraph group on the Home tab and the Sort Text dialog box displays. At this dialog box, click OK.

Quick Steps

Sort Paragraphs of Text
1. Click Sort button.
2. Make changes as needed at Sort Text dialog box.
3. Click OK.

The *Type* option at the Sort Text dialog box provides the options *Text*, *Number*, or *Date* depending on the text selected. Word attempts to determine the data type and chooses one of the three options. For example, if numbers with mathematical values are selected, Word assigns them the *Number* type. However, if a numbered list is selected, Word assigns them the *Text* type since the numbers do not represent mathematical values. Occasionally this will result in Word reorganizing a numbered list incorrectly (as 1., 10., 11., 12., 2., for example). If this occurs, change the *Type* option to *Number* to sort in correct numerical order.

Activity 3 **Sorting Paragraphs Alphabetically and Numerically** Part 1 of 1

1. Open **OnlineShop** and then save it with the name **3-OnlineShop**.
2. Sort the bulleted paragraphs alphabetically by completing the following steps:
   a. Select the four bulleted paragraphs in the section *Advantages of Online Shopping*.
   b. Click the Sort button in the Paragraph group on the Home tab.
   c. At the Sort Text dialog box, make sure that *Paragraphs* displays in the *Sort by* option box and that the *Ascending* option is selected.
   d. Click OK.
3. Sort the numbered paragraphs by completing the following steps:
   a. Select the six numbered paragraphs in the section *Online Shopping Safety Tips*.
   b. Click the Sort button in the Paragraph group.
   c. Click OK at the Sort Text dialog box.

4. Sort alphabetically the three paragraphs below the title *REFERENCES* by completing the following steps:
   a. Select the paragraphs below the title *REFERENCES*.
   b. Click the Sort button in the Paragraph group.
   c. Click the *Type* option box arrow and then click *Text* at the drop-down list.
   d. Click OK.
5. Save, print, and then close **3-OnlineShop**.

Check Your Work

Activity 4 Prepare a Document on Workshops and Training Dates   4 Parts

You will set and move tabs on the horizontal ruler and at the Tabs dialog box and type tabbed text about workshops, training dates, and a table of contents.

Setting and Modifying Tabs

Tabs allow text to be aligned at different points in the document. The default setting for tabs in Word is a left tab set every 0.5 inch. When the Tab key is pressed, the insertion point moves to the right 0.5 inch. In some situations, these default tabs are appropriate; in others, custom tabs may be needed. Two methods are available for setting tabs: set tabs on the horizontal ruler or at the Tabs dialog box.

Setting and Modifying Tabs on the Horizontal Ruler

 Tutorial

Setting and Modifying Tabs on the Horizontal Ruler

Quick Steps

Set Tabs on Horizontal Ruler
1. Click Alignment button above vertical ruler.
2. Click tab locations on horizontal ruler.

💡 *Hint* When setting tabs on the horizontal ruler, a dotted guideline displays to help align them.

💡 *Hint* Position the insertion point in any paragraph of text, and tabs for the paragraph appear on the horizontal ruler.

Use the horizontal ruler to set, move, and delete tabs. If the ruler is not visible, click the View tab and then click the *Ruler* check box in the Show group to insert a check mark. By default, tabs are set every 0.5 inch on the horizontal ruler. To set a new tab, first click the Alignment button to the left of the ruler to specify how text will be aligned on the tab. The types of tabs that can be set on the ruler are left, center, right, decimal, and bar. These tab types are represented on the ruler with the symbols shown in Table 3.1. Text is aligned at the left edge of a left tab, in the middle of a center tab, at the right edge of a right tab, and at the decimal point with a decimal tab. Setting a bar tab causes a vertical bar (line) to be inserted in the document at the point where the tab is set. Refer to Figure 3.7 on page 76 to see an example of a document with a bar tab.

When the Alignment button displays the correct tab symbol, position the mouse pointer on the ruler where the tab should be set, and then click the left mouse button to set the tab. When a new tab is set, any default tabs to the left of it are automatically deleted by Word.

If the tab symbol on the Alignment button is changed, the symbol remains in place until it is changed again or Word is closed. If Word is closed and then reopened, the Alignment button displays with the left tab symbol.

To set a tab at a specific measurement on the horizontal ruler, press and hold down the Alt key, position the mouse pointer at the desired position, and then

Table 3.1 Alignment Button Tab Symbols

Alignment Button Symbol	Type of Tab
∟	left
⊥	center
⌐	right
⊥.	decimal
		bar

click and hold down the left mouse button. This displays two measurements in the white portion of the horizontal ruler. The first measurement is the location of the mouse pointer on the ruler in relation to the left margin. The second measurement is the distance from the mouse pointer to the right margin. With the left mouse button held down, position the tab symbol at the desired location and then release the mouse button followed by the Alt key.

Tabs can be used to type text in columns. Type text and then click the Tab key to create a new column. At the end of a line, press the Enter key or press Shift + Enter. If the Enter key is used to end each line, all lines of text in columns will need to be selected to make paragraph formatting changes. To make changes to columns of text with line breaks inserted using Shift + Enter, the insertion point needs to be positioned in only one location in the columns of text.

Activity 4a Setting Left, Center, and Right Tabs on the Horizontal Ruler   Part 1 of 4

1. Press Ctrl + N to open a new blank document.
2. Type WORKSHOPS and apply bold formatting and center alignment, as shown in Figure 3.5.
3. Press the Enter key and then change the paragraph alignment back to left and turn off bold formatting.
4. Set a left tab at the 0.5-inch mark, a center tab at the 3.25-inch mark, and a right tab at the 6-inch mark by completing the following steps:
   a. Click the Show/Hide ¶ button in the Paragraph group on the Home tab to turn on the display of nonprinting characters.
   b. Make sure the horizontal ruler is visible. (If it is not, click the View tab and then click the *Ruler* check box in the Show group to insert a check mark.)
   c. Make sure the left tab symbol displays in the Alignment button above the vertical ruler.
   d. Position the mouse pointer on the 0.5-inch mark on the horizontal ruler and then click the left mouse button.

e. Position the mouse pointer on the Alignment button and then click the left mouse button until the center tab symbol displays (see Table 3.1).

f. Position the mouse pointer on the 3.25-inch mark on the horizontal ruler. Press and hold down the Alt key and then click and hold down the left mouse button. Make sure the first measurement on the horizontal ruler displays as approximately *3.25"* and then release the mouse button followed by the Alt key. (If 3.25" does not display, consider increasing the zoom.)

g. Position the mouse pointer on the Alignment button and then click the left mouse button until the right tab symbol displays (see Table 3.1).

h. Position the mouse pointer below the 6-inch mark on the horizontal ruler. Press and hold down the Alt key and then click and hold down the left mouse button. Make sure the first measurement on the horizontal ruler displays as approximately *6"* and then release the mouse button followed the Alt key.

5. Type the text in columns, as shown in Figure 3.5. Press the Tab key before typing each column entry and press Shift + Enter after typing each entry in the third column. Apply bold formatting to column headings, as shown in the figure.

6. After typing the final entry in the last column entry, press the Enter key two times.

7. Press Ctrl + Q to remove paragraph formatting (tab settings) below the columns from the current paragraph.

8. Click the Show/Hide ¶ button to turn off the display of nonprinting characters.

9. Save the document and name it **3-Tabs**.

 Check Your Work

Figure 3.5 Activity 4a

WORKSHOPS

Title	**Price**	**Date**
Quality Management	$240	Friday, February 5
Staff Development	229	Friday, February 19
Streamlining Production	175	Monday, March 1
Managing Records	150	Tuesday, March 16
Customer Service Training	150	Thursday, March 18
Sales Techniques	125	Tuesday, April 13

After a tab has been set on the horizontal ruler, it can be moved to a new location. To move a tab, position the mouse pointer on the tab symbol on the ruler, click and hold down the left mouse button, drag the symbol to the new location on the ruler, and then release the mouse button. To delete a tab from the ruler, position the mouse pointer on the tab symbol to be deleted, click and hold down the left mouse button, drag down into the document, and then release the mouse button.

Activity 4b Moving Tabs   Part 2 of 4

1. With **3-Tabs** open, position the insertion point anywhere in the first entry in the tabbed text.
2. Position the mouse pointer on the left tab symbol at the 0.5-inch mark on the horizontal ruler, click and hold down the left mouse button, drag the left tab symbol to the 1-inch mark on the ruler, and then release the mouse button. *Hint: Use the Alt key to help you position the tab symbol precisely*.

3. Position the mouse pointer on the right tab symbol at the 6-inch mark on the horizontal ruler, click and hold down the left mouse button, drag the right tab symbol to the 5.5-inch mark on the ruler, and then release the mouse button. *Hint: Use the Alt key to help you position the tab symbol precisely*.
4. Save **3-Tabs**.

 Check Your Work

 Tutorial

Setting and
Clearing Tabs at
the Tabs Dialog Box

Setting and Modifying Tabs at the Tabs Dialog Box

Use the Tabs dialog box, shown in Figure 3.6, to set tabs at specific measurements and clear one tab or all tabs. To display the Tabs dialog box, click the Paragraph group dialog box launcher. At the Paragraph dialog box, click the Tabs button in the lower left corner of the dialog box.

A left, right, center, decimal, or bar tab can be set at the Tabs dialog box. (For an example of a bar tab, refer to Figure 3.7 on page 76.) To set a tab, click the type of tab in the *Alignment* section of the dialog box, type the tab measurement in the *Tab stop position* text box, and then click the Set button. To clear an individual tab at the Tabs dialog box, select or enter the tab position and then click the Clear button. To clear all tabs, click the Clear All button.

 Quick Steps

**Set Tabs at Tabs
Dialog Box**
1. Click Paragraph
   group dialog box
   launcher.
2. Click Tabs button.
3. Specify tab positions,
   alignments, and
   leader options.
4. Click OK.

Figure 3.6 Tabs Dialog Box

Type a tab measurement in this text box.

Choose a tab alignment with options in this section.

Choose a leader symbol with options in this section.

Activity 4c Setting Left Tabs and a Bar Tab at the Tabs Dialog Box

1. With **3-Tabs** open, press Ctrl + End to move the insertion point to the end of the document.
2. Type the title TRAINING DATES and apply bold formatting and center alignment, as shown in Figure 3.7. Press the Enter key, return the paragraph alignment to left, and then turn off bold formatting.
3. Display the Tabs dialog box and then set left tabs and a bar tab by completing the following steps:
    a. Click the Paragraph group dialog box launcher.
    b. At the Paragraph dialog box, click the Tabs button in the lower left corner of the dialog box.
    c. Make sure *Left* is selected in the *Alignment* section of the dialog box.
    d. Type 1.75 in the *Tab stop position* text box.
    e. Click the Set button.
    f. Type 4 in the *Tab stop position* text box and then click the Set button.
    g. Type 3.25 in the *Tab stop position* text box, click *Bar* in the *Alignment* section, and then click the Set button.
    h. Click OK to close the Tabs dialog box.
4. Type the text in columns, as shown in Figure 3.7. Press the Tab key before typing each column entry and press Shift + Enter to end each line. After typing *February 23*, press the Enter key.
5. Clear tabs below the columns from the current paragraph by completing the following steps:
    a. Click the Paragraph group dialog box launcher.
    b. At the Paragraph dialog box, click the Tabs button.
    c. At the Tabs dialog box, click the Clear All button.
    d. Click OK.
6. Press the Enter key.
7. Remove the 8 points of spacing after the last entry in the text by completing the following steps:
    a. Position the insertion point anywhere in the *January 26* entry.
    b. Click the Line and Paragraph Spacing button in the Paragraph group on the Home tab.
    c. Click the *Remove Space After Paragraph* option.
8. Save **3-Tabs**.

3g

3h

Check Your Work

Figure 3.7 Activity 4c

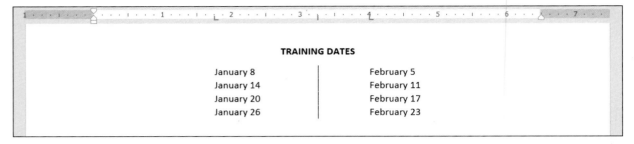

TRAINING DATES	
January 8	February 5
January 14	February 11
January 20	February 17
January 26	February 23

Four types of tabs (left, right, center, and decimal) can be set with leaders at the Tabs dialog box. Leaders are useful in a table of contents or other material where the reader's eyes should be directed across the page. Figure 3.8 shows an example of leaders. Leaders can be periods (.), hyphens (-), or underlines (_). To add leaders to a tab, click the type of leader in the *Leader* section of the Tabs dialog box.

Activity 4d Setting a Left Tab and a Right Tab with Period Leaders   Part 4 of 4

1. With **3-Tabs** open, press Ctrl + End to move the insertion point to the end of the document.
2. Type the title TABLE OF CONTENTS and apply bold formatting and center alignment, as shown in Figure 3.8.
3. Press the Enter key and then return the paragraph alignment to left and turn off bold formatting.
4. Set a left tab and then a right tab with period leaders by completing the following steps:
   a. Click the Paragraph group dialog box launcher.
   b. Click the Tabs button.
   c. At the Tabs dialog box, make sure *Left* is selected in the *Alignment* section of the dialog box.
   d. With the insertion point positioned in the *Tab stop position* text box, type 1 and then click the Set button.
   e. Type 5.5 in the *Tab stop position* text box.
   f. Click *Right* in the *Alignment* section.
   g. Click *2 ......* in the *Leader* section and then click the Set button.
   h. Click OK to close the dialog box.
5. Type the text in columns, as shown in Figure 3.8. Press the Tab key before typing each column entry and press Shift + Enter to end each line.
6. Save, print, and then close **3-Tabs**.

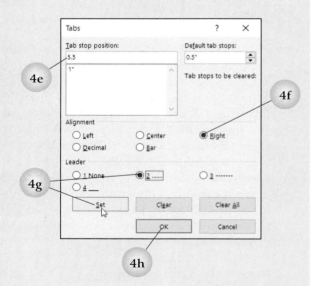

Check Your Work

Figure 3.8 Activity 4d

Activity 5 **Move and Copy Text in a Document on Online Shopping Tips**   **2 Parts**

You will open a document containing information on online shopping safety tips and then cut, copy, and paste text in the document.

Tutorial

Cutting, Copying, and Pasting Text

Cutting, Copying, and Pasting Text

When editing a document, specific text may need to be deleted, moved to a different location in the document, or copied to various locations in the document. These activities can be completed using buttons in the Clipboard group on the Home tab.

Deleting and Cutting Text

Cutting and deleting text are two ways to remove text from a document. Delete text by selecting it and then using the Delete key on the keyboard, or delete one character at a time with the Delete key or the Backspace key. To cut text, select it and then click the Cut button in the Clipboard group on the Home tab, or select it and then use the keyboard shortcut Ctrl + X. (Note: If text is accidentally cut or deleted, restore it by clicking the Undo button on the Quick Access Toolbar or with the keyboard shortcut Ctrl + Z before saving or closing the file. After a document has been saved and closed, the text cannot be restored.)

✂ Cut

When text is deleted, it is simply removed from the document. When text is cut, it is removed and stored temporarily in the Clipboard. The Clipboard holds text while it is being moved or copied to a new location in the document or to a different document.

💡 **Hint** The Clipboard content is deleted when the computer is turned off. Text you want to save permanently should be saved as a separate document.

Cutting and Pasting Text

To move text to a different location in the document, select the text, click the Cut button, position the insertion point at the location the text is to be inserted, and then click the Paste button in the Clipboard group.

📋 Paste

Selected text can also be moved using the shortcut menu. To do this, select the text and then position the insertion point inside the selected text until it turns into an arrow pointer. Click the right mouse button and then click *Cut* at the shortcut menu. Position the insertion point where the text is to be inserted, click the right mouse button, and then click *Paste* at the shortcut menu. Keyboard shortcuts are also available for cutting and pasting text. Use Ctrl + X to cut text and Ctrl + V to paste text.

Quick Steps

Move Selected Text
1. Select text.
2. Click Cut button or use Ctrl + X.
3. Position insertion point.
4. Click Paste button or use Ctrl + V.

Quick Steps

Move Text with Mouse

1. Select text.
2. Position mouse pointer in selected text.
3. Click and hold down left mouse button and drag to new location.
4. Release left mouse button.

When text is cut from a document, it will remain in the Clipboard while Word is open and can be pasted multiple times. The Clipboard holds only one item at a time. If another portion of text is cut to the Clipboard, the first selection will be removed.

Moving Text by Dragging with the Mouse

The mouse can be used to move text. To do this, select text to be moved and then click and drag the selection with the mouse pointer. As the text is being dragged, the mouse pointer will display as an arrow with a small gray box attached. Move to the location the selected text is to be inserted, and then release the button. If the selected text is inserted in the wrong location, click the Undo button immediately.

Activity 5a Cutting and Dragging Selected Text   Part 1 of 2

1. Open **ShoppingTips** and then save it with the name **3-ShoppingTips**.
2. Move a paragraph by completing the following steps:
   a. Select the paragraph that begins with *Only buy at secure sites,* including the blank line below the paragraph.
   b. Click the Cut button in the Clipboard group on the Home tab.
   c. Position the insertion point at the beginning of the paragraph that begins with *Watch for phony shopping apps.*
   d. Click the Paste button (make sure you click the Paste button and not the Paste button arrow) in the Clipboard group on the Home tab. (If the fourth and fifth paragraphs are not separated by a blank line, press the Enter key.)

3. Following steps similar to those in Step 2, move the paragraph that begins with *Never provide your social* before the paragraph that begins *Watch for phony shopping apps* and after the paragraph that begins *Only buy at secure sites.*
4. Use the mouse to select the paragraph that begins with *Do not shop online using,* including one blank line below the paragraph.
5. Move the I-beam pointer inside the selected text until it displays as an arrow pointer.
6. Click and hold down the left mouse button, drag the arrow pointer (which displays with a small gray box attached) so that the insertion point (which displays as a black vertical bar) is positioned at the beginning of the paragraph that begins *Never provide your social* and then release the mouse button.
7. Deselect the text.
8. Save **3-ShoppingTips**.

Check Your Work

Using the Paste Options Button

When text is pasted in a document, the Paste Options button displays in the lower right corner of the text. Click this button (or press the Ctrl key on the keyboard) and the Paste Options gallery displays, as shown in Figure 3.9. The gallery can also be displayed by clicking the Paste button arrow in the Clipboard group.

The Paste Options gallery contains four buttons for specifying the formatting of pasted text. The first button, Keep Source Formatting, is the default and pastes the text with the original formatting. Click the second button, Merge Formatting, and pasted text will take on the formatting of the text where it is pasted. The third button, Picture, will paste selected text as an image. Click the last button, Keep Text Only, to paste only the text and not the text formatting. Hover the mouse pointer over a button in the gallery and the live preview displays the text in the document as it will appear when pasted.

Figure 3.9 Paste Options Button Drop-Down Gallery

Answer only the minimum questions when filling out forms. Many sites put an asterisk next to the questions that must be answered, so only answer those.

Paste Options:

Set Default Paste...

Click the button that specifies the formatting for the pasted text.

Activity 5b Using the Paste Options Button

Part 2 of 2

1. With **3-ShoppingTips** open, open **Tip**.
2. In the **Tip** document, select the paragraph of text, including the blank line below the paragraph, and then click the Cut button in the Clipboard group on the Home tab.
3. Close **Tip**.
4. Press Ctrl + End to move the insertion point to the end of **3-ShoppingTips**.
5. Click the Paste button.
6. Click the Paste Options button at the end of the paragraph and then click the Merge Formatting button in the Paste Options gallery. (This changes the font so it matches the font of the other paragraphs in the document.)
7. Save, print, and then close **3-ShoppingTips**.

Watch for phony shopping apps. Counterfeit apps use a variety of methods for getting you to provide credit card information to steal your identity. Some use phishing emails that look like they are from a legitimate store with authentic-looking logos and marketing messages.

Answer only the minimum questions when filling out forms. Many sites put an asterisk next to the questions that must be answered, so only answer those.

Paste Options:

Set Default Paste...

6

Check Your Work

You will copy and paste text in a document announcing a staff meeting for the Technical Support Team.

Copying and Pasting Text

 Copy

Use copy and paste to copy text from one document and paste it into another. Or, paste copied text into one document multiple times to insert duplicate portions of text without needing to retype it. Copy selected text and then paste it in a different location using the Copy and Paste buttons in the Clipboard group on the Home tab or the keyboard shortcuts Ctrl + C and Ctrl + V.

Quick Steps

Copy Selected Text
1. Select text.
2. Click Copy button or use Ctrl + C.
3. Position insertion point.
4. Click Paste button or use Ctrl + V.

Text can also be copied and pasted using the mouse. To do this, select the text and then click inside the selected text. Hold down the left mouse button and also press and hold down the Ctrl key while dragging the selected text with the mouse. While text is being dragged, the pointer displays with a small gray box and a box containing a plus [+] symbol and a black vertical bar moves with the pointer. Position the black bar in the desired location, release the mouse button, and then release the Ctrl key to paste in the text.

Activity 6 **Copying Text**

Part 1 of 1

1. Open **StaffMtg** and then save it with the name **3-StaffMtg**.
2. Copy the text in the document to the end of the document by completing the following steps:
   a. Select all the text in the document and include one blank line below the text. *Hint:* ***Click the Show/Hide ¶ button to turn on the display of nonprinting characters. When you select the text, select one of the paragraph markers below the text.***
   b. Click the Copy button in the Clipboard group on the Home tab.
   c. Press Ctrl + End to move the insertion point to the end of the document.
   d. Click the Paste button.
3. Paste the text again at the end of the document. To do this, click the Paste button. (This inserts a copy of the text from the Clipboard.)
4. Select all the text in the document using the mouse and include one blank line below the text.
5. Move the I-beam pointer inside the selected text until it becomes an arrow pointer.
6. Click and hold down the Ctrl key and then the left mouse button. Drag the arrow pointer (which displays with a box containing a plus symbol) so the vertical black bar is positioned at the end of the document, release the mouse button, and then release the Ctrl key.
7. Deselect the text.
8. Make sure all the text fits on one page. If not, consider deleting any extra blank lines.
9. Save, print, and then close **3-StaffMtg**.

 Check Your Work

Activity 7 Create a Contract Negotiations Document   1 Part

You will use the Clipboard task pane to copy and paste paragraphs to and from
separate documents to create a contract negotiations document.

 Tutorial

Using the Clipboard
Task Pane

Quick Steps

Use the Clipboard
1. Click Clipboard
   group task pane
   launcher.
2. Select and copy or
   cut text.
3. Position insertion
   point.
4. Click option in
   Clipboard task pane.

Hint You can
copy or cut items to
the Clipboard from
various Microsoft Office
applications and then
paste them into any
Office file.

Using the Clipboard Task Pane

Use the Clipboard task pane to collect and paste multiple items. Up to 24
different items can be collected and then pasted in various locations. To display
the Clipboard task pane, click the Clipboard group task pane launcher in the
lower right corner of the Clipboard group on the Home tab. The Clipboard task
pane displays at the left side of the screen in a manner similar to what is shown in
Figure 3.10.

Select the text or object to be copied and then click the Copy button or Cut
button in the Clipboard group. Continue selecting text or items and clicking the
Copy or Cut button. To insert an item from the Clipboard task pane into the
document, position the insertion point in the desired location and then click
the option in the Clipboard task pane representing the item. Click the Paste All
button to paste all the items in the Clipboard task pane into the document. If
the copied or cut item is text, the first 50 characters display in the list box on the
Clipboard task pane. When all the items are inserted, click the Clear All button to
clear all items from the task pane.

Figure 3.10 Clipboard Task Pane

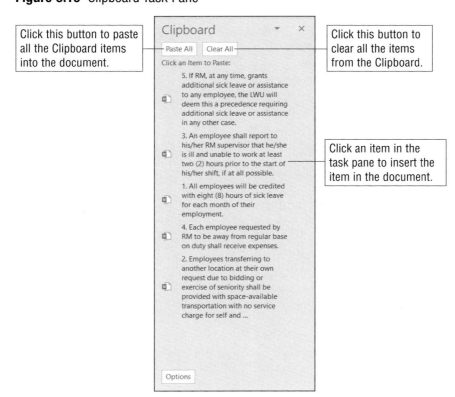

1. Open **ContractItems**.
2. Display the Clipboard task pane by clicking the Clipboard group task pane launcher in the bottom right corner of the Clipboard group on the Home tab. (If the Clipboard task pane list box contains any items, click the Clear All button at the top of the Clipboard task pane.)

②

3. Select paragraph 1 in the document (the *1.* is not selected) and then click the Copy button.
4. Select paragraph 3 in the document (the *3.* is not selected) and then click the Copy button.
5. Close **ContractItems**.
6. Paste the paragraphs by completing the following steps:
   a. Press Ctrl + N to open a new blank document. (If the Clipboard task pane does not display, click the Clipboard group task pane launcher.)
   b. Type CONTRACT NEGOTIATION ITEMS and apply bold formatting and center alignment.
   c. Press the Enter key, turn off bold formatting, and return the paragraph alignment to left.
   d. Click the Paste All button in the Clipboard task pane to paste both paragraphs in the document.
   e. Click the Clear All button in the Clipboard task pane.

6d　　　　　**6e**

7. Open **UnionContract**.
8. Select and then copy each of the following paragraphs:
   a. Paragraph 2 in the *Transfers and Moving Expenses* section.
   b. Paragraph 4 in the *Transfers and Moving Expenses* section.
   c. Paragraph 1 in the *Sick Leave* section.
   d. Paragraph 3 in the *Sick Leave* section.
   e. Paragraph 5 in the *Sick Leave* section.
9. Close **UnionContract**.
10. Make sure the insertion point is positioned at the end of the document on a new line and then paste the paragraphs by completing the following steps:
    a. Click the button in the Clipboard task pane representing paragraph 2. (When the paragraph is inserted in the document, the paragraph number changes to *3.*)
    b. Click the button in the Clipboard task pane representing paragraph 4.
    c. Click the button in the Clipboard task pane representing paragraph 3.
    d. Click the button in the Clipboard task pane representing paragraph 5.

10a

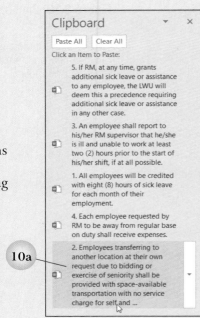

11. Click the Clear All button.
12. Close the Clipboard task pane.
13. Save the document and name it **3-NegotiateItems**.
14. Print and then close **3-NegotiateItems**.

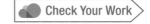
Check Your Work

Chapter Summary

- Number paragraphs using the Numbering button in the Paragraph group on the Home tab and insert bullets before paragraphs using the Bullets button in the Paragraph group on the Home tab.

- Remove all paragraph formatting from a paragraph by using the keyboard shortcut Ctrl + Q. Remove all character and paragraph formatting by clicking the Clear All Formatting button in the Font group.

- The AutoCorrect Options button displays when the AutoFormat feature inserts numbers or bullets. Click this button to display options for undoing and/or stopping automatic numbering or bulleting.

- A bulleted list with a hanging indent is automatically created when a paragraph begins with *, >, or -. The type of bullet inserted depends on the type of character entered.

- Automatic numbering and bulleting can be turned off at the AutoCorrect dialog box with the AutoFormat As You Type tab selected.

- A paragraph created in Word contains an invisible frame and a border can be added to this frame. Click the Borders button arrow in the Paragraph group on the Home tab to display a drop-down gallery of border options.

- Use options at the Borders and Shading dialog box with the Borders tab selected to add a customized border to a paragraph or selected paragraphs.

- Apply shading to selected text or paragraphs by clicking the Shading button arrow in the Paragraph group on the Home tab and then clicking a color at the drop-down gallery. Use options at the Borders and Shading dialog box with the Shading tab selected to add shading and/or a pattern to a paragraph or selected paragraphs.

- Use the Sort button in the Paragraph group on the Home tab to sort text in paragraphs alphabetically by the first character of each paragraph, which can be a number, symbol, or letter.

- By default, tabs are set every 0.5 inch. Tab settings can be changed on the horizontal ruler or at the Tabs dialog box.

- Use the Alignment button above the vertical ruler to select a left, right, center, decimal, or bar tab.

- When a tab is set on the horizontal ruler, any default tabs to the left are automatically deleted.

- After a tab has been set on the horizontal ruler, it can be moved or deleted using the mouse pointer.

- At the Tabs dialog box, any of the five types of tabs can be set at a specific measurement. Four types of tabs (left, right, center, and decimal) can be set with preceding leaders, which can be periods, hyphens, or underlines. Individual tabs or all tabs can be cleared at the Tabs dialog box.

- Cut, copy, and paste text using buttons in the Clipboard group on the Home tab, with options at the shortcut menu, or with keyboard shortcuts.

- When selected text is pasted, the Paste Options button displays in the lower right corner of the text. Click the button and the Paste Options gallery displays with buttons for specifying how text and formatting is pasted in the document.

- With the Clipboard task pane, up to 24 items can be copied and then pasted in various locations in a document or other document.

- Display the Clipboard task pane by clicking the Clipboard group task pane launcher in the Clipboard group on the Home tab.

Commands Review

FEATURE	RIBBON TAB, GROUP	BUTTON, OPTION	KEYBOARD SHORTCUT
borders	Home, Paragraph		
Borders and Shading dialog box	Home, Paragraph	, *Borders and Shading*	
bullets	Home, Paragraph		
clear all formatting	Home, Font		
clear paragraph formatting			Ctrl + Q
Clipboard task pane	Home, Clipboard		
copy text	Home, Clipboard		Ctrl + C
cut text	Home, Clipboard		Ctrl + X
numbering	Home, Paragraph		
Paragraph dialog box	Home, Paragraph		
paste text	Home, Clipboard		Ctrl + V
shading	Home, Paragraph		
Sort Text dialog box	Home, Paragraph		
Tabs dialog box	Home, Paragraph	, Tabs	

Microsoft
Word

Formatting Pages and Documents

CHAPTER 4

Performance Objectives

Upon successful completion of Chapter 4, you will be able to:

1 Change margins, page orientation, and paper size

2 Format pages at the Page Setup dialog box

3 Insert a page break, blank page, and cover page

4 Insert and remove page numbers

5 Insert and edit predesigned headers and footers

6 Insert a watermark, page background color, and page border

7 Insert section breaks

8 Create and format text in columns

9 Hyphenate words automatically and manually

10 Create a drop cap

11 Use the Click and Type feature

12 Vertically align text

13 Find and replace text

Word provides a number of options for changing the layout of a document, such as adjusting page margins, orientation, and paper size. Word also includes features that can be inserted in a document such as a page break, blank page, cover page, and watermark, as well as page numbers, headers, footers, page color, and page borders. You will learn about these features in this chapter along with other page and document formatting options such as inserting section breaks, formatting text into columns, hyphenating words, creating a drop cap, and vertically aligning text. You will also learn how to find and replace text in a document.

Data Files

Before beginning chapter work, copy the WL1C4 folder to your storage medium and then make WL1C4 the active folder.

The online course includes additional training and assessment resources.

You will open a document containing information on guidelines for online etiquette and then change the margins, page orientation, and paper size.

Changing Page Setup

The Page Setup group on the Layout tab contains a number of options for changing the layout of pages in a document. Use options in the Page Setup group to perform such actions as changing margins, orientation, and paper size and inserting page breaks. The Pages group on the Insert tab contains three buttons for inserting a cover page, blank page, or page break.

Changing Margins

Margins

Changing Margins

Change page margins with options at the Margins button drop-down list, as shown in Figure 4.1. To display this drop-down list, click the Layout tab and then click the Margins button in the Page Setup group. To change the margins, click one of the preset margins in the drop-down list. Be aware that most printers require a minimum margin (between ¼ and ⅜ inch) because they cannot print to the edge of the page.

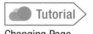

Changing Page Orientation

Orientation

Changing Page Orientation

Click the Orientation button in the Page Setup group on the Layout tab and two options display: *Portrait* and *Landscape*. At the portrait orientation, which is the default, the page is 8.5 inches wide and 11 inches tall. At the landscape orientation, the page is 11 inches wide and 8.5 inches tall. Change the page orientation and the page margins automatically shift: The left and right margin measurements become the top and bottom margin measurements.

Quick Steps

Change Margins
1. Click Layout tab.
2. Click Margins button.
3. Click margin setting.

Change Page Orientation
1. Click Layout tab.
2. Click Orientation button.
3. Click *Portrait* or *Landscape*.

Change Paper Size
1. Click Layout tab.
2. Click Size button.
3. Click paper size.

Figure 4.1 Margins Button Drop-Down List

Click the Margins button to display this drop-down list of margin options.

Click the *Custom Margins* option to display the Page Setup dialog box with the Margins tab selected.

Tutorial

Changing Paper Size

 Size

Changing Paper Size

By default, Word formats documents for printing on standard letter-sized paper that is 8.5 inches wide and 11 inches tall. Change this default setting with options at the Size button drop-down list. Display this drop-down list by clicking the Size button in the Page Setup group on the Layout tab.

Activity 1a Changing Margins, Page Orientation, and Paper Size   Part 1 of 2

1. Open **Netiquette** and then save it with the name **4-Netiquette**.
2. Click the Layout tab.
3. Click the Margins button in the Page Setup group and then click the *Narrow* option.

4. Click the Orientation button in the Page Setup group and then click *Landscape* at the drop-down list.

5. Scroll through the document and notice how the text displays on the page in landscape orientation.
6. Click the Orientation button in the Page Setup group and then click *Portrait* at the drop-down list. (This changes the orientation back to the default.)

7. Click the Size button in the Page Setup group and then click the *Executive* option (*7.25" × 10.5"*). Paper size options may vary. If this option is not available, choose an option with a similar paper size.

8. Scroll through the document and notice how the text displays on the page.
9. Click the Size button and then click *Legal (8.5" × 14")*.
10. Scroll through the document and notice how the text displays on the page.
11. Click the Size button and then click *Letter (8.5" × 11")*. (This returns the size back to the default.)
12. Save **4-Netiquette**.

 Check Your Work

Changing Margins at the Page Setup Dialog Box

Quick Steps

Change Margins at Page Setup Dialog Box

1. Click Layout tab.
2. Click Page Setup group dialog box launcher.
OR
2. Click Margins button, *Custom Margins*.
3. Specify margins.
4. Click OK.

Change Paper Size at Page Setup Dialog Box

1. Click Layout tab.
2. Click Size button.
3. Click *More Paper Sizes* at drop-down list.
4. Specify size.
5. Click OK.

The Margins button in the Page Setup group provides a number of preset margins. If these margins do not provide the desired margins, set specific margins at the Page Setup dialog box with the Margins tab selected, as shown in Figure 4.2. Display this dialog box by clicking the Page Setup group dialog box launcher on the Layout tab or by clicking the Margins button and then clicking *Custom Margins* at the bottom of the drop-down list.

To change one of the margins, select the current measurement in the *Top*, *Bottom*, *Left*, or *Right* measurement box and then type the new measurement, or click the measurement box up arrow to increase the measurement or the measurement box down arrow to decrease the measurement. As the margin measurements change at the Page Setup dialog box, the sample page in the *Preview* section shows the effects of the changes.

Changing Paper Size at the Page Setup Dialog Box

The Size button drop-down list contains a number of preset paper sizes. If these sizes do not provide the desired paper size, specify a size at the Page Setup dialog box with the Paper tab selected. Display this dialog box by clicking the Size button in the Page Setup group and then clicking *More Paper Sizes* at the bottom of the drop-down list.

Figure 4.2 Page Setup Dialog Box with the Margins Tab Selected

Notice the default settings for the top, bottom, left, and right margins.

Changes made to margins are reflected in this preview page.

Activity 1b Changing Margins and Paper Size at the Page Setup Dialog Box

Part 2 of 2

1. With **4-Netiquette** open, make sure the Layout tab is selected.
2. Click the Page Setup group dialog box launcher.
3. At the Page Setup dialog box with the Margins tab selected, click the *Top* measurement box up arrow until *0.7"* displays.
4. Click the *Bottom* measurement box up arrow until *0.7"* displays.
5. Select the current measurement in the *Left* measurement box and then type 0.75.
6. Select the current measurement in the *Right* measurement box and then type 0.75.
7. Click OK to close the dialog box.
8. Click the Size button in the Page Setup group and then click *More Paper Sizes* at the drop-down list.
9. At the Page Setup dialog box with the Paper tab selected, click the *Paper size* option box arrow and then click *Legal* at the drop-down list.
10. Click OK to close the dialog box.
11. Scroll through the document and notice how the text displays on the page.
12. Click the Size button in the Page Setup group and then click *Letter* at the drop-down list.
13. Save, print, and then close **4-Netiquette**.

Check Your Work

Activity 2 Customize a Report on Computer Input and Output Devices

3 Parts

You will open a document containing information on computer input and output devices and then insert page breaks, a blank page, a cover page, and page numbers.

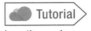

Inserting and
Removing a Page
Break

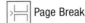 Page Break

Inserting and Removing a Page Break

With the default top and bottom margins set at 1 inch, approximately 9 inches of text prints on the page. At approximately the 10-inch mark, Word automatically inserts a page break. Insert a page break manually in a document with the keyboard shortcut Ctrl + Enter or with the Page Break button in the Pages group on the Insert tab.

A page break inserted by Word is considered a *soft page break* and a page break inserted manually is considered a *hard page break*. Soft page breaks automatically adjust if text is added to or deleted from a document. Hard page breaks do not adjust and are therefore less flexible than soft page breaks.

If text is added to or deleted from a document containing a hard page break, check the break to determine whether it is still in a desirable location. Display a hard page break, along with other nonprinting characters, by clicking the Show/Hide ¶ button in the Paragraph group on the Home tab. A hard page break displays as a row of dots with the words *Page Break* in the center. To delete a hard page break, position the insertion point at the beginning of the page break and then press the Delete key or double-click the words *Page Break* and then press the Delete key. If the display of nonprinting characters is turned off, delete a hard page break by positioning the insertion point immediately below the page break and then pressing the Backspace key.

Quick Steps

Insert Page Break
1. Click Insert tab.
2. Click Page Break button.
OR
Press Ctrl + Enter.

  Show/Hide ¶

Activity 2a Inserting and Deleting Page Breaks

Part 1 of 3

1. Open **CompDevices** and then save it with the name **4-CompDevices**.
2. Change the top margin by completing the following steps:
   a. Click the Layout tab.
   b. Click the Page Setup group dialog box launcher.
   c. At the Page Setup dialog box with the Margins tab selected, type 1.5 in the *Top* measurement box.

   d. Click OK to close the dialog box.

3. Insert a page break at the beginning of the heading *Mouse* by completing the following steps:
   a. Position the insertion point at the beginning of the heading *Mouse* (at the bottom of page 1).
   b. Click the Insert tab and then click the Page Break button in the Pages group.

4. Move the insertion point to the beginning of the title *COMPUTER OUTPUT DEVICES* (on the second page) and then insert a page break by pressing Ctrl + Enter.
5. Move the insertion point to the beginning of the heading *Printer* and then press Ctrl + Enter to insert a page break.
6. Delete a page break by completing the following steps:
   a. Click the Home tab.
   b. Turn on the display of nonprinting characters by clicking the Show/Hide ¶ button in the Paragraph group.
   c. Scroll up to see the bottom of the third page and then double-click the words *Page Break*.
   d. Press the Delete key.
   e. Click the Show/Hide ¶ button to turn off the display of nonprinting characters.
7. Save **4-CompDevices**.

Inserting and Removing a Blank Page

Inserting and Removing a Blank Page

 Blank Page

Click the Blank Page button in the Pages group on the Insert tab to insert a blank page at the position of the insertion point. This might be useful in a document where a blank page is needed for an illustration, graphic, or figure. When a blank page is inserted, Word inserts a page break and then inserts another page break to create the blank page. To remove a blank page, turn on the display of nonprinting characters and then delete the page breaks.

Inserting and Removing a Cover Page

Inserting and Removing a Cover Page

 Cover Page

Consider inserting a cover page to improve the visual appeal of a document or to prepare it for distribution to others. Use the Cover Page button in the Pages group on the Insert tab to insert a predesigned cover page and then type personalized text in the placeholders on the page. Click the Cover Page button and a drop-down list displays with visual representations of the cover pages. Scroll through the list and then click a predesigned cover page option.

A predesigned cover page contains location placeholders, in which specific text is entered. For example, a cover page might contain the placeholder *[Document title]*. Click the placeholder to select it and then type the title of the document. Delete a placeholder by clicking to select it, clicking the placeholder tab, and then pressing the Delete key. Remove a cover page by clicking the Cover Page button and then clicking *Remove Current Cover Page* at the drop-down list.

Activity 2b Inserting and Removing a Blank Page and Inserting a Cover Page

1. With **4-CompDevices** open, create a blank page by completing the following steps:
   a. Move the insertion point to the beginning of the heading *Touchpad and Touchscreen* on the second page.
   b. Click the Insert tab.
   c. Click the Blank Page button in the Pages group.
2. Insert a cover page by completing the following steps:
   a. Press Ctrl + Home to move the insertion point to the beginning of the document.
   b. Click the Cover Page button in the Pages group.
   c. Scroll down the drop-down list and then click the *Motion* option.
   d. Click the *[Document title]* placeholder and then type Computer Devices.

e. Click the *[Year]* placeholder, click the placeholder option box arrow, and then click the Today button at the bottom of the drop-down calendar.

f. Click the *[Company name]* placeholder and then type Drake Computing. (If a name appears in the placeholder, select the name and then type Drake Computing.)

g. Select the name above the company name and then type your first and last names. If instead of a name, the *[Author name]* placeholder displays above the company name, click the placeholder and then type your first and last names.

3. Remove the blank page you inserted in Step 1 by completing the following steps:

a. Move the insertion point immediately right of the period that ends the last sentence in the paragraph of text in the *Trackball* section (the last sentence on page 3).

b. Press the Delete key on the keyboard approximately six times until the heading *Touchpad and Touchscreen* displays on page 3.

4. Save **4-CompDevices**.

Trackball

A trackball is like an upside-down mouse. A mouse is move
and the user moves the ball with his or her fingers or palm.
are incorporated into the design of the trackball.

Touchpad and Touchscreen

A touchpad feels less mechanical than a mouse or trackball

3a-3b

> Check Your Work

> Tutorial

Inserting and Removing Page Numbers

Inserting and Removing Page Numbers

Word by default does not include page numbers on pages. To insert page numbers in a document, click the Page Number button in the Header & Footer group on the Insert tab. A drop-down list displays with options for placing page numbers in the top margin of the page (in the Header pane) in the bottom margin of the page (in the Footer pane), in a page margin (either in a Header or Footer pane), or at the location of the insertion point. Click or point to an option and a drop-down list will appear showing several predesigned page number formats. Scroll through the list and then click an option.

Choose a page number option other than *Current Position*, and the Header and Footer panes open. Changes can be made to the page numbering format in the Header pane or Footer pane. To do this, select the page number and then apply formatting such as a different font size, style, or color. A page number inserted in a document with the *Current Position* option is positioned in the document, not in the Header or Footer pane. Format the page number like any other text in the document.

After formatting page numbers inserted in the Header or Footer pane, click the Close Header and Footer button, or simply double-click anywhere in the document outside the header or footer. Remove page numbers from the document by clicking the Page Number button in the Header & Footer group and then clicking *Remove Page Numbers* at the drop-down list.

Activity 2c Inserting and Removing Predesigned Page Numbers

Part 3 of 3

1. With **4-CompDevices** open, insert page numbers by completing the following steps:
   a. Move the insertion point so it is positioned anywhere in the title *COMPUTER INPUT DEVICES*.
   b. If necessary, click the Insert tab.
   c. Click the Page Number button in the Header & Footer group and then point to *Top of Page*.
   d. Scroll through the drop-down list and then click the *Brackets 2* option.

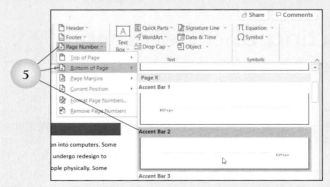

2. Click the Close Header and Footer button in the Close group on the Header & Footer Tools Design tab.
3. Scroll through the document and notice the page numbers at the top of each page except the cover page. (The cover page and text are divided by a page break. Word does not include the cover page when numbering pages.)
4. Remove the page numbering by clicking the Insert tab, clicking the Page Number button, and then clicking *Remove Page Numbers* at the drop-down list.
5. Click the Page Number button, point to *Bottom of Page*, scroll down the drop-down list, and then click the *Accent Bar 2* option.

6. Click the Close Header and Footer button.
7. Save, print, and then close **4-CompDevices**.

 Check Your Work

You will open a document containing information on the process of writing effectively, insert a predesigned header and footer, remove a header, and format and delete header and footer elements.

Inserting and Removing a Predesigned Header and Footer

Inserting Predesigned Headers and Footers

As mentioned in the last section, text that appears in the top margin of a page is called a *header* and text that appears in the bottom margin of a page is referred to as a *footer*. Headers and footers are common in manuscripts, textbooks, reports, and other publications. They typically include page numbers and other information such as the author's name, the title of the publication, and/or the chapter title.

 Header

Quick Steps

Insert Predesigned Header or Footer
1. Click Insert tab.
2. Click Header button or Footer button.
3. Click header or footer option.
4. Type text in specific placeholders in header or footer.
5. Click Close Header and Footer button.

Insert a predesigned header in a document by clicking the Insert tab and then clicking the Header button in the Header & Footer group. This displays the Header button drop-down list. At this drop-down list, click a predesigned header option and the header is inserted in the document.

A predesigned header or footer may contain location placeholders such as [Document title] or [Type here]. Click in the placeholder text to select it and type the title of the document or other personalized text. Delete a placeholder by clicking to select it and then pressing the Delete key. If the placeholder contains a tab, delete the placeholder by clicking the tab and then pressing the Delete key.

To return to the document after inserting a header or footer, double-click in the document outside the header or footer pane or click the Close Header and Footer button.

Activity 3a Inserting a Predesigned Header   Part 1 of 3

1. Open **WritingProcess** and then save it with the name **4-WritingProcess**.
2. Press Ctrl + End to move the insertion point to the end of the document.
3. Move the insertion point to the beginning of the heading *REFERENCES* and then insert a page break by clicking the Insert tab and then clicking the Page Break button in the Pages group.

4. Press Ctrl + Home to move the insertion point to the beginning of the document and then insert a header by completing the following steps:
   a. If necessary, click the Insert tab.
   b. Click the Header button in the Header & Footer group.
   c. Scroll to the bottom of the drop-down list and then click the *Sideline* option.

   d. Click the *[Document title]* placeholder and then type The Writing Process.

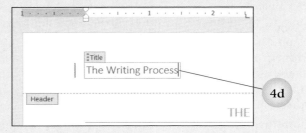

   e. Double-click in the document text. (This makes the document text active and dims the header.)
5. Scroll through the document to see how the header will print.
6. Save and then print **4-WritingProcess**.

Check Your Work

Footer

Insert a predesigned footer in the same manner as a header. Click the Footer button in the Header & Footer group on the Insert tab and a drop-down list displays that is similar to the Header button drop-down list. Click a footer and the predesigned footer is inserted in the document.

Removing a Header or Footer

Remove a header from a document by clicking the Insert tab and then clicking the Header button in the Header & Footer group. At the drop-down list, click the *Remove Header* option. Complete similar steps to remove a footer.

1. With **4-WritingProcess** open, press Ctrl + Home to move the insertion point to the beginning of the document.
2. Remove the header by clicking the Insert tab, clicking the Header button in the Header & Footer group, and then clicking the *Remove Header* option at the drop-down list.
3. Insert a footer in the document by completing the following steps:
   a. Click the Footer button in the Header & Footer group.
   b. Scroll down the drop-down list and then click *Ion (Light)*.

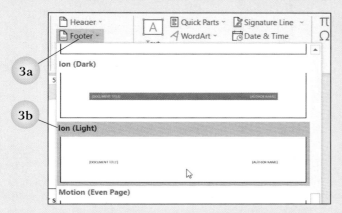

   c. Notice that Word inserted the document title at the left side of the footer. (Word remembered the document title you entered in the header.) Word also inserted your name at the right side of the footer. If the document title does not appear, click the *[DOCUMENT TITLE]* placeholder and then type THE WRITING PROCESS. If your name does not appear, click the *[AUTHOR NAME]* placeholder and then type your first and last names.
   d. Click the Close Header and Footer button to close the Footer pane and return to the document.
4. Scroll through the document to see how the footer will print.
5. Save and then print **4-WritingProcess**.

Check Your Work

Editing a Predesigned Header or Footer

Predesigned headers and footers contain elements such as page numbers, a title, and an author's name. The formatting of an element can be changed by clicking the element and then applying formatting. Delete an element from a header or footer by selecting the element and then pressing the Delete key.

1. With **4-WritingProcess** open, remove the footer by clicking the Insert tab, clicking the Footer button, and then clicking *Remove Footer* at the drop-down list.
2. Insert and then format a header by completing the following steps:
    a. Click the Header button in the Header & Footer group on the Insert tab, scroll down the drop-down list, and then click *Grid*. (This header inserts the document title and a date placeholder.)
    b. Delete the date placeholder by clicking the *[Date]* placeholder, clicking the placeholder tab, and then pressing the Delete key.
    c. Double-click in the document text.

3. Insert and then format a footer by completing the following steps:
    a. Click the Insert tab.
    b. Click the Footer button, scroll down the drop-down list, and then click *Retrospect*.
    c. Select the name in the author placeholder at the left side of the footer and then type your first and last names.
    d. Select your name and the page number, apply bold formatting, and then change the font size to 10 points.
    e. Click the Close Header and Footer button.

4. Scroll through the document to see how the header and footer will print.
5. Save, print, and then close **4-WritingProcess**.

▶ Check Your Work

Activity 4 **Format a Report on Desirable Employee Qualities** **2 Parts**

You will open a document containing information on desirable employee qualities and then insert a watermark, change the page background color, and insert a page border.

Formatting the Page Background

The Page Background group on the Design tab contains three buttons for customizing the page background. Click the Watermark button and choose a predesigned watermark from options at the drop-down list. If a document will be shared electronically or published online, consider adding a page background color with the Page Color button. Use the Page Borders button to apply a border to the background of a page. Customize the style of the page border by using options in the Borders and Shading dialog box.

Tutorial

Inserting and
Removing a
Watermark

 Watermark

Inserting a Watermark

A watermark is a lightened image that displays behind the text in a document. Use a watermark to add visual appeal or to identify a document as a draft, sample, or confidential document. Word provides a number of predesigned watermarks. View watermark designs by clicking the Watermark button in the Page Background group on the Design tab. Scroll through the list and then click an option.

 Tutorial

Applying Page
Background Color

 Page Color

Applying Page Background Color

Use the Page Color button in the Page Background group on the Design tab to apply a background color to a document. This background color is intended for documents that will be viewed on-screen or online, as color is visible on the screen but does not print. Insert a page color by clicking the Page Color button and then clicking a color at the drop-down color palette.

Activity 4a Inserting and Removing a Watermark and Applying a Page Background Color Part 1 of 2

1. Open **EmpQualities** and then save it with the name **4-EmpQualities**.
2. Insert a watermark by completing the following steps:
   a. With the insertion point positioned at the beginning of the document, click the Design tab.
   b. Click the Watermark button in the Page Background group.
   c. At the drop-down list, click the *CONFIDENTIAL 1* option.
3. Scroll through the document and notice how the watermark displays behind the text.
4. Remove the watermark and insert a different one by completing the following steps:
   a. Click the Watermark button and then click *Remove Watermark* at the drop-down list.
   b. Click the Watermark button and then click the *DO NOT COPY 1* option at the drop-down list.
5. Scroll through the document and notice how the watermark displays.
6. Move the insertion point to the beginning of the document.
7. Click the Page Color button in the Page Background group and then click the *Gray, Accent 3, Lighter 80%* option (seventh column, second row in the *Theme Colors* section).
8. Save **4-EmpQualities**.

> **Check Your Work**

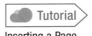

Tutorial

Inserting a Page
Border

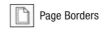

Page Borders

Quick Steps

Insert Page Border
1. Click Design tab.
2. Click Page Borders button.
3. Specify options at dialog box.
4. Click OK.

Inserting a Page Border

To improve the visual interest of a document, consider inserting a page border. When a page border is inserted in a multiple-page document, it prints on each page. To insert a page border, click the Page Borders button in the Page Background group on the Design tab. This displays the Borders and Shading dialog box with the Page Border tab selected, as shown in Figure 4.3. At this dialog box, specify the border style, color, and width.

The dialog box contains an option for inserting a page border containing an art image. To display the images available, click the *Art* option box arrow and then scroll through the drop-down list. Click an image to insert the art image page border in the document.

Changing Page Border Options

By default, a page border appears and prints 24 points from the top, left, right, and bottom edges of the page. Some printers, particularly inkjet printers, have a nonprinting area around the outside edges of the page that can interfere with the printing of a border. Before printing a document with a page border, click the File tab and then click the *Print* option. Look at the preview of the page at the right side of the Print backstage area and determine whether the entire border is visible. If a portion of the border is not visible in the preview page (generally at the bottom and right sides of the page), consider changing measurements at the Border and Shading Options dialog box, shown in Figure 4.4.

Display the Border and Shading Options dialog box by clicking the Design tab and then clicking the Page Borders button. At the Borders and Shading dialog box with the Page Border tab selected, click the Options button in the lower right corner of the dialog box. The options at the Border and Shading Options dialog box change depending on whether the Borders tab or the Page Border tab is selected when the Options button is clicked.

Figure 4.3 Borders and Shading Dialog Box with the Page Border Tab Selected

Figure 4.4 Border and Shading Options Dialog Box

Increase these measurements to move the page border away from the edge of the page or decrease these measurements to move the page border closer to the edge of the page.

Change this option to *Text* to specify the distance from the text to the page border.

If a printer contains a nonprinting area and the entire page border will not print, consider increasing the spacing from the page border to the edge of the page. Do this with the *Top*, *Left*, *Bottom*, and/or *Right* measurement boxes. The *Measure from* option box has a default setting of *Edge of page*. To fit the border more closely around the text of the document, choose the *Text* option in the option box. This option sets the top and bottom margins at *1 pt* and the side margins at *4 pt*. These measurements can be increased or decreased by clicking the arrows in the measurement boxes.

Change the *Measure from* option to *Text* and the *Surround header* and *Surround footer* options become available and the check boxes contain check marks. With check marks in the check boxes, header and footer text is positioned inside the page border. To specify that header and footer text should be positioned outside the page border, remove the check marks from the check boxes.

Activity 4b Inserting a Page Border   Part 2 of 2

1. With **4-EmpQualities** open, remove the page color by clicking the Page Color button in the Page Background group on the Design tab and then clicking the *No Color* option.
2. Insert a page border by completing the following steps:
   a. Click the Page Borders button in the Page Background group on the Design tab.
   b. At the Borders and Shading dialog box with the Page Border tab selected, click the *Box* option in the *Setting* section.
   c. Scroll down the list of line styles in the *Style* list box to the last line style and then click the third line from the end.
   d. Click the *Color* option box arrow and then click the *Orange, Accent 2* option (sixth column, first row in the *Theme Colors* section).
   e. Click OK to close the dialog box.

3. Increase the spacing from the page border to the edges of the page by completing the following steps:

a. Click the Page Borders button.

b. At the Borders and Shading dialog box with the Page Border tab selected, click the Options button in the lower right corner.

c. At the Border and Shading Options dialog box, click the *Top* measurement box up arrow until *31 pt* displays. (This is the maximum measurement allowed.)

d. Increase the measurements in the *Left, Bottom,* and *Right* measurement boxes to *31 pt.*

e. Click OK to close the Border and Shading Options dialog box.

f. Click OK to close the Borders and Shading dialog box.

4. Save **4-EmpQualities** and then print page 1.

5. Insert an art image page border and change the page border spacing options by completing the following steps:

a. Click the Page Borders button.

b. Click the *Art* option box arrow and then click the border image shown at the right (approximately one-third of the way down the drop-down list).

c. Click the Options button in the lower right corner of the Borders and Shading dialog box.

d. At the Border and Shading Options dialog box, click the *Measure from* option box arrow and then click *Text* at the drop-down list.

e. Click the *Top* measurement box up arrow until *10 pt* displays.

f. Increase the measurement in the *Bottom* measurement box to *10 pt* and the measurements in the *Left* and *Right* measurement boxes to *14 pt.*

g. Click the *Surround header* check box to remove the check mark.

h. Click the *Surround footer* check box to remove the check mark.

i. Click OK to close the Border and Shading Options dialog box.

j. Click OK to close the Borders and Shading dialog box.

6. Save, print, and then close **4-EmpQualities**.

Check Your Work

In a document on computer input devices, you will format text into columns, improve the readability by hyphenating long words, and improve the visual interest by inserting a drop cap.

Tutorial

Inserting and Deleting a Section Break

 Breaks

Quick Steps

Insert Section Break
1. Click Layout tab.
2. Click Breaks button.
3. Click section break option.

Hint When you delete a section break, the text that follows takes on the formatting of the text preceding the break.

Inserting a Section Break

Some documents may have several sections of text that need to be formatted in different ways. To help make formatting easier, insert section breaks. Formatting changes that are made to one section—such as narrower margins, a paragraph border, colored text, and so on—will only apply to that section and not to the rest of the document.

Insert a section break in a document by clicking the Breaks button in the Page Setup group on the Layout tab. Choose from four types of section breaks in the drop-down list: Next Page, Continuous, Even Page, and Odd Page. Click *New Page* to insert a section break and start a new section on the next page. Click *Continuous* to insert a section break and start a new section on the same page. Click *Even Page* or *Odd Page* to insert a section break and then start a new section on either the next even or the next odd page.

To see the locations of section breaks in a document, click the Show/Hide ¶ button on the Home tab to turn on the display of nonprinting characters. A section break is shown in the document as a double row of dots with the words *Section Break* in the middle. Word will identify the type of section break. For example, if a continuous section break is inserted, the words *Section Break (Continuous)* display in the middle of the row of dots. To delete a section break, click the Show/Hide ¶ button to turn on the display of nonprinting characters, click on the section break, and then press the Delete key.

Activity 5a **Inserting a Continuous Section Break**   Part 1 of 6

1. Open **InputDevices** and then save it with the name **4-InputDevices**.
2. Insert a continuous section break by completing the following steps:
   a. Move the insertion point to the beginning of the heading *Keyboard*.
   b. Click the Layout tab.
   c. Click the Breaks button in the Page Setup group and then click *Continuous* in the *Section Breaks* section of the drop-down list.
3. Click the Home tab, click the Show/Hide ¶ button in the Paragraph group, and then notice the section break at the end of the first paragraph of text.
4. Click the Show/Hide ¶ button to turn off the display of nonprinting characters.

5. With the insertion point positioned at the beginning of the heading *Keyboard*, change the left and right margins to 1.5 inches. (The margin changes affect only the text after the continuous section break.)
6. Save and then print **4-InputDevices**.

 Check Your Work

 Tutorial

Formatting Text into Columns

Formatting Text into Columns

When preparing a document containing text, an important point to consider is its readability. *Readability* refers to the ease with which a person can read and understand groups of words. The line length of text in a document can enhance or detract from its readability. If the line length is too long, the reader may lose his or her place and have a difficult time moving to the next line below.

To improve the readability of a document, consider formatting the text in columns. One common type is the newspaper column, which is typically used for text in newspapers, newsletters, and magazines.

Format text in one, two, or three columns with the Columns button in the Page Setup group on the Layout tab. To customize the column width and spacing, click the *More Columns* option to open the Columns dialog box. Adjust the measurement to create columns of varying widths. A document can include as many columns as will fit on the page. Word determines how many columns can be included based on the page width, the margin widths, and the size and spacing of the columns. Columns should be at least 0.5 inch in width.

🔲 Columns

Q̌uick Steps

Create Columns
1. Click Layout tab.
2. Click Columns button.
3. Click number of columns.

Activity 5b Formatting Text into Columns

Part 2 of 6

1. With **4-InputDevices** open, make sure the insertion point is positioned below the section break and then change the left and right margins back to 1 inch.
2. Delete the section break by completing the following steps:
   a. Click the Show/Hide ¶ button in the Paragraph group on the Home tab to turn on the display of nonprinting characters.
   b. Click on *Section Break (Continuous)* at the end of the first paragraph below the title in the document. (This moves the insertion point to the beginning of the section break.)

   c. Press the Delete key.
   d. Click the Show/Hide ¶ button to turn off the display of nonprinting characters.

3. Move the insertion point to the beginning of the first paragraph of text below the title and then insert a continuous section break.
4. Format the text into columns by completing the following steps:
   a. Make sure the insertion point is positioned below the section break.
   b. If necessary, click the Layout tab.
   c. Click the Columns button in the Page Setup group.
   d. Click *Two* at the drop-down list.
5. Save **4-InputDevices**.

 Check Your Work

Creating Columns with the Columns Dialog Box

Quick Steps

Create Columns at Columns Dialog Box
1. Click Layout tab.
2. Click Columns button.
3. Click *More Columns*.
4. Specify column options.
5. Click OK.

Use the Columns dialog box to create newspaper columns that are equal or unequal in width. To display the Columns dialog box, shown in Figure 4.5, click the Columns button in the Page Setup group on the Layout tab and then click *More Columns* at the drop-down list.

With options at the Columns dialog box, specify the style and number of columns, enter specific column measurements, create unequal columns, and insert a line between columns. By default, column formatting is applied to the whole document. This can be changed to *This point forward* at the *Apply to* option box at the bottom of the Columns dialog box. With the *This point forward* option, a section break is inserted and the column formatting is applied to text from the location of the insertion point to the end of the document or until another column format is encountered. The *Preview* section of the dialog box shows an example of how the columns will appear in the document.

Figure 4.5 Columns Dialog Box

Choose the number of columns in this section or with this measurement box.

Specify column width and spacing with options in this section.

Use this option box to apply column formatting to the whole document, from the insertion point to the end of the document, or to a specific section.

Click this check box to insert a line between columns.

Preview the effects of column settings in this section.

Removing Column Formatting

To remove column formatting using the Columns button, position the insertion point in the section containing columns, click the Layout tab, click the Columns button, and then click *One* at the drop-down list. Column formatting can also be removed at the Columns dialog box by selecting the *One* option in the *Presets* section.

Inserting a Column Break

Hint You can also insert a column break with the keyboard shortcut Ctrl + Shift + Enter.

When formatting text into columns, Word automatically breaks the columns to fit the page. At times, automatic column breaks may appear in undesirable locations. Insert a manual column break by positioning the insertion point where the column is to end, clicking the Layout tab, clicking the Breaks button in the Page Setup group, and then clicking *Column* at the drop-down list.

Activity 5c **Formatting Text into Columns at the Columns Dialog Box**   Part 3 of 6

1. With **4-InputDevices** open, delete the section break by completing the following steps:
   a. If necessary, click the Home tab.
   b. Click the Show/Hide ¶ button in the Paragraph group to turn on the display of nonprinting characters.
   c. Click on *Section Break (Continuous)* and then press the Delete key.
   d. Click the Show/Hide ¶ button to turn off the display of nonprinting characters.
2. Remove column formatting by clicking the Layout tab, clicking the Columns button, and then clicking *One* at the drop-down list.
3. Format the text into columns by completing the following steps:
   a. If necessary, position the insertion point at the beginning of the first paragraph of text below the title.
   b. Click the Columns button and then click *More Columns* at the drop-down list.
   c. At the Columns dialog box, click *Two* in the *Presets* section.
   d. Click the *Spacing* measurement box down arrow until *0.3"* displays.
   e. Click the *Line between* check box to insert a check mark.
   f. Click the *Apply to* option box arrow and then click *This point forward* at the drop-down list.
   g. Click OK to close the dialog box.

4. Insert a column break by completing the following steps:
   a. Position the insertion point at the beginning of the heading *Mouse*.
   b. Click the Breaks button in the Page Setup group and then click *Column* at the drop-down list.
5. Save and then print **4-InputDevices**.

4b

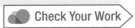
Check Your Work

Balancing Columns on a Page

In a document containing text formatted into columns, Word automatically lines up (balances) the last lines of text at the bottoms of the columns, except on the last page. Text in the last column of the last page may end far short of the bottom of the page, and the page will look unbalanced. Balance columns by inserting a continuous section break at the end of the text.

Activity 5d **Formatting and Balancing Columns of Text**   Part 4 of 6

1. With **4-InputDevices** open, delete the column break by positioning the insertion point at the beginning of the heading *Mouse*, if necessary, and then pressing the Backspace key.
2. Select the entire document and then change the font to 12-point Constantia.
3. Move the insertion point to the end of the document and then balance the columns by clicking the Layout tab, clicking the Breaks button in the Page Setup group, and then clicking *Continuous* at the drop-down list.

> A touchscreen allows the user to choose options by pressing the appropriate part of the screen. Touchscreens are widely used in bank ATMs and in kiosks at retail outlets and in tourist areas.

3

4. Apply the Green, Accent 6, Lighter 60% paragraph shading (last column, third row) to the title *COMPUTER INPUT DEVICES*.
5. Apply the Green, Accent 6, Lighter 80% paragraph shading (last column, second row) to each heading in the document.
6. Insert page numbers that print at the bottom center of each page using the *Plain Number 2* option.
7. Double-click in the document to make it active.
8. Save **4-InputDevices**.

Check Your Work

Hyphenating Words

In some Word documents, especially those with left and right margins wider than 1 inch or those with text set in columns, the right margin may appear quite ragged. To make the margin neater and more uniform, use hyphens to break longer words that fall at the end of the line. Use the hyphenation feature to hyphenate words automatically or manually.

Automatically Hyphenating Words

 Hyphenation

To automatically hyphenate words in a document, click the Layout tab, click the Hyphenation button in the Page Setup group, and then click *Automatic* at the drop-down list. Scroll through the document and check to see whether hyphens were added in appropriate locations within the words. To undo hyphenation, immediately click the Undo button on the Quick Access Toolbar.

Hint Avoid dividing words at the ends of more than two consecutive lines.

Manually Hyphenating Words

To control where hyphens appear in words during hyphenation, choose manual hyphenation. To do this, click the Layout tab, click the Hyphenation button in the Page Setup group, and then click *Manual* at the drop-down list. This displays the Manual Hyphenation dialog box, as shown in Figure 4.6. (The word in the *Hyphenate at* text box will vary.)

At this dialog box, click Yes to hyphenate the word as indicated in the *Hyphenate at* text box, click No if the word should not be hyphenated, or click Cancel to cancel hyphenation. The hyphen can be repositioned in the word in the *Hyphenate at* text box. Word shows the word with syllable breaks indicated by hyphens. Each place the word will be hyphenated displays as a blinking black bar. To hyphenate a word at a different place, click and drag the blinking black bar to the position desired and then click Yes. Continue clicking Yes or No at the Manual Hyphenation dialog box.

Quick Steps

Automatically Hyphenate Document
1. Click Layout tab.
2. Click Hyphenation button.
3. Click *Automatic*.

Manually Hyphenate Document
1. Click Layout tab.
2. Click Hyphenation button.
3. Click *Manual*.
4. Click Yes or No to hyphenate indicated words.
5. When complete, click OK.

Figure 4.6 Manual Hyphenation Dialog Box

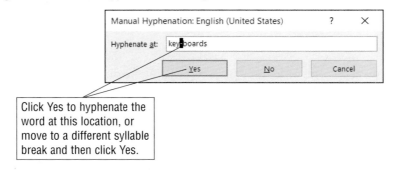

Click Yes to hyphenate the word at this location, or move to a different syllable break and then click Yes.

1. With **4-InputDevices** open, hyphenate words automatically by completing the following steps:
   a. Press Ctrl + Home.
   b. Click the Layout tab.
   c. Click the Hyphenation button in the Page Setup group and then click *Automatic* at the drop-down list.

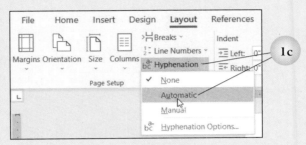

2. Scroll through the document and notice the hyphenation.
3. Click the Undo button to remove the hyphens.
4. Manually hyphenate words by completing the following steps:
   a. Click the Hyphenation button in the Page Setup group and then click *Manual* at the drop-down list.
   b. At the Manual Hyphenation dialog box, make one of the following choices:
      • Click Yes to hyphenate the word as indicated in the *Hyphenate at* text box.
      • Click and drag the hyphen in the word to break the word on a different syllable and then click Yes.
      • Click No if the word should not be hyphenated.
   c. Continue clicking Yes or No at the Manual Hyphenation dialog box.
   d. At the message indicating that hyphenation is complete, click OK.
5. Save **4-InputDevices**.

 Check Your Work

 Tutorial

Creating and Removing a Drop Cap

 Drop Cap

Quick Steps

Create Drop Cap
1. Click Insert tab.
2. Click Drop Cap button.
3. Click drop cap option.

Creating a Drop Cap

Use a drop cap to enhance the appearance of text. A drop cap is the first letter of the first word of a paragraph that is set into the paragraph with formatting that differentiates it from the rest of the paragraph. Drop caps can be used to identify the beginnings of major sections or parts of a document.

Create a drop cap with the Drop Cap button in the Text group on the Insert tab. The drop cap can be set in the paragraph or in the margin. At the Drop Cap dialog box, specify a font, the number of lines the letter should drop, and the distance the letter should be positioned from the text of the paragraph. Add a drop cap to the entire first word of a paragraph by selecting the word and then clicking the Drop Cap button.

1. With **4-InputDevices** open, create a drop cap by completing the following steps:
   a. Position the insertion point in the first word of the first paragraph below the title (the word *Engineers*).
   b. Click the Insert tab.
   c. Click the Drop Cap button in the Text group.
   d. Click *In margin* at the drop-down gallery.

2. Looking at the drop cap, you decide that you do not like it positioned in the margin and want it to be a little smaller. To change the drop cap, complete the following steps:
   a. With the *E* in the word *Engineers* selected, click the Drop Cap button and then click *None* at the drop-down gallery.
   b. Click the Drop Cap button and then click *Drop Cap Options* at the drop-down gallery.
   c. At the Drop Cap dialog box, click *Dropped* in the *Position* section.
   d. Click the *Font* option box arrow, scroll up the drop-down list, and then click *Cambria*.
   e. Click the *Lines to drop* measurement box down arrow to change the number to *2*.
   f. Click OK to close the dialog box.
   g. Click outside the drop cap to deselect it.
3. Save, print, and then close **4-InputDevices**.

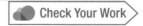

Check Your Work

Activity 6 **Create an Announcement about Supervisory Training**   **2 Parts**

You will create an announcement about upcoming supervisor training and use the Click and Type feature to center and right-align text. You also will vertically center the text on the page.

Tutorial

Using Click and Type

Using the Click and Type Feature

Word contains a Click and Type feature that allows text to be aligned left, right, or center beginning at a specific point in the document. This feature can be used to position text as it is being typed rather than typing the text and then selecting and formatting the text, which requires multiple steps.

To use the Click and Type feature, open a new blank document and move the mouse pointer slowly over the page, going from left to right. The pointer will appear as an I-beam with horizontal lines representing the text alignment. Near the left margin, the horizontal lines are left-aligned. In the center of the page, the lines are centered. At the right margin, the horizontal lines are right-aligned. Double-click in the document and begin typing. Text should automatically align to match the horizontal lines indicated on the I-beam pointer. (Note: Make sure the horizontal lines display near the mouse pointer before double-clicking the mouse button. Double-clicking when the alignment lines are not shown will insert a tab instead of changing the text alignment.)

Activity 6a Using Click and Type   Part 1 of 2

1. At a blank document, create the centered text shown in Figure 4.7 by completing the following steps:
   a. Position the I-beam pointer between the left and right margins at about the 3.25-inch mark on the horizontal ruler and at the top of the vertical ruler.
   b. When the center-alignment lines display below the I-beam pointer, double-click the left mouse button.

   c. Type the centered text shown in Figure 4.7. Press Shift + Enter to end each line except the last line.
2. Change to right alignment by completing the following steps:
   a. Position the I-beam pointer near the right margin at approximately the 1-inch mark on the vertical ruler until the right-alignment lines display at the left of the I-beam pointer.

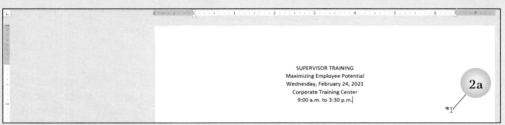

   b. Double-click the left mouse button.
   c. Type the right-aligned text shown in Figure 4.7. Press Shift + Enter to end the first line.
3. Select the centered text and then change the font to 14-point Candara bold and the line spacing to double spacing.
4. Select the right-aligned text, change the font to 10-point Candara bold, and then deselect the text.
5. Save the document and name it **4-Training**.

Check Your Work

Figure 4.7 Activity 6a

SUPERVISOR TRAINING
Maximizing Employee Potential
Wednesday, February 24, 2021
Corporate Training Center
9:00 a.m. to 3:30 p.m.

Sponsored by
Cell Systems

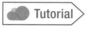

Tutorial

Changing Vertical
Alignment

Changing Vertical Alignment

Text or items in a Word document are aligned at the top of the page by default. Change this alignment with the *Vertical alignment* option box at the Page Setup dialog box with the Layout tab selected, as shown in Figure 4.8. Display this dialog box by clicking the Layout tab, clicking the Page Setup group dialog box launcher, and then clicking the Layout tab at the Page Setup dialog box.

The *Vertical alignment* option box in the *Page* section of the Page Setup dialog box contains four choices: *Top*, *Center*, *Justified*, and *Bottom*. The default setting is *Top*, which aligns text and items such as images at the top of the page. Choose *Center* to position the text in the middle of the page vertically. The *Justified* option aligns text between the top and bottom margins. The *Center* option positions text in the middle of the page vertically, while the *Justified* option adds space between paragraphs of text (not within) to fill the page from the top to the bottom margins. Choose the *Bottom* option to align text at the bottom of the page.

Quick Steps

Vertically Align Text
1. Click Layout tab.
2. Click Page Setup group dialog box launcher.
3. Click Layout tab.
4. Click *Vertical alignment* option box.
5. Click alignment.
6. Click OK.

Figure 4.8 Page Setup Dialog Box with the Layout Tab Selected

1. With **4-Training** open, click the Layout tab and then click the Page Setup group dialog box launcher.
2. At the Page Setup dialog box, click the Layout tab.
3. Click the *Vertical alignment* option box arrow in the *Page* section and then click *Center* at the drop-down list.

4. Click OK to close the dialog box.
5. Save, print, and then close **4-Training**.

Check Your Work

Activity 7 Format a Lease Agreement   3 Parts

You will open a lease agreement, search for specific text, and then search for specific text and replace it with other text.

 Find

 Replace

 Tutorial
Finding Text

Quick Steps
Find Text
1. Click Find button.
2. Type search text.
3. Click Next button.

Editing Text with Find and Replace

The Editing group on the Home tab contains the Find button and the Replace button. Use the Find button to search for specific text in a document and use the Replace button to search for and then replace specific text.

Finding Text

Click the Find button in the Editing group on the Home tab (or press the keyboard shortcut Ctrl + F) and the Navigation pane displays at the left side of the screen with the Results tab selected. With this tab selected, type search text in the search text box and any occurrence of the text in the document is highlighted. A fragment of the text surrounding the search text is shown in a thumbnail in the Navigation pane. For example, when searching for *Lessee* in **4-LeaseAgrmnt** in Activity 7a (on page 115), the screen displays as shown in Figure 4.9. Any occurrence of *Lessee* displays highlighted in yellow in the document and the Navigation pane shows thumbnails of the text surrounding the occurrences of *Lessee*.

Click a text thumbnail in the Navigation pane and the occurrence of the search text is selected in the document. Hover the mouse pointer over a text thumbnail in the Navigation pane and the page number location displays in a small box near the mouse pointer. Move to the next occurrence of the search text by clicking the Next button (contains a down arrow) below and to the right of the search text box. Click the Previous button (contains an up arrow) to move to the previous occurrence of the search text.

Click the down arrow at the right side of the search text box and a drop-down list displays. It shows options for displaying dialog boxes, such as the Find Options dialog box and the Find and Replace dialog box. It also shows options for specifying what should be found in the document, such as figures, tables, and equations.

The search text in a document can be highlighted with options at the Find and Replace dialog box with the Find tab selected. Display this dialog box by clicking the Find button arrow in the Editing group on the Home tab and then clicking *Advanced Find* at the drop-down list. Another method for displaying the Find and Replace dialog box is to click the down arrow at the right side of the search text box in the Navigation pane and then click the *Advanced Find* option at the drop-down list. To highlight found text, type the search text in the *Find what* text box, click the Reading Highlight button, and then click *Highlight All* at the drop-down list. All occurrences of the text in the document are highlighted. To remove highlighting, click the Reading Highlight button and then click *Clear Highlighting* at the drop-down list.

Figure 4.9 Navigation Pane Showing Search Results

Type the search text in this text box.

Click this option box arrow to display options for finding and replacing text.

Click this button to move to the next occurrence of the search text.

Click this button to move to the previous occurrence of the search text.

Occurrences of the search text are highlighted in the document.

Text thumbnails show instances of the search text along with the sentence or phrase it is found in.

1. Open **LeaseAgrmnt** and then save it with the name **4-LeaseAgrmnt**.
2. Find all occurrences of *lessee* by completing the following steps:
   a. Click the Find button in the Editing group on the Home tab.
   b. If necessary, click the Results tab in the Navigation pane.
   c. Type lessee in the search text box in the Navigation pane.
   d. After a moment, all occurrences of *lessee* in the document are highlighted and text thumbnails display in the Navigation pane. Click a couple of the text thumbnails in the Navigation pane to select the text in the document.
   e. Click the Previous button (contains an up arrow) to select the previous occurrence of *lessee* in the document.

3. Use the Find and Replace dialog box with the Find tab selected to highlight all occurrences of *Premises* in the document by completing the following steps:
   a. Click in the document and press Ctrl + Home to move the insertion point to the beginning of the document.
   b. Click the search option box arrow in the Navigation pane and then click *Advanced Find* at the drop-down list.
   c. At the Find and Replace dialog box with the Find tab selected (and *lessee* selected in the *Find what* text box), type Premises.
   d. Click the Reading Highlight button and then click *Highlight All* at the drop-down list.
   e. Click in the document to make it active and then scroll through the document and notice the occurrences of highlighted text.
   f. Click in the dialog box to make it active.
   g. Click the Reading Highlight button and then click *Clear Highlighting* at the drop-down list.
   h. Click the Close button to close the Find and Replace dialog box.

4. Close the Navigation pane by clicking the Close button in the upper right corner of the pane.

Finding and Replacing Text

Finding and Replacing Text

Ǫuick Steps

Find and Replace Text
1. Click Replace button.
2. Type search text.
3. Press Tab key.
4. Type replacement text.
5. Click Replace or Replace All button.

To find and replace text, click the Replace button in the Editing group on the Home tab or use the keyboard shortcut Ctrl + H. This displays the Find and Replace dialog box with the Replace tab selected, as shown in Figure 4.10. Type the search text in the *Find what* text box, press the Tab key, and then type the replacement text in the *Replace with* text box.

The Find and Replace dialog box contains several command buttons. Click the Find Next button to tell Word to find the next occurrence of the text. Click the Replace button to replace the text and find the next occurrence. If all occurrences of the text in the *Find what* text box are to be replaced with the text in the *Replace with* text box, click the Replace All button.

Figure 4.10 Find and Replace Dialog Box with the Replace Tab Selected

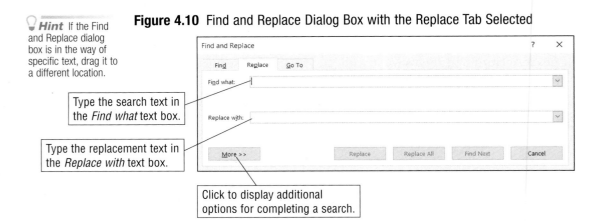

Type the search text in the *Find what* text box.

Type the replacement text in the *Replace with* text box.

Click to display additional options for completing a search.

Activity 7b Finding and Replacing Text

1. With **4-LeaseAgrmnt** open, make sure the insertion point is positioned at the beginning of the document.
2. Find all occurrences of *Lessor* and replace them with *Tracy Hartford* by completing the following steps:
   a. Click the Replace button in the Editing group on the Home tab.
   b. At the Find and Replace dialog box with the Replace tab selected and *Premises* selected in the *Find what* text box, type Lessor.
   c. Press the Tab key to move the insertion point to the *Replace with* text box.
   d. Type Tracy Hartford.
   e. Click the Replace All button.
   f. At the message stating that 11 replacements were made, click OK. (Do not close the Find and Replace dialog box.)
3. With the Find and Replace dialog box still open, complete steps similar to those in Step 2 to find all occurrences of *Lessee* and replace them with *Michael Iwami*.
4. Click the Close button to close the Find and Replace dialog box.
5. Save **4-LeaseAgrmnt**.

 Check Your Work

Specifying Search Options

The Find and Replace dialog box provides more options for completing a search. To display these options, click the More button in the lower left corner of the dialog box. This causes the Find and Replace dialog box to expand, as shown in Figure 4.11. Search Options in the dialog box are described in Table 4.1. Click check boxes to select options for customizing the search, and then click the Less button (previously the More button) to hide the options and shrink the dialog box again. If a mistake was made when replacing text, close the Find and Replace dialog box and then click the Undo button on the Quick Access Toolbar.

Figure 4.11 Expanded Find and Replace Dialog Box

Click this button to remove the display of search options.

Specify search options using the check boxes in this section.

Table 4.1 Options at the Expanded Find and Replace Dialog Box

Choose this option	To
Match case	Exactly match the case of the search text. For example, search for *Book* and select the *Match case* option and Word will stop at *Book* but not *book* or *BOOK*.
Find whole words only	Find a whole word, not a part of a word. For example, search for *her* without selecting *Find whole words only* and Word will stop at *there*, *here*, *hers*, and so on.
Use wildcards	Use special characters as wildcards to search for specific text.
Sounds like (English)	Match words that sound alike but are spelled differently, such as *know* and *no*.
Find all word forms (English)	Find all forms of the word entered in the *Find what* text box. For example, enter *hold* and Word will stop at *held* and *holding*.
Match prefix	Find only those words that begin with the letters in the *Find what* text box. For example, enter *per* and Word will stop at words such as *perform* and *perfect* but skip words such as *super* and *hyperlink*.
Match suffix	Find only those words that end with the letters in the *Find what* text box. For example, enter *ly* and Word will stop at words such as *accurately* and *quietly* but skip words such as *catalyst* and *lyre*.
Ignore punctuation characters	Ignore punctuation within characters. For example, enter *US* in the *Find what* text box and Word will stop at *U.S.*
Ignore white-space characters	Ignore spaces between letters. For example, enter *F B I* in the *Find what* text box and Word will stop at *FBI*.

1. With **4-LeaseAgrmnt** open, make sure the insertion point is positioned at the beginning of the document.
2. Find all word forms of the word *lease* and replace them with *rent* by completing the following steps:
   a. Click the Replace button in the Editing group on the Home tab.
   b. At the Find and Replace dialog box with the Replace tab selected, type lease in the *Find what* text box.
   c. Press the Tab key and then type rent in the *Replace with* text box.
   d. Click the More button.
   e. Click the *Find all word forms (English)* check box. (This inserts a check mark in the check box.)
   f. Click the Replace All button.
   g. At the message stating that Replace All is not recommended with Find All Word Forms, click OK.
   h. At the message stating that six replacements were made, click OK.
   i. Click the *Find all word forms* check box to remove the check mark.

3. Find the word *less* and replace it with the word *minus* and specify that you want Word to find only those words that end in *less* by completing the following steps:
   a. At the expanded Find and Replace dialog box, select the text in the *Find what* text box and then type less.
   b. Select the text in the *Replace with* text box and then type minus.
   c. Click the *Match suffix* check box to insert a check mark (telling Word to find only words that end in *less*).
   d. Click the Replace All button.
   e. Click OK at the message stating that two replacements were made.
   f. Click the *Match suffix* check box to remove the check mark.
   g. Click the Less button.
   h. Close the Find and Replace dialog box.

4. Save, print, and then close **4-LeaseAgrmnt**.

Check Your Work

Chapter Summary

- By default, a Word document contains 1-inch top, bottom, left, and right margins. Change margins with preset margin settings at the Margins button drop-down list or with options at the Page Setup dialog box with the Margins tab selected.

- The default page layout is portrait orientation. It can be changed to landscape orientation with the Orientation button in the Page Setup group on the Layout tab.

- The default paper size is 8.5 inches wide by 11 inches tall. It can be changed with options at the Size button drop-down list or options at the Page Setup dialog box with the Paper tab selected.

- A page break that Word inserts automatically is a *soft page break*. A page break inserted manually is a *hard page break*. Insert a hard page break using the Page Break button in the Pages group on the Insert tab or by pressing Ctrl + Enter.

- Insert a predesigned and formatted cover page by clicking the Cover Page button in the Pages group on the Insert tab and then clicking an option at the drop-down list.

- Insert predesigned and formatted page numbers by clicking the Page Number button in the Header & Footer group on the Insert tab, specifying the location of the page number, and then clicking a page numbering option.

- Insert predesigned headers and footers in a document with the Header button and the Footer button in the Header & Footer group on the Insert tab.

- A watermark is a lightened image that displays behind the text in a document. Use the Watermark button in the Page Background group on the Design tab to insert a watermark.

- Insert a page background color in a document with the Page Color button in the Page Background group on the Design tab. The page background color is designed for viewing a document on-screen and does not print.

- Click the Page Borders button in the Page Background group on the Design tab and the Borders and Shading dialog box with the Page Border tab selected displays. Use options at this dialog box to insert a page border or an art image page border in a document.

- Apply formatting to a portion of a document by inserting a continuous section break or a section break that begins a new page. Turn on the display of nonprinting characters to display section breaks.

- Set text in columns to improve the readability of documents such as newsletters and reports. Format text in columns using the Columns button in the Page Setup group on the Layout tab or with options at the Columns dialog box.

- Remove column formatting with the Columns button in the Page Setup group on the Layout tab or at the Columns dialog box. Balance column text on the last page of a document by inserting a continuous section break at the end of the text.

- Improve the appearance of text by hyphenating long words that fall at the ends of lines. Use the hyphenation feature to hyphenate words automatically or manually.

- To enhance the appearance of text, use drop caps to identify the beginnings of major sections or paragraphs. Create drop caps with the Drop Cap button in the Text group on the Insert tab.

- Use the Click and Type feature to center, right-align, and left-align text.

- Vertically align text in a document with the *Vertical alignment* option box at the Page Setup dialog box with the Layout tab selected.
- Use the Find button in the Editing group on the Home tab to search for specific text. Use the Replace button to search for specific text and replace it with other text.
- At the Find and Replace dialog box, click the Find Next button to find the next occurrence of the text. Click the Replace button to replace the text and find the next occurrence or click the Replace All button to replace all occurrences of the text.
- Click the More button at the Find and Replace dialog box to display additional search options.

Commands Review

FEATURE	RIBBON TAB, GROUP	BUTTON, OPTION	KEYBOARD SHORTCUT
blank page	Insert, Pages		
Border and Shading Options dialog box	Design, Page Background	, Options	
Borders and Shading dialog box with Page Border tab selected	Design, Page Background		
column break	Layout, Page Setup	, *Column*	Ctrl + Shift + Enter
columns	Layout, Page Setup		
Columns dialog box	Layout, Page Setup	, *More Column*	
continuous section break	Layout, Page Setup	, *Continuous*	
cover page	Insert, Pages		
drop cap	Insert, Text		
Find and Replace dialog box with Find tab selected	Home, Editing	, *Advanced Find*	
Find and Replace dialog box with Replace tab selected	Home, Editing		Ctrl + H
footer	Insert, Header & Footer		
header	Insert, Header & Footer		
hyphenate words automatically	Layout, Page Setup	, *Automatic*	
Manual Hyphenation dialog box	Layout, Page Setup	, *Manual*	
margins	Layout, Page Setup		
Navigation pane	Home, Editing		Ctrl + F

FEATURE	RIBBON TAB, GROUP	BUTTON, OPTION	KEYBOARD SHORTCUT
orientation	Layout, Page Setup		
page background color	Design, Page Background		
page break	Insert, Pages		Ctrl + Enter
page numbers	Insert, Header & Footer		
Page Setup dialog box with Margins tab selected	Layout, Page Setup	, *Custom Margins* OR	
Page Setup dialog box with Paper tab selected	Layout, Page Setup	, *More Paper Sizes*	
paper size	Layout, Page Setup		
watermark	Design, Page Background		

Microsoft®

Word Level 1

Unit 2

Enhancing and Customizing Documents

Microsoft®

Word

Inserting and Formatting Objects

Performance Objectives

Upon successful completion of Chapter 5, you will be able to:

1   Insert symbols, special characters, and the date and time

2   Insert, format, and customize images, text boxes, shapes, and WordArt

3   Insert and customize a screenshot

4   Insert, format, and modify a SmartArt graphic

Documents in Word may include special characters and symbols as well as the current date and time. The visual interest of a document can be enhanced by graphics such as images, text boxes, shapes, WordArt, and screenshots. Word's SmartArt feature can be used to insert a graphic such as a diagram or organizational chart. This chapter covers how to insert and customize these elements using buttons in the Illustrations group, the Text group, and the Symbols group on the Insert tab.

 Data Files

Before beginning chapter work, copy the WL1C5 folder to your storage medium and then make WL1C5 the active folder.

The online course includes additional training and assessment resources.

Activity 1 **Format a Document on Computer Input Devices**   **2 Parts**

In a document on computer input devices, you will insert a special character, symbols, and the date and time.

Inserting Symbols and Special Characters

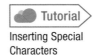

Tutorial

Inserting Symbols

Tutorial

Inserting Special Characters

 Symbol

Quick Steps

Insert Symbol
1. Click Insert tab.
2. Click Symbol button.
3. Click symbol.
OR
1. Click Insert tab.
2. Click Symbol button.
3. Click *More Symbols.*
4. Double-click symbol.
5. Click Close.

Quick Steps

Insert Special Character
1. Click Insert tab.
2. Click Symbol button.
3. Click *More Symbols.*
4. Click Special Characters tab.
5. Double-click special character.
6. Click Close.

Use the Symbol button on the Insert tab to insert special symbols in a document. Click the button and a drop-down list displays the most recently inserted symbols. Click one of the symbols in the list to insert it in the document or click the *More Symbols* option to display the Symbol dialog box, as shown in Figure 5.1. Double-click a symbol to insert it, or click it once and then click the Insert button. Click Close to exit the dialog box. Another method for selecting a symbol at the Symbol dialog box is to type the symbol code in the *Character code* text box. Click a symbol in the dialog box and the character code displays in the *Character code* text box. If a symbol is used on a regular basis, remembering the character code can be useful for inserting the symbol in a document.

At the Symbol dialog box with the Symbols tab selected, the font can be changed with the *Font* option box. When the font is changed, different symbols display in the dialog box. Click the Special Characters tab at the Symbol dialog box and a list of special characters displays along with keyboard shortcuts for creating them.

Figure 5.1 Symbol Dialog Box with the Symbols Tab Selected

Use the *Font* option box to display a specific set of characters.

Click the Special Characters tab to display a list of special characters along with keyboard shortcuts.

Click a symbol and the character code displays in this text box. If you know the symbol character code, type it in the text box.

1. Open **InputDevices** and then save it with the name **5-InputDevices**.
2. Press Ctrl + End to move the insertion point to the end of the document.
3. Type Prepared by: and then press the spacebar.
4. Type the first name Matthew and then press the spacebar.
5. Insert the last name *Viña* by completing the following steps:
   a. Type Vi.
   b. Click the Insert tab.
   c. Click the Symbol button in the Symbols group.
   d. Click *More Symbols* at the drop-down list.
   e. At the Symbol dialog box, make sure *(normal text)* appears in the *Font* option box and then double-click the *ñ* symbol (located in approximately the twelfth row).
   f. Click the Close button.
   g. Type a.
6. Press Shift + Enter.
7. Insert the keyboard symbol (⌨) by completing the following steps:
   a. Click the Symbol button and then click *More Symbols*.
   b. At the Symbol dialog box, click the *Font* option box arrow and then click *Wingdings* at the drop-down list. (You will need to scroll down the list to see this option.)
   c. Select the current number in the *Character code* text box and then type 55.
   d. Click the Insert button and then click the Close button.
8. Type SoftCell Technologies.
9. Insert the registered trademark symbol (®) by completing the following steps:
   a. Click the Symbol button and then click *More Symbols*.
   b. At the Symbol dialog box, click the Special Characters tab.
   c. Double-click the ® symbol (tenth option from the top).
   d. Click the Close button.
   e. Press Shift + Enter.
10. Select the keyboard symbol (⌨) and then change the font size to 18 points.
11. Save **5-InputDevices**.

Check Your Work

Tutorial

Inserting the Date
and Time

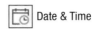 Date & Time

Quick Steps

Insert Date and Time
1. Click Insert tab.
2. Click Date & Time button.
3. Click option in list box.
4. Click OK.

Inserting the Date and Time

Use the Date & Time button in the Text group on the Insert tab to insert the current date and time in a document. Click this button and the Date and Time dialog box displays, as shown in Figure 5.2. (Your date will vary from what you see in the figure.) At the Date and Time dialog box, click the desired date and/or time format in the *Available formats* list box.

If the *Update automatically* check box does not contain a check mark, the date and/or time are inserted in the document as text that can be edited in the normal manner. The date and/or time can also be inserted as a field. The advantage to using a field is that the date and time are updated when a document is reopened. Insert a check mark in the *Update automatically* check box to insert the date and/or time as a field. The date can also be inserted as a field using the keyboard shortcut Alt + Shift + D, and the time can be inserted as a field with the keyboard shortcut Alt + Shift + T.

A date or time field will automatically update when a document is reopened. The date and time can also be updated in the document by clicking the date or time field and then clicking the Update tab that appears above the field, by right-clicking the date or time field and then clicking *Update Field* at the shortcut menu, or by pressing the F9 function key.

Figure 5.2 Date and Time Dialog Box

Click the desired option in this list box.

Insert a check mark in this check box if you want the date and/or time inserted as a field and updated each time you reopen the document.

Activity 1b Inserting the Date and Time | Part 2 of 2

1. With **5-InputDevices** open, press Ctrl + End and make sure the insertion point is positioned below the company name.
2. Insert the current date by completing the following steps:
   a. Click the Insert tab.
   b. Click the Date & Time button in the Text group.
   c. At the Date and Time dialog box, click the third option from the top in the *Available formats* list box. (Your date and time will vary from what you see in the image at the right.)
   d. Click in the *Update automatically* check box to insert a check mark.
   e. Click OK to close the dialog box.

3. Press Shift + Enter.
4. Insert the current time by pressing Alt + Shift + T.
5. Save **5-InputDevices**.
6. Update the time by clicking the time and then pressing the F9 function key.
7. Save, print, and then close **5-InputDevices**.

 Check Your Work

Activity 2 **Insert Images in a Travel Document**   **2 Parts**

You will open a document with information on an Australian tour and add visual interest to the document by inserting and formatting images.

 Tutorial

Inserting, Sizing, and Positioning an Image

 Pictures

 Online Pictures

Inserting and Formatting Images

Insert an image, such as a photo or clip art, in a Word document with buttons in the Illustrations group on the Insert tab. Use the Pictures button in the Illustrations group to insert an image from a folder on the computer's hard drive or removable drive or use the Online Pictures button to locate an online image.

Inserting an Image

Click the Pictures button in the Illustrations group on the Insert tab to display the Insert Pictures dialog box. At this dialog box, navigate to the drive and folder where images are saved, and then double-click an image to insert it in the document.

Click the Online Pictures button and the Online Pictures window displays. At this window, type the search term or topic in the search text box and then press the Enter key. Images that match the search term or topic are shown in the window. Click an image and then click the Insert button and the image is inserted in the document. Be aware that many of the images available online are copyrighted. Before using an image in a document that will be shared publicly, make sure the image is either in the public domain (and thus not copyrighted) or determine how to get permission to use the image.

Sizing and Cropping an Image

When an image is inserted in a document, the Picture Tools Format tab is active. The Size group on the Picture Tools Format tab contains buttons for changing the size of an image and cropping an image. Change the size of an image by typing a measurement in the *Shape Height* and/or *Shape Width* measurement boxes or by clicking the up or down arrows in the measurement box.

Images in Word can also be sized using the mouse. Click an image to select it and circular sizing handles display around the image. Position the mouse pointer on a sizing handle until the pointer turns into a double-headed arrow and then click and hold down the left mouse button. Drag the sizing handle in or out to decrease or increase the size of the image and then release the mouse button. Use the middle sizing handles at the left and right sides of the image to make the image wider or thinner. Use the middle sizing handles at the top and bottom of the image to make the image taller or shorter. Use the sizing handles at the corners of the image to change both the width and height at the same time.

Crop

Use the Crop button in the Size group to remove any unnecessary parts of an image. Click the Crop button and crop handles display around the image. Position the mouse pointer on a crop handle and the mouse pointer displays as a crop tool. Drag a crop handle to remove parts of the image.

Arranging an Image

The Arrange group on the Picture Tools Format tab contains buttons for positioning, aligning, and rotating images. The group also contains buttons for wrapping text around an image and specifying if an image should appear in front of or behind text or other items.

 Wrap Text

Use the Wrap Text button in the Arrange group to specify how text or other objects in the document should wrap around a selected image. The Wrap Text button drop-down list contains options for specifying square or tight wrapping, wrapping text above or below the image, and positioning the image behind or in front of text. The Layout Options button can also be used to specify text wrapping. When an image is selected, the Layout Options button displays outside the upper right corner of the image. Click the Layout Options button and then click a wrapping option at the drop-down list. Another method for specifying text wrapping is to right-click an image, point to *Wrap Text* at the shortcut menu, and click a text wrapping option at the side menu.

 Layout Options

Move an image to a specific location on the page with options at the Position button drop-down gallery in the Arrange group. Choose an option from this gallery and the image is moved to the specified location and square text wrapping is applied to it.

 Position

Rotate an image by positioning the mouse pointer on the rotation handle, a circular arrow that appears above a selected image. The pointer will display with a black circular arrow attached. Click and hold down the left mouse button, drag in the desired direction, and then release the mouse button. An image can also be rotated or flipped with options at the Rotate button drop-down gallery in the Arrange group. For example, the image can be rotated left or right or flipped horizontally or vertically.

 Rotate

Moving an Image

In addition to the Position button in the Arrange group on the Picture Tools Format tab, an image can be moved using the mouse. Before moving an image with the mouse, specify how text should wrap around the image. After specifying text wrapping, position the mouse pointer on the image until the mouse pointer displays with a four-headed arrow attached. Click and hold down the left mouse button, drag the image to the new location, and then release the mouse button.

As an image is moved to the top, left, right, or bottom margin or to the center of the document, green alignment guides display. Use these guides to help position the image on the page. If alignment guides do not display, turn them on by clicking the Align button in the Arrange group and then clicking *Use Alignment Guides* at the drop-down list. In addition to alignment guides, gridlines can be turned on to help position an image precisely. Turn on the display of gridlines by clicking the Align button and then clicking *View Gridlines*.

 Align

1. Open **Tour** and then save it with the name **5-Tour**.
2. Insert an image by completing the following steps:
   a. Click the Insert tab and then click the Pictures button in the Illustrations group.
   b. At the Insert Picture dialog box, navigate to your WL1C5 folder.
   c. Double-click the *Uluru* image file in the Content pane.

3. Crop the image by completing the following steps:
   a. Click the Crop button in the Size group on the Picture Tools Format tab.
   b. Position the mouse pointer on the bottom middle crop handle (which appears as a short black line) until the pointer turns into the crop tool (which appears as a small black T).
   c. Click and hold down the left mouse button, drag up to just below the rock (as shown at the right), and then release the mouse button.
   d. Click the Crop button in the Size group to turn the feature off.

TRAVEL ADVANTAGE

4. Change the size of the image by clicking in the *Shape Height* measurement box in the Size group, typing 3, and then pressing the Enter key.
5. Specify text wrapping by clicking the Wrap Text button in the Arrange group and then clicking *Tight* at the drop-down list.

6. Change to a different text wrapping by completing the following steps:
   a. Click the Layout Options button outside the upper right corner of the image.
   b. Click the *Behind Text* option at the side menu (second column, second row in the *With Text Wrapping* section).
   c. Close the side menu by clicking the Close button in the upper right corner of the side menu.

7. Rotate the image by clicking the Rotate button in the Arrange group and then clicking *Flip Horizontal* at the drop-down gallery.

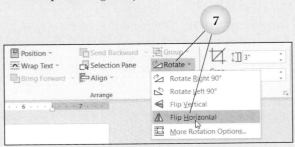

8. Position the mouse pointer on the border of the selected image until the pointer displays with a four-headed arrow attached. Click and hold down the left mouse button, drag the image up and slightly to the left until you see green alignment guides at the top margin and the center of the page, and then release the mouse button. (If the green alignment guides do not display, turn on the guides by clicking the Align button in the Arrange group on the Picture Tools Format tab and then clicking the *Use Alignment Guides* option.)

9. Save **5-Tour**.

TRAVEL ADVANTAGE
Australia Adventures Tour
Northern Territory

Check Your Work

Tutorial

Formatting an Image

 Remove Background

 Corrections

 Color

 Artistic Effects

 Transparency

 Compress Pictures

 Change Picture

 Reset Picture

Adjusting an Image

The Adjust group on the Picture Tools Format tab contains buttons for adjusting the background, color, brightness, and contrast of an image. Click the Remove Background button to display the Background Removal tab with buttons for removing unwanted portions of an image. Change the brightness and/or contrast of an image with options at the Corrections button drop-down gallery. This gallery also includes options for sharpening or softening an image. Use options at the Color button drop-down gallery to change the image color as well as the color saturation and color tone. The Color button drop-down gallery also includes the *Set Transparent Color* option. Click this option and the mouse pointer displays as a dropper tool. Click a color in the image and that color becomes transparent.

The Artistic Effects button drop-down gallery offers a variety of effects that can be applied to an image. Lighten an image with options at the Transparency button drop-down gallery. For example, make an image more transparent to display any text or other objects behind the image. Use the Compress Pictures button to compress the size of images in a document. Remove or replace an image with the Change Picture button and discard all formatting changes and reset an image with the Reset Picture button.

Applying a Picture Style

Word provides a number of predesigned picture styles that can be applied to an image. Click a picture style in the Picture Styles group or click the More Picture Styles button to display a drop-down gallery of picture styles.

Creating Alternative Text for an Image

When an image is inserted in a document, consider adding *alternative text*. Alternative text, also known as alt text, is a brief description of an image or object that can be read by a screen reader and helps a person with a visual impairment understand what the image or object represents. Create alternative text at the Alt Text task pane. Display this task pane by clicking the Alt Text button in the Accessibility group on the Picture Tools Format tab or by right-clicking the image and then clicking *Edit Alt Text* at the shortcut menu. At the Alt Text task pane, type a description of the image. If the image is only decorative and not important for understanding the content of the document, insert a check mark in the *Mark as decorative* check box. An image marked as decorative will not include any description for screen readers.

Alt Text

1. With **5-Tour** open and the image selected, apply an artistic effect by clicking the Artistic Effects button in the Adjust group and then clicking the *Watercolor Sponge* option (second column, third row).

2. Lighten the image by clicking the Transparency button in the Adjust group and then clicking the *Transparency: 30%* option (third option in the drop-down gallery).

3. After looking at the new color, artistic effect, and transparency, return to the original color and remove the artistic effect and transparency by clicking the Reset Picture button in the Adjust group.

4. Sharpen the image by clicking the Corrections button in the Adjust group and then clicking the *Sharpen: 25%* option (fourth option in the *Sharpen/Soften* section).

5. Change the contrast of the image by clicking the Corrections button in the Adjust group and then clicking the *Brightness: 0% (Normal) Contrast: +40%* option (third column, bottom row in the *Brightness/Contrast* section).

6. Compress the image by completing the following steps:
   a. Click the Compress Pictures button in the Adjust group.

   b. At the Compress Pictures dialog box, make sure check marks appear in the check boxes for both options in the *Compression options* section and then click OK.

7. Apply a picture style by clicking the More Pictures Styles button in the Picture Styles group and then clicking the *Simple Frame, Black* option (second column, second row at the drop-down gallery).

8. Add alternative text to the image by completing the following steps:
   a. Click the Alt Text button in the Accessibility group.
   b. Click in the text box in the Alt Text task pane and then type the description Uluru (also known as Ayers Rock).
   c. Click the Close button to close the task pane.

9. Click outside the image to deselect it.

10. Insert an image of Australia (with the Northern Territory highlighted) by completing the following steps:
    a. Click the Insert tab.
    b. Click the Pictures button in the Illustrations group.
    c. At the Insert Picture dialog box, with your WL1C5 folder active, double-click the *NT-Australia* image file in the Content pane.

11. Position and size the image by completing the following steps:
    a. Click the Position button in the Arrange group.
    b. Click the *Position in Top Right with Square Text Wrapping* option (third column, first row in the *With Text Wrapping* section).
    c. Click the Wrap Text button.
    d. Click the *Behind Text* option at the drop-down gallery.
    e. Click in the *Shape Height* measurement box in the Size group, type 1, and then press the Enter key.

12. Make the white background of the image transparent by completing the following steps:
    a. Click the Color button in the Adjust group.
    b. Click the *Set Transparent Color* option at the bottom of the drop-down list. (The mouse pointer turns into a dropper tool.)
    c. Position the dropper tool on the white background of the image and then click the left mouse button.

13. Click the Color button and then click the *Orange, Accent color 2 Dark* option (third column, second row in the *Recolor* section).

14. Insert an airplane image by clicking the Insert tab, clicking the Pictures button, and then double-clicking the *Airplane* image file in your WL1C5 folder.

15. With the airplane image selected, remove the background by completing the following steps:
    a. Click the Remove Background button in the Adjust group on the Picture Tools Format tab.
    b. Click the Mark Areas to Remove button. (The mouse pointer changes to a pen.)
    c. Position the mouse pointer (pen) in the blue background at the left of the tail of the airplane, press and hold down the left mouse button, drag in the blue background (left of the airplane tail), and then release the mouse button. Do not drag through any portion of the airplane. (The blue background the mouse pointer passes through should be removed.)
    d. If necessary, use the mouse pointer to drag in the blue background at the right of the tail of the airplane. (Do not drag through any portion of the airplane.
    e. If you are not satisfied with the background removal, click the Discard All Changes button and start again. If you are satisfied with the background removal, click the Keep Changes button.

16. Position the airplane by clicking the Position button and then clicking the *Position in Top Left with Square Text Wrapping* option (first column, top row in the *With Text Wrapping* section).

17. Specify text wrapping by clicking the Wrap Text button and then clicking the *Behind Text* option.

18. Change the image width by clicking in the *Shape Width* measurement box, typing 2.1, and then pressing the Enter key.

19. Save, print, and then close **5-Tour**.

Activity 3 **Customize a Report on Robots** **2 Parts**

You will open a report on robots and then add a pull quote using a predesigned text box and draw a text box and type information about an upcoming conference.

Inserting a
Text Box

 Text Box

Inserting a Text Box

Add interest or create a location in a document for text by inserting or drawing a text box. Click the Insert tab and then click the Text Box button in the Text group and a drop-down list displays with predesigned text boxes and the *Draw Text Box* option. Choose one of the predesigned text boxes, which already contain formatting, or draw a text box and then customize or apply formatting to it with options and buttons on the Drawing Tools Format tab.

Inserting a Predesigned Text Box

Quick Steps

Insert Predesigned Text Box
1. Click Insert tab.
2. Click Text Box button.
3. Click option at drop-down list.

One use for a text box in a document is to insert a pull quote. A pull quote is a quote from the text that is "pulled out" and enlarged and positioned in an attractive location on the page. Some advantages of using pull quotes are that they reinforce important concepts, summarize the message, and break up text blocks to make them easier to read. If a document contains multiple pull quotes, keep them in the order in which they appear in the text to ensure clear comprehension by readers.

A text box for a pull quote can be drawn in a document or a predesigned text box can be inserted in the document. To insert a predesigned text box, click the Insert tab, click the Text Box button, and then click the predesigned text box at the drop-down list.

Formatting a
Text Box

Formatting a Text Box

When a text box is selected, the Drawing Tools Format tab is active. This tab contains buttons for formatting and customizing the text box. Use options in the Insert Shapes group on the Drawing Tools Format tab to insert a shape in the text box or in another location in the document. Apply predesigned styles to a text box and change the shape fill, outline, and effects with options in the Shape Styles group. Change the formatting of the text in the text box with options in

Text Fill

 Text Outline

 Text Effects

the WordArt Styles group. Click the More WordArt Styles button in the WordArt Styles group and then click a style at the drop-down gallery. Further customize the formatting of text in the text box with the Text Fill, Text Outline, and Text Effects buttons in the Text group. Use options in the Arrange group to position the text box on the page, specify text wrapping in relation to the text box, align the text box with other objects in the document, and rotate the text box. Specify the text box size with the *Shape Height* and *Shape Width* measurement boxes in the Size group.

Activity 3a Inserting a Predesigned Text Box

Part 1 of 2

1. Open **Robots** and then save it with the name **5-Robots**.
2. Insert a predesigned text box by completing the following steps:
   a. Click the Insert tab.
   b. Click the Text Box button in the Text group.
   c. Scroll down the drop-down list and then click the *Ion Quote (Dark)* option.

3. Type the following text in the text box: "The task of creating a humanlike body has proven incredibly difficult."
4. Delete the line and the source placeholder in the text box by pressing the F8 function key (which turns on the Selection mode), pressing Ctrl + End (which selects text from the location of the insertion point to the end of the text box), and then pressing the Delete key.
5. With the Drawing Tools Format tab active, click the More Shape Styles button in the Shape Styles group and then click the *Subtle Effect - Blue, Accent 5* option (sixth column, fourth row in the *Theme Styles* section).
6. Click the Shape Effects button in the Shape Styles group, point to *Shadow*, and then click the *Offset: Bottom Right* option (first column, first row in the *Outer* section).

7. Position the mouse pointer on the border of the selected text box until the pointer turns into a four-headed arrow and then drag the text box so it is positioned as shown below.

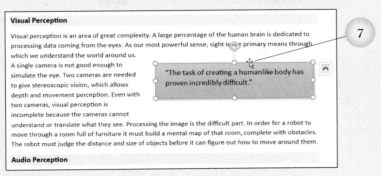

8. Click outside the text box to deselect it.
9. Save **5-Robots**.

Check Your Work

Drawing a Text Box

Quick Steps
Draw Text Box
1. Click Insert tab.
2. Click Text Box button.
3. Click *Draw Text Box*.
4. Click or drag in document to create box.

To draw a text box rather than inserting a predesigned one, click the Insert tab, click the Text Box button in the Text group, and then click *Draw Text Box* at the drop-down list. With the mouse pointer displaying as crosshairs (a plus [+] symbol), click in the document to insert the text box or position the crosshairs in the document and then drag to create the text box with the desired size and dimensions. When a text box is selected, the Drawing Tools Format tab is active. Use buttons on this tab to format a drawn text box in the same manner as a built-in text box.

Activity 3b **Inserting and Formatting a Text Box**   Part 2 of 2

1. With **5-Robots** open, press Ctrl + End to move the insertion point to the end of the document.
2. Insert a text box by completing the following steps:
   a. Click the Insert tab.
   b. Click the Text Box button and then click the *Draw Text Box* option.
   c. Position the mouse pointer (displays as crosshairs) on the insertion point and then click the left mouse button. (This inserts the text box in the document.)
3. Change the text box height and width by completing the following steps:
   a. Click in the *Shape Height* measurement box in the Size group, type 1.2, and then press the Tab key.
   b. Type 4.5 in the *Shape Width* measurement box and then press the Enter key.
4. Center the text box by clicking the Align button in the Arrange group and then clicking *Align Center* at the drop-down list.

5. Apply a shape style by clicking the More Shape Styles button in the Shape Styles group and then clicking the *Subtle Effect - Blue, Accent 1* option (second column, fourth row in the *Theme Styles* section).

6. Apply a bevel shape effect by clicking the Shape Effects button, pointing to the *Bevel* option, and then clicking the *Soft Round* option at the side menu (second column, second row in the *Bevel* section).

7. Apply a 3-D shape effect by clicking the Shape Effects button, pointing to *3-D Rotation*, and then clicking the *Perspective: Above* option (first column, second row in the *Perspective* section).

8. Insert and format text in the text box by completing the following steps:
   a. Press the Enter key two times. (The insertion point should be positioned in the text box.)
   b. Click the Home tab.
   c. Change the font size to 14 points, apply bold formatting, and change the font color to *Dark Blue* (ninth option in the *Standard Colors* section).
   d. Click the Center button in the Paragraph group.
   e. Type International Conference on Artificial Intelligence Summer 2022.
   f. Click outside the text box to deselect it. (Your text box should appear as shown at the right.)

9. Save, print, and then close **5-Robots**.

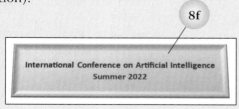

International Conference on Artificial Intelligence
Summer 2022

Check Your Work

You will create a company flyer document and increase the visual interest in the document by inserting and customizing shapes and WordArt.

 Tutorial

Inserting, Sizing, and Positioning a Shape and Line

 Tutorial

Formatting a Shape and Line

 Shapes

Quick Steps

Draw Shape
1. Click Insert tab.
2. Click Shapes button.
3. Click shape.
4. Click or drag in document to create shape.

💡 *Hint* To draw a square, choose the Rectangle shape and then press and hold down the Shift key while drawing.

Drawing Shapes

Use the Shapes button in the Illustrations group on the Insert tab to draw shapes in a document, including lines, basic shapes, block arrows, flow chart shapes, stars and banners, and callouts. Click a shape and the mouse pointer displays as crosshairs. Position the crosshairs in the document where the shape is to be inserted and then click the left mouse button or click and hold down the left mouse button, drag to create the shape, and then release the mouse button. The shape is inserted in the document and the Drawing Tools Format tab is active.

A shape selected from the *Lines* section of the drop-down list and then drawn in the document is considered a *line drawing*. A shape selected from another section of the drop-down list and then drawn in the document is considered an *enclosed object*. When drawing an enclosed object, maintain the proportions of the shape by pressing and holding down the Shift key while dragging with the mouse to create the shape.

Copying Shapes

To copy a shape, select the shape and then click the Copy button in the Clipboard group on the Home tab. Position the insertion point at the location the copied shape is to be inserted and then click the Paste button. A selected shape can also be copied by right-clicking the shape and then clicking *Copy* at the shortcut menu. Position the insertion point where the shape is to be copied, right-click and then click *Paste* at the shortcut menu. Another method for copying shapes is to press and hold down the Ctrl key while dragging a copy of the shape to the new location.

Activity 4a **Drawing and Copying Arrow Shapes** Part 1 of 2

1. At a blank document, press the Enter key two times and then draw an arrow shape by completing the following steps:
   a. Click the Insert tab.
   b. Click the Shapes button in the Illustrations group and then click the *Arrow: Striped Right* shape (fifth column, second row in the *Block Arrows* section).
   c. Position the mouse pointer (which displays as crosshairs) on the insertion point and then click the left mouse button. (This inserts the arrow shape in the document.)
2. Format the arrow by completing the following steps:
   a. Click in the *Shape Height* measurement box in the Size group, type 2.4, and then press the Tab key.
   b. Type 4.5 in the *Shape Width* measurement box and then press the Enter key.

c. Horizontally align the arrow by clicking the Align button in the Arrange group and then clicking *Distribute Horizontally* at the drop-down list.

2c

2e

d. Click the More Shape Styles button in the Shape Styles group and then click the *Intense Effect - Green, Accent 6* option (last option in the *Theme Styles* section at the drop-down gallery).

e. Click the Shape Effects button in the Shape Styles group, point to *Bevel*, and then click the *Angle* option (first column, second row in the *Bevel* section).

f. Click the Shape Outline button arrow in the Shape Styles group and then click the *Dark Blue* option (ninth option in the *Standard Colors* section).

3. Copy the arrow by completing the following steps:
   a. With the mouse pointer positioned in the arrow (mouse pointer displays with a four-headed arrow attached), press and hold down the Ctrl key and click and hold down the left mouse button. Drag down until the copied arrow appears just below the top arrow, release the mouse button, and then release the Ctrl key.
   b. Copy the selected arrow by pressing and holding down the Ctrl key and clicking and holding down the left mouse button and then dragging the copied arrow just below the second arrow.

4. Flip the middle arrow by completing the following steps:
   a. Click the middle arrow to select it.
   b. Click the Rotate button in the Arrange group on the Drawing Tools Format tab and then click the *Flip Horizontal* option at the drop-down gallery.

4b

5. Insert the text *Financial* in the top arrow by completing the following steps:
   a. Click the top arrow to select it.
   b. Type Financial.
   c. Select *Financial*.
   d. Click the Home tab.
   e. Change the font size to 16 points, apply bold formatting, and change the font color to Dark Blue (ninth option in the *Standard Colors* section).

6. Complete steps similar to those in Step 5 to insert the word *Direction* in the middle arrow.

7. Complete steps similar to those in Step 5 to insert the word *Retirement* in the bottom arrow.

8. Save the document and name it **5-FinConsult**.

9. Print the document.

Check Your Work

Tutorial

Inserting, Sizing, and Positioning WordArt

Creating and Formatting WordArt

Use the WordArt feature to distort or modify text to conform to a variety of shapes. This is useful for creating company logos, letterheads, flyer titles, and headings.

Tutorial

Formatting WordArt

WordArt

To insert WordArt in a document, click the Insert tab and then click the WordArt button in the Text group. At the drop-down list, click an option and a WordArt text box is inserted in the document containing the words *Your text here* and the Drawing Tools Format tab is active. Type the WordArt text and then format the WordArt with options on the Drawing Tools Format tab. Existing text can also be formatted as WordArt. To do this, select the text, click the WordArt button on the Insert tab, and then click the WordArt option at the drop-down list.

Quick Steps

Create WordArt Text
1. Click Insert tab.
2. Click WordArt button.
3. Click option.
4. Type WordArt text.

Activity 4b Inserting and Modifying WordArt

Part 2 of 2

1. With **5-FinConsult** open, press Ctrl + Home to move the insertion point to the beginning of the document.
2. Insert WordArt text by completing the following steps:
   a. Type Miller Financial Services and then select *Miller Financial Services*.
   b. Click the Insert tab.
   c. Click the WordArt button in the Text group and then click the option in the third column, first row (orange fill and outline).

2c

3. Format the WordArt text by completing the following steps:
   a. Make sure the WordArt text border displays as a solid line.
   b. Click the Text Fill button arrow in the WordArt Styles group on the Drawing Tools Format tab and then click the *Light Green* option (fifth option in the *Standard Colors* section).
   c. Click the Text Outline button arrow in the WordArt Styles group and then click the *Green, Accent 6, Darker 50%* option (last option in the *Theme Colors* section).

3b

d. Click the Text Effects button in the WordArt Styles group, point to *Glow*, and then click the *Glow: 5 point; Blue, Accent color 1* option (first column, first row in the *Glow Variations* section).

e. Click in the *Shape Height* measurement box in the Size group, type 1, and then press the Tab key.

f. Type 6 in the *Shape Width* measurement box in the Size group and then press the Enter key.

g. Click the Text Effects button in the WordArt Styles group, point to *Transform*, and then click the *Warp Up* option (third column, fourth row in the *Warp* section).

h. Click the Position button in the Arrange group and then click the *Position in Top Center with Square Text Wrapping* option (second column, first row in the *With Text Wrapping* section).

4. Click outside the WordArt to deselect it.

5. Move the arrows as needed to ensure they do not overlap the WordArt or each other and that they all fit on one page.

6. Save, print, and then close **5-FinConsult**.

Activity 5 Insert and Format Screenshots   2 Parts

You will create a document with screenshots of the Print and Export backstage areas and create another document with screen clippings of sample cover pages.

Inserting a Screenshot

The Illustrations group on the Insert tab contains a Screenshot button, which captures a screen or part of a screen as an image. To capture the entire screen, open a new document, click the Insert tab, click the Screenshot button in the Illustrations group, and then click the screen thumbnail at the drop-down list. (The currently active document does not appear as a thumbnail at the drop-down list—only other documents or files that are open.) Click the specific thumbnail at the drop-down list and a screenshot is inserted as an image in the open document. Once the screenshot is inserted in the document, the Picture Tools Format tab is active. Use buttons on this tab to customize the screenshot image.

Activity 5a Inserting and Formatting Screenshots

Part 1 of 2

1. Make sure that Word is the only program open and then press Ctrl + N to open a blank document.
2. Press Ctrl + N to open a second blank document, type Print Backstage Area at the left margin, and then press the Enter key.
3. Save the document and name it **5-BackstageAreas**.
4. Point to the Word button on the taskbar and then click the thumbnail representing the blank document.
5. Display the Print backstage area by clicking the File tab and then clicking the *Print* option.
6. Point to the Word button on the taskbar and then click the thumbnail representing **5-BackstageAreas**.

7. Insert and format a screenshot of the Print backstage area by completing the following steps:
   a. Click the Insert tab.
   b. Click the Screenshot button in the Illustrations group and then click the thumbnail in the drop-down list. (This inserts a screenshot of the Print backstage area in the document.)

   c. With the screenshot image selected, click the *Drop Shadow Rectangle* picture style option (fourth option in the Picture Styles gallery).
   d. Select the measurement in the *Shape Width* measurement box, type 5.5, and then press the Enter key.
8. Press Ctrl + End and then press the Enter key. (The insertion point should be positioned below the screenshot image and at the left margin. You may need to press the Enter key again so the insertion point is positioned at the left margin.)
9. Type Info Backstage Area at the left margin and then press the Enter key.
10. Point to the Word button on the taskbar and then click the thumbnail representing the blank document (with the Print backstage area displayed).
11. At the backstage area, click the *Info* option. (This displays the Info backstage area.)
12. Point to the Word button on the taskbar and then click the thumbnail representing **5-BackstageAreas**.
13. Insert and format a screenshot of the Info backstage area by completing steps similar to those in Step 7.
14. Press Ctrl + Home to move the insertion point to the beginning of the document.
15. Save, print, and then close **5-BackstageAreas**.
16. At the Info backstage area, press the Esc key to redisplay the blank document.
17. Close the blank document.

Check Your Work

To create a screenshot of only part of the image on the screen, use the *Screen Clipping* option at the Screenshot button drop-down list. Click this option and the other open document, file, or Windows Start screen or desktop displays in a dimmed manner and the mouse pointer displays as crosshairs. Using the mouse, draw a border around the specific area of the screen to be captured. The area identified is inserted in the other document as an image, the image is selected, and the Picture Tools Format tab is active.

Activity 5b   Inserting and Formatting a Screen Clipping

Part 2 of 2

1. Open **NSSLtrhd** and then save it with the name **5-NSSCoverPages**.
2. Type the text Sample Cover Pages and then press the Enter key two times.
3. Select the text you just typed, change the font to 18-point Copperplate Gothic Bold, and then center the text.
4. Press Ctrl + End to move the insertion point below the text.
5. Open **NSSCoverPg01** and then change the zoom to 50% by clicking approximately five times on the Zoom Out button at the left of the Zoom slider bar on the Status bar.
6. Point to the Word button on the taskbar and then click the thumbnail representing **5-NSSCoverPages**.
7. Insert and format a screen clipping image by completing the following steps:

   a. Click the Insert tab.
   b. Click the Screenshot button and then click the *Screen Clipping* option.
   c. When **NSSCoverPg01** displays in a dimmed manner, position the mouse crosshairs in the upper left corner of the cover page, click and hold down the left mouse button, drag down to the lower right corner of the cover page, and then release the mouse button. (See the image below and to the right.)
   d. With the cover page screen clipping image inserted in **5-NSSCoverPages**, make sure the image is selected. (The sizing handles should appear around the cover page image.)
   e. Click the Wrap Text button in the Arrange group on the Picture Tools Format tab and then click *Square* at the drop-down gallery.
   f. Select the current measurement in the *Shape Width* measurement box, type 3, and then press the Enter key.
   g. Click the Picture Border button arrow and then click the *Black, Text 1* option (second column, first row in the *Theme Colors* section).
8. Point to the Word button on the Taskbar and then click the thumbnail representing **NSSCoverPg01**.

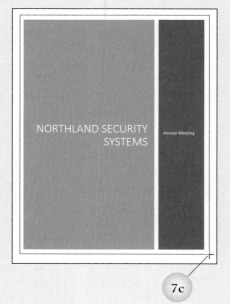

9. Close **NSSCoverPg01**.
10. Open **NSSCoverPg02** and then, if necessary, change the zoom to 50%.
11. Point to the Word button on the Taskbar and then click the thumbnail representing **5-NSSCoverPages**.
12. Insert and format a screen clipping image of the cover page by completing steps similar to those in Step 7.
13. Using the mouse, position the two cover page screenshot images side by side in the document.
14. Save, print, and then close **5-NSSCoverPages**.
15. With **NSSCoverPg02** the active document, change the zoom to 100% and then close the document.

Check Your Work

Activity 6 **Prepare and Format a SmartArt Graphic** **2 Parts**

You will prepare SmartArt process graphics that identify steps in the production process and then apply formatting to enhance the graphics.

Creating SmartArt

Hint Use SmartArt to communicate your message and ideas in a visual manner.

Use Word's SmartArt feature to insert graphics such as diagrams and organizational charts in a document. SmartArt offers a variety of predesigned graphics that are available at the Choose a SmartArt Graphic dialog box, as shown in Figure 5.3. At this dialog box, *All* is selected by default in the left panel and all the available predesigned SmartArt graphics are shown in the middle panel.

Figure 5.3 Choose a SmartArt Graphic Dialog Box

Double-click a SmartArt graphic in this panel.

Choose a SmartArt graphic category from options in this panel.

Click a SmartArt graphic in the middle panel and then read a description of it here.

Inserting, Sizing, and Positioning SmartArt

 SmartArt

Quick Steps

Insert SmartArt Graphic
1. Click Insert tab.
2. Click SmartArt button.
3. Double-click graphic.

Inserting a SmartArt Graphic

To insert a SmartArt graphic, click the Insert tab and then click the SmartArt button in the Illustrations group to open the Choose a SmartArt Graphic dialog box (see Figure 5.3). Predesigned SmartArt graphics are shown in the middle panel of the dialog box. Use the scroll bar at the right side of the middle panel to scroll down the list of choices. Click a graphic in the middle panel and its name displays in the right panel along with a description. SmartArt includes graphics for presenting a list of data; showing processes, cycles, and relationships; and presenting data in a matrix or pyramid. Double-click a graphic in the middle panel of the dialog box (or click the graphic and then click OK) and the graphic is inserted in the document.

When a SmartArt graphic is inserted in a document, a text pane may appear at the left of the graphic. Type text in the text pane or type directly in the graphic.

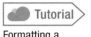

Formatting a SmartArt Graphic

Hint Limit the number of shapes and amount of text in your SmartArt graphic.

Formatting a SmartArt Graphic

Apply formatting to a SmartArt graphic with options at the SmartArt Tools Design tab. This tab becomes active when the graphic is inserted in the document. Use options and buttons on this tab to add objects, change the graphic layout, apply a style to the graphic, and reset the graphic to the original formatting.

Formatting can also be applied to a SmartArt graphic with options on the SmartArt Tools Format tab. Use options and buttons on this tab to change the sizes and shapes of objects in the graphic; apply shape styles and WordArt styles; change the shape fill, outline, and effects; and arrange and size the graphic.

Activity 6a **Inserting and Formatting SmartArt Graphics**   Part 1 of 2

1. At a blank document, insert the SmartArt graphic shown in Figure 5.4 by completing the following steps:
   a. Click the Insert tab.
   b. Click the SmartArt button in the Illustrations group.
   c. At the Choose a SmartArt Graphic dialog box, click *Process* in the left panel and then double-click the *Alternating Flow* graphic (second column, second row).

   d. If a *Type your text here* text pane does not appear at the left of the graphic, click the Text Pane button in the Create Graphic group on the SmartArt Tools Design tab to display it.
   e. With the insertion point positioned after the top bullet in the *Type your text here* text pane, type Design.
   f. Click the *[Text]* placeholder below *Design* and then type Mock-up.
   g. Continue clicking occurrences of the *[Text]* placeholder and typing text so the text pane displays as shown at the right.
   h. Close the text pane by clicking the Close button in the upper right corner of the pane. (You can also click the Text Pane button in the Create Graphic group.)

2. Change the graphic colors by clicking the Change Colors button in the SmartArt Styles group and then clicking the *Colorful Range - Accent Colors 5 to 6* option (last option in the *Colorful* section).

3. Apply a style by clicking the More SmartArt Styles button in the SmartArt Styles group and then clicking the *Inset* option (second option in the *3-D* section).

4. Copy the graphic and then change the layout by completing the following steps:
   a. Click inside the SmartArt graphic border but outside any shapes.
   b. Click the Home tab and then click the Copy button in the Clipboard group.
   c. Press Ctrl + End, press the Enter key, and then press Ctrl + Enter to insert a page break.
   d. Click the Paste button in the Clipboard group.
   e. Click inside the copied SmartArt graphic border but outside any shapes.
   f. Click the SmartArt Tools Design tab.
   g. Click the More Layouts button in the Layouts group and then click the *Continuous Block Process* layout (second column, second row).
   h. Click outside the graphic to deselect it.

5. Save the document and name it **5-SAGraphics**.

Check Your Work

Figure 5.4 Activity 6a

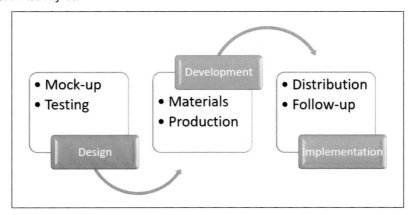

Arranging and Moving a SmartArt Graphic

 Position

 Wrap Text

Position a SmartArt graphic by clicking the Position button in the Arrange group on the SmartArt Tools Format tab. Apply text wrapping to a SmartArt graphic using options in the Arrange group, with the Layout Options button, or by right-clicking the graphic and clicking *Wrap Text* at the shortcut menu.

Move a SmartArt graphic by positioning the mouse pointer on the graphic until the pointer displays with a four-headed arrow attached, clicking and holding down the left mouse button, and then dragging the graphic to the new location. The SmartArt graphic or shapes within it can also be moved using the up, down, left, and right arrow keys on the keyboard.

Activity 6b Formatting SmartArt Graphics

Part 2 of 2

1. With **5-SAGraphics** open, format shapes by completing the following steps:
   a. Click the SmartArt graphic on the first page to select it (a border surrounds the graphic).
   b. Click the SmartArt Tools Format tab.
   c. In the SmartArt graphic, click the rectangle shape containing the word *Design*.
   d. Press and hold down the Shift key and then click the shape containing the word *Development*.
   e. With the Shift key still held down, click the shape containing the word *Implementation* and then release the Shift key. (All three shapes should now be selected.)
   f. Click the Change Shape button in the Shapes group.
   g. Click the pentagon arrow shape (seventh column, second row in the *Block Arrows* section).
   h. With the shapes still selected, click the Larger button in the Shapes group.
   i. With the shapes still selected, click the Shape Outline button arrow in the Shape Styles group and then click the *Dark Blue* option (ninth option in the *Standard Colors* section).

   j. Click inside the SmartArt graphic border but outside any shapes. (This deselects the shapes but keeps the graphic selected.)
2. Click in the *Shape Height* measurement box in, type 4, and then press the Enter key.

3. Click the Position button and then click the *Position in Middle Center with Square Text Wrapping* option (second column, second row in the *With Text Wrapping* section).
4. Click outside the SmartArt graphic to deselect it.
5. Format the bottom SmartArt graphic by completing the following steps:
   a. Press Ctrl + End to move to the end of the document and then click in the bottom SmartArt graphic to select it.
   b. Press and hold down the Shift key and then click each of the three shapes.
   c. Click the More WordArt Styles button in the WordArt Styles group on the SmartArt Tools Format tab.
   d. Click the option in the first column, first row (black fill, shadow).

   e. Click the Text Outline button arrow in the WordArt Styles group and then click the *Dark Blue* option (ninth color in the *Standard Colors* section).
   f. Click the Text Effects button in the WordArt Styles group, point to *Glow* at the drop-down list, and then click the *Glow: 5 point; Orange, Accent color 2* option (second column, first row).

   g. Click inside the SmartArt graphic border but outside any shapes.
6. Click the Position button in the Arrange group and then click the *Position in Middle Center with Square Text Wrapping* option (second column, second row in the *With Text Wrapping* section).
7. Click outside the SmartArt graphic to deselect it.
8. Save, print, and then close **5-SAGraphics**.

Check Your Work

You will prepare an organizational chart for a company and then apply formatting to enhance the appearance of the chart.

Creating an Organizational Chart with SmartArt

Quick Steps

Insert Organizational Chart
1. Click Insert tab.
2. Click SmartArt button.
3. Click *Hierarchy.*
4. Double-click organizational chart.

To visually illustrate hierarchical data, consider using a SmartArt option to create an organizational chart. To display organizational chart SmartArt options, click the Insert tab and then click the SmartArt button in the Illustrations group. At the Choose a SmartArt Graphic dialog box, click *Hierarchy* in the left panel. Organizational chart options are shown in the middle panel of the dialog box. Double-click an organizational chart and the chart is inserted in the document. Type text in a SmartArt graphic by selecting the shape and then typing text in it or type text in the *Type your text here* window at the left of the graphic. Format a SmartArt organizational chart with options and buttons on the SmartArt Tools Design tab and the SmartArt Tools Format tab, and with the Layout Options button.

Activity 7 **Creating and Formatting a SmartArt Organizational Chart** Part 1 of 1

1. At a blank document, create the SmartArt organizational chart shown in Figure 5.5. To begin, click the Insert tab.
2. Click the SmartArt button in the Illustrations group.
3. At the Choose a SmartArt Graphic dialog box, click *Hierarchy* in the left panel of the dialog box and then double-click the *Organization Chart* option (first option in the middle panel).

4. If a *Type your text here* pane displays at the left of the organizational chart, close it by clicking the Text Pane button in the Create Graphic group.
5. Delete one of the boxes in the organizational chart by clicking the border of the box in the lower right corner to select it and then pressing the Delete key. (Make sure that the selection border surrounding the box is a solid line and not a dashed line. If a dashed line appears, click the box border again. This should change the border to a solid line.)
6. With the bottom right box selected, click the Add Shape button arrow in the Create Graphic group and then click the *Add Shape Below* option.

7. Click the *[Text]* placeholder in the top box, type Blaine Willis, press Shift + Enter, and then type President. Click in each of the remaining boxes and type the text as shown in Figure 5.5. (Press Shift + Enter after typing each name.)
8. Click the More SmartArt Styles button in the SmartArt Styles group and then click the *Inset* style (second option in the *3-D* section).
9. Click the Change Colors button and then click the *Colorful Range - Accent Colors 4 to 5* option (fourth option in the *Colorful* section).

10. Click the SmartArt Tools Format tab.
11. Click the text pane control (displays with a left-pointing arrow) at the left side of the graphic border. (This displays the *Type your text here* window.)
12. Using the mouse, select all the text in the *Type your text here* window.
13. Click the Change Shape button in the Shapes group and then click the *Rectangle: Top Corners Rounded* option (eighth option in the *Rectangles* section).

14. Click the Shape Outline button arrow in the Shape Styles group and then click the *Dark Blue* option (ninth option in the *Standard Colors* section).
15. Close the *Type your text here* window.
16. Click inside the organizational chart border but outside any shapes.
17. Click in the *Shape Height* measurement box, type 4, and then press the Enter key.
18. Click in the *Shape Width* measurement box, type 6.5, and then press the Enter key.
19. Click outside the organizational chart to deselect it.
20. Save the document and name it **5-OrgChart**.
21. Print and then close the document.

Check Your Work

Figure 5.5 Activity 7

Chapter Summary

- Insert symbols with options at the Symbol dialog box with the Symbols tab selected, and insert special characters with options at the Symbol dialog box with the Special Characters tab selected.

- Click the Date & Time button in the Text group on the Insert tab to display the Date and Time dialog box. Insert the date or time with options at this dialog box or with keyboard shortcuts. If the date or time is inserted as a field, update the field by clicking the Update tab or the F9 function key.

- Insert an image, such as a photo or clip art, with buttons in the Illustrations group on the Insert tab.

- To insert an image from a folder on the computer's hard drive or removable drive, click the Insert tab and then click the Pictures button in the Illustrations group. At the Insert Picture dialog box, navigate to the specific folder and then double-click the image file.

- To insert an online image, click the Insert tab and then click the Online Pictures button. At the Online Pictures window, type the search text or topic and then press the Enter key. Click an image to select it and then click the Insert button.

- Use the *Shape Height* and *Shape Width* measurement boxes in the Size group on the Picture Tools Format tab to change the size of an image. The size of an image can also be changed with the sizing handles around a selected image.

- Use the Crop button in the Size group to remove unnecessary parts of an image. To crop an image, click the Crop button and then use the crop handles to specify what part of the image should be cropped.

- The Arrange group on the Picture Tools Format tab contains buttons for positioning, aligning, and rotating text.

- Use the Wrap Text button in the Arrange group to specify how text or other objects should wrap around a selected image. The Layout Options button that displays outside the upper right corner of a selected image can also be used to specify text wrapping.

- Move an image using options at the Position button drop-down gallery on the Picture Tools Format tab or by choosing a text wrapping style and then moving the image by dragging it with the mouse.

- Rotate a selected image using the mouse pointer on the rotation handle (circular arrow) that appears above the image.

- The Adjust group on the Picture Tools Format tab contains buttons for adjusting the background, color, brightness, and contrast of an image. An artistic effect can be applied to a selected image using the Artistic Effects button in the Adjust group. Use the *Set Transparent Color* option at the Color button drop-down gallery to make a color transparent in the selected image. Adjust the transparency of an image with options at the Transparency button drop-down gallery.

- Apply a predesigned picture style to a selected image with styles in the Picture Styles group on the Picture Tools Format tab.

- Create alternative text to describe images in a document for readers with visual impairments. Type a description of an image at the Alt Text task pane. Display this task pane by clicking the Alt Text button on the Picture Tools Format tab or right-clicking an image and then clicking *Edit Alt Text* at the shortcut menu.

- Click the Text Box button in the Text group on the Insert tab to display a drop-down list of predesigned text boxes (text boxes that already contain formatting) that can be inserted in a document.
- Draw a text box by clicking the Text Box button in the Text group on the Insert tab, clicking the *Draw Text Box* option at the drop-down list, and then clicking or dragging in the document.
- Customize a text box with buttons on the Drawing Tools Format tab.
- Draw shapes in a document by clicking the Shapes button in the Illustrations group on the Insert tab, clicking a shape at the drop-down list, and then clicking or dragging in the document to draw the shape. Customize a shape with options on the Drawing Tools Format tab.
- Copy a selected shape by clicking the Copy button in the Clipboard group on the Home tab, positioning the insertion point in the new location, and then clicking the Paste button. Another method for copying a selected shape is to press and hold down the Ctrl key while dragging the selected shape.
- Use WordArt to distort or modify text to conform to a variety of shapes. Customize WordArt with options on the Drawing Tools Format tab.
- Use the Screenshot button in the Illustrations group on the Insert tab to capture part or all of a window visible on the screen. Use buttons on the Picture Tools Format tab to customize a screenshot image.
- Use the SmartArt feature to insert predesigned graphics and organizational charts in a document. Click the SmartArt button in the Illustrations group on the Insert tab to display the Choose a SmartArt Graphic dialog box containing a variety of graphics.
- Format a SmartArt graphic with options and buttons on the SmartArt Tools Design tab and the SmartArt Tools Format tab.
- Position a SmartArt graphic by clicking the Position button in the Arrange group on the SmartArt Tools Format tab and then clicking a position option at the drop-down gallery.
- Specify how text or other objects should wrap around a SmartArt graphic with options at the Wrap Text button drop-down gallery. The Layout Options button that appears outside the upper right corner of the selected SmartArt graphic can also be used to specify text wrapping.
- Move a selected SmartArt graphic by dragging it with the mouse or using the up, down, left, and right arrow keys on the keyboard. Before moving a SmartArt graphic, apply text wrapping.
- Use a SmartArt option to create an organizational chart, which is a visual illustration of hierarchical data.

Commands Review

FEATURE	RIBBON TAB, GROUP	BUTTON, OPTION	KEYBOARD SHORTCUT
Alt Text task pane	Picture Tools Format, Accessibility		
Choose a SmartArt Graphic dialog box	Insert, Illustrations		
Date and Time dialog box	Insert, Text		
insert date as field			Alt + Shift + D
Insert Picture dialog box	Insert, Illustrations		
insert time as field			Alt + Shift + T
predesigned text box	Insert, Text		
screenshot	Insert, Illustrations		
shapes	Insert, Illustrations		
Symbol dialog box	Insert, Symbols	, More Symbols	
text box	Insert, Text		
update field			F9
WordArt	Insert, Text		

Microsoft®
Word

Managing Documents

Performance Objectives

Upon successful completion of Chapter 6, you will be able to:

1 Change the view of a document

2 Use learning tools to aid reading fluency and comprehension

3 Change page movement, display percentage, and ribbon display options

4 Hide and show white space

5 Split a window, view documents side by side, and open a new window

6 Insert a file into an open document

7 Preview and print specific text and pages in a document

8 Prepare and print envelopes and labels

9 Create a document using a template

10 Save documents in different file formats

11 Save a template and open a template using File Explorer

Word provides a number of options for managing documents, including customizing the document view, using learning tools, changing the display and display percentage, and changing ribbon display options. Managing documents can also include working with windows and performing such actions as arranging windows, splitting windows, viewing documents side by side, and opening a new window. In this chapter, you will learn these techniques, as well as saving documents in different file formats and saving and opening a template. You will also learn how to create and print envelopes and labels.

 Data Files

Before beginning chapter work, copy the WL1C6 folder to your storage medium and then make WL1C6 the active folder.

The online course includes additional training and assessment resources.

You will open a document on navigating and searching the web, change the document view, use learning tools, change page movement to side to side, change display percentages, and hide and show white space at the tops and bottoms of pages.

Tutorial

Changing the
Document View

Changing the Document View

By default, a Word document displays in Print Layout view. This view displays the document on the screen as it will appear when printed. Other views are available, such as Draft and Read Mode. Change views with buttons in the view area on the Status bar (see Figure 6.1) or with options on the View tab.

Displaying a Document in Draft View

 Draft

Change to Draft view and the document displays in a format for efficient editing and formatting. In this view, margins and other features such as headers and footers do not appear on the screen. Change to Draft view by clicking the View tab and then clicking the Draft button in the Views group.

Displaying a Document in Web Layout View

 Web Layout

To see what a document would look like as a web page, click the Web Layout button on the View tab. In Web Layout view, the document margins are wider; this can be useful for viewing objects such as tables and graphics.

Displaying a Document in Read Mode View

 Read Mode

 Read Mode

Read Mode view displays a document in a format for easy viewing and reading. Change to Read Mode view by clicking the Read Mode button in the view area on the Status bar or by clicking the View tab and then clicking the Read Mode button in the Views group. Navigate in Read Mode view using the keys on the keyboard, as shown in Table 6.1. Another way to navigate in Read Mode is to click the Next and Previous arrow buttons at the right and left sides of the screen to page forward and backward through the document.

The File, Tools, and View tabs appear in the upper left corner of the screen in Read Mode view. Click the File tab to display the backstage area. Click the Tools tab and a drop-down list displays options for finding specific text in the document, searching for information on the internet using the Smart Lookup feature, and translating text in the document.

Figure 6.1 View Buttons and the Zoom Slider Bar

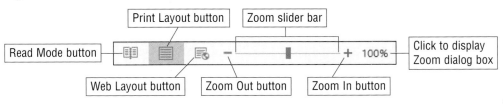

Table 6.1 Keyboard Commands in Read Mode View

Press this key	To complete this action
Page Down key, Right Arrow key, or spacebar	display next two pages
Page Up key, Left Arrow key, or Backspace key	display previous two pages
Home	display first page in document
End	display last page in document
Esc	return to previous view

Click the View tab to customize Read Mode view. Use View tab options to display the Navigation pane to navigate to specific locations in the document or to show comments inserted in the document. The View tab also includes options for making text more readable by changing column width, page color, and page layout; increasing spacing between characters, words, and lines; showing syllable breaks; and hearing text read aloud. These options are also available on the Immersive Learning Tools tab, described on the next page.

If a document contains an object such as a table, SmartArt graphic, image, or shape, zoom in on the object in Read Mode view by double-clicking it. The display size of the object increases and a button containing a magnifying glass with a plus symbol inside ( ) appears just outside the upper right corner of the object. Click the magnifying glass to zoom in and out. Click outside the object to exit the zoom view. To close Read Mode view and return to the previous view, press the Esc key or click the View tab and then click *Edit Document* at the drop-down list.

Activity 1a Changing Views
Part 1 of 3

1. Open **WebReport** and then save it with the name **6-WebReport**.
2. Display the document in Draft view by clicking the View tab and then clicking the Draft button in the Views group.

3. Click the Web Layout button in the Views group to display the document as it would appear if published as a web page.
4. Display the document in Read Mode view by clicking the Read Mode button in the view area on the Status bar.

5. If a speaker is connected to your computer, have the text read out loud by clicking the View tab and then clicking the *Read Aloud* option at the drop-down list. After listening for a short period of time, turn off the reading by clicking the View tab and then clicking the *Read Aloud* option.

6. Increase the display size of the table at the right of the screen by double-clicking the table. (If the table is not visible, click the Next button at the right of the screen to view the next page.)

7. Click the button containing a magnifying glass with a plus symbol that displays outside the upper right corner of the table. (This increases the zoom.)

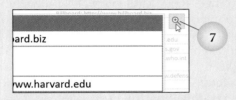

8. Click outside the table to return it to the original display size.

9. Practice navigating in Read Mode view using the actions shown in Table 6.1 (except the last action).

10. Press the Esc key to return to the Print Layout view.

Tutorial

Using Learning Tools

Using Learning Tools

The same learning tools available in Read Mode view can also be found on the Immersive Learning Tools tab, along with several additional options. Click the View tab and then click the Learning Tools button in the Immersive group and the Immersive Learning Tools tab displays as shown in Figure 6.2.

 Column Width

 Page Color

 Line Focus

 Text Spacing

 Syllables

 Read Aloud

Text in narrow columns is easier to read. Click the Column Width button on the Immersive Learning Tools tab and choose from *Very Narrow*, *Narrow*, *Moderate*, and *Wide*. Adding color to a page can also make text easier to read and reduce eye strain. Use the Page Color button to change the background color to *Sepia* (a light reddish-brown background color); or, select *Inverse* to see white text on a black background. Improve focus and comprehension by choosing the Line Focus button to read text one, three, or five lines at a time. Click the Text Spacing button to make text easier to read by increasing space between words, characters, and lines. Click the Syllables button to display syllable breaks in words, making words easier to recognize and pronounce.

If audio output is available, click the Read Aloud button to hear the text read aloud. Each word is highlighted as it is being read. A playback toolbar displays with buttons for controlling the narration, as shown in Figure 6.3. Turn off reading by clicking the Stop button on the playback toolbar or by clicking the Read Aloud button again.

Figure 6.2 Immersive Learning Tools Tab

Figure 6.3 Playback Toolbar

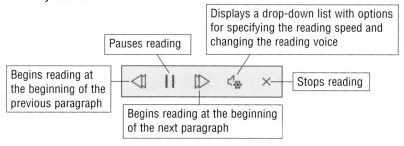

Displays a drop-down list with options for specifying the reading speed and changing the reading voice

Pauses reading

Begins reading at the beginning of the previous paragraph

Stops reading

Begins reading at the beginning of the next paragraph

Activity 1b Using Learning Tools

Part 2 of 3

1. With **6-WebReport** open, display learning tools by clicking the View tab, if necessary, and then clicking the Learning Tools button in the Immersive group.
2. Change column width by clicking the Column Width button on the Immersive Learning Tools tab and then clicking *Moderate* at the drop-down list.
3. Change page background color by clicking the Page Color button and then clicking the *Sepia* option.
4. Focus on only a few lines in the document by clicking the Line Focus button and then clicking *Five Lines* at the drop-down list.

5. Click the down arrow at the right side of the screen to scroll down five lines in the document.
6. Remove the focus by clicking the Line Focus button and then clicking *None* at the drop-down list.
7. Apply text spacing by clicking the Text Spacing button.
8. After viewing the document with extra spacing, click the Text Spacing button to turn off text spacing.
9. Click the Syllables button to display word syllable breaks.
10. After viewing the document with syllable breaks added to words, click the Syllables button to turn off syllable breaks.
11. If audio output is available, click the Read Aloud button.

12. Listen to the reading for a short time and then click the Pause button on the playback toolbar to pause the reading.
13. Click the Play button (previously the Pause button) to resume the reading.
14. Click the Next button on the playback toolbar to begin the reading with the next paragraph of text.
15. Change the reading voice by clicking the Settings button on the playback toolbar. At the drop-down list, click the *Voice Selection* option box arrow and then click *Microsoft Zira*.
16. After listening to the reading by Microsoft Zira, return to the default reading voice by clicking the Settings button, clicking the *Voice Selection* option box arrow, and then clicking *Microsoft David*.
17. Click the Stop button on the playback toolbar to turn off reading.
18. Remove the sepia page color by clicking the Page Color button and then clicking *None* at the drop-down list.
19. Close the Immersive Learning Tools tab by clicking the Close Learning Tools button.

Changing the Document Display

Word includes a number of options for changing the way a document displays on the screen. Show pages in a document like pages in a book with the Side to Side button in the Page Movement group on the View tab. Use options on the Zoom slider bar or the Zoom dialog box to change the display percentage. Show more of the document by turning off the ribbon, including tabs and commands, or turning off the display of commands but keeping the tabs visible. Another method for showing more of a document is to hide the white space that appears at the top and bottom of each page.

Changing Page Movement

Side to Side

Changing Page Movement

Paging through a document occurs by default in a vertical (up and down) manner. To view a document more like a book, with two pages visible at one time and other pages cascaded behind them, change to side-to-side page movement by clicking the Side to Side button in the Page Movement group on the View tab. Figure 6.4 shows how pages appear in the 6-WebReport document with the Side to Side button active.

Scroll through pages on a touch screen using a finger to flip through pages. If the computer screen is not a touch screen, use the horizontal scroll bar or the mouse wheel to scroll through pages. To use the horizontal scroll bar, click the Next button (right-pointing triangle) at the right side of the scroll bar to display the next page or click the Previous button (left-pointing triangle) at the left side of the scroll bar to display the previous page; drag the scroll box on the scroll bar; or click to the left or right of the scroll box. The mouse wheel can also be used to scroll through pages.

Figure 6.4 Side-to-Side Page Movement

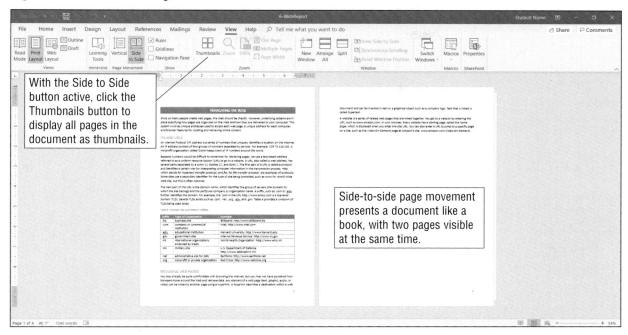

With the Side to Side button active, click the Thumbnails button to display all pages in the document as thumbnails.

Side-to-side page movement presents a document like a book, with two pages visible at the same time.

 Thumbnails

When the Side to Side button is active, the Thumbnails button appears in the Zoom group on the View tab and other options in the Zoom group are unavailable. Click the Thumbnails button and all pages in the document display as thumbnails. Click a thumbnail to move the insertion point to the beginning of the page represented by the thumbnail and that page along with the next or previous page displays side to side. Another method for displaying page thumbnails is to hold down the Ctrl key while moving the mouse wheel. Return to the default vertical page movement by clicking the Vertical button in the Page Movement group on the View tab.

 Vertical

 Tutorial

Changing the Display Percentage

Changing the Display Percentage

By default, a document displays at 100%. This display percentage can be changed with the Zoom slider bar at the right side of the Status bar (see Figure 6.1 on page 156) and with options in the Zoom group on the View tab. To change the display percentage with the Zoom slider bar, drag the button on the bar to increase or decrease the percentage. Click the Zoom Out button at the left of the slider bar to decrease the display percentage or click the Zoom In button to increase the display percentage.

 Zoom

Click the Zoom button in the Zoom group on the View tab to display the Zoom dialog box, which contains options for changing the display percentage. If the display percentage has been changed, return to the default by clicking the 100% button in the Zoom group on the View tab. Click the One Page button to display the entire page on the screen and click the Multiple Pages button to display multiple pages on the screen. Click the Page Width button and the document expands across the screen.

 100%

 One Page

 Multiple Pages

 Page Width

💡 *Hint* Click 100% at the right of the Zoom slider bar to display the Zoom dialog box.

Changing Ribbon Display Options

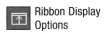
Ribbon Display Options

Use the Ribbon Display Options button in the upper right corner of the screen to view more of a document. Click the Ribbon Display Options button and a drop-down list displays with three options: *Auto-hide Ribbon, Show Tabs,* and *Show Tabs and Commands.* The default is *Show Tabs and Commands,* which displays the Quick Access Toolbar, ribbon, and Status bar on the screen. Click the first option, *Auto-hide Ribbon,* and the Quick Access Toolbar, ribbon, and Status bar are hidden, allowing more of the document to be visible on the screen. To temporarily redisplay these features, click at the top of the screen. Turn these features back on by clicking the Ribbon Display Options button and then clicking the *Show Tabs and Commands* option. Click the *Show Tabs* option at the drop-down list and the tabs display on the ribbon while the buttons and commands remain hidden.

Hiding and Showing White Space

Tutorial

Hiding and Showing White Space

Hide White Space

Show White Space

In Print Layout view, a page appears as it will when printed, including the white spaces at the top and the bottom of the page representing the document's margins. To save space on the screen in Print Layout view, the white space can be removed from view by positioning the mouse pointer at the top edge or bottom edge of a page or between pages until the pointer displays as the Hide White Space icon and then double-clicking the left mouse button. To redisplay the white space, position the mouse pointer on the thin gray line separating pages until the pointer turns into the Show White Space icon and then double-click the left mouse button.

Activity 1c Changing Views, Changing Display, and Hiding/Showing White Space   Part 3 of 3

1. With **6-WebReport** open, press Ctrl + Home to move the insertion point to the beginning of the document.
2. Change to side-to-side page movement by clicking the View tab and then clicking the Side to Side button in the Page Movement group. (This displays pages 1 and 2 side by side.)
3. Click the Next button at the right side of the horizontal scroll bar to display pages 2 and 3.
4. Display page thumbnails by clicking the Thumbnails button in the Zoom group.
5. Click the page 4 thumbnail.

6. Return to the default page movement by clicking the Vertical button in the Page Movement group.

7. Click the Zoom button in the Zoom group on the View tab.

8. At the Zoom dialog box, click the *75%* option and then click OK.

9. Return the display percentage to the default by clicking the 100% button in the Zoom group.

10. Click the Ribbon Display Options button in the upper right corner of the screen and then click *Auto-hide Ribbon* at the drop-down list.

11. Press the Page Up key until the beginning of the document displays.

12. Click at the top of the screen to temporarily redisplay the Quick Access Toolbar, ribbon, and Status bar.

13. Click the Ribbon Display Options button and then click *Show Tabs* at the drop-down list.

14. Click the Ribbon Display Options button and then click *Show Tabs and Commands* at the drop-down list.

15. Hide the white spaces at the tops and bottoms of pages by positioning the mouse pointer at the top edge of the page until the pointer turns into the Hide White Space icon and then double-clicking the left mouse button.

16. Scroll through the document and notice the appearance of pages.

17. Redisplay the white spaces at the tops and bottoms of pages by positioning the mouse pointer on any thin gray line separating pages until the pointer turns into the Show White Space icon and then double-clicking the left mouse button.

18. Close **6-WebReport**.

Activity 2 Manage Multiple Documents 7 Parts

You will arrange, maximize, restore, and minimize windows; move selected text between split windows; compare formatting of documents side by side; and print specific text, pages, and multiple copies.

Tutorial

Working with Windows

💡 *Hint* Press Ctrl + F6 to switch between open documents.

Working with Windows

Multiple documents can be opened in Word, the insertion point can be moved between documents, and information can be moved or copied from one document and pasted into another. When a new document is opened, it displays on top of any previously opened document. With multiple documents open, the window containing each document can be resized to see all or a portion of it on the screen.

Hint Press Ctrl + W or Ctrl + F4 to close the active document window.

 Switch Windows

A Word button appears on the taskbar when a document is open. If more than one document is open, another button will appear behind the first in a cascading manner. To see all documents that are currently open in Word, hover the mouse pointer over the Word button. A thumbnail of each document will appear. To make a change to a document, click the thumbnail that represents the document.

Another method for determining what documents are open is to click the View tab and then click the Switch Windows button in the Window group. The document name in the list with the check mark in front of it is the active document. The active document contains the insertion point. To make a different document active, click the document name. To switch to another document using the keyboard, type the number shown in front of the document.

Arranging Windows

Quick Steps

Arrange Windows
1. Open documents.
2. Click View tab.
3. Click Arrange All button.

 Arrange All

If several documents are open, they can be arranged so a portion of each appears. The portion that appears includes the title (if present) and the opening paragraph of each document. To arrange a group of open documents, click the View tab and then click the Arrange All button in the Window group.

Maximizing, Restoring, and Minimizing Documents

 Hint The keyboard shortcut to maximize a document is Ctrl + F10.

Maximize

Minimize

Restore

Use the Maximize and Minimize buttons in the upper right corner of the active document to change the size of a document window. The two buttons are at the left of the Close button. (The Close button is in the upper right corner of the screen and contains an X.)

If all the open documents are arranged on the screen, clicking the Maximize button in the active document causes that document to expand to fill the screen. Any other open windows will be hidden behind it. In addition, the Maximize button changes to the Restore button. To return the active document back to its original size, click the Restore button. Click the Minimize button in the active document and the document is reduced to a button on the taskbar. To maximize a document that has been minimized, hover the mouse pointer over the taskbar button and click the thumbnail of the document.

Activity 2a Arranging, Maximizing, Restoring, and Minimizing Windows   Part 1 of 7

Note: If you are using Word on a network system that contains a virus checker, you may not be able to open multiple documents at once. Continue by opening each document individually.

1. Open the following documents: **AptLease**, **CompSoftware**, **IntelProp**, and **NSS**. (To open all of the documents at one time, display the Open dialog box, hold down the Ctrl key, click each document name, release the Ctrl key, and then click the Open button.)
2. Arrange the windows by clicking the View tab and then clicking the Arrange All button in the Window group.
3. Make **AptLease** the active document by clicking the Switch Windows button in the Window group on the View tab of the document at the top of your screen and then clicking *AptLease* at the drop-down list.
4. Close **AptLease**.
5. Make **IntelProp** active and then close it.

---

6. Make **CompSoftware** active and minimize it by clicking the Minimize button in the upper right corner of the active window.
7. Maximize **NSS** by clicking the Maximize button immediately left of the Close button.
8. Close **NSS**.
9. Restore **CompSoftware** by clicking the button on the taskbar that represents the document.
10. Maximize **CompSoftware**.

Splitting a Window

A window can be split into two panes so that two different parts of a document can be seen at once. For example, show an outline for a report in one pane and the part of the report to be edited in the other pane. The original window is split into two panes that extend horizontally across the screen.

Split a window by clicking the View tab and then clicking the Split button in the Window group. This splits the window in two with a split bar and another horizontal ruler. The location of the split bar can be changed by positioning the mouse pointer on the split bar until the pointer displays as an up-and-down-pointing arrow with two small lines in the middle, holding down the left mouse button, dragging to the new location, and then releasing the mouse button.

When a window is split, the insertion point is positioned in the bottom pane. To move the insertion point to the other pane with the mouse, position the I-beam pointer in the other pane and then click the left mouse button. To remove the split bar from the document, click the View tab and then click the Remove Split button in the Window group. The split bar can also be double-clicked or dragged to the top or bottom of the screen.

Activity 2b **Moving Selected Text between Split Windows**   Part 2 of 7

1. With **CompSoftware** open, save the document and name it **6-CompSoftware**.
2. Click the View tab and then click the Split button in the Window group.
3. Move the first section below the second section by completing the following steps:

   a. Click in the top pane and then click the Home tab.
   b. Select the section *SECTION 1: PERSONAL-USE SOFTWARE* from the title to right above *SECTION 2: GRAPHICS AND MULTIMEDIA SOFTWARE*.
   c. Click the Cut button in the Clipboard group on the Home tab.
   d. Click in the bottom pane and then move the insertion point to the end of the document.
   e. Click the Paste button in the Clipboard group on the Home tab.
   f. Reverse the numbers in the two titles to *SECTION 1: GRAPHICS AND MULTIMEDIA SOFTWARE* and *SECTION 2: PERSONAL-USE SOFTWARE*.

4. Remove the split from the window by clicking the View tab and then clicking the Remove Split button in the Window group.
5. Press Ctrl + Home to move the insertion point to the beginning of the document.
6. Save **6-CompSoftware**.

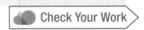

Viewing Documents Side by Side

 View Side by Side

 Synchronous Scrolling

Quick Steps

View Documents Side by Side
1. Open two documents.
2. Click View tab.
3. Click View Side by Side button.

The contents of two documents can be compared on screen by opening both documents, clicking the View tab, and then clicking the View Side by Side button in the Window group. The documents are arranged on the screen side by side, as shown in Figure 6.5. By default, synchronous scrolling is active. With this feature active, scrolling in one document causes the same scrolling in the other document. This feature is useful for comparing the text, formatting, or other features between documents. To scroll in one document and not the other, click the Synchronous Scrolling button in the Window group to turn it off.

Figure 6.5 Viewing Documents Side by Side

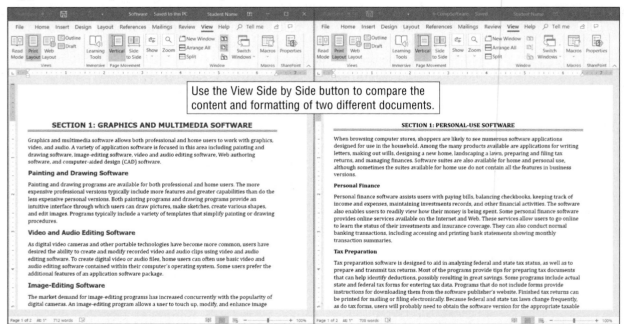

Use the View Side by Side button to compare the content and formatting of two different documents.

Activity 2c Viewing Documents Side by Side

1. With **6-CompSoftware** open, open **Software**.
2. Click the View tab and then click the View Side by Side button in the Window group.
3. Scroll through both documents simultaneously. Notice the difference between the two documents. (The titles and headings are set in different fonts and colors.) Format the title and headings in **6-CompSoftware** so they match the formatting in **Software**. *Hint: Use the Format Painter button to copy the formatting.*
4. Turn off synchronous scrolling by clicking the Synchronous Scrolling button in the Window group on the View tab.
5. Scroll through the document and notice that no scrolling occurs in the other document.
6. Make **Software** the active document and then close it.
7. Save **6-CompSoftware**.

Opening a New Window

A second copy of a document can be opened in a new window so that two copies of the same document may be viewed side by side. To do this, first open a document and then click the New Window button in the Window group on the View tab. When a new window is opened, the document name in the Title bar is followed by - *2*. The document name in the original window is followed by - *1*. Any change made to the document in one window is reflected in the document in the other window, as both windows display the exact same file.

Activity 2d Opening a New Window

1. With **6-CompSoftware** open, open a second copy of the document in a new window by clicking the New Window button in the Window group on the View tab. (Notice that the document name in the Title bar displays followed by - *2*.)
2. Click the View tab and then click the View Side by Side button in the Window group.
3. Click the Window button on the View tab and then click the Synchronous Scrolling button to turn off synchronous scrolling.
4. Click in the **6-CompSoftware - 2** window to make the document active. Look at the first paragraph of text and notice the order in which the different types of software are listed in the last sentence of the paragraph (painting and drawing software, image-editing software, video and audio editing software, and computer-aided design [CAD] software).
5. Click in the **6-CompSoftware - 1** window and then cut and paste the headings and text so each type of software is described in the order it was listed in the first paragraph.
6. Click the Save button on the Quick Access Toolbar.
7. Close the second copy of the document by clicking the Word button on the taskbar and then clicking the Close button in the upper right corner of the **6-CompSoftware - 2** thumbnail (above the Word button on the taskbar).

Inserting a File into a Document

The contents of one document can be inserted into another using the Object button in the Text group on the Insert tab. Click the Object button arrow and then click *Text from File* and the Insert File dialog box displays. This dialog box contains similar features as the Open dialog box. Navigate to the specific folder and then double-click the document to be inserted in the open document.

 Object

Activity 2e Inserting a File

1. With **6-CompSoftware** open, move the insertion point to the end of the document.
2. Insert a file into the open document by completing the following steps:
   a. Click the Insert tab.
   b. Click the Object button arrow in the Text group and then click *Text from File* at the drop-down list.
   c. At the Insert File dialog box, navigate to your WL1C6 folder and then double-click *EduComp*.
3. Save **6-CompSoftware**.

 Check Your Work

Previewing and Printing

Use options at the Print backstage area, shown in Figure 6.6, to specify what is to be printed and to preview pages before printing them. To display the Print backstage area, click the File tab and then click the *Print* option. The Quick Access Toolbar can be customized to include the Print Preview and Print button that when clicked will display the Print backstage area. Insert the button on the Quick Access Toolbar by clicking the Customize Quick Access Toolbar button at the right side of the toolbar and then clicking *Print Preview and Print* at the drop-down list.

Hint The Print backstage area can also be displayed with the keyboard shortcut Ctrl + P.

Previewing Pages

At the Print backstage area, a preview of the current page is shown (see Figure 6.6). Click the Next Page button to view the next page in the document preview, and click the Previous Page button to display the previous page. Use the Zoom slider bar to increase or decrease the size of the page and click the Zoom to Page button to fit the entire page in the viewing area.

 Zoom to Page

Figure 6.6 Print Backstage Area

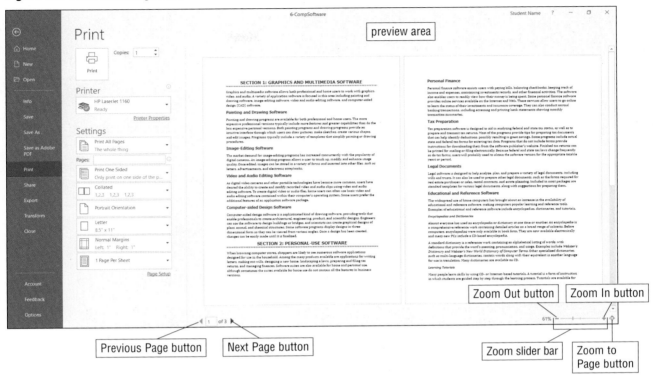

Activity 2f Previewing Pages

1. With **6-CompSoftware** open, press Ctrl + Home to move the insertion point to the beginning of the document.
2. Insert the Print Preview and Print button on the Quick Access Toolbar by clicking the Customize Quick Access Toolbar button and then clicking *Print Preview and Print* at the drop-down list.
3. Preview the document by clicking the Print Preview and Print button on the Quick Access Toolbar.
4. Click the Zoom In button (plus [+] symbol) at the right of the Zoom slider bar two times. (This increases the size of the preview page.)
5. At the Print backstage area, click the Next Page button below and to the left of the preview page. (This displays page 2 in the preview area.)
6. Click the Zoom Out button (minus [–] symbol) at the left of the Zoom slider bar until two pages of the document display in the preview area.

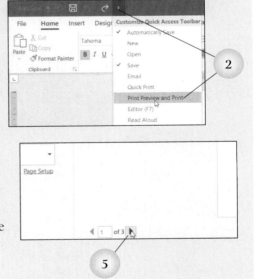

7. Change the zoom at the Zoom dialog box by completing the following steps:
   a. Click the percentage number at the left of the Zoom slider bar.
   b. At the Zoom dialog box, click the *Many pages* option in the *Zoom to* section.
   c. Click OK to close the dialog box. (Notice that all the pages in the document appear as thumbnails in the preview area.)
8. Click the Zoom to Page button at the right of the Zoom slider bar. (This returns the page to the default size.)
9. Click the Back button to return to the document.
10. Remove the Print Preview and Print button from the Quick Access Toolbar by clicking the Customize Quick Access Toolbar button and then clicking *Print Preview and Print* at the drop-down list.

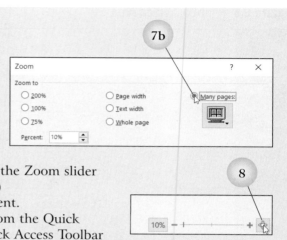

Printing Specific Text and Pages

💡 **Hint** Save a document before printing it.

Control what prints in a document with options at the Print backstage area. Click the first gallery in the *Settings* category and a drop-down list displays with options for printing. All the pages in the document may be printed; or, print only selected text, the current page, or a custom range of pages.

Print a portion of a document by selecting the text and then choosing the *Print Selection* option at the Print backstage area. With this option, only the selected text prints. (If no text is selected, this option is dimmed.) Click the *Print Current Page* option to print only the page on which the insertion point is located. Use the *Custom Print* option to identify a specific page, multiple pages, or a range of pages to print. To print specific pages, use a comma (,) to indicate *and* and use a hyphen (-) to indicate *through*. For example, to print pages 2 and 5, type 2,5 in the *Pages* text box and to print pages 6 through 10, type 6-10.

With the other galleries available in the *Settings* category of the Print backstage area, specify whether to print on one or both sides of the page, change the page orientation (portrait or landscape), specify how the pages are collated, choose a paper size, and specify document margins. The last gallery contains options for printing 1, 2, 4, 6, 8, or 16 pages of a multiple-page document on one sheet of paper. This gallery also contains the *Scale to Paper Size* option. Click this option and then use the side menu to choose the paper size to scale the document.

To print more than one copy of a document, use the *Copies* measurement box to the right of the Print button. If several copies of a multiple-page document are printed, Word collates the pages as they print so that pages appear in sequential order in each copy. For example, if two copies of a three-page document are printed, pages 1, 2, and 3 are grouped together as one copy, and then the pages print a second time. Collated copies take slightly longer to print. If copies do not need to be collated, reduce printing time by clicking the *Collated* gallery in the Print backstage area and then clicking the *Uncollated* option.

To send a document directly to the printer without displaying the Print backstage area, consider adding the Quick Print button to the Quick Access Toolbar. To do this, click the Customize Quick Access Toolbar button at the right side of the toolbar and then click *Quick Print* at the drop-down gallery. Click the Quick Print button and all the pages of the active document will print.

Activity 2g   Printing Specific Text and Pages

1. With **6-CompSoftware** open, print selected text by completing the following steps:
   a. Select the heading *Painting and Drawing Software* and the paragraph of text that follows it.
   b. Click the File tab and then click the *Print* option.
   c. At the Print backstage area, click the first gallery in the *Settings* category (displays with *Print All Pages*) and then click *Print Selection* at the drop-down list.
   d. Click the Print button.
2. Change the margins and page orientation and then print only the first page by completing the following steps:
   a. Press Ctrl + Home to move the insertion point to the beginning of the document.
   b. Click the File tab and then click the *Print* option.
   c. At the Print backstage area, click the fourth gallery (displays with *Portrait Orientation*) in the *Settings* category and then click *Landscape Orientation* at the drop-down list.
   d. Click the sixth gallery (displays with *Normal Margins*) in the *Settings* category and then click *Narrow* at the drop-down list.
   e. Click the first gallery (displays with *Print All Pages*) in the *Settings* category and then click *Print Current Page* at the drop-down list.
   f. Click the Print button. (The first page of the document prints in landscape orientation with 0.5-inch margins.)

3. Print all the pages as thumbnails on one page by completing the following steps:
   a. Click the File tab and then click the *Print* option.
   b. At the Print backstage area, click the bottom gallery (displays with *1 Page Per Sheet*) in the *Settings* category and then click *4 Pages Per Sheet* at the drop-down list.
   c. Click the first gallery (displays with *Print Current Page*) in the *Settings* category and then click *Print All Pages* at the drop-down list.
   d. Click the Print button.
4. Select the entire document, change the line spacing to 1.5 lines, and then deselect the text.
5. Print two copies of specific pages by completing the following steps:
   a. Click the File tab and then click the *Print* option.
   b. Click the fourth gallery (displays with *Landscape Orientation*) at the *Settings* category and then click *Portrait Orientation* in the drop-down list.
   c. Click in the *Pages* text box below the first gallery in the *Settings* category and then type 1,3.
   d. Click the *Copies* measurement box up arrow (located to the right of the Print button) to display *2*.
   e. Click the third gallery (displays with *Collated*) in the *Settings* category and then click *Uncollated* at the drop-down list.
   f. Click the bottom gallery (displays with *4 Pages Per Sheet*) in the *Settings* category and then click *1 Page Per Sheet* at the drop-down list.
   g. Click the Print button. (The first page of the document will print two times and then the third page will print two times.)
6. Save and then close **6-CompSoftware**.

Check Your Work

Tutorial

Preparing an
Envelope

 Envelopes

Quick Steps

Prepare Envelope
1. Click Mailings tab.
2. Click Envelopes
   button.
3. Type delivery
   address.
4. Click in *Return
   address* text box.
5. Type return address.
6. Click Add to
   Document button or
   Print button.

Preparing and Printing Envelopes

Word automates the creation of envelopes with options at the Envelopes and Labels dialog box with the Envelopes tab selected, as shown in Figure 6.7. Display this dialog box by clicking the Mailings tab and then clicking the Envelopes button in the Create group. At the dialog box, type the delivery address in the *Delivery address* text box and the return address in the *Return address* text box. Print the envelope immediately by clicking the Print button, or prepare the envelope to be printed along with a letter or other document by clicking the Add to document button.

When a return address is entered in the dialog box, Word will display the question *Do you want to save the new return address as the default return address?* At this question, click Yes to save the current return address for future envelopes or click No if the return address should not be used as the default. To omit a return address, insert a check mark in the *Omit* check box.

The Envelopes and Labels dialog box contains a *Preview* sample box and a *Feed* sample box. The *Preview* sample box shows how the envelope will appear when printed and the *Feed* sample box shows how the envelope should be fed into the printer.

Figure 6.7 Envelopes and Labels Dialog Box with the Envelopes Tab Selected

When addressing envelopes, consider following general guidelines issued by the United States Postal Service (USPS). The USPS guidelines suggest using all capital letters with no commas or periods for return and delivery addresses. Figure 6.8 shows envelope addresses that follow the USPS guidelines. Use abbreviations for street suffixes (such as *ST* for *Street* and *AVE* for *Avenue*). For a complete list of address abbreviations, visit the USPS.com website and then search for *Official USPS Abbreviations*.

Activity 3a Printing an Envelope

Part 1 of 2

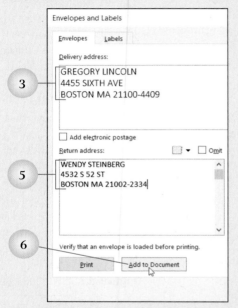

1. At a blank document, create an envelope document with the delivery address and return address shown in Figure 6.8. Begin by clicking the Mailings tab.
2. Click the Envelopes button in the Create group.
3. At the Envelopes and Labels dialog box with the Envelopes tab selected, type the delivery address shown in Figure 6.8 (the one containing the name *GREGORY LINCOLN*). (Press the Enter key to end each line in the name and address.)
4. Click in the *Return address* text box. (If any text displays in the *Return address* text box, select and then delete it.)
5. Type the return address shown in Figure 6.8 (the one containing the name *WENDY STEINBERG*). (Press the Enter key to end each line in the name and address.)
6. Click the Add to Document button.
7. At the message *Do you want to save the new return address as the default return address?*, click No.
8. Save the document and name it **6-Env**.
9. Print and then close **6-Env**. *Note: Manual feed of the envelope may be required. Please check with your instructor.*

Check Your Work

Figure 6.8 Activity 3a

WENDY STEINBERG
4532 S 52 ST
BOSTON MA 21002-2334

GREGORY LINCOLN
4455 SIXTH AVE
BOSTON MA 21100-4409

After typing a letter in Word, prepare an envelope to mail the letter by clicking the Envelopes button. Word automatically inserts the first address in the document in the *Delivery address* text box. (Note: Each line of the address must end with a press of the Enter key, and not Shift + Enter, for Word to recognize it.)

Alternately, select the delivery address in the letter document and then click the Envelopes button. When using this method, the address will be formatted exactly as it appears in the letter and may not conform to the USPS guidelines; however, these guidelines are only suggestions, not requirements.

Activity 3b Creating an Envelope in an Existing Document

Part 2 of 2

1. Open **LAProgram**.
2. Click the Mailings tab.
3. Click the Envelopes button in the Create group.
4. At the Envelopes and Labels dialog box (with the Envelopes tab selected), make sure the delivery address appears properly in the *Delivery address* text box.
5. If any text appears in the *Return address* text box, insert a check mark in the *Omit* check box (located to the right of the *Return address* option). (This tells Word not to print the return address on the envelope.)
6. Click the Print button.
7. Close **LAProgram** without saving the changes.

> Check Your Work

Activity 4 Prepare and Print Labels

2 Parts

You will create mailing labels containing different names and addresses, labels with the same name and address, and labels with an image.

Preparing and Printing Labels

Use Word's Labels feature to print text on mailing labels, file folder labels, and other types of labels. Word formats text for a variety of brands and sizes of labels that can be purchased at most office supply stores. Use the Labels feature to create a sheet of mailing labels with a different name and address on each label or with the same name and address or image on each label.

Creating Mailing Labels with Different Names and Addresses

To create a sheet of mailing labels with a different name and address on each label, click the Labels button in the Create group on the Mailings tab. At the Envelopes and Labels dialog box with the Labels tab selected, as shown in Figure 6.9, leave the *Address* text box empty and then click the New Document button to insert the labels in a new document. The insertion point is positioned in the first label. Type the name and address in the label and then press the Tab key one or two times (depending on the label) to move the insertion point to the next label. Pressing Shift + Tab will move the insertion point to the preceding label.

Changing Label Options

Click the Options button at the Envelopes and Labels dialog box with the Labels tab selected and the Label Options dialog box displays, as shown in Figure 6.10. At the Label Options dialog box, choose the type of printer, the type and brand of label, and the product number. This dialog box also provides information about the selected label, such as type, height, width, and paper size. When a label is selected, Word automatically determines the label margins. To customize these default settings, click the Details button at the Label Options dialog box.

Figure 6.9 Envelopes and Labels Dialog Box with the Labels Tab Selected

Type the label name and address in this text box.

Click the Print button to send the label directly to the printer.

Click the New Document button to insert the label in a new document.

Click the Options button to display the Label Options dialog box.

Figure 6.10 Label Options Dialog Box

Click the *Label vendors* option box arrow to display a list of available label vendors.

Choose the label product number from this list box.

Activity 4a Creating Mailing Labels with Different Names and Addresses

Part 1 of 2

1. At a blank document, click the Mailings tab.
2. Click the Labels button in the Create group.
3. At the Envelopes and Labels dialog box with the Labels tab selected, click the Options button.
4. At the Label Options dialog box, click the *Label vendors* option box arrow and then click *Avery US Letter* at the drop-down list. (You may need to scroll down the list to see this option.)
5. Scroll down the *Product number* list box and then click *5160 Address Labels*.
6. Click OK or press the Enter key.
7. At the Envelopes and Labels dialog box, click the New Document button.
8. At the document screen, type the first name and address shown in Figure 6.11 in the first label.
9. Press the Tab key two times to move the insertion point to the next label and then type the second name and address shown in Figure 6.11.
10. Continue in this manner until all the names and addresses shown in Figure 6.11 have been typed. (After typing the third name and address, you only need to press the Tab key once to move the insertion point to the first label in the second row.)
11. Save the document and name it **6-Labels**.
12. Print and then close **6-Labels**.
13. Close the blank document without saving changes.

 Check Your Work

Figure 6.11 Activity 4a

DAVID LOWRY 12033 S 152 ST HOUSTON TX 77340	MARCELLA SANTOS 394 APPLE BLOSSOM DR FRIENDSWOOD TX 77533	KEVIN DORSEY 26302 PRAIRIE DR HOUSTON TX 77316
AL AND DONNA SASAKI 1392 PIONEER DR BAYTOWN TX 77903	JACKIE RHYNER 29039 107 AVE E HOUSTON TX 77302	MARK AND TINA ELLIS 607 FORD AVE HOUSTON TX 77307

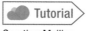 **Tutorial**

Creating Mailing
Labels with the
Same Name and
Address and an
Image

Creating Mailing Labels with the Same Name and Address

To create labels with the same name and address on each label, open a document containing the name and address, click the Mailings tab, and then click the Labels button. At the Envelopes and Labels dialog box, make sure the desired label vendor and product number are selected and then click the New Document button. Another method for creating labels with the same name and address is to display the Envelopes and Labels dialog box with the Labels tab selected, type the name and address in the *Address* text box, and then click the New Document button.

Creating Mailing Labels with an Image

Labels can be created with a graphic image, such as a company's logo and address and/or slogan. To create labels with an image, insert the image in a document, select the image, click the Mailings tab. and then click the Labels button. At the Envelopes and Labels dialog box, make sure the correct vendor and product number are selected and then click the New Document button.

Activity 4b **Creating Mailing Labels with the Same Name and Address and an Image**   **Part 2 of 2**

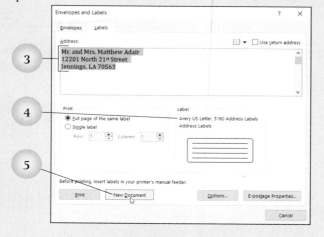

1. Open **LAProgram** and create mailing labels with the delivery address. Begin by clicking the Mailings tab.
2. Click the Labels button in the Create group.
3. At the Envelopes and Labels dialog box with the Labels tab selected, make sure the delivery address is shown properly in the *Address* text box, as shown at the right.
4. Make sure *Avery US Letter, 5160 Address Labels* displays in the *Label* section; if not, refer to Steps 3 through 6 of Activity 4a to select the label type.
5. Click the New Document button.
6. Save the mailing label document and name it **6-LAProgram**.
7. Print and then close **6-LAProgram**.
8. Close **LAProgram**.
9. At a blank document, insert an image by completing the following steps:
   a. Click the Insert tab and then click the Pictures button in the Illustrations group.
   b. At the Insert Picture dialog box, make sure your WL1C6 folder is active and then double-click the ***BGCLabels*** image file.
10. With the image selected in the document, click the Mailings tab and then click the Labels button.
11. At the Envelopes and Labels dialog box, make sure *Avery US Letter, 5160 Address Labels* displays in the *Label* section and then click the New Document button.
12. Save the document and name it **6-BGCLabels**.
13. Print and then close **6-BGCLabels**.
14. Close the document containing the image without saving changes.

 Check Your Work

Activity 5 **Create a Business Letter Using a Template**   **1 Part**

You will use a letter template provided by Word to create a business letter.

Tutorial

Creating a
Document Using a
Template

Creating a Document Using a Template

Word includes a number of document templates that are formatted for specific uses. Each Word document is based on a template document and the Normal template is the default. Choose from other available Word templates to create a variety of documents with special formatting, such as letters, calendars, and certificates.

View available templates by clicking the File tab and then clicking the *New* option. Thumbnails of various templates display in the New backstage area, as shown in Figure 6.12. Open one of the templates by double-clicking it. This opens a new document based on the template.

In addition to the templates that are shown at the New backstage area, templates can be downloaded from the internet. To do this, click in the search text box, type the search text or category, and then press the Enter key. Templates that match the search text or category display in the New backstage area. Click the template and then click the Create button or double-click the template. This downloads the template and opens a document based on it. Placeholders or content controls may appear in the document as suggested locations for personalized text. Click the placeholder or content control and then type text to personalize the document.

If a template is used on a regular basis, consider pinning it to the New backstage area. To do this, search for the template, hover the mouse pointer over it, and then click the left-pointing push pin (Pin to list) to the right of the template name. To unpin a template, click the down-pointing push pin (Unpin from list).

Quick Steps

Create Document Using Template
1. Click File tab.
2. Click *New* option.
3. Click template.
OR
1. Click File tab.
2. Click *New* option.
3. Click in search text box.
4. Type search text.
5. Press Enter.
6. Double-click template.

Figure 6.12 New Backstage Area

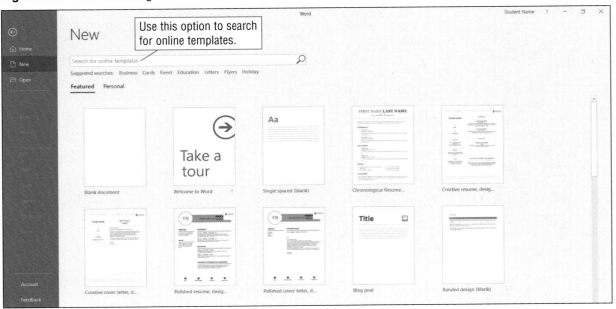

1. Click the File tab and then click the *New* option.
2. At the New backstage area, click in the search text box, type letter, and then press the Enter key.
3. When templates display that match *letter*, notice the *Category* list box at the right side of the New backstage area.
4. Click the *Business* option in the *Category* list box. (This displays only business letter templates.)
5. Search for a specific letter template by typing business letter simple design in the search text box and then pressing the Enter key.
6. Double-click the *Business letter (simple design)* template. (If this template is not available, open **BusinessLetter** from your WL1C6 folder.)

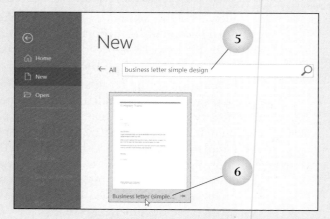

7. When the business letter document displays on the screen, click the *Company Name* content control and then type Sorenson Funds. (Clicking anywhere in the *Company Name* content control selects the entire control.)
8. Click the *Date* content control and then type the current date.
9. Click the *Street Address City, ST ZIP Code* content control. Type Ms. Jennifer Gonzalez, press the Enter key, type 12990 Boyd Street, press the Enter key, and then type Baltimore, MD 20375.
10. Click the *Recipient* content control and then type Ms. Gonzalez.
11. Insert a file in the document by completing the following steps:
    a. Click in the three paragraphs of text in the body of the letter and then press the Delete key.
    b. Click the Insert tab.
    c. Click the Object button arrow in the Text group and then click *Text from File* at the drop-down list.
    d. At the Insert File dialog box, navigate to your WL1C6 folder and then double-click **SFunds**.
    e. Press the Backspace key to delete a blank line.
12. Click the *Your Name* content control, type your first and last names, press the Enter key, and then type Financial Consultant.
13. Remove the footer by clicking the Insert tab, clicking the Footer button, and then clicking *Remove Footer* at the drop-down list.
14. Save the document and name it **6-SFunds**.
15. Print and then close **6-SFunds**.

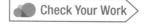

You will save an apartment lease agreement document in different file formats, including Word 97-2003 and plain text. You will also save a company document as a PDF file and then edit the file in Word.

Saving in a
Different Format

Quick Steps

Save in Different Format at Save As Dialog Box
1. Press F12 to display Save As dialog box.
2. Type document name.
3. Click *Save as type* option box.
4. Click format.
5. Click Save button.

Saving in a Different Format

When a document is saved, it is saved as a Word document with the file extension *.docx*. If the document is to be shared with someone who is using a different word processing program or a different version of Word, consider saving the document in another format. Save a document in a different file format by clicking the File tab and then clicking the *Export* option. At the Export backstage area, click the *Change File Type* option. Available file types display as shown in Figure 6.13. Save the Word document with the default file format, in a previous version of Word, in the OpenDocument Text format, or as a template. The OpenDocument Text format is an XML-based file format free from licensing and restrictions. It was designed to make word processing, spreadsheet, and presentation files easier to share across applications.

If a document is being sent to a user who does not have access to Microsoft Word, consider saving the document in plain text or rich text file format. Use the *Plain Text* option to save the document with all the formatting stripped, which is good for universal file exchange. Use the *Rich Text Format* option to save the document and preserve most of the formatting, including bold, italic, underline, bullets, and fonts. With the *Single File Web Page* option, a document can be saved as a single-page web document. Double-click the *Save as Another File Type* option and the Save As dialog box opens. Use the *Save as type* option box to specify the file format.

In addition to displaying the Save As dialog box through the Export backstage area, the dialog box can be displayed by clicking the File tab, clicking the *Save As* option, and then clicking the *Browse* option. (Pressing the F12 function key will also display the Save As dialog box.) Click the *Save as type* option box at the Save As dialog box and a drop-down list displays containing all the available file formats for saving a document. Click the specific format and then click the Save button.

Figure 6.13 Export Backstage Area with the *Change File Type* Option Selected

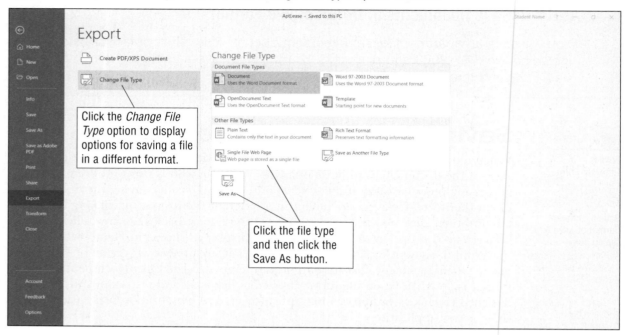

Activity 6a Saving in Different File Formats

Part 1 of 2

1. Open **AptLease** and then save it in Word 97-2003 format by completing the following steps:
   a. Click the File tab and then click the *Export* option.
   b. At the Export backstage area, click the *Change File Type* option.
   c. Click the *Word 97-2003 Document* option in the *Document File Types* section.
   d. Click the Save As button.

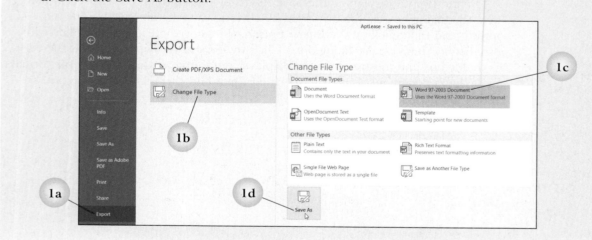

e. At the Save As dialog box with the *Save as type* option changed to *Word 97-2003 Document*, type 6-AptLease-Word97-2003 in the *File name* text box and then press the Enter key.

1e

2. At the document, notice *Compatibility Mode* after the document name.
3. Click the Design tab and notice that the Themes, Colors, and Fonts buttons are dimmed. (This is because the themes features were not available in Word 97 through 2003.)
4. Close **6-AptLease-Word97-2003**.
5. Open **AptLease**.
6. Save the document in plain text format at the Save As dialog box by completing the following steps:

6c

6d

   a. Press the F12 function key to display the Save As dialog box.
   b. At the Save As dialog box, type 6-AptLease-PlainTxt in the *File name* text box.
   c. Click the *Save as type* option box.
   d. Click *Plain Text* at the drop-down list.
   e. Click the Save button.
   f. At the File Conversion dialog box, click OK.
7. Close **6-AptLease-PlainTxt**.
8. Display the Open dialog box and, if necessary, display all the files. To do this, click the file type button at the right of the *File name* text box and then click *All Files* at the drop-down list.

8

9. Double-click **6-AptLease-PlainTxt**. At the File Conversion dialog box, click OK. (Notice that the formatting has been removed from the document.)
10. Close **6-AptLease-PlainTxt**.

> Check Your Work

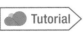

> Tutorial

Saving and Opening a Document as a PDF File

Quick Steps

Save in PDF/XPS Format
1. Click File tab.
2. Click *Export* option.
3. Click Create PDF/XPS button.
4. At Publish as PDF or XPS dialog box, specify PDF or XPS format.
5. Click Publish button.

A Word document can be saved as a PDF file or in the XPS file format. PDF stands for *portable document format* and is a file format that preserves fonts, formatting, and images in a printer-friendly version that looks the same on most computers. A person who receives a Word file saved as a PDF file does not need to have the Word application on his or her computer to open, read, and print the file. Exchanging PDF files is a popular method for collaborating, since this file type has cross-platform compatibility, allowing users to open PDF files on both Macintosh and Windows-based computers, as well as different brands of tablets and smartphones. The XML paper specification (XPS) format, which was developed by Microsoft, is a fixed-layout format with all the formatting preserved (similar to PDF).

To save a document as a PDF file or in XPS format, click the File tab, click the *Export* option, and then click the Create PDF/XPS button. This displays the Publish as PDF or XPS dialog box with the *PDF* option selected in the *Save as type* option box. To save the document in XPS format, click the *Save as type* option box and then click *XPS Document* at the drop-down list. At the Save As dialog box, type a name in the *File name* text box and then click the Publish button.

A PDF file will open in Adobe Acrobat Reader, Microsoft Edge, and Word. (A PDF file may also open in other available web browsers such as Google Chrome.) An XPS file will open in Internet Explorer and XPS Viewer. One method for opening a PDF or XPS file is to open File Explorer, navigate to the folder containing the file, right-click the file, and then point to *Open with*. This displays a side menu with the programs that can be used to open the file. A PDF file can be opened and edited in Word but an XPS file cannot.

Activity 6b Saving as a PDF File and Editing a PDF File in Word
Part 2 of 2

1. Open **NSS** and then save the document as a PDF file by completing the following steps:
   a. Click the File tab and then click the *Export* option.
   b. At the Export backstage area, click the Create PDF/XPS button.
   c. At the Publish as PDF or XPS dialog box, make sure that *PDF* is selected in the *Save as type* option box and that the *Open file after publishing* check box contains a check mark. After confirming both selections, click the Publish button.

2. Scroll through the document in Adobe Acrobat Reader and then close Adobe Acrobat Reader by clicking the Close button in the upper right corner of the window.
3. Close **NSS**.
4. In Word, open the **NSS** PDF file you saved to your WL1C6 folder. At the message telling you that Word will convert the file to an editable Word document, click OK.
5. Notice that the formatting of the text is slightly different from the original formatting and that the graphic has been moved to the second page. Edit the file by completing the following steps:
   a. Click the Design tab and then click the *Lines (Distinctive)* style set.
   b. Delete the text *We are* in the text below the first heading and replace it with Northland Security Systems is.
6. Save the file with Save As and name it **6-NSS**. (The file will be saved as a Word file.)
7. Print and then close **6-NSS**.
8. Make a screen capture of the Open dialog box and then paste it in a Word document and print the document by completing the following steps:
   a. Display the Open dialog box.
   b. Press and hold down the Alt key, press the Print Screen button on your keyboard, and then release the Alt key.
   c. Close the Open dialog box and close the Open backstage area.
   d. Press Ctrl + N to open a blank document.
   e. Click the Paste button.
   f. Print the document by pressing Ctrl + P and then clicking the Print button.
9. Close the document without saving it

You will open a summons document, save it as a template, use it to create a summons, and then find and replace text within the document. You will also save the summons document as a template in your WL1C6 folder and then use File Explorer to locate the template and open a new document based on it.

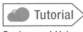

Tutorial

Saving and Using
a Template

Saving a Template

If the content of a document will be used in many other documents, consider saving the document as a template. Save a template by changing the *Save as type* option at the Save As dialog box to *Word Template*.

Saving a Template in the Custom Office Templates Folder

When the *Save as type* option is changed to a Word template, Word will save the document as a template in the Custom Office Templates folder. To use the template, click the New tab and then click the *Personal* option. This displays all custom templates. Clicking a template will open a new document based on that template.

Activity 7a **Saving and Opening a Document Based on a Template** **Part 1 of 2**

1. Open **Summons** and then save it as a template in the Custom Office Templates folder by completing the following steps:
   a. Press the F12 function key to display the Save As dialog box.
   b. At the Save As dialog box, click the *Save as type* option box and then click *Word Template* at the drop-down list. (When the *Save as type* option is changed to *Word Template*, Word automatically makes Custom Office Templates the active folder.)
   c. Select the name in the *File name* text box, type your last name followed by Summons, and then press the Enter key.

2. Close the summons template.

3. Open a document based on the summons template by completing the following steps:
   a. Click the File tab and then click the *New* option.
   b. At the New backstage area, click the *Personal* option.
   c. Click the summons template that is preceded by your last name.
4. With the summons document open, find and replace text as follows:
   a. Find *NAME1* and replace all occurrences with *AMY GARCIA*.
   b. Find *NAME2* and replace all occurrences with *NEIL CARLIN*.
   c. Find *NUMBER* and replace with *C-98002*.
5. Save the document in your WL1C6 folder and name it **6-SummonsGarcia**.
6. Print and then close **6-SummonsGarcia**.
7. Delete the summons template from the hard drive by completing the following steps:
   a. Press Ctrl + F12 to display the Open dialog box.
   b. At the Open dialog box, click the *Documents* folder in the Navigation pane.
   c. Double-click the **Custom Office Templates** folder in the Content pane.
   d. Click the summons template that begins with your last name.
   e. Click the Organize button and then click *Delete* at the drop-down list.

8. Close the Open dialog box.

 Check Your Work

Opening a Template Using File Explorer

In Word, opening a document based on a template is accomplished through the New backstage area with the *Personal* option selected. If a template is saved in a location other than the Custom Office Templates folder, File Explorer can be used to open a document based on the template. To do this, click the File Explorer icon on the taskbar, navigate to the folder containing the template, and then double-click the template. This will open a new document based on the template.

1. Open **Summons** and then save it as a template in your WL1C6 folder by completing the following steps:
   a. Click the File tab and then click the *Export* option.
   b. At the Export backstage area, click the *Change File Type* option.
   c. Click the *Template* option in the *Document File Types* section.
   d. Click the Save As button.

   e. At the Save As dialog box with *Word Template* in the *Save as type* option box, type 6-SummonsTemplate in the *File name* text box.
   f. Navigate to your WL1C6 folder and then click the Save button.
2. Close the summons template.
3. Open a document based on the summons template using File Explorer by completing the following steps:
   a. Click the File Explorer icon on the taskbar. (The taskbar displays along the bottom of the screen.)
   b. Navigate to your WL1C6 folder and then double-click *6-SummonsTemplate*.
4. With the summons document open, find and replace text as follows:
   a. Find *NAME1* and replace all occurrences with *CASEY NYE*.
   b. Find *NAME2* and replace all occurrences with *SANDRA IVERS*.
   c. Find *NUMBER* and replace with *C-99743*.
5. Save the document in your WL1C6 folder and name it **6-SummonsNye**.
6. Print and then close **6-SummonsNye**.

 Check Your Work

Chapter Summary

- Change the document view with buttons in the view area on the Status bar or with options in the Views group on the View tab.

- Print Layout is the default view but this can be changed to other views, such as Draft view, Web Layout view and Read Mode view.

- Draft view displays the document in a format for efficient editing and formatting. Change to Web Layout view to display a document as it would appear online. Read Mode view displays a document in a format for easy viewing and reading.

- The File, Tools, and View tabs display in Read Mode view. Click the File tab to display the Backstage area, the Tools tab to display a drop-down list of options for finding and searching for specific text in a document or the internet, and the View tab for changing column width and page layout, reading text in the document, and customizing reading.

- In addition to Read Mode view, options for reading a document are available on the Immersive Learning Tools tab. Display this tab by clicking the Learning Tools button in the Immersive group on the View tab. Use buttons on the Immersive Learning Tools tab to change column width, page color, focus, text spacing, and display syllable breaks in words. Click the Read Aloud button to hear a reading of the document and to control the reading with buttons on the playback toolbar.

- Use the Side to Side button in the Page Movement group on the View tab to change page movement in a document from the default of vertical to side to side, where two pages are shown at one time. On a screen without touch screen capabilities, scroll through the side to side pages using the horizontal scroll bar or the mouse wheel. Click the Vertical button on the View tab to return to the default page movement.

- Use the Zoom slider bar or buttons in the Zoom group on the View tab to change the display percentage.

- Use options at the Ribbon Display Options button drop-down list to specify if the Quick Access Toolbar, ribbon, and Status bar should be visible or hidden.

- Save space on the screen by hiding white space at the top and bottom of pages. Hide white space using the Hide White Space icon, which appears when the mouse pointer is positioned at the top or bottom edge of a page. Redisplay white space using the Show White Space icon, which appears when the mouse pointer is positioned on the thin gray line separating pages.

- Move among open documents by hovering the mouse pointer over the Word button on the taskbar and then clicking the thumbnail of the document or by clicking the View tab, clicking the Switch Windows button in the Window group, and then clicking the document name.

- View portions of all open documents by clicking the View tab and then clicking the Arrange All button in the Window group.

- Use the Minimize, Restore, and Maximize buttons in the upper right corner of the active window to reduce or increase the size of the window.

- Divide a window into two panes by clicking the View tab and then clicking the Split button in the Window group.

- View the contents of two open documents side by side by clicking the View tab and then clicking the View Side by Side button in the Window group.

- Open a new window containing the same document by clicking the View tab and then clicking the New Window button in the Window group.

- Insert a document into the open document by clicking the Insert tab, clicking the Object button arrow, and then clicking *Text from File* at the drop-down list. At the Insert File dialog box, double-click the document.

- Preview a document at the Print backstage area. Scroll through the pages in the document with the Next Page and the Previous Page buttons, which are below the preview page. Use the Zoom slider bar to increase or decrease the display size of the preview page.

- Use options at the Print backstage area to customize the print job by changing the page orientation, size, and margins; specify how many pages to print on one page; indicate the number of copies and whether to collate the pages; and specify the printer.

- Prepare and print an envelope at the Envelopes and Labels dialog box with the Envelopes tab selected.

- If the Envelopes and Labels dialog box is opened in a document containing a name and address (with each line ending with a press of the Enter key), that information is automatically inserted in the *Delivery address* text box in the dialog box.

- Use Word's labels feature to print text on mailing labels, file labels, and other types of labels. Create labels at the Envelopes and Labels dialog box with the Labels tab selected.

- Available templates are shown in the New backstage area. Double-click a template to open a document based on it. Search for templates online by typing the search text or category in the search text box and then pressing the Enter key.

- Click the *Change File Type* option at the Export backstage area and options display for saving the document in a different file format. Documents can also be saved in different file formats with the *Save as type* option box at the Save As dialog box.

- Save a document as a PDF file or in XPS format at the Publish as PDF or XPS dialog box. Display this dialog box by clicking the *Create PDF/XPS Document* option at the Export backstage area and then clicking the Create PDF/XPS button. A PDF file can be opened and edited in Word.

- Change the *Save as type* option at the Save As dialog box to *Word Template* and the Custom Office Templates folder becomes the active folder. A template saved in this folder is available at the New backstage area with the *Personal* option selected. Open a document based on a template at the New backstage area with the *Personal* option selected.

- If a template is saved in a location other than the Custom Office Templates folder, File Explorer can be used to open a document based on the template.

Commands Review

FEATURE	RIBBON TAB, GROUP/OPTION	BUTTON, OPTION	KEYBOARD SHORTCUT
arrange documents	View, Window		
Draft view	View, Views		
Envelopes and Labels dialog box with Envelopes tab selected	Mailings, Create		
Envelopes and Labels dialog box with Labels tab selected	Mailings, Create		
Export backstage area	File, *Export*		
Insert File dialog box	Insert, Text	, *Text from File*	
learning tools	View, Immersive		
maximize document			Ctrl + F10
minimize document			
New backstage area	File, *New*		
new window	View, Window		
Print backstage area	File, *Print*		Ctrl + P
Read Mode view	View, Views		
restore document to previous size			
side to side page movement	View, Page Movement		
split window	View, Window		Alt + Ctrl + S
switch windows	View, Window		
synchronous scrolling	View, Window		
vertical page movement	View, Page Movement		
view documents side by side	View, Window		
Web Layout view	View, Views		

Microsoft®

Word

Creating Tables

Performance Objectives

Upon successful completion of Chapter 7, you will be able to:

1   Create a table

2   Change the table design

3   Select cells in a table

4   Change the table layout

5   Convert text to a table and a table to text

6   Draw a table

7   Insert a Quick Table

8   Perform calculations on data in a table

9   Insert an Excel spreadsheet

Use the Tables feature in Word to organize data in tables with any number of columns and rows. The data can consist of text, values, and/or mathematical formulas. Presenting information in a table can show patterns and relationships and help with data comprehension.

This chapter will introduce the steps for creating a table in Word using the Table button drop-down grid and options at the Insert Table dialog box. You will also learn to draw a table in a document and apply formatting to tables using buttons and options on the Table Tools Design and Table Tools Layout tabs. Finally, you will learn to perform calculations in a table and practice inserting an Excel spreadsheet into a Word document to display text and numerical data.

 Data Files

Before beginning chapter work, copy the WL1C7 folder to your storage medium and then make WL1C7 the active folder.

The online course includes additional training and assessment resources.

Activity 1 Create and Format Tables with Company Information

8 Parts

You will create a table containing contact information and another containing information on employee benefit plans offered by a company. You will then change the design and layout of each table.

Tutorial

Creating a Table

Table

Quick Steps

Create Table
1. Click Insert tab.
2. Click Table button.
3. Point to create number of columns and rows.
4. Click mouse button.

OR
1. Click Insert tab.
2. Click Table button.
3. Click *Insert Table*.
4. Specify number of columns and rows.
5. Click OK.

Hint You can create a table within a table, creating a *nested* table.

Creating a Table

Tables are grids containing boxes of information called *cells*. Each cell is the intersection between a row and a column. A cell can contain text, characters, numbers, data, graphics, or formulas. Insert a table into a document by clicking the Insert tab, and then clicking the Table button in the Tables group. Move the mouse pointer down and to the right in the drop-down grid to select the number of rows and columns to include in the table. A table can also be created with options at the Insert Table dialog box. Display this dialog box by clicking the Table button in the Tables group on the Insert tab and then clicking *Insert Table* at the drop-down list.

Figure 7.1 shows an example of a table with four columns and four rows. Various parts of the table are identified in the figure. These include the gridlines, move table column markers, table move handle, and resize handle. In a table, nonprinting characters identify the ends of cells and the ends of rows. To view these characters, click the Show/Hide ¶ button in the Paragraph group on the Home tab. The end-of-cell marker appears inside each cell and the end-of-row marker appears at the end of each row of cells. These markers are identified in Figure 7.1.

Columns in a table are generally referred to using the letters A-Z while rows are numbered. When a table is inserted in a document, the insertion point is positioned in the first cell in the upper left corner of the table. This is referred to as cell A1, as it is located in column A, row 1. Cell B1 is to the right of A1, and cell A2 is directly below it.

When the insertion point is positioned in a cell in the table, move table column markers display on the horizontal ruler. These markers represent the ends of columns and can be moved to change the widths of columns. Figure 7.1 identifies move table column markers.

Figure 7.1 Table with Nonprinting Characters Displayed

Entering Text in Cells

Hint Pressing
the Tab key in a table
moves the insertion
point to the next cell.
Pressing Ctrl + Tab
moves the insertion
point to the next tab
within a cell.

With the insertion point positioned in a cell, type or edit text. Point and click with the mouse to move the insertion point from cell to cell, or press the Tab key to move to the next cell and Shift + Tab to move to the preceding cell.

Text typed in a cell automatically wraps to the next line to fit the width of the column. The Enter key can also be pressed to move to the next line within a cell. The cell expands vertically to accommodate the text, and all cells in that row also expand. Pressing the Tab key in a table causes the insertion point to move to the next cell in the table. To move the insertion point to a tab within a cell, press Ctrl + Tab. If the insertion point is in the last cell of the table, pressing the Tab key adds another row to the table. Insert a page break within a table by pressing Ctrl + Enter. The page break is inserted between rows, not within a row.

Moving the Insertion Point within a Table

To use the mouse to move the insertion point to a different cell within the table, click in the specific cell. To use the keyboard to move the insertion point to a different cell within the table, refer to the information shown in Table 7.1.

Table 7.1 Insertion Point Movement within a Table Using the Keyboard

To move the insertion point	Press
to next cell	Tab
to preceding cell	Shift + Tab
forward one character	Right Arrow key
backward one character	Left Arrow key
to previous row	Up Arrow key
to next row	Down Arrow key
to first cell in row	Alt + Home
to last cell in row	Alt + End
to top cell in column	Alt + Page Up
to bottom cell in column	Alt + Page Down

1. At a blank document, turn on bold formatting and then type the title CONTACT INFORMATION, as shown in Figure 7.2.
2. Turn off bold formatting and then press the Enter key.
3. Create the table shown in Figure 7.2 by completing the following steps:
   a. Click the Insert tab.
   b. Click the Table button in the Tables group.
   c. Move the mouse pointer down and to the right in the drop-down grid until the label above the grid displays as *3x5 Table* and then click the left mouse button.

4. Type the text in the cells as indicated in Figure 7.2. Press the Tab key to move to the next cell and press Shift + Tab to move to the preceding cell. (If you accidentally press the Enter key within a cell, immediately press the Backspace key. Do not press the Tab key after typing the text in the last cell. If you do, another row is inserted in the table. If this happens, immediately click the Undo button on the Quick Access Toolbar.)
5. Save the table and name it **7-Tables**.

Check Your Work

Figure 7.2 Activity 1a

CONTACT INFORMATION

Maggie Rivera	First Trust Bank	(203) 555-3440
Les Cromwell	Madison Trust	(602) 555-4900
Cecilia Nordyke	American Financial	(509) 555-3995
Regina Stahl	United Fidelity	(301) 555-1201
Justin White	Key One Savings	(360) 555-8963

Using the Insert Table Dialog Box

A table can also be created with options at the Insert Table dialog box, shown in Figure 7.3. To display this dialog box, click the Insert tab, click the Table button in the Tables group, and then click *Insert Table*. At the Insert Table dialog box, enter the number of columns and rows and then click OK.

Figure 7.3 Insert Table Dialog Box

Use these measurement boxes to specify the numbers of columns and rows.

Activity 1b **Creating a Table with the Insert Table Dialog Box**   **Part 2 of 8**

1. With **7-Tables** open, press Ctrl + End to move the insertion point below the table.
2. Press the Enter key two times.
3. Turn on bold formatting and then type the title OPTIONAL PLAN PREMIUM RATES, as shown in Figure 7.4.
4. Turn off bold formatting and then press the Enter key.
5. Click the Insert tab, click the Table button in the Tables group, and then click *Insert Table* at the drop-down list.
6. At the Insert Table dialog box, type 3 in the *Number of columns* measurement box. (The insertion point is automatically positioned in this measurement box.)
7. Press the Tab key (this moves the insertion point to the *Number of rows* measurement box) and then type 5.
8. Click OK.
9. Type the text in the cells as indicated in Figure 7.4. Press the Tab key to move to the next cell and press Shift + Tab to move to the preceding cell. To indent the text in cells B2 through B5 and cells C2 through C5, press Ctrl + Tab to move the insertion point to a tab within a cell and then type the text.
10. Save **7-Tables**.

Check Your Work

Figure 7.4 Activity 1b

OPTIONAL PLAN PREMIUM RATES		
Waiting Period	Basic Plan Employees	Plan 2021 Employees
60 days	0.67%	0.79%
90 days	0.49%	0.59%
120 days	0.30%	0.35%
180 days	0.23%	0.26%

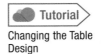
Tutorial

Changing the Table Design

Changing the Table Design

When a table is inserted in a document, the Table Tools Design tab is active. This tab contains a number of options for enhancing the appearance of the table, as shown in Figure 7.5. With options in the Table Styles group, apply a predesigned style that adds color and border lines to a table and shading to cells. Customize the formatting with options in the Table Style Options group. For example, click the *Total Row* check box to insert a total row in the table. Apply a predesigned table style with options in the Table Styles group.

Use options in the Borders group to change the look of cell borders in a table. Click the Border Styles button to display a drop-down list of available styles. Use other buttons in the Borders group to change the line style, width, and color and to add or remove borders. Apply the same border style to other cells with the Border Painter button.

Border Styles

Border Painter

Figure 7.5 Table Tools Design Tab

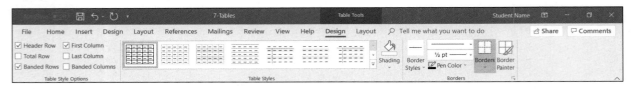

Activity 1c Applying Table Styles

Part 3 of 8

1. With **7-Tables** open, click in any cell in the top table.
2. Apply a table style by completing the following steps:
   a. Make sure the Table Tools Design tab is active.
   b. Click the More Table Styles button in the table styles gallery in the Table Styles group.
   c. Click the *Grid Table 5 Dark - Accent 5* table style (sixth column, fifth row in the *Grid Tables* section).

3. After looking at the table, you realize that the first row is not a header row and the first column should not be formatted differently from the other columns. To format the first row and the first column in the same manner as the other rows and columns, click the *Header Row* check box and the *First Column* check box in the Table Style Options group to remove the check marks.

4. Click in any cell in the bottom table and then apply the List Table 6 Colorful - Accent 5 table style (sixth column, sixth row in the *List Tables* section).

5. Add color borders to the top table by completing the following steps:
   a. Click in any cell in the top table.
   b. Click the Pen Color button arrow in the Borders group on the Table Tools Design tab and then click the *Orange, Accent 2, Darker 50%* color option (sixth column, last row in the *Theme Colors* section).
   c. Click the *Line Weight* option box arrow in the Borders group and then click *1 ½ pt* in the drop-down list. (When you choose a line weight, the Border Painter button is automatically activated.)

   d. Using the mouse (the mouse pointer appears as a pen), drag along all four sides of the table. (As you drag with the mouse, a thick brown line is inserted. If you make a mistake or the line does not appear as you intended, click the Undo button and then continue drawing along each side of the table.)

6. Click the Border Styles button arrow and then click the *Double solid lines, 1/2 pt, Accent 2* option (third column, third row in the *Theme Borders* section).

7. Drag along all four sides of the bottom table.

8. Click the Border Painter button to turn off the feature.

9. Save **7-Tables**.

Check Your Work

Selecting Cells

Data within a table can be formatted in several ways. For example, the alignment of text within cells or rows can be changed, rows or columns can be moved or copied, and character formatting, such as bold, italic, and underlining, can be applied to text. To make changes to a cell, row, or column, first select the cells.

Selecting in a Table with the Mouse

Use the mouse pointer to select a cell, row, or column or to select an entire table. Table 7.2 describes methods for selecting in a table with the mouse. To select a cell, position the mouse pointer in the *cell selection bar*, an invisible strip just inside the left edge of a cell. The pointer turns into a small black arrow pointing up and to the right. Click to select the cell. Each row in a table contains a *row selection bar*, which is the space just outside the left edge of the table. Position the mouse pointer in the row selection bar and the mouse pointer turns into a white arrow that points up and to the right. Click to select the row.

Table 7.2 Selecting in a Table with the Mouse

To select this	Do this
cell	Position the mouse pointer in the cell selection bar at the left edge of the cell until it turns into a small black arrow that points up and to the right and then click the left mouse button.
row	Position the mouse pointer in the row selection bar at the left edge of the table until it turns into an arrow that points up and to the right and then click the left mouse button.
column	Position the mouse pointer on the uppermost horizontal gridline of the table in the appropriate column until it turns into a small black arrow that points down and then click the left mouse button.
adjacent cells	Position the mouse pointer in the first cell to be selected, click and hold down the left mouse button, drag the mouse pointer to the last cell to be selected, and then release the mouse button.
all cells in a table	Click the table move handle or position the mouse pointer in the row selection bar for the first row at the left edge of the table until it turns into an arrow that points up and to the right, click and hold down the left mouse button, drag down to select all the rows in the table, and then release the left mouse button.
text within a cell	Position the mouse pointer at the beginning of the text, click and hold down the left mouse button, and then drag the mouse across the text. (When a cell is selected, its background color changes to gray. When the text within a cell is selected, only those lines containing text are selected.)

Selecting in a Table with the Keyboard

In addition to the mouse, the keyboard can be used to select specific cells within a table. Table 7.3 shows the commands for selecting specific elements of a table.

To select only the text within a cell, rather than the entire cell, position the insertion point in front of text in a cell and then press the F8 function key to turn on the Extend mode. Move the insertion point with an arrow key to select one character at a time, being careful not to select the entire cell. When a cell is selected, its background color changes to gray. When the text within a cell is selected, only those lines containing text are selected.

Table 7.3 Selecting in a Table with the Keyboard

To select	Press
next cell's contents	Tab
preceding cell's contents	Shift + Tab
entire table	Alt + 5 (on numeric keypad with Num Lock off)
adjacent cells	Press and hold down the Shift key and then press an arrow key repeatedly.
column	Position the insertion point in the top cell of the column, press and hold down the Shift key, and then press and hold down the Down Arrow key until the column is selected.

Activity 1d Selecting, Moving, and Formatting Cells in a Table

Part 4 of 8

1. With **7-Tables** open, move two rows in the top table by completing the following steps:
   a. Position the mouse pointer in the row selection bar at the left edge of the row containing the name *Cecilia Nordyke*, click and hold down the left mouse button, and then drag down to select two rows (the *Cecilia Nordyke* row and the *Regina Stahl* row).
   b. Click the Home tab and then click the Cut button in the Clipboard group.
   c. Move the insertion point so it is positioned at the beginning of the name *Les Cromwell* and then click the Paste button in the Clipboard group.

2. Move the third column in the bottom table by completing the following steps:
   a. Position the mouse pointer on the top border of the third column in the bottom table until the pointer turns into a short black arrow that points down and then click the left mouse button. (This selects the entire column.)
   b. Click the Cut button.
   c. With the insertion point positioned at the beginning of the text *Basic Plan Employees*, click the Paste button. (Moving the column removed the right border.)
   d. Insert the right border by clicking the Table Tools Design tab, clicking the Border Styles button arrow, and then clicking the *Double solid lines, 1/2 pt, Accent 2* option at the drop-down list (third column, third row in the *Theme Borders* section).
   e. Drag along the right border of the bottom table.
   f. Click the Border Painter button to turn off the feature.

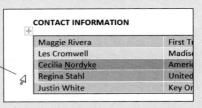

3. Apply shading to a row by completing the following steps:
   a. Position the mouse pointer in the row selection bar at the left edge of the first row in the bottom table until the pointer turns into an arrow that points up and to the right and then click the left mouse button. (This selects the entire first row of the bottom table.)

   b. Click the Shading button arrow in the Table Styles group on the Table Tools Design tab and then click the *Orange, Accent 2, Lighter 80%* color option (sixth column, second row in the *Theme Colors* section).
4. Apply a border line to the right sides of two columns by completing the following steps:
   a. Position the mouse pointer on the top border of the first column in the bottom table until the pointer turns into a short black arrow that points down and then click the left mouse button.

   b. Click the *Line Style* option box arrow and then click the top line option (a single line).
   c. Click the Borders button arrow and then click *Right Border* at the drop-down list.
   d. Select the second column in the bottom table.
   e. Click the Borders button arrow and then click *Right Border* at the drop-down list.
5. Apply italic formatting to a column by completing the following steps:
   a. Click in the first cell of the first row in the top table.
   b. Press and hold down the Shift key and then press the Down Arrow key four times. (This should select all the cells in the first column.)
   c. Press Ctrl + I.
   d. Click in any cell in the table to deselect the column.
6. Save **7-Tables**.

> **Check Your Work**

> Tutorial

Changing the Table Layout

Changing the Table Layout

To further customize a table, consider changing the layout by inserting or deleting columns and rows and specifying how text should align in cells. Change the table layout with options at the Table Tools Layout tab, shown in Figure 7.6. Use options and buttons on the tab to select specific cells, delete and insert rows and columns, merge and split cells, specify cell height and width, sort data in cells, and insert formulas.

Selecting with the Select Button

Along with selecting cells with the keyboard and mouse, specific cells can be selected with the Select button in the Table group on the Table Tools Layout tab.

Figure 7.6 Table Tools Layout Tab

Select

Position the insertion point in the specific cell, column, or row and then click the Select button. At the drop-down list, specify what is to be selected: the entire table or a column, row, or cell.

Viewing Gridlines

 View Gridlines

By default, the cells in a table are bordered by a grid of thin black horizontal and vertical lines. These borders can be modified or removed using options in the Table Tools Design tab, as described on page 196. If the design of a table is changed so that there are no visible borders, it can be difficult to see the boundaries of each cell when entering data. In this case, turn on the display of nonprinting gridlines to be used as a reference when working with the table. These gridlines appear as dashed lines on the screen, but they will not print. Turn on or off the display of nonprinting dashed gridlines with the View Gridlines button in the Table group on the Table Tools Layout tab.

Inserting and Deleting Rows and Columns

 Insert Above

 Insert Below

 Insert Left

 Insert Right

Delete

Insert or delete a row or a column with buttons in the Rows & Columns group on the Table Tools Layout tab. Click a button in the group to insert the row or column above, below, to the left, or to the right. To delete a cell, a row, a column, or the entire table, click the Delete button and then click the option identifying what is to be deleted. The shortcut menu can also be used to insert or delete a row or column. To use the shortcut menu to insert a row or column, right-click in a cell, point to the *Insert* option, and then click an insert option at the side menu. To delete a row or column, right-click in a cell and then click the *Delete Cells* option. This displays the Delete Cells dialog box with options for deleting cells, a row, or a column.

In addition to using options on the Table Tools Layout tab, rows or columns can be inserted using an Insert Control. Display the Insert Control for a row by positioning the mouse pointer just outside the left border of the table at the left edge of the row border. When the Insert Control displays (a plus symbol in a circle and a border line), click the control and a row is inserted below the Insert Control border line. To insert a column, position the mouse pointer above the column border line until the Insert Control displays and then click the control. This inserts a new column immediately left of the Insert Control border line.

Activity 1e Selecting, Inserting, and Deleting Columns and Rows   Part 5 of 8

1. Make sure **7-Tables** is open.
2. The table style applied to the bottom table removed row border gridlines. If you do not see dashed row border gridlines in the bottom table, turn on the display of nonprinting gridlines by positioning your insertion point in the table, clicking the Table Tools Layout tab, and then clicking the View Gridlines button in the Table group. (The button should appear with a gray background, indicating it is active.)
3. Select a column and apply formatting by completing the following steps:
   a. Click in any cell in the first column in the top table.
   b. Make sure the Table Tools Layout tab is active, click the Select button in the Table group, and then click *Select Column* at the drop-down list.

c. With the first column selected, press Ctrl + I to remove italic formatting and then press Ctrl + B to apply bold formatting.
4. Select a row and apply formatting by completing the following steps:
   a. Click in any cell in the first row in the bottom table.
   b. Click the Select button in the Table group and then click *Select Row* at the drop-down list.
   c. With the first row selected in the bottom table, press Ctrl + I to apply italic formatting.
5. Insert a new row in the bottom table and type text in the new cells by completing the following steps:
   a. Click in the cell containing the text *60 days*.
   b. Click the Insert Above button in the Rows & Columns group.
   c. Type 30 days in the first cell of the new row. Press the Tab key, press Ctrl + Tab, and then type 0.85% in the second cell of the new row. Press the Tab key, press Ctrl + Tab, and then type 0.81% in the third cell of the new row.

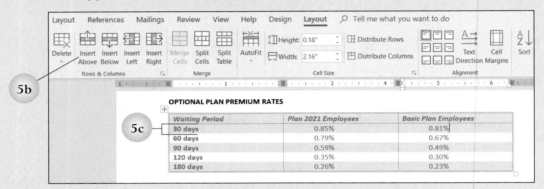

6. Insert two new rows in the top table by completing the following steps:
   a. Select the two rows of cells that begin with the names *Cecilia Nordyke* and *Regina Stahl*.
   b. Click the Insert Below button in the Rows & Columns group.
   c. Click in any cell of the top table to deselect the new rows.
7. Insert a new row in the top table by positioning the mouse pointer at the left edge of the table next to the border line below *Regina Stahl* until the Insert Control displays and then clicking the Insert Control.
8. Type the following text in the new cells:

Teresa Getty	Meridian Bank	(503) 555-9800
Michael Vazquez	New Horizon Bank	(702) 555-2435
Samantha Roth	Cascade Mutual	(206) 555-6788

CONTACT INFORMATION

Maggie Rivera	First Trust Bank	(203) 555-3440
Cecilia Nordyke	American Financial	(509) 555-3995
Regina Stahl	United Fidelity	(301) 555-1201
Teresa Getty	Meridian Bank	(503) 555-9800
Michael Vazquez	New Horizon Bank	(702) 555-2435
Samantha Roth	Cascade Mutual	(206) 555-6788
Les Cromwell	Madison Trust	(602) 555-4900
Justin White	Key One Savings	(360) 555-8963

9. Delete a row by completing the following steps:
   a. Click in the cell containing the name *Les Cromwell*.
   b. Click the Delete button in the Rows & Columns group and then click *Delete Rows* at the drop-down list.

10. Insert a new column in the top table by positioning the mouse pointer immediately above the border line between the first and second columns until the Insert Control displays and then clicking the Insert Control.

11. Type the following text in the new cells:

    B1 = Vice President
    B2 = Loan Officer
    B3 = Account Manager
    B4 = Branch Manager
    B5 = President
    B6 = Vice President
    B7 = Regional Manager

12. Save **7-Tables**.

Check Your Work

Merging and Splitting Cells and Tables

Merge Cells

Split Cells

Split Table

Click the Merge Cells button in the Merge group on the Table Tools Layout tab to merge selected cells and click the Split Cells button to split the currently active cell. Click the Split Cells button and the Split Cells dialog box displays with options for specifying the number of columns or rows into which the active cell should be split. To split one table into two tables, position the insertion point in a cell in the row that will be the first row in the new table and then click the Split Table button.

1. With **7-Tables** open, insert a new row and merge cells in the row by completing the following steps:
   a. Click in the cell containing the text *Waiting Period* (in the bottom table).
   b. Click the Insert Above button in the Rows & Columns group on the Table Tools Layout tab.
   c. With all the cells in the new row selected, click the Merge Cells button in the Merge group.
   d. Type OPTIONAL PLAN PREMIUM RATES and then press Ctrl + E to center-align the text in the cell. (The text you type will be bold and italicized.)

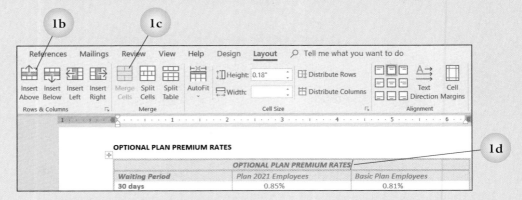

2. Select and then delete the text *OPTIONAL PLAN PREMIUM RATES* above the bottom table.
3. Insert rows and text in the top table and merge cells by completing the following steps:
   a. Click in the cell containing the text *Maggie Rivera*.
   b. Click the Table Tools Layout tab.
   c. Click the Insert Above button two times. (This inserts two rows at the top of the table.)
   d. With the cells in the top row selected, click the Merge Cells button.
   e. Type CONTACT INFORMATION, NORTH and then press Ctrl + E to center-align the text in the cell.
   f. Type the following text in the four cells in the new second row.
       Name   Title   Company   Telephone

4. Apply heading formatting to the new top row by completing the following steps:
   a. Click the Table Tools Design tab.
   b. Click the *Header Row* check box in the Table Style Options group to insert a check mark.
5. Select and then delete the text *CONTACT INFORMATION* above the top table.
6. Split a cell by completing the following steps:
   a. Click in the cell containing the telephone number *(301) 555-1201*.
   b. Click the Table Tools Layout tab.
   c. Click the Split Cells button in the Merge group.
   d. At the Split Cells dialog box, click OK. (The telephone number will wrap to a new line. You will change this in the next activity.)
   e. Click in the new cell.

f. Type x453 in the new cell. If AutoCorrect automatically capitalizes the *x*, hover the mouse pointer over the *X* until the AutoCorrect Options button displays. Click the AutoCorrect Options button and then click *Undo Automatic Capitalization* or click *Stop Auto-capitalizing First Letter of Table Cells*.

7. Split the cell containing the telephone number *(206) 555-6788* and then type x2310 in the new cell. (If necessary, make the *x* lowercase.)
8. Split the top table into two tables by completing the following steps:
   a. Click in the cell containing the name *Teresa Getty*.
   b. Click the Split Table button in the Merge group.
   c. Click in the cell containing the name *Teresa Getty* (in the first row of the new table).
   d. Click the Insert Above button in the Rows & Columns group on the Table Tools Layout tab.
   e. With the new row selected, click the Merge Cells button.
   f. Type CONTACT INFORMATION, SOUTH in the new row and then press Ctrl + E to center-align the text.
9. Save and then print **7-Tables**.
10. Delete the middle table by completing the following steps:
    a. Click in any cell in the middle table.
    b. Click the Table Tools Layout tab.
    c. Click the Delete button in the Rows & Columns group and then click *Delete Table* at the drop-down list.
11. Draw a dark-orange border at the bottom of the top table by completing the following steps:
    a. Click in any cell in the top table and then click the Table Tools Design tab.
    b. Click the *Line Weight* option box arrow in the Borders group and then click *1½ pt* at the drop-down list. (This activates the Border Painter button.)
    c. Click the Pen Color button and then click the *Orange, Accent 2, Darker, 50%* color option (sixth column, bottom row in the *Theme Colors* section).
    d. Using the mouse, drag along the bottom border of the top table.
    e. Click the Border Painter button to turn off the feature.
12. Save **7-Tables**.

Customizing Cell Size

Customizing Cells in a Table

Distribute Rows

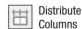
Distribute Columns

When a table is created, the column widths are equal and the row heights are equal. Both can be customized with buttons in the Cell Size group on the Table Tools Layout tab. Use the *Table Row Height* measurement box to increase or decrease the heights of rows and use the *Table Column Width* measurement box to increase or decrease the widths of columns. The Distribute Rows button will make all the selected rows the same height and the Distribute Columns button will make all the selected columns the same width.

Column width can also be changed using the move table column markers on the horizontal ruler or using the table gridlines. To change column width using the horizontal ruler, position the mouse pointer on a move table column marker until it turns into a left-and-right-pointing arrow and then drag the marker on the horizontal ruler to the specific position. Press and hold down the Shift key while dragging a table column marker and the horizontal ruler remains stationary while the table column marker moves. Press and hold down the Alt key while dragging a table column marker and measurements display on the horizontal ruler. To change column width using gridlines, position the mouse pointer on the gridline separating columns until the insertion point turns into a left-and-right-pointing arrow with a vertical double-line in the middle and then drag the gridline to the new position. Press and hold down the Alt key while dragging the gridline and column measurements display on the horizontal ruler.

Adjust row height in a manner similar to adjusting column width. Drag the adjust table row marker on the vertical ruler or drag the gridline separating rows. Press and hold down the Alt key while dragging the adjust table row marker or the row gridline and measurements display on the vertical ruler.

AutoFit Use the AutoFit button in the Cell Size group to make the column widths in a table automatically fit the contents. To do this, position the insertion point in any cell in the table, click the AutoFit button in the Cell Size group, and then click *AutoFit Contents* at the drop-down list.

Activity 1g Changing Column Width and Row Height Part 7 of 8

1. With **7-Tables** open, change the width of the first column in the top table by completing the following steps:
   a. Click in the cell containing the name *Maggie Rivera*.
   b. Position the mouse pointer on the Move Table Column marker just right of the 1.5-inch mark on the horizontal ruler until the pointer turns into a left-and-right-pointing arrow.
   c. Press and hold down the Shift key and then click and hold down the left mouse button.
   d. Drag the marker to the 1.25-inch mark, release the mouse button, and then release the Shift key.

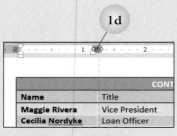

2. Complete steps similar to those in Step 1 to drag the move table column marker just right of the 3-inch mark on the horizontal ruler to the 2.75-inch mark. (Make sure the text *Account Manager* in the second column does not wrap to the next line. If it does, slightly increase the width of the column.)

3. Change the width of the third column in the top table by completing the following steps:
   a. Position the mouse pointer on the gridline separating the third and fourth columns until the pointer turns into a left-and-right-pointing arrow with a vertical double-line in the middle.
   b. Press and hold down the Alt key, click and hold down the left mouse button, drag the gridline to the left until the measurement for the third column on the horizontal ruler displays as *1.31"*, and then release the mouse button followed by the Alt key.

4. Position the mouse pointer on the gridline that separates the telephone number *(301) 555-1201* from the extension *x453* and then drag the gridline to the 5.25-inch mark on the horizontal ruler. (Make sure the phone number does not wrap down to the next line.)

5. Drag the right border of the top table to the 5.75-inch mark on the horizontal ruler.

6. Automatically fit the columns in the bottom table by completing the following steps:
   a. Click in any cell in the bottom table.
   b. Click the AutoFit button in the Cell Size group on the Table Tools Layout tab and then click *AutoFit Contents* at the drop-down list.

7. Increase the height of the first row in the bottom table by completing the following steps:
   a. Make sure the insertion point is positioned in one of the cells in the bottom table.
   b. Position the mouse pointer on the top adjust table row marker on the vertical ruler.
   c. Press and hold down the Alt key and then click and hold down the left mouse button.
   d. Drag the Adjust Table Row marker down until the first row measurement on the vertical ruler displays as *0.39"*, release the mouse button, and then release the Alt key.

8. Increase the height of the first row in the top table by completing the following steps:
   a. Click in any cell in the top table.
   b. Position the mouse pointer on the gridline at the bottom of the top row until the mouse pointer turns into an up-and-down-pointing arrow with a vertical double-line in the middle.
   c. Click and hold down the left mouse button and then press and hold down the Alt key.
   d. Drag the gridline down until the first row measurement on the vertical ruler displays as *0.39"*, release the mouse button, and then release the Alt key.

9. Save **7-Tables**.

Check Your Work

Changing Cell Alignment

The Alignment group on the Table Tools Layout tab contains a number of buttons for specifying the horizontal and vertical alignment of text in cells. Each button contains a visual representation of the alignment. Hover the mouse pointer over a button to display a ScreenTip with the button name and description.

Repeating a Header Row

Quick Steps
Repeat Header Row
1. Click in header row or select rows.
2. Click Table Tools Layout tab.
3. Click Repeat Header Rows button.

Repeat Header Rows

If a table continues over two or more pages, consider adding the header row at the beginning of each page for easier reference while reading. To repeat a header row, click in the first row (header row) and then click the Repeat Header Rows button in the Data group on the Table Tools Layout tab. To repeat more than one header row, select the rows and then click the Repeat Header Rows button.

1. With **7-Tables** open, click in the top cell in the top table (the cell containing the title *CONTACT INFORMATION, NORTH*).
2. Click the Align Center button in the Alignment group on the Table Tools Layout tab.
3. Format and align the text in the second row in the top table by completing the following steps:
   a. Select the second row.
   b. Press Ctrl + B to turn off bold formatting for the entry in the first cell and then press Ctrl + B again to turn on bold formatting for all the entries in the second row.
   c. Click the Align Top Center button in the Alignment group.
4. Click in the top cell in the bottom table and then click the Align Center button in the Alignment group.
5. Press Ctrl + End to move the insertion point to the end of the document, press the Enter key four times, and then insert a table into the current document by completing the following steps:
   a. Click the Insert tab.
   b. Click the Object button arrow in the Text group and then click *Text from File* at the drop-down list.
   c. At the Insert File dialog box, navigate to your WL1C7 folder and then double-click the *ContactsWest* document.
6. Repeat the header row by completing the following steps:
   a. Select the first two rows in the table you just inserted.
   b. Click the Table Tools Layout tab.
   c. Click the Repeat Header Rows button in the Data group.
7. Save, print, and then close **7-Tables**.

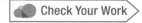

Check Your Work

Activity 2 Create and Format Tables with Employee Information   6 Parts

You will create and format a table containing information on the names and departments of employees of Tri-State Products, two tables containing additional information on employees, and a calendar quick table.

Changing Cell Margin Measurements

 Cell Margins

By default, the cells in a table contain specific margin measurements. The top and bottom margins in a cell have a default measurement of 0 inch and the left and right margins have a default measurement of 0.08 inch. Change these default measurements with options at the Table Options dialog box, shown in Figure 7.7. Display this dialog box by clicking the Cell Margins button in the Alignment group on the Table Tools Layout tab. Use the measurement boxes in the *Default cell margins* section to change the top, bottom, left, and/or right cell margin measurements.

Figure 7.7 Table Options Dialog Box

Use the measurement boxes in this section to increase and/or decrease the margin measurements in cells.

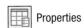 Properties

Changes to cell margins will affect all the cells in a table. To change the cell margin measurements for one cell or selected cells, position the insertion point in the cell or select the cells and then click the Properties button in the Table group on the Table Tools Layout tab (or click the Cell Size group dialog box launcher). At the Table Properties dialog box, click the Cell tab and then the Options button in the lower right corner of the dialog box. This displays the Cell Options dialog box, shown in Figure 7.8.

Before setting the new cell margin measurements, remove the check mark from the *Same as the whole table* check box. With the check mark removed, the cell margin options become available. Specify the new cell margin measurements and then click OK to close the dialog box.

Figure 7.8 Cell Options Dialog Box

Remove the check mark from this check box and the cell margin measurement boxes become available.

Activity 2a Changing Cell Margin Measurements

Part 1 of 6

1. Open **TSPTables** and then save it with the name **7-TSPTables**.
2. Change the top and bottom cell margin measurements for all the cells in the table by completing the following steps:
   a. Position the insertion point in any cell in the table and then click the Table Tools Layout tab.
   b. Click the Cell Margins button in the Alignment group.

c. At the Table Options dialog box, change the *Top* and *Bottom* measurements to 0.05 inch.

d. Click OK to close the Table Options dialog box.

3. Change the top and bottom cell margin measurements for the first row of cells by completing the following steps:

a. Select the first row of cells (the cells containing *Name* and *Department*).

b. Click the Properties button in the Table group.

c. At the Table Properties dialog box, click the Cell tab.

d. Click the Options button in the lower right corner of the dialog box.

e. At the Cell Options dialog box, click the *Same as the whole table* check box to remove the check mark.

f. Change the *Top* and *Bottom* measurements to 0.1 inch.

g. Click OK to close the Cell Options dialog box.

h. Click OK to close the Table Properties dialog box.

4. Change the left cell margin measurement for specific cells by completing the following steps:

a. Select all the rows in the table *except* the top row.

b. Click the Cell Size group dialog box launcher.

c. At the Table Properties dialog box, make sure the Cell tab is active.

d. Click the Options button.

e. At the Cell Options dialog box, remove the check mark from the *Same as the whole table* check box.

f. Change the *Left* measurement to 0.3 inch.

g. Click OK to close the Cell Options dialog box.

h. Click OK to close the Table Properties dialog box.

5. Save **7-TSPTables**.

> 🔵 Check Your Work

Changing Text Direction in a Cell

 Text Direction

Change the direction of text in a cell using the Text Direction button in the Alignment group on the Table Tools Layout tab. Each time the Text Direction button is clicked, the text in the cell rotates 90 degrees.

Changing Table Alignment and Dimensions

By default, a table aligns at the left margin. Change this alignment with options at the Table Properties dialog box with the Table tab selected, as shown in Figure 7.9. To change the alignment, click the specific alignment option in the *Alignment* section of the dialog box. Change table dimensions by clicking the

Preferred width check box to insert a check mark. This makes active both the width measurement box and the *Measure in* option box. Type a width measurement in the measurement box and specify whether the measurement type is inches or a percentage with the *Measurement in* option box.

Figure 7.9 Table Properties Dialog Box with the Table Tab Selected

Specify the horizontal alignment of the table with options in this section.

Change the table width by inserting a check mark in the *Preferred width* check box and then specifying the table width and measurement type.

Activity 2b Changing Size and Cell Alignment and Text Direction

Part 2 of 6

1. With **7-TSPTables** open, insert a new column and change text direction by completing the following steps:
   a. Click in any cell in the first column.
   b. Click the Insert Left button in the Rows & Columns group on the Table Tools Layout tab.
   c. With the cells in the new column selected, click the Merge Cells button in the Merge group.
   d. Type Tri-State Products.
   e. Click the Align Center button in the Alignment group.
   f. Click two times on the Text Direction button in the Alignment group.

   g. With *Tri-State Products* selected, click the Home tab and then increase the font size to 16 points.
2. Automatically fit the contents by completing the following steps:
   a. Click in any cell in the table.
   b. Click the Table Tools Layout tab.
   c. Click the AutoFit button in the Cell Size group and then click *AutoFit Contents* at the drop-down list.

3. Change the table width and alignment by completing the following steps:
   a. Click the Properties button in the Table group on the Table Tools Layout tab.
   b. At the Table Properties dialog box, click the Table tab.
   c. Click the *Preferred width* check box to insert a check mark.
   d. Select the measurement in the measurement box and then type 4.5.
   e. Click the *Center* option in the *Alignment* section.
   f. Click OK.
4. Select the two cells containing the text *Name* and *Department* and then click the Align Center button in the Alignment group.
5. Save **7-TSPTables**.

> Check Your Work

Changing Table Size with the Resize Handle

Quick Steps

Move Table
1. Position mouse pointer on table move handle until pointer displays with four-headed arrow attached.
2. Click and hold down left mouse button.
3. Drag table to new location.
4. Release mouse button.

Hover the mouse pointer over a table and a resize handle displays in the lower right corner. The resize handle displays as a small white square. Drag this resize handle to increase and/or decrease the size and proportion of the table.

Moving a Table

Position the mouse pointer in a table and a table move handle displays in the upper left corner. Use this handle to move the table within the document. To move a table, position the mouse pointer on the table move handle until the pointer displays with a four-headed arrow attached, click and hold down the left mouse button, drag the table to the new location, and then release the mouse button.

Activity 2c Resizing and Moving Tables   Part 3 of 6

1. With **7-TSPTables** open, insert a table into the current document by completing the following steps:
   a. Press Ctrl + End to move the insertion point to the end of the document and then press the Enter key.
   b. Click the Insert tab.
   c. Click the Object button arrow in the Text group and then click *Text from File* at the drop-down list.
   d. At the Insert File dialog box, navigate to your WL1C7 folder and then double-click the **TSPEmps** document.
2. Automatically fit the bottom table by completing the following steps:
   a. Click in any cell in the bottom table.
   b. Click the Table Tools Layout tab.
   c. Click the AutoFit button in the Cell Size group and then click *AutoFit Contents* at the drop-down list.

3. Format the bottom table by completing the following steps:
   a. Click the Table Tools Design tab.
   b. Click the More Table Styles button in the table styles gallery, scroll down the gallery, and then click the *List Table 4 - Accent 6* table style (last column, fourth row in the *List Tables* section).
   c. Click the *First Column* check box in the Table Style Options group to remove the check mark.
   d. Select the first and second rows, click the Table Tools Layout tab, and then click the Align Center button in the Alignment group.
   e. Select the second row and then press Ctrl + B to apply bold formatting.

3b

4. Size the bottom table by completing the following steps:
   a. Position the mouse pointer on the resize handle in the lower right corner of the bottom table.
   b. Click and hold down the left mouse button, drag down and to the right until the width and height of the table increase approximately 1 inch, and then release the mouse button.

TRI-STATE PRODUCTS		
Name	**Employee #**	**Department**
Whitaker, Christine	1432-323-09	Financial Services
Higgins, Dennis	1230-933-21	Public Relations
Coffey, Richard	1321-843-22	Research and Development
Lee, Yong	1411-322-76	Human Resources
Fleishmann, Jim	1246-432-90	Public Relations
Schaffer, Mitchell	1388-340-44	Purchasing
Porter, Robbie	1122-361-38	Public Relations
Buchanan, Lillian	1432-857-87	Research and Development
Kensington, Jacob	1112-473-31	Human Resources

4a-4b

5. Move the bottom table by completing the following steps:
   a. Move the mouse pointer over the bottom table and then position the mouse pointer on the table move handle that appears just outside the upper left corner of the table until the pointer displays with a four-headed arrow attached.
   b. Click and hold down the left mouse button, drag the table so it is positioned equally between the left and right margins, and then release the mouse button.

5a-5b

TRI-STATE PRODUCTS		
Name	**Employee #**	**Department**
Whitaker, Christine	1432-323-09	Financial Services
Higgins, Dennis	1230-933-21	Public Relations

6. Select the cells in the column below the heading *Employee #* and then click the Align Top Center button in the Alignment group.
7. Save **7-TSPTables**.

Check Your Work

Tutorial

Converting Text to a Table and a Table to Text

Quick Steps

Convert Text to Table
1. Select text.
2. Click Insert tab.
3. Click Table button.
4. Click *Convert Text to Table*.
5. Click OK.

Convert Table to Text
1. Click Table Tools Layout tab.
2. Click Convert to Text button.
3. Specify separator.
4. Click OK.

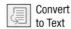
Convert to Text

Converting Text to a Table and a Table to Text

Create a table and then enter text in the cells or create the text and then convert it to a table. Converting text to a table provides formatting and layout options available on the Table Tools Design tab and the Table Tools Layout tab. When typing the text to be converted to a table, separate units of information using separator characters, such as commas or tabs. These characters identify where the text is divided into columns. To convert text, select the text, click the Insert tab, click the Table button in the Tables group, and then click *Convert Text to Table* at the drop-down list. At the Convert Text to Table dialog box, specify the separator and then click OK.

Convert a table to text by positioning the insertion point in any cell of the table, clicking the Table Tools Layout tab, and then clicking the Convert to Text button in the Data group. At the Convert Table To dialog box, specify the separator and then click OK.

Activity 2d Converting Text to a Table

Part 4 of 6

1. With **7-TSPTables** open, press Ctrl + End to move the insertion point to the end of the document. (If the insertion point does not display below the second table, press the Enter key until the insertion point displays there.)
2. Insert the document named **TSPExecs** into the current document.
3. Convert the text to a table by completing the following steps:
    a. Select the text you just inserted.
    b. Make sure the Insert tab is active.
    c. Click the Table button in the Tables group and then click *Convert Text to Table* at the drop-down list.
    d. At the Convert Text to Table dialog box, type 2 in the *Number of columns* measurement box.
    e. Click the *AutoFit to contents* option in the *AutoFit behavior* section.
    f. Click the *Commas* option in the *Separate text at* section.
    g. Click OK.

4. Select and merge the cells in the top row (the row containing the title *TRI-STATE PRODUCTS*) and then center-align the text in the merged cell.
5. Apply the List Table 4 - Accent 6 style (last column, fourth row in the *List Tables* section) and remove the check mark from the *First Column* check box in the Table Style Options group on the Table Tools Design tab.
6. Drag the table so it is centered below the table above it.
7. Apply the List Table 4 - Accent 6 style to the top table. Increase the widths of the columns so the text *Tri-State Products* is visible and the text in the second and third columns displays on one line.
8. Drag the table so it is centered above the middle table. Make sure the three tables fit on one page.

9. Click in the middle table and then convert the table to text by completing the following steps:
   a. Click the Table Tools Layout tab and then click the Convert to Text button in the Data group.
   b. At the Convert Table To dialog box, make sure *Tabs* is selected and then click OK.

10. Print **7-TSPTables**.
11. Click the Undo button to return the text to a table.
12. Save **7-TSPTables**.

Check Your Work

Drawing a Table

Eraser

In Activity 1, options in the Borders group on the Table Tools Design tab were used to draw borders around an existing table. These options can also be used to draw an entire table. To draw a table, click the Insert tab, click the Table button in the Tables group, and then click *Draw Table* at the drop-down list. Or click the Draw Table button in the Draw group on the Table Tools Layout tab; this turns the mouse pointer into a pen. Drag the pen pointer in the document to create the table. To correct an error when drawing a table, click the Eraser button in the Draw group on the Table Tools Layout tab (which changes the mouse pointer to an eraser) and then drag over any border lines to be erased. Clicking the Undo button will also undo the most recent action. To turn off the draw feature, click the Draw Table button in the Draw group or press the Esc key on the keyboard.

Activity 2e Drawing and Formatting a Table   Part 5 of 6

1. With **7-TSPTables** open, select and then delete three rows in the middle table from the row that begins with the name *Lee, Yong* through the row that begins with the name *Schaffer, Mitchell*.
2. Move the insertion point to the end of the document (outside any table) and then press the Enter key. (Make sure the insertion point is positioned below the third table.)
3. Click the Insert tab, click the Table button, and then click the *Draw Table* option at the drop-down list. (This turns the insertion point into a pen.)
4. Using the mouse, drag in the document (below the bottom table) to create the table shown at the right, drawing the outside border first. If you make a mistake, click the Undo button. You can also click the Eraser button in the Draw group on the Table Tools Layout tab and drag over a border line to erase it. Click the Draw Table button in the Draw group to turn off the draw feature.

5. After drawing the table, type Tri-State Products in the top cell, Washington Division in the cell at the left, Oregon Division in the middle bottom cell, and California Division in the cell at the right.
6. Apply the Grid Table 4 - Accent 6 table style (last column, fourth row in the *Grid Tables* section).

7. Select the table, change the font size to 12 points, apply bold formatting, and then center-align the text in the cells using the Align Center button in the Alignment group.
8. Make any adjustments needed to the border lines so the text in each cell is on one line.
9. Drag the table so it is centered and positioned below the bottom table.
10. Save **7-TSPTables**.

Check Your Work >

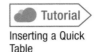

Tutorial >

Inserting a Quick Table

Inserting a Quick Table

Word includes a Quick Tables feature for inserting predesigned tables in a document. To insert a quick table, click the Insert tab, click the Table button in the Tables group, point to *Quick Tables*, and then click a table at the side menu. Additional formatting can be applied to a quick table with options on the Table Tools Design tab and the Table Tools Layout tab.

Activity 2f Inserting a Quick Table   Part 6 of 6

1. With **7-TSPTables** open, press Ctrl + End to move the insertion point to the end of the document and then press Ctrl + Enter to insert a page break.
2. Insert a quick table by clicking the Insert tab, clicking the Table button, pointing to *Quick Tables*, and then clicking the *Calendar 3* option at the side menu.

3. Edit the text in each cell so the calendar reflects the current month. (If the bottom row is empty, select and then delete the last and second to last rows.)
4. Select the entire table by clicking the Table Tools Layout tab, clicking the Select button in the Table group, and then clicking the *Select Table* option. With the table selected, change the font to Copperplate Gothic Light.
5. Drag the table so it is centered between the left and right margins.
6. Save, print, and then close **7-TSPTables**.

Check Your Work >

You will insert formulas in a Tri-State Products sales table to calculate total sales, average sales, and top sales.

Performing
Calculations in
a Table

Performing Calculations in a Table

Use the Formula button in the Data group on the Table Tools Layout tab to insert formulas that perform calculations on data in a table. The numbers in cells can be added, subtracted, multiplied, and divided. Other calculations can be performed, such as determining averages, counting items, and identifying minimum and maximum values. For more complex calculations, consider using an Excel worksheet.

fx Formula

Quick Steps

**Insert Formula
in Table**
1. Click in cell.
2. Click Table Tools
   Layout tab.
3. Click Formula button.
4. Type formula in
   Formula dialog box.
5. Click OK.

To perform a calculation on the data in a table, position the insertion point in the cell where the result of the calculation is to be inserted and then click the Formula button in the Data group on the Table Tools Layout tab. This displays the Formula dialog box, as shown in Figure 7.10. At this dialog box, accept the default formula in the *Formula* text box or type a calculation and then click OK.

Four basic operators are available for writing a formula, including the plus symbol (+) for addition, the minus symbol (–) for subtraction, the asterisk (*) for multiplication, and the forward slash (/) for division. If a calculation contains two or more operators, Word performs the operations from left to right. To change the order of operations, put parentheses around the part of the calculation to be performed first.

In the default formula, the SUM part of the formula is called a *function*. Word also provides other functions for inserting formulas. These functions are available in the *Paste function* option box in the Formula dialog box. For example, use the AVERAGE function to average numbers in cells.

Specify the numbering format with the *Number format* option box in the Formula dialog box. For example, when calculating amounts of money, specify the number of digits that should follow the decimal point.

Hint Use the
Update Field keyboard
shortcut, F9, to update
the selected field.

If changes are made to a formula, the result of the formula needs to be updated. To do this, right-click the formula result and then click *Update Field* at the shortcut menu. Another method is to click the formula result and then press the F9 function key, which is the Update Field keyboard shortcut. To update the results of all the formulas in a table, select the entire table and then press the F9 function key.

Figure 7.10 Formula Dialog Box

1. Open **TSPSalesTable** and then save it with the name **7-TSPSalesTable**.
2. Insert a formula in the table by completing the following steps:
   a. Click in cell B9. (Cell B9 is the empty cell immediately below the cell containing the amount *$375,630.*)
   b. Click the Table Tools Layout tab.
   c. Click the Formula button in the Data group.
   d. At the Formula dialog box, make sure *=SUM(ABOVE)* appears in the *Formula* text box.
   e. Click the *Number format* option box arrow and then click *#,##0* at the drop-down list (the top option in the list).
   f. Click OK to close the Formula dialog box.

   g. In the table, type a dollar symbol ($) before the number just inserted in cell B9.
3. Complete steps similar to those in Steps 2c through 2g to insert a formula in cell C9. (Cell C9 is the empty cell immediately below the cell containing the amount *$399,120.*)
4. Insert a formula that calculates the average of amounts by completing the following steps:
   a. Click in cell B10. (Cell B10 is the empty cell immediately right of the cell containing the word *Average.*)
   b. Click the Formula button in the Data group.
   c. At the Formula dialog box, delete the formula in the *Formula* text box *except* for the equals (=) sign.
   d. With the insertion point positioned immediately right of the equals sign, click the *Paste function* option box arrow and then click *AVERAGE* at the drop-down list.
   e. With the insertion point positioned between the left and right parentheses, type B2:B8. (When typing cell designations in a formula, you can type either uppercase or lowercase letters.)
   f. Click the *Number format* option box arrow and then click *#,##0* at the drop-down list (the top option in the list).
   g. Click OK to close the Formula dialog box.
   h. Type a dollar symbol ($) before the number just inserted in cell B10.
5. Complete steps similar to those in Steps 4b through 4h to insert a formula in cell C10 that calculates the average of the amounts in cells C2 through C8.

6. Insert a formula that calculates the maximum number by completing the following steps:
   a. Click in cell B11. (Cell B11 is the empty cell immediately right of the cell containing the words *Top Sales*.)
   b. Click the Formula button in the Data group.
   c. At the Formula dialog box, delete the formula in the *Formula* text box *except* for the equals sign.
   d. With the insertion point positioned immediately right of the equals sign, click the *Paste function* option box arrow and then click *MAX* at the drop-down list. (You will need to scroll down the list to locate the *MAX* option.)
   e. With the insertion point positioned between the left and right parentheses, type B2:B8.
   f. Click the *Number format* option box arrow and then click *#,##0* at the drop-down list.
   g. Click OK to close the Formula dialog box.
   h. Type a dollar symbol ($) before the number just inserted in cell B11.

7. Complete steps similar to those in Steps 6b through 6h to insert the maximum number in cell C11.
8. Save and then print **7-TSPSalesTable**.
9. Change the amount in cell B2 from *$543,241* to *$765,700*.
10. Recalculate all the formulas in the table by completing the following steps:
    a. Make sure the Table Tools Layout tab is active and then click the Select button in the Table group.
    b. Click the *Select Table* option.
    c. Press the F9 function key.
11. Save, print, and then close **7-TSPSalesTable**.

Check Your Work >

Activity 4 **Insert an Excel Worksheet** **1 Part**

You will insert an Excel worksheet in a blank document, decrease the number of rows and columns in the worksheet, insert data from a Word document, and calculate data in the worksheet.

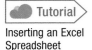

Tutorial >

Inserting an Excel Spreadsheet

Inserting an Excel Spreadsheet

An Excel spreadsheet (usually referred to as a *worksheet*) can be inserted into a Word document, which provides some Excel functions for modifying and formatting the data. To insert an Excel worksheet, click the Insert tab, click the Table button in the Tables group, and then click the *Excel Spreadsheet* option at the drop-down list. This inserts a worksheet in the document with seven columns and ten rows visible. Increase or decrease the number of visible cells by dragging the sizing handles around the worksheet. Use buttons on the Excel ribbon tabs to format the worksheet. Click outside the worksheet and the Excel ribbon tabs are removed. Double-click the table to redisplay the Excel ribbon tabs.

1. Open **SalesIncrease**.
2. Press Ctrl + N to open a blank document.
3. Insert an Excel spreadsheet into the blank document by clicking the Insert tab, clicking the Table button in the Tables group, and then clicking *Excel Spreadsheet* at the drop-down list.

4. Decrease the size of the worksheet by completing the following steps:
   a. Position the mouse pointer on the sizing handle (small black square) in the lower right corner of the worksheet until the pointer displays as a black, diagonal, two-headed arrow.
   b. Click and hold down the left mouse button, drag up and to the left, and then release the mouse button. Continue dragging the sizing handles until columns A, B, and C and rows 1 through 7 are visible.
5. Copy a table into the Excel worksheet by completing the following steps:
   a. Position the mouse pointer on the Word button on the taskbar and then click the *SalesIncrease* thumbnail.
   b. Position the mouse pointer over the table and then click the table move handle (small square containing a four-headed arrow) in the upper left corner of the table. (This selects all the cells in the table.)
   c. Click the Copy button in the Clipboard group on the Home tab.
   d. Close **SalesIncrease**.
   e. With the first cell in the worksheet active, click the Paste button in the Clipboard group.
6. Format the worksheet and insert a formula by completing the following steps:

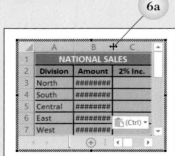

   a. Increase the width of the second column by positioning the mouse pointer on the column boundary between columns B and C and double-clicking the left mouse button.
   b. Click in cell C3, type the formula =B3*1.02, and then press the Enter key.
7. Copy the formula in cell C3 to the range C4:C7 by completing the following steps:
   a. Position the mouse pointer (white plus symbol) in cell C3, click and hold down the left mouse button, drag into cell C7, and then release the mouse button.

   b. Click the Fill button in the Editing group on the Home tab and then click *Down* at the drop-down list.
8. Click outside the worksheet to remove the Excel ribbon tabs.
9. Save the document and name it **7-Worksheet**.
10. Print and then close **7-Worksheet**.

Chapter Summary

- Use the Tables feature to create columns and rows of information. Create a table with the Table button in the Tables group on the Insert tab or with options at the Insert Table dialog box.
- A cell is the intersection between a row and a column. The lines that form the cells of the table are called *gridlines*.
- Press the Tab key to move the insertion point to the next cell or press Shift + Tab to move the insertion point to the preceding cell.
- Press Ctrl + Tab to move the insertion point to a tab within a cell.
- Move the insertion point to cells in a table using the mouse by clicking in a cell or using the keyboard commands shown in Table 7.1.
- Change the table design with options and buttons on the Table Tools Design tab.
- Refer to Table 7.2 for a list of mouse commands for selecting specific cells in a table and Table 7.3 for a list of keyboard commands for selecting specific cells in a table.
- Change the layout of a table with options and buttons on the Table Tools Layout tab.
- Select a table, column, row, or cell using the Select button in the Table group on the Table Tools Layout tab.
- Turn on and off the display of gridlines by clicking the View Gridlines button in the Table group on the Table Tools Layout tab.
- Insert and delete columns and rows with buttons in the Rows & Columns group on the Table Tools Layout tab.
- Merge selected cells with the Merge Cells button and split cells with the Split Cells button, both in the Merge group on the Table Tools Layout tab.
- Change the column width and row height using the height and width measurement boxes in the Cell Size group on the Table Tools Layout tab; by dragging move table column markers on the horizontal ruler, adjust table row markers on the vertical ruler, or gridlines in the table; or using the AutoFit button in the Cell Size group.
- Change the alignment of text in cells with buttons in the Alignment group on the Table Tools Layout tab.
- If a table spans two pages or more, a header row can be inserted at the beginning of each page. To do this, click in the header row or select the header rows and then click the Repeat Header Rows button in the Data group on the Table Tools Layout tab.
- Change cell margins with options in the Table Options dialog box.
- Change text direction in a cell with the Text Direction button in the Alignment group on the Table Tools Layout tab.
- Change the table dimensions and alignment with options at the Table Properties dialog box with the Table tab selected.
- Use the resize handle to change the size of the table and the table move handle to move the table.
- Convert text to a table with the *Convert Text to Table* option at the Table button drop-down list. Convert a table to text with the Convert to Text button in the Data group on the Table Tools Layout tab.

- Draw a table in a document by clicking the Insert tab, clicking the Table button in the Tables group, and then clicking *Draw Table* at the drop-down list. Using the mouse, drag in the document to create the table.
- Quick tables are predesigned tables that can be inserted in a document by clicking the Insert tab, clicking the Table button in the Tables group, pointing to *Quick Tables*, and then clicking a table at the side menu.
- Perform calculations on data in a table by clicking the Formula button in the Data group on the Table Tools Layout tab and then specifying the formula and number format at the Formula dialog box.
- Insert an Excel spreadsheet (worksheet) into a Word document to provide Excel functions by clicking the Insert tab, clicking the Table button in the Tables group, and then clicking *Excel Spreadsheet* at the drop-down list.

Commands Review

FEATURE	RIBBON TAB, GROUP	BUTTON, OPTION
AutoFit table contents	Table Tools Layout, Cell Size	, *AutoFit Contents*
cell alignment	Table Tools Layout, Alignment	
convert table to text	Table Tools Layout, Data	
convert text to table	Insert, Tables	, *Convert Text to Table*
delete column	Table Tools Layout, Rows & Columns	, *Delete Columns*
delete row	Table Tools Layout, Rows & Columns	, *Delete Rows*
distribute columns	Table Tools Layout, Cell Size	
distribute rows	Table Tools Layout, Cell Size	
draw table	Insert, Tables	, *Draw Table*
Formula dialog box	Table Tools Layout, Data	fx
insert column left	Table Tools Layout, Rows & Columns	
insert column right	Table Tools Layout, Rows & Columns	
Insert Excel spreadsheet	Insert, Tables	, *Excel Spreadsheet*
insert row above	Table Tools Layout, Rows & Columns	
insert row below	Table Tools Layout, Rows & Columns	
Insert Table dialog box	Insert, Tables	, *Insert Table*
merge cells	Table Tools Layout, Merge	

FEATURE	RIBBON TAB, GROUP	BUTTON, OPTION
Quick Table	Insert, Tables	▦ , *Quick Tables*
repeat header row	Table Tools Layout, Data	▦
Split Cells dialog box	Table Tools Layout, Merge	▦
table	Insert, Tables	▦
Table Options dialog box	Table Tools Layout, Alignment	▢
text direction	Table Tools Layout, Alignment	A→
view gridlines	Table Tools Layout, Table	▦

Microsoft

Word

Applying and Customizing Formatting

Performance Objectives

Upon successful completion of Chapter 8, you will be able to:

1 Create and insert custom numbers and bullets

2 Create and insert multilevel list formatting

3 Specify AutoCorrect exceptions

4 Add and delete AutoCorrect text

5 Use the AutoCorrect Options button

6 Customize AutoFormatting

7 Create custom theme colors and theme fonts

8 Save, apply, edit, and delete a custom theme

9 Reset the template theme

Word offers a number of features to apply and customize formatting and to help streamline the formatting of a document. In this chapter, you will learn how to define and insert custom numbers and bullets and to format text in a multilevel list. You will use Word's AutoCorrect and Autoformatting features and customize them for your convenience when creating documents. The Microsoft Office suite offers design themes that provide consistent formatting and help create documents with a professional and polished look. This chapter provides instruction on how to customize a theme by modifying the color and fonts and applying theme effects.

 Data Files

Before beginning chapter work, copy the WL1C8 folder to your storage medium and then make WL1C8 the active folder.

The online course includes additional training and assessment resources.

Inserting and Creating Custom Numbers and Bullets

 Numbering

Bullets

Number paragraphs or insert bullets before paragraphs using buttons in the Paragraph group on the Home tab. Use the Numbering button to insert numbers before specific paragraphs and use the Bullets button to insert bullets. To insert custom numbering or bullets, click the button arrow and then choose from the drop-down gallery that displays.

Inserting Custom Numbers

Insert numbers as text is typed or select text and then apply a numbering format. Type *1.* and then press the spacebar and Word indents the number approximately 0.25 inch. Type text after the number and then press the Enter key and Word indents all the lines in the paragraph 0.5 inch from the left margin (called a *hanging indent*). At the beginning of the next paragraph, Word inserts the number *2* followed by a period 0.25 inch from the left margin. Continue typing items and Word numbers successive paragraphs in the list. To number existing paragraphs of text, select the paragraphs and then click the Numbering button in the Paragraph group on the Home tab.

Hint If the automatic numbering or bulleting feature is on, press Shift + Enter to insert a line break without inserting a number or bullet.

Click the Numbering button in the Paragraph group and arabic numbers (1., 2., 3., etc.) are inserted in the document. This default numbering can be changed by clicking the Numbering button arrow and then clicking an option at the drop-down gallery.

To change list levels, click the Numbering button arrow, point to the *Change List Level* option at the bottom of the drop-down gallery, and then click a list level at the side menu. Set the numbering value with options at the Set Numbering Value dialog box, shown in Figure 8.1. Display this dialog box by clicking the Numbering button arrow and then clicking the *Set Numbering Value* option at the bottom of the drop-down gallery.

Figure 8.1 Set Numbering Value Dialog Box

1. Open **FDAgenda** and then save it with the name **8-FDAgenda**.
2. Restart the list numbering at 1 by completing the following steps:
   a. Select the numbered paragraphs.
   b. Click the Numbering button arrow in the Paragraph group on the Home tab and then click *Set Numbering Value* at the drop-down gallery.
   c. At the Set Numbering Value dialog box, select the number in the *Set value to* measurement box, type 1, and then press the Enter key.

3. Change the paragraph numbers to letters by completing the following steps:
   a. With the numbered paragraphs selected, click the Numbering button arrow.
   b. At the Numbering drop-down gallery, click the option that uses capital letters (second column, second row in the *Numbering Library* section [this location may vary]).

4. Add text by positioning the insertion point immediately right of the text *Introductions*, pressing the Enter key, and then typing Organizational Overview.

5. Demote the lettered list by completing the following steps:
   a. Select the lettered paragraphs.
   b. Click the Numbering button arrow, point to the *Change List Level* option, and then click the *a.* option at the side menu (*Level 2*).
6. With the paragraphs still selected, promote the list by clicking the Decrease Indent button in the Paragraph group on the Home tab. (The lowercase letters change back to capital letters.)
7. Move the insertion point to the end of the document and then type The meeting will stop for lunch, which is catered and will be held in the main conference center from 12:15 to 1:30 p.m.
8. Press the Enter key and then click the Numbering button.
9. Click the AutoCorrect Options button next to the *A.* inserted in the document and then click *Continue Numbering* at the drop-down list. (This changes the letter from *A.* to *H.*)
10. Type Future Goals, press the Enter key, type Proposals, press the Enter key, and then type Adjournment.
11. Press the Enter key and *K.* is inserted in the document. Turn off the numbering formatting by clicking the Numbering button arrow and then clicking the *None* option at the drop-down gallery.

12. Save and then print **8-FDAgenda**.
13. Select and then delete the paragraph of text in the middle of the list (the paragraph that begins *The meeting will stop*). (All the lettered items should be listed consecutively and the same amount of space should appear between them.)
14. Save **8-FDAgenda**.

 Check Your Work

Creating Custom Numbering Formats

Along with default and custom numbers, custom numbering formats can be created with options at the Define New Number Format dialog box, shown in Figure 8.2. Display this dialog box by clicking the Numbering button arrow and then clicking *Define New Number Format* at the drop-down gallery. Use options at the dialog box to specify the number style, font, and alignment. Preview the formatting in the *Preview* section.

Any number format created at the Define New Number Format dialog box is automatically included in the *Numbering Library* section of the Numbering button drop-down gallery. Remove a number format from the drop-down gallery by right-clicking the format and then clicking *Remove* at the shortcut menu.

Figure 8.2 Define New Number Format Dialog Box

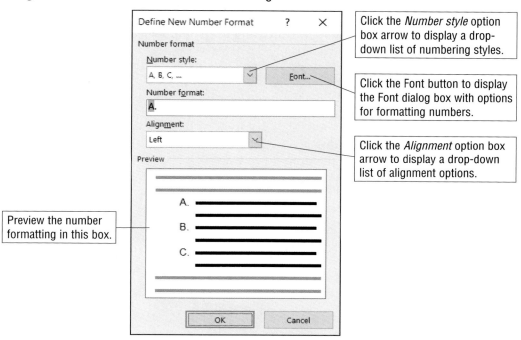

Click the *Number style* option box arrow to display a drop-down list of numbering styles.

Click the Font button to display the Font dialog box with options for formatting numbers.

Click the *Alignment* option box arrow to display a drop-down list of alignment options.

Preview the number formatting in this box.

Activity 1b Creating a Numbering Format   Part 2 of 2

1. With **8-FDAgenda** open, define a new numbering format by completing the following steps:
   a. With the insertion point positioned anywhere in the numbered paragraphs, click the Numbering button arrow in the Paragraph group on the Home tab.
   b. Click *Define New Number Format* at the drop-down list.
   c. At the Define New Number Format dialog box, click the *Number style* option box arrow and then click the *I, II, III, ...* option.
   d. Click the Font button at the right of the *Number style* list box.

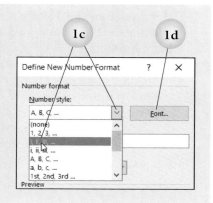

e. At the Font dialog box, scroll down the *Font* list box and then click *Calibri*.

f. Click *Bold* in the *Font style* list box.

g. Click OK to close the Font dialog box.

h. Click the *Alignment* option box arrow and then click *Right* at the drop-down list.

i. Click OK to close the Define New Number Format dialog box. (This applies the new formatting to the numbered paragraphs in the document.)

2. Insert a file into the current document by completing the following steps:

a. Press Ctrl + End to move the insertion point to the end of the document and then press the Enter key two times.

b. Click the Insert tab.

c. Click the Object button arrow in the Text group and then click *Text from File* at the drop-down list.

d. At the Insert File dialog box, navigate to your WL1C8 folder and then double-click the **PDAgenda** document.

3. Select the text below the title *PRODUCTION DEPARTMENT AGENDA*, click the Home tab, click the Numbering button arrow, and then click the roman numeral style created in Step 1.

4. Remove from the Numbering Library the numbering format you created by completing the following steps:

a. Click the Numbering button arrow.

b. In the *Numbering Library* section, right-click the roman numeral numbering format that you created.

c. Click *Remove* at the shortcut menu.

5. Save, print, and then close **8-FDAgenda**.

Check Your Work

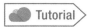 **Tutorial**

Creating Custom Bullets

Quick Steps

Define Custom Bullet
1. Click Bullets button arrow.
2. Click *Define New Bullet* at drop-down gallery.
3. Click Symbol button or Picture button.
4. Click symbol or picture.
5. Click OK.
6. Click OK.

Hint Create a picture bullet to add visual interest to a document.

Creating Custom Bullets

Click the Bullets button in the Paragraph group and a round bullet is inserted in the document. Insert custom bullets by clicking the Bullets button arrow and then clicking a bullet type at the drop-down gallery. This drop-down gallery displays the most recently used bullets along with an option for defining a new bullet.

Click the *Define New Bullet* option and the Define New Bullet dialog box displays, as shown in Figure 8.3. Use options at the dialog box to choose a symbol or picture bullet, change the font size of the bullet, and specify the alignment of the bullet. When creating a custom bullet, consider matching the theme or mood of the document to maintain a consistent look or creating a picture bullet to add visual interest.

A custom bullet created at the Define New Bullet dialog box is automatically included in the *Bullet Library* section of the Bullets button drop-down gallery. Remove a custom bullet from the drop-down gallery by right-clicking the bullet and then clicking *Remove* at the shortcut menu.

As with the level of a numbered list, the level of a bulleted list can be changed. To do this, click the item or select the items to be changed, click the Bullets button arrow, and then point to *Change List Level*. At the side menu of bullet options that displays, click a bullet. To insert a line break in the list while the automatic bullets feature is on without inserting a bullet, press Shift + Enter. (A line break can also be inserted in a numbered list without inserting a number by pressing Shift + Enter.)

Figure 8.3 Define New Bullet Dialog Box

Choose a symbol bullet by clicking the Symbol button and then clicking a symbol at the Symbol dialog box.

Apply font formatting to a bullet by clicking the Font button and then applying formatting at the Font dialog box.

Click the *Alignment* option box arrow to display a drop-down list of alignment options.

Use a picture as a bullet by clicking the Picture button and then searching for and inserting a picture from the Insert Pictures window.

Preview the bullet formatting in this box.

1. Open **TTSHawaii** and then save it with the name **8-TTSHawaii**.
2. Define and insert a picture bullet by completing the following steps:
   a. Select the four paragraphs of text below the heading *Rainy Day Activities*.
   b. Click the Bullets button arrow in the Paragraph group on the Home tab and then click *Define New Bullet* at the drop-down gallery.

   c. At the Define New Bullet dialog box, click the Picture button.
   d. At the Insert Pictures window, click the *Browse* option at the right of the *From a file* option, navigate to your WL1C8 folder, and then double-click the **Flower** image file.
   e. Click OK to close the Define New Bullet dialog box. (The new bullet is applied to the selected paragraphs.)
3. Define and insert a symbol bullet by completing the following steps:
   a. Select the six paragraphs below the heading *Kauai Sights*.
   b. Click the Bullets button arrow and then click *Define New Bullet* at the drop-down gallery.
   c. At the Define New Bullet dialog box, click the Symbol button.
   d. At the Symbol dialog box, click the *Font* option box arrow, scroll down the drop-down list, and then click *Wingdings*.

   e. Click the flower symbol shown at the right (character code 124).
   f. Click OK to close the Symbol dialog box.
   g. At the Define New Bullet dialog box, click the Font button.
   h. At the Font dialog box, click *11* in the *Size* list box.
   i. Click the *Font color* option box arrow and then click the *Light Blue, Background 2, Darker 25%* color option (third column, third row in the *Theme Colors* section).
   j. Click OK to close the Font dialog box and then click OK to close the Define New Bullet dialog box.
4. Remove the two bullets you defined from the *Bullet Library* section of the Bullets button drop-down gallery by completing the following steps:
   a. Click the Bullets button arrow.
   b. Right-click the flower picture bullet in the *Bullet Library* section and then click *Remove* at the shortcut menu.
   c. Click the Bullets button arrow.
   d. Right-click the flower symbol bullet in the *Bullet Library* section and then click *Remove* at the shortcut menu.
5. Save, print, and then close **8-TTSHawaii**.

Check Your Work

Activity 3 Apply Multilevel List Numbering to a Job Search Document

2 Parts

You will open a document containing a list of job search terms, apply multilevel list numbering to the text, and then define and apply a new multilevel list numbering style.

Applying Multilevel
List Formatting

Multilevel
List

Applying Multilevel List Formatting

Use the Multilevel List button in the Paragraph group on the Home tab to specify the type of list formatting for paragraphs of text at the left margin, first tab, second tab, and so on. To apply predesigned multilevel list formatting to text in a document, click the Multilevel List button and then click a list style at the drop-down list.

Some options at the Multilevel List button drop-down list have labels such as *Heading 1*, *Heading 2*, and so on after the numbers. Click one of these options and Word inserts the numbering and applies the heading styles to the text.

Quick Steps

Insert Multilevel List Formatting
1. Click Multilevel List button.
2. Click style at drop-down gallery.

Activity 3a Inserting Multilevel List Formatting

Part 1 of 2

1. Open **JSList** and then save it with the name **8-JSList(3a)**.
2. Select the paragraphs of text below the title and then apply multilevel list formatting by completing the following steps:
    a. Click the Multilevel List button in the Paragraph group on the Home tab.
    b. At the drop-down list, click the middle option in the top row of the *List Library* section.

   c. Deselect the text.
3. Save, print, and then close **8-JSList(3a)**.

  Check Your Work

Creating a Custom Multilevel List

The Multilevel List button drop-down list contains predesigned level formatting options. If the drop-down list does not contain the type of list formatting required, create custom list formatting. To do this, click the Multilevel List button and then click the *Define New Multilevel List* option. This displays the Define new Multilevel list dialog box, shown in Figure 8.4. At this dialog box, click a level in the *Click level to modify* list box and then specify the level format, style, position, and alignment.

Typing a Multilevel List

Select text and then apply a multilevel list or apply the list and then type the text. When typing the text, press the Tab key to move to the next level or press Shift + Tab to move to the previous level.

Figure 8.4 Define New Multilevel List Dialog Box

Click a level to modify in this list box.

Specify the list format, style, position, and alignment for the selected level.

1. Open **JSList** and then save it with the name **8-JSList(3b)**.
2. Select the paragraphs of text below the title.
3. Click the Multilevel List button in the Paragraph group on the Home tab.
4. Click the *Define New Multilevel List* option at the drop-down list.
5. At the Define new Multilevel list dialog box, make sure *1* is selected in the *Click level to modify* list box.
6. Click the *Number style for this level* option box arrow and then click *A, B, C, …* at the drop-down list.
7. Click in the *Enter formatting for number* text box, delete any text after *A*, and then type a period. (See image at the right.)
8. Click the *Aligned at* measurement box up arrow until *0.3"* displays in the measurement box.
9. Click the *Text indent at* measurement box up arrow until *0.6"* displays in the measurement box.
10. Click *2* in the *Click level to modify* list box.
11. Click the *Number style for this level* option box arrow and then click *1, 2, 3, …* at the drop-down list.
12. Click in the *Enter formatting for number* text box, delete any text after the *1*, and then type a period.
13. Click the *Aligned at* measurement box up arrow until *0.6"* displays in the measurement box.
14. Click the *Text indent at* measurement box up arrow until *0.9"* displays in the measurement box.

15. Click *3* in the *Click level to modify* list box.
16. Click the *Number style for this level* option box arrow and then click *a, b, c, ...* at the drop-down list.
17. Make sure that *a)* appears in the *Enter formatting for number* text box. (If not, delete any text after the *a* and then type a right parenthesis.)
18. Click the *Aligned at* measurement box up arrow until *0.9"* displays in the measurement box.
19. Click the *Text indent at* measurement box up arrow until *1.2"* displays in the measurement box.
20. Click OK to close the dialog box. (This applies the new multilevel list numbering to the selected text.)
21. Deselect the text.
22. Save, print, and then close **8-JSList(3b)**.

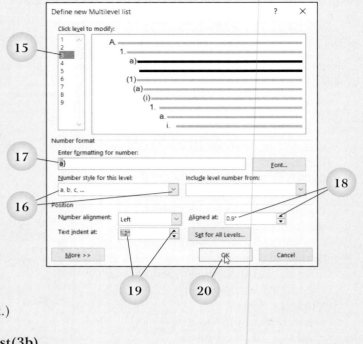

Check Your Work

Activity 4 Create a Travel Document Using AutoCorrect   **4 Parts**

You will create several AutoCorrect entries, open a letterhead document, and then use the AutoCorrect entries to type text in the document.

Tutorial

Customizing AutoCorrect

 Quick Steps

Display AutoCorrect Exceptions Dialog Box
1. Click File tab.
2. Click *Options*.
3. Click *Proofing*.
4. Click AutoCorrect Options button.
5. Click AutoCorrect tab.
6. Click Exceptions button.

Customizing AutoCorrect

Word's AutoCorrect feature corrects certain text automatically as it is typed. The types of corrections that can be made are specified with options at the AutoCorrect dialog box with the AutoCorrect tab selected, as shown in Figure 8.5.

Display this dialog box by clicking the File tab, clicking *Options*, clicking *Proofing* in the left panel, clicking the AutoCorrect Options button, and then clicking the AutoCorrect tab. At the dialog box, turn AutoCorrect features on or off by inserting or removing check marks from the check boxes. In addition, specify AutoCorrect exceptions, replace frequently misspelled words with the correctly spelled words, add frequently used words, and specify keys to quickly insert the words in a document.

Figure 8.5 AutoCorrect Dialog Box with the AutoCorrect Tab Selected

Remove the check marks from the check boxes identifying corrections that should not be made by AutoCorrect.

Click this button to display the AutoCorrect Exceptions dialog box.

Type the text shown in the first column of this list box in a document and then press the spacebar and the text is replaced by the symbol or text shown in the second column.

Specifying AutoCorrect Exceptions

The check box options at the AutoCorrect dialog box with the AutoCorrect tab selected identify the types of corrections made by AutoCorrect. Specify which corrections should not be made with options at the AutoCorrect Exceptions dialog box, shown in Figure 8.6. Display this dialog box by clicking the Exceptions button at the AutoCorrect dialog box with the AutoCorrect tab selected.

AutoCorrect usually capitalizes a word that comes after a period, since a period usually ends a sentence. This automatic capitalization may be incorrect in some cases, as when the period is used in an abbreviation. Exceptions to this general practice are shown in the AutoCorrect Exceptions dialog box with the First Letter tab selected. Many exceptions already display in the dialog box but additional exceptions can be added by typing each exception in the *Don't capitalize after* text box and then clicking the Add button.

Figure 8.6 AutoCorrect Exceptions Dialog Box

Click this tab to display a list box to add exceptions to correcting two initial capital letters in a word.

Click this tab to display a list box to add any other exceptions to corrections.

Add capitalization exceptions to this list box.

By default, AutoCorrect corrects the use of two initial capital letters in a word. If AutoCorrect should not correct these instances, display the AutoCorrect Exceptions dialog box with the INitial CAps tab selected and then type the exception text in the *Don't correct* text box. At the AutoCorrect Exceptions dialog box with the Other Corrections tab selected, type the text that should not be corrected in the *Don't correct* text box. Delete an exception from the dialog box with any of the tabs selected by clicking the text in the list box and then clicking the Delete button.

Adding and Deleting an AutoCorrect Entry

 Tutorial

Adding and Deleting an AutoCorrect Entry

Quick Steps

Add Word to AutoCorrect
1. Click File tab.
2. Click *Options*.
3. Click *Proofing*.
4. Click AutoCorrect Options button.
5. Click AutoCorrect tab.
6. Type misspelled or abbreviated word.
7. Press Tab.
8. Type correctly spelled or complete word.
9. Click Add button.
10. Click OK.

Commonly misspelled words and/or typographical errors can be added to AutoCorrect. For example, if a user consistently types *relavent* instead of *relevant*, *relavent* can be added to the AutoCorrect dialog box with the AutoCorrect tab selected with the direction to correct it to *relevant*. The AutoCorrect dialog box also contains a few symbols that can be inserted in a document. For example, type *(c)* and AutoCorrect changes the text to © (copyright symbol). Type *(r)* and AutoCorrect changes the text to ® (registered trademark symbol). The symbols display at the beginning of the AutoCorrect dialog box list box.

An abbreviation can be added to AutoCorrect that will insert the entire word (or words) in the document when it is typed. For example, in Activity 4a, the abbreviation *fav* will be added to AutoCorrect and *Family Adventure Vacations* will be inserted when *fav* is typed followed by a press of the spacebar or Enter key. The capitalization of the abbreviation can also be controlled. For example, in Activity 4a, the abbreviation *Na* will be added to AutoCorrect and *Namibia* will be inserted when *Na* is typed and *NAMIBIA* will be inserted when *NA* is typed.

AutoCorrect text can be deleted from the AutoCorrect dialog box. To do this, display the AutoCorrect dialog box with the AutoCorrect tab selected, click the word or words in the list box, and then click the Delete button.

Activity 4a **Adding Text and Specifying Exceptions to AutoCorrect**   Part 1 of 4

1. At a blank screen, click the File tab and then click *Options*.
2. At the Word Options dialog box, click *Proofing* in the left panel.
3. Click the AutoCorrect Options button in the *AutoCorrect options* section.
4. At the AutoCorrect dialog box with the AutoCorrect tab selected, add an exception to AutoCorrect by completing the following steps:
   a. Click the Exceptions button.
   b. At the AutoCorrect Exceptions dialog box, click the INitial CAps tab.
   c. Click in the *Don't correct* text box, type STudent, and then click the Add button.

    d. Click in the *Don't correct* text box, type STyle, and then click the Add button.
    e. Click OK.
5. At the AutoCorrect dialog box with the AutoCorrect tab selected, click in the *Replace* text box and then type fav.
6. Press the Tab key (which moves the insertion point to the *With* text box) and then type Family Adventure Vacations.
7. Click the Add button. (This adds *fav* and *Family Adventure Vacations* to AutoCorrect and also selects *fav* in the *Replace* text box.)

8. Type Na in the *Replace* text box. (The text *fav* is automatically removed when the typing of *Na* begins.)
9. Press the Tab key and then type Namibia.
10. Click the Add button.
11. With the insertion point positioned in the *Replace* text box, type vf.
12. Press the Tab key and then type Victoria Falls.
13. Click the Add button.
14. With the insertion point positioned in the *Replace* text box, type tts.
15. Press the Tab key and then type Terra Travel Services.
16. Click the Add button.
17. Click OK to close the AutoCorrect dialog box and then click OK to close the Word Options dialog box.
18. Open **TTSLtrhd** and then save it with the name **8-TTSAfrica**.
19. Type the text shown in Figure 8.7. Type the text exactly as shown (including applying bold formatting and centering *fav* at the beginning of the document). AutoCorrect will correct the words as they are typed.
20. Save **8-TTSAfrica**.

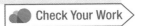

Figure 8.7 Activity 4a

fav

Na and vf Adventure

tts is partnering with fav to provide adventurous and thrilling family vacations. Our first joint adventure is a holiday trip to Na. Na is one of the most fascinating holiday destinations in Africa and offers comfortable facilities, great food, cultural interaction, abundant wildlife, and a wide variety of activities to interest people of all ages.

During the 12-day trip, you and your family will travel across Na through national parks, enjoying the beautiful and exotic scenery and watching wildlife in natural habitats. You will cruise along the Kwando and Chobe rivers and spend time at the Okapuka Lodge located near Windhoek, the capital of Na.

If you or your family member is a college student, contact one of our college travel adventure consultants to learn more about the newest Student Travel package titled "STudent STyle" that offers a variety of student discounts, rebates, and free travel accessories for qualifying participants.

tts and fav are offering a 15 percent discount if you sign up for this once-in-a-lifetime trip to Na. This exciting adventure is limited to twenty people, so don't wait to sign up.

 Tutorial

Undoing an
AutoCorrect
Correction

 AutoCorrect
Options

Using the AutoCorrect Options Button

After AutoCorrect corrects a portion of text, hover the mouse pointer near the text and a small blue box displays below it. Move the mouse pointer to this blue box and the AutoCorrect Options button displays. Click this button to display a drop-down list with the options to change the text back to the original version, stop automatically correcting the specific text, and display the AutoCorrect dialog box.

If the AutoCorrect Options button does not display, turn on the feature. To do this, display the AutoCorrect dialog box with the AutoCorrect tab selected, click the *Show AutoCorrect Options buttons* check box to insert a check mark, and then click OK to close the dialog box.

Activity 4b Using the AutoCorrect Options Button

Part 2 of 4

1. With **8-TTSAfrica** open, select and then delete the last paragraph.
2. With the insertion point positioned on the blank line below the last paragraph of text (you may need to press the Enter key), type the following text. (AutoCorrect will automatically change *Ameria* to *America*, which you will change in the next step.) Through the sponsorship of Ameria Resorts, we are able to offer you a 15 percent discount for groups of twelve or more people.
3. Change the spelling of *America* back to *Ameria* by completing the following steps:
   a. Position the mouse pointer over *America* until a blue box displays below it.
   b. Position the mouse pointer on the blue box until the AutoCorrect Options button displays.

c. Click the AutoCorrect Options button and then click the *Change back to "Ameria"* option.

4. Save and then print **8-TTSAfrica**.

3c

Check Your Work

Inserting Symbols Automatically

AutoCorrect recognizes and replaces symbols as well as text. Several symbols included in AutoCorrect are shown in the AutoCorrect dialog box and are listed first in the *Replace* text box. Table 8.1 lists these symbols along with the characters to insert them.

In addition to the symbols provided by Word, other symbols can be inserted in the AutoCorrect dialog box with the AutoCorrect button in the Symbol dialog box. To insert a symbol in the AutoCorrect dialog box, click the Insert tab, click the Symbol button in the Symbols group, and then click *More Symbols* at the drop-down list. At the Symbol dialog box, click the specific symbol and then click the AutoCorrect button in the lower left corner of the dialog box. This displays the AutoCorrect dialog box with the symbol inserted in the *With* text box and the insertion point positioned in the *Replace* text box. Type the text that will insert the symbol, click the Add button, and then click OK to close the AutoCorrect dialog box. Click the Close button to close the Symbol dialog box.

Table 8.1 AutoCorrect Symbols Available at the AutoCorrect Dialog Box

Type	To insert
(c)	©
(r)	®
(tm)	™
...	. . .
:) or :-)	☺
:| or :-|	😐
:(or :-(	☹
-->	→
<--	←
==>	→
<==	←
<=>	⇔

1. With **8-TTSAfrica** open, move the insertion point so it is positioned immediately right of the last *s* in *Resorts* (located in the last paragraph) and then type (r). (This inserts the registered trademark symbol.)
2. Move the insertion point immediately left of the *1* in *15* and then type ==>. (This inserts the ➔ symbol.)
3. Move the insertion point immediately right of the *t* in *discount* and then type <==. (This inserts the ← symbol.)
4. Insert the pound (£) currency unit symbol in AutoCorrect by completing the following steps:
    a. Click the Insert tab.
    b. Click the Symbol button and then click *More Symbols* at the drop-down list.
    c. At the Symbol dialog box, make sure that *(normal text)* displays in the *Font* option box. If it does not, click the *Font* option box arrow and then click *(normal text)* at the drop-down list (first option in the list).
    d. Scroll through the list of symbols and then click the pound (£) currency unit symbol (located in approximately the sixth or seventh row; character code *00A3*).
    e. Click the AutoCorrect button in the lower left corner of the dialog box.
    f. At the AutoCorrect dialog box, type pcu in the *Replace* text box and then click the Add button.
    g. Click OK to close the AutoCorrect dialog box.

    h. Click the Close button to close the Symbol dialog box.
5. Press Ctrl + End to move the insertion point to the end of the document and then press the Enter key.
6. Type the text shown in Figure 8.8. (Press Shift + Enter or the Enter key as indicated in the figure.) Create the pound currency unit symbol by typing pcu and then pressing the spacebar. Press the Backspace key once and then type 2,999. (Complete similar steps when typing *£2,549 (UK)*.)
7. Save **8-TTSAfrica**.

Check Your Work

Figure 8.8 Activity 4c

> **Individual price:** *(press Shift+ Enter)*
> $3,999 (US) *(press Shift+ Enter)*
> £2,999 (UK) *(press Enter)*
>
> **Individual price for groups of twelve or more:** *(press Shift+ Enter)*
> $3,399 (US) *(press Shift+ Enter)*
> £2,549 (UK)

Tutorial

Customizing
AutoFormatting

Customizing AutoFormatting

When typing text, Word provides options to automatically apply some formatting, such as changing a fraction to a fraction character (1/2 to ½), changing numbers to ordinals (1st to 1st), changing an internet or network path to a hyperlink (https://ppi-edu.net to https://ppi-edu.net), and applying bullets or numbers to text. The autoformatting options display in the AutoCorrect dialog box with the AutoFormat As You Type tab selected, as shown in Figure 8.9.

Display this dialog box by clicking the File tab and then clicking *Options*. At the Word Options dialog box, click *Proofing* in the left panel and then click the AutoCorrect Options button. At the AutoCorrect dialog box, click the AutoFormat As You Type tab. At the dialog box, remove the check marks from those options to be turned off and insert check marks for those options to be formatted automatically.

Figure 8.9 AutoCorrect Dialog Box with the AutoFormat As You Type Tab Selected

Insert check marks in the check boxes for formatting options that Word should apply automatically.

Click this tab to display options for formats that Word should apply automatically as text is being typed.

AutoCorrect

AutoCorrect | Math AutoCorrect | AutoFormat As You Type | AutoFormat | Actions

Replace as you type
- ☑ "Straight quotes" with "smart quotes"
- ☑ Fractions (1/2) with fraction character (½)
- ☐ *Bold* and _italic_ with real formatting
- ☑ Internet and network paths with hyperlinks
- ☑ Ordinals (1st) with superscript
- ☑ Hyphens (--) with dash (—)

Apply as you type
- ☑ Automatic bulleted lists
- ☑ Border lines
- ☐ Built-in Heading styles
- ☑ Automatic numbered lists
- ☑ Tables

Automatically as you type
- ☑ Format beginning of list item like the one before it
- ☑ Set left- and first-indent with tabs and backspaces
- ☐ Define styles based on your formatting

OK | Cancel

1. Make sure **8-TTSAfrica** is open.
2. Suppose that you need to add a couple of web addresses to a document and do not want the addresses automatically formatted as hyperlinks (since you are sending the document as hard copy rather than electronically). Turn off the autoformatting of web addresses by completing the following steps:
   a. Click the File tab and then click *Options*.
   b. At the Word Options dialog box, click *Proofing* in the left panel.
   c. Click the AutoCorrect Options button.
   d. At the AutoCorrect dialog box, click the AutoFormat As You Type tab.
   e. Click the *Internet and network paths with hyperlinks* check box to remove the check mark.

   f. Click OK to close the AutoCorrect dialog box.
   g. Click OK to close the Word Options dialog box.
3. Press Ctrl + End to move the insertion point to the end of the document, press the Enter key, and then type the text shown in Figure 8.10.
4. Turn on the autoformatting of web addresses that was turned off in Step 2 by completing Steps 2a through 2g (except in Step 2e, insert the check mark rather than remove it).
5. Delete *fav* from AutoCorrect by completing the following steps:
   a. Click the File tab and then click *Options*.
   b. At the Word Options dialog box, click *Proofing* in the left panel.
   c. Click the AutoCorrect Options button.
   d. At the AutoCorrect dialog box, click the AutoCorrect tab.
   e. Click in the *Replace* text box and then type fav. (This selects the entry in the list box.)
   f. Click the Delete button.
6. Complete steps similar to those in Steps 5e and 5f to delete the *Na*, *tts*, and *vf* AutoCorrect entries.

7. Delete the exceptions added to the AutoCorrect Exceptions dialog box by completing the following steps:
   a. At the AutoCorrect dialog box with the AutoCorrect tab selected, click the Exceptions button.
   b. At the AutoCorrect Exceptions dialog box, if necessary, click the INitial CAps tab.
   c. Click S*Tudent* in the list box and then click the Delete button.
   d. Click S*Tyle* in the list box and then click the Delete button.
   e. Click OK to close the AutoCorrect Exceptions dialog box.
8. Click OK to close the AutoCorrect dialog box.
9. Click OK to close the Word Options dialog box.
10. Save, print, and then close **3-TTSAfrica**.

Check Your Work

Figure 8.10 Activity 4d

For additional information on the Na adventure, as well as other exciting vacation specials, please visit our website at https://ppi-edu.net/terratravel or visit https://ppi-edu.net/famadv.

Activity 5 Apply Custom Themes to Company Documents   5 Parts

You will create custom theme colors and theme fonts and then apply theme effects. You will save the changes as a custom theme, apply the custom theme to a company services document and a company security document, and then delete the theme.

Customizing Themes

A document created in Word is based on the Normal template. This template provides a document with default layout, formatting, styles, and themes. The default template provides a number of built-in or predesigned themes. Some of these built-in themes have been used in previous chapters to apply colors, fonts, and effects to content in documents. The same built-in themes are available in Microsoft Word, Excel, Access, PowerPoint, and Outlook. Because the same themes are available across these programs, business files—such as documents, workbooks, databases, and presentations—can be branded with a consistent and professional appearance.

A theme is a combination of theme colors, theme fonts, and theme effects. Within a theme, any of these three elements can be changed with the additional buttons in the Document Formatting group on the Design tab. Apply one of the built-in themes or create a custom theme. A custom theme will display in the *Custom* section of the Themes button drop-down gallery. To create a custom theme, change the theme colors, theme fonts, and/or theme effects.

Hint Every document created in Word has a theme applied to it.

Themes

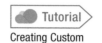 Colors

A Fonts

The Themes, Colors, and Fonts buttons in the Document Formatting group on the Design tab provide representations of the current theme. For example, the Themes button shows uppercase and lowercase *Aa* with colored squares below the letters. When the theme colors are changed, the changes are reflected in the small colored squares on the Themes button and the four squares on the Colors button. If the theme fonts are changed, the letters on the Themes button and the Fonts button reflect the change.

Creating Custom Theme Colors

☁ Tutorial

Creating Custom
Theme Colors

Quick Steps

Create Custom Theme Colors
1. Click Design tab.
2. Click Colors button.
3. Click *Customize Colors*.
4. Type name for custom theme colors.
5. Change background, accent, and hyperlink colors.
6. Click Save button.

To create custom theme colors, click the Design tab, click the Colors button, and then click *Customize Colors* at the drop-down gallery. This displays the Create New Theme Colors dialog box, similar to the one shown in Figure 8.11. Type a name for the custom theme colors in the *Name* text box and then change colors. Theme colors contain four text and background colors, six accent colors, and two hyperlink colors, as shown in the *Theme colors* section of the dialog box. Change a color in the list box by clicking the color button at the right of the color option and then clicking a color at the color palette.

After making all the changes to the colors, click the Save button. This saves the custom theme colors and also applies the color changes to the active document. Display the custom theme by clicking the Colors button. The custom theme will display at the top of the drop-down gallery in the *Custom* section.

Resetting Custom Theme Colors

If changes have been made to colors at the Create New Theme Colors dialog box, the colors can be reset by clicking the Reset button in the lower left corner of the dialog box. Clicking this button restores the colors to the default Office theme colors.

Figure 8.11 Create New Theme Colors Dialog Box

Type a name for the custom theme in the *Name* text box.

Click the Reset button to reset the colors back to the default.

Change a theme color by clicking the color button and then clicking a color at the drop-down palette.

Note: If you are running Word on a computer connected to a network in a public environment, such as a school, you may need to complete all five parts of Activity 5 during the same session. Network system software may delete your custom themes when you exit Word. Check with your instructor.

1. At a blank document, click the Design tab.
2. Click the Colors button in the Document Formatting group and then click *Customize Colors* at the drop-down gallery.
3. At the Create New Theme Colors dialog box, click the color button to the right of the *Text/Background - Light 1* option and then click the *Dark Red* option (first option in the *Standard Colors* section).

4. Click the color button to the right of the *Accent 1* option and then click the *Yellow* option (fourth option in the *Standard Colors* section).
5. You decide that you do not like the colors you have chosen and want to start over. To do this, click the Reset button in the lower left corner of the dialog box.
6. Click the color button to the right of the *Text/Background - Dark 2* option and then click the *Blue* option (eighth option in the *Standard Colors* section).
7. Change the color for the *Accent 1* option by completing the following steps:
   a. Click the color button to the right of the *Accent 1* option.
   b. Click the *More Colors* option below the color palette.
   c. At the Colors dialog box, click the Standard tab.
   d. Click the dark green color, as shown below.
   e. Click OK to close the dialog box.

8. Save the custom colors by completing the following steps:
   a. Select the current text in the *Name* text box.
   b. Type your first and last names (without a space between).
   c. Click the Save button.
9. Close the document without saving it.

8b   8c

Name: StudentName

Reset   Save   Cancel

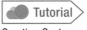 Tutorial

Creating Custom Theme Fonts

Creating Custom Theme Fonts

Quick Steps

Create Custom Theme Fonts
1. Click Design tab.
2. Click Fonts button.
3. Click *Customize Fonts*.
4. Choose fonts.
5. Type name for custom theme fonts.
6. Click Save button.

To create a custom theme font, click the Design tab, click the Fonts button, and then click *Customize Fonts* at the drop-down gallery. This displays the Create New Theme Fonts dialog box. At this dialog box, type a name for the custom fonts in the *Name* text box. Choose a font for headings and a font for body text and then click the Save button.

Activity 5b   Creating Custom Theme Fonts   Part 2 of 5

1. At a blank document, click the Design tab.
2. Click the Fonts button in the Document Formatting group and then click the *Customize Fonts* option at the drop-down gallery.
3. At the Create New Theme Fonts dialog box, click the *Heading font* option box arrow, scroll up the drop-down list, and then click *Arial*.
4. Click the *Body font* option box arrow, scroll down the drop-down list, and then click *Cambria*.
5. Save the custom fonts by completing the following steps:
   a. Select the current text in the *Name* text box.
   b. Type your first and last names (without a space between).
   c. Click the Save button.

Create New Theme Fonts   ?   X

Heading font: Sample
Arial

Body font:
Cambria

Heading
Body text body text body text. Body t

Name: StudentName

Save   Cancel

3

4

5b   5c

6. Close the document without saving it.

Applying Custom Theme Colors and Fonts

Apply custom theme colors to a document by clicking the Colors button in the Document Formatting group on the Design tab and then clicking the custom theme colors option at the top of the drop-down gallery in the *Custom* section. Complete similar steps to apply custom theme fonts.

Applying Theme Effects

The options in the Theme Effects button drop-down gallery apply sets of line and fill effects to the graphics in a document. Custom theme effects cannot be created but a theme effect can be applied to a document and the formatting can then be saved in a custom theme.

Tutorial

Saving a Custom Document Theme

Quick Steps

Save Custom Document Theme
1. Click Design tab.
2. Click Themes button.
3. Click *Save Current Theme*.
4. Type name for theme.
5. Click Save button.

Saving a Custom Document Theme

A custom document theme containing custom theme colors, fonts, and effects can be saved. To do this, create and apply custom theme colors, fonts, and theme effects to a document, click the Themes button on the Design tab, and then click *Save Current Theme* at the drop-down gallery. This displays the Save Current Theme dialog box, which has many of the same options as the Save As dialog box. Type a name for the custom document theme in the *File name* text box and then click the Save button.

Activity 5c **Applying Theme Effects and Saving a Custom Document Theme**   **Part 3 of 5**

1. Open **NSSServices** and then save it with the name **8-NSSServices**.
2. Make the following changes to the document:
   a. Apply the Title style to the company name *Northland Security Systems*.
   b. Apply the Heading 1 style to the heading *Northland Security Systems Mission*.
   c. Apply the Heading 2 style to the remaining headings, *Security Services* and *Security Software*.
   d. Apply the Word 2010 style set (the last option in the expanded style set gallery on the Design tab).
3. Apply the custom theme colors you saved by completing the following steps:
   a. Click the Colors button in the Document Formatting group on the Design tab.
   b. Click the theme colors option with your name at the top of the drop-down gallery in the *Custom* group.

4. Apply the custom theme fonts you saved by clicking the Fonts button in the Document Formatting group and then clicking the custom theme font with your name.

5. Apply a theme effect by clicking the Effects button in the Document Formatting group and then clicking *Glossy* at the drop-down gallery (last option).

6. Make the following changes to the SmartArt graphic:
   a. Click the graphic to select it. (When the graphic is selected, a gray border displays around it.)
   b. Click the SmartArt Tools Design tab.
   c. Click the Change Colors button and then click *Colorful Range - Accent Colors 5 to 6* (last option in the *Colorful* section).
   d. Click the More SmartArt Styles button in the SmartArt Styles group and then click *Cartoon* (third option in the *3-D* section).
   e. Click outside the SmartArt graphic to deselect it.
7. Save the custom theme colors and fonts, as well as the Glossy theme effect, as a custom document theme by completing the following steps:
   a. Click the Design tab.
   b. Click the Themes button in the Document Formatting group.
   c. Click the *Save Current Theme* option at the bottom of the drop-down gallery.
   d. At the Save Current Theme dialog box, type your first and last names (without a space between) in the *File name* text box and then click the Save button.

8. Save and then print **8-NSSServices**.

Editing Custom Themes

Custom theme colors and theme fonts can be edited. To edit custom theme colors, click the Design tab and then click the Colors button in the Document Formatting group. At the drop-down gallery of custom and built-in theme colors, right-click the custom theme colors and then click *Edit* at the shortcut menu. This displays the Edit Theme Colors dialog box, which contains the same options as the Create New Theme Colors dialog box. Make changes to the theme colors and then click the Save button.

To edit custom theme fonts, click the Fonts button in the Document Formatting group on the Design tab, right-click the custom theme fonts, and then click *Edit* at the shortcut menu. This displays the Edit Theme Fonts dialog box, which contains the same options as the Create New Theme Fonts dialog box. Make changes to the theme fonts and then click the Save button.

Quick Steps

Edit Custom Theme Colors or Fonts

1. Click Design tab.
2. Click Colors button or Fonts button.
3. Right-click custom theme colors or fonts.
4. Click *Edit*.
5. Make changes.
6. Click Save button.

Activity 5d Editing Custom Themes

Part 4 of 5

1. With **8-NSSServices** open, edit the theme colors by completing the following steps:
   a. If necessary, click the Design tab.
   b. Click the Colors button.
   c. Right-click the custom theme colors named with your first and last names.
   d. Click *Edit* at the shortcut menu.
   e. At the Edit Theme Colors dialog box, click the color button to the right of the *Text/ Background - Dark 2* option.
   f. Click the *More Colors* option below the color palette.
   g. At the Colors dialog box, click the Standard tab.
   h. Click the dark green color. (This is the same color you chose for *Accent 1* in Activity 5a.)
   i. Click OK to close the dialog box.
   j. Click the Save button.
2. Edit the theme fonts by completing the following steps:
   a. Click the Fonts button in the Document Formatting group.
   b. Right-click the custom theme fonts named with your first and last names and then click *Edit* at the shortcut menu.
   c. At the Edit Theme Fonts dialog box, click the *Body font* option box arrow, scroll down the drop-down list, and then click *Constantia*.
   d. Click the Save button.
3. Apply a different theme effect by clicking the Effects button and then clicking *Extreme Shadow* at the drop-down gallery (second column, last row). (This applies a shadow behind each shape.)

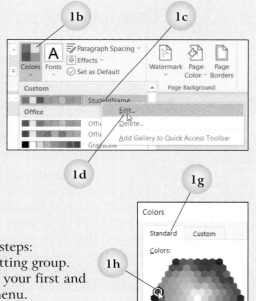

4. Save the changes to the custom theme by completing the following steps:
   a. Click the Themes button and then click *Save Current Theme* at the drop-down gallery.
   b. At the Save Current Theme dialog box, click the theme named with your first and last names in the content pane.
   c. Click the Save button.
   d. At the message stating that the theme already exists and asking if you want to replace it, click Yes.
5. Save, print, and then close **8-NSSServices**.

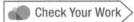

Resetting a Template Theme

Resetting Template Theme
1. Click Design tab.
2. Click Themes button.
3. Click *Reset to Theme from Template*.

If a built-in theme other than the Office default theme or a custom theme is applied to a document, the theme can be reset to the default by clicking the Themes button and then clicking the *Reset to Theme from Template* at the drop-down gallery. If the document is based on the default template provided by Word, clicking this option resets the theme to the Office default theme.

> Tutorial

Deleting a Custom Theme

Deleting Custom Themes

Delete custom theme colors from the Colors button drop-down gallery, delete custom theme fonts from the Fonts drop-down gallery, and delete custom themes at the Themes button drop-down gallery or the Save Current Theme dialog box.

Quick Steps

Delete Custom Theme Colors or Fonts
1. Click Design tab.
2. Click Colors or Fonts button.
3. Right-click custom theme.
4. Click *Delete*.
5. Click Yes.

To delete custom theme colors, click the Colors button, right-click the theme to be deleted, and then click *Delete* at the shortcut menu. At the confirmation message, click Yes. To delete custom theme fonts, click the Fonts button, right-click the theme to be deleted, and then click *Delete* at the shortcut menu. At the confirmation message, click Yes.

Delete a Custom Theme
1. Click Design tab.
2. Click Themes button.
3. Right-click custom theme.
4. Click *Delete*.
5. Click Yes.

Delete a custom theme (including custom colors, fonts, and effects) at the Themes button drop-down gallery or the Save Current Theme dialog box. To delete a custom theme from the drop-down gallery, click the Themes button, right-click the custom theme, click *Delete* at the shortcut menu, and then click Yes at the confirmation message. To delete a custom theme from the Save Current Theme dialog box, click the Themes button and then click *Save Current Theme* at the drop-down gallery. At the dialog box, click the custom theme document name, click the Organize button on the dialog box toolbar, and then click *Delete* at the drop-down list. If a confirmation message displays, click Yes.

Changing Default Settings

If formatting is applied to a document—such as a specific style set, theme, and paragraph spacing—it can be saved as the default formatting. To do this, click the Set as Default button in the Document Formatting group on the Design tab. At the message asking if the current style set and theme should be set as the default and indicating that the settings will be applied to new documents, click Yes.

1. Open **NSSSecurity** and then save it with the name **8-NSSSecurity**.
2. Apply the Title style to the company name, apply the Heading 1 style to the two headings in the document, and then apply the Word 2010 style set.
3. Apply your custom theme by completing the following steps:
   a. If necessary, click the Design tab.
   b. Click the Themes button.
   c. Click the custom theme named with your first and last names at the top of the drop-down gallery in the *Custom* section.
4. Save and then print **8-NSSSecurity**.
5. Reset the theme to the Office default theme by clicking the Themes button and then clicking *Reset to Theme from Template* at the drop-down gallery.
6. Save and then close **8-NSSSecurity**.
7. Press Ctrl + N to display a new blank document.
8. Delete the custom theme colors by completing the following steps:
   a. Click the Design tab.
   b. Click the Colors button in the Document Formatting group.
   c. Right-click the custom theme colors named with your first and last names.
   d. Click *Delete* at the shortcut menu.

   e. At the message that displays asking if you want to delete the theme colors, click Yes.
9. Complete steps similar to those in Step 8 to delete the custom theme fonts named with your first and last names.
10. Delete the custom theme by completing the following steps:
    a. Click the Themes button.
    b. Right-click the custom theme named with your first and last names.
    c. Click *Delete* at the shortcut menu.
    d. At the message asking if you want to delete the theme, click Yes.
11. Close the document without saving it.

Chapter Summary

- Use the Bullets button to insert bullets before specific paragraphs of text and use the Numbering button to insert numbers.

- Insert custom numbers by clicking the Numbering button arrow and then clicking an option at the drop-down gallery.

- Set the numbering value by clicking the Numbering button arrow and then clicking the *Set Numbering Value* option to display the dialog box.

- Define custom numbering formatting by clicking the Numbering button arrow and then clicking *Define New Number Format* to display the dialog box.

- Insert custom bullets by clicking the Bullets button arrow and then clicking an option at the drop-down gallery. Define new custom bullets by clicking the Bullets button arrow and then clicking *Define New Bullet* at the drop-down gallery to display the dialog box.

- Apply list formatting to multilevel paragraphs of text by clicking the Multilevel List button in the Paragraph group on the Home tab. Define new custom multilevel list formatting by clicking the Multilevel List button and then clicking *Define New Multilevel List* at the drop-down gallery to display the dialog box.

- When typing a multilevel list, press the Tab key to move to the next level and press Shift + Tab to move to the previous level.

- Words can be added to AutoCorrect at the AutoCorrect dialog box. Display this dialog box by clicking the File tab, clicking *Options*, clicking *Proofing*, clicking the AutoCorrect Options button, and then clicking the AutoCorrect tab.

- Specify exceptions to AutoCorrect by clicking the Exceptions button at the AutoCorrect dialog box with the AutoCorrect tab selected to display the dialog box.

- Use the AutoCorrect Options button, which displays when the mouse pointer is hovered over corrected text, to change corrected text back to the original spelling, stop automatically correcting specific text, or display the AutoCorrect dialog box.

- The AutoCorrect dialog box contains several symbols that can be inserted in a document by typing specific text or characters. To add more symbols, display the Symbol dialog box, click the specific symbol, and then click the AutoCorrect button.

- When typing text, control what Word formats automatically with options at the AutoCorrect dialog box with the AutoFormat As You Type tab selected.

- A Word document is based on the Normal template that provides a document with default layout, formatting, styles, and themes. The Normal template provides a number of predesigned themes, that are available in the Document Formatting group on the Design tab.

- A theme is a combination of theme colors, theme fonts, and theme effects. A custom theme can be created that includes custom theme colors, theme fonts, and/or theme effects.

- Create custom theme colors with options at the Create New Theme Colors dialog box. Display this dialog box by clicking the Colors button on the Design tab and then clicking *Customize Colors* at the drop-down gallery. Click the Reset button in the dialog box to return to the default Office theme colors.

- Create custom theme fonts with options at the Create New Theme Fonts dialog box. Display this dialog box by clicking the Fonts button on the Design tab and then clicking *Customize Fonts* at the drop-down gallery.
- A theme effect is a set of lines and fill effects that can be applied to a document. Custom theme effects cannot be created but a theme effect can be applied to a document and then saved in a custom theme.
- Save a custom theme by clicking the Themes button on the Design tab and then clicking *Save Current Theme* at the drop-down gallery to display the dialog box.
- Apply custom theme colors by clicking the Colors button in the Document Formatting group on the Design tab and then clicking the custom theme colors option at the top of the drop-down gallery. Complete similar steps to apply custom theme fonts.
- Edit custom theme colors by clicking the Design tab and then clicking the Colors button in the Document Formatting group. At the drop-down gallery, right-click the custom theme colors and then click *Edit* at the shortcut menu. This displays the Edit Theme Colors dialog box where changes can be made to the theme colors. Edit custom theme fonts in a similar manner.
- Click the *Reset to Theme from Template* option at the Themes button drop-down gallery to reset the theme to the Office default theme.
- Delete a custom theme at the Themes button drop-down gallery or at the Save Current Theme dialog box.
- Formatting applied to a document can be saved as the default formatting by clicking the Set as Default button in the Document Formatting group on the Design tab.

Commands Review

FEATURE	RIBBON TAB, GROUP/OPTION	BUTTON, OPTION
AutoCorrect dialog box	File, *Options*	*Proofing*, AutoCorrect Options
bullets	Home, Paragraph	
Create New Theme Colors dialog box	Design, Document Formatting	, *Customize Colors*
Create New Theme Fonts dialog box	Design, Document Formatting	, *Customize Fonts*
Define New Bullet dialog box	Home, Paragraph	, *Define New Bullet*
Define New Multilevel List dialog box	Home, Paragraph	, *Define New Multilevel List*
Define New Number Format dialog box	Home, Paragraph	, *Define New Number Format*
numbering	Home, Paragraph	
Save Current Theme dialog box	Design, Document Formatting	, *Save Current Theme*

Index

OneDrive, 13
OneDrive for Business, 13
Online Pictures button, 129
Open dialog box, 10–11
OpenDocument Text format, 181
opening
blank document, 4
documents, 10–11
multiple documents, 164–165
from recent document list, 11
Word, 4
option buttons, 6
organizational chart with SmartArt, 150–151
Orientation button, 86

P

page border, inserting and changing, 100–102
Page Break button, 90
page breaks, 90–91
Page Color button, 158
page numbers, inserting and removing, 93–94
page orientation, 86–87
pages
display options
changing display percentage, 161
changing page movement, 160–161
hiding/showing white space, 162–163
formatting background
changing page color, 99
inserting and changing page border, 100–102
inserting watermark, 99
inserting
blank page, 91–93
cover page, 91–93
page breaks, 90–91
page numbers, 93–94
predesigned headers and footers, 95–97

removing, page numbers, 93–94
setup changes
margins, 86–89
page orientation, 86–87
paper size, 87–89
view, changing, 156–158
Page Setup dialog box
margin changes, 88–89
paper size changes, 88–89
vertical alignment option box, 112–113
page size, 87, 88
Page Width button, 161
panes, dividing window into, 165–166
Paragraph dialog box, 48
change line spacing in, 55
paragraphs
alignment
buttons and keyboard shortcuts, 46
changing as you type, 46
changing at dialog box, 48
changing existing text, 46–47
default, 45
borders, 66–68
bulleting, 65
collecting and pasting with Clipboard, 82
cutting, copying and pasting text, 77–82
display paragraph symbol, 46
indenting text in, 49–52
numbering, 62–64
setting and modifying tabs, 71–77
sorting text in, 70–71
spacing
before and after, 52
changing with Paragraph Spacing button, 44–45
Paragraph Spacing button, 43
Paste button, 77
Paste Options button, 79
PDF file, saving document as, 183–184

pictures. *See also* images
inserting and customizing, 129–135
Pictures button, 129
pinning
document, 11–12
folder, 12
plain text, saving document as, 181, 183
Playback Toolbar, 158–159
plus sign, 217
points, 33
portrait orientation, 86–87
Position button, 130, 148
predesigned text box, 135–137
previewing, pages in document, 168–170
printing
document, 8–9
envelopes, 173–175
labels, 175–178
pages in document, 170–172
previewing pages, 168–170
Print backstage area, 8–9
Quick Print button, 9
Print Layout view
as default view, 156
hiding/showing white space in, 162–163
Properties button, 209
proportional typeface, 6, 33
pull quote text box, 135–137

Q

Quick Access toolbar, 5
inserting button on, 9
New button, 10
Quick Print button on, 9
Save button, 13
Undo and Redo button, 20–21
Quick Print button, 9
Quick Table, inserting, 216

R

readability, 104
Learning Tools and, 158–160

Read Aloud button, 158–160
Read Mode view, 156–157
Recent Documents list
    opening document from, 11
    pinning and unpinning
        document to, 11–12
Redo button, 20–21
Remove Background button,
    132
Remove Split button, 165
Repeat command, 53–54
Repeat Header Rows button,
    207–208
Replace button, 113
Reset Picture button, 132
resize handle, 192, 212
resizing table, 212–213
Restore button, 164
restoring, windows, 164–165
Reveal Formatting task pane,
    56–57
ribbon, 5
Ribbon Display Options button,
    162
Rich Text Format (RTF), saving
    document as, 181
Rotate button, 130
rows
    changing height in table,
        206–207
    inserting and deleting in
        table, 201–203
row selection bar, 198
ruler
    displaying, 49
    horizontal, 5
    setting/modifying tabs on,
        71–74
    view, 71
    vertical, 5

S

sans serif typeface, 32–33
Save As dialog box, 7–8, 13
Save button, 7, 13
saving documents, 7–8
    in different formats, 181–184
    changes to, 13

in PDF/XPS format, 183–184
    with Save As, 13
screen clipping, creating and
    formatting, 144–145
Screenshot button, 142
screenshots, inserting and
    formatting, 142–144
ScreenTip, 26
scrolling
    in documents, 14
    synchronous, 166
search
    finding and highlighting text,
        113–115
    specifying options, 116–118
section break
    continuous, 103–104
    inserting, 103–104
Select button, 201
Selection Mode, 18–19
serif typeface, 32–33
Set Numbering Value dialog
    box, 226–227
shading, 68–69
Shading button, 68
Sharepoint, 13
shapes
    copying, 139–140
    drawing, 139–140
Shapes button, 139
shortcuts. *See* keyboard
    shortcuts
Show/Hide ¶ button, 46, 90,
    103
Side to Side button, 160
Size button, 87
sizing
    images, 129–130
    tables, 212–213
SmartArt button, 146
SmartArt graphic
    arranging and moving,
        148–149
    Choose a SmartArt Graphic
        dialog box, 145
    creating organizational chart
        with, 150–151
    inserting and formatting,
        146–147

Smart Lookup option, 25
soft copy, 8
soft page break, 90
Sort button, 70
sorting, text in paragraphs, 70–71
Sort Text dialog box, 70–71
spacing
    changing before/after
        paragraphs, 52
    changing with Paragraph
        Spacing button,
        44–45
    line spacing changes, 54–55
special characters, inserting,
    126–127
spelling
    automatic spelling checker, 4
    spelling and grammar check,
        22–23
    Spelling task pane, 22
Split button, 165
Split Cells button, 203
Split Table button, 203
split window, 165–166
Status bar, 5
Strikethrough button, 36
styles
    applying, 42–43
    No Spacing style, 42
style set
    changing, 42–43
    customizing, 42–43
Subscript button, 36
subtraction formula, 217
suffixes, finding and replacing,
    118
SUM function, 217
superscript, AutoCorrect and, 4
Superscript button, 36
Switch Windows button, 164
Syllables button, 158
Symbol button, 126
Symbol dialog box, 126
symbols, inserting
    with AutoCorrect, 241–242
    with Symbol button, 126–
        127
Synchronous Scrolling button,
    166

Themes button, 43
time, inserting current, 128–129
Transparency button, 132
Title bar, 5
typeface. *See also* fonts
examples of, 33
monospaced, 32
proportional, 6, 33
sans serif, 32–33
serif, 32–33
typestyles, 33, 34–35

U

Underline button, 34
underline typeface, 33, 34–35
Undo button, 20–21
unpinning document, 12

V

Vertical alignment option box, 112–113
Vertical button, 161
vertically aligning text, 112–113
vertically centering text, 112–113

vertical ruler, 5
vertical scroll bar, 5, 14
view
changing, 156–158
changing display percentage, 161
Draft view, 156
hiding/showing white space, 162–163
Read Mode view, 156–157
Ribbon Display Options button, 162
Web Layout view, 156
View Gridlines button, 201
View Side by Side button, 166

W

watermark, inserting, 99
Web Layout view, 156
white space, hiding/showing, 162–163
windows
arranging, 164–165
maximizing and minimizing, 164–165
opening new, 167

restoring, 164–165
splitting, 165–166
viewing documents side by side, 166–167
Word
closing, 9
opening, 4
WordArt, creating and formatting, 141–142
word forms, finding and replacing, 118
word wrap, 4
worksheet, inserting into document, 219–220
Wrap Text button, 130, 148

X

XPS file, saving document as, 183–184

Z

Zoom In button, 156, 161
Zoom Out button, 156, 161
Zoom slider bar, 156, 161
Zoom to Page button, 168

Interior Photo Credits

Page GS-1, © lowball-jack/GettyImages, Courtesy of Paradigm Education Solutions; page *GS-2*, © irbis picture/Shutterstock.com; page *GS-3*, © th3fisa/Shutterstock.com; page *GS-4*, © goldyg/Shutterstock.com; page *GS-5*, © Pressmaster/Shutterstock.com.

Microsoft® Excel Level 1

Unit 1

Preparing and Formatting Worksheets

Microsoft

Excel®

Preparing an Excel Workbook

Performance Objectives

Upon successful completion of Chapter 1, you will be able to:

1. Identify the various elements of an Excel workbook
2. Create a worksheet
3. Enter data in a worksheet
4. Save a workbook
5. Edit data in a cell
6. Print a worksheet
7. Close a workbook and close Excel
8. Use the AutoComplete, AutoCorrect, and AutoFill features
9. Open a workbook
10. Pin and unpin a workbook and folder to and from the *Recent* option list
11. Insert a formula using the AutoSum button
12. Copy a formula using the fill handle
13. Select cells and data within cells
14. Apply basic formatting to cells in a workbook
15. Use the Tell Me feature
16. Use the Help feature

Microsoft Excel is a spreadsheet program that allows users to organize, analyze, and evaluate numerical and financial data. An Excel spreadsheet can be used for such activities as creating financial statements, preparing budgets, managing inventory, and analyzing cash flow. This chapter will introduce the basics of creating a worksheet, opening workbooks, and saving workbooks. In a worksheet, learn to enter data, as well as the use of formulas to calculate sums and averages. Learn to enter data quickly and efficiently using features such as the fill handle and to apply basic formatting to data in conventional accounting style.

 Data Files

Before beginning the chapter work, copy the EL1C1 folder to your storage medium and then make EL1C1 the active folder.

The online course includes additional training and assessment resources.

Activity 1 **Prepare a Worksheet with Employee Information** **3 Parts**

You will create a worksheet containing employee information, edit the contents, and then print, save and close the workbook.

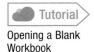

Opening a Blank
Workbook

Creating a Worksheet

Open Excel by clicking the *Excel* tile at the Windows Start menu, or by following other steps as needed depending on the operating system. At the Excel opening screen, click the *Blank workbook* template. This displays a workbook with a blank worksheet, as shown in Figure 1.1. The elements of a blank Excel worksheet are described in Table 1.1.

A file created in Excel is referred to as a *workbook*. An Excel workbook consists of an individual worksheet (or *sheet*) by default but it can contain multiple worksheets, like the sheets of paper in a notebook. Notice the tab named *Sheet1*, at the bottom of the Excel window. The area containing the gridlines in the Excel window is called the *worksheet area*. Figure 1.2 identifies the elements of the worksheet area. Create a worksheet in the worksheet area that will be saved as part of a workbook. Columns in a worksheet are labeled with letters of the alphabet and rows are labeled with numbers. The intersection of a column and a row creates a box, which is referred to as a *cell*. A cell is where data and formulas are entered.

Figure 1.1 Blank Excel Worksheet

File tab | Quick Access Toolbar | tabs | *Tell Me* text box | Title bar | ribbon

Name box | Formula bar | dialog box launcher | Collapse the Ribbon button

active cell

cell pointer

worksheet area | vertical scroll bar

sheet tab | New sheet button | horizontal scroll bar

Status bar

Table 1.1 Elements of an Excel Worksheet

Feature	Description
active cell	the currently selected cell, surrounded by a thick green border
cell pointer	when this icon appears, select cells by clicking or dragging the mouse
Collapse the Ribbon button	when clicked, removes the ribbon from the screen (Redisplay the ribbon by double-clicking a tab, except the File tab.)
dialog box launcher	click to open a dialog box with more options for that group
File tab	displays the backstage area that contains options for working with and managing files
Formula bar	displays the contents stored in the active cell
horizontal and vertical scroll bars	used to scroll left and right or up and down to view various parts of the worksheet
Name box	displays the active cell address or name assigned to the active cell
New sheet button	click to insert a new worksheet in the workbook
Quick Access Toolbar	contains buttons for commonly used commands that can be executed with a single mouse click
ribbon	contains the tabs with commands and buttons
sheet tab	identifies the current worksheet in the workbook
Status bar	displays the current mode, action messages, view buttons, and Zoom slider bar
tab	contains commands and buttons organized into groups
Tell Me text box	provides information and guidance on how to perform an action
Title bar	displays the workbook name followed by the application name
worksheet area	contains the cells used to create a worksheet

Figure 1.2 Elements of the Worksheet Area

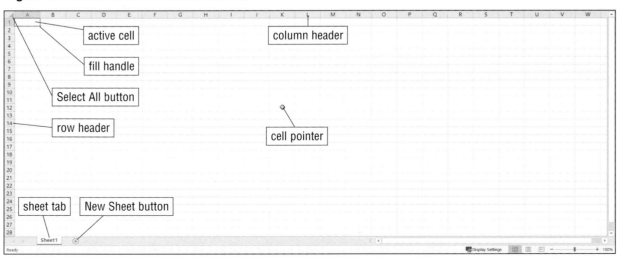

The horizontal and vertical lines that define the cells in the worksheet area are called *gridlines*. When a cell is clicked, it becomes active and a thick green border appears around it. The cell address, also called the *cell reference*, appears in the Name box. The cell reference includes the column letter and row number. For example, if the first cell of the worksheet is active, the cell reference *A1* is shown in the Name box. Any number of adjacent cells can be made active and form a range. A range is typically identified by the first cell reference and last cell reference separated by a colon. For example, the range A1:C1 contains the cells A1, B1, and C1.

Entering Data

Navigating and Scrolling

Find & Select

Entering Data in a Worksheet

Enter data such as text, a number, or a value in a cell. To enter data in a cell, make the cell active and then type the data. To make the next cell active, press the Tab key. Table 1.2 shows additional commands for making a specific cell active.

Another method for making a cell active is to use the Go To feature. To use this feature, click the Find & Select button in the Editing group on the Home tab and then click *Go To*. At the Go To dialog box, type the cell reference in the *Reference* text box and then click OK.

Before typing data into the active cell, check the Status bar. The word *Ready* should display at the left. As data is typed in a cell, the word *Ready* changes to *Enter*. Data typed in a cell is shown in the cell and in the Formula bar. If the data entered in a cell is longer than the cell can accommodate, the data overlaps the next cell to the right. (It does not become a part of the next cell—it simply overlaps it. How to change column widths to accommodate data is explained later in this chapter.)

Hint To make a cell active, position the cell pointer in the cell and then click the left mouse button.

Hint Ctrl + G is the keyboard shortcut to display the Go To dialog box.

Table 1.2 Commands for Making a Specific Cell Active

To make this cell active	Press
cell below current cell	Enter
cell above current cell	Shift + Enter
next cell	Tab
previous cell	Shift + Tab
cell at beginning of row	Home
next cell in direction of arrow	Up, Down, Left, or Right Arrow key
last cell in worksheet	Ctrl + End
first cell in worksheet	Ctrl + Home
cell in next window	Page Down
cell in previous window	Page Up
cell in window to right	Alt + Page Down
cell in window to left	Alt + Page Up

If data entered in a cell consists of text and the text does not fit in the cell, it overlaps the next cell to the right. If, however, a number is entered in a cell and the number is too long to fit in the cell, Excel changes the display of the number to number symbols *(###)*. This change is made because Excel does not want to mislead users by showing only part of a number in a cell.

Along with the keyboard, the mouse can be used to make a specific cell active. To make a specific cell active with the mouse, position the mouse pointer, which appears as a white plus symbol (⊕) (called the *cell pointer*), in the cell and then click the left mouse button. The pointer appears as a white plus sign when positioned in a cell in the worksheet and as an arrow when positioned on other elements of the Excel window, such as options and buttons on tabs and scroll bars.

Scroll through a worksheet using the horizontal and/or vertical scroll bars. Scrolling shifts the display of cells in the worksheet area but does not change the active cell. Scroll through a worksheet until the desired cell is visible and then click in the cell to make it active.

Saving a Workbook

Saving with the Same Name

Saving with a New Name

 Save

Quick Steps

Save Workbook
1. Click Save button on Quick Access Toolbar.
2. At Save As backstage area, click *Browse* option.
3. At Save As dialog box, navigate to folder.
4. Type workbook name.
5. Press Enter key.

💡 **Hint** Ctrl + S is the keyboard shortcut to save a workbook.

Save an Excel workbook, including all sheets within it, by clicking the Save button on the Quick Access Toolbar or by clicking the File tab and then clicking the *Save As* option at the backstage area. At the Save As backstage area, click the *Browse* option and the Save As dialog box displays. At the Save As dialog box, click the desired location in the Navigation pane, type a name for the workbook in the *File name* text box, and then press the Enter key or click the Save button. Bypass the Save As backstage area and go directly to the Save As dialog box by using the keyboard shortcut F12.

To save an Excel workbook in the EL1C1 folder, display the Save As dialog box, navigate to the correct drive in the Navigation pane, and then double-click *EL1C1* in the Content pane.

A workbook file name can contain up to 255 characters, including the drive letter and any folder names, and it can include spaces. Each file should have a distinct name. Excel will not allow two workbooks to be saved with the same file name in the same folder, even if one is in uppercase and one is in lowercase. (For example, one file cannot be named *EXPENSES* and another *expenses*.) Also, some symbols cannot be used in a file name, such as the following:

forward slash (/)	question mark (?)
backslash (\)	quotation mark (")
greater-than symbol (>)	colon (:)
less-than symbol (<)	asterisk (*)
pipe symbol (|)	

If changes are made to a workbook, save the file again before closing it. It is a good practice to save periodically while working with a file to be sure no changes are lost if the application crashes or freezes or if power is interrupted.

Note: If an Excel workbook is stored in a cloud location such as Microsoft OneDrive, OneDrive for Business, or SharePoint Online, any changes to it will be saved automatically with the AutoSave feature. Multiple users can edit a file and AutoSave will save the workbook every few seconds so that changes can be seen by everyone. AutoSave can be turned on or off by clicking the toggle switch in the upper left corner of the Excel screen.

1. Open Excel by clicking the *Excel* tile at the Windows Start menu. (Depending on your operating system, the steps to open Excel may vary.)
2. At the Excel opening screen, click the *Blank workbook* template. (This opens a workbook with a blank worksheet.)
3. At the blank Excel worksheet, create the worksheet shown in Figure 1.3 by completing the following steps:
   a. Press the Enter key to make cell A2 the active cell.
   b. Type Employee in cell A2.
   c. Press the Tab key. (This makes cell B2 active.)
   d. Type Location and then press the Tab key. (This makes cell C2 active.)
   e. Type Benefits and then press the Enter key to move the insertion point to cell A3.
   f. Type Avery in cell A3.
   g. Continue typing the data shown in Figure 1.3. (For commands that make specific cells active, refer to Table 1.2.)
4. After typing the data shown in the cells in Figure 1.3, save the workbook by completing the following steps:
   a. Click the Save button on the Quick Access Toolbar.
   b. At the Save As backstage area, click the *Browse* option.
   c. At the Save As dialog box, navigate to your EL1C1 folder in the Navigation pane and then double-click the *EL1C1* folder in the Content pane.
   d. Select the text in the *File name* text box and then type 1-EmpBene.
   e. Press the Enter key or click the Save button.

Check Your Work

Figure 1.3 Activity 1a

	A	B	C	D
1				
2	Employee	Location	Benefits	
3	Avery			
4	Connors			
5	Estrada			
6	Juergens			
7	Mikulich			
8	Talbot			
9				

Editing Data

Editing Data in a Cell

Edit data being typed in a cell by pressing the Backspace key to delete the character to the left of the insertion point or pressing the Delete key to delete the character to the right of the insertion point. To change the data in a cell, click in the cell to make it active and then type the new data. When a cell containing data is active, anything typed will take the place of the existing data.

If only a portion of the data in a cell needs to be edited, double-click in the cell. This makes the cell active, moves the insertion point inside the cell, and displays the word *Edit* at the left side of the Status bar. Move the insertion point using the arrow keys or the mouse and then make the needed corrections. Press the Home key to move the insertion point to the first character in the cell or Formula bar or press the End key to move the insertion point to the last character.

When the editing of data in a cell is complete, be sure to change out of the Edit mode. To do this, make another cell active by pressing the Enter key, the Tab key, or Shift + Tab. Two other ways to change out of the Edit mode and return to the Ready mode are to click in another cell and to click the Enter button on the Formula bar.

Cancel

Enter

If the active cell does not contain data, the Name box displays only the cell reference (by column letter and row number). As data is typed, two buttons become active on the Formula bar to the right of the Name box, as shown in Figure 1.4. Click the Cancel button to delete the current cell entry. (A cell entry can also be deleted by pressing the Delete key.) Click the Enter button when finished typing or editing the cell entry. Click the Enter button on the Formula bar and the word *Enter* (or *Edit*) at the left of the Status bar changes to *Ready*.

Figure 1.4 Buttons on the Formula Bar

Activity 1b Editing Data in a Cell

Part 2 of 3

1. With **1-EmpBene** open, double-click in cell A7 (contains *Mikulich*).
2. Move the insertion point immediately left of the *k* and then type c. (This changes the spelling to *Mickulich*.)
3. Click in cell A4 (contains *Connors*), type Bryant, and then press the Tab key. (Clicking only once allows you to type over the existing data.)
4. Edit cell C2 by completing the following steps:
   a. Click the Find & Select button in the Editing group on the Home tab and then click *Go To* at the drop-down list.

b. At the Go To dialog box, type c2 in the *Reference* text box and then click OK.

c. Type Classification (over *Benefits*).

5. Click in any other cell.

6. Click the Save button on the Quick Access Toolbar to save the workbook again.

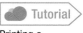 Printing a Worksheet

Printing a Worksheet

Hint Ctrl + P is the keyboard shortcut to display the Print backstage area.

With a workbook open, click the File tab and the Home backstage area displays, as shown in Figure 1.5. Use buttons and options at the backstage area to perform actions such as opening, closing, saving, and printing a workbook. Click the Back button (in the upper left corner of the backstage area) to exit the backstage area without completing an action or press the Esc key on the keyboard.

Print a worksheet from the Print backstage area, as shown in Figure 1.6. To display this backstage area, click the File tab and then click the *Print* option. The Print backstage area can also be displayed with the keyboard shortcut Ctrl + P.

Figure 1.5 Home Backstage Area

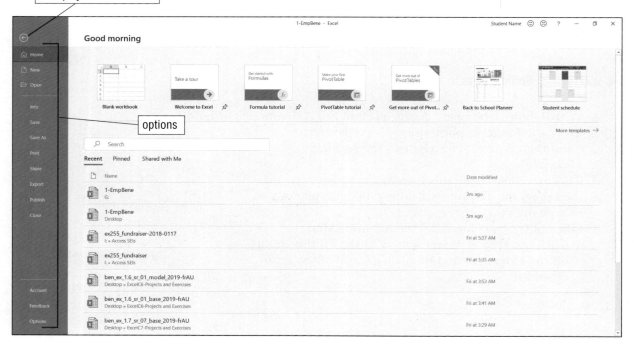

Figure 1.6 Print Backstage Area

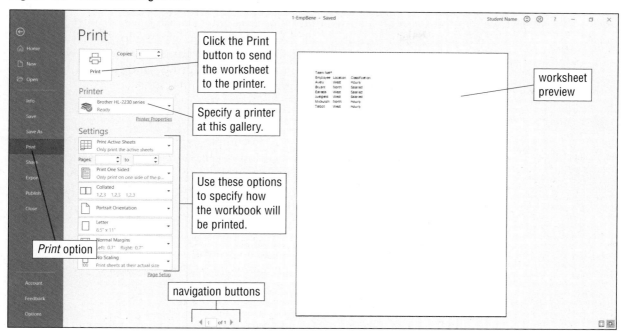

Click the Print button to send the worksheet to the printer.

Specify a printer at this gallery.

Use these options to specify how the workbook will be printed.

Print option

navigation buttons

worksheet preview

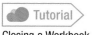
Quick Steps
Print Worksheet
1. Click File tab.
2. Click *Print* option.
3. Click Print button.

Click the Print button in the Print backstage area to send the worksheet to the printer and use the *Copies* measurement box to specify the number of copies to be printed. Below the Print button are two categories: *Printer* and *Settings*. Use the gallery in the *Printer* category to specify the printer. The *Settings* category contains a number of galleries, each with options for specifying how the workbook will be printed. Use the galleries to specify whether the pages are collated when printed; what page orientation, page size, and margins the workbook should have; and whether the worksheet will be scaled to print all rows and columns of data on one page.

Another method for printing is to click the Quick Print button on the Quick Access Toolbar to send the workbook directly to the printer. To insert this button on the Quick Access Toolbar, click the arrow button at the right of the toolbar and then click *Quick Print* at the drop-down list. To remove the button, right-click it and then click *Remove from Quick Access Toolbar* at the drop-down list.

Tutorial

Closing a Workbook and Closing Excel

Quick Steps
Close Workbook
1. Click File tab.
2. Click *Close* option.
OR
Press Ctrl + F4.

Close Excel
Click Close button.
OR
Press Alt + F4.

 Close

Closing a Workbook and Closing Excel

To close an Excel workbook without closing Excel, click the File tab and then click the *Close* option. Using the keyboard shortcut Ctrl + F4 will also close a workbook. To close Excel, click the Close button in the upper right corner of the screen. The Close button contains an *X*, and if the mouse pointer is positioned on the button, the button background changes from green to red and a ScreenTip displays with the name *Close*. Pressing the keyboard shortcut Alt + F4 will also close Excel.

Using Automatic Entering Features

Excel contains several features that help users enter data into cells more quickly and efficiently. These features include AutoComplete, which allows users to automatically complete multiple entries of the same data; AutoCorrect, which automatically corrects many common typographical errors; and AutoFill, which automatically inserts words, numbers, or formulas in a series.

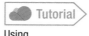

Using
AutoComplete and
AutoCorrect

Using AutoComplete

The AutoComplete feature makes it easy to complete multiple entries of the same data. As the first few characters are typed into a cell, AutoComplete predicts what will be typed next based on previous entries in the worksheet, and will automatically complete the entry based on its prediction. If the AutoComplete entry is correct, accept it by pressing the Tab key or the Enter key. If it is incorrect, simply continue typing the correct data. This feature can be very useful in a worksheet that contains repetitive data entries. For example, consider a worksheet that repeats the word *Payroll*. The second and subsequent times this word is to be inserted in a cell, simply typing the letter *P* will cause AutoComplete to insert the entire word.

Using AutoCorrect

The AutoCorrect feature automatically corrects many common typing errors. To see what symbols and words are included in AutoCorrect, click the File tab and then click *Options*. At the Excel Options dialog box, click *Proofing* in the left panel and then click the AutoCorrect Options button in the right panel. This displays the AutoCorrect dialog box with the AutoCorrect tab selected, as shown in Figure 1.7, with a list box containing the replacement data.

At the AutoCorrect dialog box, type the text shown in the first column in the list box and then press the spacebar and the text in the second column is inserted in the cell. Along with symbols, the AutoCorrect dialog box contains commonly misspelled words and common typographical errors.

Figure 1.7 AutoCorrect Dialog Box with the AutoCorrect Tab Selected

Type the text shown in the first column of this list box in a worksheet and then press the spacebar and the text is replaced by the text in the second column of this list box.

1. With **1-EmpBene** open, make cell A1 active.
2. Type text in cell A1 as shown in Figure 1.8. Insert the ® symbol by typing (r) and then pressing the Enter key. (AutoCorrect will change (r) to ®.)
3. Type the remaining text in the cells. When you type the *W* in *West* in cell B5, the AutoComplete feature will insert *West*. Accept this by pressing the Tab key. (Pressing the Tab key accepts *West* and also makes the cell to the right active.) Use the AutoComplete feature to enter *West* in cells B6 and B8 and *North* in cell B7. Use AutoComplete to enter the second and subsequent occurrences of *Salaried* and *Hourly*.
4. Click the Save button on the Quick Access Toolbar.
5. Print **1-EmpBene** by clicking the File tab, clicking the *Print* option, and then clicking the Print button at the Print backstage area. (The gridlines will not print.)

6. Close the workbook by clicking the File tab and then clicking the *Close* option at the backstage area.

 Check Your Work

Figure 1.8 Activity 1c

	A	B	C	D
1	Team Net®			
2	Employee	Location	Classification	
3	Avery	West	Hourly	
4	Bryant	North	Salaried	
5	Estrada	West	Salaried	
6	Juergens	West	Salaried	
7	Mickulich	North	Hourly	
8	Talbot	West	Hourly	
9				

Entering Data Using
the Fill Handle

Using AutoFill

When a cell is active, a thick green border surrounds it and a small green square appears in the bottom right corner. This green square is called the AutoFill *fill handle* (see Figure 1.2 on page 5). Use the fill handle to fill a range of cells with the same data or with consecutive data. For example, suppose the year 2021 is to be inserted into a row or column of cells. To do this quickly, type *2021* in the first cell, position the mouse pointer on the fill handle, click and hold down the left mouse button, drag across or down into the cells in which the year is to be inserted, and then release the mouse button.

Hint When filling cells with the fill handle, press and hold down the Ctrl key if you want to copy the same data instead of displaying the next instance in the series.

The fill handle can also be used to insert a series in a row or column of cells. For example, suppose a worksheet is being created with data for all the months in the year. Type *January* in the first cell, position the mouse pointer on the fill handle, click and hold down the left mouse button, drag down or across into 11 more cells, and then release the mouse button. Excel automatically inserts the other 11 months of the year in the proper order. When using the fill handle, the cells must be adjacent. Table 1.3 identifies the sequences inserted in cells when specific types of data are entered.

Certain sequences—such as *2, 4* and *Jan 12, Jan 13*—require that both cells be selected before using the fill handle. If only the cell containing *2* is active, the fill handle will insert *2*s in the selected cells. The list in Table 1.3 is only a sampling of what the fill handle can do. A variety of other sequences can be inserted in a worksheet using the fill handle.

Auto Fill
Options

An Auto Fill Options button appears when cells are filled with data using the fill handle. Click this button and a list of options displays for filling the cells. By default, data and formatting are filled in each cell. Use the Auto Fill Options button to choose to fill only the formatting in the cells or to fill only the data without the formatting. Other fill options include choosing to copy data into the selected cells or to fill the data as a series.

Table 1.3 AutoFill Fill Handle Series

Enter this data*	And the fill handle will insert this sequence in adjacent cells*
January	February, March, April, and so on
Jan	Feb, Mar, Apr, and so on
Jan 15, Jan 16	17-Jan, 18-Jan, 19-Jan, and so on
Monday	Tuesday, Wednesday, Thursday, and so on
Product 1	Product 2, Product 3, Product 4, and so on
Qtr 1	Qtr 2, Qtr 3, Qtr 4
2, 4	6, 8, 10, and so on

* Commas represent data in separate cells.

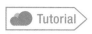

Opening a
Workbook

Opening a Workbook

Open an Excel workbook at the Open dialog box. To display this dialog box, click the File tab and then click the *Open* option. This displays the Open backstage area. Other methods of displaying the Open backstage area include using the keyboard shortcut Ctrl + O and inserting an Open button on the Quick Access Toolbar. At the Open backstage area, click the *Browse* option. At the Open dialog box, navigate to the desired folder and then double-click the workbook name in the Content pane. Bypass the Open backstage area and go directly to the Open dialog box by using the keyboard shortcut Ctrl + F12.

Opening from the
Recent Option List

Opening a Workbook from the *Recent* Option List

With the *Recent* option selected in the middle panel at the Open backstage area, a list displays with the most recently opened workbooks. Up to 50 workbook names appear in the list by default. Open a workbook from this list by clicking the workbook name.

Pinning and Unpinning Workbooks and Folders

Quick Steps

Open Workbook
1. Click File tab.
2. Click *Open* option.
3. Click *Browse* option.
4. Navigate to folder.
5. Double-click workbook name.

Pin Workbook to Recent Option List
1. Click File tab.
2. Click *Open* option.
3. Position mouse pointer over workbook name.
4. Click left-pointing push pin icon.

Unpin Workbook from Recent Option List
1. Click File tab.
2. Click *Open* option.
3. Position mouse pointer over workbook name.
4. Click down-pointing push pin icon.

If a workbook is opened on a regular basis, consider pinning it to the *Recent* option list so it can be found more easily. To pin a workbook, position the mouse pointer over the workbook name and then click the left-pointing push pin icon at the right of the workbook name. The left-pointing push pin icon changes to a down-pointing push pin icon and the pinned workbook appears in the *Pinned* category at the top of the *Recent* option list, where it can be easily found whenever the Open backstage area is displayed.

A workbook can also be pinned to the Recent list at the Excel opening screen and the Home backstage area. To unpin a workbook from the Recent or *Recent* option list, click the pin icon to change it from a down-pointing push pin icon to a left-pointing push pin icon. More than one workbook can be pinned to a list. Another method for pinning and unpinning documents is to use the shortcut menu. Right-click a workbook name and then click the option *Pin to list* or *Unpin from list*.

In addition to workbooks, folders can be pinned to a list at the Save As backstage area with the *Recent* option selected. The third panel in the Save As backstage area shows a list of the most recently opened folders and groups them into categories such as *Today*, *Yesterday*, and *Last Week*. Pin a folder or folders to the list to display them in the *Pinned* category at the top of the list.

Activity 2a **Inserting Data in Cells with the Fill Handle**   Part 1 of 3

1. Open **FillCells** by completing the following steps:
   a. Click the File tab and then click the *Open* option, if necessary.
   b. Click the *Browse* option.
   c. Navigate to the EL1C1 folder on your storage medium and then double-click *FillCells*.
2. Save the workbook with the name **1-FillCells** by completing the following steps:
   a. Press the F12 function key to display the Save As dialog box.
   b. Press the Home key on the keyboard to position the insertion point at the beginning of the name in the *File name* text box and then type 1-.
   c. Click the Save button.
3. Add data to cells as shown in Figure 1.9. Begin by making cell B1 active and then typing January.

4. Position the mouse pointer on the fill handle for cell B1, click and hold down the left mouse button, drag across into cell G1, and then release the mouse button.

5. Type a sequence and then use the fill handle to fill the remaining cells by completing the following steps:

a. Make cell A2 active and then type *Year 1*.
b. Make cell A3 active and then type *Year 3*.
c. Select cells A2 and A3 by clicking in cell A2 and holding down the left mouse button, dragging into cell A3, and then releasing the mouse button.
d. Drag the fill handle for cell A3 into cell A5. (This inserts *Year 5* in cell A4 and *Year 7* in cell A5.)

6. Use the fill handle to fill adjacent cells with a number but not the formatting by completing the following steps:
a. Make cell B2 active. (This cell contains *100* with bold formatting.)
b. Drag the fill handle for cell B2 to the right into cell E2. (This inserts *100* in cells C2, D2, and E2.)
c. Click the Auto Fill Options button at the bottom right of the selected cells.
d. Click the *Fill Without Formatting* option at the drop-down list.

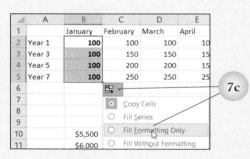

7. Use the fill handle to apply formatting only by completing the following steps:
a. Make cell B2 active.
b. Drag the fill handle into cell B5.
c. Click the Auto Fill Options button and then click *Fill Formatting Only* at the drop-down list.

8. Make cell A10 active and then type *Qtr 1*.
9. Drag the fill handle for cell A10 into cell A13.
10. Save **1-FillCells**.

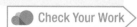

Check Your Work

Figure 1.9 Activity 2a

	A	B	C	D	E	F	G
1		January	February	March	April	May	June
2	Year 1	**100**	100	100	100	125	125
3	Year 3	**150**	150	150	150	175	175
4	Year 5	**200**	200	200	150	150	150
5	Year 7	**250**	250	250	250	250	250
6							
7							
8							
9							
10	Qtr1	$5,500	$6,250	$7,000	$8,500	$5,500	$4,500
11	Qtr2	$6,000	$7,250	$6,500	$9,000	$4,000	$5,000
12	Qtr3	$4,500	$8,000	$6,000	$7,500	$6,000	$5,000
13	Qtr4	$6,500	$8,500	$7,000	$8,000	$5,500	$6,000
14							

Entering Formulas

Quick Steps

Enter Formula Using AutoSum button
1. Click in cell.
2. Click AutoSum button.
3. Check range identified and make changes if necessary.
4. Press Enter key.

Formulas in Excel allow users to perform calculations on data and get a result in return. For example, the total cost of an item can be determined by inputting the individual costs of the item into a sum formula and the result will be the total of those costs. An active cell that contains a formula will display the results in the cell and the formula in the Formula bar. Formulas can be inserted using various methods, such as typing, using the mouse, and using buttons on the ribbon.

Formulas in Excel begin with an equals sign and may contain one or more of the following: mathematical operators (such as + or -), numerical values, references to a cell or range of cells, and/or a function (such as the SUM function, described below). For example, the formula =A1+A2 can be inserted in cell A3. When values are added to cells A1 and A2, their sum will automatically appear in cell A3. Formulas can be written that add, subtract, multiply, and/or divide values. Formulas can also be written that calculate averages, percentages, minimum and maximum values, and much more.

Tutorial

Entering Formulas Using the AutoSum Button

AutoSum

Hint You can use the keyboard shortcut Alt + = to insert the SUM function in a cell.

Using the AutoSum Button to Add Numbers

Use the AutoSum button in the Editing group on the Home tab to insert a formula for calculating the sum of numbers in a range of cells. Clicking the AutoSum button will create a formula that adds numbers automatically using the SUM function. Make active the cell in which the formula will be inserted (this cell should be empty) and then click the AutoSum button. Excel looks for a range of cells containing numbers above the active cell. If no cell above contains numbers, then Excel looks to the left of the active cell. Excel suggests the range of cells to be added. If the suggested range is not correct, drag through the range of cells with the mouse and then press the Enter key. Double-click the AutoSum button to automatically insert the SUM function with the range Excel chooses.

Activity 2b Adding Values with the AutoSum Button

Part 2 of 3

1. With **1-FillCells** open, make cell A6 active and then type Total.
2. Make cell B6 active and then calculate the sum of the cells by clicking the AutoSum button in the Editing group on the Home tab.
3. Excel inserts the formula =SUM(B2:B5) in cell B6. This is the correct range of cells, so press the Enter key.

4. Make cell C6 active and then click the AutoSum button in the Editing group.

5. Excel inserts the formula *=SUM(C2:C5)* in cell C6. This is the correct range of cells, so press the Enter key.
6. Make cell D6 active.
7. Double-click the AutoSum button. This inserts the formula *=SUM(D2:D5)* in cell D6 and inserts the sums *700*.
8. Insert the sums in cells E6, F6, and G6.
9. Save **1-FillCells**.

Check Your Work >

Using the AutoSum Button to Average Numbers

A common function in a formula is the AVERAGE function. With this function, a range of cells are added together and then the total is divided by the number of cell entries. The AVERAGE function is available on the AutoSum button. Click the AutoSum button arrow and a drop-down list displays with a number of common functions.

Tutorial

Copying Formulas

Using the Fill Handle to Copy a Formula

The same basic formula can be inserted in other cells in a worksheet. When copying a formula to other locations in a worksheet, use a relative cell reference. Copy a formula containing relative cell references and the cell references change. For example, insert the formula *=SUM(A2:C2)* in cell D2 and then copy it relatively to cell D3 and the formula in cell D3 displays as *=SUM(A3:C3)*. Use the fill handle to copy a formula relatively in a worksheet. To do this, position the mouse pointer on the fill handle until the mouse pointer turns into a thin black cross, click and hold down the left mouse button, drag and select the cells, and then release the mouse button.

Activity 2c **Inserting the AVERAGE Function and Copying a Formula Relatively**   Part 3 of 3

1. With **1-FillCells** open, make cell A14 active and then type Average.
2. Insert the average of the range B10:B13 by completing the following steps:
   a. Make cell B14 active.
   b. Click the AutoSum button arrow in the Editing group and then click *Average* at the drop-down list.
   c. Excel inserts the formula *=AVERAGE(B10:B13)* in cell B14. This is the correct range of cells, so press the Enter key.
3. Copy the formula relatively to the range C14:G14 by completing the following steps:
   a. Make cell B14 active.
   b. Position the mouse pointer on the fill handle, click and hold down the left mouse button, drag across into cell G14, and then release the mouse button.
4. Save, print, and then close **1-FillCells**.

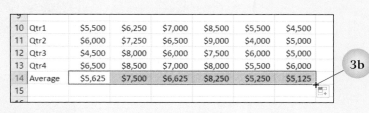

10	Qtr1	$5,500	$6,250	$7,000	$8,500	$5,500	$4,500
11	Qtr2	$6,000	$7,250	$6,500	$9,000	$4,000	$5,000
12	Qtr3	$4,500	$8,000	$6,000	$7,500	$6,000	$5,000
13	Qtr4	$6,500	$8,500	$7,000	$8,000	$5,500	$6,000
14	Average	$5,625	$7,500	$6,625	$8,250	$5,250	$5,125
15							

Check Your Work >

<table>
<tr><td>Activity 3 Format a Monthly Expenses Worksheet</td><td>2 Parts</td></tr>
</table>

You will open a workbook containing a monthly expenses worksheet and then change the column width, merge and center cells, and apply number formatting to numbers in cells.

Selecting Cells

Selecting Cells

Cells in a worksheet can be formatted in a variety of ways. For example, change the alignment of data in cells or rows or add character formatting. To identify the cells that are to be affected by the formatting, select the specific cells.

Selecting Cells Using the Mouse

Hint The first cell in a range has a white background and is the active cell.

Select specific cells, columns, or rows in a worksheet using the mouse. Table 1.4 displays the methods for selecting cells using the mouse.

Selected cells, except the active cell, display with a gray background (this may vary) rather than a white background. The active cell is the first cell in the selection block and displays in the normal manner (white background with black data). Selected cells remain selected until another cell is clicked with the mouse or an arrow key is pressed on the keyboard.

Selecting Cells Using the Keyboard

Keys on the keyboard can be used to select specific cells within a worksheet. Table 1.5 shows the commands for selecting specific cells. If a worksheet contains data, Ctrl + A selects all the cells containing data. If a worksheet contains groups of data separated by empty cells, Ctrl + A or Ctrl + Shift + spacebar selects a group of cells rather than all the cells.

Table 1.4 Selecting with the Mouse

To select this	Do this
column	Position the cell pointer on the column header (a letter) and then click the left mouse button.
row	Position the cell pointer on the row header (a number) and then click the left mouse button.
adjacent cells	Drag with the mouse into specific cells to select them.
nonadjacent cells	Press and hold down the Ctrl key while clicking the column header, row header, or specific cells.
all cells in worksheet	Click the Select All button. (Refer to Figure 1.2 on page 5.)

Table 1.5 Selecting Cells Using the Keyboard

To select	Press
cells in direction of arrow key	Shift + arrow key
from active cell to beginning of row	Shift + Home
from active cell to beginning of worksheet	Shift + Ctrl + Home
from active cell to last cell in worksheet containing data	Shift + Ctrl + End
entire column	Ctrl + spacebar
entire row	Shift + spacebar
cells containing data	Ctrl + A
groups of data separated by empty cells	Ctrl + Shift + spacebar

Selecting Data within Cells

Hint Select nonadjacent columns or rows by holding down the Ctrl key while selecting cells.

The selection commands presented in Table 1.4 and Table 1.5 select the entire cell. Specific characters within a cell can also be selected. To do this with the mouse, position the cell pointer in a cell and then double-click the left mouse button. Drag with the I-beam pointer through the data to be selected. Data selected within a cell appears with a gray background. To select data in a cell using the keyboard, press and hold down the Shift key and then press the arrow key that moves the insertion point in the desired direction. All the data the insertion point passes through will be selected. Press the F8 function key to turn on the Extend Selection mode, move the insertion point in the desired direction to select the data, and then press F8 to turn off the Extend Selection mode. When the Extend Selection mode is on, the words *Extend Selection* are shown at the left of the Status bar.

Applying Basic Formatting

Quick Steps

Change Column Width
Drag column boundary line.
OR
Double-click column boundary line.

Merge and Center Cells
1. Select cells.
2. Click Merge & Center button on Home tab.

Excel provides a wide range of formatting options that can be applied to cells in a worksheet. Some basic formatting options that are helpful when creating a worksheet include changing the column width, merging and centering cells, and formatting numbers.

Changing Column Width

If data in a cell overlaps into the next column, increase the width of the column to accommodate the data. To do this, position the mouse pointer on the gray boundary line between columns in the column header (Figure 1.2 on page 5 identifies the column header) until the pointer turns into a double-headed arrow pointing left and right and then drag the boundary to the new location. If the column contains data, double-click the column boundary line at the right to automatically adjust the width of the column to accommodate the longest entry.

A more precise way to change the width of a column is to display the Column Width dialog box, type in the desired width and then press the OK button. Open the Column Width dialog box by clicking the Format button in the Cells group and then click the *Column Width* option in the drop-down list. Alternatively, right-click the column header and then click *Column width* at the shortcut menu.

Merging and
Centering Cells

Merge &
Center

Merging and Centering Cells

In some cases, as with a title or subtitle, it may look better to merge two or more cells and then center the text within the cells instead of allowing the text to overlap into the next column. To merge cells, first check to make sure that the cells to be merged do not contain any other data. (If other cells contain data, only the data in the first cell will be placed in the newly merged cell.) Select cells to be merged and then click the Merge & Center button in the Alignment group on the Home tab.

Activity 3a Changing Column Width and Merging and Centering Cells   Part 1 of 2

1. Open **MoExps** and then save it with the name **1-MoExps**.
2. Change column widths by completing the following steps:
    a. Position the mouse pointer in the column header on the boundary line between columns A and B until the pointer turns into a double-headed arrow pointing left and right.

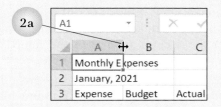

   b. Double-click the left mouse button.
   c. Position the mouse pointer in the column header on the boundary line between columns E and F and then double-click the left mouse button.
   d. Click in any cell in column F, click the Format button in the Cells group on the Home tab and then click the *Column Width* option at the drop down list.
   e. At the Column Width dialog box, type 10.25, and then click OK.
3. Merge and center cells by completing the following steps:
   a. Select the range A1:C1.
   b. Click the Merge & Center button in the Alignment group on the Home tab.

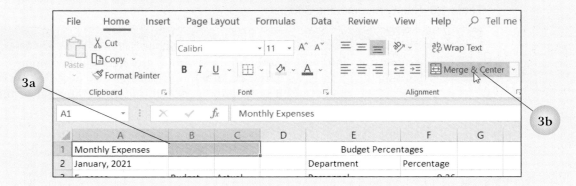

   c. Select the range A2:C2.
   d. Click the Merge & Center button.
   e. Select cells E1 and F1 and then click the Merge & Center button.
4. Save **1-MoExps**.

 Check Your Work

Formatting Numbers

Numbers in cells can be formatted to include a decimal point (45.00), comma separators (1,000,000), or symbols such as a dollar sign ($) or percentage symbol (%). As numbers are typed, Excel will recognize the formatting. For example, if *$45.50* is typed in a cell, Excel automatically applies the Currency format to the cell. If *45%* is entered in a cell, Excel automatically applies the Percentage format. Currency format, Percentage format, and other formats recognized by Excel are shown in the *Number Format* option box in the Number group on the Home tab.

Number formatting can also be applied to cells in a worksheet before or after the data is typed. To do this, select the cell or cells and then click an option in the *Number Format* option box, or click one of the buttons in the Number group on the Home tab (described in Table 1.6). For example, if the number 4500 is typed and the Accounting number formatting is applied to it, it will be formatted as $4,500.00. If the number .45 is typed and the Percentage format is applied, it will be displayed as 45%.

Use the Increase Decimal and Decrease Decimal buttons to control how many digits are displayed after the decimal point, without changing the actual value in the cell. For example, the number *1.0245* can be formatted so none or all of the digits display after the decimal point, but the value shown in the Formula bar remains the same to keep calculations accurate.

A general guideline in accounting is to insert a dollar symbol before the first amount in a column and before the total amount but not before the number amounts between them. To follow this guideline, format the first amount and total amount using the Accounting Number Format button and applying the Comma format to the number amounts between them. The Accounting number format and Comma number format are the same, except the Accounting number format includes the dollar sign. To differentiate between the two Accounting formats, steps in this textbook will use the term *Accounting format* when the Accounting Number Format button in the Number group on the Home tab is to be clicked. The term *Comma format* will be used when the Comma Style button is to be clicked.

Table 1.6 Number Formatting Buttons

Click this button		To do this
$ ⌄	Accounting Number Format	Add a dollar symbol, any necessary commas, and a decimal point followed by two digits even if none are typed; right-align the number in the cell.
%	Percent Style	Multiply the cell value by 100 and display the result with a percent symbol; right-align the number in the cell.
,	Comma Style	Add any necessary commas and a decimal point followed by two digits even if none are typed; right-align the number in the cell.
←0 .00	Increase Decimal	Increase the number of digits displayed after the decimal point in the selected cell.
.00 →0	Decrease Decimal	Decrease the number of digits displayed after the decimal point in the selected cell.

Activity 3b Formatting Numbers

1. With **1-MoExps** open, make cell B13 active and then double-click the AutoSum button. (This inserts the total of the numbers in the range B4:B12.)
2. Make cell C13 active and then double-click the AutoSum button.
3. Apply the Accounting format to cells by completing the following steps:
   a. Select cells B4 and C4.
   b. Click the Accounting Number Format button in the Number group on the Home tab.
   c. Decrease the number of digits displayed after the decimal point to none by clicking the Decrease Decimal button in the Number group two times.

d. Select cells B13 and C13.
e. Click the Accounting Number Format button.
f. Click the Decrease Decimal button two times.

4. Apply the Comma format to numbers by completing the following steps:
   a. Select the range B5:C12.
   b. Click the Comma Style button in the Number group.
   c. Click the Decrease Decimal button two times.

5. Apply the Percentage format to numbers by completing the following steps:
   a. Select the range F3:F9.
   b. Click the Percent Style button in the Number group on the Home tab.
6. Click in cell A1.
7. Save **1-MoExps**.

 Check Your Work

You will use the Tell Me feature to learn how to change the font size of text and display the Excel Help window with information about wrapping text. You will use the Help feature to learn more about entering data in cells, changing the font color, and printing a workbook.

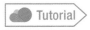

Tutorial

Using the Tell Me
Feature

Quick Steps

Use Tell Me Feature
1. Click in *Tell Me* text box.
2. Type topic or feature.
3. Click option at drop-down list.

Using the Tell Me Feature

Excel includes a Tell Me feature that provides information and guidance on how to complete certain actions. Use the Tell Me feature by clicking in the *Tell Me* text box on the ribbon to the right of the Help tab and then typing a term, or action. As text is typed in the *Tell Me* text box, a drop-down list displays with options that are refined as more text is typed. The drop-down list contains options for completing the action, displaying information on the action from sources on the web, and displaying information on the action in the Excel Help task pane.

The Tell Me drop-down list also includes a Smart Lookup option. Clicking the Smart Lookup option opens the Smart Lookup task pane, as shown in Figure 1.10, at the right side of the screen with information on the typed text from a variety of internet sources. Smart Lookup can also be accessed using the Smart Lookup button on the Review tab or by selecting a cell, right-clicking in the selected cell, and then clicking the *Smart Lookup* option at the shortcut menu.

Figure 1.10 Smart Lookup Task Pane

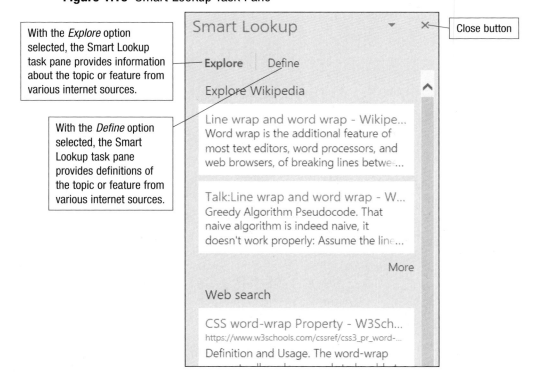

1. With **1-MoExps** open, select the range A1:E1.
2. Click in the *Tell Me* text box and then type font size.
3. At the drop-down list, click the *Font Size* option.
4. At the side menu, click the *14* option. (This increases the font size of the text in the range A1:E1, and the height of row 1 automatically adjusts to accommodate the larger text.)
5. Use the Tell Me feature to display the Help task pane with information on wrapping text by completing the following steps:
   a. Click in the *Tell Me* text box and then type wrap text.
   b. Position the mouse pointer over the *Get Help on "wrap text"* option and then click the *Wrap text in a cell* option at the side menu.

   c. At the Help task pane, read the information on wrapping text and then close the Help task pane by clicking the Close button in the upper right corner of the task pane.
6. Display information on scrolling in a workbook in the Smart Lookup task pane by completing the following steps:
   a. Click in the *Tell Me* text box and then type scrolling.
   b. Click the *Smart Lookup on "scrolling"* option. (The first time you use the Smart Lookup feature, a message may appear asking to turn on Intelligent Services. In a school setting, ask your instructor for assistance.)
   c. If two options—*Explore* and *Define*—are shown at the top of the Smart Lookup task pane, click the *Define* option. This will display a definition of the word *scrolling* in the Smart Lookup task pane.
   d. Close the Smart Lookup task pane by clicking the Close button in the upper right corner of the task pane.
7. Save, print, and then close **1-MoExps**.

Using Help

Microsoft Excel includes a Help feature that contains information about Excel features and commands. This on-screen reference manual is similar to Windows Help and the Help features in Word, PowerPoint, and Access. Click the Help button in the Help group on the Help tab to display the Help task pane, as shown in Figure 1.11.

Alternatively, type a term or action in the *Tell Me* text box, position the mouse pointer over the *Get Help on* option, and then click an option at the side menu to open the Help task pane with the selected article displayed. In the Help task pane, type a topic, feature, or question in the search text box and then press the Enter key or click the Search help button. Articles related to the search text display in the Help task pane. Click an article and the article information displays in the Help task pane.

The Help task pane contains buttons at the top, as identified in Figure 1.11. Use the Back button to navigate to the previous page in the task pane. Click the three dots button to display more options, such as *Home, Office help center*, and *Contact us*. Resize or move the task pane by clicking the down arrow left of the Close button. The Help task pane can be made larger so it is easier to read the articles. The Help task pane can also be moved to the other side of the screen or made into a window that can be moved anywhere on the screen.

Figure 1.11 Help Task Pane

Getting Help from a ScreenTip

Hover the mouse pointer over a button and a ScreenTip displays with information about the button. Some button ScreenTips display with a Help icon and the <u>Tell me more</u> hyperlink. Click the <u>Tell me more</u> hyperlink text or press the F1 function key and the Help task pane opens with information about the button feature.

Activity 4b **Using the Help Feature**   Part 2 of 3

1. At a blank screen, press Ctrl + N to display a blank workbook. (Ctrl + N is the keyboard shortcut to open a blank workbook.)
2. Click the Help tab and then click the Help button.

3. With the insertion point in the search text box in the Help task pane, type enter data and then press the Enter key.
4. When the Help task pane displays with a list of articles, click the article <u>Enter data manually in worksheet cells</u> hyperlink.
5. In the displayed article, expand some of the topics in the article and then read the information about entering data in cells.
6. Click the down arrow button in the Help task pane and then click the *Size* option at the drop-down list.

7. Resize the Help task pane to make the information in the article easier to read by moving the mouse pointer to a desired point (approximately one inch wider than it was previously) and then clicking the left mouse button.
8. Click the Back button to return to the previous page.
9. Click another article hyperlink in the Help task pane and then read in the information in the article.
10. Click the three dots button and then click the *Home* option at the drop-down list.
11. Click the Close button to close the Help task pane.
12. Click the Home tab, hover the mouse pointer over the Font Color button in the Font group until the ScreenTip displays, and then click the <u>Tell me more</u> hyperlink at the bottom of the ScreenTip.
13. Read the information that displays in the Help task pane, and then close the task pane.

Getting Help in a Dialog Box or at the Backstage Area

Some dialog boxes and the backstage area contain a Help button, labeled with a question mark (?). Click this button and the Microsoft Office support website opens in a browser window with specific information about the dialog box or backstage area. After reading the information, close the browser window and return to Excel. If a dialog box is open in Excel, close it by clicking the Close button in the upper right corner. Exit the backstage area by clicking the Back button or pressing the Esc key.

Activity 4c **Getting Help in a Dialog Box and Backstage Area**   Part 3 of 3

1. At the blank workbook, click the File tab and then click the *Print* option.
2. At the Print backstage area, click the Microsoft Excel Help button in the upper right corner of the backstage area.
3. At the Microsoft Office support website, click the hyperlink to an article on printing that interests you. Read the article and then close the window.
4. Click the Back button to return to the blank workbook.
5. At the blank workbook, click the Home tab and then click the Number group dialog box launcher.
6. At the Format Cells dialog box with the Number tab selected, click the Help button in the upper right corner of the dialog box.

7. Read the information at the Microsoft Office support website and then close the browser window to return to Excel. In Excel, close the Format Cells dialog box.
8. Close the blank workbook.

Chapter Summary

- A file created in Excel is called a *workbook* and consists of one or more individual worksheets.

- The intersection of a column and a row in a worksheet is referred to as a *cell*. Gridlines are the horizontal and vertical lines that define cells.

- When the insertion point is positioned in a cell, the cell name (also called the *cell reference*) displays in the Name box at the left of the Formula bar. The cell name includes the column letter and row number.

- If the data entered in a cell consists of text (letters) and does not fit into the cell, it overlaps the cell to the right. If the data consists of numbers and does not fit into the cell, the numbers change to number symbols (###).

- Save a workbook by clicking the Save button on the Quick Access Toolbar or by clicking the File tab and then clicking the *Save As* option. At the Save As backstage area, click the *Browse* option. At the Save As dialog box, navigate to the desired folder, type the workbook name in the *File name* text box, and then press the Enter key.

- To replace data in a cell, click in the cell and then type the new data. To edit data within a cell, double-click in the cell and then make the necessary changes.

- Print a worksheet by clicking the File tab, clicking the *Print* option, and then clicking the Print button.

- Close a workbook by clicking the File tab and then clicking the *Close* option or by using the keyboard shortcut Ctrl + F4.

- Close Excel by clicking the Close button in the upper right corner of the screen or by using the keyboard shortcut Alt + F4.

- The AutoComplete feature automatically inserts a previous entry if the character or characters being typed in a cell match a previous entry. The AutoCorrect feature corrects many common typing errors. The AutoFill fill handle adds the same or consecutive data into a range of cells.

- Open a workbook by clicking the File tab and then clicking the *Open* option. At the Open backstage area, click the *Browse* option. At the Open dialog box, double-click the workbook name.

- Workbooks can be pinned to the *Recent* option list at the Open backstage area or the Recent list at the Home backstage area so that they can be easily accessed in the future.

- Use the AutoSum button in the Editing group on the Home tab to find the total or average of data in columns or rows.

- Use the fill handle to copy a formula in a cell to adjacent cells. The fill handle is the solid box in the bottom right of an active cell.

- Select all the cells in a column by clicking the column header. Select all the cells in a row by clicking the row header. Select all the cells in a worksheet by clicking the Select All button immediately to the left of the column headers.

- Change the column width by dragging or double-clicking the column boundary line.

- Merge and center adjacent cells by selecting them and then clicking the Merge & Center button in the Alignment group on the Home tab.

- Format numbers in cells with buttons in the Number group on the Home tab.

- The Tell Me feature provides information and guidance on how to complete certain actions. The *Tell Me* text box is located on the ribbon to the right of the Help tab.

- Use the Tell Me feature, click a hyperlink in a button ScreenTip, or press F1 to display the Help task pane. At this task pane, type a topic in the search text box and then press the Enter key.

- Some dialog boxes and the backstage area contain a Help button that, when clicked, displays the Microsoft Office support website with information specific to the dialog box or backstage area.

Commands Review

FEATURE	RIBBON TAB, GROUP/OPTION	BUTTON	KEYBOARD SHORTCUT
Accounting format	Home, Number	$	
AutoSum	Home, Editing	Σ	Alt + =
close Excel		X	Alt + F4
close workbook	File, *Close*		Ctrl + F4
Comma format	Home, Number	,	
decrease decimal place	Home, Number	.00→.0	
Go To dialog box	Home, Editing	🔍	Ctrl + G
Help task pane	Help, Help	?	F1
increase decimal place	Home, Number	←.0.00	
merge and center cells	Home, Alignment		
Open backstage area	File, *Open*		Ctrl + O
Percentage format	Home, Number	%	Ctrl + Shift + %
Print backstage area	File, *Print*		Ctrl + P
Save As backstage area	File, *Save As*	💾	Ctrl + S

Microsoft®
Excel®
Inserting Formulas in a Worksheet

CHAPTER 2

Performance Objectives

Upon successful completion of Chapter 2, you will be able to:

1 Write formulas with mathematical operators

2 Type a formula in the Formula bar

3 Copy a formula

4 Determine the order of operations

5 Identify common formula and function errors

6 Use the Insert Function dialog box to insert a function in a cell

7 Write formulas with the AVERAGE, MAX, MIN, COUNT, COUNTA, NOW, and TODAY functions

8 Display formulas

9 Use absolute and mixed cell references in formulas

Excel is a powerful decision-making tool that contains data that can be manipulated in "What if?" situations. Insert a formula in a worksheet and then manipulate the data to make projections, answer specific questions, and plan for the future. For example, the owner of a company might prepare a worksheet on production costs and then determine the impact on company revenues if production is increased or decreased.

As explained in Chapter 1, formulas can be inserted into Excel worksheets to add, subtract, multiply, and/or divide values as well as calculate averages, percentages, and much more. Chapter 1 described how to use the AutoSum button to insert formulas for calculating totals and averages. In Chapter 2, you will learn to use the Formulas tab to create formulas with a variety of different functions.

 Data Files

Before beginning chapter work, copy the EL1C2 folder to your storage medium and then make EL1C2 the active folder.

The online course includes additional training and assessment resources.

31

Activity 1 Insert Formulas in a Worksheet　　　　　　　　　　**4 Parts**

You will open a worksheet containing data and then insert formulas to calculate differences, salaries, and percentages of budgets and equipment usage down time.

Entering Formulas
Using the Keyboard

💡 **Hint** After typing a formula in a cell, press the Enter key, the Tab key, or Shift + Tab.

Writing Formulas with Mathematical Operators

As explained in Chapter 1, the AutoSum button in the Editing group on the Home tab creates a formula for calculating the sum or average of values. A formula can also be written using mathematical operators. Commonly used mathematical operators and their purposes are shown in Table 2.1. When writing a formula, begin it with the equals sign (=). For example, to create a formula that divides the contents of cell B2 by the contents of cell C2 and inserts the result in cell D2, make D2 the active cell and then type *=b2/c2*. The column reference letters used in formulas can be entered as either lowercase or uppercase letters. If the column reference letters are entered in a formula in lowercase, Excel will automatically convert the column reference letters to uppercase. Formulas entered in a cell will also display in the Formula bar, where the formula can be modified.

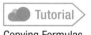

Copying Formulas

Copying a Formula with Relative Cell References

In many worksheets, the same basic formula is used repetitively. In a situation where a formula is copied to other locations in a worksheet, use a relative cell reference. Copy a formula containing relative cell references and the cell references change. For example, if the formula *=SUM(A2:C2)* is entered in cell D2 and then copied relatively into cell D3, the formula in cell D3 appears as *=SUM(A3:C3)*. (Additional information on cell references is provided later in this chapter in the section "Using an Absolute Cell Reference in a Formula.")

 Fill

Q̌uick Steps

Copy Formulas with Relative Cell References
1. Insert formula in cell.
2. Select cell containing formula and all cells to which formula is to be copied.
3. Click Fill button.
4. Click direction option.

To copy a formula with a relative cell reference, use the Fill button or the fill handle. (You used the fill handle to copy a formula in Chapter 1.) To use the Fill button, select the cell containing the formula and all the cells to which the formula is to be copied and then click the Fill button in the Editing group on the Home tab. At the Fill button drop-down list, click the direction. For example, click the *Down* option if the formula is being copied down the worksheet.

Table 2.1 Mathematical Operators

Operator	Purpose	Operator	Purpose
+	addition	/	division
-	subtraction	%	percentage
*	multiplication	^	exponentiation

1. Open **HCReports** and then save it with the name **2-HCReports**.
2. Insert a formula by completing the following steps:
   a. Make cell D3 active.
   b. Type the formula =c3-b3.
   c. Press the Enter key.
3. Copy the formula to the range D4:D10 by completing the following steps:
   a. Select the range D3:D10.
   b. Click the Fill button in the Editing group on the Home tab and then click *Down* at the drop-down list.

4. Save **2-HCReports**.
5. With the worksheet open, make the following changes to cell contents:
   - B4: Change *48,290* to *46425*
   - C6: Change *61,220* to *60000*
   - B8: Change *55,309* to *57415*
   - B9: Change *12,398* to *14115*
6. Make cell D3 active, apply the Accounting format by clicking the Accounting Number Format button in the Number group on the Home tab, and then click the Decrease Decimal button two times to decrease the digits displayed past the decimal point to none.
7. Save **2-HCReports**.

Check Your Work

○ *Hint* Use the fill handle to copy a relative version of a formula.

As explained in Chapter 1, the fill handle can be used to copy a formula up, down, left, or right within a worksheet. To use the fill handle, insert the data in the cell (text, value, formula, etc.). With the cell active, position the mouse pointer on the fill handle until the mouse pointer turns into a thin black cross. Click and hold down the left mouse button, drag and select the cells, and then release the mouse button. When dragging a cell containing a formula, a relative version of the formula is copied to the selected cells.

Checking Cell References in a Formula

To verify if a formula is using the correct cell references, double-click in a cell containing the formula and the cells referenced in the formula display with a colored border and shading in the worksheet. This feature makes it easy to identify which cells are being referenced in a formula and is helpful when trying to identify errors that may occur in a formula.

1. With **2-HCReports** open, insert a formula by completing the following steps:
   a. Make cell D15 active.
   b. Click in the Formula bar text box and then type =c15*b15.
   c. Click the Enter button on the Formula bar.
2. Copy the formula to the range D16:D20 by completing the following steps:
   a. Make sure cell D15 is still the active cell.
   b. Position the mouse pointer on the fill handle at the lower right corner of cell D15 until the pointer turns into a thin black cross.
   c. Click and hold down the left mouse button, drag into cell D20, and then release the mouse button.
3. Save **2-HCReports**.
4. Double-click in cell D20 to display the formula with cell references color coded to ensure the formula was copied relatively and then press the Enter key to exit the Edit mode.
5. Make the following changes to cell contents in the worksheet:
   B16: Change *20* to *28*
   C17: Change *18.75* to *19.10*
   B19: Change *15* to *24*
6. Select the range D16:D20 and then apply the Comma format by clicking the Comma Style button in the Number group on the Home tab.
7. Save **2-HCReports**.

| PMT | ▾ | : | × | ✓ | fx | =c15*b15 |

	A	B	C	D
1	**Highland Construction**			
2	**Customer**	**Actual**	**Planned**	**Difference**
3	Sellar Corporation	$ 30,349	$ 34,109	$ 3,760
4	Main Street Photos	46,425	48,100	1,675
5	Sunset Automotive	34,192	32,885	(1,307)
6	Linstrom Enterprises	63,293	60,000	(3,293)
7	Morcos Media	29,400	30,500	1,100
8	Green Valley Optics	57,415	58,394	979
9	Detailed Designs	14,115	13,100	(1,015)
10	Arrowstar Company	87,534	86,905	(629)
11				
12				
13				
14	**Name**	**Hours**	**Rate**	**Salary**
15	Carolyn Bentley	35	$ 23.15	=c15*b15

	A	B	C	D
13				
14	**Name**	**Hours**	**Rate**	**Salary**
15	Carolyn Bentley	35	$ 23.15	$ 810.25
16	Lindon Cassini	20	19.00	$ 380.00
17	Michelle DeFord	40	18.75	$ 750.00
18	Javier Farias	24	16.45	$ 394.80
19	Deborah Gould	15	11.50	$ 172.50
20	William Jarman	15	11.50	$ 172.50
21				

Check Your Work

 Tutorial

Entering Formulas Using the Mouse

Quick Steps

Write Formula by Pointing
1. Click in cell that will contain formula.
2. Type equals sign.
3. Click in cell to be referenced in formula.
4. Type mathematical operator.
5. Click in next cell reference.
6. Press Enter key.

Writing a Formula by Pointing

The formulas written in Activity 1a and Activity 1b used cell references such as =c3-b3. Another method for writing a formula is to "point" to the specific cells that are to be part of the formula. Creating a formula by pointing is more accurate than typing the cell reference because a mistake can be made when the cell reference is typed.

To write a formula by pointing, click in the cell that will contain the formula, type the equals sign to begin the formula, and then click in the cell to be referenced in the formula. This inserts a moving border around the cell and changes the mode from Enter to Point. (The word *Point* displays at the left side of the Status bar.) Type the mathematical operator and then click in the next cell reference. Continue in this manner until all the cell references are specified and then press the Enter key. This ends the formula and inserts the result of the calculation in the active cell. When a formula is written by pointing, the range of cells to be included in the formula can be selected.

1. With **2-HCReports** open, enter a formula by pointing that calculates the percentage of actual budget by completing the following steps:
   a. Make cell D25 active.
   b. Type an equals sign (=).
   c. Click in cell B25. (This inserts a moving border around the cell and changes the mode from Enter to Point.)
   d. Type a forward slash symbol (/).
   e. Click in cell C25.
   f. Make sure the formula in D25 is *=B25/C25* and then press the Enter key.
2. Make cell D25 active, click the fill handle and hold down the left mouse button, drag into cell D31, and then release the mouse button.

	Expense	Actual	Budget	% of Actual
23				
24	**Expense**	**Actual**	**Budget**	**% of Actual**
25	Salaries	$126,000	$124,000	=B25/C25
26	Commissions	58,000	54,500	
27	Media space	8,250	10,100	
28	Travel expenses	6,350	6,000	
29	Dealer display	4,140	4,500	
30	Payroll taxes	2,430	2,200	
31	Telephone	1,450	1,500	
32				

1a–1f

Budget	**% of Actual**
$124,000	102%
54,500	106%
10,100	82%
6,000	106%
4,500	92%
2,200	110%
1,500	97%

2

3. Save **2-HCReports**.

Check Your Work

Determining the Order of Operations

If a formula contains two or more operators, Excel uses the same order of operations used in algebra. From left to right in a formula, this order is negations (negative number—a number preceded by -) first, then percentages (%), then exponentiations (^), followed by multiplications (*), divisions (/), additions (+), and subtractions (-). To change the order of operations, put parentheses around the part of the formula that is to be calculated first. For example, if cells A1, B1, and C1 all contain the value *5*, the result of the formula *=a1+b1*c1* will be 30 (because 5*5=25 and 5+25=30). However, if parentheses are placed around the first two cell references so the formula appears as *=(a1+b1)*c1*, the result will be 50 (because 5+5=10 and 10*5=50).

Excel requires each left parenthesis to be paired with a right parenthesis. If a formula is missing a left or right parenthesis, a message box will display explaining that an error exists in the formula and providing a possible correction, which can be accepted or declined. This feature is useful when creating a formula that contains multiple layers of parentheses (called *nested parentheses*) because it will identify any missing left or right parentheses in the formula. Parentheses can also be used in various functions to further determine the order of operations.

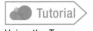
Using the Trace Error Button

When typing or editing data in a worksheet, a button may display near the active cell. The general term for this button is a *smart tag*. The display of the smart tag button varies depending on the action performed. In Activity 1d, you will insert a formula that causes a smart tag button named the Trace Error button to appear. When the Trace Error button appears, a small dark-green triangle also appears in the upper left corner of the cell. Click the Trace Error button and a drop-down list displays with options for updating the formula to include specific cells, getting help with the error, ignoring the error, editing the error in the Formula bar, and completing an error check. In Activity 1d, two of the formulas you insert return the correct results. You will click the Trace Error button, read about what Excel perceives to be the error, and then tell Excel to ignore the error.

 Trace Error

Identifying Common Formula Errors

Excel is a sophisticated program that requires data input and formula creation to follow strict guidelines in order to function properly. When guidelines that specify how data or formulas are entered are not followed, Excel will display one of many error codes. When an error is identified with a code, determining and then fixing the problem is easier than if no information is provided. Table 2.2 lists some common error codes.

Most errors in Excel result from the user incorrectly inputting data into a worksheet. However, most error messages will not display until the data is used in a formula or function. Common mistakes made while inputting data include placing text in a cell that requires a number, entering data in the wrong location, and entering numbers in an incorrect format. Other errors result from entering a formula or function improperly. A formula will often produce an error message if it is trying to divide a number by 0 or contains a circular reference (that is, when a formula within a cell uses the results of that formula in the same cell).

Table 2.2 Common Error Codes

Error Code	Meaning
#DIV/O	A formula is attempting to divide a number by 0.
#N/A	An argument parameter has been left out of a function.
#NAME?	A function name is not entered correctly.
#NUM!	An argument parameter does not meet a function's requirements.
#REF!	A referenced cell no longer exists within a worksheet.
#VALUE	The data entered is the wrong type (for example, text instead of numbers).

1. With **2-HCReports** open, enter a formula by pointing that calculates the percentage of equipment down time by completing the following steps:
   a. Make cell B45 active.
   b. Type an equals sign followed by a left parenthesis (=().
   c. Click in cell B37. (This inserts a moving border around the cell and changes the mode from Enter to Point.)
   d. Type a minus symbol (-).
   e. Click in cell B43.
   f. Type a right parenthesis followed by a forward slash ()/).
   g. Click in cell B37.
   h. Make sure the formula in cell B45 is =(B37-B43)/B37 and then press the Enter key.

2. Make cell B45 active, click the fill handle and press and hold down the left mouse button, drag into cell G45, and then release the mouse button.

3. Enter a formula by dragging to a range of cells by completing the following steps:
   a. Click in cell B46 and then click the AutoSum button in the Editing group on the Home tab.
   b. Select the range B37:D37.
   c. Click the Enter button on the Formula bar. (This inserts *7,260* in cell B46.)

4. Click in cell B47 and then complete steps similar to those in Step 3 to create a formula that totals hours available from April through June (the range E37:G37). (This inserts *7,080* in cell B47.)

5. Click in cell B46 and notice the Trace Error button. Complete the following steps to read about the error and then tell Excel to ignore it:
   a. Click the Trace Error button.
   b. At the drop-down list, click the *Help on this Error* option.
   c. Read the information in the Excel Help window and then close the window.
   d. Click the Trace Error button again and then click *Ignore Error* at the drop-down list.

6. Remove the dark-green triangle from cell B47 by completing the following steps:
   a. Click in cell B47.
   b. Click the Trace Error button and then click *Ignore Error* at the drop-down list.

7. Save, print, and then close **2-HCReports**.

1a-1h

34				
35		**EQUIPMENT USAGE REPORT**		
36	**Hours**	**January**	**February**	**March**
37	Total hours available	2,300	2,430	2,530
38	Avoidable delays	19	12	16
39	Unavoidable delays	9	8	6
40	Repairs	5	7	12
41	Servicing	6	13	7
42	Unassigned	128	95	85
43	In use	2,040	2,105	2,320
44				
45	% of down time	=(B37-B43)/B37		
46	Jan - March hours			
47	April - June hours			

3b

34					
35		**EQUIPMENT USAGE REPORT**			
36	**Hours**	**January**	**February**	**March**	**Ap**
37	Total hours available	2,300	2,430	2,530	
38	Avoidable delays	19	12	16	
39	Unavoidable delays	9	8	6	
40	Repairs	5	7	12	
41	Servicing	6	13	7	
42	Unassigned	128	95	85	
43	In use	2,040	2,105	2,320	
44					
45	% of down time	11%	13%	8%	
46	Jan - March hours	=SUM(B37:D37)			
47	April - June hours	SUM(**number1**, [number2], ...)			

5a

5b

44		
45	% of down time	11%
46	Jan - March hour	7,260
47	April - June hours	Formula Omits Adjacent Cells
48		Update Formula to Include Cells
49		
50		Help on this Error
51		Ignore Error
52		Edit in Formula Bar
53		Error Checking Options...
54		

Check Your Work

You will use the AVERAGE function to determine average test scores, use the MINIMUM and MAXIMUM functions to determine lowest and highest averages, use the COUNT function to count the number of students taking a test, and use the COUNTA function to determine the number of tests administered. You will also use date and time functions and display a formula in a cell rather than the result of a formula.

Inserting Formulas with Functions

In Activity 2b in Chapter 1, the AutoSum button was used to insert the formula =*SUM(b2:b5)* in a cell. The beginning section of the formula, =*SUM*, is called a *function*. Functions are built-in formulas. Inserting a formula takes fewer keystrokes than creating one from scratch. For example, using the =*SUM* function made it unnecessary to type a string of cell references with the plus symbol (+) between each one.

Excel provides other functions for writing formulas. A function operates on what is referred to as an *argument*. An argument may consist of a constant, a cell reference, or another function. In the formula =*SUM(b2:b5)*, the cell range *(b2:b5)* is an example of a cell reference argument. An argument may also contain a *constant*. A constant is a value entered directly into the formula. For example, in the formula =*SUM(b3:b9,100)*, the cell range *b3:b9* is a cell reference argument and *100* is a constant. In this formula, 100 is always added to the sum of the cells.

The phrase *returning the result* is used to describe when a value calculated by the formula is inserted in a cell. The term *returning* refers to the process of calculating the formula and the term *result* refers to the value inserted in the cell.

 Insert Function

Type a function in a cell in a worksheet or use the Insert Function button on the Formula bar or the Formulas tab to write the formula. Figure 2.1 shows the Formulas tab, which provides the Insert Function button and other buttons for inserting functions in a worksheet. The Function Library group on the Formulas tab contains a number of buttons for inserting functions from a variety of categories, such as *Financial*, *Logical*, *Text*, and *Date & Time*.

Click the Insert Function button on the Formula bar or the Formulas tab and the Insert Function dialog box displays, as shown in Figure 2.2. The Insert Function dialog box can also be accessed using the keyboard shortcut Shift + F3. At the Insert Function dialog box, the most recently used functions display in the *Select a function* list box. Choose a function category by clicking the *Or select a category* option box arrow and then clicking the category at the drop-down list. Use the *Search for a function* search box to locate a specific function.

Figure 2.1 Formulas Tab

| File | Home | Insert | Page Layout | **Formulas** | Data | Review | View | Help | ○ Tell me what you want to do |

| f_x Insert Function | Σ AutoSum ˅ | ☆ Recently Used ˅ | 📊 Financial ˅ | ? Logical ˅ | A Text ˅ | 📅 Date & Time ˅ | Q Lookup & Reference ˅ | θ Math & Trig ˅ | ··· More Functions ˅ | Name Manager | ◇ Define Name ˅ / Use in Formula ˅ 🗐 Create from Selection | 🗗 Trace Precedents 🗗 Trace Dependents 🗗 Remove Arrows ˅ | $\sqrt{fx}$ Show Formulas 🔺 Error Checking ˅ 🔂 Evaluate Formula | Watch Window | Calculation Options ˅ | 🔲 Calculate Now 🔲 Calculate Sheet |
| | | Function Library | | | | | | | | | Defined Names | | Formula Auditing | | Calculation | |

Figure 2.2 Insert Function Dialog Box

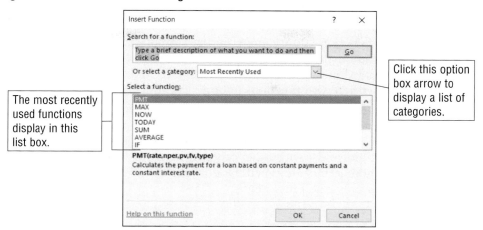

The most recently used functions display in this list box.

Click this option box arrow to display a list of categories.

With the function category selected, choose a function in the *Select a function* list box and then click OK. This displays a Function Arguments dialog box, like the one shown in Figure 2.3. At this dialog box, enter in the *Number1* text box the range of cells to be included in the formula, any constants to be included as part of the formula, or another function.

Type a cell reference or a range of cells in an argument text box or point to a cell or select a range of cells with the mouse pointer. Pointing to cells or selecting a range of cells using the mouse pointer is the preferred method of entering data into an argument text box because there is less chance of making errors. After entering a range of cells, a constant, or another function, click OK.

More than one argument can be included in a function. If the function contains more than one argument, click in the *Number2* text box or press the Tab key to move the insertion point to the *Number2* text box and then enter the second argument. If the function dialog box covers a specific cell or cells, move the dialog box by positioning the mouse pointer on the dialog box title bar, clicking and holding down the left mouse button, dragging the dialog box to a different location, and then releasing the mouse button.

Figure 2.3 Example of a Function Arguments Dialog Box

In this text box, enter the range of cells to be included in the formula.

Information about the selected function is shown here.

Click this hyperlink to display help on the function.

Excel performs over 300 functions that are divided into 13 categories: *Financial, Date & Time, Math & Trig, Statistical, Lookup & Reference, Database, Text, Logical, Information, Engineering, Cube, Compatibility,* and *Web.* Clicking the AutoSum button in the Function Library group on the Formulas tab or the Editing group on the Home tab automatically adds numbers with the SUM function. The SUM function is included in the *Math & Trig* category. In some activities in this chapter, formulas will be written with functions in other categories, including *Statistical* and *Date & Time.*

Excel includes the Formula AutoComplete feature, which displays a drop-down list of functions. To use this feature, click in the cell or in the Formula bar text box, type the equals sign, and then type the first letter of the function. This displays a drop-down list with functions that begin with the letter. The list is further refined as more letters are typed. Double-click the function, enter the cell references, and then press the Enter key.

Using Statistical Functions

Writing Formulas with Statistical Functions

Write formulas with statistical functions such as AVERAGE, MAX, MIN, and COUNT. The AVERAGE function returns the average (arithmetic mean) of the arguments. The MAX function returns the largest value in a set of values and the MIN function returns the smallest value in a set of values. Use the COUNT or COUNTA functions to count the number of cells that contain numbers or letters within the specified range.

Finding Averages A common function in a formula is the AVERAGE function. With this function, the values in a range of cells are added together and then divided by the number of cells. In Activity 2a, you will use the AVERAGE function to add all the test scores for a student and then divide that number by the total number of scores. You will use the Insert Function button to simplify the creation of the formula containing an AVERAGE function.

One of the advantages to using formulas in a worksheet is that the data can be easily manipulated to answer certain questions. In Activity 2a, you will learn how retaking certain tests affects the final average score.

Activity 2a   Averaging Test Scores in a Worksheet

Part 1 of 4

1. Open **DWTests** and then save it with the name **2-DWTests**.
2. Use the Insert Function button to find the average of test scores by completing the following steps:
   a. Make cell E4 active.
   b. Click the Insert Function button on the Formula bar.

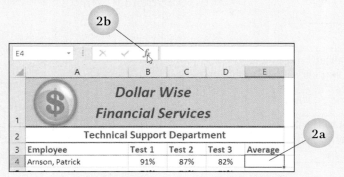

c. At the Insert Function dialog box, click the *Or select a category* option box arrow and then click *Statistical* at the drop-down list.

d. Click *AVERAGE* in the *Select a function* list box.

e. Click OK.

f. At the Function Arguments dialog box, make sure *B4:D4* displays in the *Number1* text box. (If not, type b4:d4 in the *Number1* text box.)

g. Click OK.

3. Copy the formula by completing the following steps:

a. Make sure cell E4 is still active.

b. Position the mouse pointer on the fill handle until the pointer turns into a thin black cross.

c. Click and hold down the left mouse button, drag into cell E16, and then release the mouse button.

4. Save and then print **2-DWTests**.

5. After viewing the averages of test scores, you notice that a couple of students have low averages. You decide to see what happens to these average scores if students retake the tests on which they scored the lowest. You decide that a student can score a maximum of 70% on a retake of the test. Make the following changes to test scores to see how the changes affect the test averages:

B9: Change *50* to *70*

C9: Change *52* to *70*

D9: Change *60* to *70*

B10: Change *62* to *70*

B14: Change *0* to *70*

D14: Change *0* to *70*

D16: Change *0* to *70*

6. Save and then print **2-DWTests**. (Compare the test averages of Teri Fisher-Edwards, Stephanie Flanery, Claude Markovits, and Douglas Pherson to see how retaking the tests affects their final test averages.)

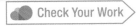

Check Your Work

When a function such as the AVERAGE function calculates cell entries, it ignores certain cell entries. The AVERAGE function will ignore text in cells and blank cells (not zeros). For example, in the worksheet containing test scores, a couple of cells contained *0%*. These entries were included in the averaging of the test scores. To exclude a particular test from the average, enter text in the cell such as *N/A* (for *not applicable*) or leave the cell blank.

Finding Maximum and Minimum Values The MAX function in a formula returns the maximum value in a cell range and the MIN function returns the minimum value in a cell range. For example, the MAX and MIN functions in a worksheet containing employee hours can be used to determine which employee worked the most hours and which worked the least. In a worksheet containing sales commissions, the MAX and MIN functions can be used to identify the salesperson who earned the highest commission and the one who earned the lowest.

Insert a MAX or a MIN function into a formula in the same manner as an AVERAGE function. In Activity 2b, you will use the Formula AutoComplete feature to insert the MAX function in cells to determine the highest test score average and the Insert Function button to insert the MIN function to determine the lowest test score average.

Activity 2b Finding Maximum and Minimum Values in a Worksheet

1. With **2-DWTests** open, type the following in the specified cells:
   A19: Highest Test Average
   A20: Lowest Test Average
   A21: Average of Completed Tests
2. Insert a formula to identify the highest test score average by completing the following steps:
   a. Make cell B19 active.
   b. Type =m. (This displays the Formula AutoComplete list.)
   c. Double-click *MAX* in the Formula AutoComplete list.
   d. Type e4:e16) and then press the Enter key.

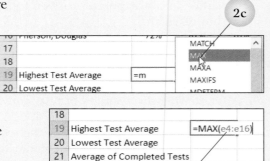

3. Insert a formula to identify the lowest test score average by completing the following steps:
   a. Make sure cell B20 is active.
   b. Click the Insert Function button on the Formula bar.
   c. At the Insert Function dialog box, make sure *Statistical* is selected in the *Or select a category* option box and then click *MIN* in the *Select a function* list box. (You will need to scroll down the list to locate *MIN*.)
   d. Click OK.
   e. At the Function Arguments dialog box, type e4:e16 in the *Number1* text box.
   f. Click OK.

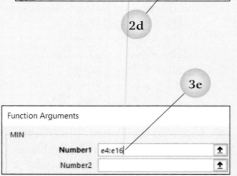

4. Insert a formula to determine the average of the completed test scores by completing the following steps:
   a. Make cell B21 active.
   b. Click the Formulas tab.
   c. Click the Insert Function button in the Function Library group.
   d. At the Insert Function dialog box, make sure *Statistical* is selected in the *Or select a category* option box and then click *AVERAGE* in the *Select a function* list box.
   e. Click OK.

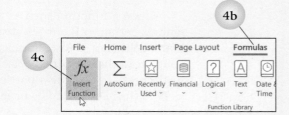

   f. At the Function Arguments dialog box, make sure the insertion point is positioned in the *Number1* text box with existing text selected, use the mouse pointer to select the range E4:E16 in the worksheet (you may need to move the dialog box to display the cells), and then click OK.

5. Save and then print **2-DWTests**.
6. Change the *70%* values (which were previously *0%*) in cells B14, D14, and D16 to *N/A*. (This will cause the average test scores for Claude Markovits and Douglas Pherson to increase and will change the average of completed tests.)
7. Save and then print **2-DWTests**.

Counting Numbers in a Range Use the COUNT function to count the numeric values in a range and use the COUNTA function to count the cells in a range containing any characters. In Activity 2c, you will use the COUNT function to specify the number of students who have completed Test 3. In the worksheet, the cells containing the text *N/A* are not counted by the COUNT function. Additionally, you will use the COUNTA function to determine how many students should have completed Test 3 by counting the cells that contain test scores and the text N/A.

Activity 2c Counting the Number of Students Taking Tests

Part 3 of 4

1. With **2-DWTests** open, make cell A22 active.
2. Type Test 3 Completed.
3. Make cell B22 active.
4. Insert a formula counting the number of students who have completed Test 3 by completing the following steps:
   a. With cell B22 active, click in the Formula bar text box.
   b. Type =c.
   c. At the Formula AutoComplete list, scroll down the list until *COUNT* displays and then double-click *COUNT*.
   d. Type d4:d16) and then press the Enter key.

5. Count the number of students who have been given Test 3 by completing the following steps:
   a. Make cell A23 active.
   b. Type Test 3 Administered.
   c. Make cell B23 active.
   d. Click the Insert Function button on the Formula bar.
   e. At the Insert Function dialog box, make sure *Statistical* is selected in the *Or select a category* option box.
   f. Scroll down the list of functions in the *Select a function* list box until *COUNTA* is visible and then double-click *COUNTA*.
   g. At the Function Arguments dialog box, type d4:d16 in the *Value1* text box and then click OK.
6. Save and then print **2-DWTests**.

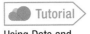

Using Date and
Time Functions

 Date & Time

 Calculate Now

Writing Formulas with the NOW and TODAY Functions

The NOW and TODAY functions are part of the *Date & Time* category of functions. The NOW function returns the current date and time in a date-and-time format. The TODAY function returns the current date in a date format. Both the NOW and TODAY functions automatically update when a workbook is opened. To access the NOW and TODAY functions, click the Date & Time button in the Function Library group on the Formulas tab. The formulas can also be accessed at the Insert Function dialog box.

The NOW and TODAY functions can also be updated without closing and then reopening the workbook. To update a workbook that contains a NOW or TODAY function, click the Calculate Now button in the Calculation group on the Formulas tab or press the F9 function key.

Displaying
Formulas

 Show
Formulas

♀ Hint Press Ctrl + `
to display the formulas
in a worksheet rather
than the results.

Displaying Formulas

In some situations, displaying the formulas in a worksheet, rather than the results, may be useful—for example, to display formulas for auditing purposes or to check formulas for accuracy. Display all the formulas in a worksheet, rather than the results, by clicking the Formulas tab and then clicking the Show Formulas button in the Formula Auditing group. The display of formulas can also be turned on with the keyboard shortcut Ctrl + `. (This symbol is the grave accent, generally to the left of the 1 key on the keyboard.) To turn off the display of formulas, press Ctrl + ` or click the Show Formulas button on the Formulas tab.

Activity 2d Using the NOW Function and Displaying Formulas

Part 4 of 4

1. With **2-DWTests** open, make cell A26 active and then type Prepared by:.
2. Make cell A27 active and then type your first and last names.
3. Insert the current date and time by completing the following steps:
   a. Make cell A28 active.
   b. Click the Date & Time button in the Function Library group on the Formulas tab and then click *NOW* at the drop-down list.
   c. At the Function Arguments dialog box stating that the function takes no argument, click OK.
4. Update the time in cell A28 by completing the following steps:
   a. Wait for 1 minute.
   b. Click the Calculate Now button in the Calculation group on the Formulas tab.
5. Click the Show Formulas button in the Formula Auditing group to turn on the display of formulas.
6. Print the worksheet with the formulas. (The worksheet will print on two pages.)
7. Press Ctrl + ` to turn off the display of formulas.
8. Save, print, and then close **2-DWTests**.

◆ Check Your Work

You will insert a formula containing an absolute cell reference that determines the effect on earnings with specific increases, insert a formula with multiple absolute cell references that determines the weighted average of scores, and use mixed cell references to determine simple interest.

Using Absolute and Mixed Cell References in Formulas

A reference identifies a cell or range of cells in a worksheet and can be relative, absolute, or mixed. A relative cell reference refers to a cell relative to a position in a formula. An absolute cell reference refers to a cell in a specific location. When a formula is copied, a relative cell reference adjusts whereas an absolute cell reference remains constant. A mixed cell reference does both: either the column remains absolute and the row is relative or the column is relative and the row remains absolute. Distinguish among relative, absolute, and mixed cell references using the dollar symbol ($). Type a dollar symbol before the column and/or row cell reference in a formula to specify that the column or row is an absolute cell reference.

Absolute Addressing

Using an Absolute Cell Reference in a Formula

In this chapter, you have learned to copy a relative formula. For example, if the formula *=SUM(A2:C2)* in cell D2 is copied relatively into cell D3, it changes to *=SUM(A3:C3)*. In some situations, a formula may contain an absolute cell reference, which always refers to a cell in a specific location. In Activity 3a, you will add a column for projected job earnings and then consider "What if?" situations using a formula with an absolute cell reference. To identify an absolute cell reference, insert a dollar symbol before the row and the column. For example, the absolute cell reference *C12* is typed as *c12* in a formula.

Activity 3a Inserting and Copying a Formula with an Absolute Cell Reference   Part 1 of 4

1. Open **CCReports** and then save it with the name **2-CCReports**.
2. Determine the effect of a 10% pay increase on actual job earnings by completing the following steps:
   a. Make cell C3 active, type the formula =b3*b12, and then press the Enter key.
   b. Make cell C3 active and then use the fill handle to copy the formula to the range C4:C10.
   c. Make cell C3 active, click the Accounting Number Format button on the Home tab, and then click the Decrease Decimal button two times.

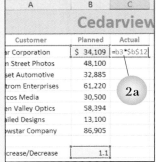

3. Save and then print **2-CCReports**.
4. With the worksheet still open, determine the effect of a 10% pay decrease on actual job earnings by completing the following steps:
   a. Make cell B12 active.
   b. Type 0.9 and then press the Enter key.
5. Save and then print the **2-CCReports**.
6. Determine the effect of a 20% pay increase on actual job earnings. (To do this, type 1.2 in cell B12 and then press the Enter key.)
7. Save and then print **2-CCReports**.

Check Your Work

In Activity 3a, you created a formula with one absolute cell reference. A formula can also be created with multiple absolute cell references. For example, in Activity 3b, you will create a formula that contains both relative and absolute cell references to determine the average of training scores based on specific weight percentages. In a weighted average, some scores have more value (weight) than others. For example, in Activity 3b, you will create a formula that determines the weighted average of training scores that gives more weight to the *Carpentry* percentages than the *Plumbing* or *Electrical* percentages.

Activity 3b Inserting and Copying a Formula with Multiple Absolute Cell References

Part 2 of 4

1. With **2-CCReports** open, insert the following formulas:
   a. Insert a formula in cell B23 that averages the percentages in the range B17:B22.
   b. Copy the formula in cell B23 to cells C23 and D23.
2. Insert a formula that determines the weighted average of training scores by completing the following steps:
   a. Make cell E17 active.
   b. Type the following formula:
      =b24*b17+c24*c17+d24*d17
   c. Press the Enter key.
   d. Copy the formula in cell E17 to the range E18:E22.
   e. With the range E17:E22 selected, click the Decrease Decimal button three times.
3. Save and then print **2-CCReports**.
4. With the worksheet still open, determine the effect on weighted training scores if the weighted values change by completing the following steps:
   a. Make cell B24 active, type 30, and then press the Enter key.
   b. Make cell D24 active, type 40, and then press the Enter key.
5. Save and then print **2-CCReports**.

Check Your Work

Tutorial

Entering and
Copying a Formula
with Mixed Cell
References

Using a Mixed Cell Reference in a Formula

The formula you created in Step 2a in Activity 3a contained a relative cell reference (b3) and an absolute cell reference (b12). A formula can also contain a mixed cell reference. As stated earlier, in a mixed cell reference, either the column remains absolute and the row is relative or the column is relative and the row remains absolute. In Activity 3c, you will insert a number of formulas—two of which will contain mixed cell references. You will insert the formula $=e29*e\$26$ to calculate withholding tax and $=e29*h\$36$ to calculate social security tax. The dollar symbol before each row number indicates that the row is an absolute reference.

Activity 3c Determining Payroll Using Formulas with Absolute and Mixed Cell References

Part 3 of 4

1. With **2-CCReports** open, make cell E29 active and then type the following formula that calculates the gross pay, including overtime (press the Enter key after typing each formula):
   $=(b29*c29+(b29*\$b\$36*d29))$
2. Copy the formula in cell E29 to the range E30:E34.
3. Make cell F29 active and then type the following formula that calculates the amount of withholding tax:
   $=e29*e\$36$
4. Copy the formula in cell F29 to the range F30:F34.
5. Make cell G29 active and then type the following formula that calculates the amount of social security tax:
   $=e29*h\$36$
6. Copy the formula in cell G29 to the range G30:G34.
7. Make cell H29 active and then type the following formula that calculates net pay:
   $=e29-(f29+g29)$
8. Copy the formula in cell H29 to the range H30:H34.
9. Select the range E29:H29 and then click the Accounting Number Format button.
10. Save **2-CCReports**.

 Check Your Work

As you learned in Activity 3c, a formula can contain a mixed cell reference. In Activity 3d, you will create the formula $=\$a41*b\$40$. In the first cell reference in the formula, $\$a41$, the column is absolute and the row is relative. In the second cell reference, $b\$40$, the column is relative and the row is absolute. The formula containing the mixed cell reference allows you to fill in the column and row data using only one formula.

Identify an absolute or mixed cell reference by typing a dollar symbol before the column and/or row reference or press the F4 function key to cycle through the various cell references. For example, type $=a41$ in a cell, press the F4 function key, and the cell reference changes to $=\$a\$41$. Press F4 again and the cell reference changes to $=a\$41$. Press F4 a third time and the cell reference changes to $=\$a41$ and press F4 a fourth time and the cell reference changes back to $=a41$.

1. With **2-CCReports** open, make cell B41 the active cell and then insert a formula containing mixed cell references by completing the following steps:
   a. Type =a41 and then press the F4 function key three times. (This changes the cell reference to *$A41*.)
   b. Type *b40 and then press the F4 function key two times. (This changes the cell reference to *B$40*.)
   c. Make sure the formula displays as =*$A41*B$40* and then press the Enter key.

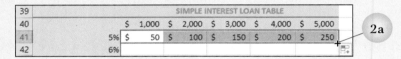

1c

2. Copy the formula to the right by completing the following steps:
   a. Make cell B41 active and then use the fill handle to copy the formula to cell F41.

39	SIMPLE INTEREST LOAN TABLE					
40		$ 1,000	$ 2,000	$ 3,000	$ 4,000	$ 5,000
41	5%	$ 50	$ 100	$ 150	$ 200	$ 250
42	6%					

2a

b. With the range B41:F41 selected, use the fill handle to copy the formula to cell F51.

39	SIMPLE INTEREST LOAN TABLE					
40		$ 1,000	$ 2,000	$ 3,000	$ 4,000	$ 5,000
41	5%	$ 50	$ 100	$ 150	$ 200	$ 250
42	6%	$ 60	$ 120	$ 180	$ 240	$ 300
43	7%	$ 70	$ 140	$ 210	$ 280	$ 350
44	8%	$ 80	$ 160	$ 240	$ 320	$ 400
45	9%	$ 90	$ 180	$ 270	$ 360	$ 450
46	10%	$ 100	$ 200	$ 300	$ 400	$ 500
47	11%	$ 110	$ 220	$ 330	$ 440	$ 550
48	12%	$ 120	$ 240	$ 360	$ 480	$ 600
49	13%	$ 130	$ 260	$ 390	$ 520	$ 650
50	14%	$ 140	$ 280	$ 420	$ 560	$ 700
51	15%	$ 150	$ 300	$ 450	$ 600	$ 750

2b

3. Save, print, and then close **2-CCReports**.

 Check Your Work

Chapter Summary

- Type a formula in a cell and the formula displays in the cell and in the Formula bar. If cell entries are changed, a formula automatically recalculates the values and inserts the result in the cell.

- Write a formula using commonly used operators, such as addition (+), subtraction (-), multiplication (*), division (/), percentage (%), and exponentiation (^). When writing a formula, begin with the equals sign (=).

- Copy a formula to other cells in a row or column with the Fill button in the Editing group on the Home tab or with the fill handle in the bottom right corner of the active cell.

- Double-click in a cell containing a formula and the cell references display with a colored border and cell shading.

- Another method for writing a formula is to point to specific cells that are part of the formula as the formula is being built.
- Excel uses the same order of operations as algebra and that order can be modified by adding parentheses around certain parts of a formula.
- If Excel detects an error in a formula, a Trace Error button appears and a small dark-green triangle displays in the upper left corner of the cell containing the formula.
- Excel provides different error codes for different formula errors. An error code helps identify an error in a formula by providing information on the specific issue.
- A function operates on an argument, which may consist of a cell reference, a constant, or another function. When a value calculated by a formula is inserted in a cell, this is referred to as *returning the result*.
- Excel performs over 300 functions that are divided into 13 categories.
- The AVERAGE function returns the average (arithmetic mean) of the arguments. The MAX function returns the largest value in a set of values and the MIN function returns the smallest value in a set of values. The COUNT function counts the number of cells containing numbers within the list of arguments. The COUNTA function counts the number of cells containing any data, numerical or alphabetical.
- The NOW function returns the current date and time and the TODAY function returns the current date.
- Turn on the display of formulas in a worksheet with the Show Formulas button in the Formula Auditing group on the Formulas tab or with the keyboard shortcut Ctrl + ` (grave accent).
- A reference identifies a cell or a range of cells in a worksheet and can be relative, absolute, or mixed. Identify an absolute cell reference by inserting a dollar symbol ($) before the column and row. Cycle through the various cell reference options by typing the cell reference and then pressing the F4 function key.

Commands Review

FEATURE	RIBBON TAB, GROUP	BUTTON	KEYBOARD SHORTCUT
cycle through cell references			F4
display formulas	Formulas, Formula Auditing		Ctrl + `
Insert Function dialog box	Formulas, Function Library		Shift + F3
SUM function	Home, Editing OR Formulas, Function Library	Σ	Alt + =
update formulas	Formulas, Calculation		F9

Microsoft® Excel®

CHAPTER 3

Formatting a Worksheet

Performance Objectives

Upon successful completion of Chapter 3, you will be able to:

1 Change column widths and row heights

2 Insert rows and columns

3 Delete cells, rows, and columns

4 Clear data in cells

5 Apply formatting to data in cells

6 Apply formatting to selected data using the Mini toolbar

7 Apply a theme and customize the theme font and colors

8 Format numbers

9 Apply formatting at the Format Cells dialog box

10 Repeat the last action

11 Automate formatting with Format Painter

12 Hide and unhide rows and columns

The appearance of a worksheet on screen and how it looks when printed is called the *format*. In Chapter 1, you learned how to apply basic formatting to cells in a worksheet. Additional types of formatting include changing column width and row height; applying character formatting such as bold, italic, and underlining; specifying number formatting; inserting and deleting rows and columns; and applying borders, shading, and patterns to cells. You can also apply formatting to a worksheet with a theme. A theme is a set of formatting choices that include colors and fonts.

Data Files

Before beginning chapter work, copy the EL1C3 folder to your storage medium and then make EL1C3 the active folder.

The online course includes additional training and assessment resources.

Activity 1 **Format a Product Pricing Worksheet**   **7 Parts**

You will open a workbook containing a worksheet with product pricing data and then format it by changing column widths and row heights, inserting and deleting rows and columns, and clearing data in cells. You will also apply font and alignment formatting as well as borders and fill.

Tutorial

Adjusting Column
Width and Row
Height

Changing Column Width

The columns in a worksheet are the same width by default. In some worksheets, column widths may need to be changed to accommodate more or less data. Change column widths using the mouse on column boundary lines or at a dialog box.

Changing Column Width Using Column Boundaries

💡 **Hint** To change
the width of all
the columns in a
worksheet, click the
Select All button and
then drag a column
boundary line to the
desired position.

As explained in Chapter 1, column width can be adjusted by dragging the column boundary line or adjusted to the longest entry by double-clicking the boundary line. When the boundary line is being dragged, the column width is shown in a box above the mouse pointer. The number that is shown represents the average number of characters in the standard font that can fit in a cell.

The width of selected adjacent columns can be changed at the same time. To do this, select the columns and then drag one of the column boundary lines within the selected columns. When the boundary line is being dragged, the column width changes for all the selected columns. To select adjacent columns, position the cell pointer on the first column header to be selected (the mouse pointer turns into a black down-pointing arrow), click and hold down the left mouse button, drag the cell pointer into the last column header, and then release the mouse button.

Activity 1a **Changing Column Width Using a Column Boundary Line**   Part 1 of 7

1. Open **CMProducts** and then save it with the name **3-CMProducts**.
2. Insert a formula in cell D2 that multiplies the price in cell B2 with the number in cell C2. Copy the formula in cell D2 to the range D3:D14.
3. Change the width of column D by completing the following steps:
   a. Position the mouse pointer on the column boundary line in the column header between columns D and E until it turns into a double-headed arrow pointing left and right.
   b. Click and hold down the left mouse button, drag the column boundary line to the right until *Width: 11.00* displays in the box, and then release the mouse button.
4. Make cell D15 active and then insert the sum of the values in the range D2:D14.
5. Change the width of columns A and B by completing the following steps:
   a. Select columns A and B. To do this, position the cell pointer on the column A header, click and hold down the left mouse button, drag the cell pointer into the column B header, and then release the mouse button.
   b. Position the cell pointer on the column boundary line between columns A and B until it turns into a double-headed arrow pointing left and right.

c. Click and hold down the left mouse button, drag the column boundary line to the right until *Width: 10.43* displays in the box, and then release the mouse button.

6. Adjust the width of column C to accommodate the longest entry by double-clicking on the column boundary line between columns C and D.

7. Save **3-CMProducts**.

5c

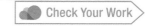

Changing Column Width at the Column Width Dialog Box

Use the *Column width* measurement box in the Column Width dialog box, shown in Figure 3.1, to specify a column width number. Increase the number to make the column wider and decrease the number to make the column narrower.

Display the Column Width dialog box by clicking the Format button in the Cells group on the Home tab and then clicking *Column Width* at the drop-down list. At the Column Width dialog box, type a measurement number (the number represents the number of characters in the standard font that can fit in the column) and then press the Enter key or click OK.

 Format

Quick Steps

Change Column Width

Drag column boundary line.
OR
Double-click column boundary line.
OR
1. Click Format button.
2. Click *Column Width.*
3. Type width.
4. Click OK.

Figure 3.1 Column Width Dialog Box

Type the column width in this measurement box.

Activity 1b Changing Column Width at the Column Width Dialog Box   Part 2 of 7

1. With **3-CMProducts** open, change the width of column A by completing the following steps:
   a. Make any cell in column A active.
   b. Click the Format button in the Cells group on the Home tab and then click *Column Width* at the drop-down list.
   c. At the Column Width dialog box, type 12.7 in the *Column width* measurement box.
   d. Click OK to close the dialog box.
2. Make any cell in column B active and then change the width of column B to 12.5 characters by completing steps similar to those in Step 1.
3. Make any cell in column C active and then change the width of column C to 8 characters by completing steps similar to those in Step 1.
4. Save **3-CMProducts**.

1c

1d

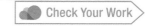

Changing Row Height

Quick Steps

Change Row Height
Drag row boundary line.
OR
1. Click Format button.
2. Click *Row Height*.
3. Type height.
4. Click OK.

Hint To change the height of all the rows in a worksheet, click the Select All button and then drag a row boundary line to the desired position.

Hint Excel measures row height in points and column width in characters.

Change row height in much the same manner as column width. Change row height using the mouse on a row boundary line or at the Row Height dialog box. Change row height using a row boundary line by positioning the cell pointer on the boundary line between rows in the row header until it turns into a double-headed arrow pointing up and down, clicking and holding down the left mouse button, dragging up or down until the row is the desired height, and then releasing the mouse button.

Change the height of adjacent rows by selecting the rows and then dragging one of the row boundary lines within the selected rows. As the boundary line is being dragged, the row height changes for all the selected rows.

As a row boundary line is being dragged, the row height displays in a box above the mouse pointer. The number that is shown represents a point measurement. Increase the point size to increase the row height; decrease the point size to decrease the row height.

Another method for changing row height is to use the *Row height* measurement box at the Row Height dialog box, shown in Figure 3.2. Display this dialog box by clicking the Format button in the Cells group on the Home tab and then clicking *Row Height* at the drop-down list.

Figure 3.2 Row Height Dialog Box

Type the row height in this measurement box.

Activity 1c Changing Row Height

1. With **3-CMProducts** open, change the height of row 1 by completing the following steps:
   a. Position the cell pointer in the row header on the row boundary line between rows 1 and 2 until it turns into a double-headed arrow pointing up and down.
   b. Click and hold down the left mouse button, drag the row boundary line down until *Height: 19.50* displays in the box, and then release the mouse button.

2. Change the height of rows 2 through 14 by completing the following steps:
   a. Select rows 2 through 14. To do this, position the cell pointer on the number *2* in the row header, click and hold down the left mouse button, drag the cell pointer to the number *14* in the row header, and then release the mouse button.
   b. Position the cell pointer on the row boundary line between rows 2 and 3 until it turns into a double-headed arrow pointing up and down.

c. Click and hold down the left mouse button, drag the row boundary line down until *Height: 16.50* displays in the box, and then release the mouse button.

3. Change the height of row 15 by completing the following steps:
   a. Make cell A15 active.
   b. Click the Format button in the Cells group on the Home tab and then click *Row Height* at the drop-down list.
   c. At the Row Height dialog box, type 20 in the *Row height* measurement box and then click OK.

4. Save **3-CMProducts**.

Check Your Work

Tutorial

Inserting Columns and Rows

Inserting and Deleting Cells, Rows, and Columns

New data may need to be included in an existing worksheet. For example, a row or several rows of new data may need to be inserted into a worksheet or data may need to be removed from a worksheet.

Inserting Rows

Hint When you insert cells, rows, or columns in a worksheet, all the references affected by the insertion automatically adjust.

A row or rows can be inserted in an existing worksheet. Insert a row with the Insert button in the Cells group on the Home tab or with options at the Insert dialog box. By default, a row is inserted above the row containing the active cell. To insert a row in a worksheet, select the row below where the row is to be inserted and then click the Insert button. To insert more than one row, select the number of rows to be inserted in the worksheet and then click the Insert button.

 Insert

Quick Steps

Insert Row
Click Insert button.
OR
1. Click Insert button arrow.
2. Click *Insert Sheet Rows*.
OR
1. Click Insert button arrow.
2. Click *Insert Cells*.
3. Click *Entire row*.
4. Click OK.

Another method for inserting a row is to make a cell active in the row below where the row is to be inserted, click the Insert button arrow, and then click *Insert Sheet Rows*. A row can also be inserted by clicking the Insert button arrow and then clicking *Insert Cells*. This displays the Insert dialog box, as shown in Figure 3.3. At the Insert dialog box, click *Entire row* and then click OK. This inserts a row above the active cell.

Figure 3.3 Insert Dialog Box

1. With **3-CMProducts** open, insert two rows at the beginning of the worksheet by completing the following steps:
   a. Make cell A1 active.
   b. Click the Insert button arrow in the Cells group on the Home tab.
   c. At the drop-down list that displays, click *Insert Sheet Rows*.
   d. With cell A1 active, click the Insert button arrow and then click *Insert Sheet Rows* at the drop-down list.
2. Type the text Capstan Marine Products in cell A1.
3. Make cell A2 active and then type Purchasing Department.
4. Change the height of row 1 to 42 points.
5. Change the height of row 2 to 21 points.
6. Insert two rows by completing the following steps:
   a. Select rows 7 and 8 in the worksheet.
   b. Click the Insert button in the Cells group on the Home tab.
7. Type the following data in the specified cells. For the cells that contain money amounts, you do not need to type the dollar symbols:
   A7: 855-495
   B7: 42.75
   C7: 5
   A8: ST039
   B8: 12.99
   C8: 25
8. Make cell D6 active and then use the fill handle to copy the formula into cells D7 and D8.
9. Save **3-CMProducts**.

 Check Your Work

Inserting Columns

Quick Steps

Insert Column
Click Insert button.
OR
1. Click Insert button arrow.
2. Click *Insert Sheet Columns*.
OR
1. Click Insert button arrow.
2. Click *Insert Cells*.
3. Click *Entire column*.
4. Click OK.

Insert columns in a worksheet in much the same way as rows. Insert a column with options from the Insert button drop-down list or with options at the Insert dialog box. By default, a column is inserted immediately to the left of the column containing the active cell. To insert a column in a worksheet, make a cell active in the column immediately to the right of where the new column is to be inserted, click the Insert button arrow, and then click *Insert Sheet Columns* at the drop-down list. To insert more than one column, select the number of columns to be inserted in the worksheet, click the Insert button arrow, and then click *Insert Sheet Columns*.

Another method for inserting a column is to make a cell active in the column immediately to the right of where the new column is to be inserted, click the Insert button arrow, and then click *Insert Cells* at the drop-down list. At the Insert dialog box that displays, click *Entire column*. This inserts a column immediately left of the active cell.

Excel includes an especially helpful and time-saving feature related to inserting columns. When columns are inserted in a worksheet, all the references affected by the insertion automatically adjust.

1. With **3-CMProducts** open, insert a column to the left of column A by completing the following steps:
   a. Click in any cell in column A.
   b. Click the Insert button arrow in the Cells group on the Home tab and then click *Insert Sheet Columns* at the drop-down list.
2. Type the following data in each specified cell:
   A3: Company
   A4: RD Manufacturing
   A8: Smithco, Inc.
   A11: Sunrise Corporation
   A15: Geneva Systems
3. Make cell A1 active and then adjust the width of column A to accommodate the longest entry.
4. Insert another column to the left of column B by completing the following steps:
   a. Make cell B1 active.
   b. Click the Insert button arrow and then click *Insert Cells* at the drop-down list.
   c. At the Insert dialog box, click *Entire column*.
   d. Click OK.
5. Type Date in cell B3 and then press the Enter key.
6. Save **3-CMProducts**.

Check Your Work

 Delete

Hint Display the Delete dialog box by positioning the cell pointer in the worksheet, clicking the right mouse button, and then clicking *Delete* at the shortcut menu.

Deleting Cells, Rows, or Columns

Specific cells in a worksheet or rows or columns in a worksheet can be deleted. To delete a row, select it and then click the Delete button in the Cells group on the Home tab. To delete a column, select it and then click the Delete button. Delete a specific cell by making it active, clicking the Delete button arrow, and then clicking *Delete Cells* at the drop-down list. This displays the Delete dialog box, shown in Figure 3.4. At the Delete dialog box, specify what is to be deleted and then click OK. Delete adjacent cells by selecting them and then displaying the Delete dialog box.

Figure 3.4 Delete Dialog Box

Choose the option that makes the desired change.

Clear

Quick Steps

Clear Data in Cells
1. Select cells.
2. Press Delete key.
OR
1. Select cells.
2. Click Clear button.
3. Click *Clear Contents*.

Clearing Data in Cells

To delete the cell contents but not the cell, make the cell active or select cells and then press the Delete key. A quick method for clearing the contents of a cell is to right-click in the cell and then click *Clear Contents* at the shortcut menu. Another method for deleting cell contents is to make the cell active or select cells, click the Clear button in the Editing group on the Home tab, and then click *Clear Contents* at the drop-down list.

Use options at the Clear button drop-down list to clear the contents of the cell or selected cells as well as the formatting and comments. Click the *Clear Formats* option to remove the formatting from the cell or selected cells but leave the data. Click the *Clear All* option to clear the contents of the cell or selected cells as well as the formatting.

Activity 1f **Deleting and Clearing Rows in a Worksheet**   Part 6 of 7

1. With **3-CMProducts** open, delete column B in the worksheet by completing the following steps:
   a. Click in any cell in column B.
   b. Click the Delete button arrow in the Cells group on the Home tab and then click *Delete Sheet Columns* at the drop-down list.

2. Delete row 5 by completing the following steps:
   a. Select row 5.
   b. Click the Delete button in the Cells group.
3. Clear row contents by completing the following steps:
   a. Select rows 7 and 8.
   b. Click the Clear button in the Editing group on the Home tab and then click *Clear Contents* at the drop-down list.

4. Type the following data in each specified cell:
   A7: Ray Enterprises
   B7: S894-T
   C7: 4.99
   D7: 30
   B8: B-3448
   C8: 25.50
   D8: 12

5. Make cell E6 active and then copy the formula into cells E7 and E8.
6. Save **3-CMProducts**.

6		855-495	$	42.75	5		$	213.75
7	Ray Enterprises	S894-T	$	4.99	30			
8		B-3448	$	25.50	12			
9		43-GB-39	$	45.00	20		$	900.00

Check Your Work

Applying Formatting

Many of the groups on the Home tab contain options for applying formatting to text in the active cell or selected cells. Use buttons and options in the Font group to apply font formatting to text and use buttons in the Alignment group to apply alignment formatting.

Figure 3.5 Font Group

Use buttons and options in the Font group to apply formatting to cells or the data in cells.

Applying Font Formatting

Applying Font Formatting

Apply a variety of formatting to cells in a worksheet with buttons and options in the Font group on the Home tab. Use buttons and options in the Font group, shown in Figure 3.5, to change the font, font size, and font color; to bold, italicize, and underline data in cells; to change the text color; and to apply a border or add fill to cells.

Use the *Font* option box in the Font group to change the font of the text in a cell and use the *Font Size* option box to specify the size of the text. Apply bold formatting to text in a cell with the Bold button, italic formatting with the Italic button, and underlining with the Underline button, or use the keyboard shortcuts Ctrl + B, Ctrl + I, and Ctrl + U.

Click the Increase Font Size button and the text in the active cell or selected cells increases to the next font size in the *Font Size* option box drop-down gallery. Click the Decrease Font Size button and the text in the active cell or selected cells decreases to the next point size.

Use the Borders button in the Font group to insert a border on any or all sides of the active cell or any or all sides of selected cells. The name of the button changes depending on the most recent border applied to a cell or selected cells. Use the Fill Color button to insert color in the active cell or in selected cells. Change the color of the text within a cell with the Font Color button.

 Bold

Italic

Underline

Increase Font Size

Decrease Font Size

Borders

Fill Color

Font Color

Formatting with the Mini Toolbar

Double-click in a cell and then select the data within it and the Mini toolbar displays above the selected data. The Mini toolbar also displays when right-clicking in a cell. The Mini toolbar contains buttons and options for applying font formatting, such as font, font size, and font color, as well as bold and italic formatting. Click a button or option on the Mini toolbar to apply formatting to selected text.

Applying Alignment Formatting

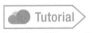
Applying Alignment Formatting

The alignment of data in cells depends on the type of data entered. Enter words or text combined with numbers in a cell and the text aligns at the left edge of the cell. Enter numbers in a cell and the numbers align at the right of the cell. Use buttons in the Alignment group to align data at the left, center, or right of the cell; align data at the top, center, or bottom of the cell; increase and/or decrease the indent of data in a cell; and change the orientation of data in a cell.

As explained in Chapter 1, selected cells can be merged by clicking the Merge & Center button. If cells are merged, the merged cell can be split into the original cells by selecting the cell and then clicking the Merge & Center button. Click the

 Merge & Center

Merge & Center button arrow and a drop-down list of options displays. Click the *Merge & Center* option to merge all the selected cells and to apply center cell alignment. Click the *Merge Across* option to merge each row of selected cells. For example, if three cells and two rows are selected, clicking the *Merge Across* option will merge the three cells in the first row and merge the three cells in the second row, resulting in two cells. Click the *Merge Cells* option to merge all the selected cells but not apply center cell alignment. Use the last option, *Unmerge Cells*, to split cells that were previously merged. If cells that are selected and then merged contain data, only the data in the upper left cell remains. Data in the other merged cells is deleted.

 Orientation

abc Wrap Text

Click the Orientation button in the Alignment group and a drop-down list displays with options for rotating data in a cell. If the data typed in a cell is longer than the cell, it overlaps the next cell to the right. To wrap the data to the next line within the cell, click the Wrap Text button in the Alignment group.

Activity 1g Applying Font and Alignment Formatting

1. With **3-CMProducts** open, make cell B1 active and then click the Wrap Text button in the Alignment group on the Home tab. (This wraps the company name within the cell.)
2. Select the range B1:C2, click the Merge & Center button arrow in the Alignment group on the Home tab, and then click *Merge Across* at the drop-down list.
3. After looking at the merged cells, you decide to merge additional cells and horizontally and vertically center the text in the cells by completing the following steps:
   a. With the range B1:C2 selected, click the Merge & Center button arrow and then click *Unmerge Cells* at the drop-down list.
   b. Select the range A1:E2.
   c. Click the Merge & Center button arrow and then click the *Merge Across* option at the drop-down list.
   d. Click the Middle Align button in the Alignment group and then click the Center button.

4. Rotate the text in the third row by completing the following steps:
   a. Select the range A3:E3.
   b. Click the Orientation button in the Alignment group and then click *Angle Counterclockwise* at the drop-down list.
   c. After looking at the rotated text, you decide to return the orientation to horizontal by clicking the Undo button on the Quick Access Toolbar.
5. Change the font, font size, and font color for the text in specific cells by completing the following steps:
   a. Make cell A1 active.
   b. Click the *Font* option box arrow in the Font group, scroll down the drop-down gallery, and then click *Bookman Old Style*.
   c. Click the *Font Size* option box arrow in the Font group and then click *22* at the drop-down gallery.

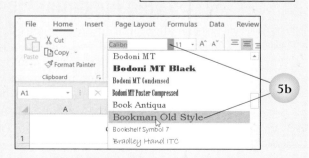

d. Click the Font Color button arrow and then click the *Dark Blue* option (ninth option in the *Standard Colors* section).

6. Make cell A2 active and then complete steps similar to those in Step 5 to change the font to Bookman Old Style, the font size to 16 points, and the font color to Dark Blue.

7. Select the range A3:E3 and then click the Center button in the Alignment group.

8. With the range A3:E3 still selected, click the Bold button in the Font group and then click the Italic button.

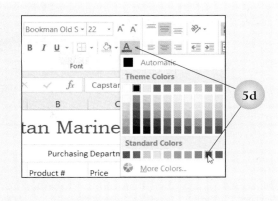

9. Select the range A3:E18 and then change the font to Bookman Old Style.

10. Use the Mini toolbar to apply formatting to selected data by completing the following steps:
    a. Double-click in cell A4.
    b. Select the letters *RD*. (This displays the Mini toolbar above the selected word.)
    c. Click the Increase Font Size button on the Mini toolbar.
    d. Double-click in cell A14.
    e. Select the word *Geneva* and then click the Italic button on the Mini toolbar.

11. Adjust columns A through E to accommodate the longest entry in each column. To do this, select columns A through E and then double-click any selected column boundary line.

12. Select the range D4:D17 and then click the Center button in the Alignment group.

13. Add a double-line bottom border to cell A2 by completing the following steps:
    a. Make cell A2 active.
    b. Click the Borders button arrow in the Font group. (The name of this button varies depending on the last option selected.)
    c. Click the *Bottom Double Border* option at the drop-down list.

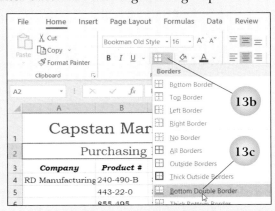

14. Add a single-line bottom border to the range A3:E3 by completing the following steps:
    a. Select the range A3:E3.
    b. Click the Borders button arrow and then click the *Bottom Border* option.

15. Apply a fill color to specific cells by completing the following steps:
    a. Select the range A1:E3.
    b. Click the Fill Color button arrow in the Font group.
    c. Click the *Blue, Accent 5, Lighter 80%* color option (ninth column, second row in the *Theme Colors* section).

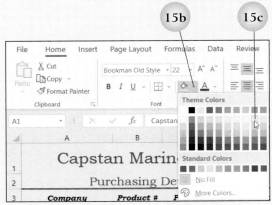

16. Select the range C5:C17 and then click the Comma Style button.

17. Select the range E5:E17 and then click the Comma Style button.

18. Save, print, and then close **3-CMProducts**.

Activity 2 Apply a Theme to a Payroll Worksheet

1 Part

You will open a workbook containing a worksheet with payroll information and then insert text in cells, apply formatting to the cells and cell contents, apply a theme, and then change the theme font and colors.

Tutorial

Applying and Modifying Themes

 Themes

Hint Apply a theme to give your worksheet a professional look.

Applying a Theme

Excel provides a number of themes that can be used to format text and cells in a worksheet. A theme is a set of formatting choices that includes a color theme (a set of colors), a font theme (a set of heading and body text fonts), and an effects theme (a set of lines and fill effects). To apply a theme, click the Page Layout tab and then click the Themes button in the Themes group. At the drop-down gallery that displays, click the desired theme. Position the mouse pointer over a theme and the live preview feature displays the worksheet with the theme formatting applied.

Activity 2 Applying a Theme

Part 1 of 1

1. Open **SBAPayroll** and then save it with the name **3-SBAPayroll**.
2. Make cell G4 active and then insert a formula that calculates the amount of social security tax. (Multiply the gross pay amount in cell E4 with the social security rate in cell H11; you will need to use the mixed cell reference H$11 when writing the formula.)
3. Copy the formula in cell G4 to the range G5:G9.
4. Make H4 the active cell and then insert a formula that calculates the net pay (gross pay minus withholding and social security tax).
5. Copy the formula in cell H4 to the range H5:H9.
6. Increase the height of row 1 to 36.00 points.
7. Make cell A1 active, click the Middle Align button in the Alignment group, click the *Font Size* option box arrow, click *18* at the drop-down gallery, and then click the Bold button.
8. Type Stanton & Barnett Associates in cell A1.
9. Select the range A2:H3 and then click the Bold button in the Font group.
10. Apply a theme and customize the font and colors by completing the following steps:
    a. Make cell A1 active.
    b. Click the Page Layout tab.
    c. Click the Themes button in the Themes group, hover the mouse pointer over individual themes at the drop-down gallery to see how they affect the formatting of the worksheet, and then click *Wisp*.

d. Click the Colors button in the Themes group and then click *Red Orange* at the drop-down gallery.

e. Click the Fonts button in the Themes group, scroll down the drop-down gallery, and then click *Trebuchet MS*.

11. Select columns A through H and adjust the width of the columns to accommodate the longest entries.

12. Save, print, and then close **3-SBAPayroll**.

 Check Your Work

Activity 3 Format an Invoices Worksheet   2 Parts

You will open a workbook containing an invoice worksheet and apply number formatting to the numbers in the cells.

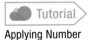 Tutorial

Applying Number
Formatting

Formatting Numbers

By default, the numbers in a cell align at the right and decimals and commas do not appear unless they are typed in the cell. Change the format of numbers with buttons in the Number group on the Home tab or with options at the Format Cells dialog box with the Number tab selected.

Formatting Numbers Using Number Group Buttons

The format symbols available for formatting numbers include a percent symbol (%), comma (,), and dollar symbol ($). For example, type *$45.50* in a cell and Excel automatically applies the Currency format to the number. Type *45%* in a cell and Excel automatically applies the Percentage format to the number. The Number group on the Home tab contains five buttons for formatting numbers in cells. (These buttons were explained in Chapter 1.)

Specify the formatting for numbers in cells in a worksheet before typing the numbers or format existing numbers in a worksheet. Use the Increase Decimal and Decrease Decimal buttons in the Number group on the Home tab to change the number of digits after the decimal point for existing numbers only.

The Number group on the Home tab also contains the *Number Format* option box. Click the *Number Format* option box arrow and a drop-down list displays common number formats. Click a format at the drop-down list to apply the number formatting to the cell or selected cells.

Activity 3a Formatting Numbers with Buttons in the Number Group

Part 1 of 2

1. Open **RPInvoices** and then save it with the name **3-RPInvoices**.
2. Make the following changes to column widths:
   a. Change the width of column C to 17.00 characters.
   b. Change the width of column D to 10.00 characters.
   c. Change the width of column E to 7.00 characters.
   d. Change the width of column F to 12.00 characters.
3. Select row 1 and then click the Insert button in the Cells group on the Home tab.
4. Change the height of row 1 to 42.00 points.
5. Select the range A1:F1 and then make the following changes:
   a. Click the Merge & Center button in the Alignment group on the Home tab.
   b. With cell A1 active, change the font size to 24 points and the font color to Green, Accent 6, Darker 50% (last column, sixth row in the *Theme Colors* section).
   c. Click the Fill Color button arrow in the Font group and then click *Gray, Accent 3, Lighter 60%* (seventh column, third row in the *Theme Colors* section).
   d. Click the Borders button arrow in the Font group and then click the *Top and Thick Bottom Border* option.
   e. With cell A1 active, type REAL PHOTOGRAPHY and then press the Enter key.
6. Change the height of row 2 to 24.00 points.
7. Select the range A2:F2 and then make the following changes:
   a. Click the Merge & Center button in the Alignment group.
   b. With cell A2 active, change the font size to 18 points.
   c. Click the Fill Color button in the Font group. (This will fill the cell with the gray color applied in Step 5c.)
   d. Click the Borders button arrow in the Font group and then click the *Bottom Border* option.
8. Make the following changes to row 3:
   a. Change the height of row 3 to 18.00 points.
   b. Select the range A3:F3, click the Bold button in the Font group, and then click the Center button in the Alignment group.
   c. With the cells still selected, click the Borders button.

9. Make the following number formatting changes:
   a. Select the range E4:E16 and then click the Percent Style button in the Number group on the Home tab.
   b. With the cells still selected, click the Increase Decimal button in the Number group. (The percentages should include one digit after the decimal point.)

9a   9b

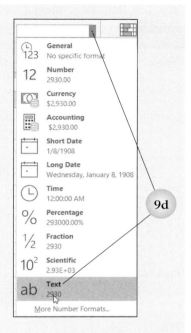

9d

   c. Select the range A4:B16.
   d. Click the *Number Format* option box arrow, scroll down the drop-down list, and then click *Text*.
   e. With the range A4:B16 still selected, click the Center button in the Alignment group.
10. Save **3-RPInvoices**.

Check Your Work

Applying Number Formatting at the Format Cells Dialog Box

In addition to using buttons in the Number group, numbers can be formatted with options at the Format Cells dialog box with the Number tab selected, as shown in Figure 3.6. Display this dialog box by clicking the Number group dialog box launcher or by clicking the *Number Format* option box arrow and then clicking *More Number Formats* at the drop-down list. The left side of the dialog box shows number categories; the default category is *General*. At this setting, no specific formatting is applied to numbers except right alignment in cells. The other number categories are described in Table 3.1.

Figure 3.6 Format Cells Dialog Box with the Number Tab Selected

Choose a category in this list box and a description of the category displays in the dialog box.

Table 3.1 Number Formatting Options at the Format Cells Dialog Box

Category	Formatting
Number	Specify the number of digits after the decimal point and whether a "thousand" separator should be used; choose the appearance of negative numbers; right-align numbers in the cell.
Currency	Apply general monetary values; add a dollar symbol as well as commas and decimal points, if needed; right-align numbers in the cell.
Accounting	Line up the currency symbols and decimal points in a column; add a dollar symbol and two digits after the decimal point; right-align numbers in the cell.
Date	Show the date as a date value; specify the type of formatting desired by clicking an option in the *Type* list box; right-align the date in the cell.
Time	Show the time as a time value; specify the type of formatting desired by clicking an option in the *Type* list box; right-align the time in the cell.
Percentage	Multiply the cell value by 100 and show the result with a percent symbol; add a decimal point followed by two digits by default; change the number of digits with the *Decimal places* option; right-align numbers in the cell.
Fraction	Specify how a fraction appears in the cell by clicking an option in the *Type* list box; right-align a fraction in the cell.
Scientific	Use for very large or very small numbers; use the letter *E* to have Excel move the decimal point a specified number of digits.
Text	Treat a number in the cell as text; the number is shown in the cell exactly as typed.
Special	Choose a number type, such as *Zip Code*, *Phone Number*, or *Social Security Number*, in the *Type* option list box; useful for tracking list and database values.
Custom	Specify a numbering type by choosing an option in the *Type* list box.

Activity 3b Formatting Numbers at the Format Cells Dialog Box

Part 2 of 2

1. With **3-RPInvoices** open, make cell F4 active, type the formula =(d4*e4)+d4, and then press the Enter key.
2. Make cell F4 active and then copy the formula to the range F5:F16.
3. Apply the Accounting format by completing the following steps:
   a. Select the range D4:D16.
   b. Click the Number group dialog box launcher.

c. At the Format Cells dialog box with the Number tab selected, click *Accounting* in the *Category* list box.

d. Make sure a *2* appears in the *Decimal places* option box and a *$* (dollar symbol) appears in the *Symbol* option box.

e. Click OK.

4. Apply the Accounting format to the range F4:F16 by completing actions similar to those in Step 3.

5. Save, print, and then close **3-RPInvoices**.

Check Your Work

Activity 4 **Format a Company Budget Worksheet** **6 Parts**

You will open a workbook containing a company budget worksheet and then apply formatting to cells with options at the Format Cells dialog box, use Format Painter to apply formatting, and hide and unhide rows and columns.

Tutorial

Applying Formatting Using the Format Cells Dialog Box

Applying Formatting Using the Format Cells Dialog Box

As explained earlier in this chapter, the Format Cells dialog box with the Number tab selected provides options for formatting numbers. This dialog box also contains other tabs with options for formatting cells.

Aligning and Indenting Data

Align and indent data in cells using buttons in the Alignment group on the Home tab or using options at the Format Cells dialog box with the Alignment tab selected, as shown in Figure 3.7. Display this dialog box by clicking the Alignment group dialog box launcher.

Use options in the *Orientation* section to rotate data. A portion of the *Orientation* section shows points on an arc. Click a point on the arc to rotate the text along that point. Or type a rotation degree in the *Degrees* measurement box. Type a positive number to rotate selected text from the lower left to the upper right side of the cell. Type a negative number to rotate selected text from the upper left to the lower right side of the cell.

If the data typed in a cell is longer than the cell, it overlaps the next cell to the right. To wrap text to the next line within a cell, insert a check mark in the *Wrap text* check box in the *Text control* section of the dialog box. Insert a check mark in the *Shrink to fit* check box to reduce the size of the text font so all the data fits within the cell. Insert a check mark in the *Merge cells* check box to combine two or more selected cells into a single cell. To enter data on more than one line within a cell, enter the data on the first line and then press Alt + Enter. Pressing Alt + Enter moves the insertion point to the next line within the same cell.

Figure 3.7 Format Cells Dialog Box with the Alignment Tab Selected

Specify horizontal and vertical alignment with options in this section.

Use options in this section to control how text fits in a cell.

Rotate text in a cell by clicking a point on the arc or by entering a number in the *Degrees* measurement box.

Activity 4a Aligning and Rotating Data in Cells at the Format Cells Dialog Box

Part 1 of 6

1. Open **HBCJobs** and then save it with the name **3-HBCJobs**.
2. Make the following changes to the worksheet:
   a. Insert a new row at the beginning of the worksheet.
   b. Change the height of row 1 to 66.00 points.
   c. Merge and center the range A1:E1.
   d. Type Harris & Briggs in cell A1 and then press Alt + Enter. (This moves the insertion point down to the next line in the same cell.)
   e. Type Construction and then press the Enter key.
   f. With cell A2 active, type Preferred, press Alt + Enter, type Customer, and then press the Enter key.
   g. Change the width of column A to 22.00 characters.
   h. Change the width of column B to 7.00 characters.
   i. Change the widths of columns C, D, and E to 10.00 characters.
3. Make cell E3 active and then type the formula =d3-c3. Copy this formula to the range E4:E11.
4. Change the number formatting for specific cells by completing the following steps:
   a. Select the range C3:E3.
   b. Click the Number group dialog box launcher.
   c. At the Format Cells dialog box with the Number tab selected, click *Accounting* in the *Category* list box.
   d. Click the *Decimal places* measurement box down arrow until *0* displays.
   e. Make sure a *$* (dollar symbol) appears in the *Symbol* option box.
   f. Click OK.

5. Select the range C4:E11, click the Comma Style button in the Number group on the Home tab, and then decrease the number of digits after the decimal point to 0.

6. Change the orientation of data in cells by completing the following steps:
   a. Select the range B2:E2.
   b. Click the Alignment group dialog box launcher.
   c. At the Format Cells dialog box with the Alignment tab selected, select *0* in the *Degrees* measurement box and then type 45.
   d. Click OK.

7. Change the vertical alignment of text in cells by completing the following steps:
   a. Select the range A1:E2.
   b. Click the Alignment group dialog box launcher.
   c. At the Format Cells dialog box with the Alignment tab selected, click the *Vertical* option box arrow.
   d. Click *Center* at the drop-down list.
   e. Click OK.

8. Change the horizontal alignment of text in cells by completing the following steps:
   a. Select the range A2:E2.
   b. Click the Alignment group dialog box launcher.
   c. At the Format Cells dialog box with the Alignment tab selected, click the *Horizontal* option box arrow.
   d. Click *Center* at the drop-down list.
   e. Click OK.

9. Change the horizontal alignment and indent of text in cells by completing the following steps:
   a. Select the range B3:B11.
   b. Click the Alignment group dialog box launcher.
   c. At the Format Cells dialog box with the Alignment tab selected, click the *Horizontal* option box arrow and then click *Right (Indent)* at the drop-down list.
   d. Click the *Indent* measurement box up arrow. (This displays *1*.)
   e. Click OK.

10. Save **3-HBCJobs**.

Changing the Font

As explained earlier in this chapter, the Font group on the Home tab contains buttons and options for applying font formatting to data in cells. The font for data in cells can also be changed with options at the Format Cells dialog box with the Font tab selected, as shown in Figure 3.8. Use options at the Format Cells dialog box with the Font tab selected to change the font, font style, font size, and font color; to change the underlining method; and to add effects such as superscript and subscript. Click the Font group dialog box launcher to display this dialog box.

Figure 3.8 Format Cells Dialog Box with the Font Tab Selected

Choose a font in this list box. Use the scroll bar at the right of the box to view the available fonts.

Choose a font style in this list box. The options in the box may vary depending on the selected font.

Choose a font size in this list box or select the current measurement in the option box and then type the measurement.

Apply font effects to text by inserting a check mark in the check box next to the desired effect.

Preview the text with the selected formatting applied.

Activity 4b **Applying Font Formatting at the Format Cells Dialog Box**   Part 2 of 6

1. With **3-HBCJobs** open, change the font and font color by completing the following steps:
   a. Select the range A1:E11.
   b. Click the Font group dialog box launcher.
   c. At the Format Cells dialog box with the Font tab selected, scroll down the *Font* option list box and then click *Garamond*.
   d. Click *12* in the *Size* list box.
   e. Click the *Color* option box arrow.
   f. At the color palette, click the *Dark Red* color (first option in the *Standard Colors* section).
   g. Click OK to close the dialog box.
2. Make cell A1 active and then change the font size to 24 points and apply bold formatting.
3. Select the range A2:E2 and then apply bold formatting.
4. Save and then print **3-HBCJobs**.

Check Your Work

Tutorial

Adding Borders to
Cells

Adding Borders to Cells

The gridlines in a worksheet do not print. As explained earlier in this chapter, use the Borders button in the Font group to add borders to cells that will print. Borders can also be added to cells with options at the Format Cells dialog box with the Border tab selected, as shown in Figure 3.9. Display this dialog box by clicking the Borders button arrow in the Font group and then clicking *More Borders* at the drop-down list.

With options in the *Presets* section, remove borders with the *None* option, add only outside borders with the *Outline* option, and add borders to the insides of selected cells with the *Inside* option. In the *Border* section of the dialog box, specify the side of the cell or selected cells to which the border is to be applied. Choose the line style for the border with options in the *Style* list box. Add color to border lines by clicking the *Color* option box arrow and then clicking a color at the color palette that displays.

Quick Steps

Add Borders to Cells
1. Select cells.
2. Click Borders button arrow.
3. Click border.
OR
1. Select cells.
2. Click Borders button arrow.
3. Click *More Borders*.
4. Use options in dialog box to apply border.
5. Click OK.

Figure 3.9 Format Cells Dialog Box with the Border Tab Selected

Activity 4c Adding Borders to Cells at the Format Cells Dialog Box   Part 3 of 6

1. With **3-HBCJobs** open, remove the 45-degree orientation you applied in Activity 4a by completing the following steps:
   a. Select the range B2:E2.
   b. Click the Alignment group dialog box launcher.
   c. At the Format Cells dialog box with the Alignment tab selected, select *45* in the *Degrees* measurement box and then type 0.
   d. Click OK.
2. Change the height of row 2 to 33.00 points.

3. Add a thick, dark red border line to cells by completing the following steps:
   a. Select the range A1:E11.
   b. Click the Borders button arrow and then click the *More Borders* option at the drop-down list.
   c. At the Format Cells dialog box with the Border tab selected, click the *Color* option box arrow and then click the *Dark Red* color (first option in the *Standard Colors* section).
   d. Click the thick single-line option in the *Style* list box in the *Line* section (sixth option in the second column).
   e. Click the *Outline* option in the *Presets* section.
   f. Click OK.

4. Add borders above and below cells by completing the following steps:
   a. Select the range A2:E2.
   b. Click the Borders button arrow and then click *More Borders* at the drop-down list.
   c. At the Format Cells dialog box with the Border tab selected, make sure the color is still Dark Red.
   d. Make sure the thick single-line option is still selected in the *Style* list box in the *Line* section.
   e. Click the top border of the sample cell in the *Border* section of the dialog box.
   f. Click the double-line option in the *Style* list box (last option in the second column).
   g. Click the bottom border of the sample cell in the *Border* section of the dialog box.
   h. Click OK.

5. Save **3-HBCJobs**.

Check Your Work

Quick Steps

Add Fill and Shading
1. Select cells.
2. Click Fill Color button
   arrow.
3. Click color.
OR
1. Select cells.
2. Click Format button.
3. Click *Format Cells.*
4. Click Fill tab.
5. Use options in dialog
   box to apply shading.
6. Click OK.

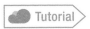

Using Format
Painter and the
Repeat Command

Quick Steps

Repeat Last Action
1. Apply formatting.
2. Move to location.
3. Press F4 or
   Ctrl + Y.

Adding Fill and Shading to Cells

To enhance the appearance of cells and data within cells, consider adding fill color. As explained earlier in this chapter, fill color can be added to cells with the Fill Color button in the Font group. Fill color can also be added to cells in a worksheet with options at the Format Cells dialog box with the Fill tab selected, as shown in Figure 3.10. Display the Format Cells dialog box by clicking the Format button in the Cells group and then clicking *Format Cells* at the drop-down list. The dialog box can also be displayed by clicking the Font group, Alignment group, or Number group dialog box launcher. At the Format Cells dialog box, click the Fill tab or right-click in a cell and then click *Format Cells* at the shortcut menu. Choose a fill color for a cell or selected cells by clicking a color choice in the *Background Color* section. To add gradient fill to a cell or selected cells, click the Fill Effects button and then click a style at the Fill Effects dialog box.

Repeating the Last Action

To apply the same formatting to other cells in a worksheet, use the Repeat command by pressing the F4 function key or the keyboard shortcut Ctrl + Y. The Repeat command repeats the last action performed.

Figure 3.10 Format Cells Dialog Box with the Fill Tab Selected

1. With **3-HBCJobs** open, add a fill color to cell A1 and repeat the formatting by completing the following steps:
   a. Make cell A1 active.
   b. Click the Format button in the Cells group and then click *Format Cells* at the drop-down list.
   c. At the Format Cells dialog box, click the Fill tab.
   d. Click the light gold color in the *Background Color* section (eighth column, second row).

   e. Click OK.
   f. Select the range A2:E2 and then press the F4 function key. (This repeats the application of the light gold fill.)
2. Select row 2, insert a new row, and then change the height of the new row to 12.00 points.
3. Add gradient fill to cells by completing the following steps:
   a. Select the range A2:E2.
   b. Click the Format button in the Cells group and then click *Format Cells* at the drop-down list.
   c. At the Format Cells dialog box, click the Fill tab, if necessary.
   d. Click the Fill Effects button.
   e. At the Fill Effects dialog box, click the *Color 2* option box arrow and then click the *Gold, Accent 4* option (eighth column, first row in the *Theme Colors* section).
   f. Click OK to close the Fill Effects dialog box.
   g. Click OK to close the Format Cells dialog box.
4. Save **3-HBCJobs**.

Check Your Work

Formatting with Format Painter

Use the Format Painter button in the Clipboard group on the Home tab to copy formatting to different locations in the worksheet. To use the Format Painter button, make active a cell or selected cells that contain the desired formatting, click the Format Painter button, and then click in the cell or selected cells to which the formatting is to be applied.

Format Painter

Click the Format Painter button and the mouse pointer displays with a paintbrush attached. To apply formatting in a single location, click the Format Painter button. To apply formatting in more than one location, double-click the Format Painter button, select the desired cells, and then click the Format Painter button to turn off the feature.

Activity 4e **Formatting with Format Painter** Part 5 of 6

1. With **3-HBCJobs** open, select the range A5:E5.
2. Click the Font group dialog box launcher.
3. At the Format Cells dialog box, click the Fill tab.
4. Click the light green color in the *Background Color* section (last column, second row).
5. Click OK to close the dialog box.
6. Use Format Painter to apply the light green color to rows by completing the following steps:
   a. With the range A5:E5 selected, double-click the Format Painter button in the Clipboard group.
   b. Select the range A7:E7.
   c. Select the range A9:E9.
   d. Select the range A11:E11.
   e. Turn off Format Painter by clicking the Format Painter button.
7. Save and then print **3-HBCJobs**.

> Check Your Work

> Tutorial

Hiding and Unhiding Columns and Rows

Hiding and Unhiding Columns and Rows

Quick Steps

Hide Columns
1. Select columns.
2. Click Format button.
3. Point to *Hide & Unhide.*
4. Click *Hide Columns.*

Hide Rows
1. Select rows.
2. Click Format button.
3. Point to *Hide & Unhide.*
4. Click *Hide Rows.*

Hint Set the column width to 0 and the column is hidden. Set the row height to 0 and the row is hidden.

If a worksheet contains columns and/or rows of data that is not being used or should not be viewed, consider hiding the columns and/or rows. To hide columns in a worksheet, select the columns, click the Format button in the Cells group on the Home tab, point to *Hide & Unhide*, and then click *Hide Columns*. To hide rows, select the rows, click the Format button in the Cells group, point to *Hide & Unhide*, and then click *Hide Rows*. To make a hidden column visible, select the columns to the left and the right of the hidden column, click the Format button in the Cells group, point to *Hide & Unhide*, and then click *Unhide Columns*. To make a hidden row visible, select the rows above and below the hidden row, click the Format button in the Cells group, point to *Hide & Unhide*, and then click *Unhide Rows*.

If the first row or column is hidden, use the Go To feature to make it visible. To do this, click the Find & Select button in the Editing group on the Home tab and then click *Go To* at the drop-down list. At the Go To dialog box, type *A1* in the *Reference* text box and then click OK. At the worksheet, click the Format button in the Cells group, point to *Hide & Unhide*, and then click *Unhide Columns* or click *Unhide Rows*.

The mouse can also be used to unhide columns or rows. If a column or row is hidden, the light-gray boundary line in the column or row header displays as a slightly thicker gray line. To unhide a column, position the mouse pointer on the

---

slightly thicker gray line in the column header until the mouse pointer changes into a left-and-right-pointing arrow with a double line in the middle. (Make sure the mouse pointer displays with two lines between the arrows. If a single line displays, only the size of the visible column will change.) Click and hold down the left mouse button, drag to the right until the column displays at the desired width, and then release the mouse button. Unhide a row in a similar manner. Position the mouse pointer on the slightly thicker gray line in the row header until the mouse pointer changes into an up-and-down-pointing arrow with a double line in the middle. Drag down until the row is visible and then release the mouse button. If two or more adjacent columns or rows are hidden, unhide each column or row separately.

Activity 4f Hiding and Unhiding Columns and Rows

1. With **3-HBCJobs** open, hide the row for Linstrom Enterprises and the row for Summit Services by completing the following steps:
   a. Click the row 7 header to select the entire row.
   b. Press and hold down the Ctrl key and then click the row 11 header to select the entire row.
   c. Click the Format button in the Cells group on the Home tab, point to the *Hide & Unhide* option, and then click the *Hide Rows* option at the side menu.

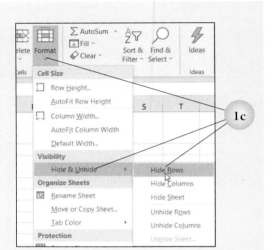

2. Hide the column containing the dollar amounts by completing the following steps:
   a. Click in cell D3 to make it the active cell.
   b. Click the Format button in the Cells group, point to the *Hide & Unhide* option, and then click the *Hide Columns* option at the side menu.

3. Save and then print **3-HBCJobs**.

4. Unhide the rows by completing the following steps:
   a. Select rows 6 through 12.
   b. Click the Format button in the Cells group, point to *Hide & Unhide*, and then click *Unhide Rows*.
   c. Click in cell A4.

5. Unhide column D by completing the following steps:
   a. Position the mouse pointer on the thicker gray line between columns C and E in the column header until the pointer turns into a left-and-right-pointing arrow with a double line in the middle.
   b. Click and hold down the left mouse button, drag to the right until *Width: 9.29* displays in a box above the mouse pointer, and then release the mouse button.

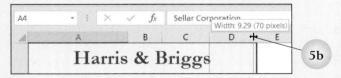

6. Save, print, and then close **3-HBCJobs**.

 Check Your Work

Chapter Summary

- Change column width using the mouse on column boundary lines or using options at the Column Width dialog box. Change row height using the mouse on row boundary lines or using options at the Row Height dialog box.

- Insert a row or column in a worksheet with the Insert button in the Cells group on the Home tab or with options at the Insert dialog box.

- Delete a selected row or column or multiple rows or columns by clicking the Delete button in the Cells group.

- Delete a specific cell by clicking the Delete button arrow and then clicking *Delete Cells* at the drop-down list. At the Delete dialog box, specify if only the cell should be deleted or an entire row or column.

- Delete the cell contents by pressing the Delete key or clicking the Clear button in the Editing group on the Home tab and then clicking *Clear Contents*.

- Apply font formatting with buttons and options in the Font group on the Home tab. Use the Mini toolbar to apply font formatting to selected data in a cell.

- Apply alignment formatting with buttons in the Alignment group on the Home tab.

- Use the Themes button in the Themes group on the Page Layout tab to apply a theme to cells in a worksheet, which includes formatting such as color, font, and effects. Use the other buttons in the Themes group to customize the theme.

- Format numbers in cells with buttons in the Number group on the Home tab or with options at the Format Cells dialog box with the Number tab selected.

- Apply formatting to cells in a worksheet with options at the Format Cells dialog box, which includes the Number, Alignment, Font, Border, and Fill tabs.

- Press the F4 function key or the keyboard shortcut Ctrl + Y to repeat the last action performed.

- Use the Format Painter button in the Clipboard group on the Home tab to apply formatting to several locations in a worksheet.

- Hide selected columns or rows in a worksheet by clicking the Format button in the Cells group on the Home tab, pointing to *Hide & Unhide*, and then clicking *Hide Columns* or *Hide Rows*.

- To make a hidden column visible, select the columns to the left and right, click the Format button in the Cells group, point to *Hide & Unhide*, and then click *Unhide Columns*.

- To make a hidden row visible, select the rows above and below, click the Format button in the Cells group, point to *Hide & Unhide*, and then click *Unhide Rows*.

Commands Review

FEATURE	RIBBON TAB, GROUP	BUTTON	KEYBOARD SHORTCUT
bold text	Home, Font	**B**	Ctrl + B
borders	Home, Font		
bottom-align (in row)	Home, Alignment		
center-align (in column)	Home, Alignment		

FEATURE	RIBBON TAB, GROUP	BUTTON	KEYBOARD SHORTCUT
clear cell or cell contents	Home, Editing		
column width	Home, Cells		
decrease font size	Home, Font		
decrease indent	Home, Alignment		
delete cells, rows, or columns	Home, Cells		
fill color	Home, Font		
font	Home, Font		
font color	Home, Font		
font size	Home, Font		
Format Painter	Home, Clipboard		
hide & unhide	Home, Cells		
increase font size	Home, Font		
increase indent	Home, Alignment		
insert cells, rows, or columns	Home, Cells		
italicize text	Home, Font		Ctrl + I
left-align (in column)	Home, Alignment		
merge and center cells	Home, Alignment		
middle-align (in row)	Home, Alignment		
number format	Home, Number		
orientation	Home, Alignment		
repeat last action			F4 or Ctrl + Y
right-align (in column)	Home, Alignment		
row height	Home, Cells		
themes	Page Layout, Themes		
top-align (in row)	Home, Alignment		
underline text	Home, Font		Ctrl + U
wrap text	Home, Alignment		

Microsoft® Excel®

Enhancing a Worksheet

Performance Objectives

Upon successful completion of Chapter 4, you will be able to:

1　Change the margins in a worksheet

2　Center a worksheet horizontally and vertically on the page

3　Change page orientation and paper size

4　Insert and remove page breaks in a worksheet

5　Print column and row titles on multiple pages

6　Scale data

7　Insert a background picture

8　Print gridlines and row and column headings

9　Set and clear a print area

10　Insert headers and footers

11　Customize a print job

12　Complete a spelling check

13　Use the Undo and Redo buttons

14　Find and replace data and cell formatting

15　Sort data

16　Filter data

Excel contains features you can use to enhance and control the formatting of a worksheet. In this chapter, you will learn how to change worksheet margins, orientation, size, and scale; print column and row titles; print gridlines; and center a worksheet horizontally and vertically on the page. You will also learn how to complete a spelling check on the text in a worksheet, find and replace specific data and formatting in a worksheet, and sort and filter data.

 Data Files

Before beginning chapter work, copy the EL1C4 folder to your storage medium and then make EL1C4 the active folder.

The online course includes additional training and assessment resources.

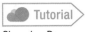

Tutorial

Changing Page
Layout Options

Formatting a Worksheet Page

An Excel worksheet has default page formatting. For example, a worksheet has left and right margins of 0.7 inch and top and bottom margins of 0.75 inch. In addition, a worksheet prints in portrait orientation and its paper size is 8.5 inches by 11 inches. These defaults, along with additional settings, can be changed and/or controlled with options on the Page Layout tab.

Changing Margins

The Page Setup group on the Page Layout tab contains buttons for changing the margins and the page orientation and size. In addition, it contains buttons for establishing a print area, inserting a page break, applying a picture background, and printing titles.

Margins

Change the worksheet margins by clicking the Margins button in the Page Setup group on the Page Layout tab. This displays a drop-down list of predesigned margin choices. If one of the predesigned choices applies the desired margins, click that option. To customize the margins, click the *Custom Margins* option at the bottom of the Margins button drop-down list. This displays the Page Setup dialog box with the Margins tab selected, as shown in Figure 4.1.

Ǫuick Steps

Change Worksheet Margins
1. Click Page Layout tab.
2. Click Margins button.
3. Click predesigned margin.
OR
1. Click Page Layout tab.
2. Click Margins button.
3. Click *Custom Margins* at drop-down list.
4. Change top, left, right, and/or bottom measurements.
5. Click OK.

Figure 4.1 Page Setup Dialog Box with the Margins Tab Selected

A worksheet page showing the cells and margins displays in the dialog box. As the top, bottom, left, or right margin measurements are increased or decreased, the sample worksheet page reflects the change. The measurement from the top of the page to the header can be increased or decreased with the *Header* measurement box and the measurement from the footer to the bottom of the page can be changed with the *Footer* measurement box. (Headers and footers are covered later in this chapter.)

Ǫuick Steps

Center Worksheet Horizontally and/or Vertically

1. Click Page Layout tab.
2. Click Margins button.
3. Click *Custom Margins*.
4. Click *Horizontally* option and/or click *Vertically* check box.
5. Click OK.

Centering a Worksheet Horizontally and/or Vertically

By default, a worksheet prints in the upper left corner of the page. A worksheet can be centered on the page by changing the margins. However, an easier method for centering a worksheet is to use the *Horizontally* and/or *Vertically* check boxes that appear in the Page Setup dialog box with the Margins tab selected. Choose one or both of these check boxes and the worksheet page in the preview section displays how the worksheet will print on the page.

Activity 1a **Changing Margins and Horizontally and Vertically Centering a Worksheet**

Part 1 of 12

1. Open **RPBudget** and then save it with the name **4-RPBudget**.
2. Insert the following formulas in the worksheet:
   a. Insert a SUM function in cell N5 that sums the range B5:M5. Copy the formula to the range N6:N10.
   b. Insert a SUM function in cell B11 that sums the range B5:B10. Copy the formula to the range C11:N11.
   c. Insert a SUM function in cell N14 that sums the range B14:M14. Copy the formula to the range N15:N19.
   d. Insert a SUM function in cell B20 that sums the range B14:B19. Copy the formula to the range C20:N20.
   e. Insert a formula in cell B21 that subtracts the total expenses from the income. (Make cell B21 active and then type the formula =b11-b20. Copy this formula to the range C21:N21.
   f. Apply the Accounting format with no digits after the decimal point to cell N5 and cell N14.
3. Click the Page Layout tab.
4. Click the Margins button in the Page Setup group and then click *Custom Margins* at the drop-down list.

5. At the Page Setup dialog box with the Margins tab selected, click the *Top* measurement box up arrow until *3.5* displays.
6. Click the *Bottom* measurement box up arrow until *1.5* displays.
7. Preview the worksheet by clicking the Print Preview button at the bottom of the Page Setup dialog box. The worksheet appears to be a little low on the page so you decide to horizontally and vertically center it by completing the following steps:
   a. Click the Page Setup hyperlink below the galleries in the *Settings* category in the Print backstage area.
   b. Click the Margins tab at the Page Setup dialog box.
   c. In the *Top* and *Bottom* measurement boxes, change the measurements to *1*.
   d. Click the *Horizontally* check box to insert a check mark.
   e. Click the *Vertically* check box to insert a check mark.
   f. Click OK to close the dialog box.
   g. Look at the preview of the worksheet (notice the entire worksheet is not visible) and then click the Back button to return to the worksheet.
8. Save **4-RPBudget**.

Changing Page Orientation

 Orientation

Click the Orientation button in the Page Setup group and a drop-down list displays with two choices: *Portrait* and *Landscape*. The two choices are represented by sample pages. A sample page that is taller than it is wide shows how the default orientation (*Portrait*) prints data on the page. The other choice, *Landscape*, rotates the data and prints it on a page that is wider than it is tall.

Changing the Paper Size

By default, an Excel worksheet paper size is 8.5 inches by 11 inches. Change this default size by clicking the Size button in the Page Setup group. At the drop-down list that appears, notice that the default setting is *Letter* and that the measurement *8.5" × 11"* displays below *Letter*. This drop-down list also contains a number of paper sizes, such as *Executive* and *Legal*, and a number of envelope sizes.

 Size

1. With **4-RPBudget** open, click the Orientation button in the Page Setup group on the Page Layout tab and then click *Landscape* at the drop-down list.

2. Click the Size button in the Page Setup group and then click *Legal* at the drop-down list.

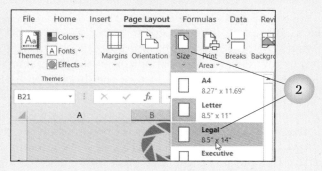

3. Preview the worksheet by clicking the File tab and then clicking the *Print* option. After viewing the worksheet in the Print backstage area, press the Esc key to return to the worksheet.
4. Save **4-RPBudget**.

Check Your Work

Tutorial

Using Page Break Preview

Inserting and Removing Page Breaks

The default left and right margins of 0.7 inch allow approximately 7 inches of cells across the page (8.5 inches minus 1.4 inches equals 7.1 inches). If a worksheet contains more than 7 inches of cells across the page, a vertical page break is inserted and the remaining columns are moved to the next page. A page break displays as a dashed line along cell borders. Figure 4.2 shows the page break in **4-RPBudget** when the paper size is set to *Letter*.

Quick Steps

Insert Page Break
1. Select column or row.
2. Click Page Layout tab.
3. Click Breaks button.
4. Click *Insert Page Break*.

A page break also displays horizontally in a worksheet. By default, a worksheet can contain approximately 9.5 inches of cells down the page. This is because the paper size is set by default at 11 inches. With the default top and bottom margins of 0.75 inch, this allows 9.5 inches of cells to print vertically on one page.

Figure 4.2 Page Break

	A	B	C	D	E	F	G	H	I	J	K	L	M	N
1						**Real Photography**								
2						Yearly Budget								
3		January	February	March	April	May	June	July	August	September	October	November	December	Total
4	**Income**													
5	Sublet Rent	$ 1,100	$ 1,100	$ 1,100	$ 1,100	$ 1,100	$ 1,100	$ 1,100	$ 1,100	$ 1,100	$ 1,100	$ 1,100	$ 1,100	$ 13,200
6	Archway Systems Contract	235	235	235	235	235	235	235	235	235	235	235	235	2,820
7	Lowell-Briggs Contract	750	750	525	525	-	-	450	450	450	575	575	575	5,625
8	Wedding Portraits	4,500	2,000	1,500	2,800	4,000	8,250	7,500	6,850	4,500	3,500	3,500	7,000	55,900
9	Senior Portraits	2,250	1,500	4,500	5,000	3,250	1,000	300	500	650	650	400	400	20,400
10	Catalog Pictures	-	-	-	-	500	500	500	500	500	-	-	-	2,500
11	*Total Income*	$ 8,835	$ 5,585	$ 7,860	$ 9,660	$ 9,085	$ 11,085	$ 10,085	$ 9,635	$ 7,435	$ 6,060	$ 5,810	$ 9,310	$ 100,445
12														
13	**Expenses**													
14	Mortgage	$ 4,230	$ 4,230	$ 4,230	$ 4,230	$ 4,230	$ 4,230	$ 4,230	$ 4,230	$ 4,230	$ 4,230	$ 4,230	$ 4,230	$ 50,760
15	Utilities	625	550	600	425	400	500	650	700	700	500	550	650	6,850
16	Insurance	375	375	375	375	375	375	375	375	375	375	375	375	4,500
17	Equipment Purchases	525	1,250	950	3,500	-	-	-	-	-	-	-	-	6,225
18	Supplies	750	750	1,500	1,250	1,500	2,500	2,250	1,750	950	850	850	2,000	16,900

page break

Breaks

Excel automatically inserts page breaks in a worksheet. To have more control over what cells print on a page, insert a page break. To insert a page break, select a column or row, click the Breaks button in the Page Setup group on the Page Layout tab, and then click *Insert Page Break* at the drop-down list. A page break is inserted immediately left of the selected column or immediately above the selected row.

To insert both horizontal and vertical page breaks at the same time, make a cell active, click the Breaks button in the Page Setup group, and then click *Insert Page Break*. This causes a horizontal page break to be inserted immediately above the active cell and a vertical page break to be inserted at the left of the active cell. To remove a page break, select the column or row or make the cell active, click the Breaks button in the Page Setup group, and then click *Remove Page Break* at the drop-down list.

A page break that is automatically inserted by Excel may not be visible in a worksheet. One way to display the page break is to display the worksheet in the Print backstage area. Return to the worksheet and the page break will display in the worksheet.

Page Break Preview

Hint You can edit a worksheet in Page Break Preview.

Excel provides a page break view that displays worksheet pages and page breaks. To display this view, click the Page Break Preview button in the view area at the right side of the Status bar or click the View tab and then click the Page Break Preview button in the Workbook Views group. This causes the worksheet to display similarly to the worksheet shown in Figure 4.3. The word *Page* along with the page number appears in gray behind the cells in the worksheet. A dashed blue line indicates a page break inserted automatically by Excel and a solid blue line indicates a page break inserted manually.

Normal

Move a page break by positioning the mouse pointer on the blue line, clicking and holding down the left mouse button, dragging the line to the desired location, and then releasing the mouse button. To return to Normal view, click the Normal button in the view area on the Status bar or click the View tab and then click the Normal button in the Workbook Views group.

Figure 4.3 Worksheet in Page Break Preview

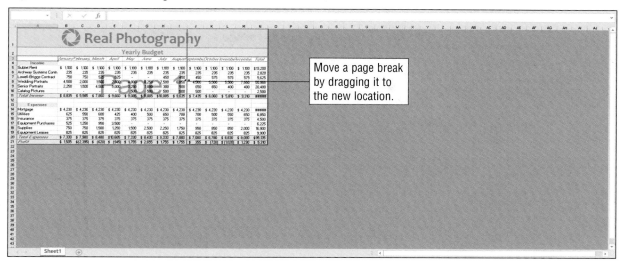

Move a page break by dragging it to the new location.

Activity 1c Inserting a Page Break in a Worksheet

1. With **4-RPBudget** open, click the Size button in the Page Setup group on the Page Layout tab and then click *Letter* at the drop-down list.
2. Click the Margins button and then click *Custom Margins* at the drop-down list.
3. At the Page Setup dialog box with the Margins tab selected, click in the *Horizontally* check box to remove the check mark, click in the *Vertically* check box to remove the check mark, and then click OK to close the dialog box.
4. Insert a page break between columns I and J by completing the following steps:
   a. Select column J.
   b. Click the Breaks button in the Page Setup group and then click *Insert Page Break* at the drop-down list. Click in any cell in column I.
5. View the worksheet in Page Break Preview by completing the following steps:
   a. Click the Page Break Preview button in the view area at the right side of the Status bar.
   b. View the pages and page breaks in the worksheet.
   c. You decide to include the first six months of the year on one page. To do this, position the mouse pointer on the vertical blue line until the mouse pointer displays as a left-and-right-pointing arrow, click and hold down the left mouse button, drag the line left so it is between columns G and H, and then release the mouse button.

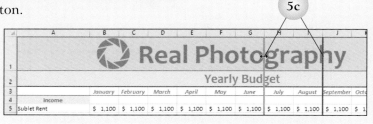

d. Click the Normal button in the view area on the Status bar.

6. Save **4-RPBudget**.

 Check Your Work

 Tutorial

Printing Column
Headers on
Multiple Pages

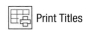 Print Titles

Quick Steps

**Print Column and
Row Titles**
1. Click Page Layout
   tab.
2. Click Print Titles
   button.
3. Type row range in
   *Rows to repeat at
   top* option.
4. Type column range
   in *Columns to repeat
   at left* option.
5. Click OK.

Printing Column and Row Titles on Multiple Pages

The columns and rows in a worksheet usually have titles. For example, in 4-RPBudget, the column titles include *Income, Expenses, January, February, March*, and so on. The row titles include the income and expenses categories. If a worksheet prints on more than one page, having column and/or row titles print on each page provides context for understanding the text and values in columns and rows. To do this, click the Print Titles button in the Page Setup group on the Page Layout tab. This displays the Page Setup dialog box with the Sheet tab selected, as shown in Figure 4.4.

At the Page Setup dialog box with the Sheet tab selected, specify the range of row cells to print on every page in the *Rows to repeat at top* text box. Type a cell range using a colon. For example, to print the range A1:J1 on every page, type *a1:j1* in the *Rows to repeat at top* text box. Type the range of column cells to print on every page in the *Columns to repeat at left* text box. To make rows and columns easy to identify on the printed page, specify that row and/or column headings print on each page.

Figure 4.4 Page Setup Dialog Box with the Sheet Tab Selected

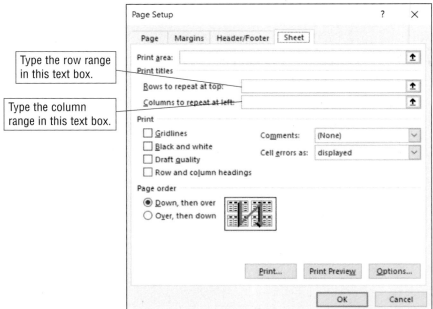

1. With **4-RPBudget** open, click the Page Layout tab and then click the Print Titles button in the Page Setup group.
2. At the Page Setup dialog box with the Sheet tab selected, click in the *Columns to repeat at left* text box.
3. Type a1:a21.
4. Click OK to close the dialog box.
5. Save and then print **4-RPBudget**.

 Check Your Work

 Tutorial

Changing Print Scaling

 Width

Scaling Data

Use buttons in the Scale to Fit group on the Page Layout tab to adjust the printed output by a percentage to fit the number of pages specified. For example, if a worksheet contains too many columns to print on one page, click the *Width* option box arrow in the Scale to Fit group on the Page Layout tab and then click *1 page*. This reduces the size of the data so all the columns appear and print on one page. Manually adjust the scale of a worksheet by clicking the up or down arrows in the *Scale* measurement box or by typing a percentage in the *Scale* measurement box and then pressing the Enter key.

1. With **4-RPBudget** open, display the Page Setup dialog box with the Sheet tab selected.
2. Select and then delete the text in the *Columns to repeat at left* text box and then click the OK button.
3. Click the *Width* option box arrow in the Scale to Fit group on the Page Layout tab and then click the *1 page* option at the drop-down list.
4. Display the Print backstage area, notice that all the cells that contain data appear on one page in the worksheet, and then return to the worksheet.

5. Change the margins by completing the following steps:
   a. Click the Margins button in the Page Setup group and then click *Custom Margins* at the drop-down list.
   b. At the Page Setup dialog box with the Margins tab selected, select the current number in the *Top* measurement box and then type 3.5.
   c. Select the current number in the *Left* measurement box and then type 0.3.
   d. Select the current number in the *Right* measurement box and then type 0.3.
   e. Click OK to close the Page Setup dialog box.
6. Specify that you want row titles to print on each page by completing the following steps:
   a. Click the Print Titles button in the Page Setup group on the Page Layout tab.
   b. Click in the *Rows to repeat at top* text box and then type a3:n3.
   c. Click OK to close the dialog box.

7. Save and then print **4-RPBudget**. (The worksheet prints on two pages and the row titles are repeated on the second page.)
8. At the worksheet, return to the default margins by clicking the Page Layout tab, clicking the Margins button, and then clicking the *Normal* option at the drop-down list.
9. Prevent titles from printing on the second and subsequent pages by completing the following steps:
   a. Click the Print Titles button in the Page Setup group.
   b. At the Page Setup dialog box with the Sheet tab selected, select and then delete the text in the *Rows to repeat at top* text box.
   c. Click OK to close the dialog box.
10. Change the scaling back to the default by completing the following steps:
    a. Click the *Width* option box arrow in the Scale to Fit group and then click *Automatic* at the drop-down list.
    b. Click the *Scale* measurement box up arrow until *100%* displays in the box.
11. Save **4-RPBudget**.

Check Your Work

Inserting a Background Picture

Insert a picture as a background for a worksheet with the Background button in the Page Setup group on the Page Layout tab. The picture displays only on the screen and does not print. To insert a picture, click the Background button in the Page Setup group and then click the *From a file* option at the Insert Pictures window. At the Sheet Background dialog box, navigate to the folder containing the picture and then double-click the picture. To remove the picture from the worksheet, click the Delete Background button.

Activity 1f **Inserting a Background Picture**   Part 6 of 12

1. With **4-RPBudget** open, insert a background picture by completing the following steps:
   a. Click the Background button in the Page Setup group on the Page Layout tab.
   b. At the Insert Pictures window, click the *From a file* option.
   c. At the Sheet Background dialog box, navigate to your EL1C4 folder and then double-click **Ship**.
   d. Scroll down the worksheet until the ship is visible.
2. Display the Print backstage area, notice that the picture does not appear in the preview worksheet, and then return to the worksheet.
3. Remove the picture by clicking the Delete Background button in the Page Setup group on the Page Layout tab.
4. Save **4-RPBudget**.

Printing Gridlines and Row and Column Headings

By default, the gridlines that create the cells in a worksheet and the row numbers and column letters that label the cells do not print. The Sheet Options group on the Page Layout tab contains check boxes for gridlines and headings. The *View* check boxes for gridlines and headings contain check marks. At these settings, gridlines and row and column headings show on the screen but do not print. To print gridlines and headings, insert check marks in the *Print* check boxes. Complex worksheets may be easier to read with the gridlines printed.

The display and printing of gridlines and headings can also be controlled with options at the Page Setup dialog box with the Sheet tab selected. Display this dialog box by clicking the Sheet Options group dialog box launcher. To print gridlines and headings, insert check marks in the check boxes in the *Print* section of the dialog box. The *Print* section contains two additional options: *Black and white* and *Draft quality*. When printing with a color printer, insert a check mark in the *Black and white* check box to print the worksheet in black and white. Insert a check mark in the *Draft quality* option to print a draft of the worksheet. With this option checked, some types of formatting, such as shading and fill, do not print.

Quick Steps

**Print Gridlines
and/or Row and
Column Headings**
1. Click Page Layout tab.
2. Click *Print* check
   boxes in *Gridlines* and/
   or *Headings* section in
   Sheet Options group.
OR
1. Click Page Layout tab.
2. Click Sheet Options
   dialog box launcher.
3. Click *Gridlines* and/
   or *Row and column
   headings* check boxes.
4. Click OK.

Activity 1g Printing Gridlines and Row and Column Headings   Part 7 of 12

1. With **4-RPBudget** open, click in the *Print* check box below *Gridlines* in the Sheet Options group on the Page Layout tab to insert a check mark.
2. Click in the *Print* check box below *Headings* in the Sheet Options group to insert a check mark.
3. Click the Margins button in the Page Setup group and then click *Custom Margins* at the drop-down list.
4. At the Page Setup dialog box with the Margins tab selected, click in the *Horizontally* check box to insert a check mark.
5. Click in the *Vertically* check box to insert a check mark.
6. Click OK to close the dialog box.
7. Save and then print **4-RPBudget**.
8. Click in the *Print* check box below *Headings* in the Sheet Options group to remove the check mark.
9. Click in the *Print* check box below *Gridlines* in the Sheet Options group to remove the check mark.
10. Save **4-RPBudget**.

Printing a Specific Area of a Worksheet

Use the Print Area button in the Page Setup group on the Page Layout tab to select and print specific areas of a worksheet. To do this, select the cells to print, click the Print Area button in the Page Setup group, and then click *Set Print Area* at the drop-down list. This inserts a border around the selected cells. Display the Print backstage area and click the Print button to print the cells within the border.

More than one print area can be specified in a worksheet. To do this, select the first group of cells, click the Print Area button in the Page Setup group, and then click *Set Print Area*. Select the next group of cells, click the Print Area button, and then click *Add to Print Area*. Clear a print area by clicking the Print Area button in the Page Setup group and then clicking *Clear Print Area* at the drop-down list.

Each area specified as a print area prints on a separate page. To print nonadjacent print areas on the same page, consider hiding columns and/or rows in the worksheet to bring the areas together.

Activity 1h Printing Specific Areas

1. With **4-RPBudget** open, print the first half of the year's income and expenses by completing the following steps:
   a. Select the range A3:G21.
   b. Click the Print Area button in the Page Setup group on the Page Layout tab and then click *Set Print Area* at the drop-down list.
   c. With the border surrounding the range A3:G21, click the File tab, click the *Print* option, and then click the Print button at the Print backstage area.
   d. Clear the print area by clicking the Print Area button in the Page Setup group and then clicking *Clear Print Area* at the drop-down list.

2. Suppose you want to print the income and expenses information as well as the totals for April. To do this, hide columns and select a print area by completing the following steps:
   a. Select columns B through D.
   b. Click the Home tab.
   c. Click the Format button in the Cells group, point to *Hide & Unhide*, and then click *Hide Columns*.
   d. Click the Page Layout tab.
   e. Select the range A3:E21. (Columns A and E are now adjacent.)
   f. Click the Print Area button in the Page Setup group and then click *Set Print Area* at the drop-down list.
3. Click the File tab, click the *Print* option, and then click the Print button.
4. Clear the print area by ensuring that the range A3:E21 is selected, clicking the Print Area button in the Page Setup group, and then clicking *Clear Print Area* at the drop-down list.
5. Unhide the columns by completing the following steps:
   a. Click the Home tab.
   b. Select columns A and E. (These columns are adjacent.)
   c. Click the Format button in the Cells group, point to *Hide & Unhide*, and then click *Unhide Columns*.
   d. Deselect the text by clicking in any cell containing data in the worksheet.
6. Save **4-RPBudget**.

Check Your Work

Inserting Headers and Footers

Text that prints at the top of each worksheet page is called a *header* and text that prints at the bottom of each worksheet page is called a *footer*. Create a header and/or footer with the Header & Footer button in the Text group on the Insert tab in Page Layout view or with options at the Page Setup dialog box with the Header/Footer tab selected.

 Header &
Footer

To create a header with the Header & Footer button, click the Insert tab, click the Text button and then click the Header & Footer button. This displays the worksheet in Page Layout view and displays the Header & Footer Tools Design tab. Use buttons on this tab, shown in Figure 4.5, to insert predesigned headers and/or footers or to insert header and footer elements such as page numbers, date, time, path name, and file name. A different header or footer can be created on the first page of the worksheet or one header or footer can be created for even pages and another for odd pages.

Quick Steps

Insert Header or Footer
1. Click Insert tab.
2. Click the Text button.
3. Click Header & Footer button.
4. Click Header button and then click predesigned header or click Footer button and then click predesigned footer.
OR
1. Click Insert tab.
2. Click the Text button.
3. Click Header & Footer button.
4. Click header or footer elements.

At the Print backstage area, preview headers and footers before printing. Click the File tab and then click the *Print* option to display the Print backstage area. A preview of the worksheet is shown at the right side of the backstage area. If the worksheet will print on more than one page, view the different pages by clicking the Next Page button or the Previous Page button. These buttons are below and to the left of the preview worksheet at the Print backstage area. Two buttons display in the bottom right corner of the Print backstage area. Click the Zoom to Page button to zoom in or out of the preview of the worksheet. Click the Show Margins button to display margin guidelines and handles on the preview page. The handles, which appear as black squares, can be used to increase or decrease the page margins and column widths. To do this, position the mouse pointer on the desired handle, click and hold down the left mouse button, drag to the new position, and then release the mouse button.

Figure 4.5 Header & Footer Tools Design Tab

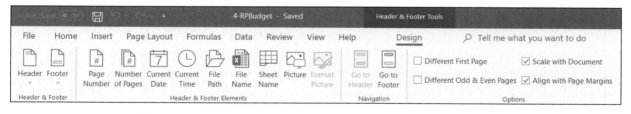

Activity 1i Inserting a Header in a Worksheet

1. With **4-RPBudget** open, create a header by completing the following steps:
   a. Click the Insert tab.
   b. Click the Text button and then click the Header & Footer button.

c. Click the Header button at the left side of the Header & Footer Tools Design tab and then click *Page 1, 4-RPBudget* at the drop-down list. (This inserts the page number in the middle header box and the workbook name in the right header box.)

2. Preview the worksheet by completing the following steps:
   a. Click the File tab and then click the *Print* option.
   b. At the Print backstage area, look at the preview worksheet at the right side of the backstage area.
   c. View the next page of the worksheet by clicking the Next Page button below and to the left of the preview worksheet.
   d. View the first page by clicking the Previous Page button left of the Next Page button.
   e. Click the Zoom to Page button in the lower right corner of the backstage area. (Notice that the preview page has zoomed in on the worksheet.)
   f. Click the Zoom to Page button again.
   g. Click the Show Margins button in the lower right corner of the backstage area. (Notice the guidelines and handles that display on the preview page.)
   h. Click the Show Margins button to remove the guidelines and handles.
   i. Click the Back button to return to the worksheet.
3. Save **4-RPBudget**.

Check Your Work

A header and/or footer can also be inserted by working in Page Layout view. In Page Layout view, the text *Add header* appears at the top of the worksheet page. Click this text and the insertion point is positioned in the middle header box. Type the header in this box or click in the left box or right box and then type the header. Create a footer in a similar manner. Scroll down the worksheet until the bottom of the page is visible and then click the text *Add footer*. Type the footer in the center footer box or click the left box or right box and then type the footer.

1. With **4-RPBudget** open, make sure the workbook displays in Page Layout view.
2. Scroll down the worksheet until the text *Add footer* is visible and then click the text.

3. Type your first and last names.
4. Click in the left footer box, click the Header & Footer Tools Design tab, and then click the Current Date button in the Header & Footer Elements group. (This inserts a date code. The date will display when you click outside the footer box.)
5. Click in the right footer box and then click the Current Time button in the Header & Footer Elements group. (This inserts the time as a code. The time will display when you click outside the footer box.)
6. View the header and footer at the Print backstage area and then return to the worksheet.
7. Modify the header by completing the following steps:
   a. Scroll to the beginning of the worksheet and display the header text.
   b. Click the page number in the middle header box. (This displays the Header & Footer Tools Design tab, changes the header to a field, and selects the field.)
   c. Press the Delete key to delete the header.
   d. Click the header text in the right header box and then press the Delete key.
   e. With the insertion point positioned in the right header box, insert the page number by clicking the Header & Footer Tools Design tab and then clicking the Page Number button in the Header & Footer Elements group.
   f. Click in the left header box and then click the File Name button in the Header & Footer Elements group.

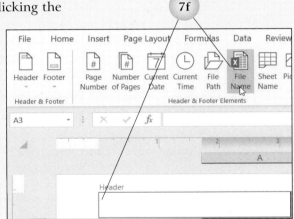

8. Click in any cell in the worksheet that contains data.
9. View the header and footer at the Print backstage area and then return to the worksheet.
10. Save **4-RPBudget**.

Check Your Work

Headers and footers can also be inserted and customized using options at the Page Setup dialog box with the Header/Footer tab selected, as shown in Figure 4.6. Display this dialog box by clicking the Page Layout tab and then clicking the Page Setup group dialog box launcher. At the Page Setup dialog box, click the Header/Footer tab. If a worksheet contains headers or footers, they will appear in the dialog box. Use the check box options in the lower left corner of the dialog box to insert different odd and even page headers and/or footers or to insert a different

Figure 4.6 Page Setup Dialog Box with the Header/Footer Tab Selected

Click this button to display the Header dialog box with options for creating the header.

Insert a check mark in this check box to create different headers and/or footers for odd pages and even pages.

Click this button to display the Footer dialog box with options for creating the footer.

Insert a check mark in this check box to create different headers and/or footers on the first page.

first page header and/or footer. The bottom two check box options are active by default. These defaults scale the header and footer text with the worksheet text and align the header and footer with the page margins.

To create different odd and even page headers, click the *Different odd and even pages* check box to insert a check mark and then click the Custom Header button. This displays the Header dialog box with the Odd Page Header tab selected. Type or insert the odd page header data in the *Left section*, *Center section*, or *Right section* text box and then click the Even Page Header tab. Type or insert the even page header data in the desired section text box and then click OK. Use the buttons above the section boxes to format the header text and insert information such as the page number, current date, current time, file name, worksheet name, and so on. Complete similar steps to create different odd and even page footers and a different first page header or footer.

Activity 1k **Creating Different Odd and Even Page Headers and Footers and a Different First Page Header and Footer**

Part 11 of 12

1. With **4-RPBudget** open, remove the page break by clicking the Page Layout tab, clicking the Breaks button in the Page Setup group, and then clicking *Reset All Page Breaks* at the drop-down list.
2. Change the margins by completing the following steps:
   a. Click the Margins button in the Page Setup group on the Page Layout tab and then click *Custom Margins* at the drop-down list.
   b. At the Page Setup dialog box with the Margins tab selected, select the current number in the *Left* measurement box and then type 3.
   c. Select the current number in the *Right* measurement box and then type 3.
   d. Click OK to close the dialog box.

3. Click the Page Setup group dialog box launcher on the Page Layout tab.
4. At the Page Setup dialog box, click the Header/Footer tab.
5. At the Page Setup dialog box with the Header/Footer tab selected, click the *Different odd and even pages* check box to insert a check mark and then click the Custom Header button.
6. At the Header dialog box with the Odd Page Header tab selected, click the Format Text button (above the *Left section* text box).
7. At the Font dialog box, click *12* in the *Size* list box and then click OK.
8. At the Header dialog box with the file name code (&[File]) highlighted in the *Left section* text box, type Yearly Budget.

9. Click the Even Page Header tab, click in the *Left section* text box, and then click the Insert Page Number button.
10. Click in the *Right section* text box and then type Yearly Budget.
11. Select the text *Yearly Budget*, click the Format Text button, click *12* in the *Size* list box, and then click OK.
12. Click OK to close the Header dialog box.

13. Click the Custom Footer button. At the Footer dialog box with the Odd Page Footer tab selected, delete the data in the *Left section* text box and then select and delete the data in the *Right section* text box. (The footer should contain only your name.)
14. Select your name, click the Format Text button, click *12* in the *Size* list box, and then click OK.
15. Click the Even Page Footer tab, type your name in the *Center section* text box, select your name, and then change the font size to 12 points.
16. Click OK to close the Footer dialog box and then click OK to close the Page Setup dialog box. (View the header and footer in the Print backstage area and then return to the worksheet.)
17. Click the Page Setup group dialog box launcher on the Page Layout tab.
18. At the Page Setup dialog box, click the Header/Footer tab.
19. Click the *Different odd and even pages* check box to remove the check mark.
20. Click the *Different first page* check box to insert a check mark and then click the Custom Header button.

21. At the Header dialog box with the Header tab selected, click the First Page Header tab.
22. Click in the *Right section* text box and then click the Insert Page Number button.
23. Click OK to close the Header dialog box and then click OK to close the Page Setup dialog box.
24. View the header and footer in the Print backstage area and then return to the worksheet.
25. Save **4-RPBudget**.

Check Your Work

Customizing Print Jobs

Use options in the *Settings* category at the Print backstage area to specify what to print. By default, the active worksheet prints. Change this by clicking the first gallery in the *Settings* category. At the drop-down list, specify if the entire workbook is to print (which is useful when a workbook contains multiple worksheets) or only selected cells. With the other galleries in the *Settings* category, specify if pages are to print on one side or both sides of the paper (this depends on the printer) and if they are to be collated. With other options, specify the worksheet orientation, size, and margins and whether the worksheet is to be scaled to fit all the columns or rows on one page.

With the *Pages* text boxes in the *Settings* category, specify the pages of the worksheet to be printed. For example, to print pages 2 and 3 of the active worksheet, type *2* in the *Pages* measurement box in the *Settings* category and then type *3* in the *to* measurement box. Or click the up- and down-pointing arrows to select page numbers.

Activity 1I **Printing Specific Pages of a Worksheet**   Part 12 of 12

1. With **4-RPBudget** open, print the first two pages of the worksheet by completing the following steps:
   a. Click the File tab and then click the *Print* option.
   b. At the Print backstage area, click in the *Pages* measurement box below the first gallery in the *Settings* category and then type 1.
   c. Click in the *to* measurement box in the *Settings* category and then type 2.
   d. Click the Print button.

2. Print selected cells by completing the following steps:
   a. Display the worksheet in Normal view.
   b. Select the range A3:D11.
   c. Click the File tab and then click the *Print* option.
   d. At the Print backstage area, select and then delete the number in the *Pages* measurement box and the number in the *to* measurement box. (These are the numbers you inserted in Steps 1b and 1c.)
   e. Click the first gallery in the *Settings* category (displays with *Print Active Sheets*) and then click *Print Selection* at the drop-down list.
   f. Click the Print button.
3. Save and then close **4-RPBudget**.

Check Your Work

Activity 2 **Format a Sales and Commissions Worksheet**　　　**3 Parts**

You will format a sales commission worksheet by inserting a formula, completing a spelling check, and finding and replacing data and cell formatting.

Tutorial

Checking Spelling

 Spelling

Quick Steps

Checking Spelling
1. Click Review tab.
2. Click Spelling button.
3. Replace or ignore selected words.

Checking Spelling

Excel provides a spelling check feature that verifies the spelling of text in a worksheet. The spelling check uses an electronic dictionary to identify misspelled words and suggest alternatives. Before checking the spelling in a worksheet, make the first cell active. The spelling check reviews the worksheet from the active cell to the last cell in the worksheet that contains data.

To use the spelling check, click the Review tab and then click the Spelling button in the Proofing group. Figure 4.7 shows the Spelling dialog box. At this dialog box, tell Excel to ignore a word or to replace a misspelled word with a word from the *Suggestions* list box using one of the available buttons.

Tutorial

Using Undo and Redo

 Undo

 Redo

Using Undo and Redo

Excel includes an Undo button on the Quick Access Toolbar that reverses certain commands or deletes the last data typed in a cell. For example, apply formatting to cells in a worksheet and then click the Undo button on the Quick Access Toolbar and the formatting is removed. To reapply the formatting, click the Redo button on the Quick Access Toolbar.

Figure 4.7 Spelling Dialog Box

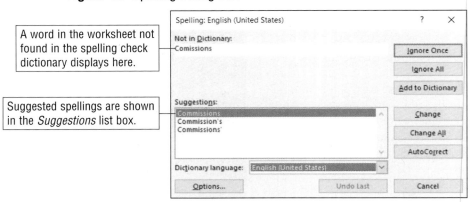

A word in the worksheet not found in the spelling check dictionary displays here.

Suggested spellings are shown in the *Suggestions* list box.

💡 **Hint** Ctrl + Z is the keyboard shortcut to undo a command and Ctrl + Y is the keyboard shortcut to redo a command.

Excel maintains actions in temporary memory. To undo an action, click the Undo button arrow and a drop-down list displays containing the actions performed on the worksheet. Click a specific action at the drop-down list and that action along with any preceding actions are undone. Click the Redo button and click a specific action at the drop-down list and that action along with any preceding actions are redone. Multiple actions must be undone or redone in sequence.

Activity 2a Spell Checking and Formatting a Worksheet

Part 1 of 3

1. Open **MRSales** and then save it with the name **4-MRSales**.
2. Complete a spelling check on the worksheet by completing the following steps:
   a. If necessary, make cell A1 active.
   b. Click the Review tab.
   c. Click the Spelling button in the Proofing group.
   d. Click the Change button as needed to correct misspelled words in the worksheet. (When the spelling check stops at the proper names *Pirozzi* and *Yonemoto*, click the Ignore All button.)
   e. At the message stating the spelling check is complete, click OK.

3. Insert a formula and then copy the formula without the formatting by completing the following steps:
   a. Make cell G4 active and then insert a formula that multiplies the sale price by the commission percentage.
   b. Copy the formula to the range G5:G26.
   c. Some of the cells contain shading that you do not want removed, so click the Auto Fill Options button at the bottom right of the selected cells and then click the *Fill Without Formatting* option at the drop-down list.

4. Make cell G27 active and then insert the sum of the range G4:G26.
5. Apply the Accounting format with no digits after the decimal point to cell G4 and cell G27.

6. Apply a theme by clicking the Page Layout tab, clicking the Themes button, and then clicking *Ion* at the drop-down gallery.

7. After looking at the worksheet with the Ion theme applied, you decide that you want to return to the original formatting. To do this, click the Undo button on the Quick Access Toolbar.

8. Save **4-MRSales**.

 Check Your Work

 Tutorial
Finding Data

 Tutorial
Replacing Data

 Tutorial
Replacing Formatting

Quick Steps

Find Data
1. Click Find & Select button.
2. Click *Find*.
3. Type data in *Find what* text box.
4. Click Find Next button.

 Find & Select

Finding and Replacing Data and Cell Formatting

Use Excel's find feature to look for specific data and either replace it with nothing or replace it with other data. This feature is particularly helpful for finding data quickly in a large worksheet. Excel also includes a find and replace feature. Use this feature to look for specific data in a worksheet and replace it with other data.

To find specific data in a worksheet, click the Find & Select button in the Editing group on the Home tab and then click *Find* at the drop-down list. This displays the Find and Replace dialog box with the Find tab selected, as shown in Figure 4.8. Type the find data in the *Find what* text box and then click the Find Next button. Continue clicking the Find Next button to move to the next occurrence of the data. If the Find and Replace dialog box blocks the view of the worksheet, use the mouse pointer on the title bar to drag the dialog box to a different location.

To find specific data in a worksheet and replace it with other data, click the Find & Select button in the Editing group on the Home tab and then click *Replace* at the drop-down list. This displays the Find and Replace dialog box with the

Figure 4.8 Find and Replace Dialog Box with the Find Tab Selected

Replace tab selected, as shown in Figure 4.9. Enter the find data in the *Find what* text box. Press the Tab key or click in the *Replace with* text box and then enter the replace data in the *Replace with* text box.

Click the Find Next button to find the next occurrence of the data. Click the Replace button to replace the data and find the next occurrence. To replace all the occurrences of the data in the *Find what* text box with the data in the *Replace with* text box, click the Replace All button. Click the Close button to close the Replace dialog box.

Display additional find and replace options by clicking the Options button. This expands the dialog box, as shown in Figure 4.10. By default, Excel will look for any data that contains the same characters as the data entered in the *Find what* text box without concern for the characters before or after the entered data. For example, in Activity 2b, you will look for sale prices of $450,000 and replace them with sale prices of $475,000. If you do not specify that you want to find only cells that contain *450000*, Excel will stop at any cell containing *450000*. For example, Excel will stop at a cell containing *$1,450,000* and a cell containing *$2,450,000*. To specify that the only data to be contained in the cell is what is entered in the *Find what* text box, click the Options button to expand the dialog box and then insert a check mark in the *Match entire cell contents* check box.

If the *Match case* option is active (contains a check mark), Excel will look for only that data that matches the case of the data entered in the *Find what* text box. Remove the check mark from this check box and Excel will find the data entered in the *Find what* text box in any case. By default, Excel will search in the current worksheet. If the workbook contains more than one worksheet, change the *Within* option to *Workbook*. By default, Excel searches by rows in a worksheet. This can be changed to by columns with the *Search* option.

Figure 4.9 Find and Replace Dialog Box with the Replace Tab Selected

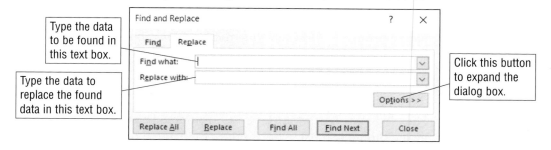

Figure 4.10 Expanded Find and Replace Dialog Box

1. With **4-MRSales** open, find all occurrences of *Land* in the worksheet and replace them with *Acreage* by completing the following steps:
   a. Click the Find & Select button in the Editing group on the Home tab and then click *Replace* at the drop-down list.
   b. At the Find and Replace dialog box with the Replace tab selected, type Land in the *Find what* text box.
   c. Press the Tab key. (This moves the insertion point to the *Replace with* text box.)
   d. Type Acreage.
   e. Click the Replace All button.
   f. At the message stating that four replacements were made, click OK.
   g. Click the Close button to close the Find and Replace dialog box.

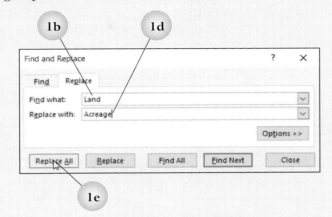

2. Find all occurrences of *$450,000* and replace them with *$475,000* by completing the following steps:
   a. Click the Find & Select button in the Editing group and then click *Replace* at the drop-down list.
   b. At the Find and Replace dialog box with the Replace tab selected, select any text in the *Find what* text box and then type 450000.
   c. Press the Tab key.
   d. Type 475000.
   e. Click the Options button to display additional options. (If additional options are already visible, skip this step.)
   f. Click the *Match entire cell contents* check box to insert a check mark.
   g. Click the Replace All button.
   h. At the message stating that two replacements were made, click OK.
   i. At the Find and Replace dialog box, click the *Match entire cell contents* check box to remove the check mark.
   j. Click the Close button to close the Find and Replace dialog box.

3. Save **4-MRSales**.

Check Your Work

Use the Format buttons at the expanded Find and Replace dialog box (see Figure 4.10 (on page 100)) to search for specific cell formatting and replace it with other formatting. Click the Format button arrow and a drop-down list displays. Click the *Format* option and the Find Format dialog box displays with the Number, Alignment, Font, Border, Fill, and Protection tabs. Specify formatting at this dialog box. Click the *Choose Format From Cell* option from the Format button drop-down list or click the Choose Format From Cell button in the Find Format dialog box and the mouse pointer displays with a pointer tool attached. Click in the cell containing the desired formatting and the formatting displays in the *Preview* box left of the Format button. Click the *Clear Find Format* option at the Find button drop-down list and any formatting in the *Preview* box is removed.

Activity 2c Finding and Replacing Cell Formatting

Part 3 of 3

1. With **4-MRSales** open, search for a light-turquoise fill color and replace it with a light-green fill color by completing the following steps:
   a. Click the Find & Select button in the Editing group on the Home tab and then click *Replace* at the drop-down list.
   b. At the Find and Replace dialog box with the Replace tab selected, make sure the dialog box is expanded. (If not, click the Options button.)
   c. Select and then delete any text in the *Find what* text box.
   d. Select and then delete any text in the *Replace with* text box.
   e. Make sure the boxes immediately before the two Format buttons display with the text *No Format Set*. (If not, click the Format button arrow and then click the *Clear Find Format* or *Clear Replace Format* option at the drop-down list. Do this for each Format button.)
   f. Click the top Format button.
   g. At the Find Format dialog box, click the Fill tab.
   h. Click the More Colors button.
   i. At the Colors dialog box with the Standard tab selected, click the light-turquoise color, as shown at the right.
   j. Click OK to close the Colors dialog box.
   k. Click OK to close the Find Format dialog box.
   l. Click the bottom Format button.
   m. At the Replace Format dialog box with the Fill tab selected, click the light-green color (last column, second row), as shown at the right.
   n. Click OK to close the dialog box.
   o. At the Find and Replace dialog box, click the Replace All button.
   p. At the message stating that 10 replacements were made, click OK.

2. Search for a light-gray fill color and replace it with a light-yellow fill color by completing the following steps:
   a. At the Find and Replace dialog box, click the top Format button.
   b. At the Find Format dialog box with the Fill tab selected, click the light-gray color (fourth column, second row), as shown at the right.
   c. Click OK to close the Find Format dialog box.
   d. Click the bottom Format button.
   e. At the Replace Format dialog box with the Fill tab selected, click the yellow color (eighth column, second row), as shown below and to the right.
   f. Click OK to close the dialog box.
   g. At the Find and Replace dialog box, click the Replace All button.
   h. At the message stating that 78 replacements were made, click OK.

3. Search for 11-point Calibri formatting and replace it with 10-point Arial formatting by completing the following steps:
   a. With the Find and Replace dialog box open, clear formatting from the top Format button by clicking the top Format button arrow and then clicking the *Clear Find Format* option at the drop-down list.
   b. Clear formatting from the bottom Format button by clicking the bottom Format button arrow and then clicking *Clear Replace Format.*
   c. Click the top Format button.
   d. At the Find Format dialog box, click the Font tab.
   e. Scroll down the *Font* list box and then click *Calibri.*
   f. Click *11* in the *Size* list box.
   g. Click OK to close the dialog box.
   h. Click the bottom Format button.
   i. At the Replace Format dialog box with the Font tab selected, scroll down the *Font* list box and then click *Arial.*
   j. Click *10* in the *Size* list box.
   k. Click OK to close the dialog box.
   l. At the Find and Replace dialog box, click the Replace All button.
   m. At the message stating that 174 replacements were made, click OK.
   n. At the Find and Replace dialog box, clear formatting from both Format buttons.
   o. Click the Close button to close the Find and Replace dialog box.
4. Save, print, and then close **4-MRSales**.

Check Your Work

Activity 3 Insert a Formula and Sort and Filter Data in a Billing Worksheet
4 Parts

You will insert a formula in a weekly billing worksheet and then sort and filter specific data in the worksheet.

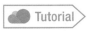

Tutorial

Sorting Data

Sorting Data

Excel is primarily a spreadsheet program but it also includes some basic database functions, such as sorting data in alphabetic or numeric order. To sort data in a worksheet, use the Sort & Filter button in the Editing group on the Home tab.

 Sort & Filter

To sort data in a worksheet, select the cells containing the data to be sorted, click the Sort & Filter button in the Editing group and then click the option representing the desired sort. The sort option names vary depending on the data in selected cells. For example, if the first column of selected cells contains text, the sort options at the drop-down list are *Sort A to Z* and *Sort Z to A*. If the selected cells contain dates, the sort options at the drop-down list are *Sort Oldest to Newest* and *Sort Newest to Oldest*. If the cells contain numbers or values, the sort options are *Sort Smallest to Largest* and *Sort Largest to Smallest*. If more than one column is selected in a worksheet, Excel sorts the data in the first selected column.

Quick Steps

Sort Data
1. Select cells.
2. Click Sort & Filter button.
3. Click sort option at drop-down list.

Activity 3a Sorting Data

Part 1 of 4

1. Open **APTBilling** and then save it with the name **4-APTBilling**.
2. Insert a formula in cell F4 that multiplies the rate by the hours. Copy the formula to the range F5:F29.
3. Sort the data in the first column in descending order by completing the following steps:
    a. Make cell A4 active.
    b. Click the Sort & Filter button in the Editing group on the Home tab.
    c. Click the *Sort Largest to Smallest* option at the drop-down list.
4. Sort in ascending order by clicking the Sort & Filter button and then clicking *Sort Smallest to Largest* at the drop-down list.
5. Save **4-APTBilling**.

 Check Your Work

Completing a Custom Sort

Quick Steps

Complete Custom Sort
1. Select cells.
2. Click Sort & Filter button.
3. Click *Custom Sort* at drop-down list.
4. Specify options at Sort dialog box.
5. Click OK.

To sort data in a column other than the first column, use options at the Sort dialog box. Select one column in a worksheet, click the Sort & Filter button, and then click the desired sort option; only the data in that column is sorted. If this data is related to data to the left or right that relationship is broken. For example, after sorting the range C4:C29 in 4-APTBilling, the client number, treatment, hours, and total no longer match the date.

Use options at the Sort dialog box to sort data and maintain the relationship among all the cells. To sort using the Sort dialog box, select the cells to be sorted, click the Sort & Filter button, and then click *Custom Sort*. This displays the Sort dialog box, shown in Figure 4.11.

Figure 4.11 Sort Dialog Box

Click this button to specify a second column for sorting.

Click this option box arrow and then specify if sorting on values, cell color, font color, or cell icon.

Click this option box arrow and then click the desired column at the drop-down list.

Click this option box arrow and then specify the sort order.

The data that displays in the *Sort by* option box will vary depending on what is selected. Generally, the data that displays is the title of the first column of selected cells. If the selected cells do not have a title, the data may display as *Column A*. Use this option to specify what column is to be sorted. Using the Sort dialog box to sort data in a column maintains the relationship among the data.

Activity 3b **Sorting Data Using the Sort Dialog Box**   Part 2 of 4

1. With **4-APTBilling** open, sort the rates in the range E4:E29 in descending order and maintain the relationship to the other data by completing the following steps:
   a. Select the range A3:F29.
   b. Click the Sort & Filter button and then click *Custom Sort*.
   c. At the Sort dialog box, click the *Sort by* option box arrow and then click *Rate* at the drop-down list.
   d. Click the *Order* option box arrow and then click *Largest to Smallest* at the drop-down list.

1c   1d

   e. Click OK to close the Sort dialog box.
   f. Deselect the cells.
2. Sort the dates in ascending order (oldest to newest) by completing steps similar to those in Step 1.
3. Save and then print **4-APTBilling**.

Check Your Work

Sorting More Than One Column

When sorting data in cells, data in more than one column can be sorted. For example, in Activity 3c, you will sort the dates from oldest to newest and the client numbers from lowest to highest. In this sort, the dates are sorted first and then the client numbers are sorted in ascending order within the same date.

To sort data in more than one column, select all the columns in the worksheet that need to remain relative and then display the Sort dialog box. At the Sort dialog box, specify the first column to be sorted in the *Sort by* option box, click the *Add Level* button, and then specify the second column in the first *Then by* option box. To sort multiple columns, add additional *Then by* option boxes by clicking the *Add Level* button.

Activity 3c **Sorting Data in Two Columns**   Part 3 of 4

1. With **4-APTBilling** open, select the range A3:F29.
2. Click the Sort & Filter button and then click *Custom Sort*.
3. At the Sort dialog box, click the *Sort by* option box arrow and then click *Date* at the drop-down list. (Skip this step if *Date* already displays in the *Sort by* option box.)
4. Make sure *Oldest to Newest* displays in the *Order* option box.
5. Click the Add Level button.
6. Click the *Then by* option box arrow and then click *Client #* at the drop-down list.
7. Click OK to close the dialog box.
8. Deselect the cells.
9. Save and then print **4-APTBilling**.

Check Your Work

 Tutorial

Filtering Data

Quick Steps

Filter List
1. Select cells.
2. Click Sort & Filter button.
3. Click *Filter* at drop-down list.
4. Click filter arrow in heading to filter.
5. Click option at drop-down list.

Filtering Data

A restriction called a *filter* can be placed temporarily on data in a worksheet to isolate specific data. To turn on filtering, make a cell containing data active, click the Sort & Filter button in the Editing group on the Home tab, and then click *Filter* at the drop-down list. This turns on filtering and causes a filter arrow to appear with each column label in the worksheet, as shown in Figure 4.12. Data does not need to be selected before turning on filtering because Excel automatically searches for column labels in a worksheet.

To filter data in a worksheet, click the filter arrow in the heading to be filtered. This causes a drop-down list to display with options to filter all the records, create a custom filter, or select an entry that appears in one or more of the cells in the column. When data is filtered, the filter arrow changes to a funnel icon. The funnel icon indicates that rows in the worksheet have been filtered. To turn off filtering, click the Sort & Filter button and then click *Filter*.

If a column contains numbers, click the filter arrow and point to *Number Filters* and a side menu displays with options for filtering numbers. For example, numbers can be filtered that are equal to, greater than, or less than a specified number; the top 10 numbers can be filtered; and numbers can be filtered that are above or below a specified number.

Figure 4.12 Filtering Data

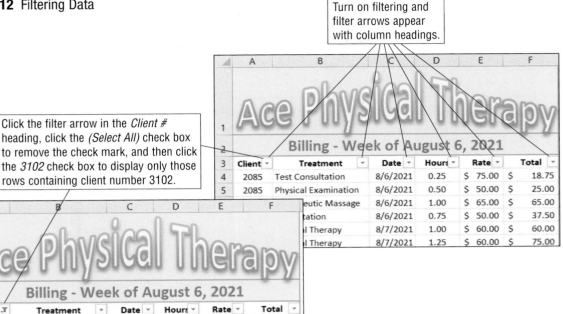

Turn on filtering and filter arrows appear with column headings.

Click the filter arrow in the *Client #* heading, click the *(Select All)* check box to remove the check mark, and then click the *3102* check box to display only those rows containing client number 3102.

Activity 3d Filtering Data

Part 4 of 4

1. With **4-APTBilling** open, click in cell A4.
2. Turn on filtering by clicking the Sort & Filter button in the Editing group on the Home tab and then clicking *Filter* at the drop-down list.
3. Filter rows for client number 3102 by completing the following steps:
   a. Click the filter arrow in the *Client #* heading.
   b. Click the *(Select All)* check box to remove the check mark. (This also removes the check marks for all the items in the list.)
   c. Scroll down the list box and then click *3102* to insert a check mark in the check box.
   d. Click OK.
4. Redisplay all the rows containing data by completing the following steps:
   a. Click the funnel icon in the *Client #* heading.
   b. Click the *(Select All)* check box to insert a check mark. (This also inserts check marks for all the items in the list.)
   c. Click OK.

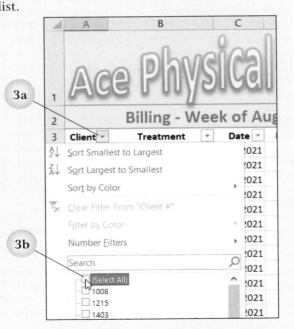

5. Filter a list of clients who receive physical therapy by completing the following steps:
   a. Click the filter arrow in the *Treatment* heading.
   b. Click the *(Select All)* check box to remove the check mark.
   c. Click the *Physical Therapy* check box to insert a check mark.
   d. Click OK.
6. Redisplay all the rows containing data by completing the following steps:
   a. Click the funnel icon in the *Treatment* heading.
   b. Click the *Clear Filter From "Treatment"* option.
7. Display the two highest rates by completing the following steps:
   a. Click the filter arrow in the *Rate* heading.
   b. Point to *Number Filters* and then click *Top 10* at the side menu.
   c. At the Top 10 AutoFilter dialog box, select the *10* in the middle measurement box and then type 2.
   d. Click OK to close the dialog box.
8. Redisplay all the rows that contain data by completing the following steps:
   a. Click the funnel icon in the *Rate* heading.
   b. Click the *Clear Filter From "Rate"* option.
9. Display totals greater than $60 by completing the following steps:
   a. Click the filter arrow in the *Total* heading.
   b. Point to *Number Filters* and then click *Greater Than*.
   c. At the Custom AutoFilter dialog box, type 60 and then click OK.
10. Print the worksheet by clicking the File tab, clicking the *Print* option, and then clicking the Print button.
11. Turn off the filtering feature by clicking the Sort & Filter button and then clicking *Filter* at the drop-down list.
12. Save and then close **4-APTBilling**.

Chapter Summary

- The Page Setup group on the Page Layout tab contains buttons for changing the margins and page orientation and size, as well as buttons for establishing the print area, inserting a page break, applying a picture background, and printing titles.

- The default left and right margins are 0.7 inch and the default top and bottom margins are 0.75 inch. Change these default margins with the Margins button in the Page Setup group on the Page Layout tab.

- Display the Page Setup dialog box with the Margins tab selected by clicking the Margins button in the Page Setup group on the Page Layout tab and then clicking *Custom Margins* at the drop-down list.

- Center a worksheet on the page with the *Horizontally* and *Vertically* check boxes at the Page Setup dialog box with the Margins tab selected.

- Click the Orientation button in the Page Setup group on the Page Layout tab to display the two orientation choices: *Portrait* and *Landscape*.

- Insert a page break by selecting the column or row, clicking the Breaks button in the Page Setup group on the Page Layout tab, and then clicking *Insert Page Break* at the drop-down list.

- To insert both horizontal and vertical page breaks at the same time, make a cell active, click the Breaks button, and then click *Insert Page Break* at the drop-down list.

- Preview the page breaks in a worksheet by clicking the Page Break Preview button in the view area on the Status bar or clicking the View tab and then clicking the Page Break Preview button in the Workbook Views group.

- Use options at the Page Setup dialog box with the Sheet tab selected to specify printing column and/or row titles on each page. Display this dialog box by clicking the Print Titles button in the Page Setup group on the Page Layout tab.

- Use buttons in the Scale to Fit group on the Page Layout tab to scale data to fit on a specific number of pages.

- Use the Background button in the Page Setup group on the Page Layout tab to insert a worksheet background picture. A background picture displays on the screen but does not print.

- Use options in the Sheet Options group on the Page Layout tab to specify whether to view and/or print gridlines and headings.

- Specify the print area by selecting cells, clicking the Print Area button in the Page Setup group on the Page Layout tab, and then clicking *Set Print Area* at the drop-down list. Add another print area by selecting the cells, clicking the Print Area button, and then clicking *Add to Print Area* at the drop-down list.

- Create a header and/or footer with the Header & Footer button in the Text group on the Insert tab, in Page Layout view, or with options at the Page Setup dialog box with the Header/Footer tab selected.

- Customize odd and even page headers and footers at the Page Setup dialog box with the Header/Footer tab selected.

- Customize a print job with options at the Print backstage area.

- To check spelling in a worksheet, click the Review tab and then click the Spelling button.

- Click the Undo button on the Quick Access Toolbar to reverse the most recent action and click the Redo button to redo a previously reversed action.
- Use options at the Find and Replace dialog box with the Find tab selected to find specific data and/or formatting in a worksheet.
- Use options at the Find and Replace dialog box with the Replace tab selected to find specific data and/or formatting and replace it with other data and/or formatting.
- Sort data in a worksheet with options at the Sort & Filter button in the Editing group on the Home tab.
- Create a custom sort with options at the Sort dialog box. Display this dialog box by clicking the Sort & Filter button and then clicking *Custom Sort* at the drop-down list.
- Temporarily isolate data by filtering it. Turn on the filter feature by clicking the Sort & Filter button in the Editing group on the Home tab and then clicking *Filter* at the drop-down list. This inserts a filter arrow with each column label. Click a filter arrow and then use options at the drop-down list to specify the filter data.

Commands Review

FEATURE	RIBBON TAB, GROUP	BUTTON, OPTION	KEYBOARD SHORTCUT
background picture	Page Layout, Page Setup		
filter data	Home, Editing		
Find and Replace dialog box with Find tab selected	Home, Editing	, *Find*	Ctrl + F
Find and Replace dialog box with Replace tab selected	Home, Editing	, *Replace*	Ctrl + H
header and footer	Insert, Text		
insert page break	Page Layout, Page Setup	, *Insert Page Break*	
margins	Page Layout, Page Setup		
orientation	Page Layout, Page Setup		
Page Layout view	View, Workbook Views		
Page Setup dialog box with Margins tab selected	Page Layout, Page Setup	, *Custom Margins*	
Page Setup dialog box with Sheet tab selected	Page Layout, Page Setup		
preview page break	View, Workbook Views		
print area	Page Layout, Page Setup		
redo an action			Ctrl + Y
remove page break	Page Layout, Page Setup	, *Remove Page Break*	

FEATURE	RIBBON TAB, GROUP	BUTTON, OPTION	KEYBOARD SHORTCUT
scale height	Page Layout, Scale to Fit		
scale to fit	Page Layout, Scale to Fit		
scale width	Page Layout, Scale to Fit		
size	Page Layout, Page Setup		
sort data	Home, Editing		
spelling check	Review, Proofing		F7
undo an action			Ctrl + Z

Microsoft® Excel® Level 1

Unit 2
Enhancing the Display of Workbooks

Microsoft®

Excel®

Moving Data within and between Workbooks

Performance Objectives

Upon successful completion of Chapter 5, you will be able to:

1 Insert and delete worksheets

2 Move, copy, and paste cells within and between worksheets

3 Move, rename, and format sheet tabs

4 Hide and unhide worksheets

5 Print a workbook containing multiple worksheets

6 Change the zoom

7 Split a worksheet into windows and freeze/unfreeze panes

8 Name a range of cells and use a range in a formula

9 Open multiple workbooks

10 Arrange, size, hide/unhide, and move workbooks

11 Move, copy, and paste data between workbooks

12 Link data between worksheets

13 Copy and paste data between programs

Up to this point, the workbooks you have worked in have consisted of single worksheets. In this chapter, you will learn to create a workbook with several worksheets and complete tasks such as copying and pasting data within and between worksheets. Moving and pasting or copying and pasting selected cells within and between worksheets is useful for rearranging data and saving time. You will also work with multiple workbooks and complete tasks such as arranging, sizing, and moving workbooks and opening and closing multiple workbooks.

 Data Files

Before beginning chapter work, copy the EL1C5 folder to your storage medium and then make EL1C5 the active folder.

The online course includes additional training and assessment resources.

Activity 1	**Manage Data in a Multiple-Worksheet Account Workbook**	**7 Parts**

You will open an account workbook containing multiple worksheets and then insert and delete worksheets and move, copy, and paste data between worksheets. You will rename and apply color to sheet tabs, hide and unhide a worksheet, and format and print multiple worksheets in the workbook.

Creating a Workbook with Multiple Worksheets

Hint Creating multiple worksheets within a workbook is helpful for saving related data.

An Excel workbook contains one worksheet by default, but additional worksheets can be added. Add additional worksheets to a workbook to store related data, such as a worksheet for expenses for individual salespeople in the company and another worksheet for the monthly payroll for all the departments within the company. Another example is to record sales statistics for each quarter in individual worksheets within a workbook.

Inserting and Renaming Worksheets

 New sheet

Quick Steps

Insert Worksheet
Click New sheet button.
OR
Press Shift + F11.

Delete Worksheet
1. Click sheet tab.
2. Click Delete button arrow.
3. Click *Delete Sheet*.
4. Click Delete button.

Inserting a New Worksheet

Insert a new worksheet in a workbook by clicking the New sheet button to the right of the Sheet1 tab at the bottom of the worksheet area. A new worksheet can also be inserted in a workbook with the keyboard shortcut Shift + F11. A new sheet tab is inserted to the right of the active tab. To move between worksheets, click the desired tab. The active sheet tab displays with a white background and the worksheet name displays in green. Any inactive tabs display with a light-gray background and gray text.

Deleting a Worksheet

If a worksheet is no longer needed in a workbook, delete it by clicking the sheet tab, clicking the Delete button arrow in the Cells group on the Home tab, and then clicking *Delete Sheet* at the drop-down list. Another method for deleting a worksheet is to right-click the sheet tab and then click *Delete* at the shortcut menu. When deleting a worksheet, Excel displays a deletion confirmation message. At this message, click the Delete button.

Selecting Multiple Worksheets

To work with more than one worksheet at a time, select the worksheets. With multiple worksheets selected, the same formatting can be applied to cells or the selected worksheets can be deleted. To select adjacent sheet tabs, click the first tab, press and hold down the Shift key, click the last tab, and then release the Shift key. To select nonadjacent sheet tabs, click the first tab, press and hold down the Ctrl key, click any other tabs to be selected, and then release the Ctrl key.

Tutorial

Copying and
Pasting Cells
between
Worksheets

 Copy

 Cut

 Paste

Quick Steps

Copy and Paste Cells
1. Select cells.
2. Click Copy button.
3. Click cell.
4. Click Paste button.

💡**Hint** Ctrl + C is
the keyboard shortcut
to copy selected data.

Copying, Cutting, and Pasting Cells

Cells in a workbook may need to be copied or moved to different locations within a worksheet or to another worksheet in the workbook. Move or copy cells in a worksheet or between worksheets or workbooks by selecting the cells and then using the Cut, Copy, and/or Paste buttons in the Clipboard group on the Home tab.

Copying and Pasting Selected Cells

Copying selected cells can be useful in worksheets that contain repetitive data. To copy cells, select the cells and then click the Copy button in the Clipboard group on the Home tab. This causes a moving dashed line border (called a *marquee*) to appear around the selected cells. To copy cells to another worksheet, click the sheet tab, click in the cell where the first selected cell is to be pasted, and then click the Paste button in the Clipboard group. Remove the moving marquee from selected cells by pressing the Esc key or double-clicking in any cell.

Selected cells in the same worksheet can be copied using the mouse and the Ctrl key. To do this, select the cells to be copied and then position the mouse pointer on any border around the selected cells until the pointer appears with a four-headed arrow attached. Press and hold down the Ctrl key, click and hold down the left mouse button, drag the outline of the selected cells to the new location, release the left mouse button, and then release the Ctrl key.

Activity 1a **Inserting, Deleting, Selecting, Copying, Pasting,
and Formatting Worksheets**

Part 1 of 7

1. Open **RPFacAccts** and then save it with the name **5-RPFacAccts**.
2. Insert a new worksheet in the workbook by completing the following steps:
   a. Click the 2ndHalfSales sheet tab to make it active.
   b. Click the New sheet button to the right of the 2ndHalfSales sheet tab. (This inserts a new worksheet to the right of the 2ndHalfSales worksheet with the name Sheet4.)
3. Delete two sheet tabs by completing the following steps:
   a. Click the 1stHalfSales sheet tab.
   b. Press and hold down the Shift key, click the 2ndHalfSales sheet tab, and then release the Shift key. (These tabs must be adjacent. If they are not, press and hold down the Ctrl key when clicking the 2ndHalfSales sheet tab.)
   c. With the two sheet tabs selected, click the Delete button arrow in the Cells group on the Home tab and then click *Delete Sheet* at the drop-down list.
   d. At the message stating that Microsoft will permanently delete the sheets, click the Delete button.

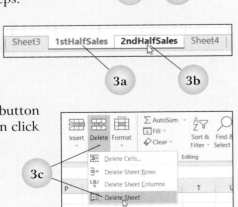

4. Copy cells from Sheet1 to Sheet4 by completing the following steps:
   a. Click the Sheet1 tab to make it the active worksheet.
   b. Select the range A1:A3 (the first three rows of data).
   c. Click the Copy button.
   d. Click the Sheet4 tab to make it the active tab.
   e. With A1 the active cell, click the Paste button.
5. Make the following changes to the new worksheet:
   a. Click in cell A3 and then type First Quarter Summary 2021.
   b. Change the width of column A to 20.00 characters.
   c. Change the width of columns B, C, and D to 12.00 characters.
   d. Type the following text in the specified cells:
      B4 January
      C4 February
      D4 March
      A5 Checks amount
      A6 Deposit amount
      A7 End-of-month balance
   e. Select the range B4:D4, click the Bold button and then click the Center button.
   f. Select the range B5:D7 and then apply the Comma format (using the Comma Style button in the Number group on the Home tab) with two digits after the decimal point.
6. Apply formatting to the cells in all four worksheets by completing the following steps:
   a. Click the Sheet1 tab to make it active and then click in cell A1 to make it the active cell.
   b. Press and hold down the Shift key, click the Sheet4 tab, and then release the Shift key. (This selects all four worksheets.)
   c. With cell A1 active, change the row height to 51.00 points.
   d. Click in cell A3.
   e. Change the font size to 14 points.
   f. Click each remaining sheet tab (Sheet2, Sheet3, and Sheet4) and notice the formatting changes applied to all the cells.
7. Change the column width for the three worksheets by completing the following steps:
   a. Click the Sheet1 tab to make it active.
   b. Press and hold down the Shift key, click the Sheet3 tab, and then release the Shift key.
   c. Select columns E, F, and G and then change the column width to 10.00 characters.
   d. Click the Sheet2 tab and then click the Sheet3 tab. Notice that the width of columns E, F, and G has changed to 10.00 characters. Click the Sheet4 tab and notice that the column width did not change.
8. Save **5-RPFacAccts**.

 Check Your Work

 Tutorial

Using Paste Options

 (Ctrl) ▼

Paste Options

Using Paste Options

When pasting cells in a worksheet, specify how the cells are pasted by clicking the Paste button arrow and then clicking a paste option button at the drop-down list. Click the Paste button (not the button arrow) and a Paste Options button displays in the lower right corner of the pasted cell(s). Display a list of paste options by clicking the button or pressing the Ctrl key. This causes a drop-down list to display, as shown in Figure 5.1. The same option buttons display when the

Figure 5.1 Paste Options Buttons

Use buttons in this section to specify how text and formulas are pasted in cells and whether to keep source column widths.

Use buttons in this section to specify how values are pasted in the worksheet.

Use buttons in this section to specify whether an image, such as a picture, is copied or linked to the worksheet.

Paste button arrow is clicked. Hover the mouse pointer over a button in the drop-down list and the descriptive name of the button displays along with the keyboard shortcut. Use buttons in this drop-down list to specify what is pasted.

Moving Selected Cells

 Tutorial

Moving Cells

Quick Steps

Move and Paste Cells
1. Select cells.
2. Click Cut button.
3. Click cell.
4. Click Paste button.

Hint Ctrl + X is the keyboard shortcut to cut selected data. Ctrl + V is the keyboard shortcut to paste data.

Selected cells and cell contents can be moved within and between worksheets. Move selected cells using the Cut and Paste buttons in the Clipboard group on the Home tab or by dragging with the mouse.

To move selected cells with buttons on the Home tab, select the cells and then click the Cut button in the Clipboard group. Click in the cell where the first selected cell is to be inserted and then click the Paste button in the Clipboard group.

To move selected cells with the mouse, select the cells and then position the mouse pointer on any border of the selected cells until the pointer appears with a four-headed arrow attached. Click and hold down the left mouse button, drag the outline of the selected cells to the new location, and then release the mouse button.

Activity 1b Copying and Moving Cells and Pasting Cells Using Paste Options   Part 2 of 7

1. With **5-RPFacAccts** open, copy cells from Sheet2 to Sheet3 using the Paste Options button by completing the following steps:
   a. Click the Sheet2 tab to make it active.
   b. Select the range C7:E9.
   c. Click the Copy button.
   d. Click the Sheet3 tab.
   e. Click in cell C7.
   f. Click the Paste button.

g. Click the Paste Options button in the lower right corner of the pasted cells and then click the Keep Source Column Widths button at the drop-down list.

h. Make Sheet2 active and then press the Esc key to remove the moving marquee.

2. Click the Sheet1 tab.

3. You realize that the sublet rent deposit was recorded on the wrong day. The correct day is January 9. To move the cells containing information on the deposit, complete the following steps:

a. Click in cell A13 and then insert a row. (The new row should appear above the row containing *Rainier Suppliers*.)

b. Select the range A7:F7.

c. Click the Cut button.

d. Click in cell A13.

e. Click the Paste button.

f. Change the date of the deposit from January 1 to January 9.

g. Select row 7 and then delete it.

4. Move cells using the mouse by completing the following steps:

a. Click the Sheet2 tab.

b. Click in cell A13 and then insert a new row.

c. Using the mouse, select the range A7:F7.

d. Position the mouse pointer on any boundary of the selected cells until it apppears with a four-headed arrow attached. Click and hold down the left mouse button, drag the outline of the selected cells to row 13, and then release the mouse button.

e. Change the date of the deposit to February 13.

f. Delete row 7.

5. Save **5-RPFacAccts**.

Check Your Work

Copying and Pasting Using the Clipboard Task Pane

Quick Steps

Copy and Paste Multiple Items
1. Click Clipboard group task pane launcher.
2. Select cells.
3. Click Copy button.
4. Repeat Steps 2 and 3 as desired.
5. Make cell active.
6. Click item in Clipboard task pane to be inserted in worksheet.
7. Repeat Step 6 as desired.

Use the Clipboard task pane to copy and paste multiple items. To use the task pane, click the Clipboard group task pane launcher in the lower right corner of the Clipboard group on the Home tab. The Clipboard task pane displays at the left side of the screen similarly to what is shown in Figure 5.2.

Select data or an object to be copied and then click the Copy button in the Clipboard group. Continue selecting cells, text, or other items and clicking the Copy button. To paste an item into a worksheet, make the desired cell active and then click the item in the Clipboard task pane. If the copied item is text, the first 50 characters appear in the task pane. To paste all the selected items into a single location, make the desired cell active and then click the Paste All button in the task pane. When all the items have been pasted into the worksheet, click the Clear All button to remove any remaining items from the task pane.

Figure 5.2 Clipboard Task Pane

Click this button to paste all the items in the Clipboard task pane into the worksheet.

Click this button to clear all the items from the Clipboard task pane.

Cut or copied items appear in this list box.

Activity 1c Copying and Pasting Cells Using the Clipboard Task Pane

Part 3 of 7

1. With **5-RPFacAccts** open, select cells for copying by completing the following steps:
   a. Display the Clipboard task pane by clicking the Clipboard group task pane launcher. (If the Clipboard task pane contains any copied data, click the Clear All button.)
   b. Click the Sheet1 tab.
   c. Select the range C15:E16.
   d. Click the Copy button.
   e. Select the range C19:E19.
   f. Click the Copy button.

2. Paste the copied cells by completing the following steps:
   a. Click the Sheet2 tab.
   b. Click in cell C15.
   c. Click the item in the Clipboard task pane representing *General Systems Developer*.
   d. Click the Sheet3 tab.
   e. Click in cell C15.
   f. Click the item in the Clipboard task pane representing *General Systems Developer*.
   g. Click in cell C19.
   h. Click the item in the Clipboard task pane representing *Parkland City Services*.
3. Click the Clear All button at the top of the Clipboard task pane.
4. Close the Clipboard task pane by clicking the Close button (contains an *X*) in the upper right corner of the task pane.
5. Save **5-RPFacAccts**.

Check Your Work

Pasting Values Only

When pasting cells that contain a value and a formula, specify what is to be pasted using button options from the Paste button or Paste Options button drop-down list. Use the buttons in the *Paste Values* section of the drop-down list to insert only the value, the value with numbering formatting, or the value with source formatting.

Activity 1d Copying and Pasting Values

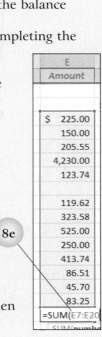

1. With **5-RPFacAccts** open, make Sheet1 the active tab.
2. Click in cell G6, type the formula =(f6-e6)+g5, and then press the Enter key.
3. Copy the formula in cell G6 to the range G7:G20.
4. Copy as a value (and not a formula) the final balance from Sheet1 to Sheet2 by completing the following steps:
   a. Click in cell G20.
   b. Click the Copy button.
   c. Click the Sheet2 tab.
   d. Click in cell G5 and then click the Paste button arrow.
   e. At the drop-down list, click the Values button in the *Paste Values* section of the drop-down list. (This inserts the value and not the formula.)
5. Click in cell G6, insert a formula that determines the balance (see Step 2), and then copy the formula to the range G7:G20.
6. Copy the amount in cell G20 and then paste the value only in cell G5 in Sheet3.
7. With Sheet3 active, make cell G6 active, insert a formula that determines the balance (see Step 2), and then copy the formula to the range G7:G20.
8. Insert formulas and apply formatting to cells in the three worksheets by completing the following steps:
   a. Click the Sheet1 tab.
   b. Press and hold down the Shift key, click the Sheet3 tab, and then release the Shift key.
   c. Click in cell D21, click the Bold button and then type Total.
   d. Click in cell E21 and then click the AutoSum button. (This inserts the formula =SUM(E13:E20).)
   e. Change the formula to =SUM(E7:E20) and then press the Enter key.
   f. Click in cell F21 and then click the AutoSum button. (This inserts the formula =SUM(F12:F20).)
   g. Change the formula to =SUM(F6:F20) and then press the Enter key.
   h. Select cells E21 and F21 and then click the Accounting Number Format button. Click in cell G5 and then click the Accounting Number Format button. (Cell G5 in Sheet1 already contains the Accounting format but cells G5 in Sheet2 and Sheet3 do not.)
   i. Click the Sheet2 tab and notice the text and formulas inserted in the worksheet, click the Sheet3 tab and notice the text and formulas, and then click the Sheet4 tab (to deselect the tabs).
9. Copy values from Sheet1 to Sheet4 by completing the following steps:
   a. Click the Sheet1 tab.
   b. Click in cell E21 and then click the Copy button.
   c. Click the Sheet4 tab.

d. Click in cell B5 and then click the Paste button.

e. Click the Paste Options button and then click the Values button in the *Paste Values* section of the drop-down list.

f. Click the Sheet1 tab.

g. Click in cell F21 and then click the Copy button.

h. Click the Sheet4 tab.

i. Click in cell B6, click the Paste button arrow, and then click the Values button at the drop-down list.

j. Click the Sheet1 tab.

k. Click in cell G20 and then click the Copy button.

l. Click the Sheet4 tab.

m. Click in cell B7, click the Paste button arrow, and then click the Values button at the drop-down list.

10. Complete steps similar to those in Step 9 to insert amounts and balances for February (from Sheet2) and March (from Sheet3).

11. Select the range B5:D5 and then click the Accounting Number Format button.

12. Save **5-RPFacAccts**.

9e

Check Your Work

Managing Worksheets

Tutorial

Moving, Copying, and Deleting a Worksheet

Quick Steps

Move or Copy Worksheet
1. Right-click sheet tab.
2. Click *Move or Copy.*
3. At Move or Copy dialog box, click worksheet name in *Before sheet* list box.
4. Click OK.
OR
Drag sheet tab to new position. (To copy, press and hold down Ctrl key while dragging.)

Right-click a sheet tab and a shortcut menu displays with options for managing worksheets, as shown in Figure 5.3. For example, remove a worksheet by clicking the *Delete* option. Move or copy a worksheet by clicking the *Move or Copy* option. Clicking this option causes a Move or Copy dialog box to display with options for specifying where to move or copy the selected sheet. By default, Excel names worksheets in a workbook *Sheet1, Sheet2, Sheet3,* and so on. To rename a worksheet, click the *Rename* option (which selects the default sheet name) and then type the new name.

In addition to the shortcut menu options, the mouse can be used to move or copy worksheets. To move a worksheet, position the mouse pointer on the sheet tab, click and hold down the left mouse button (a page icon displays next to the mouse pointer), drag the page icon to the new position, and then release the mouse button. For example, to move the Sheet2 tab after the Sheet3 tab, position the mouse pointer on the Sheet2 tab, click and hold down the left mouse button, drag the page icon after the Sheet3 tab, and then release the mouse button. To copy a worksheet, press and hold down the Ctrl key and then drag the sheet tab.

Figure 5.3 Sheet Tab Shortcut Menu

Quick Steps

Apply Color to Sheet Tab
1. Right-click sheet tab.
2. Point to *Tab Color.*
3. Click color at color palette.

Use the *Tab Color* option at the shortcut menu to apply a color to a sheet tab. Right-click a sheet tab, point to *Tab Color* at the shortcut menu, and then click a color at the color palette.

Activity 1e **Selecting, Moving, Renaming, and Changing the Color of Sheet Tabs** Part 5 of 7

1. With **5-RPFacAccts** open, move Sheet4 by completing the following steps:
   a. Right-click the Sheet4 tab and then click *Move or Copy* at the shortcut menu.
   b. At the Move or Copy dialog box, make sure *Sheet1* is selected in the *Before sheet* list box and then click OK.

2. Rename Sheet4 by completing the following steps:
   a. Right-click the Sheet4 tab and then click *Rename*.
   b. Type Summary and then press the Enter key.
3. Complete steps similar to those in Step 2 to rename Sheet1 to *January*, Sheet2 to *February*, and Sheet3 to *March*.

4. Change the color of the Summary sheet tab by completing the following steps:
   a. Right-click the Summary sheet tab.
   b. Point to *Tab Color* at the shortcut menu.
   c. Click the *Red* color option (second option in the *Standard Colors* section).
5. Follow steps similar to those in Step 4 to change the January sheet tab to Blue (eighth option in the *Standard Colors* section), the February sheet tab to Purple (last option in the *Standard Colors* section), and the March sheet tab to Green (sixth option in the *Standard Colors* section).
6. Save **5-RPFacAccts**.

● Check Your Work ▷

Hiding and Unhiding a Worksheet in a Workbook

Tutorial

Hiding and Unhiding a Worksheet

Format

In a workbook with multiple worksheets, a worksheet can be hidden that contains data that should not appear or print with the workbook. To hide a worksheet in a workbook, click the Format button in the Cells group on the Home tab, point to *Hide & Unhide*, and then click *Hide Sheet*. A worksheet can also be hidden by right-clicking a sheet tab and then clicking the *Hide* option at the shortcut menu.

Quick Steps

Hide Worksheet
1. Click Format button.
2. Point to *Hide & Unhide*.
3. Click *Hide Sheet*.
OR
1. Right-click sheet tab.
2. Click *Hide* at shortcut menu.

To make a hidden worksheet visible, click the Format button in the Cells group, point to *Hide & Unhide* and then click *Unhide Sheet*, or right-click a sheet tab and then click *Unhide* at the shortcut menu. At the Unhide dialog box, shown in Figure 5.4, double-click the name of the worksheet to be unhidden.

Figure 5.4 Unhide Dialog Box

Unhide Worksheet
1. Click Format button.
2. Point to *Hide & Unhide*.
3. Click *Unhide Sheet*.
4. Double-click hidden worksheet in Unhide dialog box.
OR
1. Right-click sheet tab.
2. Click *Unhide* at shortcut menu.
3. Double-click hidden worksheet in Unhide dialog box.

The names of hidden worksheets are shown in this list box.

Activity 1f Hiding and Unhiding a Worksheet and Formatting Multiple Worksheets   Part 6 of 7

1. With **5-RPFacAccts** open, hide the Summary worksheet by completing the following steps:
   a. Click the Summary tab.
   b. Click the Format button in the Cells group on the Home tab, point to *Hide & Unhide*, and then click *Hide Sheet*.

2. Unhide the worksheet by completing the following steps:
   a. Click the Format button, point to *Hide & Unhide*, and then click *Unhide Sheet*.
   b. At the Unhide dialog box, make sure *Summary* is selected in the *Unhide sheet* list box and then click OK.

3. Insert a header for each worksheet by completing the following steps:
   a. With the Summary tab active, press and hold down the Shift key, click the March tab, and then release the Shift key. (This selects all four tabs.)
   b. Click the Insert tab.
   c. Click the Header & Footer button in the Text group.
   d. Click the Header button in the Header & Footer group on the Header & Footer Tools Design tab and then click the option at the drop-down list that prints your name at the left side of the page (if a name other than your own appears at the left side of the page, select the name and then type your first and last names), the page number in the middle, and the date at the right.
4. With all the sheet tabs selected, center each worksheet horizontally and vertically on the page. **Hint: Do this at the Page Setup dialog box with the Margins tab selected.**
5. With all the sheet tabs still selected, change to landscape orientation. **Hint: Do this with the Orientation button on the Page Layout tab.**
6. Save **5-RPFacAccts**.

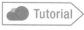 **Tutorial**

Printing Multiple
Worksheets

Quick Steps

**Print All Worksheets
in Workbook**

1. Click File tab.
2. Click *Print* option.
3. Click first gallery in *Settings* category.
4. Click *Print Entire Workbook*.
5. Click Print button.

Printing a Workbook Containing Multiple Worksheets

By default, Excel prints the currently displayed worksheet. To print all the worksheets in a workbook, display the Print backstage area, click the first gallery in the *Settings* category, click *Print Entire Workbook* at the drop-down list, and then click the Print button. Print specific worksheets in a workbook by selecting the tabs of the worksheets to be printed. With the sheet tabs selected, display the Print backstage area and then click the Print button.

1. With **5-RPFacAccts** open, click the File tab and then click the *Print* option.
2. At the Print backstage area, click the first gallery in the *Settings* category and then click *Print Entire Workbook* at the drop-down list.
3. Click the Print button.
4. Save and then close **5-RPFacAccts**.

 Check Your Work

Activity 2 **Write Formulas Using Ranges in an Equipment Usage Workbook**   **2 Parts**

You will open an equipment usage workbook, view the document at different zoom percentages, and then split the window, freeze panes and edit cells. You will also name ranges and then use the range names to write formulas in the workbook.

Changing the Zoom

 Zoom

 100%

 Zoom to Selection

Changing the Zoom

The View tab contains a Zoom group with three buttons for changing zoom settings. Click the Zoom button in the Zoom group to open the Zoom dialog box, which contains options for changing the zoom percentage. Click the 100% button in the Zoom group to return the view to 100%, which is the default. Select a range of cells and then click the Zoom to Selection button to scale the zoom setting so the selected range fills the worksheet area.

Use the zoom slider bar at the right side of the Status bar to change the zoom percentage. Click the Zoom Out button (displays with a minus symbol [–]) to decrease the zoom percentage or click the Zoom In button (displays with a plus symbol [+]) to increase the zoom percentage. Another method for increasing or decreasing zoom percentage is to click and drag the zoom slider bar button on the slider bar.

Splitting a
Worksheet

Freezing and
Unfreezing Panes

 Split

Quick Steps

Split Worksheet
1. Click View tab.
2. Click Split button.

 Freeze Panes

Hint Remove a split line by double-clicking anywhere on the split line that divides the panes.

Splitting a Worksheet and Freezing and Unfreezing Panes

Depending on the size of a worksheet and the screen display settings, all cells in a worksheet may not be visible in the worksheet area at one time. (An example of this will be seen in Activity 2a.) To more easily view all the data, it can be helpful to split the window into panes. Split a worksheet window into panes with the Split button in the Window group on the View tab. Click the Split button and the worksheet splits into four panes, as shown in Figure 5.5. The panes are separated by thick light-gray lines called *split lines*. To remove split lines from a worksheet, click the Split button to deactivate it.

A window pane will display the active cell. As the insertion point is moved through the pane, another active cell may display. This additional active cell displays when the insertion point passes over one of the split lines that creates the pane. Move through a worksheet and both active cells may display. Make a change to one active cell and the change is made in the other as well. To display only one active cell, freeze the window panes by clicking the Freeze Panes button in the Window group on the View tab and then clicking *Freeze Panes* at the drop-down list. Maintain the display of column headings while editing or typing text in cells by clicking the Freeze Panes button and then clicking *Freeze Top Row*. Maintain the display of row headings by clicking the Freeze Panes button and then clicking *Freeze First Column*. Unfreeze window panes by clicking the Freeze Panes button and then clicking *Unfreeze Panes* at the drop-down list.

The split lines that divide the window can be adjusted using the mouse. To do this, position the mouse pointer on a split line until the pointer turns into a left-and-right-pointing arrow with a double line in the middle. Click and hold down the left mouse button, drag the outline of the split line to the desired location, and then release the mouse button. To move both the horizontal and vertical split lines at the same time, position the mouse pointer on the intersection of the split lines until the pointer turns into a four-headed arrow. Click and hold down the left mouse button, drag the split lines to the desired location, and then release the mouse button.

Figure 5.5 Split Window

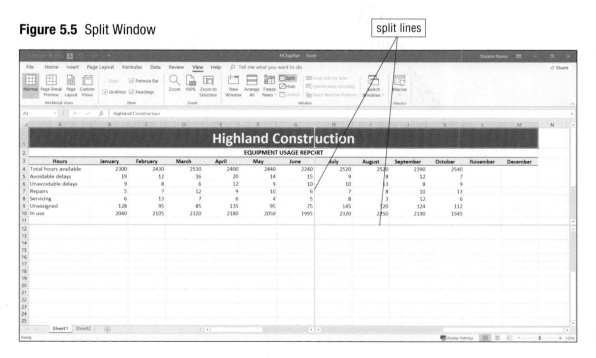

1. Open **HCEqpRpt** and then save it with the name **5-HCEqpRpt**.
2. Increase the Zoom percentage by clicking the Zoom In button at the right of the zoom slider bar two times.
3. Select the range G3:I10, click the View tab, and then click the Zoom to Selection button in the Zoom group.
4. Click the Zoom button in the Zoom group, click the *75%* option at the Zoom dialog box, and then click OK.
5. Click the 100% button in the Zoom group.
6. Make cell A1 active and then split the window by clicking the Split button in the Window group on the View tab. (This splits the window into four panes.)
7. Drag the vertical split line by completing the following steps:
   a. Position the mouse pointer on the vertical split line until the pointer turns into a left-and-right-pointing arrow with a double line in the middle.
   b. Click and hold down the left mouse button, drag to the left until the vertical split line is immediately to the right of the first column, and then release the mouse button.

8. Freeze the window panes by clicking the Freeze Panes button in the Window group on the View tab and then clicking *Freeze Panes* at the drop-down list.
9. Make cell L4 active and then type the following data in the specified cells:

L4	2310	M4	2210
L5	12	M5	5
L6	5	M6	7
L7	9	M7	8
L8	11	M8	12
L9	95	M9	120
L10	2005	M10	1830

10. Unfreeze the window panes by clicking the Freeze Panes button and then clicking *Unfreeze Panes* at the drop-down list.
11. Remove the panes by clicking the Split button in the Window group to deactivate it.
12. Save **5-HCEqpRpt**.

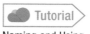

Naming and Using
a Range

Naming and Using a Range

A group of adjacent cells is referred to as a *range*. A range of cells can be formatted, moved, copied, or deleted. A range can also be named and then the insertion point can be moved to the range or the named range can be used as part of a formula.

To name a range, select the cells and then click in the Name box to the left of the Formula bar. Type a name for the range (do not use spaces) and then press the Enter key. To move the insertion point to a specific range and select the range, click the Name box arrow and then click the range name at the drop-down list.

A range can also be named using the Define Name button in the Defined Names group on the Formulas tab. Clicking the Define Name button displays the New Name dialog box. At the New Name dialog box, type a name for the range and then click OK.

A range name can be used in a formula. For example, to insert in a cell the average of all the cells in a range named *Profit*, make the cell active and then type the formula *=AVERAGE(Profit)*. Use a named range in the current worksheet or in another worksheet within the workbook.

Quick Steps

Name Range
1. Select cells.
2. Click in Name box.
3. Type range name.
4. Press Enter key.

 Define Name

💡 **Hint** Another method for moving to a range is to click the Find & Select button in the Editing group on the Home tab and then click *Go To*. At the Go To dialog box, double-click the range name.

Activity 2b Naming a Range and Using a Range in a Formula

Part 2 of 2

1. With **5-HCEqpRpt** open, click the Sheet2 tab and then type the following text in the specified cells:

   A1   EQUIPMENT USAGE REPORT
   A2   Yearly hours
   A3   Avoidable delays
   A4   Unavoidable delays
   A5   Total delay hours
   A6   (leave blank)
   A7   Repairs
   A8   Servicing
   A9   Total repair/servicing hours

2. Make the following formatting changes to the worksheet:
   a. Automatically adjust the width of column A.
   b. Center and apply bold formatting to the text in cells A1 and A2.

3. Select a range of cells in Sheet1, name the range, and then use it in a formula in Sheet2 by completing the following steps:
   a. Click the Sheet1 tab.
   b. Select the range B5:M5.
   c. Click in the Name box to the left of the Formula bar.
   d. Type adhours (for Avoidable Delays Hours) and then press the Enter key.
   e. Click the Sheet2 tab.
   f. Click in cell B3.
   g. Type the equation =sum(adhours) and then press the Enter key.

4. Click the Sheet1 tab and then complete the following steps:
   a. Select the range B6:M6.
   b. Click the Formulas tab.
   c. Click the Define Name button in the Defined Names group.
   d. At the New Name dialog box, type udhours and then click OK.
   e. Click the Sheet2 tab, make sure cell B4 is active, type the equation =sum(udhours), and then press the Enter key.

5. Click the Sheet1 tab and then complete the following steps:
   a. Select the range B7:M7 and then name the range *rhours*.
   b. Click the Sheet2 tab, make cell B7 active, type the equation =sum(rhours), and then press the Enter key.
   c. Click the Sheet1 tab.
   d. Select the range B8:M8 and then name the range *shours*.
   e. Click the Sheet2 tab, make sure cell B8 is active, type the equation =sum(shours), and then press the Enter key.

6. With Sheet2 still active, make the following changes:
   a. Make cell B5 active.
   b. Double-click the AutoSum button.
   c. Make cell B9 active.
   d. Double-click the AutoSum button.

7. Click the Sheet1 tab and then move to the adhours range by clicking the Name box arrow and then clicking *adhours* at the drop-down list.

8. Select both sheet tabs, change to landscape orientation, scale the contents to fit on one page (by changing the width to *1 page* on the Page Layout tab), and then insert a custom footer with your name, the page number, and the date.

9. With both sheet tabs selected, print both worksheets in the workbook.

10. Save and then close **5-HCEqpRpt**.

Check Your Work

Activity 3 Arrange, Size, and Copy Data between Workbooks   3 Parts

You will open, arrange, hide, unhide, size, and move multiple workbooks. You will also copy cells from one workbook and paste the contents in another workbook.

Working with Windows and Hiding and Unhiding Workbooks

Working with Windows

In Excel, multiple workbooks can be opened, a new window with the current workbook can be opened, and the open workbooks can be arranged in the Excel window. With multiple workbooks open, cell entries can be cut and pasted or copied and pasted from one workbook to another using the techniques discussed earlier in this chapter. The exception is that the destination workbook must be active before using the Paste command.

Opening Multiple Workbooks

With multiple workbooks or more than one version of the current workbook open, data can be moved or copied between workbooks and the contents of several workbooks can be compared. When a new workbook or a new window of the current workbook is opened, it is placed on top of the original workbook.

 New Window

Open a new window of the current workbook by clicking the View tab and then clicking the New Window button in the Window group. Excel adds a colon followed by the number *2* to the end of the workbook title and adds a colon followed by the number *1* to the end of the originating workbook name.

Open multiple workbooks at one time at the Open dialog box. Select adjacent workbooks by clicking the name of the first workbook to be opened, pressing and holding down the Shift key, clicking the name of the last workbook to be opened, releasing the Shift key, and then clicking the Open button. If the workbooks are nonadjacent, click the name of the first workbook to be opened, press and hold down the Ctrl key, and then click the names of any other workbooks to be opened.

 Switch Windows

To see what workbooks are currently open, click the View tab and then click the Switch Windows button in the Window group. The names of the open workbooks display in a drop-down list and the workbook name preceded by a check mark is the active workbook. To make another workbook active, click the workbook name at the drop-down list.

Another method for determining which workbooks are open is to hover the mouse over the Excel button on the taskbar. This causes a thumbnail to display of each open workbook. If more than one workbook is open, the Excel button on the taskbar displays additional layers in a cascaded manner. The layer behind the Excel button displays only a portion of the edge at the right of the button. Hovering the mouse over the Excel button on the taskbar displays thumbnails of all the workbooks above the button. To make another workbook active, click the thumbnail that represents the workbook.

Arranging Workbooks

If more than one workbook is open, arrange the workbooks at the Arrange Windows dialog box, shown in Figure 5.6. To display this dialog box, click the Arrange All button in the Window group on the View tab. At the Arrange Windows dialog box, click *Tiled* to display a portion of each open workbook. Figure 5.7 displays four tiled workbooks.

 Arrange All

Quick Steps

Arrange Workbooks
1. Click View tab.
2. Click Arrange All button.
3. At Arrange Windows dialog box, click arrangement.
4. Click OK.

Figure 5.6 Arrange Windows Dialog Box

Use options at this dialog box to choose an arrange method.

Choose the *Horizontal* option at the Arrange Windows dialog box to display the open workbooks across the screen. Choose the *Vertical* option to display the open workbooks up and down the screen. Choose the last option, *Cascade*, to display the Title bar of each open workbook. Figure 5.8 shows four cascaded workbooks.

Select the arrange option for displaying multiple workbooks based on which parts of the workbooks are most important to view simultaneously. For example, the tiled workbooks in Figure 5.7 display the company names of the workbooks.

Figure 5.7 Tiled Workbooks

Figure 5.8 Cascaded Workbooks

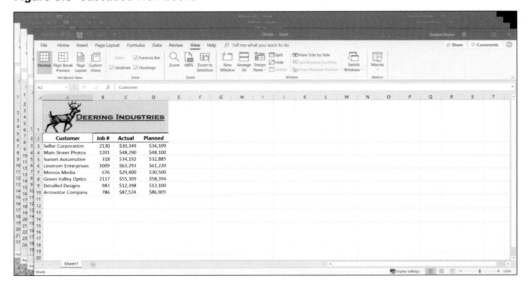

Hiding and Unhiding Workbooks

Hide

Unhide

Use the Hide button in the Window group on the View tab to hide the active workbook. If a workbook has been hidden, redisplay it by clicking the Unhide button in the Window group. At the Unhide dialog box, make sure the specific workbook is selected in the list box and then click OK.

Activity 3a Opening, Arranging, Hiding and Unhiding Workbooks   Part 1 of 3

1. Open several workbooks at the same time by completing the following steps:
   a. Display the Open dialog box with EL1C5 the active folder.
   b. Click the workbook *DIJobs*.
   c. Press and hold down the Ctrl key, click *EPSales*, click *FinCon*, click *RPFacAccts*, and then release the Ctrl key.
   d. Click the Open button in the dialog box.
2. Make **DIJobs** the active workbook by clicking the View tab, clicking the Switch Windows button, and then clicking *DIJobs* at the drop-down list.
3. Tile the workbooks by completing the following steps:
   a. Click the View tab and then click the Arrange All button in the Window group.
   b. At the Arrange Windows dialog box, make sure *Tiled* is selected and then click OK.
4. Cascade the workbooks by completing the following steps:
   a. Click the Arrange All button in the **DIJobs** workbook.
   b. At the Arrange Windows dialog box, click *Cascade* and then click OK.
5. Hide and unhide workbooks by completing the following steps:
   a. Make sure **DIJobs** is the active workbook. (The file name displays on top of each workbook file.)
   b. Click the Hide button in the Window group on the View tab.
   c. Make sure **RPFacAccts** is the active workbook. (The file name displays at the top of each workbook file.)
   d. Click the Hide button in the Window group on the View tab.
   e. At the active workbook, click the View tab and then click the Unhide button.
   f. At the Unhide dialog box, click *RPFacAccts* in the list box and then click OK.
   g. Click the Unhide button.
   h. At the Unhide dialog box, make sure **DIJobs** is selected in the list box and then click OK.
6. Close all the open workbooks (without saving changes) except **DIJobs**.
7. Open a new window with the current workbook by clicking the New Window button in the Window group on the View tab. (Notice that the new window contains the workbook name followed by a hyphen and the number *2*.)
8. Switch back and forth between the two versions of the workbook.
9. Make **DIJobs-2** the active window and then close the workbook.

Sizing and Moving Workbooks

Maximize

Minimize

Close

Restore Down

Change the size of the window using the Maximize and Minimize buttons in the upper right corner of the active workbook. The Maximize button is in the upper right corner of the active workbook immediately to the left of the Close button. (The Close button is the button containing the *X*.) The Minimize button is immediately to the left of the Maximize button.

If all the open workbooks are arranged, clicking the Maximize button causes the active workbook to expand to fill the screen. In addition, the Maximize button changes to the Restore Down button. To return the active workbook back to its original size, click the Restore Down button.

Click the Minimize button in the active workbook and the workbook is reduced and displays as a layer behind the Excel button on the taskbar. To maximize a workbook that has been minimized, click the Excel button on the taskbar and then click the thumbnail representing the workbook.

Activity 3b **Minimizing, Maximizing, and Restoring Workbooks**   Part 2 of 3

1. Make sure **DIJobs** is open.
2. Maximize **DIJobs** by clicking the Maximize button in the upper right corner of the screen immediately to the left of the Close button.
3. Open **EPSales** and **FinCon**.
4. Make the following changes to the open workbooks:
   a. Tile the workbooks.
   b. Click the **DIJobs** Title bar to make it the active workbook.
   c. Minimize **DIJobs** by clicking the Minimize button at the right side of the Title bar.
   d. Make **EPSales** the active workbook and then minimize it.
   e. Minimize **FinCon**.
5. Click the Excel button on the taskbar, click the **DIJobs** thumbnail, and then close the workbook without saving changes.
6. Complete steps similar to Step 5 to close the other two workbooks.

Moving, Linking, Copying, and Pasting Data between Workbooks

With more than one workbook open, data can be moved, linked, copied, and/or pasted from one workbook to another. To move, link, copy, and/or paste data between workbooks, use the cutting and pasting options discussed earlier in this chapter together with the information about windows.

Moving and Copying Data

Data can be moved or copied within a worksheet, between worksheets, and between workbooks and documents created in other programs, such as Word, PowerPoint, and Access. The Paste Options button provides a variety of options for pasting data in a worksheet, another workbook, or a document created in another program. In addition to being pasted, data can be linked and data can be pasted as an object or a picture object.

Activity 3c **Copying Selected Cells from One Open Worksheet to Another**   Part 3 of 3

1. Open **DIFebJobs**.
2. If you just completed Activity 3b, click the Maximize button so the worksheet fills the entire worksheet window.
3. Save the workbook and name it **5-DIFebJobs**.
4. With **5-DIFebJobs** open, open **DIJobs**.
5. Select and then copy text from **DIJobs** to **5-DIFebJobs** by completing the following steps:
   a. With **DIJobs** the active workbook, select the range A3:D10.
   b. Click the Copy button.
   c. Click the Excel button on the taskbar and then click the **5-DIFebJobs** thumbnail.
   d. Make cell A8 active and then click the Paste button.

   e. Make cell E7 active and then drag the fill handle to cell E15.
6. Print **5-DIFebJobs** centered horizontally and vertically on the page.
7. Save and then close **5-DIFebJobs**.
8. Close **DIJobs**.

 Check Your Work

Activity 4 **Linking and Copying Data within and between**   **2 Parts**
             Worksheets and Word

You will open a workbook containing four worksheets with quarterly expenses data, copy and link cells between the worksheets, and then copy and paste the worksheets into Word as picture objects.

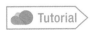
Linking Data

In addition to being copied and pasted, data can be copied and then linked within or between worksheets or workbooks. Linking data is useful for maintaining consistency and control over critical data in worksheets or workbooks. When data is linked, a change made in a linked cell is automatically made to the other cells in the link. Links can be made with individual cells or with a range of cells. When linking data, the worksheet that contains the original data is called the *source worksheet* and the worksheet that relies on the source worksheet for the data in the link is called the *dependent worksheet*.

To create a link, make active the cell containing the data to be linked (or select the cells) and then click the Copy button in the Clipboard group on the Home tab. Make active the worksheet where the cells are to be linked, click the Paste button arrow, and then click the Paste Link button in the *Other Paste Options* section in the drop-down list. Another method for creating a link is to click the Paste button, click the Paste Options button, and then click the Paste Link button in the *Other Paste Options* section in the drop-down list.

Quick Steps

Link Data between Worksheets

1. Select cells.
2. Click Copy button.
3. Click sheet tab.
4. Click in cell.
5. Click Paste button arrow.
6. Click Paste Link button.

Activity 4a Linking Cells between Worksheets

Part 1 of 2

1. Open **DWQtrlyExp** and then save it with the name **5-DWQtrlyExp**.
2. Link cells in the first-quarter worksheet to the other three worksheets by completing the following steps:
   a. With the 1st Qtr tab active, select the range C4:C10.
   b. Click the Copy button.
   c. Click the 2nd Qtr tab.
   d. Make cell C4 active.
   e. Click the Paste button arrow and then click the Paste Link button in the *Other Paste Options* section in the drop-down list.
   f. Click the 3rd Qtr tab and then make cell C4 active.
   g. Click the Paste button arrow and then click the Paste Link button.
   h. Click the 4th Qtr tab and then make cell C4 active.
   i. Click the Paste button.
   j. Click the Paste Options button and then click the Paste Link button in the *Other Paste Options* section in the drop-down list.

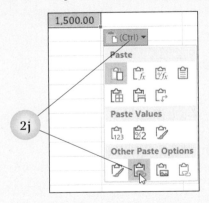

3. Click the 1st Qtr tab and then press the Esc key to remove the moving marquee.

4. Insert a formula in each worksheet that subtracts the budget amount from the variance amount by completing the following steps:
   a. Make sure the first-quarter worksheet is visible.
   b. Press and hold down the Shift key and then click the 4th Qtr tab. (This selects all four tabs.)
   c. Make cell D4 active, type the formula =c4-b4, and then press the Enter key.
   d. Copy the formula in cell D4 to the range D5:D10.
   e. Make cell D4 active and then apply the Accounting format with two digits after the decimal point and a dollar symbol.
   f. Click the 2nd Qtr tab and notice that the formula was inserted and copied in this worksheet.
   g. Click the other sheet tabs and notice the amounts in column D.
   h. Click the 1st Qtr tab.

1arter		
	Budget	Variance
	$ 126,000.00	4,000.00
	54,500.00	(3,500.00)
	10,100.00	1,850.00
	6,000.00	(350.00)
	4,500.00	360.00
	2,200.00	(230.00)
	1,500.00	50.00

4d

5. With the first-quarter worksheet active, make the following changes to the specified linked cells:

   C4: Change *$126,000* to *$128,000*

   C5: Change *54,500* to *56,000*

   C9: Change *2,200* to *2,400*

6. Click the 2nd Qtr tab and notice that the values in cells C4, C5, and C9 automatically changed (because they were linked to the first-quarter worksheet).
7. Click the other tabs and notice that the values changed.
8. Save **5-DWQtrlyExp** and then print all four worksheets in the workbook.

Check Your Work

 Tutorial

Copying and Pasting Data between Programs

Copying and Pasting Data between Programs

Microsoft Office is a suite that allows *integration*, which is the combining of data from files created by two or more programs into one file. Integration can occur by copying and pasting data between files created in different programs. For example, a worksheet can be created in Excel and specific data can be selected in the worksheet and then copied to a Word document. When pasting Excel data in a Word document, choose from among these formatting options: keep the source formatting, use destination styles, link the data, insert the data as a picture, or keep only the text.

Activity 4b Copying and Pasting Excel Data into a Word Document   Part 2 of 2

1. With **5-DWQtrlyExp** open, open the Word program.
2. In Word, open the document **DWQtrlyRpt** in your EL1C5 folder.
3. Save the Word document with the name **5-DWQtrlyRpt**.
4. Click the Excel button on the taskbar.
5. Copy the first-quarter data into the Word document by completing the following steps:
   a. Click the 1st Qtr tab.
   b. Select the range A2:D10.
   c. Click the Copy button.
   d. Click the Word button on the taskbar.

e. In the **5-DWQtrlyRpt** document, press Ctrl + End to move the insertion point below the heading.

f. Click the Paste button arrow. (This displays a drop-down list of paste option buttons.)

g. Move the mouse over the various buttons in the drop-down list to see how each option inserts the data in the document.

h. Click the Picture button. (This inserts the data as a picture object.)

i. Press Ctrl + End and then press the Enter key two times. (This moves the insertion point below the data.)

j. Click the Excel button on the taskbar.

6. Click the 2nd Qtr tab and then complete steps similar to those in Step 5 to copy and paste the second-quarter data into the Word document. Press Ctrl + End and then press the Enter key two times.

7. Click the 3rd Qtr tab and then complete steps similar to those in Step 5 to copy and paste the third-quarter data to the Word document. Press Ctrl + End and then press the Enter key two times.

8. Click the 4th Qtr tab and then complete steps similar to those in Step 5 to copy and paste the fourth-quarter data to the Word document. (The data will display on two pages.)

9. Print the document by clicking the File tab, clicking the *Print* option, and then clicking the Print button at the Print backstage area.

10. Save and close **5-DWQtrlyRpt** and then close Word.

11. In Excel, press the Esc key to remove the moving marquee and then make cell A1 active.

12. Save and then close **5-DWQtrlyExp**.

Check Your Work

Chapter Summary

- By default, an Excel workbook contains one worksheet. Add a new worksheet to a workbook by clicking the New sheet button or using the keyboard shortcut Shift + F11.

- Delete a worksheet with the Delete button in the Cells group on the Home tab or by right-clicking a sheet tab and then clicking *Delete* at the shortcut menu.

- To manage more than one worksheet at a time, first select the worksheets. Use the mouse together with the Shift key to select adjacent sheet tabs and use the mouse together with the Ctrl key to select nonadjacent sheet tabs.

- Copy or move selected cells and cell contents in and between worksheets using the Cut, Copy, and/or Paste buttons in the Clipboard group on the Home tab or by dragging with the mouse.

- Move selected cells with the mouse by dragging the outline of the selected cells to the new position.

- Copy selected cells with the mouse by pressing and holding down the Ctrl key while dragging the cells to the new position.

- When pasting data, specify how cells are to be pasted by clicking the Paste button arrow or pasting the cells and then clicking the Paste Options button. Clicking either button displays a drop-down list of paste option buttons. Click a button at the drop-down list.

- Use the Clipboard task pane to copy and paste data within and between worksheets and workbooks. Display the Clipboard task pane by clicking the Clipboard group task pane launcher.

- Manage worksheets by right-clicking a sheet tab and then clicking an option at the shortcut menu. Options include removing and renaming a worksheet.

- The mouse can be used to move or copy worksheets. To move a worksheet, drag the sheet tab with the mouse. To copy a worksheet, press and hold down the Ctrl key and then drag the sheet tab with the mouse.

- Use the *Tab Color* option at the sheet tab shortcut menu to apply a color to a sheet tab.

- Hide and unhide a worksheet by clicking the Format button in the Cells group on the Home tab and then clicking the desired option at the drop-down list or by right-clicking the sheet tab and then clicking the option at the shortcut menu.

- To print all the worksheets in a workbook, display the Print backstage area, click the first gallery in the *Settings* category, and then click *Print Entire Workbook* at the drop-down list. Print specific worksheets by selecting their tabs.

- Use buttons in the Zoom group on the View tab or the zoom slider bar at the right side of the Status bar to change the zoom percentage.

- Split the worksheet window into panes with the Split button in the Window group on the View tab. To remove a split from a worksheet, click the Split button to deactivate it.

- Freeze window panes by clicking the Freeze Panes button in the Window group on the View tab and then clicking *Freeze Panes* at the drop-down list. Unfreeze window panes by clicking the Freeze Panes button and then clicking *Unfreeze Panes* at the drop-down list.

- A selected group of cells is referred to as a *range*. A range can be named and used in a formula. Name a range by typing the name in the Name box to the left of the Formula bar or at the New Name dialog box.

- To open multiple workbooks that are adjacent, display the Open dialog box, click the name of the first workbook, press and hold down the Shift key, click the name of the last workbook, release the Shift key, and then click the Open button. To open workbooks that are nonadjacent, click the name of the first workbook, press and hold down the Ctrl key, click the names of the desired workbooks, release the Ctrl key, and then click the Open button.

- To see a list of open workbooks, click the View tab and then click the Switch Windows button in the Window group.

- Arrange multiple workbooks in a window with options at the Arrange Windows dialog box.

- Hide the active workbook by clicking the Hide button in the Window group on the View tab and unhide a workbook by clicking the Unhide button.

- Click the Maximize button in the upper right corner of the active workbook to make the workbook fill the entire window area. Click the Minimize button to reduce the workbook and display it as a layer behind the Excel button on the taskbar. Click the Restore Down button to return the workbook to its previous size.

- Data can be moved, copied, linked, and/or pasted between workbooks using options at the Paste Options button. Also, a workbook can be pasted as a link in a different Microsoft Office program, such a Word or PowerPoint. Changing the data in one program will change linked data that exists in a different program.

Commands Review

FEATURE	RIBBON TAB, GROUP	BUTTON, OPTION	KEYBOARD SHORTCUT
100% view	View, Zoom		
Arrange Windows dialog box	View, Window		
Clipboard task pane	Home, Clipboard		
copy selected cells	Home, Clipboard		Ctrl + C
cut selected cells	Home, Clipboard		Ctrl + X
freeze window panes	View, Window	, *Freeze Panes*	
hide workbook	View, Window		
hide worksheet	Home, Cells	, *Hide & Unhide, Hide Sheet*	
insert new worksheet			Shift + F11
maximize window			
minimize window			
New Name dialog box	Formulas, Defined Names		
new window	View, Window		
paste selected cells	Home, Clipboard		Ctrl + V
restore down			
split window into panes	View, Window		
switch windows	View, Window		
unfreeze window panes	View, Window	, *Unfreeze Panes*	
unhide workbook	View, Window		
unhide worksheet	Home, Cells	, *Hide & Unhide, Unhide Sheet*	
Zoom dialog box	View, Zoom		

Microsoft®

Excel®

Maintaining Workbooks

Performance Objectives

Upon successful completion of Chapter 6, you will be able to:

1 Pin and unpin workbooks at the *Recent* option list

2 Copy and move worksheets between workbooks

3 Apply and modify a cell style

4 Modify, remove, and delete a cell style

5 Insert and use hyperlinks

6 Modify, edit, and remove hyperlinks

7 Create financial forms using templates

8 Insert, edit, delete, and show comments

9 Insert formulas using financial functions

After you have worked with Excel for a period of time, you will have accumulated several workbook files. Frequently used workbooks can be pinned at the Open and Home backstage areas so you can access them without needing to browse for them. In this chapter, you will also learn more methods for creating and maintaining workbooks, such as copying or moving worksheets from one workbook to another, applying cell styles and globally changing the style, inserting hyperlinks in a workbook, and using an Excel template to create a workbook. Inserting, posting, editing, and deleting comments will also be covered.

 Data Files

Before beginning chapter work, copy the EL1C6 folder to your storage medium and then make EL1C6 the active folder.

The online course includes additional training and assessment resources.

Copy and Move Worksheets into an Equipment Rental Workbook **3 Parts**

You will manage workbooks at the Open backstage area and then open multiple workbooks and copy and move worksheets between the workbooks.

Tutorial

Managing the
Recent Option List

Managing the *Recent* Option List

As workbooks are opened and closed, Excel keeps a list of the most recently opened workbooks. To view this list, click the File tab and then click the *Open* option. This displays the Open backstage area, similar to what is shown in Figure 6.1. (The workbook names you see may vary from those in the figure.) Generally, the names of the 50 most recently opened workbooks are shown in the *Recent* option list and are organized in categories such as *Today*, *Yesterday*, and *Last Week*. To open a workbook, scroll down the list and then click the workbook name. The Excel opening screen and Home backstage area also display a list of the most recently opened workbooks.

Figure 6.1 Open Backstage Area

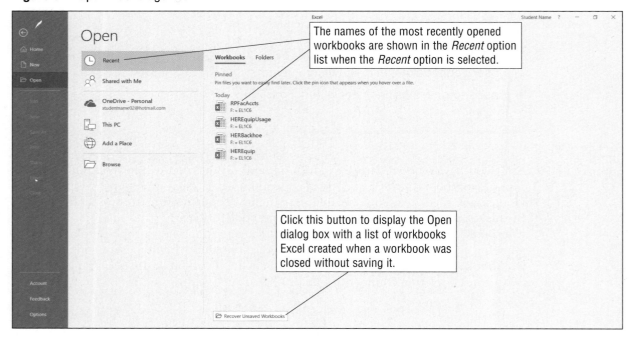

Pinning and Unpinning a Workbook

Quick Steps

Pinning/Unpinning Document
1. Click File tab.
2. Click push pin icon at right of workbook name.
OR
1. Click File tab.
2. Click *Open* option.
3. Click push pin icon at right of workbook name.

A workbook that is opened on a regular basis can be pinned to the *Recent* option list so that it can be found more easily. To pin a workbook to the *Recent* option list at the Open backstage area, hover the mouse pointer over the workbook name and then click the small left-pointing push pin icon to the right of the workbook name. The left-pointing push pin changes to a down-pointing push pin and the pinned workbook appears at the top of the list in the *Pinned* category. A workbook can also be pinned at the Home backstage area. Click the push pin icon next to a workbook name and then workbook will display in the *Pinned* tab.

To "unpin" a workbook from the *Recent* option list at the Open backstage area or the *Pinned* tab at the Home backstage area, click the push pin icon to change it from a down-pointing pin to a left-pointing pin. More than one workbook can be pinned to a list. Another method for pinning and unpinning a workbook is to use the shortcut menu. Right-click a workbook name and then click the *Pin to list* or *Unpin from list* option.

In addition to workbooks, folders can be pinned for easier access. To pin a frequently-used folder, display the Open backstage area and then click the *Folders* option. Recently opened folders are listed and grouped into categories such as *Today*, *Yesterday*, and *Last Week* to reflect the time they were last accessed. Click the push pin icon to the right of a folder and it will be pinned to the top of the list.

Recovering an Unsaved Workbook

If a workbook is closed without having been saved, it can be recovered with the Recover Unsaved Workbooks button below the *Recent* option list. Click this button and the Open dialog box displays with the names of the workbooks that Excel has saved automatically. At this dialog box, double-click the workbook name to open it.

Clearing the *Recent* Option List and the Recent List

Clear the contents (except pinned workbooks) of the *Recent* option list by right-clicking a workbook name in the list and then clicking *Clear unpinned Workbooks* at the shortcut menu. At the message asking to confirm removal of the items, click Yes. To clear a folder from the Open backstage area, right-click a folder in the list and then click *Remove from list* at the shortcut menu.

Activity 1a **Managing Workbooks at the Open Backstage Area**   Part 1 of 3

1. Open Excel.
2. Click the File tab and then click the *Open* option.
3. Make sure the *Recent* option below the heading *Open* is selected. Notice the workbook names that display in the *Recent* option list.
4. Navigate to your EL1C6 folder, open **HEREquip**, and then save it with the name **6-HEREquip**.
5. Close **6-HEREquip**.
6. Open **HEREquipUsage** and then close it.

7. Open **HERBackhoe** and then close it.
8. Pin the three workbooks to the *Recent* option list (you will use them in Activity 1b) by completing the following steps:
   a. Click the File tab and then click the *Open* option. (This displays the Open backstage area with the *Recent* option selected.)
   b. Click the left-pointing push pin icon at the right of **6-HEREquip**. (This changes the pin from left pointing to down pointing and moves the workbook to the top of the list in the *Pinned* category.)

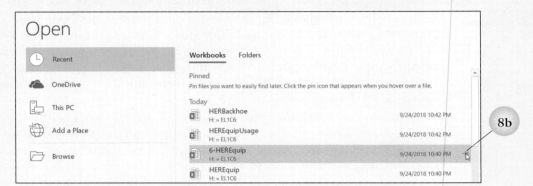

   c. Click the left-pointing push pin icon at the right of **HEREquipUsage**.
   d. Right-click *HERBackhoe* and then click *Pin to list* at the shortcut menu.
   e. Click the Back button to exit the Open backstage area.
9. Open **6-HEREquip** by clicking the File tab, clicking the *Open* option, and then clicking **6-HEREquip** in the *Recent* option list.

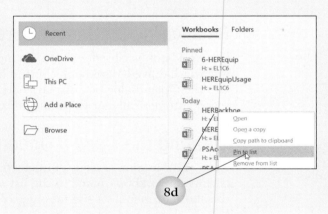

Managing Worksheets

Individual worksheets can be moved or copied within the same workbook or to another existing workbook. Exercise caution when moving sheets, since any calculations and charts based on the data in a worksheet might become inaccurate if a worksheet is moved. To duplicate a sheet in the same workbook, press and hold down the Ctrl key, click the sheet tab and hold down the left mouse button, drag to the new location, and then release the mouse button and the Ctrl key.

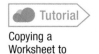

Copying a
Worksheet to
Another Workbook

Copying a Worksheet to Another Workbook

To copy a worksheet to another workbook, open both the source and the destination workbooks. Right-click the sheet tab and then click *Move or Copy* at the shortcut menu. At the Move or Copy dialog box, shown in Figure 6.2, select the name of the destination workbook in the *To book* option drop-down list, select the name of the worksheet the copied worksheet will be placed before in the *Before sheet* list box, click the *Create a copy* check box, and then click OK.

Quick Steps

Copy Worksheet to Another Workbook

1. Right-click sheet tab.
2. Click *Move or Copy*.
3. Select destination workbook.
4. Select worksheet location.
5. Click *Create a copy* check box.
6. Click OK.

Figure 6.2 Move or Copy Dialog Box

Click the name of a worksheet in this list box and the moved or copied worksheet is inserted before it.

Click this option box arrow and then click the specific workbook.

Insert a check mark in this check box to copy the worksheet.

Activity 1b Copying Worksheets to Another Workbook

Part 2 of 3

1. With **6-HEREquip** open, open **HEREquipUsage**.
2. Copy the Front Loader worksheet by completing the following steps:
   a. With **HEREquipUsage** the active workbook, right-click the Front Loader tab and then click *Move or Copy* at the shortcut menu.
   b. Click the *To book* option box arrow and then click **6-HEREquip.xlsx** at the drop-down list.
   c. Click *(move to end)* in the *Before sheet* list box.
   d. Click the *Create a copy* check box to insert a check mark.
   e. Click OK. (Excel switches to the **6-HEREquip** workbook and inserts the copied Front Loader worksheet after Sheet1.)

3. Complete steps similar to those in Step 2 to copy the Tractor worksheet to the **6-HEREquip** workbook.
4. Complete steps similar to those in Step 2 to copy the Forklift worksheet to the **6-HEREquip** workbook and insert the Forklift worksheet before the Tractor worksheet.
5. Save **6-HEREquip**.
6. Make **HEREquipUsage** the active workbook and then close it.

Check Your Work

Moving a Worksheet to Another Workbook

Quick Steps

Move Worksheet to Another Workbook
1. Right-click sheet tab.
2. Click *Move or Copy*.
3. Select destination workbook.
4. Select worksheet location.
5. Click OK.

To move a worksheet to another workbook, open both the source and the destination workbooks. Make active the worksheet to be moved in the source workbook, right-click the sheet tab, and then click *Move or Copy* at the shortcut menu. At the Move or Copy dialog box, shown in Figure 6.2 (on page 147), select the name of the destination workbook in the *To book* drop-down list, select the name of the worksheet the moved worksheet will be placed before in the *Before sheet* list box, and then click OK. To reposition a sheet tab, drag the tab to the new position.

Be careful when moving a worksheet to another workbook file. If formulas in the source workbook depend on the contents of the cells in the worksheet that is moved, they will no longer work properly.

Activity 1c Moving a Worksheet to Another Workbook

Part 3 of 3

1. With **6-HEREquip** open, open **HERBackhoe**.
2. Move Sheet1 from **HERBackhoe** to **6-HEREquip** by completing the following steps:
   a. With **HERBackhoe** the active workbook, right-click the Sheet1 tab and then click *Move or Copy* at the shortcut menu.
   b. Click the *To book* option box arrow and then click **6-HEREquip.xlsx** at the drop-down list.
   c. Click *(move to end)* in the *Before sheet* list box.
   d. Click OK.
3. With **6-HEREquip** open, make the following changes:
   a. Rename Sheet1 as *Equipment Hours*.
   b. Rename Sheet1 (2) as *Backhoe*.
4. Create a range for the front loader total hours available by completing the following steps:
   a. Click the Front Loader tab.
   b. Select the range B4:E4.
   c. Click in the Name box.
   d. Type FrontLoaderHours.
   e. Press the Enter key.
5. Complete steps similar to those in Step 4 to create the following ranges:
   a. In the Front Loader worksheet, select the range B10:E10 and name it *FrontLoaderHoursInUse*.
   b. Click the Forklift tab and then select the range B4:E4 and name it *ForkliftHours*. Also select the range B10:E10 and name it *ForkliftHoursInUse*.
   c. Click the Tractor tab and then select the range B4:E4 and name it *TractorHours*. Also select the range B10:E10 and name it *TractorHoursInUse*.
   d. Click the Backhoe tab and then select the range B4:E4 and name it *BackhoeHours*. Also select the range B10:E10 and name it *BackhoeHoursInUse*.

6. Click the Equipment Hours tab to make it the active worksheet and then insert a formula that calculates the total hours for the front loader by completing the following steps:
   a. Make cell C4 active.
   b. Type =sum(Fr.
   c. When you type *Fr*, a drop-down list displays with the front loader ranges. Double-click *FrontLoaderHours*.
   d. Type) (the closing parenthesis).

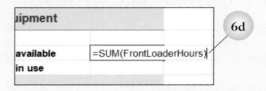

   e. Press the Enter key.
7. Complete steps similar to those in Step 6 to insert ranges in the following cells:
   a. Make cell C5 active and then insert a formula that calculates the total in-use hours for the front loader.
   b. Make cell C8 active and then insert a formula that calculates the total hours available for the forklift.
   c. Make cell C9 active and then insert a formula that calculates the total in-use hours for the forklift.
   d. Make cell C12 active and then insert a formula that calculates the total hours available for the tractor.
   e. Make cell C13 active and then insert a formula that calculates the total in-use hours for the tractor.
   f. Make cell C16 active and then insert a formula that calculates the total hours available for the backhoe.
   g. Make cell C17 active and then insert a formula that calculates the total in-use hours for the backhoe.
8. Make the following changes to specific worksheets:
   a. Click the Front Loader tab and then change the number in cell E4 from *415* to *426* and the number in cell C6 from *6* to *14*.
   b. Click the Forklift tab and then change the number in cell E4 from *415* to *426* and the number in cell D8 from *4* to *12*.
9. Select all the sheet tabs and then create a header that prints your name at the left of each worksheet, the page number in the middle, and the current date at the right.
10. Save and then print all the worksheets in **6-HEREquip**.
11. Close the workbook. (Make sure all the workbooks are closed.)
12. Make the following changes to the Open backstage area:
    a. Click the File tab and then click the *Open* option.
    b. Make sure the *Recent* option is selected.
    c. Unpin **6-HEREquip** from the *Recent* option list by clicking the down-pointing push pin icon at the right of **6-HEREquip**. (This changes the down-pointing push pin to a left-pointing push pin and moves the workbook down the list.)
    d. Unpin **HERBackhoe** and **HEREquipUsage**.
13. Click the Back button to exit the Open backstage area.

Formatting with Cell Styles

 Hint Cell styles are based on the workbook theme.

Formatting can be applied in a worksheet to highlight or accentuate certain cells. Apply formatting to a cell or selected cells with a cell style, which is a predefined set of formatting attributes, such as font, font size, alignment, borders, shading, and so forth. Excel provides a gallery of predesigned cell styles in the Styles group on the Home tab. Click the Cell Styles button to open the gallery. (On a wide-screen monitor, the gallery may already be open and some of the styles will be displayed. Click the More Styles arrow button at the right of the gallery to see all the available styles.)

 Tutorial

Applying Cell Styles

Applying a Cell Style

To apply a style, select the cell(s), click the Cell Styles button in the Styles group on the Home tab, and then click the style at the drop-down gallery, shown in Figure 6.3. Hover the mouse pointer over a style in the drop-down gallery and the cell or selected cells display with the formatting applied.

 Quick Steps

Apply Cell Style
1. Select cell(s).
2. Click Cell Styles button.
3. Click style.

Cell Styles

Figure 6.3 Cell Styles Button Drop-Down Gallery

Choose an option at this drop-down gallery to apply a predesigned style to a cell or selected cells in the worksheet.

1. Open **OEPayroll** and then save it with the name **6-OEPayroll**.
2. With Sheet1 the active worksheet, insert the necessary formulas to calculate gross pay, withholding tax amount, social security tax amount, and net pay. **Hint: Refer to Activity 3c in Chapter 2 for assistance**. Select the range D4:G4 and then click the Accounting Number Format button to insert dollar symbols.
3. Make Sheet2 active and then insert a formula that calculates the amount due. **Hint: The formula in cell F4 will be =D4*(1+E4)**. Make cell F4 active and then click the Accounting Number Format button to insert a dollar symbol.
4. Make Sheet3 active and then insert a formula in the *Due Date* column that calculates the purchase date plus the number of days in the *Terms* column. **Hint: The formula in cell F4 will be =D4+E4**.
5. Apply cell styles to cells by completing the following steps:
   a. Make Sheet1 active and then select cells A11 and A12.
   b. Click the Cell Styles button in the Styles gallery in the Styles group on the Home tab.
   c. At the drop-down gallery, hover the mouse pointer over different styles to see how the formatting affects the selected cells.
   d. Click the *Check Cell* option (second column, first row in the *Data and Model* section).
6. Select cells B11 and B12, click the Cell Styles button, and then click the *Output* option (first column, second row in the *Data and Model* section).

7. Save **6-OEPayroll**.

Tutorial

Defining a Cell Style

Quick Steps

Define Cell Style with Existing Formatting
1. Select cell containing formatting.
2. Click Cell Styles button.
3. Click *New Cell Style*.
4. Type name for new style.
5. Click OK.

Defining a Cell Style

Apply a style from the Cell Styles button drop-down gallery or create a new style. Using a style to apply formatting has several advantages. One key advantage is that it helps to ensure consistent formatting from one worksheet to another. To change the formatting, change the style and all the cells formatted with that style automatically reflect the change.

Two basic methods are available for defining a cell style. Define a style with formats already applied to a cell or display the Style dialog box, click the Format button, and then choose formatting options at the Format Cells dialog box. New styles are available only in the workbook in which they are created.

Figure 6.4 Style Dialog Box

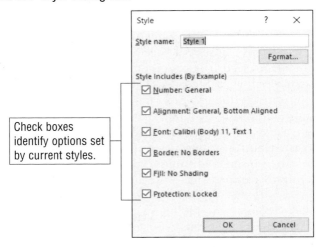

Check boxes identify options set by current styles.

To define a style with existing formatting, select the cell or cells containing the formatting, click the Cell Styles button on the Home tab, and then click the *New Cell Style* option at the bottom of the drop-down gallery. At the Style dialog box, shown in Figure 6.4, type a name for the new style in the *Style name* text box and then click OK to close the dialog box. Custom styles are shown at the top of the Cell Styles button drop-down gallery in the *Custom* section.

Activity 2b Defining and Applying a Cell Style

Part 2 of 5

1. With **6-OEPayroll** open, define a style named *C6Title* with the formatting in cell A1 by completing the following steps:
   a. Make sure Sheet1 is active and then make cell A1 active.
   b. Click the Cell Styles button in the Styles group on the Home tab and then click the *New Cell Style* option at the bottom of the drop-down gallery.

c. At the Style dialog box, type C6Title in the *Style name* text box.
d. Click OK.

2. Even though cell A1 is already formatted, the style has not been applied to it. (Later, you will modify the style and the style must be applied to the cell for the change to affect it.) Apply the C6Title style to cell A1 by completing the following steps:

a. With cell A1 active, click the Cell Styles button.
b. Click the *C6Title* style in the *Styles* gallery.

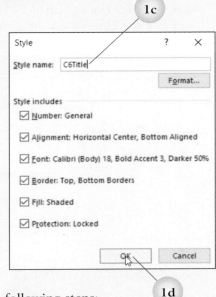

3. Apply the C6Title style to other cells by completing the following steps:
a. Click the Sheet2 tab.
b. Make cell A1 active.
c. Click the *C6Title* style at the Styles gallery. (Notice that the style does not apply row height formatting. The style applies only cell formatting.)
d. Click the Sheet3 tab.
e. Make cell A1 active.
f. Click the *C6Title* style at the Styles gallery.
g. Click the Sheet1 tab.

4. Save **6-OEPayroll**.

Check Your Work

Quick Steps

Define Cell Style
1. Click in blank cell.
2. Click Cell Styles button.
3. Click *New Cell Style*.
4. Type style name.
5. Click Format button.
6. Choose formatting options.
7. Click OK.
8. Click OK.

In addition to defining a style based on cell formatting, a custom style can be defined without first applying the formatting. To do this, display the Style dialog box, type a name for the custom style, and then click the Format button. At the Format Cells dialog box, apply the formatting and then click OK to close the dialog box. At the Style dialog box, remove the check mark from any formatting that should not be included in the style and then click OK to close the Style dialog box.

Activity 2c Defining a Cell Style without First Applying Formatting   Part 3 of 5

1. With **6-OEPayroll** open, define a custom style named *C6Subtitle* without first applying the formatting by completing the following steps:
a. With Sheet1 active, click in any empty cell.
b. Click the Cell Styles button and then click *New Cell Style* at the drop-down gallery.

c. At the Style dialog box, type C6Subtitle in the *Style name* text box.

d. Click the Format button in the Style dialog box.

e. Click the Font tab.

f. At the Format Cells dialog box with the Font tab selected, change the font to Candara, the font style to bold, the size to 12 points, and the color to White, Background 1.

g. Click the Fill tab.

h. Click the green color shown at the right (last column, fifth row).

i. Click the Alignment tab.

j. Change the horizontal alignment to center alignment.

k. Click OK to close the Format Cells dialog box.

l. Click OK to close the Style dialog box.

2. Apply the C6Subtitle custom style by completing the following steps:

a. Make cell A2 active.

b. Click the Cell Styles button and then click the *C6Subtitle* style.

c. Click the Sheet2 tab.

d. Make cell A2 active.

e. Click the Cell Styles button and then click the *C6Subtitle* style.

f. Click the Sheet3 tab.

g. Make cell A2 active.

h. Click the Cell Styles button and then click the *C6Subtitle* style.

i. Click the Sheet1 tab.

3. Apply the following predesigned cell styles:

a. With Sheet1 the active tab, select the range A3:G3.

b. Click the Cell Styles button and then click the *Heading 3* style in the *Titles and Headings* section at the drop-down gallery.

c. Select the range A5:G5.

d. Click the Cell Styles button and then click the *20% - Accent3* style.

e. Apply the 20% - Accent3 style to the range A7:G7 and the range A9:G9.

f. Click the Sheet2 tab.

g. Select the range A3:F3 and then apply the Heading 3 style.

h. Select the range A5:F5 and then apply the 20% - Accent3 style.

i. Apply the 20% - Accent3 style to every other row of cells (the range A7:F7, A9:F9, and so on, finishing with the range A17:F17).

j. Click the Sheet3 tab.

k. Select the range A3:F3 and then apply the Heading 3 style.

l. Apply the 20% - Accent3 style to the ranges A5:F5, A7:F7, and A9:F9.

4. With Sheet3 active, change the height of row 1 to 36.00 points.

5. Make Sheet2 active and then change the height of row 1 to 36.00 points.
6. Make Sheet1 active.
7. Save **6-OEPayroll** and then print only the first worksheet.

 Check Your Work

Modifying a Cell Style

 Tutorial

Modifying a Cell Style

One of the advantages to formatting cells with a style is that when the formatting is modified and all the cells formatted with that style update automatically. Modify a predesigned style and only the style in the current workbook is affected. Open a blank workbook and the cell styles available are the default styles.

To modify a style, click the Cell Styles button in the Styles group on the Home tab and then right-click the style at the drop-down gallery. At the shortcut menu, click *Modify*. At the Style dialog box, click the Format button. Make the formatting changes at the Format Cells dialog box and then click OK. Click OK to close the Style dialog box and any cells formatted with the style automatically update.

Quick Steps

Modify Cell Style
1. Click Cell Styles button.
2. Right-click style.
3. Click *Modify*.
4. Click Format button.
5. Make formatting changes.
6. Click OK.
7. Click OK.

Activity 2d **Modifying Cell Styles**   Part 4 of 5

1. With **6-OEPayroll** open, modify the C6Title custom style by completing the following steps:
   a. Click in any empty cell.
   b. Click the Cell Styles button.
   c. At the drop-down gallery, right-click the *C6Title* style in the *Custom* section and then click *Modify* at the drop-down gallery.
   d. At the Style dialog box, click the Format button.
   e. At the Format Cells dialog box, click the Font tab and then change the font to Candara.
   f. Click the Alignment tab.
   g. Click the *Vertical* option box arrow and then click *Center* at the drop-down list.
   h. Click the Fill tab.
   i. Click the light blue fill color (fifth column, third row), as shown at the right.

1c

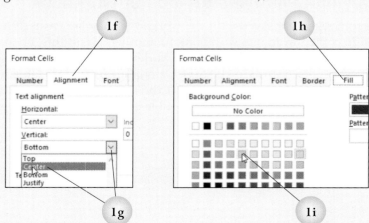
1f
1h
1g
1i

j. Click OK to close the Format Cells dialog box.

k. Click OK to close the Style dialog box.

2. Modify the C6Subtitle style by completing the following steps:

   a. Click in any empty cell.

   b. Click the Cell Styles button.

   c. At the drop-down gallery, right-click the *C6Subtitle* style in the *Custom* section and then click *Modify*.

   d. At the Style dialog box, click the Format button.

   e. At the Format Cells dialog box, click the Font tab and then change the font to Calibri.

   f. Click the Fill tab.

   g. Click the dark blue fill color, as shown at the right (fifth column, sixth row).

   h. Click OK to close the Format Cells dialog box.

   i. Click OK to close the Style dialog box.

3. Modify the predefined 20% - Accent3 style by completing the following steps:

   a. Click the Cell Styles button.

   b. At the drop-down gallery, right-click the *20% - Accent3* style and then click *Modify*.

   c. At the Style dialog box, click the Format button.

   d. At the Format Cells dialog box, click the Fill tab.

   e. Click the light blue fill color, as shown at the right (fifth column, second row).

   f. Click OK to close the Format Cells dialog box.

   g. Click OK to close the Style dialog box.

4. Click each sheet tab and notice the formatting changes made by the modified styles.

5. Change the name of Sheet1 to *Weekly Payroll*, the name of Sheet2 to *Invoices*, and the name of Sheet3 to *Overdue Accounts*.

6. Apply a different color to each of the three sheet tabs.

7. Save and then print all the worksheets in **6-OEPayroll**.

Check Your Work

 Tutorial

Copying Cell
Styles to Another
Workbook

Ǫuick Steps

**Copy Cell Styles to
Another Workbook**

1. Open workbook containing styles.
2. Open workbook to be modified.
3. Click Cell Styles button.
4. Click *Merge Styles* option.
5. Double-click name of workbook that contains styles.

Copying Cell Styles to Another Workbook

Custom styles are saved with the workbook they are created in. However, styles can be copied from one workbook to another. To do this, open the workbook containing the styles and open the workbook the styles will be copied into. Click the Cell Styles button in the Styles group on the Home tab and then click the *Merge Styles* option at the bottom of the drop-down gallery. At the Merge Styles dialog box, shown in Figure 6.5, double-click the name of the workbook that contains the styles to be copied.

Figure 6.5 Merge Styles Dialog Box

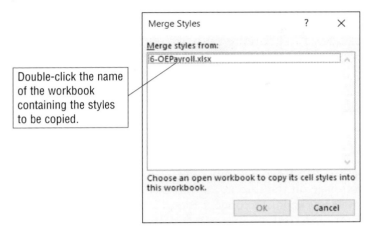

Double-click the name of the workbook containing the styles to be copied.

Removing a Cell Style

Remove formatting applied by a style by applying the Normal style, which is the default. To do this, select the cells, click the Cell Styles button, and then click the *Normal* style at the drop-down gallery.

Deleting a Cell Style

To delete a style, click the Cell Styles button in the Styles group on the Home tab. At the drop-down gallery, right-click the style to be deleted and then click *Delete* at the shortcut menu. Formatting applied by the deleted style is removed from cells in the workbook. The Normal cell style cannot be deleted.

Activity 2e **Copying Cell Styles to Another Workbook**   Part 5 of 5

1. With **6-OEPayroll** open, open **OEPlans**.
2. Save the workbook and name it **6-OEPlans**.
3. Copy the styles in **6-OEPayroll** into **6-OEPlans** by completing the following steps:
   a. With **6-OEPlans** as the active workbook, click the Cell Styles button in the Styles group on the Home tab.
   b. Click the *Merge Styles* option at the bottom of the drop-down gallery.
   c. At the Merge Styles dialog box, double-click **6-OEPayroll.xlsx** in the *Merge styles from* list box.
   d. At the message asking if you want to merge styles that have the same names, click Yes.

4. Apply the C6Title custom style to cell A1 and the C6Subtitle custom style to cell A2.
5. Increase the height of row 1 to 36.00 points.
6. Save, print, and then close **6-OEPlans**.
7. Close **6-OEPayroll**.

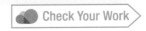
Check Your Work

You will open a facilities account workbook and then insert hyperlinks to a website, to cells in other worksheets in the workbook, and to another workbook. You will modify and edit hyperlinks and then remove a hyperlink from the workbook.

Tutorial

Inserting Hyperlinks

Quick Steps

Insert Hyperlink
1. Click Insert tab.
2. Click Link button.
3. Make changes at Insert Hyperlink dialog box.
4. Click OK.

Link

Inserting Hyperlinks

A hyperlink can serve a number of purposes in a workbook: Click it to navigate to a web page on the internet or a specific location in the workbook, to display a different workbook, to open a file in a different program, to create a new document, or to link to an email address. Create a customized hyperlink by clicking in a cell in a workbook, clicking the Insert tab, and then clicking the Link button in the Links group. This displays the Insert Hyperlink dialog box, shown in Figure 6.6. At this dialog box, identify what is to be linked and the location of the link. Click the ScreenTip button to customize the hyperlink ScreenTip.

Linking to an Existing Web Page or File

At the Insert Hyperlink dialog box, link to a web page on the internet by typing a web address or by using the Existing File or Web Page button in the *Link to* section. To link to an existing web page, type the address of the web page, such as *www.paradigmeducation.com*.

By default, the automatic formatting of hyperlinks is turned on and the web address is formatted as a hyperlink. (The text is underlined and the color changes to blue.) Turn off the automatic formatting of hyperlinks at the AutoCorrect dialog box. Display this dialog box by clicking the File tab, clicking *Options*, and then clicking *Proofing* in the left panel of the Excel Options dialog box. Click the AutoCorrect Options button to display the AutoCorrect dialog box. At this dialog

Figure 6.6 Insert Hyperlink Dialog Box

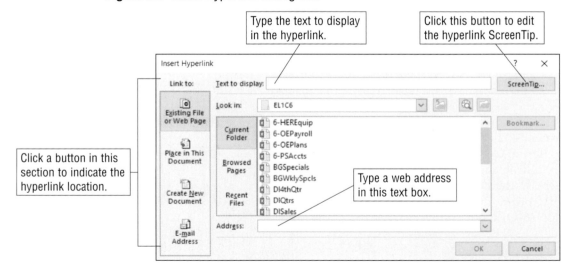

box, click the AutoFormat As You Type tab and then remove the check mark from the *Internet and network paths with hyperlinks* check box.

A hyperlink can be inserted that links to any of several sources, such as another Excel workbook, a Word document, or a PowerPoint presentation. To link an Excel workbook to a workbook or file in another application, display the Insert Hyperlink dialog box and then click the Existing File or Web Page button in the *Link to* section. Use buttons in the *Look in* section to navigate to the folder containing the file and then click the file name. Make other changes in the Insert Hyperlink dialog box as needed and then click OK.

Navigating Using Hyperlinks

Navigate to a hyperlinked location by clicking the hyperlink in the worksheet. Hover the mouse pointer over the hyperlink and a ScreenTip displays with the address of the hyperlinked location. To display specific information in the ScreenTip, click the ScreenTip button at the Insert Hyperlink dialog box, type the text in the Set Hyperlink ScreenTip dialog box, and then click OK.

Activity 3a **Linking to a Website and Another Workbook**   Part 1 of 3

1. Open **PSAccts** and then save it with the name **6-PSAccts**.
2. Insert a hyperlink to information about Pyramid Sales, a fictitious company (the hyperlink will connect to the publishing company website), by completing the following steps:
   a. Make cell A13 active in the Summary sheet.
   b. Click the Insert tab and then click the Link button in the Links group.
   c. At the Insert Hyperlink dialog box, if necessary, click the Existing File or Web Page button in the *Link to* section.
   d. Type www.paradigmeducation.com in the *Address* text box. (*http://* will automatically be added to the address)
   e. Select the text in the *Text to display* text box and then type Company information.
   f. Click the ScreenTip button in the upper right corner of the dialog box.

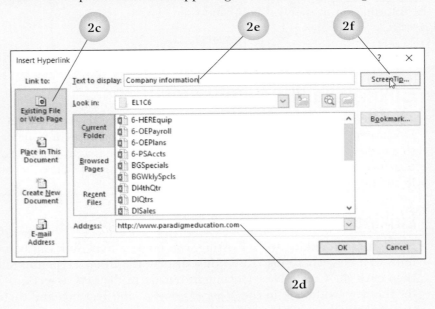

g. At the Set Hyperlink ScreenTip dialog box, type View the company website. and then click OK.

h. Click OK to close the Insert Hyperlink dialog box.

3. Navigate to the company website (in this case, the publishing company website) by clicking the <u>Company information</u> hyperlink in cell A13.

4. Close the web browser.

5. Create a link to another workbook by completing the following steps:

a. Make cell A11 active, type Semiannual sales, and then press the Enter key.

b. Make cell A11 active and then click the Link button.

c. At the Insert Hyperlink dialog box, make sure the Existing File or Web Page button is selected.

d. If necessary, click your *Look in* option box arrow and then navigate to your EL1C6 folder.

e. Double-click **PSSalesAnalysis**.

6. Click the <u>Semiannual sales</u> hyperlink to open **PSSalesAnalysis**.

7. Look at the information in the workbook and then close it.

8. Save **6-PSAccts**.

 Check Your Work

Linking to a Place in the Workbook

To create a hyperlink to another location in the workbook, click the Place in This Document button in the *Link to* section in the Edit Hyperlink dialog box. To link to a cell within the same worksheet, type the cell name in the *Type the cell reference* text box. To link to another worksheet in the workbook, click the worksheet name in the *Or select a place in this document* list box.

Linking to a New Workbook

In addition to linking to an existing workbook, a hyperlink can be inserted that links to a new workbook. To do this, display the Insert Hyperlink dialog box and then click the Create New Document button in the *Link to* section. Type a name for the new workbook in the *Name of new document* text box and then specify if the workbook will be edited now or later.

Linking Using a Graphic

A graphic—such as an image, picture, or text box—can be used to create a hyperlink to a file or website. To create a hyperlink with a graphic, select the graphic, click the Insert tab, and then click the Link button. Or right-click the graphic and then click *Link* at the shortcut menu. At the Insert Hyperlink dialog box, specify the location to be linked to and the text to display in the hyperlink.

Linking to an Email Address

At the Insert Hyperlink dialog box, a hyperlink can be inserted that links to an email address. To do this, click the E-mail Address button in the *Link to* section, type the address in the *E-mail address* text box, and then type a subject for the email in the *Subject* text box. Click in the *Text to display* text box and then type the text to display in the worksheet.

Activity 3b **Linking to a Place in a Workbook, Linking to Another Workbook, and Linking from a Graphic** Part 2 of 3

1. With **6-PSAccts** open, create a link from the balance in cell B8 to the balance in cell G20 in the January worksheet by completing the following steps:
   a. Make cell B8 active.
   b. Click the Link button.
   c. At the Insert Hyperlink dialog box, click the Place in This Document button in the *Link to* section.
   d. Select the text in the *Type the cell reference* text box and then type g20.
   e. Click *January* in the *Or select a place in this document* list box.
   f. Click OK to close the Insert Hyperlink dialog box.

2. Make cell C8 active and then complete steps similar to those in Steps 1b through 1f except click *February* in the *Or select a place in this document* list box.
3. Make cell D8 active and then complete steps similar to those in Steps 1b through 1f except click *March* in the *Or select a place in this document* list box.
4. Click the hyperlinked amount in cell B8. (This makes cell G20 active in the January worksheet.)
5. Click the Summary sheet tab.
6. Click the hyperlinked amount in cell C8. (This makes cell G20 active in the February worksheet.)
7. Click the Summary sheet tab.
8. Click the hyperlinked amount in cell D8. (This makes cell G20 active in the March worksheet.)
9. Click the Summary sheet tab.

10. Use the first pyramid graphic image in cell A1 to create a link to the company web page by completing the following steps:

   a. Right-click the first pyramid graphic image in cell A1 and then click *Link* at the shortcut menu.

   b. At the Insert Hyperlink dialog box, if necessary, click the Existing File or Web Page button in the *Link to* section.

   c. Type www.paradigmeducation.com in the *Address* text box.

   d. Click the ScreenTip button in the upper right corner of the dialog box.

   e. At the Set Hyperlink ScreenTip dialog box, type View the company website. and then click OK.

   f. Click OK to close the Insert Hyperlink dialog box.

11. Make cell A5 active.

12. Navigate to the company website (the publishing company website) by clicking the first pyramid graphic image.

13. Close the web browser.

14. Save **6-PSAccts**.

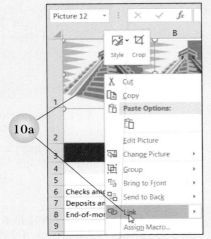

Check Your Work

Tutorial

Modifying, Editing, and Removing a Hyperlink

Modifying, Editing, and Removing a Hyperlink

The hyperlink text or destination can be modified. To do this, right-click the hyperlink and then click *Edit Hyperlink* at the shortcut menu. At the Edit Hyperlink dialog box, make changes and then close the dialog box. The same options are provided at the Edit Hyperlink dialog box as the Insert Hyperlink dialog box.

    The hyperlinked text in a cell can also be modified. To do this, make the cell active and then make the changes, such as applying a different font or font size, changing the text color, and adding a text effect. Remove a hyperlink from a workbook by right-clicking the cell containing the hyperlink and then clicking *Remove Hyperlink* at the shortcut menu.

Activity 3c **Modifying, Editing, and Removing a Hyperlink**   Part 3 of 3

1. With **6-PSAccts** open, modify the <u>Semiannual sales</u> hyperlink by completing the following steps:

   a. Position the mouse pointer on the <u>Semiannual sales</u> hyperlink in cell A11, click the right mouse button, and then click *Edit Hyperlink* at the shortcut menu.

   b. At the Edit Hyperlink dialog box, select the text *Semiannual sales* in the *Text to display* text box and then type Customer sales analysis.

    c. Click the ScreenTip button in the upper right corner of the dialog box.

    d. At the Set Hyperlink ScreenTip dialog box, type Click this hyperlink to display the workbook containing customer sales analysis.

    e. Click OK to close the Set Hyperlink ScreenTip dialog box.

    f. Click OK to close the Edit Hyperlink dialog box.

2. Click the <u>Customer sales analysis</u> hyperlink.

3. After looking at the **PSSalesAnalysis** workbook, close it.

4. With cell A11 active, edit the <u>Customer sales analysis</u> hyperlink text by completing the following steps:

    a. Click the Home tab.

    b. Click the Font Color button arrow and then click the *Dark Red* color option (first option in the *Standard Colors* section).

    c. Click the Bold button.

    d. Click the Underline button. (This removes underlining from the text.)

5. Remove the <u>Company information</u> hyperlink by right-clicking in cell A13 and then clicking *Remove Hyperlink* at the shortcut menu.

6. Press the Delete key to remove the contents of cell A13.

7. Save, print only the first worksheet (the Summary worksheet), and then close **6-PSAccts**.

Activity 4 **Create a Billing Statement Using a Template;**   **3 Parts**
Posting, Editing and Deleting Comments

You will open a Billing Statement template provided by Excel, add data, and then save the template as an Excel workbook. You will also post, edit, and delete comments in the Billing statement workbook.

Using Templates

Using Excel Templates

Excel provides a number of template worksheet forms for specific uses. Use Excel templates to create a variety of worksheets with specialized formatting, such as balance sheets, billing statements, loan amortizations, sales invoices, and time cards. Display installed templates by clicking the File tab and then clicking the *New* option. This displays the New backstage area, as shown in Figure 6.7.

Click a template in the New backstage area and a preview of the template displays in a window. Click the Create button in the template window and a workbook based on the template opens and displays on the screen.

Locations for personalized text are shown in placeholders in the worksheet. To enter information in the worksheet, position the mouse pointer (white plus symbol [+]) in the location the data is to be typed and then click the left mouse button. After typing the data, click the next location. The insertion point can also be moved to another cell using the commands learned in Chapter 1. For example, press the Tab key to make the next cell active or press Shift + Tab to make the previous cell active. If the computer is connected to the internet, a number of templates offered by Microsoft can be downloaded.

Quick Steps

Use Excel Template

1. Click File tab.
2. Click *New* option.
3. Double-click template.

Figure 6.7 New Backstage Area

> Use this option to search for templates online.

> The templates shown in this section of the New backstage area will vary from what is shown in this figure.

Activity 4a Preparing a Billing Statement Using a Template

Part 1 of 3

1. Click the File tab and then click the *New* option.
2. At the New backstage area, click in the search text box, type billing statement, and then press the Enter key.
3. Double-click the *Billing statement* template (see image below). If you are unable to access online templates, open the **BillingStatement** file in your EL1C6 folder.

4. Make cell B1 active and then type IN-FLOW SYSTEMS.
5. Click in the cell to the right of *Street Address* (cell C2) and then type 320 Milander Way.

6. Click in each of the cells for the labels specified below and then type the text indicated:

    Address 2 (cell C3): P.O. Box 2300
    City, ST ZIP Code (cell C4): Boston, MA 02188
    Phone (cell G2): (617) 555-3900
    Fax (cell G3): (617) 555-3945
    E-mail (cell G4): inflow@ppi-edu.net
    Statement # (cell C6): 5432
    Date (cell C7): =TODAY()
    Customer ID (cell C8): 25-345
    Name (cell G6): Aidan Mackenzie
    Company Name (cell G7): Stanfield Enterprises
    Street Address (cell G8): 9921 South 42nd Avenue
    Address 2 (cell G9): P.O. Box 5540
    City, ST ZIP Code (cell G10): Boston, MA 02193
    Type (cell C13): System Unit
    Invoice # (cell D13): 7452
    Description (cell E13): Calibration Unit
    Amount (cell F13): 950
    Payment (cell G13): 200
    Customer Name (cell C22): Stanfield Enterprises
    Amount Enclosed (cell C27): 750

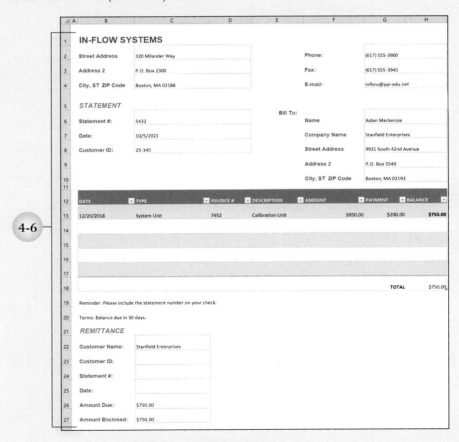

7. Save the completed invoice and name it **6-Billing**.

Tutorial

Inserting, Editing, and Printing Comments

Inserting and Managing Comments

Excel includes a comment feature that allows users to post, edit, reply, and delete comments. A comment is a pop-up box that is attached to a cell and contains text pertaining to the contents of the cell, as shown in Figure 6.8. Other users can post replies to a comment, starting a dialog between users to assist in reviewing a workbook. A cell that contains a comment will show a colored comment icon in the upper right corner of a cell, alerting the reader that a comment exists. Display a comment by hovering the mouse over the cell that contains a comment. Insert and manage comments with buttons in the Comments group on the Review tab, a shown in Firgure 6.9

Inserting a New Comment

New Comment

Insert a new comment in a cell by first making the desired cell active and then clicking the New Comment button in the Comments group on the Review tab. When a new comment is inserted, a comment pop-up box will appear, with the insertion point in a text box. Type the comment in the text box that is regarding the contents of the cell.

A new comment can also be inserted using the shortcut menu. Insert a new comment using the shortcut menu by right-clicking a cell and then clicking the *New Comment* option on the shortcut menu.

Quick Steps

Insert New Comment
1. Click in cell.
2. Click Review tab.
3. Click New Comment button.
4. Type comment.
OR
1. Right-click cell.
2. Click *New Comment* option.
3. Type comment.

Posting a Comment

Once a comment is typed into the text box of the comment pop-up box, click the Post button to post the comment. Once a comment has been posted, other users can reply to it and additional comments can be added to the worksheet.

Figure 6.8 Comment Box

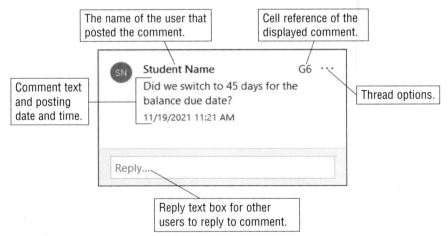

The name of the user that posted the comment.

Cell reference of the displayed comment.

Comment text and posting date and time.

Thread options.

Student Name   G6 ···

Did we switch to 45 days for the balance due date?
11/19/2021 11:21 AM

Reply...

Reply text box for other users to reply to comment.

Figure 6.9 Review Tab

1. With 6-Billing open, insert a new comment by completing the following steps:
   a. Make cell C3 active.
   b. Click the Review tab.
   c. Click the New Comment button in the Comments group.

   d. Type Please enter the new P.O. Box for the Billing department here.
   e. Click the Post button.
2. Insert a new comment indicating that the contact person for Stanfield Enterprises has changed by completing the following steps:
   a. Right-click cell G6.
   b. Click the *New Comment* option at the shortcut menu.
   c. Type Check with Stanfield Enterprises to learn the name of their new contact person.
   d. Click the Post button.

3. Insert a new comment about the payment amount by completing the following steps:
   a. Click in cell G13.
   b. Click the New Comment button.
   c. Type Ask Roger if this is the correct payment previously sent by Stanfield Enterprises.
   d. Click the Post button.
4. Insert a new comment about the balance due by completing the following steps:
   a. Click in cell B20.
   b. Click the New Comment button.
   c. Type Did we switch to 45 days for the balance due date?
   d. Click the Post button.
5. Save **6-Billing**.

Editing and Deleting a Comment

After a comment has been posted, it can be edited by using the Edit button in the comment box. Click in a cell that contains a posted comment and then position the mouse pointer anywhere inside the comment box and an Edit button appears in the lower right corner of the comment box. Click the Edit button and then use the mouse and keyboard to make edits to the comment text.

 Delete

  If a comment is no longer needed or has been entered in the wrong cell, delete it using the Delete button in the Comment group on the Review tab or using the *Delete Comment* option at the shortcut menu. All comments in a thread can be deleted by clicking the Thread options button (shown as three dots in the upper right corner of the comment box) and then clicking the *Delete thread* option at the drop-down list.

Viewing and Managing Comments at the Comments Task Pane

 Show
Comments

Quick Steps

Open Comments Task Pane
1. Click Review tab.
2. Click Show Comments button.

In a large worksheet, locating every cell that contains a comment may be difficult. To view all comments at a glance, open the Comments task pane, as shown in figure 6.10. Open the Comments task pane by clicking the Show Comments button in the Comments group on the Review tab. Comments will appear in the Comments task pane in order first by row number, then by column letter. Comments can be edited, deleted and replied to in the Comments task pane. If a worksheet contains more comments than can be shown at one time in the Comments task pane, a scroll bar is added to the task pane. Close the Comments task pane by clicking the Close button in the task pane or by clicking the Show Comments button.

Figure 6.10 Comments task pane

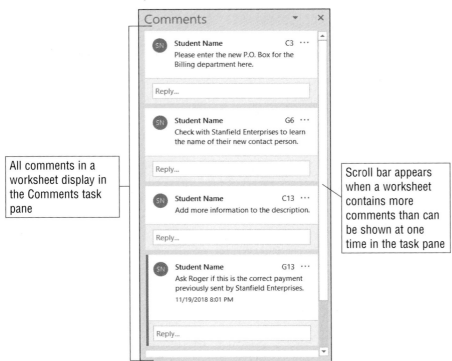

All comments in a worksheet display in the Comments task pane

Scroll bar appears when a worksheet contains more comments than can be shown at one time in the task pane

1. With 6-Billing open, edit the comment in cell G6 by completing the following steps:
   a. Click in cell G6.
   b. Position the mouse pointer anywhere in the Comment box.
   c. Click the Edit button.
   d. Move the insertion point to just before the period, press the spacebar, and then type in the Accounts department.
   e. Click the Save button.
2. Click the Show Comments button in the Comments group.
3. With the Comments task pane displayed, edit the comment in cell G13 by completing the following steps:
   a. Click the comment box with the cell reference G13 in the upper right corner.
   b. Click the Edit button.
   c. Change the text *Roger* to *Richard*.
   d. Click the Save button.
4. Click the first comment box in the Comments task pane and then click the Delete button in the Comments group.
5. Change the settings in the Page Setup dialog box in order to print the comments by completing the following steps:
   a. Click the Page Layout tab.
   b. Click the Page Setup group dialog box launcher.
   c. At the Page Setup dialog box, click the Sheet tab.
   d. Click the Comments option box arrow and then click *At end of sheet* at the drop-down list.

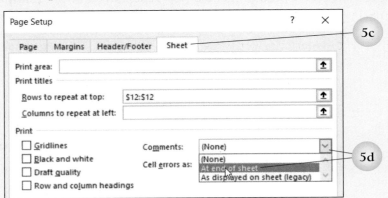

   e. Click OK.
6. Click the Close button in the Comments task pane.
7. Save, print, and then close **6-Billing**.

You will use the PMT financial function to calculate payments and the FV financial function to find the future value of an investment.

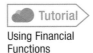

Using Financial
Functions

Writing Formulas with Financial Functions

Excel provides a number of financial functions that can be used in formulas. Use financial functions to determine different aspects of a financial loan or investment, such as the payment amount, present value, future value, interest rate, and number of payment periods. Each financial function requires some of the variables listed below to return a result. Two such financial functions are the PMT function and FV function. The PMT function calculates the payment for a loan based on constant payments and a constant interest rate. The FV function calculates the future value of an investment. Financial functions use some of the following arguments:

- **Rate:** The rate is the interest rate for a payment period. The rate may need to be modified for the function to produce the desired results. For example, most rate values are given as an APR (annual percentage rate), which is the percentage rate for one year, not a payment period. So a percentage rate may be given as 12% APR but if the payment period is a month, then the percentage rate for the function is 1%, not 12%. If a worksheet contains the annual percentage rate, enter the cell reference in the function argument and specify that it should be divided by 12 months. For example, if cell B6 contains the annual interest rate, enter *b6/12* as the Rate argument.

- **Nper:** The Nper is the number of payment periods in an investment. The Nper may also need to be modified depending on what information is provided. For example, if a loan duration is expressed in years but the payments are made monthly, the Nper value needs to be adjusted accordingly. A five-year loan has an Nper of 60 (five years times 12 months in each year).

- **Pmt:** The Pmt is the payment amount for each period. This argument describes the payment amount for a period and is commonly expressed as a negative value because it is an outflow of cash. However, the Pmt value can be entered as a positive value if the present value (Pv) or future value (Fv) is entered as a negative value. Whether the Pmt value is positive or negative depends on who created the workbook. For example, a home owner lists the variable as outflow, while the lending institution lists it as inflow.

- **Pv:** The Pv is the present value of an investment, expressed in a lump sum. The Pv argument is generally the initial loan amount. For example, if a person is purchasing a new home, the Pv is the amount of money he or she borrowed to buy the home. Pv can be expressed as a negative value, which denotes it as an investment instead of a loan. For example, if a bank issues a loan to a home buyer, it enters the Pv value as negative because it is an outflow of cash.

- **Fv:** The Fv is the future value of an investment, expressed in a lump sum amount. The Fv argument is generally the loan amount plus the amount of interest paid during the loan. In the example of a home buyer, the Fv is the sum of payments, which includes both the principle and interest paid on the loan. In the example of a bank, the Fv is the total amount received after a loan has been paid off. Fv can also be expressed as either a positive or negative value, depending on which side of the transaction is being reviewed.

Finding the Periodic Payments for a Loan

The PMT function finds the payment for a loan based on constant payments and a constant interest rate. In Activity 5a, the PMT function will be used to determine monthly payments for equipment and a used van as well as monthly income from selling equipment. The formulas created with the PMT function will include Rate, Nper, and Pv arguments. The Nper argument is the number of payments that will be made on the loan or investment, Pv is the current value of amounts to be received or paid in the future, and Fv is the value of the loan or investment at the end of all periods.

 Financial

To write the PMT function, click the Formulas tab, click the Financial button in the Function Library group, and then click the PMT function at the drop-down list. This displays the Function Arguments dialog box with options for inserting cell designations for Rate, Nper, and Pv. (These are the arguments displayed in bold formatting in the Function Arguments dialog box. The dialog box also contains the Fv and Type functions, which are dimmed.)

Activity 5a Calculating Payments

Part 1 of 2

1. Open **RPReports** and then save it with the name **6-RPReports**.
2. The owner of Real Photography is interested in purchasing a new developer and needs to determine monthly payments on three different models. Insert a formula that calculates monthly payments and then copy that formula by completing the following steps:
   a. Make cell E5 active.
   b. Click the Formulas tab.
   c. Click the Financial button in the Function Library group, scroll down the drop-down list, and then click *PMT*.

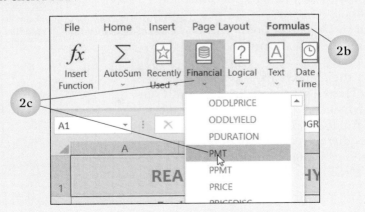

d. At the Function Arguments dialog box, type c5/12 in the *Rate* text box. (This tells Excel to divide the interest rate by 12 months.)

e. Press the Tab key. (This moves the insertion point to the *Nper* text box.)

f. Type d5. (This is the total number of months for the investment.)

g. Press the Tab key. (This moves the insertion point to the *Pv* text box.)

h. Type b5. (This is the purchase price of the developer.)

i. Click OK. (This closes the dialog box and inserts the monthly payment of *($316.98)* in cell E5. Excel shows the result of the PMT function as a negative number since the loan represents money going out of the company—a negative cash flow.)

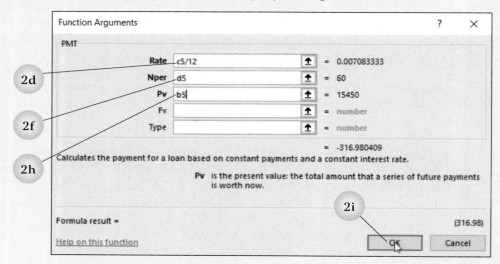

j. Copy the formula in cell E5 into cells E6 and E7.

3. The owner is interested in purchasing a used van for the company and wants an idea of what monthly payments would be at various terms and rates. Insert a formula that calculates monthly payments for a three-year loan at 5% interest by completing the following steps:

a. Make cell E12 active.

b. Make sure the Formulas tab is active.

c. Click the Financial button, scroll down the drop-down list, and then click *PMT*.

d. At the Function Arguments dialog box, type c12/12 in the *Rate* text box. (This tells Excel to divide the interest rate by 12 months.)

e. Press the Tab key.

f. Type d12 in the *Nper* text box. (This is the total number of months for the investment.)

g. Press the Tab key.

h. Type b12 in the *Pv* text box.

i. Click OK. (This closes the dialog box and inserts the monthly payment of *($299.71)* in cell E12.)

j. Copy the formula in cell E12 to the range E13:E15.

Term in Months	Monthly Payments
36	($299.71)
36	($449.56)
36	($599.42)
36	($749.27)

3j

4. The owner has discovered that the interest rate for a used van will be 6.25% instead of 5%. Change the percentages in the range C12:C15 to 6.25%.

5. The owner is selling a camera and wants to determine the monthly payments for a two-year loan at 4.5% interest. Determine monthly payments on the camera (income to Real Photography) by completing the following steps:
   a. Make cell E20 active.
   b. Make sure the Formulas tab is active.
   c. Click the Financial button, scroll down the drop-down list, and then click *PMT*.
   d. At the Function Arguments dialog box, type c20/12 in the *Rate* text box.
   e. Press the Tab key.
   f. Type d20 in the *Nper* text box.
   g. Press the Tab key.
   h. Type -b20 in the *Pv* text box. (Enter the *Pv* cell reference preceded by a hyphen because the sale of the camera represents an outflow of an asset. Excel displays the result of the PMT function as a positive number since the camera payments represent a positive cash inflow.)
   i. Click OK. (This closes the dialog box and inserts the monthly income of *$185.92* in cell E20.)
6. Save, print, and then close **6-RPReports**.

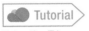
Tutorial

Finding the Future Value of a Series of Payments

Using the FV Function to Find the Future Value of an Investment

The FV function calculates the future value of a series of equal payments or an annuity. Use this function to determine information such as how much money can be earned in an investment account with a specific interest rate and over a specific period of time.

Activity 5b Finding the Future Value of an Investment

Part 2 of 2

1. Open **RPInvest** and then save it with the name **6-RPInvest**.
2. The owner of Real Photography has decided to save the money needed to purchase a new developer and wants to compute how much money can be earned by investing in an investment account that returns 7.5% annual interest. The owner determines that $1,200 per month can be invested in the account for three years. Complete the following steps to determine the future value of the investment account:
   a. Make cell B6 active.
   b. Click the Formulas tab.
   c. Click the Financial button in the Function Library group.
   d. At the drop-down list, scroll down the list and then click *FV*.
   e. At the Function Arguments dialog box, type b3/12 in the *Rate* text box.
   f. Press the Tab key.
   g. Type b4 in the *Nper* text box.
   h. Press the Tab key.
   i. Type b5 in the *Pmt* text box.
   j. Click OK. (This closes the dialog box and also inserts the future value of *$48,277.66* in cell B6.)
3. Save and then print **6-RPInvest**.
4. The owner decides to determine the future return after two years. To do this, change the amount in cell B4 from *36* to *24* and then press the Enter key. (This recalculates the future investment amount in cell B6.)
5. Save, print, and then close **6-RPInvest**.

Chapter Summary

- Pin a frequently used workbook at the *Recent* options list at the Open backstage area or at the Home backstage area.

- Pinned workbooks will remain at the Open backstage area in the *Recent* options list or at the Home backstage area until unpinned.

- To move or copy a worksheet to another existing workbook, open both the source workbook and the destination workbook and then open the Move or Copy dialog box.

- Use options from the Cell Styles button drop-down gallery to apply predesigned styles to a cell or selected cells.

- Automate the formatting of cells in a workbook by defining and then applying cell styles. A style is a predefined set of formatting attributes.

- Define a cell style with formats already applied to a cell or display the Style dialog box, click the Format button, and then choose formatting options at the Format Cells dialog box.

- To apply a style, select the desired cell or cells, click the Cell Styles button in the Styles group on the Home tab, and then click the style at the drop-down gallery.

- Modify a style and all the cells to which it is applied update automatically. To modify a style, click the Cell Styles button in the Styles group on the Home tab, right-click the style, and then click *Modify* at the shortcut menu.

- Custom styles are saved in the workbook they are created in but can be copied to another workbook. Do this with options at the Merge Styles dialog box.

- Remove any new style formatting in a cell by applying the Normal style to the cell.

- Delete cell styles at the Cell Styles drop-down gallery by right-clicking a style and then clicking *Delete*.

- With options at the Insert Hyperlink dialog box, create a hyperlink to a web page, another workbook, a location within a workbook, a new workbook, or an email address. Or create a hyperlink using a graphic.

- Hyperlinks can be modified, edited, and removed.

- Excel provides templates for creating forms. Search for and download templates at the New backstage area.

- Templates contain unique areas called placeholders where information is entered at the keyboard. These areas vary depending on the template.

- Comments are a feature that allows users to provide commentary on a specific cell.

- A comment must be posted before another comment is created or before another user replies to the comment.

- Display all of the comments in a worksheet by opening the Comments task pane.

- Financial functions are available in Excel that calculate an aspect of a financial loan or investment.

- Financial functions generally use Nper, FV, PV, and Pmt as function arguments.

- Use the PMT function to determine the payments on a loan or investment.

- Use the FV function to determine the future value on a loan or investment.

Commands Review

FEATURE	RIBBON TAB, GROUP/OPTION	BUTTON, OPTION	KEYBOARD SHORTCUT
cell styles	Home, Styles		
delete comment	Review, *Comments*		
financial functions	Financial, Function Library		
Insert Hyperlink dialog box	Insert, Links		Ctrl + K
Merge Styles dialog box	Home, Styles	, *Merge Styles*	
New backstage area	File, *New*		
new comment	Review, *Comments*		
Open backstage area	File, *Open*		Ctrl + O
show comments	Review, *Comments*		
Style dialog box	Home, Styles	, *New Cell Style*	

Microsoft®

Excel®

Creating Charts and Inserting Formulas

Performance Objectives

Upon successful completion of Chapter 7, you will be able to:

1   Create a chart with data in an Excel worksheet

2   Size, move, edit, format, and delete charts

3   Print a selected chart and print a worksheet containing a chart

4   Change a chart design

5   Change a chart location

6   Insert, move, size, and delete chart elements and shapes

7   Use the Quick Analysis feature

8   Format a chart at a task pane

9   Write formulas with the IF logical function

In previous chapters, you learned how to create and format worksheets in Excel to display and organize data. While a worksheet does an adequate job of representing data, some data are better represented visually with a chart. A chart, which is sometimes referred to as a *graph*, is a picture of numeric data. In this chapter, you will learn to create and customize charts in Excel. You will also learn how to write formulas using logical functions.

 Data Files

Before beginning chapter work, copy the EL1C7 folder to your storage medium and then make EL1C7 the active folder.

The online course includes additional training and assessment resources.

Creating Charts

Creating a Chart

To provide a visual representation of data, consider inserting data in a chart. Use buttons in the Charts group on the Insert tab to create a variety of charts, such as a column chart, line chart, pie chart, and much more. Excel provides 17 basic chart types, as described in Table 7.1.

Table 7.1 Types of Charts

Chart	Description
Column	Displays values in vertical bars; useful for comparing items or showing how values vary over time.
Line	Shows trends and overall change across time at even intervals. Emphasizes the rate of change across time rather than the magnitude of change.
Pie	Shows proportions and the relationship of the parts to the whole.
Bar	Shows individual figures at a specific time or shows variations between components but not in relationship to the whole.
Area	Similar to a line chart, but with the area below the line filled in. Emphasizes the magnitude of change over time.
X Y (Scatter)	Shows the relationships among numeric values in several data series or plots the interception points between x and y values. Shows uneven intervals of data and is commonly used for scientific data.
Map	Compares values and shows categories across geographical regions.
Stock	Shows four values for a stock: open, high, low, and close.
Surface	Shows trends in values across two dimensions in a continuous curve.
Radar	Emphasizes differences and amounts of change over time as well as variations and trends. Each category has a value axis radiating from the center point. Lines connect all values in the same series.
Treemap	Provides a hierarchical view of data and compares proportions within the hierarchy.
Sunburst	Displays hierarchical data. Each level is represented by one ring; the innermost ring is the top of the hierarchy.
Histogram	Condenses a data series into a visual representation by grouping data points into logical ranges called *bins*.

continues

Table 7.1 Types of Charts—*continued*

Chart	Description
Box & Whisker	Displays medians, quartiles, and extremes of a data set on a number line to show the distribution of data. Lines extending vertically are called *whiskers* and indicate variability outside the upper and lower quartiles.
Waterfall	Illustrates how an initial value is affected by a series of positive and negative values.
Funnel	Shows values over multiple stages in a process; typically, the values decrease, making the shape of the chart resemble a funnel.
Combo	Combines two or more chart types to make data easy to understand.

Quick Steps

Create Chart
1. Select cells.
2. Click Insert tab.
3. Click chart button.
4. Click chart style.

Recommended Charts

To create a chart, select the cells in the worksheet to be charted, click the Insert tab, and then click a specific chart button in the Charts group. At the drop-down gallery, click a specific chart style. Excel will make a recommendation on the type of chart that will best illustrate the data. To let Excel recommend a chart, select the data, click the Insert tab, and then click the Recommended Charts button. This displays the data in a chart in the Insert Chart dialog box. Customize the recommended chart with options in the left panel of the dialog box. Click the OK button to insert the recommended chart in the worksheet. Another method for inserting a recommended chart is to use the keyboard shortcut Alt + F1.

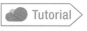
Tutorial

Resizing, Positioning, and Moving Charts

Sizing and Moving a Chart

By default, a chart is inserted in the same worksheet as the selected cells. Figure 7.1 shows the worksheet and chart that will be created in Activity 1a. The chart is inserted in a box, which can be sized or moved within the worksheet.

Figure 7.1 Activity 1a Chart

Change the size of the chart using the sizing handles (white circles) on the chart borders. Drag the top-middle and bottom-middle sizing handles to increase or decrease the height of the chart; use the left-middle and right-middle sizing handles to increase or decrease the width; and use the corner sizing handles to increase or decrease the height and width at the same time. To increase or decrease the size of the chart but maintain its proportions, press and hold down the Shift key while dragging one of the chart's corner borders.

To move the chart, make sure it is selected (a border with sizing handles appears around the chart), position the mouse pointer on a border until the pointer displays with a four-headed arrow attached, click and hold down the left mouse button, drag to the new position, and then release the mouse button.

Editing Chart Data

Editing Data and Adding a Data Series

The cells selected to create a chart are linked to it. To change the data for a chart, edit the data in the specific cells and the corresponding sections of the chart update automatically. If data is added to cells within the range of cells used for the chart, called the *source data*, the new data will be included in the chart. If a data series is added in cells next to or below the source data, click in the chart to display the source data with sizing handles and then drag with a sizing handle to include the new data.

Activity 1a Creating a Chart   Part 1 of 3

1. Open **SalesChart** and then save it with the name **7-SalesChart**.
2. Select the range A1:E4.
3. Let Excel recommend a chart type by completing the following steps:
   a. Click the Insert tab.
   b. Click the Recommended Charts button in the Charts group.

c. At the Insert Chart dialog box, look at the options in the left panel and then click OK.
4. Slightly increase the size of the chart and maintain its proportions by completing the following steps:
   a. Position the mouse pointer on the sizing handle in the lower right corner of the chart border until the pointer turns into a two-headed arrow pointing diagonally.
   b. Press and hold down the Shift key and then click and hold down the left mouse button.

c. Drag out approximately 0.5 inch. Release the mouse button and then release the Shift key.

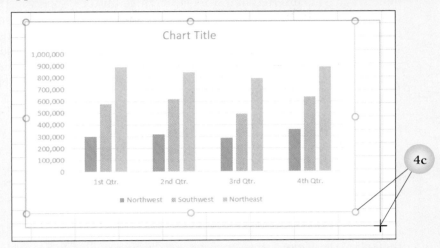

5. Move the chart below the cells containing data by completing the following steps:
   a. Make sure the chart is selected. (When the chart is selected, the border surrounding it displays with sizing handles.)
   b. Position the mouse pointer on the chart border until the pointer displays with a four-headed arrow attached.
   c. Click and hold down the left mouse button, drag the chart to row 6 below the cells containing data, and then release the mouse button.

	A	B	C	D	E
1	Region	1st Qtr.	2nd Qtr.	3rd Qtr.	4th Qtr.
2	Northwest	300,560	320,250	287,460	360,745
3	Southwest	579,290	620,485	490,125	635,340
4	Northeast	890,355	845,380	795,460	890,425
5					
6			Chart Title		
7					
8	1,000,000				

5c

6. Make the following changes to the specified cells:
   a. Make cell B2 active and then change *300,560* to *421,720*.
   b. Make cell D2 active and then change *287,460* to *397,460*.
7. Add a new data series by typing data in the following cells:

   A5   Southeast
   B5   290,450
   C5   320,765
   D5   270,450
   E5   300,455

8. Add the new data series to the chart by completing the following steps:
   a. Click in a blank area of the chart. (This selects the data source, which is the range A1:E4.)
   b. Position the mouse pointer on the sizing handle in the lower right corner of cell E4 until the pointer displays as a two-headed diagonally pointing arrow.
   c. Click and hold down the left mouse button, drag down into cell E5, and then release the mouse button. (This incorporates data row 5 in the chart.)
9. Save **7-SalesChart**.

4	Northeast	890,355	845,380	795,460	890,425
5	Southeast	290,450	320,765	270,450	300,455
6					
7			Chart Title		
8	1,000,000				

8c

Check Your Work

Formatting with Chart Buttons

When a chart is inserted in a worksheet, three buttons appear at the right of the chart border. Click the top button, Chart Elements, and a side menu displays chart elements, as shown in Figure 7.2. The check boxes containing check marks indicate the elements that are currently part of the chart. Add a new element to the chart by inserting a check mark in the check box for that element and remove an element by removing the check mark. Remove the Chart Elements side menu by clicking one of the other chart buttons or by clicking the Chart Elements button.

Excel offers a variety of chart styles that can be applied to a chart. Click the Chart Styles button at the right of the chart and a side menu gallery of styles displays, as shown in Figure 7.3. Scroll down the gallery, hover the mouse pointer over a style option, and the style formatting is applied to the chart. Click the chart style that applies the desired formatting. Remove the Chart Styles side menu gallery by clicking one of the other chart buttons or by clicking the Chart Styles button.

In addition to offering a variety of chart styles, the Chart Styles button side menu gallery offers a variety of chart colors. Click the Chart Styles button and then click the Color tab to the right of the Style tab. Click a color option at the color palette. Hover the mouse pointer over a color option to view how the color change affects the elements in the chart.

Use the bottom button, Chart Filters, to isolate specific data in the chart. Click the button and a side menu displays, as shown in Figure 7.4. Specify the series or categories to display in the chart. To do this, remove the check marks from those elements that should not appear in the chart. After removing the specific check marks, click the Apply button at the bottom of the side menu. Click the Names tab at the Chart Filters button side menu and options display for turning on/off the display of column and row names.

Chart
Elements

Chart Styles

Chart Filters

Figure 7.2 Chart Elements Button Side Menu

Figure 7.3 Chart Styles Button Side Menu Gallery

Click the Chart Elements button to display this side menu. Add or remove chart elements by inserting or removing check marks from check boxes.

Chart Elements
- Axes
- Axis Titles
- Chart Title
- Data Labels
- Data Table
- Error Bars
- Gridlines
- Legend
- Trendline

Click the Chart Styles button to display this side menu gallery of chart style options.

Figure 7.4 Chart Filters Button Side Menu

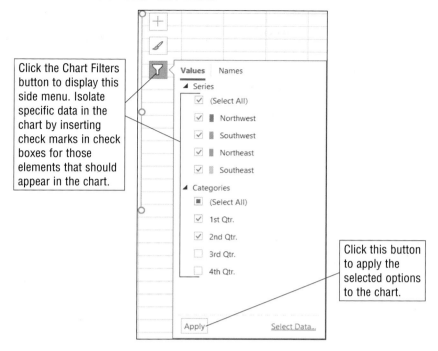

Click the Chart Filters button to display this side menu. Isolate specific data in the chart by inserting check marks in check boxes for those elements that should appear in the chart.

Click this button to apply the selected options to the chart.

Activity 1b Formatting with Chart Buttons

Part 2 of 3

1. With **7-SalesChart** open, make the chart active by clicking inside it but outside any elements.
2. Insert and remove chart elements by completing the following steps:
   a. Click the Chart Elements button outside the upper right corner of the chart.
   b. At the side menu, click the *Chart Title* check box to remove the check mark.
   c. Click the *Data Table* check box to insert a check mark.
   d. Hover the mouse pointer over *Gridlines* in the Chart Elements button side menu and then click the right-pointing triangle.
   e. At the side menu, click the *Primary Major Vertical* check box to insert a check mark.

   f. Click the *Legend* check box to remove the check mark.

3. Apply a different chart style by completing the following steps:
   a. Click the Chart Styles button outside the upper right corner of the chart (immediately below the Chart Elements button). (Clicking the Chart Styles button removes the Chart Elements button side menu.)
   b. At the side menu gallery, click the *Style 3* option (third option in the gallery).
4. Display only the first-quarter and second-quarter sales by completing the following steps:
   a. Click the Chart Filters button outside the upper right corner of the chart (immediately below the Chart Styles button). (Clicking the Chart Filters button removes the Chart Styles button side menu gallery.)
   b. Click the *3rd Qtr.* check box in the *Categories* section to remove the check mark.
   c. Click the *4th Qtr.* check box in the *Categories* section to remove the check mark.
   d. Click the Apply button at the bottom of the side menu.
   e. Click the Chart Filters button to remove the side menu.

5. Save **7-SalesChart**.

 Tutorial

Printing a Chart

Printing a Chart

In a worksheet containing data in cells and in a chart, print only the chart by selecting it, displaying the Print backstage area, and then clicking the Print button. With the chart selected, the first gallery in the *Settings* category automatically changes to *Print Selected Chart*. A preview of the chart is shown at the right side of the Print backstage area.

1. With **7-SalesChart** open, make sure the chart is selected.
2. Click the File tab and then click the *Print* option.
3. At the Print backstage area, look at the preview of the chart in the preview area and notice that the first gallery in the *Settings* category is set to *Print Selected Chart*.
4. Click the Print button.
5. Save and then close **7-SalesChart**.

Check Your Work

Activity 2 **Create a Department Expenditures Bar Chart and Column Chart**   **2 Parts**

You will open a workbook containing expenditure data by department and then create a bar chart with the data. You will then change the chart type, layout, and style; add chart elements; and move the chart to a new worksheet.

 Tutorial

Changing Chart Design

Changing the Chart Design

Along with the buttons at the upper right corner of the chart, buttons and options on the Chart Tools Design tab can be used to apply formatting to change the chart design. This tab, shown in Figure 7.5, appears when a chart is inserted in a worksheet or a chart is selected. Use buttons and options on the tab to add chart elements, change the chart type, specify a different layout or style for the chart, and change the location of the chart so it appears in a separate worksheet.

Figure 7.5 Chart Tools Design Tab

Changing the Chart Style

Quick Steps

Change Chart Type and Style
1. Make chart active.
2. Click Chart Tools Design tab.
3. Click Change Chart Type button.
4. Click chart type.
5. Click chart style.
6. Click OK.

Change Chart Type

Excel offers a variety of custom charts and varying styles for each chart type. A chart style was applied to a chart in Activity 1b using the Chart Styles button outside the right border of the chart. The style of a chart can also be changed with options in the Chart Styles group on the Chart Tools Design tab. To do this, click a chart style in the Chart Styles group or click the More Chart Styles button and then click the desired chart style.

Another method for applying a chart style is to use options at the Change Chart Type dialog box. Display this dialog box by clicking the Change Chart Type button in the Type group. The dialog box displays with the All Charts tab selected, as shown in Figure 7.6. Click a chart type in the left panel of the dialog box, click the chart style in the row of options at the top right, and then click a specific chart layout below the row of styles. Click the Recommended Charts tab to display chart styles recommended for the data by Excel.

Switching Rows and Columns

Switch Row/Column

Quick Steps

Switch Rows and Columns
1. Make chart active.
2. Click Chart Tools Design tab.
3. Click Switch Row/ Column button.

When creating a chart, Excel uses row headings for grouping data along the bottom of the chart (the horizontal axis) and column headings for the legend (the area of a chart that identifies the data in the chart). Change this order by clicking the Switch Row/Column button in the Data group on the Chart Tools Design tab. Click this button and Excel uses the column headings to group data along the horizontal axis and the row headings for the legend.

Figure 7.6 Change Chart Type Dialog Box

1. Open **DIDeptExp** and then save it with the name **7-DIDeptExp**.
2. Create a bar chart by completing the following steps:
   a. Select the range A3:G9.
   b. Click the Insert tab.
   c. Click the Insert Column or Bar Chart button in the Charts group.
   d. Click the *3-D Clustered Bar* option (first option in the *3-D Bar* section).
3. With the Chart Tools Design tab active, change the chart type by completing the following steps:
   a. Click the Change Chart Type button in the Type group.
   b. At the Change Chart Type dialog box, click the *Column* option in the left panel.
   c. Click the *3-D Clustered Column* option in the top row (fourth option from left).
   d. Click OK to close the Change Chart Type dialog box.
4. With the chart selected and the Chart Tools Design tab active, click the Switch Row/Column button in the Data group.

5. Save **7-DIDeptExp**.

Check Your Work

Changing Chart Layout and Colors

 Quick Layout

Change Colors

The Chart Tools Design tab contains options for changing the chart layout and chart colors. Click the Quick Layout button in the Chart Layouts group and a drop-down gallery of layout options displays. Hover the mouse pointer over a layout option and the chart reflects the layout. Change the colors used in the chart by clicking the Change Colors button in the Chart Styles group and then clicking a color option at the drop-down gallery.

Changing the Chart Location

Quick Steps

Change Chart Location
1. Make chart active.
2. Click Chart Tools Design tab.
3. Click Move Chart button.
4. Click *New sheet* option.
5. Click OK.

Move Chart

Create a chart and it is inserted in the currently open worksheet as an embedded object. Change the location of a chart with the Move Chart button in the Location group on the Chart Tools Design tab. Click this button and the Move Chart dialog box displays, as shown in Figure 7.7. To move the chart to a new sheet in the workbook, click the *New sheet* option; Excel automatically names the new sheet *Chart1*. As explained earlier in the chapter, pressing Alt + F1 will insert a recommended chart in the active worksheet. To insert a recommended chart into a separate worksheet, press the F11 function key.

A chart that is moved to a separate sheet can be moved back to the original sheet or to a different sheet within the workbook. To move a chart to a different sheet, click the Move Chart button in the Location group. At the Move Chart dialog box, click the *Object in* option box arrow and then click the sheet at the drop-down list. Click OK and the chart is inserted in the specified sheet as an object that can be moved, sized, and formatted.

Adding, Moving, and Deleting Chart Elements

Tutorial

Removing, Modifying, and Adding Chart Elements

Add Chart Element

Quick Steps

Delete Chart Element
1. Click chart element.
2. Press Delete key.
OR
1. Right-click chart element.
2. Click *Delete*.

In addition to adding chart elements with the Chart Elements button at the right of a selected chart, chart elements can be added with the Add Chart Element button on the Chart Tools Design tab. Click this button and a drop-down list of elements displays. Point to a category of elements and then click the desired element at the side menu.

A chart element can be moved and/or sized. To move a chart element, click the element to select it and then move the mouse pointer over the border until the pointer turns into a four-headed arrow. Click and hold down the left mouse button, drag the element to the new location, and then release the mouse button. To size a chart element, click to select the element and then use the sizing handles to increase or decrease the size. To delete a chart element, click the element to select it and then press the Delete key. A chart element can also be deleted by right-clicking it and then clicking *Delete* at the shortcut menu.

Figure 7.7 Move Chart Dialog Box

1. With **7-DIDeptExp** open, make sure the Chart Tools Design tab is active. (If it is not, make sure the chart is selected and then click the Chart Tools Design tab.)
2. Change the chart style by clicking the *Style 5* option in the Chart Styles group (fifth option from the left).

3. Change the chart colors by clicking the Change Colors button in the Chart Styles group and then clicking the *Colorful Palette 3* option (third option in the *Colorful* group).
4. Change the chart layout by clicking the Quick Layout button in the Chart Layouts group and then clicking the *Layout 1* option (first option in the drop-down gallery).

5. Add axis titles by completing the following steps:
   a. Click the Add Chart Element button in the Chart Layouts group on the Chart Tools Design tab.
   b. Point to *Axis Titles* and then click *Primary Horizontal* at the side menu.
   c. Type Department and then press the Enter key. (The word *Department* will appear in the Formula bar.)
   d. Click the Add Chart Element button, point to *Axis Titles*, and then click *Primary Vertical* at the side menu.
   e. Type Expenditure Amounts and then press the Enter key.
6. Click in the *Chart Title* placeholder text at the top of the chart, type Half-Yearly Expenditures, and then press the Enter key.
7. Delete the *Expenditure Amounts* axis title by clicking anywhere in it and then pressing the Delete key.
8. Move the legend by completing the following steps:
   a. Click in the legend to select it.
   b. Move the mouse pointer over the legend border until the pointer turns into a four-headed arrow.
   c. Click and hold down the left mouse button, drag up until the top border of the legend aligns with the top gridline in the chart, and then release the mouse button.

9. Move the chart to a new location by completing the following steps:
   a. Click the Move Chart button in the Location group.
   b. At the Move Chart dialog box, click the *New sheet* option and then click OK. (The chart is inserted in a worksheet named *Chart1*.)

10. Save **7-DIDeptExp**.
11. Print the Chart1 worksheet.
12. Move the chart from Chart1 to Sheet2 by completing the following steps:
   a. Make sure that Chart1 is the active worksheet and that the chart is selected (not just an element in the chart).
   b. Make sure the Chart Tools Design tab is active.
   c. Click the Move Chart button in the Location group.
   d. At the Move Chart dialog box, click the *Object in* option box arrow and then click *Sheet2* at the drop-down list.
   e. Click OK.

13. Change the amounts in Sheet1 by completing the following steps:
   a. Click the Sheet1 tab.
   b. Make cell B7 active and then change the amount from *10,540* to *19,750*.
   c. Make cell D8 active and then change the amount from *78,320* to *63,320*.
   d. Make cell G8 active and then change the amount from *60,570* to *75,570*.
   e. Make cell A2 active.
   f. Click the Sheet2 tab and notice that the chart displays the updated amounts.
14. Click outside the chart to deselect it.
15. Insert a header in the Sheet2 worksheet that prints your name at the left, the current date in the middle, and the workbook file name at the right.
16. Display the worksheet at the Print backstage area and make sure it will print on one page. If the chart does not fit on the page, return to the worksheet and then move and/or decrease the size of the chart until it fits on one page.
17. Print the active worksheet (Sheet2).
18. Save and then close **7-DIDeptExp**.

Check Your Work

Activity 3 Create a Population Comparison Line Chart   2 Parts

You will open a workbook containing population comparison data for Seattle and Portland and then create a line chart with the data. You will move the chart to a new worksheet, format the chart elements, and insert a shape in the chart.

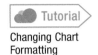

Changing Chart Formatting

Customize the formatting of a chart and its elements with options on the Chart Tools Format tab, as shown in Figure 7.8. Use buttons in the Current Selection group to identify specific elements in the chart and then apply formatting. Insert a shape in a chart with options in the Insert Shapes group and format shapes with options in the Shape Styles group. Apply WordArt formatting to data in a chart with options in the WordArt Styles group. Arrange, align, and size a chart with options in the Arrange and Size groups.

Formatting a Selection

Identify a specific element in a chart for formatting by clicking the *Chart Elements* option box arrow in the Current Selection group on the Chart Tools Format tab and then clicking the element at the drop-down list. This selects the specific element in the chart. Click the Reset to Match Style button to return the formatting of the element back to the original style. Use buttons in the Shape Styles group to apply formatting to a selected object and use buttons in the WordArt Styles group to apply formatting to selected data.

Figure 7.8 Chart Tools Format Tab

Activity 3a Creating and Formatting a Line Chart   Part 1 of 2

1. Open **PopComp** and then save it with the name **7-PopComp**.
2. Create a line chart and add a chart element by completing the following steps:
   a. Select the range A2:I4.
   b. Click the Insert tab.
   c. Click the Insert Line or Area Chart button in the Charts group.
   d. Click the *Line with Markers* option at the drop-down list (fourth column, first row in the *2-D Line* section).
   e. Click the Chart Elements button at the upper right corner of the chart.
   f. Hover the mouse pointer over the *Data Table* option at the side menu, click the right-pointing triangle, and then click *No Legend Keys* at the side menu.
   g. Click the Chart Elements button to remove the side menu.
3. Move the chart to a new sheet by completing the following steps:
   a. Click the Move Chart button in the Location group on the Chart Tools Design tab.
   b. At the Move Chart dialog box, click the *New sheet* option.
   c. Click OK.

4. Format the *Portland* line by completing the following steps:
   a. Click the Chart Tools Format tab.
   b. Click the *Chart Elements* option box arrow in the Current Selection group and then click *Series "Portland"* at the drop-down list.
   c. Click the Shape Fill button arrow in the Shape Styles group and then click the *Green* color (sixth color in the *Standard Colors* section).

   d. Click the Shape Outline button arrow in the Shape Styles group and then click the *Green* color (sixth color in the *Standard Colors* section).
5. Type a title for the chart and format the title by completing the following steps:
   a. Click the *Chart Elements* option box arrow in the Current Selection group and then click *Chart Title* at the drop-down list.
   b. Type Population Comparison between Seattle and Portland and then press the Enter key.
   c. Click the *Fill: Black, Text color 1; Shadow* WordArt style in the WordArt Styles group (first style in the WordArt Styles gallery).

6. Format the legend by completing the following steps:
   a. Click the *Chart Elements* option box arrow and then click *Legend* at the drop-down list.
   b. Click the *Colored Outline - Blue, Accent 1* shape style in the Shape Styles group (second shape style).
7. Save **7-PopComp**.

Check Your Work

Inserting a Shape

The Insert Shapes group on the Chart Tools Format tab contains options for inserting shapes in a chart. Click a shape option and the mouse pointer turns into crosshairs (thin black plus symbol [+]). Click in the chart or drag with the mouse to create the shape in the chart. The shape is inserted in the chart and the Drawing Tools Format tab is active. This tab contains many of the same options as the Chart Tools Format tab. For example, a shape style or WordArt style can be applied to the shape and the shape can be arranged and sized. Size a shape by clicking the up and down arrows at the right sides of the *Shape Height* and *Shape Width* measurement boxes in the Size group on the Drawing Tools Format tab. Or select the current measurement in the *Shape Height* or *Shape Width* measurement box and then type a specific measurement.

Creating Alternative Text for an Image

Alternative text, also known as alt text, is a brief description of an object, such as a chart, that can be read by a screen reader to help a person with a visual impairment understand what objects are included in a worksheet. Create alternative text at the Alt Text task pane. Display this task pane by clicking the Alt Text button in the Accessibility group on the Chart Tools Format tab. Or, right-click a chart and then click *Edit Alt Text* at the shortcut menu. At the Alt Text task pane, type a description of the chart. If the chart is only decorative and not important for understanding the content of the worksheet, insert a check mark in the *Mark as decorative* check box. A chart marked as decorative will not include any description for screen readers.

Alt Text

Activity 3b Inserting and Customizing a Shape and Adding Alt Text to a Chart   Part 2 of 2

1. With **7-PopComp** open, create a shape similar to the one shown in Figure 7.9 by completing the following steps:
    a. Click the More Shapes button in the Insert Shapes group on the Chart Tools Format tab.
    b. Click the *Callout: Up Arrow* shape (last column, second row in the *Block Arrows* section).
    c. Click in the chart to insert the shape.
    d. Click in the *Shape Height* measurement box in the Size group on the Drawing Tools Format tab, type 1.5, and then press the Enter key.
    e. Click in the *Shape Width* measurement box, type 1.5, and then press the Enter key.
    f. Apply a shape style by clicking the More Shape Styles button in the Shape Styles group and then clicking the *Subtle Effect - Blue, Accent 1* option (second column, fourth row in the *Theme Styles* section).
    g. Type Largest disparity in the shape, press the Enter key, and then type (184,411).
    h. Select the text you just typed.
    i. Click the Home tab.
    j. Click the Bold button in the Font group.
    k. Click the *Font Size* option box arrow and then click *14*.
    l. Click the Center button in the Alignment group.
2. With the shape selected, drag the shape so it is positioned as shown in Figure 7.9.
3. Select the entire chart and then create alternative text for the chart by completing the following steps:
    a. Click the Drawing Tools Format tab.
    b. Click the Alt Text button in the Accessibility group.

c. At the Alt Text task pane, click in the description text box and then type Chart showing a comparison between the population of Seattle and Portland.

d. Close the Alt Text task pane.

4. Save **7-PopComp**, print the Chart1 worksheet, and then close the workbook.

3c

Check Your Work

Figure 7.9 Activity 3 Chart

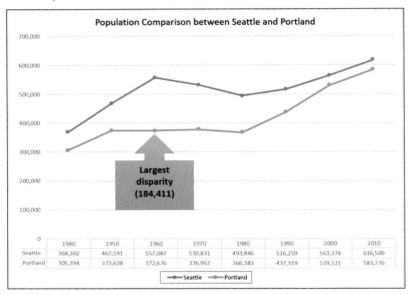

Activity 4 Create a Costs Pie Chart and Treemap Chart   2 Parts

You will create a pie chart and a treemap chart, add data labels, apply a style, format chart elements, and then size and move the treemap chart.

Tutorial

Using Quick Analysis to Create a Chart

Using the Quick Analysis Feature

A variety of methods are available for adding visual elements to a worksheet, including charts, sparklines, and conditional formatting. The Quick Analysis feature consists of a toolbar that has buttons and options for inserting all of these visual elements plus common formulas in one location. When a range is selected, Excel determines how the data in the range can be analyzed and then provides buttons and options for inserting relevant visual elements or formulas. When a range of data that is used to create a pie chart is selected, the Quick Analysis Toolbar provides buttons and options for inserting many different visual elements or formulas but also specifically including a pie chart.

A Quick Analysis button appears at the bottom right corner of the selected range and when clicked, displays the Quick Analysis Toolbar, as shown in Figure 7.10. The Quick Analysis Toolbar includes the *Formatting*, *Charts*, *Totals*, *Tables*, and *Sparklines*

Hint Ctrl + Q is the keyboard shortcut to display the Quick Analysis Toolbar for selected cells.

options. Each option provides buttons that relate to how the data can be analyzed. Click a button to insert an element or formula into the worksheet.

Figure 7.10 Quick Analysis Toolbar

Applying Formatting at a Task Pane

Display Task Pane
1. Select chart or specific element.
2. Click Chart Tools Format tab.
3. Click Format Selection button.

To view and apply more formatting options for charts, display the formatting task pane by clicking the Format Selection button in the Current Selection group on the Chart Tools Format tab. The task pane displays at the right side of the screen and the name of and contents in the task pane vary depending on what is selected. If the entire chart is selected, the Format Chart Area task pane displays, as shown in Figure 7.11. Format the chart by clicking formatting options in the task pane. Display additional formatting options by clicking the icons at the top of the task pane. For example, click the Effects icon in the Format Chart Area task pane and options display for applying shadow, glow, soft edges, and three-dimensional formatting.

Format Selection

Click a chart element and then click the Format Selection button and the task pane name and options change. Another method for displaying the task pane is to right-click a chart or chart element and then click the format option at the shortcut menu. The name of the format option varies depending on the selected element.

Figure 7.11 Format Chart Area Task Pane

Display additional formatting options by clicking icons in this section of the task pane.

Click the Format Selection button with the chart selected to display this task pane. Apply formatting to the chart with options in the task pane.

Click an option to expand it and display additional options.

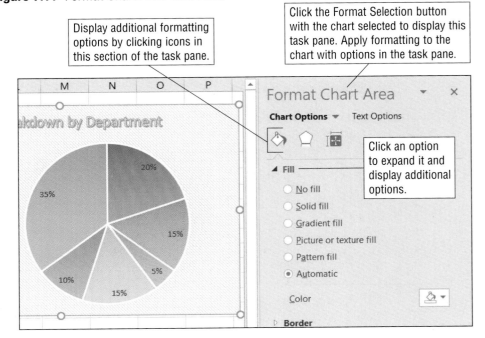

Changing Chart Height and Width Measurements

Quick Steps

Change Chart Height and/or Width
1. Make chart active.
2. Click Chart Tools Format tab.
3. Insert height and/or width with *Shape Height* and/or *Shape Width* measurement boxes.

A chart that is inserted into the current worksheet (not a separate new worksheet) can be sized by selecting it and dragging a sizing handle. A chart can also be sized with the *Shape Height* and *Shape Width* measurement boxes in the Size group on the Chart Tools Format tab. Click the up or down arrow at the right side of the measurement box to increase or decrease the size or click in the measurement box and then type a specific measurement. Another method for changing a chart size is to use options at the Format Chart Area task pane. Display this task pane by clicking the Size group task pane launcher on the Chart Tools Format tab.

Activity 4a   Deleting a Chart and Creating and Formatting a Pie Chart   Part 1 of 2

1. Open **DIDeptCosts** and then save it with the name **7-DIDeptCosts**.
2. Create the pie chart shown in Figure 7.11 by completing the following steps:
   a. Select the range A3:B9.
   b. Click the Quick Analysis button at the bottom right corner of the selected range.
   c. Click the *Charts* option.
   d. Click the Pie button.
3. Insert data labels in the chart by completing the following steps:
   a. Click the Chart Elements button outside the upper right border of the chart.
   b. Hover the mouse pointer over the *Data Labels* option and then click the right-pointing triangle.
   c. Click *Inside End* at the side menu.
   d. Click the Chart Elements button to hide the side menu.
4. Click the *Style 6* option in the Chart Styles group on the Chart Tools Design tab.
5. Type a title and then apply a WordArt style to it by completing the following steps:
   a. Click the Chart Tools Format tab.
   b. Click the *Chart Elements* option box arrow in the Current Selection group.
   c. Click *Chart Title* at the drop-down list.
   d. Type Costs Breakdown by Department and then press the Enter key.
   e. Click the More WordArt Styles button in the WordArt Styles group.
   f. Click the option in the fourth column, third row (white fill with orange outline).

6. Use the Format Legend task pane to apply formatting to the legend by completing the following steps:
   a. Click the *Chart Elements* option box arrow and then click *Legend* at the drop-down list.
   b. Click the Format Selection button in the Current Selection group.
   c. At the Format Legend task pane, click the *Left* option in the *Legend Options* section to select it.

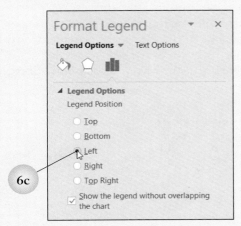

   d. Click the Effects icon in the task pane. (This changes the options in the task pane.)
   e. Click *Shadow* to expand the shadow options in the task pane.
   f. Click the Shadow button to the right of *Presets* and then click the *Offset: Bottom Right* option (first option in the *Outer* section).

   g. Click the Fill & Line icon in the task pane.
   h. Click *Fill* to expand the fill options in the task pane.
   i. Click the *Gradient fill* option.
   j. Close the task pane by clicking the Close button in the upper right corner of the task pane.

7. Use the Format Chart Area task pane to apply formatting to the chart by completing the following steps:
   a. Click inside the chart but outside any chart elements.
   b. Click the Format Selection button in the Current Selection group.
   c. Make sure the Fill & Line icon in the Format Chart Area task pane is selected. (If not, click the icon.)
   d. Make sure the *Fill* option is expanded. (If not, click *Fill*.)
   e. Click the *Gradient fill* option.
   f. Click the Size & Properties icon in the task pane.
   g. Click *Size* to expand the size options in the task pane.
   h. Select the current measurement in the *Height* measurement box, type 3.5, and then press the Enter key.
   i. Select the current measurement in the *Width* measurement box, type 5.5, and then press the Enter key.
   j. Close the task pane.

8. Save **7-DIDeptCosts** and then print only the chart.
9. Change the chart style by completing the following steps:
   a. Click the Chart Tools Design tab.
   b. Click the More Chart Styles button in the Chart Styles group.
   c. Click the *Style 9* option at the drop-down gallery.
10. Move the chart so it is positioned below the cells containing data.
11. Click outside the chart to deselect it.
12. Display the Print backstage area, make sure the chart fits on one page with the data, and then click the Print button.
13. Save **7-DIDeptCosts**.

Check Your Work

Deleting a Chart

Delete a chart created in Excel by clicking the chart to select it and then pressing the Delete key. If a chart has been moved to a different worksheet in the workbook, deleting the chart will delete the chart but not the worksheet. To delete the worksheet and the chart, position the mouse pointer on the sheet tab, click the right mouse button, and then click *Delete* at the shortcut menu. At the message box indicating that the selected sheet will be permanently deleted, click the Delete button.

Activity 4b **Deleting a Chart and Creating and Formatting a Treemap Chart** Part 2 of 2

1. With **7-DIDeptCosts** open, click the Sheet2 tab.
2. Delete the column chart by completing the following steps:
   a. Click the column chart to select it. (Make sure the chart is selected, not a specific element in the chart.)
   b. Press the Delete key.
3. Create a treemap chart by completing the following steps:
   a. Select the range A2:C8.
   b. Click the Insert tab.
   c. Click the Insert Hierarchy Chart button in the Charts group.
   d. Click the *Treemap* option (first option).

4. Click the *Style 4* option in the Chart Styles group on the Chart Tools Design tab (fourth option from the left).
5. Click the Change Colors button in the Chart Styles group and then click the *Colorful Palette 3* option in the *Colorful* section of the drop-down gallery.
6. Click the Add Chart Element button, position the mouse pointer over the *Legend* option, click the right-pointing triangle, and then click the *None* option.

7. Click in the *Chart Title* placeholder text and then type Proportionate Departmental Expenses.
8. Change the chart height and width by completing the following steps:
   a. Make the entire chart active and then click the Chart Tools Format tab.
   b. Click in the *Shape Height* measurement box, type 5, and then press the Enter key.
   c. Click in the *Shape Width* measurement box, type 4, and then press the Enter key.
9. Move the chart so it is positioned below the cells containing data.
10. Click outside the chart to deselect it.
11. Center the worksheet horizontally and vertically.
12. Save, print, and then close **7-DIDeptCosts**.

Check Your Work

Activity 5 Insert Formulas with the IF Logical Function 3 Parts

You will write formulas using the IF logical function to calculate sales bonuses, determine pass/fail grades based on averages, and identify discounts and discount amounts.

Tutorial

Using Logical IF Functions

Writing Formulas with the Logical IF Function

A question that can be answered true or false is considered a *logical test*. The **IF function** can be used to create a logical test that performs a particular action if the answer is true (condition met) and another action if the answer is false (condition not met).

For example, an IF function can be used to write a formula that calculates a salesperson's bonus as 10% if he or she sells more than $99,999 worth of product and 0% if he or she does not sell more than $99,999 worth of product. When writing a formula with an IF function, think about the words *if* and *then*. For example, the formula written out for the bonus example would look like this:

> *If* the salesperson sells more than $99,999 of product, *then* the salesperson receives a bonus of 10%.

> *If* the salesperson does not sell more than $99,999 of product, *then* the salesperson receives a bonus of 0%.

When writing a formula with an IF function, use commas to separate the condition and the action. The formula for the bonus example would look like this: *=IF(sales>99999,sales*0.1,0)*. The formula contains three parts:

- the condition or logical test: *IF(sales>99999*
- the action taken if the condition or logical test is true: *sales*0.1*
- the action taken if the condition or logical test is false: *0*

In Activity 5a, you will write a formula with cell references rather than cell data. You will write a formula with an IF function that determines the following:

> *If* the sales amount is greater than the quota amount, *then* the salesperson will receive a 15% bonus.

> *If* the sales amount is not greater than the quota amount, *then* the salesperson will not receive a bonus.

Written with cell references in the activity, the formula looks like this: *=IF(C4>B4,C4*0.15,0)*. In this formula, the condition, or logical test, is whether the number in cell C4 is greater than the number in cell B4. If the condition is true and the number is greater, then the number in cell C4 is multiplied by 0.15 (providing a 15% bonus). If the condition is false and the number in cell C4 is less than the number in cell B4, then nothing happens (no bonus). Notice how commas are used to separate the logical test from the action.

1. Open **CMPReports** and then save it with the name **7-CMPReports**.
2. Write a formula with the IF function that determines if a sales quota has been met and if it has, inserts the bonus of 15% of actual sales. (If the quota has not been met, the formula will insert a 0.) Write the formula by completing the following steps:
   a. Make cell D4 active.
   b. Type =if(c4>b4,c4*0.15,0) and then press the Enter key.

	A	B	C	D	
1	**Capstan Marine Products**				
2			Sales Department		2b
3	Salesperson	Quota	Actual Sales	Bonus	
4	Allejandro	$ 95,500.00	$	=if(c4>b4,c4*0.15,0)	
5	Crispin	137,000.00	129,890.00		

   c. Make cell D4 active and then use the fill handle to copy the formula to the range D5:D9.
3. Print the worksheet.
4. Revise the formula so it inserts a 20% bonus if the quota has been met by completing the following steps:
   a. Make cell D4 active.
   b. Click in the Formula bar, edit the formula so it displays as *=IF(C4>B4,C4*0.2,0)*, and then click the Enter button on the Formula bar.
   c. Copy the formula in cell D4 to the range D5:D9.
   d. Make cell D4 active and then apply the Accounting format with a dollar symbol ($) and two digits after the decimal point.
5. Save **7-CMPReports**.

 Check Your Work

Writing Formulas with an IF Function Using the Function Arguments Dialog Box

 Logical

A formula containing an IF function can be typed directly into a cell or the Function Arguments dialog box can be used to help write the formula. To use the Function Arguments dialog box to write a formula with the IF function, click the Formulas tab, click the Logical button in the Function Library group, and then click *IF* at the drop-down list. This displays the Function Arguments dialog box, shown in Figure 7.12. The Function Arguments dialog box displays the information you will type in the three argument text boxes for Activity 5b.

At the Function Arguments dialog box, click in the *Logical_test* text box and information about the *Logical_test* argument displays in the dialog box. In this text box, type the cell designation followed by what is evaluated. In the figure, the *Logical_test* text box contains *b14>599*, indicating that what is being evaluated is whether the amount in cell B14 is greater than $599. The *Value_if_true* text box contains *b14*0.95*, indicating that if the logical test is true, then the amount in cell B14 is multiplied by 0.95. (The discount for any product price greater than $599 is 5%, and multiplying the product price by 0.95 determines the price after the 5% discount is applied.) The *Value_if_ false* text box contains *b14*, indicating that if the logical test is false (the product price is not greater than $599), then the amount from cell B14 is simply inserted.

Figure 7.12 Function Arguments Dialog Box

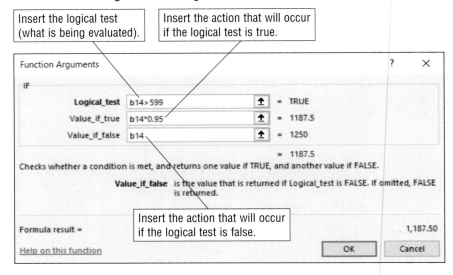

Insert the logical test (what is being evaluated).

Insert the action that will occur if the logical test is true.

Insert the action that will occur if the logical test is false.

Activity 5b **Writing a Formula with an IF Function Using the Function Arguments Dialog Box**

Part 2 of 3

1. With **7-CMPReports** open, insert a formula with an IF function using the Function Arguments dialog box by completing the following steps:
   a. Make cell C14 active.
   b. Click the Formulas tab.
   c. Click the Logical button in the Function Library group.
   d. Click *IF* at the drop-down list.
   e. At the Function Arguments dialog box, type b14>599 in the *Logical_test* text box and then press the Tab key.
   f. Type b14*0.95 in the *Value_if_true* text box and then press the Tab key.
   g. Type b14 in the *Value_if_ false* text box.

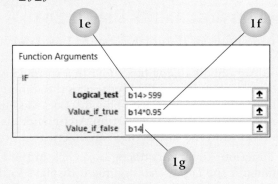

   h. Click OK to close the Function Arguments dialog box.
2. Copy the formula in cell C14 to the range C15:C26.
3. Apply the Accounting format with a dollar symbol and two digits after the decimal point to cell C14.
4. Save **7-CMPReports**.

 Check Your Work

Writing IF Statements Containing Text

When writing a formula with an IF statement, if text is to be inserted in a cell rather than a value, put quotation marks around the text. For example, in Step 2 of Activity 5c, you will write a formula with an IF function that looks like this when written out:

> *If* the new employee averages more than 79 on the quizzes, **then** he or she passes.

> *If* the new employee does not average more than 79 on the quizzes, **then** he or she fails.

In Activity 5c, you will write the formula so the word *PASS* is inserted in a cell if the average of the new employee quizzes is greater than 79 and the word *FAIL* is inserted if the condition is not met. The formula would be *=IF(E31>79, "PASS", "FAIL")*. The quotation marks before and after *PASS* and *FAIL* identify the data as text rather than values.

The Function Arguments dialog box can be used to write a formula with an IF function that contains text. For example, in Step 3 of Activity 5c, you will write a formula with an IF function using the Function Arguments dialog box that looks like this when written out:

> *If* the product price is greater than $599, **then** insert YES.

> *If* the product price is not greater than $599, **then** insert NO.

To create the formula in Step 3 using the Function Arguments dialog box, display the dialog box and then type *b14>599* in the *Logical_test* text box, *YES* in the *Value_if_true* text box and *NO* in the *Value_if_false* text box. When you press the Enter key after typing *YES* in the *Value_if_true* text box, Excel automatically inserts quotation marks around the text. Excel will do the same thing for *NO* in the *Value_if_false* text box.

Activity 5c Writing IF Statements Containing Text   Part 3 of 3

1. With **7-CMPReports** open, insert quiz averages by completing the following steps:
   a. Make cell E31 active and then insert a formula that calculates the average of the test scores in the range B31:D31.
   b. Copy the formula in cell E31 to the range E32:E35.
2. Write a formula with an IF function that inserts the word *PASS* if the new employee quiz average is greater than 79 and inserts the word *FAIL* if the quiz average is not greater than 79. Write the formula by completing the following steps:
   a. Make cell F31 active.
   b. Type =if(e31>79,"PASS","FAIL") and then press the Enter key.

   c. Copy the formula in cell F31 to the range F32:F35.

3. Write a formula with an IF function using the Function Arguments dialog box that inserts the word *YES* in the cell if the product price is greater than $599 and inserts the word *NO* if the price is not greater than $599. Write the formula by completing the following steps:

   a. Make cell D14 active.
   b. Click the Formulas tab.
   c. Click the Logical button in the Function Library group.
   d. Click *IF* at the drop-down list.
   e. Type b14>599 in the *Logical_test* text box and then press the Tab key.
   f. Type YES in the *Value_if_true* text box and then press the Tab key.
   g. Type NO in the *Value_if_false* text box.
   h. Click OK to close the Function Arguments dialog box.
   i. Copy the formula in cell D14 to the range D15:D26.

4. Save and then print **7-CMPReports**.
5. Press Ctrl + ` to turn on the display of formulas.
6. Print the worksheet again. (The worksheet will print on two pages.)
7. Press Ctrl + ` to turn off the display of formulas.
8. Save and then close **7-CMPReports**.

Check Your Work

Chapter Summary

- A chart is a visual presentation of data. Excel provides 17 basic chart types: Column, Line, Pie, Bar, Area, X Y (Scatter), Map, Stock, Surface, Radar, Treemap, Sunburst, Histogram, Box & Whisker, Waterfall, Funnel, and Combo.

- To create a chart, select the cells, click the Insert tab, and then click a specific chart button in the Charts group. Click the Recommended Charts button in the Charts group and Excel will recommend a type of chart for the data.

- A chart is inserted in the same worksheet as the selected cells by default.

- Change the size of a chart using the mouse by dragging one of the sizing handles that display around the border of the chart. When changing the chart size, maintain the proportions of the chart by pressing and holding down the Shift key while dragging a sizing handle.

- Move a chart by positioning the mouse pointer on the chart border until the pointer displays with a four-headed arrow attached and then dragging with the mouse.

- The cells selected to create a chart are linked to the chart. Changes made to the data are reflected in the chart.

- Three buttons appear outside the right border of a selected chart. Use the Chart Elements button to insert or remove chart elements, use the Chart Styles button to apply chart styles, and use the Chart Filters button to isolate specific data in the chart.

- Print a chart by selecting it, displaying the Print backstage area, and then clicking the Print button.

- When a chart is inserted in a worksheet, the Chart Tools Design tab is active. Use buttons and options on this tab to add chart elements, change the chart type, specify a different layout or style for the chart, and change the location of the chart.

- Choose a chart style with options in the Chart Styles group on the Chart Tools Design tab or at the Change Chart Type dialog box.

- Click the Switch Row/Column button in the Data group on the Chart Tools Design tab to change what Excel uses to determine the grouping of data along the horizontal axis and legend.

- Use the Quick Layout button in the Chart Layouts group on the Chart Tools Design tab to change the chart layout.

- Use the Change Colors button in the Chart Styles group on the Chart Tools Design tab to apply different colors to a chart.

- Create a chart and it is inserted in the currently open worksheet. The chart can be moved to a new worksheet in the workbook with the *New sheet* option at the Move Chart dialog box.

- Add chart elements with the Add Chart Element button in the Chart Layouts group on the Chart Tools Design tab.

- Move a chart element by selecting it and then dragging it with the mouse. Use the sizing handles around a chart element to change its size. Delete a chart element by selecting it and then pressing the Delete key or by right-clicking the element and then clicking *Delete* at the shortcut menu.

- Customize the formatting of a chart and chart elements with options on the Chart Tools Format tab. Use these options to identify specific elements in the chart for formatting, insert a shape, apply formatting to a shape, apply WordArt formatting to data in a chart, insert alt text, and arrange, align, and size a chart.

- Insert a shape by clicking it in the Insert Shapes group on the Chart Tools Format tab and then clicking or dragging in the chart.

- Create alternate text for an object such as a chart and the text is read by a screen reader, helping people with a visual impairment understand what objects are included in the worksheet.

- Excel provides additional formatting options at a formatting task pane. A formatting task pane displays at the right side of the screen; the name and the contents in the task pane vary depending on whether the entire chart or an element in the chart is selected. Display a task pane by clicking the chart or element in the chart and then clicking the Format Selection button in the Current Selection group on the Chart Tools Format tab.

- Change the size of a chart with the *Shape Height* and *Shape Width* measurement boxes on the Chart Tools Format tab or at the Format Chart Area task pane.

- To delete a chart in a worksheet, click the chart to select it and then press the Delete key. To delete a chart created in a separate sheet, position the mouse pointer on the chart sheet tab, click the right mouse button, and then click *Delete*.

- A logical test is a question that can be answered with true or false. Use the IF function to create a logical test that performs one action if the answer is true (condition met) or another action if the answer is false (condition not met).

Commands Review

FEATURE	RIBBON TAB, GROUP	BUTTON	KEYBOARD SHORTCUT
add chart element	Chart Tools Design, Chart Layouts		
Change Chart Type dialog box	Chart Tools Design, Type		
change colors	Chart Tools Design, Chart Styles		
chart or chart element task pane	Chart Tools Format, Current Selection		
logical functions	Formulas, Function Library		
Move Chart dialog box	Chart Tools Design, Location		
quick layout	Chart Tools Design, Chart Layouts		
recommended chart	Insert, Charts		Alt + F1
recommended chart in separate sheet			F11
switch row/column	Chart Tools Design, Data		

Microsoft®
Excel®

Adding Visual Interest to Workbooks

Performance Objectives

Upon successful completion of Chapter 8, you will be able to:

1 Insert symbols and special characters

2 Insert, size, move, and format images

3 Create and insert screenshots

4 Draw, format, and copy shapes

5 Insert, format, and type text in text boxes

6 Insert, format, and modify icons and 3D models

7 Insert, format, size, move, and delete SmartArt graphics

8 Insert, format, size, and move WordArt

Microsoft Excel includes a variety of features that you can use to enhance the appearance of a workbook. Some of the methods for adding visual appeal that you will learn in this chapter include inserting and modifying images, screenshots, shapes, text boxes, icons, 3D models, SmartArt, and WordArt.

Data Files

Before beginning the chapter work, copy the EL1C8 folder to your storage medium and then make EL1C8 the active folder.

The online course includes additional training and assessment resources.

Activity 1 Insert Symbols, Images, and Shapes in a Financial Analysis Workbook   5 Parts

You will open a financial analysis workbook and then insert symbols and move, size, and format an image in the workbook. You will also insert an arrow shape, type and format text in the shape, and then copy the shape.

Tutorial

Inserting Symbols and Special Characters

  Symbol

Quick Steps

Insert Symbol
1. Click in cell.
2. Click Insert tab.
3. Click Symbol button.
4. Double-click symbol.
5. Click Close.

Insert Special Character
1. Click in cell.
2. Click Insert tab.
3. Click Symbol button.
4. Click Special Characters tab.
5. Double-click special character.
6. Click Close.

💡 **Hint** Increase or decrease the size of the Symbol dialog box by positioning the mouse pointer on the lower right corner until the pointer displays as a two-headed arrow and then dragging with the mouse.

Inserting Symbols and Special Characters

Use the Symbol button on the Insert tab to insert symbols in a worksheet. Click the button and the Symbol dialog box displays, as shown in Figure 8.1. At the dialog box, double-click a symbol to insert it, click the symbol and then click the Insert button, or type the code in the *Character code* text box. Click the Close button to exit the dialog box.

At the Symbol dialog box with the Symbols tab selected, additional symbols are available with different fonts. Change the font by clicking the *Font* option box arrow and then clicking a font at the drop-down list. Click the Special Characters tab at the Symbol dialog box and a list of special characters displays. Insert a special character by double-clicking a character and then clicking the Close button or by clicking the character, clicking the Insert button, and then clicking the Close button.

Figure 8.1 Symbol Dialog Box with the Symbols Tab Selected

Click this tab to display a list of special characters.

Use the *Font* option box to select a font with a set of characters.

This section of the dialog box displays the most recently used symbols.

The *Character code* text box displays the code that can be entered at the keyboard to insert the symbol.

1. Open **SMFFinCon** and then save it with the name **8-SMFFinCon**.
2. Insert a symbol by completing the following steps:
   a. Double-click in cell A2.
   b. Delete the *e* at the end of *Qualite*.
   c. With the insertion point positioned immediately right of the *t* in *Qualit*, click the Insert tab.
   d. Click the Symbol button in the Symbols group.
   e. At the Symbol dialog box, scroll down the list box and then click the *é* symbol (located in approximately the ninth through eleventh rows). (You can also type *00E9* in the *Character code* text box to select the symbol.)
   f. Click the Insert button and then click the Close button.

3. Insert a special character by completing the following steps:
   a. With cell A2 selected and in Edit mode, move the insertion point so it is positioned immediately right of *Group*.
   b. Click the Symbol button in the Symbols group.
   c. At the Symbol dialog box, click the Special Characters tab.
   d. Double-click the ® *Registered* symbol (tenth option from the top).
   e. Click the Close button.

4. Insert a symbol by completing the following steps:
   a. With cell A2 selected and in Edit mode, move the insertion point so it is positioned immediately left of the *Q* in *Qualité*.
   b. Click the Symbol button in the Symbols group.
   c. At the Symbol dialog box, click the *Font* option box arrow and then click *Wingdings* at the drop-down list. (You will need to scroll down the list to see this option.)
   d. Click the ❖ symbol (located in approximately the fifth or sixth row). (You can also type *118* in the *Character code* text box to select the symbol.)
   e. Click the Insert button and then click the Close button.

5. Click in cell A3.
6. Save **8-SMFFinCon**.

Check Your Work

Figure 8.2 Picture Tools Format Tab

 Tutorial

Inserting an Image

 Pictures

Inserting an Image

Insert an image, such as a picture or clip art image, in an Excel workbook with buttons in the Illustrations group on the Insert tab. Click the Pictures button to display the Insert Picture dialog box with options for inserting an image from a folder on the computer or a removable drive. Or click the Online Pictures button and search for images online. When an image is inserted in a worksheet, the Picture Tools Format tab appears, as shown in Figure 8.2.

 Tutorial

Modifying Images

 Compress Pictures

Quick Steps

Insert Image
1. Click Insert tab.
2. Click Pictures button.
3. Navigate to folder.
4. Double-click image.

Customizing and Formatting an Image

Use buttons in the Adjust group on the Picture Tools Format tab to remove unwanted parts of an image, correct the image brightness and contrast, change the image color, apply artistic effects to the image, change to a different image, and restore the original image formatting. Use the Compress Pictures button in the Adjust group to compress the size of an image file and reduce the amount of space the image requires on the storage medium. Use buttons in the Picture Styles group to apply a predesigned style to the image, change the image border, or apply other effects to the image. Use the Alt Text button in the Accessibility group to add alternate text for the image. With options in the Arrange group, position the image on the page, specify how text will wrap around the image, align the image with other elements in the worksheet, and rotate the image. Use the Crop button in the Size group to remove any unwanted parts of the image and use the *Shape Height* and *Shape Width* measurement boxes to specify the image size.

In addition to options at the Picture Tools Format tab, options at the shortcut menu can be used to format an image. Display this menu by right-clicking the image. Use options at the shortcut menu to change the image, choose text wrapping around the image, insert alt text, size and position the image, and display the Format Picture task pane.

Sizing and Moving an Image

Change the size of an image with the *Shape Height* and *Shape Width* measurement boxes in the Size group on the Picture Tools Format tab or with the sizing handles around the selected image. To change size with a sizing handle, position the mouse pointer on a sizing handle until the pointer turns into a double-headed arrow and then drag in or out to decrease or increase the size of the image. Use the middle sizing handles at the left and right sides of the image to make the image wider or thinner. Use the middle sizing handles at the top and bottom of the image to make the image taller or shorter. Use the sizing handles at the corners of the image to change both the width and height at the same time. Press and hold down the Shift key while dragging a sizing handle to maintain the proportions of the image.

Move an image by positioning the mouse pointer on the image border until the pointer displays with a four-headed arrow attached and then dragging the image to the new location. Rotate the image by positioning the mouse pointer on the white round rotation handle until the pointer displays as a circular arrow. Click and hold down the left mouse button, drag in the desired direction, and then release the mouse button.

1. With **8-SMFFinCon** open, insert an image by completing the following steps:
   a. Click the Insert tab and then click the Pictures button in the Illustrations group.
   b. At the Insert Picture dialog box, navigate to your EL1C8 folder and then double-click **WallStreet**.

2. Change the size of the image by clicking in the *Shape Height* measurement box in the Size group on the Picture Tools Format tab, typing 1.8, and then pressing the Enter key.

3. Remove the yellow background from the image by completing the following steps:
   a. Click the Remove Background button in the Adjust group.
   b. Click the Keep Changes button in the Close group on the Background Removal tab.

4. Change the color by clicking the Color button in the Adjust group and then clicking the *Blue, Accent color 1 Light* option (second column, third row in the *Recolor* section).

5. Apply a correction by clicking the Corrections button in the Adjust group and then clicking the *Brightness: +20% Contrast: +20%* option (fourth column, fourth row in the *Brightness/Contrast* section).

6. Apply an artistic effect by clicking the Artistic Effects button in the Adjust group and then clicking the *Glow Edges* option (last option in the drop-down gallery).

7. Move the image by completing the following steps:
   a. Position the mouse pointer on the image (displays with a four-headed arrow attached).
   b. Click and hold down the left mouse button, drag the image to the upper left corner of the worksheet, and then release the mouse button.

8. Save and then print **8-SMFFinCon**.

Check Your Work

Formatting an Image at the Format Picture Task Pane

In addition to the Picture Tools Format tab, the Format Picture task pane provides options for formatting an image. Click the Picture Styles group task pane launcher or the Size group task pane launcher and the Format Picture task pane displays at the right side of the screen. Click the Picture Styles group task pane launcher and the task pane displays with the Effects icon selected; click the Size group task pane launcher and the Size & Properties icon is selected. Two other icons are also available in this task pane: the Fill & Line icon and the Picture icon. The formatting options may need to be expanded. For example, click *Size* with the Size & Properties icon selected and options for changing the size of the image display. Close the task pane by clicking the Close button in the upper right corner.

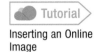

Tutorial

Inserting an Online Image

Online Pictures

Quick Steps

Insert Online Image
1. Click Insert tab.
2. Click Online Pictures button.
3. Type search word or topic.
4. Press Enter key.
5. Double-click image.

Inserting an Online Image

Use the Bing Image Search feature to search for images online. To use this feature, click the Insert tab and then click the Online Pictures button in the Illustrations group. This displays the Online Pictures window, shown in Figure 8.3. Click in the search text box, type the search term or topic, and then press the Enter key. Images that match the search term or topic display in the window. To insert an image, click the image and then click the Insert button or double-click the image. This downloads the image to the document. Customize the image with options and buttons on the Picture Tools Format tab.

Figure 8.3 Online Pictures Window

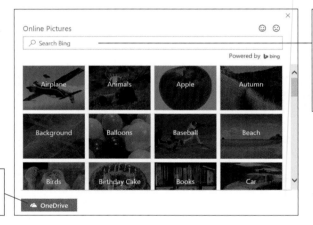

Type a search term or topic in this search box to search for images online using the Bing search engine.

Click this button to search for images in your OneDrive account.

Activity 1c Inserting and Formatting an Image   Part 3 of 5

1. With **8-SMFFinCon** open, delete the Wall Street sign image by clicking the image and then pressing the Delete key.
2. Insert a different image by completing the following steps:
   a. Make cell A1 active.
   b. Click the Insert tab and then click the Online Pictures button in the Illustrations group.

c. At the Online Pictures window, type stock market clip art in the search box and then press the Enter key.

d. Double-click the graph image shown below and to the right. (If this image is not available online, click the Pictures button on the Insert tab. At the Insert Picture dialog box, navigate to your EL1C8 folder and then double-click *StockMarket*.)

3. Display the Format Picture task pane with the Size & Properties icon selected by clicking the Size group task pane launcher on the Picture Tools Format tab.

4. If necessary, click *Size* in the task pane to display the sizing options.

5. Change the height of the image by selecting the current measurement in the *Height* measurement box, typing 1.65, and then pressing the Enter key. (The width automatically changes to maintain the proportions of the image.)

6. Change the properties of the image by clicking *Properties* in the Format Picture task pane to expand the options and then clicking the *Move and size with cells* option. (With this option selected, changing the size of the row also changes the size of the image.)

7. Make a correction to the image by completing the following steps:

a. Click the Picture icon at the top of the task pane.

b. Click *Picture Corrections* to expand the options.

c. Select the current percentage in the *Brightness* text box and then type -25.

d. Select the current percentage in the *Contrast* text box, type 40, and then press the Enter key.

8. Close the Format Picture task pane by clicking the Close button in the upper right corner.

9. Create alternative text for the image by completing the following steps:

a. Click the Alt Text button in the Accessibility group on the Picture Tools Format tab.

b. At the Alt Text task pane, click in the description text box and then type Chart containing an up-pointing arrow.

c. Close the Alt Text task pane.

10. Click outside the image to deselect it.

11. Increase the height of row 1 to 126.00 points and notice that the image size increases with the row height.

12. Save **8-SMFFinCon**.

Check Your Work

Creating and
Inserting a
Screenshot

 Screenshot

Quick Steps

Insert Screenshot
1. Open window to be captured.
2. Make Excel active.
3. Open workbook.
4. Click Insert tab.
5. Click Screenshot button.
6. Click window at drop-down list.
OR
1. Click Screenshot button and then *Screen Clipping*.
2. Drag to specify capture area.

Creating and Inserting a Screenshot

The Illustrations group on the Insert tab contains a Screenshot button that can be used to capture all or part of the contents of a screen as an image. This is useful for capturing information from a web page or a file in another program. To create a screenshot, open the web page or file to be captured so that it is visible on the screen. Next, make Excel active and open a workbook. Click the Insert tab, click the Screenshot button, and then look in the drop-down list to see thumbnails of windows open in other programs. Click the thumbnail of the screen to be captured and the screenshot is inserted as an image in the open workbook, the image is selected, and the Picture Tools Format tab is active. Use buttons on this tab to customize the screenshot image.

A screenshot can also be made of a specific portion of the screen by clicking the *Screen Clipping* option at the Screenshot button drop-down list. Click this option and the open web page, file, or Windows desktop displays in a dimmed manner and the mouse pointer displays as crosshairs (a plus symbol [+]). Using the mouse, draw a border around the specific area of the screen to be captured. The area identified is inserted in the workbook as an image, the image is selected, and the Picture Tools Format tab is active.

Activity 1d Inserting and Formatting a Screenshot   Part 4 of 5

1. With **8-SMFFinCon** open, make sure that no other programs are open.
2. Open Word and then open **SMFProfile** from your EL1C8 folder.
3. Click the Excel button on the taskbar.
4. Insert a screenshot of the table in the Word document by completing the following steps:
   a. Click the Insert tab.
   b. Click the Screenshot button in the Illustrations group and then click *Screen Clipping* at the drop-down list.
   c. When **SMFProfile** displays in a dimmed manner, position the mouse crosshairs in the upper left corner of the table, click and hold down the left mouse button, drag down to the lower right corner of the table, and then release the mouse button. (This creates a screenshot of the entire table.)

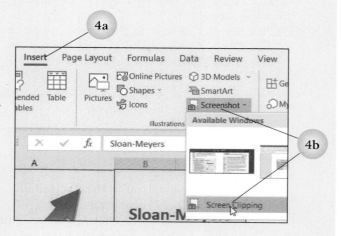

5. With the screenshot image inserted in **8-SMFFinCon**, make the following changes:
   a. Click in the *Shape Width* measurement box in the Size group on the Picture Tools Format tab, type 3.7, and then press the Enter key.

b. Click the Corrections button and then click the *Sharpen: 25%* option (fourth option in the *Sharpen/Soften* section).

c. Click the Corrections button and then click the *Brightness: 0% (Normal) Contrast: -40%* (third column, first row in the *Brightness/Contrast* section).

d. Using the mouse, drag the screenshot image one row below the data in row 10.

6. Make cell A4 active.
7. Save **8-SMFFinCon**.
8. Click the Word button on the taskbar, close **SMFProfile**, and then close Word.

Check Your Work

Inserting and Formatting a Shape

Tutorial

Inserting a Shape

Tutorial

Formatting a Shape

 Shapes

Quick Steps

Insert Shape
1. Click Insert tab.
2. Click Shapes button.
3. Click shape option at drop-down list.
4. Click or drag in worksheet.

Copy Shape
1. Select shape.
2. Click Copy button.
3. Position insertion point in new location.
4. Click Paste button.
OR
1. Select shape.
2. Press and hold down Ctrl key.
3. Drag shape to new location.

Chapter 7 covered how to insert shapes in a chart with options on the Chart Tools Format tab. Shapes can also be inserted in a worksheet with the Shapes button in the Illustrations group on the Insert tab. Use the Shapes button to draw shapes in a worksheet, including lines, basic shapes, block arrows, flow chart symbols, callouts, stars, and banners. Click a shape and the mouse pointer displays as crosshairs. Click in the worksheet or position the crosshairs where the shape is to begin, click and hold down the left mouse button, drag to create the shape, and then release the mouse button. Click or drag in the worksheet and the shape is inserted and the Drawing Tools Format tab, shown in Figure 8.4, becomes active. Use options and buttons on this tab to choose a shape, apply a style to a shape, arrange a shape, and change the size of a shape.

Choose a shape in the *Lines* section of the Shapes button drop-down list and the shape that is drawn is considered a line drawing. Choose an option in another section of the drop-down list and the shape drawn is considered an enclosed object. When drawing an enclosed object, maintain the proportions of the shape by pressing and holding down the Shift key while dragging with the mouse. Text can be typed in an enclosed object and then formatted using buttons in the WordArt Styles group (or options on the Home tab).

Copy a shape in a worksheet by selecting the shape and then clicking the Copy button in the Clipboard group on the Home tab. Make active the cell where the shape is to be copied and then click the Paste button. A shape can also be copied by pressing and holding down the Ctrl key while dragging the shape to the new location.

Figure 8.4 Drawing Tools Format Tab

1. With **8-SMFFinCon** open, create the larger arrow shown in Figure 8.5 by completing the following steps:

   a. Click the Insert tab.

   b. Click the Shapes button in the Illustrations group and then click the *Arrow: Up* shape (third column, first row in the *Block Arrows* section).

   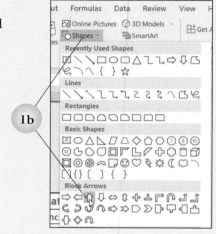

   c. Position the mouse pointer (appears as crosshairs) near the upper left corner of cell D1 and then click the left mouse button. (This inserts the arrow in the worksheet.)

   d. Click in the *Shape Height* measurement box and then type 3.7.

   e. Click in the *Shape Width* measurement box, type 2.1, and then press the Enter key.

   f. If necessary, drag the arrow so it is positioned as shown in Figure 8.5. (To drag the arrow, position the mouse pointer on the border of the selected arrow until the pointer displays with a four-headed arrow attached, click and hold down the left mouse button, drag the arrow to the new position, and then release the mouse button.)

   g. Click the More Shape Styles button in the Shape Styles group on the Drawing Tools Format tab and then click the *Intense Effect - Blue, Accent 1* option (second column, last row in the *Theme Styles* section).

   h. Click the Shape Effects button in the Shape Styles group, point to *Glow*, and then click the *Glow: 11 point; Orange, Accent color 2* option (second column, third row in the *Glow Variations* section).

2. Insert text in the arrow by completing the following steps:
   a. With the arrow selected, type McGuire Mutual Shares 5.33%.
   b. Select the text you just typed (*McGuire Mutual Shares 5.33%*).
   c. Click the More WordArt Styles button in the WordArt Styles group and then click the option in the fourth column, third row (orange outline with white fill).
   d. Press Ctrl + E to center the text.

3. With the arrow selected, copy it by completing the following steps:
   a. Press and hold down the Ctrl key.
   b. Position the mouse pointer on the arrow border until the pointer displays with a square box and plus symbol attached.
   c. Click and hold down the left mouse button and drag to the right so the outline of the arrow is positioned at the right of the existing arrow.
   d. Release the mouse button and then release the Ctrl key.
4. Format the second arrow by completing the following steps:
   a. With the second arrow selected, click in the *Shape Height* measurement box on the Drawing Tools Format tab and then type 2.
   b. Click in the *Shape Width* measurement box, type 1.6, and then press the Enter key.
   c. Select the text *McGuire Mutual Shares 5.33%* and then type SR Linus Fund 0.22%.
   d. Drag the arrow so it is positioned as shown in Figure 8.5.
5. Change to landscape orientation. (Make sure the cells containing the data, screenshot image, and arrows will print on the same page.)
6. Save, print, and then close **8-SMFFinCon**.

> Check Your Work

Figure 8.5 Activity 1e

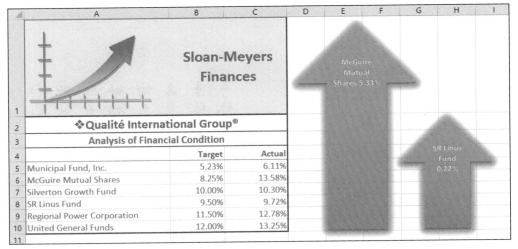

You will open a division sales workbook and then insert, move, and size an image, an icon, and a 3D model. You will also insert a text box and then format the text.

Tutorial

Inserting and
Modifying Text
Boxes

 Text Box

Inserting and Modifying Text Boxes

To draw a text box in a worksheet, click the Insert tab and then click the Text Box button in the Text group. This causes the mouse pointer to display as a long, thin, upside-down cross (↓). Position the pointer in the worksheet and then drag to create the text box. When a text box is selected, the Drawing Tools Format tab displays with options for customizing it.

Click a text box to select it and a dashed border and sizing handles display around it. To delete the text box, click the border again to change the dashed lines to solid lines and then press the Delete key.

Tutorial

Inserting and
Modifying an Icon

Quick Steps

Draw Text Box
1. Click Insert tab.
2. Click Text Box button.
3. Click or drag in worksheet to create text box.

Insert Icons
1. Click Insert tab.
2. Click Icons button.
3. Click icon.
4. Click Insert button.

Icons

Inserting and Customizing Icons

Use the Icons button in the Illustrations group on the Insert tab to insert an icon in a Word document. An icon is a simple graphic used to represent a concept or idea, such as emotions, weather, nature, the arts, and so on. Icons can be used to highlight or label data in a worksheet. These simple graphics draw the eye to important information and can be understood at a glance. Click the Icons button on the Insert tab and the Insert Icons window opens, as shown in Figure 8.6. At this window, scroll down the list box to view the various icons or click a category in the left panel to display a specific category of icons. To insert an icon in a document, double-click the icon in the list box or click the icon and then click the Insert button.

Figure 8.6 Insert Icons Window

Click a category in this panel to display icons relating to the category.

Click an option in this list box and then click the Insert button to insert the icon into the worksheet.

When an icon is inserted and selected in a worksheet, the Graphics Tools Format tab is active, as shown in Figure 8.7. Use options on this tab to apply a graphic style, fill, outline, and effect; type alternate text for the icon; position, align, group, rotate, and size the icon; and apply text wrapping.

Icons, like other images, can be formatted with options at the Format Graphic task pane. Display this task pane by clicking the Graphics Styles group or Size group task pane launcher. The task pane contains four icons: Fill & Line, Effects, Size & Properties, and Picture. Use options at the Format Graphic task pane to format an icon in a manner similar to formatting an image, shape, and text box.

Figure 8.7 Graphics Tools Format Tab

Activity 2a Inserting and Customizing an Icon and a Text Box   Part 1 of 2

1. Open **HPDivSales** and then save it with the name **8-HPDivSales**.
2. Insert and format an icon by completing the following steps:
   a. Click in cell A2.
   b. Click the Insert tab.
   c. Click the Icons button in the Illustrations group.

   d. At the Insert Icons window, click *Arts* at the left side of the window.
   e. Click the video camera icon shown below and then click the Insert button.

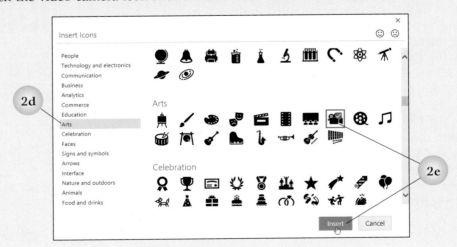

f. With the Icon selected, click the Rotate button in the Arrange group and then click the *Flip Horizontal* option at the drop-down list.

g. Click the More Graphic Styles button in the Graphics Styles group and then click the *Transparent, Colored Outline - Dark 1* option at the drop-down gallery (first column, last row).

h. Move the icon it so it is positioned as shown in Figure 8.8.

3. Draw a text box by completing the following steps:
   a. Click the Insert tab.
   b. Click the Text Box button in the Text group.
   c. Drag to cell A1 to draw a text box the approximate size and shape shown below.

4. Format the text box by completing the following steps:
   a. Click the Drawing Tools Format tab.
   b. Click the Shape Fill button arrow in the Shape Styles group and then click *No Fill* at the drop-down gallery.
   c. Click the Shape Outline button arrow in the Shape Styles group and then click *No Outline* at the drop-down gallery.

5. Insert text in the text box by completing the following steps:
   a. With the text box selected, click the Home tab.
   b. Click the *Font* option box arrow and then click *Lucida Calligraphy* at the drop-down gallery. (Scroll down the gallery to display this font.)
   c. Click the *Font Size* option box arrow and then click *24* at the drop-down gallery.
   d. Click the Font Color button arrow and then click *Blue, Accent 1, Darker 50%* (fifth column, last row in the *Theme Colors* section).
   e. Click the Align Right button in the Alignment group.
   f. Type Hummingbird Productions.

6. Move the text box so the text is positioned in cell A1, as shown in Figure 8.8.

7. Save **8-SPDivSales**.

Figure 8.8 Activity 2a

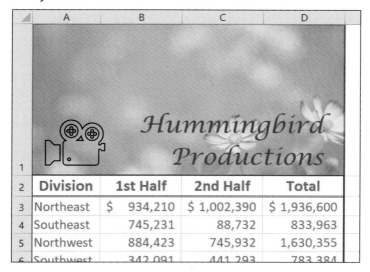

⊿	A	B	C	D
1				
2	**Division**	**1st Half**	**2nd Half**	**Total**
3	Northeast	$ 934,210	$ 1,002,390	$ 1,936,600
4	Southeast	745,231	88,732	833,963
5	Northwest	884,423	745,932	1,630,355
6	Southwest	342,091	441,293	783,384

Tutorial

Inserting and
Modifying 3D
Models

Quick Steps

Insert 3D Model
1. Click Insert tab.
2. Click 3D Models
   button.
3. Click category.
4. Click model.
5. Click Insert button.

⬡ 3D Model

Inserting and Customizing 3D Models

A 3D model is a graphic file of an image shown in three dimensions. The model can be rotated or tilted to allow viewing from various angles or to display a specific portion or feature. Microsoft's Remix 3D library includes a collection of free 3D models that can be inserted into a Word document, PowerPoint presentation, or Excel worksheet. Access these images by clicking the 3D Models button in the Illustrations group on the Insert tab. At the Online 3D Models window, shown in Figure 8.9, click a category to view all 3D models within the category or type a keyword(s) in the search text box and then press the Enter key. Insert a 3D model in a worksheet by double-clicking the model or clicking the model and then clicking the Insert button.

Figure 8.9 Online 3D Models Window

Click a category to
display 3D model
in the category.

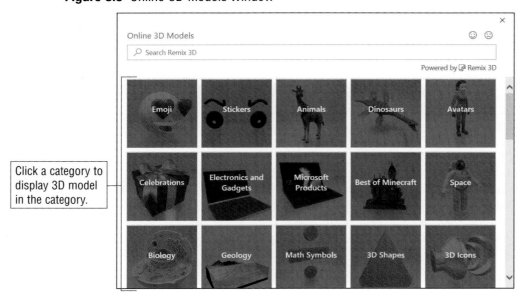

When a 3D model is inserted in a document, the 3D Model Tools Format tab is active. Use buttons in the Adjust group to insert a different 3D model or reset the selected model to its original size and position. The 3D Model Views group includes a gallery of preset views for the model. Click the Alt Text button in the Accessibility group and the Alt Text task pane displays, where a description of the model can be added. Use options in the Arrange group to position the model, apply text wrapping, send the model forward or backward, and align the model. Change the height and width of the model with options in the Size group.

Pan & Zoom

The Size group also contains the Pan & Zoom button. Click this button to lock the position of the 3D model and a button (a magnifying glass with a plus symbol inside) will display at the right of the selected model. Position the mouse pointer on this button, hold down the left mouse button, and then drag up to increase the size of the model (zoom in) or drag down to decrease the size (zoom out). Use the 3D control in the middle of the model to freely rotate the model. Pan the model by clicking and dragging within the frame to change the model's position within the frame. Turn off the pan and zoom feature by clicking the Pan & Zoom button to deactivate it.

Use the 3D control that displays in the middle of a selected 3D model to rotate or tilt the model. To use the 3D control, position the mouse pointer on the control, click and hold down the left mouse button, and then drag with the mouse to rotate or tilt the model.

Options for formatting and customizing a 3D model are available at the Format 3D Model task pane. Display the task pane by clicking the 3D Model Views group or Size group task pane launcher. The task pane displays with four icons: Fill & Line, Effects, Size & Properties, and 3D Model.

Click the Fill & Line icon to display options for formatting the border line and fill of the 3D model. Use options at the task pane with the Effects icon selected to apply formatting effects, such as shadow, reflection, glow, and soft edges, and to format and rotate the model. Click the Size & Properties icon to display options for adjusting the size of the 3D model, or click the 3D Model icon to specify the rotation and camera view.

Activity 2b Inserting and Customizing a 3D Model

Part 2 of 2

1. With **8-HPDivSales** open, click in cell E1.
2. Insert a 3D model from the Remix 3D library by completing the following steps:
   a. Click the Insert tab.
   b. Click the 3D Models button in the Illustrations group.
   c. At the Online 3D Models window, click the *Animals* category.
   d. Scroll down and click the hummingbird model.
   e. Click the Insert button.
   Note: If you do not have access to the Online 3D Models window, open Bird3D *from your EL1C8 folder. This workbook contains the 3D hummingbird model. Copy the model and then paste it into 8-DivSales.*

2d

3. Change the size of the model at the Format 3D Model task pane by completing the following steps:
   a. Click the Size group task pane launcher.
   b. Select the value in the *Width* measurement box.
   c. Type 3 and then press the Enter key.
4. Change the view of the model by clicking the *Right* view (fifth option) in the 3D Model Views gallery.

5. Reset the bird model by clicking the Reset 3D Model button in the Adjust group.
6. Use the 3D control that displays in the middle of the bird model by positioning the mouse pointer on the 3D control, pressing and holding down the left mouse button, and then dragging with the mouse to rotate the model. Rotate the model so it displays as shown in Figure 8.10.
7. Zoom in and pan the model by completing the following steps:
   a. Click the Pan & Zoom button in the Size group on the 3D Model Tools Format tab.
   b. Position the mouse pointer on the button that displays as a magnifying glass with a plus symbol inside (at the right of the model), press and hold down the left mouse button, and then drag down to decrease the size of the model so it displays as shown in Figure 8.10.
   c. Position the mouse inside the model and then pan the hummingbird within the frame by click-dragging it to the position as shown in Figure 8.10.
   d. Click the Pan & Zoom button to deactivate it.
   e. Move the model to the upper left corner of cell A1.
8. Close the Format 3D Model task pane.
9. Save, print, and then close **8-HPDivSales**.

Figure 8.10 Activity 2b

	A	B	C	D
1				
2	Division	1st Half	2nd Half	Total
3	Northeast	$ 934,210	$ 1,002,390	$ 1,936,600

Activity 3 **Insert and Format SmartArt Graphics in a** **4 Parts**
Company Sales Workbook

You will open a workbook that contains two company sales worksheets. You will insert and format a SmartArt cycle graphic in one worksheet and a SmartArt relationship graphic in the other. You will also create and format WordArt text.

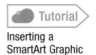

Tutorial

Inserting a
SmartArt Graphic

Inserting a SmartArt Graphic

Use the SmartArt feature included in Excel to insert graphics, such as diagrams and organizational charts, in a worksheet. SmartArt offers a variety of predesigned graphics that are available at the Choose a SmartArt Graphic dialog box, shown in Figure 8.11. Display this dialog box by clicking the Insert tab and then clicking the SmartArt button in the Illustrations group. At the dialog box, *All* is selected in the left panel and all the predesigned graphics are available in the middle panel. Use the scroll bar at the right side of the middle panel to scroll down the list of graphic choices. Click a graphic in the middle panel and the name of the graphic displays in the right panel along with a description of the graphic type. SmartArt includes graphics for presenting lists of data; showing data processes, cycles, and relationships; and presenting data in a matrix or pyramid. Double-click a graphic in the middle panel of the dialog box and the graphic is inserted in the worksheet.

SmartArt

Quick Steps

Insert SmartArt
Graphic
1. Click Insert tab.
2. Click SmartArt button.
3. Double-click graphic.

Entering Data in a SmartArt Graphic

Some SmartArt graphics are designed to include text. Type text in a graphic by selecting a shape in the graphic and then typing text in the shape, or display a text pane and then type text in the pane. Display the text pane by clicking the Text Pane button in the Create Graphic group on the SmartArt Tools Design tab. Turn off the display of the pane by clicking the Text Pane button or clicking the Close button in the upper right corner of the pane.

Text Pane

💡 **Hint** Generally, you would use a SmartArt graphic to represent text and a chart to represent numbers.

Figure 8.11 Choose a SmartArt Graphic Dialog Box

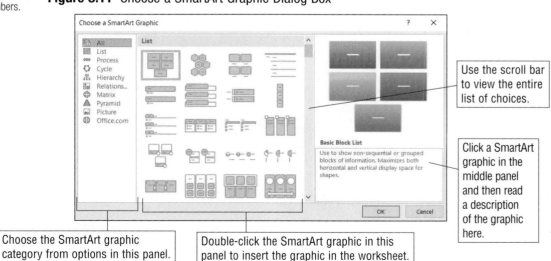

Use the scroll bar to view the entire list of choices.

Click a SmartArt graphic in the middle panel and then read a description of the graphic here.

Choose the SmartArt graphic category from options in this panel.

Double-click the SmartArt graphic in this panel to insert the graphic in the worksheet.

Tutorial

Modifying a
SmartArt Graphic

Sizing, Moving, and Deleting a SmartArt Graphic

Increase or decrease the size of a SmartArt graphic by dragging one of the sizing handles that display around the selected graphic. Use the corner sizing handles to increase or decrease the height and width at the same time. Use the middle sizing handles to increase or decrease the height or width of the SmartArt graphic.

To move a SmartArt graphic, select it and then position the mouse pointer on the graphic border until the pointer displays with a four-headed arrow attached. Click and hold down the left mouse button, drag the graphic to the new position, and then release the mouse button. Delete a graphic by selecting it and then pressing the Delete key.

Activity 3a Inserting, Moving, and Sizing a SmartArt Graphic in a Worksheet   Part 1 of 4

1. Open **EPCoSales** and then save it with the name **8-EPCoSales**.
2. Create the SmartArt graphic shown in Figure 8.12. To begin, click the Insert tab.
3. Click the SmartArt button in the Illustrations group.
4. At the Choose a SmartArt Graphic dialog box, click *Cycle* in the left panel.
5. Double-click *Radial Cycle* in the middle panel (as shown in the image at the right).
6. If the text pane is not open, click the Text Pane button in the Create Graphic group. (The text pane will display at the left of the SmartArt graphic.)
7. With the insertion point positioned after the top bullet in the text pane, type Evergreen Products.
8. Click in the *[Text]* placeholder below *Evergreen Products* and then type Seattle.
9. Click in the next *[Text]* placeholder and then type Olympia.
10. Click in the next *[Text]* placeholder and then type Portland.
11. Click in the next *[Text]* placeholder and then type Spokane.
12. Click the Text Pane button to close the text pane.
13. Drag the SmartArt graphic so it is positioned as shown in Figure 8.12. To drag the graphic, position the mouse pointer on the graphic border until the pointer displays with a four-headed arrow attached. Click and hold down the left mouse button, drag the graphic to the new position, and then release the mouse button.
14. Use the sizing handles around the SmartArt graphic to increase or decrease the size so it displays as shown in Figure 8.12.
15. Save **8-EPCoSales**.

Check Your Work

Figure 8.12 Activity 3a

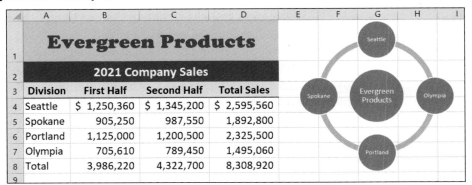

	A	B	C	D	E	F	G	H	I
1	**Evergreen Products**								
2		**2021 Company Sales**							
3	**Division**	**First Half**	**Second Half**	**Total Sales**					
4	Seattle	$ 1,250,360	$ 1,345,200	$ 2,595,560					
5	Spokane	905,250	987,550	1,892,800					
6	Portland	1,125,000	1,200,500	2,325,500					
7	Olympia	705,610	789,450	1,495,060					
8	Total	3,986,220	4,322,700	8,308,920					
9									

Changing the SmartArt Graphic Design

Hint To restore the SmartArt default layout and color, click the Reset Graphic button in the Reset group on the SmartArt Tools Design tab.

Double-click a SmartArt graphic at the Choose a SmartArt Graphic dialog box and the graphic is inserted in the worksheet and the SmartArt Tools Design tab is active. Use options and buttons on this tab to add objects, change the graphic layout, apply a style to the graphic, and reset the original formatting of the graphic.

Activity 3b Changing the SmartArt Graphic Design   Part 2 of 4

1. With **8-EPCoSales** open, make sure the SmartArt Tools Design tab is active and then click the *Spokane* circle shape in the graphic to select it.
2. Click the Right to Left button in the Create Graphic group. (This switches *Olympia* and *Spokane*.)
3. Click the More SmartArt Styles button in the SmartArt Styles group and then click the *Polished* option at the drop-down list (first column, first row in the *3-D* section).

4. Click the Change Colors button in the SmartArt Styles group, scroll down the drop-down gallery, and then click the *Gradient Range - Accent 6* option (third option in the *Accent 6* section).
5. Click outside the SmartArt graphic to deselect it.
6. Change to landscape orientation. (Make sure the graphic fits on the first page.)
7. Save **8-EPCoSales** and then print the Total Sales worksheet.

Check Your Work

Changing the SmartArt Graphic Formatting

Click the SmartArt Tools Format tab and options display for formatting a SmartArt graphic. Use buttons on this tab to insert and customize shapes; apply a shape style; apply WordArt styles; and specify the position, alignment, rotation, wrapping style, height, and width of a graphic.

Activity 3c Changing the SmartArt Graphic Formatting

1. With **8-EPCoSales** open, click the Seattle Sales sheet tab.
2. Create the SmartArt graphic shown in Figure 8.13. To begin, click the Insert tab and then click the SmartArt button in the Illustrations group.
3. At the Choose a SmartArt Graphic dialog box, click *Relationship* in the left panel and then double-click *Gear* in the middle panel.

4. Click in the *[Text]* placeholder in the bottom gear and then type Quality Products.
5. Click in the *[Text]* placeholder in the left gear and then type Customized Plans.
6. Click in the *[Text]* placeholder in the top gear and then type Exemplary Service.
7. Click inside the SmartArt graphic border but outside any specific shape.
8. Click the More SmartArt Styles button in the SmartArt Styles group and then click the *Inset* option (second column, first row in the *3-D* section).
9. Click the Change Colors button and then click the *Gradient Loop - Accent 6* option (fourth option in the *Accent 6* section).
10. Click the SmartArt Tools Format tab.
11. Click in the *Height* measurement box in the Size group and then type 4.
12. Click in the *Width* measurement box, type 4.5, and then press the Enter key.

13. Click the bottom gear to select it.

14. Click the Shape Fill button arrow in the Shape Styles group and then click the *Green, Accent 6, Darker 50%* option (last column, last row in the *Theme Colors* section).
15. Click the top gear to select it.
16. Click the Shape Fill button arrow and then click the *Green, Accent 6, Darker 25%* option (last column, fifth row in the *Theme Colors* section).
17. Change to landscape orientation.
18. Move the SmartArt graphic so it fits on the first page and displays as shown in Figure 8.13.
19. Click outside the SmartArt graphic to deselect it.
20. Save **8-EPCoSales** and then print the Seattle Sales worksheet.

Check Your Work

Figure 8.13 Activity 3c

Tutorial

Creating WordArt

 WordArt

Quick Steps

Create WordArt
1. Click Insert tab.
2. Click Text button.
3. Click WordArt button.
4. Click WordArt style at drop-down list.
5. Type text.

Creating, Sizing, and Moving WordArt

Use the WordArt feature to distort or modify text so it conforms to a variety of shapes. This is useful for creating company logos and headings. Change the font, style, and alignment of text with WordArt and use fill patterns and colors, customize border lines, and add shadow and three-dimensional effects.

To insert WordArt in an Excel worksheet, click the Insert tab, click the Text button, click the WordArt button at the drop-down list, and then click an option at the drop-down list. This inserts the text *Your text here* in the worksheet, formatted in the WordArt option selected at the drop-down list. Type text and then use the options and buttons on the Drawing Tools Format tab to format the WordArt.

Hint To remove a WordArt style from text and retain the text, click the More WordArt Styles button in the WordArt Styles group on the Drawing Tools Format tab and then click *Clear WordArt.*

WordArt text inserted in a worksheet is surrounded by white sizing handles. Use these sizing handles to change the height and width of the WordArt text. To move WordArt text, position the mouse pointer on the border of the WordArt text box until the pointer displays with a four-headed arrow attached and then drag the outline of the text box to the new location.

Make WordArt text conform to a variety of shapes using the *Transform* option from the Text Effects button drop-down list. Apply a transform shape and a small yellow circle displays below the WordArt text. Use this circle to change the slant of the WordArt text.

Activity 3d Inserting and Formatting WordArt

Part 4 of 4

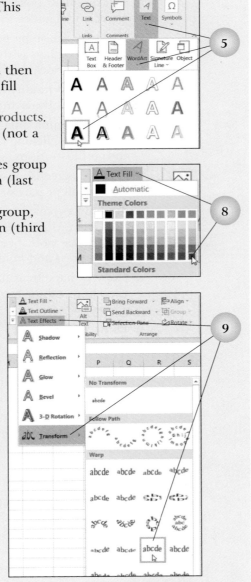

1. With **8-EPCoSales** open, click the Total Sales sheet tab.
2. Make cell A1 active and then press the Delete key. (This removes the text from the cell.)
3. Increase the height of row 1 to 138 points.
4. Click the Insert tab.
5. Click the Text button, click the WordArt button, and then click the option in the first column, third row (black fill with white outline).
6. Type Evergreen, press the Enter key, and then type Products.
7. Click the WordArt border to change it to a solid line (not a dashed line).
8. Click the Text Fill button arrow in the WordArt Styles group and then click the *Green, Accent 6, Darker 50%* option (last column, last row in the Theme Colors section).
9. Click the Text Effects button in the WordArt Styles group, point to *Transform*, and then click the *Warp Up* option (third column, fourth row in the *Warp* section).
10. Position the mouse pointer (turns into a white arrow) on the small yellow circle immediately below the *d* in *Products*, click and hold down the left mouse button, drag up approximately 0.25 inch, and then release the mouse button. (This changes the slant of the text.)
11. Drag the WordArt text so it is positioned in cell A1.
12. If necessary, size the SmartArt graphic and position it so it prints on one page with the data.
13. Click the Seattle Sales sheet tab and then complete steps similar to those in Steps 2 through 11 to insert *Evergreen Products* as WordArt in cell A1.
14. Make sure the SmartArt graphic fits on one page with the data. If necessary, decrease the size of the graphic.
15. Save **8-EPCoSales** and then print both worksheets.
16. Close **8-EPCoSales**.

Check Your Work

Chapter Summary

- Insert symbols with options at the Symbol dialog box with the Symbols tab or Special Characters tab selected.

- Use buttons in the Illustrations group on the Insert tab to insert an image such as a picture, clip art image, screenshot, shape, or SmartArt graphic.

- Insert an image by clicking the Insert tab, clicking the Pictures button in the Illustrations group, and then double-clicking an image at the Insert Picture dialog box.

- Insert an image in a worksheet and the Picture Tools Format tab is active. It provides options for adjusting the image, applying preformatted styles to the image, and arranging and sizing the image.

- Change the size of an image with the *Shape Height* and *Shape Width* measurement boxes in the Size group on the Picture Tools Format tab or with the sizing handles that display around a selected image.

- Move an image by positioning the mouse pointer on the image border until the pointer displays with a four-headed arrow attached and then dragging the image to the new location.

- Format and modify an image by displaying the Format Picture task pane and using the options and buttons to alter the image.

- Insert an online image with options at the Online Pictures window. Display this window by clicking the Insert tab and then clicking the Online Pictures button in the Illustrations group.

- Use the Screenshot button in the Illustrations group on the Insert tab to capture all or part of the contents of a screen as an image.

- To draw a shape in a workbook, click the Insert tab, click the Shapes button in the Illustrations group, and then click a shape at the drop-down list. Click or drag in the worksheet to insert the shape. To maintain the proportions of the shape, press and hold down the Shift key while dragging in the worksheet.

- Copy a shape by using the Copy and Paste buttons in the Clipboard group on the Home tab or by pressing and holding down the Ctrl key while dragging the shape.

- Draw a text box in a worksheet by clicking the Insert tab, clicking the Text Box button in the Text group, and then clicking or dragging in the worksheet. Use options on the Drawing Tools Format tab to format and customize the text box.

- Use the Icons button to insert simple images into a worksheet. Customize the appearance of an icon using buttons and options on the Graphics Tools Format tab and at the Format Graphic task pane.

- Insert a 3D model into a worksheet by clicking the 3D Model button in the Illustrations group on the Insert tab. Customize the appearance of a 3D model using the object control inside the model and also by using buttons and options on the 3D Models Tool Format tab and at the Format 3D Model task pane.

- Insert a SmartArt graphic in a worksheet by clicking the Insert tab, clicking the SmartArt button in the Illustrations group, and then double-clicking a graphic at the Choose a SmartArt Graphic dialog box. Customize a SmartArt graphic with options on the SmartArt Tools Design tab and SmartArt Tools Format tab.

- Use WordArt to create, distort, and modify text and to make it conform to a variety of shapes. Insert WordArt in a worksheet with the WordArt button in the Text button drop-down list on the Insert tab. Customize WordArt text with options on the Drawing Tools Format tab.

Commands Review

FEATURE	RIBBON TAB, GROUP	BUTTON
alternative text	Picture Tools Format, Accessibility	
Choose a SmartArt Graphic dialog box	Insert, Illustrations	
Insert Icons window	Insert, Illustrations	
Insert Picture dialog box	Insert, Illustrations	
Insert WordArt button drop-down list	Insert, Text	
Online 3D Models window	Insert, Illustrations	
Online Pictures window	Insert, Illustrations	
screenshot	Insert, Illustrations	
Shapes button drop-down list	Insert, Illustrations	
Symbol dialog box	Insert, Symbols	
text box	Insert, Text	

Index

fill handle to copy formula, 18

with functions, 38–44

mixed cell references in, 47–48

ranges in, 130–131

Trace Error button, 36

writing

with AVERAGE, MIN, MAX, COUNT functions, 40–43

with financial functions, 170–173

with IF logical function, 200–204

with mathematical operators, 32–37

with NOW and TODAY function, 44

by pointing, 34–35

with statistical functions, 40–43

Formula tab, 38

Fraction, as category in Format Cells dialog box, 66

Freeze Panes button, 128–129

Function Arguments dialog box, 39, 201–202

Function Library group, 38

functions

argument, 38

AVERAGE, 18, 40–41

constants, 38

COUNT, 43

COUNTA, 43

defined, 38

FV, 170

identifying common errors, 36

inserting formulas with, 38–44

MAX, 41–43

MIN, 41–43

NOW, 44

PMT, 170

SUM, 17

TODAY, 44

writing formulas

with financial functions, 170–173

finding future value of investment, 173

finding periodic payments for loan, 171–173

with IF logical function, 200–204

with statistical functions, 40–43

funnel chart, 179

future value, 171

finding, 173

Fv, in financial functions, 171

FV function, 170

G

Go To feature, 6

graphic, linking using, 161–162

Graphics Tools Format Tab, 219

gridlines, 6

printing, 89

H

Header & Footer button, 91

Header & Footer Tools Design tab, 91–92

headers, inserting, 91–96

headings, printing row and column headings, 89

Help feature

in dialog box or backstage area, 28

Help Task Pane, 26

ScreenTips, 27

Hide button, 134

hiding

columns and rows, 75–76

worksheet, 125–126

histogram chart, 178

horizontal scroll bar, 4, 5, 7

hyperlinks

automatic formatting of, 158–159

editing, 162–163

inserting, 158–163

linking

to existing web page or file, 158–160

to new workbook, 160–162

to place in workbook, 160–162

using email address, 161

using graphic, 161–162

modifying, 162–163

navigating using, 159

purposes of, 148

removing, 162–163

I

icons, inserting and customizing, 218–221

Icons button, 218

IF function, writing formulas with, 200–204

IF statements

writing, containing text, 203–204

images

compress and crop, 210

creating alternative text for, 193–194

customizing and formatting, 210–211

formatting with Format Picture task pane, 212

inserting, 210–213

inserting and formatting clip art images, 212–213

sizing and moving, 210

Increase Decimal button, 22, 64

Increase Font Size button, 59

indenting, data, 67–68

Info backstage area, 10

Insert button, 55

Insert dialog box, 55

Insert Function button, 38

Insert Function dialog box, 38–39

Insert Hyperlink dialog box, 158

inserting

background picture, 88

clip art, 212–213

columns, 56–57

comments, 166–167

data in cells with fill handle, 14, 15–16

footers, 91–96

formulas

AutoSum, 17–18

fill handle to copy, 18

with functions, 38–44

headers, 91–96

hyperlinks, 158–163

icons, 218–221

images, 210–213

new worksheet, 116–118

page breaks, 83–86

rows, 55–56

screenshots, 214–215

shapes, 192–194, 215–217

SmartArt graphic, 224–228

Size button, 83
sizing
    chart, 179–180
    image, 210
    SmartArt graphic, 225
    WordArt, 229
    workbook, 135
SmartArt button, 224
SmartArt graphic
    changing design of, 226
    changing formatting of,
        227–228
    entering data in, 224
    sizing, moving and deleting,
        225
SmartArt Graphic dialog box,
    224
Smart Lookup task pane, 24–25
smart tag, 36
Sort dialog box, 104–105
Sort & Filter button, 104, 106
sorting data, 104–106
    custom sort, 104–106
    more than one column, 106
source data, 180
source worksheet, 137
Special, as category in Format
        Cells dialog box, 66
special characters, inserting,
        208–209
Spelling button, 97
spelling checker, 97, 98–99
Spelling dialog box, 98
Split button, 129
split lines, 129
statistical functions, writing
        formulas with, 40–43
Status bar, 4, 5, 6
stock chart, 178
Style dialog box, 152
subtraction
    inserting and copying formula,
        33
    order of operations, 35
    writing formula with, 32
SUM function, 17, 40
sunburst chart, 178
surface chart, 178
Switch Row/Column button, 186
Switch Windows button, 132
Symbol button, 208
Symbol dialog box, 208
symbols, inserting, 208–209

T

tab, 4, 5
Tell Me feature, 4, 5
    using, 24–25
templates, for worksheets,
        163–165
Text, as category in Format Cells
        dialog box, 66
text, rotating, 68–69
Text Box button, 218
text boxes, drawing and
        formatting, 218–221
Text Pane button, 224
theme
    applying, 62–63
    defined, 62
Themes button, 62
3D Model button, 221
3D Models, inserting and
        customizing, 221–223
tiled workbook, 132–133
Time, as category in Format
        Cells dialog box, 66
Title bar, 4, 5
TODAY function, writing
        formulas with, 44
Trace Error button, 36
treemap chart, 178, 199

U

Underline button, 59
Undo button, 97–98
Unfreeze Panes, 128–129
Unhide button, 134
Unhide dialog box, 125–126
unhiding, columns and rows,
        75–76
unpinning, workbook to *Recent*
        option list, 145

V

VALUE error code, 36
vertical scroll bar, 4, 5, 7

W

waterfall chart, 179
web page, linking to existing,
        158–160
Width option box, 87
windows

arranging workbooks in,
        132–134
    cascaded workbooks, 133
    hiding/unhiding workbooks,
        134
    opening multiple workbooks,
        132, 134
    opening new window, 132
    sizing and moving workbooks,
        135
    splitting worksheet into,
        128–129
    tiled workbooks, 132–133
WordArt, inserting and
        formatting, 228–229
WordArt button, 228
Word document, copying and
        pasting Excel data
        into, 138–139
workbook
    arranging, 132–134
    automatic entering features,
        12–14
    cascaded, 133
    closing, 11
    copying
        cell styles to another
            workbook, 156, 157
        worksheet to another,
            146–147
    creating, 4–8
        with multiple worksheets,
            116–118
    defined, 4
    deleting worksheet in, 116–
        118
    hide/unhiding, 134
    hide worksheet in, 125–126
    inserting new worksheet,
        116–118
    linking
        to new workbook, 160–162
        to place in, 160–162
    maintaining, 144–149
    managing at Open Backstage
        Area, 144–146
    maximizing, 135
    minimizing, 135
    moving, 135
        and copying data between,
            136
        worksheet to another,
            148–149
    naming, 6

Interior Photo Credits

Page GS-1, © lowball-jack/GettyImages, Courtesy of Paradigm Education Solutions; *page GS-2*, © irbis picture/Shutterstock.com; page *GS-3*, © th3fisa/Shutterstock.com; page *GS-4*, © goldyg/Shutterstock.com; page *GS-5*, © Pressmaster/Shutterstock.com.

Microsoft® Access® Level 1

Unit 1

Creating Tables and Queries

Microsoft®
Access®

Managing and Creating Access Tables

Performance Objectives

Upon successful completion of Chapter 1, you will be able to:

1 Open and close objects in a database

2 Insert and delete records in a table

3 Insert, delete, and move fields in a table

4 Hide, unhide, freeze, and unfreeze fields

5 Adjust table column width

6 Preview and print a table

7 Change page layout

8 Design and create a table

9 Rename a field, caption, or description

10 Insert Quick Start fields

11 Assign a field size or default value

Managing information is an integral part of operating a business. Information can come in a variety of forms, such as data about customers, including names, addresses, and telephone numbers; product data; or purchasing and sales data. Most companies manage data using system software. Microsoft Access is a database management system offered as part of the suite of applications in Microsoft Office 365. With Access, you can organize, store, maintain, retrieve, sort, and print all types of business data.

This chapter contains just a few ideas on how to manage data with Access. A properly designed and maintained database management system can help a company operate smoothly.

 Data Files

Before beginning chapter work, copy the AL1C1 folder to your storage medium and then make AL1C1 the active folder.

The online course includes additional review and assessment resources.

You will open a database and open and close objects in the database, including a table, a query, a form, and a report.

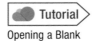
Tutorial

Opening a Blank Database

Exploring a Database

A database is comprised of a series of objects (such as tables, queries, forms, and/or reports) used to enter, manage, view, and print data. Data in a database is organized into tables, which contain information for related items (such as customers, employees, orders, or products).

To create a new database or open a previously created database, click the Windows Start button and then click the Access tile. (These steps may vary depending on your system configuration.) This displays the Access opening screen, as shown in Figure 1.1. At this screen, open a recently opened database, a blank database, a database from the Open backstage area, or a database based on a template.

Quick Steps

Create New Database
1. Open Access.
2. Click *Blank desktop database* template.
3. Type database name.
4. Click Create button.

Create

To create a new blank database, click the *Blank database* template. At the Blank database window, type a name for the database in the *File Name* text box, and then click the Create button. To save the database in a particular location, click the Browse button at the right side of the *File Name* text box. At the File New Database dialog box, navigate to the location or folder, type the database name in the *File name* text box, and then click OK.

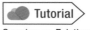
Tutorial

Opening an Existing Database

Opening a Database

A previously saved database can be opened at the Open dialog box. To display this dialog box, display the Open backstage area and then click the *Browse* option.

Figure 1.1 Access Opening Screen

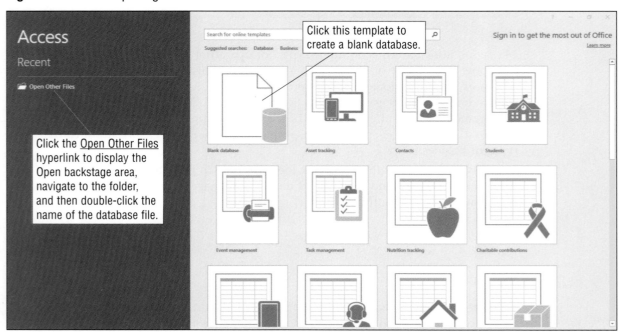

Display the Open backstage area by clicking the <u>Open Other Files</u> hyperlink at the Access opening screen. Or, click the File tab at the blank Access screen and then click the *Open* option. Other methods for displaying the Open backstage area include using the keyboard shortcut, Ctrl + O, or inserting an Open button on the Quick Access Toolbar.

At the Open backstage area, click the *Browse* option and the Open dialog box displays. At the Open dialog box, navigate to the desired location, such as the drive containing your storage medium, open the folder containing the database, and then double-click the database name in the Content pane. When a database is open, the Access screen looks similar to what is shown in Figure 1.2. Refer to Table 1.1 for descriptions of the Access screen elements.

Only one Access database can be open at a time. If a new database is opened in the current Access window, the existing database closes. However, multiple instances of Access can be opened and a database can be opened in each instance. In other applications in the Microsoft Office suite, a revised file must be saved after changes are made to the file. In an Access database, any changes made to data are saved automatically when moving to a new record, closing a table, or closing the database.

Enabling Content

A security warning message bar may appear below the ribbon if Access determines the file being opened did not originate from a trusted location on the computer and may contain viruses or other security hazards. This often occurs when an Access database is copied from another medium (such as an external drive or cloud storage location). Active content in the file is disabled until the Enable Content button is clicked. The message bar closes when the database is identified as a trusted source. Before making any changes to the database, the Enable Content button must be clicked.

Figure 1.2 Access Screen

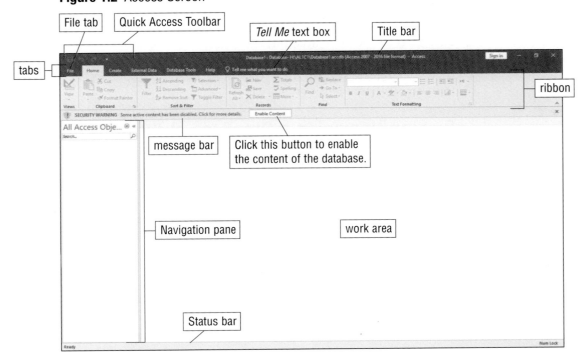

Table 1.1 Access Screen Elements

Feature	Description
File tab	when clicked, displays the backstage area that contains options for working with and managing databases
message bar	displays security alerts if the database being opened contains potentially unsafe content
Navigation pane	lists the names of objects within the database grouped by categories
Quick Access Toolbar	contains buttons for commonly used commands
ribbon	contains tabs with commands and buttons divided into groups
Status bar	displays messages, the current view, and view buttons
tabs	contain commands and features organized into groups
Tell Me text box	provides information as well as guidance on how to perform a function
Title bar	contains the database name followed by the program name
work area	displays opened objects

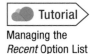

Managing the
Recent Option List

Opening a Database from the *Recent* Option List

At the Open backstage area with the *Recent* option selected, a list of the most recently opened databases displays. Access shows 50 of the most recently opened databases and groups them into categories such as *Today*, *Yesterday*, and perhaps another category such as *Last Week*. Click the database name in the *Recent* option list to open the database.

(Note: If opening a database from a OneDrive account, Access requires that a copy of the database be saved to a location such as the computer's hard drive or a USB flash drive. Any changes made to the database will be saved to the local copy of the database but not the database in the OneDrive account. To save a database back to the OneDrive account, the database will need to be uploaded by opening a web browser, going to OneDrive.com, logging in to the OneDrive account, and then clicking the Upload link. Microsoft constantly updates the OneDrive.com website, so these steps may vary.)

Pinning/Unpinning a Database at the *Recent* Option List

If a database is opened on a regular basis, consider pinning it to the *Recent* option list. To pin a database to the *Recent* option list at the Open backstage area, hover the mouse pointer over the database name and then click the small left-pointing push pin icon to the right of the database name. The left-pointing push pin changes to a down-pointing push pin and the pinned database is inserted into a new category named *Pinned*. The *Pinned* category appears at the top of the *Recent* option list. The next time the Open backstage area displays, the pinned database is in the *Pinned* category. A database can also be pinned to the Recent list at the Access opening screen. When a database is pinned, it is found at the top of the Recent list as well as the *Recent* option list at the Open backstage area.

To unpin a database from the Recent or *Recent* option list, click the pin icon to change it from a down-pointing push pin to a left-pointing push pin. More than one database can be pinned to a list. Another method for pinning and unpinning databases is to use the shortcut menu. Right-click a database name and then click the *Pin to list* or *Unpin from list* option.

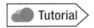

Opening and
Closing an Object

Opening and Closing Objects

The Navigation pane at the left side of the Access screen lists the objects contained in the database. Some common objects found in a database include tables, queries, forms, and reports. Refer to Table 1.2 for descriptions of these four types of objects.

Control what is shown in the pane by clicking the menu bar at the top of the Navigation pane and then clicking an option at the drop-down list or by clicking the button on the menu bar containing the down arrow. (The name of this button changes depending on what is selected.) For example, to display a list of all saved objects in the database, click the *Object Type* option at the drop-down list. This view lists the objects grouped by type: *Tables, Queries, Forms*, and *Reports*. To open an object, double-click the object in the Navigation pane. The object opens in the work area and a tab displays with the object name at the left side of the object. An object can also be opened with the shortcut menu by right-clicking the object in the Navigation pane and then clicking the *Open* option at the shortcut menu.

Shutter Bar
Open/Close
Button

To view more of an object, consider closing the Navigation pane by clicking the Shutter Bar Open/Close Button in the upper right corner of the Navigation pane or by pressing the F11 function key. Click the button or press the F11 function key again to reopen the Navigation pane. More than one object can be opened in the work area. Each object opens with a visible tab. Navigate to objects by clicking the object tab.

Hint Hide the Navigation pane by clicking the Shutter Bar Open/Close Button or by pressing the F11 function key.

To close an object, click the Close button (X) for that object (depending on the version of Access, this button will be located on the object tab or at the right corner of the work area) or use the keyboard shortcut Ctrl + F4. The shortcut menu can also be used to close an object by right-clicking the object tab and then clicking *Close* at the shortcut menu. Close multiple objects by right-clicking an object tab and then clicking *Close All* at the shortcut menu.

Closing a Database
and Closing Access

Closing a Database

To close a database, click the File tab and then click the *Close* option. Close Access by clicking the Close button in the upper right corner of the screen or with the keyboard shortcut Alt + F4.

  Close

Table 1.2 Database Objects

Object Type	Description
table	Organizes data in fields (columns) and records (rows). A database must contain at least one table. The table is the base upon which other objects are created.
query	Displays data from a table or related tables that meets a conditional statement and/or performs calculations. For example, all records from a specific month can be shown or only those records containing a specific city.
form	Allows fields and records to be presented in a layout different from the datasheet. Used to facilitate data entry and maintenance.
report	Prints data from tables or queries.

1. Open Access by clicking the Windows Start button and then clicking the Access tile in the Start menu.
2. At the Access opening screen, click the <u>Open Other Files</u> hyperlink.
3. At the Open backstage area, click the *Browse* option.
4. At the Open dialog box, navigate to the AL1C1 folder on your storage medium and then double-click *1-SampleDatabase*. (This database contains data on orders, products, and suppliers for a specialty hiking and backpacking outfitters store named Pacific Trek.)
5. Click the Enable Content button in the message bar if a security warning message appears. (The message bar will display immediately below the ribbon.)
6. With the database open, click the Navigation pane menu bar and then click *Object Type* in the *Navigate To Category* section of the drop-down list. Click the Navigation pane menu bar again and then click *All Access Objects* in the *Filter By Group* section. (This option lists the objects grouped by type: *Tables, Queries, Forms,* and *Reports.*)

7. Double-click *Suppliers* in the Tables group in the Navigation pane. This opens the Suppliers table in the work area, as shown in Figure 1.3.
8. Close the Suppliers table by clicking the Close button for the table. (Note that the Close button for an object will be located on the object tab or in the corner of the work area, as shown in the image below. Be careful not to confuse it with the Close button for the Access window, which closes the application.)

9. Double-click *OrdersOver$500* in the Queries group in the Navigation pane. A query displays data that meets a conditional statement. This query displays orders that meet the criterion of being more than $500.
10. Close the query by clicking the Close button for the query object (located on the object tab or in the right corner of the work area).
11. Right-click *SuppliersNotVancouver* in the Queries group in the Navigation pane and then click *Open* at the shortcut menu. This query displays information about suppliers but excludes those in Vancouver.

12. Right-click the SuppliersNotVancouver tab in the work area and then click *Close* at the shortcut menu.
13. Double-click *Orders* in the Forms group in the Navigation pane. This opens an order form. A form is used to view and edit data in a table one record at a time.
14. Double-click *Orders* in the Reports group in the Navigation pane. The Orders form is still open and the report opens in the work area over the Orders form. The Orders report displays information about orders and order amounts.

15. Close the Navigation pane by clicking the Shutter Bar Open/Close Button in the upper right corner of the pane.
16. After viewing the report, click the Shutter Bar Open/Close Button again to open the Navigation pane.
17. Right-click the Orders tab and then click *Close All* at the shortcut menu. (This closes both open objects.)
18. Close the database by clicking the File tab and then clicking the *Close* option.
19. Close Access by clicking the Close button in the upper right corner of the screen.

Figure 1.3 Suppliers Table

Activity 2 Manage Tables in a Database   7 Parts

Pacific Trek is an outfitting store specializing in hiking and backpacking gear. Information about the store, including suppliers and products, is contained in a database. You will open the database and then insert and delete records; insert, move, and delete fields; preview and print tables; rename and delete a table; and create two new tables for the database. Additionally, you will modify field columns, change page layout, insert Quick Start fields, and modify field properties.

Managing Tables

In a new database, tables are the first objects created, since all other database objects rely on a table as the source for their data. Managing the tables in the database is important for keeping the database up to date and may include inserting or deleting records, inserting or deleting fields, renaming fields, creating a hard copy of the table by printing the table, and renaming and deleting tables.

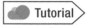

Tutorial

Adding and Deleting Records in a Table

Adding and Deleting Records

When a table is opened, it displays in Datasheet view in the work area. The Datasheet view displays the contents of a table in a column and row format similar to an Excel worksheet. Columns contain field data, with the field names in the header row at the top of the table, and rows contain records. A Record Navigation bar displays at the bottom of the screen just above the Status bar and contains buttons to navigate in the table. Figure 1.4 identifies the buttons and other elements on the Record Navigation bar.

To add a new record to the open table, make sure the Home tab is active and then click the New button in the Records group. This moves the insertion point to the first field in the blank row at the bottom of the table and the *Current Record* box on the Record Navigation bar indicates what record is being created (or edited). A new record can also be added by clicking the New (blank) record button on the Record Navigation bar.

When working in a table, press the Tab key to make the next field in the current record active or press Shift + Tab to make the previous field in the current record active. Make a field active with the mouse by clicking in the field. When typing data for the first field in the record, another row of cells is automatically inserted below the current row and a pencil icon appears in the record selector bar at the beginning of the current record. The pencil icon indicates that the record is being edited and that the changes to the data have not been saved. When data is entered in the last field and the insertion point is moved out of the field, the pencil icon is removed, indicating that the data has been saved.

To delete a record, click in one of the fields in the record, make sure the Home tab is active, click the Delete button arrow, and then click *Delete Record* at the drop-down list. At the message asking to confirm the deletion, click Yes. Click in a field in a record and the Delete button is dimmed unless specific data is selected.

Data entered in a table is automatically saved; however, changes to the layout of a table are not automatically saved. For example, if a column is deleted in a table, a deletion confirmation message will display when the table is closed.

 New

 Delete

Quick Steps

Add New Record
1. Open table.
2. Click New button on Home tab.
3. Type data.
OR
1. Open table.
2. Click New (blank) record button on Record Navigation bar.
3. Type data.

Quick Steps

Delete Record
1. Click field in record.
2. Click Delete button arrow.
3. Click *Delete Record*.
4. Click Yes.

Figure 1.4 Record Navigation Bar

1. Open Access.
2. At the Access opening screen, click the <u>Open Other Files</u> hyperlink.
3. At the Open backstage area, click the *Browse* option.
4. At the Open dialog box, navigate to the AL1C1 folder on your storage medium and then double-click *1-PacTrek*.
5. Click the Enable Content button in the message bar if a security warning message appears. (The message bar will display immediately below the ribbon.)
6. With the database open, make sure the Navigation pane lists object types. (If it does not, click the Navigation pane menu bar and then click *Object Type* at the drop-down list.)
7. Double-click *Suppliers* in the Tables group in the Navigation pane. (This opens the table in Datasheet view.)
8. With the Suppliers table open and the Home tab active, add a new record by completing the following steps:

   a. Click the New button in the Records group on the Home tab. (This moves the insertion point to the first field in the blank record at the bottom of the table and the *Current Record* box in the Record Navigation bar indicates what record you are creating or editing.)

   b. Type 38. (This inserts *38* in the field immediately below *99*.)
   c. Press the Tab key (to make the next field in the current record active) and then type Hadley Company.
   d. Press the Tab key and then type 5845 Jefferson Street.
   e. Press the Tab key and then type Seattle.
   f. Press the Tab key and then type WA.
   g. Press the Tab key and then type 98107.
   h. Press the Tab key and then type hcompany@ppi-edu.net.
   i. Press the Tab key and then type Jurene Miller.

SupplierID	SupplierNam	StreetAddre	City	Prov/State	PostalCode	EmailAddr	Contact	Click to Add
10	Hopewell, Inc.	5600 Carver Ro	Port Moody	BC	V3H 1A4	hopewell@p	Jacob Hopewel	
25	Langley Corpor	805 First Avenu	Burnaby	BC	V3J 1C9	langley@ppi	Mandy Shin	
31	Sound Supplie:	2104 Union Stre	Seattle	WA	98105	ssupplies@p	Regan Levine	
35	Emerald City Pi	1059 Pike Stree	Seattle	WA	98102	ecproducts@	Howard Greer	
42	Fraser Valley P	3894 Old Yale R	Abbotsford	BC	V2S 1A9	fvproducts@	Layla Adams	
54	Manning, Inc.	1039 South 22n	Vancouver	BC	V5K 1R1	manning@pr	Jack Silversteir	
68	Freedom Corpc	14 Fourth Aven	Vancouver	BC	V5K 2C7	freedom@pr	Opal Northwoc	
70	Rosewood, Inc	998 North 42nc	Vancouver	BC	V5K 2N8	rosewood@r	Clint Rivas	
84	Macadam, Inc.	675 Third Stree	Vancouver	BC	V5K 2R9	macadam@r	Hans Reiner	
99	KL Distribution	402 Yukon Driv	Bellingham	WA	98435	kldist@ppi-e	Noland Dannis	
38	Hadley Compai	5845 Jefferson	Seattle	WA	98107	hcompany@	Jurene Miller	

9. Close the Suppliers table by clicking the table's Close button. (The text you entered was automatically saved by Access.)
10. Open the Products table by double-clicking *Products* in the Tables group in the Navigation pane. (This opens the table in Datasheet view.)
11. Insert two new records by completing the following steps:
   a. Click the New button in the Records group and then enter the data for a new record as shown in Figure 1.5. (See the record that begins with *901-S*.)

b. After typing the last field entry in the record for product number 901-S, press the Tab key. This moves the insertion point to the blank field below *901-S*.

c. Type the new record as shown in Figure 1.5. (See the record that begins with *917-S*.)

12. With the Products table open, delete a record by completing the following steps:

a. Click in the field containing the data *780-2*.

b. Click the Delete button arrow in the Records group (notice that the button is dimmed) and then click *Delete Record* at the drop-down list.

c. At the message asking if you want to delete the record, click Yes.

13. Close the Products table by clicking the Close button for the table.

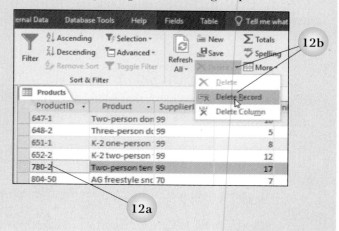

Check Your Work

Figure 1.5 Activity 2a, Step 11

ProductID	Product	SupplierID	UnitsInStock	UnitsOnOrde	ReorderLevel	Click to Add
602-XR	Binoculars, 8 x 42	35	3	5	5	
602-XT	Binoculars, 10.5 x 45	35	5	0	4	
602-XX	Binoculars, 10 x 50	35	7	0	5	
647-1	Two-person dome tent	99	10	15	15	
648-2	Three-person dome tent	99	5	0	10	
651-1	K-2 one-person tent	99	8	0	10	
652-2	K-2 two-person tent	99	12	0	10	
804-50	AG freestyle snowboard, X50	70	7	0	10	
804-60	AG freestyle snowboard, X60	70	8	0	5	
897-L	Lang blunt snowboard	70	8	0	7	
897-W	Lang blunt snowboard, wide	70	4	0	3	
901-S	Solar battery pack	38	16	0	15	
917-S	Silo portable power pack	38	8	0	10	
*						

Step 11

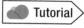

Managing Fields in Datasheet View

Quick Steps

Insert New Field
1. Open table.
2. Click in first cell below *Click to Add*.
3. Type data.

Inserting, Moving, and Deleting Fields

When managing a database, an additional field may need to be added to a table. For example, a field column may need to be added for contact information, one for cell phone numbers, or for the number of items in stock. To insert a new field column in a table, open the table in Datasheet view and then click in the first cell below *Click to Add* in the header row. Type the data in the cell, press the Down Arrow key, and then type the data for the second row. Continue in this manner until all data has been entered for the new field. In addition to pressing the Down Arrow key, move the insertion point down to the next cell by clicking in the cell or by pressing the Tab key.

Quick Steps

Move Field
1. Select column.
2. Position mouse pointer on field name in header row.
3. Click and hold down left mouse button.
4. Drag to new location.
5. Release mouse button.

Delete Field
1. Click in field.
2. Click Delete button arrow.
3. Click *Delete Column*.
4. Click Yes.

A new field column is added to the right of existing field columns. Move a field column by positioning the mouse pointer on the field name in the header row until the pointer displays as a down-pointing black arrow and then click the left mouse button. This selects the entire field column. With the field column selected, position the mouse pointer on the field name; click and hold down the left mouse button; drag to the left or right until a thick, black vertical line displays in the desired location; and then release the mouse button. The thick, black vertical line indicates where the field column will be positioned when the mouse button is released. In addition, the pointer displays with the outline of a gray box attached to it, indicating that a move operation is being performed.

Delete a field column in a manner similar to deleting a row. Click in one of the fields in the column, make sure the Home tab is active, click the Delete button arrow, and then click *Delete Column* at the drop-down list. At the message asking to confirm the deletion, click Yes.

Activity 2b Inserting, Moving, and Deleting Fields

1. With **1-PacTrek** open, add a new field to the Suppliers table by completing the following steps:
    a. Double-click *Suppliers* in the Tables group in the Navigation pane.
    b. Click in the field immediately below *Click to Add* in the header row.
    c. Type (604) 555-3843 and then press the Down Arrow key.
    d. Type the remaining telephone numbers as shown below and at the right.

2. Move the *Field1* field column so it is positioned immediately left of the *EmailAddress* field column by completing the following steps:
    a. Position the mouse pointer on the *Field1* field name in the header row until the pointer displays as a down-pointing black arrow and then click the left mouse button. (This selects the field column.)
    b. Position the mouse pointer on the *Field1* field name. Click and hold down the left mouse button; drag to the left until the thick, black vertical line displays immediately left of the *EmailAddress* field column; and then release the mouse button.

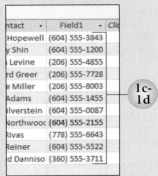

3. Delete the *Contact* field by completing the following steps:
    a. Position the mouse pointer on the *Contact* field name in the header row until the pointer displays as a down-pointing black arrow and then click the left mouse button. (This selects the field column.)
    b. Click the Delete button arrow in the Records group and then click *Delete Column* at the drop-down list.

    c. At the message asking if you want to permanently delete the selected field(s) click Yes.
4. Close the Suppliers table. At the message asking if you want to save the changes to the layout of the table, click Yes.

Check Your Work

Hiding, Unhiding,
Freezing, and
Unfreezing Field
Columns

 More

Hiding, Unhiding, Freezing, and Unfreezing Field Columns

A field column in a table can be hidden if the column is not needed for data entry or editing purposes or to make viewing easier for two nonadjacent field columns containing data to be compared. To hide a field column, click in any field in the column, click the More button in the Records group on the Home tab, and then click *Hide Fields* at the drop-down list. Hide adjacent field columns by selecting the columns, clicking the More button in the Records group, and then clicking *Hide Fields* at the drop-down list. To unhide field columns, click the More button and then click *Unhide Fields*. At the Unhide Columns dialog box, insert a check mark in the check boxes for those field columns that should remain visible.

Another method for comparing field columns side by side is to freeze a column. Freezing a field column is also helpful when not all of the columns of data are visible at one time. To freeze a field column, click in any field in the column, click the More button, and then click *Freeze Fields* at the drop-down list. To freeze adjacent field columns, select the columns first, click the More button, and then click *Freeze Fields* at the drop-down list. To unfreeze all field columns in a table, click the More button and then click *Unfreeze All Fields* at the drop-down list.

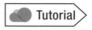

Adjusting Field
Column Width

Quick Steps

Adjust Field Column Width
1. Click More button.
2. Click *Field Width*.
3. Type measurement.
4. Click OK.
OR
1. Click More button.
2. Click *Field Width*.
3. Click Best Fit button.
OR
Double-click column boundary line.
OR
Select field columns and then double-click column boundary line.
OR
Drag column boundary line to new position.

Adjusting Field Column Width

Field columns have a default width of 13.111 characters, which is the approximate number of characters that will be visible in a field in the column. Depending on the data entered in a field in a field column, not all of the data will be visible. Or data entered in a field may take up only a portion of the field. Change a field's column width with options at the Column Width dialog box. Display the dialog box by clicking the More button in the Records group on the Home tab and then clicking the *Field Width* option. Enter a measurement in the *Column Width* measurement box or click the Best Fit button to adjust the column width to accommodate the longest entry.

The width of a field column also can be adjusted to accommodate the longest entry by positioning the mouse pointer on the column boundary line at the right side of the column in the header row until the pointer turns into a left-and-right-pointing arrow with a vertical line in the middle and then double-clicking the left mouse button. Adjust the widths of adjacent field columns by selecting the columns first and then double-clicking one of the selected column boundary lines in the header row. To select adjacent field columns, position the mouse pointer on the first field name to be selected in the header row until the pointer turns into a down-pointing black arrow, click and hold down the left mouse button, drag to the last field name to be selected, and then release the mouse button. With the field columns selected, double-click one of the field column boundary lines.

Another method for adjusting the width of a field column is to drag a boundary line to the desired position. To do this, position the mouse pointer on the column boundary line (until the pointer turns into a left-and-right-pointing arrow with a vertical line in the middle), click and hold down the left mouse button, drag until the field column is the desired width, and then release the mouse button.

Activity 2c Hiding, Unhiding, Freezing, and Unfreezing Field Columns
and Changing Field Column Widths

1. With **1-PacTrek** open, open the Suppliers table.
2. Hide the *PostalCode* field column by clicking the *PostalCode* field name in the header row, clicking the More button in the Records group on the Home tab, and then clicking *Hide Fields* at the drop-down list.

3. Unhide the field column by clicking the More button and then clicking *Unhide Fields* at the drop-down list. At the Unhide Columns dialog box, click the *PostalCode* check box to insert a check mark, and then click the Close button.
4. Adjust the width of the *SupplierID* field column by completing the following steps:
   a. Click the *SupplierID* field name in the header row.
   b. Click the More button in the Records group on the Home tab.
   c. Click the *Field Width* option.
   d. Type 11 in the *Column Width* measurement box.
   e. Click OK.

5. Adjust the *SupplierName* field column by completing the following steps:
   a. Click the *SupplierName* field name in the header row.
   b. Click the More button in the Records group.
   c. Click the *Field Width* option.
   d. Click the Best Fit button.

6. Select the remaining columns and adjust the column widths by completing the following steps:
   a. Position the mouse pointer on the *StreetAddress* field name in the header row until the pointer turns into a down-pointing black arrow, click and hold down the left mouse button, drag to the *EmailAddress* field name, and then release the mouse button.
   b. With the columns selected, double-click one of the column boundary lines in the header row.
   c. Click in any field in the table to deselect the field columns.
7. Increase the width of the *EmailAddress* field column by positioning the mouse pointer on the column boundary line in the header row at the right side of the *EmailAddress* field column until it turns into a left-and-right-pointing arrow with a vertical line in the middle, clicking and holding down the left mouse button, dragging all the way to the right side of the screen, and then releasing the mouse button. (Check the horizontal scroll bar at the bottom of the table and notice that the scroll bar contains a scroll box.)
8. Position the mouse pointer on the scroll box on the horizontal scroll bar and then drag to the left until the *SupplierID* field is visible.
9. Freeze the *SupplierID* field column by clicking in any field in the *SupplierID* field column, clicking the More button in the Records group, and then clicking *Freeze Fields* at the drop-down list.

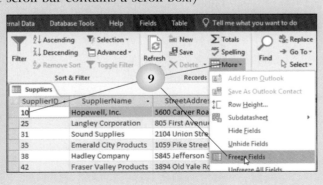

10. Using the mouse, drag the scroll box along the horizontal scroll to the right and left to see that the *SupplierID* field column remains visible on the screen.
11. Unfreeze the field column by clicking the More button in the Records group and then clicking *Unfreeze All Fields* at the drop-down list.
12. Double-click the column boundary line in the header row at the right side of the *EmailAddress* field column.
13. Close the Suppliers table and click Yes at the message that asks if you want to save the changes to the layout.
14. Open the Products table and then complete steps similar to those in Step 6 to select and then adjust the field column widths.
15. Close the Products table and click Yes at the message that asks if you want to save the changes to the layout.

 Check Your Work

 Tutorial

Renaming and Deleting Objects

Quick Steps

Rename Table
1. Right-click table name in Navigation pane.
2. Click *Rename*.
3. Type new name.
4. Press Enter key.

Delete Table
1. Right-click table name in Navigation pane.
2. Click *Delete*.
3. Click Yes, if necessary.

Renaming and Deleting a Table

Managing tables might include actions such as renaming and deleting a table. Rename a table by right-clicking the table name in the Navigation pane, clicking *Rename* at the shortcut menu, typing the new name, and then pressing the Enter key. Delete a table from a database by clicking the table name in the Navigation pane, clicking the Delete button in the Records group on the Home tab, and then clicking Yes at the message asking to confirm the deletion. Another method is to right-click the table in the Navigation pane, click *Delete* at the shortcut menu, and then click Yes at the message. If a table is deleted from the computer's hard drive, the message asking to confirm the deletion does not display. This is because Access automatically sends the deleted table to the Recycle Bin, where it can be retrieved if necessary.

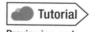 Tutorial

Previewing and Printing a Table

Quick Steps

Print Table
1. Click File tab.
2. Click *Print*.
3. Click *Quick Print*.
OR
1. Click File tab.
2. Click *Print*.
3. Click *Print*.
4. Click OK.

Printing Tables

Click the File tab and then click the *Print* option to display the Print backstage area as shown in Figure 1.6. Click the *Quick Print* option to send the table directly to the printer without making any changes to the printer setup or the table formatting. Click the *Print* option to display the Print dialog box, with options for specifying the printer, page range, and specific records to print. Click OK to close the dialog box and send the table to the printer. By default, Access prints a table on letter-size paper in portrait orientation.

Figure 1.6 Print Backstage Area

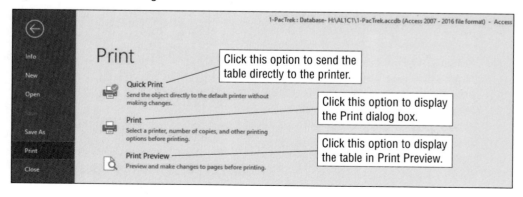

Previewing a Table

Quick Steps

Preview Table
1. Click File tab.
2. Click *Print* option.
3. Click *Print Preview* option.

Print Preview

Print

Close Print Preview

Before printing a table, consider displaying the table in Print Preview to see how the table will print on the page. To display a table in Print Preview, as shown in Figure 1.7, click the *Print Preview* option at the Print backstage area.

Use options in the Zoom group on the Print Preview tab to increase or decrease the size of the page display. The size of the page display can also be changed using the Zoom slider bar at the right side of the Status bar. If a table spans more than one page, use buttons on the Navigation bar to move to the next or previous page.

Print a table from Print Preview by clicking the Print button at the left side of the Print Preview tab. Click the Close Print Preview button to close Print Preview and continue working in the table without printing it.

Changing Page Size and Margins

Size

Margins

By default, Access prints a table in standard letter size (8.5 inches wide and 11 inches tall). Click the Size button in the Page Size group on the Print Preview tab and a drop-down list displays with options for changing the page size to legal, executive, envelope, and so on. Access uses default top, bottom, left, and right margins of 1 inch. Change these default margins by clicking the Margins button in the Page Size group and then clicking one of the predesigned margin options.

Figure 1.7 Print Preview

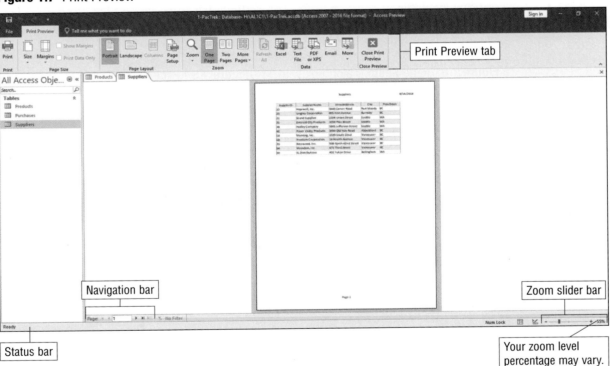

Changing Page Layout

The Print Preview tab contains the Page Layout group with buttons for controlling how data is printed on the page. By default, Access prints a table in portrait orientation, which prints the text on the page so that it is taller than it is wide (like a page in this textbook). If a table contains a number of columns, changing to landscape orientation allows more columns to fit on a page. Landscape orientation rotates the printout to be wider than it is tall. To change from the default portrait orientation to landscape orientation, click the Landscape button in the Page Layout group on the Print Preview tab.

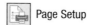
Landscape

Page Setup

Click the Page Setup button in the Page Layout group and the Page Setup dialog box displays as shown in Figure 1.8. At the Page Setup dialog box with the Print Options tab selected, notice that the default margins are 1 inch. Change these defaults by typing different numbers in the margin measurement boxes. By default, the table name prints at the top center of the page and the current date prints in the upper right corner of the page. In addition, the word *Page* followed by the page number prints at the bottom of the page. To specify that the name of the table, date, and page number should not print, remove the check mark from the *Print Headings* option at the Page Setup dialog box with the Print Options tab selected.

Quick Steps

Display Page Setup Dialog Box
1. Click File tab.
2. Click *Print* option.
3. Click *Print Preview* option.
4. Click Page Setup button.

Click the Page tab at the Page Setup dialog box and the dialog box displays as shown in Figure 1.9. Change the orientation with options in the *Orientation* section and change the paper size with options in the *Paper* section. Click the *Size* option box arrow and a drop-down list displays with paper sizes similar to the options available at the *Size* button drop-down list in the Page Size group on the Print Preview tab. Specify the printer with options in the *Printer for (table name)* section of the dialog box.

Figure 1.8 Page Setup Dialog Box with Print Options Tab Selected

Figure 1.9 Page Setup Dialog Box with Page Tab Selected

Enter measurements in these measurement boxes to change the page margins.

Remove the check mark from this check box to specify that the table name, date, and page number should not print.

Click this option to change the page orientation to landscape.

Change the paper size with this option.

1. With **1-PacTrek** open, open the Suppliers table.
2. Preview and then print the Suppliers table in landscape orientation by completing the following steps:

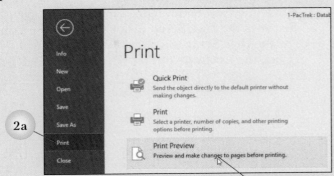

   a. Click the File tab and then click the *Print* option.
   b. At the Print backstage area, click the *Print Preview* option.
   c. Click the Two Pages button in the Zoom group on the Print Preview tab. (This displays two pages of the table.)
   d. Click the Zoom button arrow in the Zoom group on the Print Preview tab and then click *75%* at the drop-down list.

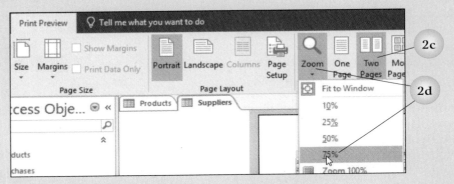

   e. Position the mouse pointer on the Zoom slider bar button at the right side of the Status bar, click and hold down the left mouse button, drag to the right until *100%* displays at the right of the Zoom slider bar, and then release the mouse button.

   f. Return the display to a full page by clicking the One Page button in the Zoom group on the Print Preview tab.
   g. Click the Margins button in the Page Size group on the Print Preview tab and then click the *Narrow* option at the drop-down list. (Notice how the data will print on the page with the narrow margins.)

   h. Change the margins back to the default by clicking the Margins button in the Page Size group and then clicking the *Normal* option at the drop-down list.
   i. Change to landscape orientation by clicking the Landscape button in the Page Layout group.
   j. Print the table by clicking the Print button at the left side of the Print Preview tab and then clicking OK at the Print dialog box.
3. Close the Suppliers table.

4. Open the Products table and then print the table by completing the following steps:
   a. Click the File tab and then click the *Print* option.
   b. At the Print backstage area, click the *Print Preview* option.
   c. Click the Page Setup button in the Page Layout group on the Print Preview tab. (This displays the Page Setup dialog box with the Print Options tab selected.)
   d. At the Page Setup dialog box, click the Page tab.
   e. Click the *Landscape* option.

   f. Click the Print Options tab.
   g. Select the current measurement in the *Top* measurement box and then type 0.5.
   h. Select the current measurement in the *Bottom* measurement box and then type 0.5.
   i. Select the current measurement in the *Left* measurement box and then type 1.5.
   j. Click OK to close the dialog box.
   k. Click the Print button on the Print Preview tab and then click OK at the Print dialog box. (This table will print on two pages.)
5. Close the Products table.
6. Rename the Purchases table by right-clicking *Purchases* in the Navigation pane, clicking *Rename* at the shortcut menu, typing Orders, and then pressing the Enter key.
7. Delete the Orders table by right-clicking *Orders* in the Tables group in the Navigation pane and then clicking *Delete* at the shortcut menu. If a message displays asking if you want to permanently delete the table, click Yes.

Check Your Work

Designing a Table

Tables are the first objects created in a new database and all other objects in a database rely on tables for data. Designing a database involves planning the number of tables needed and the fields that will be included in each table. Each table in a database should contain information about only one subject. For example, the Suppliers table in the 1-PacTrek database contains data only about suppliers and the Products table contains data only about products.

Database designers often create a visual representation of the database's structure in a diagram similar to the one shown in Figure 1.10. Each table is represented by a box with the table name at the top. Within each box, the fields that will be stored in the table are listed with the field names that will be used when the table is created.

Notice that one field in each table has an asterisk next to its name. The field with the asterisk is called the *primary key field*. A primary key field holds data that uniquely identifies each record in a table and is usually an identification number. The lines drawn between each table in Figure 1.10 are called *join lines*, and they represent links established between tables (called *relationships*) so that data can be extracted from one or more tables. The join lines point to a common field name included in each table that is to be linked. (Joining tables is covered in Chapter 2.) A database with related tables is called a *relational database*.

The join line in the database diagram connects the *SupplierID* field in the Suppliers table with the *SupplierID* field in the Products table and another join line connects the *SupplierID* field in the Suppliers table with the *SupplierID* field in the Orders table. A join line connects the *ProductID* field in the Products table with the *ProductID* field in the Orders table.

Hint Join tables to minimize or eliminate data duplication.

Consider certain design principles when designing a database. The first principle is to reduce redundant (duplicate) data. Redundant data increases the amount of data entry required, increases the chances for errors and inconsistencies, and takes up additional storage space. The Products table contains a *SupplierID* field and that field reduces the duplicate data needed in the table by keeping the data in one table instead of two and then joining the tables by a common field.

Figure 1.10 Database Diagram

Suppliers	Products	Orders
*SupplierID	*ProductID	*OrderID
SupplierName	Product	SupplierID
StreetAddress	SupplierID	ProductID
City	UnitsInStock	UnitsOrdered
Prov/State	UnitsOnOrder	OrderAmount
PostalCode	ReorderLevel	OrderDate
EmailAddress		
Contact		

For example, rather than typing the supplier information in the Suppliers table *and* the Products table, type the information once in the Suppliers table and then join the tables with the connecting field *SupplierID*. If information is needed on suppliers as well as specific information about products, the information can be drawn into one object, such as a query or report using data from both tables. When creating the Orders table, the *SupplierID* field and the *ProductID* field will be used rather than typing all the information for the suppliers and the product description. Typing a two-letter unique identifier number for a supplier greatly reduces the amount of typing required to create the Orders table. Inserting the *ProductID* field in the Orders table eliminates the need to type the product description for each order; instead, a unique five-, six-, or seven-digit identifier number is typed.

Tutorial

Creating a Table in Datasheet View

💡 *Hint* A database table contains fields that can describe a person, customer, client, object, place, idea, or event.

Creating a Table

Creating a new table generally involves determining fields, assigning a data type to each field, modifying properties, designating the primary key field, and naming the table. This process is referred to as defining the table structure.

The first step in creating a table is to determine the fields. A field, commonly called a column, is one piece of information about a person, place, or item. Each field contains data about one aspect of the table subject, such as a company name or product number. All fields for one unit, such as a customer or product, are considered a record. For example, in the Suppliers table in the 1-PacTrek database, a record is all of the information pertaining to one supplier. A collection of records becomes a table.

When designing a table, determine the fields to be included based on how the information will be used. When organizing fields be sure to consider not only the current needs for the data but also any future needs. For example, a company may need to keep track of customer names, addresses, and telephone numbers for current mailing lists. In the future, the company may want to promote a new product to customers who purchase a specific type of product. For this information to be available at a later date, a field that identifies product type must be included in the database. When organizing fields, consider all potential needs for the data but also try to keep the fields logical and manageable.

 Table

A table can be created in Datasheet view or Design view. To create a table in Datasheet view, open the database (or create a new database), click the Create tab, and then click the Table button in the Tables group. This inserts a blank table in the work area with the tab labeled *Table1*, as shown in Figure 1.11. Notice the column with the field name *ID* has been created automatically. Access creates *ID* as an AutoNumber data type field in which the field value is assigned automatically by Access as each record is entered in the table. In many tables, this AutoNumber data type field is used to create the unique identifier for the table. For example, in Activity 2e, you will create an Orders table and use the *ID* AutoNumber data type field to assign automatically a number to each order, since each order must contain a unique number.

💡 *Hint* Assign a data type to each field that determines the type of information that can be entered into the field.

When creating a new field (column), determine the type of data to be inserted in the field. For example, one field might contain text such as a name or product description, another field might contain an amount of money, and another might contain a date. The data type defines the type of information Access will allow to be entered into the field. For example, Access will not allow alphabetic characters to be entered into a field with a data type set to Date & Time.

Figure 1.11 Blank Table in Datasheet View

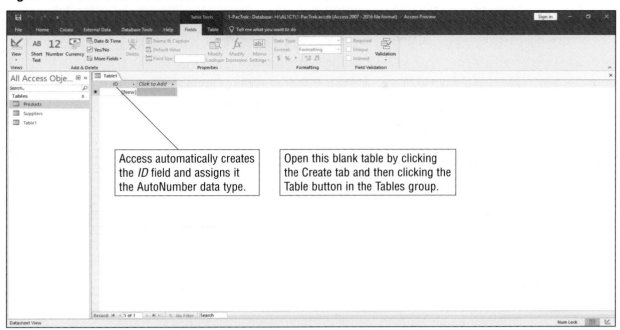

Access automatically creates the *ID* field and assigns it the AutoNumber data type.

Open this blank table by clicking the Create tab and then clicking the Table button in the Tables group.

 More Fields

The Add & Delete group on the Table Tools Fields tab contains five buttons for assigning data types plus a More Fields button. Descriptions of the five data types assigned by the buttons are provided in Table 1.3.

Table 1.3 Data Types

Button	Description
Short Text	Alphanumeric data up to 255 characters in length—for example, a name, an address, or a value such as a telephone number or social security number that is used as an identifier and not for calculating.
Number	Positive or negative values that can be used in calculations; not to be used for values that will calculate monetary amounts (see Currency).
Currency	Values that involve money; Access will not round off during calculations.
Date & Time	Used to ensure dates and times are entered and sorted properly.
Yes/No	Data in the field will be either *Yes* or *No*, *True* or *False*, *On* or *Off*.

In Activity 2e, you will create the Orders table, as shown in Figure 1.12. Looking at the diagram in Figure 1.10 (on page 21), you will assign the following data types to the columns:

OrderID:	AutoNumber (Access automatically assigns this data type to the first column)
SupplierID:	Short Text (the supplier numbers are identifiers, not numbers for calculating)
ProductID:	Short Text (the product numbers are identifiers, not numbers for calculating)
UnitsOrdered:	Number (the unit numbers are values for calculating)
Amount:	Currency
OrderDate:	Date & Time

Click a data type button and Access inserts a field to the right of the *ID* field and selects the field heading *Field1*. Type a name for the field; press the Enter key; and Access selects the next field heading, named *Click to Add*, and displays a drop-down list of data types. This drop-down list contains the same five data types as the buttons in the Add & Delete group as well as additional data types. Click the data type at the drop-down list, type the field name, and then press the Enter key. Continue in this manner until all field names have been entered for the table. When naming a field, consider the following guidelines:

- Each field must have a unique name.
- The name should describe the contents of the field.
- A field name can contain up to 64 characters.
- A field name can contain letters and numbers. Some symbols are permitted but others are excluded, so avoid using symbols other than the underscore (to separate words) and the number symbol (to indicate an identifier number).

💡 **Hint** Avoid using spaces in field names.

- Do not use spaces in field names. Although a space is an accepted character, most database designers avoid using spaces in field names and object names. Use field compound words for field names or the underscore character as a word separator. For example, a field name for a person's last name could be named *LastName*, *Last_Name*, or *LName*.
- Abbreviate field names so that they are as short as possible but still easily understood. For example, a field such as *CompanyName* could be shortened to *CoName* and a field such as *EmailAddress* could be shortened to *Email*.

Activity 2e Creating a Table and Entering Data

Part 5 of 7

1. With **1-PacTrek** open, create a new table and specify data types and field names by completing the following steps:
   a. Click the Create tab.
   b. Click the Table button in the Tables group.
   c. Click the Short Text button in the Add & Delete group.

   d. With the *Field1* field name selected, type SupplierID and then press the Enter key. (This displays a drop-down list of data types below the *Click to Add* heading.)

e. Click the *Short Text* option at the drop-down list.

f. Type ProductID in the next field name and then press the Enter key.

g. Click *Number* at the drop-down list, type UnitsOrdered in the next field name, and then press the Enter key.

h. Click *Currency* at the drop-down list, type OrderAmount for the next field, and then press the Enter key.

i. Click *Date & Time* at the drop-down list and then type OrderDate. (Do not press the Enter key since this is the last field in the table.)

2. Enter the first record in the table, as shown in Figure 1.12, by completing the following steps:

a. Click two times in the first field below the *SupplierID* field name. (The first time you click the mouse button, the row is selected. Clicking the second time makes only the field below *SupplierID* active.)

b. Type the data in the fields as shown in Figure 1.12. Press the Tab key to move to the next field or press Shift + Tab to move to the previous field. Access will automatically insert the next number in the sequence in the first field column (the *ID* field column). When typing the money amounts in the *OrderAmount* field column, you do not need to type the dollar symbol or the comma. Access will automatically insert them when you make the next field active. Make sure to proofread the data after you type it to ensure it is accurate. ***Note: Since the ID field has the Autonumber data type applied, Access automatically inserts (New) in the row after the last record. Even though (New) appears in the field, the row does not contain a new record and the information in the row does not print.***

3. When the 14 records have been entered, click the Save button on the Quick Access Toolbar.

4. At the Save As dialog box, type Orders and then press the Enter key. (This saves the table with the name *Orders*.)

5. Close the Orders table by clicking the Close button for the table.

 Check Your Work

Figure 1.12 Activity 2e

ID	SupplierID	ProductID	UnitsOrdered	OrderAmount	OrderDate	Cli
1	54	101-S3	10	$1,137.50	1/5/2021	
2	68	209-L	25	$173.75	1/5/2021	
3	68	209-XL	25	$180.00	1/5/2021	
4	68	209-XXL	20	$0.00	1/5/2021	
5	68	210-M	15	$0.00	1/5/2021	
6	68	210-L	25	$0.00	1/5/2021	
7	31	299-M2	10	$0.00	1/19/2021	
8	31	299-M3	10	$0.00	1/19/2021	
9	31	299-M5	10	$0.00	1/19/2021	
10	31	299-W1	8	$0.00	1/19/2021	
11	31	299-W3	10	$0.00	1/19/2021	
12	31	299-W4	10	$0.00	1/19/2021	
13	31	299-W5	10	$0.00	1/19/2021	
14	35	602-XR	5	$0.00	1/19/2021	
(New)			0	$0.00		

Renaming a Field

Click a data type button or click a data type at the data type drop-down list and the default field name (such as *Field1*) is automatically selected. With the default field name selected, type a name for the field. To change a field name, right-click the name, click *Rename Field* at the shortcut menu (which selects the current field name), and then type the new name.

Tutorial

Modifying Field
Properties in
Datasheet View

Name &
Caption

Inserting a Name, Caption, and Description

When creating a table that others will use, consider providing additional information so users understand the fields in the table and what should be entered in each one. Along with the field name, provide a caption and description for each field with options at the Enter Field Properties dialog box, shown in Figure 1.13. Display this dialog box by clicking the Name & Caption button in the Properties group on the Table Tools Fields tab.

At the Enter Field Properties dialog box, type the name for the field in the *Name* text box. To provide a more descriptive name for the field, type the descriptive name in the *Caption* text box. The text typed will become the field caption but the actual field name will still be part of the table structure. Creating a caption is useful if the field name is abbreviated or to show spaces between words in a field name. The field name is what Access uses for the table and the caption is what users see.

The *Description* text box is another source for providing information about the field to others using the database. Type information in the text box that specifies what should be entered in the field. The text typed in the *Description* text box displays at the left side of the Status bar when a field in a column is active. For example, type *Enter the total amount of the order* in the *Description* text box for the *OrderAmount* field and that text will display at the left side of the Status bar when a field in the column is active.

Figure 1.13 Enter Field Properties Dialog Box

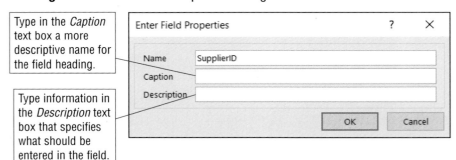

Type in the *Caption* text box a more descriptive name for the field heading.

Type information in the *Description* text box that specifies what should be entered in the field.

1. With **1-PacTrek** open, open the Orders table.
2. Access automatically named the first field *ID*. You want to make the field name more descriptive, so you decide to rename it. To do this, right-click the *ID* field name and then click *Rename Field* at the drop-down list.
3. Type OrderID and then press the Enter key.
4. To provide more information for others using the table, you decide to add information for the *SupplierID* field by creating a caption and description. To do this, complete the following steps:
   a. Click the *SupplierID* field name in the header row. (This selects the entire column.)
   b. Click the Table Tools Fields tab.
   c. Click the Name & Caption button in the Properties group. (At the Enter Field Properties dialog box, notice that *SupplierID* is already inserted in the *Name* text box.)
   d. At the Enter Field Properties dialog box, click in the *Caption* text box and then type Supplier Number.
   e. Click in the *Description* text box and then type Supplier identification number.
   f. Click OK to close the dialog box. (Notice that the field name now reads *Supplier Number*.)
5. Click the *ProductID* field name in the header row and then complete steps similar to those in Steps 4c through 4f to create the caption *Product Number* and the description *Product identification number*.
6. Click the *OrderAmount* field name in the header row and then complete steps similar to those in Steps 4c through 4f to create the caption *Order Amount* and the description *Total amount of order*.
7. Click the Save button on the Quick Access Toolbar to save the changes to the Orders table.
8. Close the Orders table.

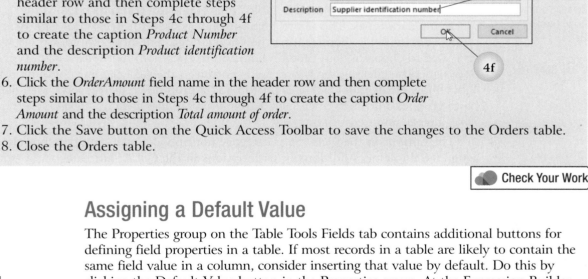

> Check Your Work

Assigning a Default Value

The Properties group on the Table Tools Fields tab contains additional buttons for defining field properties in a table. If most records in a table are likely to contain the same field value in a column, consider inserting that value by default. Do this by clicking the Default Value button in the Properties group. At the Expression Builder dialog box, type the default value and then click OK.

Default Value

For example, in Activity 2g, you will create a new table in the 1-PacTrek database containing information on customers, most of whom live in Vancouver, British Columbia. You will create a default value of *Vancouver* for the *City* field and a default value of *BC* for the *Prov/State* field. You can replace the default value with different text, so if a customer lives in Abbotsford instead of Vancouver, simply type *Abbotsford* in the *City* field instead.

Assigning a Field Size

The default field size property varies depending on the data type. For example, the Short Text data type assigns a maximum length of 255 characters that can be entered in the field. This number can be decreased depending on what data will be entered in the field. The field size can also be changed to control how much data is entered to help reduce errors. For example, if the two-letter state abbreviation is to be inserted in a state field, a field size of 2 characters can be assigned to the field. If someone entering data into the table tries to type more than two letters, Access will not accept the additional text. To change the field size, click in the *Field Size* text box in the Properties group on the Table Tools Fields tab and then type the number.

Changing the AutoNumber Data Type Field

Access automatically applies the AutoNumber data type to the first field in a table and assigns a unique number to each record in the table. In many cases, letting Access automatically assign a number to a record is a good idea. Some situations may arise, however, when the unique value in the first field should be something other than a number.

To change the AutoNumber data type for the first field, click the *Data Type* option box arrow in the Formatting group on the Table Tools Fields tab and then click the data type at the drop-down list.

Creating a Table Using Quick Start Fields

AB Short Text

Inserting Quick Start Fields

The Add & Delete group on the Table Tools Fields tab contains buttons for specifying data types. The Short Text button was used to specify the data type for the *SupplierID* field when creating the Orders table. The field drop-down list was also used to choose a data type. In addition to these two methods, a data type can be assigned by clicking the More Fields button in the Add & Delete group on the Table Tools Fields tab. Click this button and a drop-down list displays with data types grouped into categories such as *Basic Types*, *Number*, *Large Number*, *Date and Time*, *Yes/No*, and *Quick Start*.

The options in the *Quick Start* category not only define a data type but also assign a field name. Additionally, with options in the *Quick Start* category, a group of related fields can be added in one step. For example, click the *Name* option in the *Quick Start* category and Access inserts the *LastName* field in one column and the *FirstName* field in the next column. Both fields are automatically assigned a Short Text data type. Click the *Address* option in the *Quick Start* category and Access inserts five fields, including *Address*, *City*, *StateProvince*, *ZIPPostal*, and *CountryRegion*—all with the Short Text data type assigned.

Activity 2g Creating a Customers Table, Inserting Quick Start Fields
and Modifying Field Properties   **Part 7 of 7**

1. The owners of Pacific Trek have decided to
   publish a semiannual product catalog and
   have asked customers who want to
   receive the catalog to fill out a form and
   include on the form whether or not they
   want to receive notices of upcoming
   sales in addition to the catalog. Create a
   table to store the data for customers by
   completing the following steps:
   a. With **1-PacTrek** open, click the Create
      tab.
   b. Click the Table button in the Tables
      group.
   c. With the *Click to Add* field active, click
      the More Fields button in the Add &
      Delete group on the Table Tools Fields
      tab.
   d. Scroll down the drop-down list and
      then click *Name* in the *Quick Start*
      category. (This inserts the captions
      Last Name and *First Name* in the table.
      The actual field names are *LastName*
      and *FirstName*.)

   e. Click *Click to Add* immediately right of the *First Name* field name in the header row.
      (Although the data type drop-down list displays, you are going to use the More Fields
      button rather than the drop-down list to create the next fields.)
   f. Click the More Fields button, scroll down the drop-down list, and then click *Address* in
      the *Quick Start* category. (This inserts five more fields in the table.)
   g. Scroll to the right in the table until *Click to Add* is visible in the header row following
      the *Country Region* field name. (You can scroll in the table using the horizontal scroll bar
      to the right of the Record Navigation bar.)
   h. Click *Click to Add* and then click *Yes/No* at the drop-
      down list.
   i. With the name *Field1* selected, type Mailers. (When
      entering records in the table, you will insert a check
      mark in the field check box if a customer wants to
      receive sales promotion mailers. If a customer
      does not want to receive the mailers, you will
      leave the check box blank.)

2. Rename and create a caption and description for
   the *ID* field by completing the following steps:
   a. Scroll to the beginning of the table and then click
      the *ID* field name in the header row.
   b. Click the Name & Caption button in the Properties group on the Table Tools Fields tab.

c. At the Enter Field Properties dialog box, select the text *ID* in the *Name* text box and then type CustomerID.

d. Press the Tab key and then type Customer Number in the *Caption* text box.

e. Press the Tab key and then type Access will automatically assign the record the next number in the sequence.

f. Click OK to close the Enter Field Properties dialog box. (Notice the description at the left side of the Status bar.)

3. Add a description to the *Last Name* field by completing the following steps:

a. Click the *Last Name* field name in the header row.

b. Click the Name & Caption button in the Properties group.

c. At the Enter Field Properties dialog box, notice that Access named the field *LastName* but provided the caption *Last Name*. You do not want to change the name and caption so press the Tab key two times to make the *Description* text box active and then type Customer last name.

d. Click OK to close the dialog box.

4. You know that a customer's last name will not likely exceed 30 characters, so you decide to limit the field size. To do this, click in the *Field Size* text box in the Properties group (this selects *255*), type 30, and then press the Enter key.

5. Click the *First Name* field name in the header row and then complete steps similar to those in Steps 3 and 4 to add the description *Customer first name* and change the field size to 30 characters.

6. Since most of Pacific Trek's customers live in the city of Vancouver, you decide to make it the default field value. To do this, complete the following steps:

a. Click the *City* field name in the header row.

b. Click the Default Value button in the Properties group.

c. At the Expression Builder dialog box, type Vancouver.

d. Click OK to close the dialog box.

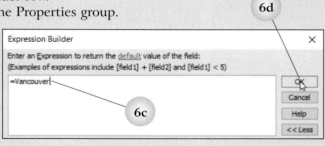

7. Change the *State Province* field name and insert a default value by completing the following steps:

a. Right-click the *State Province* field name in the header row and then click *Rename Field* at the shortcut menu.

b. Type Province.

c. Click the Default Value button.

d. Type BC in the Expression Builder dialog box and then click OK.

8. Click the *ZIP Postal* field name in the header row and then limit the field size to 7 characters by clicking in the *Field Size* text box (which selects *255*), typing 7, and then pressing the Enter key.

9. Since most customers want to be sent the sales promotional mailers, you decide to insert a check mark as the default value in the check boxes in the *Yes/No* column. To do this, complete the following steps:
   a. Click the *Mailers* field name in the header row.
   b. Click the Default Value button in the Properties group.
   c. At the Expression Builder dialog box, press the Backspace key two times to delete *No* and then type Yes.
   d. Click OK to close the dialog box.
10. Delete the *Country Region* field by clicking the *Country Region* field name in the header row and then clicking the Delete button in the Add & Delete group.
11. Save the table by completing the following steps:
   a. Click the Save button on the Quick Access Toolbar.
   b. At the Save As dialog box, type Customers and then press the Enter key.
12. Enter the six records in the table shown in Figure 1.14. To remove a check mark in the *Mailers* column, press the spacebar.
13. Adjust the field column widths to accommodate the longest entry in each column by completing the following steps:
   a. Position the mouse pointer on the *Customer Number* field name in the header row until the pointer turns into a down-pointing black arrow, click and hold down the left mouse button, drag to the *Mailers* field name, and then release the mouse button.
   b. With the columns selected, double-click one of the column boundary lines in the header row.
14. Click the Save button on the Quick Access Toolbar to save the Customers table.
15. Print the Customers table by completing the following steps:
   a. Click the File tab and then click the *Print* option.
   b. At the Print backstage area, click the *Print Preview* option.
   c. Click the Landscape button in the Page Layout group on the Print Preview tab.
   d. Click the Print button at the left side of the Print Preview tab.
   e. At the Print dialog box, click OK.
16. Close the Customers table.
17. Open the Orders table.
18. Adjust the field column widths to accommodate the longest entry in each column.
19. Click the Save button to save the Orders table.
20. Print the table in landscape orientation (refer to Step 15) and then close the table.
21. Close **1-PacTrek**.

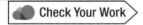 Check Your Work

Figure 1.14 Activity 2g

Customer Number	Last Name	First Name	Address	City	State Province	ZIP Postal	Mailers
1	Blakely	Mathias	7433 224th Ave E	Vancouver	BC	V5K 2M7	☑
2	Donato	Antonio	18225 Victoria Dr	Vancouver	BC	V5K 1H4	☐
3	Girard	Stephanie	430 Deer Lake Pl	Burnaby	BC	V3J 1E4	☑
4	Hernandez	Angelica	1233 E 59th Ave	Vancouver	BC	V5K 3H3	☑
5	Ives-Keller	Shane	9055 Gilber Rd	Richmond	BC	V6Y 1B2	☐
6	Kim	Keung	730 West Broadway	Vancouver	BC	V5K 5B2	☑
(New)				Vancouver	BC		☑

Chapter Summary

- Microsoft Access is a database management system software program that can organize, store, maintain, retrieve, sort, and print all types of business data.

- In Access, open an existing database by clicking the <u>Open Other Files</u> hyperlink at the Access opening screen. At the Open backstage area, click the *Browse* option. At the Open dialog box, navigate to the location of the database and then double-click the database.

- Some common objects found in a database include tables, queries, forms, and reports.

- The Navigation pane displays at the left side of the Access screen and lists the objects that are contained in the database.

- Open a database object by double-clicking the object in the Navigation pane or by right-clicking the object and then clicking *Open* at the shortcut menu.

- Close an object by clicking the object's Close button or right-clicking the object tab and then clicking *Close* at the shortcut menu.

- When a table is open, the Record Navigation bar displays at the bottom of the screen and contains buttons for viewing records in the table.

- Insert a new record in a table by clicking the New button in the Records group on the Home tab or by clicking the New (blank) record button in the Record Navigation bar.

- Delete a record by clicking in a field in the record to be deleted, clicking the Delete button arrow on the Home tab, and then clicking *Delete Record* at the drop-down list.

- Add a field column to a table by clicking in the first field below *Click to Add* and then typing the data.

- Move a field column by selecting the column and then using the mouse to drag a thick, black, vertical line (representing the column) to the desired location.

- Delete a field column by clicking in any field in the column, clicking the Delete button arrow, and then clicking *Delete Column* at the drop-down list.

- Data entered in a table is automatically saved while changes to the layout of a table are not automatically saved.

- Hide, unhide, freeze, and unfreeze field columns with options at the More button drop-down list. Display this list by clicking the More button in the Records group on the Home tab.

- Adjust the width of a field column with options at the Column Width dialog box. Display the dialog box by clicking the More button and then clicking *Field Width* at the drop-down list. Enter a column measurement in the *Column Width* measurement box or click the Best Fit button.

- Adjust the width of a field column by dragging the column boundary line in the header row. Or adjust the width of a column (or selected columns) to accommodate the longest entry by double-clicking the column boundary line.

- Rename a table by right-clicking the table name in the Navigation pane, clicking *Rename*, and then typing the new name. Delete a table by right-clicking the table name in the Navigation pane and then clicking *Delete*.

- Print a table by clicking the File tab, clicking the *Print* option, and then clicking the *Quick Print* option. Preview a table before printing by clicking the *Print Preview* option at the Print backstage area.

- Use buttons and options on the Print Preview tab to change the page size, orientation, and margins.
- The first principle in database design is to reduce redundant data, because redundant data increases the amount of data entry required and the potential for errors, as well as takes up additional storage space.
- A data type defines the type of data Access will allow in the field. Assign a data type to a field with buttons in the Add & Delete group on the Table Tools Fields tab, by clicking an option from the field drop-down list, or with options at the More Fields button drop-down list.
- Rename a field by right-clicking the field name, clicking *Rename Field* at the shortcut menu, and then typing the new name.
- Type a name, caption, and description for a field with options at the Enter Field Properties dialog box.
- Use options in the *Quick Start* category in the More Fields button drop-down list to define a data type and assign a field name to a group of related fields.
- Insert a default value in a field with the Default Value button and assign a field size with the *Field Size* text box in the Properties group on the Table Tools Fields tab.
- Use the *Data Type* option box in the Formatting group on the Table Tools Fields tab to change the AutoNumber data type for the first column in a table.

Commands Review

FEATURE	RIBBON TAB, GROUP/OPTION	BUTTON, OPTION	KEYBOARD SHORTCUT
close Access			Alt + F4
close database	File, *Close*		
create table	Create, Tables		
Currency data type	Table Tools Fields, Add & Delete		
Date & Time data type	Table Tools Fields, Add & Delete		
delete column	Home, Records	, *Delete Column*	
delete record	Home, Records	, *Delete Record*	
Enter Field Properties dialog box	Table Tools Fields, Properties		
Expression Builder dialog box	Table Tools Fields, Properties		
freeze column	Home, Records	, *Freeze Fields*	
hide column	Home, Records	, *Hide Fields*	

FEATURE	RIBBON TAB, GROUP/OPTION	BUTTON, OPTION	KEYBOARD SHORTCUT
landscape orientation	File, *Print*		
new record	Home, Records		Ctrl + +
next field			Tab
Number data type	Table Tools Fields, Add & Delete	12	
page margins	File, *Print*		
Page Setup dialog box	File, *Print*		
page size	File, *Print*		
portrait orientation	File, *Print*		
previous field			Shift + Tab
Print backstage area	File, *Print*		
Print dialog box	File, *Print*	*Print*	Ctrl + P
Print Preview	File, *Print*	*Print Preview*	
Short Text data type	Table Tools Fields, Add & Delete	AB	
unfreeze column	Home, Records	, *Unfreeze Fields*	
unhide column	Home, Records	, *Unhide Fields*	
Yes/No data type	Table Tools Fields, Add & Delete	☑	

Microsoft®

Access®

Creating Relationships between Tables

Performance Objectives

Upon successful completion of Chapter 2, you will be able to:

1 Define a primary key field in a table

2 Create a one-to-many relationship

3 Specify referential integrity

4 Print, edit, and delete relationships

5 Edit, insert, and delete records

6 Create a one-to-one relationship

7 View and edit a subdatasheet

Access is a relational database program you can use to create tables that are related or connected within the same database. When a relationship is established between tables, you can view and edit records in related tables with a subdatasheet. In this chapter, you will learn how to identify a primary key field in a table that is unique to that table, how to join tables by creating a relationship between them, and how to view and edit subdatasheets.

Data Files

Before beginning chapter work, copy the AL1C2 folder to your storage medium and then make AL1C2 the active folder.

The online course includes additional training and assessment resources.

Activity 1 Establish Relationships between Tables　　4 Parts

You will specify the primary key fields in a table, establish one-to-many relationships between tables, specify referential integrity, and print the relationships. You will also insert, edit, and delete records and edit and delete a relationship.

Relating Tables

Hint Defining a relationship between tables is one of the most powerful features of a relational database management system.

Generally, a database management system fits into one of two categories: a file management system (also sometimes referred to as a *flat file database*) or a relational database management system. A flat file management system stores all data in a single directory and cannot contain multiple tables. This type of management system is a simple way to store data but becomes inefficient as more data is added. In a relational database management system, like Access, relationships are defined between sets of data, allowing greater flexibility in manipulating data and eliminating data redundancy (entering the same data in more than one place).

In Activity 1, you will define relationships between tables in the Pacific Trek database. Because the tables in the database will be related, information on the same product does not need to be repeated in multiple tables. If you used a flat file management system to maintain product information, you would need to repeat that product description each time.

Determining Relationships

Taking time to plan a database is extremely important. Creating a database with related tables takes even more consideration. Determine how to break down the required data and what tables to create to eliminate redundancies. One idea to help determine what tables are necessary in a database is to think of the word *about*. For example, the Pacific Trek store needs a table *about* products, another *about* suppliers, and another *about* orders. A table should be about only one subject, such as products, suppliers, or orders.

Along with determining the necessary tables for a database, determine the relationship between those tables. The ability to relate, or "join," tables is what makes Access a relational database management system. As explained in Chapter 1, database designers often create a visual representation of the database's structure in a diagram. The database diagram for the Pacific Trek database is shown in Figure 2.1. (Some of the fields in tables have been modified slightly from the database used in Chapter 1.)

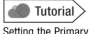
Tutorial

Setting the Primary Key Field

Setting the Primary Key Field

A database table can contain two different types of key fields: a primary key field and a foreign key field. In the database diagram in Figure 2.1, notice that one field in each table contains an asterisk. The asterisk indicates a primary key field, which is a field that holds data that uniquely identifies each record in a table. For example, the *SupplierID* field in the Suppliers table contains a unique supplier number for each record in the table and the *ProductID* field in the Products table contains a unique product number for each product. A table can have only one primary key field and it is the field by which the table is sorted whenever the table is opened.

Figure 2.1 Pacific Trek Database Diagram

When a new record is added to a table, Access checks to ensure that there is no existing record with the same data in the primary key field. If there is, Access displays an error message indicating there are duplicate values and does not allow the record to be saved. When adding a new record to a table, Access expects a value in each record in the table. This is is referred to as *entity integrity*. If a value is not entered in a field, Access enters a null value, but a null value cannot be given to a primary key field. Access will not allow a database to be closed that contains a primary key field with a null value.

By default, Access includes the *ID* field as the first field in a table, assigns the AutoNumber data type, and identifies the field as the primary key field. The AutoNumber data type assigns the first record a field value of *1* and each new record is assigned the next sequential number. Use this default field as the primary key field or define a different primary key field. To determine what field is the primary key field or to define a primary key field, display the table in Design view. To do this, open the table and then click the View button at the left side of the Home tab. A table also can be opened in Design view by clicking the View button arrow and then clicking *Design View* at the drop-down list. To add or remove a primary key designation from a field, click the field in the *Field Name* column and then click the Primary Key button in the Tools group on the Table Tools Design tab. A key icon is inserted in the field selector bar (the blank column to the left of the field names) for the field. Figure 2.2 shows the Products table in Design view with the *ProductID* field identified as the primary key field.

Typically, a primary key field in one table becomes the foreign key field in a related table. For example, the primary key field *SupplierID* in the Suppliers table is considered the foreign key field in the Orders table. In the Suppliers table, each entry in the *SupplierID* field must be unique since it is the primary key field but the same supplier number may appear more than once in the *SupplierID* field in the Orders table (for instance, in a situation when more than one product is ordered from the same supplier).

Data in the foreign key field must match data in the primary key field of the related table. For example, any supplier number entered in the *SupplierID* field in the Orders table must also be contained in the Suppliers table. In other words, an order would not be placed by a supplier that does not exist in the Suppliers table. Figure 2.3 identifies the primary and foreign key fields in the tables in the Pacific Trek database. Primary key fields are identified with *(PK)* and foreign key fields are identified with *(FK)* in the figure.

Figure 2.2 Products Table in Design View

A key icon in the field selector bar specifies the primary key field.

Figure 2.3 Pacific Trek Database Diagram with Primary and Foreign Key Fields Identified

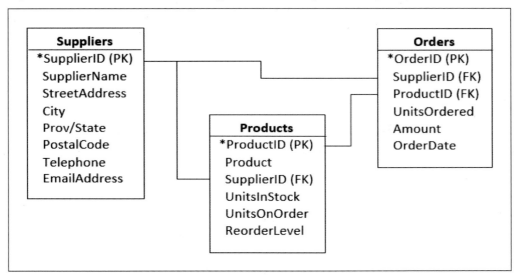

Activity 1a Defining a Primary Key Field

Part 1 of 4

1. Open Access.
2. At the Access opening screen, click the <u>Open Other Files</u> hyperlink at the left side of the screen.
3. At the Open backstage area, click the *Browse* option.
4. At the Open dialog box, navigate to your AL1C2 folder and then double-click the database **2-PacTrek**.
5. Click the Enable Content button in the message bar if the security warning message appears. (The message bar will display immediately below the ribbon.)
6. Open the Products table.

7. View the primary key field by completing the following
steps:
   a. Click the View button at the left side of the Home
   tab. (This displays the table in Design view.)
   b. In Design view, notice the *Field Name*, *Data Type*, and
   Description columns and the information for each
   field. The first field, *ProductID*, is the primary key field
   and is identified by the key icon in the field selector bar.
   c. Click the View button to return to Datasheet view.
   d. Close the Products table.

8. Open the Suppliers table, click the View button to display the table in Design view, and
then notice the *SupplierID* field is defined as the primary key field.
9. Click the View button to return to Datasheet view and then close the table.
10. Open the Orders table. (The first field in the Orders table has been changed from the
AutoNumber data type field automatically assigned by Access to a Short Text data type field.)
11. Define the *OrderID* field as the primary key field by completing the following steps:
    a. Click the View button at the left side of
    the Home tab.
    b. With the table in Design view and
    the *OrderID* field selected in the *Field
    Name* column, click the Primary Key
    button in the Tools group on the Table
    Tools Design tab.
    c. Click the Save button on the Quick
    Access Toolbar.
    d. Click the View button to return the
    table to Datasheet view.
12. Move the *OrderDate* field by completing
the following steps:
    a. Click the *OrderDate* field name in the
    header row. (This selects the column.)
    b. Position the mouse pointer on the field name in the header row; click and hold down
    the left mouse button; drag to the left until the thick, black vertical line displays
    immediately left of the *ProductID* field; and then release the mouse button.

13. Adjust the column widths.
14. Save and then close the Orders table.

Check Your Work

Creating a One-to-
Many Relationship

Creating a One-to-Many Relationship

In Access, one table can be related to another. Establishing this relationship is is generally referred to as performing a join. When tables with a common field are joined, data can be extracted from both tables as if they were one large table. Relating tables helps to ensure the integrity of the data by avoiding the need to enter the same data in multiple tables. For example, in Activity 1b, a relationship will be established between the Suppliers table and the Products table. The relationship will ensure that a supplier number cannot be entered in the Products table without first being entered in the Suppliers table. This type of relationship is called a *one-to-many relationship*, which means that one record in the Suppliers table will match zero, one, or many records in the Products table.

In a one-to-many relationship, the table containing the "one" is referred to as the *primary table* and the table containing the "many" is referred to as the *related table*. Access follows a set of rules that provide referential integrity, which enforces consistency between related tables. These rules are enforced when data is updated in related tables. The referential integrity rules ensure that a record added to a related table has a matching record in the primary table.

Relationships

Quick Steps

Create One-to-Many Relationship
1. Click Database Tools tab.
2. Click Relationships button.
3. Add tables.
4. Drag "one" field from primary table to "many" field in related table.
5. At Edit Relationships dialog box, click Create button.
6. Click Save button.

To create a one-to-many relationship, open the database containing the tables to be related. Click the Database Tools tab and then click the Relationships button in the Relationships group. This displays the Show Table dialog box, as shown in Figure 2.4. (If the Show Table dialog box is not visible, click the Show Table button in the Relationships group.) At the Show Table dialog box, each table that will be related must be added to the Relationships window. To do this, click the first table name to be included and then click the Add button (or double-click the table name). This inserts the fields of the table in a table field list box. Continue in this manner until all necessary tables (in table field list boxes) have been added to the Relationships window and then click the Close button.

At the Relationships window, such as the one shown in Figure 2.5, use the mouse to drag the common field from the primary table's table field list box (the "one") to the related table's table field list box (the "many"). This displays the Edit Relationships dialog box, as shown in Figure 2.6. At the Edit Relationships dialog box, check to make sure the correct field name is in the *Table/Query* and *Related Table/Query* list boxes and the relationship type at the bottom of the dialog box is *One-To-Many*.

Figure 2.4 Show Table Dialog Box

Figure 2.5 Relationships Window

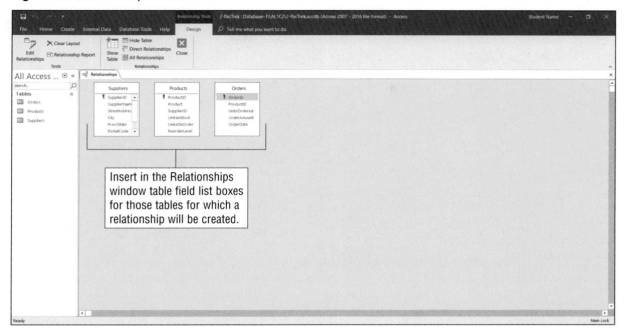

Insert in the Relationships window table field list boxes for those tables for which a relationship will be created.

Figure 2.6 Edit Relationships Dialog Box

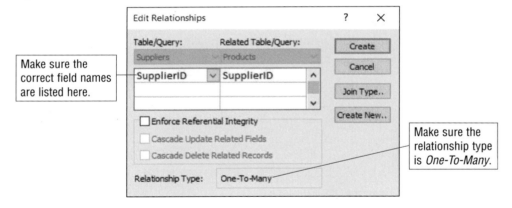

Make sure the correct field names are listed here.

Make sure the relationship type is *One-To-Many*.

Specify the relationship options by choosing *Enforce Referential Integrity*, as well as *Cascade Update Related Fields* and/or *Cascade Delete Related Records*, and then click the Create button. This closes the Edit Relationships dialog box and opens the Relationships window showing the relationship between the tables.

Relationships are indicated with a black line connecting the table field list boxes, as shown in Figure 2.7. The number 1 at one end of the line signifies the "one" side of the relationship and the infinity symbol (∞) at the other end signifies the "many" side of the relationship. The black line, called the *join line*, is thick at both ends if the *Enforce Referential Integrity* option is chosen. If this option is not chosen, the line is thin at both ends. Click the Save button on the Quick Access Toolbar to save the relationship. After saving, click the X to close the Relationships window.

Figure 2.7 One-to-Many Relationship

This is an example of a one-to-many relationship, where 1 identifies the "one" side of the relationship and the infinity symbol (∞) identifies the "many" side.

💡 **Hint** Referential integrity ensures that a record exists in the "one" table before the record can be entered in the "many" table.

Specifying Referential Integrity Choose *Enforce Referential Integrity* at the Edit Relationships dialog box to ensure that the relationships between records in related tables are valid. Referential integrity can be set if the field from the primary table is a primary key field and the related fields have the same data type. When referential integrity is established, a value for the primary key field must first be entered in the primary table before it can be entered in the related table.

If only *Enforce Referential Integrity* is selected and the related table contains a record, a primary key field value in the primary table cannot be changed. A record in the primary table cannot be deleted if its key value equals a foreign key field in the related table. Select *Cascade Update Related Fields* and, if changes are made to the primary key field value in the primary table, Access will automatically update the matching value in the related table. Choose *Cascade Delete Related Records* and, if a record is deleted in the primary table, Access will delete any related records in the related table.

In Activity 1b, you will create one-to-many relationships between tables in the 2-PacTrek database, as shown in Figure 2.8.

Figure 2.8 Relationships in the 2-PacTrek Database

A one-to-many relationship with referential integrity enforced and updated and deleted records cascaded.

A one-to-many relationship with referential integrity enforced. (Notice the join line is thick in the middle, indicating that updated and deleted records are not cascaded.)

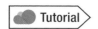

Tutorial

Creating a
Relationship Report

Relationship
Report

Quick Steps

Create Relationship Report

1. Click Database Tools tab.
2. Click Relationships button.
3. Click Relationship Report button.

Creating and Printing a Relationship Report Once all relationships have been created in a database, printing a hard copy of the relationships is a good idea. The documentation is a quick reference of all of the table names, fields within each table, and relationships between tables. To create and print a relationship report, display the Relationships window and then click the Relationship Report button in the Tools group. This opens a relationship report in Print Preview. Click the Print button in the Print group on the Print Preview tab and then click OK at the Print dialog box. After printing the relationship report, click the Close button to close the relationship report.

Activity 1b Relating Tables

1. With **2-PacTrek** open, click the Database Tools tab and then click the Relationships button in the Relationships group. (The Show Table dialog box should display in the Relationships window. If it does not display, click the Show Table button in the Relationships group on the Relationship Tools Design tab.)

2. At the Show Table dialog box with the Tables tab selected, add the Suppliers, Products, and Orders tables to the Relationships window by completing the following steps:
   a. Click *Suppliers* in the list box and then click the Add button.

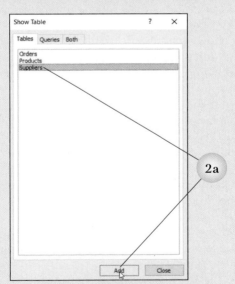

   b. Click *Products* in the list box and then click the Add button.
   c. Double-click *Orders* in the list box.
3. Click the Close button to close the Show Table dialog box.

---

4. At the Relationships window, drag the *SupplierID* field from the Suppliers table field list box to the Products table field list box by completing the following steps:
   a. Position the mouse pointer on the *SupplierID* field in the Suppliers table field list box.
   b. Click and hold down the left mouse button, drag the mouse pointer (with a field icon attached) to the *SupplierID* field in the Products table field list box, and then release the mouse button. (This displays the Edit Relationships dialog box.)

5. At the Edit Relationships dialog box, make sure *SupplierID* displays in the *Table/Query* and *Related Table/Query* list boxes and the relationship type at the bottom of the dialog box displays as *One-To-Many*.
6. Enforce the referential integrity of the relationship by completing the following steps:
   a. Click the *Enforce Referential Integrity* check box to insert a check mark. (This makes the other two options available.)
   b. Click the *Cascade Update Related Fields* check box to insert a check mark.
   c. Click the *Cascade Delete Related Records* check box to insert a check mark.

7. Click the Create button. (This closes the Edit Relationships dialog box and displays the Relationships window, showing a black join line [thick on the ends and thin in the middle] connecting the *SupplierID* field in the Suppliers table field list box to the *SupplierID* field in the Products table field list box. A *1* appears on the join line on the Suppliers table side and an infinity symbol [∞] appears on the join line on the Products table side.)
8. Click the Save button on the Quick Access Toolbar to save the relationship.
9. Create a one-to-many relationship between the Products table and the Orders table with the *ProductID* field by completing the following steps:
   a. Position the mouse pointer on the *ProductID* field in the Products table field list box.
   b. Click and hold down the left mouse button, drag the mouse pointer (with a field icon attached) to the *ProductID* field in the Orders table field list box, and then release the mouse button.

c. At the Edit Relationships dialog box, make sure *ProductID* displays in the *Table/Query* and *Related Table/Query* list boxes and the relationship type displays as *One-To-Many*.

d. Click the *Enforce Referential Integrity* check box to insert a check mark. (Do not insert check marks in the other two check boxes.)

e. Click the Create button.

10. Click the Save button on the Quick Access Toolbar to save the relationships.

11. Print the relationships by completing the following steps:

a. At the Relationships window, click the Relationship Report button in the Tools group. This opens the relationship report in Print Preview. (If a security notice displays, click the Open button.)

b. Click the Print button in the Print group at the left side of the Print Preview tab.

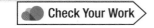

c. Click OK at the Print dialog box.

d. Close the report by clicking the report's Close button.

e. At the message asking if you want to save changes to the design of the report, click No.

12. Close the Relationships window by clicking the Close button for the window.

Check Your Work

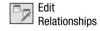 Show Table

Showing Tables Once a relationship is established between tables and the Relationships window is closed, clicking the Relationships button displays the Relationships window without the Show Table dialog box. To display the Show Table dialog box, click the Show Table button in the Relationships group.

Pacific Trek offers a discount on one product each week. Keep track of this information by creating a Discounts table that includes the discount item for each week of the first three months of the year. A new record will be added to this field each week when the discount item is chosen. (In Activity 1c, you will create the Discounts table shown in Figure 2.9 on page 49 and then relate the Products table with the Discounts table using the *ProductID* field.)

Tutorial

Editing and
Deleting a
Relationship

Edit Relationships

Quick Steps

Edit Relationship
1. Click Database Tools tab.
2. Click Relationships button.
3. Click Edit Relationships button.
4. Make changes at Edit Relationships dialog box.
5. Click OK.

Editing a Relationship A relationship between tables can be edited or deleted. To edit a relationship, open the database containing the tables with the relationship, click the Database Tools tab, and then click the Relationships button in the Relationships group. This displays the Relationships window with the related tables. Click the Edit Relationships button in the Tools group to display the Edit Relationships dialog box. The dialog box will be similar to the one shown in Figure 2.6 on page 41. Identify the relationship to be edited by clicking the *Table/Query* option box arrow and then clicking the table name containing the "one" field. Click the *Related Table/Query* option box arrow and then click the table name containing the "many" field.

To edit a specific relationship, position the mouse pointer on the middle portion of the join line that connects the related tables and then click the right mouse button. At the shortcut menu, click the *Edit Relationship* option. This displays the Edit Relationships dialog box with the specific related field in both list boxes.

Deleting a Relationship To delete a relationship between tables, display the related tables in the Relationships window. Position the mouse pointer on the middle portion of the join line connecting the related tables and then click the right mouse button. At the shortcut menu, click *Delete*. At the message asking to confirm the deletion, click Yes.

Activity 1c Creating a Table and Creating and Editing Relationships   Part 3 of 4

1. With **2-PacTrek** open, create the Discounts table shown in Figure 2.9 on page 49 by completing the following steps:
   a. Click the Create tab.
   b. Click the Table button in the Tables group.
   c. Click the Short Text button in the Add & Delete group. (This creates and then selects *Field1* at the right of the *ID* column.)

    d. Type ProductID and then press the Enter key.

    e. Click the *Short Text* option at the drop-down list and then type DiscountAmount.

    f. Click the *ID* field name (in the first column), click the *Data Type* option box arrow in the Formatting group, and then click *Date/Time* at the drop-down list.

    g. Right-click the *ID* field name, click *Rename Field* at the shortcut menu, type Week, and then press the Enter key.

    h. Type the 13 records in the Discounts table shown in Figure 2.9 on page 49.

2. After typing the records, save the table by completing the following steps:

    a. Click the Save button on the Quick Access Toolbar.

    b. At the Save As dialog box, type Discounts and then press the Enter key.

3. Close the Discounts table.

4. Display the Relationships window and add the Discounts table to the window by completing the following steps:

    a. Click the Database Tools tab and then click the Relationships button in the Relationships group.

    b. Display the Show Table dialog box by clicking the Show Table button in the Relationships group.

    c. At the Show Table dialog box, double-click the *Discounts* table.

    d. Click the Close button to close the Show Table dialog box.

5. At the Relationships window, create a one-to-many relationship between the Products table and the Discounts table with the *ProductID* field by completing the following steps:

    a. Drag the *ProductID* field from the Products table field list box to the *ProductID* field in the Discounts table field list box.

b. At the Edit Relationships dialog box, make sure *ProductID* displays in the *Table/Query* and *Related Table/Query* list boxes and the relationship type at the bottom of the dialog box displays as *One-To-Many*.

c. Click the *Enforce Referential Integrity* check box to insert a check mark.

d. Click the *Cascade Update Related Fields* check box to insert a check mark.

e. Click the *Cascade Delete Related Records* check box to insert a check mark.

f. Click the Create button. (At the Relationships window, notice the join line between the Products table and the Discounts table. If a message occurs stating that the relationship cannot be created, click OK. Open the Discounts table, check to make sure the product numbers are entered correctly in the *ProductID* field, and then close the Discounts table. Try again to create the relationship.)

6. Edit the one-to-many relationship between the *ProductID* field in the Products table and the Orders table and specify that you want to cascade updated and related fields and cascade and delete related records by completing the following steps:

a. Click the Edit Relationships button in the Tools group on the Relationship Tools Design tab.

b. At the Edit Relationships dialog box, click the *Table/Query* option box arrow and then click *Products* at the drop-down list.

c. Click the *Related Table/Query* option box arrow and then click *Orders* at the drop-down list.

d. Click the *Cascade Update Related Fields* check box to insert a check mark.

e. Click the *Cascade Delete Related Records* check box to insert a check mark.

f. Click OK.

7. Click the Save button on the Quick Access Toolbar to save the relationship.

8. Print the relationships by completing the following steps:

a. Click the Relationship Report button in the Tools group.

b. Click the Print button in the Print group.

c. Click OK at the Print dialog box.

d. Close the report by clicking the Close button.

e. At the message asking if you want to save changes to the design of the report, click No.

9. Delete the relationship between the Products table and the Discounts table by completing the following steps:
   a. Position the mouse pointer on the thin portion of the join line connecting the *ProductID* field in the Products table field list box with the *ProductID* field in the Discounts table field list box and then click the right mouse button.
   b. Click the *Delete* option at the shortcut menu.

   c. At the message asking if you are sure you want to permanently delete the selected relationship from your database, click Yes.
10. Click the Save button on the Quick Access Toolbar to save the relationship.
11. Print the relationships by completing the following steps:
    a. Click the Relationship Tools Design tab and then click the Relationship Report button.
    b. Click the Print button.
    c. Click OK at the Print dialog box.
    d. Close the report by clicking the Close button.
    e. At the message asking if you want to save changes to the design of the report, click No.
12. Close the Relationships window.

Check Your Work

Figure 2.9 Discounts Table in Datasheet View

Week	ProductID	DiscountAmc	Click to Add
1/7/2021	155-45	20%	
1/14/2021	652-2	15%	
1/21/2021	443-1A	20%	
1/28/2021	202-CW	15%	
2/4/2021	804-60	10%	
2/11/2021	652-2	15%	
2/18/2021	101-S1B	5%	
2/25/2021	560-TL	20%	
3/4/2021	652-2	20%	
3/11/2021	602-XX	15%	
3/18/2021	100-05	10%	
3/25/2021	652-2	15%	
4/1/2021	202-CW	15%	

Inserting and Deleting Records in Related Tables In the relationship established in Activity 1b, a record must first be added to the Suppliers table before a related record can be added to the Products table. This is because the *Enforce Referential Integrity* option was selected at the Edit Relationships dialog box. Because the two options, *Cascade Update Related Fields* and *Cascade Delete Related Records*, were also selected, records in the Suppliers table (the primary table) can be updated or deleted and related records in the Products table (the related table) are automatically updated or deleted.

Activity 1d Editing, Inserting, and Deleting Records   Part 4 of 4

1. With **2-PacTrek** open, open the Suppliers table.
2. Change two supplier numbers in the Suppliers table (Access will automatically change them in the Products table and the Orders table) by completing the following steps:
   a. Double-click the field value *15* in the *SupplierID* field.
   b. Type 33.
   c. Double-click the field value *42* in the *SupplierID* field.
   d. Type 51.
   e. Click the Save button on the Quick Access Toolbar.
   f. Close the Suppliers table.
   g. Open the Products table and notice that supplier number *15* changed to *33* and supplier number *42* changed to *51*.
   h. Close the Products table.
3. Open the Suppliers table and then add the following records:

SupplierID	16		SupplierID	28
SupplierName	Olympic Suppliers		SupplierName	Gorman Company
StreetAddress	1773 50th Avenue		StreetAddress	543 26th Street
City	Seattle		City	Vancouver
Prov/State	WA		Prov/State	BC
PostalCode	98101		PostalCode	V5K 3C5
Telephone	(206) 555-9488		Telephone	(778) 555-4550
EmailAddress	olysuppliers@ppi-edu.net		EmailAddress	gormanco@ppi-edu.net

4. Delete the record for supplier number 38 (Hadley Company). At the message stating that relationships that specify cascading deletes are about to cause records in this table and related tables to be deleted, click Yes.

5. Display the table in Print Preview, change to landscape orientation, and then print the table.

6. Close the Suppliers table.

7. Open the Products table and then add the following records to the table:

ProductID	701-BK	*ProductID*	703-SP
Product	Basic first aid kit	*Product*	Medical survival pack
SupplierID	33	*SupplierID*	33
UnitsInStock	8	*UnitsInStock*	8
UnitsOnOrder	0	*UnitsOnOrder*	0
ReorderLevel	5	*ReorderLevel*	5
ProductID	185-10	*ProductID*	185-50
Product	Trail water filter	*Product*	Trail filter replacement cartridge
SupplierID	51	*SupplierID*	51
UnitsInStock	4	*UnitsInStock*	14
UnitsOnOrder	10	*UnitsOnOrder*	0
ReorderLevel	10	*ReorderLevel*	10

8. Display the Products table in Print Preview, change to landscape orientation, change the top and bottom margins to 0.5 inch and then print the table. (The table will print on three pages.)

9. Close the Products table.

10. Open the Orders table and then add the following record:

OrderID	1033
OrderDate	2/15/2021
ProductID	185-10
UnitsOrdered	10
Amount	$310.90

11. Print and then close the Orders table.

12. Close **2-PacTrek**.

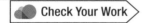 Check Your Work

---

Activity 2 Create Relationships and Display Subdatasheets in a Database   2 Parts

You will open a company database and then create one-to-many relationships between tables, as well as a one-to-one relationship. You will also display and edit subdatasheets.

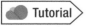 Tutorial

Creating a One-to-One Relationship

Creating a One-to-One Relationship

A one-to-one relationship can be created between tables in which each record in the first table matches only one record in the second table and one record in the second table matches only one record in the first table. (One-to-one relationships exist between primary key fields.) A one-to-one relationship is not as common as a one-to-many relationship, since the type of information used to create the relationship can be stored in one table. A one-to-one relationship is generally used to break a large table with many fields into two smaller tables.

In Activity 2a, you will create a one-to-one relationship between the Employees table and the Benefits table in the Griffin database. Each record in the Employees table and each record in the Benefits table pertains to one employee. These two tables could be merged into one but the data in each table is easier to manage when separated. Figure 2.10 shows the relationships you will define between the tables in the Griffin database. The Benefits table and the Departments table have been moved down so you can more easily see the relationships.

Figure 2.10 Griffin Database Table Relationships

A one-to-one relationship between the *EmpID* field in the Employees table and the Benefits table.

A one-to-many relationship between the *EmpID* field in the Employees table and the Absences table.

A one-to-many relationship between the *DeptID* field in the Departments table and the Employees table.

Activity 2a Creating One-to-Many and One-to-One Relationships

Part 1 of 2

1. Open **2-Griffin** and enable the content.
2. Click the Database Tools tab.
3. Click the Relationships button.
4. At the Show Table dialog box with the Tables tab selected, add all of the tables to the Relationships window by completing the following steps:
   a. Double-click *Employees* in the list box. (This inserts the table in the Relationships window.)
   b. Double-click *Benefits* in the list box.
   c. Double-click *Absences* in the list box.
   d. Double-click *Departments* in the list box.
   e. Click the Close button to close the Show Table dialog box.
5. At the Relationships window, create a one-to-many relationship with the *EmpID* field in the Employees table as the "one" and the *EmpID* field in the Absences table the "many" by completing the following steps:

a. Position the mouse pointer on the *EmpID* field in the Employees table field list box.
b. Click and hold down the left mouse button, drag the mouse pointer (with a field icon attached) to the *EmpID* field in the Absences table field list box, and then release the mouse button. (This displays the Edit Relationships dialog box.)

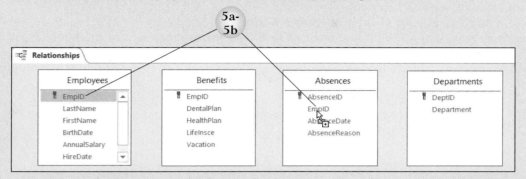

c. At the Edit Relationships dialog box, make sure *EmpID* displays in the *Table/Query* and *Related Table/Query* list boxes and the relationship type at the bottom of the dialog box displays as *One-To-Many*.
d. Click the *Enforce Referential Integrity* check box to insert a check mark.
e. Click the *Cascade Update Related Fields* check box to insert a check mark.
f. Click the *Cascade Delete Related Records* check box to insert a check mark.
g. Click the Create button. (A *1* appears at the Employees table field list box side and an infinity symbol [∞] appears at the Absences table field list box side of the black line.)
6. Complete steps similar to those in Step 5 to create a one-to-many relationship with the *DeptID* field in the Departments table the "one" and the *DeptID* field in the Employees table the "many." (You may need to scroll down the Employees table field list box to see the *DeptID* field.)
7. Create a one-to-one relationship with the *EmpID* field in the Employees table and the *EmpID* field in the Benefits table by completing the following steps:
a. Position the mouse pointer on the *EmpID* field in the Employees table field list box.
b. Click and hold down the left mouse button, drag the mouse pointer to the *EmpID* field in the Benefits table field list box, and then release the mouse button. (This displays the Edit Relationships dialog box; notice at the bottom of the dialog box that the relationship type displays as *One-To-One*.)
c. Click the *Enforce Referential Integrity* check box to insert a check mark.
d. Click the *Cascade Update Related Fields* check box to insert a check mark.
e. Click the *Cascade Delete Related Records* check box to insert a check mark.
f. Click the Create button. (Notice that a *1* appears at both the side of the Employees table field list box and at the side of the Benefits table field list box, indicating a one-to-one relationship.)

8. Click the Save button on the Quick Access Toolbar to save the relationships.
9. Print the relationships by completing the following steps:
   a. Click the Relationship Report button in the Tools group.
   b. Click the Print button in the Print group.
   c. Click OK at the Print dialog box.
   d. Close the report by clicking the Close button.
   e. At the message asking if you want to save changes to the design of the report, click No.
10. Close the Relationships window.
11. Add a record to and delete a record from the Employees and Benefits tables by completing the following steps:
    a. Open the Employees table.
    b. Click the New button in the Records group on the Home tab and then type the following data in the specified field:

EmpID	1096
LastName	Schwartz
FirstName	Bryan
BirthDate	5/21/1983
AnnualSalary	$45,000.00
HireDate	1/15/2010
DeptID	IT

    c. Delete the record for Trevor Sargent (employee number 1005). At the message stating that relationships that specify cascading deletes are about to cause records in this table and related tables to be deleted, click Yes.
    d. Print and then close the Employees table.
12. Open the Benefits table and notice that the record for Trevor Sargent is deleted but the new employee record you entered in the Employees table is not reflected in the Benefits table. Add a new record for Bryan Schwartz with the following information:

EmpID	1096
Dental Plan	(Press spacebar to remove check mark.)
Health Plan	(Leave check mark.)
Life Insurance	$100,000.00
Vacation	2 weeks

13. Print and then close the Benefits table.

 Check Your Work

 Tutorial

Viewing a
Subdatasheet

Displaying Related Records in Subdatasheets

When a relationship is established between tables, records in related tables can be viewed and edited with a subdatasheet. Figure 2.11 shows the Employees table with the subdatasheet displayed for employee Kate Navarro. The subdatasheet contains the fields in the Benefits table related to Kate Navarro. Use this subdatasheet to view and edit information in both the Employees table and Absences table. Changes made to fields in a subdatasheet affect the table and any related tables.

Quick Steps

Display Subdatasheet
1. Open table.
2. Click expand indicator at left side of record.
3. Click table at Insert Subdatasheet dialog box.
4. Click OK.

Access automatically inserts a plus symbol (referred to as an *expand indicator*) before each record in a table that is joined to another table by a one-to-many relationship. Click the expand indicator and, if the table is related to only one other table, a subdatasheet containing fields from the related table displays below the record, as shown in Figure 2.11. To close the subdatasheet, click the minus symbol (referred to as a *collapse indicator*) preceding the record. (The plus symbol turns into the minus symbol when a subdatasheet displays.)

If a table has more than one relationship defined, clicking the expand indicator will display the Insert Subdatasheet dialog box, as shown in Figure 2.12. At this dialog box, click the table in the Tables list box and then click OK. The Insert Subdatasheet dialog box can also be displayed by clicking the More button in the Records group on the Home tab, pointing to *Subdatasheet*, and then clicking *Subdatasheet*. Display subdatasheets for all records by clicking the More button, pointing to *Subdatasheet*, and then clicking *Expand All*. Close all subdatasheets by clicking the More button, pointing to *Subdatasheet*, and then clicking *Collapse All*.

If a table is related to two or more tables, specify the subdatasheet at the Insert Subdatasheet dialog box. To display a different subdatasheet, remove the subdatasheet first, before selecting the next subdatasheet. Do this by clicking the More button, pointing to *Subdatasheet*, and then clicking *Remove*.

Figure 2.11 Table with Subdatasheet Displayed in Datasheet View

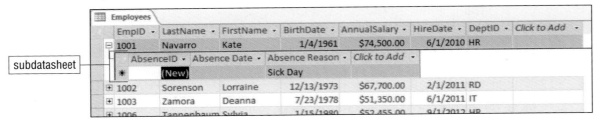

Figure 2.12 Insert Subdatasheet Dialog Box

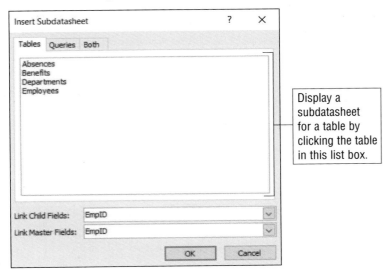

1. With **2-Griffin** open, open the Employees table.
2. Display a subdatasheet by clicking the expand indicator (plus symbol) at the left side of the first row (the row for Kate Navarro).
3. Close the subdatasheet by clicking the collapse indicator (minus symbol) at the left side of the record for Kate Navarro.
4. Display subdatasheets for all of the records by clicking the More button in the Records group, pointing to *Subdatasheet*, and then clicking *Expand All*.

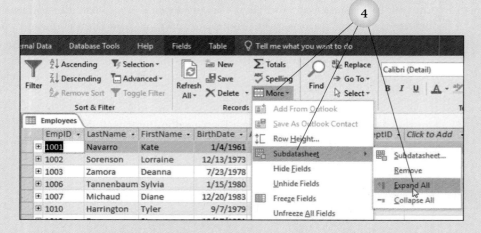

5. Remove the display of all subdatasheets by clicking the More button, pointing to *Subdatasheet*, and then clicking *Collapse All*.
6. Remove the connection between the Employees table and Absences table by clicking the More button, pointing to *Subdatasheet*, and then clicking *Remove*. (Notice that the expand indicators [plus symbols] no longer display before each record.)

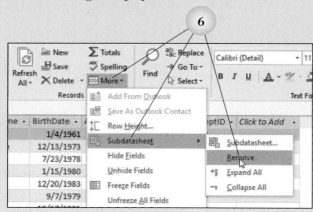

7. Suppose that the employee, Diane Michaud, has moved to a different department and has had an increase in salary. You would like to update her record in the tables. Display the Benefits subdatasheet and make changes to fields in the Employees table and Benefits table by completing the following steps:

   a. Click the More button, point to *Subdatasheet*, and then click *Subdatasheet* at the side menu.

   b. At the Insert Subdatasheet dialog box, click *Benefits* in the list box and then click OK.

   c. Change the department ID for the record for *Diane Michaud (EmpID 1007)* from *DP* to *A*.

   d. Change the salary from *$56,250.00* to *$57,500.00*.

   e. Click the expand indicator (plus symbol) at the left side of the record for Diane Michaud.

   f. Insert a check mark in the *Dental Plan* check box and change the vacation from 3 weeks to 4 weeks.

   g. Click the collapse indicator (minus symbol) at the left side of the record for Diane Michaud.

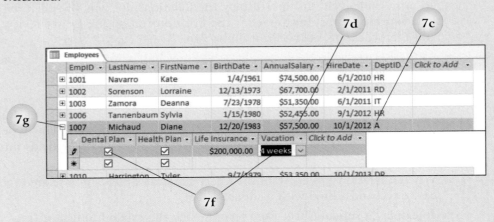

8. Click the Save button on the Quick Access Toolbar.
9. Print and then close the Employees table.
10. Open, print, and then close the Benefits table.
11. Close **2-Griffin**.

Check Your Work

Chapter Summary

- Access is a relational database software program in which tables can be created that are related or connected.

- When planning a table, take time to determine how to break down the required data and what relationships need to be defined to eliminate data redundancies.

- Generally, one field in a table must be unique so that one record can be distinguished from another. A field with a unique value is considered a primary key field.

- A table can have only one primary key field and it is the field by which the table is sorted whenever it is opened.

- In a field defined as a primary key field, duplicate values are not allowed. Access also expects a value in each record in the primary key field.

- Typically, a primary key field in one table becomes the foreign key field in a related table. Data in a foreign key field must match data in the primary key field of the related tables.

- Tables are related by performing a join. When tables that have a common field are joined, data can be extracted from both tables as if they were one large table.

- A one-to-many relationship can be created between tables. In this relationship, a record must be added to the "one" table before it can be added to the "many" table.

- To print table relationships, display the Relationships window, click the Relationship Report button, click the Print button on the Print Preview tab, and then click OK at the Print dialog box.

- At the Relationships window, click the Show Table button to display the Show Table dialog box.

- A relationship between tables can be edited or deleted.

- A one-to-one relationship can be created between tables in which each record in the first table matches only one record in the related table. This type of relationship is generally used to break a large table with many fields into two smaller tables.

- When a relationship is established between tables, fields in a related table can be viewed and edited with a subdatasheet.

- To display a subdatasheet for a record, click the expand indicator (plus symbol) at the left of the record in Datasheet view. To display subdatasheets for all records, click the More button in the Records group on the Home tab, point to *Subdatasheet*, and then click *Expand All*.

- Display the Insert Subdatasheet dialog box by clicking the More button in the Reports group on the Home tab, pointing to *Subdatasheet*, and then clicking *Subdatasheet*.

- Turn off the display of a subdatasheet by clicking the collapse indicator (minus symbol) at the left of the record. To turn off the display of subdatasheets for all records, click the More button, point to *Subdatasheet*, and then click *Collapse All*.

Commands Review

FEATURE	RIBBON, GROUP	BUTTON, OPTION
Edit Relationships dialog box	Relationship Tools Design, Tools	
Insert Subdatasheet dialog box	Home, Records	, *Subdatasheet, Subdatasheet*
primary key field	Table Tools Design, Tools	
print relationships report	Relationship Tools Design, Tools	
Relationships window	Database Tools, Relationships	
Show Table dialog box	Relationship Tools Design, Relationships	

Microsoft® Access®

CHAPTER 3

Performing Queries

Performance Objectives

Upon successful completion of Chapter 3, you will be able to:

1 Design queries to extract specific data from tables

2 Modify queries

3 Design queries with *Or* and *And* criteria

4 Use the Simple Query Wizard to create and modify queries

5 Create and format a calculated field

6 Use aggregate functions in queries

7 Create a crosstab query, find duplicates, and find unmatched queries

One of the primary uses of a database is to extract the specific information needed to answer questions and make decisions. A company might need to know how much inventory is currently on hand, which products have been ordered, which accounts are past due, or which customers live in a particular city. You can extract specific information from a table or multiple tables by creating and running a query. You will learn how to perform a variety of queries on information in tables in this chapter.

 Data Files

Before beginning chapter work, copy the AL1C3 folder to your storage medium and then make AL1C3 the active folder.

The online course includes additional training and assessment resources.

You will design and run a number of queries including queries with fields from one table and queries with fields from more than one table. You will also use the Simple Query Wizard to design queries and create and format a calculated field.

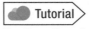 Tutorial

Creating a Query in
Design View

💡 **Hint** The first
step in designing a
query is to choose the
fields that you want to
include in the query
results datasheet.

Designing Queries

Being able to extract (pull out) specific data from a table is one of the most important functions of a database. Extracting data in Access is referred to as performing a query. The word *query* means "question" and to perform a query means to ask a question. Access provides several methods for designing a query. In this chapter, you will learn how to design your own query; use the Simple Query Wizard; create a calculated field; use aggregate functions in a query; and use the Crosstab Query Wizard, Find Duplicates Query Wizard, and Find Unmatched Query Wizard.

Designing a query consists of identifying the table or tables containing the data to be extracted, the field or fields from which the data will be drawn, and the criteria for selecting the data.

Specifying Tables and Fields for a Query

 Query Design

⏱ *Quick Steps*

Design Query
1. Click Create tab.
2. Click Query Design button.
3. Click table at Show Table dialog box.
4. Click Add button.
5. Add any additional tables.
6. In query design grid, click option box arrow in field in *Field* row.
7. Click field at drop-down list.
8. Insert criterion.
9. Click Run button.
10. Save query.

To design a query, open a database, click the Create tab, and then click the Query Design button in the Queries group. This displays a query window in the work area and also displays the Show Table dialog box, as shown in Figure 3.1.

Figure 3.1 Query Window with Show Table Dialog Box

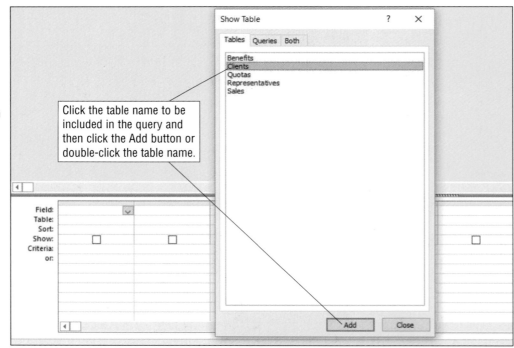

In the Show Table dialog box, click the name of the table to be included in the query and then click the Add button; or simply double-click the table name. This inserts a field list box for the table. Add any other tables required for the query. When all tables have been added, click the Close button. A sample query window is shown in Figure 3.2.

To insert a field in the query design grid, click the option box arrow in the field in the *Field* row and then click the specific field at the drop-down list. Or, double-click a field in a table field list box to insert it in the first available field in the *Field* row in the query design grid.

A third method for inserting a field in the query design grid is to drag a field from the table field list box to the desired location in the query design grid. To do this, position the mouse pointer on the field in the table field list box, click and hold down the left mouse button, drag to the specific field in the *Field* row in the query design grid, and then release the mouse button.

Tutorial

Adding a Criteria Statement to a Query

Establish Query Criterion

1. At query window, click in field in *Criteria* row in query design grid.
2. Type criterion and then press Enter key.
3. Click Run button.

! Run

Adding a Criteria Statement to a Query

Unless a criterion statement is added to a query in the *Criteria* row, the query will return (*return* is the term used for the query results) all records with the fields specified in the query design grid. While returning this information may be helpful, the information could easily be found in the table or tables. The value of performing a query is to extract specific information from a table or tables. To extract specific information, add a criterion statement to the query. To do this, click in the field in the *Criteria* row in the column containing the field name in the query design grid and then type the criterion. With the fields and criterion established, click the Run button in the Results group on the Query Tools Design tab. Access searches the specified tables for records that match the criterion and then displays those records in the query results datasheet.

Figure 3.2 Query Window

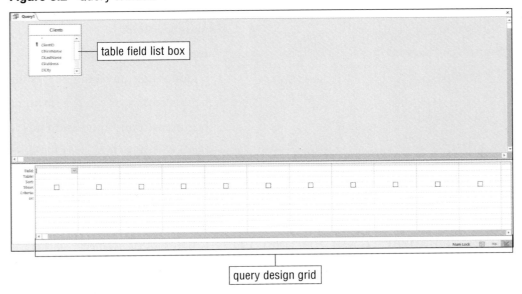

Hint Insert fields in the *Field* row in the query design grid in the order in which you want the fields to appear in the query results datasheet.

For example, to determine how many purchase orders were issued on a specific date, double-click the *PurchaseOrderID* field in the table field list box (which inserts *PurchaseOrderID* in the first field in the *Field* row in the query design grid) and then double-click the *OrderDate* field in the table field list box (which inserts *OrderDate* in the second field in the *Field* row in the query design grid). In this example, both fields are needed, so the purchase order ID is displayed along with the specific order date. After inserting the fields, add the criterion statement. The criterion statement for this example would be something like *#1/15/2021#*. After inserting the criterion, click the Run button in the Results group and the query returns only purchase orders for 1/15/2021 in the query results datasheet. If the criterion statement for the date was not added to the query, the query would return all purchase orders for all of the dates.

Hint Access inserts quotation marks around text criteria and pound symbols around date criteria.

Access makes writing a criterion statement fairly simple by inserting the necessary symbols in the criterion. Type a city name, such as *Indianapolis*, in the *Criteria* row for a *City* field and then press the Enter key and Access changes the criterion to "*Indianapolis*". The quotation marks are inserted by Access and are necessary for the query to run properly. Let Access put the proper symbols around the criterion data in the field in the *Criteria* row or type the criterion with the symbols. Table 3.1 shows some examples of criteria statements, including what is typed and what is returned.

In the criteria examples, the asterisk is used as a wildcard character, which is a symbol that can be used to indicate any character. This is consistent with many other software applications. Two of the criteria examples in Table 3.1 use less-than and greater-than symbols. These symbols can be used for fields containing numbers, values, dates, amounts, and so forth. In the next several activities, you will design queries to extract specific information from different tables in databases.

Table 3.1 Criteria Examples

Typing This Criterion	Returns a Field Value Result That
"Smith"	matches *Smith*
"Smith" Or "Larson"	matches either *Smith* or *Larson*
Not "Smith"	is not *Smith* (anything but "Smith")
"s*"	begins with *S* or *s* and ends in anything
"*s"	begins with anything and ends in *S* or *s*
"[A-D]*"	begins with *A*, *B*, *C*, or *D* and ends in anything
#01/01/2021#	matches the date 01/01/2021
<#04/01/2021#	is less than (before) 04/01/2021
>#04/01/2021#	is greater than (after) 04/01/2021
Between #01/01/2021# And #03/31/2021#	is between 01/01/2021 and 03/31/2021

1. Open **3-Dearborn** from your AL1C3 folder and enable the content.
2. Create the following relationships and enforce referential integrity and cascade fields and records for each relationship:
   a. Create a one-to-many relationship with the *ClientID* field in the Clients table field list box the "one" and the *ClientID* field in the Sales table field list box the "many."
   b. Create a one-to-one relationship with the *RepID* field in the Representatives table field list box the "one" and the *RepID* field in the Benefits table field list box the "one."
   c. Create a one-to-many relationship with the *RepID* field in the Representatives table field list box the "one" and the *RepID* field in the Clients table field list box the "many."
   d. Create a one-to-many relationship with the *QuotaID* field in the Quotas table field list box the "one" and the *QuotaID* field in the Representatives table field list box the "many."
3. Click the Save button on the Quick Access Toolbar.
4. Print the relationships by completing the following steps:
   a. Click the Relationship Report button in the Tools group on the Relationship Tools Design tab.
   b. At the relationship report window, click the Landscape button in the Page Layout group on the Print Preview tab.
   c. Click the Print button at the left side of the Print Preview tab.
   d. At the Print dialog box, click OK.
5. Close the relationship report window without saving the report.
6. Close the Relationships window.
7. Extract records of those clients in Indianapolis by completing the following steps:
   a. Click the Create tab.
   b. Click the Query Design button in the Queries group.
   c. At the Show Table dialog box with the Tables tab selected, click *Clients* in the list box, click the Add button, and then click the Close button.

   d. Insert fields from the Clients table field list box into the *Field* row in the query design grid by completing the following steps:

   1) Click the option box arrow at the right of the first field in the *Field* row in the query design grid and then click *Client* at the drop-down list.
   2) Click in the next field in the *Field* row (to the right of *Client*) in the query design grid, click the option box arrow, and then click *ClAddress* at the drop-down list.
   3) Click in the next field in the *Field* row (to the right of *ClAddress*), click the option box arrow, and then click *ClCity* at the drop-down list.
   4) Click in the next field in the *Field* row (to the right of *ClCity*), click the option box arrow, and then click *ClState* at the drop-down list.

5) Click in the next field in the *Field* row (to the right of *ClState*), click the option box arrow, and then click *ClZIP* at the drop-down list.

e. Insert the query criterion statement telling Access to display only those suppliers in Indianapolis by completing the following steps:
   1) Click in the *ClCity* field in the *Criteria* row in the query design grid. (This positions the insertion point in the field.)
   2) Type Indianapolis and then press the Enter key. (This changes the criterion to "*Indianapolis*".)

f. Return the results of the query by clicking the Run button in the Results group on the Query Tools Design tab. (This displays the results in the query results datasheet.)

g. Save the results of the query by completing the following steps:
   1) Click the Save button on the Quick Access Toolbar.
   2) At the Save As dialog box, type Clients_Indianapolis and then press the Enter key or click OK.

h. Print the query results datasheet by clicking the File tab, clicking the *Print* option, and then clicking the *Quick Print* option.

i. Close the query.

8. Extract those records with quota identification numbers greater than 2 by completing the following steps:
   a. Click the Create tab and then click the Query Design button.
   b. Double-click *Representatives* in the Show Table dialog box and then click the Close button.
   c. In the query window, double-click *RepName*. (This inserts the field in the first field in the *Field* row in the query design grid.)
   d. Double-click *QuotaID*. (This inserts the field in the second field in the *Field* row in the query design grid.)

e. Insert the query criterion by completing the following steps:
   1) Click in the *QuotaID* field in the *Criteria* row in the query design grid.
   2) Type >2 and then press the Enter key. (Access will automatically insert quotation marks around *2* since the data type for the field is identified as *Short Text* [rather than *Number*].)

Field:	RepName	QuotaID
Table:	Representatives	Representatives
Sort:		
Show:	☑	☑
Criteria:		>"2"
or:		

8e2

   f. Return the results of the query by clicking the Run button.
   g. Save the query, typing QuotaID>2 as the query name.
   h. Print and then close the query.

9. Extract those sales greater than $99,999 by completing the following steps:
   a. Click the Create tab and then click the Query Design button.
   b. Double-click *Sales* in the Show Table dialog box and then click the Close button.
   c. At the query window, double-click *ClientID*. (This inserts the field in the first field in the *Field* row in the query design grid.)
   d. Insert the *SalesAmount* field in the second field in the *Field* row.
   e. Insert the query criterion by completing the following steps:
      1) Click in the *SalesAmount* field in the *Criteria* row in the query design grid.
      2) Type >99999 and then press the Enter key. (Access will not insert quotation marks around *99999* since the field is identified as *Currency*.)

Field:	ClientID	SalesAmount
Table:	Sales	Sales
Sort:		
Show:	☑	☑
Criteria:		>99999
or:		

9e2

   f. Return the results of the query by clicking the Run button.
   g. Save the query, typing Sales>$99999 as the query name.
   h. Print and then close the query.

10. Extract records of those representatives with a telephone number that begins with the 765 area code by completing the following steps:
   a. Click the Create tab and then click the Query Design button.
   b. Double-click *Representatives* in the Show Table dialog box and then click the Close button.
   c. Insert the *RepName* field in the first field in the *Field* row.
   d. Insert the *RepTelephone* field in the second field in the *Field* row.
   e. Insert the query criterion by completing the following steps:
      1) Click in the *RepTelephone* field in the *Criteria* row.
      2) Type "(765*" and then press the Enter key. (You need to type the quotation marks in this criterion because the criterion contains a left parenthesis.)

Field:	RepName	RepTelephone
Table:	Representatives	Representatives
Sort:		
Show:	☑	☑
Criteria:		Like "(765*"
or:		

10e2

   f. Return the results of the query by clicking the Run button.
   g. Save the query, typing Reps_765AreaCode as the query name.
   h. Print and then close the query.

Check Your Work

Tutorial

Creating a Query in Design View Using Multiple Tables

In Activity 1a, each query was performed on fields from one table. Queries can also be performed on fields from multiple tables. In Activity 1b, queries will be performed on tables containing yes/no check boxes. When designing a query, both records that contain a check mark and records that do not contain a check mark can be extracted. To extract records that contain a check mark, click in the field in the *Criteria* row in the query design grid, type a *1*, press the Enter key, and Access changes the *1* to *True*. To extract records that do not contain a check mark, type *0* in the field in the *Criteria* row, press the Enter key, and Access changes the *0* to *False*.

The Zoom box can be used when entering a criterion in a query to provide a larger area for typing. To display the Zoom box, press Shift + F2 or right-click in the specific field in the *Criteria* row and then click *Zoom* at the shortcut menu. Type the criterion in the Zoom box and then click OK.

Activity 1b Performing Queries on Related Tables

1. With **3-Dearborn** open, extract information on representatives hired between January 2014 and June 2014 and include the representatives' names by completing the following steps:
   a. Click the Create tab and then click the Query Design button.
   b. Double-click *Representatives* in the Show Table dialog box.
   c. Double-click *Benefits* in the Show Table dialog box and then click the Close button.
   d. At the query window, double-click *RepName* in the Representatives table field list box.
   e. Double-click *HireDate* in the Benefits table field list box.
   f. Insert the query criterion in the Zoom box by completing the following steps:
      1) Click in the *HireDate* field in the *Criteria* row.
      2) Press Shift + F2 to display the Zoom box.
      3) Type Between 1/1/2014 And 6/30/2014.
      4) Click OK.
   g. Return the results of the query by clicking the Run button.
   h. Save the query, typing Hires_2014JantoJun as the query name.
   i. Print and then close the query.

2. Extract records of those representatives who were hired in 2015 by completing the following steps:
   a. Click the Create tab and then click the Query Design button.
   b. Double-click *Representatives* in the Show Table dialog box.
   c. Double-click *Benefits* in the Show Table dialog box and then click the Close button.
   d. Double-click *RepID* in the Representatives table field list box.
   e. Double-click *RepName* in the Representatives table field list box.
   f. Double-click *HireDate* in the Benefits table field list box.

g. Insert the query criterion by completing the following steps:
   1) Click in the *HireDate* field in the *Criteria* row.
   2) Type *2015 and then press the Enter key.
h. Return the results of the query by clicking the Run button.
i. Save the query, typing Hires_2015 as the query name.
j. Print and then close the query.

Field:	RepID	RepName	HireDate
Table:	Representatives	Representatives	Benefits
Sort:			
Show:	☑	☑	☑
Criteria:			Like "*2015"
or:			

2g2

3. Suppose you need to determine sales for a company but you can only remember that the company name begins with *Blue*. Create a query that finds the company and identifies the sales by completing the following steps:
   a. Click the Create tab and then click the Query Design button.
   b. Double-click *Clients* in the Show Table dialog box.
   c. Double-click *Sales* in the Show Table dialog box and then click the Close button.
   d. Insert the *ClientID* field from the Clients table field list box in the first field in the *Field* row in the query design grid.
   e. Insert the *Client* field from the Clients table field list box in the second field in the *Field* row.
   f. Insert the *SalesAmount* field from the Sales table field list box in the third field in the *Field* row.
   g. Insert the query criterion by completing the following steps:
      1) Click in the *Client* field in the *Criteria* row.
      2) Type Blue* and then press the Enter key.

Field:	ClientID	Client	SalesAmount
Table:	Clients	Clients	Sales
Sort:			
Show:	☑	☑	☑
Criteria:		Like "Blue*"	
or:			

3g2

   h. Return the results of the query by clicking the Run button.
   i. Save the query, typing Sales_BlueRidge as the query name.
   j. Print and then close the query.
4. Close **3-Dearborn**.
5. Display the Open dialog box with your AL1C3 folder active.
6. Open **3-PacTrek** and enable the content.
7. Extract information on products ordered between February 1, 2021, and February 28, 2021, by completing the following steps:
   a. Click the Create tab and then click the Query Design button.
   b. Double-click *Products* in the Show Table dialog box.
   c. Double-click *Orders* in the Show Table dialog box and then click the Close button.
   d. Insert the *ProductID* field from the Products table field list box in the first field in the *Field* row.
   e. Insert the *Product* field from the Products table field list box in the second field in the *Field* row.
   f. Insert the *OrderDate* field from the Orders table field list box in the third field in the *Field* row.
   g. Insert the query criterion by completing the following steps:
      1) Click in the *OrderDate* field in the *Criteria* row.
      2) Type Between 2/1/2021 And 2/28/2021 and then press the Enter key.

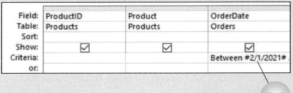

Field:	ProductID	Product	OrderDate
Table:	Products	Products	Orders
Sort:			
Show:	☑	☑	☑
Criteria:			Between #2/1/2021#...
or:			

7g2

h. Return the results of the query by clicking the Run button.

i. Save the query, typing Orders_February as the query name.

j. Print and then close the query.

8. Close **3-PacTrek**.

9. Open **3-CopperState** and enable the content.

10. Display the Relationships window and create the following additional relationships (enforce referential integrity and cascade fields and records):

a. Create a one-to-many relationship with the *AgentID* field in the Agents table field list box the "one" and the *AgentID* field in the Assignments table field list box the "many."

b. Create a one-to-many relationship with the *OfficeID* field in the Offices table field list box the "one" and the *OfficeID* field in the Assignments table field list box the "many."

c. Create a one-to-many relationship with the *OfficeID* field in the Offices table field list box the "one" and the *OfficeID* field in the Agents table field list box the "many."

11. Save and then print the relationships.

12. Close the relationship report without saving it and then close the Relationships window.

13. Extract records of clients that have uninsured motorist coverage by completing the following steps:

a. Click the Create tab and then click the Query Design button.

b. Double-click *Clients* in the Show Table dialog box.

c. Double-click *Coverage* in the Show Table dialog box and then click the Close button.

d. Insert the *ClientID* field from the Clients table field list box in the first field in the *Field* row.

e. Insert the *ClFirstName* field from the Clients table field list box in the second field in the *Field* row.

f. Insert the *ClLastName* field from the Clients table field list box in the third field in the *Field* row.

g. Insert the *UninsMotorist* field from the Coverage table field list box in the fourth field in the *Field* row. (You may need to scroll down the Coverage table field list box to see the *UninsMotorist* field.)

h. Insert the query criterion by clicking in the *UninsMotorist* field in the *Criteria* row, typing 1, and then pressing the Enter key. (Access changes the *1* to *True*.)

Field:	ClientID	ClFirstName	ClLastName	UninsMotorist
Table:	Clients	Clients	Clients	Coverage
Sort:				
Show:	☑	☑	☑	☑
Criteria:				True
or:				

13h

i. Click the Run button.

j. Save the query, typing Coverage_UninsuredMotorist as the query name.

k. Print and then close the query.

14. Extract records of claims in January over $999 by completing the following steps:

a. Click the Create tab and then click the Query Design button.

b. Double-click *Clients* in the Show Table dialog box.

c. Double-click *Claims* in the Show Table dialog box and then click the Close button.

d. Insert the *ClientID* field from the *Clients* table field list box in the first field in the *Field* row.

e. Insert the *ClFirstName* field from the Clients table field list box in the second field in the *Field* row.

f. Insert the *ClLastName* field from the Clients table field list box in the third field in the *Field* row.

g. Insert the *ClaimID* field from the Claims table field list box in the fourth field in the *Field* row.

h. Insert the *DateOfClaim* field from the Claims table field list box in the fifth field in the *Field* row.

i. Insert the *AmountOfClaim* field from the Claims table field list box in the sixth field in the *Field* row.
j. Click in the *DateOfClaim* field in the *Criteria* row, type Between 1/1/2021 And 1/31/2021, and then press the Enter key.
k. With the insertion point positioned in the *AmountOfClaim* field in the *Criteria* row, type >999 and then press the Enter key.

Field:	ClientID	ClFirstName	ClLastName	ClaimID	DateOfClaim	AmountOfClaim
Table:	Clients	Clients	Clients	Claims	Claims	Claims
Sort:						
Show:	☑	☑	☑	☑	☑	☑
Criteria:					Between #1/1/2021#.	>999
or:						

14j   14k

l. Click the Run button.
m. Save the query, typing Claims_2021Jan>$999 as the query name.
n. Print and then close the query.

 Check Your Work

 Tutorial

Sorting Data and
Hiding Fields in
Query Results

Sorting in a Query

When designing a query, the sort order of a field or fields can be specified. Click in a field in the *Sort* row and an option box arrow displays at the right side of the field. Click this option box arrow and a drop-down list displays with the choices *Ascending*, *Descending*, and *(not sorted)*. Click *Ascending* to sort from lowest to highest or click *Descending* to sort from highest to lowest.

 Quick Steps

Sort Fields in Query
1. At query window, click in field in *Sort* row in query design grid.
2. Click option box arrow in field.
3. Click *Ascending* or *Descending*.

Hiding Fields in a Query

By default, each check box in the fields in the *Show* row in the query design grid contains a check mark, indicating that the column will be included in the query results datasheet. If a specific field is needed for the query but not needed when viewing the query results, remove the check mark from the field in the *Show* row to hide the field in the query results datasheet.

Arranging Fields in a Query

Use buttons in the Query Setup group on the Query Design Tools tab to insert a new field column in or delete an existing field column from the query design grid. To insert a field column, click in a field in the column that will display immediately to the right of the new column and then click the Insert Columns button in the Query Setup group on the Query Design Tools tab. To remove a column, click in a field in the column to be deleted and then click the Delete Columns button in the Query Setup group. Complete similar steps to insert or delete a row in the query design grid.

Columns in the query design grid can be rearranged by selecting the field column and then dragging the column to the desired position. To select a column in the query design grid, position the mouse pointer at the top of the column

Insert Columns

Delete Columns

until the pointer turns into a small, black, down-pointing arrow and then click the left mouse button. Position the mouse pointer at the top of the selected column until the mouse displays as a pointer, click and hold down the left mouse button, drag to the desired position in the query design grid, and then release the mouse button. While the column is being dragged, a thick, black, vertical line displays identifying the location where the column will be inserted.

Activity 1c Performing Queries on Related Tables and Sorting in Field Values   Part 3 of 8

1. With **3-CopperState** open, extract information on clients with agents from the West Bell Road Glendale office and sort the information alphabetically by client last name by completing the following steps:
   a. Click the Create tab and then click the Query Design button.
   b. Double-click *Assignments* in the Show Table dialog box.
   c. Double-click *Clients* in the Show Table dialog box and then click the Close button.
   d. Insert the *OfficeID* field from the Assignments table field list box in the first field in the *Field* row.
   e. Insert the *AgentID* field from the Assignments table field list box in the second field in the *Field* row.
   f. Insert the *ClFirstName* field from the Clients table field list box in the third field in the *Field* row.
   g. Insert the *ClLastName* field from the Clients table field list box in the fourth field in the *Field* row.
   h. Click in the *OfficeID* field in the *Criteria* row, type GW, and then press the Enter key.
   i. Sort the *ClLastName* field column in ascending alphabetical order (A–Z) by completing the following steps:
      1) Click in the *ClLastName* field in the *Sort* row. (This displays an option box arrow in the field.)
      2) Click the option box arrow in the field in the *Sort* row and then click *Ascending*.

   j. Specify that you do not want the *AgentID* field to show in the query results by clicking in the check box in the *AgentID* field in the *Show* row to remove the check mark.
   k. Click the Run button.
   l. Save the query, typing Clients_GW as the query name.
   m. Print and then close the query.
2. Close **3-CopperState**.
3. Open **3-PacTrek**.
4. Extract information on orders less than $1,500 by completing the following steps:
   a. Click the Create tab and then click the Query Design button.
   b. Double-click *Products* in the Show Table dialog box.
   c. Double-click *Orders* in the Show Table dialog box and then click the Close button.
   d. Insert the *ProductID* field from the Products table field list box in the first field in the *Field* row.
   e. Insert the *SupplierID* field from the Products table field list box in the second field in the *Field* row.

f. Insert the *UnitsOrdered* field from the Orders table field list box in the third field in the *Field* row.

g. Insert the *OrderAmount* field from the Orders table field list box in the fourth field in the *Field* row. (You may need to scroll down the table field list box to display this field.)

h. Insert the query criterion by completing the following steps:

1) Click in the *OrderAmount* field in the *Criteria* row.

2) Type <1500 and then press the Enter key.

Field:	ProductID	SupplierID	UnitsOrdered	OrderAmount
Table:	Products	Products	Orders	Orders
Sort:				
Show:	☑	☑	☑	☑
Criteria:				<1500
or:				

4h2

i. Sort the *OrderAmount* field column values from highest to lowest by completing the following steps:

1) Click in the *OrderAmount* field in the *Sort* row. (This displays an option box arrow in the field.)

2) Click the option box arrow in the field in the *Sort* row and then click *Descending*.

UnitsOrdered	OrderAmount
Orders	Orders
	Ascending
	Descending
	(not sorted)
☑	

4i2

j. Return the results of the query by clicking the Run button.

k. Save the query, typing Orders<$1500 as the query name.

l. Print and then close the query.

5. Close **3-PacTrek**.

6. Open **3-Dearborn**.

7. Design a query by completing the following steps:

a. Click the Create tab and then click the Query Design button.

b. Double-click *Representatives* in the Show Table dialog box.

c. Double-click *Clients* in the Show Table dialog box.

d. Double-click *Sales* in the Show Table dialog box and then click the Close button.

e. Insert the *RepID* field from the Representatives table field list box in the first field in the *Field* row.

f. Insert the *RepName* field from the Representatives table field list box in the second field in the *Field* row.

g. Insert the *ClientID* field from the Clients table field list box in the third field in the *Field* row.

h. Insert the *SalesAmount* field from the Sales table field list box in the fourth field in the *Field* row.

8. Move the *RepName* field column by completing the following steps:

a. Position the mouse pointer at the top of the *RepName* field column until the pointer turns into a small, black, down-pointing arrow and then click the left mouse button. (This selects the entire column.)

8a

Field:	RepID	RepName	ClientID
Table:	Representatives	Representatives	Clients
Sort:			
Show:	☑	☑	☑
Criteria:			
or:			

b. Position the mouse pointer at the top of the selected column until the pointer turns into a white arrow.

c. Click and hold down the left mouse button; drag to the right until a thick, black horizontal line displays between the *ClientID* field column and the *SalesAmount* field column; and then release the mouse button.

8c

RepID	RepName	ClientID	SalesAmount
Representatives	Representatives	Clients	Sales
☑	☑	☑	☑

9. Delete the *RepID* field column by clicking in a field in the column and then clicking the Delete Columns button in the Query Setup group.
10. Insert a new field column and insert a new field in the column by completing the following steps:

   a. Click in a field in the *SalesAmount* field column and then click the Insert Columns button in the Query Setup group.

   b. Click the option box arrow in the *Field* row in the new field column and then click *Clients.Client* at the drop-down list.

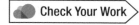

11. Hide the *ClientID* field so it is not included in the query results by clicking the *Show* check box in the *ClientID* field in the *Show* row to remove the check mark.
12. Insert the query criterion that extracts information on sales over $100,000 by completing the following steps:

   a. Click in the *SalesAmount* field in the *Criteria* row.

   b. Type >100000 and then press the Enter key.

13. Sort the *SalesAmount* field column values from highest to lowest by completing the following steps:

   a. Click in the *SalesAmount* field in the *Sort* row.

   b. Click the option box arrow in the field in the *Sort* row and then click *Descending*.

14. Return the results of the query by clicking the Run button.
15. Save the query, typing Sales>$100000 as the query name.
16. Print and then close the query.

> **Check Your Work**

Modifying a Query

A query can be modified and used for a new purpose. For example, if a query is designed to return sales of more than $100,000, the query can be used to find sales that are less than $100,000. Rather than design a new query, open the existing query, make any needed changes, and then run the query.

To modify an existing query, double-click the query in the Navigation pane. (This opens the query in Datasheet view.) Click the View button to display the query in Design view. A query can also be opened in Design view by right-clicking the query in the Navigation pane and then clicking *Design View* at the shortcut menu. Make changes to the query and then click the Run button in the Results group. Click the Save button on the Quick Access Toolbar to save the query with the same name. To save the query with a new name, click the File tab, click the *Save As* option, click the *Save Object As* option, and then click the Save As button. At the Save As dialog box, type a name for the query and then press the Enter key.

If a database contains a number of queries, the queries can be listed together in the Navigation pane. To do this, click the option box arrow in the Navigation pane menu bar and then click *Object Type* at the drop-down list. This groups objects in categories, such as *Tables* and *Queries*.

Quick Steps

Modify Query

1. Double-click query in Navigation pane.
2. Click View button.
3. Make changes to query.
4. Click Run button.
5. Click Save button.

Hint Save time designing a new query by modifying an existing query.

Renaming and Deleting a Query

If a query has been modified, consider renaming it. To do this, right-click the query name in the Navigation pane, click *Rename* at the shortcut menu, type the new name, and then press the Enter key. If a query is no longer needed in the database, delete it by clicking the query name in the Navigation pane, clicking the Delete button in the Records group on the Home tab, and then clicking the Yes button at the deletion message. Another method is to right-click the query in the Navigation pane, click *Delete* at the shortcut menu, and then click Yes at the deletion message. If a query is being deleted from a file on the computer's hard drive, the deletion message will not display. This is because Access automatically sends the deleted query to the Recycle Bin, where it can be retrieved if necessary.

Activity 1d Modifying and Deleting Queries   Part 4 of 8

1. With **3-Dearborn** open, find sales less than $100,000 by completing the following steps:
   a. Double-click *Sales>$100000* in the Queries group in the Navigation pane.
   b. Click the View button in the Views group to switch to Design view.
   c. Click in the field in the *Criteria* row containing the text *>100000* and then edit the text so it reads *<100000*.

Field:	RepName	Client	SalesAmount
Table:	Representatives	Clients	Sales
Sort:			Descending
Show:	☑	☑	☑
Criteria:			<100000
or:			

1c

   d. Click the Run button.
2. Save the query with a new name by completing the following steps:
   a. Click the File tab, click the *Save As* option, click the *Save Object As* option, and then click the Save As button.
   b. At the Save As dialog box, type *Sales<$100000* and then click OK or press the Enter key.
   c. Print and then close the query.
3. Modify an existing query and find employees with three weeks of vacation by completing the following steps:
   a. Right-click *Hires_2014JantoJun* in the Queries group in the Navigation pane and then click *Design View* at the shortcut menu.
   b. Click in the *HireDate* field in the *Field* row.
   c. Click the option box arrow in the field and then click *Vacation* at the drop-down list.
   d. Select the current text in the *Vacation* field in the *Criteria* row, type *3 weeks*, and then press the Enter key.
   e. Click the Run button.
   f. Save and then close the query.

4. Rename the query by completing the following steps:
   a. Right-click *Hires_2014JantoJun* in the Navigation pane and then click *Rename* at the shortcut menu.
   b. Type Reps_3WeeksVacay and then press the Enter key.
   c. Open, print, and then close the query.
5. Delete the *Sales>$99999* query by right-clicking the query name in the Navigation pane and then clicking *Delete* at the shortcut menu. If a deletion message displays, click Yes.

 Check Your Work

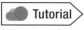 Tutorial

Designing a Query
with *Or* Criteria

 Tutorial

Designing a Query
with *And* Criteria

💡 **Hint** A query
can be designed that
combines *And* and *Or*
statements.

Designing Queries with *Or* and *And* Criteria

The query design grid contains an *or* row for designing a query that instructs Access to display records matching any of the criteria. Multiple criterion statements on different rows in a query become an *Or* statement, which means that any of the criterion can be met for a record to be included in the query results datasheet. For example, to display a list of employees with three weeks of vacation *or* four weeks of vacation, type *3 weeks* in the *Vacation* field in the *Criteria* row and then type *4 weeks* in the field immediately below *3 weeks* in the *or* row. Other examples include finding clients that live in *Muncie* or *Lafayette* and finding representatives with quotas of *1* or *2*.

When designing a query, criteria statements can be entered into more than one field in the *Criteria* row. Multiple criteria all entered in the same row become an *And* statement, for which each criterion must be met for Access to select the record. For example, a query can be designed to return clients in the Indianapolis area with sales greater than $100,000.

Activity 1e Designing Queries with *Or* and *And* Criteria

Part 5 of 8

1. With **3-Dearborn** open, modify an existing query and find employees with three weeks or four weeks of vacation by completing the following steps:
   a. Double-click the *Reps_3WeeksVacay* query in the Navigation pane.
   b. Click the View button in the Views group to switch to Design view.
   c. Click in the empty field below "*3 weeks*" in the *or* row, type 4 weeks, and then press the Enter key.
   d. Click the Run button.
2. Save the query with a new name by completing the following steps:
   a. Click the File tab, click the *Save As* option, click the *Save Object As* option, and then click the Save As button.

Field:	RepName	Vacation
Table:	Representatives	Benefits
Sort:		
Show:	☑	☑
Criteria:		"3 weeks"
or:		"4 weeks"

1c

   b. At the Save As dialog box, type Reps_3or4WeeksVacay and then press the Enter key.
   c. Print and then close the query.
3. Design a query that finds records of clients in the Indianapolis area with sales over $100,000 by completing the following steps:
   a. Click the Create tab and then click the Query Design button.

b. Double-click *Clients* in the Show Table dialog box.
c. Double-click *Sales* in the Show Table dialog box and then click the Close button.
d. Insert the *Client* field from the Clients table field list box in the first field in the *Field* row.
e. Insert the *ClCity* field from the Clients table field list box in the second field in the *Field* row.
f. Insert the *SalesAmount* field from the Sales table field list box in the third field in the *Field* row.
g. Insert the query criteria by completing the following steps:
   1) Click in the *ClCity* field in the *Criteria* row.
   2) Type Indianapolis and then press the Enter key.
   3) With the insertion point positioned in the *SalesAmount* field in the *Criteria* row, type >100000 and then press the Enter key.

h. Click the Run button.
i. Save the query, typing Sales_Indianapolis>$100000 as the query name.
j. Print and then close the query.
4. Close **3-Dearborn**.
5. Open **3-PacTrek**.
6. Design a query that finds products available from supplier numbers 25, 31, and 42 by completing the following steps:
   a. Click the Create tab and then click the Query Design button.
   b. Double-click *Suppliers* in the Show Table dialog box.
   c. Double-click *Products* in the Show Table dialog box and then click the Close button.
   d. Insert the *SupplierID* field from the Suppliers table field list box in the first field in the *Field* row.
   e. Insert the *SupplierName* field from the Suppliers table field list box in the second field in the *Field* row.
   f. Insert the *Product* field from the Products table field list box in the third field in the *Field* row.
   g. Insert the query criteria by completing the following steps:
      1) Click in the *SupplierID* field in the *Criteria* row.
      2) Type 25 and then press the Down Arrow key. (This makes the field below *25* active.)
      3) Type 31 and then press the Down Arrow key. (This makes the field below *31* active.)
      4) Type 42 and then press the Enter key.

h. Click the Run button.
i. Save the query, typing Suppliers_25-31-42 as the query name.
j. Print and then close the query.

7. Design a query that finds the number of ski hats or gloves on order by completing the following steps:
   a. Click the Create tab and then click the Query Design button.
   b. Double-click *Orders* in the Show Table dialog box.
   c. Double-click *Suppliers* in the Show Table dialog box.
   d. Double-click *Products* in the Show Table dialog box and then click the Close button.
   e. Insert the *OrderID* field from the Orders table field list box in the first field in the *Field* row.
   f. Insert the *SupplierName* field from the Suppliers table field list box in the second field in the *Field* row.
   g. Insert the *Product* field from the Products table field list box in the third field in the *Field* row.
   h. Insert the *UnitsOrdered* field from the Orders table field list box in the fourth field in the *Field* row.
   i. Insert the query criteria by completing the following steps:
      1) Click in the *Product* field in the *Criteria* row.
      2) Type *ski hat* and then press the Down Arrow key. (You need to type the asterisk before and after *ski hat* so the query will find any product that includes the words *ski hat* in the description, no matter what text comes before or after the words. When you press the Down Arrow key, Access changes the criteria to *Like* "**ski hat**".)
      3) Type *gloves* and then press the Enter key.

   j. Click the Run button.
   k. Save the query, typing Orders_HatsGloves as the query name.
   l. Print and then close the query.
8. Design a query that finds boots, sleeping bags, or backpacks and the suppliers that produce them by completing the following steps:
   a. Click the Create tab and then click the Query Design button.
   b. Double-click *Products* in the Show Table dialog box.
   c. Double-click *Suppliers* in the Show Table dialog box and then click the Close button.
   d. Insert the *ProductID* field from the Products table field list box in the first field in the *Field* row.
   e. Insert the *Product* field from the Products table field list box in the second field in the *Field* row.
   f. Insert the *SupplierName* field from the Suppliers table field list box in the third field in the *Field* row.
   g. Insert the query criteria by completing the following steps:
      1) Click in the *Product* field in the *Criteria* row.

2) Type *boots* and then press the Down Arrow key.
3) Type *sleeping bag* and then press the Down Arrow key.
4) Type *backpack* and then press the Enter key.

h. Click the Run button.
i. Save the query, typing Products_ Equipment as the query name.
j. Print and then close the query.

9. Close **3-PacTrek**.
10. Open **3-CopperState**.
11. Design a query that finds clients who have only liability auto coverage by completing the following steps:

a. Click the Create tab and then click the Query Design button.
b. Double-click *Clients* in the Show Table dialog box.
c. Double-click *Coverage* in the Show Table dialog box and then click the Close button.
d. Insert the *ClientID* field from the Clients table field list box in the first field in the *Field* row.
e. Insert the *ClFirstName* field from the Clients table field list box in the second field in the *Field* row.
f. Insert the *ClLastName* field from the Clients table field list box in the third field in the *Field* row.
g. Insert the *Medical* field from the Coverage table field list box in the fourth field in the *Field* row.
h. Insert the *Liability* field from the Coverage table field list box in the fifth field in the *Field* row.
i. Insert the *Comprehensive* field from the Coverage table field list box in the sixth field in the *Field* row.
j. Insert the *UninsMotorist* field from the Coverage table field list box in the seventh field in the *Field* row. (You may need to scroll down the Coverage table field list box to see the *UninsMotorist* field.)
k. Insert the *Collision* field from the Coverage table field list box in the eighth field in the *Field* row. (You may need to scroll down the Coverage table field list box to see the *Collision* field.)
l. Insert the query criteria by completing the following steps:
1) Click in the *Medical* field in the *Criteria* row, type 0, and then press the Enter key. (Access changes the *0* to *False*.)
2) With the insertion point in the *Liability* field in the *Criteria* row, type 1 and then press the Enter key. (Access changes the *1* to *True*.)

Field:	ProductID	Product	SupplierName
Table:	Products	Products	Suppliers
Sort:			
Show:	☑	☑	☑
Criteria:		Like "*boots*"	
or:		Like "*sleeping bag*"	
		Like "*backpack*"	

8g2 8g4 8g3

Field:	ClientID	ClFirstName	ClLastName	Medical	Liability
Table:	Clients	Clients	Clients	Coverage	Coverage
Sort:					
Show:	☑	☑	☑	☑	☑
Criteria:				False	True
or:					

1l11 1l12

3) With the insertion point in the *Comprehensive* field in the *Criteria* row, type 0 and then press the Enter key.

4) With the insertion point in the *UninsMotorist* field in the *Criteria* row, type 0 and then press the Enter key.

5) With the insertion point in the *Collision* field in the *Criteria* row, type 0 and then press the Enter key.

m. Click the Run button.

n. Save the query, typing Coverage_LiabilityOnly as the query name.

o. Print the query in landscape orientation.

p. Close the query.

12. Close **3-CopperState**.

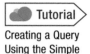

Creating a Query Using the Simple Query Wizard

Quick Steps

Create Query Using Simple Query Wizard

1. Click Create tab.
2. Click Query Wizard button.
3. Make sure *Simple Query Wizard* is selected in list box and then click OK.
4. Follow query steps.
5. Click Finish button.

The Simple Query Wizard provides steps for preparing a query. To use this wizard, open the database, click the Create tab, and then click the Query Wizard button in the Queries group. At the New Query dialog box, make sure *Simple Query Wizard* is selected in the list box and then click OK. At the first Simple Query Wizard dialog box, shown in Figure 3.3, specify the table(s) in the *Tables/Queries* option box. After specifying the table(s), insert the fields to be included in the query in the *Selected Fields* list box and then click the Next button.

At the second Simple Query Wizard dialog box, specify a detail or summary query and then click the Next button. At the third (and last) Simple Query Wizard dialog box, shown in Figure 3.4, type a name for the completed query or accept the name provided by the wizard. The third Simple Query Wizard dialog box also includes options for choosing to open the query to view the information or to modify the query design. To extract specific information, be sure to choose the *Modify the query design* option. After making any necessary changes, click the Finish button.

If the query design is not modified in the last Simple Query Wizard dialog box, the query displays all records for the fields identified in the first Simple Query Wizard dialog box.

Figure 3.3 First Simple Query Wizard Dialog Box

Figure 3.4 Last Simple Query Wizard Dialog Box

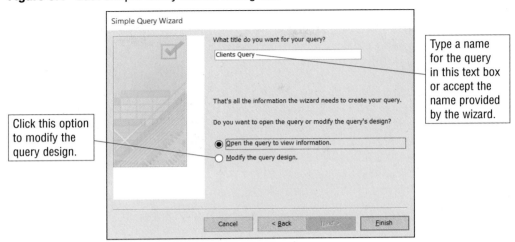

Type a name for the query in this text box or accept the name provided by the wizard.

Click this option to modify the query design.

Activity 1f Creating Queries Using the Simple Query Wizard

1. Open **3-Dearborn** and then use the Simple Query Wizard to create a query that returns client names along with sales by completing the following steps:

   a. Click the Create tab and then click the Query Wizard button in the Queries group.

   b. At the New Query dialog box, make sure *Simple Query Wizard* is selected in the list box and then click OK.

   c. At the first Simple Query Wizard dialog box, click the *Tables/Queries* option box arrow and then click *Table: Clients*.

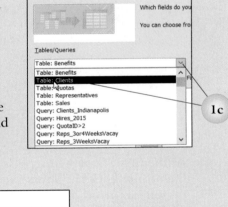

   d. With *ClientID* selected in the *Available Fields* list box, click the One Field button (the button containing the greater-than symbol, >). This inserts the *ClientID* field in the *Selected Fields* list box.

   e. Click *Client* in the *Available Fields* list box and then click the One Field button.

f. Click the *Tables/Queries* option box arrow and then click *Table: Sales*.

g. Click *SalesAmount* in the *Available Fields* list box and then click the One Field button.

h. Click the Next button.

i. At the second Simple Query Wizard dialog box, click the Next button.

j. At the last Simple Query Wizard dialog box, select the name in the *What title do you want for your query?* text box, type Clients_Sales, and then press the Enter key.

k. When the results of the query display, print the results.

2. Close the query.

3. Close **3-Dearborn**.

4. Open **3-PacTrek**.

5. Create a query that returns the products on order, order amounts, and supplier names by completing the following steps:

a. Click the Create tab and then click the Query Wizard button.

b. At the New Query dialog box, make sure *Simple Query Wizard* is selected in the list box and then click OK.

c. At the first Simple Query Wizard dialog box, click the *Tables/Queries* option box arrow and then click *Table: Suppliers*.

d. With *SupplierID* selected in the *Available Fields* list box, click the One Field button. (This inserts the *SupplierID* field in the *Selected Fields* list box.)

e. With *SupplierName* selected in the *Available Fields* list box, click the One Field button.

f. Click the *Tables/Queries* option box arrow and then click *Table: Orders*.

g. Click *ProductID* in the *Available Fields* list box and then click the One Field button.

h. Click *OrderAmount* in the *Available Fields* list box and then click the One Field button.

i. Click the Next button.

j. At the second Simple Query Wizard dialog box, click the Next button.

k. At the last Simple Query Wizard dialog box, select the text in the *What title do you want for your query?* text box, type Products_OrderAmounts, and then press the Enter key.

l. When the results of the query display, print the results.

m. Close the query.

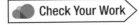

To extract specific information when using the Simple Query Wizard, tell the wizard that the query design is to be modified. This displays the query window with the query design grid, where query criteria can be entered.

1. With **3-PacTrek** open, use the Simple Query Wizard to create a query that returns suppliers outside British Columbia by completing the following steps:

   a. Click the Create tab and then click the Query Wizard button.

   b. At the New Query dialog box, make sure *Simple Query Wizard* is selected and then click OK.

   c. At the first Simple Query Wizard dialog box, click the *Tables/Queries* option box arrow and then click *Table: Suppliers*.

   d. Insert the following fields in the *Selected Fields* list box:

   SupplierName
   StreetAddress
   City
   Prov/State
   PostalCode

   e. Click the Next button.

   f. At the last Simple Query Wizard dialog box, select the current text in the *What title do you want for your query?* text box and then type Suppliers_NotBC.

   g. Click the *Modify the query design* option and then click the Finish button.

   h. At the query window, complete the following steps:

   1) Click in the *Prov/State* field in the *Criteria* row in the query design grid.

   2) Type Not BC and then press the Enter key.

   i. Specify that the fields are to be sorted in descending order by postal code by completing the following steps:

   1) Click in the *PostalCode* field in the *Sort* row.

   2) Click the option box arrow in the field and then click *Descending*.

   j. Click the Run button. (This returns suppliers that are not in British Columbia and sorts the records by postal code in descending order.)

   k. Save, print, and then close the query.

2. Close **3-PacTrek**.
3. Open **3-Dearborn**.
4. Use the Simple Query Wizard to create a query that returns clients in Muncie by completing the following steps:
   a. Click the Create tab and then click the Query Wizard button.
   b. At the New Query dialog box, make sure *Simple Query Wizard* is selected and then click OK.
   c. At the first Simple Query Wizard dialog box, click the *Tables/Queries* option box arrow and then click *Table: Clients*. (You may need to scroll up the list to see this table.)
   d. Insert the following fields in the *Selected Fields* list box:

   > Client
   > ClAddress
   > ClCity
   > ClState
   > ClZIP

   e. Click the Next button.
   f. At the last Simple Query Wizard dialog box, select the current text in the *What title do you want for your query?* text box and then type Clients_Muncie.
   g. Click the *Modify the query design* option and then click the Finish button.
   h. At the query window, complete the following steps:
      1) Click in the *ClCity* field in the *Criteria* row in the query design grid.
      2) Type Muncie and then press the Enter key.

Field:	[Client]	[ClAddress]	[ClCity]	[ClState]	[ClZIP]
Table:	Clients	Clients	Clients	Clients	Clients
Sort:					
Show:	☑	☑	☑	☑	☑
Criteria:			"Muncie"		
or:					

4h2

   i. Click the Run button. (This displays clients in Muncie.)
   j. Save, print, and then close the query.
5. Close **3-Dearborn**.
6. Open **3-CopperState**.
7. Use the Simple Query Wizard to display clients that live in Phoenix with claims over $500 by completing the following steps:
   a. Click the Create tab and then click the Query Wizard button.
   b. At the New Query dialog box, make sure *Simple Query Wizard* is selected in the list box and then click OK.
   c. At the first Simple Query Wizard dialog box, click the *Tables/Queries* option box arrow and then click *Table: Clients*.
   d. Insert the following fields in the *Selected Fields* list box:

   > ClientID
   > ClFirstName
   > ClLastName
   > ClAddress
   > ClCity
   > ClState
   > ClZIP

   e. Click the *Tables/Queries* option box arrow and then click *Table: Claims*.

f. With *ClaimID* selected in the *Available Fields* list box, click the One Field button.

g. Click *AmountOfClaim* in the *Available Fields* list box and then click the One Field button.

h. Click the Next button.

i. At the second Simple Query Wizard dialog box, click the Next button.

j. At the last Simple Query Wizard dialog box, select the current text in the *What title do you want for your query?* text box and then type Claims_Phoenix>$500.

k. Click the *Modify the query design* option and then click the Finish button.

l. At the query window, complete the following steps:

1) Click in the *ClCity* field in the *Criteria* row in the query design grid.

2) Type Phoenix and then press the Enter key.

3) Click in the *AmountOfClaim* field in the *Criteria* row. (You may need to scroll to the right to see this field.)

4) Type >500 and then press the Enter key.

ClCity	ClState	ClZIP	ClaimID	AmountOfClaim
Clients	Clients	Clients	Claims	Claims
☑	☑	☑	☑	☑
"Phoenix"				>500

712   714

m. Click the Run button. (This displays clients in Phoenix with claims greater than $500.)

n. Save the query, print the query in landscape orientation, and then close the query.

8. Close **3-CopperState**.

Check Your Work

Tutorial

Performing Calculations in a Query

Performing Calculations in a Query

In a query, values from a field can be calculated by inserting a calculated field in a field in the *Field* row in the query design grid. To insert a calculated field, click in a field in the *Field* row, type a field name followed by a colon, and then type the equation. For example, to determine pension contributions as 3% of an employee's annual salary, type *PensionContribution:[AnnualSalary]*0.03* in the field in the *Field* row. Use brackets to specify field names and use mathematical operators to perform the equation. Some basic operators include the plus (+) for addition, the hyphen (-) for subtraction, the asterisk (*) for multiplication, and the forward slash (/) for division.

Type a calculation in a field in the *Field* row or in the Expression Builder dialog box. To display the Expression Builder dialog box, open the query in Design view, click in the field where the calculated field expression is to be inserted, and then click the Builder button in the Query Setup group on the Query Tools Design tab. Type field names in the Expression Builder and click OK and the equation is inserted in the field with the correct symbols. For example, type *AnnualSalary*0.03* in the Expression Builder and *Expr1: [AnnualSalary]*0.03* is inserted in the field in the *Field* row when OK is clicked. If a name is not typed for the field, Access creates the alias *Expr1* for the field name. Provide a specific name for the field, such as *PensionContribution*, by typing the name in the Expression Builder, followed by a colon, and then typing the expression.

Builder

Property Sheet

If the results of the calculation should display as currency, apply numeric formatting and define the number of digits past the decimal point using the Property Sheet task pane. In Design view, click the Property Sheet button in the Show/Hide group on the Query Tools Design tab and the Property Sheet task pane displays at the right side of the screen. Click in the *Format* property box, click the option box arrow, and then click *Currency* at the drop-down list.

Activity 1h Creating and Formatting a Calculated Field in a Query

1. Open **3-MRInvestments** and enable the content.
2. Create a query that returns employer pension contributions at 3% of employees' annual salary by completing the following steps:
   a. Click the Create tab and then click the Query Design button.
   b. Double-click *Employees* in the Show Table dialog box and then click the Close button.
   c. Insert the *EmpID* field from the Employees table field list box in the first field in the *Field* row.
   d. Insert the *FirstName* field in the second field in the *Field* row.
   e. Insert the *LastName* field in the third field in the *Field* row.
   f. Insert the *AnnualSalary* field in the fourth field in the *Field* row.
   g. Click in the fifth field in the *Field* row.
   h. Type PensionContribution:[AnnualSalary]*0.03 and then press the Enter key.
   i. Click in the *PensionContribution* field and then click the Property Sheet button in the Show/Hide group.
   j. Click in the *Format* property box, click the option box arrow, and then click *Currency* at the drop-down list.
   k. Click the Close button in the upper right corner of the Property Sheet task pane.
   l. Click the Run button.
   m. Save the query, typing Benefits_PensionContri as the query name.
   n. Print and then close the query.
3. Modify *PensionContributionsQuery* and use the Expression Builder to write an equation finding the total amount of annual salary plus a 3% employer pension contribution by completing the following steps:
   a. Right-click *Benefits_PensionContri* in the Queries group in the Navigation pane and then click *Design View* at the shortcut menu.
   b. Click in the field in the *Field* row containing *PensionContribution:[AnnualSalary]*0.03*.
   c. Click the Builder button in the Query Setup group on the Query Tools Design tab.
   d. In the Expression Builder, select the existing expression *PensionContribution: [AnnualSalary]*0.03*.
   e. Type Salary&Pension:[AnnualSalary]*1.03 and then click OK.

4. Click the Run button.
5. Save the query by completing the following steps:
   a. Click the File tab, click the *Save As* option, click the *Save Object As* option, and then click the Save As button.
   b. At the Save As dialog box, type Benefits_Salary&Pension and then click OK.
6. Print and then close the query.
7. Close **3-MRInvestments**.
8. Open **3-PacTrek**.
9. Create a query that returns orders and total order amounts by completing the following steps:
   a. Click the Create tab and then click the Query Design button.
   b. Double-click *Products* in the Show Table dialog box.
   c. Double-click *Orders* in the Show Table dialog box and then click the Close button.
   d. Insert the *Product* field from the Products table field list box in the first field in the *Field* row.
   e. Insert the *OrderID* field from the Orders table field list box in the second field in the *Field* row.
   f. Insert the *UnitsOrdered* field from the Orders table field list box in the third field in the *Field* row.
   g. Insert the *OrderAmount* field from the Orders table field list box in the fourth field in the *Field* row.
   h. Click in the fifth field in the *Field* row.
   i. Click the Builder button.
   j. Type Total:OrderAmount*UnitsOrdered in the Expression Builder and then click OK.
   k. Click the Run button.
   l. Adjust the width of the columns to fit the longest entries.
   m. Save the query, typing Orders_TotalAmount as the query name.
   n. Print and then close the query.
10. Close **3-PacTrek**.

9j

Expression Builder   ✕

Enter an Expression to define the <u>calculated query field</u>:
(Examples of expressions include [field1] + [field2] and [field1] < 5)

Total:OrderAmount*UnitsOrdered

OK

Cancel

 Check Your Work

Activity 2   Create Aggregate Functions and Crosstab Queries,   6 Parts
Find Duplicates, and Find Unmatched Queries

You will create an aggregate functions query that determines the total, average, minimum, and maximum order amounts and then calculate total and average order amounts grouped by supplier. You will also use the Crosstab Query Wizard, Find Duplicates Query Wizard, and Find Unmatched Query Wizard to design queries.

Designing Queries with Aggregate Functions

An *aggregate function*—such as Sum, Avg, Min, Max, or Count—can be included in a query to calculate statistics from numeric field values of all the records in the table. When an aggregate function is used, Access displays one row in the query results datasheet with the formula result for the function used. For example, in a table with a numeric field containing annual salary amounts, the Sum function can be used to calculate the total of all salary amount values.

Σ Totals

To use aggregate functions, click the Totals button in the Show/Hide group on the Query Tools Design tab. Access adds a *Total* row to the query design grid with a drop-down list of functions. Access also inserts the words *Group By* in the field in the *Total* row. Click the option box arrow and then click an aggregate function at the drop-down list. In Activity 2a, Step 1, you will create a query in Design view and use aggregate functions to find the total of all sales, average sales, maximum and minimum sales, and total number of sales. The completed query is shown in Figure 3.5. Access automatically determines the column heading names.

Quick Steps

Design Query with Aggregate Function
1. At query window, click Totals button.
2. Click option box arrow in field in the *Total* row.
3. Click aggregate function.

Figure 3.5 Query Results for Activity 2a, Step 1

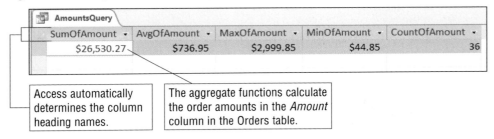

| Access automatically determines the column heading names. | The aggregate functions calculate the order amounts in the *Amount* column in the Orders table. |

Activity 2a Using Aggregate Functions   Part 1 of 6

1. Open **3-PacTrek** and then create a query with aggregate functions that determines total, average, maximum, and minimum order amounts, as well as the total number of orders, by completing the following steps:
   a. Click the Create tab and then click the Query Design button.
   b. At the Show Table dialog box, make sure *Orders* is selected in the list box, click the Add button, and then click the Close button.
   c. Insert the *OrderAmount* field in the first, second, third, fourth, and fifth fields in the *Field* row. (You may need to scroll down the Orders table field list box to see the *OrderAmount* field.)

d. Click the Totals button in the Show/Hide group on the Query Tools Design tab. (This adds a *Total* row to the query design grid between *Table* and *Sort* with the default option of *Group By*.)

e. Specify a Sum function for the first field in the *Total* row by completing the following steps:
   1) Click in the first field in the *Total* row.
   2) Click the option box arrow in the field.
   3) Click *Sum* at the drop-down list.

f. Complete steps similar to those in Step 1e to insert *Avg* in the second field in the *Total* row.

g. Complete steps similar to those in Step 1e to insert *Max* in the third field in the *Total* row.

h. Complete steps similar to those in Step 1e to insert *Min* in the fourth field in the *Total* row.

i. Complete steps similar to those in Step 1e to insert *Count* in the fifth field in the *Total* row.

j. Click the Run button. (Notice the headings that Access assigns to the columns.)

k. Adjust the widths of the columns.

l. Save the query, typing Orders_Statistics as the query name.

m. Print and then close the query.

2. Close **3-PacTrek**.

3. Open **3-CopperState**.

4. Create a query with aggregate functions that determines total, average, maximum, and minimum claim amounts by completing the following steps:

   a. Click the Create tab and then click the Query Design button.

   b. At the Show Table dialog box, double-click *Claims*.

   c. Click the Close button to close the Show Table dialog box.

   d. Insert the *AmountOfClaim* field in the first, second, third, and fourth fields in the *Field* row.

   e. Click the Totals button in the Show/Hide group.

   f. Click in the first field in the *Total* row, click the option box arrow in the field, and then click *Sum* at the drop-down list.

   g. Click in the second field in the *Total* row, click the option box arrow, and then click *Avg* at the drop-down list.

h. Click in the third field in the *Total* row, click the option box arrow, and then click *Max* at the drop-down list.

i. Click in the fourth field in the *Total* row, click the option box arrow, and then click *Min* at the drop-down list.

j. Click the Run button. (Notice the headings that Access chooses for the columns.)

k. Automatically adjust the widths of the columns.

l. Save the query, typing Claims_Amounts as the query name.

m. Print the query in landscape orientation and then close the query.

Use the *Group By* field in the *Total* row to add a field to the query that groups records for statistical calculations. For example, to calculate the total of all orders for a specific supplier, add the *SupplierID* field to the query design grid with the *Total* row set to *Group By*. In Activity 2b, Step 1, you will create a query in Design view and use aggregate functions to find the total of all order amounts and the average order amounts grouped by supplier number.

Activity 2b Using Aggregate Functions and Grouping Records

1. With **3-CopperState** open, determine the sum and average of client claims by completing the following steps:

a. Click the Create tab and then click the Query Design button.

b. At the Show Table dialog box, double-click *Clients* in the list box.

c. Double-click *Claims* in the list box and then click the Close button.

d. Insert the *ClientID* field from the Clients table field list box to the first field in the *Field* row.

e. Insert the *AmountOfClaim* field from the Claims table field list box to the second field in the *Field* row.

f. Insert the *AmountOfClaim* field from the Claims table field list box to the third field in the *Field* row.

g. Click the Totals button in the Show/ Hide group.

h. Click in the second field in the *Total* row, click the option box arrow, and then click *Sum* at the drop-down list.

i. Click in the third field in the *Total* row, click the option box arrow, and then click *Avg* at the drop-down list.

j. Make sure *Group By* displays in the first field in the *Total* row.

k. Click the Run button.

l. Adjust column widths.

m. Save the query, typing Claims_AmountsSumAvg as the query name.

n. Print and then close the query.

2. Close **3-CopperState**.

3. Open **3-PacTrek**.

4. Determine the total and average order amounts for each supplier by completing the following steps:

a. Click the Create tab and then click the Query Design button.

b. At the Show Table dialog box, make sure *Orders* is selected in the list box and then click the Add button.

c. Click *Suppliers* in the list box, click the Add button, and then click the Close button.

d. Insert the *OrderAmount* field from the Orders table field list box to the first field in the *Field* row. (You may need to scroll down the Orders table field list box to see the *OrderAmount* field.)

e. Insert the *OrderAmount* field from the Orders table field list box to the second field in the *Field* row.

f. Insert the *SupplierID* field from the Suppliers table field list box to the third field in the *Field* row.

g. Insert the *SupplierName* field from the Suppliers table field list box to the fourth field in the *Field* row.

h. Click the Totals button.

i. Click in the first field in the *Total* row, click the option box arrow, and then click *Sum* at the drop-down list.

j. Click in the second field in the *Total* row, click the option box arrow, and then click *Avg* at the drop-down list.

k. Make sure *Group By* displays in the third and fourth fields in the *Total* row.

l. Click the Run button.

m. Adjust column widths.

n. Save the query, typing Suppliers_Amounts as the query name.

o. Print and then close the query.

> 🌥 Check Your Work

🌥 Tutorial >

Creating a Crosstab Query

Creating a Crosstab Query

A crosstab query calculates aggregate functions, such as Sum and Avg, in which field values are grouped by two fields. A wizard is included that provides the steps to create the query. The first field selected displays one row in the query results datasheet for each group. The second field selected displays one column in the query results datasheet for each group. A third field is specified that is the numeric field to be summarized. The cell at the intersection of each row and column holds a value that is the result of the specified aggregate function for the designated row and column group.

Quick Steps

Create Crosstab Query
1. Click Create tab.
2. Click Query Wizard button.
3. Double-click *Crosstab Query Wizard*.
4. Complete wizard steps.

Create a crosstab query from fields in one table. To include fields from more than one table, first create a query containing the fields, and then create the crosstab query. For example, in Activity 2c, Step 2, you will create a new query that contains fields from each of the three tables in the Pacific Trek database. Using this query, you will use the Crosstab Query Wizard to create a query that summarizes the order amounts by supplier name and product ordered. The results of that crosstab query are shown in Figure 3.6. The first column displays the supplier names, the second column displays the total amounts for each supplier, and the remaining columns display the amounts by suppliers for specific items.

Figure 3.6 Crosstab Query Results for Activity 2c, Step 2

Order amounts are grouped by supplier name and individual product.

SupplierName	Total Of Orde	Binoculars, 8	Cascade R4 j	Cascade R4 j	Cascade R4 j	Cascade R4 j	Deluxe map c	Eight-piece s
Bayside Supplies	$224.00							$99.75
Cascade Gear	$3,769.00		$1,285.00	$1,285.00	$599.50	$599.50		
Emerald City Products	$2,145.00	$2,145.00						
Fraser Valley Products	$3,892.75							
Freedom Corporation	$1,286.65							
Hopewell, Inc.	$348.60							
KL Distributions	$4,288.35							
Langley Corporation	$593.25							
Macadam, Inc.	$175.70						$129.75	
Manning, Inc.	$4,282.25							
Sound Supplies	$5,524.72							

Activity 2c Creating Crosstab Queries

Part 3 of 6

1. With **3-PacTrek** open, create a query containing fields from the three tables by completing the following steps:
   a. Click the Create tab and then click the Query Design button.
   b. At the Show Table dialog box with *Orders* selected in the list box, click the Add button.
   c. Double-click *Products* in the list box.
   d. Double-click *Suppliers* in the list box and then click the Close button.
   e. Insert the following fields to the specified fields in the *Field* row:
      1) From the Products table field list box, insert the *ProductID* field in the first field in the *Field* row.
      2) From the Products table field list box, insert the *Product* field in the second field in the *Field* row.
      3) From the Orders table field list box, insert the *UnitsOrdered* field in the third field in the *Field* row.
      4) From the Orders table field list box, insert the *OrderAmount* field in the fourth field in the *Field* row.
      5) From the Suppliers table field list box, insert the *SupplierName* field in the fifth field in the *Field* row.
      6) From the Orders table field list box, insert the *OrderDate* field in the sixth field in the *Field* row.

   f. Click the Run button to run the query.
   g. Save the query, typing Items_Ordered as the query name.
   h. Close the query.

2. Create a crosstab query that summarizes the orders by supplier name and by product ordered by completing the following steps:
   a. Click the Create tab and then click the Query Wizard button.
   b. At the New Query dialog box, double-click *Crosstab Query Wizard* in the list box.

   c. At the first Crosstab Query Wizard dialog box, click the *Queries* option in the *View* section and then click *Query: Items_Ordered* in the list box.

   d. Click the Next button.
   e. At the second Crosstab Query Wizard dialog box, click *SupplierName* in the *Available Fields* list box and then click the One Field button. (This inserts *SupplierName* in the *Selected Fields* list box and specifies that you want the *SupplierName* field for the row headings.)

   f. Click the Next button.
   g. At the third Crosstab Query Wizard dialog box, click *Product* in the list box. (This specifies that you want the *Product* field for the column headings.)

   h. Click the Next button.
   i. At the fourth Crosstab Query Wizard dialog box, click *OrderAmount* in the *Fields* list box and then click *Sum* in the *Functions* list box.
   j. Click the Next button.
   k. At the fifth Crosstab Query Wizard dialog box, select the current text in the *What do you want to name your query?* text box and then type Orders_Crosstab.

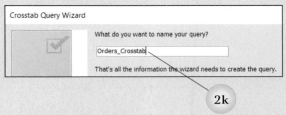

   l. Click the Finish button.
3. Display the query in Print Preview, change to landscape orientation, change the left margin to 0.4 inch and the right margin to 0.5 inch, and then print the query. (The query will print on four pages.)
4. Close the query.
5. Close **3-PacTrek**.

6. Open **3-CopperState**.
7. Create a crosstab query from fields in one table that summarizes clients' claims by completing the following steps:
   a. Click the Create tab and then click the Query Wizard button.
   b. At the New Query dialog box, double-click *Crosstab Query Wizard* in the list box.
   c. At the first Crosstab Query Wizard dialog box, click *Table: Claims* in the list box.
   d. Click the Next button.
   e. At the second Crosstab Query Wizard dialog box, click the One Field button. (This inserts the *ClaimID* field in the *Selected Fields* list box.)
   f. Click the Next button.
   g. At the third Crosstab Query Wizard dialog, make sure *ClientID* is selected in the list box and then click the Next button.
   h. At the fourth Crosstab Query Wizard dialog box, click *AmountOfClaim* in the *Fields* list box and click *Sum* in the *Functions* list box.
   i. Click the Next button.
   j. At the fifth Crosstab Query Wizard dialog box, click the Finish button.
8. Change to landscape orientation and then print the query. The query will print on two pages.
9. Close the query.
10. Close **3-CopperState**.

 Check Your Work

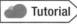 Tutorial

Creating a Find
Duplicates Query

Creating a Find Duplicates Query

Use a find duplicates query to search a specified table or query for duplicate field values within a designated field or fields. Create this type of query, for example, if a record (such as a product record) may have been entered two times inadvertently (perhaps under two different product numbers). A find duplicates query has many applications. Here are a few other examples of how to use a find duplicates query:

Quick Steps

**Create Find
Duplicates Query**
1. Click Create tab.
2. Click Query Wizard button.
3. Double-click *Find Duplicates Query Wizard*.
4. Complete wizard steps.

- In an orders table, find records with the same customer number to identify loyal customers.

- In a customers table, find records with the same last name and mailing address so only one mailing will be sent to a household to save on printing and postage costs.

- In an employee expenses table, find records with the same employee number to determine which employee is submitting the most claims.

Access provides the Find Duplicates Query Wizard to build the query based on the selections made in a series of dialog boxes. To use this wizard, open a database, click the Create tab, and then click the Query Wizard button. At the New Query dialog box, double-click *Find Duplicates Query Wizard* in the list box and then complete the steps provided by the wizard.

In Activity 2d, you will assume that you have been asked to update the address for a supplier in the Pacific Trek database. Instead of updating the address, you create a new record. You will then use the Find Duplicates Query Wizard to find duplicate field values in the Suppliers table.

1. Open **3-PacTrek** and then open the Suppliers table.
2. Add the following record to the table:

   SupplierID   29
   SupplierName   Langley Corporation
   StreetAddress   1248 Larson Avenue
   City   Burnaby
   Prov/State   BC
   PostalCode   V5V 9K2
   Email   lc@ppi-edu.net
   Telephone   (604) 555-1200

3. Close the Suppliers table.
4. Use the Find Duplicates Query Wizard to find any duplicate supplier names by completing the following steps:
   a. Click the Create tab and then click the Query Wizard button.
   b. At the New Query dialog box, double-click *Find Duplicates Query Wizard*.
   c. At the first wizard dialog box, click *Table: Suppliers* in the list box.
   d. Click the Next button.
   e. At the second wizard dialog box, click *SupplierName* in the *Available fields* list box and then click the One Field button. (This moves the *SupplierName* field to the *Duplicate-value fields* list box.)
   f. Click the Next button.
   g. At the third wizard dialog box, click the All Fields button (the button containing the two greater-than symbols, >>). This moves all the fields to the *Additional query fields* list box. You are doing this because if you find a duplicate supplier name, you want to view all the fields to determine which record is accurate.
   h. Click the Next button.
   i. At the fourth (and last) wizard dialog box, type Suppliers_Duplicate in the *What do you want to name your query?* text box.

4c

4e

4i

   j. Click the Finish button.
   k. Change to landscape orientation and then print the query.

5. As you look at the query results, you realize that an inaccurate record was entered for the Langley Corporation, so you decide to delete one of the records. To do this, complete the following steps:

a. Select the row with a supplier ID of *29*.
b. Click the Home tab and then click the Delete button in the Records group.
c. At the message asking you to confirm the deletion, click Yes.
d. Close the query.
6. Change the street address for Langley Corporation by completing the following steps:
a. Open the Suppliers table in Datasheet view.
b. Change the address for Langley Corporation from *805 First Avenue* to *1248 Larson Avenue*. Do not make any changes to the other fields.
c. Close the Suppliers table.

> **Check Your Work**

The Find Duplicates Query can be used to find accidental duplications in database records, as shown in Activity 2d. This query is also useful for finding other types of information. In Activity 2e, the duplicate entries found by the wizard are not mistaken entries but rather indicate repeated use of the same supplier. This information could be used to negotiate for better prices or to ask for discounts.

Activity 2e Finding Duplicate Orders   Part 5 of 6

1. With **3-PacTrek** open, create a query with the following fields (in the order shown) from the specified tables:

SupplierID	Suppliers table
SupplierName	Suppliers table
ProductID	Orders table
Product	Products table

2. Run the query.
3. Save the query with the name *Suppliers_Orders* and then close the query.
4. Use the Find Duplicates Query Wizard to find the suppliers you order from the most by completing the following steps:

a. Click the Create tab and then click the Query Wizard button.
b. At the New Query dialog box, double-click *Find Duplicates Query Wizard*.
c. At the first wizard dialog box, click the *Queries* option in the *View* section and then click *Query: Suppliers_Orders*. (You may need to scroll down the list to display this query.)

d. Click the Next button.
e. At the second wizard dialog box, click *SupplierName* in the *Available fields* list box and then click the One Field button.
f. Click the Next button.
g. At the third wizard dialog box, click the Next button.
h. At the fourth (and last) wizard dialog box, type Suppliers_OrderCount in the *What do you want to name your query?* text box.

Find Duplicates Query Wizard

What do you want to name your query?

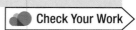
Suppliers_OrderCount

4h

i. Click the Finish button.
j. Adjust the widths of the columns to fit the longest entries.
k. Save and then print the query.
5. Close the query.

> Check Your Work

> Tutorial

Creating a Find Unmatched Query

Quick Steps

Create Find Unmatched Query
1. Click Create tab.
2. Click Query Wizard button.
3. Double-click *Find Unmatched Query Wizard*.
4. Complete wizard steps.

Creating a Find Unmatched Query

Create a find unmatched query to compare two tables and produce a list of the records in one table that have no matching record in the other table. This type of query can be useful, for instance, to produce a list of customers who have never placed orders or a list of invoices that have no record of payment. Access provides the Find Unmatched Query Wizard to build the query.

In Activity 2f, you will use the Find Unmatched Query Wizard to find all of the products that have no units on order. This information is helpful in identifying which products are not selling and might need to be discontinued or returned. To use the Find Unmatched Query Wizard, click the Create tab and then click the Query Wizard button in the Queries group. At the New Query dialog box, double-click *Find Unmatched Query Wizard* in the list box and then follow the wizard steps.

Activity 2f Creating a Find Unmatched Query

Part 6 of 6

1. With **3-PacTrek** open, use the Find Unmatched Query Wizard to find all products that do not have units on order by completing the following steps:
   a. Click the Create tab and then click the Query Wizard button.
   b. At the New Query dialog box, double-click *Find Unmatched Query Wizard*.
   c. At the first wizard dialog box, click *Table: Products* in the list box. (This is the table containing the fields you want to see in the query results.)
   d. Click the Next button.
   e. At the second wizard dialog box, make sure *Table: Orders* is selected in the list box. (This is the table containing the related records.)
   f. Click the Next button.

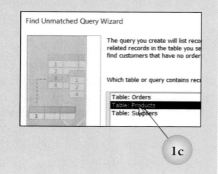

Find Unmatched Query Wizard

The query you create will list reco related records in the table you se find customers that have no order

Which table or query contains rec

Table: Orders
Table: Products
Table: Suppliers

1c

g. At the third wizard dialog box, make sure *ProductID* is selected in both the *Fields in 'Products'* list box and in the *Fields in 'Orders'* list box.

h. Click the Next button.

i. At the fourth wizard dialog box, click the All Fields button to move all of the fields from the *Available fields* list box to the *Selected fields* list box.

j. Click the Next button.

k. At the fifth wizard dialog box, click the Finish button. (Let the wizard determine the query name: *Products Without Matching Orders*.)

1g

2. Print the query in landscape orientation and then close the query.
3. Close **3-PacTrek**.

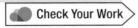

Chapter Summary

- One of the most important uses of a database is to select the information needed to answer questions and make decisions. Data can be extracted from an Access database by performing a query, which can be accomplished by designing a query or using a query wizard.

- Designing a query consists of identifying the table, the field or fields from which the data will be drawn, and the criterion or criteria for selecting the data.

- In designing a query, type the criterion (or criteria) statement for extracting the specific data. Access inserts any necessary symbols in the criterion when the Enter key is pressed.

- In a criterion, quotation marks surround field values and pound symbols (#) surround dates. Use the asterisk (*) as a wildcard character.

- A query can be performed on fields within one table or on fields from related tables.

- When designing a query, the sort order of a field or fields can be specified.

- An existing query can be modified and used for a new purpose rather than creating a new one from scratch.

- Enter a criterion in the *or* row in the query design grid to instruct Access to display records that match any of the criteria.

- Multiple criteria entered in the *Criteria* row in the query design grid become an *And* statement, where each criterion must be met for Access to select the record.

- The Simple Query Wizard provides the steps for preparing a query.

- A calculated field can be inserted in a field in the *Field* row when designing a query. If the results of the calculation should display as currency, apply numeric formatting and decimal places using the Format property box at the Property Sheet task pane. Display the task pane by clicking the Property Sheet button in the Show/Hide group on the Query Tools Design tab.

- Include an aggregate function (such as Sum, Avg, Min, Max, or Count) to calculate statistics from numeric field values. Click the Totals button in the Show/Hide group on the Query Tools Design tab to display the aggregate function list.
- Use a *Group By* field in the *Total* row to add a field to a query for grouping records for statistical calculations.
- Create a crosstab query to calculate aggregate functions (such as Sum and Avg), in which fields are grouped by two. Create a crosstab query from fields in one table. To include fields from more than one table, create a query first and then create the crosstab query.
- Use a find duplicates query to search a specified table for duplicate field values within a designated field or fields.
- Create a find unmatched query to compare two tables and produce a list of the records in one table that have no matching records in the other related table.

Commands Review

FEATURE	RIBBON TAB, GROUP	BUTTON, OPTION
add *Total* row to query design	Query Tools Design, Show/Hide	Σ
Crosstab Query Wizard	Create, Queries	, *Crosstab Query Wizard*
Expression Builder dialog box	Query Tools Design, Query Setup	
Find Duplicates Query Wizard	Create, Queries	, *Find Duplicates Query Wizard*
Find Unmatched Query Wizard	Create, Queries	, *Find Unmatched Query Wizard*
New Query dialog box	Create, Queries	
Property Sheet task pane	Query Tools Design, Show/Hide	
query results	Query Tools Design, Results	!
query window	Create, Queries	
Simple Query Wizard	Create, Queries	, *Simple Query Wizard*

Microsoft®

Access®

Creating and Modifying Tables in Design View

Performance Objectives

Upon successful completion of Chapter 4, you will be able to:

1 Create a table in Design view

2 Assign a default value for a field

3 Use the Input Mask Wizard and the Lookup Wizard

4 Validate field entries

5 Insert, move, and delete fields in Design view

6 Insert a *Total* row

7 Sort records in a table

8 Print selected records in a table

9 Apply text formatting

10 Complete a spelling check

11 Find and replace data in records in a table

12 Use the Help and Tell Me features

In Chapter 1, you learned how to create a table in Datasheet view. A table can also be created in Design view, where the table's structure and properties are established before entering data. In this chapter, you will learn how to create a table in Design view and use the Input Mask Wizard and Lookup Wizards; insert, move, and delete fields in Design view; sort records; check spelling in a table; find and replace data; apply text formatting to a table; and use the Help and Tell Me features.

 Data Files

Before beginning chapter work, copy the AL1C4 folder to your storage medium and then make AL1C4 the active folder.

The online course includes additional training and assessment resources.

Tutorial

Creating a Table in Design View

Tutorial

Modifying Field Properties in Design View

Table

View

Ŏuick Steps

Create Table in Design View
1. Open database.
2. Click Create tab.
3. Click Table button.
4. Click View button.
5. Type name for table.
6. Press Enter key or click OK.
7. Type field names, specify data types, and include descriptions.
8. Click Save button.

Creating a Table in Design View

In Datasheet view, a table is created by assigning each column a data type and typing the field name. Once the columns are defined, the data is entered into records. A table can also be created in Design view, where field properties can be set before entering data.

To display a table in Design view, open the database, click the Create tab, and then click the Table button. This opens a new blank table in Datasheet view. Display the table in Design view by clicking the View button at the left side of the Table Tools Fields tab in the Views group. Click the View button in a new table and Access displays the Save As dialog box. Type a name for the table and then press the Enter key or click OK. The Properties table in Design view in the SunProperties database is shown in Figure 4.1.

In Design view, each row in the top section of the work area represents one field in the table and is used to define the field name, the field data type, and a description. The *Field Properties* section in the lower half of the work area displays the properties for the active field. The properties vary depending on the active field. In the lower right corner of Design view, Help information is available for the active field or property in the Design window. In Figure 4.1, the *PropID* field name is active in Design view, so information on field names is available in the Help area.

Define each field in the table in the rows in the top section of Design view. When a table is created in Design view, Access automatically assigns the first field the name *ID* and assigns the AutoNumber data type. Leave this field name as *ID* or type a new name and accept the AutoNumber data type or change to a different data type. To create a new field in the table, click in a field in the *Field Name* column, type the field name, and then press the Tab key or Enter key. This makes the field in the *Data Type* column active. Click the option box arrow in the field in the *Data Type* column and then click the data type at the drop-down list. In Chapter 1, you created tables in Datasheet view and assigned data types of Short Text, Date/Time, Currency, and Yes/No. The drop-down list in the *Data Type* column includes these data types plus additional types, as described in Table 4.1.

Click the specific data type at the drop-down list and then press the Tab key and the field in the *Description* column becomes active. In the field, type a description that provides useful information to someone entering data in the table. For example, consider identifying the field's purpose or contents or providing instructional information for data entry. The description typed in the field in the *Description* column displays in the Status bar when the table's field is active in the table in Datasheet view.

Figure 4.1 Properties Table in Design View

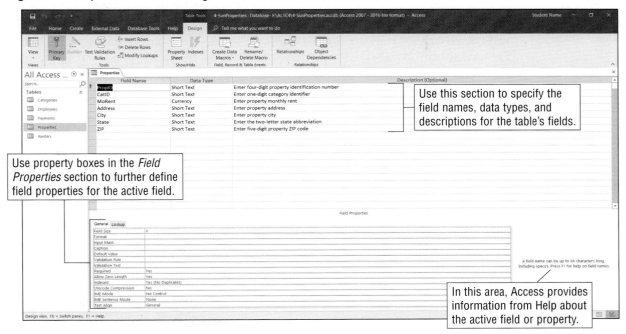

Use this section to specify the field names, data types, and descriptions for the table's fields.

Use property boxes in the *Field Properties* section to further define field properties for the active field.

In this area, Access provides information from Help about the active field or property.

Table 4.1 Data Types

Data Type	Description
Short Text	Used for alphanumeric data up to 255 characters in length—for example, a name, address, or value (such as a telephone number or social security number) that is used as an identifier and not for calculating.
Long Text	Used for alphanumeric data up to 65,535 characters in length.
Number	Used for positive and negative values that can be used in calculations. Do not use for values that will calculate monetary amounts (see Currency).
Date/Time	Used to ensure dates and times are entered and sorted properly.
Currency	Used for values that involve money. Access will not round off during calculations.
AutoNumber	Used to automatically number records sequentially (increments of 1); each new record is numbered as it is typed.
Yes/No	Used for values of *Yes* or *No*, *True* or *False*, or *On* or *Off*.
OLE Object	Used to embed or link objects created in other Office applications.
Hyperlink	Used to store a hyperlink, such as a URL.
Attachment	Used to add file attachments to a record such as a Word document or Excel workbook.
Calculated	Used to display the Expression Builder dialog box, where an expression is entered to calculate the value of the calculated column.
Lookup Wizard	Used to enter data in the field from another existing table or to display a list of values in a drop-down list from which the user chooses.

Save

When creating the table, continue typing field names, assigning data types to fields, and typing field descriptions. When the table design is completed, save the table by clicking the Save button on the Quick Access Toolbar. Return to Datasheet view by clicking the View button in the Views group on the Table Tools Design tab. In Datasheet view, type the records for the table.

Activity 1a Creating a Renters Table in Design View

Part 1 of 9

1. Open Access and then open **4-SunProperties** from your AL1C4 folder.
2. Click the Enable Content button in the message bar.
3. View the Properties table in Design view by completing the following steps:
   a. Open the Properties table.
   b. Click the View button in the Views group on the Home tab.

3b

   c. Click each field name and then look at the information in the *Field Properties* section.
   d. Click in various fields or properties in the work area and then read the information in the Help area in the lower right corner of Design view.
   e. Click the View button to return the table to Datasheet view.
   f. Close the Properties table.
4. Create a new table in Design view, as shown in Figure 4.2, by completing the following steps:
   a. Click the Create tab and then click the Table button in the Tables group.
   b. Click the View button in the Views group on the Table Tools Fields tab.
   c. At the Save As dialog box, type Renters and then press the Enter key.
   d. Type RenterID in the first field in the *Field Name* column and then press the Tab key.
   e. Change to the Short Text data type by clicking the option box arrow in the field in the *Data Type* column and then clicking *Short Text* at the drop-down list.
   f. Change the field size from the default of 255 characters to 3 characters by selecting *255* in the *Field Size* property box in the *Field Properties* section and then typing 3.

g. Click in the *Description* column for the *RenterID* field, type Enter three-digit renter identification number, and then press the Tab key.

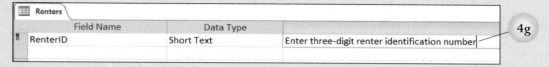

h. Type RenFirstName in the second field in the *Field Name* column and then press the Tab key.
i. Select *255* in the *Field Size* property box in the *Field Properties* section and then type 20.
j. Click in the *Description* column for the *RenFirstName* field, type Enter renter's first name, and then press the Tab key.
k. Type RenLastName in the third field in the *Field Name* column and then press the Tab key.
l. Change the field size to 30 characters (at the *Field Size* property box).
m. Click in the *Description* column for the *RenLastName* field, type Enter renter's last name, and then press the Tab key.
n. Enter the remaining field names, data types, and descriptions as shown in Figure 4.2. (Change the field size to 4 characters for the *PropID* field, 5 characters for the *EmpID* field, and 3 characters for the *RenCreditScore* field.)
o. After all of the fields are entered, click the Save button on the Quick Access Toolbar.
p. Make sure the *RenterID* field is identified as the primary key field. (A key icon displays in the *RenterID* field selector bar.)
q. Click the View button to return the table to Datasheet view.
5. Enter the records in the Renters table as shown in Figure 4.3.
6. After all of the records are entered, adjust the column widths.
7. Save, print in landscape orientation, and then close the Renters table.

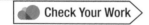

Figure 4.2 Activity 1a Renters Table in Design View

Field Name	Data Type	
RenterID	Short Text	Enter three-digit renter identification number
RenFirstName	Short Text	Enter renter's first name
RenLastName	Short Text	Enter renter's last name
PropID	Short Text	Enter four-digit property identification number
EmpID	Short Text	Enter five-digit employee identification number
RenCreditScore	Short Text	Enter renter's current credit score
LeaseBegDate	Date/Time	Enter beginning date of lease
LeaseEndDate	Date/Time	Enter ending date of lease

Figure 4.3 Activity 1a Renters Table in Datasheet View

RenterID	RenFirstName	RenLastName	PropID	EmpID	RenCreditScore	LeaseBegDate	LeaseEndDate	Clic
110	Greg	Hamilton	1029	04-14	624	1/1/2021	12/31/2021	
111	Julia	Perez	1013	07-20	711	1/1/2021	12/31/2021	
115	Dana	Rozinski	1026	02-59	538	2/1/2021	1/31/2022	
117	Miguel	Villegas	1007	07-20	695	2/1/2021	1/31/2022	
118	Mason	Ahn	1004	07-23	538	3/1/2021	2/28/2022	
119	Michelle	Bertram	1001	03-23	621	3/1/2021	2/28/2022	
121	Travis	Jorgenson	1010	04-14	590	3/1/2021	2/28/2022	
123	Richard	Terrell	1014	07-20	687	3/1/2021	2/28/2022	
125	Rose	Wagoner	1015	07-23	734	4/1/2021	3/31/2022	
127	William	Young	1023	05-31	478	4/1/2021	3/31/2022	
129	Susan	Lowrey	1002	04-14	634	4/1/2021	3/31/2022	
130	Ross	Molaski	1027	03-23	588	5/1/2021	4/30/2022	
131	Danielle	Rubio	1020	07-20	722	5/1/2021	4/30/2022	
133	Katie	Smith	1018	07-23	596	5/1/2021	4/30/2022	
134	Carl	Weston	1009	03-23	655	6/1/2021	5/31/2022	
135	Marty	Lobdell	1006	04-14	510	6/1/2021	5/31/2022	
136	Nadine	Paschal	1022	05-31	702	6/1/2021	5/31/2022	

Assigning a Default Value

Chapter 1 covered how to specify a default value for a field in a table in Datasheet view using the Default Value button in the Properties group on the Table Tools Fields tab. In addition to this method, a default value for a field can be specified in Design view with the *Default Value* property box in the *Field Properties* section. Click in the *Default Value* property box and then type the field value.

In Activity 1b, a health insurance field will be created with a Yes/No data type. Since most of the agents of Sun Properties have signed up for health insurance benefits, the default value for the field will be set to *Yes*. If a new field containing a default value is added to an existing table, the existing records do not reflect the default value. Only new records entered in the table reflect the default value.

Tutorial

Creating an Input Mask

Hint An input mask is a set of characters that control what can and cannot be entered in a field.

Build

Creating an Input Mask

To maintain consistency and control data entered in a field, consider using the *Input Mask* property box to set a pattern for how data is entered in the field. For example, a pattern can be set for a zip code field that requires that the nine-digit zip code is entered in the field rather than the five-digit zip code. Or, a pattern can be set for a telephone field that requires that the three-digit area code is entered with the telephone number. Access includes an Input Mask Wizard that provides the steps for creating an input mask. The Input Mask is available for fields with a data type of Short Text or Date/Time.

Use the Input Mask Wizard when assigning a data type to a field. In Design view, click in the *Input Mask* property box in the *Field Properties* section and then run the Input Mask Wizard by clicking the Build button (contains three black dots) that appears at the right side of the *Input Mask* property box. This displays the first Input Mask Wizard dialog box, as shown in Figure 4.4. In the *Input Mask* list box, choose which input mask the data should look like and then click the Next button. At the second Input Mask Wizard dialog box, as shown in

Figure 4.5, specify the appearance of the input mask and the placeholder character and then click the Next button. At the third Input Mask Wizard dialog box, specify if the data should be stored with or without the symbol in the mask and then click the Next button. At the fourth dialog box, click the Finish button.

The input mask controls how data is entered into a field. In some situations, such as establishing an input mask to enter the date in the Medium Date format, what is entered will not match what Access displays. An input mask with the Medium Date data type format will require that the date be entered as *12-Sep-21* but, after the date is entered, Access will change the display to *09/12/2021*. Use the *Format* property box to match how Access displays the date with the input mask. Click in the *Format* property box, click the option box arrow in the property box and then click *Medium Date* at the drop-down list.

Figure 4.4 First Input Mask Wizard Dialog Box

Choose the input mask from this list box.

Figure 4.5 Second Input Mask Wizard Dialog Box

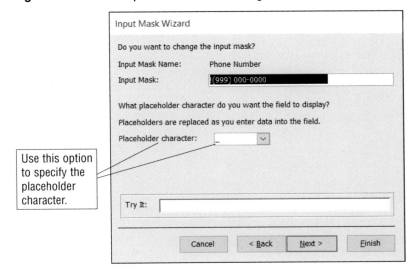

Use this option to specify the placeholder character.

1. With **4-SunProperties** open, create the Employees table in Design view as shown in Figure 4.6. Begin by clicking the Create tab and then clicking the Table button.
2. Click the View button to switch to Design view.
3. At the Save As dialog box, type Employees and then press the Enter key.
4. Type EmpID in the first field in the *Field Name* column and then press the Tab key.
5. Change to the Short Text data type by clicking the option box arrow in the *Data Type* column and then clicking *Short Text* at the drop-down list.
6. Change the field size from the default of 255 characters to 5 characters by selecting *255* in the *Field Size* property box in the *Field Properties* section and then typing 5.
7. Click in the *Description* column for the *EmpID* field, type Enter five-digit employee identification number, and then press the Tab key.

8. Type EmpFirstName in the second field in the *Field Name* column and then press the Tab key.
9. Select *255* in the *Field Size* property box in the *Field Properties* section and then type 20.
10. Click in the *Description* column for the *EmpFirstName* field, type Enter employee's first name, and then press the Tab key.
11. Complete steps similar to those in Steps 8 through 10 to create the *EmpLastName*, *EmpAddress*, and *EmpCity* fields as shown in Figure 4.6 (on page 111). Change the field size for the *EmpLastName* field and *EmpAddress* field to 30 characters and change the *EmpCity* field to 20 characters.
12. Create the *EmpState* field with a default value of *CA,* since all employees live in California, by completing the following steps:
    a. Type EmpState in the field below the *EmpCity* field in the *Field Name* column and then press the Tab key.
    b. Click in the *Default Value* property box in the *Field Properties* section and then type CA.
    c. Click in the *Description* column for the *EmpState* field, type CA automatically entered as state, and then press the Tab key.

General	Lookup	
Field Size		255
Format		
Input Mask		
Caption		
Default Value		CA
Validation Rule		
Validation Text		
Required		No

12b

13. Type EmpZIP and then press the Tab key.
14. Select *255* in the *Field Size* property box in the *Field Properties* section and then type 5.
15. Click in the *Description* column for the *EmpZIP* field, type Enter employee's five-digit ZIP code, and then press the Tab key.
16. Type EmpTelephone and then press the Tab key.
17. Create an input mask for the telephone number by completing the following steps:
    a. Click the Save button on the Quick Access Toolbar to save the table. (You must save the table before using the Input Mask Wizard.)

b. Click in the *Input Mask* property box in the *Field Properties* section.
c. Click the Build button (contains three black dots) at the right side of the *Input Mask* property box.

17b   17c

d. At the first Input Mask Wizard dialog box, make sure *Phone Number* is selected in the *Input Mask* list box and then click the Next button.
e. At the second Input Mask Wizard dialog box, click the *Placeholder character* option box arrow and then click # at the drop-down list.

17d

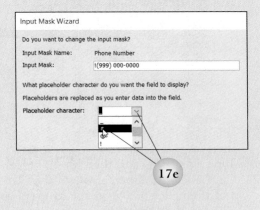

17e

f. Click the Next button.
g. At the third Input Mask Wizard dialog box, click the *With the symbols in the mask, like this* option.
h. Click the Next button.
i. At the fourth Input Mask Wizard dialog box, click the Finish button.

17g

18. Click in the *Description* column for the *EmpTelephone* field, type Enter employee's telephone number, and then press the Tab key.
19. Type HireDate and then press the Tab key.
20. Click the option box arrow in the *Date Type* column and then click *Date/Time*.
21. Create an input mask for the date by completing the following steps:
    a. Click the Save button on the Quick Access Toolbar to save the table.
    b. Click in the *Input Mask* property box in the *Field Properties* section.
    c. Click the Build button (contains three black dots) at the right side of the *Input Mask* property box.

d. At the first Input Mask Wizard dialog box, click *Medium Date* in the *Input Mask* list box and then click the Next button.

e. At the second Input Mask Wizard dialog box, click the Next button.

f. At the third Input Mask Wizard dialog box, click the Finish button.

g. Click in the *Format* property box.

h. Click the option box arrow in the *Format* property box and then click *Medium Date* at the drop-down list.

21d

21h

22. Click in the *Description* column for the *HireDate* field, type Enter employee's hire date and then press the Tab key.

23. Type HealthIns and then press the Tab key.

24. Click the option box arrow in the *Data Type* column and then click *Yes/No* at the drop-down list.

25. Click in the *Default Value* property box in the *Field Properties* section, delete the text *No*, and then type Yes.

26. Click in the *Description* column for the *HealthIns* field, type Leave check mark if employee is signed up for health insurance, and then press the Tab key.

27. Type DentalIns and then press the Tab key.

28. Click the option box arrow in the *Data Type* column and then click *Yes/No* at the drop-down list. (The text in the *Default Value* property box will remain as *No*.)

25

29. Click in the *Description* column for the *DentalIns* field, type Insert a check mark if employee is signed up for dental insurance, and then press the Tab key.

30. After all of the fields are entered, click the Save button on the Quick Access Toolbar.

31. Click the View button to return the table to Datasheet view.

32. Enter the records in the Employees table as shown in Figure 4.7.

33. After all of the records are entered, adjust the widths of the columns in the table.

34. Save, print, and then close the Employees table.

Check Your Work

Figure 4.6 Activity 1b Employees Table in Design View

Field Name	Data Type	
EmpID	Short Text	Enter five-digit employee identification number
EmpFirstName	Short Text	Enter employee's first name
EmpLastName	Short Text	Enter employee's last name
EmpAddress	Short Text	Enter employee's address
EmpCity	Short Text	Enter employee's city
EmpState	Short Text	CA automatcially entered as state
EmpZIP	Short Text	Enter employee's five-digit ZIP code
EmpTelephone	Short Text	Enter employee's telephone number
HireDate	Date/Time	Enter employee's hire date
HealthIns	Yes/No	Leave check mark if employee is signed up for health insurance
DentalIns	Yes/No	Insert a check mark if employee is signed up for dental insurance

Figure 4.7 Activity 1b Employees Table in Datasheet View

EmpID	EmpFirstName	EmpLastName	EmpAddress	EmpCity	EmpState	EmpZIP	EmpTelephone	HireDate	HealthIns	DentalIns
02-59	Christina	Solomon	12241 East 51st	Citrus Heights	CA	95611	(916) 555-8844	01-Feb-08	✓	✓
03-23	Douglas	Ricci	903 Mission Road	Roseville	CA	95678	(916) 555-4125	01-Mar-09	✓	
03-55	Tatiana	Kasadev	6558 Orchard Drive	Citrus Heights	CA	95610	(916) 555-8534	15-Nov-11	✓	
04-14	Brian	West	12232 142nd Avenue East	Citrus Heights	CA	95611	(916) 555-0967	01-Apr-12	✓	✓
04-32	Kathleen	Addison	21229 19th Street	Citrus Heights	CA	95621	(916) 555-3408	01-Feb-13	✓	✓
05-20	Teresa	Villanueva	19453 North 42nd Street	Citrus Heights	CA	95611	(916) 555-2302	15-Jul-14	✓	✓
05-31	Marcia	Griswold	211 Haven Road	North Highlands	CA	95660	(916) 555-1449	01-May-15		
06-24	Tiffany	Gentry	12312 North 20th	Roseville	CA	95661	(916) 555-0043	15-Apr-17	✓	✓
06-33	Joanna	Gallegos	6850 York Street	Roseville	CA	95747	(916) 555-7446	01-Jul-18		
07-20	Jesse	Scholtz	3412 South 21st Street	Fair Oaks	CA	95628	(916) 555-4204	15-Feb-19	✓	
07-23	Eugene	Bond	530 Laurel Road	Orangevale	CA	95662	(916) 555-9412	01-Mar-20	✓	
*					CA				✓	

Tutorial

Applying a
Validation Rule in
Design View

Tutorial

Applying a
Validation Rule in
Datasheet View

Validating Field Entries

Use the *Validation Rule* property box in the *Field Properties* section in Design view to enter a statement containing a conditional test that is checked each time data is entered into a field. If data is entered that fails to satisfy the test, Access rejects the entry and returns an error message. Such errors can be reduced by entering a conditional statement in the *Validation Rule* property box that checks each entry against the acceptable range. Customize the error message that will display if incorrect data is entered in the field by typing that message in the *Validation Text* property box.

A validation rule and validation text can also be applied to a field in Datasheet view by selecting the field and then clicking the Table Tools Fields tab. Click the Validation button in the Field Validation group and then click *Field Validation Rule* at the drop-down list. Type the conditional statement in the Expression Builder dialog box and then click OK. Create validation text by clicking the Validation button and then clicking *Field Validation Message*. Type the message in the Enter Validation Message dialog box and then click OK.

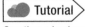
Tutorial

Creating a Lookup
Field

Using the Lookup Wizard

Like the Input Mask Wizard, the Lookup Wizard can be used to control data entered in a field. Use the Lookup Wizard to confine data entered into a field to a specific list of items. For example, in Activity 1c, the Lookup Wizard will be used to restrict the new *EmpCategory* field to one of three choices: *Salaried*, *Hourly*, and *Temporary*. When entering data, clicking in the field displays an option box arrow. Click the option box arrow and then click an option at the drop-down list.

Figure 4.8 First Lookup Wizard Dialog Box

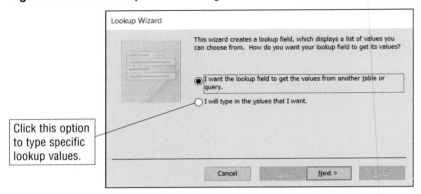

Click this option to type specific lookup values.

Figure 4.9 Second Lookup Wizard Dialog Box

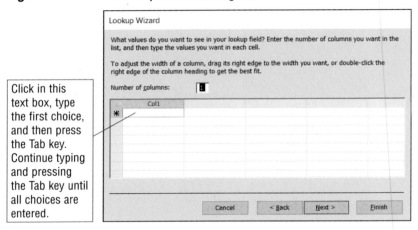

Click in this text box, type the first choice, and then press the Tab key. Continue typing and pressing the Tab key until all choices are entered.

Use the Lookup Wizard when assigning a data type to a field. Click in the field in the *Data Type* column, click the option box arrow, and then click *Lookup Wizard* at the drop-down list. This displays the first Lookup Wizard dialog box, as shown in Figure 4.8. At this dialog box, indicate that specific field choices will be entered by clicking the *I will type in the values that I want* option and then click the Next button. At the second Lookup Wizard dialog box, shown in Figure 4.9, click in the blank text box below *Col1* and then type the first choice. Press the Tab key and then type the second choice. Continue in this manner until all choices have been entered and then click the Next button. At the third Lookup Wizard dialog box, make sure the proper name is in the *What label would you like for your lookup column?* text box and then click the Finish button.

Tutorial

Managing Fields in Design View

Inserting, Moving, and Deleting Fields in Design View

As shown in Chapter 1, field management tasks such as inserting, moving, and deleting fields can be completed in Datasheet view. These tasks can also be completed in Design view.

To insert a new field in a table in Design view, position the insertion point in a field in the row that will be immediately *below* the new field and then click the Insert Rows button in the Tools group on the Table Tools Design tab. Another option is to position the insertion point in text in the row that will be immediately *below* the new field, click the right mouse button, and then click *Insert Rows* at the shortcut menu. A row in the Design view creates a field in the table.

 Insert Rows

A field in a table can be moved to a different location in Datasheet view or Design view. To move a field in Design view, click the field selector bar at the left side of the row to be moved. With the row selected, position the mouse pointer in the field selector bar at the left side of the selected row, click and hold down the left mouse button, drag the mouse pointer with a gray square attached until a thick black line displays in the desired position, and then release the mouse button.

Delete a field in a table and all data entered in that field is also deleted. When a field is deleted, the deletion cannot be undone with the Undo button. Delete a field only if all data associated with it should be removed from the table. To delete a field in Design view, click in the field selector bar at the left side of the row to be deleted and then click the Delete Rows button in the Tools group. At the confirmation message, click Yes. A row can also be deleted by positioning the mouse pointer in the row to be deleted, clicking the right mouse button, and then clicking *Delete Rows* at the shortcut menu.

Inserting a *Total* Row

A *Total* row can be added to a table in Datasheet view and then used to perform functions such as finding the sum, average, maximum, minimum, count, standard deviation, or variance results in a numeric column. To insert a *Total* row, click the Totals button in the Records group on the Home tab. Access adds a row to the bottom of the table with the label *Total*. Click in the *Total* row, click the option box arrow that displays, and then click a specific function at the drop-down list.

Activity 1c **Validating Field Entries; Using the Lookup Wizard; and Inserting, Moving, and Deleting a Field**   **Part 3 of 9**

1. With **4-SunProperties** open, open the Employees table.
2. Insert a new field in the Employees table and apply a validation rule by completing the following steps:
   a. Click the View button to switch to Design view.
   b. Click in the empty field immediately below the *DentalIns* field in the *Field Name* column and then type LifeIns.
   c. Press the Tab key.
   d. Click the option box arrow in the field in the *Data Type* column and then click *Currency* at the drop-down list.
   e. Click in the *Validation Rule* property box, type <=100000, and then press the Enter key.
   f. With the insertion point positioned in the *Validation Text* property box, type Enter a value that is equal to or less than $100,000.

2e   2f

General	Lookup	
Format	Currency
Decimal Places	Auto
Input Mask	
Caption	
Default Value	0
Validation Rule	<=100000
Validation Text	Enter a value that is equal to or less than $100,000
Required	No
Indexed	No
Text Align	General

   g. Click in the *LifeIns* field in the *Description* column and then type Enter optional life insurance amount.
   h. Click the Save button on the Quick Access Toolbar. Since the validation rule was created *after* data was entered into the table, Access displays a warning message indicating that some data may not be valid. At this message, click No.
   i. Click the View button to switch to Datasheet view.

3. Click in the first empty field in the *LifeIns* column, type 200000, and then press the Down Arrow key.
4. Access displays the error message prompting you to enter an amount that is equal to or less than $100,000. At this error message, click OK.
5. Edit the amount in the field to be *100000* and then press the Down Arrow key.
6. Type the following entries in the remaining fields in the *LifeIns* column:

Record 2	25000	Record 7	100000
Record 3	0	Record 8	50000
Record 4	50000	Record 9	25000
Record 5	50000	Record 10	0
Record 6	0	Record 11	100000

7. Insert the *EmpCategory* field in the Employees table and use the Lookup Wizard to specify field choices by completing the following steps:
   a. Click the View button to change to Design view.
   b. Click in the *EmpFirstName* field in the *Field Name* column.
   c. Click the Insert Rows button in the Tools group.
   d. With the insertion point positioned in the new empty field in the *Field Name* column, type EmpCategory.
   e. Press the Tab key. (This moves the insertion point to the *Data Type* column.)
   f. Click the option box arrow in the field in the *Data Type* column and then click *Lookup Wizard* at the drop-down list.
   g. At the first Lookup Wizard dialog box, click the *I will type in the values that I want* option and then click the Next button.

h. At the second Lookup Wizard dialog box, click in the blank text box below *Col1*, type Salaried, and then press the Tab key.

i. Type Hourly and then press the Tab key.

j. Type Temporary.

k. Click the Next button.

l. At the third Lookup Wizard dialog box, click the Finish button. *Note: After completing the Lookup Wizard, the data type for* **EmpCategory** *will change to Short Text*.

m. Press the Tab key and then type Click option box arrow and then click employee category in the *Description* column.

8. Click the Save button on the Quick Access Toolbar.

9. Click the View button to switch to Datasheet view.

10. Insert information in the *EmpCategory* column by completing the following steps:

a. Click in the first empty field in the new *EmpCategory* column.

b. Click the option box arrow in the field and then click *Hourly* at the drop-down list.

c. Click in the next empty field in the *EmpCategory* column, click the option box arrow, and then click *Salaried* at the drop-down list.

d. Continue entering information in the *EmpCategory* column by completing similar steps as in 10a-10b. Choose the following in the specified record:

Record 3: *Hourly*
Record 4: *Salaried*
Record 5: *Temporary*
Record 6: *Hourly*
Record 7: *Salaried*
Record 8: *Temporary*
Record 9: *Hourly*
Record 10: *Salaried*
Record 11: *Salaried*

11. Print the Employees table. (The table will print on two pages.)

12. After looking at the printed table, you decide to move the *EmpCategory* field. Move the *EmpCategory* field in Design view by completing the following steps:

a. With the Employees table open, click the View button to switch to Design view.

b. Click in the field selector bar at the left side of the *EmpCategory* field to select the row.

c. Position the mouse pointer in the *EmpCategory* field selector bar, click and hold down the left mouse button, drag down until a thick black line displays below the *EmpTelephone* field, and then release the mouse button.

13. Delete the *DentalIns* field by completing the following steps:
    a. Click in the field selector bar at the left side of the *DentalIns* field. (This selects the row.)
    b. Click the Delete Rows button in the Tools group.
    c. At the message asking if you want to permanently delete the field and all of the data in the field, click Yes.
14. Click the Save button on the Quick Access Toolbar.
15. Click the View button to switch to Datasheet view.
16. Print the Employees table. (The table will print on two pages.)
17. Close the Employees table.
18. Open the Payments table and then insert a new field in Design view by completing the following steps:
    a. Click the View button to switch to Design view.
    b. Click in the empty field immediately below the *PymntAmount* field in the *Field Name* column and then type LateFee.
    c. Press the Tab key.
    d. Click the option box arrow in the field in the *Data Type* column and then click *Currency* at the drop-down list.
    e. Press the Tab key and then type Enter a late fee amount if applicable in the Description column.
    f. Click the Save button on the Quick Access Toolbar.
    g. Click the View button to switch to Datasheet view.
19. Apply a validation rule and message for the LateFee field by completing the following steps:
    a. Click the *LateFee* column heading to select the column.
    b. Click the Table Tools Fields tab, click the Validation button in the Field Validation group, and then click *Field Validation Rule* at the drop-down list.
    c. Type <=50 in the Expression Builder dialog box and then click OK.
    d. Click Yes at the message that displays.
    e. Click the Validation button and then click *Field Validation Message*.
    f. Type Late fee must be $50 or less and then click OK.
20. Insert late fees for the last three records by completing the following steps:
    a. Click in the *LateFee* field for record 15, type 25, and then press the Down Arrow key.
    b. With the *LateFee* field for record 16 active, type 25 and then press the Down Arrow key.
    c. With the *LateFee* field for record 17 active, type 50 and then press the Up Arrow key.

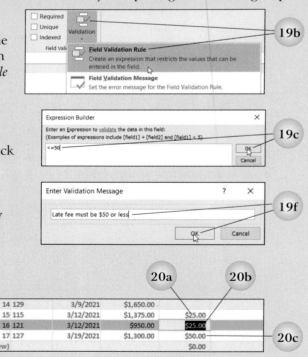

21. Insert a *Total* row by completing the following steps:

   a. In Datasheet view, click the Totals button in the Records group on the Home tab.

   b. Click in the empty field in the *PymntAmount* column in the *Total* row.

   c. Click the option box arrow in the field and then click *Sum* at the drop-down list.

   d. Click in the empty field in the *LateFee* column in the *Total* row.

   e. Click the option box arrow in the field and then click *Sum* at the drop-down list.

   f. Click in any other field.

22. Save, print, and then close the Payments table.

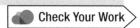

PymntIt	RenterID	PymntDate	PymntAmount	LateFee	Click to Add
1	130	3/1/2021	$1,800.00		
2	111	3/1/2021	$1,900.00		
3	136	3/1/2021	$1,250.00		
4	110	3/1/2021	$1,300.00		
5	135	3/2/2021	$1,900.00		
6	123	3/2/2021	$1,000.00		
7	117	3/2/2021	$1,100.00		
8	114	3/3/2021	$1,400.00		
9	131	3/3/2021	$1,200.00		
10	118	3/3/2021	$900.00		
11	125	3/5/2021	$1,650.00		
12	119	3/5/2021	$1,500.00		
13	133	3/8/2021	$1,650.00		
14	129	3/9/2021	$1,650.00		
15	115	3/12/2021	$1,375.00	$25.00	
16	121	3/12/2021	$950.00	$25.00	
17	127	3/19/2021	$1,300.00	$50.00	
(New)				$0.00	
Total					

21a

21c

> **Check Your Work**

 Tutorial

Sorting Records in a Table

 Ascending

 Descending

Sorting Records

The Sort & Filter group on the Home tab contains two buttons for sorting data in records. Click the Ascending button to sort data in the active field and text is sorted in alphabetical order from A to Z, numbers are sorted from lowest to highest, and dates are sorted from earliest to latest. Click the Descending button to sort data in the active field and text is sorted in alphabetical order from Z to A, numbers from highest to lowest, and dates from latest to earliest.

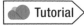 **Tutorial**

Printing Specific Records in a Table

Quick Steps

Sort Records
1. Open table in Datasheet view.
2. Click field in column.
3. Click Ascending or Descending button.

Print Selected Records
1. Open table and select records.
2. Click File tab.
3. Click *Print* option.
4. Click next *Print* option.
5. Click *Selected Record(s)*.
6. Click OK.

Printing Specific Records

Specific records in a table can be printed by selecting the records and then displaying the Print dialog box. Display this dialog box by clicking the File tab, clicking the *Print* option, and then clicking the next *Print* option in the center panel. At the Print dialog box, click the *Selected Record(s)* option in the *Print Range* section and then click OK.

To select specific records, open the table in Datasheet view, click the record selector for the first record, click and hold the left mouse button, drag to select the specific records, and then release the mouse button. The record selector is the light gray square at the left side of the record. When the mouse pointer is positioned on the record selector, the pointer turns into a right-pointing black arrow.

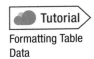

Formatting Table Data

A table in Datasheet view can be formatted with options available in the Text Formatting group on the Home tab as shown in Figure 4.10 and described in Table 4.2. (Some of the buttons in the Text Formatting group are dimmed and unavailable. These buttons are only available for fields formatted as rich text.) Alignment buttons such as Align Left, Center, or Align Right, apply formatting to data in the currently active column. Click one of the other options or buttons in the Text Formatting group and the formatting is applied to data in all columns and rows.

Figure 4.10 Text Formatting Group on the Home Tab

Table 4.2 Text Formatting Buttons and Option Boxes

Button/Option Box	Name	Description
Calibri (Detail)	*Font*	Change the text font.
11	*Font Size*	Change the text size.
B	Bold	Bold the text.
I	Italic	Italicize the text.
U	Underline	Underline the text.
A ▾	Font Color	Change the text color.
	Background Color	Apply a background color to all fields.
	Align Left	Align all text in the currently active column at the left side of the fields.
	Center	Center all text in the currently active column in the center of the fields.
	Align Right	Align all text in the currently active column at the right side of the fields.
	Gridlines	Specify whether to display vertical and/or horizontal gridlines.
	Alternate Row Color	Apply a specified color to alternating rows in the table.

When creating a table, a data type is specified for a field, such as the Short Text, Date/Time, or Currency data type. To format text in a field rather than all of the fields in a column or the entire table, choose the Long Text data type and then specify rich text formatting. For example, in Activity 1d, specific credit scores will be formatted in the *RenCreditScore* column. To be able to format specific scores, the data type will be changed to Long Text with rich text formatting. Use the Long Text data type only for fields containing text—not for fields containing currency amounts, numbers, or dates.

By default, the Long Text data type uses plain text formatting. To change to rich text, click in the *Text Format* property box in the *Field Properties* section (displays with the text *Plain Text*), click the option box arrow at the right side of the property box, and then click *Rich Text* at the drop-down list.

Activity 1d Sorting, Printing, and Formatting Records and Fields in Tables Part 4 of 9

1. With **4-SunProperties** open, open the Renters table.
2. With the table in Datasheet view, sort records in ascending alphabetical order by last name by completing the following steps:
   a. Click in any last name in the *RenLastName* column in the table.
   b. Click the Ascending button in the Sort & Filter group on the Home tab.
   c. Print the Renters table in landscape orientation.

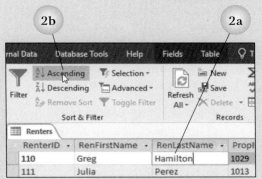

3. Sort records in descending order (highest to lowest) by credit score number by completing the following steps:
   a. Click in any number in the *RenCreditScore* column.
   b. Click the Descending button in the Sort & Filter group.
   c. Print the Renters table in landscape orientation.
4. Close the Renters table without saving the changes.
5. Open the Properties table.
6. Sort and then print selected records with a specific apartment property type by completing the following steps:
   a. Click in any entry in the *CatID* column.
   b. Click the Ascending button in the Sort & Filter group.
   c. Position the mouse pointer on the record selector of the first record with a category ID of *A*, click and hold down the left mouse button, drag to select the four records with a category ID of *A*, and then release the mouse button.
   d. Click the File tab and then click the *Print* option.
   e. Click the next *Print* option in the center panel.

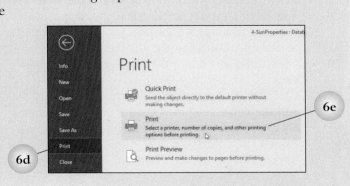

f. At the Print dialog box, click the *Selected Record(s)* option in the *Print Range* section.

g. Click OK.

7. With the Properties table open, apply the following text formatting:

a. Click in any field in the *CatID* column and then click the Center button in the Text Formatting group on the Home tab.

b. Click in any field in the *PropID* column and then click the Center button in the Text Formatting group.

c. Click the Bold button in the Text Formatting group. (This applies bold to all text in the table.)

d. Click the Font Color button arrow and then click the *Dark Blue* color option (fourth column, first row in the *Standard Colors* section).

e. Adjust the column widths.

f. Save, print, and then close the Properties table.

8. Open the Payments table and apply the following text formatting:

a. With the first field active in the *PymntID* column, click the Center button.

b. Click in any field in the *RenterID* column and then click the Center button.

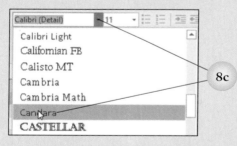

c. Click the *Font* option box arrow in the Text Formatting group, scroll down the drop-down list, and then click *Candara*. (Fonts are listed in alphabetical order in the drop-down list.)

d. Click the *Font Size* option box arrow and then click *12* at the drop-down list.

e. Click the Alternate Row Color button arrow and then click the *Green 2* color option (seventh column, third row in the *Standard Colors* section).

f. Adjust the column widths.

g. Save, print, and then close the Payments table.

9. Open the Renters table and then apply the following formatting to columns in the table:
   a. With the first field active in the *RenterID* column, click the Center button.
   b. Click in any field in the *PropID* column and then click the Center button.
   c. Click in any field in the *EmpID* column and then click the Center button.
   d. Click in any field in the *RenCreditScore* column and then click the Center button.
10. Change the data type for the *RenCreditScore* field to Long Text with rich text formatting and apply formatting by completing the following steps:
    a. Click the View button to switch to Design view.
    b. Click in the *RenCreditScore* field in the *Data Type* column, click the option box arrow in the field, and then click *Long Text* at the drop-down list.
    c. Click in the *Text Format* property box in the *Field Properties* section (displays with the words *Plain Text*), click the option box arrow in the property box, and then click *Rich Text* at the drop-down list.

General	Lookup	
Format		
Caption		
Default Value		
Validation Rule		
Validation Text		
Required	No	
Allow Zero Length	Yes	
Indexed	No	
Unicode Compression	Yes	
IME Mode	No Control	
IME Sentence Mode	None	
Text Format	Plain Text	
Text Align	Plain Text	
Append Only	Rich Text	

10c

    d. At the message stating that the field will be converted to rich text, click the Yes button.
    e. Click the Save button on the Quick Access Toolbar.
    f. Click the View button to switch to Datasheet view.
    g. Double-click the field value *538* in the *RenCreditScore* column in the row for Dana Rozinski. (Double-clicking in the field selects the field value *538*.)
    h. With *538* selected, click the Font Color button in the Text Formatting group. (This changes the color of the number to standard red. If the font color does not change to red, click the Font Color button arrow and then click the *Red* option [second column, bottom row in the *Standard Colors* section].)
    i. Change the font to standard red for any credit scores below 600.
    j. Save and print the Renters table in landscape orientation and then close the table.

Check Your Work

Tutorial

Completing a
Spelling Check

Hint Begin a
spelling check with the
keyboard shortcut F7.

 Spelling

Quick Steps

Complete Spelling
Check
1. Open table in
   Datasheet view.
2. Click Spelling button.
3. Change or ignore
   spelling.
4. Click OK.

Completing a Spelling Check

The spelling feature in Access finds misspelled words and suggests replacement words. It also finds duplicate words and irregular capitalizations. When checking the spelling of an object in a database, such as a table, the words in a table are compared with the words in the spelling dictionary. If a match is found, the word is passed over. If no match is found, then the word is selected and possible replacements are suggested.

To complete a spelling check, open a table in Datasheet view and then click the Spelling button in the Records group on the Home tab. If no match is found for a word in the table, the Spelling dialog box displays with replacement options. Figure 4.11 displays the Spelling dialog box with the word *Citruis* selected and possible replacements display in the *Suggestions* list box. Use options in the Spelling dialog box, to ignore the word (for example, if a proper name is selected), change to one of the replacement options, or add the word to the dictionary or AutoCorrect feature. A spelling check also can be completed on other objects in a database, such as a query, form, and report. (Forms and reports are covered in later chapters.)

Figure 4.11 Spelling Dialog Box

The spelling check selects this word in the table and suggests possible replacements in this list box.

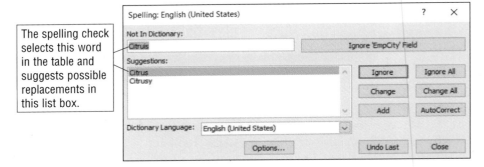

Activity 1e Checking Spelling in a Table

Part 5 of 9

1. With **4-SunProperties** open, open the Employees table.
2. Add the following record to the Employees table. (Type the misspelled words as shown below. You will correct the spelling in a later step.)

EmpID	02-72
EmpFirstName	Roben
EmpLastName	Wildre
EmpAddress	9945 Valley Avenue
EmpCity	Citruis Heights
EmpState	(CA automatically inserted)
EmpZIP	95610
EmpTelephone	9165556522
EmpCategory	(choose *Salaried*)
HireDate	01may20
HealthIns	No (Remove check mark)
LifeIns	50000

3. Save the Employees table.

4. Click in the first field in the *EmpID* column.
5. Click the Spelling button in the Records group on the Home tab.
6. The name *Kasadev* is selected. This is a proper name, so click the Ignore button to leave the name as written.
7. The name *Roben* is selected. Although this is a proper name, it is spelled incorrectly. Click *Robin* (the proper spelling) in the *Suggestions* list box and then click the Change button.
8. The name *Wildre* is selected. Although this is a proper name, it is spelled incorrectly. The proper spelling *(Wilder)* is selected in the *Suggestions* list box, so click the Change button.
9. The word *Citruis* is selected. The proper spelling *(Citrus)* is selected in the *Suggestions* list box, so click the Change button.
10. At the message stating that the spelling check is complete, click OK.
11. Print the Employees table and then close the table.

 Check Your Work

 Tutorial
Finding Data

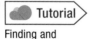 Tutorial
Finding and Replacing Data

 Find

Finding and Replacing Data

To find a specific entry in a field in a table, consider using options at the Find and Replace dialog box with the Find tab selected, as shown in Figure 4.12. Display this dialog box by clicking the Find button in the Find group on the Home tab or with the keyboard shortcut Ctrl + F. At the Find and Replace dialog box, enter the data to be found in the *Find What* text box. By default, Access looks only in the specific column where the insertion point is positioned. Click the Find Next button to find the next occurrence of the data or click the Cancel button to close the Find and Replace dialog box.

The *Look In* option defaults to the column where the insertion point is positioned. This can be changed to search the entire table by clicking the *Look In* option box arrow and then clicking the table name at the drop-down list. The *Match* option has a default setting of *Whole Field*. This can be changed to *Any Part of Field* or *Start of Field*. The *Search* option has a default setting of *All*, which means that Access will search all of the data in a specific column. This can be changed to *Up* or *Down*. To find data that contains specific uppercase and lowercase letters, insert a check mark in the *Match Case* check box and Access will return results that match the case formatting of the text entered in the *Find What* text box.

Quick Steps
Find Data in Table
1. Click Find button.
2. Type data in *Find What* text box.
3. Click Find Next button.

Use the Find and Replace dialog box with the Replace tab selected to search for specific data and replace it with other data. Display this dialog box by clicking the Replace button in the Find group on the Home tab or with the keyboard shortcut Ctrl + H.

Figure 4.12 Find and Replace Dialog Box with Find Tab Selected

Enter the data to be found in this text box.

Activity 1f Finding and Replacing Data, Creating Relationships, and Performing Queries

1. With **4-SunProperties** open, open the Properties table.
2. Find records containing the zip code *95610* by completing the following steps:
   a. Click in the first field in the *ZIP* column.
   b. Click the Find button in the Find group on the Home tab.
   c. At the Find and Replace dialog box with the Find tab selected, type *95610* in the *Find What* text box.
   d. Click the Find Next button. (Access finds and selects the first occurrence of *95610*. If the Find and Replace dialog box covers the data, position the mouse pointer on the dialog box title bar, click and hold down the left mouse button, and then drag the dialog box to a different location on the screen.)
   e. Continue clicking the Find Next button until a message displays stating that Access has finished searching the records. At this message, click OK.
   f. Click the Cancel button to close the Find and Replace dialog box.
3. Suppose a new zip code has been added to the city of North Highlands and you need to change to this new zip code for some of the North Highlands properties. Complete the following steps to find *95660* and replace it with *95668*:
   a. Click in the first field in the *ZIP* column.
   b. Click the Replace button in the Find group.

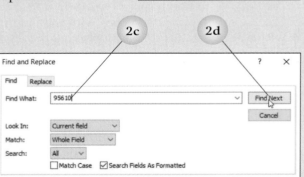

c. At the Find and Replace dialog box with the Replace tab selected, delete the existing text in the *Find What* text box, and then type 95660 in the *Find What* text box.

d. Press the Tab key. (This moves the insertion point to the *Replace With* text box.)

e. Type 95668 in the *Replace With* text box.

f. Click the Find Next button.

g. When Access selects the first occurrence of *95660*, click the Replace button.

h. When Access selects the second occurrence of *95660*, click the Find Next button.

i. When Access selects the third occurrence of *95660*, click the Replace button.

j. When Access selects the fourth occurrence of *95660*, click the Find Next button.

k. When Access selects the fifth occurrence of *95660*, click the Find Next button.

l. When Access selects the sixth occurrence of *95660*, click the Replace button.

m. Access goes back and selects the first occurrence of *95660* (record 1003) in the table. Click the Cancel button to close the Find and Replace dialog box.

4. Print and then close the Properties table.

5. Open the Relationships window and then create the following relationships (enforce referential integrity and cascade fields and records):

a. Create a one-to-many relationship with the *CatID* field in the Categories table field list box the "one" and the *CatID* field in the Properties table field list box the "many."

b. Create a one-to-many relationship with the *EmpID* field in the Employees table field list box the "one" and the *EmpID* field in the Renters table field list box the "many."

c. Create a one-to-many relationship with the *PropID* field in the Properties table field list box the "one" and the *PropID* field in the Renters table field list box the "many."

d. Create a one-to-many relationship with the *RenterID* field in the Renters table field list box the "one" and the *RenterID* field in the Payments table field list box the "many."

e. Save the relationships and then print the relationship report in landscape orientation.

f. Close the relationship report without saving it and then close the Relationships window.

6. Design a query that returns employees with health insurance benefits with the following specifications:

a. Insert the Employees table in the query window.

b. Insert the *EmpID* field in the first field in the *Field* row.

c. Insert the *EmpFirstName* field in the second field in the *Field* row.

d. Insert the *EmpLastName* field in the third field in the *Field* row.

e. Insert the *HealthIns* field in the fourth field in the *Field* row.

f. Click in the check box in the *EmpID* field in the *Show* row to remove the check mark. (This hides the EmpID numbers in the query results.)

g. Extract those employees with health benefits. (Type 1 in the *HealthIns* field in the *Criteria* row.)

h. Run the query.

i. Save the query, typing Emp_wHealthIns as the query name.

j. Print and then close the query.

7. Design a query that returns all properties in the city of Citrus Heights with the following specifications:
   a. Insert the Properties table and the Categories table field list box in the query window.
   b. Insert the *PropID* field from the Properties table field list box in the first field in the *Field* row.
   c. Insert the *Category* field from the Categories table in the second field in the *Field* row.
   d. Insert the *Address*, *City*, *State*, and *ZIP* fields from the Properties table field list box to the third, fourth, fifth, and sixth fields in the *Field* row, respectively.
   e. Extract those properties in the city of Citrus Heights.
   f. Run the query.
   g. Save the query, typing Prop_CitrusHeights as the query name.
   h. Print and then close the query.
8. Design a query that returns rent payments made between 3/1/2021 and 3/5/2021 with the following specifications:
   a. Insert the Payments table and the Renters table in the query window.
   b. Insert the *PymntID*, *PymntDate*, and *PymntAmount* fields from the Payments table field list box in the first, second, and third fields in the *Field* row fields, respectively.
   c. Insert the *RenFirstName* and *RenLastName* fields from the Renters table field list box in the fourth and fifth fields in the *Field* row, respectively.
   d. Extract those payments made between 3/1/2021 and 3/5/2021.
   e. Run the query.
   f. Save the query, typing Pymnts_March1to5 as the query name.
   g. Print and then close the query.
9. Design a query that returns properties in Citrus Heights or Orangevale that rent for less than $1,501 a month as well as the type of property with the following specifications:
   a. Insert the Categories table and the Properties table in the query window.
   b. Insert the *Category* field from the Categories table field list box.
   c. Insert the *PropID*, *MoRent*, *Address*, *City*, *State*, and *ZIP* fields from the Properties table field list box.
   d. Extract those properties in Citrus Heights or Orangevale that rent for less than $1,501.
   e. Run the query.
   f. Save the query, typing Prop_CitrusOrange<$1501 as the query name.
   g. Print the query in landscape orientation and then close the query.
10. Design a query that returns properties in Citrus Heights assigned to employee identification number *07-20* with the following specifications:
   a. Insert the Employees table and Properties table in the query window.
   b. Insert the *EmpID*, *EmpFirstName*, and *EmpLastName* fields from the Employees table field list box.
   c. Insert the *Address*, *City*, *State*, and *ZIP* fields from the Properties table field list box.
   d. Extract those properties in Citrus Heights assigned to employee identification number 07-20.
   e. Run the query.
   f. Save the query, typing Emp_07-20Citrus as the query name.
   g. Print and then close the query.

Check Your Work

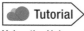
Using the Help and Tell Me Features

Microsoft Access includes a Help feature that contains information about Access features and commands. This on-screen reference manual is similar to Windows Help and the Help features in Word, PowerPoint, and Excel. The Tell Me feature provides information and guidance on how to complete a function.

Getting Help at the Help Task Pane

Hint Press the F1 function key to display the Help task pane.

Click the Help button in the Help group on the Help tab or press the F1 function key to display the Help task pane, as shown in Figure 4.13. In this task pane, type a topic, feature, or question in the search text box and then press the Enter key. Articles related to the search text display in the Help task pane. Open an article by clicking the article's hyperlink.

The Help task pane contains buttons above the search text box. Use the Back and three dots buttons to navigate within the task pane. Click the Move and Size button (displays as a down arrow at the top right of the task pane) to show sizing and moving options for the Help task pane.

Getting Help on a Button

Position the mouse pointer on a button and a ScreenTip displays with information about the button. Some button ScreenTips display with a Help icon and the text *Tell me more*. Click this hyperlinked text or press the F1 function key and the Help task pane opens with information about the button feature.

Figure 4.13 Help Task Pane

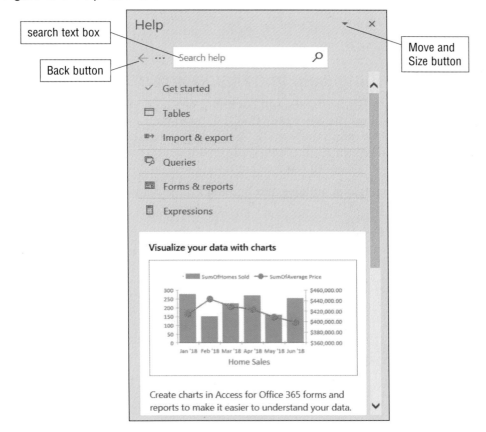

1. With **4-SunProperties** open, click the Help tab and then click the Help button in the Help group.
2. At the Help task pane, type input mask in the search text box and then press the Enter key.
3. When the list of articles displays, click the <u>Control data entry formats with input masks</u> hyperlink. (If this article is not available, choose a similar article.)
4. Read the information on creating an input mask.
5. Close the Help task pane by clicking the Close button in the upper right corner of the task pane.
6. Click the Create tab.
7. Hover the mouse over the Table button and then click the <u>Tell me more</u> hyperlink at the bottom of the ScreenTip.
8. At the Help task pane, read the information on tables and then close the task pane.

Getting Help in a Dialog Box or Backstage Area

Some dialog boxes and backstage areas provide a Help button that, when clicked, displays the Microsoft Office support website with information about the dialog box or backstage area. After reading the information, close the browser window and return to Access.

1. With **4-SunProperties** open, click the Database Tools tab.
2. Click the Relationships button. (Make sure the Show Table dialog box displays. If it does not, click the Show Table button in the Relationships group.)
3. Click the Help button in the upper right corner of the Show Table dialog box.

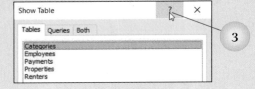

4. Look at the information at the Microsoft Office support website and then close the window.
5. Close the Show Table dialog box and then close the Relationships window.
6. Click the File tab and then click the *Open* option.
7. At the Open backstage area, click the Microsoft Access Help button in the upper right corner.
8. Look at the information at the Microsoft Office support website and then close the window.
9. Press the Esc key to return to the database.

Using the Tell Me Feature

Hint Alt + Q is the keybord shortcut to make the *Tell Me* text box active.

Access includes a Tell Me feature that provides information as well as guidance on how to complete a function. To use Tell Me, click in the *Tell Me* text box on the ribbon to the right of the View tab and then type the function. Type text in the *Tell Me* text box and a drop-down list displays with options that are refined as the text is typed. The drop-down list displays options for completing the function or for displaying information on the function in the Help task pane.

Activity 1i Using the Tell Me Feature   Part 9 of 9

1. With **4-SunProperties** open, open the query named *Prop_CitrusHeights*.
2. Use the Tell Me feature to display the Find and Replace dialog box with the Replace tab selected and apply vertical gridlines by completing the following steps:
   a. Click in the *Tell Me* text box.
   b. Type replace.
   c. Click the *Replace* option at the drop-down list. (This displays the Find and Replace dialog box with the Replace tab selected.)
   d. Click the Cancel button to close the Find and Replace dialog box.
   e. Click in the *Tell Me* text box.
   f. Type gridlines.
   g. Click the arrow at the right side of the *Gridlines* option at the drop-down list.
   h. Click the *Gridlines: Vertical* option at the side menu.
3. Save, print, and then close the Prop_CitrusHeights query.
4. Close the **4-SunProperties** database.

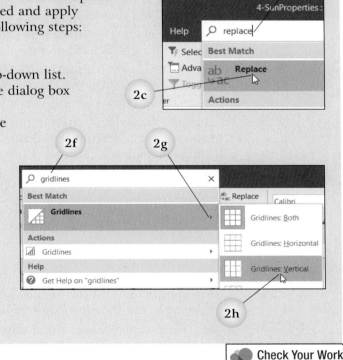

> **Check Your Work**

Chapter Summary

- A table can be created in Datasheet view or Design view. Click the View button on the Table Tools Fields tab or the Home tab to switch between Datasheet view and Design view.

- Define each field in a table in the rows in the top section of Design view. Access automatically assigns the first field the name *ID* and assigns the AutoNumber data type.

- In Design view, specify a field name, data type, and description for each field.

- Assign a data type in Design view by clicking in a specific field in the *Data Type* column, clicking the option box arrow at the right side of the field, and then clicking the data type at the drop-down list.

- Create a default value for a field in Design view with the *Default Value* property box in the *Field Properties* section.

- Use the Input Mask Wizard to set a pattern for how data is entered in a field. Use the *Format* property box to control what displays in a field.

- Use the *Validation Rule* property box in the *Field Properties* section in Design view to enter a statement containing a conditional test. Customize the error message if the data entered violates the validation rule by typing that message in the *Validation Text* property box. In Datasheet view, use the Validation button in the Field Validation group on the Table Tools Fields tab to apply a validation rule and message.

- Use the Lookup Wizard to confine data entered in a field to a specific list of items.

- Insert a field in Design view by clicking in the row immediately below where the new field is to be inserted and then clicking the Insert Rows button.

- Move a field in Design view by clicking in the field selector bar of the field to be moved and then dragging to the new position.

- Delete a field in Design view by clicking in the field selector bar at the left side of the field to be deleted and then clicking the Delete Rows button.

- Insert a *Total* row in a table in Datasheet view by clicking the Totals button in the Records group on the Home tab, clicking the option box arrow in the *Total* row field, and then clicking a function at the drop-down list.

- Click the Ascending button in the Sort & Filter group on the Home tab to sort records in ascending order and click the Descending button to sort records in descending order.

- To print specific records in a table, select the records, display the Print dialog box, make sure *Selected Record(s)* is selected, and then click OK.

- Apply formatting to a table in Datasheet view with options and buttons in the Text Formatting group on the Home tab. Depending on the option or button selected, formatting is applied to all of the data in a table or data in a specific column in the table.

- To format text in a specific field, change the data type to Long Text and then specify rich text formatting. Do this in Design view with the *Text Format* property box in the *Field Properties* section.

- Use the spelling feature to find misspelled words in a table and consider possible replacement words. Begin checking the spelling in a table by clicking the Spelling button in the Records group on the Home tab.

- Use options at the Find and Replace dialog box with the Find tab selected to search for specific field entries in a table. Use options at the Find and Replace dialog box with the Replace tab selected to search for specific data and replace it with other data.
- Click the Help tab and then click the Help button or press the F1 function key to display the Help task pane. At the Help task pane, type a topic in the search text box and then press the Enter key.
- The ScreenTip for some buttons displays with a Help icon and the text *Tell me more*. Click this hyperlinked text or press the F1 function key and the Help task pane opens with information about the button.
- Some dialog boxes and backstage areas contain a Help button that links to the Microsoft Office support website to provide more information about available functions and features.
- The Tell Me feature, located on the ribbon, provides information and guidance on how to complete a function.

Commands Review

FEATURE	RIBBON TAB, GROUP	BUTTON	KEYBOARD SHORTCUT
align text left	Home, Text Formatting		
align text right	Home, Text Formatting		
alternate row color	Home, Text Formatting		
background color	Home, Text Formatting		
bold formatting	Home, Text Formatting	B	
center text	Home, Text Formatting		
delete field	Table Tools Design, Tools		
Design view	Home, Views OR Table Tools Fields, Views		
Find and Replace dialog box with Find tab selected	Home, Find		Ctrl + F
Find and Replace dialog box with Replace tab selected	Home, Find		Ctrl + H
font	Home, Text Formatting	Calibri (Detail)	
font color	Home, Text Formatting	A	
font size	Home, Text Formatting	11	
gridlines	Home, Text Formatting		
Help task pane	Help, Help		F1

FEATURE	RIBBON TAB, GROUP	BUTTON	KEYBOARD SHORTCUT
insert field	Table Tools Design, Tools		
italic formatting	Home, Text Formatting	*I*	
sort records ascending	Home, Sort & Filter		
sort records descending	Home, Sort & Filter		
spelling check	Home, Records	ABC	F7
Tell Me feature			Alt + Q
Total row	Home, Records	Σ	
underline formatting	Home, Text Formatting	U	

Microsoft®

Access® Level 1

Unit 2

Creating Forms and Reports

Creating Forms

Performance Objectives

Upon successful completion of Chapter 5, you will be able to:

1 Create a form using the Form button

2 Change views in a form

3 Print a form

4 Navigate in a form

5 Delete a form

6 Add records to and delete records from a form

7 Sort records in a form

8 Create a form with a related table

9 Manage control objects in a form

10 Format a form

11 Apply conditional formatting to data in a form

12 Add an existing field to a form

13 Insert a calculation in a form

14 Create a split form and multiple items form

15 Create a form using the Form Wizard

In this chapter, you will learn how to create forms from database tables, improving the data display and making data entry easier. Access offers several methods for presenting data on the screen for easier data entry. You will create a form using the Form button, create a split form and multiple items form, and use the Form Wizard to create a form. You will also learn how to customize control objects, insert control objects and fields, and apply formatting to a form.

 Data Files

Before beginning chapter work, copy the AL1C5 folder to your storage medium and then make AL1C5 the active folder.

The online course includes additional training and assessment resources.

Creating a Form

💡 **Hint** A form allows you to focus on a single record at a time.

Access offers a variety of options for presenting data in a clear and attractive format. For instance, data can be viewed, added, or edited in a table in Datasheet view. When data is entered in a table in Datasheet view, multiple records are visible at the same time. If a record contains several fields, not all of the fields in the record may be visible at the same time. Create a form, however, and all of the fields for a record are generally visible on the screen.

💡 **Hint** Save a form before making changes or applying formatting to it.

A form is an object used to enter and edit data in a table or query. It is a user-friendly interface for viewing, adding, editing, and deleting records. A form is also useful in helping to prevent incorrect data from being entered and it can be used to control access to specific data. Several methods are available for creating forms. This chapter covers creating forms using the Form, Split Form, and Multiple Items buttons, as well as the Form Wizard.

Tutorial

Creating a Form Using the Form Button

  Form

Creating a Form Using the Form Button

The simplest method for creating a form is to click a table in the Navigation pane, click the Create tab, and then click the Form button in the Forms groups. Figure 5.1 shows the form that will be created in Activity 1a. Access creates the form using all fields in the table in a vertical layout and opens the form in Layout view with the Form Layout Tools Design tab active.

Quick Steps

Create Form with Form Button
1. Click table in Navigation pane.
2. Click Create tab.
3. Click Form button.

Changing Views

Click the Form button to create a form and the form opens in Layout view. This is one of three views for working with forms. Use the Form view to enter and manage records. Use the Layout view to view the data and modify the appearance and contents of the form. Use the Design view to view the form's structure and modify it. Change views with the View button in the Views group on the Form Layout Tools Design tab or with buttons in the view area at the right side of the Status bar. An existing form can be opened in Layout view by right-clicking the form name in the Navigation pane and then clicking *Layout View* at the shortcut menu.

  Form View

  Layout View

  Design View

Printing a Form

Print all of the records in a form by clicking the File tab, clicking the *Print* option, and then clicking the *Quick Print* option. To print a specific record in a form, click the File tab, click the *Print* option, and then click the *Print* option at the Print backstage area. At the Print dialog box, click the *Selected Record(s)* option and then click OK. Print a range of records by clicking the *Pages* option in the *Print Range*

Figure 5.1 Form Created with the Sales Table

Quick Steps

Print Specific Record
1. Click File tab.
2. Click *Print* option.
3. Click next *Print* option.
4. Click *Selected Record(s)*.
5. Click OK.

section of the Print dialog box and then entering the beginning record number in the *From* text box and the ending record number in the *To* text box.

Before printing a form, display the form in Print Preview. If column shading displays on the second page without any other data, decrease the width of the column. To do this, click the Columns button in the Page Layout group on the Print Preview tab. At the Page Setup dialog box with the Columns tab selected, decrease the measurement in the *Width* measurement box, and then click OK.

Deleting a Form

If a form is no longer needed in a database, delete the form. Delete a form by clicking the form name in the Navigation pane, clicking the Delete button in the Records group on the Home tab, and then clicking the Yes button at the confirmation message. Another method is to right-click the form name in the Navigation pane, click *Delete* at the shortcut menu, and then click Yes at the message. If a form is being deleted from a computer's hard drive, the confirmation message will not display. This is because Access automatically sends the deleted form to the Recycle Bin, where it can be restored if necessary.

Tutorial

Navigating in Objects

Navigating in a Form

When a form displays in Form view or Layout view, navigation buttons display along the bottom of the form in the Record Navigation bar, as identified in Figure 5.1. Use these navigation buttons to display the first, previous, next, or last record in the form or add a new record. Navigate to a specific record by clicking in the *Current Record* box, selecting the current number, typing the number of the record to view, and then pressing the Enter key. The keyboard can also be used to navigate in a form. Press the Page Down key to move forward or the Page Up key to move back a single record. Press Ctrl + Home to go to the first record or press Ctrl + End to display the last record.

1. Display the Open dialog box with your AL1C5 folder active.
2. Open **5-Dearborn** and enable the content.
3. Create a form with the Sales table by completing the following steps:
   a. Click *Sales* in the Tables group in the Navigation pane.
   b. Click the Create tab.
   c. Click the Form button in the Forms group.
4. Switch to Form view by clicking the View button in the Views group on the Form Layout Tools Design tab.
5. Navigate in the form by completing the following steps:
   a. Click the Next record button in the Record Navigation bar to display the next record.
   b. Click in the *Current Record* box, select its contents, type 15, and then press the Enter key.
   c. Click the First record button in the Record Navigation bar to display the first record.
6. Save the form by completing the following steps:
   a. Click the Save button on the Quick Access Toolbar.
   b. At the Save As dialog box, with *Sales* inserted in the *Form Name* text box, click OK.
7. Print the current record in the form by completing the following steps:
   a. Click the File tab and then click the *Print* option.
   b. At the Print backstage area, click the *Print* option.
   c. At the Print dialog box, click the *Selected Record(s)* option in the *Print Range* section and then click OK.
8. Close the Sales form.
9. Delete the RepBenefits form by right-clicking *RepBenefits* in the Navigation pane, clicking *Delete* at the shortcut menu, and then clicking Yes at the confirmation message.

Check Your Work

Adding and
Deleting Records in
a Form

 New (blank)
record

 Delete

Quick Steps

Add Record
Click New (blank)
record button on
Record Navigation bar.
OR
1. Click Home tab.
2. Click New button.

Delete Record
1. Click Home tab.
2. Click Delete button
   arrow.
3. Click *Delete Record.*
4. Click Yes.

Adding and Deleting Records

Add a new record to the form by clicking the New (blank) record button (contains a right-pointing arrow and a yellow asterisk) on the Record Navigation bar along the bottom of the form. A new record can also be added to a form by clicking the Home tab and then clicking the New button in the Records group.

To delete a record, display the record, click the Home tab, click the Delete button arrow in the Records group, and then click *Delete Record* at the drop-down list. At the confirmation message, click the Yes button. Add records to or delete records from the table from which the form was created and the form will reflect the additions or deletions. Also, if additions or deletions are made to the form, the changes are reflected in the table from which the form was created.

Sorting Records

Sort data in a form by clicking in the field containing data on which to sort and then clicking the Ascending button or Descending button in the Sort & Filter group on the Home tab. Click the Ascending button to sort text in alphabetic order from A to Z, numbers from lowest to highest, and dates from earliest to latest. Click the Descending button to sort text in alphabetic order from Z to A, numbers from highest to lowest, and dates from latest to earliest.

Activity 1b Adding, Deleting, and Sorting Records in a Form   **Part 2 of 7**

1. With **5-Dearborn** open, open the Sales table (not the form) and add a new record by completing the following steps:
   a. Click the New (blank) record button in the Record Navigation bar.

1a

   b. At the new blank record, type the following information in the specified fields. (Move to the next field by pressing the Tab key or the Enter key; move to the previous field by pressing Shift + Tab.)

SalesID	(This is an AutoNumber field, so press the Tab key.)
ClientID	127
CalendarYear	2021
Sales	176420

2. Close the Sales table.
3. Open the Sales form.
4. Click the Last record button on the Record Navigation bar and notice that the new record you added to the table also has been added to the form.

5. Delete the second record (*SalesID 3*) in the form by completing the following steps:
   a. Click the First record button in the Record Navigation bar.
   b. Click the Next record button in the Record Navigation bar.
   c. With Record 2 active, click the Delete button arrow in the Records group on the Home tab and then click *Delete Record* at the drop-down list.

   d. At the confirmation message, click the Yes button.
6. Click the New (blank) record button in the Record Navigation bar and then type the following information in the specified fields:

SalesID	(Press the Tab key.)
ClientID	103
CalendarYear	2021
Sales	110775

7. Sort the records in the form by completing the following steps:
   a. Click in the field containing *103* and then click the Ascending button in the Sort & Filter group on the Home tab.
   b. Click in the field containing *$289,563.00* and then click the Descending button in the Sort & Filter group.
   c. Click in the field containing *36* and then click the Ascending button.
8. Close the Sales form.

Creating a Form with a Related Table

Creating a Form with a Related Table

When the form was created with the Sales table, the form contained only the Sales table fields. If a form is created with a table that has a one-to-many relationship established, Access adds a datasheet to the form that is based on the related table.

For example, in Activity 1c, the form shown in Figure 5.2 will be created from the Representatives table and, since it is related to the Clients table by a one-to-many relationship, Access inserts a datasheet at the bottom of the form containing all of the records in the Clients table. Notice the datasheet at the bottom of the form.

If only a single one-to-many relationship has been created in a database, the datasheet for the related table displays in the form. If multiple one-to-many relationships have been created in a table, Access will not display any datasheets in a form created with that table.

Figure 5.2 Representatives Form with Clients Datasheet

Activity 1c Creating a Form with a Related Table

Part 3 of 7

1. With **5-Dearborn** open, create a form with the Representatives table by completing the following steps:
   a. Click *Representatives* in the Tables group in the Navigation pane.
   b. Click the Create tab.
   c. Click the Form button in the Forms group.
2. Insert a new record in the Clients table for representative *12* (Catherine Singleton) by completing the following steps:
   a. Click two times on the Next record button in the Record Navigation bar at the bottom of the form window (not the Record Navigation bar in the Clients datasheet) to display the record for Catherine Singleton.
   b. Click in the cell immediately below *127* in the *ClientID* field in the Clients datasheet.

c. Type the following information in the specified fields:

ClientID	129	*State*	IN
Client	Dan-Built Construction	*ZipCode*	460339050
StreetAddress	903 James Street	*Telephone*	3175551122
City	Carmel	*Email*	dc@ppi-edu.net

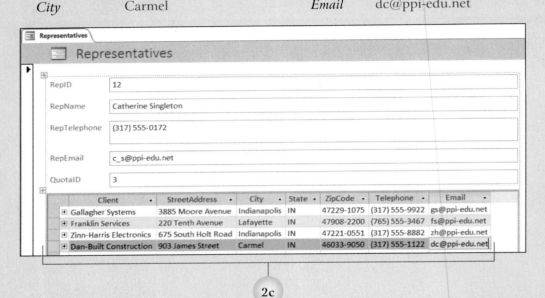

2c

3. Click the Save button on the Quick Access Toolbar and then, at the Save As dialog box with *Representatives* in the *Form Name* text box, click OK.
4. Print the current record in the form by completing the following steps:
   a. Click the File tab and then click the *Print* option.
   b. At the Print backstage area, click the *Print* option.
   c. At the Print dialog box, click the *Selected Record(s)* option in the *Print Range* section and then click OK.
5. Close the Representatives form.

 Check Your Work

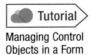 Tutorial

Managing Control
Objects in a Form

💡 *Hint* Almost all
changes can be made
to a form in Layout
view.

Managing Control Objects

A form, like a table in a Word document, is made up of cells that are arranged in rows and columns. Each cell in a form can contain one control object, which is an object that displays a title or description, accepts data, or performs an action. For example, a cell can contain a label control object that displays a field name from the table used to create the form, a text box control that displays and accepts data, or a logo control that displays a logo image. Control objects are contained in the *Form Header* and *Detail* sections of the form. (Refer to Figure 5.1 on page 137.) The control objects in the *Detail* section are contained within a form table.

Manage control objects with buttons on the Form Layout Tools ribbon with the Design tab, Arrange tab, or Format tab selected. When a form is opened in Layout view, the Form Layout Tools Design tab is active.

Inserting Data in a Control Object

Use buttons in the Header/Footer group on the Form Layout Tools Design tab to insert a logo, form title, or date and time. Click the Logo button and the Insert Picture dialog box displays. Browse to the folder containing the image and then double-click the image file. Click the Title button and the current title is selected. Type the new title and then press the Enter key. Click the Date and Time button in the Header/Footer group and the Date and Time dialog box displays. At this dialog box, choose a date and time format and then click OK. The date and time are inserted at the right side of the *Form Header* section.

Sizing Control Objects

When Access creates a form from a table, the cells in the first column in the *Detail* section of the form contain the label control objects with the field names from the table. The second column of cells contains the text box control objects with the field values entered in the table. The control objects in the *Form Header* section and the columns in the *Detail* section can be sized by dragging the border of a selected control object or with the *Width* property box in the Property Sheet task pane with the Format tab selected.

To size a control object by dragging, select the object (displays with an orange border) and then position the mouse pointer on the left or right border of the object until the pointer displays as a left-and-right pointing arrow. Click and hold down the left mouse button, drag left or right to change the width of the column, and then release the mouse button. Complete similar steps to change the height of a control object. When dragging a border, a line and character count displays at the left side of the Status bar. Use the line and character count numbers to move the border to a precise location. When dragging the border of a label control or text box control object, the entire column width is sized.

In addition to dragging a control object border, the column width can be adjusted with the *Width* property box in the Property Sheet task pane with the Format tab selected and the height can be adjusted with the *Height* property box. Display this task pane by clicking the Property Sheet button in the Tools group. In the Property Sheet task pane with the Format tab selected, select the current measurement in the *Width* or *Height* property box, type the new measurement, and then press the Enter key. Close the Property Sheet task pane by clicking the Close button in the upper right corner of the task pane.

Deleting a Control Object

To delete a control object from the form, click the object and then press the Delete key. Or, right-click the object and then click *Delete* at the shortcut menu. To delete a form row, right-click an object in the row to be deleted and then click *Delete Row* at the shortcut menu. To delete a column, right-click one of the objects in the column to be deleted and then click *Delete Column* at the shortcut menu.

Inserting Control Objects

The Controls group on the Form Layout Tools Design tab contains a number of control objects that can be inserted in a form. By default, the Select button is active. With this button active, use the mouse pointer to select control objects. A new label control and text box control object can be inserted in a form by

| abl | Text Box

clicking the Text Box button in the Controls group and then clicking in the desired position in the form. Click the label control object, select the default text, and then type the label text.

Text can be entered in a label control object in Layout view, but not in a text box control object. In Form view, data can be entered in a text box control object but text in a label control object cannot be edited. The Controls group contains a number of additional buttons for inserting control objects in a form, such as a hyperlink, combo box, or image.

Activity 1d Creating a Form and Customizing the Design of a Form

1. With **5-Dearborn** open, create a form with the Clients table and delete the accompanying datasheet by completing the following steps:
   a. Click *Clients* in the Tables group in the Navigation pane.
   b. Click the Create tab.
   c. Click the Form button.
   d. Click in the *SalesID* field in the datasheet that displays below the form.
   e. Click the table move handle in the upper left corner of the datasheet (see image at right).
   f. Press the Delete key.

2. Insert a logo image in the *Form Header* section by completing the following steps:
   a. Right-click the logo object that displays in the *Form Header* section (to the left of the title *Clients*) and then click *Delete* at the shortcut menu.
   b. Click the Logo button in the Header/Footer group on the Form Layout Tools Design tab.
   c. At the Insert Picture dialog box, navigate to your AL1C5 folder and then double-click the file named ***DearbornLogo***.

3. Change the title by completing the following steps:
   a. Click the Title button in the Header/Footer group. (This selects *Clients* in the *Form Header* section.)
   b. Type Dearborn Clients Form and then press the Enter key.

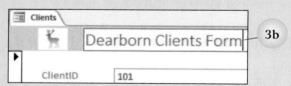

4. Insert the date and time in the *Form Header* section by completing the following steps:
   a. Click the Date and Time button in the Header/Footer group.
   b. At the Date and Time dialog box, click OK.
5. Size the control object containing the title by completing the following steps:
   a. Click any field outside the title and then click the title to select the control object.
   b. Position the mouse pointer on the right border of the selected object until the pointer displays as a black left-and-right-pointing arrow.

c. Click and hold down the left mouse button, drag to the left until the right border is immediately right of the title, and then release the mouse button.

6. Size and move the control objects containing the date and time by completing the following steps:
   a. Click the date to select the control object.
   b. Press and hold down the Shift key, click the time, and then release the Shift key. (Both control objects should be selected.)
   c. Position the mouse pointer on the left border of the selected objects until the pointer displays as a black left-and-right-pointing arrow.
   d. Click and hold down the left mouse button, drag to the right until the border is immediately left of the date, and then release the mouse button.

   e. Position the mouse pointer in the selected objects until the pointer displays with a four-headed arrow attached.
   f. Click and hold down the left mouse button, drag the outline of the date and time objects to the left until the outline displays near the title, and then release the mouse button.
7. Decrease the size of the second column of cells containing control objects in the *Detail* section by completing the following steps:
   a. Click the text box control object containing the client number *101*. (This selects and inserts an orange border around the object.)
   b. Position the mouse pointer on the right border of the selected object until the pointer displays as a black left-and-right-pointing arrow.
   c. Click and hold down the left mouse button, drag to the left until *Lines: 1 Characters: 30* displays at the left side of the Status bar, and then release the mouse button.

8. Insert a label control object by completing the following steps:
   a. Click the Label button in the Controls group.
   b. Click immediately right of the text box control object containing the telephone number *(765) 555-5565*. (This inserts the label to the right of the *Telephone* text box control object.)
   c. With the insertion point positioned inside the label, type Type the telephone number without symbols or spaces and then press the Enter key.
9. Change the width and height of the new label control object by completing the following steps:
   a. Click the Property Sheet button in the Tools group.
   b. In the Property Sheet task pane that displays, if necessary, click the Format tab.
   c. Select the current measurement in the fixed *Width* property box, type 2, and then press the Enter key.
   d. With the current measurement selected in the *Height* property box, type 0.4.
   e. Close the Property Sheet task pane by clicking the Close button in the upper right corner of the task pane.

10. Delete the control object containing the time by clicking the time to select the object and then pressing the Delete key.
11. Click the Save button on the Quick Access Toolbar.
12. At the Save As dialog box with *Clients* in the *Form Name* text box, click OK.

Moving a Form Table

Hint You can move a control object by dragging it to a new location.

The control objects in the *Detail* section in a form in Layout view are contained in cells within the form table. Click in a control object and the table move handle is visible. The table move handle is a small square with a four-headed arrow inside that displays in the upper left corner of the table. (Refer to Figure 5.1 on page 137.) To move the table, position the mouse pointer on the table move handle, click and hold down the left mouse button, drag the table to the new position, and then release the mouse button.

Tutorial

Arranging Control Objects in a Form

Arranging a Control Object

The Form Layout Tools Arrange tab contains options for selecting, inserting, deleting, arranging, merging, and splitting cells. When a label control object was inserted to the right of the *Telephone* text box control object in Activity 1d, empty cells were inserted in the form above and below the new label control object. Select a control object or cell by clicking in the object or cell. Select adjacent control objects or cells by pressing and holding down the Shift key while clicking in each of the objects or cells. To select nonadjacent control objects or cells, press and hold down the Ctrl key while clicking in each of the objects or cells.

 Select Row

 Select Column

Select a row of cells by clicking the Select Row button in the Rows & Columns group or by right-clicking in a cell and then clicking *Select Entire Row* at the shortcut menu. To select a column of cells, click the Select Column button in the Rows & Columns group or right-click an object or cell and then click *Select Entire Column* at the shortcut menu. A column of cells can also be selected by positioning the mouse pointer at the top of the column until the pointer displays as a small, black, down arrow and then clicking the left mouse button.

The Rows & Columns group contains buttons for inserting a row or column of blank cells. To insert a new row, select a cell in a row and then click the Insert Above button to insert a row of blank cells above the current row or click the Insert Below button to insert a row of blank cells below the current row. Complete similar steps to insert a new column of blank cells to the left or right of the current column.

Insert Above

Insert Below

Merge adjacent selected cells by clicking the Merge button in the Merge/Split group on the Form Layout Tools Arrange tab. A cell can contain only one control object. So, merging two cells, each containing a control object, is not possible. A cell containing a control object can be merged with an empty cell or cells. Split a cell by clicking in the cell to make it active and then clicking the Split Vertically button or Split Horizontally button in the Merge/Split group. When a cell is split, an empty cell is created to the right of the cell or below the cell.

Merge

Split Vertically

Split Horizontally

A row of cells can be moved up or down by selecting the row and then clicking the Move Up button in the Move group or the Move Down button. Use the Control Margins button in the Position group to increase or decrease margins within cells. The Position group also contains a Control Padding button for increasing or decreasing spacing between cells.

Control Margins

Control Padding

The Table group at the left side of the Form Layout Tools Arrange tab contains buttons for applying gridlines to cells and changing the layout of the cells to a stacked or columnar layout.

1. With the Clients form in **5-Dearborn** open in Layout view, select and merge cells by completing the following steps:
   a. Click to the right of the text box control object containing the text *101*. (This selects the empty cell.)
   b. Press and hold down the Shift key, click to the right of the text box control object containing the text *Muncie*, and then release the Shift key. (This selects five adjacent cells.)
   c. Click the Form Layout Tools Arrange tab.
   d. Click the Merge button in the Merge/Split group.

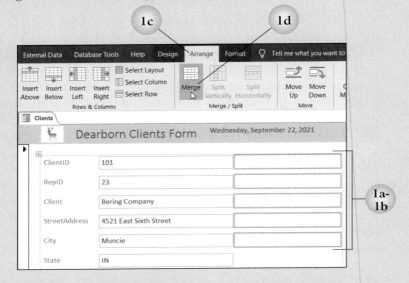

2. With the cells merged, insert an image control object and then insert an image by completing the following steps:
   a. Click the Form Layout Tools Design tab.
   b. Click the Image button in the Controls group.
   c. Move the mouse pointer (which displays as crosshairs with an image icon next to the crosshairs) to the location of the merged cell until the cell displays with pink fill color and then click the left mouse button.

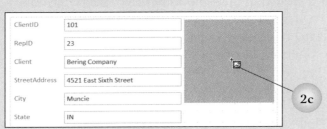

   d. At the Insert Picture dialog box, navigate to your AL1C5 folder and then double-click *Dearborn*.

3. Move down a row of cells by completing the following steps:
   a. Click the Form Layout Tools Arrange tab.
   b. Click in the control object containing the text *Telephone*.
   c. Click the Select Row button in the Rows & Columns group.
   d. Click the Move Down button in the Move group.
4. Decrease the margins within cells, increase the spacing (padding) between cells in the form, and apply gridlines by completing the following steps:
   a. If necessary, click the Form Layout Tools Arrange tab.
   b. Click the Select Layout button in the Rows & Columns group. (This selects all cells in the form table.)
   c. Click the Control Margins button in the Position group and then click *Narrow* at the drop-down list.

d. Click the Control Padding button in the Position group and then click *Medium* at the drop-down list.

e. Click the Gridlines button in the Table group and then click *Top* at the drop-down list.

f. Click the Gridlines button in the Table group, point to *Color*, and then click the *Orange, Accent 2, Darker 50%* option (sixth column, bottom row in the *Theme Colors* section).

5. Move the form table by completing the following steps:

a. Position the mouse pointer on the table move handle (which displays as a small square with a four-headed arrow inside in the upper left corner of the table).

b. Click and hold down the left mouse button, drag the form table up and to the left so it is positioned close to the top left border of the *Detail* section, and then release the mouse button.

6. Click in the control object containing the field name *ClientID*.

7. Save the Clients form.

> **Check Your Work**

Formatting a Form

💡 **Hint** Themes available in Access are the same as the themes available in Word, Excel, and PowerPoint.

Formatting a Form

Apply formatting to enhance the appearance of a form. Format a form by applying a theme, theme colors, and theme fonts; applying formatting with options on the Form Layout Tools Format tab; and applying conditional formatting that meets a specific criterion.

Applying Themes

 Themes

Access provides a number of themes for formatting objects in a database. A theme is a set of formatting choices that include a color theme (a set of colors) and a font theme (a set of heading and body text fonts). To apply a theme to a form, click the Themes button in the Themes group on the Form Layout Tools Design tab and then click a theme at the drop-down gallery. Position the mouse pointer over a theme and the live preview feature will display the form with the theme formatting applied. When a theme is applied, any new objects created in the database will be formatted with that theme.

 Colors

Further customize the formatting of a form with the Colors button and the Fonts button in the Themes group on the Form Layout Tools Design tab. To customize the theme colors, click the Colors button in the Themes group and then click an option at the drop-down list. Change the theme fonts by clicking the Fonts button in the Themes group and then clicking an option at the drop-down list.

A Fonts

Formatting with the Form Layout Tools Format Tab

 Object

 Select All

Click the Form Layout Tools Format tab and buttons and options display for applying formatting to a form or specific cells in a form. To apply formatting to a specific cell, click the cell in the form or click the Object button arrow in the Selection group and then click the control object at the drop-down list. To format all cells in the form, click the Select All button in the Selection group. This selects all cells in the form, including cells in the *Form Header* section. To select all of the cells in the *Detail* section (and not the *Form Header* section), click in a cell in the *Detail* section and then click the table move handle.

Use options and buttons in the Font, Number, Background, and Control Formatting groups to apply formatting to a cell or selected cells in a form. Use options and buttons in the Font group to change the font, change the font size, apply text effects (such as bold and underline), and change the alignment of data in cells. If the form contains data with a Number or Currency data type, use buttons in the Number group to apply specific formatting to numbers. Insert a background image in the form using the Background Image button and apply formatting to cells with buttons in the Control Formatting group. Depending on what is selected in the form, some of the buttons may not be active.

Background Image

Activity 1f Formatting a Form

Part 6 of 7

1. With the Clients form in **5-Dearborn** open and in Layout view, apply a theme by completing the following steps:
   a. Click the Form Layout Tools Design tab.
   b. Click the Themes button and then click the *Facet* option (second column, first row in the *Office* section).
2. Change the theme fonts by clicking the Fonts button in the Themes group and then clicking *Gill Sans MT* at the drop-down gallery. (You will need to scroll down the list to display *Gill Sans MT*.)

3. Change the theme colors by clicking the Colors button in the Themes group and then clicking *Orange* at the drop-down gallery.

4. Change the font and font size of text in the form table by completing the following steps:
   a. Click in any cell containing a control object in the form table.
   b. Select all cells in the form table by clicking the table move handle in the upper left corner of the *Detail* section.
   c. Click the Form Layout Tools Format tab.
   d. Click the *Font* option box arrow, scroll down the drop-down list, and then click *Tahoma*. (Fonts are alphabetized in the drop-down list.)
   e. Click the *Font Size* option box arrow and then click *10* at the drop-down list.

5. Apply formatting and change the alignment of the first column of cells by completing the following steps:
   a. Click in the control object containing the field name *ClientID*, press and hold down the Shift key, click in the bottom control object containing the field name *Telephone*, and then release the Shift key.
   b. Click the Bold button in the Font group.
   c. Click the Shape Fill button in the Control Formatting group and then click the *Brown, Accent 3, Lighter 60%* option (seventh column, third row in the *Theme Colors* section).

   d. Click the Shape Outline button in the Control Formatting group and then click the *Brown, Accent 3, Darker 50%* option (seventh column, bottom row in the *Theme Colors* section).
   e. Click the Align Right button in the Font group.
6. Apply shape fill to the second column of cells by completing the following steps:
   a. Click in the text box control object containing the text *101*.
   b. Position the mouse pointer at the top border of the selected cell until the pointer displays as a small, black, down arrow and then click the left mouse button. (Make sure all of the cells in the second column are selected.)

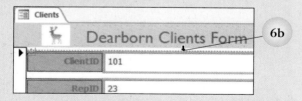

   c. Click the Shape Fill button in the Control Formatting group and then click the *Brown, Accent 3, Lighter 80%* option (seventh column, second row in the *Theme Colors* section).

7. Remove the gridlines by completing the following steps:
   a. Click the Form Layout Tools Arrange tab.
   b. Click the Select Layout button in the Rows & Columns group.
   c. Click the Gridlines button in the Table group and then click *None* at the drop-down list.
8. Click the Save button on the Quick Access Toolbar to save the Clients form.
9. Insert a background image by completing the following steps:
   a. Click the Form Layout Tools Format tab.
   b. Click the Background Image button in the Background group and then click *Browse* at the drop-down list.
   c. Navigate to your AL1C5 folder and then double-click **Mountain**.
   d. View the form and background image in Print Preview. (To display Print Preview, click the File tab, click the *Print* option, and then click the *Print Preview* option.)
   e. After viewing the form in Print Preview, return to the form by clicking the Close Print Preview button.
10. Click the Undo button on the Quick Access Toolbar to remove the background image. (If this does not remove the image, close the form without saving it and then reopen the form.)
11. Save the Clients form.

7c

Check Your Work

Tutorial

Applying Conditional Formatting to a Form

 Conditional Formatting

Quick Steps

Apply Conditional Formatting
1. Click Form Layout Tools Format tab.
2. Click Conditional Formatting button.
3. Click New Rule button.
4. Specify formatting.
5. Click OK.
6. Click OK.

Applying Conditional Formatting

Use the Conditional Formatting button in the Control Formatting group on the Form Layout Tools Format tab to apply formatting to data that meets a specific criterion. For example, conditional formatting can be applied to display sales amounts higher than a certain number in a different color, or to display certain state names in a specific color. Conditional formatting can also be applied that inserts data bars that visually compare data among records. The data bars provide a visual representation of the comparison. For example, in Activity 1g, data bars will be inserted in the *Sales* field that provide a visual representation of how the sales amount in one record compares to the sales amounts in other records.

To apply conditional formatting, click the Conditional Formatting button in the Control Formatting group and the Conditional Formatting Rules Manager dialog box displays. At this dialog box, click the New Rule button and the New Formatting Rule dialog box displays, as shown in Figure 5.3. In the *Select a rule type* list box, choose the *Check values in the current record or use an expression* option if the conditional formatting is applied to a field in the record that matches a specific condition. Click the *Compare to other records* option to insert data bars in a field in all records that compare the data among the records.

Apply conditional formatting to a field by specifying the field and field condition with options in the *Edit the rule description* section of the dialog box. Specify the type of formatting to be applied to data in a field that meets the specific criterion. For example, in Activity 1g, conditional formatting will be applied that changes the shape fill to a light green for all *City* fields containing the text *Indianapolis*. When all changes have been made at the dialog box, click OK to close the dialog box and then click OK to close the Conditional Formatting Rules Manager dialog box.

To insert data bars in a field, click the Conditional Formatting button, click the New Rule button at the Conditional Formatting Rules Manager dialog box, and then click the *Compare to other records* option in the *Select a rule type* list box. This changes the options in the dialog box, as shown in Figure 5.4. Make specific changes in the *Edit the rule description* section.

Figure 5.3 New Formatting Rule Dialog Box with the *Check values in the current record or use an expression* Option Selected

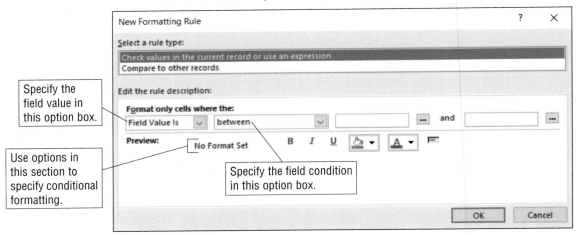

Figure 5.4 New Formatting Rule Dialog Box with the *Compare to other records* Option Selected

1. With the Clients form in **5-Dearborn** open and in Layout view, apply conditional formatting so that the *City* field displays all Indianapolis entries with a light green shape fill by completing the following steps:
   a. Click in the text box control object containing the text *Muncie*.
   b. Click the Form Layout Tools Format tab.
   c. Click the Conditional Formatting button in the Control Formatting group.
   d. At the Conditional Formatting Rules Manager dialog box, click the New Rule button.

   e. At the New Formatting Rule dialog box, click the option box arrow for the option box containing the word *between* and then click *equal to* at the drop-down list.
   f. Click in the text box to the right of the *equal to* option box and then type Indianapolis.
   g. Click the Background color button arrow and then click the *Green 3* option (seventh column, fourth row).
   h. Click OK to close the New Formatting Rule dialog box.
   i. Click OK to close the Conditional Formatting Rules Manager dialog box.

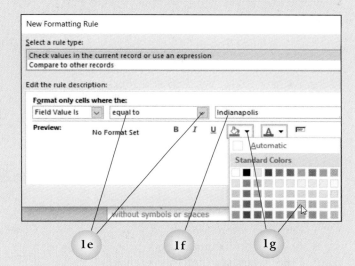

2. Click the Home tab and then click the View button to switch to Form view.
3. Click the Next record button to display the next record in the form. Continue clicking the Next record button to view records and notice that *Indianapolis* entries display with a light green shape fill.
4. Click the First record button in the Record Navigation bar.
5. Click the Save button on the Quick Access Toolbar.
6. Print page 2 of the form by completing the following steps:
   a. Click the File tab and then click the *Print* option.
   b. At the Print backstage area, click the *Print* option.
   c. At the Print dialog box, click the *Pages* option in the *Print Range* section, type 2 in the *From* text box, press the Tab key, and then type 2 in the *To* text box.
   d. Click OK.
7. Close the Clients form.
8. Open the Sales form and switch to Layout View by clicking the View button in the Views group on the Home tab.

9. With the text box control object containing the sales ID number *1* selected, drag the right border to the left until *Lines: 1 Characters: 21* displays at the left side of the Status bar.

10. Change the alignment of text by completing the following steps:
    a. Right-click the selected text box control object (the object containing *1*) and then click *Select Entire Column* at the shortcut menu.
    b. Click the Form Layout Tools Format tab.
    c. Click the Align Right button in the Font group.
11. Apply data bars to the *Sales* field by completing the following steps:
    a. Click in the text box control object containing the amount *$289,563.00*.
    b. Make sure the Form Layout Tools Format tab is active.
    c. Click the Conditional Formatting button.
    d. At the Conditional Formatting Rules Manager dialog box, click the New Rule button.
    e. At the New Formatting Rule dialog box, click the *Compare to other records* option in the *Select a rule type* list box.
    f. Click the *Bar color* option box arrow and then click the *Green 4* option (seventh column, fifth row).
    g. Click OK to close the New Formatting Rule dialog box and then click OK to close the Conditional Formatting Rules Manager dialog box.

12. Click the Next record button in the Record Navigation bar to display the next record. Continue clicking the Next record button and notice the data bars in the *Sales* field.
13. Click the First record button in the Record Navigation bar.
14. Click the Save button on the Quick Access Toolbar.

15. Print page 1 of the form by completing the following steps:
    a. Click the File tab and then click the *Print* option.
    b. At the Print backstage area, click the *Print* option.
    c. At the Print dialog box, click the *Selected Record(s)* option in the *Print Range* section and then click OK.
16. Close the Sales form.
17. Close **5-Dearborn**.

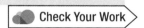 Check Your Work

---

Activity 2   **Add Fields, Create a Split Form and Multiple Items**   **6 Parts**
                 Form, and Use the Form Wizard

You will open the Skyline database, create a form and add related fields and a calculation to the form, create a split and multiple items form, and create a form using the Form Wizard.

 Tutorial

Adding an Existing
Field to a Form

 Add Existing
Fields

💡**Hint** Alt + F8 is
the keyboard shortcut
to display the Field List
task pane.

💡**Hint** Use the Field
List task pane to add
fields from a table or
query to a form.

Quick Steps

**Add Existing Field
to Form**
1. Click Add Existing
   Fields button on
   Form Layout Tools
   Design tab.
2. Drag field from Field
   List task pane to
   specific location in
   form.

Adding an Existing Field

A field can be inserted into an existing form by opening the form in Layout view and then clicking the Add Existing Fields button in the Tools group on the Form Layout Tools Design tab. Clicking the Add Existing Field button displays the Field List task pane at the right side of the screen. This task pane, shown in Figure 5.5, displays the fields available in the current view, fields available in related tables, and fields available in other tables.

In the *Fields available for this view* section, Access displays all fields in any tables used to create the form. So far, forms in activities have been created using all fields in one table. In the *Fields available in related tables* section, Access displays tables that are related to the table(s) used to create the form. To display the fields in the related table, click the expand button (plus symbol in a square) that displays to the left of the table name in the Field List task pane and the list expands to display all of the field names.

To add a field to the form, double-click the field in the Field List task pane. This inserts the field below the active control object in the form. Another method for inserting a field is to drag the field from the Field List task pane into the form. To do this, position the mouse pointer on the field in the Field List task pane, click and hold down the left mouse button, drag into the form, and then release the mouse button. A pink insert indicator bar displays when dragging the field into the existing fields in the form. Drag over an empty cell and the cell displays with pink fill. When the pink insert indicator bar is in the desired position or the cell is selected, release the mouse button.

Multiple fields can be inserted in a form from the Field List task pane. To do this, press and hold down the Ctrl key while clicking specific fields and then drag the fields into the form. Dragging a field from a table in the *Fields available in other tables* section displays the Specify Relationship dialog box. To move a field from the Field List task pane to the form, the field must be in a table that is related to the table(s) used to create the form.

Figure 5.5 Field List Task Pane

Inventory table fields used to create the Inventory form

Suppliers table related to the Inventory table

other tables in the database not related to the Inventory table

Activity 2a Adding Existing Fields to a Form

Part 1 of 6

1. Open **5-Skyline** from your AL1C5 folder and enable the content.
2. Create a form with the Inventory table by clicking *Inventory* in the Tables group in the Navigation pane, clicking the Create tab, and then clicking the Form button.
3. With the text box control object containing the text *001* selected, drag the right border to the left until the selected object is approximately one-half the original width.

4. With the text box control object still selected, click the Form Layout Tools Arrange tab and then click the Split Horizontally button in the Merge/Split group. (This splits the text box control object into one object and one empty cell.)
5. You decide that you want to add the supplier name to the form so the name displays when entering data in the form. Add the *SupplierName* field by completing the following steps:
   a. Click the Form Layout Tools Design tab.
   b. Click the Add Existing Fields button in the Tools group.
   c. Click the Show all tables hyperlink in the Field List task pane.
   d. Click the expand button immediately left of the Suppliers table name in the *Fields available in related tables* section of the Field List task pane.

   e. Position the mouse pointer on the *SupplierName* field, click and hold down the left mouse button, drag into the form until the pink insert indicator bar displays immediately right of the text box control containing the *2* (the text box control at the right side of the *SupplierID* label control), and then release the mouse button. Access inserts the field as a Lookup field (a down arrow displays at the right side of the field).

f. Change the *SupplierName* field from a Lookup field to a text box by clicking the Options button that displays below the field and then clicking *Change to Text Box* at the drop-down list. (This removes the down arrow at the right side of the field.)

g. Close the Field List task pane by clicking the Close button in the upper right corner of the task pane.

6. Insert a logo image in the *Form Header* section by completing the following steps:
   a. Right-click the logo object that displays in the *Form Header* section (to the left of the title *Inventory*) and then click *Delete* at the shortcut menu.
   b. Click the Logo button.
   c. At the Insert Picture dialog box, navigate to your AL1C5 folder and then double-click the file named **Cityscape**.

7. Change the title by completing the following steps:
   a. Click the Title button. (This selects *Inventory* in the *Form Header* section.)
   b. Type Skyline Inventory Input Form and then press the Enter key.

8. Insert the date and time in the *Form Header* section by clicking the Date and Time button and then clicking OK at the Date and Time dialog box.

9. Click in any field outside the title, click the title to select the control object, and then drag the right border of the title control object to the left until the border displays near the title.

10. Select the date and time control objects, drag in the left border until the border displays near the date and time, and then drag the objects so they are positioned near the title.

11. Scroll through the records in the form.

12. Click the First record button in the Record Navigation bar.

13. Click the Save button on the Quick Access Toolbar and save the form with the name *Inventory*.

14. Print the current record.

15. Close the Inventory form.

Check Your Work

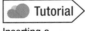
Tutorial

Inserting a Calculation in a Form

Inserting a Calculation in a Form

A calculation can be inserted in a form in a text box control object. To insert a text box control object as well as a label control object, click the Text Box button in the gallery in the Controls group on the Form Layout Tools Design tab, and then click in the location in the form where the two objects are to display. Click in the label control box and then type a label for the calculated field.

Insert a calculation by clicking in the text box control object and then clicking the Property Sheet button in the Tools group on the Form Layout Tools Design tab. This displays the Property Sheet task pane at the right side of the screen. The Property Sheet task pane contains options for setting the form's properties. To insert a calculation in the text box, click the Data tab in the Property Sheet task pane, click in the *Control Source* property box, and then type the calculation.

Type a calculation in the *Control Source* property box using mathematical operators such as the plus symbol (+) for addition, hyphen (-) for subtraction, the asterisk (*) for multiplication, and the forward slash symbol (/) for division. Type field names in the calculation inside square brackets. A field name must be typed in the calculation as it appears in the source object. For example, in Activity 2b the calculation =[AmountTotal]-[AmountPaid] will be inserted in a text box control object to determine the amount due on banquet reservations. Notice that the calculation begins with the equals sign, the field names are typed inside brackets, and the hyphen is used to indicate subtraction. This calculation will subtract the amount paid for a banquet event from the banquet event total amount.

If a calculation result is currency, apply currency formatting to the text box control object. Apply currency formatting by clicking the Form Layout Tools Format tab and then clicking the Apply Currency Format button in the Number group.

Activity 2b Inserting a Calculation in a Form

1. With **5-Skyline** open, create a form with the AmountDue query using the Form button.
2. With the form open in Layout view, insert a text box control by completing the following steps:
   a. Click the Text Box button in the gallery in the Controls group on the Form Layout Tools Design tab.
   b. Position the crosshairs below the *AmountPaid* field (the pink insert indicator bar displays below the field) and then click the left mouse button. (This inserts a label control object and a text box control object in the form.)

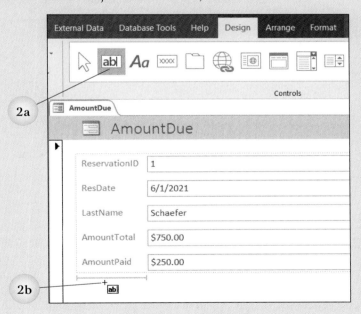

3. Name the new field by clicking in the label control object, double-clicking the text in the label control object, and then typing AmountDue.
4. Click in the text box control object and then insert a calculation by completing the following steps:
   a. Click the Property Sheet button in the Tools group on the Form Layout Tools Design tab.
   b. At the Property Sheet task pane, click the Data tab.
   c. Click in the *Control Source* property box.
   d. Type =[AmountTotal]-[AmountPaid] and then press the Enter key.
   e. Close the Property Sheet task pane by clicking the Close button in the upper right corner of the task pane.

5. With the text box control object still selected, apply currency formatting by completing the following steps:
   a. Click the Form Layout Tools Format tab.
   b. Click the Apply Currency Format button in the Number group.

6. Scroll through the records in the form by clicking the Next record button and then click the First record button.
7. Save the form with the name *BanquetAmountsDue*.
8. Print the first page of the form.
9. Close the BanquetAmountsDue form.

 Check Your Work

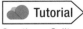 **Tutorial**

Creating a Split Form and Multiple Items Form

 More Forms

Quick Steps

Create Split Form
1. Click table.
2. Click Create tab.
3. Click More Forms button.
4. Click *Split Form*.

Creating a Split Form

Another method for creating a form is to use the *Split Form* option at the More Forms button drop-down list in the Forms group on the Create tab. Use this option to create a form and Access splits the screen in the work area and provides two views of the form. The top half of the work area displays the form in Layout view and the bottom half of the work area displays the form in Datasheet view. The two views are connected and are synchronous, which means that displaying or modifying a specific field in the Layout view portion will cause the same action to occur in the field in the Datasheet view portion. Figure 5.6 displays the split form that will be created in Activity 2c.

Figure 5.6 Split Form

The Suppliers table is used to create a split form, with the top half of the work area displaying the form in Layout view and the bottom half displaying the form in Datasheet view.

Activity 2c Creating a Split Form

1. With **5-Skyline** open, create a split form with the Suppliers table by completing the following steps:
   a. Click *Suppliers* in the Tables group in the Navigation pane.
   b. Click the Create tab.
   c. Click the More Forms button in the Forms group and then click *Split Form* at the drop-down list.

   d. Click several times on the Next record button in the Record Navigation bar. (As you display records, notice that the current record in the Form view in the top portion of the window is the same record selected in Datasheet view in the lower portion of the window.)
   e. Click the First record button.

2. Apply a theme by clicking the Themes button in the Themes group on the Form Layout Tools Design tab and then clicking *Integral* at the drop-down gallery (fourth column, first row in the *Office* section).

3. Insert a logo image in the *Form Header* section by completing the following steps:
   a. Right-click the logo object that displays in the *Form Header* section (to the left of the title *Suppliers*) and then click *Delete* at the shortcut menu.
   b. Click the Logo button.
   c. At the Insert Picture dialog box, navigate to your AL1C5 folder and then double-click **Cityscape**.

4. Change the title by completing the following steps:
   a. Click the Title button.
   b. Type Skyline Suppliers Input Form and then press the Enter key.
   c. Click in any field outside the title, click the title again to select the control object, and then drag the right border to the left until the border displays near the title.

5. Click the text box control object containing the supplier identification number *1* and then drag the right border of the text box control object to the left until *Lines: 1 Characters: 25* displays at the left side of the Status bar.

6. Click the text box control object containing the city *Cape Coral* and drag the right border of the text box control object to the left until *Lines: 1 Characters: 25* displays at the left side of the Status bar.

7. Insert a new record in the Suppliers form by completing the following steps:
   a. Click the View button to switch to Form view.
   b. Click the New (blank) record button in the Record Navigation bar.
   c. Click in the *SupplierID* field in the Form view portion of the window and then type the following information in the specified fields:

SupplierID	8
SupplierName	Jackson Produce
ContactName	Marshall Jackson
SuAddress	5790 Cypress Avenue
SuCity	Fort Myers
SuState	FL
SuZIP	33917
SuTelephone	2395555002

8. Click the Save button on the Quick Access Toolbar and save the form with the name *Suppliers*.
9. Print the current form by completing the following steps:
   a. Click the File tab and then click the *Print* option.
   b. At the Print backstage area, click the *Print* option.
   c. At the Print dialog box, click the Setup button.
   d. At the Page Setup dialog box, click the *Print Form Only* option in the *Split Form* section of the dialog box and then click OK.
   e. At the Print dialog box, click the *Selected Record(s)* option and then click OK.
10. Close the Suppliers form.

9d

 Check Your Work

Creating a Multiple Items Form

Quick Steps

Create Multiple Items Form
1. Click table.
2. Click Create tab.
3. Click More Forms button.
4. Click *Multiple Items*.

When a form is created with the Form button, a single record displays. Use the *Multiple Items* option at the More Forms button drop-down list to create a form that displays multiple records. The advantage to creating a multiple items form over displaying the table in Datasheet view is that the form can be customized using buttons on the Form Layout Tools ribbon with the Design, Arrange, or Format tab selected.

Activity 2d Creating a Multiple Items Form   Part 4 of 6

1. With **5-Skyline** open, create a multiple items form by completing the following steps:
   a. Click *Orders* in the Tables group in the Navigation pane.
   b. Click the Create tab.
   c. Click the More Forms button and then click *Multiple Items* at the drop-down list.
2. Delete the existing logo and then insert the **Cityscape** image as the logo.
3. Type Skyline Orders as the title.
4. Click in any field outside the title, click the title again to select the control object, and then drag the right border to the left until the border displays near the title.
5. Save the form with the name *Orders*.
6. Print the first page of the form by completing the following steps:
   a. Click the File tab and then click the *Print* option.
   b. At the Print backstage area, click the *Print* option.
   c. At the Print dialog box, click the *Pages* option in the *Print Range* section.
   d. Type 1 in the *From* text box, press the Tab key, and then type 1 in the *To* text box.
   e. Click OK.
7. Close the Orders form.

 Check Your Work

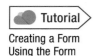
Form Wizard

Quick Steps

**Create Form Using
Form Wizard**
1. Click Create tab.
2. Click Form Wizard
   button.
3. Choose options at
   each Form Wizard
   dialog box.

Hint With the
Form Wizard, you can
be more selective
about which fields you
insert in a form.

Creating a Form Using the Form Wizard

Access offers a Form Wizard that provides steps for creating a form. To create a form using the Form Wizard, click the Create tab and then click the Form Wizard button in the Forms group. At the first Form Wizard dialog box, shown in Figure 5.7, specify the table or query and then the fields to be included in the form. To select the table or query, click the *Table/Queries* option box arrow and then click the table or query at the drop-down list. Select a field in the *Available Fields* list box and then click the One Field button (the button containing the greater-than [>] symbol). This inserts the field in the *Selected Fields* list box. Continue in this manner until all of the fields have been inserted in the *Selected Fields* list box. To insert all of the fields into the *Selected Fields* list box at one time, click the All Fields button (the button containing two greater-than symbols). After specifying the fields, click the Next button.

At the second Form Wizard dialog box, specify the layout for the records. Choose from these layout type options: *Columnar*, *Tabular*, *Datasheet*, and *Justified*. Click the Next button and the third and final Form Wizard dialog box displays. It offers a title for the form and also provides the option *Open the form to view or enter information*. Make any necessary changes in this dialog box and then click the Finish button.

Figure 5.7 First Form Wizard Dialog Box

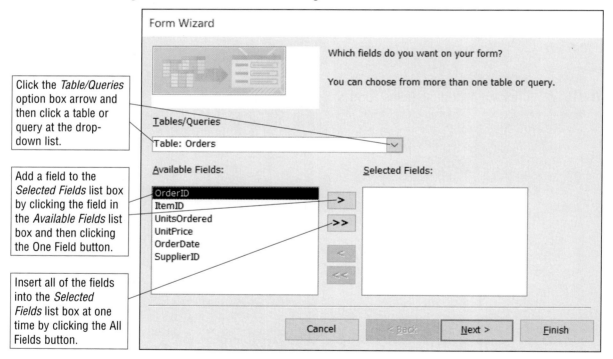

Click the *Table/Queries* option box arrow and then click a table or query at the drop-down list.

Add a field to the *Selected Fields* list box by clicking the field in the *Available Fields* list box and then clicking the One Field button.

Insert all of the fields into the *Selected Fields* list box at one time by clicking the All Fields button.

1. With **5-Skyline** open, create a form with the Form Wizard by completing the following steps:
   a. Click the Create tab.
   b. Click the Form Wizard button in the Forms group.
   c. At the first Form Wizard dialog box, click the *Tables/Queries* option box arrow and then click *Table: Employees* at the drop-down list.
   d. Specify that you want all of the fields included in the form by clicking the All Fields button (the button containing the two greater-than symbols).

   e. Click the Next button.
   f. At the second Form Wizard dialog box, click the *Justified* option and then click the Next button.
   g. At the third and final Form Wizard dialog box, click the Finish button.
2. Format the field headings by completing the following steps:
   a. Click the View button to switch to Layout view.
   b. Click the *EmpID* label control object. (This selects the object.)

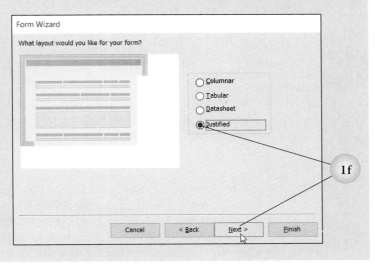

c. Press and hold down the Ctrl key and then click each of the following label control objects: *EmpFirstName*, *EmpLastName*, *EmpAddress*, *EmpCity*, *EmpState*, *EmpZIP*, *EmpTelephone*, *HireDate*, and *HealthIns*.

d. With all of the label control objects selected, release the Ctrl key.

e. Click the Form Layout Tools Format tab.

f. Click the Shape Fill button and then click the *Aqua Blue 2* option (ninth column, third row in the *Standard Colors* section).

g. Click the Form Layout Tools Design tab and then click the View button to switch to Form view.

3. In Form view, click the New (blank) record button and then add the following records:

EmpID	13
EmpFirstName	Carol
EmpLastName	Thompson
EmpAddress	6554 Willow Drive, Apt. B
EmpCity	Fort Myers
EmpState	FL
EmpZIP	33915
EmpTelephone	2395553719
HireDate	10/1/2021
HealthIns	(Click the check box to insert a check mark.)

EmpID	14
EmpFirstName	Eric
EmpLastName	Hahn
EmpAddress	331 South 152nd Street
EmpCity	Cape Coral
EmpState	FL
EmpZIP	33906
EmpTelephone	2395558107
HireDate	10/1/2021
HealthIns	(Leave blank.)

4. Click the Save button on the Quick Access Toolbar.

5. Print the record for Eric Hahn and then print the record for Carol Thompson.

6. Close the Employees form.

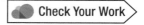 Check Your Work

In Activity 2e, the Form Wizard was used to create a form with all of the fields in one table. If tables are related, a form can be created using fields from related tables. At the first Form Wizard dialog box, choose fields from the selected table and then choose fields from a related table. To change to a related table, click the *Tables/Queries* option box arrow and then click the name of the related table.

1. With **5-Skyline** open, create a form with related tables by completing the following steps:
   a. Click the Create tab.
   b. Click the Form Wizard button.
   c. At the first Form Wizard dialog box, click the *Tables/Queries* option box arrow and then click *Table: Banquets*.
   d. Click *ResDate* in the *Available Fields* list box and then click the One Field button. (This inserts *ResDate* in the *Selected Fields* list box.)
   e. Click *AmountTotal* in the *Available Fields* list box and then click the One Field button.
   f. With *AmountPaid* selected in the *Available Fields* list box, click the One Field button.
   g. Click the *Tables/Queries* option box arrow and then click *Table: Events* at the drop-down list.
   h. Click *Event* in the *Available Fields* list box and then click the One Field button.
   i. Click the *Tables/Queries* option box arrow and then click *Table: Employees* at the drop-down list.
   j. Click *EmpLastName* in the *Available Fields* list box and then click the One Field button.
   k. Click the Next button.
   l. At the second Form Wizard dialog box, click the Next button.
   m. At the third Form Wizard dialog box, click the Next button.
   n. At the fourth Form Wizard dialog box, select the text in the *What title do you want for your form?* text box, type Upcoming Banquets, and then click the Finish button.
2. When the first record displays, print the record.
3. Save and then close the form.
4. Close **5-Skyline**.

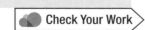

Check Your Work

Chapter Summary

- Creating a form generally improves the ease of entering data into a table. Some methods for creating a form include using the Form, Split Form, and Multiple Items buttons or the Form Wizard.

- A form is an object used to enter and edit data in a table or query and to help prevent incorrect data from being entered in a database.

- The simplest method for creating a form is to click a table in the Navigation pane, click the Create button, and then click the Form button in the Forms group.

- Create a form and it displays in Layout view. Use this view to display data and modify the appearance and contents of the form. Other form views include Form view and Design view. Use Form view to enter and manage records and use Design view to view and modify the structure of the form.

- Open an existing form in Layout view by right-clicking the form in the Navigation pane and then clicking *Layout View* at the shortcut menu.

- Print a form with options at the Print dialog box. To print an individual record, display the Print dialog box, click the *Selected Record(s)* option, and then click OK.

- Delete a form with the Delete button in the Records group on the Home tab or by right-clicking the form in the Navigation pane and then clicking *Delete* at the shortcut menu. A message may display asking to confirm the deletion.

- Navigate in a form with buttons in the Record Navigation bar.

- Add a new record to a form by clicking the New (blank) record button in the Record Navigation bar or by clicking the Home tab and then clicking the New button in the Records group.

- Delete a record from a form by displaying the record, clicking the Home tab, clicking the Delete button arrow, and then clicking *Delete Record* at the drop-down list.

- If a form is created with a table that has a one-to-many relationship established, Access adds a datasheet at the bottom of the form.

- A form is made up of cells arranged in rows and columns and each cell can contain one control object. Customize control objects with buttons on the Form Layout Tools ribbon with the Design tab, Arrange tab, or Format tab selected. These tabs are available when a form displays in Layout view.

- Apply a theme to a form with the Themes button in the Themes group on the Form Layout Tools Design tab. Use the Colors and Fonts buttons in the Themes group to further customize a theme.

- Use buttons in the Header/Footer group on the Form Layout Tools Design tab to insert a logo, form title, and the date and time.

- Control objects can be sized, deleted, and inserted in Layout view.

- Use buttons in the Rows & Columns group on the Form Layout Tools Arrange tab to select or insert rows or columns of cells.

- The Controls group on the Form Layout Tools Design tab contains control objects that can be inserted in a form.

- Merge cells in a form by selecting cells and then clicking the Merge button in the Merge/Split group on the Form Layout Tools Arrange tab. Split selected cells by clicking the Split Vertically or Split Horizontally button.

- Format cells in a form with buttons on the Form Layout Tools Format tab.

- Use the Conditional Formatting button in the Control Formatting group on the Form Layout Tools Format tab to apply formatting to data that matches a specific criterion.
- Click the Add Existing Fields button in the Tools group on the Form Layout Tools Design tab to display the Field List task pane. Add fields to the form by double-clicking a field or dragging the field from the task pane to the form.
- Insert a calculation in a form by inserting a text box control object, displaying the Property Sheet task pane with the Data tab selected, and then typing the calculation in the *Control Source* property box. If a calculation result is currency, apply currency formatting with the Apply Currency Format button on the Form Layout Tools Format tab.
- Create a split form by clicking the More Forms button on the Create tab and then clicking *Split Form* in the drop-down list. Access displays the form in Layout view in the top portion of the work area and in Datasheet view in the bottom portion of the work area. The two views are connected and synchronous.
- Create a Multiple Items form by clicking the More Forms button on the Create tab and then clicking *Multiple Items* in the drop-down list.
- The Form Wizard provides steps for creating a form such as specifying the fields to be included in the form, a layout for the records, and a name for the form.
- A form can be created with the Form Wizard that contains fields from tables connected by a one-to-many relationship.

Commands Review

FEATURE	RIBBON TAB, GROUP	BUTTON, OPTION	KEYBOARD SHORTCUT
Conditional Formatting Rules Manager dialog box	Form Layout Tools Format, Control Formatting		
Field List task pane	Form Layout Tools Design, Tools		
form	Create, Forms		
Form Wizard	Create, Forms		
multiple items form	Create, Forms	, *Multiple Items*	
Property Sheet task pane	Form Layout Tools Design, Tools		Alt + Enter
split form	Create, Forms	, *Split Form*	

Microsoft®

Access®

Creating Reports and Mailing Labels

CHAPTER

6

Performance Objectives

Upon successful completion of Chapter 6, you will be able to:

1 Create a report using the Report button

2 Modify the record source

3 Select, edit, size, move, and delete control objects

4 Sort records

5 Find data

6 Display and customize a report in Print Preview

7 Delete a report

8 Format a report

9 Apply conditional formatting to data in a report

10 Group and sort records in a report

11 Insert a calculation in a report

12 Create a report using the Report Wizard

13 Create mailing labels using the Label Wizard

In this chapter, you will learn how to prepare reports from data in a table or query using the Report button in the Reports group on the Create tab and using the Report Wizard. You will also learn how to manage control objects, format, and insert a calculation in a report and create mailing labels using the Label Wizard.

 Data Files

Before beginning chapter work, copy the AL1C6 folder to your storage medium and then make AL1C6 the active folder.

 The online course includes additional training and assessment resources.

You will create reports with the Report button using tables and queries. You will change the report views; select, move, and size control objects; sort records; customize reports; apply conditional formatting; group and sort fields; and insert a calculation in a report.

Tutorial

Creating a Report

Create Report
1. Click table or query in Navigation pane.
2. Click Create tab.
3. Click Report button.

Creating a Report

Create a report in a database to control what data appears on the page when printed and how the data is formatted. Reports generally answer specific questions (queries). For example, a report could answer the question *What customers have submitted claims?* or *What products do we currently have on order?* The record source for a report can be a table or query. Create a report with the Report button in the Reports group or use the Report Wizard that provides steps for creating a report.

Creating a Report with the Report Button

Report

Hint Create a report to control what data appears on the page when printed.

To create a report with the Report button, click a table or query in the Navigation pane, click the Create tab, and then click the Report button in the Reports group. This displays the report in columnar style in Layout view with the Report Layout Tools Design tab active, as shown in Figure 6.1. Access creates the report using all of the fields in the table or query.

Figure 6.1 Report Created with Sales Table

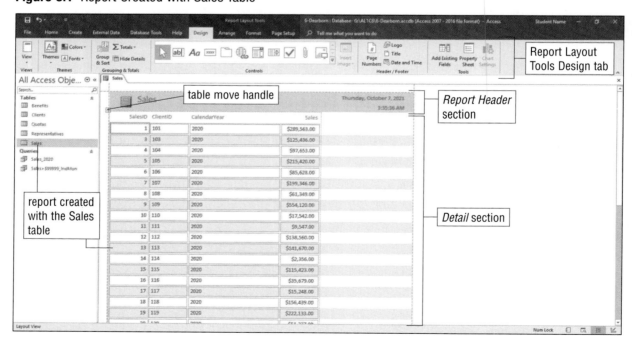

Modifying the Record Source

The record source for a report is the table or query used to create the report. If changes are made to the record source, such as adding or deleting records, those changes are reflected in the report. For example, in Activity 1a, a report will be created based on the Sales table. A record will be added to the Sales table (the record source for the report) and the added record will display in the Sales report.

Activity 1a Creating Reports with the Report Button   Part 1 of 5

1. Open **6-Dearborn** from your AL1C6 folder and enable the content.
2. Create a report based on the Sales table by completing the following steps:
   a. Click *Sales* in the Tables group in the Navigation pane.
   b. Click the Create tab.
   c. Click the Report button in the Reports group.

   d. Save the report by clicking the Save button on the Quick Access Toolbar and then clicking OK at the Save As dialog box. (This saves the report with the default name *Sales*.)
   e. Close the Sales report.
3. Add a record to the Sales table by completing the following steps:
   a. Double-click *Sales* in the Tables group in the Navigation pane. (Make sure you open the Sales table and not the Sales report.)
   b. Click the New button in the Records group on the Home tab.
   c. Press the Tab key to accept the default number in the *SalesID* field.
   d. Type 127 in the *ClientID* field and then press the Tab key.
   e. Type 2021 in the *CalendarYear* field and then press the Tab key.
   f. Type 176420 in the *Sales* field.
   g. Close the Sales table.
4. Open the Sales report and then scroll down to the bottom. Notice that the new record you added to the Sales table displays in the report.
5. Close the Sales report.

6. Use the Sales_2020 query to create a report by completing the following steps:
   a. Click *Sales_2020* in the Queries group in the Navigation pane.
   b. Click the Create tab.
   c. Click the Report button in the Reports group.
7. Access automatically inserted a total amount for the *Sales* column of the report. Delete this amount by scrolling down to the bottom of the report, clicking the total amount at the bottom of the *Sales* column, and then pressing the Delete key. (This deletes the total amount but not the underline above the amount.)
8. Save the report by clicking the Save button on the Quick Access Toolbar, typing 2020Sales in the *Report Name* text box in the Save As dialog box, and then clicking OK.

 Check Your Work

Modifying a Report

Make modifications to a report to address specific needs. For example, select, size, move, edit, or delete control objects in a report; sort records in ascending or descending order, and find data in a report. Use options in Print Preview to customize a report and, if the report is no longer needed, delete the report.

 Tutorial

Managing Control
Objects in a Report

Managing Control Objects

A report, like a form, is comprised of control objects, such as logos, titles, labels, and text boxes. Select a control object in a report by clicking the object and the object displays with an orange border. Click in a cell in the report and Access selects all of the objects in the column except the column heading. Select adjacent control objects by pressing and holding down the Shift key and then clicking objects, or select nonadjacent control objects by pressing and holding down the Ctrl key and then clicking objects.

Like a form, a report contains a *Header* section and a *Detail* section. Select all of the control objects in the report in both the *Header* and *Detail* sections by pressing Ctrl + A. Control objects in the *Detail* section are contained in a report table. To select the control objects in the report table, click in any cell in the report and then click the table move handle. The table move handle is a small square with a four-headed arrow inside that displays in the upper left corner of the table as shown in Figure 6.1 (on page 174). Move the table and all of the control objects within the table by dragging the table move handle using the mouse.

Change the size of control objects by dragging the border of a selected control object or with the *Width* and *Height* property boxes in the Property Sheet task pane with the Data tab selected. To change the size of a control object by dragging, select the object (displays with an orange border) and then, using the mouse, drag a left or right border to increase or decrease the width or drag a top or bottom border to increase or decrease the height of the control object. When dragging the border of a control object, a line and character count displays at the left side of the Status bar. Use the line and character count numbers to adjust the width and/or height of the object by a precise line and character count number.

The width and height of a control object or column of control objects can be adjusted with the *Width* and *Height* property boxes in the Property Sheet task pane. Display this task pane by clicking the Property Sheet button in the Tools group. In the Property Sheet task pane, click the Data tab, select the current measurement in the *Width* or *Height* property box, type the new measurement, and then press the Enter key.

A selected control object can be moved by positioning the mouse pointer in the object until the pointer displays with a four-headed arrow attached. Click and hold down the left mouse button, drag to the new location, and then release the mouse button. To move a column of selected control objects, position the mouse pointer in the column heading until the pointer displays with a four-headed arrow attached and then click and drag to the new location. While dragging a control object(s), a pink insert indicator bar displays indicating where the control object(s) will be positioned when the mouse button is released.

Some control objects in a report, such as a column heading or title, are label control objects. Edit a label control by double-clicking in the label control object and then making the specific changes. For example, to rename a label control, double-click in the label control and then type the new name.

Sorting Records

Sort data in a report by clicking in the field containing the data to be sorted and then clicking the Ascending button or the Descending button in the Sort & Filter group on the Home tab. Click the Ascending button to sort text in alphabetic order from A to Z, numbers from lowest to highest, and dates from earliest to latest. Click the Descending button to sort text in alphabetic order from Z to A, numbers from highest to lowest, and dates from latest to earliest.

Finding Data in a Report

 Find

Find specific data in a report with options at the Find dialog box. Display this dialog box by clicking the Find button in the Find group on the Home tab. At the Find dialog box, enter the search data in the *Find What* text box.

The *Match* option at the Find dialog box is set at *Whole Field* by default. At this setting, the data entered must match the entire entry in a field. To search for partial data in a field, change the *Match* option to *Any Part of Field* or *Start of Field*. If the text entered in the *Find What* text box needs to match the case in a field entry, click the *Match Case* check box to insert a check mark.

Access searches the entire report by default. This can be changed to *Up* to tell Access to search from the currently active field to the beginning of the report or *Down* to search from the currently active field to the end of the report. Click the Find Next button to find data that matches the data in the *Find What* text box.

Displaying and Customizing a Report in Print Preview

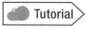

Customizing a Report in Print Preview

 Print Preview

When a report is created, the report displays in the work area in Layout view. In addition to Layout view, three other views are available: Report, Print Preview, and Design. Use Print Preview to display the report as it will appear when printed. To change to Print Preview, click the Print Preview button in the view area at the right side of the Status bar. Another method for displaying the report in Print Preview is to click the View button arrow in the Views group on the Home tab or Report Layout Tools Design tab and then click *Print Preview* at the drop-down list.

In Print Preview, send the report to the printer by clicking the Print button on the Print Preview tab. Use options in the Page Size group to change the page size and margins. To print only the report data and not the column headings, report title, shading, and gridlines, insert a check mark in the *Print Data Only* check box. Use options in the Page Layout group to specify the page orientation, specify the number and size of columns, and display the Page Setup dialog box. Click the Page Setup button and the Page Setup dialog box displays with options for customizing margins, orientation, size, and columns. The Zoom group contains options and buttons for specifying a zoom percentage and for displaying one, two, or multiple pages of the report.

Deleting a Report

Quick Steps

Delete Report
1. Click report name in Navigation pane.
2. Click Delete button on Home tab.
3. Click Yes.
OR
1. Right-click report name in Navigation pane.
2. Click *Delete*.
3. Click Yes.

If a report is no longer needed in a database, delete the report. Delete a report by clicking the report name in the Navigation pane, clicking the Delete button in the Records group on the Home tab, and then clicking the Yes button at the confirmation message. Another method is to right-click the report in the Navigation pane, click *Delete* at the shortcut menu, and then click Yes at the message. If a report is being deleted from the computer's hard drive, the confirmation message will not display. This is because Access automatically sends the deleted report to the Recycle Bin, where it can be retrieved at a later time, if necessary.

Activity 1b Adjusting Control Objects, Renaming Labels, Finding and Sorting Data, Displaying a Report in Print Preview, and Deleting a Report

Part 2 of 5

1. With the 2020Sales report open, reverse the order of the *RepName* and *Client* columns by completing the following steps:
   a. Make sure the report displays in Layout view.
   b. Click the *RepName* column heading.
   c. Press and hold down the Shift key, click in the first control object below the *RepName* column heading (the control object containing *Linda Foster*), and then release the Shift key.
   d. Position the mouse pointer inside the *RepName* column heading until the pointer displays with a four-headed arrow attached.
   e. Click and hold down the left mouse button, drag to the left until the vertical pink insert indicator bar displays to the left of the *Client* column, and then release the mouse button.
2. Sort the data in the *Sales* column in descending order by completing the following steps:
   a. Click in any field in the *Sales* column.
   b. Click the Home tab.
   c. Click the Descending button in the Sort & Filter group.
3. Rename the *RepName* label control as *Representative* by double-clicking in the label control object containing the text *RepName*, selecting *RepName*, and then typing Representative.

4. Double-click in the *Sales* label control and then rename it *Sales 2020*.
5. Move the report table by completing the following steps:
   a. Click in a cell in the report.
   b. Position the mouse pointer on the table move handle (the small square with a four-headed arrow inside that displays in the upper left corner of the table).
   c. Click and hold down the left mouse button, drag the report table to the right until it is centered between the left and right sides of the *Detail* section, and then release the mouse button. (When you drag with the mouse, you will see only outlines of some of the control objects.)

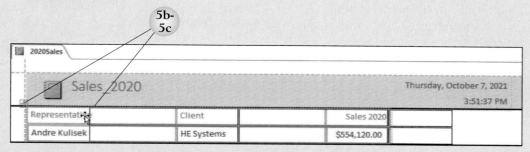

6. Display the report in Print Preview by clicking the Print Preview button in the view area at the right side of the Status bar.

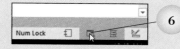

7. Click the One Page button in the Zoom group to display the entire page. (Even though the button displays with a darker gray background and appears to be active, you need to click it to display the entire page.)
8. Click the Zoom button arrow in the Zoom group and then click *50%* at the drop-down list.
9. Click the One Page button in the Zoom group.
10. Print the report by clicking the Print button on the Print Preview tab and then clicking OK at the Print dialog box.
11. Close Print Preview by clicking the Close Print Preview button at the right side of the Print Preview tab.
12. Save and then close the 2020Sales report.
13. Create a report with the Representatives table by completing the following steps:
    a. Click *Representatives* in the Tables group in the Navigation pane.
    b. Click the Create tab.
    c. Click the Report button in the Reports group.
14. Adjust the width of the second column by completing the following steps:
    a. Click in the *RepName* column heading.
    b. Drag the right border of the selected column heading to the left until *Lines: 1 Characters: 18* displays at the left side of the Status bar, and then release the mouse button.
15. Complete steps similar to those in Step 14 to decrease the width of the third column (*RepTelephone*) to *Lines: 1 Characters: 15* and the fourth column (*RepEmail*) to *Lines: 1 Characters: 16*.

16. Adjust the width of the *QuotaID* column and the width and height of the title control object by completing the following steps:
    a. Click in the *QuotaID* column heading.
    b. Click the Property Sheet button in the Tools group and, if necessary, click the Format tab.
    c. Select the current measurement in the *Width* property box, type 0.9, and then press the Enter key.
    d. Click *Representatives* in the title control object.
    e. Select the current measurement in the *Width* property box, type 2, and then press the Enter key.
    f. With the current measurement selected in the *Height* property box, type 0.6.
    g. Close the Property Sheet task pane by clicking the Close button in the upper right corner of the task pane.
17. Search for fields containing a quota of *2* by completing the following steps:
    a. Click in the *RepID* column heading.
    b. Click the Home tab and then click the Find button in the Find group.
    c. At the Find dialog box, type 2 in the *Find What* text box.
    d. Make sure the *Match* option is set to *Whole Field*. (If not, click the *Match* option box arrow and then click *Whole Field* at the drop-down list.)
    e. Click the Find Next button.
    f. Continue clicking the Find Next button until a message displays stating that Access has finished searching the records. Click OK at the message.
    g. Click the Cancel button to close the Find dialog box.

18. Suppose you want to find information on a representative and you remember the first name but not the last name. Search for a field containing the first name *Lydia* by completing the following steps:
    a. Click in the *RepID* column heading.
    b. Click the Find button in the Find group.
    c. At the Find dialog box, type Lydia in the *Find What* text box.
    d. Click the *Match* option box arrow and then click *Any Part of Field* at the drop-down list.
    e. Click the Find Next button. (Access will find and select the representative name *Lydia Alvarado*.)
    f. Click the Cancel button to close the Find dialog box.
19. Click the control object at the bottom of the *RepID* column containing the number *17* and then press the Delete key. (This does not delete the underline above the amount.)

20. Switch to Print Preview by clicking the View button arrow in the Views group on the Home tab and then clicking *Print Preview* at the drop-down list.
21. Click the Margins button in the Page Size group and then click *Normal* at the drop-down list.

22. Decrease column width (so gray shading does not print on a second page) by completing the following steps:
    a. Click the Columns button in the Page Layout group on the Print Preview tab.
    b. Select the current measurement in the *Width* measurement box in the *Column Size* section of the dialog box and then type 7.5.
    c. Click OK to close the dialog box.

23. Print the report by clicking the Print button at the left side of the Print Preview tab and then clicking OK at the Print dialog box.
24. Close Print Preview by clicking the Close Print Preview button.
25. Save the report with the name *Representatives*.
26. Close the Representatives report.
27. Delete the Sales report by right-clicking *Sales* in the Reports group in the Navigation pane, clicking *Delete* at the shortcut menu, and then clicking Yes at the confirmation message.

Check Your Work

Formatting a Report

Customize a report in much the same manner as customizing a form. When a report is created, the report displays in Layout view and the Report Layout Tools Design tab is active. Customize control objects in the *Detail* section and the *Header* section with buttons on the Report Layout Tools ribbon with the Design tab, Arrange tab, Format tab, or Page Setup tab selected.

Totals

The Report Layout Tools Design tab contains many of the same options as the Form Layout Tools Design tab. Use options on this tab to apply a theme, insert controls, insert header or footer data, and add existing fields. Use the Totals button in the Grouping & Totals group to perform calculations, such as finding the sum, average, maximum, or minimum of the numbers in a column. To use the Totals button, click in the column heading of the column containing the data to be totaled, click the Totals button, and then click a function at the drop-down list.

Hint The themes available in Access are the same as the themes available in Word, Excel, and PowerPoint.

The Report Layout Tools Arrange tab contains options for inserting and selecting rows, splitting cells horizontally and vertically, moving data up or down, controlling margins, and changing the padding between cells. The options on the Report Layout Tools Arrange tab are the same as the options on the Form Layout Tools Arrange tab.

Select and format data in a report with options on the Report Layout Tools Format tab. The options on this tab are the same as the options on the Form Layout Tools Format tab. Use options to apply formatting to a report or specific objects in a report. To apply formatting to a specific object, click the object in the report or click the Object button arrow in the Selection group on the Report Layout Tools Format tab and then click the object at the drop-down list. To format all objects in the report, click the Select All button in the Selection group. This selects all objects in the report, including objects in the *Header* section. To select all of the objects in the report table, click the table move handle.

Background

Use options and buttons in the Font, Number, Background, and Control Formatting groups to apply formatting to a cell or selected cells in a report. Use options and buttons in the Font group to change the font, apply a different font size, apply text effects (such as bold and underline), and change the alignment of data in objects. Insert a background image in the report using the Background button and apply formatting to cells with buttons in the Control Formatting group. Depending on what is selected in the report, some of the buttons may not be active.

The buttons on the Report Layout Tools Page Setup tab are also available in Print Preview. For example, the Print Preview tab contains buttons for changing the page size and page layout of the report and displaying the Page Setup dialog box.

Applying
Conditional
Formatting to a
Report

Conditional
Formatting

Applying Conditional Formatting to a Report

Apply conditional formatting to a report in the same manner as applying conditional formatting to a form (covered in Chapter 5). Click the Conditional Formatting button in the Control Formatting group on the Report Layout Tools Format tab and the Conditional Formatting Rules Manager dialog box displays. Click the New Rule button and then use options in the New Formatting Rule dialog box to specify the conditional formatting.

1. With **6-Dearborn** open, open the 2020Sales report.
2. Display the report in Layout view.
3. Click the Themes button in the Themes group
   on the Report Layout Tools Design tab and then
   click *Ion* at the drop-down gallery.
4. Click the Title button in the Header/Footer
   group (which selects the current title), type
   2020 Sales, and then press the Enter key.
5. Insert a row of empty cells in the report by
   completing the following steps:
   a. Click in the *Representative* cell.
   b. Click the Report Layout Tools Arrange tab.
   c. Click the Insert Above button in the Rows &
      Columns group.
6. Merge the cells in the new row by
   completing the following steps:
   a. Click in the empty cell immediately
      above the *Representative* cell.
   b. Press and hold down the Shift key,
      click immediately above the *Sales
      2020* cell, and then release the Shift
      key. (This selects three cells.)
   c. Click the Merge button in the
      Merge/Split group.
   d. Type Dearborn 2020 Sales in the new
      cell.
7. Split a cell by completing the following
   steps:
   a. Click in the *2020 Sales* title in the
      Header section.
   b. Split the cell containing the title by clicking the Split Horizontally button in the
      Merge/Split group.
   c. Click in the empty cell immediately right of the cell containing the title *2020 Sales* and
      then press the Delete key. (Deleting the empty cell causes the date and time to move to
      the left in the *Header* section.)
8. Change the report table margins and padding by completing the following steps:
   a. Click in any cell in the *Detail* section and then click the table move handle in the upper
      left corner of the *Dearborn 2020 Sales* cell. (This selects all of the control objects in the
      report table in the *Detail* section.)
   b. Click the Control Margins button in the
      Position group and then click *Narrow* at the
      drop-down list.
   c. Click the Control Padding button in the
      Position group and then click *Medium* at the
      drop-down list.

9. Click in the *Dearborn 2020 Sales* cell and then drag down the bottom border so all of the text in the cell is visible.
10. Change the font for all of the data in the report by completing the following steps:
    a. Press Ctrl + A to select all control objects in the report. (An orange border displays around selected objects.)
    b. Click the Report Layout Tools Format tab.
    c. Click the *Font* option box arrow in the Font group and then click *Cambria* at the drop-down list. (You may need to scroll down the list to find *Cambria*.)

11. Apply bold formatting and change the alignment of the column headings by completing the following steps:
    a. Click *Dearborn 2020 Sales* to select the control object.
    b. Press and hold down the Shift key, click *Sales 2020*, and then release the Shift key. (This selects four cells.)
    c. Click the Bold button in the Font group.
    d. Click the Center button in the Font group.

12. Format and apply conditional formatting to the amounts by completing the following steps:
    a. Click the first field value below the *Sales 2020* column heading. (This selects all of the amounts in the column.)
    b. Click the Decrease Decimals button in the Number group two times.

    c. Click the Conditional Formatting button in the Control Formatting group.
    d. At the Conditional Formatting Rules Manager dialog box, click the New Rule button.

e. At the New Formatting Rule dialog box, click the option box arrow for the second option box in the *Edit the rule description* section and then click *greater than* at the drop-down list.

f. Click in the text box immediately right of the option box containing *greater than* and then type 199999.

g. Click the Background color button arrow and then click the *Green 2* color option (seventh column, third row).

h. Click OK.

i. At the Conditional Formatting Rules Manager dialog box, click the New Rule button.

j. At the New Formatting Rule dialog box, click the option box arrow for the second option box in the *Edit the rule description* section and then click *less than* at the drop-down list.

k. Click in the text box immediately right of the option box containing *less than* and then type 200000.

l. Click the Background color button arrow and then click the *Maroon 2* color option (sixth column, third row in the *Standard Colors* section).

m. Click OK to close the New Formatting Rule dialog box.

n. Click OK to close the Conditional Formatting Rules Manager dialog box.

13. Sum the totals in the *Sales 2020* column by completing the following steps:

a. Click in the *Sales 2020* column heading.

b. Click the Report Layout Tools Design tab.

c. Click the Totals button in the Grouping & Totals group and then click *Sum* at the drop-down list.

14. Click in the *Sales 2020* sum amount (at the bottom of the *Sales 2020* column) and then drag down the bottom border so the entire amount is visible in the cell.

15. Change the top margin by completing the following steps:

a. Click in the *Representative* column heading and then click the Report Layout Tools Page Setup tab.

b. Click the Page Setup button in the Page Layout group.
c. At the Page Setup dialog box with the Print Options tab selected, select the current measurement in the *Top* measurement box and then type **0.5**.
d. Click OK to close the Page Setup dialog box.

16. Change the page size by clicking the Size button in the Page Size group and then clicking *Legal* at the drop-down list.
17. Display the report in Print Preview by clicking the File tab, clicking the *Print* option, and then clicking the *Print Preview* option.
18. Click the One Page button in the Zoom group and notice that the entire report will print on one legal-sized page.
19. Click the Close Print Preview button to return to the report.
20. Change the page size by clicking the Report Layout Tools Page Setup tab, clicking the Size button in the Page Size group, and then clicking *Letter* at the drop-down list.
21. Insert and then remove a background image by completing the following steps:
    a. Click the Report Layout Tools Format tab.
    b. Click the Background Image button in the Background group and then click *Browse* at the drop-down list.
    c. At the Insert Picture dialog box, navigate to your AL1C6 folder and then double-click **Mountain**.
    d. Scroll through the report and notice how the image displays in the report.
    e. Click the Undo button on the Quick Access Toolbar to remove the background image. (You may need to click the Undo button more than once.)
22. Print the report by clicking the File tab, clicking the *Print* option, and then clicking the *Quick Print* option.
23. Save and then close the report.

> Check Your Work

Grouping and Sorting Records in a Report

Tutorial

Grouping and Sorting Records in a Report

 Group & Sort

 Add a group

Quick Steps
Group and Sort Records
1. Open report in Layout view.
2. Click Group & Sort button.
3. Click Add a group button.
4. Click group field.

A report presents database information in a printed form and generally contains data that answers a specific question. To make the data in a report easy to understand, divide the data into groups. For example, data can be divided in a report by regions, sales, dates, or any other division that helps clarify the data for the reader. Access contains a group and sort feature for dividing data into groups and sorting the data.

Click the Group & Sort button in the Grouping & Totals group on the Report Layout Tools Design tab and the Group, Sort, and Total pane displays at the bottom of the work area, as shown in Figure 6.2. Click the Add a group button in the Group, Sort, and Total pane and Access adds a new grouping level row to the pane, along with a list of available fields. Click the field by which data is to be grouped in the report and Access adds the grouping level in the report. With options in the grouping level row, change the group, specify the sort order, and expand the row to display additional options.

Figure 6.2 Group, Sort, and Total Pane

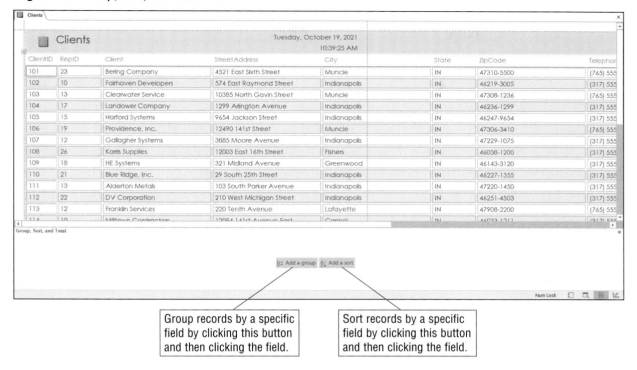

Group records by a specific field by clicking this button and then clicking the field.

Sort records by a specific field by clicking this button and then clicking the field.

When a grouping level is specified, Access automatically sorts that level in ascending order (from A to Z or lowest to highest). Additional data can be sorted within the report by clicking the Add a sort button in the Group, Sort, and Total pane. This inserts a sorting row in the pane below the grouping level row, along with a list of available fields. At this list, click the field by which to sort. For example, in Activity 1d, one of the reports will be grouped by city (which will display in ascending order) and then the client names will display in alphabetic order within the city.

To delete a grouping or sorting level in the Group, Sort, and Total pane, click the Delete button at the right side of the level row. After specifying the grouping and sorting levels, close the Group, Sort, and Total pane by clicking the Close button in the upper right corner of the pane or by clicking the Group & Sort button in the Grouping & Totals group.

Add a sort

Hint Grouping allows you to separate groups of records visually.

Activity 1d Grouping and Sorting Records in a Report   Part 4 of 5

1. With **6-Dearborn** open, create a report with the Clients table using the Report button on the Create tab.
2. Click in each column heading individually and then decrease the size of each column so the right border is just right of the longest entry.
3. Change to landscape orientation by completing the following steps:
   a. Click the Report Layout Tools Page Setup tab.
   b. Click the Landscape button in the Page Layout group.
4. Group the report by representative ID and then sort by clients by completing the following steps:
   a. Click the Report Layout Tools Design tab.
   b. Click the Group & Sort button in the Grouping & Totals group.

c. Click the Add a group button in the Group, Sort, and Total pane.

d. Click the *RepID* field in the list box.
e. Scroll through the report and notice that the records are grouped by the *RepID* field. Also, notice that the client names within each *RepID* field group are not in alphabetic order.
f. Click the Add a sort button in the Group, Sort, and Total pane.
g. Click the *Client* field in the list box.
h. Scroll through the report and notice that client names are now alphabetized within *RepID* field groups.
i. Close the Group, Sort, and Total pane by clicking the Group & Sort button in the Grouping & Totals group.

5. Save the report with the name *RepIDGroupedRpt*.
6. Change column width and print the first page of the report by completing the following steps:
   a. Click the File tab, click the *Print* option, and then click the *Print Preview* option.
   b. Click the Columns button on the Print Preview tab, select the current measurement in the *Width* measurement box, type 10, and then click OK. (The Email field will not fully display.)
   c. Click the Print button on the Print Preview tab.
   d. At the Print dialog box, click the *Pages* option in the *Print Range* section.
   e. Type 1 in the *From* text box, press the Tab key, and then type 1 in the *To* text box.
   f. Click OK.
7. Close the RepIDGroupedRpt report.
8. Create a report with the Sales>$99999_IndMun query using the Report button on the Create tab. Make sure the report displays in Layout view.
9. Group the report by city and then sort by clients by completing the following steps:
   a. Click the Group & Sort button in the Grouping & Totals group on the Report Layout Tools Design tab.
   b. Click the Add a group button in the Group, Sort, and Total pane.
   c. Click the *City* field in the list box.
   d. Click the Add a sort button in the Group, Sort, and Total pane.
   e. Click the *Client* field in the list box.
   f. Close the Group, Sort, and Total pane by clicking the Group & Sort button.
10. Print the first page of the report.
11. Save the report, name it *Sales>$99999_IndMun*, and then close the report.
12. Close **6-Dearborn**.
13. Open **6-WarrenLegal** from your AL1C6 folder and enable the content.

14. Design a query that extracts records from three tables with the following specifications:
    a. Add the Billing, Clients, and Rates tables to the query window.
    b. Insert the *LastName* field from the Clients table field list box in the first field in the *Field* row.
    c. Insert the *BillDate* field from the Billing table field list box in the second field in the *Field* row.
    d. Insert the *BilledHours* field from the Billing table field list box in the third field in the *Field* row.
    e. Insert the *Rate* field from the Rates table field list box in the fourth field in the *Field* row.
    f. Click in the fifth field in the *Field* row, type Total: [BilledHours]*[Rate], and then press the Enter key.

g. Run the query.
h. Save the query, typing Clients_Billing as the query name, and then close the query.
15. Create a report with the Clients_Billing query using the Report button on the Create tab.
16. Click in each column heading individually and then decrease the size of each column so the right border is near the longest entry.
17. Apply currency formatting to the numbers in the *Total* column by completing the following steps:
    a. Click the Report Layout Tools Format tab.
    b. Click in the first field below the *Total* column (the field containing the number *350*).
    c. Click the Apply Currency Format button in the Number group.
    d. If necessary, increase the size of the *Total* column so the entire amounts (including the dollar symbols ($)) are visible.

18. Group the report by last name and then sort by date by completing the following steps:
    a. Click the Report Layout Tools Design tab.
    b. Click the Group & Sort button.
    c. Click the Add a group button in the Group, Sort, and Total pane.
    d. Click the *LastName* field in the list box.
    e. Click the Add a sort button in the Group, Sort, and Total pane.
    f. Click the *BillDate* field in the list box.
    g. Close the Group, Sort, and Total pane by clicking the Close button in the upper right corner of the pane.
19. Scroll to the bottom of the report and delete the total amount in the *Rate* column and the line above the total. (Click the line and then press the Delete key.)
20. Save the report with the name *Clients_BillingRpt*.
21. Close the report.

Inserting a Calculation in a Report

Like a form, a calculation can be inserted in a report in a text box control object. To insert a text box control object as well as a label control object, click the Text Box button in the gallery in the Controls group on the Report Layout Tools Design tab, and then click in a location in the report where the two objects are to display. Click in the label control box and then type a label for the calculated field.

Insert a calculation by clicking in the text box control object and then clicking the Property Sheet button in the Tools group on the Report Layout Tools Design tab. At the Property Sheet task pane, click the Data tab, click in the *Control Source* property box, and then type the calculation. Type a calculation in the *Control Source* property box using mathematical operators and type field names in the calculation inside square brackets. Begin the calculation with an equals sign (=). A field name must be typed in the calculation as it appears in the source object.

If a calculation result is currency, apply currency formatting to the text box control object. Apply currency formatting by clicking the Report Layout Tools Format tab and then clicking the Apply Currency Format button in the Number group.

Quick Steps

Insert Calculation in Report
1. Click Text Box button on Report Layout Tools Design tab.
2. Click in report to insert label and text box control objects.
3. Click in text box control object.
4. Click Property Sheet button in Tools group.
5. Click Data tab.
6. Click in *Control Source* property box.
7. Type calculation.
8. Click Close button.

Activity 1e Inserting a Calculation in a Report   Part 5 of 5

1. With **6-WarrenLegal** open, open the Clients_BillingRpt report in Layout view.
2. Insert label and text box control objects by completing the following steps:
   a. Click the Text Box button in the gallery in the Controls group on the Report Layout Tools Design tab.
   b. Position the crosshairs to the right of the *Total* field name and then click the left mouse button. (This inserts a label control object and text box object in the report.)

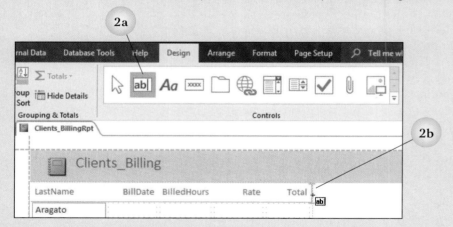

3. Name the new field by clicking in the label control object, double-clicking the text in the label control object, and then typing Total + 9% Tax.

4. Click in the text box control object and then insert a calculation by completing the following steps:

   a. Click the Property Sheet button in the Tools group on the Report Layout Tools Design tab.

   b. At the Property Sheet task pane, click the Data tab.

   c. Click in the *Control Source* property box.

   d. Type =[Total]*1.09 and then press the Enter key.

   e. Close the Property Sheet task pane by clicking the Close button in the upper right corner of the task pane.

5. With the text box control object still selected, apply currency formatting by clicking the Report Layout Tools Format tab and then clicking the Apply Currency Format button.

6. Save and then print the report. (The report will print on three pages.)

7. Close the Clients_BillingRpt report and then close **6-WarrenLegal**.

Check Your Work

Activity 2   Use Wizards to Create Reports and Labels   3 Parts

You will create reports using the Report Wizard and prepare mailing labels using the Label Wizard.

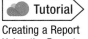

Creating a Report
Using the Report
Wizard

  Report Wizard

Creating a Report Using the Report Wizard

Access offers a Report Wizard that provides the steps for creating a report. To create a report using the wizard, click the Create tab and then click the Report Wizard button in the Reports group. At the first Report Wizard dialog box, shown in Figure 6.3, choose a table or query with options from the *Tables/Queries* option box. Specify the fields to be included in the report by inserting them in the *Selected Fields* list box and then clicking the Next button.

At the second Report Wizard dialog box, shown in Figure 6.4, specify the grouping level of data in the report. To group data by a specific field, click the field in the list box at the left side of the dialog box and then click the One Field button. Use the button containing the left-pointing arrow to remove an option as a grouping level. Use the up and down arrows to change the priority of the field.

Hint Use the Report Wizard to select specific fields and specify how data is grouped and sorted.

Specify a field on which to sort and the sort order with options at the third Report Wizard dialog box, shown in Figure 6.5. To specify a field on which to sort, click the option box arrow for the option box preceded by the number *1* and then click the field name. The default sort order is ascending. This can be changed to descending by clicking the button at the right side of the option box. After identifying the field and sort order, click the Next button.

Figure 6.3 First Report Wizard Dialog Box

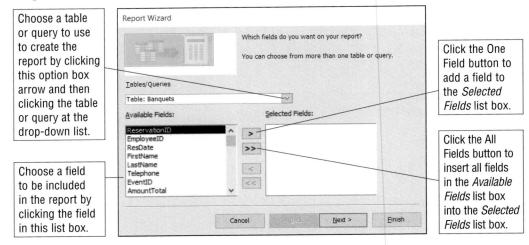

Choose a table or query to use to create the report by clicking this option box arrow and then clicking the table or query at the drop-down list.

Choose a field to be included in the report by clicking the field in this list box.

Click the One Field button to add a field to the *Selected Fields* list box.

Click the All Fields button to insert all fields in the *Available Fields* list box into the *Selected Fields* list box.

Figure 6.4 Second Report Wizard Dialog Box

Use these buttons to increase or decrease the field priority level.

Preview field priorities in this preview box.

Quick Steps

Create Report Using Report Wizard
1. Click Create tab.
2. Click Report Wizard button.
3. Choose options at each Report Wizard dialog box.

Use options at the fourth Report Wizard dialog box, shown in Figure 6.6, to specify the layout and orientation of the report. The *Layout* section has the default setting of *Stepped*, which can be changed to *Block* or *Outline*. By default, the report will print in portrait orientation. Change to landscape orientation by clicking the *Landscape* option in the *Orientation* section of the dialog box. Access will adjust field widths in the report, so all of the fields fit on one page. To specify that field widths should not be adjusted, remove the check mark from the *Adjust the field width so all fields fit on a page* option.

At the fifth and final Report Wizard dialog box, type a name for the report and then click the Finish button.

Figure 6.5 Third Report Wizard Dialog Box

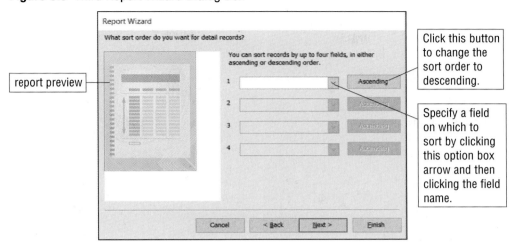

report preview

Click this button to change the sort order to descending.

Specify a field on which to sort by clicking this option box arrow and then clicking the field name.

Figure 6.6 Fourth Report Wizard Dialog Box

report preview

Choose a layout for the report in this section.

Choose an orientation for the report in this section.

Activity 2a Creating a Report Using the Report Wizard

Part 1 of 3

1. Open **6-Skyline** from your AL1C6 folder and enable the content.
2. Create a report using the Report Wizard by completing the following steps:
   a. Click the Create tab.
   b. Click the Report Wizard button in the Reports group.
   c. At the first Report Wizard dialog box, click the *Tables/Queries* option box arrow and then click *Table: Inventory* at the drop-down list.
   d. Click the All Fields button to insert all of the Inventory table fields in the *Selected Fields* list box.
   e. Click the Next button.

f. At the second Report Wizard dialog box, make sure *SupplierID* displays in blue at the top of the preview page at the right side of the dialog box and then click the Next button.

g. At the third Report Wizard dialog box, click the Next button. (You want to use the sorting defaults.)

h. At the fourth Report Wizard dialog box, click the *Block* option in the *Layout* section and then click the Next button.

i. At the fifth Report Wizard dialog box, make sure *Inventory* displays in the *What title do you want for your report?* text box and then click the Finish button. (The report displays in Print Preview.)

3. With the report in Print Preview, click the Print button at the left side of the Print Preview tab and then click OK at the Print dialog box. (The report will print on two pages.)

4. Close Print Preview.

5. Switch to Report view by clicking the View button on the Report Design Tools Design tab.

6. Close the Inventory report.

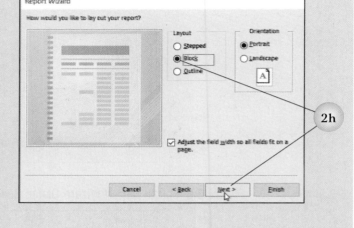

Check Your Work

If a report is created with fields from only one table, options are specified in five Report Wizard dialog boxes. If a report is created with fields from more than one table, options are specified in six Report Wizard dialog boxes. After choosing the tables and fields at the first dialog box, the second dialog box asks how the data will be viewed. For example, if fields are selected from a Suppliers table and an Orders table, the second Report Wizard dialog box will ask if the data is to be viewed "by Suppliers" or "by Orders."

Activity 2b Creating a Report with Fields from Two Tables

Part 2 of 3

1. With **6-Skyline** open, create a report with the Report Wizard by completing the following steps:

   a. Click the Create tab.

   b. Click the Report Wizard button.

   c. At the first Report Wizard dialog box, click the *Tables/Queries* option box arrow and then click *Table: Events* at the drop-down list.

   d. Click the *Event* field in the *Available Fields* list box and then click the One Field button.

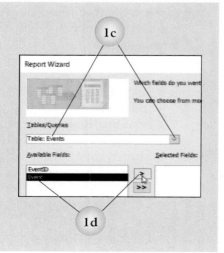

e. Click the *Tables/Queries* option box arrow and then click *Table: Banquets* at the drop-down list.
f. Insert the following fields in the *Selected Fields* list box:
    ResDate
    FirstName
    LastName
    AmountTotal
    AmountPaid
g. After inserting the fields, click the Next button.

h. At the second Report Wizard dialog box, make sure *by Events* is selected and then click the Next button.
i. At the third Report Wizard dialog box, click the Next button. (The report preview shows that the report will be grouped by event.)
j. At the fourth Report Wizard dialog box, click the Next button. (You want to use the sorting defaults.)
k. At the fifth Report Wizard dialog box, click the *Block* option in the *Layout* section, click *Landscape* in the *Orientation* section, and then click the Next button.
l. At the sixth Report Wizard dialog box, select the current name in the *What title do you want for your report?* text box and then type BanquetEvents.

m. Click the Finish button.
2. Close Print Preview and then change to Layout view.
3. Print and then close the BanquetEvents report.
4. Close **6-Skyline**.

Check Your Work

Tutorial

Creating Mailing
Labels

 Labels

Ǫuick Steps

**Create Mailing Labels
Using Label Wizard**
1. Click table.
2. Click Create tab.
3. Click Labels button.
4. Choose options at
   each Label Wizard
   dialog box.

Creating Mailing Labels

Access includes a mailing label wizard that provides the steps for creating mailing labels with fields in a table. To create mailing labels, click a table, click the Create tab, and then click the Labels button in the Reports group. At the first Label Wizard dialog box, shown in Figure 6.7, specify the label size, unit of measure, and label type and then click the Next button. At the second Label Wizard dialog box, shown in Figure 6.8, specify the font name, size, weight, and color and then click the Next button.

Figure 6.7 First Label Wizard Dialog Box

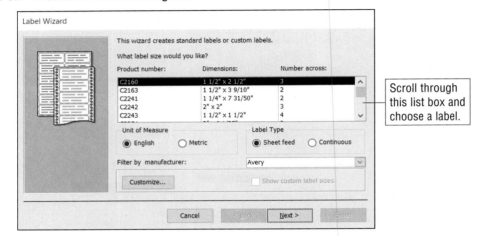

Scroll through this list box and choose a label.

Figure 6.8 Second Label Wizard Dialog Box

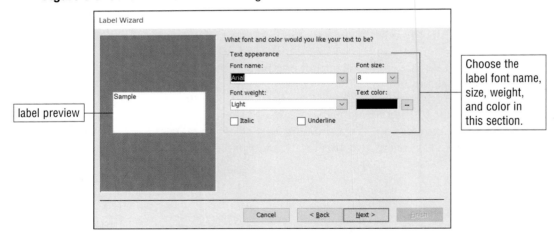

label preview

Choose the label font name, size, weight, and color in this section.

Specify the fields to be included in the mailing labels at the third Label Wizard dialog box, shown in Figure 6.9. To do this, click the field in the *Available fields* list box and then click the One Field button. This moves the field to the *Prototype label* box. Insert the fields in the *Prototype label* box as the text should display on the label. After inserting the fields in the *Prototype label* box, click the Next button.

At the fourth Label Wizard dialog box, shown in Figure 6.10, specify a field from the database by which the labels will be sorted. To sort labels (for example, by last name, postal code, etc.), insert that field in the *Sort by* list box and then click the Next button.

At the last Label Wizard dialog box, type a name for the label report and then click the Finish button. After a few moments, the labels display on the screen in Print Preview. Print the labels and/or close Print Preview.

Figure 6.9 Third Label Wizard Dialog Box

Figure 6.10 Fourth Label Wizard Dialog Box

1. Open **6-WarrenLegal** and enable the content.
2. Click *Clients* in the Tables group in the Navigation pane.
3. Click the Create tab and then click the Labels button in the Reports group.
4. At the first Label Wizard dialog box, make sure *English* is selected in the *Unit of Measure* section, *Avery* is selected in the *Filter by manufacturer* list box, *Sheet feed* is selected in the *Label Type* section, and *C2160* is selected in the *Product number* list box and then click the Next button.

5. At the second Label Wizard dialog box, if necessary, change the font size to 10 points and then click the Next button.
6. At the third Label Wizard dialog box, complete the following steps to insert the fields in the *Prototype label* box:
   a. Click *FirstName* in the *Available fields* list box and then click the One Field button.
   b. Press the spacebar, make sure *LastName* is selected in the *Available fields* list box, and then click the One Field button.
   c. Press the Enter key. (This moves the insertion point down to the next line in the *Prototype label* box.)
   d. With *StreetAddress* selected in the *Available fields* list box, click the One Field button.
   e. Press the Enter key.
   f. With *City* selected in the *Available fields* list box, click the One Field button.
   g. Type a comma (,) and then press the spacebar.
   h. With *State* selected in the *Available fields* list box, click the One Field button.
   i. Press the spacebar.
   j. With *ZipCode* selected in the *Available fields* list box, click the One Field button.

   k. Click the Next button.

7. At the fourth Label Wizard dialog box, sort by zip code. To do this, click *ZipCode* in the *Available fields* list box and then click the One Field button.
8. Click the Next button.
9. At the last Label Wizard dialog box, click the Finish button. (The Label Wizard automatically names the label report *Labels Clients*.)
10. Print the labels by clicking the Print button at the left side of the Print Preview tab and then click OK at the Print dialog box.
11. Close Print Preview.
12. Switch to Report view by clicking the View button on the Report Design Tools Design tab.
13. Close the labels report and then close **6-WarrenLegal**.

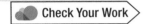

Check Your Work

Chapter Summary

- Create a report with data in a table or query to control how data appears on the page and how the data is formatted when printed.
- Create a report with the Report button in the Reports group on the Create tab.
- Four views are available for viewing a report: Report view, Print Preview, Layout view, and Design view.
- Use options on the Print Preview tab to specify how a report prints.
- In Layout view, a report control object can be selected and then sized or moved.
- One method for changing column width in a report is to click a column heading and then drag the border to the desired width.
- Sort data in a record using the Ascending button or Descending button in the Sort & Filter group on the Home tab.
- Customize a report with options on the Report Layout Tools ribbon with the Design tab, Arrange tab, Format tab, or Page Setup tab selected.
- To make data in a report easier to understand, divide the data into groups using the Group, Sort, and Total pane. Display this pane by clicking the Group & Sort button in the Grouping & Totals group on the Report Layout Tools Design tab.
- Insert a calculation in a report by inserting a text box object, displaying the Property Sheet task pane with the Data tab selected, and then typing the calculation in the *Control Source* property box. If a calculation result is currency, apply currency formatting with the Apply Currency Format button on the Report Layout Tools Format tab.
- Use the Report Wizard to provide the steps for creating a report. Begin the wizard by clicking the Create tab and then clicking the Report Wizard button in the Reports group.
- Create mailing labels with fields in a table using the Label Wizard. Begin the wizard by clicking a table, clicking the Create tab, and then clicking the Labels button in the Reports group.

Commands Review

FEATURE	RIBBON TAB, GROUP	BUTTON	KEYBOARD SHORTCUT
Conditional Formatting Rules Manager dialog box	Report Layout Tools Format, Control Formatting		
Find dialog box	Home, Find		Ctrl + F
Group, Sort, and Total pane	Report Layout Tools Design, Grouping & Totals		
Labels Wizard	Create, Reports		
Property Sheet task pane	Report Layout Tools Design, Tools		Alt + Enter
report	Create, Reports		
Report Wizard	Create, Reports		
sort data in ascending order	Home, Sort & Filter		
sort data in descending order	Home, Sort & Filter		

Performance Objectives

Upon successful completion of Chapter 7, you will be able to:

1 Filter records using the Filter button

2 Remove a filter

3 Filter on specific values, by selection, by shortcut menu, and using the *Filter By Form* option

4 View object dependencies

5 Compact and repair a database

6 Encrypt a database with a password

7 View and customize document properties

8 Save a database in an earlier version of Access

9 Save a database object as a PDF or XPS file

10 Back up a database

Data in a database object can be filtered to view specific records without having to change the design of the object. In this chapter, you will learn how to filter data by selection, by shortcut menu, and by form, as well as how to remove a filter. You will also learn how to view object dependencies, compact and repair a database, encrypt a database with a password, view and customize database properties, save a database in an earlier version of Access, save a database object as a PDF or XPS file, and back up a database.

 Data Files

Before beginning chapter work, copy the AL1C7 folder to your storage medium and then make AL1C7 the active folder.

The online course includes additional training and assessment resources.

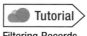
Tutorial

Filtering Records

Filtering Records

A set of restrictions, called a *filter*, can be put on records in a table, query, form, or report to isolate temporarily specific records. A filter, like a query, displays specific records without having to change the design of the table, query, form, or report. Access provides a number of buttons and options for filtering data. Filter data using the Filter button in the Sort & Filter group on the Home tab, right-click specific data in a record and then specify a filter, and use the Selection and Advanced buttons in the Sort & Filter group.

Quick Steps

Filter Records
1. Open object.
2. Click in entry in field to filter.
3. Click Filter button.
4. Select sorting option at drop-down list.

 Filter

Filtering Using the Filter Button

Use the Filter button in the Sort & Filter group on the Home tab to filter records in an object (a table, query, form, or report). To use this button, open the object, click in any entry in the field column to be filtered, and then click the Filter button. This displays a drop-down list with sorting options and a list of all of the field entries, as shown in Figure 7.1. In a table, display this drop-down list by clicking the filter arrow at the right side of a column heading. To filter on a specific

Figure 7.1 *City* Field Drop-down List

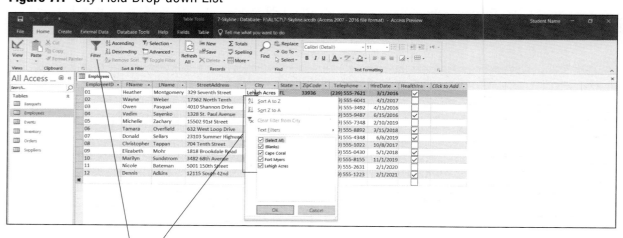

To filter on the *City* field, click in any entry in the field and then click the Filter button. This displays a drop-down list with sorting options and a list of all field entries.

criterion, click the *(Select All)* check box to remove all check marks from the list of field entries. Click the item to filter by in the list box and then click OK.

Open a table, query, or form and the Record Navigation bar contains the dimmed words *No Filter* preceded by a filter icon with a delete symbol (X). If records are filtered, *Filtered* displays in place of *No Filter*, the delete symbol is removed, and the text and filter icon display with an orange background. In a report, apply a filter to records and the word *Filtered* displays at the right side of the Status bar.

Removing a Filter

When data is filtered, the underlying data in the object is not deleted. Switch back and forth between the data and filtered data by clicking the Toggle Filter button in the Sort & Filter group on the Home tab. Click the Toggle Filter button to turn off the filter and all of the data in the table, query, or form displays and the message *Filtered* in the Record Navigation bar changes to *Unfiltered*.

Clicking the Toggle Filter button may redisplay all of the data in an object, but it does not remove the filter. To remove the filter, click in the field column containing the filter and then click the Filter button in the Sort & Filter group on the Home tab. At the drop-down list that displays, click *Clear filter from xxx* (where *xxx* is the name of the field). Remove all of the filters from an object by clicking the Advanced button in the Sort & Filter group and then clicking the *Clear All Filters* option. When all filters are removed (cleared) from an object, the *Unfiltered* message in the Record Navigation bar changes to *No Filter*.

Toggle Filter

Quick Steps

Remove Filter
1. Click in an entry in field containing filter.
2. Click Filter button.
3. Click *Clear filter from (name of field)*.
OR
1. Click Advanced button.
2. Click *Clear All Filters* at drop-down list.

Activity 1a Filtering Records in a Table and Form   Part 1 of 4

1. Open **7-Skyline** from your AL1C7 folder and enable the content.
2. Filter records in the Employees table by completing the following steps:
   a. Open the Employees table.
   b. Click in any entry in the *EmCity* field.
   c. Click the Filter button in the Sort & Filter group on the Home tab. (This displays a drop-down list of options for sorting and filtering the *EmCity* field.)

d. Click the *(Select All)* check box in the filter drop-down list box. (This removes all check marks from the list options.)

e. Click the *Fort Myers* check box in the list box. (This inserts a check mark in the check box.)

f. Click OK. (Access displays only those records with a city field entry of *Fort Myers* and also displays *Filtered* and the filter icon with an orange background in the Record Navigation bar.)

g. Print the filtered records by pressing Ctrl + P (the keyboard shortcut to display the print dialog box) and then clicking OK at the Print dialog box.

3. Toggle the display of filtered data by clicking the Toggle Filter button in the Sort & Filter group on the Home tab. (This redisplays all of the data in the table.)

4. Remove the filter by completing the following steps:

a. Click in any entry in the *EmCity* field.

b. Click the Filter button in the Sort & Filter group.

c. Click the *Clear filter from EmCity* option at the drop-down list. (Notice that the message on the Record Navigation bar changes to *No Filter* and dims the words.)

5. Save and then close the Employees table.

6. Create a form by completing the following steps:

a. Click *Orders* in the Tables group in the Navigation pane.

b. Click the Create tab and then click the Form button in the Forms group.

c. Click the Form View button in the view area at the right side of the Status bar.

d. Save the form with the name *Orders*.

7. Filter the records to show only those records with a supplier identification number of 2 by completing the following steps:

a. Click in the *SupplierID* field containing the text *2*.

b. Click the Filter button in the Sort & Filter group.

c. At the filter drop-down list, click *(Select All)* to remove all of the check marks from the list options.

d. Click the *2* option to insert a check mark.

e. Click OK.

f. Navigate through the records and notice that only the records with a supplier identification number of 2 display.

8. Close the Orders form.

 Check Your Work

Filtering on Specific Values

Quick Steps

Filter on Specific Value
1. Click in entry in field.
2. Click Filter button on Home tab.
3. Point to filter option.
4. Click specific value.

When filtering on a specific field, a list of unique values for that field can be displayed. Click the Filter button for a field containing text and the drop-down list for the specific field will contain a *Text Filters* option. Click this option and a values list displays next to the drop-down list. The options in the values list vary depending on the type of data in the field. Click the Filter button for a field containing number values and the option in the drop-down list displays as *Number Filters*. If filtering dates, the Filter button's drop-down list displays as *Date Filters*. Use the options in the values list to refine a filter for a specific field. For example, the values list can be used to show only money amounts within a specific range or order dates from a certain time period. The values list can also be used to find fields that are "equal to" or "not equal to" data in the current field.

Activity 1b Filtering Records in a Query and Report   Part 2 of 4

1. With **7-Skyline** open, create a query in Design view with the following specifications:
   a. Add the Banquets and Events tables to the query window.
   b. Insert the *ResDate* field from the Banquets table field list box in the first field in the *Field* row.
   c. Insert the *ResFirstName* field from the Banquets table field list box in the second field in the *Field* row.
   d. Insert the *ResLastName* field from the Banquets table field list box in the third field in the *Field* row.
   e. Insert the *ResTelephone* field from the Banquets table field list box in the fourth field in the *Field* row.
   f. Insert the *Event* field from the Events table field list box in the fifth field in the *Field* row.
   g. Insert the *EmployeeID* field from the Banquets table field list box in the sixth field in the *Field* row.
   h. Run the query.
   i. Save the query, typing BanquetReservations as the query name.
2. Filter records of reservations on or before June 15, 2021, in the query by completing the following steps:
   a. With the BanquetReservations query open, make sure the first entry is selected in the *ResDate* field.
   b. Click the Filter button in the Sort & Filter group on the Home tab.
   c. Point to the *Date Filters* option in the drop-down list box.
   d. Click *Before* in the values list.

---

e. At the Custom Filter dialog box, type 6/15/2021 and then click OK.

f. Print the filtered query by pressing Ctrl + P and then clicking OK at the Print dialog box.

3. Remove the filter by clicking the filter icon at the right side of the *ResDate* column heading and then clicking *Clear filter from ResDate* at the drop-down list.

4. Save and then close the BanquetReservations query.

5. Create and format a report by completing the following steps:

   a. Click *BanquetReservations* in the Queries group in the Navigation pane.

   b. Click the Create tab and then click the Report button in the Reports group.

   c. Delete the total amount and line at the bottom of the *ResDate* column.

   d. Delete the page number control object at the bottom of the report.

   e. With the report in Layout view, decrease the column widths so the right side column border displays near the longest entry in each column.

   f. Move the date and time control objects so they align with the last column in the report.

   g. Click the Report View button in the view area at the right of the Status bar.

   h. Save the report with the name *BanquetReport*.

6. Filter the records to show all records of events except *Other* events by completing the following steps:

   a. Click in the first entry in the *Event* field.

   b. Click the Filter button.

   c. Point to the *Text Filters* option in the drop-down list box and then click *Does Not Equal* at the values list.

   d. At the Custom Filter dialog box, type Other and then click OK.

7. Further refine the filter by completing the following steps:

   a. Click in the first entry in the *EmployeeID* field.

   b. Click the Filter button.

   c. At the filter drop-down list, click the *(Select All)* check box to remove all of the check marks from the list options.

   d. Click the *03* check box to insert a check mark.

   e. Click OK.

8. Print the filtered report by pressing Ctrl + P and then clicking OK at the Print dialog box.

9. Save and then close the BanquetReport report.

Filtering by Selection

Click in a field in an object and then click the Selection button in the Sort & Filter group on the Home tab and a drop-down list displays with options for filtering on the data in the field. For example, click in a field containing the city name *Fort Myers* and then click the Selection button and a drop-down list displays as shown in Figure 7.2. Click one of the options at the drop-down list to filter records.

Specific data can be selected in an object and then filtered by the selected data. For example, in Activity 1c, the word *peppers* will be selected in the entry *Green peppers* and then records will be filtered containing the word *peppers*.

Filtering by Shortcut Menu

Right-click in a field entry and a shortcut menu displays with options to sort the text, display a values list, or filter on a specific value. For example, right-click in the field entry *Birthday* in the *Event* field and the shortcut menu displays, as shown in Figure 7.3. Click a sort option to sort text in the field in ascending or descending order, point to the *Text Filters* option to display a values list, or click one of the values filters at the bottom of the menu. The shortcut menu can also be displayed by selecting specific text within a field entry and then right-clicking the selection.

Figure 7.2 Selection Button Drop-Down List

Figure 7.3 Filtering Shortcut Menu

Right-click in a field entry to display a shortcut menu with sorting and filtering options.

ResDate ▾	ResFirstNar ▾	ResLastNar ▾	ResTelephon ▾	Event	EmployeeID ▾
6/9/2021	Joanne	Blair	(239) 555-7783	Birthday	03
6/17/2021	Jason	Haley	(239) 555-6641	Birthday	06
6/22/2021	Heidi	Thompson	(941) 555-3215	Birthday	01
6/30/2021	Kirsten	Simpson	(941) 555-4425	Birthday	02
6/16/2021	Aaron	Williams	(239) 555-3821	Bar mitzvah	04
6/29/2021	Robin	Gehring	(239) 555-0126	Bar n	
6/10/2021	Tim	Drysdale	(941) 555-0098	Bat n	
6/8/2021	Bridget	Kohn	(239) 551-1299	Other	
6/10/2021	Gabrielle	Johnson	(239) 555-1882	Other	
6/15/2021	Tristan	Strauss	(941) 555-7746	Other	
6/17/2021	Lillian	Krakosky	(239) 555-8890	Other	
6/29/2021	David	Fitzgerald	(941) 555-3792	Other	
6/1/2021	Terrance	Schaefer	(239) 555-6239	Wedd	
6/10/2021	Cliff	Osborne	(239) 555-7823	Wedd	
6/2/2021	David	Hooper	(941) 555-2338	Wedd	
6/23/2021	Anthony	Wiegand	(239) 555-7853	Wedd	
6/30/2021	Shane	Rozier	(239) 555-1033	Wedd	
6/1/2021	Andrea	Wyatt	(239) 555-4282	Wedd	
6/15/2021	Janis	Semala	(239) 555-0476	Wedding reception	06

Shortcut menu:
- Cut
- Copy
- Paste
- Sort A to Z
- Sort Z to A
- Clear filter from Event
- Text Filters ▸
- Equals "Bar mitzvah"
- Does Not Equal "Bar mitzvah"
- Contains "Bar mitzvah"
- Does Not Contain "Bar mitzvah"

Activity 1c Filtering Records by Selection

Part 3 of 4

1. With **7-Skyline** open, open the Inventory table.
2. Filter only those records with a supplier number of 6 by completing the following steps:
   a. Click in the first entry containing *6* in the *SupplierID* field.
   b. Click the Selection button in the Sort & Filter group on the Home tab and then click *Equals "6"* at the drop-down list.
   c. Print the filtered table by pressing Ctrl + P and then clicking OK at the Print dialog box.
   d. Click the Toggle Filter button in the Sort & Filter group.
3. Filter any records in the *Item* field containing the word *peppers* by completing the following steps:
   a. Click in an entry in the *Item* field containing the text *Green peppers*.
   b. Using the mouse, select the word *peppers*.
   c. Click the Selection button and then click *Contains "peppers"* at the drop-down list.
   d. Print the filtered table by pressing Ctrl + P and then clicking OK at the Print dialog box.
4. Close the Inventory table without saving the changes.

5. Open the BanquetReservations query.
6. Filter the records so that all but those containing *Birthday* in the *Event* field display by completing the following steps:
   a. Right-click in the first *Birthday* entry in the *Event* field.
   b. Click *Does Not Equal "Birthday"* at the shortcut menu.

c. Print the filtered query.
   d. Click the Toggle Filter button.
7. Filter the records so that only those containing the word *mitzvah* in the *Event* field display by completing the following steps:
   a. Click in an entry in the *Event* field containing the entry *Bar mitzvah*.
   b. Using the mouse, select the word *mitzvah*.
   c. Right-click in the selected word and then click *Contains "mitzvah"* at the shortcut menu.
   d. Print the filtered query.
8. Close the BanquetReservations query without saving the changes.

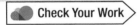

Using the *Filter By Form* Option

Advanced

Quick Steps

Use *Filter By Form* Option
1. Click Advanced button.
2. Click *Filter By Form*.
3. Click in empty field below column to filter.
4. Click arrow.
5. Click item to filter.

The Advanced button in the Sort & Filter group on the Home tab contains additional options for filtering records, including *Filter By Form*. Click this option and a blank record displays in a Filter by Form window in the work area. In the Filter by Form window, the Look for tab and the Or tab display at the bottom of the form. The Look for tab is active by default and tells Access to look for whatever data is inserted in a field. Click in the empty field below the column and an arrow displays at the right side of the field. Click the arrow and then click the item by which to filter. Click the Toggle Filter button to display the desired records. Add an additional value to a filter by clicking the Or tab at the bottom of the form.

1. With **7-Skyline** open, open the Banquets table.
2. Filter records by a specific employee ID number by completing the following steps:
   a. Click the Advanced button in the Sort & Filter group on the Home tab and then click *Filter By Form* at the drop-down list.

   b. At the Filter by Form window, click in the empty field below the *EmployeeID* column heading.
   c. Click the arrow at the right side of the field and then click *03* at the drop-down list.
   d. Click the Toggle Filter button in the Sort & Filter group.
3. Print the filtered table by completing the following steps:
   a. Click the File tab, click the *Print* option, and then click the *Print Preview* option.
   b. Change the orientation to landscape and the left and right margins to 0.5 inch.
   c. Click the Print button and then click OK at the Print dialog box.
   d. Click the Close Print Preview button.
4. Close the Banquets table without saving the changes.
5. Open the Inventory table.
6. Filter records by the supplier number 2 or 7 by completing the following steps:
   a. Click the Advanced button and then click *Filter By Form* at the drop-down list.
   b. At the Filter by Form window, click in the empty field below the *SupplierID* column heading.
   c. Click the arrow at the right side of the field and then click *2* at the drop-down list.
   d. Click the Or tab at the bottom of the form.
   e. If necessary, click in the empty field below the *SupplierID* column heading.
   f. Click the arrow at the right side of the field and then click *7* at the drop-down list.
   g. Click the Toggle Filter button.

   h. Print the filtered table.
   i. Click the Toggle Filter button to redisplay all records in the table.
   j. Click the Advanced button and then click *Clear All Filters* at the drop-down list.
7. Close the Inventory table without saving the changes.

> Check Your Work

<table>
<tr>
<td>Activity 2</td>
<td>View Object Dependencies, Manage a Database, and Save a Database in a Different File Format</td>
<td>4 Parts</td>
</tr>
</table>

You will view object dependencies in the Skyline database, compact and repair the database, encrypt it with a password, view and customize database properties, save an object in the database as a PDF file, save the database in a previous version of Access, and back up the database.

Tutorial

Viewing Object
Dependencies

Quick Steps

**View Object
Dependencies**
1. Open database.
2. Click object in
   Navigation pane.
3. Click Database Tools
   tab.
4. Click Object
   Dependencies
   button.

Object
Dependencies

Viewing Object Dependencies

The structure of a database is comprised of table, query, form, and report objects. Tables are related to other tables by the relationships that have been created. Queries, forms, and reports draw the source data from the records in the tables to which they have been associated, and forms and reports can include subforms and subreports, which further expand the associations between objects. A database with a large number of interdependent objects is more complex to work with than a simpler database. Viewing a list of the objects within a database and viewing the dependencies between objects can be beneficial to ensure an object is not deleted or otherwise modified, causing an unforeseen effect on another object.

View the structure of a database—including tables, queries, forms, and reports, as well as relationships—at the Object Dependencies task pane. Display this task pane by opening the database, clicking an object in the Navigation pane, clicking the Database Tools tab, and then clicking the Object Dependencies button in the Relationships group. The Object Dependencies task pane, shown in Figure 7.4, displays the objects in the Skyline database that depend on the Banquets table.

Figure 7.4 Object Dependencies Task Pane

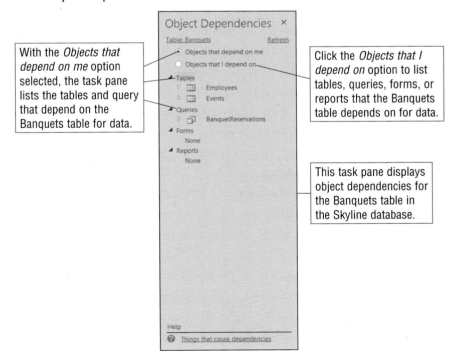

With the *Objects that depend on me* option selected, the task pane lists the tables and query that depend on the Banquets table for data.

Click the *Objects that I depend on* option to list tables, queries, forms, or reports that the Banquets table depends on for data.

This task pane displays object dependencies for the Banquets table in the Skyline database.

By default, *Objects that depend on me* is selected in the Object Dependencies task pane and the list box displays the names of the objects for which the selected object is the source. Next to each object in the task pane list box is an expand button (a right-pointing, white triangle). Clicking the expand button next to an object shows the other objects that depend on it. For example, if a query is based on the Banquets and Events tables and the query is used to generate a report, clicking the expand button next to the query name will show the report name. Clicking an object name in the Object Dependencies task pane opens the object in Design view.

Activity 2a Viewing Object Dependencies

Part 1 of 4

1. With **7-Skyline** open, display the structure of the database by completing the following steps:
   a. Click *Banquets* in the Tables group in the Navigation pane.
   b. Click the Database Tools tab and then click the Object Dependencies button in the Relationships group. (This displays the Object Dependencies task pane. By default, *Objects that depend on me* is selected and the task pane lists the names of the objects for which the Banquets table is the source.)

   c. Click the expand button (the right-pointing, white triangle that turns pink when you hover your mouse pointer over it) to the left of *Employees* in the *Tables* section. (This displays all of the objects that depend on the Employees table.)
   d. Click the *Objects that I depend on* option near the top of the Object Dependencies task pane.

   e. Click *Events* in the Tables group in the Navigation pane. (Make sure to click *Events* in the Navigation pane and not the Object Dependencies task pane.)
   f. Click the <u>Refresh</u> hyperlink in the upper right corner of the Object Dependencies task pane.
   g. Click the *Objects that depend on me* option near the top of the Object Dependencies task pane.
2. Close the Object Dependencies task pane.

Using Options at the Info Backstage Area

The Info backstage area contains options for compacting and repairing a database, encrypting a database with a password, and viewing and customizing database properties. Display the Info backstage area, shown in Figure 7.5, by opening a database and then clicking the File tab.

Compacting and Repairing a Database

To optimize the performance of a database, compact and repair it on a regular basis. When working in a database on an ongoing basis, data in it can become fragmented, causing the amount of space the database takes on the storage medium or in the folder to be larger than necessary. To compact and repair a database, open the database, click the File tab and then click the Compact & Repair Database button or click the Compact and Repair Database button in the Tools group on the Database Tools tab.

A database can be compacted and repaired each time it is closed. To do this, click the File tab and then click *Options*. At the Access Options dialog box, click the *Current Database* option in the left panel. Click the *Compact on Close* check box to insert a check mark and then click OK to close the dialog box. Before compacting and repairing a database in a multi-user environment, make sure that no other user has the database open.

Figure 7.5 Info Backstage Area

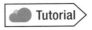

Tutorial

Encrypting a
Database with a
Password

 Encrypt with
Password

 Decrypt
Database

Quick Steps

**Open Database in
Exclusive Mode**
1. Display Open dialog
   box.
2. Click database.
3. Click Open button
   arrow.
4. Click *Open Exclusive*.

**Encrypt Database
with Password**
1. Open database in
   Exclusive mode.
2. Click File tab.
3. Click Encrypt with
   Password button.
4. Type password,
   press Tab key, and
   type password again.
5. Click OK.

💡 **Hint** When
encrypting a database
with a password,
use a password that
combines uppercase
and lowercase letters,
numbers, and symbols.

Encrypting a Database with a Password

To prevent unauthorized access to a database, encrypt the database with a password to ensure that it can be opened only by someone who knows the password. Be careful when encrypting a database with a password because if the password is lost, the database will not open.

To encrypt a database with a password, the database must be opened in Exclusive mode. To do this, display the Open dialog box, navigate to the folder containing the database, and then click the database to select it. Click the Open button arrow (in the lower right corner of the dialog box) and then click *Open Exclusive* at the drop-down list. When the database opens, click the File tab and then click the Encrypt with Password button at the Info backstage area. This displays the Set Database Password dialog box, as shown in Figure 7.6. At this dialog box, type a password in the *Password* text box, press the Tab key, and then type the password again. The typed text will display as asterisks. Click OK to close the Set Database Password dialog box.

To remove a password from a database, open the database in Exclusive mode, click the File tab, and then click the Decrypt Database button. At the Unset Database Password dialog box, type the password and then click OK.

Figure 7.6 Set Database Password Dialog Box

Type a password in
the *Password* text box.

Retype the same
password in the
Verify text box.

Activity 2b Compacting and Repairing a Database and Encrypting with a Password   Part 2 of 4

1. With **7-Skyline** open, compact and repair the database by completing the following steps:
   a. Click the File tab. (This displays the Info backstage area.)
   b. Click the Compact & Repair Database button.
2. Close **7-Skyline**.
3. Open the database in Exclusive mode by completing the following steps:
   a. Display the Open dialog box and make AL1C7 the active folder.
   b. Click **7-Skyline** in the Content pane to select it.

c. Click the Open button arrow (in the lower right corner of the dialog box) and then click *Open Exclusive* at the drop-down list.

4. Encrypt the database with a password by completing the following steps:
   a. Click the File tab.
   b. At the Info backstage area, click the Encrypt with Password button.
   c. At the Set Database Password dialog box, type your first and last names in all lowercase letters with no space, press the Tab key, and then type your first and last names again in lowercase letters.
   d. Click OK to close the dialog box.
   e. If a message displays with information about encrypting with a block cipher, click OK.

5. Close **7-Skyline**.
6. Display the Open dialog box with AL1C7 the active folder and then open **7-Skyline** in Exclusive mode.
7. At the Password Required dialog box, type your password and then click OK.
8. Remove the password by completing the following steps:
   a. Click the File tab.
   b. Click the Decrypt Database button.
   c. At the Unset Database Password dialog box, type your first and last names in lowercase letters and then press the Enter key.

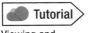

Viewing and Customizing Database Properties

Each database has associated properties, such as the type of file; its location; and when it was created, accessed, and modified. These properties can be viewed and modified at the Properties dialog box. To view properties for the currently open database, click the File tab to display the Info backstage area and then click the <u>View and edit database properties</u> hyperlink at the right side of the backstage area. This displays the Properties dialog box, similar to what is shown in Figure 7.7.

The Properties dialog box for an open database contains tabs with information about the database. With the General tab selected, the dialog box provides information about the database type, size, and location. Click the Summary tab to see fields such as *Title*, *Subject*, *Author*, *Category*, *Keywords*, and *Comments*. Some fields contain data and others are blank. Text can be inserted, edited, or deleted in the fields. Move the insertion point to a field by clicking in the field or by pressing the Tab key until the insertion point is positioned in the field.

Figure 7.7 Properties Dialog Box

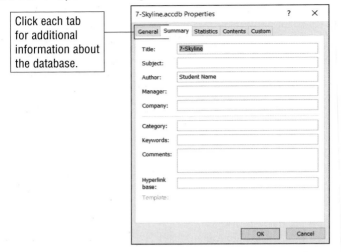

Click each tab for additional information about the database.

7-Skyline.accdb Properties

General | Summary | Statistics | Contents | Custom

Title: 7-Skyline
Subject:
Author: Student Name
Manager:
Company:

Category:
Keywords:
Comments:

Hyperlink base:
Template:

OK   Cancel

Click the Statistics tab to view information such as the dates the database was created, modified, accessed, and printed. With the Content tab selected, the *Document contents* section lists the objects in the database, including tables, queries, forms, reports, macros, and modules.

Use options at the Properties dialog box with the Custom tab selected to add custom properties to the database. For example, a property can be added to include the date the database was completed, information on the department in which the database was created, and much more. The list box below the *Name* option box displays the predesigned properties provided by Access. Choose a predesigned property from this list box or create a custom property.

To choose a predesigned property, click a predesigned property in the list box, specify what type of property it is (such as value, date, number, yes/no), and then type a value. For example, to specify the department in which the database was created, click *Department* in the list box, make sure the *Type* displays as *Text*, click in the *Value* text box, and then type the name of the department.

Activity 2c Viewing and Customizing Database Properties   Part 3 of 4

1. With **7-Skyline** open, click the File tab and then click the <u>View and edit database properties</u> hyperlink at the right side of the backstage area.

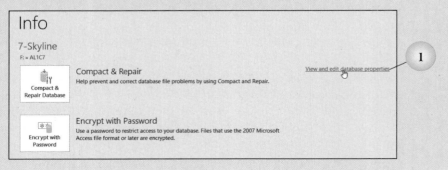

Info

7-Skyline
F: » AL1C7

Compact & Repair
Help prevent and correct database file problems by using Compact and Repair.

Compact & Repair Database

Encrypt with Password
Use a password to restrict access to your database. Files that use the 2007 Microsoft Access file format or later are encrypted.

Encrypt with Password

View and edit database properties   1

2. At the 7-Skyline.accdb Properties dialog box, click the General tab and then read the information in the dialog box.
3. Click the Summary tab and then type the following text in the specified text boxes:

Title	7-Skyline database
Subject	Restaurant and banquet facilities
Author	(*Type your first and last names.*)
Category	restaurant
Keywords	restaurant, banquet, event, Fort Myers
Comments	This database contains information on Skyline Restaurant employees, banquets, inventory, and orders.

4. Click the Statistics tab and read the information in the dialog box.
5. Click the Contents tab and notice that the *Document contents* section of the dialog box displays the objects in the database.
6. Click the Custom tab and then create custom properties by completing the following steps:
   a. Click the *Date completed* option in the *Name* list box.
   b. Click the *Type* option box arrow and then click *Date* at the drop-down list.
   c. Click in the *Value* text box and then type the current date in this format: *dd/mm/yyyy*.
   d. Click the Add button.
   e. With the insertion point positioned in the *Name* text box, type Course.
   f. Click the *Type* option box arrow and then click *Text* at the drop-down list.
   g. Click in the *Value* text box, type your current course number, and then press the Enter key.
   h. Click OK to close the dialog box.
7. Click the Back button to return to the database.

 Check Your Work

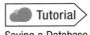
Saving a Database and Database Object in Different Formats

Access 2003 and earlier versions save a database with a different file extension. To save an Access database in Access 2003 or earlier, open the database, click the File tab, and then click the *Save As* option. This displays the Save As backstage area, as shown in Figure 7.8. Click the *Access 2002-2003 Database* option in the *Save Database As* section and then click the Save As button at the bottom of the *Save Database As* section. This displays the Save As dialog box with the *Save as type* option set to *Microsoft Access Database (2002-2003)*. At this dialog box, click the Save button.

With an object open in a database, clicking the *Save Object As* option in the *File Types* section of the Save As backstage area displays options for saving the object. Click the *Save Object As* option to save the selected object in the database or click the *PDF or XPS* option to save the object as a PDF or XPS file. The letters *PDF* stand for *portable document format*, a file format developed by Adobe Systems that captures all of the elements of a file as an electronic image. An XPS file is a Microsoft file format for publishing content in an easily viewable format. The letters *XPS* stand for *XML paper specification* and the letters *XML* stand for *extensible markup language*, which is a set of rules for encoding files electronically.

Saving an Object as a PDF or XPS File

To save an object as a PDF or XPS file, open the object, click the File tab, and then click the *Save As* option. At the Save As backstage area, click the *Save Object As* option in the *File Types* section, click the *PDF or XPS* option in the *Save the current database object* section, and then click the Save As button. This displays the Publish as PDF or XPS dialog box with the *Save as type* option set at *PDF*. Click the Publish button and the object is saved as a PDF file. To specify that the object should open in Adobe Acrobat Reader, click the *Open file after publishing* check box to insert a check box. With this check box active, the object will open in Adobe Acrobat Reader when the Publish button is clicked.

Figure 7.8 Save As Backstage Area with *Save Database As* Option Selected

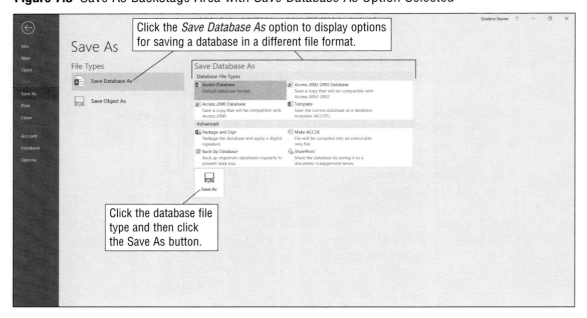

A PDF file can be opened in Adobe Acrobat Reader, Microsoft Edge, or Microsoft Word. (A PDF file may also open in other available web browsers such as Google Chrome.) An XPS file can be opened in Internet Explorer or XPS Viewer. One method for opening a PDF or XPS file is to open File Explorer, navigate to the folder containing the file, right-click on the file, and then point to *Open with*. This displays a side menu with the programs that will open the file.

Tutorial

Backing Up a Database

Backing Up a Database

Databases often contain important company information, and loss of this information can cause major problems. Backing up a database is important to minimize the chances of losing critical company data and is especially important when several people update and manage a database.

To back up a database, open the database, click the File tab, and then click the *Save As* option. At the Save As backstage area, click the *Back Up Database* option in the *Advanced* section and then click the Save As button. This displays the Save As dialog box with a default database file name, which is the original database name followed by the current date, in the *File name* text box. Click the Save button to save the backup database while keeping the original database open.

Quick Steps

Back Up Database
1. Click File tab.
2. Click *Save As* option.
3. Click *Back Up Database* option.
4. Click Save As button.
5. Click Save button.

Activity 2d Saving an Object as a PDF File, Saving a Database in a Previous Version, and Backing Up a Database
Part 4 of 4

1. With **7-Skyline** open, save the Orders table as a PDF file by completing the following steps:
   a. Open the Orders table.
   b. Click the File tab and then click the *Save As* option.
   c. At the Save As backstage area, click the *Save Object As* option in the *File Types* section.
   d. Click the *PDF or XPS* option in the *Save the current database object* section.
   e. Click the Save As button.

   f. At the Publish as PDF or XPS dialog box, make sure your AL1C7 folder is active and then click the *Open file after publishing* check box to insert a check mark. (Skip this step if the check box already contains a check mark.)
   g. Click the Publish button.

h. When the Orders table opens in Adobe Acrobat Reader, scroll through the file and then close the file by clicking the Close button in the upper right corner of the screen.

2. Close the Orders table.

3. Save the database in a previous version of Access by completing the following steps:
   a. Click the File tab and then click the *Save As* option.
   b. At the Save As backstage area, click the *Access 2002-2003 Database* option in the *Save Database As* section.
   c. Click the Save As button.

d. At the Save As dialog box, make sure your AL1C7 folder is active, type 7-Skyline-2002-2003format, and then click the Save button. (This saves the database with the file extension *.mdb*.)

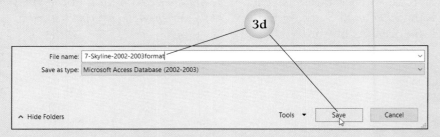

e. Notice that the Title bar displays the database file name *7-Skyline-2002-2003format : Database (Access 2002 - 2003 file format)*.

4. Close the database.

5. Open **7-Skyline**.

6. Create a backup of the database by completing the following steps:
   a. Click the File tab and then click the *Save As* option.
   b. At the Save As backstage area, click the *Back Up Database* option in the *Advanced* section and then click the Save As button.
   c. At the Save As dialog box, notice that the database name in the *File name* text box displays the original file name followed by the current date (year, month, day).
   d. Make sure your AL1C7 folder is active and then click the Save button. (This saves the backup copy of the database to your folder and the original database remains open.)

7. Close **7-Skyline**.

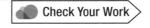

Chapter Summary

- A set of restrictions called a filter can be put on records in a table or form. A filter is used to select specific field values.
- Filter records with the Filter button in the Sort & Filter group on the Home tab.
- Click the Toggle Filter button in the Sort & Filter group to switch back and forth between data and filtered data.
- Remove a filter by clicking the Filter button in the Sort & Filter group and then clicking the *Clear filter from xxx* (where *xxx* is the name of the field).
- Another method for removing a filter is to click the Advanced button in the Sort & Filter group and then click *Clear All Filters*.
- Display a list of filter values by clicking the Filter button and then pointing to *Text Filters* (if the data is text), *Number Filters* (if the data is numbers), or *Date Filters* (if the data is dates).
- Filter by selection by clicking the Selection button in the Sort & Filter group.
- Right-click in a field entry to display a shortcut menu with filtering options.
- Filter by form by clicking the Advanced button in the Sort & Filter group and then clicking *Filter By Form* at the drop-down list. This displays a blank record with two tabs: Look for and Or.
- View the structure of a database and relationships between objects at the Object Dependencies task pane. Display this task pane by clicking the Database Tools tab and then clicking the Object Dependencies button in the Relationships group.
- Click the Compact & Repair Database button at the Info backstage area or in the Tools group on the Database Tools tab to optimize database performance.
- To prevent unauthorized access to a database, encrypt the database with a password. To encrypt a database, the database must be opened in Exclusive mode using the Open button drop-down list in the Open dialog box. While in Exclusive mode, encrypt a database with a password using the Encrypt with Password button at the Info backstage area.
- To view properties for the current database, click the <u>View and edit database properties</u> hyperlink at the Info backstage area. The Properties dialog box displays with a number of tabs containing information about the database.
- Save a database in Access 2003 or earlier using options in the *Save Database As* section of the Save As backstage area.
- To save a database object as a PDF or XPS file, display the Save As backstage area, click the *Save Object As* option, click the *PDF or XPS* option, and then click the Save As button.
- Back up a database to maintain critical data. Back up a database with the *Back Up Database* option at the Save As backstage area.

Commands Review

FEATURE	RIBBON TAB, GROUP/OPTION	BUTTON, OPTION
filter	Home, Sort & Filter	
filter by form	Home, Sort & Filter	, *Filter By Form*
filter by selection	Home, Sort & Filter	
Info backstage area	File, *Info*	
Object Dependencies task pane	Database Tools, Relationships	
remove filter	Home, Sort & Filter	, *Clear filter from xxx* OR , *Clear All Filters*
toggle filter	Home, Sort & Filter	

Microsoft® Access®

Exporting and Importing Data

Performance Objectives

Upon successful completion of Chapter 8, you will be able to:

1. Export Access data to Excel
2. Export Access data to Word
3. Merge Access data with a Word document
4. Export an Access object to a PDF or XPS file
5. Import data to a new table
6. Link data to a new table
7. Use the Office Clipboard

Microsoft Office is a suite of applications that allows for easy data exchange. In this chapter, you will learn how to export data from Access to Excel and Word, merge Access data with a Word document, export an Access object to a PDF or XPS file, import and link Excel data to a new table, and copy and paste data between applications and programs.

 Data Files

Before beginning chapter work, copy the AL1C8 folder to your storage medium and then make AL1C8 the active folder.

The online course includes additional training and assessment resources.

Activity 1 Export Data to Excel and Export and Merge Data to Word

5 Parts

You will export a table and query to Excel, export a table and report to Word, and export an Access object to a PDF file. You will also merge data in an Access table and query with a Word document.

Exporting Data

One of the advantages of using the Microsoft Office suite is the ability to exchange data between programs. Access, like other programs in the suite, offers a feature to export data from Access into Excel and/or Word. The Export group on the External Data tab contains buttons for exporting a table, query, form, or report to other programs, such as Excel and Word.

Tutorial

Exporting Access
Data to Excel

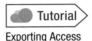
Excel

Hint Store data in Access and analyze it using Excel.

Exporting Access Data to Excel

Use the Excel button in the Export group on the External Data tab to export data in a table, query, or form to an Excel workbook. Click the object containing the data to be exported to Excel, click the External Data tab, and then click the Excel button in the Export group. The Export - Excel Spreadsheet dialog box displays, as shown in Figure 8.1.

At the dialog box, Access uses the name of the object as the Excel workbook name. This can be changed by selecting the current name and then typing a new name. The file format also can be changed with the *File format* option. Click the

Quick Steps

Export Access Data to Excel
1. Click table, query, or form.
2. Click External Data tab.
3. Click Excel button in Export group.
4. Make changes at Export - Excel Spreadsheet dialog box.
5. Click OK.

Insert a check mark in this check box to export all object formatting and layout.

Insert a check mark in this check box to open the file in the destination program.

Figure 8.1 Export - Excel Spreadsheet Dialog Box

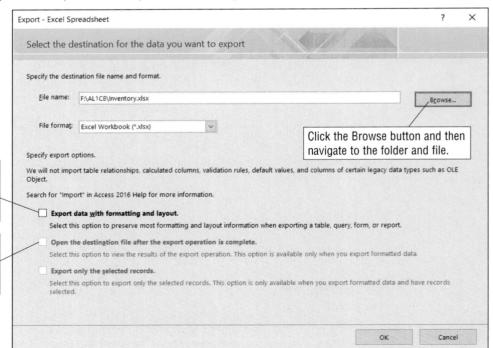

Hint Data exported from Access to Excel is saved as an Excel workbook with the .xlsx file extension.

Hint You can export only one database object at a time.

Export data with formatting and layout check box to insert a check mark. This exports all data formatting to the Excel workbook. To open Excel with the exported data, click the *Open the destination file after the export operation is complete* option to insert a check mark.

When all changes have been made, click OK. This opens Excel with the data in a workbook. Make changes to the workbook and then save, print, and close the workbook. When Excel is closed, Access displays with a dialog box, asking if the export step should be saved. At this dialog box, insert a check mark in the *Save export steps* check box to save the export steps or leave the check box blank and then click the Close button.

Activity 1a Exporting a Table and Query to Excel   Part 1 of 5

1. Open **8-Hilltop** from your AL1C8 folder and enable the content.
2. Save the Inventory table as an Excel workbook by completing the following steps:
   a. Click *Inventory* in the Tables group in the Navigation pane.
   b. Click the External Data tab and then click the Excel button in the Export group.
   c. At the Export - Excel Spreadsheet dialog box, click the Browse button.
   d. At the File Save dialog box, navigate to your AL1C8 folder and then click the Save button.
   e. Click the *Export data with formatting and layout* option to insert a check mark in the check box.
   f. Click the *Open the destination file after the export operation is complete* option to insert a check mark in the check box.
   g. Click OK.

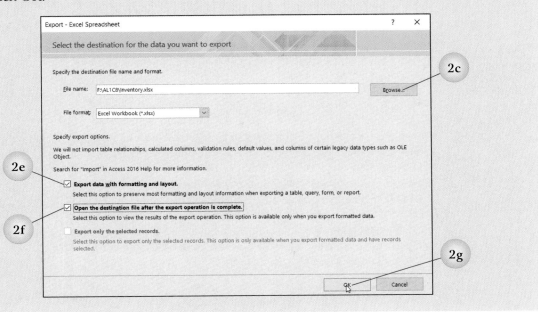

h. When the data displays on the screen in Excel as a worksheet, select the range A2:A11 and then click the Center button in the Alignment group on the Home tab.

i. Select the range D2:F11 and then click the Center button.

j. Click the Save button on the Quick Access Toolbar.

k. Print the worksheet by pressing Ctrl + P and then clicking the Print button at the Print backstage area.

l. Close the worksheet and then close Excel.

3. In Access, click the Close button to close the dialog box.

4. Design a query that extracts records from three tables with the following specifications:

a. Add the Invoices, Customers, and Rates tables to the query window.

b. Insert the *BillingDate* field from the Invoices table field list box in the first field in the *Field* row.

c. Insert the *Customer* field from the Customers table field list box in the second field in the *Field* row.

d. Insert the *BillingHours* field from the Invoices table field list box in the third field in the *Field* row.

e. Insert the *Rate* field from the Rates table field list box in the fourth field in the *Field* row.

f. Click in the fifth field in the *Field* row, type Total: [BillingHours]*[Rate], and then press the Enter key.

g. Run the query.

h. If necessary, adjust the column width of the *Customer* field to display all records.

i. Save the query, typing CustomerInvoices as the query name.

j. Close the query.

5. Export the CustomerInvoices query to Excel by completing the following steps:

a. Click *CustomerInvoices* in the Queries group in the Navigation pane.

b. Click the External Data tab and then click the Excel button.

c. At the Export - Excel Spreadsheet dialog box, click the *Export data with formatting and layout* option to insert a check mark in the check box.

d. Click the *Open the destination file after the export operation is complete* option to insert a check mark in the check box.

e. Click OK.

f. When the data displays on the screen in Excel as a worksheet, select the range C2:C31 and then click the Center button in the Alignment group on the Home tab.

g. Click the Save button on the Quick Access Toolbar.

h. Print the worksheet by pressing Ctrl + P and then clicking the Print button at the Print backstage area.

i. Close the worksheet and then close Excel.

6. In Access, click the Close button to close the dialog box.

Exporting Access Data to Word

Tutorial

Exporting Access Data to Word

 More

Export data from Access to Word in a similar manner as exporting to Excel. To export data to Word, click the object in the Navigation pane, click the External Data tab, click the More button in the Export group, and then click *Word* at the drop-down list. At the Export - RTF File dialog box, make changes and then click OK. Word automatically opens and the data displays in a Word document that is saved automatically with the same name as the database object. The difference is that the file extension *.rtf* is added to the name. An RTF file is saved in rich-text format, which preserves formatting such as fonts and styles. A document saved with the .rtf extension can be exported in Word and other Windows word processing or desktop publishing programs.

Quick Steps

Export Data to Word
1. Click object in Navigation pane.
2. Click External Data tab.
3. Click More button in Export group.
4. Click *Word*.
5. Make changes at Export - RTF File dialog box.
6. Click OK.

Activity 1b Exporting a Table and Report to Word   Part 2 of 5

1. With **8-Hilltop** open, click *Invoices* in the Tables group in the Navigation pane.
2. Click the External Data tab, click the More button in the Export group, and then click *Word* at the drop-down list.

3. At the Export - RTF File dialog box, click the Browse button.
4. At the File Save dialog box, make sure your AL1C8 folder is active and then click the Save button.
5. At the Export - RTF File dialog box, click the *Open the destination file after the export operation is complete* check box to insert a check mark.

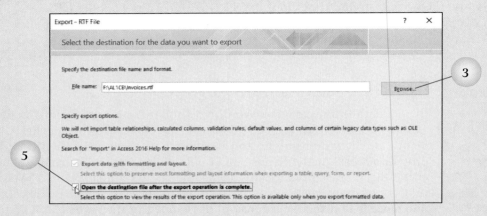

6. Click OK.
7. With **Invoices** open in Word, print the file by pressing Ctrl + P and then clicking the Print button at the Print backstage area.
8. Close **Invoices** and then close Word.
9. In Access, click the Close button to close the dialog box.
10. Create a report with the Report Wizard by completing the following steps:
    a. Click the Create tab and then click the Report Wizard button in the Reports group.
    b. At the first Report Wizard dialog box, insert the following fields in the *Selected Fields* list box:
        From the Customers table:
            Customer
        From the Equipment table:
            Equipment
        From the Invoices table:
            BillingDate
            BillingHours

    c. After inserting the fields, click the Next button.
    d. At the second Report Wizard dialog box, make sure *by Customers* is selected in the list box at the left and then click the Next button.
    e. At the third Report Wizard dialog box, click the Next button.
    f. At the fourth Report Wizard dialog box, click the Next button.
    g. At the fifth Report Wizard dialog box, click *Block* in the *Layout* section and then click the Next button.
    h. At the sixth and final Report Wizard dialog box, select the current name in the *What title do you want for your report?* text box, type CustomerReport, and then click the Finish button.
    i. When the report displays in Print Preview, click the Print button at the left of the Print Preview tab and then click OK at the Print dialog box.
    j. Save and then close the CustomerReport report.

11. Export the CustomerReport report to Word by completing the following steps:
   a. Click *CustomerReport* in the Reports group in the Navigation pane.
   b. Click the External Data tab, click the More button, and then click *Word* at the drop-down list.
   c. At the Export - RTF File dialog box, click the *Open the destination file after the export operation is complete* option to insert a check mark in the check box and then click OK.
   d. When the data displays on the screen in Word, print the document by pressing Ctrl + P and then clicking the Print button at the Print backstage area.
   e. Save and then close the CustomerReport document.
   f. Close Word.
12. In Access, click the Close button to close the dialog box.

Check Your Work

Tutorial

Merging Access Data with a Word Document

Merging Access Data with a Word Document

Data from an Access table or query can be merged with a Word document. When merging data, the data in the Access table is considered the data source and the Word document is considered the main document. When the merge is completed, the merged document displays in Word.

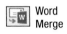

Word Merge

To merge data in a table, click the table in the Navigation pane, click the External Data tab, and then click the Word Merge button. When merging Access data, either type the text in the main document or merge Access data with an existing Word document.

Activity 1c Merging Access Table Data with a Word Document   Part 3 of 5

1. With **8-Hilltop** open, click *Customers* in the Tables group in the Navigation pane.
2. Click the External Data tab.
3. Click the Word Merge button in the Export group.

4. At the Microsoft Word Mail Merge Wizard dialog box, make sure *Link your data to an existing Microsoft Word document* is selected and then click OK.
5. At the Select Microsoft Word Document dialog box, make sure your AL1C8 folder is active and then double-click the document named **8-HilltopLetter**.
6. Click the Word button on the taskbar.
7. Click the Maximize button in the *8-HilltopLetter* Title bar and then close the Mail Merge task pane.

8. Press the Down Arrow key six times (not the Enter key) and then type the current date.
9. Press the Down Arrow key four times and then insert fields for merging from the Customers table by completing the following steps:
   a. If necesssary, click the Mailings tab.
   b. Click the Insert Merge Field button arrow in the Write & Insert Fields group and then click *Customer* in the drop-down list. (This inserts the «Customer» field in the document.)

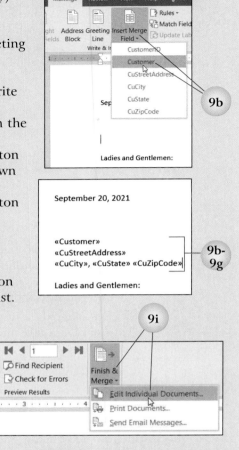

   c. Press the Enter key, click the Insert Merge Field button arrow, and then click *CuStreetAddress* in the drop-down list.
   d. Press the Enter key, click the Insert Merge Field button arrow, and then click *CuCity* in the drop-down list.
   e. Type a comma (,) and then press the spacebar.
   f. Click the Insert Merge Field button arrow and then click *CuState* in the drop-down list.
   g. Press the spacebar, click the Insert Merge Field button arrow, and then click *CuZipCode* in the drop-down list.
   h. Replace the letters *XX* at the bottom of the letter with your initials.
   i. Click the Finish & Merge button in the Finish group and then click *Edit Individual Documents* in the drop-down list.
   j. At the Merge to New Document dialog box, make sure *All* is selected and then click OK.
   k. When the merge is completed, save the new document and name it **8-HilltopLtrs** in your AL1C8 folder.
10. Print just the first two pages (two letters) of **8-HilltopLtrs**.
11. Close **8-HilltopLtrs** and then close **8-HilltopLetter** without saving the changes.
12. Close Word.
13. Close **8-Hilltop**.

Check Your Work

A query in a database can be used to merge with a Word document. In Activity 1c, a table was merged with an existing Word document. A table or query also can be merged and then the Word document typed.

In Activity 1c, a number of merge fields were inserted for the inside address of a letter. Another method for inserting fields for the inside address is to insert the «AddressBlock» field, which inserts all of the fields required for the inside address. The «AddressBlock» field is an example of a composite field, which groups a number of fields together. Insert the «AddressBlock» composite field by clicking the Address Block button in the Write & Insert Fields group on the Mailings tab. Clicking the button displays the Insert Address Block dialog box with a preview of how the fields will be inserted in the document to create the inside address. The dialog box also contains buttons and options for customizing the fields. Click OK and the «AddressBlock» field is inserted in the document.

In Activity 1c, the «AddressBlock» composite field could not be used because the *Customer* field was not recognized by Word as a field for the inside address. In Activity 1d, a query will be created that contains the *FirstName* and *LastName* fields, which Word recognizes and uses for the «AddressBlock» composite field.

Activity 1d Performing a Query and then Merging with a Word Document   Part 4 of 5

1. Open **8-CopperState** from your AL1C8 folder and enable the content.
2. Perform a query with the Query Wizard and modify the query by completing the following steps:
   a. Click the Create tab and then click the Query Wizard button in the Queries group.
   b. At the New Query dialog box, make sure *Simple Query Wizard* is selected and then click OK.
   c. At the first Simple Query Wizard dialog box, click the *Tables/Queries* option box arrow and then click *Table: Clients*.
   d. Click the All Fields button to insert all of the fields in the *Selected Fields* list box.
   e. Click the Next button.
   f. At the second Simple Query Wizard dialog box, make the following changes:
      1) Select the current name in the *What title do you want for your query?* text box and then type ClientsPhoenix.
      2) Click the *Modify the query design* option.
      3) Click the Finish button.
   g. At the query window, click in the *City* field in the *Criteria* row, type Phoenix, and then press the Enter key.
   h. Click the Run button in the Results group. (Only clients living in Phoenix will display.)
   i. Save and then close the query.

3. Click *ClientsPhoenix* in the Queries group in the Navigation pane.
4. Click the External Data tab and then click the Word Merge button in the Export group.
5. At the Microsoft Word Mail Merge Wizard dialog box, click the *Create a new document and then link the data to it* option and then click OK.
6. Click the Word button on the taskbar.
7. Click the Maximize button in the Document1 Title bar and then close the Mail Merge task pane.

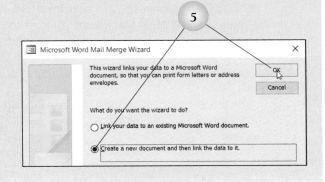

8. Complete the following steps to type text and insert the «AddressBlock» composite field in the blank Word document:

a. Click the Home tab and then click the *No Spacing* style in the Styles group.

b. Press the Enter key six times.

c. Type the current date.

d. Press the Enter key four times.

e. Click the Mailings tab.

f. Insert the «AddressBlock» composite field by clicking the Address Block button in the Write & Insert Fields group on the Mailings tab and then clicking OK at the Insert Address Block dialog box. (This inserts the «AddressBlock» composite field in the document.)

g. Press the Enter key two times and then type the salutation Ladies and Gentlemen:.

h. Press the Enter key two times and then type the following paragraphs of text (press the Enter key two times after typing the first paragraph):

> At the Grant Street West office of Copper State Insurance, we have hired two additional insurance representatives as well as one support staff member to ensure that we meet all your insurance needs. To accommodate the new staff, we have moved to a larger office just a few blocks away. Our new address is 3450 Grant Street West, Suite 110, Phoenix, AZ 85003. Our telephone number, (602) 555-6300, has remained the same.
>
> If you have any questions or concerns about your insurance policies or want to discuss adding or changing current coverage, please stop by or give us a call. We are committed to providing our clients with the most comprehensive automobile insurance coverage in the county.

i. Press the Enter key two times and then type the following complimentary close at the left margin (press the Enter key four times after typing *Sincerely,*):

> Sincerely,
>
>
>
> Lou Galloway
> Manager (Press the Enter key two times after typing *Manager*.)
>
> XX (Type your initials instead of XX.)
> 8-CSLtrs

j. Click the Finish & Merge button in the Finish group on the Mailings tab and then click *Edit Individual Documents* in the drop-down menu.

k. At the Merge to New Document dialog box, make sure *All* is selected, and then click OK.

l. When the merge is complete, save the new document in your AL1C8 folder and name it **8-CSLtrs**.

9. Print the first two pages (two letters) of **8-CSLtrs**.

10. Close **8-CSLtrs**.

11. Save the main document as **8-CSMainDoc** in your AL1C8 folder and then close the document.

12. Close Word.

 Check Your Work

Exporting an Access Object to a PDF or XPS File

With the PDF or XPS button in the Export group on the External Data tab, an Access object can be exported to a PDF or XPS file. As explained in Chapter 7, the letters *PDF* stand for *portable document format*, which is a file format that captures all of the elements of a file as an electronic image. The letters *XPS* stand for *XML paper specification* and the letters *XML* stand for *extensible markup language*, which is a set of rules for encoding files electronically. PDF and XPS files both have a fixed layout, so they can be shared or displayed for viewing without worry that content will be modified or formatting will be lost.

To export an Access object to a PDF or XPS file, click the object, click the External Data tab, and then click the PDF or XPS button in the Export group. This displays the Publish as PDF or XPS dialog box with the *PDF* option selected in the *Save as type* option box. To save the Access object in XPS file format, click the *Save as type* option box and then click *XPS Document* at the drop-down list. At the Save As dialog box, type a name in the *File name* text box and then click the Publish button.

To open a PDF or XPS file in a web browser, open the browser and then press Ctrl + O to display the Open dialog box. At the Open dialog box, change the *Files of type* to *All Files*, navigate to the folder containing the file, and then double-click the file.

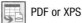
Activity 1e Exporting an Access Object to a PDF File

Part 5 of 5

1. With **8-CopperState** open, export the Coverage table to a PDF file by completing the following steps:
   a. Click *Coverage* in the Tables group in the Navigation pane.
   b. Click the External Data tab.
   c. Click the PDF or XPS button in the Export group.
   d. At the Publish as PDF or XPS dialog box, navigate to your AL1C8 folder and make sure the *Save as type* option box displays with *PDF*. (If not, click the option box and then click *PDF* at the drop-down list.)
   e. Click the *Open file after publishing* check box to insert a check mark and then click the Publish button.
   f. When the Coverage table data displays in Adobe Acrobat Reader, scroll through the file to see how it looks.
   g. Print the PDF file by clicking the Print button on the menu bar and then clicking the Print button at the Print dialog box.
   h. Close Adobe Acrobat Reader by clicking the Close button in the upper right corner of the window.
2. In Access, click the Close button to close the dialog box.

Importing and Linking Data to a New Table

In addition to exporting Access data to Excel or Word, data from other
applications can be imported into an Access table. For example, data from an
Excel worksheet can be imported to create a new table in a database. Data in the
original application is not connected to the data imported into an Access table.
If changes are made to data in the original application, those changes are not
reflected in the Access table. To connect the imported data with the data in the
original application, link the data.

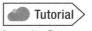

Importing Data to a New Table

New Data
Source

Quick Steps

Import Data into New Table
1. Click External Data tab.
2. Click New Data
   Source button.
3. Click location and
   application.
4. Click Browse button.
5. Double-click file name.
6. Click OK.
7. Make choices at each
   wizard dialog box.

Importing Data to a New Table

To import data, click the External Data tab, click the New Data Source button
in the Import & Link group, and then click a location and application from
which to retrieve data. At the Import dialog box that displays, click the Browse
button, double-click the file name, and then click OK. This activates the Import
Wizard and displays the first wizard dialog box. The appearance of the dialog box
varies depending on the file selected. Complete the steps of the Import Wizard,
specifying information such as the range of data, whether the first row contains
column headings, whether to store the data in a new table or existing table, the
primary key, and the name of the table.

Activity 2a Importing an Excel Worksheet to an Access Table   Part 1 of 2

1. With **8-CopperState** open, import an Excel
   worksheet into a new table in the database
   by completing the following steps:
   a. Click the External Data tab.
   b. Click the New Data Source button in the
      Import & Link group, point to the *From
      File* option at the-drop down menu, and
      then click the *Excel* option at the side
      menu.

c. At the Get External Data - Excel Spreadsheet dialog box, click the Browse button and then make your AL1C8 folder active.

d. Double-click *8-Policies* in the list box.

e. Click OK at the Get External Data - Excel Spreadsheet dialog box.

f. At the first Import Spreadsheet Wizard dialog box, make sure the *First Row Contains Column Headings* check box contains a check mark and then click the Next button.

g. At the second Import Spreadsheet Wizard dialog box, click the Next button.

h. At the third Import Spreadsheet Wizard dialog box, click the *Choose my own primary key* option (which inserts *PolicyID* in the option box to the right of the option) and then click the Next button.

i. At the fourth Import Spreadsheet Wizard dialog box, type Policies in the *Import to Table* text box and then click the Finish button.

j. At the Get External Data - Excel Spreadsheet dialog box, click the Close button.

2. Open the new Policies table in Datasheet view.

3. Print and then close the Policies table.

Check Your Work

Tutorial

Linking Data to a New Table

Linking Data to an Excel Worksheet

Imported data is not connected to the source program. If the data will only be used in Access, import it. However, to update the data in a program other than Access, link the data. Changes made to linked data in the source program file are reflected in the destination program file. For example, an Excel worksheet can be linked with an Access table and, when changes are made to the Excel worksheet, the changes are reflected in the Access table.

To link Excel data to a new table, click the External Data tab, click the New Data Source button in the Import & Link group, point to *From File* at the drop-down list, and then click the *Excel* option at the side menu. At the Get External Data - Excel Spreadsheet dialog box, click the Browse button, double-click the file name, click the *Link to a data source by creating a linked table* option, and then click OK. This activates the Link Wizard and displays the first wizard dialog box. Complete the steps of the Link Wizard, specifying the same basic information as the Import Wizard.

⏱ *Quick Steps*

Link Data to Excel Worksheet
1. Click External Data tab.
2. Click New Data Source button.
3. Point to *From File*.
4. Click *Excel*.
5. Click Browse button.
6. Double-click file name.
7. Click *Link to a data source by creating a linked table*.
8. Click OK.
9. Make choices at each wizard dialog box.

Activity 2b Linking an Excel Worksheet to an Access Table   Part 2 of 2

1. With **8-CopperState** open, click the External Data tab, click the New Data Source button in the Import & Link group, point to *From File* at the drop-down list, and then click *Excel* at the side menu.
2. At the Get External Data - Excel Spreadsheet dialog box, click the Browse button, make sure your AL1C8 folder is active, and then double-click **8-Policies**.
3. At the Get External Data - Excel Spreadsheet dialog box, click the *Link to the data source by creating a linked table* option and then click OK.

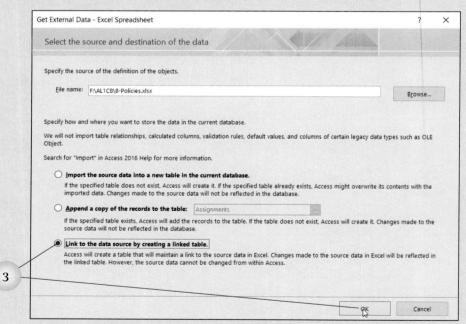

4. At the first Link Spreadsheet Wizard dialog box, make sure the *First Row Contains Column Headings* option contains a check mark and then click the Next button.
5. At the second Link Spreadsheet Wizard dialog box, type LinkedPolicies in the *Linked Table Name* text box and then click the Finish button.
6. At the message stating the linking is finished, click OK.
7. Open the new LinkedPolicies table in Datasheet view.
8. Close the LinkedPolicies table.
9. Open Excel, open the **8-Policies** workbook, click the Enable Editing button, if necessary, and then make the following changes:
   a. Change the amount *$745* in cell C3 to *$850*.
   b. Add the following information in the specified cells:

       A26: 190-C-28
       B26: 3120
       C26: 685
10. Save, print, and then close **8-Policies**.
11. Close Excel.
12. With Access as the active program and **8-CopperState** open, open the LinkedPolicies table. Notice the changes you just made in Excel are reflected in the table.
13. Close the LinkedPolicies table.
14. Close **8-CopperState**.

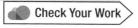
Check Your Work

Activity 3 Collect Data in Word and Paste It into an Access Table   1 Part

You will open a Word document containing Hilltop customer names and addresses and then copy the data and paste it into an Access table.

Tutorial

Using the Office Clipboard

Quick Steps

Display Clipboard Task Pane
Click Clipboard group task pane launcher.

Using the Office Clipboard

Use the Office Clipboard to collect and paste multiple items. Up to 24 different items can be collected and pasted in Access or other applications in the Office suite. To copy and paste multiple items, display the Clipboard task pane, shown in Figure 8.2, by clicking the Clipboard group task pane launcher on the Home tab.

Select the data or object to be copied and then click the Copy button in the Clipboard group on the Home tab. Continue selecting text or items and clicking the Copy button. To insert an item from the Clipboard task pane to a field in an Access table, make the destination field active and then click the button in the task pane representing the item. If the copied item is text, the first 50 characters display in the Clipboard task pane. After items have been inserted, click the Clear All button to remove any remaining items from the Clipboard task pane.

Data can be copied from one object to another in an Access database or from a file in another application to an Access database. In Activity 3, data from a Word document will be copied and then pasted into an Access table. Data also can be collected from other applications, such as PowerPoint and Excel.

Figure 8.2 Office Clipboard Task Pane

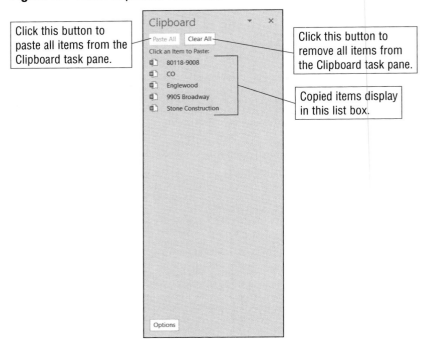

Click this button to paste all items from the Clipboard task pane.

Click this button to remove all items from the Clipboard task pane.

Copied items display in this list box.

Activity 3 Collecting Data in Word and Pasting It into an Access Table

Part 1 of 1

1. Open **8-Hilltop** and then open the Customers table.
2. Copy data from Word and paste it into the Customers table by completing the following steps:
   a. Open Word, make AL1C8 the active folder, and then open **8-HilltopCustomers**.
   b. If necessary, click the Enable Editing button, and then make sure the Home tab is active.
   c. Click the Clipboard group task pane launcher to display the Clipboard task pane. (If the Clipboard contains any items, click the Clear All button.)
   d. Select the first company name, *Stone Construction*, and then click the Copy button in the Clipboard group.

   e. Select the street address, *9905 Broadway*, and then click the Copy button.
   f. Select the city, *Englewood* (selecting only the city and not the comma after the city), and then click the Copy button.

g. Select the state, *CO* (selecting only the two letters and not the space after the letters), and then click the Copy button.

h. Select the zip code, *80118-9008*, and then click the Copy button.

i. Click the Access button on the taskbar. (Make sure the Customers table is open and displays in Datasheet view.)

j. Click in the first empty field in the *CustomerID* field column and then type 178.

k. Display the Clipboard task pane by clicking the Home tab and then clicking the Clipboard group task pane launcher.

l. Close the Navigation pane by clicking the Shutter Bar Open/Close Button.

m. Click in the first empty field in the *Customer* field column and then click *Stone Construction* in the Clipboard task pane.

2m

n. Click in the *CuStreetAddress* field and then click *9905 Broadway* in the Clipboard task pane.

o. Click in the *CuCity* field and then click *Englewood* in the Clipboard task pane.

p. Click in the *CuState* field and then click *CO* in the Clipboard task pane.

q. Click in the *CuZipCode* field, make sure the insertion point is positioned at the left side of the field, and then click *80118-9008* in the Clipboard task pane.

r. Click the Clear All button in the Clipboard task pane. (This removes all entries from the Clipboard.)

3. Complete steps similar to those in 2d through 2q to copy the information for Laughlin Products and paste it into the Customers table. (The customer ID number is 255.)

4. Click the Clear All button in the Clipboard task pane.

5. Close the Clipboard task pane by clicking the Close button (X) in the upper right corner of the task pane.

6. Save, print, and then close the Customers table.

7. Open the Navigation pane by clicking the Shutter Bar Open/Close Button.

8. Make Word the active program, close **8-HilltopCustomers** without saving changes, and then close Word.

9. Close **8-Hilltop**.

2r

Clipboard ▾ ✕

Paste All   Clear All

Click an Item to Paste:

📋 80118-9008

📋 CO

📋 Englewood

📋 9905 Broadway

📋 Stone Construction

Check Your Work

Chapter Summary

- Use the Excel button in the Export group on the External Data tab to export data in a table, query, or form to an Excel worksheet.

- Export data in a table, query, form, or report to a Word document by clicking the More button and then clicking *Word* at the drop-down list. Access exports the data to an RTF (rich-text format) file.

- Access data can be merged with a Word document. The Access data is the data source and the Word document is the main document. To merge data, click the table or query, click the External Data tab, and then click the Word Merge button in the Export group.

- Export an Access object to a PDF or XPS file with the PDF or XPS button in the Export group on the External Data tab.

- Click the New Data Source button in the Import group on the External Data tab, point to *From File*, and then click *Excel* to import Excel data to an Access table.

- Imported data can be linked so that changes made to the data in the source program file are reflected in the destination source file.

- To link imported data, click the *Link to the data source by creating a linked table* option at the Get External Data dialog box.

- Use the Clipboard task pane to collect up to 24 different items in Access or other programs and paste them in various locations.

- Display the Clipboard task pane by clicking the Clipboard group task pane launcher on the Home tab.

Commands Review

FEATURE	RIBBON TAB, GROUP	BUTTON, OPTION
Clipboard task pane	Home, Clipboard	
export object to Excel	External Data, Export	
export object to PDF or XPS	External Data, Export	
export object to Word	External Data, Export	, *Word*
import data	External Data, Import & Link	
merge Access data with Word	External Data, Export	

Index

A

Access
exporting object to PDF or XPS file, 233
merging data in Word document, 229–230
opening, 4
screen elements, 5–6
Access Help Window, 127–128
Add a group button, 186
Add a sort button, 187
Add Existing Fields button, 157
Address Block button, 230
Advanced button, 209
aggregate function, designing queries with, 89–92
Align Left button, 118
Align Right button, 118
Alternate Row Color button, 118
And criteria, queries designed with, 76–80
Ascending button, 117, 139, 177
Attachment data type, 103
AutoNumber data type, 22, 23, 103
assigning, 37
changing, 28

B

Background button, 182
Background Color button, 118
Background Image button, 151
backing up database, 219–220
backstage area, getting help in, 128–129
Back Up Database option, 219
Bold button, 118
Build button, 106
Builder button, 87

C

Calculated data type, 103
calculator
inserting in form, 160–162

inserting in report, 190–191
Caption text box, 26
Cascade Update Related Fields, 41, 50
Center button, 118
Clear All button, 237–238
Close button, 7
Close Print Preview button, 17
closing
database, 7–9
objects, 7–9
collapse indicator, 55
Colors button, 150
columns. *See also* fields
hiding, unhiding, freezing and unfreezing, 14–16
width changes, 14–16
compacting, database, 213–215
Compact & Repair Database button, 213–215
conditional formatting
of forms, 153–157
of reports, 182–186
Conditional Formatting button, 153, 182
Control Margins button, 147
control objects
arranging in form, 147–150
defined, 142
deleting, 143
inserting, 143–144
modifying
in forms, 143–144
in reports, 176–177
moving form table, 147
sizing, 143
Control Padding button, 147
Control Source property box, 160–161
Copy button, 237
Create button, 4
Create tab, 62, 136
criterion statement
adding, 63–64
criteria examples, 64

queries with *Or* and *And* criteria, 76–80
crosstab query, 92–95
Crosstab Query Wizard, 92
Currency data type, 23, 103
Current Record box, 10
customizing
database properties, 215–217
forms, 142–169
reports
layout view, 182–191
in print preview, 177–178

D

data
collecting data in Word and pasting in Access table, 238–239
exporting
to Excel, 224–227
to Word, 227–229
filtering
by Filter button, 202–203
by *Filter By Form* option, 209–210
in query and report, 205–206
records in table and form, 203–205
removing a filter, 203
by selection, 207–209
by shortcut menu, 207–208
on specific values, 205
finding and replacing, 123–126
formatting in table data, 118–119
grouping and sorting in reports, 186–189
importing into new table, 234–235
inserting in form header, 143
linking, to Excel worksheet, 236–237

types of, 7
viewing object dependencies, 211–212
object tab, 9
Office Clipboard, using, 237–239
OLE Object data type, 103
OneDrive
opening database from, 6
one-to-many relationships
creating, 52–54
relating tables in, 40–51
one-to-one relationships, creating, 51–54
opening
database, 4–5, 8–9
objects, 7–9
Or criteria, queries designed with, 76–80
orientation
landscape, 18
portrait, 18

P

page layout, changing, 18–20
Page Setup button, 18
Page Setup dialog box, 18
page size, changing, 17
password, encrypting database with, 214–215
paste data, 237–239
PDF file format
exporting Access object to, 233
saving object as, 218–220
PDF or XPS button, 233
pinning, database file, 6–7
portrait orientation, 18
Previous record button, 10, 137
primary key, 36–39
Primary Key button, 37
primary key field
defining, 36–39
determining, 37
function of, 21
primary table, 40
Print Backstage area, 16
Print button, 17

printing
forms, 136–137
records and fields in tables, 119–121
relationships, 43
specific records, 117
tables, 16–20
changing page layout, 18–20
changing page size and margins, 17
previewing, 17
Print Preview, displaying and customizing report in, 177–178
Print Preview button, 17, 177
Properties dialog box, 215–216
Property Sheet task pane, 87

Q

query
crosstab query, 92–95
as database object, 7
defined, 62
deleting, 75
description of, 7
designing, 62–80
adding criterion statement to, 63–64
with aggregate function, 89–92
arranging fields in, 71–72
with *Or* and *And* criteria, 76–80
overview, 62–64
showing/hiding fields in, 71
sorting fields in, 71–74
exporting, to Excel, 224–227
filtering records in, 205–206
find duplicate query, 95–98
find unmatched query, 98–99
inserting calculated fields, 86–88
merging query data with Word document, 230–232
modifying, 74–76

performing, 62
calculations in, 86–88
on related tables, 68–71
with Simple Query Wizard, 80–86
on tables, 65–67
renaming, 75
Query Design button, 62
Query Wizard button, 80
Quick Access toolbar, 5, 6
Quick Print option, 16
Quick Start fields, 28–31

R

Recent option list
opening database from, 6
pinning/unpinning database file, 6–7
Record Navigation bar, 9, 137
buttons on, 10
records
adding, 10–12
collapse indicator, 55
defined, 22
deleting, 10–12
in related tables, 50–51
displaying related records in subdatasheets, 54–57
expand indicator, 55
forms
adding and deleting, 139–140
sorting, 139–140
inserting, 10–12
in related tables, 50–51
modifying record source in report, 175
printing specific, 117
in reports
grouping and sorting, 186–189
sorting, 177
sorting, printing and formatting in tables, 119–121
sorting data in, 117
record selector bar, 9
referential integrity

Interior Photo Credits

PowerPoint®

Unit 1

Creating and Formatting Presentations

Microsoft® PowerPoint®

Preparing a PowerPoint Presentation

Performance Objectives

Upon successful completion of Chapter 1, you will be able to:

1 Open a presentation

2 Pin and unpin presentations and folders

3 Run a slide show

4 Plan a presentation

5 Close a presentation

6 Create a presentation using a design theme template

7 Insert slides, insert text in slides, and change slide layouts

8 Change presentation views

9 Save a presentation

10 Navigate and edit slides

11 Preview and print a presentation

12 Apply a design theme and a color variant to a presentation

13 Delete a presentation

14 Prepare a presentation from a blank presentation

15 Prepare a presentation in Outline view

16 Add slide transitions, transition sounds, and timings to a presentation

In any presentation, visual aids strengthen the impact of the message. Microsoft PowerPoint is a presentation graphics program that can be used to create a slide show presentation that includes many types of visual aids, including graphics, photos, videos, animations, and text formatted in attractive and appealing ways. Copies of slides can also be printed to use as handouts during a presentation. PowerPoint makes it easy to organize and present information.

 Data Files

Before beginning chapter work, copy the PC1 folder to your storage medium and then make PC1 the active folder.

The online course includes additional training and assessment resources.

You will open a presentation on using color in publications, run the slide show, and then close the presentation. You will also pin and unpin the presentation to the *Recent* options list.

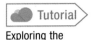

Exploring the
PowerPoint Screen

Creating a Presentation

PowerPoint provides several methods for creating a presentation. Create a presentation using a theme template or starting with a blank presentation. The steps to follow when creating a presentation will vary depending on the chosen method, but will often follow these basic steps:

1. Open PowerPoint.
2. Choose a theme template or start with a blank presentation.
3. Type the text for each slide, adding additional elements, such as images, as needed.
4. Apply a design theme if desired to add color and style.
5. Save the presentation.
6. Print slides, handouts, notes pages, or an outline of the presentation as needed.
7. Run the slide show.
8. Close the presentation.
9. Close PowerPoint.

Once a presentation has been created, the PowerPoint window displays in Normal view. Options in the window will vary depending on the type of presentation being created. However, the PowerPoint window contains some consistent elements, as shown in Figure 1.1. Many of these elements are similar to those in other Microsoft Office programs, such as Word and Excel. For example, the PowerPoint window, like the Word and Excel windows, contains a File tab, Quick Access Toolbar, tabs, ribbon, vertical and horizontal scroll bars, and Status bar. The PowerPoint window elements are described in Table 1.1.

PowerPoint, like other Microsoft Office programs, provides enhanced ScreenTips for buttons and options. Hover the mouse pointer over a button or option and, after approximately one second, an enhanced ScreenTip will display the name of the button or option, any shortcut command if one is available, and a description of that button or option.

Figure 1.1 PowerPoint Window

Table 1.1 PowerPoint Window Elements

Feature	Description
Collapse the Ribbon button	when clicked, removes the ribbon from the screen (To redisplay the ribbon, click any tab [except the File tab] and then click the Pin the Ribbon button [previously the Collapse the Ribbon button])
File tab	when clicked, displays the backstage area with options for working with and managing presentations
I-beam pointer	used to move the insertion point or to select text
insertion point	indicates the location of the next character entered at the keyboard
placeholder	location on a slide that holds text or objects
Quick Access Toolbar	contains buttons for commonly used commands
ribbon	area containing the tabs with options and buttons divided into groups
scroll box	indicates the location of the slide in relation to the other slides in the presentation
slide pane	displays the slide and slide contents
slide thumbnails pane	area on the left of the screen that displays slide thumbnails
Status bar	displays the slide number and number of slides; accessibility issues, if any; and the view area
tabs	contain commands and features organized into groups
Tell Me feature	provides information as well as guidance on how to complete a function
Title bar	displays presentation name followed by the program name
vertical scroll bar	allows scrolling up and down through a presentation
view area	a feature of the Status bar that contains buttons for changing the presentation view or slide display percentage

Opening a Presentation

After a presentation has been saved and then closed, it can be opened from a variety of locations including the PowerPoint opening screen, the Open dialog box, the *Recent* option list at the Open backstage area, or from the Home backstage area.

Opening a Presentation from the Open Backstage Area and the Open Dialog Box

At the PowerPoint opening screen, click the *Open* option or click the <u>More presentations</u> hyperlink at the bottom right corner of the window. This displays the Open backstage area, shown in Figure 1.2. The backstage area contains a list of recently opened PowerPoint presentations organized by the date they were last accessed. Click a file to open it, or click the *Browse* option to browse for files in the Open dialog box.

Access the Open backstage area while working in PowerPoint by clicking the File tab and then clicking the *Open* option, or by using the keyboard shortcut Ctrl + O. An Open button can also be added to the Quick Access Toolbar at the top left corner of the PowerPoint window. Go directly to the Open dialog box without displaying the Open backstage area by pressing Ctrl + F12. At the Open dialog box, navigate to a specific location, open the folder containing the file, and then double-click the file name in the Content pane.

Figure 1.2 Open Backstage Area

Opening a Presentation from the *Recent* Option List

At the Open backstage area with the *Recent* option selected, PowerPoint displays 50 of the most recently opened presentations and groups them into categories such as *Today, Yesterday,* and sometimes *Last Week.* The Home backstage area also contains a list of the most recently opened presentations. Click a presentation name in the *Recent* option list at the Open backstage area or the Recent list at the Home backstage area to open the presentation.

Pinning and Unpinning Presentations and Folders

If a presentation is opened on a regular basis, consider pinning it so it can be found more easily. At the Open backstage area, hover the mouse pointer over the presentation name in the *Recent* option list and then click the left-pointing push pin icon at the right of the presentation name. The presentation will appear at the top of the list in the *Pinned* category, with the push pin icon pointing down. A presentation can also be pinned at the Home backstage area. Click the push pin icon next to a presentation name, and the presentation will display in the *Pinned* tab.

To unpin a document from the *Recent* option list at the Open backstage area or the Pinned list at the Home backstage area, click the push pin icon to the right of the presentation name. More than one presentation can be pinned to a list. Another method for pinning and unpinning presentations is to right-click a presentation name in the *Recent* option list or Recent list and then click the *Pin to list* or *Unpin from list* option.

In addition to presentations, folders can be pinned to a list at the Open backstage area. Click the Folders tab at the Open backstage area with the *Recent* option selected and the most recently opened folders display grouped into categories such as *Today, Yesterday,* and *Older.* Pinned folders will display in the *Pinned* category at the top of the list where they can be easily accessed.

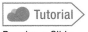
Running a Slide Show

When a presentation is opened, the presentation displays in Normal view. A presentation can be edited and customized in this view. To run the slide show, click the Start From Beginning button on the Quick Access Toolbar, click the Slide Show button in the view area on the Status bar, or click the Slide Show tab and then click the From Beginning button in the Start Slide Show group. Navigate through the slides in the slide show by clicking the left mouse button.

Closing a Presentation

To remove a presentation from the screen, close the presentation. Close a presentation by clicking the File tab and then clicking the *Close* option or with the keyboard shortcut Ctrl + F4. If any changes are made to the presentation, a message will display asking if the presentation should be saved.

1. Open PowerPoint by clicking the PowerPoint tile at the Windows Start menu. (Depending on your operating system, the steps to open PowerPoint may vary.)
2. At the PowerPoint opening screen, click the *Open* option.
3. At the Open backstage area, click the *Browse* option.
4. At the Open dialog box, navigate to the PC1 folder on your storage medium and then double-click **ColorInfo**. (Note: The file may open in Protected View. If so, click Enable Editing to be allowed to make changes to the file.)
5. Run the slide show by completing the following steps:
   a. Click the Start From Beginning button on the Quick Access Toolbar.

   b. Read the information in the first slide in the presentation and then click the left mouse button.
   c. Continue reading the information in the slides and clicking the left mouse button to advance the slides.
   d. At the black screen with the *End of slide show* message, click the left mouse button. (This returns the presentation to Normal view.)
6. Close the presentation by clicking the File tab and then clicking the *Close* option. (If a message displays asking if you want to save changes, click the No button.)
7. Pin **ColorInfo** to the *Recent* option list by completing the following steps:
   a. Click the File tab and then click the *Open* option.
   b. At the Open backstage area with the *Recent* option selected, hover your mouse over the **ColorInfo** presentation name at the top of the *Recent* option list and then click the push pin icon to the right of the presentation name.

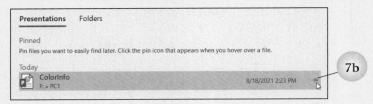

   c. Click the Back button to return to the blank presentation screen. (The Back button is in the upper left corner of the backstage area and displays as a circle with a left-pointing arrow.)
8. Close PowerPoint by clicking the Close button in the upper right corner of the screen.
9. Open PowerPoint by clicking the PowerPoint tile at the Windows Start menu. (These steps may vary; check with your instructor.)
10. At the PowerPoint opening screen, click the *Open* option and notice that **ColorInfo** is pinned in the *Pinned* section of the *Recent* option list. Open the presentation by clicking **ColorInfo** at the top of the list.
11. Close **ColorInfo**.
12. Unpin **ColorInfo** from the *Recent* option list by completing steps 7a through 7c.

You will use a design theme template to create a presentation, insert text in slides in the presentation, choose a slide layout, insert new slides, change views, navigate through the presentation, edit text in slides, type a note in the notes pane, and then print the presentation.

Planning a Presentation

When planning a presentation, first define the purpose of the presentation. Is the intent to inform, educate, sell, motivate, and/or entertain? Also consider the audience who will be listening to and watching the slide show. What are their interests or concerns about this topic, and what do they need from the presentation? Determine the content of the presentation and the medium that will be used to convey the message. Will a computer monitor be used to display the presentation or will the presentation be projected onto a screen? Consider these guidelines when preparing the content of a presentation:

- **Focus on one main topic or idea for the presentation.** Do not try to cover too many topics — this may strain the audience's attention or cause confusion. Identifying the main point of the presentation will help to stay focused and convey a clear message to the audience.

- **Show one idea per slide.** Each slide in a presentation should convey only one main idea. Too many thoughts or ideas on a slide may confuse the audience and cause you to stray from the purpose of the slide. Determine the specific message you want to convey and then outline the message to organize your ideas.

- **Determine the display medium.** Is the presentation going to be presented on a computer or will the slides be projected onto a screen? To help determine which type of output to use, consider the availability of equipment, the size of the room where the presentation will be given, and the number of people who will be attending the presentation.

- **Maintain a consistent layout.** Using a consistent layout and color scheme for slides in a presentation will create continuity and cohesiveness. Do not get carried away by using too many colors, pictures, and/or other graphic elements.

- **Keep slides simple.** Keep slides uncluttered so that they are easy for the audience to read. Keep words and other items, such as bullets, to a minimum.

- **Determine the output needed.** Will you be providing audience members with handouts? If so, what format will the handouts take? Will they show the slides either with or without space for taking notes or an outline of the slide content?

Opening a
Presentation Based
on a Template

Creating a Presentation Using a Design Theme Template

PowerPoint provides built-in design theme templates for creating slides for a presentation. These design theme templates include formatting options such as color, background, fonts, and so on. Choose a design theme template at the New backstage area shown in Figure 1.3. Display the New backstage area by clicking the *New* option at the PowerPoint opening screen, or by clicking the File tab

Figure 1.3 New Backstage Area

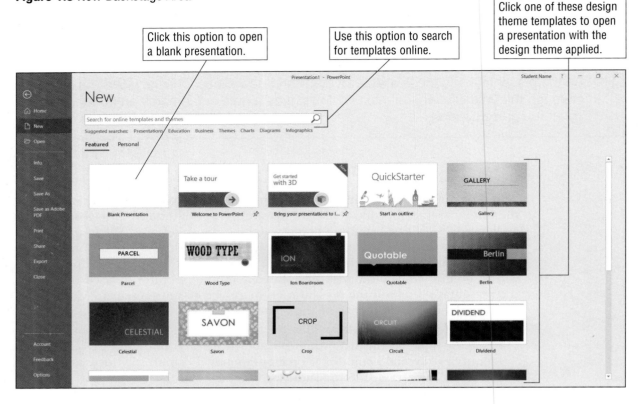

Click this option to open a blank presentation.

Use this option to search for templates online.

Click one of these design theme templates to open a presentation with the design theme applied.

and then clicking the *New* option. At this backstage area, click the design theme template or search for a template online by typing a category in the search text box or by clicking one of the categories below the search text box.

Click a design theme template at the New backstage area and a window opens containing a slide with the design theme applied as well as theme color variants. The color variants display at the right side of the window and provide color options for the theme. To change the color of the theme, click the color variant and then click the Create button. This opens a presentation with the design theme and the new theme colors applied.

Quick Steps

Create Presentation Using Design Theme Template
1. Click File tab.
2. Click *New* option.
3. Click design theme template.
4. Click color variant.
5. Click Create button.

Inserting Text in a Placeholder

Choose a blank presentation template or design theme template at the New backstage area and a slide displays in the slide pane in Normal view. The slide displays with the default Title Slide layout. This layout contains placeholders for entering the slide title and subtitle. To insert text in a placeholder, click in the placeholder. This positions the insertion point inside the placeholder, removes the placeholder label (the text inside the placeholder), and makes the placeholder active. An active placeholder displays surrounded by a dashed border with sizing handles and a white rotation handle, as shown in Figure 1.4.

With the insertion point positioned in a placeholder, type the text. Edit text in a placeholder in the same manner as editing text in a Word document. Press the Backspace key to delete the character immediately left of the insertion point and press the Delete key to delete the character immediately right of the insertion point. Use the arrow keys on the keyboard to move the insertion point in a specific direction.

Figure 1.4 Slide Placeholders

Inserting a New Slide

Choosing a Slide Layout

 New Slide

Inserting Slides

Create a new slide in a presentation by clicking the New Slide button in the Slides group on the Home tab or by pressing Ctrl + M. By default, PowerPoint inserts a new slide with the Title and Content layout. However, if a slide with a different layout is selected in the slide thumbnails pane, the layout of the selected slide is applied to the new slide. Choose a different slide layout for a new slide by clicking the New Slide button arrow and then clicking the layout option at the drop-down list. Click the top portion of the New Slide button and a new slide is inserted in the presentation with the default layout. Click the bottom portion (the New Slide button arrow) to display the drop-down list of layout options.

Changing a Slide Layout

 Layout

Changing a Slide Layout

Choose a blank presentation template or design theme template to create a presentation and the slide displays in the Title Slide layout. Change the slide layout with the Layout button in the Slides group on the Home tab. Click the Layout button and a drop-down list of layout options displays. Click a layout at the drop-down list and that layout is applied to the current slide.

Inserting and Deleting Text in Slides

Selecting Text

Inserting, Selecting, and Deleting Text in Slides

Text in a slide may need to be edited, moved, copied, or deleted. Specific text in a slide may need to be replaced with other text. Text is generally inserted in a slide placeholder. Placeholders can be moved, sized, and/or deleted.

To insert or delete text in an individual slide, open the presentation, edit the text as needed, and then save the presentation. To delete more than one character, consider selecting the text first. This will help reduce the number of times the Delete key or Backspace key needs to be pressed. Several methods can be used for selecting text, as described in Table 1.2.

Table 1.2 Selecting Text

To select	Perform this action
text the mouse pointer passes through	Click and drag the mouse.
an entire word	Double-click in the word.
an entire bulleted item	Click the bullet.
an entire paragraph	Triple-click in the paragraph.
all text in a selected placeholder	Click the Select button in the Editing group on the Home tab and then click *Select All*, or press Ctrl + A.

Text in a slide is positioned inside a placeholder. Slide layouts provide placeholders for text and display a label suggesting the type of text to be entered in the slide. For example, the Title and Content slide layout contains a placeholder with the label *Click to add title* and a second placeholder with the label *Click to add text*. Click in the placeholder and the insertion point is positioned inside the placeholder, the default label is removed, and the placeholder is selected.

Saving to a
Removable Disk

Saving a Presentation

After creating or editing a presentation, save it for future use by clicking the File tab and then clicking the *Save* or *Save As* option. At the backstage area, choose a location where the file is to be saved or click the *Browse* option to navigate to a specific folder. Files may be saved to a location on the computer, to a removable device such as a USB flash drive, or to a cloud storage location such as OneDrive. At the backstage area or in the dialog box, enter a unique name for the file that will allow it to be easily identified later. Certain symbols cannot be used in a file name, including /, ?, \, ", >, :, <, ;, *, and |.

Saving with the
Same Name

 Save

Quick Steps

**Save Changes to
Presentation**
1. Click File tab.
2. Click *Save*.

Saving Changes to a Presentation

Save a presentation whenever edits are made by clicking the File tab and then clicking the *Save* option, clicking the Save button on the Quick Access Toolbar, or using the keyboard shortcut Ctrl + S. Consider saving changes to a presentation on a periodic basis to ensure that no changes are lost if the application freezes or crashes or if power is interrupted. If a presentation is stored in a cloud location such as OneDrive, changes will be saved automatically with the AutoSave feature. AutoSave can be turned on or off by clicking the toggle switch in the upper left corner of the PowerPoint screen.

Saving a Presentation with a New Name

Quick Steps

**Save Presentation
with New Name**
1. Click File tab.
2. Click *Save As*.
3. Click *Browse*.
4. Navigate to folder.
5. Type name in *File
   name* text box.
6. Click Save.

To save a new version of a presentation while keeping the original, click the File tab and then click the *Save As* option. (Do not click *Save*, or changes will be saved to the existing file.) At the Save As backstage area, click the *Browse* option to display the Save As dialog box. Navigate to the folder where the presentation is to be saved, type a new name for the presentation in the *File name* text box, and then press the Enter key or click the Save button.

1. With PowerPoint open, click the File tab and then click the *New* option.
2. At the New backstage area, scroll down the list of design theme templates and then click the *Organic* design theme template.
3. At the window, click the Create button.

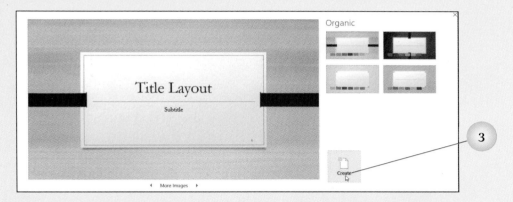

4. Click in the *Click to add title* placeholder and then type Career Finders.
5. Click in the *Click to add subtitle* placeholder and then type Resume Writing.

6. Click the New Slide button in the Slides group on the Home tab. (This inserts a slide with the Title and Content slide layout.)

7. Click in the *Click to add title* placeholder and then type Resume Styles.
8. Click in the *Click to add text* placeholder and then type Chronological resume.
9. Press the Enter key (this moves the insertion point to the next line and inserts a bullet) and then type Functional resume.
10. Press the Enter key and then type Hybrid resume.

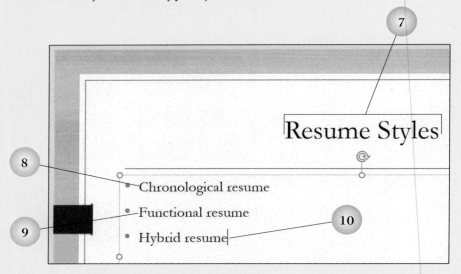

11. Click the New Slide button in the Slides group.
12. Click in the *Click to add title* placeholder and then type Resume Sections.
13. Click in the *Click to add text* placeholder and then type Contact information.
14. Press the Enter key and then type Summary or job objective statement.
15. Press the Enter key and then type Work history.
16. Press the Enter key and then type Education details.
17. Press the Enter key and then type References.

18. Click the New Slide button arrow and then click the *Title Only* layout option.

19. Click in the *Click to add title* placeholder and then type Career Finders.
20. Click the Layout button in the Slides group on the Home tab and then click the *Title Slide* layout option.

21. Click in the *Click to add subtitle* placeholder and then type Contact us by calling 1-800-555-2255.
22. Click in the slide pane, but outside the slide. (This deselects the placeholder.)
23. Save the presentation by completing the following steps:
    a. Click the Save button on the Quick Access Toolbar.

    b. At the Save As backstage area, click the *Browse* option.
    c. At the Save As dialog box, navigate to the PC1 folder on your storage medium.
    d. Select the text in the *File name* text box and then type 1-Resumes (*1* for Chapter 1 and *Resumes* because that is the topic of the presentation).
    e. Press the Enter key or click the Save button.

Check Your Work

Tutorial

Changing Views

 Normal

 Outline View

 Slide Sorter

 Notes Page

 Reading View

 Slide Sorter

 Reading View

 Normal

 Slide Show

 Notes

Changing Views

PowerPoint provides a variety of viewing options. Change the view with buttons in the view area on the Status bar or with options in the Presentation Views group on the View tab. The viewing choices include:

- **Normal view.** This is the default view and displays two panes: The slide pane and the slide thumbnails pane. Enter text in a slide in the slide pane and manage slides in the slide thumbnails pane.
- **Outline view.** In Outline view, the slide thumbnails pane changes to an outline pane where text is typed for slides.
- **Slide Sorter view.** Choosing Slide Sorter view displays slides in the presentation as thumbnails. In this view, add, move, rearrange, and delete slides.
- **Notes Page view.** Changing to Notes Page view displays an individual slide on a page with any added notes displayed below the slide.
- **Reading view.** Use Reading view to deliver a presentation to people viewing the presentation on their own computers. In this view, a slide show can be played in the PowerPoint window without switching to a full-screen slide show.
- **Slide Show view.** Use Slide Show view to run a slide show. Choose this view and each slide fills the entire screen.

The view area on the Status bar contains four buttons for changing the view: Normal, Slide Sorter, Reading View, and Slide Show. The active button displays with a darker gray background. The Status bar also contains a Notes button. Click the Notes button and a notes pane displays at the bottom of the slide in the slide pane.

 Tutorial

Navigating to Slides

 Previous Slide

 Next Slide

Navigating in a Presentation

In Normal view, change slides by clicking the Previous Slide or Next Slide button at the bottom of the vertical scroll bar. Or, change to a different slide using the mouse pointer on the vertical scroll bar. To do this, position the mouse pointer on the scroll box on the vertical scroll bar, hold down the left mouse button, drag up or down until a box displays with the desired slide number, and then release the button.

Keyboard keys can also be used to display slides in a presentation. In Normal view, press the Down Arrow or Page Down key to show the next slide or press the Up Arrow or Page Up key to show the previous slide in the presentation. Press the Home key to show the first slide in the presentation and press the End key to show the last slide in the presentation. Navigate in the slide thumbnails pane by clicking the slide thumbnail. Navigate in Slide Sorter view by clicking the slide or using the arrow keys on the keyboard.

1. With **1-Resumes** open, navigate within the presentation by completing the following steps:
   a. Make sure no placeholders are selected.
   b. Press the Home key to display Slide 1 in the slide pane.
   c. Click the Next Slide button at the bottom of the vertical scroll bar.

   d. Press the End key to display the last slide in the slide pane.
   e. Click the Slide Sorter button in the view area on the Status bar.

   f. Click Slide 1. (Notice that the active slide displays with an orange border.)
   g. Double-click Slide 3. (This closes Slide Sorter view and displays the presentation in Normal view with Slide 3 active.)
2. Insert text in slides by completing the following steps:
   a. Click in the bulleted text. (This positions the insertion point inside the placeholder.)
   b. Move the insertion point so it is positioned immediately right of *Education details*.
   c. Press the Enter key and then type Professional affiliations.

   d. Click Slide 4 in the slide thumbnails pane. (This displays Slide 4 in the slide pane.)
   e. Click in the text containing the telephone number and move the insertion point so it is positioned immediately right of the telephone number. Press the spacebar and then type or visit our website at https://ppi-edu.net/careerfinders.

3. Type a note in the notes pane by completing the following steps:
   a. Click Slide 2 in the slide thumbnails pane.
   b. Click the Notes button on the Status bar.
   c. Click in the *Click to add notes* placeholder in the notes pane.
   d. Type Distribute resume examples to the audience.

   e. Display the slide in Notes Page view by clicking the View tab and then clicking the Notes Page button in the Presentation Views group. (Notice the note you typed displays below the slide in this view.)

   f. Return to Normal view by clicking the Normal button in the view area on the Status bar.
   g. Click the Notes button on the Status bar to close the notes pane.
   h. Press the Home key to make Slide 1 the active slide.
4. Save the presentation by clicking the Save button on the Quick Access Toolbar.

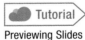
Previewing and Printing a Presentation

A PowerPoint presentation can be printed in a variety of formats. Print each slide on a separate piece of paper; print each slide at the top of the page, leaving the bottom of the page for notes; print a specific number of slides (up to nine slides) on a single piece of paper; or print the slide titles and topics in outline form. Use options in the Print backstage area, shown in Figure 1.5, to specify what is to be printed. To display the Print backstage area, click the File tab and then click the *Print* option or use the keyboard shortcut Ctrl + P.

Click the Print button to send the presentation to the printer and specify the number of copies to be printed with the *Copies* measurement box. Below the Print button are two categories: *Printer* and *Settings*. Use the gallery in the *Printer* category to specify the printer. Click the first gallery in the *Settings* category and options display for specifying what is to be printed, such as all of the presentation or specific slides in the presentation. The *Settings* category also contains a number of galleries that describe how the slides will print.

Figure 1.5 Print Backstage Area

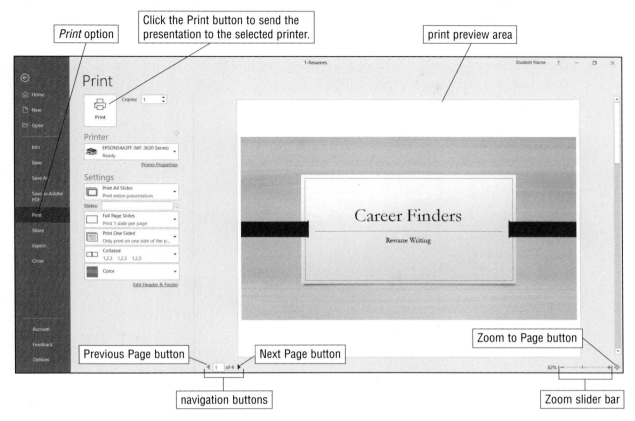

In the *Settings* category, print a range of slides using the hyphen and print specific slides using a comma. For example, to print Slides 2 through 6, type *2-6* in the *Slides* text box. To print Slides 1, 3, and 7, type *1,3,7*. A hyphen and comma can be combined. For example, to print Slides 1 through 5 and Slide 8, type *1-5,8* in the *Slides* text box.

A preview of how a slide or slides will print displays at the right side of the Print backstage area. If a color printer is selected, the slide or slides at the right side of the Print backstage area display in color, and if a black-and-white printer is selected, the slide or slides will display in grayscale. Use the Next Page button (right-pointing arrow) below and to the left of the page to view the next slide in the presentation; click the Previous Page button (left-pointing arrow) to display the previous slide in the presentation; use the Zoom slider bar to increase or decrease the size of the slide; and click the Zoom to Page button to fit the slide in the viewing area in the Print backstage area. (You may need to scroll down the backstage area to display these options. One method for scrolling down the backstage area is to click the Page Down button on the keyboard.)

A presentation can be printed as individual slides, handouts, notes pages, or an outline. If a presentation is printed as handouts or an outline, PowerPoint will automatically print the current date in the upper right corner of the page and the page number in the lower right corner. If the presentation is printed as notes pages, PowerPoint will automatically print the page number in the lower right corner. PowerPoint does not insert the date or page number when individual slides are printed.

1. With **1-Resumes** open, click the File tab and then click the *Print* option.
2. Click the Next Page button (below and to the left of the slide in the viewing area) two times to display Slide 3 in the print preview area. (If the Next Page button is not visible, click the Page Down button to scroll down the backstage area.)

3. Click the Previous Page button two times to display Slide 1.
4. Change the zoom by completing the following steps:
   a. Position the mouse pointer on the Zoom slider bar button (at the bottom right of the Print backstage area), drag the button to the right to increase the size of the slide in the print preview area of the Print backstage area, and then to the left to decrease the size of the slide.
   b. Click the percentage at the left of the Zoom slider bar. (This displays the Zoom dialog box.)
   c. Click the *50%* option in the Zoom dialog box and then click OK.
   d. Click the Zoom to Page button to the right of the Zoom slider bar. (This changes the size of the slide to fill the print preview area.)

5. Print the presentation as a handout with four slides displayed horizontally on the page by completing the following steps:
   a. At the Print backstage area, click the second gallery (displays with *Full Page Slides*) in the *Settings* category and then click *4 Slides Horizontal* in the *Handouts* section.

   b. Click the Print button.
6. Print Slide 2 as a notes page by completing the following steps:
   a. Click the File tab and then click the *Print* option.
   b. At the Print backstage area, click in the *Slides* text box in the *Settings* category, and then type 2.
   c. Click the second gallery (displays with *4 Slides Horizontal*) in the *Settings* category and then click *Notes Pages* in the *Print Layout* section.
   d. Click the Print button.

7. Print Slides 1, 2, and 4 by completing the following steps:
   a. Click the File tab and then click the *Print* option.
   b. At the Print backstage area, click in the *Slides* text box in the *Settings* category and then type 1-2,4.
   c. Click the second gallery (displays with *Notes Pages*) in the *Settings* category and then click *4 Slides Horizontal* in the *Handouts* section.
   d. Click the Print button.
8. Close the presentation by clicking the File tab and then clicking the *Close* option.

 Check Your Work

Activity 3 **Open a Presentation, Navigate in a Slide Show, and Change the Presentation Design Theme** **3 Parts**

You will open a presentation, run the slide show using buttons on the Slide Show toolbar, apply a different design theme and color variant to the presentation, and then delete a presentation.

 Tutorial

Navigating in a Slide Show

 Tutorial

Changing the Display when Running a Slide Show

 Tutorial

Displaying Slide Show Help and Hiding Slides during a Slide Show

 Tutorial

Using Pen Button Options during a Slide Show

 From Beginning

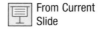 From Current Slide

Using the Slide Show Toolbar

As discussed earlier in this chapter, run a slide show by clicking the Start From Beginning button on the Quick Access Toolbar, by clicking the Slide Show button in the view area on the Status bar, or by clicking the Slide Show tab and then clicking the From Beginning button in the Start Slide Show group. This group also contains a From Current Slide button. Use this button to begin running the slide show with the currently active slide rather than the first slide in the presentation.

PowerPoint offers a number of options for navigating through slides in a slide show. Click the left mouse button to advance slides in a slide show, right-click in a slide and then choose options from a shortcut menu, or use buttons on the Slide Show toolbar. The Slide Show toolbar displays in the lower left corner of a slide when running the slide show. Figure 1.6 identifies the buttons on the Slide Show toolbar. To display the Slide Show toolbar, run the slide show and then hover the mouse pointer over the buttons. Click the Next button (displays with a right arrow) on the toolbar to display the next slide and click the Previous button (displays with a left arrow) to display the previous slide.

Click the Pen button (displays with a pen icon) on the Slide Show toolbar and a pop-up list displays with the following options: *Laser Pointer, Pen, Highlighter, Eraser,* and *Erase All Ink on Slide,* along with a row of color options. Click the *Laser Pointer* option and the pointer displays as a red, glowing circle, which can be used to point to specific locations on the slide. Use the *Pen* option to draw in the slide,

Figure 1.6 Slide Show Toolbar

Figure 1.6 Slide Show Toolbar

Quick Steps

Run Slide Show

1. Click Start From Beginning button on Quick Access Toolbar.
2. Click left mouse button to advance slides.

OR

1. Click Slide Show button on Status bar.
2. Click left mouse button to advance slides.

OR

1. Click Slide Show tab.
2. Click From Beginning button.
3. Click left mouse button to advance slides.

Within the figure:

- Click the Previous button to display the previous slide.
- Click the Pen button to display a pop-up list of options for using the laser pointer, pen, or highlighter when running the slide show.
- Click the Zoom into the slide button to zoom in on a specific area on the slide.
- Click the More slide show options button to display options for customizing the slide show.
- Click the See all slides button to display all slides in the presentation as thumbnails.
- Click the Next button to display the next slide.

and use the *Highlighter* option to highlight specific items in the slide. Select the *Pen* or *Highlighter* option and then drag the mouse in the slide to draw or highlight items. Erase the drawing or highlighting in a slide by clicking the Pen button on the Slide Show toolbar, clicking the *Eraser* option, and then clicking or dragging the mouse pointer (displays as an eraser) to erase the drawing or highlighting. To erase all drawing or highlighting on the slide, click the Pen button and then click the *Erase All Ink on Slide* option.

Change the pen or highlighter color by clicking the Pen button and then clicking a color option in the color row. Draw in a slide with the pen or highlighter and PowerPoint will ask if the ink annotations are to be kept or discarded. Reply to this message, and return the laser pointer, pen, or highlighter option back to the mouse pointer by pressing the Esc key on the keyboard.

Click the See all slides button on the Slide Show toolbar and all slides in the slide show display on the screen. Use this feature to display all of the slides in the slide show and/or move to a different slide by clicking the slide.

Zoom in on a portion of a slide by clicking the Zoom into the slide button (contains an image of a magnifying glass) on the Slide Show toolbar. Clicking this button creates a magnification area and dims the remainder of the slide. Drag the magnification area with the mouse to specify what is to be magnified and then click the left mouse button. Return to the normal zoom by pressing the Esc key or right-clicking the slide.

Click the More slide show options button (the last button on the Slide Show toolbar; depicting three dots) and a pop-up list displays with a variety of options. The pop-up list contains options for displaying a custom show or switching to Presenter view; changing the screen display, display settings, and arrow options; and pausing or ending the show. Click the *Help* option and the Slide Show Help dialog box displays, as shown in Figure 1.7. This dialog box contains various tabs that describe the keyboard options available when running a slide show.

Quick Steps

Use Pen or Highlighter During Slide Show

1. Run slide show.
2. Display slide.
3. Click Pen button on Slide Show toolbar.
4. Click *Pen* or *Highlighter* option.
5. Drag to draw line or highlight text.

💡 **Hint** If you use the pen or highlighter on a slide when running a slide show, choose an ink color that the audience can see easily.

In addition to the options on the Slide Show toolbar, right-click in a slide and a shortcut menu displays with many of the same options as the options that display when the More slide show options button is clicked.

When running a slide show, the mouse pointer is set, by default, to be hidden automatically after three seconds of inactivity. The mouse pointer will appear again when the mouse is moved. Change this default setting by clicking the More slide show options button on the Slide Show toolbar, clicking *Arrow Options*, and then clicking *Visible* to make the mouse pointer always visible or *Hidden* if the mouse pointer should not display at all when running the slide show. The *Automatic* option is the default setting.

If the mouse pointer displays as the pen or highlighter, return to the regular pointer by pressing the Esc key or clicking the More slide show options button on the Slide Show toolbar, clicking *Arrow Options* at the pop-up list, and then clicking *Visible*.

Figure 1.7 Slide Show Help Dialog Box

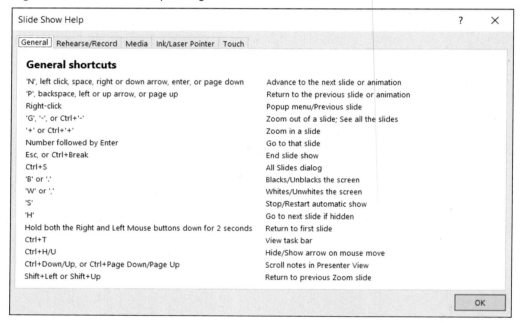

Activity 3a Opening a Presentation and Navigating in a Slide Show

Part 1 of 3

1. Click the File tab and then click the *Open* option.
2. At the Open backstage area, click the *Browse* option.
3. At the Open dialog box, navigate to the PC1 folder on your storage medium and then double-click *PlanningPres*.
4. Save the presentation by completing the following steps:
   a. Click the File tab and then click the *Save As* option.
   b. At the Save As backstage area, click the *Browse* option.
   c. At the Save As dialog box, make sure the PC1 folder on your storage medium is active and then type 1-PlanningPres in the *File name* text box.
   d. Press the Enter key or click the Save button.

5. Run the slide show by completing the following steps:
   a. Click the Slide Show button in the view area on the Status bar.
   b. When Slide 1 fills the screen, move the mouse to display the Slide Show toolbar. (This toolbar displays in a dimmed manner in the lower left corner of the slide.)
   c. Click the Next button (contains a right arrow) to display the next slide.

   d. Continue clicking the Next button until a black screen displays.
   e. Click the left mouse button. (This displays the presentation in Normal view.)
6. Run the slide show from the current slide by completing the following steps:
   a. Click Slide 4 in the slide thumbnails pane. (This makes Slide 4 active.)
   b. Click the Slide Show tab.
   c. Click the From Current Slide button in the Start Slide Show group.

7. With Slide 4 active, zoom in on the step text by completing these steps:
   a. Move the mouse to display the Slide Show toolbar.
   b. Click the Zoom into the slide button (the button displays as a magnifying glass) on the Slide Show toolbar.
   c. Using the mouse, drag the magnification area so it displays the step text and then click the left mouse button.
   d. Press the Esc key to return to the normal zoom.
8. Click the See all slides button on the Slide Show toolbar and then click the Slide 2 thumbnail.

9. With Slide 2 active, use the pen to draw in the slide by completing the following steps:
   a. Move the mouse to display the Slide Show toolbar.
   b. Click the Pen button on the Slide Show toolbar and then click the *Pen* option at the pop-up list. (This changes the mouse pointer to a small circle.)

c. Click and hold down the left mouse button and draw a circle around the text *Step 1*.

d. Click and hold down the left mouse button and draw a line below the word *identify*.

e. Press the Esc key to return the mouse pointer to an arrow.

10. Erase the pen markings by clicking the Pen button on the Slide Show toolbar and then clicking *Erase All Ink on Slide* at the pop-up list.

11. Click the Next button to display Slide 3.

12. Click the Pen button and then click *Highlighter*.

13. Click the Pen button and then click the *Light Green* color (seventh option).

14. Click and hold down the left mouse button and drag through the text *Assess your target audience*.

15. Press the Esc key to return the mouse pointer to an arrow.

16. Press the Esc key to end the slide show. Click the Discard button at the message asking if you want to keep or discard the ink annotations.

17. With Slide 3 active, click the Slide Show button on the Status bar to start the slide show.

18. Click the Pen button on the Slide Show toolbar and then click *Laser Pointer* at the pop-up list.

19. Use the laser pointer to point to various locations on the slide.

20. Press the Esc key to return the mouse pointer to an arrow.

21. Click the Next button on the Slide Show toolbar. (This displays Slide 4.)

22. Turn on the highlighter and then use the mouse to drag through the words *best format* to highlight them.

23. Press the Esc key to return the mouse pointer to an arrow.

24. Continue clicking the left mouse button to move through the presentation.

25. At the black screen, click the left mouse button.

26. At the message asking if you want to keep your ink annotations, click the Keep button.

27. Save the presentation with a new name by completing the following steps:

a. Click the File tab and then click the *Save As* option.

b. At the Save As backstage area, click the *Browse* option.

c. At the Save As dialog box, make sure the PC1 folder on your storage medium is the active folder, type 1-PlanningPres-Ink in the *File name* text box, and then press the Enter key.

28. Print Slide 4 as a handout.

29. Close **1-PlanningPres-Ink**.

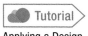
Applying a Design Theme and Color Variant

PowerPoint provides a variety of built-in design theme templates that can be used when creating slides for a presentation. Choose a design theme template at the New backstage area or with options in the Themes group on the Design tab. Click the Design tab and themes display in the themes gallery in the Themes group. Click one of these themes to apply it to the current presentation. Click the More Themes button at the right side of the themes gallery to display additional themes. Click the up arrow or down arrow at the right side of the themes gallery to scroll through the list. Hover the mouse pointer over a theme and the active slide in the presentation displays with the theme formatting applied. This is an example of the live preview feature, which displays how theme formatting will affect the presentation.

Each design theme contains color variations that display in the Variants group on the Design tab. These are the same theme color variants that display when applying a theme template at the New backstage area. Click a color variant in the Variants group to apply the colors to the slides in the presentation.

Hover the mouse pointer over a theme in the theme gallery and a ScreenTip displays (after approximately a second) containing the theme name. Theme names in PowerPoint are similar to those in Word, Excel, Access, and Outlook and apply similar formatting. With the availability of the themes across these programs, business files such as documents, workbooks, and presentations can be "branded" with a consistent and uniform appearance.

More Themes

Quick Steps

Apply Design Theme
1. Click Design tab.
2. Click theme in themes gallery.

Hint Design themes were designed by professional graphic artists who understand the use of color, space, and design.

Activity 3b **Applying a Design Theme and Color Variant**   Part 2 of 3

1. Open **1-PlanningPres**.
2. Make sure Slide 1 is active and that the presentation displays in Normal view.
3. Apply a different design theme to the presentation by completing the following steps:
   a. Click the Design tab.
   b. Hover the mouse pointer over the *Ion* theme in the themes gallery in the Themes group and notice the theme formatting applied to the slide in the slide pane.
   c. Click the *Ion* option.

4. Run the slide show and notice the formatting applied by the theme.
5. With the presentation displayed in Normal view, apply a different design theme by clicking the *Facet* theme in the themes gallery in the Themes group on the Design tab.

6. Apply a color variant by clicking the fourth option in the Variants group.
7. Run the slide show.
8. Print the presentation as a handout by completing the following steps:
   a. Click the File tab and then click the *Print* option.
   b. At the Print backstage area, click the second gallery (displays with *Full Page Slides*) in the *Settings* category and then click *6 Slides Horizontal* in the *Handouts* section.
   c. Click the Print button.
9. Save and then close **1-PlanningPres**.

Variants

Check Your Work

Deleting a Presentation

Quick Steps

Delete Presentation
1. Display Open dialog box.
2. Navigate to folder or drive.
3. Click presentation.
4. Click Organize button.
5. Click *Delete*.
6. Click Yes.

File management tasks in PowerPoint can be performed at the Open dialog box or Save As dialog box. To delete a PowerPoint presentation, display the Open dialog box, click the presentation to be deleted in the Content pane, click the Organize button on the toolbar, and then click *Delete* at the drop-down list. At the message asking to confirm the deletion, click the Yes button. The presentation file must be closed to be deleted. Another method for deleting a presentation is to right-click the presentation in the Content pane of the Open or Save As dialog box and then click the *Delete* option at the shortcut menu.

If a presentation is deleted from a folder on the computer's hard drive, the confirmation message does not display. This is because the deleted presentation is sent to the Recycle Bin where it can be restored, if needed.

Activity 3c Deleting a PowerPoint Presentation

Part 3 of 3

1. Click the File tab and then click the *Open* option.
2. At the Open backstage area, click the *Browse* option.
3. At the Open dialog box, make sure the PC1 folder on your storage medium is the active folder and then click **PlanningPres** in the Content pane.
4. Click the Organize button on the toolbar and then click *Delete* at the drop-down list.
5. At the message asking if you are sure you want to delete the presentation, click Yes. (If you are deleting the presentation from a folder on your computer's hard drive, the confirmation message will not display because the presentation is sent automatically to the Recycle Bin.)
6. Click the Cancel button to close the Open dialog box.
7. Close PowerPoint.

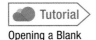

Tutorial

Opening a Blank Presentation

Quick Steps

Prepare Presentation from Blank Presentation
1. Click File tab.
2. Click *New* option.
3. Click *Blank Presentation*.

Tutorial

Entering Text in the Outline Pane

Preparing a Presentation from a Blank Presentation

To create a presentation without a design theme applied, open a blank presentation. Open a blank presentation at the PowerPoint opening screen, the Home backstage area, or the New backstage area by clicking the *Blank Presentation* template. Another method for opening a new blank presentation is to use the keyboard shortcut Ctrl + N.

Preparing a Presentation in Outline View

Text can be inserted in a slide by typing the text in the outline pane. Display this pane by clicking the View tab and then clicking the Outline View button in the Presentation Views group. The outline pane replaces the slide thumbnails pane at the left side of the screen. A slide number displays in the pane followed by a small slide icon. When typing text in the outline pane, press the Tab key to move the insertion point to the next tab. This moves the insertion point and also changes the formatting. The formatting will vary depending on the theme applied. Press Shift + Tab to move the insertion point to the previous tab. Moving the insertion point back to the left margin will create a new slide.

Activity 4a Preparing a Presentation in Outline View   Part 1 of 3

1. Open PowerPoint.
2. At the PowerPoint opening screen, click the *Blank Presentation* template.
3. At the blank presentation, click the View tab and then click the Outline View button in the Presentation Views group.

4. At the top of the outline pane, find the icon for Slide 1 (a small rectangle with an orange border) and then click immediately right of the icon.
5. Type the first slide title shown in Figure 1.8 (*Computer Technology*) and then press the Enter key. (The text you type displays immediately right of the slide icon in the outline pane.)
6. Type the second slide title shown in Figure 1.8 (*The Motherboard*) and then press the Enter key.
7. Press the Tab key, type the text after the first bullet in Figure 1.8 (*Buses*), and then press the Enter key.
8. Continue typing the text below the title *The Motherboard* as it displays in Figure 1.8, pressing the Enter key after each item.
9. After typing *Expansion slots*, press the Enter key and then press Shift + Tab to move the insertion point back to the previous tab to create a new slide.
10. Type the third slide title shown in Figure 1.8 (*Input Devices*), press the Enter key, and then press the Tab key.
11. Continue typing the text as shown in Figure 1.8. Press the Tab key to move the insertion point to the next tab or press Shift + Tab to move the insertion point back to a previous tab.

12. After typing all of the information as shown in Figure 1.8, click the Normal button in the Presentation Views group on the View tab.
13. Click the Notes button on the Status bar to close the notes pane.
14. Click Slide 1 in the slide thumbnails pane. (This displays Slide 1 in the slide pane.)
15. Apply a design theme by completing the following steps:
    a. Click the Design tab.
    b. Click the *Ion* option in the themes gallery.
    c. Click the fourth option in the Variants group (the orange color variant).
16. Save the presentation and name it **1-Computers**.
17. Run the slide show.

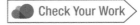
Check Your Work

Figure 1.8 Activity 4a

> 1 Computer Technology
> 2 The Motherboard
>   • Buses
>   • System clock
>   • Microprocessor
>   • ROM and RAM
>   • Power supply
>   • Ports
>   • Expansion slots
> 3 Input Devices
>   • Keyboard
>   • Mouse
>   • Trackball
>   • Touchpad and touchscreen
>   • Pen and tablet
>   • Scanner
> 4 Output Devices
>   • Monitor
>   • Printer
>   • Laser
>   • Ink jet
>   • Speakers

Adding Slide Transitions and Transition Sounds

Interesting slide transitions and transition sounds can be applied to a presentation. A transition is how one slide is removed from the screen during a slide show and the next slide is displayed. Transitions such as cut, fade, push, wipe, split, reveal, and random bars can be applied to a presentation. To add transitions and transition sounds, open a presentation, and then click the Transitions tab. This displays transition buttons and options, as shown in Figure 1.9.

Transitions and transition sounds apply by default to the active slide. To apply transitions and transition sounds to all slides in the presentation, click the Apply To All button in the Timing group. In Slide Sorter view, select all slides by pressing Ctrl + A (or by clicking the Home tab, clicking the Select button, and then clicking *Select All* at the drop-down list) and then apply the transition and/or transition sounds.

Figure 1.9 Transitions Tab

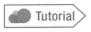
Adding Slide Transitions

To add a transition to a slide, click an option in the gallery in the Transition to This Slide group on the Transitions tab and the transition plays in the slide in the slide pane. Use the up and down arrows at the right of the transitions gallery to display additional transitions. Click the More Transitions button at the right of the transitions gallery and a drop-down list displays with additional options. Use the *Duration* measurement box in the Timing group to specify the duration of slide transitions when running the slide show. Click the *Duration* measurement box up or down arrows to change the duration time. Or, select the current time in the measurement box and then type the specific time. Use the Apply To All button in the Timing group to apply a transition to all slides in the presentation.

Use options in the Effect Options button drop-down gallery to change transition effects. The options in the drop-down gallery vary depending on the transition applied. The Effect Options button is in the Transition to This Slide group on the Transitions tab.

When a transition is applied to slides in a presentation, animation icons display below the slide numbers in the slide thumbnails pane and in Slide Sorter view. Click an animation icon for a particular slide and the slide will display the transition effect.

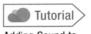
Adding Sound to Slide Transitions

To add a sound effect to slide transitions in a presentation, click the *Sound* option box arrow and then click a sound at the drop-down list. Preview a transition and/or transition sound applied to a slide by clicking the Preview button at the left side of the Transitions tab.

Removing Slide Transitions and Transition Sounds

Remove a transition from a slide by clicking the *None* option in the transitions gallery in the Transition to This Slide group. To remove transitions from all slides, click the Apply To All button in the Timing group. To remove a transition sound from a slide, click the *Sound* option box arrow and then click *[No Sound]* at the drop-down gallery. To remove sound from all slides, click the Apply To All button.

Activity 4b Adding Slide Transitions and Transition Sounds to a Presentation   Part 2 of 3

1. With **1-Computers** open, click the Transitions tab.
2. Apply transitions and a transition sound to all slides in the presentation by completing the following steps:
   a. Click the More Transitions button at the right of the transitions gallery in the Transition to This Slide group.

b. Click the *Fall Over* option in the *Exciting* section.
c. Click the Effect Options button in the Transition to This Slide group and then click *Right* at the drop-down list.

d. Click in the *Duration* measurement box in the Timing group, type 1, and then press the Enter key.

e. Click the *Sound* option box arrow in the Timing group and then click *Chime* at the drop-down list.

f. Click the Apply To All button in the Timing group.

3. Run the slide show. (Notice the transitions and transition sound as you move from slide to slide.)
4. With the presentation in Normal view and the Transitions tab active, remove the transitions and transition sound by completing the following steps:
   a. Click the More Transitions button in the Transition to This Slide group and then click the *None* option in the *Subtle* section.
   b. Click the *Sound* option box arrow and then click *[No Sound]* at the drop-down list.
   c. Click the Apply To All button.
5. Apply transitions and transition sounds to specific slides by completing the following steps:
   a. Make sure the presentation displays in Normal view.
   b. Click Slide 1 in the slide thumbnails pane.
   c. Hold down the Shift key and then click Slide 2 in the slide thumbnails pane. (Slides 1 and 2 will display with orange backgrounds.)
   d. Click the More Transitions button at the right of the transitions gallery and then click the *Ferris Wheel* option in the *Dynamic Content* section.
   e. Click the *Sound* option box arrow and then click the *Breeze* option.
   f. Click Slide 3 in the slide thumbnails pane.
   g. Hold down the Shift key and then click Slide 4.
   h. Click the More Transitions button at the right of the transitions gallery and then click the *Glitter* option in the *Exciting* section.
   i. Click the *Sound* option box arrow and then click the *Wind* option.
6. Run the slide show from the beginning.
7. Remove the transitions and transition sounds from all slides. (Refer to Step 4.)
8. Save **1-Computers**.

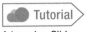
Tutorial

Advancing Slides
Automatically

Quick Steps

**Advance Slides
Automatically**
1. Click Transitions tab.
2. Click *After* check
   box.
3. Insert number
   of seconds in
   measurement box.
4. Click *On Mouse Click*
   check box.
5. Click Apply To All
   button.

Advancing Slides Automatically

Slides in a slide show can be advanced after a specific number of seconds by selecting options in the Timing group on the Transitions tab. To advance slides automatically, click the *After* check box and then insert the number of seconds in the measurement box. Or, select the current time in the measurement box and then type the time, or click the up or down arrows to increase or decrease the time. Click the *On Mouse Click* check box to remove the check mark. To apply the transition time to all slides in the presentation, click the Apply To All button. In Slide Sorter view, the transition time displays below each affected slide.

Activity 4c Advancing Slides Automatically

1. With **1-Computers** open, make sure the Transitions tab is active.
2. Click the *On Mouse Click* check box in the Timing group to remove the check mark.
3. Click in the *After* check box in the Timing group to insert a check mark.
4. Click the *After* measurement box up arrow until *00:04.00* displays in the box.
5. Click the Apply To All button.

6. Run the slide show from the beginning. (Each slide will advance automatically after four seconds.)
7. At the black screen, click the left mouse button.
8. Print the presentation as an outline by completing the following steps:
   a. Click the File tab and then click the *Print* option.
   b. At the Print backstage area, click the second gallery (displays with *Full Page Slides*) in the *Settings* category and then click *Outline* in the *Print Layout* section.
   c. Click the Print button.
9. Save and then close **1-Computers**.

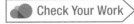
Check Your Work

Chapter Summary

- PowerPoint is a presentation graphics program used for creating slides for an on-screen presentation.

- Open a presentation at the Open dialog box. Display this dialog box by clicking the File tab and then clicking the *Open* option. At the Open backstage area, click the *Browse* option.

- A presentation can be pinned to or unpinned from the *Recent* option list at the Open backstage area or the Recent list at the Home backstage area.

- Start running a slide show by clicking the Start From Beginning button on the Quick Access Toolbar, by clicking the Slide Show button in the view area on the Status bar, or by clicking the View tab and then clicking the From Beginning button.

- Close a presentation by clicking the File tab and then clicking the *Close* option or with the keyboard shortcut Ctrl + F4.

- Before creating a presentation in PowerPoint, plan the presentation by defining the purpose and determining the content and display medium.

- Built-in presentation design theme templates are available at the New backstage area. Display this backstage area by clicking the File tab and then clicking the *New* option.

- To insert text in a slide, click in a placeholder and then type the text.

- Insert a new slide in a presentation with the Title and Content layout by clicking the New Slide button in the Slides group on the Home tab. Insert a new slide with a specific layout by clicking the New Slide button arrow and then clicking the layout at the drop-down list.

- A slide layout provides placeholders for specific data in a slide. Choose a slide layout by clicking the Layout button in the Slides group on the Home tab and then clicking a layout option at the drop-down list.

- Save a presentation by clicking the Save button on the Quick Access Toolbar or clicking the File tab and then clicking the *Save As* option. At the Save As backstage area, click the *Browse* option. At the Save As dialog box, navigate to the location where the presentation is to be saved and then type a name for the presentation.

- View a presentation in one of the following six views: Normal view, which is the default view and displays two panes—the slide thumbnails pane and the slide pane; Outline view, which displays the outline pane for typing text in slides; Slide Sorter view, which displays all slides in the presentation in slide thumbnails; Reading view, which delivers a presentation to people viewing it on their computers; Notes Page view, which displays an individual slide with any added notes displayed below the slide; and Slide Show view, which runs the slide show.

- Navigate to various slides in a presentation using the mouse and/or keyboard. Navigate in the presentation using the Previous Slide and Next Slide buttons at the bottom of the vertical scroll bar, the scroll box on the vertical scroll bar, arrow keys on the keyboard, or the Page Up and Page Down keys on the keyboard.

- Click the File tab and the backstage area displays options for working with and managing presentations.

- Use options at the Print backstage area to print presentations with each slide on a separate piece of paper; each slide at the top of the page, leaving room for notes; all or a specific number of slides on a single piece of paper; or slide titles and topics in outline form.

- When a slide show is running, the Slide Show toolbar displays in the lower left corner of the slide. This toolbar contains buttons and options for running a slide show. Use the buttons to navigate to slides, make ink notations on slides, display slide thumbnails, zoom in on a specific location in a slide, and display a Help menu.

- Apply a design theme to a presentation by clicking the Design tab and then clicking the theme in the themes gallery in the Themes group. Apply a color variation to a theme by clicking an option in the Variants group on the Design tab.

- Delete a presentation at the Open or Save As dialog box by clicking the presentation file name in the Content pane, clicking the Organize button on the toolbar, and then clicking *Delete* at the drop-down list. Another method for deleting a presentation it to right-click a presentation file name in the Content pane of the Open or Save As dialog box and then click *Delete* at the shortcut menu.

- Open a blank presentation by displaying the PowerPoint opening screen, the Home backstage area, or the New backstage area and then clicking the *Blank Presentation* template or with the keyboard shortcut Ctrl + N.

- Type text in a slide in the slide pane or in the outline pane. Display the outline pane by clicking the View tab and then clicking the Outline View button.

- Enhance a presentation by adding slide transitions (how one slide is removed from the screen and replaced with the next slide) and transition sounds. Add transitions and transition sounds to a presentation with options on the Transitions tab.

- Advance slides automatically in a slide show by removing the check mark from the *On Mouse Click* check box on the Transitions tab, inserting a check mark in the *After* check box, and then specifying the time in the *After* measurement box.

- Click the Apply To All button to apply transitions, transition sounds, and/or time settings to all slides in a presentation.

Commands Review

FEATURE	RIBBON TAB, GROUP/OPTION	BUTTON	KEYBOARD SHORTCUT
close presentation	File, *Close*		Ctrl + F4
design theme	Design, Themes		
New backstage area	File, *New*		
new slide	Home, Slides		Ctrl + M
Normal view	View, Presentation Views		
Notes Page view	View, Presentation Views		
Open backstage area	File, *Open*		Ctrl + O
Outline view	View, Presentation Views		
Print backstage area	File, *Print*		Ctrl + P
run slide show	Slide Show, Start Slide Show OR Quick Access Toolbar		F5
Save As backstage area	File, *Save* OR *Save As*		Ctrl + S
slide layout	Home, Slides		
Slide Sorter view	View, Presentation Views		
transition	Transitions, Transition to This Slide		
transition duration	Transitions, Timing		
transition sound	Transitions, Timing		

Microsoft®

PowerPoint®

Modifying a Presentation and Using Help and Tell Me

CHAPTER 2

Performance Objectives

Upon successful completion of Chapter 2, you will be able to:

1 Check spelling

2 Use the Thesaurus

3 Find and replace text in slides

4 Cut, copy, and paste text in slides

5 Rearrange text in the outline pane

6 Size and rearrange placeholders

7 Insert, delete, move, and copy slides

8 Copy slides between presentations

9 Duplicate slides

10 Reuse slides

11 Create and manage sections

12 Customize the Quick Access Toolbar

13 Use the Help and Tell Me features

When preparing a presentation, modify the contents by finding and replacing specific text or copying and pasting text in slides. Improve the quality of a presentation by completing a spelling check to ensure that the words in the presentation are spelled correctly and use the Thesaurus to find synonyms and antonyms. Additional modifications that can be made to a presentation include sizing and rearranging placeholders and rearranging, inserting, deleting, or copying slides. In this chapter, you will learn how to make these modifications to a presentation as well as how to create sections within a presentation and use the Help and Tell Me features.

 Data Files

Before beginning chapter work, copy the PC2 folder to your storage medium and then make PC2 the active folder.

The online course includes additional training and assessment resources.

<table>
<tr><td>

Activity 1 **Check Spelling, Use the Thesaurus, and Manage Text in a Design Presentation**

</td><td>**2 Parts**</td></tr>
</table>

You will open a presentation on steps for planning a design publication, complete a spelling check on the text in the presentation, use the Thesaurus to find synonyms, and find and replace specific text in slides.

Checking Spelling

Checking Spelling

When preparing a presentation, perform a spelling check on text in slides using PowerPoint's spelling checker feature. The spelling checker feature compares words in slides in a presentation with words in its dictionary. If a match is found, the word is passed over. If a match is not found, the Spelling task pane displays replacement suggestions. At this task pane, choose to change the word or ignore it and leave it as written. To perform a spelling check, click the Review tab and then click the Spelling button in the Proofing group. Pressing the F7 function key will also start the spelling checker.

Spelling

Quick Steps

Complete Spelling Check
1. Click Review tab.
2. Click Spelling button.
3. Change or ignore errors.
4. Click OK.

When checking the spelling in the presentation in Activity 1a, the spelling checker will stop at the misspelled word *Layuot* and display the Spelling task pane as shown in Figure 2.1. The buttons available in the Spelling task pane are described in Table 2.1.

Figure 2.1 Spelling Task Pane

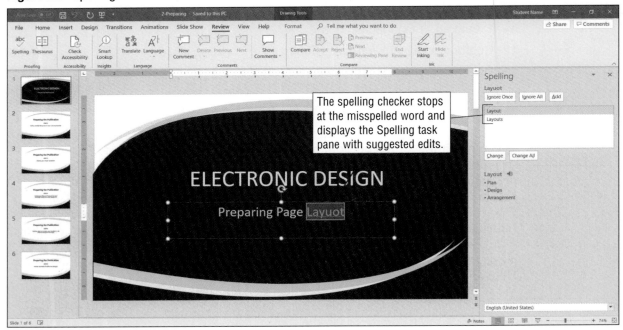

The spelling checker stops at the misspelled word and displays the Spelling task pane with suggested edits.

Table 2.1 Spelling Task Pane Options

Button	Function
Ignore Once	skips that occurrence of the word
Ignore All	skips that occurrence of the word and all other occurrences of the word in the presentation
Add	adds the selected word to the main spelling check dictionary
Delete	deletes the currently selected word(s)
Change	replaces the selected word with the word selected in the task pane list box
Change All	replaces the selected word and all other occurrences of it in the presentation with the word selected in the task pane list box

Tutorial

Using the
Thesaurus

Thesaurus

Q̃uick Steps

Use the Thesaurus
1. Click word.
2. Click Review tab.
3. Click Thesaurus button.
4. Position mouse pointer on replacement word in Thesaurus task pane.
5. Click down arrow at right of word.
6. Click *Insert*.

Using the Thesaurus

Use the Thesaurus to find synonyms, antonyms, and related words for a particular word. Synonyms are words that have the same or nearly the same meaning and antonyms are words with the opposite meanings.

To use the Thesaurus, click in the word, click the Review tab, and then click the Thesaurus button in the Proofing group. This displays the Thesaurus task pane with information about the word where the insertion point is positioned. Hover the mouse over the synonym or antonym, click the down arrow at the right of the word, and then click *Insert* at the drop-down list. Another method for displaying and inserting a synonym for a word is to right-click the word, point to *Synonyms*, and then click the replacement word at the side menu.

Activity 1a Checking the Spelling in a Presentation   Part 1 of 2

1. Open **Preparing** and then save it with the name **2-Preparing**.
2. With the presentation in Normal view, run a spelling check by completing the following steps:
   a. Click the Review tab.
   b. Click the Spelling button in the Proofing group.
   c. The spelling checker selects the misspelled word *Layuot* and displays the Spelling task pane. The proper spelling (*Layout*) is selected in the Spelling task pane list box, so click the Change button (or the Change All button) to correct the misspelling.

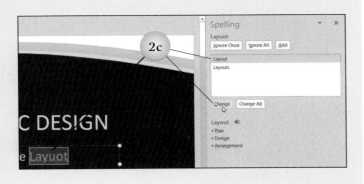

d. The spelling checker selects the misspelled word *Clerly*. The correct spelling is selected in the Spelling task pane list box, so click the Change button (or the Change All button).

e. When the spelling checker selects the misspelled word *massege*, click *message* in the Spelling task pane list box and then click the Change button (or the Change All button).

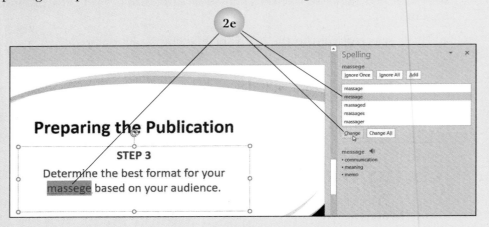

f. The spelling checker selects the misspelled word *fo*. The correct spelling is selected in the Spelling task pane list box, so click the Change button (or the Change All button).

g. At the message stating that the spell check is complete, click OK.

3. Make Slide 2 active and then use the Thesaurus to find a synonym for *point* by completing the following steps:

a. Click in the word *point*.

b. Click the Review tab, if necessary, and then click the Thesaurus button in the Proofing group.

c. At the Thesaurus task pane, if necessary, scroll down the task pane list box to display *purpose* (below *purpose (n.)*).

d. Hover your mouse pointer over the word *purpose* in the task pane, click the down arrow, and then click *Insert* at the drop-down list.

e. Close the Thesaurus task pane by clicking the Close button (contains an *X*) in the upper right corner of the task pane.

4. Make Slide 6 active and right-click in the word *Gather*.

5. Point to *Synonyms* at the short-cut menu and then click *Collect* at the side menu.

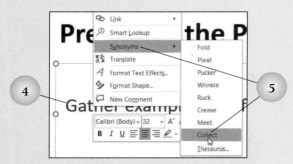

6. Save **2-Preparing**.

Check Your Work

Managing Text and Placeholders

Text in a placeholder in a slide can be edited, modified, and rearranged. For example, text can be replaced with other text and text can be cut, copied, and pasted to other locations. The placeholder containing text or other objects can be modified by resizing it or moving it to another location.

Finding and Replacing Text in Slides

Tutorial

Finding and
Replacing Text

 Find

 Replace

Quick Steps

Find Text
1. Click Find button.
2. Type search text.
3. Click Find Next button.

Replace Text
1. Click Replace button.
2. Type search text.
3. Press Tab key.
4. Type replacement text.
5. Click Replace All button.

Use the Find feature to look for specific text in slides in a presentation and use the Find and Replace feature to look for specific text in slides in a presentation and replace it with other text. Begin a search by clicking the Find button in the Editing group on the Home tab. This displays the Find dialog box, as shown in Figure 2.2. In the *Find what* text box, type the text to be found and then click the Find Next button. Continue clicking this button until a message displays indicating that the search is complete. At this message, click OK.

Use options at the Replace dialog box, shown in Figure 2.3, to search for text and replace it with other text. Display this dialog box by clicking the Replace button in the Editing group on the Home tab. Type the text to be found in the *Find what* text box, press the Tab key, and then type the replacement text in the *Replace with* text box. Click the Find Next button to find the next occurrence of the text and then click the Replace button to replace it with the new text, or click the Replace All button to replace all occurrences in the presentation.

Both the Find dialog box and the Replace dialog box contain two additional options. Insert a check mark in the *Match case* check box to specify that the text in the presentation should exactly match the case of the text in the *Find what* text box. For example, search for *Planning* and PowerPoint will stop at *Planning* but not *planning* or *PLANNING*. Insert a check mark in the *Find whole words only* check box to specify that the text to be found is a whole word only and not part of a word. For example, if you search for *plan* and do not check the *Find whole words only* option, PowerPoint will stop at ex*plan*ation, *plan*ned, *plan*ning, and so on.

Figure 2.2 Find Dialog Box

Figure 2.3 Replace Dialog Box

1. With **2-Preparing** open, make Slide 1 active.
2. Find all occurrences of *Preparing* in the presentation and replace them with *Planning* by completing the following steps:
   a. With Slide 1 active, click the Replace button in the Editing group on the Home tab.
   b. At the Replace dialog box, type Preparing in the *Find what* text box.
   c. Press the Tab key.
   d. Type Planning in the *Replace with* text box.
   e. Click the Replace All button.

   f. At the message stating that six replacements were made, click OK.
   g. Click the Close button to close the Replace dialog box.
3. Find all occurrences of *Publication* and replace them with *Newsletter* by completing steps similar to those in Step 2.
4. Save the presentation.
5. Apply a transition and transition sound of your choosing to all slides in the presentation.
6. Run the slide show.
7. Print Slide 1 by completing the following steps:
   a. Click the File tab and then click the *Print* option.
   b. At the Print backstage area, click in the *Slides* text box in the *Settings* category and then type 1.
   c. Click the Print button.
8. Print the presentation as a handout with six slides displayed horizontally on the page. (Change the second gallery in the *Settings* category to *6 Slides Horizontal* and delete the *1* in the *Slides* text box.)
9. Save and then close **2-Preparing**.

Check Your Work

Activity 2 Cut, Copy, Paste, Rearrange, and Manage   5 Parts
Slides in a Network Presentation

You will open a network evaluation presentation and then cut, copy, and paste text in slides; rearrange text in the slide thumbnails pane; size and rearrange placeholders in slides; and manage slides by inserting, deleting, moving, and copying them. You will also copy slides between presentations.

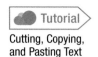

Tutorial

Cutting, Copying, and Pasting Text

 Cut

 Paste

 Copy

Cutting, Copying, and Pasting Text in Slides

Use buttons in the Clipboard group on the Home tab and/or shortcut menu options to cut, copy, and paste text in slides. For example, to move text in a slide, click in the placeholder containing the text to be moved, select the text, and then click the Cut button in the Clipboard group or use the keyboard shortcut Ctrl + X. Position the insertion point where the text is to be inserted and then click the Paste button in the Clipboard group or use the keyboard shortcut Ctrl + V.

To cut and paste with the shortcut menu, select the text to be moved, right-click in the selected text, and then click *Cut* at the shortcut menu. Position the insertion point where the text is to be inserted, right-click in the placeholder, and then click *Paste* at the shortcut menu. Complete similar steps to copy and paste text, except click the Copy button instead of the Cut button, use the keyboard shortcut Ctrl + C, or click the *Copy* option at the shortcut menu instead of the *Cut* option.

Activity 2a Cutting, Copying, and Pasting Text in Slides   Part 1 of 5

1. Open **NetworkSystem** and then save it with the name **2-NetworkSystem**.
2. Insert a new slide by completing the following steps:
   a. Make Slide 4 active.
   b. Click the New Slide button in the Slides group on the Home tab.
   c. Click in the title placeholder and then type TIME.
3. Cut text from Slide 3 and paste it into Slide 5 by completing the following steps:
   a. Make Slide 3 active.
   b. Click in the bulleted text in the slide pane.
   c. Using the mouse, select the bottom three lines of bulleted text. (The bullets will not be selected.)
   d. With the text selected, click the Cut button in the Clipboard group on the Home tab.

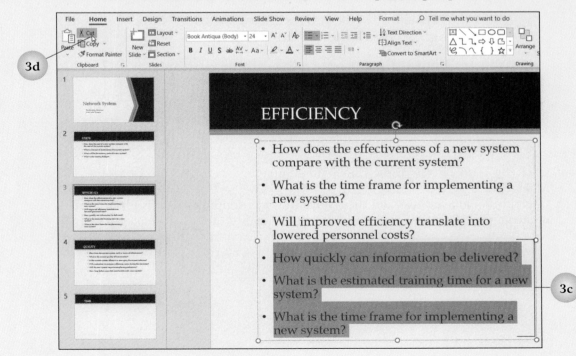

 e. Make Slide 5 the active slide (contains the title *TIME*).

 f. Click in the text placeholder.

 g. Click the Paste button in the Clipboard group.

 h. With the insertion point positioned below the third bulleted item following a bullet, press the Backspace key two times. (This removes the bullet and deletes the blank line below the third bullet.)

4. Insert a new slide by completing the following steps:

 a. With Slide 5 the active slide, click the New Slide button.

 b. Click in the title placeholder and then type EASE OF USE.

5. Cut text from Slide 4 and paste it into Slide 6 by completing the following steps:

 a. Make Slide 4 active.

 b. Click in the bulleted text.

 c. Select the bottom three bulleted items.

 d. Click the Cut button.

 e. Make Slide 6 active (contains the title *EASE OF USE*).

 f. Click in the text placeholder.

 g. Click the Paste button.

 h. With the insertion point positioned below the third bulleted item following a bullet, press the Backspace key two times.

6. Copy text from Slide 3 to Slide 5 by completing the following steps:

 a. Make Slide 3 active.

 b. Click in the bulleted text.

 c. Position the mouse pointer over the last bullet until the pointer turns into a four-headed arrow and then click the left mouse button. (Clicking the bullet selects the bulleted text.)

 d. Click the Copy button in the Clipboard group.

 e. Make Slide 5 active.

 f. Click in the bulleted text and then move the insertion point so it is positioned immediately right of the question mark at the end of the second bulleted item.

g. Press the Enter key. (This moves the insertion point down to the next line and inserts another bullet.)

h. Click the Paste button.

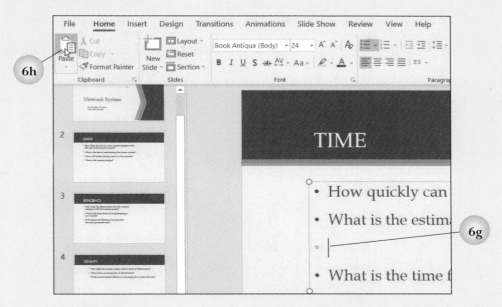

i. If there is a blank line between the third and fourth bullets, press the Backspace key two times to remove it.

7. Save **2-NetworkSystem**.

 Check Your Work

 Tutorial

Rearranging Text Using the Outline Pane

Rearranging Text Using the Outline Pane

Text in slides can be moved and copied in the outline pane. Display the outline pane by clicking the View tab and then clicking the Outline View button in the Presentation Views group or with the keyboard shortcut Ctrl + Shift + Tab. To move text in the outline pane, position the mouse pointer on the slide icon or bullet at the left of the text until the mouse pointer turns into a four-headed arrow. Click and hold down the left mouse button, drag the mouse pointer (a thin horizontal line displays) to the new location, and then release the mouse button.

Position the mouse pointer on the slide icon and then click the left mouse button and all of the text in the slide is selected. Click a bullet and all text following that bullet is selected.

Dragging selected text with the mouse moves the selected text to a new location in the presentation. Selected text can also be copied. To do this, click the slide icon or the bullet to select the text. Position the mouse pointer in the selected text, press and hold down the Ctrl key, and then click and hold down the left mouse button. Drag the mouse pointer (displays with a light gray box and a plus symbol attached) to the new location, release the mouse button, and then release the Ctrl key.

1. With **2-NetworkSystem** open, make Slide 1 active.
2. Press Ctrl + Shift + Tab to display the outline pane.
3. Move the first bulleted item in Slide 4 in the outline pane to the end of the list by completing the following steps:
   a. Position the mouse pointer on the first bullet below *QUALITY* until it turns into a four-headed arrow.
   b. Click and hold down the left mouse button, drag the mouse pointer down until a thin horizontal line displays below the last bulleted item, and then release the mouse button.

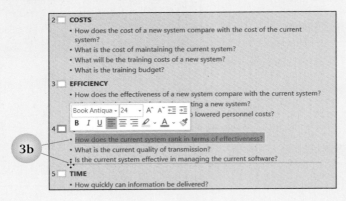

4. Copy and paste text by completing the following steps:
   a. In the outline pane, move the insertion point to the end of the text in Slide 6 and then press the Enter key. (This inserts a new bullet in the slide.)
   b. If necessary, scroll up the outline pane until the last bulleted item in Slide 2 is visible in the outline pane as well as the last bullet in Slide 6. (You may need to increase the width of the outline pane to display both bulleted items.)
   c. Position the mouse pointer near the last bulleted item in Slide 2 until it turns into a four-headed arrow and then click the left mouse button. (This selects the text.)
   d. Position the mouse pointer in the selected text, click and hold down the left mouse button, press and hold down the Ctrl key, and then drag down until the mouse pointer and light gray vertical line display on the blank line below the text in Slide 6.
   e. Release the mouse button and then release the Ctrl key.
5. Press Ctrl + Shift + Tab to return to the slide thumbnails pane.
6. Click the Notes button on the Status bar to close the notes pane.
7. Save **2-NetworkSystem**.

Check Your Work

Modifying Placeholders

Clicking in a placeholder selects the placeholder and displays white sizing handles and a white rotation handle around the placeholder border. Use the sizing handles to increase or decrease the size of the placeholder by positioning the mouse pointer on a sizing handle until the pointer turns into a double-headed arrow and then dragging the placeholder border to the desired size. To move a placeholder, position the mouse pointer on the placeholder border until the mouse pointer displays with a four-headed arrow attached. Click and hold down the left mouse button, drag the placeholder to the new position, and then release the mouse button.

Dragging a selected placeholder with the mouse moves the placeholder. To copy a placeholder, press and hold down the Ctrl key while dragging the placeholder. When the placeholder is in position, release the mouse button, and then release the Ctrl key. If an unwanted change is made to the size and/or location of a placeholder, click the Reset button in the Slides group on the Home tab to return the formatting of the placeholder back to the default.

When dragging a placeholder on a slide, guidelines may display. Use the guidelines to help position placeholders. For example, use the guidelines to help align a title placeholder with a subtitle placeholder.

If a placeholder is no longer necessary, delete the placeholder. To delete a placeholder, click in the placeholder, click the border to change it to a solid line border, and then press the Delete key.

Activity 2c Sizing and Rearranging Placeholders   Part 3 of 5

1. With **2-NetworkSystem** open, make Slide 1 active.
2. Size and move a placeholder by completing the following steps:
   a. Click in the subtitle *Evaluating Current Network System*.
   b. Position the mouse pointer on the sizing handle (small, white circle) in the middle of the right border until the pointer turns into a left-and-right-pointing arrow.
   c. Click and hold down the left mouse button, drag to the right until the subtitle text appears on one line, and then release the mouse button.

   d. Position the mouse pointer on the border of the placeholder until the pointer turns into a four-headed arrow.
   e. Click and hold down the left mouse button, drag the placeholder up and to the left so the placeholder is positioned as shown at the right, and then release the mouse button. Use the guideline to the left of and above the placeholder to align the subtitle placeholder with the title placeholder.

3. Make Slide 4 active.

4. Size and move a placeholder by completing the following steps:
   a. Click in the bulleted text.
   b. Position the mouse pointer on the sizing handle in the middle of the right border until the pointer turns into a left-and-right-pointing arrow.
   c. Click and hold down the left mouse button, drag to the left until the right border is positioned just to the right of the question mark in the first bulleted item, and then release the mouse button.

   d. Drag the middle sizing handle on the bottom border up until the bottom border of the placeholder is positioned just below the last bulleted item.
   e. Position the mouse pointer on the border of the placeholder until the pointer turns into a four-headed arrow.
   f. Click and hold down the left mouse button, drag the placeholder to the left until the vertical guideline displays left of the title, and then release the mouse button.

5. Save **2-NetworkSystem**.

Managing Slides

Editing a presentation may require reorganizing slides, inserting new slides, or deleting existing slides. Manage slides in the slide thumbnails pane or in Slide Sorter view. Switch to Slide Sorter view by clicking the Slide Sorter button in the view area on the Status bar or by clicking the View tab and then clicking the Slide Sorter button in the Presentation Views group.

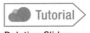
Deleting Slides

Ọuick Steps

Insert Slide
1. Click Home tab.
2. Click New Slide button.

Delete Slide
1. Click slide in slide thumbnails pane.
2. Press Delete key.

Inserting and Deleting Slides

As explained in Chapter 1, clicking the New Slide button in the Slides group on the Home tab inserts a new slide in the presentation immediately following the currently active slide. A new slide can also be inserted in Slide Sorter view. To do this, click the slide that should immediately precede the new slide and then click the New Slide button in the Slides group. Delete a slide in Normal view by clicking the slide thumbnail in the slide thumbnails pane and then pressing the Delete key. A slide can also be deleted by switching to Slide Sorter view, clicking the slide thumbnail, and then pressing the Delete key.

Rearranging Slides

Hint Press
Ctrl + X to cut the
selected slide and then
press Ctrl + V to paste
the cut slide.

Rearranging Slides

Rearrange slides in a presentation in Normal view or Slide Sorter view. In Normal view, click a slide in the slide thumbnails pane and then position the mouse pointer on the selected slide. Click and hold down the left mouse button, drag the pointer up or down until the slide thumbnail is in the new location, and then release the mouse button. Complete similar steps to move a slide in Slide Sorter view. Click the desired slide and hold down the left mouse button, drag the slide to the new location, and then release the mouse button.

Copying a Slide

Hint Press
Ctrl + C to copy the
selected slide and then
press Ctrl + V to paste
the copied slide.

Copying a Slide

When creating slides in a presentation, some slides may contain similar text, objects, and/or formatting. Rather than creating new slides in these presentations, consider copying an existing slide. To do this, display the presentation in Slide Sorter view, position the mouse on the slide to be copied, press and hold down the Ctrl key, and then click and hold down the left mouse button. Drag the copy of the slide thumbnail to the location where it is to be inserted, release the mouse button, and then release the Ctrl key. Slides can also be copied using the Ctrl key in the slide thumbnails pane in Normal view.

In addition to copying slides using the Ctrl key, slides can be copied in Normal view or Slide Sorter view with buttons in the Clipboard group on the Home tab. To copy a slide, click the slide thumbnail and then click the Copy button in the Clipboard group. Click the slide thumbnail of the slide that will precede the copied slide and then click the Paste button in the Clipboard group.

Activity 2d **Moving and Copying Slides**   Part 4 of 5

1. With **2-NetworkSystem** open in Normal view, move slides by completing the following steps:
   a. Click Slide 3 (*EFFICIENCY*) in the slide thumbnails pane.
   b. Position the mouse pointer on Slide 3, click and hold down the left mouse button, drag the slide thumbnail up between Slides 1 and 2, and then release the mouse button.
   c. Click Slide 4 (*QUALITY*) in the slide thumbnails pane.
   d. Position the mouse pointer on Slide 4, click and hold down the left mouse button, drag the slide thumbnail down below Slide 6, and then release the mouse button.
2. Move and copy slides in Slide Sorter view by completing the following steps:
   a. Click the Slide Sorter button in the view area on the Status bar.
   b. Click Slide 4 (*TIME*) to make it the active slide. (The slide thumbnail displays with an orange border.)

1b

c. Position the mouse pointer on Slide 4, click and hold down the left mouse button, drag the slide thumbnail between Slides 1 and 2, and then release the mouse button.

d. Click Slide 1 to make it the active slide.
e. Position the mouse pointer on Slide 1 (*Network System*), click and hold down the left mouse button, and then press and hold down the Ctrl key.
f. Drag the slide thumbnail down and to the right of Slide 6.

g. Release the mouse button and then release the Ctrl key.
3. Click the Normal button in the view area on the Status bar.
4. Save **2-NetworkSystem**.

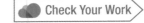
Check Your Work

Copying a Slide between Presentations

Slides can be copied between presentations as well as within them. To copy a slide, click the slide thumbnail of the slide to be copied (either in Slide Sorter view or in the slide thumbnails pane in Normal view) and then click the Copy button in the Clipboard group on the Home tab. Open the presentation into which the slide is to be copied (in either Normal view or Slide Sorter view). Click in the location where the slide is to be positioned and then click the Paste button. The copied slide will take on the design theme of the presentation into which it is copied.

1. With **2-NetworkSystem** open, open the file named **EvalNetwork** in your PC2 folder.
2. Copy Slide 2 from **EvalNetwork** to the **2-NetworkSystem** file by completing the following steps:
   a. With **EvalNetwork** active, click Slide 2 in the slide thumbnails pane to make it the active slide.
   b. Click the Copy button in the Clipboard group on the Home tab.
   c. Position the mouse pointer on the PowerPoint button on the taskbar and then click the **2-NetworkSystem** thumbnail.
   d. Click Slide 4 (*COSTS*) in the slide thumbnails pane.
   e. Click the Paste button.
   f. Position the mouse pointer on the PowerPoint button on the taskbar and then click the **EvalNetwork** thumbnail.
3. Copy Slide 3 from the **EvalNetwork** to **2-NetworkSystem** by completing the following steps:
   a. With **EvalNetwork** active, click Slide 3 in the slide thumbnails pane.
   b. Position the mouse pointer on Slide 3 and then click the right mouse button. (This displays a shortcut menu.)
   c. Click *Copy* at the shortcut menu.
   d. Position the mouse pointer on the PowerPoint button on the taskbar and then click the **2-NetworkSystem** thumbnail.
   e. Right-click Slide 3 in the slide thumbnails pane.
   f. Click the Use Destination Theme button in the *Paste Options* section.

4. Position the mouse pointer on the PowerPoint button on the taskbar and then click the **EvalNetwork** thumbnail.
5. Close the presentation.
6. With **2-NetworkSystem** open, delete Slide 9 by completing the following steps:
   a. If necessary, scroll down the slide thumbnails pane until Slide 9 is visible.
   b. Click to select Slide 9.
   c. Press the Delete key.
7. Save the presentation.
8. Print the presentation as a handout with four slides displayed horizontally per page.
9. Close **2-NetworkSystem**.

<table>
<tr><td>

Activity 3 **Insert and Manage Slides in an Adventure
Tours Presentation**

</td><td>**4 Parts**</td></tr>
</table>

You will open a presentation on Adventure Tours and then insert additional slides
by duplicating existing slides in the presentation and reusing slides from another
presentation. You will then divide the presentation into sections, rearrange
sections, and print a section. You will also make customizations to the Quick
Access Toolbar.

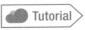

Tutorial

Duplicating Slides

Quick Steps

Duplicate Slides
1. Select slides in slide
   thumbnails pane.
2. Click New Slide
   button arrow.
3. Click *Duplicate
   Selected Slides* at
   drop-down list.

Duplicating Slides

In Activity 2, the Copy and Paste buttons in the Clipboard group and options
from a shortcut menu were used to copy slides in a presentation. Slides can also
be copied in a presentation using the *Duplicate Selected Slides* option from the New
Slide button drop-down list or by clicking the Copy button arrow and then
clicking *Duplicate* at the drop-down list. In addition to duplicating slides, the
Duplicate option from the Copy button drop-down list can be used to duplicate a
selected object in a slide, such as a placeholder.

A single slide or multiple selected slides can be duplicated. To select adjacent
(sequential) slides, click the first slide in the slide thumbnails pane, press and hold
down the Shift key, and then click the last slide. This will select all slides between
that first slide and the last slide. To select nonadjacent (nonsequential) slides,
press and hold down the Ctrl key while clicking each slide.

Activity 3a **Duplicating Selected Slides**   Part 1 of 4

1. Open **AdvTours** and then save it with
   the name **2-AdvTours**.
2. Make sure the presentation displays in
   Normal view.
3. Select and then duplicate slides by
   completing the following steps:
   a. Click Slide 1 in the slide
      thumbnails pane.
   b. Press and hold down the Ctrl key.
   c. Click Slide 3, Slide 4, and then
      Slide 5.
   d. Release the Ctrl key.
   e. Click the New Slide button arrow
      in the Slides group on the Home
      tab and then click *Duplicate Selected
      Slides* at the drop-down list.
4. With Slide 6 active in the slide pane,
   change *Fiji Tour* to *Costa Rica Tour*.

5. Make Slide 7 active, select *Fiji* in the title and then type Costa Rica. Select and delete the existing bulleted text and then type the following bulleted text:
   - Round-trip airfare from Los Angeles to San Jose, Costa Rica
   - 8 days and 7 nights in Costa Rica
   - Monthly tours
   - Prices from $1099 to $1599

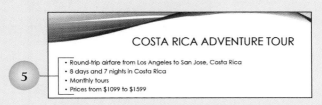

6. Make Slide 8 active, select and delete the existing bulleted text, and then type the following bulleted text:
   - San Jose, Emerald Suites
   - Tortuguero, Plantation Spa and Resort
   - Fortuna, Pacific Resort
   - Jaco, Monteverde Cabanas

7. Make Slide 9 active, select and delete the existing bulleted text, and then type the following bulleted text:
   - San Jose city tour
   - Rainforest tram
   - Canal cruise
   - Forest hike

8. Save **2-AdvTours**.

 Check Your Work

 Tutorial

Reusing Slides

Quick Steps

Reuse Slides
1. Click New Slide button arrow.
2. Click *Reuse Slides*.
3. Click Browse button.
4. Navigate to folder.
5. Double-click presentation.
6. Click slide in Reuse Slides task pane.

Reusing Slides

Reusing slides is another method for copying slides from one presentation to another. Click the New Slide button arrow and then click the *Reuse Slides* option at the drop-down list to display the Reuse Slides task pane at the right side of the screen, as shown in Figure 2.4. Depending on the PowerPoint version being used, a Reuse Slides button may display in the Slides group on the Home tab and the Insert tab. At the Reuse Slides task pane, click the Browse button and the Browse dialog box displays. At this dialog box, navigate to the desired folder and then double-click the presentation. This inserts the presentation slides in the Reuse Slides task pane. Click a slide in the Reuse Slides task pane to insert it into the currently open presentation.

By default, the slides inserted from the Reuse Slides task pane will take on the formatting of the current presentation. To retain the original formatting of the slides when inserted into the current presentation, insert a check mark in the *Keep source formatting* check box at the bottom of the Reuse Slides task pane.

Figure 2.4 Reuse Slides Task Pane

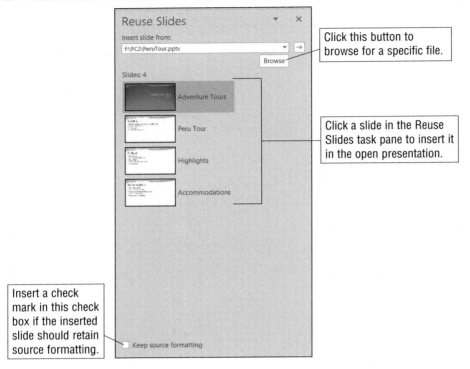

Click this button to browse for a specific file.

Click a slide in the Reuse Slides task pane to insert it in the open presentation.

Insert a check mark in this check box if the inserted slide should retain source formatting.

Activity 3b Reusing Slides

Part 2 of 4

1. With **2-AdvTours** open, click the New Slide button arrow in the Slides group on the Home tab and then click *Reuse Slides* at the drop-down list (or click the Reuse Slides button in the Slides group, if it is available). (This displays the Reuse Slides task pane at the right side of the screen.)
2. Click the Browse button in the Reuse Slides task pane.
3. At the Browse dialog box, navigate to your PC2 folder and then double-click *PeruTour*.
4. In the slide thumbnails pane, scroll down the slide thumbnails until Slide 9 displays and then click below Slide 9. (This inserts a thin, horizontal line below the Slide 9 thumbnail in the slide thumbnails pane.)
5. Click the first slide thumbnail (*Adventure Tours*) in the Reuse Slides task pane. (This inserts the slide in the open presentation immediately below Slide 9.)
6. Click the second slide thumbnail (*Peru Tour*) in the Reuse Slides task pane.
7. Click the fourth slide thumbnail (*Accommodations*) in the Reuse Slides task pane.
8. Click the third slide thumbnail (*Highlights*) in the Reuse Slides task pane.
9. Close the Reuse Slides task pane by clicking the Close button (contains an *X*) in the upper right corner of the task pane.
10. Save **2-AdvTours**.

 Check Your Work

Tutorial

Creating Sections
within a Presentation

Creating Sections within a Presentation

When working on a presentation with others in a group or working in a presentation containing numerous slides, consider dividing related slides in the presentation into sections. Dividing a presentation into sections allows for easy navigating and editing of slides within the presentation.

Create a section by selecting the first slide in the slide thumbnails pane, clicking the Section button in the Slides group on the Home tab, and then clicking *Add Section* at the drop-down list. Type a name for the new section at the Rename Section dialog box. Once a section has been named, the name will display as a title bar above the first slide in the section in the slide thumbnails pane.

Rename, remove, move, collapse, and expand sections with options in the Section button drop-down list or by right-clicking the section title bar and then clicking an option at the shortcut menu. Different formatting can be applied to an individual section by clicking the section title bar to select that section and then applying the formatting.

Creating sections within a presentation provides the option to print only certain sections of the presentation. To print a section of a presentation, click the File tab, click the *Print* option, click the first gallery in the *Settings* category, click the section at the drop-down list, and then click the Print button.

 Section

Quick Steps

Create Section
1. Select first slide for new section.
2. Click Section button.
3. Click *Add Section*.

Activity 3c Creating and Printing Sections

Part 3 of 4

1. With **2-AdvTours** open, create a section for slides about Fiji by completing the following steps:
   a. Click Slide 1 in the slide thumbnails pane.
   b. Click the Section button in the Slides group on the Home tab and then click *Add Section* at the drop-down list.
   c. At the Rename Section dialog box, type Fiji Tour and then click the Rename button.

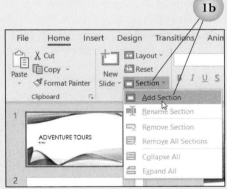

2. Create a section for slides about Costa Rica by completing the following steps:
   a. Click Slide 6 in the slide thumbnails pane.
   b. Click the Section button and then click *Add Section* at the drop-down list.
   c. At the Rename Section dialog box, type Costa Rica and then press the Enter key.
3. Complete steps similar to those in Step 2 to create a section beginning with Slide 10 and type Peru Tour as the section name.

4. Rename the *Costa Rica* section by completing the following steps:
   a. Right-click in the section title bar that displays *Costa Rica* in the slide thumbnails pane.
   b. Click *Rename Section* at the shortcut menu.
   c. At the Rename Section dialog box, type Tour at the end of the title. (The section name should display as *Costa Rica Tour*.)
   d. Click the Rename button.
5. Change the design theme of a section by completing the following steps:
   a. Click the *Fiji Tour* section title bar at the top of the slide thumbnails pane. (This selects all five slides in the *Fiji Tour* section.)
   b. Click the Design tab.
   c. Click the More Themes button in the themes gallery.
   d. Click the *Wisp* theme at the drop-down gallery. (Note: The location of the design theme may vary from what is shown in the image below.)

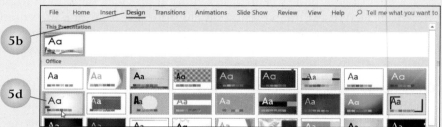

6. Complete steps similar to those in Steps 5a through 5d to apply the Ion Boardroom design theme to the *Costa Rica Tour* section.
7. Move the Peru Tour section above the *Costa Rica Tour* section by completing the following steps:
   a. Click the Home tab, click the Section button in the Slides group, and then click *Collapse All* at the drop-down list.
   b. Position the mouse pointer on the *Peru Tour* section title bar, click and hold down the left mouse button, drag the title bar up until the title displays above the *Costa Rica Tour* section title bar, and then release the mouse button.

8. Display only slides in the *Costa Rica Tour* section by double-clicking the *Costa Rica Tour* section title bar in the slide thumbnails pane. (Notice that only Slides 10 through 13 display in the slide thumbnails pane and that the slides in the *Fiji Tour* and *Peru Tour* sections are hidden.)
9. Redisplay the *Fiji Tour* section slides by double-clicking the *Fiji Tour* section title bar in the slide thumbnails pane.
10. Display all sections by clicking the Section button in the Slides group and then clicking *Expand All* at the drop-down list.

11. Print only the *Costa Rica Tour* section by completing the following steps:
   a. Click the File tab and then click the *Print* option.
   b. At the Print backstage area, click the first gallery in the *Settings* category and then click *Costa Rica Tour* in the *Sections* section (at the bottom of the drop-down list).
   c. Click the second gallery (contains the text *Full Page Slides*) in the *Settings* category and then click *4 Slides Horizontal* in the *Handouts* section.
   d. Click the Print button.
12. Complete steps similar to those in Step 11 to print only the *Peru Tour* section.
13. Save **2-AdvTours**.

11b

Check Your Work

 Tutorial

Customizing the Quick Access Toolbar

Customizing the Quick Access Toolbar

 Save

 Undo

 Redo

 Start From Beginning

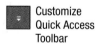 Customize Quick Access Toolbar

The Quick Access Toolbar contains buttons for some of the most commonly performed tasks. By default, the toolbar contains the Save, Undo, Redo, and Start From Beginning buttons. Buttons can be added to or deleted from the Quick Access Toolbar. To add or delete a button, click the Customize Quick Access Toolbar button at the right of the toolbar. At the drop-down list, options with a check mark display on the toolbar and options without a check mark do not. Click an option to add or remove a check mark to specify what buttons should appear on the toolbar.

Click the Customize Quick Access Toolbar button and then click the *More Commands* option at the drop-down list and the PowerPoint Options dialog box displays with *Quick Access Toolbar* selected in the left panel. Use options at this dialog box to add buttons from a list of PowerPoint commands. Click the Reset button at the dialog box to reset the Quick Access Toolbar back to the default.

By default, the Quick Access Toolbar displays above the ribbon tabs. Display the Quick Access Toolbar below the ribbon by clicking the Customize Quick Access Toolbar button and then clicking the *Show Below the Ribbon* option at the drop-down list.

Activity 3d Customizing the Quick Access Toolbar

Part 4 of 4

1. With **2-AdvTours** open, add a New button to the Quick Access Toolbar by clicking the Customize Quick Access Toolbar button and then clicking *New* at the drop-down list.
2. Add an Open button to the Quick Access Toolbar by clicking the Customize Quick Access Toolbar button and then clicking *Open* at the drop-down list.

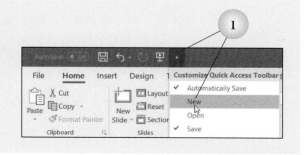

1

3. Add a Print Preview and Print button to the Quick Access Toolbar by clicking the Customize Quick Access Toolbar button and then clicking *Print Preview and Print* at the drop-down list.
4. Move the Quick Access Toolbar below the ribbon by clicking the Customize Quick Access Toolbar button and then clicking the *Show Below the Ribbon* option at the drop-down list.
5. Click the Print Preview and Print button on the Quick Access Toolbar. (This displays the Print backstage area.)
6. Click the Back button to close the Print backstage area and return to the presentation.
7. Close **2-AdvTours**.
8. Click the New button on the Quick Access Toolbar to open a new blank presentation.
9. Click the Open button on the Quick Access Toolbar to display the Open backstage area.
10. Press the Esc key to return to the blank presentation and then close the presentation.
11. Move the Quick Access Toolbar back to the original position by clicking the Customize Quick Access Toolbar button and then clicking the *Show Above the Ribbon* option at the drop-down list.
12. Remove the New button by clicking the Customize Quick Access Toolbar button and then clicking *New* at the drop-down list.
13. Remove the Open button by right-clicking the button and then clicking *Remove from Quick Access Toolbar* at the drop-down list.
14. Remove the Print Preview and Print button from the Quick Access Toolbar.

Activity 4 Use the PowerPoint Help and Tell Me Features and Create a Presentation   2 Parts

You will use the Help feature to learn more about PowerPoint features. You will also use the Help feature to find information on keyboard shortcuts and then use that information to create a presentation. You will use the Tell Me feature to change the font color for the presentation title.

Using the Help Feature

Help

Quick Steps
Use Help Feature
1. Press F1.
2. Type topic or feature name.
3. Press Enter key.
4. Click article hyperlink.

Using the Help Feature

Microsoft PowerPoint includes a Help feature that contains information about PowerPoint features and commands. This on-screen reference manual is similar to Windows Help and the Help features in Word, Excel, and Access.

Display the Help task pane by pressing the F1 function key or by clicking the Help tab and then clicking the Help button. In the Help task pane, type a topic, feature name, or question in the search text box, and then press the Enter key. Articles related to the search text display in the task pane. Click an article hyperlink and the article information displays in the task pane.

Getting Help from a ScreenTip

Hover the mouse pointer over a certain button and a ScreenTip displays with information about the button. Some button ScreenTips display with a Help icon and the text <u>Tell me more</u>. Click this hyperlinked text or press the F1 function key and the Help task pane displays with information about the button feature.

Getting Help in a Dialog Box or Backstage Area

Some dialog boxes and the backstage area contain a help button. Click this button to display the Microsoft Office support website with information about the dialog box or backstage area. After reading and/or printing the information, close the Microsoft Office support website by clicking the Close button in the upper right corner of the window.

Activity 4a Using the Help Feature and Creating a Presentation   Part 1 of 2

1. Open **Shortcuts** and then save the presentation with the name **2-Shortcuts**.
2. Press the F1 function key.
3. At the Help task pane, type basic tasks for creating a presentation in the search text box and then press the Enter key.
4. When the list of articles displays, click the <u>Basic tasks for creating a PowerPoint presentation</u> hyperlink. (If your Help task pane does not display this hyperlink, click a similar hyperlink.)
5. Read the information in the article.
6. Close the Help task pane by clicking the Close button in the upper right corner of the task pane.
7. Hover the mouse over the New Slide button in the Slides group on the Home tab and then click the <u>Tell me more</u> hyperlinked text at the bottom of the ScreenTip.
8. At the Help task pane, read the information on adding, rearranging, duplicating, and deleting slides and then click the Close button in the upper right corner of the task pane.
9. Click the File tab and then click the *Open* option.
10. At the Open backstage area, click the Microsoft PowerPoint Help button in the upper right corner of the backstage area.
11. Look at the information that displays at the Microsoft Office support website and then close the window.
12. Click the Back button to return to the presentation.
13. Click the Help tab and then click the Help button.

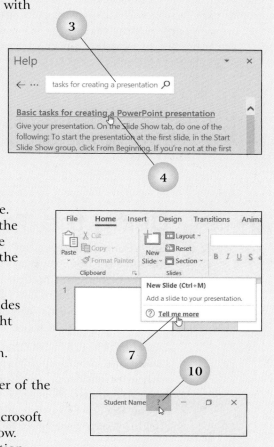

14. At the Help task pane, type keyboard shortcuts in the search text box and then press the Enter key.
15. When the list of articles displays, click the <u>Use keyboard shortcuts to create PowerPoint presentations</u> hyperlink.
16. Scroll down to the *Quick links* section and then click the <u>Select and edit text and objects</u> hyperlink.
17. Scroll down to the *Delete and copy text and objects* section.
18. With Slide 1 active, click in the title placeholder in the slide pane and then type PowerPoint Help.
19. Click in the subtitle placeholder and then type Keyboard Shortcuts.
20. Make Slide 2 active and then insert a new slide.
21. Type the text Cut, Copy, Paste Text as the title for the new slide.
22. Click in the *Click to add text* placeholder and then type the three items shown below. Type the keyboard shortcut for each item after the colon. (Hint: Find shortcuts for cutting, copying, and pasting text in the Help task pane or hover the mouse pointer over each of the three buttons in the Clipboard group on the Home tab.)
    Cut selected object or text:
    Copy selected object or text:
    Paste cut or copied object or text:
23. Close the Help task pane.
24. Apply the Facet design theme with the blue variant to the presentation.
25. Apply a transition and transition sound of your choosing to all slides in the presentation.
26. Save **2-Shortcuts**.

Using the Tell Me Feature

Using the Tell Me
Feature

PowerPoint includes a Tell Me feature that provides information as well as guidance on how to complete various functions in the program. To get help finding or using a function in PowerPoint, click in the *Tell Me* text box on the ribbon to the right of the Help tab and then type the function. A drop-down list displays with options for completing the function. The drop-down list will also include links to find more information online or through the Help feature.

The drop-down list also includes a *Smart Lookup* option. Clicking the *Smart Lookup* option will open the Smart Lookup task pane at the right of the screen with information on the function from a variety of sources on the internet. Smart Lookup can also be accessed with the Smart Lookup button in the Insights group on the Review tab or by selecting text, right-clicking the selected text, and then clicking *Smart Lookup* at the shortcut menu.

1. With **2-Shortcuts** open, make Slide 1 active.
2. Select the title *PowerPoint Help* by triple-clicking in the title.
3. Use the Tell Me feature to change the font color and increase the font size for the title by completing the following steps:
   a. Click in the *Tell Me* text box.
   b. Type font color.
   c. Click the *Font Color* option arrow at the drop-down list.
   d. At the side menu of color options, click the *Dark Blue* option (ninth option in the *Standard Colors* section).
   e. With the title still selected, click in the *Tell Me* text box.
   f. Type font size.
   g. Click the *Increase Font Size* option at the drop-down list.
   h. Click in the slide to deselect the text.

4. Use the Tell Me feature to display the Help task pane with information on the Quick Access Toolbar by completing the following steps:
   a. Click in the *Tell Me* text box.
   b. Type Quick Access Toolbar.
   c. Point to the *Get Help on "Quick Access Toolbar"* option.
   d. Click the *Customize the Quick Access Toolbar* option at the side menu.
   e. At the Help task pane, look at the information in the article on customizing the Quick Access Toolbar and then close the task pane by clicking the Close button in the upper right corner of the task pane.
5. Display information in the Smart Lookup task pane on tips for preparing a presentation by completing the following steps:
   a. Click in the *Tell Me* text box.
   b. Type tips for preparing a presentation.
   c. Click the *Smart Lookup on "tips for preparing a presentation"* option (not all of the text may be visible).
   d. Look at the information in the Smart Lookup task pane on tips for preparing a presentation.
   e. Close the Smart Lookup task pane by clicking the Close button in the upper right corner of the task pane.

6. Print the presentation as a handout with six slides displayed horizontally per page.
7. Save and then close **2-Shortcuts**.

Check Your Work

Chapter Summary

- Use the spelling checker feature to check the spelling of the text in a presentation. Begin a spelling check by clicking the Review tab and then clicking the Spelling button in the Proofing group.

- Use the Thesaurus to find synonyms and antonyms for words in a presentation. Display synonyms in the Thesaurus task pane or by right-clicking a word and then pointing to *Synonyms* at the shortcut menu.

- Display the Find dialog box by clicking the Find button in the Editing group on the Home tab. Display the Replace dialog box by clicking the Replace button in the Editing group on the Home tab.

- Click in a placeholder to select that placeholder and position the insertion point inside the placeholder.

- Cut and paste or copy and paste text in slides using buttons in the Clipboard group or with options from the shortcut menu.

- Use the mouse to move text in the outline pane by selecting and then dragging text to a new location. To copy text to a new location, press and hold down the Ctrl key while dragging.

- Use the sizing handles that display around a selected placeholder to increase or decrease the size of the placeholder. Use the mouse to drag a selected placeholder to a new location in the slide.

- Use the New Slide button on the Home tab or Insert tab to insert a slide in a presentation.

- Delete a selected slide by pressing the Delete key. Move or delete a selected slide in Normal view in the slide thumbnails pane or in Slide Sorter view.

- Copy a selected slide by pressing and holding down the Ctrl key while dragging the slide to the new location. Use the Copy and Paste buttons in the Clipboard group on the Home tab to copy a slide between presentations.

- Select adjacent slides in the slide thumbnails pane or in Slide Sorter view by clicking the first slide, pressing and holding down the Shift key, and then clicking the last slide. Select nonadjacent slides by pressing and holding down the Ctrl key while clicking each slide.

- Duplicate slides in a presentation by selecting the slides in the slide thumbnails pane, clicking the New Slide button arrow, and then clicking the *Duplicate Selected Slides* option or clicking the Copy button arrow and then clicking *Duplicate* at the drop-down list.

- Copy slides from a presentation into the open presentation with options at the Reuse Slides task pane. Display this task pane by clicking the New Slide button arrow and then clicking *Reuse Slides* at the drop-down list (or click the Reuse Slides button in the Slides group, if it is available).

- Divide a presentation into sections to easily navigate and edit slides in a presentation.

- Customize the Quick Access Toolbar by clicking the Customize Quick Access Toolbar button at the right of the toolbar and then clicking the button or option at the drop-down list. Buttons can be added to or deleted from the Quick Access Toolbar and the toolbar can be displayed below the ribbon.

- Press the F1 function key or click the Help button on the Help tab to display the Help task pane.

- Some dialog boxes and the backstage area contain a Help button that, when clicked, will display the Microsoft Office support website with information specific to the dialog box or backstage area.
- Use the Tell Me feature to provide information and guidance on how to complete a function.

Commands Review

FEATURE	RIBBON TAB, GROUP	BUTTON, OPTION	KEYBOARD SHORTCUT
copy text or slide	Home, Clipboard		Ctrl + C
create section	Home, Slides		
cut text or slide	Home, Clipboard		Ctrl + X
duplicate slide	Home, Slides	, *Duplicate Selected Slides*	
Find dialog box	Home, Editing		Ctrl + F
Help task pane	Help, Help		F1
paste text or slide	Home, Clipboard		Ctrl + V
Replace dialog box	Home, Editing		Ctrl + H
Reuse Slides task pane	Home, Slides	, *Reuse Slides*	
spelling checker	Review, Proofing		F7
Tell Me feature	*Tell Me* text box		Alt + Q
Thesaurus task pane	Review, Proofing		Shift + F7

Microsoft®
PowerPoint®

CHAPTER 3

Formatting Slides

Performance Objectives

Upon successful completion of Chapter 3, you will be able to:

1 Apply font and paragraph formatting to text in slides
2 Apply formatting with the Mini toolbar and Format Painter
3 Replace fonts
4 Customize columns
5 Customize bullets and numbers
6 Customize placeholders
7 Change slide size and page setup
8 Modify design themes
9 Customize slide backgrounds
10 Create custom design themes including custom theme colors and theme fonts
11 Delete custom design themes

The Font and Paragraph groups on the Home tab contain a number of buttons and options for formatting text in slides. PowerPoint also provides a Mini toolbar and a Format Painter to format text. The design theme colors and fonts provided by PowerPoint can be modified and custom design themes can be created. You will learn to use these features in this chapter along with how to change slide size and page setup options.

 Data Files

Before beginning chapter work, copy the PC3 folder to your storage medium and then make PC3 the active folder.

The online course includes additional training and assessment resources.

You will open an e-commerce presentation, apply font and paragraph formatting, apply formatting with Format Painter, apply column formatting to text in placeholders, and rotate text in placeholders.

Formatting a Presentation

PowerPoint provides a variety of design themes that can be applied to a presentation. These themes contain formatting options such as font, color, and graphics effects. In some situations, the formatting provided by a theme is appropriate; in other situations, specific formatting can be applied to enhance the presentation.

Applying Font Formatting

Applying Font Formatting at the Font Dialog Box

Applying Font Formatting

The Font group on the Home tab contains a number of buttons and options for applying font formatting to text in a slide. Use these buttons and options to change the font, font size, and font color, as well as apply font effects. Table 3.1 describes the buttons and options in the Font group along with any keyboard shortcuts for applying font formatting.

Changing Fonts Design themes apply a certain font (or fonts) to text in slides. A different font or font size can be applied to text to change the mood of a presentation, enhance the visual appearance of slides, or increase the readability of the text. Change the font with the *Font* and *Font Size* option boxes in the Font group on the Home tab.

Select text and then click the *Font* option box arrow and a drop-down gallery displays with font options. Hover the mouse pointer over a font option and the selected text in the slide displays with the font applied. Continue hovering the mouse pointer over different font options to see how the selected text displays in the specified font. The *Font* option drop-down gallery is an example of the live preview feature, which displays text with different formatting before actually applying the formatting. The live preview feature is also available at the *Font Size* option drop-down gallery and the Font Color button drop-down gallery.

Fonts may be decorative or plain and generally fall into one of two categories: serif fonts or sans serif fonts. A serif is a small line at the end of a character stroke. A serif font is easier to read and is generally used for large blocks of text. A sans serif font does not have serifs (*sans* is French for *without*). Sans serif fonts are generally used for titles and headings.

Hint Consider using a sans serif font for titles and headings and a serif font for body text.

Hint Use options at the Font dialog box with the Character Spacing tab selected to increase or decrease spacing between characters and to apply kerning to text.

In addition to option boxes and buttons in the Font group on the Home tab, use options at the Font dialog box, shown in Figure 3.1, to apply character formatting to text. Display the Font dialog box by clicking the Font group dialog box launcher or with the keyboard shortcut Ctrl + Shift + F. (The dialog box launcher is the small button containing a diagonal arrow in the lower right corner of the group.) Use options at the Font dialog box to choose a font, font style, and font size and to apply special text effects in slides such as superscript, subscript, and double strikethrough.

Table 3.1 PowerPoint Home Tab Font Group Option Boxes and Buttons

Button/Option Box	Name	Function	Keyboard Shortcut
B	Bold	Applies or removes bold formatting to or from selected text.	Ctrl + B
Aa	Change Case	Changes the case of selected text.	Shift + F3
AV	Character Spacing	Adjusts spacing between selected characters.	
A◇	Clear All Formatting	Clears all character formatting from selected text.	Ctrl + Spacebar
A˅	Decrease Font Size	Decreases font size of selected text to next smaller size.	Ctrl + Shift + <
Calibri (Body)	*Font*	Changes selected text to a different font.	
A˅	Font Color	Changes the font color for selected text.	
24	*Font Size*	Changes selected text to a different font size.	
A^	Increase Font Size	Increases font size of selected text to next larger size.	Ctrl + Shift + >
I	Italic	Applies or removes italic formatting to or from selected text.	Ctrl + I
ab	Strikethrough	Inserts or removes a line through the middle of selected text.	
✎	Text Highlight Color	Applies or removes highlight formatting to or from selected text.	
S	Text Shadow	Applies or removes shadow formatting to or from selected text.	
U	Underline	Applies or removes underline formatting to or from selected text.	Ctrl + U

Figure 3.1 Font Dialog Box

Click this option box arrow and then choose a font at the drop-down list.

Click this option box arrow and then choose a font style at the drop-down list.

Click the Font color button and then choose a color at the color palette.

Use these measurement box arrows to increase or decrease the font size, or click the number and type the font size.

Insert a check mark for these effects to be applied to text.

Tutorial

Formatting with the Mini Toolbar

Formatting with the Mini Toolbar When text is selected, the Mini toolbar displays above the selected text. Click a button or option on the Mini toolbar to apply formatting to selected text. The option to display the Mini toolbar can be turned off. To do this, click the File tab and then click *Options*. At the PowerPoint Options dialog box with the *General* option selected in the left panel, click the *Show Mini Toolbar on selection* check box to remove the check mark.

Activity 1a Applying Font Formatting to Text

1. Open **EComm** and then save it with the name **3-EComm**.
2. Apply the Ion Boardroom design theme with the green variant by completing the following steps:
   a. Click the Design tab.
   b. Click the More Themes button at the right of the themes gallery.
   c. Click the *Ion Boardroom* theme. (Make sure you click the Ion Boardroom theme and not the Ion theme.)
   d. Click the green color variant in the Variants group.
3. Change the font formatting of the Slide 1 subtitle by completing the following steps:
   a. With Slide 1 active, click in the subtitle and then select *ONLINE SERVICES*.
   b. Click the Home tab.
   c. Click the *Font* option box arrow, scroll down the drop-down gallery, and then click *Cambria*.

   d. Click the *Font Size* option box arrow and then click *40* at the drop-down gallery.
   e. Click the Bold button in the Font group.
   f. Click the Text Shadow button in the Font group
   g. Click the Font Color button arrow and then click the *Dark Red, Accent 1, Darker 25%* option (fifth column, fifth row in the *Theme Colors* section).

4. Change the size of the title text by completing the following steps:
   a. Click in the title *ELECTRONIC COMMERCE* and then click the placeholder border to change the border line to a solid line.
   b. Click the Decrease Font Size button in the Font group.

4b

5. Change the case of the title text in Slide 2 by completing the following steps:
   a. Make Slide 2 active.
   b. Click in the title *ELECTRONIC COMMERCE* and then click the placeholder border to change the border line to a solid line.
   c. Click the Change Case button in the Font group and then click *Capitalize Each Word* at the drop-down list.

5c

6. Apply and then clear formatting from text by completing the following steps:
   a. Make Slide 3 active.
   b. Click in the bulleted text.
   c. Select the text *m-commerce* (in parentheses), but do not select the parentheses.
   d. Click the Underline button in the Font group on the Home tab.
   e. Click the Bold button in the Font group.
   f. After applying underlining and bold formatting, remove the formatting by clicking the Clear All Formatting button in the Font group.
   g. With the text still selected, click the Italic button in the Font group and then click in the placeholder to deselect the text.

6d   6f

6e

7. Highlight text in Slide 3 by completing the following steps:
   a. Click the Text Highlight Color button arrow in the Font group and then click *Turquoise* (third column, first row).
   b. Position the mouse pointer at the beginning of the fourth bulleted item, click and hold down the left mouse button, drag through the text *Electronic commerce venue*, and then release the mouse button.
   c. Click the Text Highlight Color button to turn off highlighting.

7a

8. Apply italic formatting with the Mini toolbar by completing the following steps:
   a. Select *B2C* in the second bulleted item and then click the Italic button on the Mini toolbar.
   b. Select *B2B* in the third bulleted item and then click the Italic button on the Mini toolbar.

7b

8a

9. Save **3-EComm**.

 Check Your Work

Formatting with Format Painter

 Format
Painter

Quick Steps

**Format with Format
Painter**
1. Click text containing
   formatting.
2. Double-click Format
   Painter button.
3. Select or click text.
4. Click Format Painter
   button.

💡 **Hint** You can also
turn off Format Painter
by pressing the Esc
key.

If character and/or paragraph formatting is applied to text in a slide and the same formatting should be applied to other text in the presentation, use Format Painter. With Format Painter, the same formatting can be applied in more than one location in a slide or slides. To use Format Painter, apply specific formatting to text, position the insertion point anywhere in the formatted text, and then double-click the Format Painter button in the Clipboard group on the Home tab. Using the mouse, select the additional text to apply the formatting. After applying the formatting in the new locations, click the Format Painter button to deactivate it. To apply formatting in only one other location, click the Format Painter button one time. The first time text is selected and the formatting is applied, the Format Painter button is deactivated.

Activity 1b Formatting with Format Painter

1. With **3-EComm** open, make sure Slide 3 is active.
2. Apply formatting to the title by completing the following steps:
   a. Click in the title and then click the title placeholder border to change the border line to a solid line.
   b. Click the Font group dialog box launcher on the Home tab.
   c. At the Font dialog box, click the *Latin text font* option box arrow, scroll down the drop-down list, and then click *Candara*.
   d. Click the *Font style* option box arrow and then click *Bold Italic* at the drop-down list.
   e. Select the current measurement in the *Size* measurement box and then type 40.
   f. Click OK to close the dialog box.

3. Click in the title.
4. Double-click the Format Painter button in the Clipboard group on the Home tab.

5. Make Slide 8 active.
6. Using the mouse, select the title *Advantages of Online Shopping*. (The mouse pointer displays as an I-beam with a paintbrush attached. Instead of selecting the whole title, you can also click each word in the title to apply the formatting. However, clicking individual words will not format the spaces between the words in multiple-word titles.)
7. Make Slide 9 active and then select the title.
8. Make Slide 10 active and then select the title.
9. Click the Format Painter button to deactivate it.
10. If necessary, deselect the text.
11. Save **3-EComm**.

Check Your Work

Tutorial

Replacing Fonts

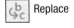 Replace

Quick Steps

Replace Fonts
1. Click Replace button arrow.
2. Click *Replace Fonts*.
3. At Replace Font dialog box, click *Replace* option box arrow and click font.
4. Press Tab.
5. Click *With* option box arrow and click font.
6. Click Replace button.
7. Click Close button.

Replacing Fonts

Search for a specific font in the presentation and replace all occurrences of that font with a different font using options at the Replace Font dialog box. Display the Replace Font dialog box by clicking the Replace button arrow in the Editing group on the Home tab and then clicking the *Replace Fonts* option at the drop-down list. At the Replace Font dialog box, click the *Replace* option box arrow and then click a font to replace at the drop-down list. Click the *With* option box arrow and then click a font with which to replace the existing font at the drop-down list. Click the Replace button to replace all the fonts and then click the Close button to close the Replace Font dialog box.

1. With **3-EComm** open, make Slide 1 active.
2. Replace the Century Gothic font with Candara in the entire presentation by completing the following steps:
   a. Click the Replace button arrow in the Editing group on the Home tab and then click *Replace Fonts* at the drop-down list.
   b. At the Replace Font dialog box, click the *Replace* option box arrow and then click *Century Gothic* at the drop-down list.
   c. Click the *With* option box arrow, scroll down the drop-down list, and then click *Candara*.
   d. Click the Replace button.
   e. Click the Close button.

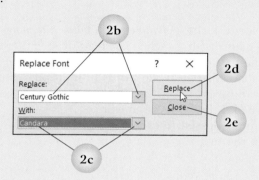

3. Scroll through the slides to view the Candara font that has been applied to titles and bulleted text in each slide.
4. Save **3-EComm**.

 Check Your Work

 Tutorial
Changing Alignment

Formatting Paragraphs

The Paragraph group on the Home tab contains a number of buttons for applying paragraph formatting to text in a slide, such as applying bullets and numbers, increasing and decreasing list levels, changing the horizontal and vertical alignment of text, changing line spacing, and rotating text in a placeholder. Table 3.2 describes the buttons in the Paragraph group along with any keyboard shortcuts.

 Tutorial
Changing Line Spacing

 Tutorial
Increasing and Decreasing Indent

Fitting Contents in a Placeholder

 Tutorial
Fitting Contents in a Placeholder

 AutoFit Options

If text in a placeholder exceeds the size of the placeholder, use the AutoFit Options button to decrease the spacing between bulleted items or decrease the font size to ensure that all the text fits in the placeholder. The AutoFit Options button displays in the lower left corner of the placeholder when text no longer fits inside the placeholder. Click the AutoFit Options button to display a list of options such as *Autofit Text to Placeholder, Stop Fitting Text to This Placeholder, Split Text Between Two Slides, Continue on a New Slide, Change to Two Columns*, and *Control AutoCorrect Options*.

Table 3.2 Buttons in the Paragraph Group on the Home Tab

Button	Name	Function	Keyboard Shortcut
	Bullets	Adds or removes bullets to or from selected text.	
	Numbering	Adds or removes numbers to or from selected text.	
	Decrease List Level	Moves text to the previous tab (level).	Shift + Tab
	Increase List Level	Moves text to the next tab (level).	Tab
	Line Spacing	Increases or reduces spacing between lines of text.	
	Align Left	Left-aligns text.	Ctrl + L
	Center	Center-aligns text.	Ctrl + E
	Align Right	Right-aligns text.	Ctrl + R
	Justify	Justifies text.	
	Add or Remove Columns	Splits text into two or more columns.	
	Text Direction	Rotates or stacks text.	
	Align Text	Changes the alignment of text within a text box.	
	Convert to SmartArt Graphic	Converts selected text to a SmartArt graphic.	

Creating and Customizing Columns

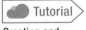

Tutorial

Creating and Customizing Columns

Add or Remove Columns

Hint Split text into columns to make it attractive and easy to read.

Click the Add or Remove Columns button in the Paragraph group to specify one-, two-, or three-column formatting for text. To format text in more than three columns or to control spacing between columns, click the *More Columns* option at the drop-down list. This displays the Columns dialog box, as shown in Figure 3.2. With options at this dialog box, specify the number of columns and the amount of spacing between them.

Figure 3.2 Columns Dialog Box

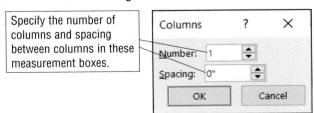

Specify the number of columns and spacing between columns in these measurement boxes.

1. With **3-EComm** open, change bullets by completing the following steps:
   a. Make Slide 3 active.
   b. Click in the bulleted text.
   c. Select the bulleted text.
   d. Click the Bullets button arrow in the Paragraph group on the Home tab and then click the *Filled Square Bullets* option at the drop-down gallery.

2. Change bullets to letters by completing the following steps:
   a. Make Slide 8 active.
   b. Click in the bulleted text.
   c. Select the bulleted text.
   d. Click the Numbering button arrow in the Paragraph group on the Home tab and then click the *A. B. C.* option at the drop-down gallery.

   e. With the lettered text selected, change to numbers by clicking the Numbering button arrow and then clicking the *1. 2. 3.* option at the drop-down gallery.

3. Decrease and increase list levels and change font color by completing the following steps:
   a. With Slide 8 active and the numbered text selected, click the Increase List Level button in the Paragraph group.
   b. With the text still selected, click the Font Color button arrow in the Font group on the Home tab and then click *Teal, Accent 5, Darker 50%* at the drop-down gallery (ninth column, last row in the *Theme Colors* section).

c. Make Slide 10 active.

d. Click in the bulleted text.

e. Move the insertion point so it is positioned immediately left of the *N* in *Nordstrom*.

f. Click the Decrease List Level button in the Paragraph group.

g. Move the insertion point so it is positioned immediately left of the *M* in *Macy's*.

h. Press Shift + Tab.

i. Move the insertion point so it is positioned immediately left of the first *L.* in *L.L. Bean*.

j. Click the Increase List Level button in the Paragraph group.

k. Move the insertion point so it is positioned immediately left of the *T* in *The Gap*.

l. Press the Tab key.

m. Use the Increase List Level button or Tab key to indent *Bloomingdale's, Expedia, Travelocity,* and *Orbitz* to the next level.

4. Increase the size of the text and make sure the content fits within the Slide 10 placeholder by completing the following steps:

a. With Slide 10 active, select all the bulleted items and then change the font size to 16 points.

b. Click in the bulleted text to deselect the text.

c. Click the AutoFit Options button in the lower left corner of the placeholder and then click *AutoFit Text to Placeholder* at the drop-down list. (This decreases the spacing between the bulleted items to ensure all items fit in the placeholder.)

5. Change the line spacing of text by completing the following steps:

a. Make Slide 3 active.

b. Click in the bulleted text and then select the bulleted text.

c. Click the Line Spacing button in the Paragraph group and then click *1.5* at the drop-down list.

d. Make Slide 8 active.

e. Click in the numbered text and then select the numbered text.

f. Click the Line Spacing button and then click *2.0* at the drop-down list.

6. Change paragraph alignment by completing the following steps:

a. Make Slide 3 active, click in the title, and then click the Center button in the Paragraph group.

b. Make Slide 8 active, click in the title, and then click the Center button.

c. Make Slide 9 active, click in the title, and then click the Center button.

d. Make Slide 10 active, click in the title, and then click the Center button.

7. Change the vertical alignment of text by completing the following steps:
   a. Make Slide 3 active.
   b. Click in the bulleted text.
   c. Click the Align Text button in the Paragraph group on the Home tab and then click *Middle* at the drop-down list.
8. Split text into two columns by completing the following steps:
   a. Make Slide 9 active.
   b. Click in the bulleted text and then select the bulleted text.
   c. Click the Add or Remove Columns button in the Paragraph group and then click *Two Columns* at the drop-down list.
   d. Select the first sentence in the first bulleted paragraph (*Clear selling terms.*) and then click the Bold button.
   e. Select and then bold the first sentence in each of the remaining bulleted paragraphs in Slide 9.
   f. Drag the bottom border of the bulleted text placeholder up until two bulleted items display in each column.
9. Save **3-EComm**.

 Check Your Work

 Tutorial

Changing
Paragraph Spacing

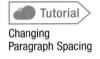 Line
Spacing

Customizing Paragraphs

Control paragraph alignment, indenting, and spacing with options at the Paragraph dialog box. Display the dialog box, shown in Figure 3.3, by clicking the Paragraph group dialog box launcher on the Home tab. The dialog box can also be displayed by clicking the Line Spacing button in the Paragraph group and then clicking *Line Spacing Options* at the drop-down list. Use options at this dialog box to specify text alignment, paragraph indentation, spacing before and after paragraphs, and line spacing.

Figure 3.3 Paragraph Dialog Box

1. With **3-EComm** open, change line and paragraph spacing by completing the following steps:
   a. Make Slide 3 active.
   b. Click in the bulleted text and then select the text.
   c. Click the Paragraph group dialog box launcher.
   d. In the *Indentation* section at the Paragraph dialog box, click the *Before text* measurement box up arrow three times. (This inserts *0.6"* in the measurement box.)
   e. In the *Spacing* section, click the *After* measurement box up arrow two times. (This inserts *12 pt* in the box.)
   f. Click the *Line Spacing* option box arrow and then click *Multiple* at the drop-down list.
   g. Select the current measurement in the *At* measurement box and then type 1.8.
   h. Click OK.

2. Format text into columns by completing the following steps:
   a. Make Slide 10 active.
   b. Click in the bulleted text and then select the text.
   c. Click the Add or Remove Columns button in the Paragraph group and then click *More Columns* at the drop-down list.
   d. At the Columns dialog box, click the *Number* measurement box up arrow. (This inserts a *2* in the measurement box.)
   e. Click the *Spacing* measurement box up arrow until *0.5"* displays in the measurement box.
   f. Click OK.
   g. With the text still selected, click the Paragraph group dialog box launcher.
   h. In the *Spacing* section at the Paragraph dialog box, click the *After* measurement box up arrow three times. (This inserts *18 pt* in the measurement box.)
   i. Click OK.
3. With the bulleted text selected, change the font size to 20 points.
4. Save **3-EComm**.

Tutorial

Rotating Text

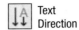

Text
Direction

Rotating Text

To make specific text stand out or to enhance the appearance of text, consider rotating or stacking text by changing the text direction. For example, text can be rotated so that it displays vertically in the placeholder. Rotate text in a placeholder using the Text Direction button. Click the Text Direction button in the Paragraph group on the Home tab and then click an option at the drop-down gallery.

Activity 1f Rotating Text

1. With **3-EComm** open, make Slide 8 active.
2. Modify the slide so it displays as shown in Figure 3.4 by completing the following steps:
   a. Click in the numbered text and then select the text.
   b. Click the Bullets button arrow and then click the *Hollow Square Bullets* option.
   c. With the text selected, change the font size to 20 points.
   d. Decrease the size of the bulleted text placeholder so the placeholder borders display just outside the text.
   e. Drag the placeholder to the middle of the slide until the guideline (a vertical dashed line) displays and then release the mouse button. (Refer to Figure 3.4 for the position of the placeholder.)

   f. Click in the title *Advantages of Online Shopping*.
   g. Delete the text *of Online Shopping*.
   h. Select *Advantages* and then change the font size to 54 points.
   i. Drag the right border of the placeholder to the left so it is positioned just outside the text.
   j. Click the Text Direction button in the Paragraph group and then click *Rotate all text 270°*.

k. Using the sizing handles around the title placeholder, increase the height and decrease the width of the placeholder and then drag the placeholder so the title displays as shown in Figure 3.4. Use the horizontal guideline (a dashed line) to help you vertically center the placeholder on the slide.

l. With the title placeholder selected, click the Font Color button arrow in the Font group and then click *Dark Red, Accent 1, Darker 25%* at the drop-down gallery (fifth column, fifth row in the *Theme Colors* section).

3. Apply a transition and transition sound to all slides in the presentation.
4. Print the presentation as a handout with six slides displayed horizontally per page.
5. Save and then close **3-EComm**.

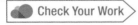

Figure 3.4 Activity 1f, Slide 8

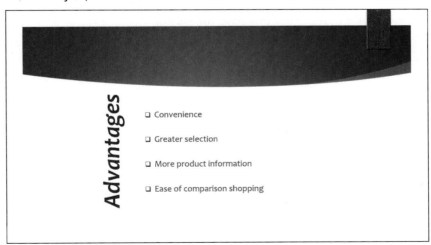

Activity 2 **Customize Bullets, Numbers, and Placeholders;**   **4 Parts**
Change Slide Size and Page Setup in a Color Presentation

You will open a presentation on using colors in publications, create and apply custom bullets and numbering, customize placeholders, change slide size, and change the page setup.

Tutorial ▷

Customizing Bullets

▤ ⌄ Bullets

Q̇uick Steps

Customize Bullets
1. Select placeholder containing numbered or bulleted text.
2. Click Bullets button arrow.
3. Click *Bullets and Numbering*.
4. Make changes.
5. Click OK.

💡 **Hint** Choose a custom bullet that matches the theme or mood of the presentation.

Customizing Bullets

Each design theme contains a Title and Content slide layout with bullets. The appearance and formatting of the bullets vary within each design theme. Use the bullet style provided by the design theme or create custom bullets. Customize bullets with options at the Bullets and Numbering dialog box with the Bulleted tab selected, as shown in Figure 3.5. Display this dialog box by selecting a placeholder containing bulleted text (or select bulleted text), clicking the Bullets button arrow in the Paragraph group on the Home tab, and then clicking *Bullets and Numbering* at the drop-down gallery.

At the Bullets and Numbering dialog box, choose one of the predesigned bullets from the list box, change the size of the bullets (measured by percentage in relation to the size of the text), change the bullet color, and/or specify an image or symbol to use as a bullet. Click the Picture button at the bottom of the dialog box and the Insert Pictures window displays. Click the *From a File* option, navigate to the desired folder in the Insert Picture dialog box, and then double-click the image. Click the *Online Pictures* option at the Insert Pictures window to search for images online, and click the *From Icons* option to search for icons at the Insert Icons window. Click the Customize button at the bottom of the Bullets and Numbering dialog box and the Symbol dialog box displays. Choose a symbol bullet option at the Symbol dialog box and then click OK. Image or symbol bullets are particularly effective for adding visual interest to a presentation.

To insert a new bullet point in a bulleted list, press the Enter key. To move the insertion point down to the next line without inserting a new bullet, press Shift + Enter. A new bullet will be inserted the next time the Enter key is pressed.

Figure 3.5 Bullets and Numbering Dialog Box with Bulleted Tab Selected

1. Open **ColorPres** and then save it with the name **3-ColorPres**.
2. Increase the list level of text and create custom bullets by completing the following steps:
   a. Make Slide 2 active.
   b. Select the second, third, and fourth bulleted paragraphs.
   c. Click the Increase List Level button.
   d. With the three bulleted paragraphs still selected, click the Bullets button arrow and then click *Bullets and Numbering* at the drop-down list.
   e. At the Bullets and Numbering dialog box with the Bulleted tab selected, select the current number (*100*) in the *Size* measurement box and then type 75.
   f. Click the Picture button in the bottom right corner of the dialog box.
   g. At the Insert Pictures window, click the *From a File* option.
   h. At the Insert Picture dialog box, navigate to your PC3 folder and then double-click the **Bullet** image file.
3. Insert symbol bullets by completing the following steps:
   a. Make Slide 3 active.
   b. Click in the placeholder containing the bulleted text and then click the placeholder border to change the border to a solid line.
   c. Click the Bullets button arrow and then click *Bullets and Numbering* at the drop-down list.
   d. At the Bullets and Numbering dialog box with the Bulleted tab selected, click the *Size* measurement box down arrow until 90 displays.
   e. Click the Customize button in the bottom right corner of the dialog box.
   f. At the Symbol dialog box, make sure *(normal text)* displays in the *Font* option box. If it does not, click the *Font* option box arrow and then click the *(normal text)* option (the first option in the drop-down list).
   g. Double-click the current number in the *Character code* text box and then type 221E.
   h. Click OK.

i. At the Bullets and Numbering dialog box, click the Color button and then click *Blue, Accent 5* (ninth column, first row in the *Theme Colors* section).

j. Click OK to close the Bullets and Numbering dialog box. (This applies the blue infinity symbol bullets to the selected text.)

4. Increase the spacing between the bullets and the text by completing the following steps:

a. With the placeholder containing the bulleted text still selected, click the Paragraph group dialog box launcher.

b. At the Paragraph dialog box, select the current measurement in the *By* measurement box (in the *Indentation* section), type 0.5, and then press the Enter key.

5. Save **3-ColorPres**.

Check Your Work

Customizing Numbers

Click the Numbering button arrow in the Paragraph group and several numbering options display in a drop-down gallery. Customize numbers with options at the Bullets and Numbering dialog box with the Numbered tab selected, as shown in Figure 3.6. Display this dialog box by selecting a placeholder containing a bulleted or numbered list, clicking the Numbering button arrow and then clicking *Bullets and Numbering* at the drop-down gallery. Use options at this dialog box to change the size and color of the numbers as well as the starting number.

To insert a new numbered item in a numbered list, press the Enter key. To move the insertion point down to the next line without inserting the next number, press Shift + Enter. The next number will be inserted the next time the Enter key is pressed.

Figure 3.6 Bullets and Numbering Dialog Box with Numbered Tab Selected

1. With **3-ColorPres** open, create and insert custom numbers by completing the following steps:
   a. Make Slide 4 active.
   b. Select the placeholder containing the bulleted text. (Make sure the placeholder border displays as a solid line.)
   c. Click the Numbering button arrow in the Paragraph group on the Home tab and then click the *Bullets and Numbering* option at the drop-down list.
   d. At the Bullets and Numbering dialog box with the Numbered tab selected, click the *1. 2. 3.* option (second column, first row).
   e. Select the measurement in the *Size* measurement box and then type 80.
   f. Click the Color button and then click *Blue, Accent 5* (ninth column, first row in the *Theme Colors* section).
   g. Click OK.

   h. Make Slide 5 active.
   i. Select the placeholder containing the bulleted text. (Make sure the placeholder border displays as a solid line.)
   j. Click the Numbering button arrow and then click the *Bullets and Numbering* option at the drop-down list.
   k. At the Bullets and Numbering dialog box with the Numbered tab selected, click the *1. 2. 3.* option (second column, first row).
   l. Select the number in the *Size* measurement box and then type 80.
   m. Click the Color button and then click *Blue, Accent 5* (ninth column, first row in the *Theme Colors* section).
   n. Click the *Start at* measurement box up arrow until 6 displays.
   o. Click OK.

2. Add a transition and transition sound to all slides in the presentation.
3. Run the slide show.
4. Save **3-ColorPres**.

Check Your Work

Customizing
Placeholders Using
the Ribbon

 Quick
Styles

 Arrange

 Shape
Fill

 Shape
Outline

 Shape
Effects

Hint You can also
use options on the
Drawing Tools Format
tab to customize a
placeholder.

Quick Steps

**Apply Color with
Eyedropper**
1. Click object.
2. Click Shape Fill
   button arrow.
3. Click *Eyedropper*.
4. Click color.

Customizing Placeholders

Customize a placeholder in a slide with buttons in the Drawing group on the Home tab. Use options in the Drawing group to choose a shape, arrange the placeholder, apply a quick style, change the shape fill and outline colors, and apply a shape effect.

Click the Quick Styles button in the Drawing group and a drop-down gallery of styles displays. Choose a quick style from this gallery or click the *Other Theme Fills* option to display a side menu with additional fills. Arrange, align, and rotate a placeholder with options at the Arrange button drop-down list. Use the Shape Fill button to apply a fill to a placeholder. Click the Shape Fill button arrow and a drop-down gallery displays with options for applying a color, picture, gradient, or texture to the placeholder. Use the Shape Outline button to apply an outline to a placeholder and specify the outline color, weight, and style. Use the Shape Effects button to choose from a variety of effects such as shadow, reflection, glow, and soft edges.

Both the Shape Fill and Shape Outline buttons in the Drawing group contain drop-down galleries with the *Eyedropper* option. Use the eyedropper to capture an exact color from one object and apply it to another object in the slide. To use the eyedropper to apply a fill color, click the object to which the fill color is to be applied, click the Shape Fill button arrow, and then click *Eyedropper* at the drop-down gallery. The mouse pointer displays as an eyedropper. Position the tip of the eyedropper on the desired color and then click the mouse button. The color clicked is applied to the selected object. Move the eyedropper and a live preview box displays above and to the right of the eyedropper. Use this live preview box to help choose the specific color. To pick a color outside the slide pane, press and hold down the Ctrl key, click and hold down the left mouse button, and then drag outside the slide pane. Position the tip of the eyedropper on the desired color and then release the mouse button and the Ctrl key. The *Eyedropper* option is also available with the Shape Outline and Font Color buttons on the Home tab as well as with buttons on other tabs that apply color.

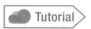

Customizing
Placeholders at the
Format Shape Task
Pane

Customizing Placeholders at the Format Shape Task Pane

With options in the Format Shape task pane, apply shape options to a placeholder or apply text options to the text within a placeholder. Display the Format Shape task pane by clicking the Drawing group task pane launcher on the Home tab. The Shape Options tab in the Format Shape task pane displays three icons: Fill & Line, Effects, and Size & Properties, each with different options for formatting a placeholder. After clicking an icon, the icon options may need to be expanded. For example, click the *Fill* option with the Fill & Line icon selected on the Shape Options tab to display options for applying a fill to a placeholder, as shown in Figure 3.7. The Text Options tab in the Format Shape task pane displays three icons: Text Fill & Outline, Text Effects, and Textbox, each with different options for formatting text within a placeholder.

Align text in a placeholder with options at the Format Shape task pane with the Size & Properties icon selected and options in the *Text Box* section displayed. (If necessary, click the *Text Box* option to expand the list.) Use options in the *Text Box* section to align text in a placeholder as well as change text direction, autofit contents, and change internal margins.

Figure 3.7 Format Shape Task Pane with Shape Options Tab Selected

Click an icon to display options related to the icon.

Click a tab to display different options in the task pane list box.

Click an option to expand or collapse the list of formatting options.

Format Shape

Shape Options   Text Options

Fill
- No fill
- Solid fill
- ● Gradient fill
- Picture or texture fill
- Pattern fill
- Slide background fill

Preset gradients

Type   Linear

Direction

Angle   90°

Gradient stops

Color

Position   0%

Transparency   0%

Brightness   95%

☑ Rotate with shape

▷ Line

Text can be moved within a placeholder with the margin measurements in the Format Shape task pane. Display the margin measurements by clicking the Size & Properties icon and then scrolling down the task pane list box to the *Text Box* section. Use the *Left margin*, *Right margin*, *Top margin*, and *Bottom margin* measurement boxes to specify internal margins for text inside a placeholder.

Activity 2c Customizing Placeholders

Part 3 of 4

1. With **3-ColorPres** open, customize the title placeholder in Slide 1 by completing the following steps:
   a. If necessary, make Slide 1 active.
   b. Click in the title to make the title placeholder active.
   c. If necessary, click the Home tab.
   d. Click the Quick Styles button in the Drawing group.
   e. Click the *Subtle Effect - Gold, Accent 4* option at the drop-down gallery (fifth column, fourth row).
   f. Click the Shape Outline button arrow in the Drawing group and then click *Green, Accent 6* (last column, first row in the *Theme Colors* section).

g. Click the Shape Outline button arrow, point to *Weight*, and then click *3 pt* at the side menu.

h. Click the Shape Effects button, point to *Bevel*, and then click *Slant* at the side menu (fourth column, first row in the *Bevel* section).

i. Click the Quick Styles button in the Drawing group, point to *Other Theme Fills* at the bottom of the drop-down gallery, and then click *Style 9* at the side menu (first column, third row).

2. Change the alignment of the text within the placeholder by completing the following steps:

a. With the title placeholder active, click the Drawing group task pane launcher.

b. At the Format Shape task pane, make sure the Shape Options tab is selected, and then click the Size & Properties icon.

c. Click the *Text Box* option to display the list of options.

d. Click the *Vertical alignment* option box arrow and then click *Middle* at the drop-down list.

e. Click the *Top margin* measurement box up arrow until *0.3″* displays in the measurement box.

f. Close the Format Shape task pane by clicking the Close button in the upper right corner of the task pane.

3. Customize the subtitle placeholder by completing the following steps:
   a. Click in the subtitle text to make the subtitle placeholder active.
   b. Click the Shape Fill button arrow in the Drawing group, point to *Texture*, and then click *Blue tissue paper* at the drop-down gallery (first column, fifth row).
   c. Click the Shape Effects button, point to *Bevel*, and then click *Slant* at the side menu (fourth column, first row in the *Bevel* section).

4. You decide the texture fill does not match the theme of the presentation. Change the subtitle placeholder fill by completing the following steps:
   a. With the subtitle placeholder active, click the Drawing group task pane launcher.
   b. At the Format Picture task pane, make sure the Shape Options tab is selected, click the Fill & Line icon, and then make sure the options in the *Fill* section are displayed.
   c. Click the *Gradient fill* option.
   d. Click the Preset gradients button and then click *Light Gradient - Accent 6* (sixth column, first row).

5. At the Format Shape task pane, click the Size & Properties icon, make sure the options in the *Text Box* section are displayed, click the *Vertical alignment* option box arrow, and then click *Middle* at the drop-down list.
6. Make Slide 3 active and then change the spacing after paragraphs by completing the following steps:
   a. Select the bulleted text.
   b. Click the Paragraph group dialog box launcher.
   c. In the *Spacing* section at the Paragraph dialog box, click the *After* measurement box up arrow two times to display *12 pt* in the measurement box.
   d. Click OK to close the dialog box.
7. Customize and arrange the placeholder by completing the following steps:
   a. With the bulleted text selected and the Format Shape task pane open, click the Fill & Line icon, make sure the options in the *Fill* section are displayed, and then click the *Solid fill* option.
   b. Click the Color button and then click *Blue, Accent 5, Lighter 80%* (ninth column, second row in the *Theme Colors* section).

c. Click the Effects icon and then click the *Shadow* option to display the list of options.

d. Click the Presets button and then click *Offset: Bottom Right* (first column, first row in *Outer* section).

e. Click the Color button and then click *Blue, Accent 5, Darker 50%* (ninth column, last row in the *Theme Colors* section).

f. Click the *Distance* measurement box up arrow until *15 pt* displays.

g. Click the Size & Properties icon.

h. Click the *Size* option to display the list of options.

i. Click the *Height* measurement box down arrow until *2.8″* displays in the measurement box.

j. Scroll down the task pane and, if necessary, click the *Text Box* option to display the list of options.

k. Change the left and top margin measurements to 0.2 inches.

l. Click the Arrange button in the Drawing group on the Home tab, point to *Align* in the drop-down list, and then click *Distribute Vertically* at the side menu.

8. Make Slide 2 active, click in the bulleted text, and then customize and arrange the placeholder by completing the steps in Step 7. When completing Step 7i, change the height of the placeholder in Slide 2 to 3 inches.

9. Close the Format Shape task pane.

10. Make Slide 1 active and then use the eyedropper to apply fill color from the subtitle placeholder to the title placeholder by completing the following steps:

a. Click in the title placeholder.

b. Click the Shape Fill button arrow in the Drawing group on the Home tab, and then click the *Eyedropper* option at the drop-down gallery.

c. Position the tip of the eyedropper on the green color above the word *Publications* in the subtitle placeholder and then click the left mouse button.

11. Run the slide show.

12. Print the presentation as a handout with six slides displayed horizontally per page.

13. Save **3-ColorPres**.

Changing Slide Size

Slide Size

Changing Slide Size and Page Setup

Control the page setup and the size and orientation of slides using options in the Slide Size dialog box, as shown in Figure 3.8. Display the Slide Size dialog box by clicking the Slide Size button in the Customize group on the Design tab and then clicking *Custom Slide Size* at the drop-down list. With options in the dialog box, change the slide orientation, specify how slides are sized, change the slide size ratio, and change the starting slide number. By default, slides are sized for an on-screen show with a widescreen 16:9 ratio. If a widescreen size (16:9) presentation is changed to a standard size (4:3) presentation, the slide content will need to be maximized or scaled down to fit in the new slide size. Click the *Slides sized for* option box arrow and a drop-down list displays with options for changing the slide size ratio and choosing other paper sizes. The Slide Size dialog box also contains options for changing the orientation of notes, handouts, and outline pages.

Figure 3.8 Slide Size Dialog Box

Activity 2d **Changing Slide Orientation and Page Setup**   Part 4 of 4

1. With **3-ColorPres** open, change the slide size by completing the following steps:
   a. Click the Design tab.
   b. Click the Slide Size button in the Customize group and then click *Standard (4:3)* at the drop-down list.

   c. At the Microsoft PowerPoint dialog box, click the Ensure Fit button.
2. Run the slide show to view how the slides appear in the standard size.

3. Change the slide orientation by completing the following steps:
   a. Click the Slide Size button in the Customize group and then click *Custom Slide Size* at the drop-down list.
   b. At the Slide Size dialog box, click the *Portrait* option in the *Slides* section, and then click OK.
   c. Click the Ensure Fit button at the Microsoft PowerPoint dialog box.
4. Run the slide show to view how the slides appear in portrait orientation.
5. After running the slide show, change the page setup by completing the following steps:
   a. Click the Slide Size button and then click *Custom Slide Size* at the drop-down list.
   b. At the Slide Size dialog box, click the *Landscape* option in the *Slides* section.
   c. Click the *Slides sized for* option box arrow and then click *On-screen Show (16:10)*. (Notice that the slide height changed from *10* to *6.25* in the *Height* measurement box.)
   d. Click OK.
   e. Click the Maximize button at the Microsoft PowerPoint dialog box.
6. Run the slide show.
7. Specify slide width and height and change slide numbering by completing the following steps:
   a. Click the Slide Size button and then click *Custom Slide Size* at the drop-down list.
   b. At the Slide Size dialog box, click the *Width* measurement box down arrow until *9 in* displays.
   c. Click the *Height* measurement box down arrow until *6 in* displays.
   d. Click the *Number slides from* measurement box up arrow until *6* displays.
   e. Click OK.
   f. Click the Ensure Fit button at the Microsoft PowerPoint dialog box.
8. Notice that the slide numbering in the slide thumbnails pane begins with Slide 6.
9. Run the slide show.
10. Save and then close **3-ColorPres**.

Check Your Work

Activity 3 **Modify the Design Theme and Slide Background of a Network Presentation**   **1 Part**

You will open a network presentation, apply a design theme, and then change the theme colors and fonts. You will also apply and customize a background style.

Tutorial

Changing and Modifying Design Themes

💡 **Hint** Themes are shared across Office programs such as PowerPoint, Word, Excel, and Access.

Changing and Modifying Design Themes

A design theme is a set of formatting choices that includes a color theme (a set of colors), a font theme (heading and text fonts), and an effects theme (a set of lines and fill effects). Click the More Variants button in the Variants group on the Design tab to display options for changing design theme colors, fonts, and effects.

A theme contains specific color formatting that can be changed with color options. Change color options by clicking the More Variants button in the Variants group, pointing to the *Colors* option, and then clicking a color option in the side menu. Each theme applies specific fonts and these fonts can be changed by pointing to the *Fonts* option at the More Variants button drop-down gallery and then choosing an option at the side menu. Each font group in the side menu contains two choices: The first choice is the font that is applied to slide titles and the second choice is the font that is applied to slide subtitles and text. If a presentation contains graphic elements such as illustrations, images, or text boxes, specify theme effects by pointing to the *Effects* option at the More Variants button drop-down gallery and then choosing an option at the side menu.

Tutorial

Formatting the Slide Background

🖊️ Format Background

Quick Steps

Change Slide Background
1. Click Design tab.
2. Click Format Background button.
3. Make changes at Format Background task pane.

Formatting the Slide Background

Format the slide background with background styles or with options at the Format Background task pane. Display background styles by clicking the More Variants button in the Variants group on the Design tab and then pointing to the *Background Styles* option. Apply a background style by clicking an option at the side menu.

Click the Format Background button in the Customize group on the Design tab to display the Format Background task pane, as shown in Figure 3.9. Use options in the Format Background task pane to apply fill, effects, or a picture to the slide background. Apply the slide background to all slides in the presentation by clicking the Apply to All button at the bottom of the task pane. If changes are made to the slide background, reset the background to the default by clicking the Reset Background button at the bottom of the Format Background task pane.

Some of the design themes provided by PowerPoint contain a background graphic. The background graphic can be removed from slides by inserting a check mark in the *Hide background graphics* check box in the *Fill* section of the Format Background task pane with the Fill icon selected and then clicking the Apply to All button.

Figure 3.9 Format Background Task Pane

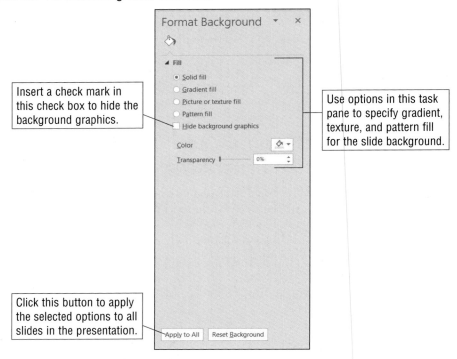

Insert a check mark in this check box to hide the background graphics.

Use options in this task pane to specify gradient, texture, and pattern fill for the slide background.

Click this button to apply the selected options to all slides in the presentation.

Activity 3 Changing Theme Colors, Theme Fonts, and Slide Backgrounds   Part 1 of 1

1. Open **NetworkPres** and then save it with the name **3-NetworkPres**.
2. Apply a design theme by completing the following steps:
   a. Click the Design tab.
   b. Click the More Themes button at the right of the themes gallery in the Themes group and then click *Dividend* at the drop-down gallery.
3. Change the theme colors by clicking the More Variants button in the Variants group, pointing to *Colors*, scrolling down the color options in the side menu, and then clicking *Marquee*.

4. Change the theme fonts by clicking the More Variants button, pointing to *Fonts*, scrolling down the side menu, and then clicking *Calibri-Cambria*.

5. Change the background style by clicking the More Variants button, pointing to *Background Styles*, and then clicking *Style 5* at the side menu (first column, second row).

6. With Slide 1 active, run the slide show to view the formatting applied by the design theme, theme colors, theme fonts, and background style.

7. With Slide 1 still active, apply and customize the background style of all slides by completing the following steps:

   a. Click the Format Background button in the Customize group on the Design tab.

   b. At the Format Background task pane with the Fill icon selected and the fill options displayed in the *Fill* section, click the *Picture or texture fill* option.

   c. Click the Texture button (below the Online button) and then click the *Stationery* option (first column, fourth row).

   d. Double-click the number that displays in the *Transparency* measurement box and then type 25.

   e. Click the Apply to All button at the bottom of the task pane.

   f. Close the Format Background task pane.

8. Run the slide show to view the background formatting.

9. Apply an artistic effect to all slides in the presentation by completing the following steps:

   a. Make Slide 2 active.

   b. Click the Format Background button in the Customize group on the Design tab.

   c. Click the Effects icon in the Format Background task pane.

   d. Click the Artistic Effects button and then click the *Paint Brush* option (third column, second row).

   e. Click the Apply to All button.

10. Run the slide show to view the artistic effect applied to all slides in the presentation.

11. Change the background to a gradient fill rather than an artistic effect by completing the following steps:
    a. Click the Fill icon in the Format Background task pane.
    b. Click the *Gradient fill* option.
    c. Click the Preset gradients button and then click *Light Gradient - Accent 2* (second column, first row).
    d. Click the *Type* option box arrow and then click *Radial* at the drop-down list.
    e. Click the Direction button and then click the *From Bottom Left Corner* option (second option from the left).
    f. Double-click the number that displays in the *Position* measurement box and then type 25.
    g. Click the Apply to All button.
12. Look at the slides in the slide thumbnails pane to view the gradient fill applied to all slides.
13. Apply a pattern fill to Slide 1 by completing the following steps:
    a. If necessary, make Slide 1 the active slide.
    b. At the Format Background task pane, click the *Pattern fill* option.
    c. Click the *Divot* option in the *Pattern* section (first column, seventh row).
    d. Click the Background button and then click the *Green, Accent 2, Lighter 80%* option (sixth column, second row in the *Theme Colors* section).
14. After viewing the pattern fill in the slide pane, reset the slide background of Slide 1 to the gradient fill background by clicking the Reset Background button at the bottom of the Format Background task pane.
15. Close the Format Background task pane.
16. Run the slide show to view the background formatting.
17. Print the presentation as a handout with six slides displayed horizontally per page.
18. Save and then close **3-NetworkPres**.

Check Your Work

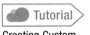

Activity 4 **Create and Apply Custom Design Themes**   **4 Parts**
to Presentations

You will create custom theme colors and custom theme fonts and then save the changes as a custom design theme. You will then apply the custom design theme to a job search presentation and a resume writing presentation.

Creating Custom Design Themes

If the default themes, theme colors, and theme fonts do not provide the necessary formatting for a presentation, create custom theme colors, custom theme fonts, and a custom design theme. A custom design theme will display in the *Custom* section of the Themes drop-down gallery. To create a custom design theme, change the theme colors, theme fonts, and/or theme effects.

Click the More Variants button in the Variants group on the Design tab and the options at the drop-down gallery display a visual representation of the current theme. If the theme colors are changed, the colors are reflected in the small color squares on the *Colors* option. If the theme fonts are changed, the *A* on the *Fonts* option reflects the change.

Creating Custom Theme Colors

To create custom theme colors, click the Design tab, click the More Variants button, point to the *Colors* option, and then click *Customize Colors* at the side menu. This displays the Create New Theme Colors dialog box, similar to the one shown in Figure 3.10. Theme colors contain four text and background colors, six accent colors, and two hyperlink colors, as shown in the *Theme colors* section of the dialog box. Change a theme color by clicking the color button at the right of the color option and then clicking the desired color at the color palette. If changes are made to colors at the Create New Theme Colors dialog box, clicking the Reset button in the lower left corner of the dialog box will change the colors back to the default.

Figure 3.10 Create New Theme Colors Dialog Box

Click this button to reset colors back to the default.

Change a theme color by clicking the color button and then clicking the color at the drop-down palette.

Save custom theme colors by clicking in the *Name* text box, typing a name for the custom theme colors, and then clicking the Save button. This saves the custom theme colors and applies the color changes to the currently open presentation.

Apply custom theme colors to a presentation by clicking the More Variants button in the Variants group, pointing to the *Colors* option, and then clicking the custom theme colors at the top of the drop-down gallery in the *Custom* section.

Activity 4a Creating Custom Theme Colors

Note: If you are running PowerPoint on a computer connected to a network in a public environment such as a school, you may need to complete all four parts of Activity 4 during the same session. Network system software may delete your custom themes when you close PowerPoint. Check with your instructor.

1. At a blank presentation, click the Design tab, click the More Themes button in the Themes group, and then click *Wisp* at the drop-down gallery.
2. Click the third option in the Variants group (light blue color).
3. Create custom theme colors by completing the following steps:
   a. Click the More Variants button in the Variants group, point to the *Colors* option, and then click the *Customize Colors* option at the side menu.
   b. At the Create New Theme Colors dialog box, click the color button at the right of the *Text/Background - Dark 2* option and then click the *Dark Blue, Accent 3, Darker 25%* option (seventh column, fifth row in the *Theme Colors* section).
   c. Click the color button at the right of the *Text/Background - Light 2* option and then click the *Purple, Accent 4, Lighter 80%* option (eighth column, second row in the *Theme Colors* section).

   d. Click the color button at the right of the *Accent 1* option and then click the *Purple, Accent 4, Darker 50%* option (eighth column, last row in the *Theme Colors* section).
4. Save the custom colors by completing the following steps:
   a. Select the text in the *Name* text box.
   b. Type your first and last names.
   c. Click the Save button.
5. Save the presentation and name it **3-CustomTheme**.

Tutorial

Creating Custom Theme Fonts

To create custom theme fonts, click the Design tab, click the More Variants button in the Variants group, point to the *Fonts* option, and then click *Customize Fonts* at the side menu. This displays the Create New Theme Fonts dialog box, similar to the one shown in Figure 3.11. At this dialog box, choose a heading font and body font. Type the name of the custom theme fonts in the *Name* text box and then click the Save button.

Quick Steps

Create Custom Theme Fonts

1. Click Design tab.
2. Click More Variants button.
3. Point to *Fonts*.
4. Click *Customize Fonts*.
5. Choose fonts.
6. Type name for custom theme fonts.
7. Click Save button.

Figure 3.11 Create New Theme Fonts Dialog Box

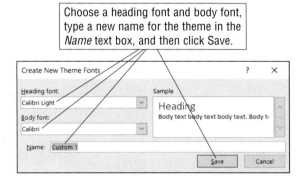

Choose a heading font and body font, type a new name for the theme in the *Name* text box, and then click Save.

Activity 4b Creating Custom Theme Fonts

Part 2 of 4

1. With **3-CustomTheme** open, create custom theme fonts by completing the following steps:
   a. If necessary, click the Design tab.
   b. Click the More Variants button in the Variants group, point to the *Fonts* option, and then click the *Customize Fonts* option at the side menu.
   c. At the Create New Theme Fonts dialog box, click the *Heading font* option box arrow and then click *Candara*.
   d. Click the *Body font* option box arrow, scroll down the drop-down list, and then click *Constantia*.
2. Save the custom theme fonts by completing the following steps:
   a. Select the current text in the *Name* text box.
   b. Type your first and last names.
   c. Click the Save button.
3. Save **3-CustomTheme**.

Tutorial

Saving and
Deleting a Custom
Design Theme

Quick Steps

Save Custom Design
Theme
1. Click Design tab.
2. Click More Themes
   button.
3. Click *Save Current
   Theme*.
4. Type name for
   custom theme.
5. Click Save button.

Saving a Custom Design Theme

When theme colors and fonts have been customized, save these as a custom design theme. To do this, click the More Themes button in the Themes group on the Design tab and then click *Save Current Theme*. This displays the Save Current Theme dialog box with the Document Themes folder active on the computer's hard drive, which contains many of the same options as the Save As dialog box. Type a name for the custom design theme in the *File name* text box and then click the Save button. To apply a custom design theme, click the More Themes button in the Themes group, and then click the theme in the *Custom* section of the drop-down gallery.

Activity 4c Saving and Applying a Custom Design Theme

Part 3 of 4

1. With **3-CustomTheme** open, save the custom theme colors and fonts as a custom design theme by completing the following steps:
   a. If necessary, click the Design tab.
   b. Click the More Themes button in the Themes group.
   c. Click the *Save Current Theme* option at the bottom of the drop-down gallery.
   d. At the Save Current Theme dialog box with the Document Themes folder active on the computer's hard drive, type C3 and then type your last name in the *File name* text box.
   e. Click the Save button.

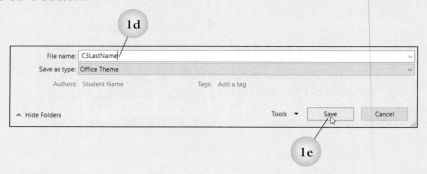

2. Close **3-CustomTheme**.
3. Open **JobSearch** and then save it with the name **3-JobSearch**.
4. Apply your custom design theme by completing the following steps:
   a. Click the Design tab, if necessary.
   b. Click the More Themes button in the Themes group.
   c. Click the custom design theme that begins with *C3* followed by your last name. (The theme will display in the *Custom* section of the drop-down gallery.)

5. Run the slide show to view how the slides display with the custom design theme applied.
6. Print Slide 1 of the presentation.
7. Save and then close **3-JobSearch**.
8. Open **ResumePres** and then save it with the name **3-ResumePres**.

---

9. Apply your custom design theme (the theme beginning with *C3* followed by your last name) to the presentation.
10. Run the slide show.
11. Print Slide 1 of the presentation.
12. Save and then close **3-ResumePres**.

Editing Custom Themes

Tutorial

Editing Custom Themes

*Q*uick Steps

Edit Custom Theme Colors or Fonts
1. Click Design tab.
2. Click More Variants button.
3. Point to *Colors* or *Fonts* option.
4. Right click custom theme.
5. Click *Edit.*
6. Make changes.
7. Click Save button.

Delete Custom Theme Colors or Fonts
1. Click Design tab.
2. Click More Variants button.
3. Point to *Colors* or *Fonts* option.
4. Right-click custom theme.
5. Click *Delete.*
6. Click Yes.

Delete Custom Design Theme
1. Click Design tab.
2. Click More Themes button.
3. Right-click custom theme.
4. Click *Delete.*
5. Click Yes.

Editing Custom Themes

Custom theme colors and custom theme fonts can be edited. To edit the custom theme colors, click the More Variants button in the Variants group on the Design tab and then point to the *Colors* option. At the side menu of custom and built-in themes, right-click the custom theme and then click *Edit* at the shortcut menu. This displays the Edit Theme Colors dialog box, which contains the same options as the Create New Theme Colors dialog box shown in Figure 3.10 (on page 97). Make the changes to the theme colors and then click the Save button.

To edit custom theme fonts, click the More Variants button, point to the *Fonts* option, right-click the custom theme fonts, and then click *Edit* at the shortcut menu. This displays the Edit Theme Fonts dialog box that contains the same options as the Create New Theme Fonts dialog box shown in Figure 3.11 (on page 99). Make the changes and then click the Save button.

Deleting Custom Themes

Delete custom theme colors from the *Colors* option side menu, delete custom theme fonts from the *Fonts* option side menu, and delete custom design themes from the More Themes button drop-down gallery or the Save Current Theme dialog box. To delete custom theme colors, click the More Variants button in the Variants group, point to the *Colors* option, right-click the theme to be deleted, and then click *Delete* at the shortcut menu. At the message asking to confirm the deletion, click Yes. Complete similar steps to delete custom theme fonts.

Delete a custom design theme by clicking the More Themes button in the Themes group on the Design tab, right-clicking the custom design theme, and then clicking *Delete* at the shortcut menu. A custom design theme can also be deleted at the Save Current Theme dialog box. To display this dialog box, click the More Themes button in the Themes group on the Design tab and then click *Save Current Theme* at the drop-down gallery. At the Save Current Theme dialog box, click the custom design theme file name, click the Organize button on the toolbar, and then click *Delete* at the drop-down list. At the message asking to confirm the deletion, click Yes.

1. Open a new, blank presentation and delete the custom theme colors by completing the following steps:
   a. Click the Design tab.
   b. Click the More Variants button in the Variants group and then point to the *Colors* option.
   c. Right-click the custom theme colors named with your first and last names.
   d. Click *Delete* at the shortcut menu.

   e. At the message asking if you want to delete the theme colors, click Yes.
2. Complete steps similar to those in Step 1 to delete the custom theme fonts you created named with your first and last names.
3. Delete the custom design theme by completing the following steps:
   a. Click the More Themes button in the Themes group.
   b. Right-click the custom design theme that begins with *C3* followed by your last name.
   c. Click *Delete* at the shortcut menu.
   d. At the message asking if you want to delete the theme, click Yes.
4. Close the presentation without saving it.

Chapter Summary

- The Font group on the Home tab contains buttons and options for applying character formatting to text in slides.

- Change the font with the *Font* option box and the *Font Size* option box in the Font group.

- Some options, such as the *Font* and *Font Size* options, contain the live preview feature, which displays how the formatting affects selected text before actually applying the formatting to the text.

- Character formatting can also be applied with options at the Font dialog box. Display this dialog box by clicking the Font group dialog box launcher.

- Select text in a slide and the Mini toolbar displays above the selected text. Apply formatting using the buttons and options on this toolbar.

- Use Format Painter to apply formatting to more than one location in a slide or slides.

- The Paragraph group on the Home tab contains a number of buttons for applying paragraph formatting to text in slides.

- Customize paragraph formatting with options at the Paragraph dialog box with the Indents and Spacing tab selected. Display this dialog box by clicking the Paragraph group dialog box launcher on the Home tab or by clicking the Line Spacing button in the Paragraph group and then clicking *Line Spacing Options* at the drop-down list.

- Use the Add or Remove Columns button in the Paragraph group on the Home tab or options at the Columns dialog box to format selected text into columns. Display the Columns dialog box by clicking the Add or Remove Columns button and then clicking *More Columns* at the drop-down list.

- Use the Text Direction button or options at the Format Shape task pane to rotate or stack text in a slide. Display the Format Shape task pane by clicking the Drawing group task pane launcher on the Home tab.

- The Shape Options tab in the Format Shape task pane displays three icons: Fill & Line, Effects, and Size & Properties, each with different options for formatting a placeholder.

- Customize bullets and numbering with options at the Bullets and Numbering dialog box. Display this dialog box by clicking the Bullets button arrow or the Numbering button arrow and then clicking *Bullets and Numbering* at the drop-down list.

- Click the Quick Styles button in the Drawing group on the Home tab to apply formatting to a placeholder. The Drawing group also contains the Shape Fill, Shape Outline, and Shape Effects buttons for customizing a placeholder, and the Arrange button for arranging slide elements.

- Click the Slide Size button and then click *Custom Slide Size* at the drop-down list to display the Slide Size dialog box. Use options at this dialog box to change the slide size and ratio, the starting slide number, and the orientation of slides, notes, handouts, and outline pages.

- Use the Format Background task pane to customize the background of slides. Display this task pane by clicking the Format Background button in the Customize group on the Design tab.

- Create custom theme colors and fonts with options by clicking the More Variants button in the Variants group on the Design tab, pointing to the *Colors* option, and then clicking *Customize Colors* at the side menu to display the dialog box.

- Save a custom design theme at the Save Current Theme dialog box. Display this dialog box by clicking the More Themes button in the Themes group on the Design tab and then clicking *Save Current Theme*.

- Edit custom theme colors with options at the Edit Theme Colors dialog box and edit custom theme fonts with options at the Edit Theme Fonts dialog box.

- Delete custom theme colors or fonts by clicking the More Variants button in the Variants group on the Design tab, pointing to the *Colors* or the *Fonts* option, right-clicking the custom theme, clicking the *Delete* option, and then clicking Yes.

- Delete a custom design theme by clicking the More Themes button in the Themes group on the Design tab, right-clicking the custom theme, and then clicking *Delete* at the shortcut menu.

Commands Review

FEATURE	RIBBON TAB, GROUP	BUTTON, OPTION	KEYBOARD SHORTCUT
Bullets and Numbering dialog box with Bulleted tab selected	Home, Paragraph	, Bullets and Numbering	
Bullets and Numbering dialog box with Numbered tab selected	Home, Paragraph	, Bullets and Numbering	
Columns dialog box	Home, Paragraph	, More Columns	
Create New Theme Colors dialog box	Design, Variants	, Colors, Customize Colors	
Create New Theme Fonts dialog box	Design, Variants	, Fonts, Customize Fonts	
Font dialog box	Home, Font		Ctrl + Shift + F
Format Background task pane	Design, Customize		
Format Painter	Home, Clipboard		
Format Shape task pane	Home, Drawing		
Paragraph dialog box	Home, Paragraph		
Save Current Theme dialog box	Design, Themes	, Save Current Theme	
slide size	Design, Customize		

Microsoft®
PowerPoint®

Inserting Elements in Slides

Performance Objectives

Upon successful completion of Chapter 4, you will be able to:

1 Insert, format, select, and align a text box
2 Set the default text box format
3 Set tabs in a text box
4 Insert, format, and copy shapes
5 Display rulers, gridlines, and guides
6 Merge, group, and ungroup objects
7 Insert, crop, size, position, and format an image
8 Insert an image as a slide background
9 Copy objects within and between presentations
10 Insert, size, format, and position an icon
11 Create and insert a screenshot
12 Create and format WordArt text
13 Insert symbols, headers, footers, the current date, and slide numbers

An audience may overlook a presentation consisting only of text-heavy slides. Adding visual elements, where appropriate, can help by adding interest and impact to the information. In this chapter, you will learn how to create and add visual elements on slides such as text boxes, shapes, images, icons, screenshots, and WordArt text. These elements will make the delivery of your presentation a dynamic experience for your audience.

 Data Files

Before beginning chapter work, copy the PC4 folder to your storage medium and then make PC4 the active folder.

The online course includes additional training and assessment resources.

Tutorial

Inserting and Formatting Text Boxes

 Text Box

Inserting and Formatting Text Boxes

Many slide layouts contain placeholders for entering text and other elements in a slide. Along with placeholders, a text box can be inserted and formatted in a slide. To insert a text box in a slide, click the Insert tab, click the Text Box button in the Text group, and the mouse pointer displays as a thin, down-pointing arrow. Using the mouse, click and drag in the slide to create the text box. Or, click in a slide to insert a small text box at that location.

Formatting a Text Box

Quick Steps

Draw Text Box
1. Click Insert tab.
2. Click Text Box button.
3. Click or drag in slide to create box.

When a text box is inserted in a slide, the Home tab displays. Use options in the Drawing group to format the text box by applying a Quick Style or adding a shape fill, outline, or effect. Format a text box in a manner similar to formatting a placeholder. Formatting can also be applied to a text box with options on the Drawing Tools Format tab. Click this tab and the ribbon displays as shown in Figure 4.1. The Shape Styles group contains the same options as the Drawing group on the Home tab. Use other options on the tab to apply WordArt formatting to text and arrange and size the text box.

Move a text box in the same way as a placeholder. Click the text box to select it, position the mouse pointer on the text box border until the pointer displays with a four-headed arrow, and then click and drag the text box to the new position. Change the size of a selected text box using the sizing handles that display around the box. Use the *Shape Height* and *Shape Width* measurement boxes in the Size group on the Drawing Tools Format tab to adjust the size of the text box to a specific height and width measurement.

Hint Use a text box to place text anywhere in a slide. Text in inserted text boxes does not appear in the Outline view.

PowerPoint provides a task pane with a variety of options for formatting a placeholder. The same task pane is available with options for formatting and customizing a text box. Click the Shape Styles group task pane launcher and the Format Shape task pane displays at the right side of the screen with options for formatting the text box fill, effects, and size; options for formatting an image in the text box; and options for formatting text in a text box. Click the WordArt

Figure 4.1 Drawing Tools Format Tab

Styles group task pane launcher and the Format Shape task pane displays text formatting options. Click the Size group task pane launcher and the Format Shape task pane displays size and position options.

The same formatting applied to a placeholder can also be applied to a text box. For example, use the buttons in the Paragraph group on the Home tab to align text horizontally and vertically in a text box, change text direction, set text in columns, and set internal margins for the text in the text box.

Selecting Multiple Objects

Quick Steps
Select All Text Boxes
1. Click Select button.
2. Click *Select All.*
OR
Press Ctrl + A.

 Select

 Align

Hint To select an object that is behind another object, select the top object and then press the Tab key to cycle through and select the other objects.

Multiple text boxes and other objects can be selected in a slide and then the objects can be formatted, aligned, and arranged in the slide. To select all objects in a slide, click the Select button in the Editing group on the Home tab and then click *Select All* at the drop-down list. Or, select all objects in a slide with the keyboard shortcut Ctrl + A. To select specific text boxes or objects in a slide, click the first object, press and hold down the Shift key, and then click each of the other objects.

Aligning Text Boxes

Use the Align button in the Arrange group on the Drawing Tools Format tab to align the edges of multiple objects in a slide. Click the Align button and a drop-down list of alignment options displays, including options for aligning objects vertically and horizontally and distributing objects in the slide.

Activity 1a **Inserting and Formatting Text Boxes** Part 1 of 14

1. Open **AddisonReport** and then save it with the name **4-AddisonReport**.
2. Insert a new slide with the Blank layout by completing the following steps:
   a. Click the New Slide button arrow in the Slides group on the Home tab.
   b. Click *Blank* at the drop-down list.
3. Insert and format the *Safety* text box shown in Figure 4.2 (on page 110) by completing the following steps:
   a. Click the Insert tab.
   b. Click the Text Box button in the Text group.
   c. Click in the slide. (This inserts a small text box in the slide.)
   d. Type Safety.
   e. Select the text and then change the font to Copperplate Gothic Bold and the font size to 36 points.

f. Click the Text Direction button in the Paragraph group on the Home tab and then click *Stacked* at the drop-down list.

g. Click the Drawing Tools Format tab.

h. Click the More Shape Styles button in the Shape Styles group and then click the *Subtle Effect - Aqua, Accent 5* option (sixth column, fourth row in the *Theme Styles* section).

i. Click the Shape Outline button arrow in the Shape Styles group and then click the *Blue* color (eighth option in the *Standard Colors* section).

j. Click the Shape Outline button arrow, point to *Weight*, and then click the *1½ pt* option.

k. Click the Shape Effects button, point to *Bevel*, and then click the *Round* option (first option in the *Bevel* section).

l. Click the More WordArt Styles button in the WordArt Styles group and then click the option in the first column, third row (black outline with white fill).

m. Click in the *Shape Height* measurement box, type 4, and then press the Enter key.

n. Drag the text box so it is positioned as shown in Figure 4.2 (on page 110).

4. Insert and size the other text box shown in Figure 4.2 by completing the following steps:

a. Click the Insert tab.

b. Click the Text Box button in the Text group.

c. Drag in the slide to create a text box. (Drag to the approximate width of the text box in Figure 4.2.)

d. Type the text shown in the text box in Figure 4.2 in a single column. Type the text in the first column and then type the text in the second column. (Your text will display as shown at the right in one column, in a smaller font, and with different line spacing than in Figure 4.2.)

e. Select the text and then change the font size to 32 points.

f. Click the Line Spacing button in the Paragraph group and then click *2.0* at the drop-down list. (The text will flow off the slide.)

g. Click the Add or Remove Columns button in the Paragraph group and then click *Two Columns* at the drop-down list. (The text in the slide will not display in two columns until you complete step 7i.)

5. Click the Drawing Tools Format tab.

6. Apply a WordArt style by completing the following steps:
   a. Click the More WordArt Styles button in the WordArt Styles group.
   b. Click the option in the first column, third row (black outline with white fill).

7. Change the height, width, and internal margin measurements of the text box and turn off Autofit in the Format Shape task pane by completing the following steps:

   a. Click the Size group task pane launcher.
   b. At the Format Shape task pane, click the Size & Properties icon if it is not selected.
   c. If necessary, click *Text Box* in the task pane to display the text box options.
   d. Click the *Do not Autofit* option.
   e. Select the current measurement in the *Left margin* measurement box and then type 0.8.
   f. Select the current measurement in the *Right margin* measurement box and then type 0.
   g. Select the current measurement in the *Top margin* measurement box, type 0.2, and then press the Enter key.
   h. If necessary, click *Size* at the top of the task pane to display the size options.
   i. Select the current measurement in the *Height* measurement box and then type 4.
   j. Select the current measurement in the *Width* measurement box, type 8, and then press the Enter key.

8. Apply fill formatting with options in the Format Shape task pane by completing the following steps:
   a. Click the Fill & Line icon in the task pane.
   b. If necessary, click *Fill* to display the fill options.
   c. Click the *Gradient fill* option to select it. (Notice the options available for customizing the gradient fill.)
   d. Click the *Pattern fill* option to select it. (Notice the options available for applying a pattern fill.)
   e. Click the *Picture or texture fill* option to select it.
   f. Click the File button in the *Insert picture from* section.
   g. At the Insert Picture dialog box, navigate to your PC4 folder and then double-click the **Ship** image file.

h. Select the current percentage in the *Transparency* measurement box, type 10, and then press the Enter key.

i. Close the task pane by clicking the Close button in the upper right corner of the task pane.

9. Click in the slide outside the text box.

10. Arrange the text boxes by completing the following steps:

a. Press Ctrl + A to select both text boxes.

b. Click the Drawing Tools Format tab.

c. Click the Align button in the Arrange group and then click *Align Bottom* at the drop-down list.

d. Drag both boxes to the approximate location in the slide as shown in Figure 4.2.

11. Save **4-AddisonReport**.

12. Print only Slide 2 by completing the following steps:

a. Press Ctrl + P to display the Print backstage area.

b. Click in the *Slides* text box in the *Settings* category and then type 2.

c. Click the Print button.

13. Click in the slide to deselect the text boxes, then select only the text box containing the image of the ship.

14. Make sure the Drawing Tools Format tab is active, click the More Shape Styles button in the Shape Styles group, and then click the *Moderate Effect - Aqua, Accent 5* option (sixth column, fifth row).

15. Click the Shape Outline button arrow in the Shape Styles group, and then click the *Blue* color (eighth option in the *Standard Colors* section).

16. Click the Shape Outline button arrow, point to *Weight*, and then click the *1½ pt* option.

17. Click the Shape Effects button, point to *Bevel*, and then click the *Round* option (first option in the *Bevel* section).

18. Save **4-AddisonReport**.

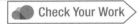

Check Your Work

Figure 4.2 Activity 1a, Slide 2

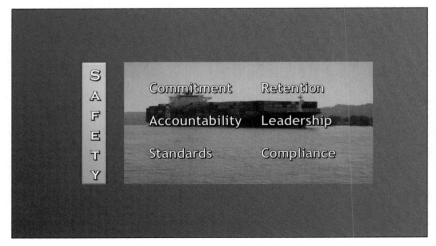

Setting the Default Text Box Format

The Format Shape task pane can be displayed using the shortcut menu. To do this, position the mouse pointer on the border of the text box until the pointer displays with a four-headed arrow and then click the right mouse button. At the shortcut menu, click the *Size and Position* option to display the Format Shape task pane with the Size & Properties icon active. Click the *Format Shape* option at the shortcut menu and the Format Shape task pane displays with the Fill & Line icon active. Formatting applied to a text box can become the default for other text boxes in the current presentation by clicking the *Set as Default Text Box* option at the shortcut menu.

Activity 1b Formatting a Text Box and Setting the Default Text Box   Part 2 of 14

1. With **4-AddisonReport** open, make sure Slide 2 is the active slide and then complete the following steps:
   a. Click the Insert tab, click the Text Box button, and then click in the lower right corner of the slide.
   b. Type Default text box. (In the next step you will change the default text box. You will then use the text box you just inserted to return to the original default text box.)
2. Set as the default the text box containing the word *SAFETY* by completing the following steps:
   a. Position the mouse pointer on the border of the text box containing the word *SAFETY* until the pointer displays with a four-headed arrow and then click the right mouse button.
   b. Click the *Set as Default Text Box* option at the shortcut menu.
3. Make Slide 1 active.
4. Insert a text box by clicking the Insert tab, clicking the Text Box button, and then clicking between the company name and the left side of the slide.
5. Type 2021 in the text box.
6. Change the *Autofit* option, wrap text in the text box, and change the size of the text box by completing the following steps:
   a. Position the mouse pointer on the border of the text box until the pointer displays with a four-headed arrow and then click the right mouse button.
   b. Click the *Size and Position* option at the shortcut menu.
   c. At the Format Shape task pane with the Size & Properties icon selected, click *Text Box* if the text box options do not display, scroll to the bottom of the task pane list box, and then click in the *Wrap text in shape* check box to insert a check mark.
   d. Click the *Shrink text on overflow* option to select it.
   e. Scroll up to the top of the task pane and then click *Size* if the size options do not display.
   f. Select the current measurement in the *Height* measurement box in the *Size* section and then type 2.4.
   g. Select the current measurement in the *Width* measurement box, type 0.8, and then press the Enter key.

2b

6d

6c

7. With the text box selected, change the shape of the text box by completing the following steps:
   a. Click the Drawing Tools Format tab.
   b. Click the Edit Shape button in the Insert Shapes group, point to *Change Shape*, and then click the *Rectangle: Beveled* option (last column, second row in the *Basic Shapes* section).

8. Precisely position the text box by completing the following steps:
   a. If necessary, scroll down the Format Shape task pane to the *Position* section and then click *Position* to display the options.
   b. Select the current measurement in the *Horizontal position* measurement box and then type 1.8.
   c. Select the current measurement in the *Vertical position* measurement box, type 2, and then press the Enter key.
9. Close the Format Shape task pane.
10. Return to the original text box by completing the following steps:
    a. Make Slide 2 active.
    b. Click in the text box containing the words *Default text box*.
    c. Position the mouse pointer on the border of the text box until the pointer displays with a four-headed arrow and then click the right mouse button.
    d. Click the *Set as Default Text Box* option at the shortcut menu.
    e. Press the Delete key to delete the text box.
11. Save **4-AddisonReport**.

Check Your Work

Setting Tabs in a Text Box

💡 *Hint* Setting tabs helps you align text in a slide.

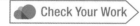 Left Tab

Center Tab

Right Tab

Decimal Tab

Text inside a text box can be aligned in columns using tabs. A text box, by default, contains left alignment tabs that display as gray marks along the bottom of the horizontal ruler. (If the ruler is not visible, display the horizontal ruler as well as the vertical ruler by clicking the View tab and then clicking the *Ruler* check box in the Show group to insert a check mark.) These default left alignment tabs can be changed to center, right, or decimal. To change to a different tab alignment, click the Alignment button that displays at the left of the horizontal ruler. Continue clicking the Alignment button to cycle though the tab alignment options. Display the necessary tab alignment symbol and then click a location on the horizontal ruler. When a tab is set on the horizontal ruler, any default tabs to the left of the new tab are deleted. Move tabs on the horizontal ruler using the mouse to drag the tab to the new position. To delete a tab, use the mouse to drag the tab down and off of the ruler.

Tabs can also be set with options at the Tabs dialog box. To display this dialog box, click the Paragraph group dialog box launcher. At the Paragraph dialog box, click the Tabs button in the lower left corner. At the Tabs dialog box, type a tab position in the *Tab stop position* measurement box, choose a tab alignment with options in the *Alignment* section, and then click the Set button. Clear a specific tab by typing the tab position in the *Tab stop position* measurement box and then clicking the Clear button. Clear all tabs from the horizontal ruler by clicking the Clear All button. When all changes have been made, click OK to close the Tabs dialog box and then click OK to close the Paragraph dialog box.

Activity 1c Creating a Text Box and Setting Tabs

1. With **4-AddisonReport** open, make Slide 1 active and then click the Home tab.
2. Click the New Slide button arrow and then click the *Title Only* layout.
3. Click in the title placeholder and then type Executive Officers.
4. Draw a text box by completing the following steps:
   a. Click the Insert tab.
   b. Click the Text Box button in the Text group.
   c. Draw a text box in the slide that is approximately 10 inches wide and 0.5 inch tall. (Refer to Figure 4.3 on the next page.)
5. Change tabs in the text box by completing the following steps:
   a. If necessary, display the horizontal ruler by clicking the View tab and then clicking the *Ruler* check box in the Show group to insert a check mark.

   b. With the insertion point inside the text box, check the Alignment button at the left of the horizontal ruler and make sure the left tab symbol displays.
   c. Position the tip of the mouse pointer on the horizontal ruler below the 0.5-inch mark and then click the left mouse button.
   d. Click the Alignment button to display the center tab symbol.
   e. Click immediately below the 5-inch mark on the horizontal ruler.

   f. Click the Alignment button to display the right tab symbol.
   g. Click the horizontal ruler immediately below the 9.5-inch mark. (You may need to expand the size of the text box to set the tab at the 9.5-inch mark.)
6. Type the text in the text box as shown in Figure 4.3. Make sure you press the Tab key before typing text in the first column. (This moves the insertion point to the first tab, which is a left alignment tab.) Bold the three column headings—*Name*, *Title*, and *Number*.
7. When you are finished typing the text in the text box, press Ctrl + A to select all of the text in the text box and then change the font size to 24 points.
8. With the text in the text box still selected, drag the left alignment marker on the horizontal ruler from the 0.5-inch mark to the 0.25-inch mark and then drag the center alignment marker on the horizontal ruler from the 5-inch mark on the ruler to the 5.5-inch mark.

9. Click the Line Spacing button in the Paragraph group on the Home tab and then click the *1.5* option.
10. Position the text box as shown in Figure 4.3.
11. Save **4-AddisonReport**.

 Check Your Work

Figure 4.3 Activity 1c, Slide 2

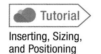 Tutorial

Inserting, Sizing, and Positioning Shapes

 Tutorial

Formatting Shapes

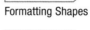 Tutorial

Copying and Rotating Shapes

 Shapes

Quick Steps

Insert Shape
1. Click Insert tab.
2. Click Shapes button.
3. Click shape at drop-down list.
4. Click or drag in slide to create shape.

Inserting, Formatting, and Copying Shapes

Draw shapes in a slide with shapes in the Drawing group or with the Shapes button in the Illustrations group on the Insert tab. Use the Shapes button drop-down list to draw shapes including lines, basic shapes, block arrows, flow chart symbols, callouts, stars, and banners. Click a shape and the mouse pointer displays as crosshairs (plus sign). Click in the slide to insert the shape, or position the crosshairs in the slide and then click and drag to create the shape.

Apply formatting to a shape in a manner similar to formatting a text box. Format a shape with buttons in the Drawing group on the Home tab, with buttons on the Drawing Tools Format tab, using options in the Format Shape task pane, or with options at the shortcut menu. When drawing an enclosed object, maintain the proportions of the shape by holding down the Shift key while dragging with the mouse to create the shape. The formatting applied to a shape can be saved as the default formatting. To do this, right-click the border of the shape and then click *Set as Default Shape*.

To copy a shape, select the shape and then click the Copy button in the Clipboard group on the Home tab. Position the insertion point at the new location and then click the Paste button. A selected shape can also be copied by pressing and holding down the Ctrl key while dragging the shape to the new location. Rotate a shape using the rotation handle above the selected shape or with the Rotate button in the Arrange group on the Drawing Tools Format tab.

Displaying Rulers, Gridlines, and Guides

PowerPoint provides a number of features for positioning objects such as placeholders, text boxes, and shapes. Display horizontal and vertical rulers, gridlines, and/or drawing guides and use Smart Guides as shown in Figure 4.4. Turn the horizontal and vertical rulers on and off with the *Ruler* check box in the Show group on the View tab as you did in Activity 1c. The Show group also contains a *Gridlines* check box. Insert a check mark in this check box and gridlines display in the active slide. Gridlines are intersecting lines that create a grid on the slide and are useful for aligning objects. Gridlines can also be turned on and off with the keyboard shortcut Shift + F9.

Turn on drawing guides to help position objects on a slide. Drawing guides are a horizontal dashed line and a vertical dashed line that display on the slide in the slide pane as shown in Figure 4.4. To turn on the drawing guides, display the Grid and Guides dialog box shown in Figure 4.5. Display this dialog box by clicking the Show group dialog box launcher on the View tab. At the dialog box, insert a check mark in the *Display drawing guides on screen* check box. Drawing guides can also be displayed by clicking the *Guides* check box in the Show group on the View tab to insert a check mark. By default, the horizontal and vertical drawing guides intersect in the middle of the slide. Drawing guides and gridlines display on the slide but do not print.

Figure 4.4 Rulers, Gridlines, Drawing Guides, and Smart Guides

Figure 4.5 Grid and Guides Dialog Box

Insert a check mark in this check box to snap objects into alignment with the gridlines.

Insert a check mark in this check box to display gridlines.

Insert a check mark in this check box to display drawing guides.

PowerPoint includes Smart Guides, which appear when objects that are close together are moved on a slide. Use these guides to help align and evenly space the objects on the slide.

Turn on gridlines by inserting a check mark in the *Gridlines* check box on the View tab or by inserting a check mark in the *Display grid on screen* check box at the Grid and Guides dialog box. The horizontal and vertical spacing between the gridlines is 0.08 inch by default. This measurement can be changed with the *Spacing* option at the Grid and Guides dialog box.

An object can be positioned precisely in a slide by dragging the object with the mouse pointer or by using the arrow keys on the keyboard. PowerPoint can also snap objects to the nearest intersection of gridlines. Snap objects to gridlines by clicking the *Snap objects to grid* check box at the Grid and Guides dialog box to insert a check mark. Smart Guides display when shapes are moved and aligned. To turn off the display of Smart Guides, click the *Display smart guides when shapes are aligned* check box in the Grid and Guides dialog box to remove the check mark.

Activity 1d Inserting, Formatting, and Copying Shapes

Part 4 of 14

1. With **4-AddisonReport** open, make Slide 3 active and then insert a new slide by clicking the New Slide button arrow and then clicking the *White Background* layout at the drop-down list.
2. Turn on the display of gridlines by clicking the View tab and then clicking *Gridlines* to insert a check mark in the check box.

3. Click in the title placeholder and then type Production Percentages.
4. Turn on the drawing guides by completing the following steps:
   a. Make sure the View tab is active and then click the Show group dialog box launcher.
   b. At the Grid and Guides dialog box, make sure the *Snap objects to grid* check box does not contain a check mark. If necessary, click the check box to remove the check mark.

c. Make sure the *Display grid on screen* check box contains a check mark.

d. Click the *Display drawing guides on screen* check box to insert a check mark.

e. Click OK.

5. Insert the left-most arrow in the slide, as shown in Figure 4.6 (on page 119), by completing the following steps:

a. Click outside the title placeholder to deselect it.

b. Click the Insert tab.

c. Click the Shapes button in the Illustrations group and then click the *Arrow: Up* shape (third column, first row in the *Block Arrows* section).

d. Position the crosshairs at the intersection of the horizontal drawing guide and the third vertical gridline from the left.

e. Click and hold down the left mouse button, drag down and to the right until the crosshairs are positioned on the intersection of the fifth vertical line from the left and the first horizontal line from the bottom, and then release the mouse button. (Your arrow should be the approximate size shown in Figure 4.6.)

f. With the arrow selected and the Drawing Tools Format tab active, click the Shape Fill button arrow in the Shape Styles group, and then click *Aqua, Accent 5* at the drop-down gallery (ninth column, first row in the *Theme Colors* section).

g. Click the Shape Outline button arrow and then click *Dark Blue* at the drop-down gallery (ninth option in the *Standard Colors* section).

h. Apply a shape style to the arrow by clicking the More Shape Styles button in the Shapes Styles group and then clicking the *Subtle Effect - Blue, Accent 1* option (second column, fourth row).

i. Click the Shape Effects button in the Shape Styles group, point to *Bevel*, and then click the *Soft Round* option (second column, second row in the *Bevel* section).

6. Insert text in the arrow by completing the following steps:

a. With the arrow selected, type Plant 3, press the Enter key, and then type 48%.

b. Click the Home tab, click the Align Text button in the Paragraph group, and then click the *Top* option at the drop-down list.

7. Copy the arrow by completing the following steps:

a. Position the mouse pointer on the border of the selected arrow until the mouse pointer displays with a four-headed arrow.

b. Press and hold down the Ctrl key, click and hold down the left mouse button, drag the arrow to the intersection of the horizontal and vertical drawing guides, and then release the Ctrl key and the mouse button.

8. Copy the arrow again by completing Step 7a and 7b, but drag the new arrow so the tip of the arrow is positioned at the intersection of the horizontal drawing guide and the fourth vertical line from the right. Watch for the Smart Guides to display indicating that the arrows are aligned and evenly spaced (see image below).

9. Increase the height of the middle and right arrows by completing the following steps:
   a. Click the middle arrow to select it.
   b. Use the mouse to drag the top middle sizing handle up to the next horizontal gridline.
   c. Click the right arrow and then drag the top middle sizing handle up to the second horizontal gridline (see Figure 4.6).
   d. Change the text in the middle arrow to *Plant 1 72%* and change the text in the right arrow to *Plant 2 91%* (see Figure 4.6).

10. Turn off the gridlines and drawing guides by completing the following steps:
    a. Click the View tab.
    b. Click the Show group dialog box launcher.
    c. Click the *Display grid on screen* option to remove the check mark.
    d. Click the *Display drawing guides on screen* check box to remove the check mark.
    e. Click OK.
11. Change the slide layout by clicking the Home tab, clicking the Layout button in the Slides group, and then clicking the *Title Only* layout.
12. Set the formatting of the arrow shape as the default by completing the following steps:
    a. Click the left arrow shape.
    b. Position the mouse pointer on the arrow shape border until the pointer displays with a four-headed arrow and then click the right mouse button.
    c. Click the *Set as Default Shape* option at the shortcut menu.
13. Draw a shape by completing the following steps:
    a. Click the Insert tab, click the Shapes button, and then click the *Rectangle: Beveled* option (first column, third row in the *Basic Shapes* section).
    b. Click in the lower right corner of the slide.
    c. Change the height and width of the shape to 0.6 inch.
    d. Type AI in the shape. (Note that *I* in *AI* is the capital letter i, not the number 1.)
    e. Position the shape in the slide as shown in Figure 4.6.
14. Save **4-AddisonReport**.

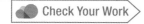
Check Your Work

Figure 4.6 Activity 1d, Slide 4

Merging Shapes

Merge
Shapes

Use the Merge Shapes button on the Drawing Tools Format tab to merge shapes to create custom shapes that are not available with the default shapes. To merge shapes, draw the shapes in the slide, select the shapes, and then click the Merge Shapes button in the Insert Shapes group on the Drawing Tools Format tab. At the drop-down list, choose one of the following options: *Union*, *Combine*, *Fragment*, *Intersect*, and *Subtract*. Each option merges the shapes in a different manner.

Activity 1e Merging Shapes

Part 5 of 14

1. With **4-AddisonReport** open, make sure Slide 4 is active and then insert a slide from another presentation by completing the following steps:
   a. Click the Home tab.
   b. Click the New Slide button arrow and then click *Reuse Slides* at the drop-down list.
   c. At the Reuse Slides task pane, click the Browse button.
   d. At the Browse dialog box, navigate to your PC4 folder and then double-click **IEC**.
   e. Click the second slide thumbnail in the Reuse Slides task pane.
   f. Close the Reuse Slides task pane by clicking the Close button in the upper right corner of the task pane.
2. The slide you inserted contains a circle shape and four rectangle shapes. Merge the shapes to create an image for the International Energy Consortium by completing the following steps:
   a. Click the slide in the slide pane and then press Ctrl + A to select all of the shapes in the slide.
   b. Click the Drawing Tools Format tab.
   c. Click the Merge Shapes button in the Insert Shapes group.
   d. Hover your mouse over each option in the drop-down list to view how the option merges the shapes in the slide, and then click the *Subtract* option. (This merges the shapes into one shape.)

3. Apply formatting to the shape and type text in the shape by completing the following steps:
   a. Click the Shape Fill button arrow in the Shape Styles group and then click the *White, Text 1* option (second column, first row in the *Theme Colors* section).
   b. Click the Text Fill button arrow in the WordArt Styles group and then click the *Black, Background 1* option (first column, first row in the *Theme Colors* section).
   c. Type the following in the shape pressing the Enter key to end each line as shown:

   > International Energy
   > Consortium
   > Global Summit
   > March 8 to 10, 2021
   > Paris, France

   d. Select the text you just typed and then change the font size to 20 points.
4. Save **4-AddisonReport**.

Grouping and Ungrouping Objects

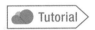

Grouping and Ungrouping Objects

Quick Steps

Group Objects
1. Select objects.
2. Click Drawing Tools Format tab.
3. Click Group button.
4. Click *Group*.

  Group

💡 **Hint** Group objects so you can move, size, flip, or rotate objects at the same time.

To apply the same formatting or make the same adjustments to the size or rotation of objects, group the objects. When objects are grouped, any formatting applied such as a shape fill, effect, or shape style, is applied to each object within the group. To group objects, select the objects to be included in the group by clicking each object while holding down the Shift key or, using the mouse, click and drag a border around all the objects. With the objects selected, click the Drawing Tools Format tab, click the Group button in the Arrange group, and then click *Group* at the drop-down list.

An individual object within a group can be formatted. To do this, click any object in the group and the group border displays around the objects. Click the individual object and then apply the desired formatting. To ungroup objects, click the group to select it, click the Drawing Tools Format tab, click the Group button in the Arrange group, and then click *Ungroup* at the drop-down list.

Activity 1f **Grouping and Formatting Objects**   Part 6 of 14

1. With **4-AddisonReport** open, make Slide 3 active.
2. Group the objects and apply formatting by completing the following steps:
   a. Using the mouse, click and drag a border around the two text boxes in the slide to select them.
   b. Click the Drawing Tools Format tab.
   c. Click the Group button in the Arrange group and then click *Group* at the drop-down list.

d. Click the More Shape Styles button in the Shape Styles group and then click the *Subtle Effect - Blue, Accent 1* option (second column, fourth row).

e. Click the Shape Outline button arrow and then click the *Dark Blue* color (ninth color in the *Standard Colors* section).

f. Click the Shape Outline button arrow, point to *Weight*, and then click *4½ pt*.

3. With the text boxes selected, ungroup the text boxes by clicking the Group button in the Arrange group and then clicking *Ungroup* at the drop-down list.

4. Click outside the selected text boxes to deselect them. Click the border of the text box containing the columns of text, click the More WordArt Styles button in the WordArt Styles group, and then click the option in the first column, third row (black outline with white fill).

5. Make Slide 4 active and then group and apply formatting to the shapes by completing the following steps:

a. Using the mouse, click and drag a border around the three arrows in the slide to select the arrows.

b. Click Drawing Tools Format tab, click the Group button in Arrange group and then click *Group* at the drop-down list.

c. Click the More Shape Styles button in the Shape Styles group and then click the *Subtle Effect - Blue, Accent 1* option (second column, fourth row).

6. Make Slide 1 active, click the text box containing the text *2021*, click the Quick Styles button in the Drawing group on the Home tab, and then click the *Subtle Effect - Blue, Accent 1* option (second column, fourth row).

7. Save **4-AddisonReport**.

 Check Your Work

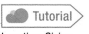 Tutorial

Inserting, Sizing, and Positioning an Image

 Pictures

Inserting an Image

Insert an image such as a picture or clip art in a slide using the buttons in the Images group on the Insert tab. To insert an image in a presentation, click the Insert tab and then click the Pictures button in the Images group. At the Insert Picture dialog box, navigate to the folder containing the image and then double-click the image. Use buttons on the Picture Tools Format tab to format and customize the image.

 Tutorial

Formatting an Image

Quick Steps

Insert Image
1. Click Insert tab.
2. Click Pictures button.
3. Navigate to folder.
4. Double-click image.

Customizing and Formatting an Image

When an image that has been inserted in a slide is selected, the Picture Tools Format tab becomes active, as shown in Figure 4.7. Use buttons on this tab to apply formatting to the image. Use options in the Adjust group on the Picture Tools Format tab to crop or remove unwanted portions of the image, correct the brightness and contrast, change the image color, apply artistic effects, adjust the transparency of the image, compress the size of the image file, change to a different image, and reset the image back to its original formatting. Use buttons in the Picture Styles group to apply a predesigned style to the image, change the image border, or apply other effects to the image.

Figure 4.7 Picture Tools Format Tab

Alt Text

Use the Alt Text button in the Accessibility group to add alternative text to an image. Alternative text, or alt text, is a text description of an image that can be read by a screen reader to help a person with a visual impairment understand what the image represents. Click the Alt Text button to display the Alt Text task pane and then type a description in the task pane. Another method for displaying the Alt Text task pane is to right-click an image and then click *Edit Alt Text* at the shortcut menu. If the image is only decorative and not important for understanding the content of the presentation, insert a check mark in the *Mark as decorative* check box at the Alt Text task pane. An image marked as decorative will not include any description for screen readers.

The Arrange group contains options for positioning the image, specifying how text will wrap around it, aligning the image with other elements in the document, and rotating the image. Use options in the Size group to crop the image and change the image size.

Sizing, Cropping, Rotating, and Positioning an Image

Change the size of an image with the *Shape Height* and *Shape Width* measurement boxes in the Size group on the Picture Tools Format tab or with the sizing handles that display around the selected image. To change the size with a sizing handle, position the mouse pointer on a sizing handle until the pointer turns into a double-headed arrow and then click and hold down the left mouse button. Drag the sizing handle in or out to decrease or increase the size of the image and then release the mouse button. Use the middle sizing handles at the left or right of the image to make the image wider or thinner. Use the middle sizing handles at the top or bottom of the image to make the image taller or shorter. Use the sizing handles at the corners of the image to change both the width and height at the same time.

 Crop

The Size group on the Picture Tools Format tab contains a Crop button. Use this button to remove portions of an image. Click the Crop button and the mouse pointer displays with the crop tool attached, which is a black square with overlapping lines, and the image displays with cropping handles around the border. Drag a cropping handle to remove a portion of the image.

💡 **Hint** Insert a picture from your camera by downloading the picture to your computer and then copying or inserting the picture into PowerPoint.

Move a selected image by dragging it to the new location. Move the image by positioning the mouse pointer on the image border until the mouse pointer turns into a four-headed arrow. Click and hold down the left mouse button, drag the image to the new position, and then release the mouse button. The arrow keys on the keyboard can be used to move the image in the desired direction. Press an arrow key on the keyboard to move the image in a specific direction.

Use the rotation handle to rotate an image by positioning the mouse pointer on the white, round rotation handle until the pointer displays as a circular arrow. Click and hold down the left mouse button, drag in the desired direction, and then release the mouse button.

In addition to using sizing handles to size an image and using the mouse to drag an image, an object can be sized and positioned with options at the Format Picture task pane with the Size & Properties icon selected. Display this task pane by selecting an object and then clicking the Size group task pane launcher on the Picture Tools Format tab.

Arranging Images

Bring Forward

Send Backward

Use the Bring Forward and Send Backward buttons in the Arrange group on the Drawing Tools Format tab or the Picture Tools Format tab to layer one object on top of another. Click the Bring Forward button and the selected object is moved forward one layer. For example, if three objects are layered on top of each other, select the object at the bottom of the layers and then click the Bring Forward button to move the object in front of the second object (but not the first object). To move an object to the top layer, select the object, click the Bring Forward button arrow, and then click the *Bring to Front* option at the drop-down list. To move the selected object back one layer, click the Send Backward button. To move the selected object behind all other objects, click the Send Backward button arrow and then click the *Send to Back* option at the drop-down list.

Activity 1g **Inserting and Formatting Images**   Part 7 of 14

1. With **4-AddisonReport** open, make Slide 4 active.
2. Insert a new slide by clicking the New Slide button arrow and then clicking *Blank* at the drop-down list.
3. Insert a text box by completing the following steps:
   a. Click the Insert tab and then click the Text Box button in the Text group.
   b. Click in the middle of the slide.
   c. Change the font to Arial Black and the font size to 36 points.
   d. Click the Center button in the Paragraph group.
   e. Type Alternative, press the Enter key, and then type Energy Resources.
   f. Click the border of the text box and then click the Drawing Tools Format tab.
   g. Click the Align button in the Arrange group and then click *Distribute Horizontally* at the drop-down list.
   h. Click the Align button and then click *Distribute Vertically* at the drop-down list.

4. Insert an image by completing the following steps:
   a. Click the Insert tab.
   b. Click the Pictures button in the Images group.
   c. At the Insert Picture dialog box, navigate to your PC4 folder and then double-click the **Mountain** image file.
5. You decide to insert an image of the ocean rather than a mountain. Change the image by completing the following steps:
   a. With the image of the mountain selected, click the Change Picture button in the Adjust group and then click *From a File* at the drop-down list.
   b. At the Insert Picture dialog box, make sure your PC4 folder is selected and then double-click the **Ocean** image file.
6. Crop the image by completing the following steps:
   a. With the image selected, click the Crop button in the Size group on the Picture Tools Format tab.
   b. Position the mouse pointer (displays with the crop tool attached) on the cropping handle in the middle of the right side of the image.

c. Click and hold down the left mouse button and then drag to the left approximately 0.25 inch. (Use the guideline on the horizontal ruler to crop the image 0.25 inch.)

d. Click the Crop button to turn off cropping.

e. Click the Crop button arrow, point to the *Crop to Shape* option at the drop-down list, and then click the *Oval* shape (first option in the *Basic Shapes* section of the side menu).

7. Click in the *Shape Height* measurement box in the Size group, type 5, and then press the Enter key.

8. Click the Send Backward button in the Arrange group. (This moves the image behind the text in the text box.)

9. Align the image by completing the following steps:

a. Click the Align button in the Arrange group on the Picture Tools Format tab and then click the *Distribute Horizontally* option.

b. Click the Align button and then click the *Distribute Vertically* option.

10. Format the image by completing the following steps:

a. Click the Artistic Effects button in the Adjust group and then click the *Cutout* option (first column, last row).

b. Click the Corrections button in the Adjust group and then click the *Soften: 25%* option (second option in the *Sharpen/Soften* section).

c. Click the Transparency button in the Adjust group and then click the *Transparency: 50%* option (fourth option).

d. Click the Picture Border button arrow in the Picture Styles group and then click the *Dark Blue* color (ninth option in the *Standard Colors* section).

11. After viewing the effects applied to the image, reset the image to the original formatting by clicking the Reset Picture button arrow in the Adjust group and then clicking *Reset Picture* at the drop-down list.

12. Format the image by completing the following steps:
    a. Click the Corrections button in the Adjust group and then click the *Brightness: -20% Contrast: +40%* option (second column, last row in the *Brightness/Contrast* section).
    b. Click the Corrections button and then click the *Sharpen: 25%* option (fourth option in the *Sharpen/Soften* section).
    c. Click the More Picture Styles button in the Picture Styles group and then click the *Soft Edge Oval* option at the drop-down gallery. (See image below as the location may vary.)

    d. Click the Compress Pictures button in the Adjust group. At the Compress Pictures dialog box, click OK.
13. Add alternative text to the image by completing the following steps:
    a. Click the Alt Text button in the Accessibility group.
    b. At the Alt Text task pane that displays, click in the description text box and then type Pacific Ocean, Washington State Coast.
    c. Click the Close button to close the Alt Text task pane.
14. Make Slide 4 active and then insert a new slide by clicking the New Slide button arrow in the Slides group on the Home tab, and then clicking *Two Content* at the drop-down list.

15. Click in the title placeholder and then type Technology.
16. Click in the content placeholder at the right side of the slide.
17. Click the Bullets button in the Paragraph group to turn off bullets.
18. Turn on bold formatting and turn off text shadow formatting.
19. Type Equipment and then press the Enter key two times.
20. Type Software and then press the Enter key two times.
21. Type Personnel.
22. Insert an image by completing the following steps:
    a. Click the Pictures button in the middle of the placeholder at the left side of the slide.
    b. At the Insert Picture dialog box, navigate to your PC4 folder and then double-click the *Computer* image file.

23. Scale, rotate, and position the computer image by completing the following steps:

a. With the image selected, click the Rotate button in the Arrange group on the Picture Tools Format tab and then click *Flip Horizontal* at the drop-down list.

b. Click the Size group task pane launcher.

c. At the Format Picture task pane with the Size & Properties icon selected, if necessary, click *Size* to expand the options.

d. Select *0°* in the *Rotation* measurement box and then type -10.

e. Select the current percentage in the *Scale Height* measurement box and then type 65.

f. If necessary, click *Position* to expand the options.

g. Select the current measurement in the *Horizontal position* measurement box and then type 3.1.

h. Select the current measurement in the *Vertical position* measurement box, type 2.2, and then press the Enter key.

i. Close the Format Picture task pane.

24. Save **4-AddisonReport**.

Check Your Work

 Tutorial

Inserting an Image as a Slide Background

Quick Steps

Insert Image as Slide Background
1. Click Design tab.
2. Click Format Background button.
3. Click *Picture or texture fill* option.
4. Click File button.
5. Navigate to folder.
6. Double-click image.
7. Click Close button.

Inserting an Image as a Slide Background

Insert an image, such as a picture or clip art, as a slide background by clicking the Design tab and then clicking the Format Background button in the Customize group. This displays the Format Background task pane with the Fill icon selected. Click the *Picture or texture fill* option in the *Fill* section of the task pane and then click the File button. At the Insert Picture dialog box, navigate to the folder containing the image and then double-click the image. To display the image background on all slides, click the Apply to All button at the Format Background task pane.

Use options in the Format Background task pane to apply formatting to the background image. When an image is inserted in a slide, the Format Background task pane (with the Fill icon selected) includes options for hiding background graphics, applying a texture, changing the image transparency, and offsetting the image on the slide either at the left, right, top, or bottom. Click the Effects icon and then click the Artistic Effects button and a drop-down palette of artistic options displays. Click the Picture icon and options display in the task pane for correcting the sharpness, softness, brightness, and contrast of the image and for changing the color saturation and tone of the image.

1. With **4-AddisonReport** open, make Slide 7 active.
2. Click the New Slide button arrow and then click the *Title Only* layout at the drop-down list.
3. Insert an image background on Slide 8 by completing the following steps:
   a. Click the Design tab.
   b. Click the Format Background button in the Customize group.
   c. At the Format Background task pane, click the *Picture or texture fill* option in the *Fill* section to select it.
   d. Click the File button in the task pane below the text *Insert picture from*.
   e. At the Insert Picture dialog box, navigate to your PC4 folder and then double-click the *EiffelTower* image file.
4. Apply formatting to the image background by completing these steps:
   a. Click the *Hide background graphics* check box to insert a check mark.
   b. Select the current percentage in the *Transparency* measurement box, type 5, and then press the Enter key.
   c. Select the current percentage in the *Offset top* measurement box, type -50, and then press the Enter key. (Decreasing the negative number displays more of the top of the Eiffel Tower.)
   d. Click the Effects icon in the task pane and then, if necessary, click *Artistic Effects* to display the formatting options.
   e. Click the Artistic Effects button and then click the *Glow Diffused* option (fourth column, second row).
   f. Click the Picture icon and, if necessary, expand the *Picture Corrections* section.
   g. Select the current percentage in the *Contrast* measurement box, type 25, and then press the Enter key.
   h. If necessary, expand the *Picture Color* section.
   i. Select the current percentage in the *Saturation* measurement box, type 80, and then press the Enter key.
5. Remove the artistic effect by clicking the Effects icon, clicking the Artistic Effects button, and then clicking the *None* option (first option).
6. Close the Format Background task pane.
7. Click in the title placeholder, type European, press the Enter key, and then type Division 2023. Drag the placeholder so it is positioned attractively on the slide in the upper left corner.
8. Save **4-AddisonReport**.

Check Your Work

Copying Objects within and between Presentations

Objects can be copied within a presentation and also between presentations. To copy an object, select the object and then click the Copy button in the Clipboard group on the Home tab. Make the slide in which the object is to be pasted active or open another presentation and then click the Paste button in the Clipboard group. Another method for copying an object is to right-click the object and then click *Copy* at the shortcut menu. To paste the object, make active the slide in which the object is to be pasted, click the right mouse button, and then click *Paste* at the shortcut menu.

Activity 1i Copying an Object within and between Presentations   Part 9 of 14

1. With **4-AddisonReport** open, make Slide 1 active.
2. Open the **Addison** presentation.
3. Click the image in Slide 1, click the Copy button in the Clipboard group, and then close **Addison**.
4. With **4-AddisonReport** open, click the Home tab and then click the Paste button in the Clipboard group. (This inserts the image in Slide 1.)
5. With the image selected, make Slide 2 active and then click the Paste button.
6. Decrease the size and position of the image on Slide 2 by completing the following steps:
    a. Click the Picture Tools Format tab.
    b. Click in the *Height* measurement box, type 0.8, and then press the Enter key.
    c. Drag the image so that it is positioned in the upper right corner of the slide.
7. Copy the image to other slides by completing the following steps:
    a. With the image selected in Slide 2, click the Home tab and then click the Copy button.
    b. Make Slide 3 active and then click the Paste button.
    c. Paste the image in Slide 5 and Slide 7.
8. Save **4-AddisonReport**.

 Check Your Work

Inserting an Online Image

Quick Steps

Insert Online Image
1. Click Insert tab.
2. Click Online Pictures button.
3. Type search term or topic.
4. Press Enter key.
5. Double-click image.

Use the Bing Image Search feature to search for images online. To use this feature, click the Insert tab and then click the Online Pictures button. This displays the Online Pictures window. Click a category in the window or click in the search text box, type the search term or topic, and then press the Enter key. Images that match the search term or topic display in the window. To insert an image, double-click the image or click the image and then click the Insert button. This downloads the image to the slide. Customize the image with options and buttons on the Picture Tools Format tab.

Tutorial

Inserting and
Formatting an Icon

 Icons

Inserting and Formatting an Icon

An icon is another visual element that can be added to a presentation to communicate a message or improve the appearance of the presentation. Insert an icon by clicking the Icons button in the Illustrations group on the Insert tab. At the Insert Icons window shown in Figure 4.8, click an icon and then click the Insert button to insert the icon in the active slide. When an icon has been inserted in a slide and is selected, the Graphics Tools Format tab becomes active. Use options on this tab to arrange, size, change, and apply styles to the icon.

Q̌uick Steps

Insert Icon
1. Click Insert tab.
2. Click Icons button.
3. Click icon.
4. Click Insert button.

Figure 4.8 Insert Icons Window

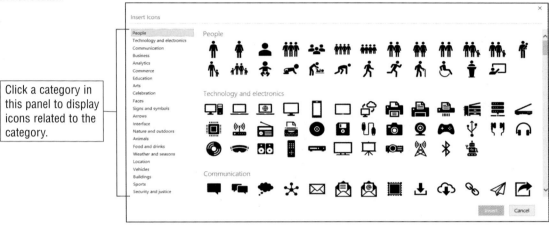

Click a category in this panel to display icons related to the category.

Activity 1j Inserting and Formatting an Icon

1. With **4-AddisonReport** open, make Slide 8 active.
2. Click the New Slide button arrow and then click *Title and Content* at the drop-down list.
3. Click in the title placeholder and then type Divisions.
4. Click in the content placeholder and then type the bulleted text as shown below:

5. Insert an icon by completing the following steps:
   a. Click the Insert tab.
   b. Click the Icons button in the Illustrations group.
   c. At the Insert Icons window, click the *Location* category in the left panel. (You may need to scroll down the panel to see this category.)
   d. Click the compass image (shown at the right) and then click the Insert button.
6. Format the compass icon by completing the following steps:
   a. With the icon selected, click in the *Shape Height* measurement box in the Size group on the Graphics Tools Format tab, type 5, and then press the Enter key.
   b. Click the More Graphics Styles button in the Graphics Styles group and then click the *Colored Fill - Accent 5, Dark 1 Outline* option (sixth column, third row).
   c. Click the Graphics Effects button in the Graphics Styles group, point to the *Glow* option, and then click the *Glow: 5 point; Orange, Accent color 6* option (last column, first row).
   d. Using the mouse pointer, drag the image to the position shown in Figure 4.9.
7. Save **4-AddisonReport**.

Check Your Work

Figure 4.9 Activity 1j, Slide 9

Inserting and
Formatting
Screenshot and
Screen Clipping
Images

 Screenshot

Insert Screenshot
Image
1. Open presentation.
2. Open another file.
3. Display information.
4. Make presentation active.
5. Click Insert tab.
6. Click Screenshot button.
7. Click window at drop-down list.
OR
6. Click Screenshot button.
7. Click *Screen Clipping*.
8. Drag to specify capture area.

Creating Screenshot Images

The Images group on the Insert tab contains a Screenshot button for capturing the contents or a portion of a screen as an image. This is useful for capturing information from a web page or from a file in another program. To capture the entire screen, display a web page, or open a file, make PowerPoint active, and then open a presentation. Click the Insert tab, click the Screenshot button, and then click the specific screen thumbnail at the drop-down list. The currently active presentation does not display as a thumbnail at the drop-down list. Instead, any other open file or program displays. If no other file or program is open, the Windows desktop displays. Click a thumbnail at the drop-down list and a screenshot of the screen is inserted as an image in the active slide in the open presentation, the image is selected, and the Picture Tools Format tab is active. Use options and buttons on this tab to customize the screenshot image.

In addition to making a screenshot of an entire screen, make a screenshot of a specific portion of the screen by clicking the *Screen Clipping* option at the Screenshot button drop-down list. Click this option and the open web page, file, or Windows desktop displays in a dimmed manner and the mouse pointer displays as crosshairs. Using the mouse, draw a border around a specific area of the screen. The identified area is inserted in the active slide in the presentation as an image, the image is selected, and the Picture Tools Format tab is active.

Activity 1k Inserting and Formatting a Screenshot

1. With **4-AddisonReport** open, make sure that no other programs are open.
2. Make sure Slide 9 is active and then insert a new slide by clicking the New Slide button arrow and then clicking the *Title Only* layout.
3. Click in the title placeholder and then type Draft Invitation.
4. Open Word and then open the document named **AddIndInvite** from your PC4 folder.
5. Make sure the entire invitation displays in the Word window. If necessary, decrease the size of the invitation using the Zoom Out button on the Status bar.
6. Click the PowerPoint button on the taskbar.
7. Insert a screenshot of the draft invitation in the Word document by completing the following steps:
   a. Click the Insert tab.
   b. Click the Screenshot button in the Images group and then click *Screen Clipping* at the drop-down list.

c. When the invitation displays in a dimmed manner, position the mouse crosshairs in the upper left corner of the invitation, click and hold down the left mouse button, drag down to the lower right corner of the invitation, and then release the mouse button.

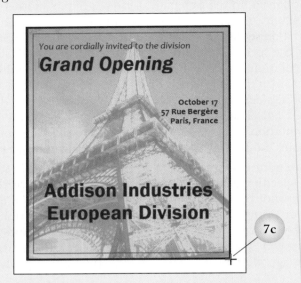

8. With the screenshot image inserted in the slide in the presentation, make the following changes:
   a. Click in the *Shape Width* measurement box in the Size group on the Picture Tools Format tab, type 4.5, and then press the Enter key.
   b. Click the Corrections button in the Adjust group and then click the *Sharpen: 25%* option (fourth option in the *Sharpen/Soften* section).

   c. Using the mouse, drag the screenshot image so it is centered in the slide.
9. Click outside the screenshot image to deselect it.
10. Save **4-AddisonReport**.
11. Click the Word button, close **AddIndInvite**, and then close Word.

Creating and Formatting WordArt Text

Use the WordArt feature to insert preformatted, decorative text in a slide and to modify text to conform to a variety of shapes. Consider using WordArt to create a company logo, letterhead, flyer title, or heading. Insert WordArt in a slide by clicking the Insert tab and then clicking the WordArt button in the Text group. This displays the WordArt drop-down list as shown in Figure 4.10. Click a WordArt style at the drop-down list and a text box is inserted in the slide containing the text *Your Text Here*. Type the WordArt text and then use the options and buttons on the Drawing Tools Format tab to customize the WordArt text.

Apply predesigned formatting to WordArt text with a WordArt style. Customize the text with the Text Fill, Text Outline, and Text Effects buttons in the WordArt Styles group. Use the Text Fill button to change the fill color; the Text Outline button to change the text outline color, width, and style; and the Text Effects button to apply a variety of text effects and shapes.

Click the Text Effects button and then point to *Transform* and a side menu displays with shaping and warping options as shown in Figure 4.11. Use these options to conform the WordArt text to a specific shape.

Quick Steps

Create WordArt Text
1. Click Insert tab.
2. Click WordArt button.
3. Click WordArt style.
4. Type WordArt text.

 WordArt

 Text Fill

 Text Outline

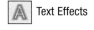 Text Effects

Hint Edit WordArt by double-clicking the WordArt text.

Figure 4.10 WordArt Drop-down List

Click the WordArt button to display this drop-down list of predesigned WordArt text options.

Figure 4.11 Text Effects *Transform* Side Menu

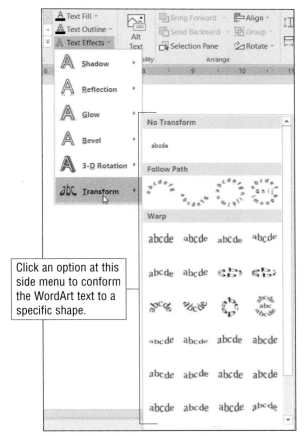

Click an option at this side menu to conform the WordArt text to a specific shape.

1. With **4-AddisonReport** open, make sure Slide 10 and the Home tab are active.
2. Click the New Slide button arrow and then click the *Blank* layout.
3. Click the Insert tab.
4. Click the WordArt button in the Text group and then click the option in the second column, third row (white fill with black outline and aqua shadow).
5. Type Addison Industries, press the Enter key, and then type 2021.
6. Click the WordArt text border to change the border from a dashed line to a solid line. (This selects the text box.)
7. Click the Text Outline button arrow in the WordArt Styles group and then click the *Dark Blue* color (ninth option in the *Standard Colors* section).
8. Click the Text Effects button, point to *Glow*, and then click *Glow: 11 point; Blue, Accent color 1* at the side menu (first column, third row).
9. Click the Text Effects button, point to *Transform*, and then click the *Triangle: Up* option (third column, first row in the *Warp* section).

10. Click in the *Shape Height* measurement box, type 5, and then press the Enter key.
11. Click in the *Shape Width* measurement box, type 10, and then press the Enter key.
12. Click the Align button in the Arrange group and then click *Distribute Horizontally*.
13. Click the Align button and then click *Distribute Vertically*.
14. Save **4-AddisonReport**.

Check Your Work

Inserting Symbols

 Symbol

Insert symbols in a slide using options at the Symbol dialog box. Display this dialog box by clicking the Symbol button in the Symbols group on the Insert tab. At the Symbol dialog box, choose a symbol font with the *Font* option in the dialog box, click a symbol in the list box, click the Insert button, and then click the Close button. The symbol is inserted in the slide at the location of the insertion point.

Activity 1m   Inserting Symbols in a Presentation

Part 13 of 14

1. With **4-AddisonReport** open, insert a symbol by completing the following steps:
   a. Make Slide 2 active.
   b. Click in the text box containing the names, titles, and telephone numbers.
   c. Delete the *n* in *Pena* (the last name of the fourth person).
   d. Click the Insert tab and then click the Symbol button in the Symbols group.
   e. At the Symbol dialog box, click the *Font* option box arrow, scroll down the drop-down list and then click the *Trebuchet MS* option.
   f. Double-click the current number in the *Character code* text box and then type 00F1.
   g. Click the Insert button and then click the Close button.
2. Save **4-AddisonReport**.

◀ Check Your Work ▶

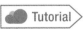
Inserting Headers and Footers

 Header & Footer

 Date & Time

 Slide Number

If a presentation is printed as a handout or an outline, PowerPoint automatically prints the current date in the upper right corner of the page and the page number in the lower right corner. Print the presentation as notes pages and PowerPoint automatically prints the page number on individual slides. The date and page numbers are considered header and footer elements. These existing header and footer elements can be modified or additional elements can be inserted using options in the Header and Footer dialog box. Display the Header and Footer dialog box shown in Figure 4.12 by clicking the Header & Footer button in the Text group on the Insert tab, clicking the Date & Time button in the Text group, or clicking the Slide Number button in the Text group. Another method for displaying the Header and Footer dialog box is to display the Print backstage area and then click the <u>Edit Header & Footer</u> hyperlink below the galleries in the *Settings* category.

The Header and Footer dialog box has two tabs, the Slide tab and the Notes and Handouts tab, and the options in the dialog box are similar with either tab selected. Use options in the dialog box to insert the date and time, a header, a footer, and page numbers. Insert the date and time in a presentation and then choose the *Update automatically* option to update the date and time when the presentation is opened. Choose the date and time formatting by clicking the *Update automatically* option box arrow and then clicking the desired formatting at the drop-down list. Choose the *Fixed* option and then type the desired date and/or time in the *Fixed* text box. Type header text in the *Header* text box and type footer text in the *Footer* text box.

To print the slide number on slides, insert a check mark in the *Slide number* check box in the Header and Footer dialog box with the Slide tab selected. To include page numbers on handouts, notes pages, or outline pages, insert a check mark in the *Page number* check box in the Header and Footer dialog box with the Notes and Handouts tab selected. Apply changes to all slides or all handouts, notes pages, and outline pages by clicking the Apply to All button in the lower right corner of the dialog box.

Figure 4.12 Header and Footer Dialog Box with the Notes and Handouts Tab Selected

Insert a check mark in this check box to insert the date and/or time.

To update the time when a presentation is opened, click *Update automatically* and then choose the formatting at the option box drop-down list.

Text typed in the *Header* text box or *Footer* text box will print when the presentation is printed as notes pages, handouts, or an outline.

Activity 1n Inserting Headers and Footers

1. With **4-AddisonReport** open, insert slide numbers on each slide in the presentation by completing the following steps:
   a. Make Slide 1 active.
   b. Click the Insert tab.
   c. Click the Slide Number button in the Text group.
   d. At the Header and Footer dialog box with the Slide tab selected, click the *Slide number* check box to insert a check mark.
   e. Click the Apply to All button.
   f. Scroll through the slides to view the slide number in the lower right corner of each slide, except for the first slide.

2. Insert your name as a footer on each slide (except the first slide) in the presentation by completing the following steps:
   a. Click the Header & Footer button in the Text group.
   b. Click the *Footer* check box to insert a check mark, click in the *Footer* text box, and then type your first and last names.
   c. Make sure a check mark displays in the *Slide number* check box.
   d. Click the Apply to All button.
   e. Run the slide show to confirm that your name displays at the bottom left of each slide (except the first slide).

3. You decide that you also want your name to print as a footer on handouts pages. To do this, complete the following steps:
   a. Click the Header & Footer button.
   b. At the Header and Footer dialog box, click the Notes and Handouts tab.
   c. Click the *Footer* check box to insert a check mark, click in the *Footer* text box, and then type your first and last names.
   d. Click the Apply to All button.

4. Insert the current date as a header that prints on handout pages by completing the following steps:
   a. Click the Date & Time button in the Text group.
   b. At the Header and Footer dialog box, click the Notes and Handouts tab.
   c. Click the *Date and time* check box to insert a check mark.
   d. Click the Apply to All button.

5. Insert the presentation name as a header that prints on handouts pages by completing the following steps:
   a. Click the File tab and then click the *Print* option.
   b. At the Print backstage area, click the Edit Header & Footer hyperlink below the galleries in the *Settings* category.
   c. At the Header and Footer dialog box, click the Notes and Handouts tab, if necessary.

d. Click the *Header* check box to insert a check mark, click in the *Header* text box, and then type 4-AddisonReport.

e. Click the Apply to All button.

f. Click the second gallery in the *Settings* category and then click *6 Slides Horizontal* at the drop-down list. (If a number displays in the *Slides* text box, delete the number.)

g. Display the next handout page by clicking the Next Page button at the bottom of the Print backstage area.

h. Click the Previous Page button to display the first handout page.

i. Click the Print button to print the presentation as a handout with six slides displayed horizontally per page.

6. Save and then close **4-AddisonReport**.

Check Your Work

Chapter Summary

- Insert a text box in a slide using the Text Box button in the Text group on the Insert tab. Format a text box with options in the Drawing group on the Home tab, with options on the Drawing Tools Format tab, with options at the shortcut menu, or with options at the Format Shape task pane.

- Select all objects in a slide by clicking the Select button in the Editing group on the Home tab and then clicking *Select All* or by using the keyboard shortcut Ctrl + A.

- Align selected objects using options from the Align button in the Arrange group on the Drawing Tools Format tab.

- Set tabs in a text box by clicking the Alignment button at the left of the horizontal ruler until the desired tab alignment symbol displays and then clicking a location on the ruler. Set left, center, right, and/or decimal tabs.

- Insert a shape in a slide by clicking a shape in the Drawing group on the Home tab and then clicking or clicking and dragging in the slide. Or, click the Shapes button in the Illustrations group on the Insert tab, click a shape at the drop-down list and then click or click and drag in the slide.

- Use options in the Shapes button drop-down list to draw a line, basic shapes, block arrows, flow chart symbols, callouts, stars, and banners.

- Copy a shape by selecting the shape, clicking the Copy button in the Clipboard group, positioning the insertion point in the new position, and then clicking the Paste button in the Clipboard group. A shape can also be copied by holding down the Ctrl key and then dragging the shape to the new location.

- Turn the horizontal and vertical rulers on and off with the *Ruler* check box in the Show group on the View tab and turn gridlines on and off with the *Gridlines* check box. Turn gridlines as well as drawing guides and the snap-to-grid feature on and off with options at the Grid and Guides dialog box.

- Group objects together to apply the same formatting to all the objects in that group. To group objects, select the objects, click the Group button in the Arrange group on the Drawing Tools Format tab, and then click *Group* at the drop-down list.

- Size images with the *Shape Height* and *Shape Width* measurement boxes on the Picture Tools Format tab or with the sizing handles that display around a selected image.

- Use the Crop button in the Size group on the Picture Tools Format tab to remove portions of an image.

- Press an arrow key on the keyboard to move a selected image in a specific direction.

- Specify the order in which objects are to be layered with the Bring Forward and Send Backward buttons in the Adjust group on the Drawing Tools Format tab or the Picture Tools Format tab.

- Insert an image in a slide with the Pictures button in the Images group on the Insert tab.

- Insert an image as a slide background using options at the Format Background task pane. Display this task pane by clicking the Format Background button in the Customize group on the Design tab.

- Size objects with options at the Format Shape or Format Picture task pane with the Size & Properties icon selected.

- Insert an online image using the Online Pictures window. Display this window by clicking the Online Pictures button in the Images group on the Insert tab or clicking the Online Pictures button in a layout content placeholder.

- Insert an icon in a slide with the Icons button in the Illustrations group on the Insert tab. At the Insert Icons window, click an icon and then click the Insert button. Format an icon with options on the Graphics Tools Format tab.

- Use the Screenshot button in the Images group on the Insert tab to capture the contents of a screen or a portion of a screen.

- Use the WordArt feature to distort or modify text to conform to a variety of shapes. Insert WordArt with the WordArt button in the Text group on the Insert tab. Format WordArt using options and buttons on the Drawing Tools Format tab.

- Insert symbols in a slide with options at the Symbol dialog box. Display this dialog box by clicking the Symbol button in the Symbols group on the Insert tab.

- Click the Header & Footer button, the Date & Time button, or the Slide Number button in the Text group on the Insert tab to display the Header and Footer dialog box. Another method for displaying this dialog box is to click the Edit Header & Footer hyperlink at the Print backstage area.

Commands Review

FEATURE	RIBBON TAB, GROUP	BUTTON, OPTION	KEYBOARD SHORTCUT
date and time	Insert, Text		
Format Background task pane	Design, Customize		
Format Picture task pane	Picture Tools Format, Picture Styles OR Size		
Grid and Guides dialog box	View, Show		
gridlines	View, Show	*Gridlines*	Shift + F9
guides	View, Show	*Guides*	
header and footer	Insert, Text		
icon	Insert, Illustrations		
Insert Picture dialog box	Insert, Images		
Online Pictures window	Insert, Images		
rulers	View, Show	*Ruler*	
screenshot	Insert, Images		
shape	Insert, Illustrations OR Home, Drawing		
slide number	Insert, Text		
Symbol dialog box	Insert, Symbols		
text box	Insert, Text		
WordArt	Insert, Text		

Microsoft® PowerPoint®

Unit 2

Customizing and Enhancing Presentations

Microsoft®
PowerPoint®
Creating Tables, SmartArt Graphics, Charts, and Photo Albums

CHAPTER 5

Performance Objectives

Upon successful completion of Chapter 5, you will be able to:

1 Create a table

2 Modify the design and layout of a table

3 Insert an image in a table

4 Insert an Excel spreadsheet

5 Draw a table

6 Create SmartArt graphics

7 Modify the design and layout of SmartArt

8 Convert text and WordArt to SmartArt

9 Convert a SmartArt graphic to text or shapes

10 Create and format charts

11 Modify the design and layout of charts

12 Select and format chart elements

13 Create, edit, and format a photo album

PowerPoint allows you to present information using different formats. Use the Tables feature to create and design tables for organizing data in columns and rows. For an even more impressive presentation, use the SmartArt feature and choose from a variety of predesigned charts and graphics that can be customized with different colors and formats. Use the Photo Album feature to attractively display personal or business photographs and then format the appearance of the images in the presentation.

 Data Files

Before beginning chapter work, copy the PC5 folder to your storage medium and then make PC5 the active folder.

The online course includes additional training and assessment resources.

Activity 1 **Create a Company Sales Conference Presentation**   **14 Parts**

You will create a sales conference presentation for Nature's Way that includes tables, a column chart, a pie chart, and three SmartArt graphics.

Tutorial

Creating a Table

Table

Quick Steps

Insert Table

1. Click Insert Table button in content placeholder.
2. Type number of columns.
3. Press Tab key.
4. Type number of rows.
5. Click OK.
OR
1. Click Insert tab.
2. Click Table button.
3. Position mouse pointer in grid until correct number for columns and rows displays above grid and then click left mouse button.

Hint Add a row to the bottom of a table by positioning the insertion point in the last cell and then pressing the Tab key.

Creating a Table

A *table* presents data in columns and rows of cells. Each cell is a box containing information in the form of text, characters, numbers, data, graphics, or formulas. To add a table to a PowerPoint presentation, insert a new slide that contains a content placeholder. Click the Insert Table button in the content placeholder and the Insert Table dialog box displays. At the Insert Table dialog box, type the number of columns, press the Tab key, type the number of rows, and then press the Enter key or click OK. A table can also be inserted using the Table button in the Tables group on the Insert tab. Click the Table button, position the mouse pointer in the grid until the correct number for columns and rows displays above the grid, and then click the left mouse button.

In a table, columns are labeled alphabetically from left to right, starting with the letter *A*, and rows are numbered from top to bottom, beginning with the number *1*. Each cell is designated with a letter and a number according to the column and row it is found in. When a table is inserted in a slide, the insertion point is positioned in cell A1, the first cell in the upper left corner of the table. Cell B1 is to the right of A1, and cell A2 is directly below it.

Entering Text in Cells

With the insertion point positioned in a cell, type or edit text. Move the insertion point to any other cell in the table by pointing and clicking with the mouse. Navigate from cell to cell using the arrow keys on the keyboard, or press the Tab key to move to the next cell and Shift + Tab to move to the previous cell.

Text typed in a cell automatically wraps to the next line to fit the width of the column. The Enter key can also be pressed to move to the next line within a cell. The cell expands vertically to accommodate the text, and all cells in that row also expand. Pressing the Tab key in a table causes the insertion point to move to the next cell. To move the insertion point to a tab position within a cell, press Ctrl + Tab. If the insertion point is in the last cell of a table, pressing the Tab key will add another row to the bottom of the table.

Selecting Cells

Formatting can be applied to an entire table or to specific cells, rows, or columns in a table. To identify cells for formatting, select the cells using the mouse or the keyboard. Press the Tab key to select the next cell or press Shift + Tab to select the previous cell. Refer to Table 5.1 for additional methods for selecting in a table.

Table 5.1 Selecting in a Table

To select this	Do this
A cell	Position the mouse pointer at the left of the cell until the pointer turns into a small, black, diagonally pointing arrow and then click the left mouse button.
A column	Position the mouse pointer outside the table at the top of the column until the pointer turns into a small, black, down-pointing arrow and then click the left mouse button. Drag to select multiple columns.
A row	Position the mouse pointer outside the table at the left edge of the row until the pointer turns into a small, black, right-pointing arrow and then click the left mouse button. Drag to select multiple rows.
All cells in a table	With the insertion point positioned in the table, drag to select all cells or press Ctrl + A.
Text within a cell	Position the mouse pointer at the beginning of the text, click and hold down the left mouse button, drag the mouse across the text, and then release the mouse button. (When a cell is selected, the cell background color changes to gray. When text within a cell is selected, only those lines containing text are highlighted in gray.)

Activity 1a Creating a Table

Part 1 of 14

1. Open **Conference** and then save it with the name **5-Conference**.
2. Make Slide 3 active.
3. Insert a table in the slide and enter text into the cells by completing the following steps:
   a. Click the Insert Table button in the middle of the slide in the content placeholder.
   b. At the Insert Table dialog box, select the current number in the *Number of columns* measurement box and then type 2.
   c. Press the Tab key.
   d. Type 5 in the *Number of rows* measurement box.
   e. Click OK or press the Enter key.
   f. Type the text as shown in the table below. Press the Tab key to move the insertion point to the next cell or press Shift + Tab to move the insertion point to the previous cell. Do not press the Tab key after typing the last cell entry.

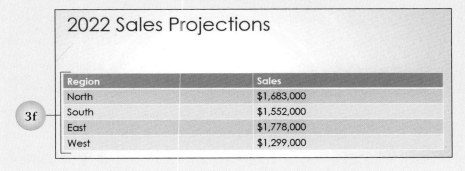

Region	Sales
North	$1,683,000
South	$1,552,000
East	$1,778,000
West	$1,299,000

4. Apply formatting to text in specific cells by completing the following steps:

   a. With the insertion point positioned in the table, press Ctrl + A to select all of the text in the table.

   b. Click the Home tab and then change the font size to 32 points.

   c. Set the text below the headings in a smaller point size by positioning the mouse pointer at the left edge of the second row (to the left of the cell containing *North*) until the pointer turns into a small, black, right-pointing arrow. Click and hold down the left mouse button, drag down so the remaining rows are selected, and then release the mouse button. Change the font size to 28 points.

   d. Click outside the table to deselect it.

5. Save **5-Conference**.

 Tutorial

Changing the Table Design

 Shading

 Borders

 Effects

 Draw Table

 Eraser

Changing the Table Design

When a table is inserted in a slide, the Table Tools Design tab is active. This tab contains a number of options for enhancing the appearance of the table, as shown in Figure 5.1. With options in the Table Styles group, select a predesigned style that applies color and border lines to a table. Maintain further control over the predesigned style formatting applied to columns and rows with options in the Table Style Options group. For example, to format the first column differently than the other columns in a table, insert a check mark in the *First Column* check box.

Apply additional design formatting to cells in a table with the Shading, Borders, and Effects buttons in the Table Styles group and the options in the WordArt Styles group. Draw a table or draw additional rows and/or columns in a table by clicking the Draw Table button in the Draw Borders group. Click this button and the mouse pointer turns into a pencil. Drag in the table to create the columns and rows. Click the Eraser button and the mouse pointer turns into an eraser. Drag through the column and/or row borders to erase the lines.

Figure 5.1 Table Tools Design Tab

1. With **5-Conference** open, make sure Slide 3 is active, click in a cell in the table, and then click the Table Tools Design tab.
2. Click the *First Column* check box in the Table Style Options group to insert a check mark. (This applies bold formatting to the text in the first column and applies darker shading to the cells.)
3. Click the More Table Styles button in the Table Styles group and then click the *Themed Style 1 - Accent 1* option (second column, first row in the *Best Match for Document* section).

4. Select the first row of the table and then apply the following formatting options:
   a. Click the Quick Styles button in the WordArt Styles group and then click the option in the fourth column, third row (lime-green outline with white fill).
   b. Click the Text Fill button arrow in the WordArt Styles group and then click the *Lime, Accent 3, Lighter 80%* option (seventh column, second row in the *Theme Colors* section).

   c. Click the Text Outline button arrow in the WordArt Styles group and then click the *Green, Accent 1, Lighter 80%* option (fifth column, second row in the *Theme Colors* section).
5. Click the *Pen Weight* option box arrow in the Draw Borders group and then click the *2¼ pt* option. (This activates the Draw Table button.)
6. Click the Pen Color button in the Draw Borders group and then click the *Green, Accent 1, Darker 25%* option (fifth column, fifth row in the *Theme Colors* section).
7. Draw along the border that separates the two columns from the top of the first row to the bottom of the last row.
8. Draw along the border that separates the first row from the second row.
9. Click the Draw Table button to deactivate the tool.
10. Save **5-Conference**.

Tutorial

Changing the Table
Layout

💡**Hint** If you make
a mistake while
formatting a table,
immediately click the
Undo button on the
Quick Access Toolbar.

Changing the Table Layout

To further customize a table, consider changing the table layout by inserting or deleting columns or rows and specifying cell alignments. Change the table layout with options on the Table Tools Layout tab, shown in Figure 5.2. Use options and buttons on the tab to select specific cells, delete and insert rows and columns, merge and split cells, specify cell and table height and width, specify text alignment in cells, and arrange elements in a slide.

Figure 5.2 Table Tools Layout Tab

Activity 1c Modifying the Table Layout

1. With **5-Conference** open, make sure Slide 3 is active.
2. Click in any cell in the table and then click the Table Tools Layout tab.
3. Click in the cell containing the word *East*.
4. Click the Insert Above button in the Rows & Columns group.

5. Type Central in the new cell at the left, press the Tab key, and then type $1,024,000 in the new cell at the right.
6. Click in the cell containing the word *Region*.
7. Click the Insert Left button in the Rows & Columns group.
8. Click the Merge Cells button in the Merge group.
9. Type Sales Projections in the new cell.
10. Click the Text Direction button in the Alignment group and then click *Rotate all text 270°* at the drop-down list.
11. Click the Center button in the Alignment group and then click the Center Vertically button in the Alignment group.
12. Click in the *Width* measurement box in the Cell Size group, type 1.2, and then press the Enter key.

13. Click the Table Tools Design tab.
14. With the insertion point positioned in the cell containing the text *Sales Projections*, click the Borders button arrow in the Table Styles group and then click *Bottom Border* at the drop-down list.

15. Click in the cell containing the text *Sales* and then click the Table Tools Layout tab.
16. Click in the *Height* measurement box in the Cell Size group and then type 0.7.
17. Click in the *Width* measurement box in the Cell Size group, type 2.5, and then press the Enter key.
18. Click in the cell containing the text *Region*.
19. Click in the *Width* measurement box in the Cell Size group, type 4, and then press the Enter key.
20. Click in the *Height* measurement box in the Table Size group, type 4.2, and then press the Enter key.

21. Click the Select button in the Table group and then click *Select Table* at the drop-down list.
22. Click the Center button and then click the Center Vertically button in the Alignment group.

23. After looking at the text in the cells, you decide that you want the text in the second column left-aligned. To do this, complete the following steps:
    a. Click in the cell containing the text *Region*.
    b. Click the Select button in the Table group and then click *Select Column* at the drop-down list.
    c. Click the Align Left button in the Alignment group.
    d. Click in any cell in the table.
24. Align the table by completing the following steps:
    a. Click the Align button in the Arrange group on the Table Tools Layout tab and then click *Distribute Horizontally* at the drop-down list.

    b. Click the Align button and then click *Distribute Vertically* at the drop-down list.
    c. Looking at the table, you decide that it should be moved down in the slide. To do this, position the mouse pointer on the table border until the pointer displays with a four-headed arrow. Click and hold down the left mouse button, drag down approximately 0.5 inch, and then release the mouse button.

25. Insert an image in the table by completing the following steps:
    a. Click the Insert tab.
    b. Click the Pictures button in the Images group.
    c. At the Insert Picture dialog box, navigate to your PC5 folder and then double-click the **Sales** image file.
    d. With the image selected, click the Color button on the Picture Tools Format tab and then click the *Green, Accent color 1 Dark* option (second column, second row in the *Recolor* section).
    e. Click in the *Shape Height* measurement box in the Size group, type 2.5, and then press the Enter key.
    f. Drag the image so it is positioned in the table as shown in Figure 5.3.
    g. Click outside the image to deselect it.
26. Save **5-Conference**.

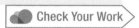

Figure 5.3 Activity 1c, Slide 3

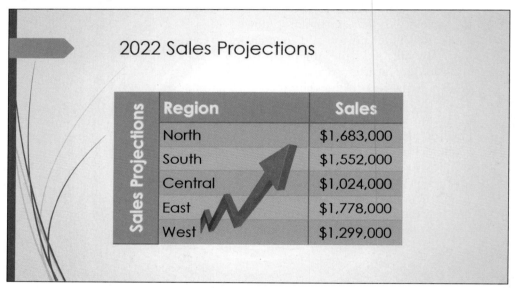

Inserting an Excel Spreadsheet

In addition to a table, an Excel worksheet can be inserted in a slide, which provides some Excel functions in PowerPoint. To insert an Excel worksheet, click the Insert tab, click the Table button in the Tables group, and then click the *Excel Spreadsheet* option. This inserts a small worksheet in the slide with two columns and two rows visible, and the ribbon displays with Excel tabs. Increase the number of visible cells by dragging the sizing handles around the selected worksheet. Click outside the worksheet and the cells display as an object that can be formatted with options on the Drawing Tools Format tab. To format the worksheet with Excel options, double-click the worksheet and the Excel tabs display.

1. With **5-Conference** open, make sure Slide 3 is active and then insert a new slide with the Title Only layout.
2. Click in the title placeholder and then type Projected Increase.
3. Insert an Excel worksheet by clicking the Insert tab, clicking the Table button in the Tables group, and then clicking *Excel Spreadsheet*.

4. Increase the size of the worksheet by completing the following steps:
   a. Position the mouse pointer on the sizing handle (small black square) in the lower right corner of the worksheet until the pointer displays as a black, diagonal, two-headed arrow.
   b. Click and hold down the left mouse button, drag down and to the right, and then release the mouse button. Continue dragging the sizing handle and releasing the mouse button until columns A, B, and C and rows 1 through 6 are visible.
5. Copy a Word table into the Excel worksheet by completing the following steps:
   a. Open Word and then open **NWSalesInc** from your PC5 folder.
   b. Hover your mouse pointer over the table and then click the table move handle (small square containing a four-headed arrow) in the upper left corner of the table. (This selects all cells in the table.)
   c. Click the Copy button in the Clipboard group on the Home tab.
   d. Click the PowerPoint button on the taskbar.
   e. With Slide 4 and the first cell in the worksheet active, click the Paste button in the Clipboard group on the Home tab.
6. Size and position the worksheet object by completing the following steps:
   a. Click outside the worksheet to remove the Excel ribbon tabs.
   b. With the worksheet object selected, click the Drawing Tools Format tab.
   c. Click in the *Shape Width* measurement box, type 7, and then press the Enter key.
   d. Using the mouse, drag the worksheet object so it is centered on the slide.
7. Format the worksheet and insert a formula by completing the following steps:
   a. Double-click in the worksheet. (This displays the Excel ribbon tabs.)
   b. Click in cell C2, type the formula =B2*1.02, and then press the Enter key.

8. Copy the formula in C2 to cells C3 through C6 by completing the following steps:
   a. Position the mouse pointer (white plus symbol) in cell C2, click and hold down the left mouse button, drag down to cell C6, and then release the mouse button.
   b. Click the Fill button in the Editing group on the Home tab and then click *Down* at the drop-down list.

   c. With cells C2 through C6 selected, click the Decrease Decimal button in the Number group two times.
9. Click outside the worksheet to remove the Excel ribbon tabs.

10. Make the following changes to the table:
    a. Click the Drawing Tools Format tab.
    b. Click the Align button and then click *Distribute Horizontally* at the drop-down list.
    c. Click the Align button and then click *Distribute Vertically* at the drop-down list.
11. Click the Word button on the taskbar, close the document, and then close Word.
12. Save **5-Conference**.

> ● Check Your Work >

Drawing a Table

A table can be drawn in a slide using the *Draw Table* option at the Table button drop-down list. Click the Table button and then click the *Draw Table* option and the mouse pointer displays as a pen. Drag in the slide to create the table. Use buttons on the Table Tools Design tab and Table Tools Format tab to format the table.

Activity 1e **Drawing a Table**   Part 5 of 14

1. With **5-Conference** open, make sure Slide 4 is active.
2. Draw a table and then split the table into two columns and two rows by completing the following steps:
    a. Click the Insert tab, click the Table button in the Tables group, and then click the *Draw Table* option at the drop-down list.
    b. Position the mouse pointer (displays as a pen) below the worksheet and then drag to create a table that is approximately 7 inches wide and 1 inch tall.
    c. Click the Table Tools Layout tab and then click the Split Cells button in the Merge group.
    d. At the Split Cells dialog box, press the Tab key, type 2, and then click OK. (This splits the table into two columns and two rows.)
    e. Select the current measurement in the *Height* measurement box in the Table Size group and then type 1.
    f. Select the current measurement in the *Width* measurement box in the Table Size group, type 7, and then press the Enter key.

3. With the table selected, make the following formatting changes:
    a. Click the Table Tools Design tab.
    b. Click the More Table Styles button in the Table Styles group and then click the *Themed Style 2 - Accent 1* option (second column, second row in the *Best Match for Document* section).
    c. Click the Effects button in the Table Styles group, point to *Cell Bevel*, and then click the *Relaxed Inset* option (second column, first row in the *Bevel* section).

152   PowerPoint | Unit 2   Chapter 5 | Creating Tables, SmartArt Graphics, Charts, and Photo Albums

d. Click the Home tab, click the Bold button, and then click the Center button.

e. Click the Align Text button and then click *Middle* at the drop-down list.

f. Make sure the table is positioned evenly between the bottom of the top table and the bottom of the slide.

g. Click the Arrange button in the Drawing group, point to *Align*, and then click *Distribute Horizontally* at the side menu.

4. Type Maximum in the first cell in the table, press the Tab key, and then type $1,813,560.

5. Press the Tab key and then type Minimum.

6. Press the Tab key and then type $1,044,480.

7. Click outside the table to deselect it.

8. Save **5-Conference**.

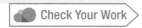

Check Your Work

Creating SmartArt

Tutorial

Inserting, Sizing, and Positioning SmartArt

 SmartArt

Quick Steps

Insert SmartArt Graphic

1. Click Insert a SmartArt Graphic button in content placeholder.
2. Double-click graphic.
OR
1. Click Insert tab.
2. Click SmartArt button.
3. Double-click graphic.

Use the SmartArt feature to insert graphics such as diagrams and organizational charts in a slide. SmartArt offers a variety of predesigned graphics that are available at the Choose a SmartArt Graphic dialog box, shown in Figure 5.4. Display the Choose a SmartArt Graphic dialog box by clicking the Insert a SmartArt Graphic button in a content placeholder or by clicking the Insert tab and then clicking the SmartArt button in the Illustrations group. At the dialog box, *All* is selected in the left panel and all available predesigned graphics are shown in the middle panel. Use the scroll bar at the right of the middle panel to scroll down the list of graphic choices.

Figure 5.4 Choose a SmartArt Graphic Dialog Box

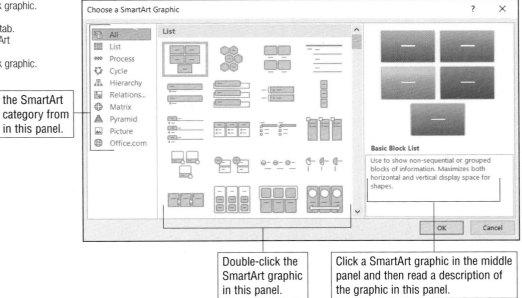

Choose the SmartArt graphic category from options in this panel.

Double-click the SmartArt graphic in this panel.

Click a SmartArt graphic in the middle panel and then read a description of the graphic in this panel.

Click a graphic in the middle panel and the name and description of the graphic displays in the right panel. SmartArt includes graphics for presenting a list of data; showing processes, cycles, and relationships; and presenting data in a matrix or pyramid. Double-click a graphic in the middle panel of the dialog box and the graphic is inserted in the slide.

When a graphic is inserted in the slide, a text pane may display at the left of the graphic. Type text in the text pane or directly in the graphic. Apply design formatting to a graphic with options on the SmartArt Tools Design tab, shown in Figure 5.5. This tab is active when the graphic is selected in the slide. Use options and buttons on this tab to change the graphic layout, apply a style to the graphic, and reset the graphic back to the original formatting.

Figure 5.5 SmartArt Tools Design Tab

Activity 1f Inserting and Modifying a SmartArt Graphic

1. With **5-Conference** open, make sure Slide 4 is active and then insert a new slide with the Title and Content layout.
2. Click in the title placeholder and then type Division Reorganization.
3. Click the Insert a SmartArt Graphic button in the middle of the slide in the content placeholder.
4. At the Choose a SmartArt Graphic dialog box, click *Hierarchy* in the left panel of the dialog box.
5. Double-click the *Horizontal Hierarchy* option shown below.

6. If a *Type your text here* pane displays at the left of the organizational chart, close the pane by clicking the Text Pane button in the Create Graphic group.
7. Delete one of the boxes in the organizational chart by clicking the border of the top box at the right side of the slide (the top box of the three stacked boxes) and then pressing the Delete key. (Make sure that the selection border that surrounds the box is a solid line and not a dashed line. If a dashed line displays, click the box border again. This should change it to a solid line.)

8. Click the *[Text]* placeholder in the first box at the left, type Andrew Singh, press Shift + Enter, and then type Director. Click in each of the remaining box placeholders and type the text as shown below. (Press Shift + Enter after each name.)

9. Click inside the SmartArt border, but outside of any shape, and then click the SmartArt Tools Design tab.
10. Click the More SmartArt Styles button in the SmartArt Styles group and then click the *Polished* option (first option in the *3-D* section).
11. Click the Change Colors button in the SmartArt Styles group and then click the *Colorful Range - Accent Colors 3 to 4* option (third option in the *Colorful* section).
12. Change the layout of the organizational chart by clicking the More Layouts button in the Layouts group and then clicking *Table Hierarchy* (third column, second row in the drop-down gallery). Your slide should now look like the slide shown in Figure 5.6.

13. Save **5-Conference**.

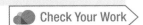

Check Your Work

Figure 5.6 Activity 1f, Slide 5

Formatting
SmartArt

Hint Move
selected shape(s) with
the up, down, left, or
right arrow keys on the
keyboard.

Formatting SmartArt

Apply formatting to a SmartArt graphic with options on the SmartArt Tools
Format tab, shown in Figure 5.7. Use options and buttons on this tab to change
the size and shape of objects in the graphic; apply shape styles and WordArt
styles; change the shape fill, outline, and effects; and arrange and size the graphic.
Move the graphic by positioning the mouse pointer on the graphic border until
the pointer turns into a four-headed arrow, clicking and holding down the left
mouse button, dragging the graphic to the new location, and then releasing the
mouse button.

Figure 5.7 SmartArt Tools Format Tab

Activity 1g Inserting and Formatting a SmartArt Graphic

Part 7 of 14

1. With **5-Conference** open, make
   Slide 1 active and then insert a
   new slide with the Blank layout.
2. Click the Insert tab and then
   click the SmartArt button in the
   Illustrations group.
3. At the Choose a SmartArt Graphic
   dialog box, click *Relationship* in the
   left panel.
4. Double-click the *Basic Venn* option
   shown at the right. (You will need
   to scroll down the list to locate this
   graphic.)

5. Click in the top shape and type Health.
6. Click in the shape at the left and type Happiness.
7. Click in the shape at the right and type Harmony.
8. Click inside the SmartArt border but outside of any shape.
9. Click the Change Colors button in the SmartArt Styles group and then click the *Colorful Range - Accent Colors 3 to 4* option (third option in the *Colorful* section).
10. Click the More SmartArt Styles button in the SmartArt Styles group and then click the *Cartoon* option (third option in the *3-D* section).

11. Click the SmartArt Tools Format tab.
12. Click the More WordArt Styles button in the WordArt Styles group and then click the option in the third column, fourth row (green pattern fill with green outline).

13. Click the Text Outline button arrow in the WordArt Styles group and then click the *Green, Accent 1, Darker 50%* option (fifth column, last row in the *Theme Colors* section).
14. Click in the *Height* measurement box in the Size group and then type 6.
15. Click in the *Width* measurement box in the Size group, type 9, and then press the Enter key.

16. Save **5-Conference**.

Check Your Work

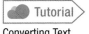 Tutorial

Converting Text
and WordArt to a
SmartArt Graphic

 Convert to
SmartArt
Graphic

Converting Text and WordArt to a SmartArt Graphic

A SmartArt graphic can be created using text or WordArt. To do this, select the placeholder containing the text or WordArt and then click the Convert to SmartArt Graphic button in the Paragraph group on the Home tab. Click the SmartArt graphic at the drop-down gallery or click the *More SmartArt Graphics* option and then choose a SmartArt graphic at the Choose a SmartArt Graphic dialog box.

 Tutorial

Inserting Text in the
Text Pane

 Text Pane

Inserting Text in the Text Pane

Enter text in a SmartArt shape by clicking in the shape and then typing the text or by typing text in the Text pane. Display the Text pane by clicking the Text Pane button in the Create Graphic group on the SmartArt Tools Design tab.

Activity 1h Creating a SmartArt Graphic with Text and WordArt

1. With **5-Conference** open, make Slide 7 active. (This slide contains WordArt text.)
2. Click in the WordArt text.
3. If necessary, click the Home tab.
4. Click the Convert to SmartArt Graphic button in the Paragraph group.
5. Click the *More SmartArt Graphics* option.
6. At the Choose a SmartArt Graphic dialog box, click *Cycle* in the left panel and then double-click *Diverging Radial* in the middle panel.

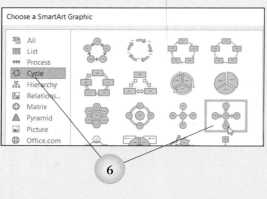

7. Click the Add Shape button in the Create Graphic group on the SmartArt Tools Design tab and then type Supplies in the new shape.
8. Change the order of the text in the shapes at the left and right sides of the graphic by clicking the Right to Left button in the Create Graphic group.

9. Click the Change Colors button in the SmartArt Styles group and then click the *Colorful - Accent Colors* option (first option in the *Colorful* section).

10. Click the More SmartArt Styles button in the SmartArt Styles group and then click the *Inset* option (second option in the *3-D* section).

11. Click the SmartArt Tools Format tab.

12. Click the middle circle (contains the text *Central Division*).

13. Click the Larger button in the Shapes group three times.

14. Click inside the SmartArt border but outside of any shape.

15. Click in the *Height* measurement box in the Size group and then type 6.6.

16. Click in the *Width* measurement box, type 8.2, and then press the Enter key.

17. With the SmartArt graphic selected, click the Align button in the Arrange group and then click *Distribute Horizontally*.

18. Click the Align button in the Arrange group and then click *Distribute Vertically*.

19. Click the Home tab.

20. Click the Bold button in the Font group.

21. Make Slide 9 active.

22. Click in the bulleted text and, if necessary, click the Home tab.

23. Click the Convert to SmartArt Graphic button in the Paragraph group and then click the *Vertical Block List* option (second column, first row).

24. Click the shape containing the text *Sales over $2 million* and then click the Demote button in the Create Graphic group on the SmartArt Tools Design tab.

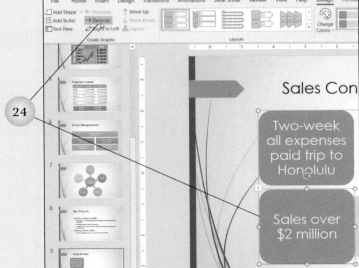

25. Click in the text *One-week all expenses paid trip to Las Vegas* and then click the Promote button in the Create Graphic group.

26. Click the Text Pane button in the Create Graphic group to display the *Type your text here* text pane.
27. Click immediately right of the *s* in *Vegas* in the text pane and then press the Enter key.
28. Press the Tab key and then type Sales over $1 million.
29. Close the text pane by clicking the Close button in the upper right corner of the pane.
30. Click the More SmartArt Styles button in the SmartArt Styles group and then click the *Inset* option (second column, first row in the *3-D* section).
31. Save **5-Conference**.
32. Print Slides 7 and 9.

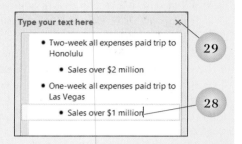

Check Your Work >

Tutorial >

Converting SmartArt to Text and to Shapes

Converting
SmartArt to Text
and to Shapes

 Reset Graphic

 Convert

To remove all formatting from a SmartArt graphic, click the Reset Graphic button in the Reset group on the SmartArt Tools Design tab. Use the Convert button to convert a SmartArt graphic to text or shapes. Click the Convert button and then click the *Convert to Text* option to convert the SmartArt graphic to bulleted text or click the *Convert to Shapes* option to convert a SmartArt graphic to shapes. Once the SmartArt graphic has been converted to shapes, those shapes can be moved, sized, or deleted independently from the other shapes.

Activity 1i Converting SmartArt to Text and to Shapes   Part 9 of 14

1. With **5-Conference** open, make sure Slide 9 is active.
2. Click to select the SmartArt graphic.
3. Click the SmartArt Tools Design tab.
4. Click the Reset Graphic button in the Reset group.
5. With the SmartArt graphic still selected, click the Convert button in the Reset group and then click *Convert to Text*.
6. Make Slide 7 active.
7. Click to select the SmartArt graphic.
8. Click the SmartArt Tools Design tab, click the Convert button in the Reset group, and then click *Convert to Shapes*.
9. Select and then delete each of the arrows that points from the middle circle to each of the outer circles.
10. Save **5-Conference**.

Check Your Work >

Chart

Creating a Chart

A chart is a visual presentation of data. A variety of charts can be created in a slide, including bar and column charts, pie charts, area charts, and many more. To create a chart, click the Insert Chart button in a content placeholder or click the Insert tab and then click the Chart button in the Illustrations group. This displays the Insert Chart dialog box, as shown in Figure 5.8. Choose the chart type from the list in the left panel of the dialog box, select a style for the chart, and then click OK.

When a chart is inserted in a slide, a new window opens with a worksheet containing sample data, as shown in Figure 5.9. Enter data for the chart into the worksheet by clicking in each cell and typing over the sample text. The chart in the slide will reflect the new data. Use the arrow keys to move from cell to cell, click in a cell with the mouse, or press the Tab key to move to the next cell and Shift + Tab to move to the previous cell. Press the Enter key to move down to the next cell in the column.

The sample worksheet contains a range of data in rows and columns, shaded with a light fill color. More columns and rows may be added to the range as needed to create the chart. Simply type data in cells outside the data range and the table will expand automatically. To turn off the AutoExpansion feature and prevent the table from being further expanded, click the AutoCorrect Options button that displays in the lower right corner of the table.

If the sample worksheet contains more columns and rows than necessary to fill out the chart, the data range can also be decreased. To do this, position the mouse pointer on the small blue square icon in the lower right corner of the data range until the pointer displays as a diagonally pointing two-headed arrow and then drag up to decrease the number of rows in the range and/or drag left to decrease the number of columns.

Chart data can also be entered in Excel by clicking the Edit Data in Microsoft Excel button that displays in the worksheet window. Once all data is entered, click the Close button in the upper right corner of the worksheet. The worksheet window closes and the chart in the slide is active.

Figure 5.8 Insert Chart Dialog Box

Figure 5.9 Sample Chart

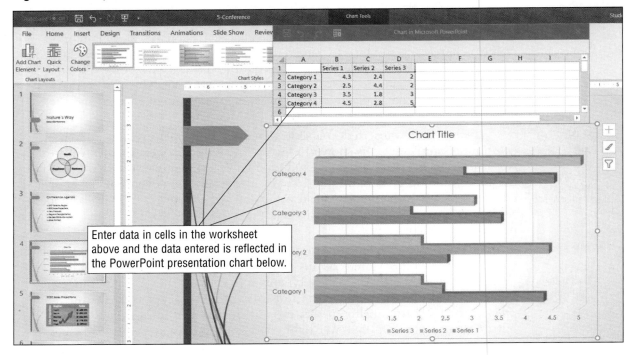

Enter data in cells in the worksheet above and the data entered is reflected in the PowerPoint presentation chart below.

Activity 1j Creating a Chart

1. With **5-Conference** open, make Slide 3 active and then insert a new slide with the Blank layout.
2. Click the Insert tab and then click the Chart button in the Illustrations group.
3. At the Insert Chart dialog box, click *Bar* in the left panel.
4. Double-click the *3-D Clustered Bar* option at the top of the dialog box (fourth option).

5. In the worksheet, position the mouse pointer in the bottom right corner of the cell D5 border until the mouse pointer displays as a diagonally pointing two-headed arrow. Click and hold down the left mouse button, drag to the left until the border is at the right side of column C, and then release the mouse button.

6. Type the text in cells as shown below by completing the following steps:
   a. Click in cell B1 in the worksheet, type 1st Half, and then press the Tab key.
   b. With cell C1 active, type 2nd Half and then press the Tab key.
   c. Click in cell A2, type North, and then press the Tab key.
   d. Type $853,000 and then press the Tab key.
   e. Type $970,000 and then press the Enter key.
   f. Continue typing the remaining data in cells as indicated below. (The data range will automatically expand to include row 6.)

	A	B	C	D
1		1st Half	2nd Half	Series 3
2	North	$853,000	$970,000	
3	South	$750,000	$910,000	
4	Central	$720,000	$750,000	
5	East	$880,000	$950,000	
6	West	$830,000	$900,000	
7				

6a-6f

7. Click the Close button in the upper right corner of the worksheet window.

7

8. Save **5-Conference**.

Check Your Work

Formatting with Chart Buttons

 Tutorial

Formatting with Chart Buttons

 Chart Elements

 Chart Styles

 Chart Filters

When a chart is inserted in a slide, three buttons display to the right of the chart area: the Chart Elements button, the Chart Styles button, and the Chart Filters button. Click the top button, Chart Elements, and a side menu displays with a list of chart elements such as axis title, chart title, data labels, data table, gridlines, and a legend. Click the check box next to each element to indicate which items should be included in the chart.

Click the Chart Styles button and a side menu opens with options for changing the style and color of the chart. At the Style tab, scroll through the gallery of styles and click to choose a chart style. At the Color tab, view a palette of color schemes and click to choose an option for a colorful or monochromatic look.

Use the Chart Filters button to isolate specific data in a chart. Click the button and then, at the side menu that displays, specify the series or categories to include in the chart. To do this, remove check marks from those elements that should not appear in the chart. After removing the check marks, click the Apply button at the bottom of the side menu. Click the Names tab at the Chart Filters button side menu to show options for turning the display of column and row names on or off.

1. With **5-Conference** open, make sure Slide 4 is the active slide and that the chart in the slide is selected. (Make sure the entire chart is selected and not just an element in the chart.)
2. Insert and remove chart elements by completing the following steps:
   a. Click the Chart Elements button outside the upper right of the chart.
   b. At the side menu, click the *Chart Title* check box to remove the check mark.
   c. Click the *Data Table* check box to insert a check mark.
   d. Hover your mouse pointer over *Gridlines* in the Chart Elements button side menu and then click the right-pointing arrow.
   e. At the next side menu, click the *Primary Major Horizontal* check box to insert a check mark.
   f. Click the *Legend* check box to remove the check mark.
   g. Hover your mouse pointer over *Axis Titles* in the Chart Elements button side menu and then click the right-pointing arrow.
   h. At the next side menu, click the *Primary Vertical* check box to insert a check mark.
   i. With *Axis Title* selected in the rotated text box at the left side of the chart, type Region.

3. Apply a different chart style by completing the following steps:
   a. Click the chart border to redisplay the chart buttons.
   b. Click the Chart Styles button to the right of the chart below the Chart Elements button.
   c. At the side menu gallery, click the *Style 3* option (third option in the gallery).
   d. Click the Color tab at the top of the side menu and then click the *Colorful Palette 2* option (second row in the *Colorful* section).

   e. Click the Chart Styles button to remove the side menu.

Chapter 5 | Creating Tables, SmartArt Graphics, Charts, and Photo Albums

4. Remove the horizontal axis title by completing the following steps:
   a. Click the Chart Elements button.
   b. Hover your mouse pointer over *Axes* in the Chart Elements button side menu and then click the right-pointing arrow.
   c. At the other side menu that displays, click the *Primary Horizontal* check box to remove the check mark.
   d. Click the Chart Elements button to remove the side menu.
5. Display only the North and South sales by completing the following steps:
   a. Click the Chart Filters button below the Chart Styles button.
   b. Click the *Central* check box in the *Categories* section to remove the check mark.
   c. Click the *East* check box in the *Categories* section to remove the check mark.
   d. Click the *West* check box in the *Categories* section to remove the check mark.
   e. Click the Apply button at the bottom of the side menu.
   f. Click the Chart Filters button to remove the side menu.
   g. After viewing only the *North* and *South* sales, redisplay the other regions by clicking the Chart Filters button, clicking the *Central*, *East*, and *West* check boxes to insert check marks, and then clicking the Apply button.
   h. Click the Chart Filters button to remove the side menu.
6. Save **5-Conference**.

⬤ Check Your Work ⟩

⬤ Tutorial ⟩

Changing the Chart Design

Changing the Chart Design

 Change Chart Type

 Quick Layout

 Change Colors

 Select Data

 Switch Row/ Column

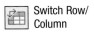 Edit Data

The design of a chart can also be customized with options on the Chart Tools Design tab, shown in Figure 5.10. Use options on this tab to add a chart element, change the chart layout and colors, apply a chart style, select, edit, or refresh data and switch rows and columns, or change the chart type.

Click the Quick Layout button in the Chart Layouts group to display a drop-down gallery of layout options for a chart and add an element to the chart with the Add Chart Element button. Apply predesigned chart styles with options in the Chart Styles group and use the Change Colors button to change the color of the selected element or chart.

Use options in the Data group on the Chart Tools Design tab to change the grouping of the data in the chart, select specific data, edit data, and refresh data that has been updated. Click the Select Data button in the Data group and the worksheet linked to the chart will open, along with the Select Data Source dialog box. At the dialog box, click the Switch Row/Column button to change the grouping of the selected data. Filter data at the dialog box by removing the check mark from those items that should not appear in the chart. To edit data in the chart, click the Edit Data button and the worksheet opens. Make edits to cells in the worksheet and then click the Close button.

Figure 5.10 Chart Tools Design Tab

Quick Steps

Change Chart Type and Style
1. Make chart active.
2. Click Chart Tools Design tab.
3. Click Change Chart Type button.
4. Click chart type.
5. Click chart style.
6. Click OK.

After creating a chart, the chart type can be changed by clicking the Change Chart Type button in the Type group on the Chart Tools Design tab. This displays the Change Chart Type dialog box. This dialog box contains the same options as the Insert Chart dialog box shown in Figure 5.8. At the Change Chart Type dialog box, click the chart type in the left panel and click the chart style in the right panel.

Activity 1I **Changing the Chart Design**   Part 12 of 14

1. With **5-Conference** open, make sure Slide 4 is active and the chart is selected. Click the Chart Tools Design tab.
2. Looking at the chart, you decide that the bar chart was not the best choice for the data and decide to change to a column chart. Do this by completing the following steps:
   a. Click the Change Chart Type button in the Type group on the Chart Tools Design tab.
   b. At the Change Chart Type dialog box, click the *Column* option in the left panel.
   c. Click the *3-D Clustered Column* option (fourth option at the top of the dialog box).

   d. Click OK to close the dialog box.
3. Add a legend to the chart by clicking the Add Chart Element button in the Chart Layouts group, pointing to *Legend,* and then clicking *Left* at the side menu.

4. Change to a different layout by clicking the Quick Layout button in the Chart Layouts group and then clicking the *Layout 10* option (the last option).
5. Click the Add Chart Element button, point to *Chart Title* at the drop-down list, and then click *Above Chart* at the side menu.

6. Type 2021 Regional Sales as the chart title.
7. Click the chart border to deselect the chart title.
8. Click the *Style 1* option in the chart styles gallery in the Chart Styles group (first option).
9. Select data and switch rows and columns by completing the following steps:
   a. Click the Select Data button in the Data group. (This opens a worksheet window and displays the Select Data Source dialog box.)
   b. Click the Switch Row/Column button in the Select Data Source dialog box.
   c. Click OK. (This switches the grouping of the data from *Region* to *Half Yearly Sales*.)

10. After viewing the chart, switch the rows and columns back to the original groupings by dragging the worksheet window so the Switch Row/Column button is visible in the Data group on the Chart Tools Design tab, clicking in the chart, and then clicking the Switch Row/Column button.
11. Close the worksheet by clicking the Close button in the upper right corner of the window.
12. Click the Edit Data button in the Data group.
13. Click in cell B4 (the cell containing the amount *$720,000*), type 650000, and then press the Enter key. (When you press the Enter key, a dollar symbol is automatically inserted in front of the number and a thousand separator comma is inserted.)
14. Click in cell B6 (the cell containing the amount *$830,000*), type 730000, and then press the Enter key.
15. Click the Close button in the upper right corner of the worksheet window.
16. Save **5-Conference**.

Check Your Work

Tutorial

Changing Chart
Formatting

Hint Right-click
text in a chart element
to display the Mini
toolbar.

Format
Selection

Hint Chart
elements can be
repositioned for
easier viewing.

Formatting a Chart and Chart Elements

Apply formatting to a chart or chart elements using options in the Drawing group on the Home tab. Apply a predesigned style to a chart or chart element with the Quick Styles button. Use other buttons in the group to add fill and outline color and apply effects.

In addition to the buttons in the Drawing group on the Home tab, a chart and chart elements can be formatted using options on the Chart Tools Format tab, as shown in Figure 5.11. First, select the element to be formatted. Do this by clicking the element in the chart or by clicking the Chart Elements button in the Current Selection group on the Chart Tools Format tab and then clicking the element in the drop-down list. With the element selected, click the Format Selection button in the Current Selection group and a task pane displays with formatting options. Insert shapes with options in the Insert Shapes group. Click the More Shapes button to view a drop-down list of available shapes, such as circles, arrows, rectangles and stars. Select a shape by clicking it in the drop-down list and then click inside the chart to add the shape. Click the Change Shape button to change the shape to a different shape.

The Shape Styles group on the Chart Tools Format tab contains predesigned styles that can be applied to elements in the chart. Click the More Shape Styles button to display a gallery of shape styles. Use the buttons at the right side of the Shape Styles group to format the selected element with a fill, outline, or other effect. The WordArt Styles group contains predesigned styles for text. Use the buttons at the right side of the WordArt Styles group to apply fill color, an outline color, or an effect to text in a chart. Use options in the Arrange group to specify the layering, alignment, rotation, and size of a chart or chart element.

Additional formatting options are available at various task panes. Display a task pane by clicking the Format Selection button or by clicking a group task pane launcher. The Shape Styles, WordArt Styles, and Size groups on the Chart Tools Format tab each contain a task pane launcher. The task pane that opens varies depending on the chart or chart element selected.

Figure 5.11 Chart Tools Format Tab

Activity 1m Formatting a Chart and Chart Elements
Part 13 of 14

1. With **5-Conference** open, make sure Slide 4 is active and the chart is selected.
2. Reposition and format the legend by completing the following steps:
   a. Click the Chart Elements button at the right of the chart.
   b. Hover your mouse pointer over *Legend*, click the right-pointing arrow at the right of *Legend* in the side menu, and then click the *Right* option at the other side menu.

c. Click the Chart Elements button again to remove the side menu.
d. Click the legend to select it.
e. If necessary, click the Home tab.
f. Click the Quick Styles button in the Drawing group and then click the *Subtle Effect - Lime, Accent 3* option (fourth column, fourth row).
g. Click the Shape Outline button arrow in the Drawing group and then click the *Green, Accent 1, Darker 50%* option (fifth column, last row in the *Theme Colors* section).
h. Increase the size of the legend by dragging down the bottom middle sizing handle about 0.25 inch.

3. Format the title by completing the following steps:
   a. Click the Chart Tools Format tab.
   b. Click the *Chart Elements* option box arrow in the Current Selection group and then click *Chart Title* at the drop-down list.
   c. Click the More Shape Styles button at the right of the gallery in the Shape Styles group and then click the *Intense Effect - Green, Accent 1* option (second column, last row).
   d. Click the Shape Effects button, point to *Bevel*, and then click the *Cross* option (third column, first row in the *Bevel* section).

4. Customize the chart wall and floor by completing the following steps:
   a. Click the *Chart Elements* option box arrow in the Current Selection group and then click *Back Wall* at the drop-down list.
   b. Click the Format Selection button in the Current Selection group. (This displays the Format Wall task pane with the Fill & Line icon selected.)

   c. If necessary, click *Fill* to display the options.
   d. Click the *Gradient fill* option.
   e. Click the Preset gradients button and then click the *Light Gradient - Accent 3* option (third column, first row).
   f. Click the *Chart Elements* option box arrow and then click *Floor*. (This displays the Format Floor task pane.)
   g. Click the *Solid fill* option.

5. Customize the 1st Half data series by completing the following steps:
   a. Click the *Chart Elements* option box arrow and then click *Series "1st Half"* at the drop-down list.
   b. Click the Effects icon at the Format Data Series task pane.
   c. Click *3-D Format* to display the options.
   d. Click the Material button in the task pane.
   e. Click the *Dark Edge* option at the drop-down list (first option in the *Special Effect* section).
   f. Click the Bottom bevel button and then click the *Hard Edge* option (third column, third row in the *Bevel* section).

6. Complete steps similar to those in Step 5a through Step 5f to format the *Series "2nd Half"* chart element.

7. Customize the chart by completing the following steps:
   a. Click the *Chart Elements* option box arrow in the Current Selection group and then click *Chart Area* at the drop-down list.
   b. Click the Fill & Line icon and make sure fill options display in the Format Chart Area task pane. (If necessary, click *Fill* to expand the options.)
   c. Click the *Picture or texture fill* option.
   d. Click the Texture button (located below the Online button).
   e. Click the *Parchment* option (last column, third row).
   f. Scroll down the task pane to the *Border* section and, if necessary, click *Border* to expand the options.
   g. Click the *Solid line* option in the *Border* section.
   h. Click the Size & Properties icon.
   i. If necessary, click *Size* to display the options.
   j. Select the current measurement in the *Height* measurement box and then type 6.
   k. Select the current measurement in the *Width* measurement box, type 9, and then press the Enter key.
   l. Click *Position* to display the options.
   m. Select the current measurement in the *Horizontal position* measurement box and then type 2.5.
   n. Select the current measurement in the *Vertical position* measurement box, type 0.8, and then press the Enter key.
   o. Close the task pane by clicking the Close button in the upper right corner of the task pane.

8. Save **5-Conference**.

Check Your Work

Another method for formatting a chart or chart elements is to use options at the shortcut menu. Some of the options on the shortcut menu vary depending on the chart or chart element selected. Some common options include deleting the element, editing data, rotating the element, and adding data labels. To display the shortcut menu, right-click the element or the chart. In addition to the shortcut menu, the Mini toolbar also displays. The Mini toolbar contains options for applying fill color and outline color.

Activity 1n Creating and Formatting a Pie Chart

Part 14 of 14

1. With **5-Conference** open, make Slide 6 active and then insert a new slide with the Blank layout.
2. Click the Insert tab and then click the Chart button in the Illustrations group.
3. At the Insert Chart dialog box, click *Pie* in the left panel.
4. Double-click the *3-D Pie* option at the top of the dialog box (second option).
5. Type the text in cells in the worksheet as shown at the right.
6. When all data is entered, click the Close button in the upper right corner of the worksheet window.
7. Click the Chart Styles button at the right of the pie chart, click the *Style 3* chart style, and then click the Chart Styles button again to remove the side menu.

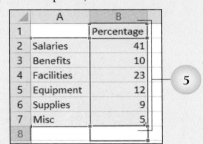

8. Move the data labels to the outside of the pie by completing the following steps:
   a. Click the Chart Elements button at the right of the chart.
   b. Hover your mouse pointer over the *Data Labels* option in the side menu and then click the right-pointing arrow.
   c. Click the *Outside End* option.
   d. Click the Chart Elements button to remove the side menu.

9. Apply formatting to the legend by completing the following steps:
   a. Hover your mouse just above the word *Salaries* in the legend until the mouse pointer displays with a four-headed arrow attached and then click the right mouse button.
   b. Click the Fill button on the Mini toolbar and then click *Tan, Background 2* (third column, first row in the *Theme Colors* section).
   c. Click the Outline button on the Mini toolbar and then click the *Green, Accent 1, Darker 50%* option (fifth column, last row in the *Theme Colors* section).
   d. Increase the size of the legend by dragging the bottom middle sizing handle down about 0.25 inch.

10. Edit the title by completing the following steps:
   a. Right-click the title *Percentage* and then click *Edit Text* in the shortcut menu.
   b. With the insertion point positioned in the title, press the End key to move the insertion point to the right of *Percentage*, press the spacebar, and then type of 100k Division Budget.

11. Click outside the title but inside the chart to select the chart.
12. Click the Chart Tools Format tab.
13. Change the chart height to 6.5 inches and the chart width to 9 inches.
14. Click the Align button in the Arrange group and then click *Distribute Horizontally*.
15. Click the Align button in the Arrange group and then click *Distribute Vertically*.
16. Apply a transition and transition sound of your choosing to all slides in the presentation.
17. Save **5-Conference**.
18. Run the slide show.
19. Print the presentation as a handout with six slides displayed horizontally per page.
20. Close **5-Conference**.

Check Your Work

Activity 2   Create and Format a Travel Photo Album   3 Parts

You will use the photo album feature to create a presentation containing travel photographs. You will also apply formatting and insert elements in the presentation.

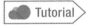
Tutorial

Creating a Photo Album

Photo Album

Creating a Photo Album

Use PowerPoint's photo album feature to create a presentation containing personal or business pictures. Customize and format the appearance of pictures by applying interesting layouts, frame shapes, and themes and insert elements such as captions and text boxes. To create a photo album, click the Insert tab and then click the Photo Album button in the Images group. Or, click the Photo Album button arrow and then click *New Photo Album* at the drop-down list. This displays the Photo Album dialog box, as shown in Figure 5.12.

To insert pictures in the photo album, click the File/Disk button to display the Insert New Pictures dialog box. At this dialog box, navigate to the necessary folder and then select photos to be inserted in the album. Photos can be selected one at a time by double-clicking each file. To select multiple images, click the first image and then hold the Shift key down and click the last image in the folder; or, hold the Ctrl key down while clicking to select specific images in the folder. At the Photo Album dialog box, pictures in the album are listed by file name in the order they will appear in the presentation. A preview of each picture can be seen in the *Preview* area of the dialog box. When all pictures have been inserted in the Photo Album dialog box, click the Create button. This creates the photo album as a presentation and displays the first slide. The first slide includes the title *Photo Album* and the user's name.

Figure 5.12 Photo Album Dialog Box

Insert a picture by clicking the File/Disk button and then double-clicking the picture at the Insert New Pictures dialog box.

Choose a picture and then preview it in this *Preview* box.

Activity 2a Creating a Travel Photo Album

Part 1 of 3

1. At a blank screen, click the Insert tab and then click the Photo Album button in the Images group.
2. At the Photo Album dialog box, click the File/Disk button.
3. At the Insert New Pictures dialog box, navigate to your PC5 folder and then double-click the *Nightscape* image file.
4. At the Photo Album dialog box, click the File/Disk button, and then double-click the *Stonehenge* image file at the Insert New Pictures dialog box.
5. Insert the following additional images: **WhiteHorse**, **Colosseum**, **Siena**, and **VictoriaBC**.
6. Click the Create button. (This opens a presentation with each image in a separate slide. The first slide contains the default text *Photo Album* followed by your name (or the user name for the computer).
7. Save the presentation and name it **5-Album**.
8. Run the slide show.

Check Your Work

Quick Steps

Edit Photo Album
1. Click Insert tab.
2. Click Photo Album
   button arrow.
3. Click *Edit Photo
   Album*.
4. Make changes at
   Edit Photo Album
   dialog box.
5. Click Update button.

Hint Search for
predesigned photo
album templates using
the search text box at
the New backstage
area.

Editing and Formatting a Photo Album

To make changes to a photo album presentation, open the presentation, click the Insert tab, click the Photo Album button arrow in the Images group, and then click *Edit Photo Album* at the drop-down list. This displays the Edit Photo Album dialog box, which contains the same options as the Photo Album dialog box in Figure 5.12 (on page 173).

Editing the Album Content Rearrange the order of pictures in the presentation by clicking the check box next to a file name or names in the *Pictures in album* list box and then clicking the arrow buttons below the list to move the selected picture(s) up or down in order. Remove a picture from the album by clicking the check box next to it and then clicking the Remove button. (Slides can also be rearranged and removed from the presentation in the usual manner in the Normal or Slide Sorter view.)

Use buttons below the *Preview* box in the Edit Photo Album dialog box to rotate the picture in the slide and increase or decrease the contrast or brightness of the picture. Display all pictures in the photo album in black and white by inserting a check mark in the *ALL pictures black and white* check box.

Pictures in the album will be sized by default as *Fit to slide*. At this setting, one picture will fill most of the slide. Change this setting to fit one, two, or four pictures on each slide, with or without titles, by clicking the *Picture layout* option box arrow in the dialog box and choosing an option at the drop-down list. Change the *Picture layout* option to something other than the default of *Fit to slide* and the *Frame shape* option becomes available. Click the *Frame shape* option box arrow and a drop-down list displays with options for applying a rounded, simple, or double frame around the picture, or a soft or shadow effect frame.

Editing the Album Layout Apply a theme to the photo album presentation by clicking the Browse button at the right of the *Theme* option box and then double-clicking the theme in the Choose Theme dialog box. This dialog box contains the predesigned themes provided by PowerPoint.

To add captions to pictures, change the *Picture layout* to show one, two, or four images per slide and then click the *Captions below ALL pictures* check box. PowerPoint will insert the file name for each picture as the caption. The captions can be edited in the slide.

Click the New Text Box button in the Edit Photo Album dialog box and a new slide containing a text box is inserted in the presentation. Type inside the text box to add information, such as an introduction to the photo album or descriptions of individual photos. Once all changes have been made to the photo album, click the Update button at the bottom right side of the dialog box.

1. With **5-Album** open, make sure the Insert tab is active, click the Photo Album button arrow in the Images group, and then click *Edit Photo Album* at the drop-down list.
2. At the Edit Photo Album dialog box, make the following changes:
   a. Click the *ALL pictures black and white* check box to insert a check mark.
   b. Click in the *VictoriaBC* check box in the *Pictures in album* list box to insert a check mark and then click the up-pointing arrow button below the list box two times. (This moves *VictoriaBC* so it is positioned between *WhiteHorse* and *Colosseum*).

   c. Click the Rotate button below the *Preview* box (the first button from the left below the image preview). Click the Rotate button three more times to return the image to the original orientation.
   d. Click the *VictoriaBC* check box in the *Pictures in album* list box to remove the check mark.
   e. Click the *Nightscape* check box in the *Pictures in album* list box to insert a check mark and then click the Increase Contrast button below the *Preview* box two times (the third button from the left below the image preview).

   f. Click the *Nightscape* check box to remove the check mark.
   g. Click the *Stonehenge* check box in the *Pictures in album* list box to insert a check mark, click the Increase Contrast button below the *Preview* box two times and then click the Increase Brightness button (fifth button to the right of the Remove button) two times.
   h. Click the *Picture layout* option box arrow and then click *1 picture* at the drop-down list.
   i. Click the *Frame shape* option box arrow and then click *Center Shadow Rectangle* at the drop-down list.
   j. Click the Browse button at the right of the *Theme* option box. At the Choose Theme dialog box, double-click **Facet**.
   k. Click the *Captions below ALL pictures* check box to insert a check mark.
   l. Click the *Stonehenge* check box in the *Pictures in album* list box to remove the check mark and then click the *Siena* check box in the *Pictures in album* list box to insert a check mark.

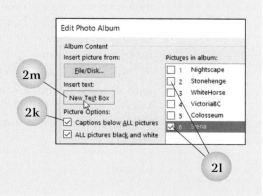

   m. Click the New Text Box button at the left of the list box. (This inserts a new slide containing a text box at the end of the presentation.)
   n. Click the Update button in the lower right corner of the dialog box.

3. At the presentation, make the following formatting changes:
   a. Click the Design tab.
   b. Click the blue variant in the Variants group (second variant).
4. With Slide 1 active, make the following changes:
   a. Select the text *Photo Album* and then type Travel Album.
   b. Select any text after the word *by* and then type your first and last names.
   c. Click the Insert tab and then click the Pictures button.
   d. At the Insert Picture dialog box, navigate to your PC5 folder and then double-click the **FCTLogo** image file.
   e. Change the height of the logo to 2 inches and then position the logo attractively in the slide.
5. Make Slide 2 active and then edit the caption by completing the following steps:
   a. Click in the caption *Nightscape*.
   b. Select *Nightscape* and then type New York City at Night.

6. Complete steps similar to those in Step 5 to change the following captions:
   a. In Slide 3, change *Stonehenge* to *Stonehenge, Wiltshire County*.
   b. In Slide 4, change *WhiteHorse* to *White Horse, Wiltshire County*.
   c. In Slide 5, change *VictoriaBC* to *Victoria, British Columbia*.
   d. In Slide 6, change *Colosseum* to *Colosseum, Rome*.
   e. In Slide 7, change *Siena* to *Siena, Italy*.
7. Make Slide 8 active and then make the following changes:
   a. Select the text *Text Box* and then type Call First Choice Travel at 213-555-4500 to book your next travel tour.
   b. Select the text, change the font size to 48 points, apply the standard blue font color, and center align the text.
   c. Change the width of the placeholder to 9 inches. (Do this at the *Shape Width* measurement box on the Drawing Tools Format tab.)
8. Apply a transition and transition sound of your choosing to all slides in the presentation.
9. Run the slide show.
10. Save **5-Album**.

Check Your Work

Formatting Pictures

If slides are formatted in the presentation instead of using the Edit Photo Album dialog box, some of those changes may be lost if changes are made at the Edit Photo Album dialog box and the Update button is clicked. Consider making initial editing and formatting changes at the Edit Photo Album dialog box and then make any final editing and formatting changes in the presentation slides.

Since a picture in a slide in a photo album is an object, it can be formatted with options on the Drawing Tools Format tab or the Picture Tools Format tab. With options on the Drawing Tools Format tab, insert shapes, apply a shape style to the picture and caption (if one exists), apply a WordArt style to caption text, and arrange and size the picture. Use options on the Picture Tools Format tab to adjust the color of the picture, apply a picture style, and arrange and size the pictures.

1. With **5-Album** open, make Slide 2 active.
2. Change the pictures back to color by completing the following steps:
   a. Click the Insert tab.
   b. Click the Photo Album button arrow in the Images group and then click *Edit Photo Album* at the drop-down list.
   c. At the Edit Photo Album dialog box, click the *ALL pictures black and white* check box to remove the check mark.
   d. Click the Update button.
3. Format the picture in Slide 2 by completing the following steps:
   a. Make Slide 2 active and then click the picture to select it.
   b. Click the Drawing Tools Format tab.
   c. Click the More Shape Styles button in the Shape Styles group and then click the *Subtle Effect - Turquoise, Accent 1* option (second column, fourth row).

4. Apply the same style to the pictures in Slides 3 through 7 by making each slide active, clicking the picture, and then pressing the F4 function key. (Pressing the F4 function key repeats the style formatting.)
5. Make Slide 2 active and then apply a WordArt style to the caption text by completing the following steps:
   a. With Slide 2 active, click the picture to select it.
   b. Click the Drawing Tools Format tab.
   c. Click the More WordArt Styles button in the WordArt Styles group and then click the option in the third column, first row (blue fill with darker blue outline).

6. Apply the same WordArt style to the caption text in Slides 3 through 7 by making each slide active, clicking the picture, and then pressing the F4 function key.
7. Make Slide 8 active and then change the width of the placeholder to 9 inches.
8. Run the slide show.
9. Print the presentation as a handout with four slides displayed horizontally per page.
10. Save and then close **5-Album**.

Check Your Work

Chapter Summary

- Use the Table button in the Tables group on the Insert tab to create a table, insert an Excel worksheet, and draw a table in a slide.

- Change the table design with options and buttons on the Table Tools Design tab. Change the table layout with options and buttons on the Table Tools Layout tab.

- Use the SmartArt feature to insert predesigned graphics, such as diagrams and organizational charts, in a slide.

- Use options and buttons on the SmartArt Tools Design tab to change the graphic layout, apply a style to the graphic, and reset the graphic back to the original formatting.

- Use options and buttons on the SmartArt Tools Format tab to change the size and shape of objects in the graphic; apply shape styles; change the shape fill, outline, and effects; and arrange and size the graphic.

- Insert text directly into a SmartArt graphic shape or at the Text pane. Display this pane by clicking the Text Pane button in the Create Graphic group on the SmartArt Tools Design tab.

- Text or WordArt can be converted to a SmartArt graphic and a SmartArt graphic can be converted to text or shapes.

- A chart is a visual presentation of data. To create a chart, display the Insert Chart dialog box by clicking the Insert Chart button in a content placeholder or clicking the Chart button in the Illustrations group on the Insert tab.

- Enter chart data in a separate worksheet. When entering data, use the arrow keys to move from cell to cell, click in a cell with the mouse, press the Tab key to make the next cell active, press Shift + Tab to make the previous cell active, and press the Enter key to make the cell below active.

- Modify a chart design with options and buttons on the Chart Tools Design tab.

- Cells in the worksheet used to create a chart are linked to the chart in the slide. To edit chart data, click the Edit Data button on the Chart Tools Design tab and then make changes to the text in the worksheet.

- Customize the format of a chart and chart elements with options and buttons on the Chart Tools Format tab. A style can be applied to a shape in a chart, a WordArt style can be applied to text in a chart, and a chart can be sized and arranged in the slide.

- Use the Photo Album feature in the Images group on the Insert tab to create a presentation containing pictures and then edit and format the pictures.

- At the Photo Album dialog box (or the Edit Photo Album dialog box), insert pictures and then use options to customize the photo album.

- Use options on the Drawing Tools Format tab and the Picture Tools Format tab to format pictures in a photo album presentation.

Commands Review

FEATURE	RIBBON TAB, GROUP	BUTTON, OPTION
Choose a SmartArt Graphic dialog box	Insert, Illustrations	
convert bulleted text to SmartArt	Home, Paragraph	
convert SmartArt to text or shapes	SmartArt Tools Design, Reset	
create photo album	Insert, Images	
edit photo album	Insert, Images	, *Edit Photo Album*
Insert Chart dialog box	Insert, Illustrations	
Insert Table dialog box	Insert, Tables	, *Insert Table*
Text pane	SmartArt Tools Design, Create Graphic	

Microsoft®
PowerPoint®
Using Slide Masters and Action Buttons

Performance Objectives

Upon successful completion of Chapter 6, you will be able to:

1. Format slides in Slide Master view
2. Apply themes and backgrounds in Slide Master view
3. Delete placeholders and slide master layouts
4. Insert elements in Slide Master view
5. Create and rename a custom slide layout
6. Insert placeholders and custom prompts in Slide Master view
7. Insert a new slide master
8. Preserve a slide master
9. Save a presentation as a template
10. Customize handouts pages in Handout Master view
11. Customize notes pages in Notes Master view
12. Change zoom, manage windows, and view presentations in color and grayscale
13. Insert action buttons
14. Apply actions to objects
15. Insert, edit, and remove hyperlinks
16. Create a zoom to section summary slide

To make design or formatting changes that affect all slides in a PowerPoint presentation, consider making the changes in a slide master in the Slide Master view. Along with the Slide Master view, changes can be made to all handouts pages with options in the Handout Master view and all notes pages in the Notes Master view. This chapter will also cover ways to manage and view presentations on the screen. Further customize presentations by adding action buttons and hyperlinks that connect to slides within the same presentation, another presentation, a website, or to another program, and use the Zoom feature to create a summary slide with thumbnails that can be used to move to a specific section or slide when running a slide show.

 Data Files

Before beginning chapter work, copy the PC6 folder to your storage medium and then make PC6 the active folder.

The online course includes additional training and assessment resources.

You will apply formatting to a blank presentation in Slide Master view, insert slides in the presentation, insert elements in Slide Master view, insert a custom slide layout, and insert a new slide master.

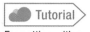

Tutorial

Formatting with a Slide Master

Quick Steps

Display Slide Master View
1. Click View tab.
2. Click Slide Master button.

Slide Master

Hint Create a consistent look for your slides by customizing them in Slide Master view.

Close
Master View

Customizing Slide Masters

To apply formatting or other changes to multiple slides in a presentation, make the changes in a slide master. Customize a slide master by changing the theme, theme colors, or theme fonts; inserting or changing the location of placeholders; applying a background style; and changing the page setup and slide orientation.

If formatting or other changes are made to an individual slide in Normal view, that slide's link to the slide master is broken. Changes made in Slide Master view will not affect the individually formatted slide. For this reason, make global formatting changes in Slide Master view before editing individual slides in a presentation.

To display Slide Master view, click the View tab and then click the Slide Master button in the Master Views group. This makes the Slide Master tab active, opens a blank slide master in the slide pane, and inserts slide master thumbnails in the slide thumbnails pane. The largest thumbnail in the pane is the slide master, and the other thumbnails represent associated layouts. Position the mouse pointer on a slide thumbnail and the name of the thumbnail displays in a ScreenTip by the thumbnail along with information on what slides in the presentation use the slide master. Figure 6.1 shows a blank presentation in Slide Master view. To specify the slide master or layout that will be customized, click the specific thumbnail in the slide thumbnails pane. With the slide master layout active in the slide pane, make the changes and then click the Close Master View button.

Figure 6.1 Slide Master View

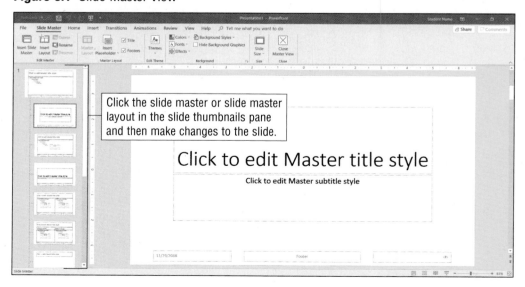

Applying Themes to Slide Masters

Themes

Colors

Fonts

Effects

Apply themes, theme colors, theme fonts, and theme effects to a slide master using buttons in the Edit Theme group and the Background group on the Slide Master tab. Click the Themes button and a drop-down gallery displays with available predesigned themes as well as any custom themes. Click a theme and the theme formatting is applied to the slide master. Use the Colors button in the Background group to change theme colors, use the Fonts button to change theme fonts, and apply a theme effect using the Effects button.

Activity 1a Formatting a Slide Master

Part 1 of 6

1. Open a blank presentation.
2. Click the View tab and then click the Slide Master button in the Master Views group.
3. Scroll up the slide thumbnails pane and then click the top (and largest) slide master thumbnail in the slide thumbnails pane (*Office Theme Slide Master*). This displays the slide master layout in the slide pane.
4. Click the Themes button in the Edit Theme group on the Slide Master tab.
5. Click the *Retrospect* option.
6. Click the Colors button in the Background group and then click the *Blue* option at the drop-down gallery.
7. Click the Fonts button in the Background group, scroll down the drop-down gallery, and then click the *Arial Black-Arial* option.
8. Change the font color for the title style by completing the following steps:
   a. Click the *Click to edit Master title style* placeholder border in the slide master in the slide pane.
   b. Click the Home tab.
   c. Click the Font Color button arrow in the Font group and then click the *Black, Text 1* option (second column, first row in the *Theme Colors* section).
9. Change the font size and color and apply custom bullets by completing the following steps:
   a. Select the text *Edit Master text styles*.
   b. With the Home tab active, click the *Font Size* option box arrow and then click *24* at the drop-down gallery.
   c. Click the Font Color button arrow and then click the *Light Blue, Background 2, Darker 50%* option (third column, fourth row in the *Theme Colors* section).

d. Click the Bullets button arrow in the Paragraph group and then click *Bullets and Numbering* at the drop-down gallery.

e. At the Bullets and Numbering dialog box, click the *Hollow Square Bullets* option.

f. Select *100* in the *Size* measurement box and then type 80.

g. Click the Color button and then click the *Light Blue, Background 2, Darker 50%* option (third column, fourth row in the *Theme Colors* section).

h. Click OK to close the dialog box.

i. Click the Paragraph group dialog box launcher.

j. At the Paragraph dialog box, select the measurement in the *By* measurement box in the *Indentation* section and then type 0.4.

k. Click OK to close the dialog box.

10. Click the Slide Master tab.

11. Click the Close Master View button.

12. Save the presentation and name it **6-TravelMaster**.

Applying and Formatting Backgrounds

In addition to the theme colors, fonts, and effects buttons, the Background group on the Slide Master tab contains the Background Styles button and the *Hide Background Graphics* check box. To change the background graphic for slides, display the presentation in Slide Master view and then click the specific slide master layout in the slide thumbnails pane. Click the Background Styles button and then click a background at the drop-down gallery. Or, click the *Format Background* option at the drop-down gallery and then make changes at the Format Background task pane. To remove the background graphic from slides, click the *Hide Background Graphics* check box to insert a check mark.

Deleting Placeholders

In Slide Master view, if a placeholder is removed from a slide layout it is then removed from all slides based on that layout. To remove a placeholder from a layout, display the presentation in Slide Master view, click the specific slide layout thumbnail, click the placeholder border (make sure the border displays as a solid line), and then press the Delete key. The title placeholder can also be removed from a slide layout by clicking the *Title* check box in the Master Layout group to remove the check mark. Remove footer placeholders by clicking the *Footer* check box to remove the check mark.

Quick Steps

Delete Slide Master Layout
1. Display presentation in Slide Master view.
2. Click slide layout thumbnail.
3. Click Delete button.

 Delete

Deleting Slide Master Layouts

In Slide Master view, a slide master displays for each available layout. If a particular layout will not be used in the presentation, the slide layout can be deleted. To do this, display the presentation in Slide Master view, click the specific slide layout thumbnail in the slide thumbnails pane, and then click the Delete button in the Edit Master group.

1. With **6-TravelMaster** open, click the View tab and then click the Slide Master button in the Master Views group.
2. Apply a picture to the background of the title slide layout (the picture will appear only on slides with this layout applied) by completing the following steps:
   a. Make sure the second slide layout thumbnail (*Title Slide Layout*) is selected in the slide thumbnails pane.
   b. Click the *Click to edit Master title style* placeholder border, click the Home tab, change the font size to 48 points, apply the Black, Text 1 font color (second column, first row in the *Theme Colors* section), and click the Center button in the Paragraph group.
   c. Click the Slide Master tab and then make sure the *Hide Background Graphics* check box in the Background group contains a check mark.
   d. Click the Background Styles button in the Background group and then click *Format Background* at the drop-down list.
   e. At the Format Background task pane, click the *Picture or texture fill* option.
   f. Click the File button.
   g. At the Insert Picture dialog box, navigate to your PC6 folder and then double-click the **Stonehenge** image file.
   h. Close the Format Background task pane.
   i. Drag the master title placeholder so it is positioned above the stones and centered horizontally. (Make sure the bottom border of the placeholder is positioned above the stones.)

   j. Delete the master subtitle placeholder by clicking the placeholder border (make sure the border displays as a solid line) and then pressing the Delete key.
   k. Click the thin horizontal line below the stones and then press the Delete key.
3. Delete slide layouts that you will not be using in the presentation by completing the following steps:
   a. Click the fourth slide layout thumbnail (*Section Header Layout*) in the slide thumbnails pane.
   b. Scroll down the pane until the last slide layout thumbnail is visible.
   c. Press and hold down the Shift key, click the last slide layout thumbnail, and then release the Shift key.
   d. Click the Delete button in the Edit Master group. (The slide thumbnails pane should now contain only one slide master and two associated layouts.)

4. Click the Close Master View button.
5. Delete the slide that is currently active in the slide pane. (After you delete the slide, a gray background displays with the text *Click to add first slide*. The presentation does not contain any slides, just formatting.)
6. Save **6-TravelMaster**.

Inserting Slides in a Customized Presentation

If slides in a presentation have been customized in Slide Master view, the presentation formatting can be used in other presentations. To do this, either save the formatted presentation as a template or save the presentation in the normal manner, open the presentation, save it with a new name, and then type text in slides. Slides can also be inserted into the current presentation using the Reuse Slides task pane. (You learned about this task pane in Chapter 2.) To use this task pane, click the Home tab, click the New Slide button arrow, and then click *Reuse Slides* at the drop-down list. This displays the Reuse Slides task pane at the right side of the screen. Click the Browse button and, at the Browse dialog box, navigate to the necessary folder and then double-click the presentation. Insert slides into the current presentation by clicking specific slides in the task pane.

Activity 1c   **Inserting Slides in a Presentation**   Part 3 of 6

1. With **6-TravelMaster** open, save it with the name **6-England**.
2. With the Home tab active, click the New Slide button arrow, and then click the *Title Slide* option.
3. Click in the title placeholder and then type Wiltshire, England.

4. Insert slides into the current presentation from an existing presentation by completing the following steps:
   a. Click the New Slide button arrow and then click the *Reuse Slides* option.
   b. Click the Browse button in the Reuse Slides task pane.
   c. At the Browse dialog box, navigate to your PC6 folder and then double-click *TravelEngland*.
   d. Click the *Wiltshire* slide in the Reuse Slides task pane. (This inserts the slide in the presentation and applies the custom formatting to the slide.)
   e. Click the *Ancient Stone Circles* slide in the Reuse Slides task pane.
   f. Click the *Ancient Wiltshire* slide in the Reuse Slides task pane.
   g. Click the *White Horses* slide in the Reuse Slides task pane.
   h. Click the Close button in the upper right corner of the Reuse Slides task pane.

5. With Slide 5 active, format the bulleted text in two columns by completing the following steps:
   a. Click in the bulleted text.
   b. Press Ctrl + A to select all of the bulleted text.
   c. Click the Line Spacing button in the Paragraph group and then click the *2.0* option.
   d. Click the Add or Remove Columns button in the Paragraph group and then click the *Two Columns* option.
6. With Slide 5 active, insert a new slide by completing the following steps:
   a. Click the New Slide button arrow and then click the *Title Slide* option.
   b. Click in the title placeholder and then type Call Lucy at 213-555-4500.
7. Save **6-England**.

Check Your Work

Inserting Elements in a Slide Master

A header, footer, or the date and time can be inserted in a presentation that will print on every slide in the presentation. These elements can also be inserted in a slide master. To insert a header or footer in a slide master, display the presentation in Slide Master view, click the Insert tab, and then click the Header & Footer button in the Text group. At the Header and Footer dialog box with the Slide tab selected, make the changes, click the Notes and Handouts tab, make the changes, and then click the Apply to All button. A picture, clip art image, shape, SmartArt graphic, or chart can also be inserted in Slide Master view. These elements are inserted in Slide Master view in the same manner as inserting them in Normal view.

Activity 1d **Inserting Elements in Slide Master View**   Part 4 of 6

1. With **6-England** open, display the presentation in Slide Master view by clicking the View tab and then clicking the Slide Master button in the Master Views group.
2. Insert a header, a footer, and the date and time by completing the following steps:
   a. Click the slide master thumbnail (the top slide thumbnail in the slide thumbnails pane).
   b. Click the Insert tab.
   c. Click the Header & Footer button in the Text group.
   d. At the Header and Footer dialog box with the Slide tab selected, click the *Date and time* check box to insert a check mark.
   e. Make sure the *Update automatically* option is selected. (With this option selected, the date and/or time will automatically update each time you open the presentation.)
   f. Click the *Slide number* check box to insert a check mark.
   g. Click the *Footer* check box to insert a check mark, click in the *Footer* text box, and then type your first and last names.
   h. Click the Notes and Handouts tab.
   i. Click the *Date and time* check box to insert a check mark.
   j. Make sure the *Update automatically* option is selected.
   k. Click the *Header* check box to insert a check mark, click in the *Header* text box, and then type the name of your school.
   l. Click the *Footer* check box to insert a check mark, click in the *Footer* text box, and then type your first and last names.
   m. Click the Apply to All button.

3. Insert the First Choice Travel logo in the upper right corner of the slide master by completing the following steps:

   a. Click the Pictures button in the Images group.

   b. At the Insert Picture dialog box, navigate to your PC6 folder and then double-click the *FCTLogo* image file.

   c. Click in the *Height* measurement box in the Size group on the Picture Tools Format tab, type 0.6, and then press the Enter key.

   d. Drag the logo to position it in the upper right corner of the slide as shown at the right.

   e. Click outside the logo to deselect it.

4. If necessary, click the Slide Master tab.

5. Click the Close Master View button.

6. Run the slide show to view the logo and other elements in the slides.

7. Save **6-England**.

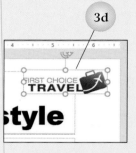

Check Your Work

Creating and Renaming a Custom Slide Layout

 Insert Layout

A custom slide layout can be created in Slide Master view and then further customized by inserting or deleting elements and applying formatting to placeholders and text. To create a new slide layout, click the Insert Layout button in the Edit Master group on the Slide Master tab. This inserts in the slide pane a new slide containing a master title placeholder and footer placeholders. Customize the layout by inserting or deleting placeholders and applying formatting to placeholders.

PowerPoint automatically assigns the name *Custom Layout* to a custom slide layout. If another custom slide layout is created, PowerPoint will name it *1_Custom Layout*, and so on. Consider renaming a custom layout with a name that describes that layout. To rename a layout, make sure the specific slide layout is active and then click the Rename button in the Edit Master group. At the Rename Layout dialog box, type the name for the layout and then click the Rename button.

 Rename

Inserting Placeholders

 Insert Placeholder

A placeholder can be inserted in a predesigned or custom slide layout. Insert a placeholder by clicking the Insert Placeholder button arrow in the Master Layout group and then clicking the specific placeholder option at the drop-down list. If the slide master layout is selected, the Insert Placeholder button is dimmed. If a placeholder is deleted from the slide master, it can be reinserted with options at the Master Layout dialog box. Display this dialog box by clicking the Master Layout button. Any placeholder that has been removed from the slide master is listed in the dialog box as an active option with an empty check box. Reinsert the placeholder by clicking the check box to insert a check mark in the box and then clicking OK to close the dialog box.

 Master Layout

Creating Custom Prompts

Some placeholders in a custom layout may contain generic text such as *Click to add Master title style* or *Click to edit Master text styles*. In Slide Master view, this generic text can be replaced with custom text. For example, custom text may describe what should be inserted in the placeholder. Insert a custom prompt by clicking the Insert Placeholder button in the Master Layout group on the Slide Master tab and then clicking the type of placeholder to be inserted in the slide. After clicking the placeholder type, the mouse pointer will display as crosshairs. Click and drag in the slide to create the placeholder and then customize the text in the placeholder.

Activity 1e Inserting a Layout and Placeholder

1. With **6-England** open, click the View tab and then click the Slide Master button in the Master Views group.
2. Click the bottom slide layout thumbnail in the slide thumbnails pane.
3. Click the Insert Layout button in the Edit Master group. (This inserts in the slide pane a new slide with a master title placeholder, the logo, and the footer information.)
4. Remove the footer by clicking the *Footers* check box in the Master Layout group to remove the check mark.
5. Format and move the placeholder by completing the following steps:
   a. Click the *Click to edit Master title style* placeholder border.
   b. Click the Home tab, change the font size to 28 points, apply the Light Blue, Background 2, Darker 50% font color (third column, fourth row in the *Theme Colors* section), and then click the Center button in the Paragraph group.
   c. Move the placeholder so it is positioned along the bottom of the slide, just above the bottom blue border line (as shown below).

6. Click the Slide Master tab.
7. Insert a picture placeholder by completing the following steps:
   a. Click the Insert Placeholder button arrow in the Master Layout group.
   b. Click *Picture* at the drop-down list.
   c. Click in the slide to insert a placeholder.
   d. With the Drawing Tools Format tab active, click in the *Shape Height* measurement box and then type 3.5.

e. Click in the *Shape Width* measurement box, type 12, and then press the Enter key.

f. Drag the placeholder so it is positioned about 0.5 inch below the thin black line in the slide and centered horizontally. (The picture placeholder will overlap the title placeholder.)

g. Click in the word *Picture* in the placeholder. (This removes the word *Picture* and positions the insertion point in the placeholder.)

h. Type Insert company logo and then click outside the placeholder.

8. Rename the custom slide layout by completing the following steps:

a. Click the Rename button in the Edit Master group on the Slide Master tab.

b. At the Rename Layout dialog box, select the text in the *Layout name* text box and then type Logo.

c. Click the Rename button.

9. Click the Close Master View button.

10. Insert a slide using the new slide layout by completing the following steps:

a. Make Slide 6 active.

b. Click the New Slide button arrow.

c. Click *Logo* at the drop-down list.

d. Click the Pictures button in the slide.

e. At the Insert Picture dialog box, navigate to your PC6 folder and then double-click the **FCTLogo** image file.

f. Click in the title placeholder and then type Monthly special: 20% discount on Wiltshire tour.

11. Save **6-England**.

Check Your Work

Inserting a New Slide Master

Insert Slide Master

A PowerPoint presentation can contain more than one slide master (and associated layouts). To insert a new slide master, display the presentation in Slide Master view and then click the Insert Slide Master button in the Edit Master group. This inserts a new slide master and all associated layouts below the existing slide master and layouts in the slide thumbnails pane. A slide master and all associated layouts can also be inserted with a design theme applied. To do this, click below the existing slide master and associated layouts, click the Themes button in the Edit Theme group, and then click the theme at the drop-down gallery. A slide master containing the chosen design theme is inserted below the existing thumbnails.

Preserving Slide Masters

If all of the slide layouts that follow a slide master are deleted, PowerPoint will automatically delete the slide master. A slide master can be protected from being deleted by preserving the master. To do this, click the slide master thumbnail and then click the Preserve button in the Edit Master group. If a slide master is inserted using the Insert Slide Master button, the Preserve button is automatically active. When a slide master is preserved, a preservation icon (a push pin) appears below the slide number in the slide thumbnails pane.

Changing Page Setup

Click the Slide Size button in the Size group on the Slide Master tab and a drop-down list displays with options for choosing standard or widescreen size. In addition to these two options, the drop-down list also includes the *Custom Slide Size* option. Click this option and the Slide Size dialog box displays. This is the same dialog box covered in Chapter 3. The dialog box contains options for changing slide width, height, and numbering, as well as applying slide orientation to slides, notes, handouts, and outline pages.

Activity 1f **Applying a Second Slide Master**   Part 6 of 6

1. With **6-England** open, preserve the Retrospect slide master by completing the following steps:
   a. Click the View tab and then click the Slide Master button in the Master Views group.
   b. Click the first slide master (*Retrospect Slide Master*) in the slide thumbnails pane.
   c. Click the Preserve button in the Edit Master group. (This inserts a preservation icon [a push pin] below the slide number in the slide thumbnails pane).

2. Insert a second slide master by completing the following steps:
   a. Click below the bottom slide layout in the slide thumbnails pane. (You want the second slide master and associated layouts to be inserted below the original slide master and not take the place of the original.)
   b. Click the Themes button in the Edit Theme group and then click *Facet* at the drop-down gallery.
   c. In the slide thumbnails pane, notice that the slide master and associated layouts are below the original slide master and associated layouts and that a preservation icon displays below the second slide master.
   d. Click the new slide master (*Facet Slide Master*) in the slide thumbnails pane.
   e. Click the Colors button in the Background group and then click the *Blue* option.
   f. Click the Fonts button and then click the *Arial Black-Arial* option.

3. Click the first layout below the new slide master (*Title Slide Layout*) and then select and delete the master subtitle placeholder.

4. Click the third layout below the new slide master (*Section Header Layout*), scroll down to the bottom of the slide thumbnails pane, press and hold down the Shift key, click the bottom thumbnail, release the Shift key, and then click the Delete button in the Edit Master group. (This deletes all but two of the layouts associated with the new slide master.)

5. Click the Close Master View button.

6. Insert a new slide by completing the following steps:
   a. Make Slide 7 active.
   b. Click the New Slide button arrow and then click *Title Slide* in the *Facet* section.

   c. Click in the title placeholder and then type New York City Tour.

7. Insert a new slide by completing the following steps:
   a. With Slide 8 active, click the New Slide button. (This inserts a slide with the Facet Title and Content layout.)
   b. Click in the title placeholder and then type Manhattan Tour.
   c. Click in the text placeholder and then type the following bulleted text:
      Times Square
      Madison Square Garden
      Greenwich Village
      Soho
      Little Italy
      Battery Park

8. Insert slides using the Reuse Slides task pane by completing the following steps:
   a. Click the New Slide button arrow and then click *Reuse Slides* at the drop-down list.
   b. Click the Browse button in the Reuse Slides task pane.
   c. At the Browse dialog box, navigate to your PC6 folder and then double-click **FCTNewYork**.
   d. Click the *Dinner Cruise* slide in the Reuse Slides task pane. (This inserts the slide in the presentation and applies the custom formatting to that slide.)
   e. Click the *City Pass* slide in the Reuse Slides task pane.
   f. Click the *Museum Passes* slide in the Reuse Slides task pane.
   g. Click the Close button in the upper right corner of the Reuse Slides task pane to close the task pane.

9. Assume that the presentation is going to be inserted into a larger presentation and that the starting slide will be Slide 12 (instead of Slide 1). Change the beginning slide number by completing the following steps:

a. Click the View tab and then click the Slide Master button.

b. Click the top slide master in the slide thumbnails pane.

c. Click the Slide Size button in the Size group and then click *Custom Slide Size* at the drop-down list.

d. At the Slide Size dialog box, select the current number in the *Number slides from* measurement box and then type 12.

e. Click OK to close the dialog box.

f. Click the second slide master in the slide thumbnails pane (*Facet Slide Master* thumbnail).

g. Click the Insert tab and then click the Slide Number button in the Text group.

h. At the Header and Footer dialog box with the Slide tab selected, click the *Slide number* check box to insert a check mark and then click the Apply to All button.

i. Click the Slide Master tab.

j. Click the Close Master View button.

10. Make Slide 12 active (the first slide in the presentation) and then run the slide show.

11. Print the presentation as a handout with six slides displayed horizontally per page.

12. Save and then close **6-England**.

Activity 2 Save a Template and Create a Travel Presentation with the Template
4 Parts

You will save a travel presentation as a template and then use that template to create and format a travel presentation. You will insert elements in the presentation in Handout Master view and Notes Master view, change the presentation zoom, manage presentation windows, and view the presentation in grayscale and black and white.

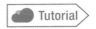
Saving a Presentation as a Template

If custom formatting will be used for future presentations, consider saving the presentation as a template. The advantage to saving a presentation as a template is that the template cannot accidentally be overwritten. Save a custom template in the Custom Office Templates folder in the Documents folder on the hard drive. Check to determine the default custom template folder location by displaying the PowerPoint Options dialog box with *Save* selected in the left panel. (Display this dialog box by clicking the File tab, clicking *Options*, and then clicking *Save* in the left panel of the dialog box.) The *Default personal templates location* option should display the Custom Office Templates folder in the Documents folder as the default location. If this is not the default location, check with your instructor.

To save a presentation as a template, display the Save As dialog box, click the *Save as type* option button, and then click *PowerPoint Template* at the drop-down list. Type a name for the template in the *File name* text box and then click the Save button.

To create a presentation based on a template, click the File tab and then click the *New* option. At the New backstage area, click the *Personal* option above the design theme thumbnails and thumbnails for templates saved in the Custom Office Templates folder display. Open a template by double-clicking the template thumbnail. PowerPoint opens a presentation based on the template, not the original template file.

By default, PowerPoint saves a template in the Custom Office Templates folder in the Documents folder on the computer's hard drive. In addition to this folder, a template can be saved to a specific folder and then a presentation based on the template can be opened using File Explorer, which is a file management application included with Microsoft Windows. To use File Explorer, click the File Explorer icon on the taskbar and, at the window that displays, navigate to the folder containing the template and then double-click the template.

If a template is no longer needed, delete the template at the Custom Office Templates folder. Open this folder by displaying the Open dialog box, navigating to the Documents folder, and then double-clicking the Custom Office Templates folder. Click the template file to be deleted, click the Organize button, and then click *Delete* at the drop-down list.

Quick Steps

Save Presentation as Template
1. Display Save As dialog box.
2. Click *Save as type* option.
3. Click *PowerPoint Template*.
4. Type presentation name.
5. Click Save button.

Open Presentation Based on Template
1. Click File tab.
2. Click *New*.
3. Click *Personal*.
4. Double-click template thumbnail.

Activity 2a Saving a Presentation as a Template   Part 1 of 4

Note: If you are using PowerPoint in a school setting on a network system, you may need to complete Activity 2a and 2b on the same day. Or, you may need to save a template to your PC6 folder and then use File Explorer to open a presentation based on the template. Check with your instructor for any specific instructions.

1. Open **6-TravelMaster**.
2. Press the F12 function key to display the Save As dialog box.
3. At the Save As dialog box, type XXXTravelTemplate in the *File name* text box. (Type your initials in place of the *XXX*.)
4. Click the *Save as type* option box and then click *PowerPoint Template* at the drop-down list.
5. Click the Save button.
6. Close **XXXTravelTemplate**.

7. Open the template and save it as a presentation by completing the following steps:
   a. Click the File tab and then click the *New* option.
   b. At the New backstage area, click the *Personal* option. (Note: If *Custom* displays rather than *Personal*, click the *Custom* option and then click the *Custom Office Templates* option to display the template.)
   c. Double-click the **XXXTravelTemplate** thumbnail.
8. Save the presentation with the name **6-ParisTour**.

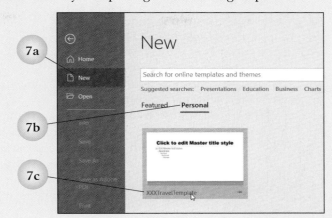

Check Your Work

Tutorial

Customizing the Handout Master

 Handout Master

Customizing the Handout Master

When a presentation is printed as handouts or an outline, PowerPoint will automatically print the current date in the upper right corner of the page and the page number in the lower right corner. Customize handouts with options in the Handout Master view. Display a presentation in Handout Master view by clicking the View tab and then clicking the Handout Master button in the Master Views group. Use options on the Handout Master tab to move, size, and format header and footer placeholders; change page orientation; add or remove placeholders; and specify the number of slides to be printed on each page.

With buttons in the Page Setup group, change the handout orientation, display the Slide Size dialog box with options for changing the size and orientation of the handouts page, and specify the number of slides to be printed on the handouts page. By default, a handouts page will contain a header, footer, date, and page number placeholder. Remove any of these placeholders by removing the check mark before the placeholder check boxes in the Placeholders group.

Click the Themes button in the Edit Theme group and the options in the drop-down gallery are dimmed, indicating that the themes are not available for the handouts pages. If a background style is applied to the handout master, theme colors can be changed by clicking the Colors button in the Background group and then clicking a color theme at the drop-down gallery. Apply theme fonts by clicking the Fonts button and then clicking a font theme at the drop-down gallery.

 Background Styles

Apply a background style to the handouts page by clicking the Background Styles button in the Background group and then clicking one of the predesigned styles. Or, click the *Format Background* option at the Background Styles button drop-down list and then make changes at the Format Background task pane. Remove any background graphics by clicking the *Hide Background Graphics* check box to insert a check mark.

1. With **6-ParisTour** open and in Normal view, click the New Slide button arrow in the Slides group on the Home tab and then click *Reuse Slides* at the drop-down list.
2. Click the Browse button in the Reuse Slides task pane.
3. Navigate to your PC6 folder and then double-click *ParisTour*.
4. Insert the second, third, fourth, and fifth slides from the Reuse Slides task pane into the current presentation.
5. Close the Reuse Slides task pane.
6. Edit the Title Slide Layout in Slide Master view by completing the following steps:
   a. Click the View tab and then click the Slide Master button.
   b. Click the second thumbnail in the slide thumbnails pane (*Title Slide Layout*).
   c. Click the Background Styles button in the Background group and then click *Format Background* at the drop-down list.
   d. At the Format Background task pane, click the File button.
   e. At the Insert Picture dialog box, navigate to your PC6 folder and then double-click the *EiffelTower* image file.
   f. Close the Format Background task pane.
   g. If necessary, click the *Hide Background Graphics* check box in the Background group to insert a check mark.

   h. Select the text *Click to edit Master title style*, click the Home tab, click the Font Color button arrow, and then click the *Turquoise, Accent 2, Lighter 60%* option (sixth column, third row in the *Theme Colors* section).
   i. Click the Slide Master tab.
   j. Click the Close Master View button.
   k. Make Slide 1 active and then type Paris Tour in the title placeholder.
   l. Size and move the text placeholder so *Paris Tour* is in a blue area of the slide (not over the tower).
7. Make Slide 5 active and then create a new slide with the Title Slide layout. Type Call Greg at 213-555-4500 in the title placeholder. (Leave the placeholder in the default location.)
8. Save **6-ParisTour**.
9. Click the View tab and then click the Handout Master button in the Master Views group.

10. Click the Handout Orientation button in the Page Setup group and then click *Landscape* at the drop-down list.

11. Click in the Header placeholder on the page and then type your first and last names.
12. Click in the Footer placeholder and then type Paris Tour.
13. Click the Background Styles button and then click *Style 9* at the drop-down list (first column, last row).
14. Click the Colors button in the Background group and then click the *Blue* option.
15. Click the Fonts button in the Background group, scroll down the drop-down gallery, and then click the *Arial Black-Arial* option.
16. Edit the header text by completing the following steps:
    a. Click in the Header placeholder.
    b. Move the insertion point so it is positioned immediately to the right of the last character in your last name.
    c. Type a comma, press the spacebar, and then type your course number and title.
    d. Click in the handouts page outside of any placeholder.
17. Click the Close Master View button.
18. Save **6-ParisTour**.

> Check Your Work

Tutorial

Customizing the Notes Master

Notes Master

Customizing the Notes Master

If notes are inserted in a presentation, the presentation can be printed as notes pages with the notes printed below the slides. To insert or format text or other elements as notes on all slides in a presentation, consider making the changes in the Notes Master view. Display this view by clicking the View tab and then clicking the Notes Master button in the Master Views group. This displays a notes page along with the Notes Master tab. Many of the buttons and options on this tab are the same as those on the Handout Master tab.

Activity 2c **Customizing the Notes Master**   Part 3 of 4

1. With **6-ParisTour** open, click the View tab and then click the Notes Master button in the Master Views group.
2. Click the *Body* check box in the Placeholders group to remove the check mark.

3. Click the Fonts button in the Background group, scroll down the drop-down gallery, and then click the *Arial Black-Arial* option.
4. Click the Insert tab.
5. Click the Text Box button in the Text group.
6. Click in the notes pane area, which is located just below the slide.
7. Type Visit https://ppi-edu.net/first-choice for a listing of all upcoming tours.

8. Size and position the text box below the slide as shown below and to the right.
9. Click the Insert tab and then click the Pictures button in the Images group.
10. At the Insert Picture dialog box, navigate to your PC6 folder and then double-click the **FCTLogo** image file.
11. Change the height of the logo to 0.5 inch. (This changes the width to approximately 1.72 inches.)
12. Drag the logo so it is positioned below the text as shown below.

13. Click the Notes Master tab and then click the Close Master View button.
14. Print Slides 2 and 4 as notes pages by completing the following steps:
    a. Display the Print backstage area.
    b. Click the second gallery in the *Settings* category and then click *Notes Pages* in the *Print Layout* section.
    c. Click in the *Slides* text box below the first gallery in the *Settings* category and then type 2,4.
    d. Click the Print button.
15. Save **6-ParisTour**.

Check Your Work

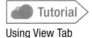
Tutorial

Using View Tab Options

Using View Tab Options

The View tab contains buttons for displaying a presentation in various views such as Normal, Slide Sorter, Slide Master, Handout Master, and Notes Master. In addition to viewing buttons, the View tab also includes options for showing or hiding the ruler and gridlines; opening the Notes pane below the slide pane; zooming in or out in the slide; viewing the slide in color, grayscale, or black and white; and working with windows.

Tutorial

Changing the
Display of a Slide
in the Slide Pane

 Zoom

 Fit to Window

Changing the Display Percentage

Change the display size of the slide in the slide pane or the slides in the slide thumbnails pane with the Zoom button on the View tab or with the Zoom slider bar at the right side of the Status bar. Click the Zoom button on the View tab and the Zoom dialog box displays. Use options in this dialog box to increase or decrease the display size of slides in the slide pane or slide thumbnails pane. Click the Fit to Window button in the Zoom group on the View tab to zoom the slide to fill the slide pane.

To change the zoom with the Zoom slider bar, use the mouse to drag the slider bar button to the left to decrease the display size or to the right to increase the display size. Click the Zoom Out button (the minus symbol at the left of the Zoom slider bar) to decrease the zoom percentage or click the Zoom In button (the plus symbol at the right of the Zoom slider bar) to increase the zoom percentage. Click the Zoom level button, which displays as a percentage number at the right of the slider bar, and the Zoom dialog box displays.

Managing Windows

Use buttons in the Window group on the View tab to work with presentation windows. Work in two locations in the same presentation by opening the presentation and then opening a new window with the same presentation. This is helpful for viewing and editing slides in two different locations in the presentation. Open a new window by clicking the New Window button in the Window group.

 New Window

 Arrange All

 Cascade

If more than one presentation is open, the presentations can be arranged so a portion of each presentation is visible. Click the Arrange All button in the Window group and each open presentation displays as a tile on the screen. Click the Cascade button in the Window group and the open presentations are displayed in a layered manner with the title bar of each presentation visible. Slides can be copied from one presentation to another when the presentations are arranged on the screen by dragging a slide from the slide thumbnails pane in one presentation to the slide thumbnails pane in the other presentation.

With more than one presentation open, switch between presentations by clicking the Switch Windows button in the Window group. Click this button and a drop-down list with the names of the open presentations displays with a check mark in front of the active presentation. Make another presentation active by clicking the presentation name at the drop-down list.

 Switch Windows

 Move Split

 Maximize

 Minimize

 Restore Down

Increase or decrease the viewing area of each section of the presentation window with the Move Split button. Click this button and the mouse pointer displays as a four-headed arrow. Use the arrow keys on the keyboard to increase or decrease the viewing area of the slide pane and slide thumbnails pane. Click the left mouse button to deactivate the feature. Use the Maximize and Minimize buttons in the upper right corner of the active presentation to change the size of the window. If all open presentations are arranged in the window, click the Maximize button in the active presentation to fill the screen. In addition, the Maximize button changes to the Restore Down button. To return the active presentation back to its size before it was maximized, click the Restore Down button. Click the Minimize button in the active presentation to reduce the presentation to a button on the taskbar.

Viewing in Color and Grayscale

Color

Grayscale

Black and White

By default, the slides in a presentation are viewed in color. This can be changed to grayscale or black and white with buttons in the Color/Grayscale group on the View tab. Click the Grayscale button and the slides in the presentation display in grayscale and the Grayscale tab becomes active. This tab contains a variety of options for changing the grayscale properties, such as light grayscale, inverse grayscale, and gray or black with grayscale fill. Return to the color view by clicking the Back to Color View button on the Grayscale tab. Click the Black and White button in the Color/Grayscale group and the slides in the presentation display in black and white and the Black And White tab becomes active. This tab contains many of the same options as the Grayscale tab.

Activity 2d **Viewing a Presentation**   Part 4 of 4

1. With **6-ParisTour** open, make Slide 1 active and then click the slide in the slide pane.
2. Click the View tab.
3. Increase and decrease the zoom by completing the following steps:
   a. Click the Zoom button in the Zoom group.
   b. At the Zoom dialog box, click the *33%* option and then click OK.
   c. Click the Zoom button, click the *100%* option in the Zoom dialog box, and then click OK.
   d. Click the Slide 2 thumbnail in the slide thumbnails pane.
   e. Click the Zoom button, click the *66%* option in the Zoom dialog box, and then click OK. (Because the slide was active in the slide thumbnails pane, the percentage changed for the thumbnails in the pane.)
   f. Position the mouse pointer on the Zoom slider bar button (at the right side of the Status bar), drag the button to the right to increase the size of the slide in the slide pane, and then drag the slider bar to the left to decrease the size of the slide.
   g. Click the Zoom level button (the percentage number at the right of the Zoom slider bar). This displays the Zoom dialog box.
   h. Click the *100%* option in the Zoom dialog box and then click OK.
   i. Click the Fit to Window button in the Zoom group on the View tab.
4. View the slides in grayscale by completing the following steps:
   a. Click the Grayscale button in the Color/Grayscale group on the View tab.
   b. Click the slide in the slide pane.
   c. Click the buttons in the Change Selected Object group on the Grayscale tab to display the slides in varying grayscale options.
   d. Click the Back To Color View button.
5. View the slides in black and white by completing the following steps:
   a. Click the View tab and then click the Black and White button in the Color/Grayscale group.
   b. Click some of the buttons in the Change Selected Object group on the Black And White tab to display the slides with varying black and white options applied.
   c. Click the Back To Color View button.

3b

3i

4a

6. Open another presentation and then arrange the presentations by completing the following steps:
   a. Open **ParisTravelInfo** from your PC6 folder.
   b. Click the View tab and then click the Cascade button in the Window group. (This arranges the two presentations with the presentations overlapping with the title bar for each presentation visible.)
   c. Click the Switch Windows button in the Window group and then click the *6-ParisTour* option at the drop-down list.
   d. Click the View tab and then click the Arrange All button in the Window group to arrange the two presentations in two side-by-side windows.

7. Copy a slide from one presentation to another by completing the following steps:
   a. Click Slide 2 (*Accommodations*) in the slide thumbnails pane of **ParisTravelInfo** and hold down the left mouse button.
   b. Drag the slide so it is positioned below the Slide 5 thumbnail in the slide thumbnails pane in **6-ParisTour** (an orange line will display) and then release the mouse button.

8. Click the Close button in the upper right corner of the **ParisTravelInfo** presentation.
9. Click the Maximize button in the upper right corner of the presentation window. (The Maximize button is immediately to the left of the Close button.)
10. Use the Move Split button by completing these steps:
    a. Click the Move Split button in the Window group. (The mouse displays as a four-headed arrow.)
    b. Press the Right Arrow key on the keyboard several times and notice the slide thumbnails pane increasing in size.
    c. Press the Left Arrow key several times.

    d. Press the Up Arrow key several times and notice that the slide in the slide pane decreases in size and the notes pane displays.
    e. Press the Down Arrow key until the slide in the slide pane returns to the original size and the notes pane has closed.
    f. Click in the slide to turn off the split feature.
11. With the View tab active, click the Grayscale button in the Color/Grayscale group and then click the Light Grayscale button in the Change Selected Object group.
12. Print the presentation by completing the following steps:
    a. Display the Print backstage area.
    b. If any text displays in the *Slides* text box, select and then delete the text.
    c. If you are using a color printer, click the *Color* gallery at the bottom of the *Settings* category and then click *Grayscale*. (Skip this step if you are using a black and white printer.)
    d. Click the second gallery in the *Settings* category and then click *4 Slides Horizontal* in the *Handouts* section.
    e. Click the Print button.
13. Click the Back To Color View button on the Grayscale tab.
14. Make Slide 1 active and then run the slide show.
15. Save and then close **6-ParisTour**.

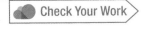
Check Your Work

You will open a job search presentation and then insert action buttons that connect to the next slide, the first slide, a website, and another presentation. You will also create a hyperlink from text, an image, and a chart in a slide to a website, a Word document, and another presentation.

Inserting Action
Buttons

Quick Steps

Insert Action Button
1. Make slide active.
2. Click Insert tab.
3. Click Shapes button.
4. Click action button.
5. Click or drag in slide to create button.
6. Make changes at Action Settings dialog box.
7. Click OK.

💡 **Hint** Apply formatting to an action button with options on the Drawing Tools Format tab.

Inserting Action Buttons

Action buttons are drawn objects on a slide that have a routine attached to them which is activated when the viewer or the presenter clicks the button. For example, an action button can be inserted in a slide that connects to the next slide in the presentation, a file in another program, or a specific web page. Creating an action button is a two-step process. The button is drawn in the slide using an Action Button shape in the Shapes button drop-down list and then the action that will take place is defined with options in the Action Settings dialog box. Customize an action button in the same manner as customizing a drawn object. When the viewer or presenter moves the mouse over an action button during a presentation, the pointer changes to a hand with the index finger pointing upward to indicate clicking will result in an action.

To see the available action buttons, click the Insert tab and then click the Shapes button in the Illustrations group. Action buttons are at the bottom of the drop-down list. Hover the mouse pointer over a button and the name and the action it performs display in a ScreenTip above the button. The action attached to an action button occurs when the button is clicked during the running of the slide show.

Activity 3a Inserting Action Buttons

1. Open **JobSearch** and then save it with the name **6-JobSearch**.
2. Make the following changes to the presentation:
   a. Apply the Dividend design theme.
   b. Click the Insert tab and then click the Header & Footer button in the Text group.
   c. At the Header and Footer dialog box with the Slide tab selected, click the *Date and time* check box and make sure *Update automatically* is selected.
   d. Click the *Slide number* check box to insert a check mark.
   e. Click the Notes and Handouts tab.
   f. Click the *Date and time* check box and make sure *Update automatically* is selected.
   g. Click the *Header* check box to insert a check mark, click in the *Header* text box, and then type the name of your school.
   h. Click the *Footer* check box to insert a check mark, click in the *Footer* text box, and then type your first and last names.
   i. Click the Apply to All button.

3. Insert an action button in Slide 1 that will advance to the next slide by completing the following steps:

   a. Make sure Slide 1 is active.

   b. Click the Insert tab and then click the Shapes button in the Illustrations group.

   c. Scroll down the drop-down list and then click the *Action Button: Go Forward or Next* button (second button in the *Action Buttons* group).

   d. Move the crosshairs to the lower right corner of the slide and then drag to create a button that is approximately 0.5 inch in height and width (see below).

   e. At the Action Settings dialog box, click OK. (The default setting is *Hyperlink to Next Slide*.)

4. Insert an action button in Slide Master view that will advance to the next slide by completing the following steps:

   a. Display the presentation in Slide Master view.

   b. Click the top slide master thumbnail (*Dividend Slide Master*).

   c. Click the Insert tab and then click the Shapes button in the Illustrations group.

   d. Scroll down the drop-down list and then click the *Action Button: Go Forward or Next* button (second button in the *Action Buttons* group).

   e. Move the crosshairs to the lower right corner of the slide master and then drag to create a button as shown below.

   f. At the Action Settings dialog box, click OK.

   g. Click the Slide Master tab and then click the Close Master View button.

5. Make Slide 1 active and then run the slide show, clicking the action button to advance slides. When you click the action button on the last slide (Slide 9) nothing happens because it is the last slide. Press the Esc key to end the slide show.

6. Change the action button on Slide 9 by completing the following steps:

   a. Make Slide 9 active.

   b. Click the Insert tab and then click the Shapes button in the Illustrations group.

c. Scroll down the drop-down list and then click the *Action Button: Go Home* button (fifth button in the *Action Buttons* group).

d. Drag to create a button on top of the previous action button. (Make sure it completely covers the previous action button.)

e. At the Action Settings dialog box with the *Hyperlink to: First Slide* option selected, click OK.

f. Deselect the button.

7. Make Slide 1 active and then run the slide show. Navigate through the slide show by clicking the action button. When you click the action button on the last slide, the first slide displays. End the slide show by pressing the Esc key.

8. Save **6-JobSearch**.

6c

Check Your Work

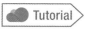

Tutorial

Applying an Action to an Object

Action

Applying an Action to an Object

An action can be applied to an object within a slide, such as an image or shape. The object will then become like a button, which can be clicked to open a link, run an application, play a sound, move to a different slide, or perform some other type of action during the presentation. To apply an action to an object, first select the object in the slide, click the Insert tab, and then click the Action button. This displays the Action Settings dialog box, where the particular action can be selected.

At the Action Settings dialog box, use options in the *Hyperlink to* drop-down list to link an object to another PowerPoint presentation, another file, or to a website. Navigate to the other presentation or file or enter the URL for the website as directed, and then click OK to complete the link. Objects can also be linked to other slides within the same presentation, such as *Next Slide, Previous Slide*, and so on, by using options at the *Hyperlink to* drop-down list.

Activity 3b Linking to Another Presentation and a Website

Part 2 of 5

1. With **6-JobSearch** open, add an action button that will link to another presentation by completing the following steps:

a. Make Slide 4 active.

b. Click the Insert tab and then click the Shapes button in the Illustrations group.

c. Scroll down the drop-down list and then click *Action Button: Help* (eleventh button in the *Action Buttons* section).

d. Draw the action button to the left of the existing button in the lower right corner of the slide.

e. At the Action Settings dialog box, click the *Hyperlink to* option.

f. Click the *Hyperlink to* option box arrow and then click *Other PowerPoint Presentation* at the drop-down list.

1e

1f

g. At the Hyperlink to Other PowerPoint Presentation dialog box, navigate to your PC6 folder and then double-click ***Contacts***.

h. At the Hyperlink to Slide dialog box, click OK.

i. Click OK to close the Action Settings dialog box.

2. Apply an action to the image in Slide 5 that links to a website by completing the following steps:

a. Make Slide 5 active and then click the image to select it.

b. Click the Insert tab and then click the Action button in the Links group.

c. At the Action Settings dialog box, click the *Hyperlink to* option.

d. Click the *Hyperlink to* option box arrow, and then click *URL* at the drop-down list.

e. At the Hyperlink to URL dialog box, type www.usajobs.gov in the *URL* text box and then click OK.

f. Click OK to close the Action Settings dialog box.

g. Click outside the image to deselect it.

3. Run the slide show by completing the following steps:

a. Make sure you are connected to the internet.

b. Make Slide 1 active.

c. Click the Slide Show button in the view area on the Status bar.

d. Navigate through the slide show to Slide 4.

e. Click the action button in Slide 4 containing the question mark. (This opens Slide 1 of **Contacts**.)

f. Navigate through the three slides in **Contacts**. Continue clicking the mouse button until you return to Slide 4 of **6-JobSearch**.

g. Advance to Slide 5 and then click the image. (If you are connected to the internet, the job site of the United States Federal Government opens in your web browser.)

h. Search for information on a specific job title that interests you and then click a few hyperlinks at the website.

i. When you have finished viewing the website, close your web browser.

j. Continue viewing the remainder of the slide show by clicking the action button in the lower right corner of each slide.

k. When Slide 1 displays, press the Esc key to end the slide show.

4. Save **6-JobSearch**.

 Check Your Work

Inserting Hyperlinks

Inserting Hyperlinks

Link

Quick Steps

Insert Hyperlink
1. Click Insert tab.
2. Click Link button.
3. Make changes at Insert Hyperlink dialog box.
4. Click OK.

Inserting Hyperlinks

Hyperlinks can be created with options at the Action Settings dialog box or with options at the Insert Hyperlink dialog box shown in Figure 6.2. To display this dialog box, select a key word, phrase, or object in a slide, click the Insert tab, and then click the Link button in the Links group, or press Ctrl + K, which is the keyboard shortcut to display the Insert Hyperlink dialog box. Link to a website, another presentation, a place in the current presentation, a new presentation, or to an email address. To insert a hyperlink to a website or an existing presentation, click the Existing File or Web Page button in the *Link to* group at the Insert Hyperlink dialog box.

Figure 6.2 Insert Hyperlink Dialog Box

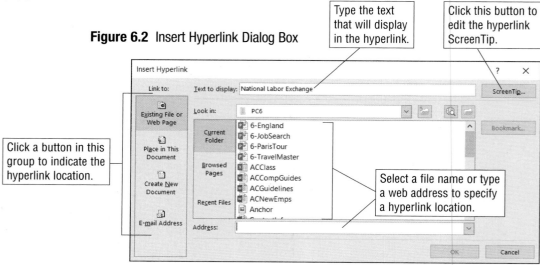

Type the text that will display in the hyperlink.

Click this button to edit the hyperlink ScreenTip.

Click a button in this group to indicate the hyperlink location.

Select a file name or type a web address to specify a hyperlink location.

Activity 3c **Inserting Hyperlinks to a Website**

Part 3 of 5

1. With **6-JobSearch** open, insert a new slide by completing the following steps:
   a. Make Slide 5 active.
   b. Click the Home tab.
   c. Click the New Slide button arrow and then click the *Title and Content* layout option.
   d. Type Internet Job Resources as the slide title.
   e. Click the text placeholder, type National Labor Exchange, press the Enter key, and then type Monster.
2. Add a hyperlink to the National Labor Exchange site by completing the following steps:
   a. Select the text *National Labor Exchange* in Slide 6.
   b. Click the Insert tab and then click the Link button in the Links group.
   c. At the Insert Hyperlink dialog box, type www.us.jobs in the *Address* text box. (PowerPoint automatically inserts *http://* at the beginning of the address.)
   d. Click OK to close the Insert Hyperlink dialog box.

2c

3. Add a hyperlink to the Monster website by completing the following steps:
   a. Select the text *Monster* in Slide 6.
   b. Click the Link button in the Links group.
   c. At the Insert Hyperlink dialog box, type www.monster.com in the *Address* text box. (PowerPoint automatically inserts *http://* at the beginning of the address.)
   d. Click OK to close the Insert Hyperlink dialog box.
4. Save **6-JobSearch**.

3c

Check Your Work

Hint Hyperlinks are active only when running the slide show, not when creating the presentation.

In addition to linking to a website, a hyperlink can be created that links to another location in the presentation with the Place in This Document button in the *Link to* group at the Insert Hyperlink dialog box. Click the slide to link to in the presentation in the *Select a place in this document* list box. Use the Create New Document button in the Insert Hyperlink dialog box to create a hyperlink to a new presentation. Click this button, type a name for the new presentation, and specify if the new presentation is to be edited now or later.

A graphic such as an image, picture, chart, or text box can be used as a hyperlink to a file or website. To create a hyperlink with a graphic, select the graphic, click the Insert tab, and then click the Link button or right-click the graphic and then click *Hyperlink* at the shortcut menu. At the Insert Hyperlink dialog box, specify what to link to and the text to display in the hyperlink.

Insert a hyperlink to an email address using the E-Mail Address button in the *Link to* group in the Insert Hyperlink dialog box. Click the button and the options change in the Insert Hyperlink dialog box. With options that display, type the email address in the *E-mail address* text box, type a subject for the email in the *Subject* text box, and type the text to display in the presentation in the *Text to display* text box. To use this feature, the email address must be set up in Outlook.

Navigate to a hyperlink by clicking the hyperlink in the slide when running the slide show. Hover the mouse over the hyperlink and a ScreenTip displays with the hyperlink. To include specific information in the ScreenTip, click the ScreenTip button in the Insert Hyperlink dialog box, type the text in the Set Hyperlink ScreenTip dialog box, and then click OK.

Activity 3d Inserting Hyperlinks to Another Presentation and to a Word Document   Part 4 of 5

1. With **6-JobSearch** open, make Slide 3 active.
2. Create a link to another presentation by completing the following steps:
   a. Move the insertion point immediately to the right of the word *Picture*, press the Enter key, press Shift + Tab, and then type Resume design.
   b. Select *Resume design*.
   c. Make sure the Insert tab is active and then click the Link button in the Links group.

d. At the Insert Hyperlink dialog box, make sure the Existing File or Web Page button is selected.
e. If necessary, click the *Look in* option box arrow and then navigate to your PC6 folder.
f. Scroll down the list box and then double-click ***DesignResume***.

3. Create a hyperlink from a graphic to a Word document by completing the following steps:
a. Make Slide 4 active.
b. Right-click the small image in the upper right corner of the slide and then click *Link* at the shortcut menu.
c. At the Insert Hyperlink dialog box, make sure the Existing File or Web Page button is selected.
d. If necessary, click the *Look in* option box arrow and then navigate to your PC6 folder.
e. Scroll down the list box and then double-click ***ContactInfo***.

4. Run the slide show by completing the following steps:
a. Make sure you are connected to the internet.
b. Make Slide 1 active.
c. Click the Slide Show button in the view area on the Status bar.
d. Navigate through the slides to Slide 3 and then click the Resume design hyperlink in the slide.

e. Run the **DesignResume** slide show that opens. Continue clicking the mouse button until you return to Slide 3 of **6-JobSearch**.
f. Click the mouse button to advance to Slide 4.
g. Open the Word document by clicking the small image in the upper right corner of the slide.

h. Look at the information in the Word document and then click the Close button in the upper right corner of the Word window.

i. Continue running the slide show to Slide 6.

j. At Slide 6, click the <u>National Labor Exchange</u> hyperlink.

k. Scroll through the website and then close the web browser.

l. Click the <u>Monster</u> hyperlink.

m. Scroll through the website and then close the web browser.

n. Continue viewing the remainder of the presentation using the Action buttons. (When Slide 1 displays, press the Esc key to end the slide show.)

5. Save **6-JobSearch**.

The hyperlinked text or the hyperlink destination can be edited. To do this, right-click the hyperlink and then click *Edit Link* at the shortcut menu. At the Edit Hyperlink dialog box, make changes and then close the dialog box. The Edit Hyperlink dialog box contains the same options as the Insert Hyperlink dialog box.

In addition to modifying the hyperlink, the hyperlinked text can be edited. For example, a different font, font size, text color, or text effect can be applied to the hyperlink text. Remove a hyperlink from a slide by right-clicking the hyperlinked text and then clicking *Remove Link* at the shortcut menu.

Activity 3e Modifying, Editing, and Removing a Hyperlink   Part 5 of 5

1. With **6-JobSearch** open, make Slide 4 active and then modify the hyperlink in the image by completing the following steps:

a. Right-click the small image in the upper right corner of the slide and then click *Edit Link* at the shortcut menu.

b. At the Edit Hyperlink dialog box, click the ScreenTip button in the upper right corner of the dialog box.

c. At the Set Hyperlink ScreenTip dialog box, type Click this image to display information on typing contact information.

d. Click OK to close the Set Hyperlink ScreenTip dialog box.

e. Click OK to close the Edit Hyperlink dialog box.

Set Hyperlink ScreenTip ? ×

ScreenTip text:
Click this image to display information on typing contact information.

OK   Cancel

1c

1d

2. Make Slide 3 active and then remove the <u>Resume design</u> hyperlink by right-clicking the hyperlinked text (the text is dimmed and barely visible) and then clicking *Remove Link* at the shortcut menu.

3. Run the slide show and click the hyperlinks as they appear in the slides.

4. Print the presentation as a handout with six slides displayed horizontally per page.

5. Save and then close **6-JobSearch**.

<table>
<tr><td>

Activity 4 **Create a Zoom to Section Summary Slide in a Vacations Presentation**

</td><td>**1 Part**</td></tr>
</table>

You will create sections in a travel presentation and then create a summary slide containing thumbnails linked to the first slide of each section in the presentation.

 Tutorial

Create a Zoom to
Section Summary
Slide

 Zoom

Quick Steps

**Zoom to Slide
or Section**
1. Create sections.
2. Click Insert tab.
3. Click Zoom button.
4. Click zoom option.

Zoom to Slide or Section

The Zoom feature allows a slide show to be presented in a non-linear format. Instead of running a slide show starting with Slide 1 and running to the last slide, the Zoom feature will insert linked slide thumbnails within the presentation that allows back and forth movement between different slides or sections in any order in a slide show. The Zoom feature can also be used to create an interactive table of contents for quick access to different sections in a presentation.

Display zoom options by clicking the Zoom button in the Links group on the Insert tab. At the drop-down list that displays, click the *Summary Zoom* option to create a new slide containing a table of contents of thumbnails of the sections or slides selected. This allows sections of a slide show to be viewed in any order. Click the *Section Zoom* option to create a link to selected sections in the presentation. Once the slides in the section in the slide show have run, the slide show will return to the original slide. The *Slide Zoom* option can be used to create a link to individual slides in a presentation. A slide zoom can also be created by dragging a slide from the slide thumbnails pane and adding it to the slide currently displayed in the slide pane.

When a linked slide is inserted as a thumbnail in a slide, the thumbnail can be formatted with options on the Zoom Tools Format tab shown in Figure 6.3. Edit the summary slide, reset the thumbnail layouts, apply a custom image for the thumbnails, and change zoom transitions with options in the Zoom Options group. Apply formatting to the thumbnails with options in the Zoom Styles group, add alt text with options in the Accessibility group, arrange the thumbnails in the slide with options in the Arrange group, and change the height and width of the thumbnails with options in the Size group.

Figure 6.3 Zoom Tools Format tab

Activity 4 **Create a Zoom to Section Summary Slide**   **Part 1 of 1**

1. Open **VacationAdv** and save it with the name **6-VacationAdv**.
2. With Slide 1 active, insert a new slide with the Title Only layout.
3. Click in the title placeholder and then type Tour Options.

4. Click outside the title placeholder and then insert a slide with slide zoom links by completing the following steps:
   a. Click the Insert tab.
   b. Click the Zoom button in the Links group and then click *Slide Zoom* at the drop-down list.
   c. At the Insert Slide Zoom dialog box, insert a check mark in the *Fiji Tour*, *Peru Tour*, and *Costa Rica Tour* check boxes.
   d. Click the Insert button at the bottom of the Insert Slide Zoom dialog box.

5. Arrange the three thumbnails in the slide so they do not overlap each other.
6. Run the slide show beginning with Slide 1. When Slide 2 displays, click the *Peru Tour* slide thumbnail link.
7. Continue running the slide show to the end and then press the Esc key to end the slide show.
8. Delete Slide 2.
9. Create sections in the presentation by completing the following steps:
   a. Make Slide 1 active, click the Home tab, click the Section button in the Slides group tab and then click *Add Section* at the drop-down list.
   b. Type Vacation Adventures in the Rename Section dialog box and then click the Rename button.
   c. Make Slide 2 active, click the Section button and then click *Add Section* at the drop-down list.
   d. Type Fiji Tour in the Rename Section dialog box and then click the Rename button.
   e. Make Slide 7 active, click the Section button, and then click *Add Section* at the drop-down list.
   f. Type Peru Tour in the Rename Section dialog box and then click the Rename button.
   g. Make Slide 11 active, click the Section button, and then click *Add Section* at the drop-down list.
   h. Type Costa Rica Tour in the Rename Section dialog box and then click the Rename button.

10. Create a zoom to section summary slide by completing the following steps:
    a. Make Slide 1 active and then click the Insert tab.
    b. Click the Zoom button in the Links group and then click the *Summary Zoom* option at the drop-down list.
    c. At the Insert Summary Zoom dialog box, remove the check mark from the *1. Vacation Adventures* check box and then make sure a check mark displays in the *2. Fiji Tour*, *7. Peru Tour*, and *11. Costa Rica Tour* check boxes.
    d. Click the Insert button at the bottom of the Insert Summary Zoom dialog box.
11. Apply formatting to the summary slide by completing the following steps:
    a. Type Vacation Options as the slide title.
    b. Click in the content placeholder and then click the placeholder border that surrounds all three slide thumbnails. (This selects all the content within the placeholder and not one individual slide thumbnail.)
    c. Click the Zoom Tools Format tab.
    d. Click the *Duration* measurement box up arrow in the Zoom Options group two times (this displays *01.50* in the measurement box).

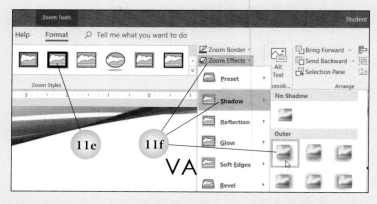

    e. Click the *Double Frame, Black* zoom style in the Zoom Styles group (seventh option from the left).
    f. Click the Zoom Effects button in the Zoom Styles group, point to *Shadow* at the drop-down list, and then click *Offset: Bottom Right* at the side menu (first column, first row in the *Outer* section).
    g. Click the first slide thumbnail (*FIJI TOUR*), click the Zoom Border button in the Zoom Styles group, and then click *Red, Accent 1* at the drop-down gallery (fifth column, first row in the *Theme Colors* section).
    h. Click the second slide thumbnail (*Peru Tour*) and then apply the Orange, Accent 2 zoom border color (sixth column, first row in the *Theme Colors* section).
    i. Click the third slide thumbnail (*Costa Rica Tour*) and then apply the Gold, Accent 3 zoom border color (seventh column, first row in the *Theme Colors* section).
    j. Arrange the three thumbnails in the slide so they do not overlap each other.
12. Run the slide show beginning with Slide 1. When the summary slide displays (*VACATION OPTIONS*), click the *FIJI TOUR* slide thumbnail. This displays the first slide in the Fiji Tour section.

13. Continue running the slide show through the Fiji Tour section. Notice that once the slides in the Fiji Tour section have all displayed, the slide show automatically returns to the summary slide (*VACATION OPTIONS*).
14. Click the *Costa Rica Tour* slide thumbnail and then view the slides in the Costa Rica Tour section.

15. When the slide show returns to the summary slide, press the Esc key to end the slide show.
16. Print only Slide 2 (*VACATION OPTIONS*).
17. Save and then close **6-VacationAdv**.

 Check Your Work

Chapter Summary

- Display a presentation in Slide Master view by clicking the View tab and then clicking the Slide Master button in the Master Views group. In Slide Master view, slide master thumbnails are shown in the slide thumbnails pane.

- Use buttons in the Background group on the Slide Master tab to change theme colors and fonts, apply a predesigned background style, display the Format Background task pane with options for applying background styles, and hide background graphics.

- Delete a placeholder by clicking in the placeholder, clicking the placeholder border, and then pressing the Delete key.

- Delete a slide master in Slide Master view by clicking the slide master thumbnail in the slide thumbnails pane and then clicking the Delete button in the Edit Master group on the Slide Master tab.

- Create a custom slide layout by clicking the Insert Layout button in the Edit Master group on the Slide Master tab. Rename the custom slide layout with the Rename button in the Edit Master group.

- Insert a placeholder in a slide layout or custom slide layout by clicking the Insert Placeholder button arrow in the Master Layout group on the Slide Master tab and then clicking the placeholder at the drop-down list.

- In Slide Master view, create a custom prompt by selecting generic text in a placeholder and then typing the specific text.

- Click the Insert Slide Master button in Slide Master view to insert a new slide master and associated slide layouts. A new slide master can also be inserted by applying a design theme using the Themes button in the Edit Theme group on the Slide Master tab.

- Save a presentation as a template by changing the *Save as type* option at the Save As dialog box to *PowerPoint Template*.

- Open a presentation based on a template by clicking the *Personal* option at the New backstage area and then double-clicking the template thumbnail.

- Customize handouts with options on the Handout Master tab. Display this tab by clicking the Handout Master button on the View tab.

- Customize notes pages with options on the Notes Master tab. Display this tab by clicking the Notes Master button on the View tab.

- In addition to changing views, use buttons on the View tab to show/hide the ruler and/or gridlines; change the zoom; view slides in color, grayscale, or black and white; and work with multiple windows.

- Action buttons are drawn objects in a slide that have an attached routine, such as displaying the next slide, the first slide, a website, or another PowerPoint presentation.

- Create an action button by clicking the Insert tab, clicking the Shapes button, clicking the specific button at the drop-down list, and then clicking or dragging in the slide to create the button.

Chapter 6 | Using Slide Masters and Action Buttons

- Apply an action to text or an object in a slide by selecting the text or object, clicking the Insert tab, and then clicking the Action button.
- Use options at the Insert Hyperlink dialog box to create a hyperlink to a web page, another presentation, a location within a presentation, a new presentation, or to an email.
- A hyperlink can be created using a graphic and can be modified, edited, or removed.
- Use the Zoom feature to insert linked slide thumbnails in a presentation for back and forth movement between different slides or sections.
- To use the Zoom feature, click the Insert tab, click the Zoom button in the Links group, and then choose an option at the drop-down list. Use options at the drop-down list to create an interactive table of contents, link to a specific slide in the presentation, and link to a specific section in a presentation.
- When a linked slide thumbnail is inserted in a slide, the Zoom Tools Format tab containing options for formatting a linked slide thumbnail is active.

Commands Review

FEATURE	RIBBON TAB, GROUP/OPTION	BUTTON	KEYBOARD SHORTCUT
action buttons	Insert, Illustrations		
Action Settings dialog box	Insert, Links		
arrange all windows	View, Window		
cascade windows	View, Window		
Handout Master view	View, Master Views		
Insert Hyperlink dialog box	Insert, Links		Ctrl + K
Move split	View, Window		
New backstage area	File, *New*		
Notes Master view	View, Master Views		
Slide Master view	View, Master Views		
Switch Windows	View, Window		
Zoom dialog box	View, Zoom		
Zoom to slide or section	Insert, Links		

Microsoft®

PowerPoint®
Applying Custom Animation and Setting Up Shows

CHAPTER

7

Performance Objectives

Upon successful completion of Chapter 7, you will be able to:

1. Apply, modify, and remove animations to text and objects
2. Apply a build effect to bulleted lists
3. Animate shapes, images, SmartArt, and chart elements
4. Draw motion paths
5. Apply an animation trigger
6. Set up a slide show to loop continuously
7. Set specific timings for slides and record narration
8. Hide and unhide slides
9. Use ink tools to draw and highlight on slides
10. Create, run, edit, and print a custom slide show
11. Insert and format 3D models
12. Apply the Morph transition effect
13. Insert and customize audio and video files
14. Create and insert a screen recording

Animation, or movement, can add visual appeal and interest to a slide show when used appropriately. PowerPoint provides a number of animation effects that can be applied to elements in a slide. In this chapter, you will learn how to apply animation effects, use ink tools on slides, insert 3D models, use the Morph slide transition, insert audio and video files, and make a screen recording to create dynamic presentations.

In some situations, you may want to prepare an automated slide show that runs on a continuous loop. A presentation can be customized to run continuously with a specific amount of time set for each slide to remain on the screen. A custom slide show can be created to present only specific slides in a presentation. In this chapter, you will learn how to prepare automated presentations and how to create and edit custom slide shows.

 Data Files

Before beginning chapter work, copy the PC7 folder to your storage medium and then make PC7 the active folder.

The online course includes additional training and assessment resources.

You will open a marketing presentation, apply animation effects to the title slide, and then apply animation effects in Slide Master view to the remaining slides. You will modify, reorder, and remove some of the animation effects and then apply custom animation effects, such as entrance and emphasis effects, to elements in slides.

Tutorial

Applying and Removing Animations

Applying and Removing Animations

Animate items such as text or objects in a slide to add visual interest to a slide show. PowerPoint includes a number of animations that can be applied to items in a slide and the animations can be modified to fit specific needs. For example, items in a slide may be animated to appear one at a time to help the audience focus on each topic or point as it is being presented. An animation can be applied and then customized to specify the direction from which items enter a slide and the rate of speed for the entrance. As a general rule, try not to overwhelm the audience with too much animation. The audience should remember the content of the slide show rather than the visual effects.

Quick Steps

Apply Animation
1. Click item.
2. Click Animations tab.
3. Click More Animations button.
4. Click animation at drop-down gallery.

To animate an item, click the item, click the Animations tab, click the More Animations button in the Animation group, and then click an animation option at the drop-down gallery. Once an animation is applied, animation effects can be specified using options in the Effect Options button drop-down gallery. Some of the animation effect options may include the direction from which the item appears and whether bulleted text or SmartArt appear as one object, all at once, or by paragraph or object.

 Effects Options

Use options in the Timing group on the Animations tab to specify when the animation starts on a slide, the duration of the animation, the delay between animations, and the order in which animations appear on the slide. To view the animation applied to a slide without running the slide show, click the Preview button on the Animations tab and the animation effect displays in the slide pane. When animation effects are applied to items in a slide, an animation icon (small shooting star) appears below the slide number in the slide thumbnails pane.

Hint You can animate text, objects, graphics, SmartArt diagrams, charts, hyperlinks, and sound.

 Preview

Whenever an animation is inserted or modified, PowerPoint automatically shows a preview of the animation in the slide pane. This preview feature can be turned off by clicking the Preview button arrow and then clicking *AutoPreview* at the drop-down list to remove the check mark.

1. Open **MarketPres** and then save it with the name **7-MarketPres**.
2. Make sure Slide 1 is active and then apply animations to the title and subtitle by completing the following steps:
   a. Click in the title *DOUGLAS CONSULTING*.
   b. Click the Animations tab.
   c. Click the *Fade* animation in the Animation group.

   d. Click in the subtitle *Marketing Report*.
   e. Click the *Fade* animation in the Animation group.
   f. Click the Preview button on the Animations tab to see the animation effects in the slide pane.
3. Apply animations to Slides 2 through 4 in Slide Master view by completing the following steps:
   a. Click the View tab and then click the Slide Master button in the Master Views group.
   b. Click the third slide master layout in the slide thumbnails pane (*Title and Content Layout*).
   c. Click in the text *Click to edit Master title style*.
   d. Click the Animations tab and then click the *Fly In* animation in the Animation group.
   e. Click the Effect Options button in the Animation group and then click *From Top* at the drop-down gallery.
   f. Click in the bulleted text *Click to edit Master text styles*.
   g. Click the *Fly In* animation in the Animation group.
   h. Click the Slide Master tab and then click the Close Master View button.

4. Make Slide 1 active and then run the slide show. Click the mouse button to advance items in slides and to move to the next slide. Notice how the bulleted text in Slides 2 through 4 displays one item at a time.
5. Save **7-MarketPres**.

To remove an animation effect from an item, click the item in the slide in the slide pane, click the Animations tab, and then click the *None* option in the Animation group. An animation effect can also be removed from an item by clicking the item in the slide pane, clicking the assigned animation number icon, and then pressing the Delete key. To apply a different animation to an item, make sure to delete any existing animations first. If the first animation is not deleted, both animations will be assigned to the item.

Activity 1b Removing Animations

1. With **7-MarketPres** open, make Slide 1 active and then remove the animation from the title and subtitle by completing the following steps:
   a. Click in the title *DOUGLAS CONSULTING*.
   b. Click the Animations tab.
   c. Click the *None* option in the Animation group.
   d. Click in the subtitle *Marketing Report*.
   e. Click the *None* option in the Animation group.

2. Remove the animation effects for Slides 2 through 4 by completing the following steps:
   a. Click the View tab and then click the Slide Master button in the Master Views group.
   b. Click the third slide master layout in the slide thumbnails pane (*Title and Content Layout*).
   c. Click in the text *Click to edit Master title style*.
   d. Click the Animations tab and then click the *None* option in the Animation group.
   e. Click in the text *Click to edit Master text styles*.
   f. Click the *None* option in the Animation group.
   g. Click the Slide Master tab and then click the Close Master View button.
3. Make Slide 1 active and then run the slide show.
4. Save **7-MarketPres**.

Modifying
Animations

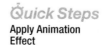

Q̌uick Steps

Apply Animation Effect
1. Click item.
2. Click Animations tab.
3. Click Add Animation button.
4. Click animation effect.

Applying Animation Effects

The Add Animation button in the Advanced Animation group on the Animations tab provides four types of animation effects that can be applied to an item. An effect can be applied that specifies how an item enters and exits the slide, an emphasis effect can be applied to an item, and a motion path can be created that will dictate the specific pattern for an item to move on, or even off, the slide.

To apply an entrance effect to an item, click the Add Animation button in the Advanced Animation group and then click the animation effect in the *Entrance* section of the drop-down gallery. Customize the entrance effect by clicking the Effect Options button in the Animation group and then clicking the specific

Add Animation

Quick Steps

Apply Effects with Animation Painter
1. Click item.
2. Apply animation effect.
3. Click item with animation effect.
4. Double-click Animation Painter button.
5. Click each item to apply the animation effect.
6. Click Animation Painter button to deactivate it.

 Animation Painter

entrance effect. Additional entrance effects are available at the Add Entrance Effect dialog box. Display this dialog box by clicking the Add Animation button and then clicking *More Entrance Effects* at the drop-down gallery. Complete similar steps to apply an exit effect and an emphasis effect. Display additional emphasis effects by clicking the Add Animation button and then clicking *More Emphasis Effects*. Display additional exit effects by clicking the Add Animation button and then clicking *More Exit Effects*.

Applying Animations with Animation Painter

An animation that has been applied to one item in a slide can also be applied to other items in the presentation with the Animation Painter. To use the Animation Painter, apply an animation to an item, position the insertion point in the animated item, and then double-click the Animation Painter button in the Advanced Animation group on the Animations tab. Using the mouse, select or click each additional item in the presentation that should have the same animation. After applying the animation to the items in the presentation, click the Animation Painter button to deactivate it. To apply animation to only one other item in a presentation, click the Animation Painter button once. The first time an item is selected or clicked, the animation is applied and the Animation Painter is deactivated.

Activity 1c **Applying Animation Effects**   Part 3 of 6

1. With **7-MarketPres** open, apply an animation effect to the title and subtitle in Slide 1 by completing the following steps:
   a. Make Slide 1 active.
   b. Click in the title *DOUGLAS CONSULTING*.
   c. Click the Animations tab.
   d. Click the Add Animation button in the Advanced Animation group and then click the *Wipe* animation in the *Entrance* section of the drop-down gallery.

e. Click the Effect Options button in the Animation group and then click *From Top* at the drop-down gallery.

f. Click in the subtitle *Marketing Report*.

g. Click the Add Animation button and then click the *Zoom* animation in the *Entrance* section.

2. Apply an animation effect to the titles in Slides 2 through 4 by completing the following steps:

a. Click the View tab and then click the Slide Master button in the Master Views group.

b. Click the third slide master layout in the slide thumbnails pane (*Title and Content Layout*).

c. Click in the text *Click to edit Master title style*.

d. Click the Animations tab, click the Add Animation button in the Advanced Animation group, and then click the *More Emphasis Effects* option at the drop-down gallery.

e. At the Add Emphasis Effect dialog box, click the *Grow With Color* option in the *Moderate* section.

f. Click OK to close the dialog box.

g. Click the Slide Master tab and then click the Close Master View button.

3. Apply an animation effect to the bulleted text in Slide 2 and then use the Animation Painter to apply the animation effect to Slides 3 and 4 by completing the following steps:

a. Make Slide 2 active.

b. Click in the bulleted text to make the placeholder active.

c. Click the Animations tab, click the Add Animation button, and then click the *Split* animation in the *Entrance* section.

d. Click in the bulleted text.

e. Double-click the Animation Painter button in the Advanced Animation group.

f. Make Slide 3 active.

g. Click in the bulleted text. (The mouse pointer displays as an arrow with a paintbrush attached. The animations are applied to all four bulleted items.)

h. Make Slide 4 active and then click in the bulleted text.

i. Click the Animation Painter button to deactivate it.

4. Click the Preview button on the Animations tab to view the animation effects.

5. Run the slide show by clicking the Start From Beginning button on the Quick Access Toolbar. Click the mouse button to advance slide elements and to move to the next slide.

6. Save **7-MarketPres**.

Modifying Animation Effects

An animation effect applied to an item can be modified with options in the Timing group on the Animations tab. Use the *Start* option box drop-down list to specify when the item should be inserted in the slide. Generally, items display in a slide when the mouse button is clicked. Click the *Start* option box arrow and then click *With Previous* or *With Next* at the drop-down list to make the item appear in the slide with the previous or next item.

Use the *Duration* measurement box to specify the number of seconds an animation takes to play. Click the *Duration* measurement box up arrow to increase the duration of the animation and click the down arrow to decrease the duration. The duration time can also be changed by selecting the current time in the *Duration* measurement box and then typing a specific time.

Use the *Delay* measurement box to specify the number of seconds an animation delays before playing after the previous animation has finished playing. Click the *Delay* measurement box up arrow to increase the delay time and click the down arrow to decrease the time. The delay time can also be changed by selecting the current time in the *Delay* measurement box and then typing a specific time.

Reordering Items

Quick Steps

Reorder Animation Item
1. Click item in slide.
2. Click Move Earlier button or Move Later button.

When an animation effect is applied to an item, an animation number appears next to the item in the slide in the slide pane. This number indicates the order in which the item will display in the slide. When more than one item displays in the slide, the order can be changed with options in the *Reorder Animation* section of the Timing group on the Animations tab. Click the Move Earlier button to move an item before another item or click the Move Later button to move an item after another item.

Activity 1d **Removing, Modifying, and Reordering Animation Effects**   Part 4 of 6

1. With **7-MarketPres** open, make Slide 1 active.
2. Modify the start setting for the animation effect you applied to the slide title by completing the following steps:
   a. Click in the title placeholder.

b. Click the *Start* option box arrow in the Timing group on the Animations tab.

c. Click *With Previous* at the drop-down list. (The title animation effect will begin as soon as the slide displays, without you having to click the mouse button. Notice that the number *1* to the left of the item in the slide changes to a *0*.)

3. Change the animation effect applied to the subtitle and modify the new animation effect by completing the following steps:

a. Click in the subtitle *Marketing Report*.

b. Click the More Animations button in the Animation group and then click the *None* option in the drop-down gallery.

c. Click the Add Animation button in the Advanced Animation group and then click the *Grow/Shrink* animation in the *Emphasis* section.

d. Click the *Start* option box arrow and then click *With Previous* at the drop-down list.

e. Click the *Duration* measurement box down arrow four times. (This displays *01.00* in the measurement box.)

4. Remove animations from slide titles in Slide Master view by completing the following steps:

a. Click the View tab and then click the Slide Master button in the Master Views group.

b. Click the third slide master layout in the slide thumbnails pane (*Title and Content Layout*).

c. Click in the text *Click to edit Master title style*.

d. Click the Animations tab.

e. Click the More Animations button in the Animation group and then click the *None* option.

f. Click the Slide Master tab and then click the Close Master View button.

5. Remove animations from the bulleted text in Slides 2 through 4 by completing the following steps:

a. Make Slide 2 active.

b. Click in the bulleted text.

c. Click the Animations tab and then click the *None* option in the Animation group.

d. Make Slide 3 active, click in the bulleted text, and then click the *None* option in the Animation group.

e. Make Slide 4 active, click in the bulleted text, and then click the *None* option in the Animation group.

6. Make Slide 2 active and then apply and customize animation effects by completing the following steps:

a. Click in the title *Department Reports*.

b. Click the Add Animation button in the Advanced Animation group and then click the *More Entrance Effects* option at the drop-down gallery.

c. At the Add Entrance Effect dialog box, scroll down the list box and then click *Spiral In* in the *Exciting* section.

d. Click OK to close the dialog box.

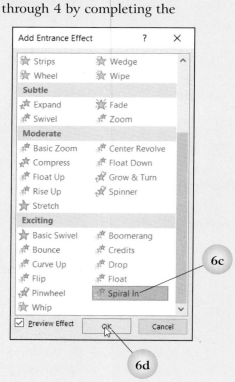

e. Click the bulleted text.

f. Click the Add Animation button and then click the *Zoom* animation in the *Entrance* section.

g. Click the image in the slide.

h. Click the Add Animation button and then click the *Zoom* animation in the *Entrance* section.

7. Click the Preview button at the left side of the Animations tab to view the animation effects.

8. After viewing the animation effects, you decide that you want the image to animate before the bulleted text and you want the animation effects to begin with the previous animation (instead of with a mouse click). With Slide 2 active, complete the following steps:

a. Click the image. (The number 5 will display outside the upper left corner of the image placeholder because the image is the fifth item to enter the slide.)

b. Click the Move Earlier button in the *Reorder Animation* section of the Timing group. (The number to the left of the image changes to *2* because you moved the image animation before the three bulleted items.)

c. Click the *Start* option box arrow in the Timing group and then click *With Previous* at the drop-down list.

d. Click in the title *Department Reports*.

e. Click the *Start* option box arrow and then click *With Previous* at the drop-down list.

9. Make Slide 3 active and then apply the same animation effects you applied in Slide 2. (Do this by completing steps similar to those in Steps 6a through 6h and Steps 8a through 8e.)

10. Make Slide 4 active and then apply the same animation effects you applied in Slide 2. (Do this by completing steps similar to those in Steps 6a through 6f and Steps 8d through 8e.)

11. Make Slide 1 active and then run the slide show.

12. Save **7-MarketPres**.

Customizing Animation Effects at the Animation Pane

Quick Steps

Reorder Animation Items

1. Click item in Animation Pane.
2. Click Move Earlier button or Move Later button.

Remove Animation Effect

1. Click item in Animation Pane.
2. Click down arrow.
3. Click *Remove*.

 Animation Pane

The Animation Pane provides options for customizing and modifying animation effects. Display the Animation Pane, shown in Figure 7.1, by clicking the Animation Pane button in the Advanced Animation group on the Animations tab. When an animation is applied to an item, the item name or description is listed in the Animation Pane. Hover the mouse pointer over an item and a description of the animation effect applied to the item displays in a box below the item. Click the down arrow at the right side of an item in the Animation Pane and a drop-down list displays with options for customizing or removing the animation effect.

When an effect is applied to an item, the item name and/or description is listed in the Animation Pane preceded by a number. This number indicates the order in which the item will appear in the slide. When more than one item is listed in the Animation Pane, the order of an item can be changed by clicking the item and then clicking the Move Earlier or Move Later button at the top of the Animation Pane.

Figure 7.1 Animation Pane

Click the Play All button (the name of the button varies) to preview the animation effects applied to the current slide.

Use these buttons to change the order of animation effects.

When an animation effect is applied to an item, the item is listed in this section.

All animation effects applied to a slide can be played by clicking the Play All button at the top of the pane. (The name of the button varies depending on the contents of the Animation Pane and what is selected in the pane.) The animation effects play in the slide in the slide pane and a time indicator displays along the bottom of the Animation Pane with a vertical line indicating the progression of time (in seconds). Play only the selected animation effect in the Animation Pane by clicking the animation effect in the pane and then clicking the Play From button at the top of the pane.

Activity 1e Removing, Customizing, and Reordering Animation Effects in the Animation Pane

Part 5 of 6

1. With **7-MarketPres** open, make Slide 1 active.
2. Click in the title *DOUGLAS CONSULTING*, click the Animations tab, and then click the *None* option in the Animation group.
3. With the title placeholder selected, click the Add Animation button in the Advanced Animation group and then click the *Grow & Turn* animation in the *Entrance* section.
4. Click the *Duration* measurement box down arrow two times. (This displays *00.50* in the measurement box.)
5. Click in the subtitle *Marketing Report*, click the More Animations button in the Animation group, and then click the *None* option.
6. With the subtitle placeholder selected, click the Add Animation button in the Advanced Animation group and then click the *Grow & Turn* animation in the *Entrance* section.
7. Click the *Duration* measurement box down arrow two times. (This displays *00.50* in the measurement box.)

8. Modify the start setting for the slide title animation effect in the Animation Pane by completing the following steps:
   a. Click the Animation Pane button in the Advanced Animation group on the Animations tab. (This displays the Animation Pane at the right side of the screen.)

8a

   b. Click the Title 1 item in the Animation Pane.
   c. Click the down arrow at the right side of the item and then click *Start With Previous* at the drop-down list.

8c

9. Remove animations from slides using the Animation Pane by completing the following steps:
   a. Make Slide 2 active.
   b. Click the Picture 3 item in the Animation Pane.
   c. Click the down arrow at the right side of the item and then click *Remove* at the drop-down list.
   d. Click the image in the slide pane, click the Add Animation button, and then click the *Pulse* animation in the *Emphasis* section.

9c

10. Make Slide 3 active and then complete steps similar to those in Steps 9b through 9d to remove the animation effect from the image and add the *Pulse* emphasis animation effect.

11. With the Picture 3 image selected in the Animation Pane, click the Play From button at the top of the pane to view the animation effect applied to the image.

12. Play all animation effects applied to the slide by clicking in the blank area below the animation effects in the Animation Pane (this deselects the Picture 3 animation effect) and then click the Play All button (previously the Play From button) at the top of the pane.

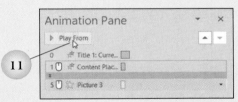

11

13. After viewing the animation effect, you decide that you want the image to animate before the title and bulleted text and you want the animation effect to begin with the previous animation. With Slide 3 active, complete the following steps:
   a. Click the Picture 3 item in the Animation Pane.
   b. Click the up arrow at the top of the Animation pane two times. (This moves the Picture 3 item above the Title 1 and the Content Placeholder items.)

   13b

   c. Click the down arrow at the right of the Picture 3 item and then click *Start With Previous* at the drop-down list.

14. Reorder animation effects in Slide 2 to match the changes made to Slide 3.
15. Close the Animation Pane.
16. Make Slide 1 active and then run the slide show.
17. Save **7-MarketPres**.

Applying Sound to Animations

Enhance an animation by adding a sound to the animation. To apply a sound, click the Animation Pane button to display the Animation Pane, click the animated item in the Animation Pane, click the down arrow at the right of the item, and then click *Effect Options* at the drop-down list. At the dialog box (the name of the dialog box varies depending on the animation applied) with the Effect tab selected, click the *Sound* option box arrow and then click a sound at the drop-down list. Sound can also be added to an animation by clicking the animated item in the slide in the slide pane, clicking the Animation group dialog box launcher, and then choosing the sound effect at the dialog box.

Applying a Build Effect

Hint You can group text (in a bulleted text placeholder) at the effect options dialog box by first, second, third, fourth, or fifth levels.

In Activity 1a, a build effect was applied to bulleted text in a slide. A build displays important points on a slide one point at a time, keeping the audience's attention focused on the current point. A build can be further customized by causing a previous point to dim when the next point displays. To customize a build, click the Animation Pane button to display the Animation Pane, click the bulleted item in the Animation Pane, click the down arrow at the right side of the item, and then click *Effect Options* at the drop-down list. At the effect options dialog box (the name of the dialog box will vary) with the Effect tab selected, choose a color option with the *After animation* option box.

Activity 1f Applying Sound and a Build to Animations

1. With **7-MarketPres** open, make Slide 2 active and then apply sound and a build to the bulleted text by completing the following steps:
   a. Click in the bulleted text.
   b. Open the Animation Pane by clicking the Animation Pane button in the Advanced Animation group on the Animations tab.
   c. Click the down arrow at the right side of the Content Placeholder item in the Animation Pane and then click *Effect Options* at the drop-down list.
   d. At the Zoom dialog box, make sure the Effect tab is selected, click the *Sound* option box arrow, scroll down the list box, and then click the *Chime* option.
   e. Click the *After animation* option box arrow and then click the light gray color (last option).
   f. Click OK to close the dialog box.
2. Click in the bulleted text in the slide.
3. Double-click the Animation Painter button.
4. Make Slide 3 active and then click in the bulleted text.
5. Make Slide 4 active and then click in the bulleted text.
6. Click the Animation Painter button to deactivate it.
7. Close the Animation Pane.
8. Make Slide 1 active and then run the slide show.
9. Save and then close **7-MarketPres**.

Activity 2   Apply Custom Animation Effects to Elements in Slides in an Online Learning Presentation   6 Parts

You will open an online learning presentation and then apply animation effects to shapes, an image, elements in SmartArt graphics, and elements in a chart. You will also draw a motion path in a slide and insert an animation trigger.

Animating Shapes and Images

Animate individual shapes or objects, such as images, in a slide in the same way a title, text, or objects in a content placeholder are animated. More than one shape can be selected and then the same animation effects can be applied to the shapes. To select more than one shape, click the first shape, press and hold down the Shift key, click any additional shapes, and then release the Shift key.

Activity 2a   Animating Shapes and an Image   Part 1 of 6

1. Open **OLLearn** and then save it with the name **7-OLLearn**.
2. Make Slide 8 active (this slide contains one large object with three smaller objects hidden behind it) and then animate objects and apply exit effects by completing the following steps:
   a. Click the Animations tab and then click the Animation Pane button in the Advanced Animation group.
   b. Click the large green shape in the slide.
   c. Click the Add Animation button in the Advanced Animation group and then click the *More Exit Effects* option.
   d. At the Add Exit Effect dialog box, click the *Spiral Out* option in the *Exciting* section. (You will need to scroll down the list to see this option.) Watch the animation effect in the slide and then click OK.

   e. Click the large green shape to select it and then drag it up the slide to make a portion of the three shapes behind it visible.
   f. Click the small shape at the left, click the Add Animation button, and then click the *More Entrance Effects* option.
   g. At the Add Entrance Effect dialog box, click *Spinner* in the *Moderate* section, and then click OK.

   h. Select the middle shape, press and hold down the Shift key, click the shape at the right, and then release the Shift key. (This selects both shapes.)
   i. Click the Add Animation button and then click the *More Entrance Effects* option.
   j. At the Add Entrance Effect dialog box, click *Spinner* in the *Moderate* section and then click OK. (Notice that the two objects are numbered *3* in the Animation Pane and are set to enter the slide at the same time. You will change this in the next step.)

k. Click the small shape at the right, click the *Start* option box arrow in the Timing group, and then click *On Click* at the drop-down list.

l. Apply emphasis to the middle shape by clicking the middle shape, clicking the Add Animation button, and then clicking the *Grow/Shrink* option in the *Emphasis* section of the drop-down gallery.

m. Click the large green shape to select it and then reposition it over the three smaller shapes.

n. Click the Preview button to play the animation effects in the slide.

3. Make Slide 9 active and apply and customize animation effects and change animation order by completing the following steps:

a. Click in the text *Online learning continues to evolve!* (this selects the text box), click the Add Animation button, and then click *Grow & Turn* in the *Entrance* section.

b. Click in the text *Stay tuned!* (this selects the text box), click the Add Animation button, and then click the *Swivel* option in the *Entrance* section.

c. Click the image to select it.

d. Click the Add Animation button and then click the *Spin* animation in the *Emphasis* section.

e. Click the Effect Options button in the Animation group and then click *Two Spins* at the drop-down gallery.

f. Click the *Duration* measurement box down arrow until *01.00* displays.

g. Click the Move Earlier button in the Timing group. This moves the image item in the list box above the *Stay tuned!* text box item.

h. Click the Preview button to play the animation effects in the slide.

4. Save **7-OLLearn**.

Animating a SmartArt Graphic

Animation effects can be applied to a SmartArt graphic and then customized to specify whether the entire SmartArt graphic displays at once or the individual elements in the graphic display one at a time. Specify a sequence for displaying elements in a SmartArt graphic with the Effect Options button in the Animation group.

When an animation effect is applied to a SmartArt graphic, animations can be applied to individual elements in the graphic. To do this, click the Effect Options button and then click the *One by One* option at the drop-down list. Display the Animation Pane and then expand the list of SmartArt graphic objects by clicking the small double arrows in the gray shaded box below the item in the Animation Pane. Click an individual item in the Animation Pane and then click an animation in the Animation group.

1. With **7-OLLearn** open, make Slide 4 active and then animate objects in the SmartArt graphic by completing the following steps:
    a. Click the shape in the SmartArt graphic containing the word *Convenient*. (Make sure white sizing handles display around the shape. White sizing handles will also display around the entire SmartArt graphic.)
    b. With the Animations tab active, click the *Float In* animation in the Animation group.
    c. Click the Effect Options button in the Animation group and then click *One by One* at the drop-down gallery. (This will allow you to apply different effects to the objects in the SmartArt graphic.)
    d. Click the Animation Pane button in the Advanced Animation group to display the Animation Pane, if necessary.
    e. Expand the list of SmartArt graphic objects in the Animation Pane by clicking the small double arrows in the gray shaded box below the Content Placeholder item. (This expands the list to show four items.)
    f. Click the item in the Animation Pane that begins with the number *2*.
    g. Click the More Animations button in the Animation group and then click the *Grow & Turn* animation in the *Entrance* section.
    h. Click the item in the Animation Pane that begins with the number *4*.
    i. Click the More Animations button in the Animation group and then click the *Grow & Turn* animation in the *Entrance* section.
2. Click the Preview button on the Animations tab to view the animation effects applied to the SmartArt graphic objects.
3. Make Slide 6 active and then apply animation effects by completing the following steps:
    a. Click the shape in the SmartArt graphic containing the text *Multi-Media*. (Make sure white sizing handles display around the shape. White sizing handles will also display around the entire SmartArt graphic.)
    b. Click the Add Animation button and then click the *More Entrance Effects* option.
    c. At the Add Entrance Effect dialog box, click the *Circle* option in the *Basic* section.
    d. Click OK to close the dialog box.
    e. Click the Effect Options button in the Animation group and then click *Out* in the *Direction* section of the drop-down list.
    f. Click the Effect Options button again and then click *One by One* in the *Sequence* section of the drop-down list.
    g. Click the *Duration* measurement box down arrow until *00.50* displays.
4. Click the Play Selected button at the top of the Animation Pane to view the animation effects applied to the SmartArt graphic objects.
5. Save **7-OLLearn**.

Animating a Chart

Like a SmartArt graphic, a chart or elements in a chart can be animated to create a more dramatic effect as data is presented. A chart can be animated to bring in one element at a time, allowing the presenter to discuss each piece of data as it displays. As with SmartArt graphics, animation can be applied to the entire chart, to individual chart elements, or to a series or category within the chart. For example, a column chart can be animated to have one column or series of columns appear at a time.

Activity 2c **Animating Elements in a Chart**   Part 3 of 6

1. With **7-OLLearn** open, make Slide 3 active and then animate chart elements by completing the following steps:
    a. Click in the chart placeholder to select the chart. (Make sure you do not have a chart element selected and that the Animations tab is active.)
    b. Click the Add Animation button and then click the *More Entrance Effects* option.
    c. At the Add Entrance Effect dialog box, click the *Dissolve In* option in the *Basic* section.
    d. Click OK to close the dialog box.
    e. In the Animation Pane, click the down arrow at the right of the Content Placeholder item in the list box, and then click *Effect Options* at the drop-down list.
    f. At the Dissolve In dialog box, click the *Sound* option box arrow, scroll down the drop-down list, and then click the *Click* option.
    g. Click the Timing tab.
    h. Click the *Duration* option box arrow and then click *1 seconds (Fast)* at the drop-down list.
    i. Click the Chart Animation tab.
    j. Click the *Group chart* option box arrow and then click *By Category* at the drop-down list.

    k. Click OK to close the dialog box.
2. Make Slide 7 active and then apply a build animation effect to the bulleted text by completing the following steps:
    a. Click in the bulleted text.
    b. Click the *Fly In* animation in the Animation group on the Animations tab.

c. Click the Effect Options button and then click *From Right* at the drop-down gallery.

d. Make sure the Animation Pane displays, click the down arrow at the right of the Content Placeholder item in the pane, and then click *Effect Options* at the drop-down list.

e. At the Fly In dialog box, make sure the Effect tab is selected, click the *After animation* option box arrow, and then click the light green color (second from the right).

f. Click OK to close the dialog box.

3. Save **7-OLLearn**.

Creating a Motion Path

Quick Steps

Insert Motion Path
1. Click item in slide.
2. Click Animations tab.
3. Click Add Animation button.
4. Click path in *Motion Paths* section.

Draw Motion Path
1. Click item in slide.
2. Click Animations tab.
3. Click Add Animation button.
4. Click *Custom Path* in *Motion Paths* section.
5. Drag in slide to create path.
6. Double-click mouse button.

Create a motion path for an object to cause it to move in a certain way when running the slide show. To create a motion path, click the object and then click the Add Animation button in the Advanced Animation group. In the *Motion Paths* section of the drop-down gallery, click an option to specify whether the object will move in a straight line, arc, turn, shape, or loop.

To further customize the direction or type of movement, click the Effect Options button in the Animation group. For example, to move an item in a straight line to the left, click the Add Animation button and then click the *Lines* option in the *Motion Paths* section of the drop-down gallery. Click the Effect Options button in the Animation group and then click *Left* at the drop-down gallery.

Other options for a motion path can be found by clicking the Add Animation button and then clicking *More Motion Paths* at the drop-down gallery. To draw a motion path freehand, select the object in the slide, click the Add Animation button, and then click the *Custom Path* option in the *Motion Paths* section of the drop-down gallery. Using the mouse, drag in the slide to create the path. When the path is completed, double-click the mouse button.

1. With **7-OLLearn** open, make Slide 1 active and then apply a motion path to the image by completing the following steps:
   a. Click the image.
   b. Click the Add Animation button and then click the *More Motion Paths* option.
   c. At the Add Motion Path dialog box, scroll down the list box and then click the *Spiral Right* option in the *Lines Curves* section.
   d. Click OK to close the dialog box.
   e. Click the *Start* option box arrow in the Timing group and then click *With Previous* at the drop-down list.
   f. Click the *Duration* measurement box up arrow in the Timing group until *03.00* displays in the measurement box.
   g. Click the *Delay* measurement box up arrow in the Timing group until *01.00* displays in the measurement box.
   h. Click outside the image to deselect it.
2. Make Slide 5 active and then animate the star on the map by completing the following steps:
   a. Click the star object in the slide below the heading *North America*.
   b. Click the Add Animation button, scroll down the drop-down gallery, and then click the *Custom Path* option in the *Motion Paths* section.
   c. Position the mouse pointer (displays as crosshairs) on the star, click and hold down the left mouse button, drag a path through each of the five locations on the map ending back in the original location in the star object, release the mouse button, and then double-click the mouse button.
3. Run the slide show and click the mouse to advance slides and elements on slides as needed.
4. Save **7-OLLearn**.

Applying a Trigger

Use the Trigger button in the Advanced Animation group to make an animation effect occur by clicking an item on the slide during a slide show. A trigger creates a link between two items and provides additional information about that item. For example, a trigger can be applied to a bulleted item to cause another item, such as a picture or chart, to appear. When running the slide show, hover the mouse pointer over the item containing the trigger until the mouse pointer displays as a hand and then click the mouse button to display the trigger item.

The advantage to applying a trigger to an item is that the presenter can control whether or not the item displays when running the slide show. For example, suppose a presentation contains product sales information and the presenter wants to provide additional specific sales data to one group but not another. When presenting to the group that should view the additional sales data, the trigger can be clicked to display the data. When presenting to the other group, the trigger is not clicked, and the sales data remains hidden.

To insert a trigger, apply an animation effect to both items, display the Animation Pane, and then click the item that will become the trigger. Click the Trigger button in the Advanced Animation group, point to *On Click of*, and then click the item to be triggered at the side menu.

 Trigger

Activity 2e Inserting Triggers

1. With **7-OLLearn** open, make Slide 2 active.
2. Apply animation effects to the text and charts by completing the following steps:
   a. Click in the bulleted text.
   b. Click the Animations tab.
   c. Click the *Split* animation in the Animation group.
   d. Select the pie chart at the left. (To do this, click in the chart and then click within the chart border but not on a specific item in the chart. Make sure the chart is selected and not an individual chart element.)
   e. Click the *Split* animation in the Animation group.
   f. Select the middle pie chart and then click the *Split* animation. (Make sure you select the chart and not a chart element.)
   g. Select the pie chart at the right and then click the *Split* animation. (Make sure you select the chart and not a chart element.)
3. Make sure the Animation Pane displays.
4. Apply a trigger to the first bulleted item that, when clicked, will display the chart at the left by completing the following steps:
   a. Click the *Chart 5* item in the Animation Pane.
   b. Click the Trigger button in the Advanced Animation group, point to *On Click of*, and then click *Content Placeholder 2* at the side menu.

   c. Click the *Chart 6* item in the Animation Pane, click the Trigger button, point to *On Click of*, and then click *Content Placeholder 2* at the side menu.
   d. Click the *Chart 7* item in the Animation Pane, click the Trigger button, point to *On Click of*, and then click *Content Placeholder 2* at the side menu.
5. Close the Animation Pane.

6. Run the slide show by completing the following steps:
   a. Run the slide show from the beginning and when you get to Slide 2, click the mouse button until the first bulleted item displays (the item that begins with *Traditional*).
   b. Hover your mouse pointer over the bulleted text until the pointer turns into a hand and then click the left mouse button. (This displays the first chart.)

   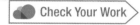

   c. Position the mouse pointer in the white background of the slide and then click the left mouse button to display the second bulleted item (the item that begins with *Hybrid*).
   d. Hover your mouse pointer over the text in the second bulleted item until the pointer turns into a hand and then click the left mouse button. (This displays the middle chart.)
   e. Position the mouse pointer in the white background of the slide and then click the left mouse button to display the third bulleted item (the item that begins with *Internet*).
   f. Hover your mouse pointer over the text in the third bulleted item until the pointer turns into a hand and then click the left mouse button. (This displays the third chart.)
   g. Continue running the remaining slides in the slide show.
7. Save **7-OLLearn**.
8. Print the presentation as a handout with all nine slides displayed horizontally on the page.

Check Your Work

Setting Up a Slide Show

Control how the slide show is played with options at the Set Up Show dialog box, shown in Figure 7.2. At the dialog box, choose options for how a slide show is played, such as whether it will run with or without animation and narration, whether slides should advance manually or with automatic timing, and which monitor and resolution should be used. Click the Slide Show tab and then click the Set Up Slide Show button to display the dialog box. Other options for setting up a slide show can be found on the Slide Show tab as well as the Transitions tab.

Figure 7.2 Set Up Show Dialog Box

Click this option to set up the slide show on a continuous loop.

Click this option to present the slide show without narration.

Click this option to present the slide show without animation effects.

Quick Steps

Run Slide Show without Animation
1. Click Slide Show tab.
2. Click Set Up Slide Show button.
3. Click *Show without animation.*
4. Click OK.

Running a Slide Show without Animation

A slide show can be run without the animations. To do this, display the Set Up Show dialog box, click the *Show without animation* check box to insert a check mark, and then click OK. Changes made to the Set Up Show dialog box are saved with the presentation.

Activity 2f **Running a Slide Show without Animation**   Part 6 of 6

1. With **7-OLLearn** open, specify that you want to run the slide show without animation by completing the following steps:
   a. Click the Slide Show tab.
   b. Click the Set Up Slide Show button in the Set Up group.
   c. At the Set Up Show dialog box, click the *Show without animation* check box to insert a check mark.
   d. Click OK to close the dialog box.
2. Run the slide show to see that the animation effects do not play.
3. Specify that you want the slide show to run with animations by completing the following steps:
   a. Click the Set Up Slide Show button on the Slide Show tab.
   b. At the Set Up Show dialog box, click the *Show without animation* check box to remove the check mark and then click OK.
4. Save and then close **7-OLLearn**.

Activity 3 **Prepare a Self-Running Adventure Slide Show,**   **7 Parts**
Use Ink Tools, and Create Custom Slide Shows

You will open a travel tour presentation and then customize it to be an automated slide show set on a continuous loop. You will also record slide narrations, hide slides, use Presenter view when running the slide show, present the slide show online, use ink tools, and create and edit custom slide shows.

Looping a Slide Show Continuously

Quick Steps

Loop Slide Show Continuously
1. Click Slide Show tab.
2. Click Set Up Slide Show button.
3. Click *Loop continuously until 'Esc'.*
4. Click OK.

Setting Up a Slide Show to Loop Continuously

In some situations, such as a trade show or convention, a slide show can be set to run and also restart automatically. An automated slide show is set up on a continuous loop and does not require someone to advance the slides or restart the slide show. To design an automated slide show, display the Set Up Show dialog box and then insert a check mark in the *Loop continuously until 'Esc'* option. With this option active, the slide show will continue running until the Esc key is pressed.

Hint Use an automated slide show to communicate information without a presenter.

---

1. Open **AdvTours** and then save it with the name **7-AdvTours**.
2. Insert slides by completing the following steps:
   a. Click below the last slide thumbnail in the slide thumbnails pane.
   b. Make sure the Home tab is selected, click the New Slide button arrow, and then click *Reuse Slides* at the drop-down list.
   c. At the Reuse Slides task pane, click the Browse button.
   d. At the Browse dialog box, navigate to your PC7 folder and then double-click *PeruTour*.
   e. Click each slide in the Reuse Slides task pane in order beginning with the top slide.
   f. Close the Reuse Slides task pane.
3. Apply a transition and transition sound and specify a time for automatically advancing slides by completing the following steps:
   a. Click the Transitions tab.
   b. Click the *On Mouse Click* check box in the Timing group to remove the check mark.
   c. Click the *After* check box to insert a check mark.
   d. Click the *After* measurement box up arrow until *00:05.00* displays.
   e. Click the *Fade* slide transition in the Transition to This Slide group.
   f. Click the *Sound* option box arrow in the Timing group and then click *Breeze* at the drop-down list.
   g. Click the Apply To All button.

4. Set up the slide show to run continuously by completing the following steps:
   a. Click the Slide Show tab.
   b. Click the Set Up Slide Show button in the Set Up group.
   c. At the Set Up Show dialog box, click the *Loop continuously until 'Esc'* check box to insert a check mark. (Make sure *All* is selected in the *Show slides* section and *Using timings, if present* is selected in the *Advance slides* section.)

   d. Click OK to close the dialog box.

5. Click Slide 1 to select it and then run the slide show. (The slides will advance automatically after five seconds.)
6. After viewing the slide show, press the Esc key.
7. Save **7-AdvTours**.

 Check Your Work

 Tutorial

Setting Timings for
Slide Show

Quick Steps

**Set Specific Times
for Slides**
1. Click Slide Show tab.
2. Click Rehearse
   Timings button.
3. Using Recording
   toolbar, specify time
   for each slide.
4. Click Yes.

 Rehearse
Timings

Hint Enter a
specific recording
time by selecting
the time in the *Slide
Time* measurement
box, typing the time,
and then pressing the
Enter key.

Setting Specific Times for Slides

Applying the same time to all slides is not very practical unless the same amount of text appears on every slide. In most cases, some slides should be left on the screen longer than others. To decide how long each slide should remain on view, rehearse the presentation and record the timing using the Recording toolbar, shown in Figure 7.3. Begin a rehearsal by clicking the Slide Show tab and then clicking the Rehearse Timings button in the Set Up group. The first slide in the presentation will be shown in Slide Show view with the Recording toolbar in the upper left corner of the slide.

When the slide displays on the screen, the timer on the Recording toolbar begins. Click the Next button on the Recording toolbar when the slide has displayed for the appropriate amount of time. To stop the timer, click the Pause button. Click the Resume Recording button to resume the timer. Use the Repeat button on the Recording toolbar to reset the time for the current slide. Continue through the presentation until the slide show is complete. After the last slide, a confirmation message displays showing the total time for the slide show. At this message, click Yes to approve the timing recorded during the rehearsal, or click No to delete the times. A slide show can be run without the rehearsed timings by clicking the Slide Show tab and then clicking the *Use Timings* check box to remove the check mark.

The recorded timing for each slide, along with the duration time of the transition, displays below each slide in Slide Sorter view. For example, if a presentation includes a transition duration time of 1:00, this time is added to the rehearsed timing. If 5 seconds is recorded for Slide 1, the time below the slide in Slide Sorter view will display as 00.06.

The slide times recorded for individual slides can be edited with the *After* measurement box in the Advance Slide section in the Timing group on the Transitions tab. Make the slide active in the slide pane or click the slide in the Slide Sorter view and then click the up or down arrow to increase or decrease the slide duration.

Figure 7.3 Recording Toolbar

1. With **7-AdvTours** open, remove the automatic times for slides by completing the following steps:
   a. Click the Transitions tab.
   b. Click the *After* measurement box down arrow in the Timing group until *00:00.00* displays.
   c. Click the *After* check box to remove the check mark.
   d. Click the Apply To All button in the Timing group.
   e. Click the Slide Show tab.
   f. Click the Set Up Slide Show button.
   g. At the Set Up Show dialog box, click the *Loop continuously until 'Esc'* check box to remove the check mark.
   h. Click OK to close the dialog box.
2. Set times for the slides to display during a slide show by completing the following steps:
   a. Make Slide 1 active.
   b. Click the Slide Show tab and then click the Rehearse Timings button in the Set Up group.
   c. The first slide displays in Slide Show view and the Recording toolbar displays. Wait until the time for the current slide reaches *:04* (4 seconds) and then click the Next button. (If you miss the time, click the Repeat button to reset the clock back to *0* for the current slide.)

   d. Set the times for the remaining slides as follows:

   > Slide 2 = 5 seconds
   > Slide 3 = 6 seconds
   > Slide 4 = 5 seconds
   > Slide 5 = 6 seconds
   > Slide 6 = 3 seconds
   > Slide 7 = 6 seconds
   > Slide 8 = 7 seconds
   > Slide 9 = 7 seconds

   e. After the last slide displays, click Yes at the message asking if you want to save the new slide timings. (The slide times may include one additional second for each slide.)
   f. If necessary, click the Normal button in the view area on the Status bar.
3. Click the Set Up Slide Show button to display the Set Up Show dialog box, click the *Loop continuously until 'Esc'* check box to insert a check mark, and then click OK to close the dialog box.
4. Run the slide show. (The slide show will start and run continuously.) Watch the slide show until it has started for the second time and then end the show by pressing the Esc key.
5. Save **7-AdvTours**.

Recording Narration

Quick Steps

Record Narration
1. Click Slide Show tab.
2. Click Record Slide Show button.
3. Click Start Recording button.
4. Narrate slides.

 Record Slide Show

A narration can be recorded for a presentation that will play when the slide show is running. To record a narration, first ensure that a microphone is connected to the computer, and then click the Record Slide Show button in the Set Up group on the Slide Show tab. This displays the presentation in Narration view, similar to what is shown in Figure 7.4. In Narration view, click the RECORD button in the upper left corner of the screen to record a narration of the slide. Stop, replay, or pause the recording with additional buttons in the upper left corner of the screen.

Narration view also includes options to view any slide notes, to clear the recordings on the current slide or all slides in the presentation, and to display microphone and camera options. Ink tools are available below the image of the slide. These ink tools can be used to emphasize points or objects in the slide during the narration and become part of the recording.

Click the Record Slide Show button arrow and a drop-down list displays with three options. Click the *Record from Beginning* option to begin recording the narration with the first slide in the presentation or click the *Record from Current Slide* option to begin recording the narration with the currently active slide. Position the mouse on the third option, *Clear*, and a side menu displays with options for clearing the narration and/or the timing on the current slide or all slides.

By default, recorded narration will play whenever a slide show is presented. To run the slide show without narration, display the Set Up Show dialog box and then click the *Show without narration* check box in the *Show options* section to insert a check mark.

Figure 7.4 Narration View

REPLAY button

Show/Hide NOTES button

Click the CLEAR button for options to clear recordings.

Click the SETTINGS button for microphone and camera options.

RECORD button

STOP button

Return to previous slide button

Accommodations

⬦ Lima, Plaza del Sol
⬦ Tarapoto, Miraflora Hotel
⬦ Chachapoyas, El Mundo Hotel & Suites
⬦ Chiclayo, Mariel Resort
⬦ Mancora, Del Bosque Plaza

slide timing

Use ink tools to emphasize points or objects during a recording.

Advance to next slide button

This is an optional activity. Before beginning the activity, check with your instructor to determine if you have a microphone available for recording.

1. With **7-AdvTours** open, save it with the name **7-AdvTours-NarrateSlide**.
2. Make Slide 9 active and then narrate the slide by completing the following steps:
   a. Click the Slide Show tab.
   b. Click the Record Slide Show button arrow in the Set Up group and then click *Record from Current Slide* at the drop-down list.
   c. In Narration view, click the RECORD button in the upper left corner of the screen.

   d. After PowerPoint counts down to begin the recording, speak the following text into the microphone: *Call Adventure Tours today to receive an additional ten percent savings when you book a Fiji or Peru tour.*
   e. Once you are finished speaking, click the STOP button in the upper left corner of the screen.
   f. Press the Esc key to return the presentation to Normal view.
3. Make Slide 1 active and then run the slide show. If your computer has speakers, you will hear your narration when Slide 9 displays. After viewing the slide show at least once, press the Esc key to end it.
4. Save and then close **7-AdvTours-NarrateSlide**.
5. Open **7-AdvTours** and then save it with the name **7-AdvTours-Narration**.
6. Remove the timings and the continuous loop option by completing the following steps:
   a. Click the Slide Show tab.
   b. Click the Record Slide Show button arrow, point to *Clear* at the drop-down list, and then click *Clear Timings on All Slides* at the side menu.
   c. Click the Set Up Slide Show button.
   d. At the Set Up Show dialog box, click the *Loop continuously until 'Esc'* check box to remove the check mark.
   e. Click OK to close the dialog box.

7. Make Slide 1 active and then record narration by completing the following steps:
   a. Click the Record Slide Show button in the Set Up group on the Slide Show tab.
   b. In Narration view, click the RECORD button and then either read the information or provide your own narrative of the slide and then click the left mouse button. (You can also click the Advance to next slide button at the right of the slide.)
   c. Continue narrating each slide (either using some of the information in the slides or creating your own narration). Try using the ink tools during the recording of at least two of the slides.
   d. After you narrate the last slide (about accommodations for the Peru tour), press the Esc key to end the presentation and return to Normal view.

8. Make Slide 1 active and then run the slide show. If your computer has speakers, you will hear your narration as the slide show runs.

9. Run the slide show without narration by completing the following steps:
   a. Click the Set Up Slide Show button in the Set Up group on the Slide Show tab.
   b. At the Set Up Show dialog box, click the *Show without narration* check box to insert a check mark.
   c. Click OK.
   d. Run the slide show beginning with Slide 1. (The slide show will still run automatically with the timing established when you were recording your narration but without the narration.)

10. Save and then close **7-AdvTours-Narration**.

Hiding Slides

Hiding and Unhiding Slides

Hide Slide

Quick Steps
Hide or Unhide Slide
1. Make slide active.
2. Click Slide Show tab.
3. Click Hide Slide button.

A slide show may be presented to a number of different groups or departments. In some situations the presenter may want to hide specific slides in a slide show depending on the audience. To hide a slide in a slide show, make the slide active, click the Slide Show tab, and then click the Hide Slide button in the Set Up group. When a slide is hidden, a slash appears over the slide number in the slide thumbnails pane and the slide in the slide thumbnails pane is dimmed. The slide is visible in the slide thumbnails pane in Normal view and also in the Slide Sorter view. To remove the hidden icon and redisplay the slide when running a slide show, click the slide in the slide thumbnails pane, click the Slide Show tab, and then click the Hide Slide button.

Managing Monitors

If two monitors are connected to the computer or PowerPoint is running on a laptop with dual-display capabilities, specify which monitor to use when running the slide show with the *Monitor* option in the Monitors group on the Slide Show tab. By default, PowerPoint automatically chooses a monitor to run the slide show. Change the monitor for viewing the slide show by clicking the *Monitor* option box arrow and then clicking the monitor at the drop-down list.

Using Presenter View

Insert a check mark in the *Use Presenter View* check box in the Monitors group on the Slide Show tab if PowerPoint is running on a computer with two monitors or on a laptop with dual-display capabilities. With this option active, the slide show will run in full-screen view on one monitor and in a special speaker view on the other, similar to what is shown in Figure 7.5. The buttons below the slide in Presenter view are the same buttons as those in Slide Show view. Other options in Presenter View include the display of slide durations, a preview of the next slide in the slide show, a notes pane, and navigation buttons.

Figure 7.5 Presenter View

Use this button to turn on the display of the taskbar to switch between programs.

Switch between Presenter View and Slide Show monitors or duplicate the slide show on both monitors with this button.

END SLIDE SHOW button

slide show duration

Pause button

Restart button

Use these buttons to mark in a slide show, view all slides, zoom into an element in a slide, change the screen to black, and show additional slide show options.

Previews the next slide in the slide show.

Displays any notes attached to a slide.

navigation buttons

Increase or decrease the notes text size with these buttons.

Activity 3d Hiding Slides and Using Presenter View

Part 4 of 7

1. Open **7-AdvTours**.
2. Remove the continuous loop option and remove timings by completing the following steps:
   a. Click the Slide Show tab.
   b. Click the Set Up Slide Show button.
   c. At the Set Up Show dialog box, click the *Loop continuously until 'Esc'* check box to remove the check mark.
   d. Click OK to close the dialog box.
   e. Click the Transitions tab.
   f. Click the *After* measurement box down arrow until *00:00* displays in the box.
   g. Click the *After* check box to remove the check mark.
   h. Make sure the *On Mouse Click* check box contains a check mark.
   i. Click the Apply To All button.
3. Hide Slide 2 by completing the following steps:
   a. Click Slide 2 in the slide thumbnails pane.
   b. Click the Slide Show tab and then click the Hide Slide button in the Set Up group.
4. Run the slide show to see that Slide 2 does not display (since it is hidden).
5. Unhide Slide 2 by clicking Slide 2 in the slide thumbnails pane and then clicking the Hide Slide button in the Set Up group on the Slide Show tab.

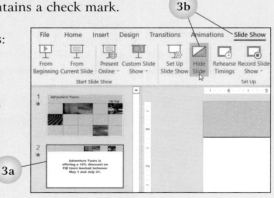

If you have two monitors connected to your computer, you can run the slide show in Presenter View. Complete these optional steps only if you have two monitors connected to your computer.

6. Make sure the Slide Show tab is active and then click the *Use Presenter View* check box in the Monitors group to insert a check mark.
7. Run the slide show from Slide 1.
8. Click the See all slides button below the slide.

9. Click the Slide 3 thumbnail.
10. Click the Return to previous slide button at the bottom of the Presenter View screen to make Slide 2 active.
11. Click the Pen button below the slide and then click *Highlighter* at the pop-up list.
12. Using the mouse, drag through the text *May 1*.
13. Press the Esc key to turn the highlighter to a mouse pointer, and then press the Esc key to end the presentation.
14. At the message asking if you want to keep the ink annotations, click the Discard button.
15. Save **7-AdvTours**.

Presenting a Slide Show Online

PowerPoint includes the Present Online feature for sharing a slide show with others over the internet by sending a link to the people who will view the slide show, which can be watched in their browsers. To use this feature, a network service is required to host the slide show. Microsoft provides the Office Presentation Service, which is available to anyone with a Windows Live ID, such as a OneDrive account, and Microsoft Office.

To present a presentation online, click the Present Online button in the Start Slide Show group on the Slide Show tab. At the Present Online window, click the CONNECT button, and, if necessary, enter a Windows Live ID user name and password. When PowerPoint has connected to an account and prepared the presentation, the Present Online window will display with a unique link PowerPoint created for the presentation. Click the Copy Link hyperlink in the Present Online window to copy the unique link, and then paste the link into an email that will be sent to the people who will be viewing the slide show. If the person presenting the slide show online has an Outlook account, clicking the Send in Email hyperlink opens Outlook and the link can be pasted in the message window.

After everyone has opened the presentation link in a web browser, click the START PRESENTATION button in the Present Online window. People viewing the slide show do not need PowerPoint installed on their computers to view the slide show since the slide show will run through their web browsers. When the slide show has ended, click the End Online Presentation button on the Present Online tab. At the confirmation message, click the End Online Presentation button. The Present Online tab provides options for running the slide show, managing monitors, sharing the slide show through OneNote, and sending the unique link to more people. Depending on the PowerPoint version, the Present Online window can also be accessed by clicking the File tab, clicking the *Share* option, clicking *Present Online*, and then clicking the Present Online button.

When presenting a slide show online, the presenter can allow the viewers to download the presentation. To do this, the presenter would click the *Enable remote viewers to download the presentation* check box at the Present Online window before clicking the CONNECT button.

Quick Steps

Present Online
1. Click Slide Show tab.
2. Click Present Online button.
3. Click CONNECT button.
4. If necessary, enter Windows Live ID user name and password.
5. Click Copy Link hyperlink.
6. Open email.
7. Paste link into email and send email.
8. Click START PRESENTATION button.

Present Online

This is an optional activity. To complete this activity, you will need a Windows Live ID account. Depending on your system configuration and what services are available, these steps will vary.

1. With **7-AdvTours** open, click the Slide Show tab and then click the Present Online button in the Start Slide Show group.
2. At the Present Online window, click the CONNECT button.
3. If necessary, type your user name and password into the Windows Security dialog box.
4. At the Present Online window with the unique link selected, click the Copy Link hyperlink.
5. Send the link to colleagues by opening your email account, pasting the link into a new message window, and then sending the email to the viewers. Or, if you are using Microsoft Outlook, click the Send in Email hyperlink and Microsoft Outlook opens in a new message window with the link inserted in the message. In Outlook, send the link to people you want to view the presentation.
6. When everyone has received the link, click the START PRESENTATION button at the Present Online window.
7. Run the slide show.
8. When the slide show has ended, press the Esc key and then click the End Online Presentation button on the Present Online tab.
9. At the message stating that all remote viewers will be disconnected if you continue, click the End Online Presentation button.

Using Ink Tools

Using Ink Tools

Similar to drawing and highlighting in slides during a slide show, as completed in Chapter 1, draw or highlight items in slides in Normal view with options on the Ink Tools Pens tab, as shown in Figure 7.6. Display this tab by clicking the Start Inking button in the Ink group on the Review tab. The Ink Tools Pens tab contains options for drawing and highlighting on slides; erasing markings on slides; selecting multiple options such as ink marks, shapes, and text boxes; selecting a variety of pen and highlighter colors; changing the color and thickness of the pen or highlighter; and converting drawings to shapes. The ink tools feature is useful when using a pen, stylus, or finger when drawing on a tablet or touchscreen computer. Hide ink markings on slides by clicking the Hide Ink button in the Ink group on the Review tab. This hides the ink markings in all slides in a presentation without deleting the markings. Click the Hide Ink button again to redisplay ink markings.

Start Inking

Hide Ink

Some versions of PowerPoint may have a Draw tab that includes similar options for drawing and highlighting on a slide as the Ink Tools Pens tab. If the Draw tab displays on the ribbon, the Start Inking button will not display on the Review tab. The following activity assumes the Start Inking button is available. To remove the Draw tab from the ribbon, click the File tab and then click *Options*. At the PowerPoint Options dialog box, click the *Customize Ribbon* option in the left

Figure 7.6 Ink Tools Pens Tab

panel. Click the *Draw* check box in the list box at the right to remove the check mark and then click OK to close the dialog box. Complete similar steps to add the Draw tab to the ribbon except insert a check mark in the *Draw* check box.

Activity 3f Using Ink Tools

Note: This activity assumes the Start Inking button is available on the Review tab. If your version of PowerPoint 365 does not include a Start Inking button, turn on the Draw tab, and then instead of completing the steps in Activity 3f, practice using the buttons and options on the Draw tab. Delete any ink markings on the slides before proceeding to the next activity.

1. With **7-AdvTours** open, make Slide 2 active.
2. Click the Review tab.
3. Click the Start Inking button in the Ink group.
4. With the Ink Tools Pens tab active, draw and highlight on the slide by completing the following steps:
   a. Click the More Pens button in the Pens group.
   b. Click the *Red Pen (1.0 mm)* option at the drop-down list (second column, second row in the *Built-In Pens* section).
   c. Using the mouse, draw a line below the text *15% discount*.
   d. Click the More Pens button in the Pens group.

   e. Click the *Yellow Highlighter (4.0 mm)* option at the drop-down list (sixth column, first row in the *Favorite Pens* section).
   f. Using the mouse, draw through the text *May 1 and July 31*.
5. Erase drawing and highlighting on the slide by completing the following steps:
   a. Click the Eraser button arrow in the Write group.
   b. Click *Stroke Eraser* at the drop-down list.
   c. Click the mouse pointer (displays with an eraser attached) in the red line below the text *15% discount*.
   d. Click the Eraser button arrow and then click *Medium Eraser* at the drop-down list.
   e. Using the mouse, which displays as a white box, drag over the text *and July 31.* to erase the yellow highlighting. (The text *May 1* should remain highlighted.)
   f. Press the Esc key to change the mouse pointer to an arrow.
6. Make Slide 5 active.

7. Convert drawings to shapes and select shapes by completing the following steps:
    a. Click the More Pens button in the Pens group and then click the *Orange Pen (0.35 mm)* option at the drop-down list (first column, third row in the *Built-In Pens* section).
    b. Click the Thickness button in the Pens group and then click *4½ pt* at the drop-down gallery.
    c. Using the mouse, draw a rectangle around the text *Coral reef cruise* in the second bulleted item. If you are not satisfied with the appearance of the rectangle, click the Undo button on the Quick Access Toolbar, select the orange pen again, and then redraw the rectangle.

    d. Click the Select Objects button in the Write group.
    e. Hover the mouse pointer over the orange rectangle until the mouse pointer displays with a four-headed arrow attached and then click the border to select it.
    f. Click the Convert Your Ink button that appears at the right of the selected rectangle and then click the *Convert Text and Shapes* option at the side menu. Notice that PowerPoint converted the drawn rectangle into a more precise rectangle and made the Drawing Tools Format tab active.

8. Run the slide show beginning with Slide 1 to see the highlighting and rectangle applied to the slides.
9. Save **7-AdvTours**.

Check Your Work

Creating a Custom Slide Show

A custom slide show is a slide show within a slide show. Creating a custom slide show might be useful in situations where only a select number of slides will be presented to a particular audience. To create a custom slide show, click the Slide Show tab, click the Custom Slide Show button in the Start Slide Show group, and then click *Custom Shows* at the drop-down list. At the Custom Shows dialog box, click the New button and the Define Custom Show dialog box displays, similar to what is shown in Figure 7.7.

At the Define Custom Show dialog box, type a name for the custom slide show in the *Slide show name* text box. To insert a slide in the custom slide show, click the check box for the specific slide in the *Slides in presentation* list box to insert a check mark and then click the Add button. This inserts the slide in the *Slides in custom show* list box. Continue in this manner until all specific slides have been added to the custom slide show. A check mark can be inserted in all of the specific slide check boxes first and then clicking the Add button will add all the slides in the *Slides in custom show* list box at once.

To change the order of the slides in the *Slides in custom show* list box, click one of the arrow keys to move the selected slide up or down in the list box. When all slides have been inserted in the *Slides in custom show* list box and are arranged in the desired order, click OK. More than one custom slide show can be created in a presentation.

**Create Custom
Slide Show**
1. Click Slide Show tab.
2. Click Custom Slide
   Show button.
3. Click *Custom Shows*.
4. Click New button.
5. Make changes at
   Define Custom Show
   dialog box.
6. Click OK.

**Run Custom
Slide Show**
1. Click Slide Show tab.
2. Click Custom Slide
   Show button.
3. Click custom show.

**Edit Custom
Slide Show**
1. Click Slide Show tab.
2. Click Custom Slide
   Show button.
3. Click *Custom Shows*.
4. Click custom show
   name.
5. Click Edit button.
6. Make changes at
   Define Custom Show
   dialog box.
7. Click OK.

Figure 7.7 Define Custom Show Dialog Box

Running a Custom Slide Show

To run a custom slide show within a slide show, click the Custom Slide Show button on the Slide Show tab and then click the custom slide show's name at the drop-down list. A custom slide show can also be run by displaying the Set Up Show dialog box and then clicking the *Custom show* option. If the presentation contains more than one custom slide show, click the *Custom show* option box arrow and then click the custom slide show's name at the drop-down list.

Editing a Custom Slide Show

Hint Create
custom slide shows
to customize a
presentation for a
variety of audiences.

A custom slide show is saved with the presentation and can be edited. To edit a custom slide show, open the presentation, click the Custom Slide Show button on the Slide Show tab, and then click *Custom Shows* at the drop-down list. At the Custom Shows dialog box, click the custom slide show name to be edited and then click the Edit button. At the Define Custom Show dialog box, make changes to the custom slide show, such as adding or removing slides or changing the order of slides and then click the OK button.

Quick Steps

**Print Custom
Slide Show**
1. Display Print
   backstage area.
2. Click first gallery in
   Settings category.
3. Click custom show
   at drop-down list.
4. Click Print button.

Printing a Custom Slide Show

Print a custom slide show with options in the *Settings* category of the Print backstage area. To do this, click the File tab and then click the *Print* option to display the Print backstage area. Click the first gallery in the *Settings* category and then click the custom slide show in the *Custom Shows* section.

Activity 3g Creating, Editing, Running, and Printing Custom Slide Shows   Part 7 of 7

1. With **7-AdvTours** open, save the presentation with the name **7-AdvTours-Custom**.
2. Create two custom slide shows by completing the following steps:
   a. Click the Slide Show tab, click the Custom Slide Show button, and then click
      Custom Shows at the drop-down list.
   b. At the Custom Shows dialog box, click the New button.

   c. At the Define Custom Show dialog box, select the text in the *Slide show name* text box and then type PeruTourCustom.

   d. Click the Slide 6 check box in the *Slides in presentation* list box to insert a check mark and then click the Add button. (This adds the slide to the *Slides in custom show* list box.)

   e. Click the check boxes for Slides 7, 8, and 9 in the list box to insert check marks and then click the Add button.

   f. Click OK to close the Define Custom Show dialog box.

   g. At the Custom Shows dialog box, click the New button.

   h. At the Define Custom Show dialog box, select the text in the *Slide show name* text box and then type FijiTourCustom.

   i. Add Slides 1 through 5 to the *Slides in custom show* list box.

   j. Click OK to close the dialog box.

   k. Click the Close button to close the Custom Shows dialog box.

3. Run the custom slide shows by completing the following steps:

   a. Click the Custom Slide Show button on the Slide Show tab and then click *PeruTourCustom* at the drop-down list.

   b. Click the left mouse button to advance slides.

   c. Click the Custom Slide Show button, click *FijiTourCustom* at the drop-down list, and then view the slide show. (Click the left mouse button to advance the slides.)

4. Edit the FijiTourCustom custom slide show by completing the following steps:

   a. Click the Custom Slide Show button and then click *Custom Shows* at the drop-down list.

   b. At the Custom Shows dialog box, click *FijiTourCustom* in the list box and then click the Edit button.

   c. At the Define Custom Show dialog box, click Slide 2 in the *Slides in custom show* list box and then click the Down button at the right of the list box three times. (This moves the slide to the bottom of the list.)

   d. Click OK to close the dialog box.

   e. Click the Close button to close the Custom Shows dialog box.

5. Run the FijiTourCustom slide show.
6. Print the FijiTourCustom slide show by completing the following steps:
   a. Click the File tab and then click the *Print* option.
   b. At the Print backstage area, click the first gallery in the *Settings* category and then click *FijiTourCustom* in the *Custom Shows* section.
   c. Click the second gallery in the *Settings* category and then click *6 Slides Horizontal* at the drop-down list.
   d. Click the Print button.
7. Save and then close **7-AdvTours-Custom**.

6b

Check Your Work

Activity 4 Format a Company Division Presentation   **1 Part**

You will open a company division presentation, insert and copy a 3D model, format the 3D models, and then run the slide show using the Morph transition.

 Tutorial

Inserting and Formatting 3D Models

 3D Models

Quick Steps

Insert 3D Model
1. Click Insert tab.
2. Click 3D Models button.
3. Click 3D model category.
4. Double-click 3D model.

💡 **Hint** The file size for a 3D animated model is quite large and may take some time to download.

Inserting and Formatting 3D Models

PowerPoint provides options for inserting a 3D model, which is a graphic file of an image that can be rotated or tilted to show different portions of the image. Microsoft's Remix 3D library includes a collection of free 3D models that can be inserted in a presentation. Access the library by clicking the 3D Models button in the Illustrations group on the Insert tab. At the Online 3D Models window, browse 3D models in a number of categories. Some 3D models include a "runner" badge in the lower left corner of the model indicating that the model includes animation. Insert a 3D model in a document by double-clicking it or by clicking the model and then clicking the Insert button. To use a 3D model file saved in another location, click the 3D Models button arrow and then click the *From a File* option to navigate to the folder where the 3D model file is saved.

When a 3D model is inserted in a presentation, the 3D Model Tools Format tab, shown in Figure 7.8, becomes active. Use buttons in the Adjust group to insert a different 3D model or reset the selected model to its original size and position. The 3D Model Views group includes a gallery of preset views for the model. Click the Alt Text button in the Accessibility group and the Alt Text task pane displays where a description of the model can be added. Use options in the Arrange group to position the model, apply text wrapping, send the model forward or backward, and align the model. Change the height and width of the model with options in the Size group. The Size group also contains the Pan & Zoom button. Click this button and a button (a magnifying glass with a plus symbol inside) displays at the right of the selected model. Position the mouse pointer on this button, click and hold down the left mouse button, and then drag up to increase the size of the model (pan in) or drag down to decrease the size (pan out). To turn off the pan feature, click the Pan & Zoom button to deactivate it. When an animated 3D model is selected, two additional buttons display on the 3D Model

Figure 7.8 3D Model Tools Format Tab

Tools Format tab–Pause and Scenes. Click the Scenes button to display a drop-down list of different animation movement options.

Use the 3D control in the middle of a selected 3D model to rotate or tilt the model. To use the 3D control, position the mouse pointer on the control, click and hold down the left mouse button, and then drag with the mouse to rotate or tilt in different directions.

A 3D model can be animated by selecting the model and then clicking the Animations tab. This displays options in the Animation group such as *Arrive*, *Turntable*, *Swing*, *Jump & Turn*, and *Leave*. Effect options can also be applied to the animation of a 3D model.

Hint Halt the animation of an animated 3D model by clicking the Pause button on the 3D Model Tools Format tab, right-clicking the model and then clicking *Pause*, or by pressing the spacebar while the model is selected.

Applying the Morph Slide Transition

The Morph slide transition allows for smooth movement of animations, images, or objects between slides in a slide show. To effectively use the Morph transition, create a number of slides in a presentation that have at least one object in common. This can be accomplished by using the duplicate slides feature or copying and pasting the object to each slide.

 Effect Options

Apply the Morph transition by clicking the Transitions tab and then clicking the *Morph* option in the Transition to This Slide group. Change Morph effect options by clicking the Effect Options button in the Transition to This Slide group and then clicking the *Objects* option to move entire objects in the slide, the *Words* option to move individual words, or the *Characters* option to move individual letters. Apply the Morph transition to all slides in the presentation by clicking the Apply To All button in the Timing group.

Activity 4 Inserting a 3D Model and Applying the Morph Transition   Part 1 of 1

1. Open **ISDivisions** and then save it with the name **7-ISDivisions**.
2. Make Slide 2 active and then insert a 3D model by completing the following steps:
   a. Click the Insert tab.
   b. Click the 3D Models button in the Illustrations group.
   c. At the Online 3D Models window, click in the search text box, type globe, and then press the Enter key.
   d. Double-click the globe model shown at the right. (If this 3D model is not available, double-click a similar globe model.) *Note: If you do not have access to the Online 3D Models window, open Globe3D from your PC7 folder. This presentation contains the 3D globe model. Copy the model and then paste it into 7-ISDivisions.*

3. Format and copy the model by completing the following steps:
   a. With the globe model selected in Slide 2, click the 3D Model Tools Format tab.
   b. Click in the *Shape Height* measurement box in the Size group, type 4, and then press the Enter key.
   c. Drag the model to the right so it does not overlap any text.
   d. Click the Home tab and then click the Copy button.
   e. Make Slide 3 active and then click the Paste button.
   f. Paste the model in Slides 4 and 5. The globe model should be in the exact same location in Slides 2 through 5.
4. Make Slide 2 active, click the model to make it active, and then click the 3D Model Tools Format tab.
5. Hover the mouse pointer over the 3D control in the middle of the globe model, click and hold down the left mouse button, and then drag with the mouse to rotate the model around so that North America is visible. (Make sure you rotate the model around in the frame and not move the model to another location in the slide.)

6. Insert and format a star shape in the slide by completing the following steps:
   a. Click the Insert tab, click the Shapes button in the Illustrations group, click the *Star: 5 Points* option (fourth column, first row in the *Stars and Banners* section), and then click in the slide.
   b. With the shape selected and the Drawing Tools Format tab selected, click in the *Shape Height* measurement box in the Size group and then type 0.2.
   c. Click in the *Shape Width* measurement box, type 0.2, and then press the Enter key.
   d. Drag the star so it is positioned in the approximate location of San Francisco, California in the model, as shown at the right.

7. Make Slide 3 active, click the globe model to select it, and then click the 3D Model Tools Format tab.
8. Click the More 3D Model Views button in the 3D Model Views group and then click the *Above Front* option at the drop-down gallery (first column, second row).
9. Use the 3D control in the middle of the globe model to rotate the model so that Europe is more visible.
10. Insert and format the same star you inserted in Step 6 and position the star in the approximate location of Paris, France in the model (shown at the right).
11. Make Slide 4 active and then complete steps similar to Steps 4 and 5 or Steps 7 through 9 to rotate the globe to show Asia and then insert the star with the same formatting used in Step 6 at the approximate location of Tokyo, Japan in the model (shown at right).

12. Make Slide 5 active and then complete steps similar to Steps 4 and 5 or Steps 7 through 9 to rotate the globe to show Africa and then insert the star with the same formatting used in Step 6 at the approximate location of Nairobi, Kenya in the model (shown at the right).

13. Apply animation to the 3D model in Slide 5 by completing the following steps:
    a. Click the 3D globe model in Slide 5 to make it active.
    b. Click the Animations tab.
    c. Click the *Jump & Turn* option in the Animation group.
14. Apply the Morph transition to all slides in the presentation by completing the following steps:
    a. Make Slide 1 active.
    b. Click the Transitions tab.
    c. Click the *Morph* option in the Transition to This Slide group.
    d. Click the *After* check box in the Timing group to insert a check mark.
    e. Click in the *After* measurement box, type 3, and then press the Enter key.
    f. Click the Apply To All button in the Timing group.
15. Run the slide show beginning with Slide 1. Watch the rotation and movement of the globe 3D model and star as the slides transition. At the end of the slide show, press the Esc key to return to Normal view.
16. Print the presentation as a handout with six slides displayed horizontally per page.
17. Save and then close **7-ISDivisions**.s

Check Your Work

Activity 5 **Insert Audio and Video Files in an Eco-Tours Presentation** **5 Parts**

You will open a presentation and then insert an audio file, a video file, and an image with motion. You will also customize the audio and video file formatting and playback options. You will then create a screen recording of an animation in a slide.

Inserting Audio and Video Files

Adding audio and/or video files to a presentation will turn a slide show into a true multimedia experience for the audience. Including a variety of elements in a presentation will stimulate interest in the slide show and keep the audience motivated.

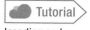

Inserting and Modifying an Audio File

 Audio

Inserting an Audio File

To add an audio file to a presentation, click the Insert tab, click the Audio button in the Media group, and then click *Audio on My PC* at the drop-down list. At the Insert Audio dialog box, navigate to the folder containing the audio file and then double-click the audio file.

If a recording device is attached to the computer, audio can be recorded for the presentation by clicking the Audio button and then clicking *Record Audio* at the drop-down list. At the Record Sound dialog box, type a name for the audio file, click the Record button, and then record the audio.

When an audio file is inserted in a presentation, the Audio Tools Format tab and the Audio Tools Playback tab are available. The Audio Tools Format tab contains options that are similar to options on the Picture Tools Format tab such as adjusting the audio file image in the slide, applying a picture style, and arranging and sizing the audio file image. The Audio Tools Playback tab contains options for previewing the audio file, inserting a bookmark at a specific time in the audio file, specifying fade in and fade out times, and specifying how to play the audio file.

Activity 5a Inserting an Audio File   Part 1 of 5

1. Open **EcoTours** and then save it with the name **7-EcoTours**.
2. Insert an audio file that plays music at the end of the presentation by completing the following steps:
   a. Make Slide 8 active and then click the Insert tab.
   b. Click the Audio button in the Media group, and then click *Audio on My PC* at the drop-down list.
   c. At the Insert Audio dialog box, navigate to your PC7 folder and then double-click the **AudioFile-01** audio file.
   d. With the Audio Tools Playback tab active, click the *Start* option box arrow in the Audio Options group and then click *Automatically* at the drop-down list.
   e. Click the *Loop until Stopped* check box in the Audio Options group to insert a check mark.
   f. Click the *Hide During Show* check box to insert a check mark.

3. Click the Start from Beginning button on the Quick Access Toolbar to run the slide show starting with Slide 1. When the last slide displays, listen to the audio file and then press the Esc key to return to Normal view.
4. Save **7-EcoTours**.

Inserting a Video File

Inserting a video file in a presentation is a similar process to inserting an audio file. Click the Video button in the Media group on the Insert tab and then click *Video on My PC* at the drop-down list to display the Insert Video dialog box. At this dialog box, navigate to the folder containing the video file and then double-click the file.

Quick Steps
Insert Video File
1. Click Insert tab.
2. Click Video button.
3. Click *Video on My PC.*
4. Double-click video file.

The Video button drop-down list also includes the *Online Video* option. Click this option to display the Insert Video window. At this window, search for videos online using the *YouTube* search option or paste an embedded code into the *From a Video Embed Code* option to insert a video from a website. To embed code from an online video, locate and copy the embedded code of the video, paste the embedded code in the *From a Video Embed Code* section of the Insert Video window, and then click the Insert button. Another way to insert a video in a presentation is to click the Insert Video button in the content placeholder on a slide. This displays the Insert Video window with the additional option to browse for a file on the computer.

When a video file is inserted in a presentation, the Video Tools Format tab and the Video Tools Playback tab display. The Video Tools Format tab contains options for adjusting the video file color and frame, applying video styles, and arranging and sizing the video file. The Video Tools Playback tab contains options similar to the options on the Audio Tools Playback tab. Formatting can also be applied to a video with options in the Format Video task pane.

Optimizing and Compressing Video Files

If a video with an older file format is inserted in a presentation, the Info backstage area may contain an Optimize Compatibility button. Optimize compatibility of a video file to increase the likelihood that the video file will play on multiple devices.

Compress Media

When a video file is inserted in a presentation, consider compressing the file to improve playback performance and save disk space. If a presentation contains a video file, the Info backstage area contains the Compress Media button. Click this button and a drop-down list displays with options for specifying the compressed quality of the video. Click the *Full HD (1080p)* option to save space and maintain the quality of the video. Click the *HD (720p)* option and the compressed video file will be comparable to a video file streamed over the internet. Choose the last option, *Standard (480p)*, to compress the file when space is limited, such as when sending the presentation as an email attachment.

Showing and Hiding Media Controls

When a slide with an audio or video file displays during a slide show, media controls appear along the bottom of the audio icon or video window. Use these media controls to play the audio or video file, move to a specific location in the file, or change the volume. The media controls display when the mouse pointer is moved over the audio icon or video window. Media controls can be turned off by clicking the Slide Show tab and then clicking the *Show Media Controls* check box in the Set Up group to remove the check mark.

Activity 5b Inserting a Video File

Part 2 of 5

1. With **7-EcoTours** open, make Slide 8 active.
2. You will insert a video file in the slide that contains audio, so delete the audio file you inserted in Activity 5a by clicking the audio file icon in the middle of Slide 8 and then pressing the Delete key.
3. Insert a video file by completing the following steps:
   a. Click the Insert tab.

b. Click the Video button in the Media group and then click *Video on My PC* at the drop-down list.
c. At the Insert Video dialog box, navigate to your PC7 folder and then double-click the **Wildlife** video file.
d. Click the Play button in the Preview group (on the left of the Video Tools Format tab) to preview the video file. (The video plays for approximately 30 seconds.)

4. Format the video by completing the following steps:
   a. Make sure the video image is selected on the slide and the Video Tools Format tab is selected.
   b. Click the *Beveled Frame, Gradient* option in the Video Styles group (fourth option).
   c. Click the Video Shape button in the Video Styles group and then click *Rectangle: Rounded Corners* at the drop-down gallery (second option in the *Rectangles* section).
   d. Click the Poster Frame button in the Adjust group and then click *Image from File* at the drop-down list.

e. At the Insert Pictures window, click the *From a File* option, navigate to your PC7 folder, and then double-click the **Olympics** image file.
f. Click the Corrections button in the Adjust group and then click *Brightness: 0% (Normal) Contrast: +20%* at the drop-down gallery (third column, fourth row).
g. Click the Rotate button in the Arrange group and then click *Flip Horizontal* at the drop-down list.
h. Click the Size group task pane launcher to display the Format Video task pane.
i. With the Size & Properties icon selected, make sure the *Size* options display.
j. Select the current measurement in the *Height* measurement box and then type 4.9.
k. Click *Position* to display the options.
l. Select the current measurement in the *Horizontal position* measurement box and then type 2.3.
m. Select the current measurement in the *Vertical position* measurement box and then type 1.8.
n. Close the Format Video task pane.
o. Click the Video Tools Playback tab.
p. Click the Volume button in the Video Options group and then click *Low* at the drop-down list.
q. Click the *Loop until Stopped* check box in the Video Options group to insert a check mark.

5. Make Slide 1 active and then run the slide show. When the slide containing the video file displays, move the mouse over the video file window and then click the play button at the bottom left of the window.

6. After viewing the video a couple of times, press the Esc key two times.

7. Specify that you want the video window to fill the slide, the video to automatically start when the slide displays, the video to play only once, and the display of media controls turned off by completing the following steps:

   a. Make sure Slide 8 is active, click the video file window, and then click the Video Tools Playback tab.

   b. Click the *Play Full Screen* check box in the Video Options group to insert a check mark and click the *Loop until Stopped* check box to remove the check mark.

   c. Click the *Start* option box arrow in the Video Options group and then click *Automatically* at the drop-down list.

   d. Click the Slide Show tab.

   e. Click the *Show Media Controls* check box in the Set Up group to remove the check mark.

8. Make Slide 1 active and then run the slide show. When the slide displays containing the video, the video will automatically begin. When the video is finished playing, press the Esc key to return to Normal view.

9. Print Slide 8.

10. Compress the video file by completing the following steps:

    a. Make Slide 8 active and then click the video file window.

    b. Click the File tab.

    c. Click the *Info* option.

    d. At the Info backstage area, click the Optimize Compatibility button.

    e. When the optimization is complete, click the Close button in the Optimize Media Compatibility dialog box.

    f. Click the Compress Media button and then click *Standard (480p)* at the drop-down list.

    g. At the Compress Media dialog box, wait until the compression is complete (notice the progress bar along the bottom of the dialog box) and then the initial size of the video file and the number of megabytes saved by the compression.

    h. Click the Close button to close the dialog box and then click the Back button to return to the presentation.

11. Save **7-EcoTours**.

Complete these optional steps to insert a video from the internet into a slide.

12. With Slide 8 active, insert a new slide with the Blank layout.

13. Click the Insert tab, click the Video button, and then click *Online Video* at the drop-down list.

14. Click in the *Search YouTube* box, type Antarctica wildlife, and then press the Enter key.

15. At the search results window, double-click a video that interests you.

16. Size and position the video window in the slide to better fill the slide.

17. Make Slide 1 active and then run the slide show. When the slide with the video file you inserted displays, click the Play button in the video window. When the video is finished playing, press the Esc key to return to Normal view.

18. Save **7-EcoTours**.

Trimming a Video File

Quick Steps

Trim Video File
1. Insert video file.
2. Click Video Tools Playback tab.
3. Click Trim Video button.
4. Specify start time and/or end time.
5. Click OK.

 Trim Video

Use the Trim Video button on the Video Tools Playback tab to trim the beginning and end of a video. This might be helpful in a situation where a portion of the video should be removed that is not pertinent to the message in the presentation. Trimming is limited to a portion of the beginning and end of the video.

To trim a video, insert the video file in the slide, click the Video Tools Playback tab, and then click the Trim Video button in the Editing group. At the Trim Video dialog box, specify the start and/or end time for the video. To trim the start of the video, insert a specific time in the *Start Time* measurement box or drag the green start point marker on the slider bar below the video. Zero in on a very specific starting point by clicking the Next Frame button or the Previous Frame button to advance the video a single frame at a time. Complete similar steps to trim the ending of the video except use the red end point marker on the slider bar or insert the specific ending time in the *End Time* measurement box.

Activity 5c **Trimming a Video**   Part 3 of 5

1. With **7-EcoTour** open, make Slide 8 active.
2. Trim the first part of the video that shows the running horses by completing the following steps:
   a. Click the video to select it and then click the Video Tools Playback tab.
   b. Click the Trim Video button in the Editing group.
   c. At the Trim Video dialog box, position the mouse pointer on the green start point marker on the slider bar until the pointer displays as a left-and-right-pointing arrow. Click and hold down the left mouse button, drag the start point marker to approximately the *00:04.0* time, and then release the mouse button.
   d. Click the Next Frame button until the first image of the birds displays and the horses have completely disappeared off the screen. (Depending on where you dragged the start point marker, you may need to click the Previous Frame button.)
   e. Click the OK button.

3. Click the *Fade In* measurement box up arrow in the Editing group until *01.00* displays and then click the *Fade Out* measurement box up arrow until *01.00* displays.
4. Run the slide show and then press the Esc key to return to Normal view.
5. Save **7-EcoTours**.

Playing an Audio File throughout a Slide Show

An audio file can be inserted in a presentation to play when a specific slide displays; or, it can be set up to play continually through all of the slides when running the slide show. An audio file that plays continually will work well for automated presentations that are set to run in a continuous loop.

 Play in Background

To specify that the audio file plays throughout the presentation, click the Play in Background button in the Audio Styles group on the Audio Tools Playback tab. When this button is clicked, the *Start* option box in the Audio Options group changes to *Automatically*, and a check mark is inserted in the *Play Across Slides* check box, the *Loop until Stopped* check box, and the *Hide During Show* check box. To automate the presentation, display the Set Up Show dialog box and then insert a check mark in the *Loop continuously until 'Esc'* check box.

Activity 5d **Playing an Audio File throughout a Slide Show**   Part 4 of 5

1. With **7-EcoTours** open, make Slide 8 active and then make the following changes:
   a. Select and then delete the video file.
   b. Apply the Title Only slide layout.
   c. Type the title Let the adventure begin! and then change the font size to 54 points and the font color to Dark Blue.
   d. Distribute the title placeholder vertically on the slide. (Do this by clicking the Align button on the Drawing Tools Format tab and then clicking *Distribute Vertically* at the drop-down list.)
2. Make Slide 1 active and then insert an audio file that plays through all slides by completing the following steps:
   a. Click the Insert tab, click the Audio button in the Media group, and then click *Audio on My PC* at the drop-down list.
   b. At the Insert Audio dialog box, navigate to your PC7 folder and then double-click the **AudioFile-02** audio file.
   c. With the Audio Tools Playback tab active, click the Play in Background button in the Audio Styles group. (Notice that when you click the Play in Background button, the *Start* option box in the Audio Options group changes to *Automatically*, and a check mark is inserted in the *Play Across Slides* check box, the *Loop until Stopped* check box, and the *Hide During Show* check box.)
   d. Click the Volume button in the Audio Options group and then click *Medium* at the drop-down list.
3. Specify that you want slides to automatically advance after five seconds by completing the following steps:
   a. Click the Transitions tab.
   b. Click the *After* measurement box up arrow in the Timing group until *00:05.00* displays.
   c. Click the *On Mouse Click* check box to remove the check mark.
   d. Click the Apply To All button.
4. Set up the slide show to run continuously by completing the following steps:
   a. Click the Slide Show tab.
   b. Click the Set Up Slide Show button.

c. At the Set Up Show dialog box, click the *Loop continuously until 'Esc'* check box to insert a check mark.

d. Click OK to close the dialog box.

5. If necessary, make Slide 1 active and then run the slide show. When the slide show begins for the second time, press the Esc key to return to Normal view.

6. Save and then close **7-EcoTours**.

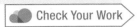 Check Your Work

Creating a Screen Recording

PowerPoint includes a screen recording feature that will record actions as they are being performed on the screen. A screen recording is automatically inserted into the active slide as a video file, and the Video Tools Format tab and Video Tools Playback tab are available. Format a screen recording in the same manner as formatting a video file.

Screen
Recording

Create a screen recording by opening any necessary files (other PowerPoint presentations, different applications, or an internet browser), clicking the Insert tab, and then clicking the Screen Recording button in the Media group. At the Screen Recording toolbar, click the Select Area button. When the mouse pointer displays as crosshairs, click and hold down the left mouse button, drag to select the screen area that will be used in the screen recording, and then release the mouse button. Once the area is selected, click the Record button on the Screen Recording toolbar, as shown in Figure 7.9. A countdown to begin the recording displays, along with an explanation of how to end the recording. When the countdown is complete, the screen recording will record all mouse movements and actions performed on the screen. Click the Stop button on the Screen Recording toolbar or press the Windows logo key + Shift + Q to end the recording. The recording is automatically inserted in the active slide.

A screen recording file is saved with the presentation. To make the recording available for other presentations, save it as a separate file by right-clicking the recording and then clicking *Save Media As* at the shortcut menu. At the Save Media As dialog box, navigate to the desired folder, type a name for the recording in the *File name* text box, and then click the Save button. Insert the recording into a different presentation with the Video button in the Media group.

Figure 7.9 Screen Recording Toolbar

Click the Stop button to end recording. This button becomes active when a recording begins.

Use the Select Area button to determine the section of the screen to be used during the recording.

Click the Record button to begin recording. This button becomes a Pause button once recording begins.

Record   00:00:00   Select Area   Audio   Record Pointer

Click the Record Pointer button to include the mouse pointer in the screen recording.

time duration of recording

Click the Audio button to include audio in the recording.

1. Open **Animations** and save it with the name **7-Animations**.
2. Make Slide 6 active.
3. Open **MotionPath**. Make sure no other applications are open except for **7-Animations** and **MotionPath**.
4. Click the PowerPoint button on the taskbar and then click **7-Animations**.
5. Create a screen recording of the steps to insert a custom motion path in a slide by completing the following steps:
   a. Click the Insert tab.
   b. Click the Screen Recording button in the Media group.
   c. When the Screen Recording toolbar displays, click the Select Area button.
   d. Using the mouse, drag to select the entire PowerPoint window for the **MotionPath** file.
   e. Click the Record button on the Screen Recording toolbar.
   f. After PowerPoint counts down to begin the recording, click the moon image in the **MotionPath** window to select it.

   g. Click the Animations tab.
   h. Click the More Animations button in the Animations group.
   i. Scroll down the drop-down list and then click *Custom Path* in the *Motion Paths* section.
   j. Using the mouse, click and drag the moon clockwise around the Earth image, ending in the original location, release the mouse button, and then double-click the mouse button.
   k. Press the Windows logo key + Shift + Q to end the screen recording. If your keyboard does not have a Windows logo key, display the Screen Recording toolbar by moving the arrow pointer to the top of the screen, and then clicking the Stop Recording button on the toolbar to end the recording.
6. Format the screen recording by completing the following steps:
   a. With the Video Tools Format tab active, click in the *Shape Height* measurement box, type 4.5, and then press the Enter key.
   b. Drag the screen recording down so it is positioned below the title and centered vertically on the slide.
7. View the screen recording by clicking the Play button in the Preview group.
8. Save the screen recording to your storage medium by completing the following steps:
   a. Right-click in the screen recording.
   b. Click the *Save Media as* option at the shortcut menu.
   c. At the Save Media As dialog box, navigate to your PC7 folder.
   d. Type 7-Motion in the *File name* text box.
   e. Click the Save button.
9. Make Slide 1 active and then run the slide show. When the slide with the screen recording displays, click the Play button in the video window. When the video is finished playing, press the Esc key to return to Normal view.
10. Print Slide 6.
11. Save and then close **7-Animations**.
12. Close **MotionPath** without saving changes.

Chapter Summary

- Apply animation to an item in a slide with options in the Animation group on the Animations tab. Specify animation effects with options from the Effect Options button drop-down gallery.

- Click the Preview button on the Animations tab to view the animation effects without running the slide show.

- Remove an animation effect from an item in a slide by clicking the *None* option in the Animation group on the Animations tab.

- The Add Animation button in the Advanced Animation group on the Animations tab provides four types of animation effects—entrance, exit, emphasis, and motion paths.

- Use the Animation Painter button in the Advanced Animation group on the Animations tab to apply the same animation to items in more than one location in a slide or slides.

- Use options in the Timing group on the Animations tab to determine when an animation starts on a slide, the duration of the animation, the delay between animations, and the order in which animations appear on the slide.

- Use the Animation Pane to customize animation effects. Display the pane by clicking the Animation Pane button in the Advanced Animation group on the Animations tab.

- Apply a sound to an animation with the *Sound* option box at the effect options dialog box with the Effect tab selected. The name of the dialog box varies depending on the animation effect selected.

- A build displays important points on a slide one point at a time. A build can be applied that dims the previous bulleted point with the *After animation* option box at the effect options dialog box with the Effect tab selected.

- Specify a path an item is to follow when it displays on the slide with options in the *Motion Paths* section of the Add Animation button drop-down gallery. To draw a motion path, choose the *Custom path* option at the drop-down gallery.

- Use the Trigger button in the Advanced Animation group to specify that an animation effect occurs during a slide show by clicking an item on the slide.

- Customize a slide show with options in the Set Up Show dialog box. Display the dialog box by clicking the Slide Show tab and then clicking the Set Up Slide Show button.

- To prepare an automated slide show, insert a check mark in the *Loop continuously until 'Esc'* check box at the Set Up Show dialog box.

- To apply specific times to slides, click the Rehearse Timings button in the Set Up group on the Slide Show tab. Use buttons on the Recording toolbar to set, pause, or repeat times.

- To record narration for a presentation, click the Record Slide Show button in the Set Up group on the Slide Show tab and then click the RECORD button in Narration view.

- Hide or unhide a slide in a slide show by clicking the Hide Slide button in the Set Up group on the Slide Show tab.

- Specify on which monitor to run the slide show with the *Monitor* option in the Monitors group on the Slide Show tab.

- If PowerPoint is running on a computer with two monitors or on a laptop with dual-display capabilities, the slide show can be run in full-screen view on one monitor and in Presenter view on the other monitor.

- Use the Present Online feature to share a slide show with others over the internet. Send a link to the people who will view the slide show and then everyone can watch the slide show in their web browsers.

- Draw or highlight text or objects in slides while in Normal view using options on the Ink Tools Pens tab. Display the Ink Tools Pens tab by clicking the Start Inking button in the Ink group on the Review tab.

- Create a custom slide show, which is a slide show within a slide show, with options in the Define Custom Show dialog box. Display this dialog box by clicking the Slide Show tab, clicking the Custom Slide Show button, clicking *Custom Shows* at the drop-down list, and then clicking the New button at the Custom Shows dialog box.

- To run a custom slide show, click the Custom Slide Show button in the Start Slide Show group on the Slide Show tab and then click the custom show at the drop-down list.

- Print a custom slide show at the Print backstage area by clicking the first gallery in the *Settings* category and then clicking the custom show in the *Custom Shows* section.

- A 3D model can be rotated or tilted to show different portions of the model. Insert a 3D model with the 3D Models button in the Illustrations group on the Insert tab, and format a 3D model with options on the 3D Model Tools Format tab.

- Apply the Morph transition to create smooth movement of animations, images, or objects between slides in a slide show.

- Insert an audio file in a slide by clicking the Audio button in the Media group on the Insert tab and then clicking *Audio on My PC*. Use options on the Audio Tools Format tab and the Audio Tools Playback tab to format and customize the audio file.

- Insert a video file in a slide by clicking the Video button in the Media group on the Insert tab and then clicking *Video on My PC*. Use options on the Video Tools Format tab and the Video Tools Playback tab to format and customize the video file.

- When a slide show runs, media controls display along the bottom of an audio icon or video window in a slide when the mouse is moved over the icon or window. Turn on or off the display of these media controls with the *Show Media Controls* check box in the Set Up group on the Slide Show tab.

- Compress a video file to improve playback performance and save disk space. Compress a video file by clicking the File tab, clicking the *Info* option, clicking the Compress Media button, and then clicking the specific compression.

- Use the Trim Video button on the Video Tools Playback tab to trim the beginning and/or end of a video.

- Create and insert a screen recording by clicking the Screen Recording button in the Media group on the Insert tab, selecting the recording area, beginning the recording, and then formatting the recording that is inserted in the selected slide.

Commands Review

FEATURE	RIBBON TAB, GROUP/OPTION	BUTTON, OPTION
3D models	Insert, Illustrations	
add animations	Animations, Advanced Animation	
Animation Painter	Animations, Advanced Animation	
Animation Pane	Animations, Advanced Animation	
animations	Animations, Animation	
compress video file	File, *Info*	
Define Custom Show dialog box	Slide Show, Start Slide Show	, *Custom Shows*, New
hide ink	Review, Ink	
hide or unhide slide	Slide Show, Set Up	
ink tools	Review, Ink	
insert audio file	Insert, Media	
insert video file	Insert, Media	
optimize video file	File, *Info*	
present online	Slide Show, Start Slide Show	
record narration	Slide Show, Set Up	
Recording toolbar	Slide Show, Set Up	
screen recording	Insert, Media	
Set Up Show dialog box	Slide Show, Set Up	
Trim Video dialog box	Video Tools Playback, Editing	

Microsoft®
PowerPoint®

Integrating, Sharing, and Protecting Presentations

CHAPTER 8

Performance Objectives

Upon successful completion of Chapter 8, you will be able to:

1 Import a Word outline into a presentation
2 Copy and paste data between programs and use the Clipboard
3 Export a presentation to Word
4 Save a presentation in different file formats
5 Share presentations with others
6 Embed and link objects
7 Download templates
8 Compare and combine presentations
9 Insert, edit, and delete comments
10 Manage presentation properties
11 Protect a presentation
12 Inspect a presentation and check for accessibility and compatibility issues
13 Manage autorecover versions of presentations
14 Customize PowerPoint options

Share data between programs in the Microsoft Office suite by importing and exporting, copying and pasting, copying and embedding, or copying and linking data. The method for sharing data depends on the data and whether it is static or dynamic. Use options at the Export backstage area to create a video or handout of a presentation and save a presentation in a variety of file formats. If PowerPoint is used in a collaborative environment, comments can be inserted in a presentation and then the presentation can be shared with others using a cloud sharing application such as OneDrive or via email. Use options at the Info backstage area to manage presentation properties, password protect a presentation, insert a digital signature, inspect a presentation, and manage versions. In this chapter, you will learn how to complete these tasks as well as how to download online design templates.

 Data Files

Before beginning chapter work, copy the PC8 folder to your storage medium and then make PC8 the active folder.

The online course includes additional training and assessment resources.

Activity 1 **Import a Word Outline, Copy and Paste Objects**   **9 Parts**
between Programs, and Save the Presentation
in Different File Formats

You will create a PowerPoint presentation using a Word document, copy and paste an Excel chart and a Word table into slides in the presentation, save the presentation in different file formats, save slides as images, and then share the presentation using email.

Tutorial

Importing a Word
Outline

Q̇uick Steps

Import Word Outline
1. Open blank
   presentation.
2. Click New Slide
   button arrow.
3. Click *Slides from
   Outline*.
4. Double-click
   document.

Importing a Word Outline

A Word document containing text formatted as an outline with heading styles can be imported into a PowerPoint presentation. Text formatted with a Heading 1 style becomes the title of a new slide. Text formatted with a Heading 2 style becomes first-level text, paragraphs formatted with a Heading 3 style become second-level text, and so on.

To import a Word outline, open a blank presentation, click the New Slide button arrow in the Slides group on the Home tab, and then click *Slides from Outline* at the drop-down list. At the Insert Outline dialog box, navigate to the folder containing the Word document and then double-click the document. If text in the Word document does not have heading styles applied, PowerPoint creates an outline based on each paragraph of text in the document.

Activity 1a **Importing a Word Outline**   Part 1 of 9

1. At a blank presentation, click the New Slide button arrow in the Slides group on the Home tab and then click *Slides from Outline* at the drop-down list.
2. At the Insert Outline dialog box, navigate to your PC8 folder and then double-click *ATTopFive*. (Note: It may take several seconds for the slides to display in the presentation.)
3. Click the Design tab and then apply the Parallax design theme.
4. Change the background by completing these steps:
   a. Click the Format Background button in the Customize group on the Design tab.
   b. At the Format Background task pane, click the *Solid fill* option.
   c. Click the Color button and then click the *White, Background 1* option (first column, first row in the *Theme Colors* section).
   d. Click the Apply to All button.
   e. Close the task pane.
5. Delete Slide 1.

6. Format the new Slide 1 by completing the following steps:
   a. Change the slide layout by clicking the Home tab, clicking the Layout button in the Slides group, and then clicking *Title Only* at the drop-down list.
   b. Drag the placeholder containing the text *Adventure Tours* to the bottom of the slide and center it horizontally in the slide.
   c. Insert the **FCTLogo** image from your PC8 folder (do this with the Pictures button on the Insert tab), and then increase the size of the logo so it fills a good portion of the white area of the slide.
7. Make Slide 2 active and then apply the Title Only layout.
8. Make Slide 3 active and then format the bulleted text line spacing as 2.0 lines.
9. Make Slide 4 active and then format the bulleted text line spacing as 1.5 lines.
10. Save the presentation and name it **8-ATTopFive**.

Tutorial

Copying and Pasting between Programs

Copying and Pasting Data

Use the Copy and Paste buttons in the Clipboard group on the Home tab to copy data such as text or an object from one program and then paste it into another program. For example, in Activity 1b, an Excel chart will be copied and then pasted into a PowerPoint slide. A copied object, such as a chart, can be moved and sized like any other object.

Activity 1b Copying an Excel Chart to a PowerPoint Slide   Part 2 of 9

1. With **8-ATTopFive** open, make Slide 2 active.
2. Open Excel and then open **Top5Tours**.
3. Click in the chart to select it. (Make sure you select the chart and not just an element in the chart.)
4. Click the Copy button in the Clipboard group on the Home tab.

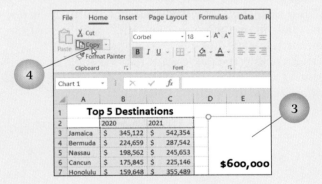

5. Close **Top5Tours** and then close Excel.
6. In PowerPoint, with Slide 2 active, click the Paste button in the Clipboard group on the Home tab.
7. Move the chart so it is centered below the title *Top Five Destinations*.
8. Make Slide 1 active and then run the slide show.
9. Print only Slide 2.
10. Save **8-ATTopFive**.

Use the Clipboard task pane to collect and paste multiple items. Up to 24 different items can be collected and then pasted in various locations. Turn on the display of the Clipboard task pane by clicking the Clipboard group task pane launcher. The Clipboard task pane displays at the left side of the screen.

Select data or an object to be copied and then click the Copy button in the Clipboard group. Continue selecting text or items and clicking the Copy button. To insert an item, position the insertion point in the specific location and then click the item in the Clipboard task pane representing that item. When all items are inserted, click the Clear All button to remove any remaining items from the Clipboard task pane. To paste all items from the Clipboard task pane at once, click the Paste All button.

Activity 1c Collecting and Pasting Text Between a Document and a Presentation

Part 3 of 9

1. With **8-ATTopFive** open, make Slide 4 active and then insert a new slide with the Title and Content layout.
2. Click in the title placeholder and then type Spring Treks.
3. Copy text from Word by completing the following steps:
   a. Open Word and then open **AdvTrek**.
   b. Click the Clipboard group task pane launcher to display the Clipboard task pane.
   c. If the Clipboard task pane contains any data, click the Clear All button at the top of the task pane.
   d. Select the text *Yucatan Adventure – 10 days* (including the paragraph mark following the text—consider turning on the display of nonprinting characters) and then click the Copy button in the Clipboard group.
   e. Select the text *Mexico Adventure – 14 days* and then click the Copy button.
   f. Select the text *Caribbean Highlights – 16 days* and then click the Copy button.
   g. Select the text *California Delights – 7 days* and then click the Copy button.
   h. Select the text *Canyon Adventure – 10 days* and then click the Copy button.
   i. Select the text *Canadian Parks – 12 days* and then click the Copy button.
   j. Select the text *Royal Canadian Adventure – 14 days* and then click the Copy button.
4. Click the PowerPoint button on the taskbar and then paste items from the Clipboard task pane by completing the following steps:
   a. With Slide 5 active, click in the *Click to add text* placeholder.
   b. Click the Clipboard group task pane launcher to display the Clipboard task pane.
   c. Click the *California Delights* item in the Clipboard task pane.

   d. Click the *Canadian Parks* item in the Clipboard task pane.
   e. Click the *Caribbean Highlights* item in the Clipboard task pane.

f. Click the *Mexico Adventure* item in the Clipboard task pane.

g. Click the *Yucatan Adventure* item in the Clipboard task pane. (Press the Backspace key two times to remove
the bullet and the blank line below *Yucatan Adventure*.)

5. Clear the Clipboard task pane by clicking the Clear All button at the top of the task pane.

6. Close the Clipboard task pane by clicking the Close button (contains an *X*) in the upper right corner of the task pane.

7. Make Slide 1 active and then run the slide show.

8. Print the presentation as a handout with four slides displayed horizontally per page. (Make sure the first gallery in the *Settings* category displays as *Print All Slides*.)

9. Save **8-ATTopFive**.

10. Make Word the active program, close the Clipboard task pane, close **AdvTrek**, and then close Word.

 Check Your Work

 Tutorial

Exporting
Presentations

Exporting Presentations

The Export backstage area contains a number of options for saving and exporting a presentation. Options at the Export backstage area include saving a presentation as a PDF or XPS file, creating a video of a presentation, packaging a presentation for a disc, creating handouts, and saving a presentation in a different file format.

Saving a Presentation as a PDF or XPS File

Q̌uick Steps

Save Presentation as PDF/XPS File
1. Open presentation.
2. Click File tab.
3. Click *Export* option.
4. Click *Create PDF/ XPS Document* option.
5. Click Create PDF/ XPS button.
6. Specify PDF or XPS format.
7. Click Publish button.

The portable document format (PDF), is a file format developed by Adobe Systems that captures all the elements of a presentation as an electronic image. The XPS file format is a similar format developed by Microsoft. The letters XPS stand for *XML paper specification*, and the letters XML stand for *extensible markup language*, which is a set of rules for encoding presentations electronically. To save a presentation in PDF or XPS format, click the File tab, click the *Export* option, make sure the *Create PDF/XPS Document* option is selected, and then click the Create PDF/XPS button. This displays the Publish as PDF or XPS dialog box with the *PDF* option selected in the *Save as type* option box. To save the presentation in XPS format, click the *Save as type* option box and then click *XPS Document* at the drop-down list. At the Save As dialog box, type a name in the *File name* text box and then click the Publish button.

A PDF file can be opened in Adobe Reader, Microsoft Edge, and Microsoft Word. An XPS file can be opened in Adobe Reader, Internet Explorer, and XPS Viewer. One method for opening a PDF or XPS file is to open File Explorer, navigate to the folder containing the file, right-click the file, and then point to *Open with*. This displays a side menu with the programs that will open the file.

Creating a Video of a Presentation

Q̌uick Steps

Save Presentation as Video
1. Open presentation.
2. Click File tab.
3. Click *Export* option.
4. Click *Create a Video* option.
5. Click Create Video button.

Create a video that incorporates all of a presentation's recorded timings and narrations and preserves animations and transitions using the *Create a Video* option. The information at the right side of the Export backstage area describes creating a video and provides a hyperlink to get help on burning a slide show video to a DVD or uploading it to the Web. Click the <u>Get help burning your slide show video to DVD or uploading it to the web</u> hyperlink for information on burning a slide show video to disc and publishing a slide show video to YouTube.

Packaging a Presentation

Quick Steps

Package Presentation for CD
1. Open presentation.
2. Click File tab.
3. Click *Export* option.
4. Click *Package Presentation for CD* option.
5. Click Package for CD button.
6. Click Copy to CD button or Copy to Folder button.

Use the *Package Presentation for CD* option to copy a presentation and include all of the linked files, embedded items, and fonts. Click the *Package Presentation for CD* option and then click the Package for CD button and the Package for CD dialog box displays. At this dialog box, type a name for the CD and specify the files to be copied. The presentation can be copied to a CD or to a specific folder.

Activity 1d **Saving a Presentation as a PDF File, as a Video, and Packaged for a CD** Part 4 of 9

1. With **8-ATTopFive** open, save the presentation as a PDF file by completing the following steps:
   a. Click the File tab and then click the *Export* option.
   b. Make sure the *Create PDF/XPS Document* option is selected.
   c. Click the Create PDF/XPS button.

   d. At the Publish as PDF or XPS dialog box, make sure the *Save as type* option is set to PDF, insert a check mark in the *Open file after publishing* check box, and then click the Publish button. (In a few moments the presentation opens as a PDF file in Adobe Acrobat Reader.)
   e. Scroll through the presentation in Adobe Acrobat Reader.
   f. Click the Close button in the upper right corner of the window to close Adobe Acrobat Reader.

2. Save **8-ATTopFive** as a video by completing the following steps:
   a. Click the File tab and then click the *Export* option.
   b. Click the *Create a Video* option.
   c. Click the Create Video button.
   d. At the Save As dialog box, click the Save button. (Saving as a video takes a minute or so. The Status bar tracks the saving progress.)

3. When the video has been saved, play the video by completing the following steps:
   a. Click the File Explorer button on the taskbar.
   b. Navigate to your PC8 folder and then double-click the mp4 file **8-ATTopFive**. (This opens the presentation video in a viewing window.)
   c. Watch the presentation video and, when it is finished, click the Close button in the upper right corner of the window.
   d. Close File Explorer.
4. With **8-ATTopFive** open, package the presentation by completing the following steps:
   a. Click the File tab and then click the *Export* option.
   b. Click the *Package Presentation for CD* option.
   c. Click the Package for CD button.
   d. At the Package for CD dialog box, select the text in the *Name the CD* text box and type ATTopFiveforCD.
   e. Click the Options button.

   f. At the Options dialog box, make sure the *Embedded TrueType fonts* check box contains a check mark and then click OK.
   g. Click the Copy to Folder button.
   h. At the Copy to Folder dialog box, click the Browse button.
   i. Navigate to your PC8 folder.
   j. Click the Select button.
   k. At the Copy to Folder dialog box, click OK.
   l. At the message asking if you want to include linked files in the presentation, click Yes.
   m. When a window displays with the folder name and files, close the window by clicking the Close button in the upper right corner of the window.

   n. Close the Package for CD dialog box by clicking the Close button.

Check Your Work

Exporting a Presentation to a Word Document

Hint Export a presentation to Word to gain greater control over formatting handouts.

Slides can be printed as handouts in PowerPoint; however, exporting a presentation to Word provides greater control over the formatting of the handouts. Use the *Create Handouts* option at the Export backstage area to export a PowerPoint presentation to a Word document. Open the presentation, click the File tab, click the *Export* option, click the *Create Handouts* option, and then click the Create Handouts button. This displays the Send to Microsoft Word dialog box, shown in Figure 8.1. At this dialog box, select the page layout to use in Word and then click OK.

The first four page layout options will export slides as they appear in PowerPoint with lines to the right or below the slides. The last option will export the text only as an outline. Select the *Paste link* option and the Word document will be updated automatically whenever changes are made to the PowerPoint presentation.

Figure 8.1 Send to Microsoft Word Dialog Box

Click the specific layout for the display of slides in the Word document.

Click the *Paste link* option to connect the slides in the Word document and the PowerPoint presentation.

Activity 1e Exporting a Presentation to Word

1. Make sure **8-ATTopFive** is open, click the File tab, and then click the *Export* option.
2. At the Export backstage area, click the *Create Handouts* option.
3. Click the Create Handouts button.
4. At the Send to Microsoft Word dialog box, click the *Blank lines next to slides* option and then click OK.
5. If necessary, click the Word button on the taskbar.
6. In Word, select the first column (the column that contains *Slide 1*, *Slide 2*, and so on) and then turn on bold formatting. (The presentation was inserted in a table in Word.)

7. Select the third column (contains the lines) and then apply the Red font color.
8. Save the document and name it **8-ATTopTours**.
9. Print and then close **8-ATTopTours**.
10. Close Word.

11. In PowerPoint, export **8-ATTopFive** as an outline by completing the following steps:
    a. Click the File tab and then click the *Export* option.
    b. At the Export backstage area, click the *Create Handouts* option.
    c. Click the Create Handouts button.
    d. At the Send to Microsoft Word dialog box, click the *Outline only* option and then click OK.
    e. If necessary, click the Word button on the taskbar.
    f. In Word, scroll through the document and then close Word without saving the document.
12. In PowerPoint, save **8-ATTopFive**.

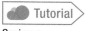

Saving a Presentation in a Different Format

Saving a Presentation in a Different Format

Quick Steps

Save Presentation in Different Format
1. Click File tab.
2. Click *Export* option.
3. Click *Change File Type* option.
4. Click format.
5. Click Save As button.

A presentation is saved, by default, as a PowerPoint presentation with the .pptx file extension. If the presentation will be used by someone who is using a different presentation program or a different version of PowerPoint, the presentation may need to be saved in another format. At the Export backstage area, click the *Change File Type* option and the backstage area displays as shown in Figure 8.2.

With options in the *Presentation File Types* section, a PowerPoint presentation can be saved with the default file format (.pptx) or in a previous version of PowerPoint. Use the *OpenDocument Presentation* option to save a presentation and make it available to open in other applications. The OpenDocument format enables files to be exchanged, retrieved, and edited with any OpenDocument-compliant software.

Figure 8.2 Export Backstage Area with *Change File Type* Option Selected

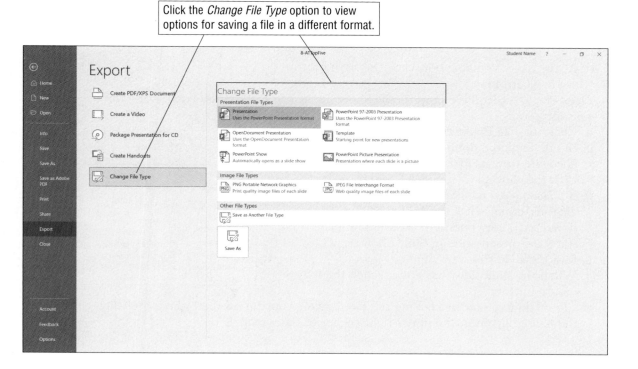

Save a presentation as a template to use the presentation as a basis for creating other presentations. (Saving a presentation as a template was explained in Chapter 6.) Save a presentation in the PowerPoint Show format and the presentation automatically starts when it is opened. When a presentation is saved using the *PowerPoint Picture Presentation* option, the contents of the presentation are flattened to a single picture per slide. A presentation saved in this format can be opened and viewed but not edited.

Activity 1f Saving a Presentation in Different Formats Part 6 of 9

1. Make sure that **8-ATTopFive** is open.
2. Save the presentation as a PowerPoint Show by completing the following steps:
   a. Click the File tab and then click the *Export* option.
   b. At the Export backstage area, click the *Change File Type* option.
   c. Click the *PowerPoint Show* option in the *Presentation File Types* section and then click the Save As button.

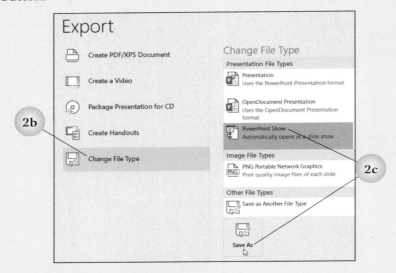

   d. At the Save As dialog box, click the Save button.
3. Close **8-ATTopFive**.
4. Open the **8-ATTopFive** PowerPoint Show file in File Explorer by completing the following steps:
   a. Click the File Explorer button.
   b. In File Explorer, double-click the drive representing your storage medium.
   c. Navigate to your PC8 folder and then double-click the slide show file, **8-ATTopFive**.
   d. If a *How do you want to open this file?* window displays, double-click the *Microsoft Office PowerPoint Viewer* option in the window. (This starts the presentation in Slide Show view.)
   e. Run the slide show.
   f. When the slide show has ended, click the left mouse button.

   g. Close File Explorer by clicking the File Explorer button on the taskbar and then clicking the Close button in the upper right corner of the window.

5. Open **8-ATTopFive** (make sure you open the presentation file and not the slide show, PDF, or XPS file) and then save it as a previous version of PowerPoint by completing the following steps:
   a. Click the File tab and then click the *Export* option.
   b. Click the *Change File Type* option.
   c. Click *PowerPoint 97-2003 Presentation* in the *Presentation File Types* section and then click the Save As button.
   d. At the Save As dialog box, type 8-ATTopFive-2003format in the *File name* text box and then click the Save button.
   e. At the Microsoft PowerPoint Compatibility Checker dialog box, click the Continue button.
   f. At the presentation, notice that the file name at the top of the screen is followed by the words *[Compatibility Mode]*.
6. Close **8-ATTopFive-2003format**.
7. Open **8-ATTopFive** (make sure you open the presentation file and not the slide show, PDF, or XPS file) and then save it in OpenDocument Presentation format by completing the following steps:
   a. Click the File tab and then click the *Export* option.
   b. Click the *Change File Type* option.
   c. Click *OpenDocument Presentation* in the *Presentation File Types* section and then click the Save As button.
   d. At the Save As dialog box, make sure *8-ATTopFive* displays in the *File name* text box and then click the Save button.
   e. When a message displays stating that the presentation may contain features that are not compatible with the format, click Yes.
   f. Run the slide show and notice that formatting remained the same.
8. Close **8-ATTopFive**.
9. Open **8-ATTopFive** (the presentation file and not the slide show, PDF, or XPS file) and then save it as a picture presentation by completing the following steps:
   a. Click the File tab and then click the *Export* option.
   b. Click the *Change File Type* option.
   c. Click *PowerPoint Picture Presentation* in the *Presentation File Types* section and then click the Save As button.
   d. At the Save As dialog box, type 8-ATTopFive-Picture in the *File name* text box and then click the Save button.
   e. At the message stating that a copy of the presentation has been saved, click OK.
   f. Close **8-ATTopFive**.
   g. Open **8-ATTopFive-Picture**.
   h. Click Slide 1 in the slide pane and notice how the entire slide is selected rather than a specific element in the slide. In this format you cannot edit a slide.
10. Close **8-ATTopFive-Picture**.

Save slides in a presentation as images in PNG or JPEG format with options in the *Image File Types* section of the Export backstage area. Save slides as PNG images for print quality, and save slides as JPEG images if the slide images will be posted to the internet. To save a slide or all slides as images, click either the *PNG Portable Network Graphics* option or the *JPEG File Interchange Format* option in the *Image File Types* section and then click the Save As button. At the Save As dialog box, type a name for the slide or presentation and then click the Save button. At the message that displays, click the All Slides button if every slide in the presentation is to be saved as an image or click the Just This One button if only the current slide is to be saved as an image. Click the All Slides button and a message displays indicating that all slides in the presentation were saved as separate files in a folder. The name of the folder is the name typed in the *File name* text box in the Save As dialog box.

Activity 1g Saving Slides as Images

1. Open **8-ATTopFive** (the presentation file and not the slide show, PDF, or XPS file).
2. Click the File tab and then click the *Export* option.
3. At the Export backstage area, click the *Change File Type* option.
4. Click the *PNG Portable Network Graphics* option in the *Image File Types* section and then click the Save As button.
5. At the Save As dialog box, make sure **8-ATTopFive** displays in the *File name* text box and then click the Save button.
6. At the message that displays, click the All Slides button.

7. At the message stating that each slide has been saved as a separate file in the 8-ATTopFive folder, click OK.
8. Open Word.
9. At a blank document, change the font size to 18 points, turn on bold formatting, change the alignment to center, and then type Adventure Tours.
10. Press the Enter key two times and then insert one of the slides saved in PNG format by completing the following steps:
    a. Click the Insert tab and then click the Pictures button in the Illustrations group.
    b. At the Insert Picture dialog box, navigate to the 8-ATTopFive folder in your PC8 folder and then double-click the *Slide3* image file.

11. Format the image in the document by completing the following steps:
    a. Click in the *Shape Height* measurement box in the Size group on the Picture Tools Format tab, type 2.8, and then press the Enter key.
    b. Click the *Drop Shadow Rectangle* option in the Picture Styles group (fourth option).
12. Press Ctrl + End to move the insertion point to the end of the document, press the Enter key, and then complete steps similar to those in Steps 10 and 11 to insert and format the **Slide4** image file in the document.

13. Save the document and name it **8-ATTours**.
14. Print and then close **8-ATTours**.
15. Close Word.
16. Capture an image of the Open dialog box and insert the image in a PowerPoint slide by completing the following steps:
    a. Press Ctrl + N to open a new blank presentation.
    b. Click the Layout button in the Slides group on the Home tab and then click *Blank* at the drop-down list.
    c. Press Ctrl + F12 to display the Open dialog box.
    d. At the Open dialog box, navigate to your PC8 folder.
    e. Click the option button at the right of the *File name* text box (the option button contains the text *All PowerPoint Presentations*) and then click *All Files* at the drop-down list.

16e

    f. Make sure all of your activity files are visible. You may need to scroll down the list box or resize the dialog box to see the files.
    g. Press and hold down the Alt key, press the Print Screen key, and then release the Alt key. (This captures an image of the Open dialog box and not the entire screen. You many need to press and hold down the Alt key, the FN key, and then press the Print Screen key.)
    h. Click the Cancel button to close the Open dialog box.
    i. Click the Paste button. (This inserts the image of the Open dialog box into the slide.)
17. Print the slide as a full page slide.
18. Close the presentation without saving it.
19. Save **8-ATTopFive**.

Check Your Work

Sharing Presentations

PowerPoint provides several options for sharing presentations. Options for sending and sharing presentations are available by clicking the File tab and then clicking the *Share* option. Depending on the system and version of Office, a number of options will be available for sharing, including sending a link to a presentation in the cloud, sending a presentation as an email attachment, providing a copy of a presentation as an Adobe PDF file, or sharing it as a live online presentation.

Sharing in the Cloud

Hint Microsoft OneDrive is cloud storage for saving files in one place, sharing them with others, and accessing them from any device connected to the internet.

PowerPoint presentations, like other files, can be stored and shared online through a file hosting service such as Microsoft OneDrive or another shared location such as a website or Microsoft SharePoint library. This is commonly referred to as cloud storage or cloud sharing.

To share a PowerPoint presentation in the cloud, first save the presentation to a OneDrive account (or other shared location). Display sharing options by clicking the File tab and then clicking the *Share* option at the backstage area, by clicking the Share button in the upper right corner of the PowerPoint window, or by clicking the File tab, clicking the *Info* option, and then clicking the Share button under the presentation name. At the window or task pane that displays, follow the instructions to send a link and invite others to view the presentation by typing in the email addresses of people to be invited. By default, anyone who is invited to view the presentation can also make edits to it. This option can be changed so that people can only view, but not edit, the presentation.

Once a presentation has been uploaded to the cloud, a link to the presentation can be shared with others by pasting it into an email, instant message, on a social media site, and so on. To do this, click *Copy Link* or <u>Get a sharing link</u> and specify whether recipients of the link will be able to edit or only view the presentation. Copy the link and then paste it in the specific locations.

Activity 1h Inviting People to View Your Presentation

Note: To complete this optional activity, you need to be connected to the internet and have a OneDrive account.

1. With **8-ATTopFive** open, save the presentation to your OneDrive folder and name it **8-ATTopFive-Shared**. To do this, click the File tab, click the *Save As* option, and then double-click the OneDrive account in the middle panel. At the Save As dialog box with the OneDrive account folder active, type 8-ATTopFive-Shared in the *File name* text box and then click the Save button.
2. With **8-ATTopFive-Shared** open, click the File tab and then click the *Share* option.
3. With the insertion point positioned in the *Enter a name or email address* text box (displays above the blue line) in the Share window, type the email address for your instructor and/or the email address of a classmate or friend.
4. Click the Link settings option near the top of the window to specify who can edit the presentation.
5. Click the *Allow editing* check box to remove the check mark.
6. Click the Apply button.
7. Click the Send button.
8. At the message that displays stating the link to the presentation was sent, click the Close button.
9. Check with your instructor, classmate, and/or friend to see if they were able to open the email containing the link to your PowerPoint presentation.
10. If you have **8-ATTopFive** saved on a removable device, close **8-ATTopFive-Shared** saved to your OneDrive folder and then reopen **8-ATTopFive** from your removable device.

Sharing by Email, Fax, or Online Presentation

A copy of a presentation can also be emailed to others as an attachment. Each recipient will receive a separate copy of the presentation, rather than accessing a shared file in the cloud. To do this, either open an email and then attach the file, or click the Share button in the upper right corner of the PowerPoint window to view options for emailing the file using an Outlook email account.

Presentations can be converted to PDF or XPS format before being attached to an email. PDF and XPS files have the advantage of being easily viewable and transferable on many platforms, and the content cannot be easily changed.

As an alternative to email, send a file as an internet fax. To use this option, the sender must be signed up with a fax service provider.

Click the *Present Online* option at the Share backstage area to share a presentation during a live online meeting using Office Presentation Service or another application such as Skype for Business. This process is described in Chapter 7.

Activity 1i Sending a Presentation as an Email Attachment

Note: Before completing this optional activity, check with your instructor to determine if you have Outlook set up as your email provider.

1. With **8-ATTopFive** open, click the Share button in the upper right corner of the PowerPoint window.
2. At the Share window, click the PDF option in the *Attach a copy instead* section.
3. At the Outlook window, type your instructor's email address in the *To* text box.
4. Click the Send button.

Activity 2 Embed and Link Excel Charts to a Presentation 3 Parts

You will open a company funds presentation and then copy an Excel pie chart and embed it in a PowerPoint slide. You will also copy and link an Excel column chart to a slide and then update the chart in Excel.

Embedding and Linking Objects

One of the reasons the Microsoft Office suite is used extensively in business is because it allows data from one program to be seamlessly integrated into another program. For example, a chart depicting sales projections created in Excel can easily be added to a slide in a PowerPoint presentation to the company board of directors on the new budget forecast.

Integration is the process of adding content from other sources to another file. Integrating content is different than simply copying and pasting it. While it makes sense to copy and paste objects from one program to another when the content is not likely to change, if the content is dynamic, the copy and paste method becomes problematic and inefficient. To illustrate this point, assume one of the outcomes from the presentation to the board of directors is a revision to the sales projections, which means that the chart originally created in Excel has to be updated to reflect the new projections. If the first version of the chart was copied and pasted into PowerPoint, it would need to be deleted and then the revised chart in Excel would need to be copied and pasted into the slide again. Both Excel and PowerPoint would need to be opened and edited to reflect this change in projection. In this case, copying and pasting the chart would not be efficient.

To eliminate the inefficiency of the copy and paste method, objects can be integrated between programs. An object can be text in a presentation; data in a table, a chart, a picture, a slide; or any combination of data. The program that was used to create the object is called the *source* and the program the object is linked or embedded to is called the *destination*.

Embedding and linking are two methods for integrating data in addition to the copy and paste method. When an object is embedded, the content in the object is stored in both the source and the destination programs. When editing an embedded object in the destination program, the source program in which the program was created opens. If the content in the object is changed in the source program, the change is not reflected in the destination program and vice versa.

Linking inserts a code into the destination file connecting the destination to the name and location of the source object. The object itself is not stored within the destination file. When linking, if a change is made to the content in the source program, the destination program reflects the change automatically. The decision to integrate data by embedding or linking will depend on whether the data is dynamic or static. If the data is dynamic, then linking the object is the most efficient method of integration.

Embedding Objects

Embedding Objects

An object that is embedded is stored in both the source *and* the destination programs. The content of the object can be edited in *either* the source or the destination; however, a change made in one will not be reflected in the other. The difference between copying and pasting and copying and embedding is that an embedded object can be edited with the source program's editing tabs and options.

Since an embedded object is edited within the source program, the source program must reside on the computer when the presentation is opened for editing. If a presentation will be edited on another computer, check before embedding any objects to verify that the other computer has the same programs.

Quick Steps

Embed Object
1. Open source program.
2. Select object.
3. Click Copy button.
4. Open destination program.
5. Click Paste button arrow.
6. Click *Paste Special*.
7. Click source of object.
8. Click OK.

To embed an object, open both programs and both files. In the source program, click the object and then click the Copy button in the Clipboard group on the Home tab. Click the button on the taskbar representing the destination program file and then position the insertion point at the location where the object is to be embedded. Click the Paste button arrow in the Clipboard group and then click *Paste Special* at the drop-down list. At the Paste Special dialog box, click the source of the object in the *As* list box and then click OK.

Edit an embedded object by double-clicking the object. This displays the object's source program tabs and options. Make changes and then click outside the object to exit the source program tabs and options. Animation effects can be applied to an embedded object with the same techniques learned in Chapter 7.

1. Open **FundsPres** and then save it with the name **8-FundsPres**.
2. Open Excel and then open **Funds01**, located in your PC8 folder.
3. Click in the chart to select it. (Make sure the entire chart is selected and not an element in the chart.)
4. Click the Copy button in the Clipboard group on the Home tab.
5. Click the PowerPoint button on the taskbar.
6. Make Slide 4 active.
7. Click the Paste button arrow and then click *Paste Special* at the drop-down list.

8. At the Paste Special dialog box, click *Microsoft Office Graphic Object* in the *As* list box and then click OK.

9. Click the Chart Tools Format tab.
10. Change the height of the chart to 5.5 inches and change the width to 9 inches.
11. Center the pie chart in the slide below the title.
12. Save **8-FundsPres**.
13. Click the Excel button on the taskbar, close the workbook, and then close Excel.

Check Your Work

Tutorial

Linking Objects

Linking Objects

Hint Since linking does not increase the size of the file in the destination program, consider linking objects if file size is a consideration.

If the content of the object to be integrated between programs is likely to change, link the object from the source program to the destination program. Linking the object establishes a direct connection between the source and destination programs. The object is stored in the source program only. The destination program will have a code inserted into it that indicates the name and location of the source of the object. Whenever the presentation containing the link is opened, a message displays saying that the presentation contains links and the user is then prompted to update the links.

To link an object, open both programs and open both program files. In the source program file, click the object and then click the Copy button in the Clipboard group on the Home tab. Click the button on the taskbar representing the destination program file and then position the insertion point in the desired location. Click the Paste button arrow in the Clipboard group on the Home tab and then click *Paste Special* at the drop-down list. At the Paste Special dialog box, click the source program for the object in the *As* list box, click the *Paste link* option at the left of the *As* list box, and then click OK.

Activity 2b Linking an Excel Chart to a Presentation

Part 2 of 3

1. With **8-FundsPres** open, open Excel and then open **Funds02** from your PC8 folder.
2. Save the workbook with the name **8-MMFunds**.
3. Copy and link the chart to a slide in the presentation by completing the following steps:
   a. Click in the chart to select it. (Make sure you select the chart and not just an element in the chart.)
   b. Click the Copy button in the Clipboard group on the Home tab.
   c. Click the PowerPoint button on the taskbar.
   d. Make Slide 5 active.
   e. Click the Paste button arrow and then click *Paste Special* at the drop-down list.
   f. At the Paste Special dialog box, click the *Paste link* option.
   g. Make sure *Microsoft Excel Chart Object* is selected in the *As* list box and then click OK.
   h. Click the Drawing Tools Format tab, change the height of the chart to 5 inches, and then drag the chart so it is centered on the slide.

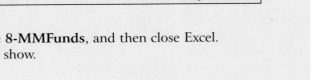

4. Click the Excel button on the taskbar, close **8-MMFunds**, and then close Excel.
5. Make Slide 1 active and then run the slide show.
6. Save and then close **8-FundsPres**.

Check Your Work

Editing Linked Objects

Edit linked objects in the source program in which they were created. Open the document, workbook, or presentation containing the object; make the changes as required; and then save and close the file. If both the source and destination programs are open at the same time, the changed content is reflected immediately in both programs.

1. Open Excel and then open **8-MMFunds**.
2. Make the changes as indicated to data in the following cells:
   a. Cell B2: Change *13%* to *17%*.
   b. Cell B3: Change *9%* to *12%*.
   c. Cell B6: Change *10%* to *14%*.
3. Click the Save button on the Quick Access Toolbar to save the edited workbook.
4. Close **8-MMFunds** and then close Excel.
5. In PowerPoint, open **8-FundsPres**.
6. At the message stating that the presentation contains links, click the Update Links button.
7. Make Slide 5 active and then notice the updated changes in the chart data.
8. Print the presentation as a handout with six slides displayed horizontally per page.
9. Save and then close **8-FundsPres**.

Check Your Work

Activity 3 **Download and Apply a Design Template to a**   **10 Parts**
Presentation and Prepare a Presentation for Sharing

You will download a design template and apply the template to a company presentation. You will compare and combine the presentation with another presentation; insert, edit, and delete comments in the presentation; insert and modify the presentation properties; encrypt the presentation with a password; inspect the presentation; complete an accessibility check on the presentation; check the compatibility of elements in the presentation; and customize PowerPoint options.

Tutorial

Downloading and
Applying a Design
Template

Ŏuick Steps
Download Template
1. Click File tab.
2. Click *New*.
3. Click in search text box.
4. Type key word or phrase.
5. Press Enter key.
6. Double-click template.

Downloading Templates

A number of PowerPoint templates are available for downloading at the New backstage area. To search for and download a template, click the File tab and then click the *New* option to display the New backstage area. Click in the search text box, type a keyword or phrase, and then press the Enter key or click the Start searching button at the right side of the search text box. PowerPoint searches an online templates gallery and displays templates that match the key word or phrase. To download a template, double-click the template or click once on the template to display a download window. At this window, read information about the template and view additional template images by clicking the right- or left-pointing arrows below the template image. To download the template, click the Create button. When a template is downloaded, a presentation based on the template opens and the downloaded template is added to the New backstage area.

Many presentations opened from a downloaded template contain predesigned slides. Use these slides to help create a presentation or delete the predesigned slides and create a presentation using just the template layouts.

To make the downloaded template (not a customized version of the template) available for future presentations, pin the template to the New backstage area. To do this, display the New backstage area, hover the mouse pointer over the template to be pinned, and then click the push pin. Complete the same steps to unpin a template from the New backstage area.

If a customized template is saved to the Custom Office Templates folder, it can be applied to an existing presentation. To do this, open the presentation, click the Design tab, click the More Themes button in the Themes group, and then click the *Browse for Themes* option at the drop-down list. At the Choose Theme or Themed Document dialog box, navigate to the Custom Office Templates folder in the Documents folder on the computer's hard drive and then double-click the template in the dialog box Content pane.

Activity 3a Downloading and Applying a Design Template

Note: Check with your instructor before downloading a design template. To download a template, you must have access to the internet and access to the hard drive. If you do not have access to the design template or cannot download it, open ISPres, save it with the name 8-ISPres, apply a design theme of your choosing, and then continue to Step 8.

1. At a blank PowerPoint screen, click the File tab and then click the *New* option.
2. At the New backstage area, click in the search text box, type marketing, and then press the Enter key.

3. Scroll down the backstage list box and view some of the templates.
4. Click in the search text box, type red radial lines, and then press the Enter key.
5. Click the *Red radial lines presentation (widescreen)* template.
6. Click the Create button. (This downloads the template and opens a presentation based on the template.)
7. Delete the sample slides in the presentation by completing the following steps:
   a. With the first slide selected in the slide thumbnails pane, scroll down the slide thumbnails pane to the last slide, press and hold down the Shift key, click the last slide, and then release the Shift key. (This selects all of the slides in the presentation.)
   b. Press the Delete key. (When you press the Delete key, the slides are deleted and a gray screen displays with the text *Click to add first slide*.)

8. Save the presentation as a template to the Custom Office Templates folder by completing the following steps:

a. Press the F12 function key to display the Save As dialog box.

b. Click the *Save as type* option box and then click *PowerPoint Template* at the drop-down list. (Make sure the Custom Office Templates folder in the Documents folder on the computer's hard drive is active.)

c. Click in the *File name* text box, type XXX-ISTemplate (type your initials in place of the *XXX*) and then click the Save button.

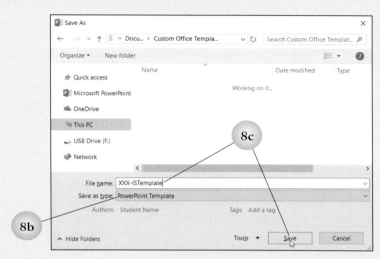

d. Close the **XXX-ISTemplate** file.

9. Open **ISPres** from your PC8 folder and then save the presentation with the name **8-ISPres**.

10. Apply **XXX-ISTemplate** to the presentation by completing the following steps:

a. Click the Design tab.

b. Click the More Themes button in the Themes group.

c. Click the *Browse for Themes* option at the drop-down list.

d. At the Choose Theme or Themed Document dialog box, double-click the *Custom Office Templates* folder in the Content pane.

e. Double-click **XXX-ISTemplate** (where your initials display in place of the **XXX**).

11. Run the slide show.

12. Print the presentation as a handout with all nine slides displayed horizontally on the page.

13. Save **8-ISPres**.

Check Your Work

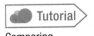

Tutorial

Comparing
and Combining
Presentations

Comparing and Combining Presentations

Use the Compare button in the Compare group on the Review tab to compare two PowerPoint presentations to determine the differences between the presentations. When the presentations are compared, options are available for combining only specific changes, accepting only specific changes, and rejecting some or all of the changes.

To compare and combine presentations, open the first presentation, click the Review tab, and then click the Compare button in the Compare group. This displays the Choose File to Merge with Current Presentation dialog box. At this dialog box, navigate to the folder containing the presentation to be compared with the current presentation, click the presentation name in the Content pane, and then click the Merge button. (The presentation name can also be double-clicked.)

Click the Merge button (or double-click the presentation name) and a Reviewing task pane with the heading *Revisions* displays at the right side of the screen containing changes to slides and the presentation. The *DETAILS* option is selected in the Reviewing task pane and the task pane displays with the *Slide Changes* section and the *Presentation Changes* section. Click a revision in either section of the task pane and the revision mark in the slide or slide thumbnails pane is selected. A revision mark displays in a slide indicating a difference between slides in the two presentations. If a difference occurs to the entire presentation, such as a difference between design themes, the revision mark will be at the left side of the screen near the top of the slide thumbnails pane. Click a revision in the Reviewing task pane or click a revision mark in the slide or slide thumbnails pane to expand the revision mark to display a revision check box followed by information about the change.

To accept a change, click the revision check box and then click the Accept button in the Compare group. A change can also be accepted by clicking the Accept button arrow. Clicking the Accept button arrow displays a drop-down list with options to accept the current change, accept all changes to the current slide, or accept all changes to the presentation. To reject a change, click the Reject button in the Compare group. Click the Reject button arrow for options for rejecting the current change, rejecting all changes to the current slide, or rejecting all changes to the presentation.

Use the Previous and Next buttons in the Compare group to navigate to changes in the presentation. Click the Reviewing Pane button to turn the display of the Reviewing task pane on or off. When finished comparing the presentations, click the End Review button and the review ends and the accept or reject decisions that were made are applied.

Quick Steps

**Compare
and Combine
Presentations**
1. Click Review tab.
2. Click Compare button.
3. Navigate to folder containing presentation to be compared.
4. Click presentation.
5. Click Merge button.
6. Accept or reject changes.
7. Click End Review button.

 Compare

 Accept

 Reject

 Previous

 Next

 Reviewing Pane

 End Review

Activity 3b Comparing and Combining Presentations

Part 2 of 10

1. With **8-ISPres** open, click the Review tab and then click the Compare button in the Compare group.
2. At the Choose File to Merge with Current Presentation dialog box, navigate to your PC8 folder, click *ISSalesMeeting* in the Content pane, and then click the Merge button in the lower right corner of the dialog box.

3. Notice the Reviewing task pane (with the heading *Revisions*) at the right side of the screen with the *DETAILS* option selected. This option contains a *Slide Changes* section and a *Presentation Changes* section. A message displays in the *Slide Changes* section indicating that the current slide (Slide 1) contains a change to the slide properties and title. The *Presentation Changes* section displays with *Theme (1 - 9)*.

4. Click the *Title 1: International Securities* revision in the *Slide Changes* section of the task pane.

5. Click the revision check box before the text *All changes to Title 1* at the side menu to insert a check mark.

6. You do not want to change the title name, so click the Reject button in the Compare group to reject this change.

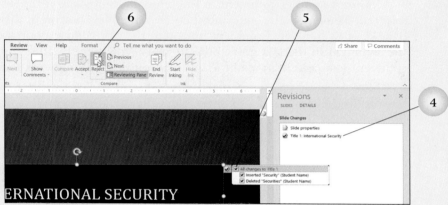

7. Click the Next button in the Compare group.

8. With the chart selected in Slide 3, click the Accept button arrow in the Compare group and then click the *Accept All Changes to This Slide* option.

9. Click the Next button in the Compare group.

10. Accept the remaining changes to the presentation by clicking the Accept button arrow and then click the *Accept All Changes to the Presentation* option.

11. Click the Next button until Slide 9 is active.

12. Notice the check mark at the left of the text *Inserted Picture 3* in Slide 9. This picture was inserted in the slide from **ISSalesMeeting**.

13. Click the Next button.

14. At the message stating that was the last change and asking if you want to continue reviewing from the beginning, click the Cancel button.

15. Click the End Review button in the Compare group.

16. At the message asking if you are sure you want to end the review, click Yes.

17. Save **8-ISPres**.

Check Your Work

Managing Comments

If a presentation is to be sent to others for review, specific questions or additional information can be included in the presentation by inserting a comment. To insert a comment, make a specific slide active and then position the insertion point where the comment is to appear or select an element in the slide on which to comment. Click the Review tab and then click the New Comment button in the Comments group. This displays an orange active icon at the location of the insertion point or next to the selected element and opens the Comments task pane with a text entry box in the pane. Type the comment in the text entry box and then click outside the text entry box, press the Tab key, or press the Enter key.

To insert another comment in the presentation, position the insertion point or select an element in the slide and then click the New button in the Comments task pane or click the New Comment button in the Comments group and then type the comment in the text entry box. To view a comment in a presentation, click the comment icon and then read the information in the Comments task pane.

To move between comments in a presentation, click the Next or Previous buttons in the upper right corner of the Comments task pane. Or, click the Previous or Next buttons in the Comments group on the Review tab.

Other methods for displaying the Comments task pane include clicking the Comments button at the right side of the ribbon or clicking the Show Comments button in the Comments group on the Review tab. When the Comments task pane is open, the Show Comments button is active (displays with a gray background). Turn off the display of the Comments task pane by clicking the Comments button on the ribbon, clicking the Show Comments button, or by clicking the Close button in the upper right corner of the Comments task pane.

To print comments, display the Print backstage area and then click the second gallery in the *Settings* category. (This is the gallery containing the text *Full Page Slides*.) At the drop-down list, make sure the *Print Comments* option is preceded by a check mark. Comments print on a separate page after the presentation is printed.

Quick Steps

Insert Comment
1. Click Review tab.
2. Click New Comment button.
3. Type comment text.

 New Comment

 Next

 Previous

 Comments

Show Comments

Activity 3c Inserting Comments

Part 3 of 10

1. With **8-ISPres** open, make Slide 2 active and then insert a comment by completing the following steps:
   a. Position the insertion point immediately to the right of the word *Australia*.
   b. Click the Review tab.
   c. Click the New Comment button in the Comments group.
   d. Type the following in the text entry box in the Comments task pane: Include information on New Zealand division.
2. Make Slide 3 active and then insert a comment by completing the following steps:
   a. Click in the chart to select it. (Make sure you select the entire chart and not a chart element.)

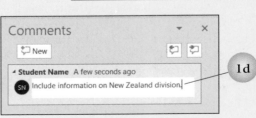

b. Click the New button in the Comments task pane.

c. Type the following in the text entry box: Include a chart showing profit amounts.

3. Make Slide 5 active, position the insertion point immediately to the right of the word *line* at the end of the third bulleted item, and then insert the comment Provide detailed information on how this goal will be accomplished.

4. Make Slide 8 active, position the insertion point immediately to the right of the word *Singapore* in the second bulleted item, and then insert the comment Who will be managing the Singapore office?

5. Click the Previous button in the Comments task pane to display the comment box in Slide 5.

6. Click the Previous button in the Comments group on the Review tab to display the comment box in Slide 3.

7. Click the Next button in the Comments task pane to display the comment in Slide 5.

8. Click the Next button in the Comments group on the Review tab to display the comment in Slide 8.

9. Click the Show Comments button in the Comments group on the Review tab to turn off the display of the Comments task pane.

10. Print the presentation and the comments by completing the following steps:

a. Click the File tab and then click the *Print* option.

b. At the Print backstage area, click the second gallery in the *Settings* category, make sure the *Print Comments* option is preceded by a check mark, and then click the *9 Slides Vertical* option.

c. Click the Print button.

11. Make Slide 1 active and then run the slide show.

12. Save **8-ISPres**.

Check Your Work

Hint Move a comment in a slide by selecting the comment icon and then dragging it to the new location.

  Delete

To edit a comment, click the comment in the Comments task pane, click in the text entry box and then edit the comment. Reply to a comment by clicking the comment in the Comments task pane, clicking in the reply entry box and then typing the response. To delete a comment from a slide, click the comment icon and then click the Delete button in the Comments task pane or the Delete button in the Comments group on the Review tab. A comment can also be deleted by right-clicking the comment icon and then clicking *Delete Comment* at the shortcut menu. Delete all comments in a presentation by clicking the Delete button arrow in the Comments group and then clicking *Delete All Comments in This Presentation* at the drop-down list.

1. With **8-ISPres** open, make Slide 8 active and then edit the comment by completing the following steps:
   a. Click the comment icon to the right of *Singapore*. (This displays the Comments task pane.)
   b. Click the comment text in the text entry box in the Comments task pane (this selects the comment text) and then type Check with Sandy Cates to determine who will be appointed branch manager.
2. Delete the comment in Slide 3 by completing the following steps:
   a. Click the Previous button in the upper right corner of the Comments task pane two times to display Slide 3 and the comment in the slide.
   b. Click the Delete button (contains an *X*) in the upper right corner of the comment box.
3. Close the Comments task pane.
4. Print the presentation as a handout with all nine slides displayed horizontally on the page and make sure the comments print.
5. Save **8-ISPres**.

1a

2a

2b

Check Your Work

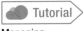

Managing
Presentation
Information and
Properties

Managing Presentation Information

If a presentation will be distributed or shared with others, check the presentation information and decide if presentation properties should be inserted in the presentation file, if the presentation should be protected with a password, and if the compatibility of the presentation should be checked or versions of the presentation should be accessed. These tasks and others can be completed at the Info backstage area shown in Figure 8.3. Display this backstage area by clicking the File tab and then clicking the *Info* option.

Managing Presentation Properties

Each presentation created has certain properties associated with it, such as the type and location of the presentation and when the presentation was created, modified, and accessed. View and modify presentation properties at the Info backstage area and at the Properties dialog box.

Property information about a presentation displays at the right side of the Info backstage area. Add or update a presentation property by hovering the mouse pointer over the information at the right of the property (a rectangular box with a light orange border displays) and then typing the information. The *Related Dates* section contains dates when the presentation was created and when it was last modified and printed. The *Related People* section contains the name of the author of the presentation and options for adding additional author names. Click the folder below the *Related Documents* section to see the contents of the folder where the current presentation is saved.

Figure 8.3 Info Backstage Area

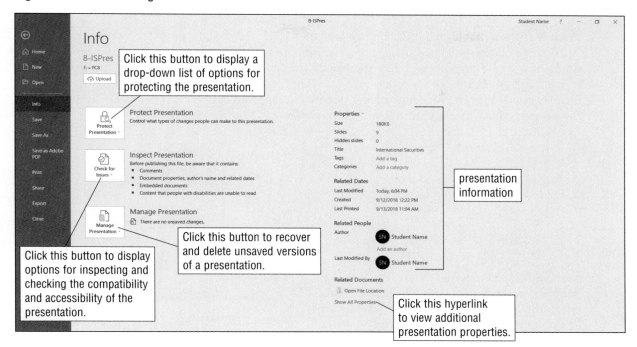

View additional presentation properties by clicking the <u>Show All Properties</u> hyperlink. Presentation properties can also be managed at the presentation Properties dialog box shown in Figure 8.4. (The name of the dialog box reflects the name of the open presentation.) Display this dialog box by clicking the Properties button at the top of the property information and then clicking *Advanced Properties* at the drop-down list. Inserting text in some of the text boxes can help organize and identify the presentation.

Figure 8.4 Properties Dialog Box

1. With **8-ISPres** open, click the File tab and then click the *Info* option.
2. At the Info backstage area, hover your mouse pointer over the text *International Securities* at the right of the *Title* property, click the left mouse button (this selects the text), and then type IS Sales Meeting.
3. Display the 8-ISPres Properties dialog box by clicking the Properties button at the top of the property information and then clicking *Advanced Properties* at the drop-down list.

4. At the 8-ISPres Properties dialog box with the Summary tab selected, press the Tab key (this makes the *Subject* text box active) and then type IS Corporate Sales Meeting.
5. Click in the *Category* text box and then type sales meeting.
6. Press the Tab key to make the *Keywords* text box active and then type International Securities, sales, divisions.
7. Press the Tab key to make the *Comments* text box active and then type This is a presentation prepared for the corporate sales meeting.
8. Click OK to close the dialog box.
9. Save **8-ISPres**.

Protecting a Presentation

Protect Presentation

Click the Protect Presentation button in the middle panel at the Info backstage area and a drop-down list displays with the options: *Always Open Read-Only*, *Encrypt with Password*, *Add a Digital Signature*, and *Mark as Final*. The drop-down list may also include the *Restrict Access* option. Use this option to allow viewing of a presentation while restricting the user's ability to edit, copy, or print the presentation. This option requires access to an information rights management account. Click the *Always Open Read-Only* option to restrict others from editing a presentation. To allow editing of a presentation marked as read-only, click the Edit Anyway button that appears below the ribbon when the presentation is opened.

Click the *Mark as Final* option to save the presentation as a read-only presentation. When that option is clicked, a message displays indicating that the presentation will be marked and then saved. At this message, click OK. This displays another message indicating that the presentation has been marked as final and that editing is complete. The message further indicates that when a presentation is marked as final, the status property is set to *Final*; typing, editing commands, and proofing marks are turned off; and that the presentation can be identified by the Mark As Final icon that displays, at the left side of the Status bar. At this message, click OK.

After a presentation is marked as final, a message displays above the ruler indicating that the author has marked the presentation as final and includes an Edit Anyway button. Click this button to edit the presentation. When a presentation is marked as final an additional message displays to the right of the Protect Presentation button at the Info backstage area stating "This presentation has been marked as final to discourage editing."

Encrypting a Presentation

Protect a presentation with a password by clicking the Protect Presentation button at the Info backstage area and then clicking the *Encrypt with Password* option at the drop-down list. At the Encrypt Document dialog box, type a password in the text box (the text will display as round bullets) and then press the Enter key or click OK. At the Confirm Password dialog box, type the password again (the text will display as round bullets) and then press the Enter key or click OK. When a password is applied to a presentation, the message *A password is required to open this document* displays to the right of the Protect Presentation button.

If a presentation is encrypted with a password, keep a copy of the password in a safe place because Microsoft cannot retrieve lost or forgotten passwords. Change a password by removing the original password and then creating a new one. To remove a password, open the password-protected presentation, display the Encrypt Document dialog box, and then remove the password (round bullets) in the *Password* text box.

Activity 3f **Marking a Presentation as Final and Encrypting with a Password** Part 6 of 10

1. With **8-ISPres** open, click the File tab and then click the *Info* option.
2. At the Info backstage area, click the Protect Presentation button and then click *Mark as Final* at the drop-down list.
3. At the message stating the presentation will be marked as final and saved, click OK.
4. At the next message, click OK.
5. Notice the message bar above the ruler.
6. Close the presentation.
7. Open **8-ISPres**, click the Edit Anyway button on the yellow message bar, and then save the presentation.

8. Encrypt the presentation with a password by completing the following steps:
   a. Click the File tab and then click the *Info* option.
   b. At the Info backstage area, click the Protect Presentation button and then click *Encrypt with Password* at the drop-down list.
   c. At the Encrypt Document dialog box, type your initials in uppercase letters. (Your text will display as round bullets.)
   d. Press the Enter key.
   e. At the Confirm Password dialog box, type your initials again in uppercase letters (your text will display as bullets) and then press the Enter key.
9. Click the Back button to return to the presentation.
10. Save and then close **8-ISPres**.
11. Open **8-ISPres**. At the Password dialog box, type your initials in uppercase letters and then press the Enter key.
12. Change the password by completing the following steps:
    a. Click the File tab and then click the *Info* option.
    b. At the Info backstage area, click the Protect Presentation button and then click *Encrypt with Password* at the drop-down list.
    c. At the Encrypt Document dialog box, delete the round bullets in the *Password* text box, type your first name in lowercase letters, and then press the Enter key.
    d. At the Confirm Password dialog box, type your first name again in lowercase letters and then press the Enter key.
    e. Press the Esc key to return to the document.
13. Save and then close **8-ISPres**.
14. Open **8-ISPres**. At the Password dialog box, type your first name in lowercase letters and then press the Enter key.
15. Remove the password protection by completing the following steps:
    a. Click the File tab and then click the *Info* option.
    b. At the Info backstage area, click the Protect Presentation button and then click *Encrypt with Password* at the drop-down list.
    c. At the Encrypt Document dialog box, delete the round bullets in the *Password* text box and then press the Enter key.
    d. Press the Esc key to return to the presentation.
16. Save **8-ISPres**.

Adding a Digital Signature

Add a digital signature, which is an electronic stamp that vouches for a presentation's authenticity. When a digital signature is added, the presentation is locked so that it cannot be edited or changed unless the digital signature is removed. To add a digital signature, a digital signature must be obtained from a commercial certification authority. With the commercial digital signature obtained, add it to a presentation by clicking the Protect Presentation button at the Info backstage area and then clicking *Add a Digital Signature* at the drop-down list.

Inspecting a Presentation

Check for Issues

Use options from the Check for Issues button drop-down list at the Info backstage area to inspect a presentation for personal and hidden data and to check a presentation for compatibility and accessibility issues. Click the Check for Issues button and a drop-down list displays with the options *Inspect Document*, *Check Accessibility*, and *Check Compatibility*.

PowerPoint includes a document inspector feature that inspects a presentation for personal data, hidden data, and metadata. Metadata is data that describes other data, such as presentation properties. If a presentation is shared with others, some personal or hidden data may need to be removed before sharing the presentation. To check a presentation for personal or hidden data, click the File tab and then click the *Info* option. At the Info backstage area, click the Check for Issues button and then click the *Inspect Document* option at the drop-down list. This displays the Document Inspector dialog box.

By default, the document inspector checks all of the items listed in the dialog box. To exclude items for inspection, remove the check mark preceding the item. For example, if a presentation contains comments, click the *Comments* check box to remove the check mark. Click the Inspect button near the bottom of the dialog box, and the document inspector scans the presentation to identify information.

When the inspection is complete, the results display in the dialog box. A check mark before an option indicates that the inspector did not find the specific item. If an exclamation point is inserted before an option, the inspector found and lists the items. To remove the found items, click the Remove All button at the right of the option. Click the Reinspect button to ensure that the specific items were removed and then click the Close button.

Quick Steps

Inspect Presentation
1. Click File tab.
2. Click *Info* option.
3. Click Check for Issues button.
4. Click *Inspect Document*.
5. Remove check marks from items that should not be inspected.
6. Click Inspect button.
7. Click Close button.

Activity 3g Inspecting a Presentation

Part 7 of 10

1. With **8-ISPres** open, click the File tab and then click the *Info* option.
2. At the Info backstage area, click the Check for Issues button and then click *Inspect Document* at the drop-down list.

3. At the Document Inspector dialog box, you decide that you do not want to check the presentation for XML data, so scroll down the dialog box and click the *Custom XML Data* check box to remove the check mark.

4. Click the Inspect button.
5. Read through the inspection results and then remove all comments by clicking the Remove All button at the right of the *Comments* section.

6. Click the Close button to close the Document Inspector dialog box.
7. Click the Back button to return to the presentation. (If necessary, close the Comments task pane.)
8. Save **8-ISPres**.

Checking the Accessibility of a Presentation

Quick Steps
Check Accessibility
1. Click File tab.
2. Click *Info* option.
3. Click Check for Issues button.
4. Click *Check Accessibility.*
OR
1. Click Review tab.
2. Click Check Accessibility button.
OR
Click accessibility message on Status bar.

Check Accessibility

When preparing a presentation, it is important to make sure the content is accessible to people of all abilities. People with a visual impairment, for instance, may use a screen reader to hear the text of a presentation read aloud. However, some visual elements such as graphics or animations cannot be understood by the screen reader. To make these elements accessible, an alternative text description should be added, as described in Chapter 4.

PowerPoint includes an accessibility checker to help identify such accessibility issues. To use this feature, click the Check for Issues button at the Info backstage area and then click *Check Accessibility*. Depending on the type of issues found in the presentation, errors, warnings, and/or tips will display in the Accessibility Checker task pane, along with explanations for how to fix the problems and why to fix the problem. An error message means that content will not be readable, while a warning indicates that it will be difficult to read or understand.

To correct an accessibility issue, click the item in the Accessibility Checker task pane, click the down arrow that displays at the right of the item, and then click an option in the *Recommended Actions* section of the drop-down list. For example, to add alternative text to an image, click the *Add a description* option. This displays the Alt Text task pane to the right of the Accessibility Checker task pane. Click in the Alt Text task pane description text box and then type a description of the item.

1. With **8-ISPres** open, click the File tab and then click the *Info* option.
2. At the Info backstage area, click the Check for Issues button and then click *Check Accessibility* at the drop-down list.
3. Notice the Accessibility Checker task pane at the right side of the screen. Click *Missing alternative text* in the *Errors* section to display the item that is missing alternative text.
4. Click *Content Placeholder 7 (Slide 3)* in the task pane and then read the information in the task pane describing why and how to fix the error.
5. Add alternative text to describe the chart by completing the following steps:
   a. Click the down arrow at the right of *Content Placeholder 7 (Slide 3)* and then click the *Add a description* option at the drop-down list.
   b. At the Alt Text task pane at the right of the Accessibility Checker task pane, click in the description text box and then type Pie chart showing percentage of profit by division: North America 32%, Europe 25%, Asia 17%, Australia 14%, and Africa 12%..
   c. Close the Alt Text task pane by clicking the Close button in the upper right corner of the task pane.
6. Click the remaining items in the Accessibility Checker task pane in the *Warnings* and *Tips* sections and then read the information in the task pane.
7. Close the Accessibility Checker task pane by clicking the Close button in the upper right corner of the task pane.
8. Save **8-ISPres**.

Checking the Compatibility of a Presentation

Quick Steps

Check Compatibility
1. Click File tab.
2. Click *Info* option.
3. Click Check for Issues button.
4. Click *Check Compatibility*.
5. Click OK.

Use the Check for Issues button drop-down option, *Check Compatibility*, to check a presentation and identify elements that are either not supported or will act differently in earlier versions of PowerPoint or Microsoft Office.

To run the compatibility checker, open a presentation, display the Info backstage area, click the Check for Issues button, and then click *Check Compatibility* at the drop-down list. This displays the Microsoft PowerPoint Compatibility Checker dialog box that provides a summary of the elements in the presentation that are not compatible with previous versions of PowerPoint and indicates what will happen if the presentation is saved and then opened in a previous version. Click OK to close the dialog box.

Opening an Autorecover Presentation

Quick Steps

Open an Autorecover Backup Presentation
1. Click File tab.
2. Click *Info* option.
3. Click presentation name at right of Manage Presentation button.

By default, a presentation that is open in PowerPoint will be automatically saved every 10 minutes. This automatic backup feature can help users recover changes made to a presentation in case it was accidentally closed without having been saved, if the application freezes or crashes, or if power is interrupted.

To open an autorecover backup presentation, click the File tab, click the *Info* option, and then click the autorecover presentation at the right of the Manage Presentation button. An autorecovered presentation opens as a read-only presentation and a message bar displays above the horizontal ruler that includes a Restore button. Click the Restore button and a message displays indicating that the selected version will overwrite the last saved version. At this message, click OK.

Manage Presentations

When a presentation is saved, any autorecovered files are deleted. However, if a presentation is closed after 10 minutes without saving or if the power is disrupted, PowerPoint keeps the backup file in the *UnsavedFiles* folder on the hard drive. Access this folder by clicking the Manage Presentation button at the Info backstage area and then clicking *Recover Unsaved Presentations*. At the Open dialog box, double-click the specific backup file to be opened. The *UnsavedFiles* folder can also be accessed by clicking the File tab, clicking the *Open* option, and then clicking the Recover Unsaved Presentations button below the *Recent* option list.

Delete an autorecover backup file by right-clicking the file at the Info backstage area, and then clicking *Delete This Version* at the shortcut menu. At the confirmation message, click Yes. To delete all unsaved files, click the Manage Presentation button and then click *Delete All Unsaved Presentations* at the drop-down list. Click Yes at the confirmation message.

Activity 3i Checking the Compatibility of Elements in a Presentation and Recovering Unsaved Versions of the Presentation

1. With **8-ISPres** open, click the File tab and then click the *Info* option.
2. Click the Check for Issues button and then click *Check Compatibility* at the drop-down list.
3. At the Microsoft PowerPoint Compatibility Checker dialog box, read the information in the *Summary* list box.
4. Click OK to close the dialog box.
5. Click the File tab, click the *Info* option, and then check to see if any versions of your presentation are listed to the right of the Manage Presentation button. If so, click the version (or the first version, if more than one displays). This opens the autorecover presentation as read-only.
6. Close the read-only presentation.
7. Click the File tab, click the *Info* option, click the Manage Presentation button, and then click *Recover Unsaved Presentations* at the drop-down list.
8. At the Open dialog box, check to see if recovered presentation file names display along with the date and time, and then click the Cancel button to close the Open dialog box.
9. Save the presentation.

Tutorial

Customizing
PowerPoint Options

Customizing PowerPoint Options

Customize PowerPoint with options at the PowerPoint Options dialog box, shown in Figure 8.5. Display this dialog box by clicking the File tab and then clicking *Options*. Click an option at the left side of the dialog box to view specific options for customizing PowerPoint. For example, click the *General* option in the left panel to see options for turning the display of the Mini toolbar on or off when text is selected, enabling or disabling live preview, and changing the user name and password.

Click the *Proofing* option at the PowerPoint Options dialog box and the dialog box displays with options for customizing the spell checker, such as specifying what should or should not be checked during a spelling check and creating a custom spell check dictionary. Click the AutoCorrect Options button and the AutoCorrect dialog box displays with options for changing how PowerPoint corrects and formats text as it is typed.

Click the *Save* option at the PowerPoint Options dialog box and the dialog box displays with options for customizing how presentations are saved. The format in which files are saved can be changed from the default of *PowerPoint Presentation* to a macro-enabled PowerPoint presentation, a 97-2003 presentation, a strict open XML presentation, or an OpenDocument presentation. Use other options to specify, by minutes, how often PowerPoint automatically saves a presentation, whether or not to save an autorecover version of a presentation if a presentation is closed without first saving it, and a default location for saving presentations.

Figure 8.5 PowerPoint Options Dialog Box

PowerPoint Options		? ✕
General	General options for working with PowerPoint.	
Proofing		
Save	**User Interface options**	
Language	When using multiple displays:ⓘ	Click each of the options in this panel to display customization features and commands.
Ease of Access	● Optimize for best appearance	
Advanced	○ Optimize for compatibility (application restart required)	
Customize Ribbon	☑ Show Mini Toolbar on selection ⓘ	
Quick Access Toolbar	☑ Enable Live Preview ⓘ	
Add-ins	ScreenTip style: Show feature descriptions in ScreenTips ▾	
Trust Center	**Personalize your copy of Microsoft Office**	
	User name: Student Name	
	Initials: SN	
	☐ Always use these values regardless of sign in to Office.	
	Office Background: No Background ▾	
	Office Theme: Colorful ▾	
	Office intelligent services	
	Intelligent services bring the power of the cloud to the Office apps to help save you time and produce better results. To provide these services, Microsoft needs to be able to collect your search terms and document content.	
	☐ Enable services	
	About intelligent services Privacy statement	
	PowerPoint Designer	
	Turn on "Office intelligent services" above to get personalized design suggestions.	
	☑ Automatically show me design ideas	
	About PowerPoint Designer	
		OK Cancel

1. With **8-ISPres** open, insert new slides in the presentation by completing the following steps:
   a. Click below the bottom slide in the slide thumbnails pane.
   b. Click the New Slide button arrow and then click *Reuse Slides* at the drop-down list.
   c. At the Reuse Slides task pane, click the Browse button.
   d. At the Browse dialog box, navigate to your PC8 folder and then double-click *ISPresAfrica*.
   e. Click each of the three slides in the Reuse Slides task pane to insert the slides into the current presentation.
   f. Close the Reuse Slides task pane.
2. Make Slide 1 active.
3. Change PowerPoint options by completing the following steps:
   a. Click the File tab and then click *Options*.
   b. At the PowerPoint Options dialog box, click the *Save* option in the left panel.
   c. Specify that you want presentations saved in the 97-2003 format by clicking the *Save files in this format* option box arrow and then clicking *PowerPoint Presentation 97-2003* at the drop-down list.
   d. Click the down arrow for the *Save AutoRecover information every* measurement box containing *10* until *1* displays.

   e. Click the *Proofing* option in the left panel of the PowerPoint Options dialog box.
   f. Click the *Ignore words in UPPERCASE* check box to remove the check mark.
   g. Click the *Ignore words that contain numbers* check box to remove the check mark.

   h. Click OK to close the PowerPoint Options dialog box.

4. Complete a spelling check of the presentation and make changes as needed.
5. Save the presentation, print six slides displayed horizontally per page, and then close the presentation.
6. Press Ctrl + N to open a new blank presentation.
7. Press the F12 function key to display the Save As dialog box.
8. At the Save As dialog box, notice that the *Save as type* option is set to *PowerPoint 97-2003 Presentation* because you changed the default format at the PowerPoint Options dialog box.
9. Click Cancel to close the dialog box.
10. Display the PowerPoint Options dialog box and then make the following changes:
    a. Click the *Save* option in the left panel.
    b. Click the *Save files in this format* option box arrow and then click *PowerPoint Presentation* at the drop-down list.
    c. Change the number in the *Save AutoRecover information every* measurement box to *10*.
    d. Click the *Proofing* option in the left panel of the PowerPoint Options dialog box.
    e. Click the *Ignore words in UPPERCASE* check box to insert a check mark.
    f. Click the *Ignore words that contain numbers* check box to insert a check mark.
    g. Click OK to close the PowerPoint Options dialog box.
    h. At the message stating that you are changing the default file format to Office Open XML and asking if you want to change this setting for all Microsoft Office applications, click No.
11. Close the blank presentation.

Check Your Work

Chapter Summary

- Create a PowerPoint presentation by importing a Word document containing text with heading styles applied using the *Slides from Outline* option at the New Slides drop-down list.

- Use the Copy and Paste buttons in the Clipboard group to copy data from one program to another.

- Use the Clipboard task pane to collect and paste up to 24 items and paste the items into a presentation or other program files.

- At the Export backstage area, create a PDF or XPS file of a presentation, create a video, package the presentation in a folder or on a CD, or create handouts.

- Click the *Change File Type* option at the Export backstage area and options display for saving a presentation in a different file format such as a previous version of PowerPoint, a PowerPoint show, an OpenDocument presentation, or as images.

- Use sharing options to send a link to a presentation in the cloud, send a presentation as an email attachment, provide a copy of a presentation as a PDF file, or share a presentation as an online presentation.

- Sharing options are available at the Share backstage area, using the Share button in the upper right corner of the PowerPoint window, and with the Share button in the Info backstage area.

- An object created in one program in the Microsoft Office suite can be copied, embedded, or linked in another program in the suite. The program containing the original object is called the *source program* and the program the object is pasted to is called the *destination program*.

- An embedded object is stored in both the source and the destination programs. A linked object is stored in the source program only. Link an object if the contents in the destination program should reflect any changes made to the object stored in the source program.
- Download online templates at the New backstage area.
- Use the Compare button in the Compare group on the Review tab to compare two presentations. Use options in the Compare group to accept or reject differences and display the next or previous change.
- Insert, edit, and delete comments with buttons in the Comments group on the Review tab or with options at the Comments task pane. Display the task pane by clicking the New Comment button or the Show Comments button in the Comments group on the Review tab.
- View and modify presentation properties at the Info backstage area and at the presentation properties dialog box. Display the presentation properties dialog box by clicking the Properties button at the Info backstage area and then clicking *Advanced Properties* at the drop-down list.
- Use options from the Protect Presentation button drop-down list at the Info backstage area to specify a presentation as read-only, encrypt with a password, restrict editing, add a digital signature, and mark as final.
- Use options from the Check for Issues button drop-down list at the Info backstage area to inspect a document for personal and hidden data, check a presentation for content that a person with disabilities, such as a visual impairment, might find difficult to read, and check the compatibility of the presentation with previous versions of PowerPoint.
- Use the Manage Presentation button at the Info backstage area to recover or delete unsaved presentations.
- PowerPoint automatically saves a presentation every 10 minutes. When a presentation is saved, any autorecover backup presentation(s) are deleted.
- Customize PowerPoint with options at the PowerPoint Options dialog box. Display this dialog box by clicking the File tab and then clicking *Options*.

Commands Review

FEATURE	RIBBON TAB, GROUP/OPTION	BUTTON, OPTION
Accessibility Checker task pane	File, *Info*	, *Check Accessibility*
Clipboard task pane	Home, Clipboard	
compare presentations	Review, Compare	
Document Inspector dialog box	File, *Info*	, *Inspect Document*
Encrypt Document dialog box	File, *Info*	, *Encrypt with Password*
Export backstage area	File, *Export*	
insert comment	Review, Comments	
Insert Outline dialog box	Home, Slides	, *Slides from Outline*
Microsoft PowerPoint Compatibility Checker dialog box	File, *Info*	, *Check Compatibility*
Package for CD dialog box	File, *Export, Package Presentation for CD*	
Paste Special dialog box	Home, Clipboard	, *Paste Special*
Publish as PDF or XPS dialog box	File, *Export, Create PDF/XPS Document*	
Send to Microsoft Word dialog box	File, *Export, Create Handouts*	
Share backstage area	File, *Share*	

Index

Interior Photo Credits

Page GS-1, © lowball-jack/GettyImages, Courtesy of Paradigm Education Solutions; *page GS-2*, © irbis picture/Shutterstock.com; *page GS-3*, © th3fisa/Shutterstock.com; page GS-4, © goldyg/Shutterstock.com; *page GS-5*, © Pressmaster/Shutterstock.com.